PSYCHOLOGY

PSYCH

PRINCIPLES
AND
APPLICATIONS

OLOGY

SECOND EDITION

STEPHEN WORCHEL
WAYNE SHEBILSKE

TEXAS A & M UNIVERSITY

PRENTICE-HALL
ENGLEWOOD CLIFFS, NEW JERSEY 07632

Library of Congress Cataloging-in-Publication Data

Worchel, Stephen.
  Psychology, principles and application.

  Includes bibliographies and indexes.
  1. Psychology.   2. Psychology, Applied.
I. Shebilske, Wayne.   II. Title.
BF121.W66 1986   150   85-24374
ISBN 0-13-732694-7

To some people whose support, understanding, and
patience have helped us appreciate and value learning about
others: our parents—Phil and Libby, Larry and Eileen; our
siblings—Harvey and Jason, Sheila, Gary, Steve, Kevin,
Mark, and Mike; our wives—Frances, Ann; and our
children—Leah and Jessica, Sherry, Lisa, and Laurie.

PSYCHOLOGY: PRINCIPLES AND APPLICATIONS, Second Edition
Stephen Worchel/Wayne Shebilske

Development Editor: Alison D. Gnerre
Production Editor: Linda Benson
Book Design & Page Layout: Kenny Beck
Photo Research: Yvonne Gerin
Assistant Art Director: Linda Conway
Cover Design: Christine Gehring-Wolfe
Cover Photo: Fred Burrell
Manufacturing Buyer: Barbara Kelly Kittle

*Acknowledgments appear on p. 658, which constitutes
a continuation of the copyright page.*

Printed in the United States of America

10 9 8 7 6 5 4 3 2 1

ISBN 0-13-732694-7 01

Prentice-Hall International (UK) Limited, *London*
Prentice-Hall of Australia Pty. Limited, *Sydney*
Prentice-Hall Canada Inc., *Toronto*
Prentice-Hall Hispanoamericana, S.A., *Mexico*
Prentice-Hall of India Private Limited, *New Delhi*
Prentice-Hall of Japan, Inc., *Tokyo*
Prentice-Hall of Southeast Asia Pte. Ltd., *Singapore*
Editora Prentice-Hall do Brasil, Ltda., *Rio de Janeiro*
Whitehall Books Limited, *Wellington, New Zealand*

4 Perception and Cognition 96

5 Alternate States of Consciousness 122

9 Adolescence, Adulthood, and Aging   264

10 Motivation   294

11 Emotions and Stress   330

12 Personality: Theories and Assessment 370

13 Abnormal Psychology 410

14 Therapy 458

15 Interpersonal Relations 496

PREFACE

"Keeping up with the times" seems to be an occupation that engages us all. Even as our first edition was going to press, there were significant events occurring in the world and in the field of psychology that led us to wish "we could have included that." At the global level, expeditions into space were becoming increasingly frequent and of greater duration. A dazzling array of experiments was being carried out in space by crews composed of people of different nationalities, sexes, backgrounds, and expertise. The union of a human sperm and egg was conducted in a test tube. An artificial heart was implanted in a patient. The first woman candidate of a major United States political party ran for national office. Along with these dramatic new events, old and often tragic problems plagued our world. Tens of thousands of people starved to death in Ethiopia while negotiations went on between governments as to how food should be supplied to these people. Terrorism reached new heights with the bombing of embassies in Beirut and the hijacking of airplanes. Indira Ghandi was assassinated by Sikh extremists in India, and fighting escalated in Central America.

Each of these events posed new and perplexing questions about human behavior and human relations. What would be the composition of a group that could work most effectively in space? What are the ethical bounds of medicine and how do we make decisions about such ethics? How do mood and attitude affect a patient's adjustment to a new medical procedure? Why can't we control crime, terrorism, and human suffering? How can machines be designed to address human needs, and how will human needs change as new technology is developed?

Psychology is the scientific study of human behavior. By discovering how and why people behave, believe, think, and learn we will be in a better position to understand our own world and anticipate the changes that will occur in it.

The problem that we as textbook writers have is how to present the richness of the field in a way that is meaningful and understandable but still gives a fair picture of psychology. This problem is not unlike the one that you face when someone says, "Tell me about yourself." Where do you start? How do you tell your story so that you present an interesting and exciting picture of yourself but still include information about your daily routine?

In writing about psychology we have tried to keep two goals in mind. Our first goal is to teach the theories and research support that constitute the principles of psychology. We do not, however, want to stop here, for while theories and research are interesting, they serve another important purpose. Psychology can be the looking-glass through which we can examine and understand events in our history and our daily lives. Therefore, our second goal in this text has been to show how psychology can be applied to everyday life. In doing this, we attempted in this edition, as in the first edition, to present current events in psychology and in our world. For example, in this edition we have given greater coverage to the interplay between psychological variables and health. Chapter 17 specifically addresses the effect of our environment on our physical health.

We have stressed application in two ways. First, we begin each chapter with a short account of an incident from history or current events. We chose these events because they represented a wide range of human behaviors. Some involve famous people (President Truman, Helen Keller), others involve people who will never make the pages of history books (Hondo Crouch, Raun Kaufman), while others focus on current figures (Geraldine Ferraro).

In some cases, the behaviors include common activities such as making decisions and raising a family, while in other cases the behaviors involve the unusual and the bizarre, such as cannibalism. We refer back to these incidents throughout the chapter to show how psychology can help explain and give insight into the events that occurred. Second, in addition to using the incidents, we also present many examples from everyday life to show how psychology can help us understand ourselves and others.

The incidents and applications are also aimed at presenting psychology in an understandable way. Many people have come to think of science as a set of abstract concepts that are difficult to master. The incidents and applications, however, bring these principles to life and thus make them easier to remember.

Features of the Second Edition

While this edition clearly builds on the earlier edition, we have made many changes based on the comments of readers and reviewers and on the recent changes in the field of psychology. First, we added material to present a more balanced approach and to "fill in the holes" that existed in the first edition. For example, in Chapter 12, we followed the discussion of Freud with sections on Jung and Adler to illustrate some of the approaches to personality spawned by psychodynamic theory. Similarly, we included a new section on thirst following an examination of hunger in Chapter 10. Second, we were particularly sensitive to new emphases and theories in psychology. For example, in Chapter 2 we updated our review of the rapidly growing information on neurotransmitters.

We have not only updated the chapters but added discussion of new theories. In Chapter 14, we added new material focussing on social support systems and community psychology. Also in this chapter, we pay particular attention to prevention as well as treatment of psychological disturbances. In Chapter 11, we examine the somatic theory of emotions. Furthermore, many of the major fields of psychology have placed greater emphasis on how information is processed, stored, and retrieved. Rather than simply devote a chapter to cognitive psychology, we have highlighted this cognitive focus in many of the chapters. For example, cognitive processes are examined as they relate to perception (Chapter 4), learning (Chapter 6), memory (Chapter 7), development (Chapters 8 and 9), emotion (Chapter 11), attribution (Chapter 15), and environment (Chapter 17). While this focus was present in the earlier edition, it is even stronger in the new one. For example, in Chapter 6, we added sections on animal cognition, concept formation, and problem solving.

Third, we have added a new chapter on perception (Chapter 4). This chapter covers such topics as the perceptual development of children, the role of organization in vision, perceptual constancies, depth perception, and visual illusions. In addition, there are sections on how our cognitive processes affect our perception of art, speech perception, and reading.

Fourth, in this edition, we have become even more concerned with helping the student learn the material. This concern is quickly evident in Chapter 1 where we present a lengthy box with the most recent research on learning from textbooks. Throughout the text we added new figures and summary charts to present a concise picture of the material. We added a figure to Chapter 4 depicting important issues raised by the Gibsonian ecological approach to perception. In Chapter 11, there are figures depicting each of the major theories of emotion. There is a summary chart in

Chapter 12 that compares the major theories of personality and identifies their major points.

Fifth, we have taken greater care to demonstrate the interrelationships between areas and theories in psychology. While these efforts are evident in each chapter, one example is the new section on the neurological basis for learning and memory in Chapter 6; this section builds on the discussion of biology and behavior in Chapter 2.

Finally, we have continued our commitment to presenting the application of psychology. There is new material on stress (Chapter 11), psychology and law (Chapters 5, 7, and 16), environment (Chapter 17), health (Chapters 2, 4, 5, and 17), work and task performance (Chapters 3, 12, and 16), prejudice and discrimination (Chapters 7 and 16), sports (Chapters 4 and 17), working mothers and day care (Chapter 8), and drug abuse (Chapters 2 and 5).

While chapters are ordered according to a plan, each one stands on its own. We have tried to make each topic understandable without outside help, because many instructors ask students to read topics before they lecture on them. We also hope students will find the book to be a valuable starting point for doing term papers in other courses. To this end, we have supplied more references than will probably be needed in an introductory course. These references help make the text a source book for people wanting a starting point to examine topics in depth. With this purpose in mind, we have retained the classic research and integrated the current. We have also listed suggested readings that expand upon topics covered in each chapter.

Learning Aids

The chapters are clearly divided into sections, with each one focussing on a particular issue in a subfield. Figures, tables, and illustrations are used to highlight important points. Summaries at the end of the chapters are designed to review major issues. Terms appear in colored print the first time they are used, and a definition is given at that point in the text. The terms are repeated in color print in the summary at the end of each chapter. The glossary at the end of the book serves as a review of main terms used in the field of psychology.

Finally, we have explicitly shown how psychological principles can be applied to learning from text books. In Chapter 1, we devote a lengthy box to this topic, and in Chapter 7 we examine ways to increase reading speed without sacrificing comprehension.

Supplements

An excellent *Study Guide with Practice Tests,* written by John Tucker of John Tyler Community College, provides a variety of review materials for each chapter, which should help the student understand the text content and improve test performance. A software study guide, the *Interactive Study Guide,* also provides review material in a modified video game format. This *Interactive Study Guide* is available for the IBM-PC and Apple-II series microcomputers and is provided without charge to instructors using this text.

The *Instructor's Resource Manual,* by Robert Wildblood of East Stroudsberg University, contains detailed chapter outlines, chapter objectives, additional lecture material, and suggested classroom demonstrations. The *Test Item File,* by Thomas Lombardo and Karen Christoff of the University of Mississippi, contains over two thousand questions which test conceptual understanding as well as factual recall. Test preparation and typing can be obtained through the Prentice-Hall phone-in testing service. A computer version of the *Test Item File* is available for many mainframe and personal computers.

Approximately 130 transparencies, many in full color, and 200 slides are also available to instructors for qualified adoptions. These include illustrations from the text as well as other nontext material. See your Prentice-Hall representative for details.

Acknowledgments

Although we as authors must be ultimately responsible for the contents of this text there are many people who made valuable contributions to the project. These people not only helped shape the book, but they turned what could have been a tedious and sometimes dreary job into an enjoyable and educational experience. In general, we would like to thank all those people for working as part of our team.

More specifically, we would like to thank John Isley, Psychology Editor, who was reckless enough to sign the project and who, despite our most diabolical efforts, never lost faith in us. These same qualities were equally evident as we worked on the second edition. We appreciate your guidance, patience, and expertise. Susanna Lesan has stuck by us through two editions. Her editorial input and insight have encouraged us and often brought us out of the depths of despair. Thanks for having the courage, wit, and patience to go it again. Alison Gnerre, development editor, did a very comprehensive and sensitive job of editing our chapters for the second edition. Linda Benson expertly guided us through the production of the second edition. She laughed with us, cried with us, and always seemed in control when we thought the second edition was only an illusion. We would also like to thank Paul Rosengard, Marilyn Coco, and Carol Ayres, and others at Prentice-Hall who contributed so much of their time and effort and gently helped us conquer our most fearsome problems.

Closer to home, there were many people who not only helped with various phases of the book, but who also cheerfully suffered our moods and anguish during the project. Thanks to M. Elizabeth Wetmore for taking some photographs and writing the appendix, and to Gora Lerma, Llyn Ellison, Carol Littowitz, Bill Webb, Kerry Marsh, Vicki Corrington, Therese Ausems, Susie Marten, and Laura Holmes, who helped type and edit the manuscript. We would like to express our appreciation to the many students at the University of Virginia and Piedmont Community College who read and offered comments on parts of the manuscript. In addition I (Steve Worchel) would like to thank my colleagues and students at the University of Athens, Greece, where I was a Fulbright Research Fellow. Not only were they generous in opening up their libraries and facilities to me, but they also broadened my perspective on psychology.

One of the most important parts of our team was the reviewers. Your efforts and help were tremendous—not only did you help shape the manuscript, but you taught us a great deal about psychology. Although you often reigned as anonymous critics, your help and guidance were much needed and greatly appreciated. The reviewers of the second edition included:

David Barkmeier, Northeastern University

Dennis Carmody, St. Peter's College

D. Bruce Carter, Syracuse University

Charles Carver, University of Miami

Karen Christoff, University of Mississippi

Helen Crawford, The University of Wyoming

Karen Duffy, State University College of New York at Geneseo

William Edell, University of Massachusetts

Irene Hanson Frieze, University of Pittsburgh

William C. Gordon, University of New Mexico

Leonard Hamilton, Rutgers–The State University

Therese Herman-Sissons, Montclair State College

Jan Heyn, Roanoke College

William A. Johnston, University of Utah

Robert J. Lueger, Marquette University

Gil Meyer, Illinois Valley Community College

Richard Miller, Western Kentucky University

Michael O'Boyle, Iowa State University

Paul Olczak, State University College at Geneseo

Pat Patterson, DeVry Institute of Technology

Sharyl Peterson, St. Norbert College

John Pittenger, University of Arkansas at Little Rock

Antonio E. Puente, University of North Carolina at Wilmington

Howard Reid, State University College–Buffalo

Nicholas Rohrman, Colby College

Richard Schiffman, Rutgers–The State University

Jack Shilkret, Anne Arundel Community College

R. Lance Shotland, The Pennsylvania State University

Charles Slem, California Polytechnic State University

Steven M. Smith, Texas A & M University

Ishmael Stagner, Brigham Young University–Hawaii

Robert Welch, University of Kansas

Jeremy Wolfe, Massachusetts Institute of Technology

Finally, we would like to express our generally unspoken appreciation to our families. Frances and Ann not only offered constant encouragement, patiently listened to our anguished bellowing, ran the households while we frantically wrote "just one more page," and helped create a working environment; they also served as our most compassionate critics and confidants, helped gather material for the book, and offered invaluable suggestions. Our children, Leah, Jessica, Sherry, Lisa, and Laurie, too often, but with good cheer, took a back seat to "the book." Your encouragement, your smiles, and your understanding sustained us. Thanks.

S. W.

W. S.

ONE

INTRODUCTION

On September 28, 1976, the host of a morning radio show in Texas opened with a sad announcement:

"A bit of the twinkle in the eyes of Texas is missing today. Hondo Crouch died yesterday. Hondo was widely known as the mayor of Luckenbach, Texas. He was also the owner of Luckenbach and the chief of police and the city manager. Hondo put Luckenbach on the world's map. He held a world's fair there. Recording artists made their albums there. Chili-cookoffs, tobacco-spitting contests, cow-chip throwing competitions, and no-talent shows were staged there. But mainly Hondo Crouch was there. He was the village attraction." (Patterson, 1979, p. 223)

This is an unusual eulogy about an unusual man. Nothing was really special about Hondo Crouch, yet everything seemed special to him. John Russell Crouch was born in 1915 in the obscure town of Hondo, Texas. Young John Russell lived an uneventful childhood. Most people thought that he would follow the pattern of other young men from Hondo; after high school most of the boys went to work for the railroad.

But John Russell always told people, "I'm different." And indeed, he was. As a child, he was fascinated by the way humans could propel themselves across a body of water. There was no lake or swimming hole near Hondo, so John Russell bought a swimming instruction book with cereal box tops and taught himself to swim by lying on a piano bench, kicking his feet, and moving his arms while reading the book. When it rained, John Russel would practice his swimming in the swollen creeks or in a local cattle-watering tank. When he was 18, he and a friend hitchhiked to Austin and entered the state swimming meet. John Russell won so many events that spectators and other contestants at the meet kept asking, "Who is this Hondo guy?" As a result, John Russell not only came away from the meet with a number of gold medals, he also earned a nickname that stayed with him all his life—he became known as Hondo Crouch.

Hondo's performance caught the eye of the University of Texas swimming coach, who offered him a place on the swimming team. Understandably, Hondo was a little frightened and insecure at the university, but this was masked by his remarkable swimming ability. Hondo also hid his insecurity with his keen sense of humor; he became a renowned practical joker. For example, he kept a family of baby skunks in a cigar box in his room and would carry them in his pocket when the swimming team went on road trips. When he got to the cash register in a restaurant, he would pull out one of the skunks and ask the cashier to "please hold this for me" while he searched in his pocket for money. Through his jokes and swimming Hondo became widely known; he was twice named All-American and had hopes of swimming in the Olympics. But his dreams of an Olympic medal were shattered when he hurt his back while playing water polo in 1940.

After serving in the Army, Hondo returned to the Texas ranch country that he loved so well. He married Helen Stieler, whose father owned a 22,000-acre ranch and was known as the Goat King of the world. Helen was everything that Hondo was not. She was self-assured and refined. Helen (or Shatzie, as Hondo called her) had a serious nature that was in sharp contrast to Hondo's fun-loving spirit.

Hondo worked for Shatzie's father, learning the ranching business and getting to know the land. He became part of the land, and the wild animals were his companions. He loved to tell stories about the animals he came into contact with. In a story for a local newspaper, he observed: ''The ground is cracking and clumsy baby ants are fallin' in 'em. That's why Mama ants raises so many youngsters to feed some to the cracks they can't stay out of. Ain't nature wonderful? You probably didn't know this went on, because not many folks lay on their bellies across deer and coon trails in the forest at night watchin' baby ants fall in big dark cracks. That's where I do alot of my spare thinkin' '' (Patterson, 1979, p. 71).

Hondo and Shatzie had four children, and Hondo delighted in teaching them everything from manners to lessons about nature. As with the rest of his life, his teaching methods were often unorthodox. In order to get his children to drink their milk, Hondo would wrap a nickel in wax paper and drop it into the bottom of the glass; the children eagerly gulped their milk to get the prize.

Hondo worked hard and saved his money. In 1953 he bought a 3,000-acre ranch. The land was hilly and rocky, dotted with sagebrush and small oak trees. Life as a rancher presented a constant challenge to Hondo; there never seemed to be enough grass or water, and it was a struggle to keep the land clear. The weather was hot and dry, but a 3-month drought could give way to a flood with a single day's rain. Hondo loved the challenge of the harsh environment, and he was constantly experimenting to find the best breed of animal for his land. His experiments often resulted in personal triumphs that he could boast about for years.

Although his ranch prospered, it was not

ranching that made Hondo Crouch the center of attention in the Texas Hill Country. While he loved the land, Hondo had a need to be with people. He became a writer for the Fredericksburg newspaper. Under the name Peter Cedarstacker, he used wit and humor to comment on issues of local interest. In addition to his writing, Hondo brought his humor to life on stage. He formed an acting team, and every summer the team would put on plays in the fallen-down dance hall in the ghost town of Waring, Texas. Hondo was a natural actor and he always seemed to know how to make the audience laugh.

Hondo was a grown man who never outgrew being a little boy. However, all was not happiness and jokes in Hondo's life. His favorite son, Kerry, went to the University of Texas in 1967. Kerry was a talented artist and a warm, sensitive young man. He idolized his father and this admiration was returned by Hondo. When Kerry was 21 years old, Hondo received a call from a doctor in Austin. Kerry had developed a severe psychological disorder known as schizophrenia. The once-happy, playful boy now lived in a world of his own. He was unable to interact with other people, and he heard voices and saw strange figures. Hondo was crushed. He blamed drugs and Kerry's "hippie" friends for the problem. He loved Kerry very much, but was hurt so deeply that he could not bear to visit him in the hospital. Kerry spent much of the next 8 years in hospitals and jails; despite urgings from family and friends, Hondo never visited his son.

Hondo's spirit was broken by this tragedy and his only wish after learning about his son's condition was to die soon. His will to live was restored, however, by a small advertisement in the Fredericksburg paper:

"Town for sale; Luckenbach. Benno Engle, owner." The town of Luckenbach stood at the end of Hondo's ranch. Its main street (the only street in town) was 200 feet long, and the whole town consisted of a general store, which had a saloon in one section and a post office in the other. (A white line painted down the center of the floor separated the saloon from the post office.) Hondo had often admired the little town and the thought of owning it stirred his imagination. He would put Luckenbach on the map; it would be a town where anyone could feel at home. Most of all, it would give Hondo a place where he could once again be the center of everyone's attention. He bought the town and hung a sign over the general store entrance: "Everybody's Somebody in Luckenbach."

Hondo assumed his role as mayor and foreign minister of Luckenback and became a champion of the downtrodden. Chili contests were popular in Texas, but women were traditionally excluded. Hondo formed the "Hell Hath No Fury (Like a Woman Scorned) Society" and staged the first women's chili cookoff. In 1973 Hondo held Luckenbach's first "Great World's Fair," which attracted 10,000 people. Contests included tobacco-spitting, chicken-frying, cow-chip throwing, and armadillo races. Hondo encouraged aspiring entertainers to come to Luckenbach; Willie Nelson and Jerry Jeff Walker, who were unknown at the time, performed at the fair and became close friends of Hondo.

Hondo and his creative humor and insight received national attention. The Clown Prince of Texas had found his kingdom in Luckenbach. Here Hondo, the man who was really no one special, discovered a way to make all those who visited his town feel a little special.

WHAT IS PSYCHOLOGY?

Even as a young boy Hondo believed he was different from other people. Indeed, in many respects Hondo was unique. His thoughts, feelings, and actions were different from everyone else's. In fact, each of us is unique. But despite this uniqueness, we all have a large number of things in common. We all learn (some faster than others); we all talk (some more than others); we all have goals that we are trying to reach; each of us experiences emotions such as love, hate, and happiness; and we all interact with other people and belong to groups. Most of us take our thoughts, feelings, and actions for granted. We rarely question how we see objects, learn new material, or feel emotions. We seldom wonder why we are attracted to certain people or why we have bizarre dreams. The exception to this occurs when something goes wrong. We begin to question how learning occurs if we see our child having difficulty reading or writing. We begin to question why people feel emotions when we find ourselves in a deep sadness or depression. The news that his son was suffering from schizophrenia forced Hondo to examine his relationships and struggle to explain Kerry's plight.

In a sense, psychologists are constantly asking questions and searching for answers about why and how people behave, believe, and act as they do. Psychology, like any science, has the goals of describing, predicting, and explaining events; the events at the heart of psychology are behaviors, both physical and mental. Thus psychology is a science of behavior, but it is more. Psychology has a strong applied side, in which its knowledge is used to solve problems, create a more fulfilling social and physical environment, and help people adjust to the demands of their changing world. **Psychology,** then, can be defined as the scientific study of behavior and the applications gained from that knowledge. As we will see in this book, psychology is an exciting partnership between science and application, with each opening up new directions and challenges for the other (Chavis & Stucky, 1983; Hatch, 1982). As one student said, "Of all the fields I have studied at the university, psychology is the one that is really about *me*. In psychology I am the center of attention; its findings apply directly to me."

Wilhelm Wundt, a German psychologist, founded the first psychology laboratory in Leipzig, Germany, in 1879.

THE HISTORY OF PSYCHOLOGY

Tracing the origins of psychology is somewhat like trying to find where the wind begins. As far back as written history goes, our ancestors wondered about why people act as they do and what makes some behave differently from others. It has been suggested that spirits and demons inhabit people's bodies and direct their behaviors; body fluids such as black bile were believed to influence people's personalities and emotions. While interest in and guesses about the causes of human behavior have a long history, attempts to scientifically study behavior are rather recent. In fact, we need look back only slightly over 100 years to find the roots of the family tree of psychology: The most cited date for the "birth" of psychology is 1879. The clearest way to examine the psychology family tree is to study the schools of thought or approaches that have developed over the last century.

Structuralism

In 1879 Wilhelm Wundt went to Leipzig, Germany, to start the first psychological laboratory. There he developed techniques for studying the laws of the human mind. Most of his techniques involved analyzing sights, sounds, and other sensations, because Wundt believed that sensations are the "atoms" of thought. Many students came to study with Wundt; one of the most famous was Edward Bradford Titchener, who set up his own laboratory in the United States at Cornell University.

Besides setting up psychological laboratories, Wundt and Titchener are credited with developing an analytical approach to studying how we experience the world the way we do. This approach, which is called **structuralism,** is based on identifying the elements of human experience and finding out how those elements combine to form thoughts and feelings. Titchener identified three categories of elements: sensations (such as sights and sounds), feelings (such as joy and sorrow), and images (such as memories and dreams). The main research tool of structuralism is the method of **analytic introspection,** which is a way of isolating the elementary sensations of which experiences are made.

You would have to go through a rigorous training program to learn analytic introspection. As a trainee, you would learn to break down your experiences into their most basic elements. To get some idea of how this works, imagine yourself standing in front of a window looking at a house, trees, and sky. You would divide the window scene into separate patches of colors and brightnesses. You might notice different shades of blue and green in the sky and trees, and you might see that the light tan house

If you were a trainee in analytic introspection, you would not just describe the scene shown here as boy, lake, trees, mountains, sky. You would learn to notice patches of brightness and darkness and how different colors are affected by shadows or bright sunlight, and you would incorporate these data into your description of the scene.

LEARNING FROM TEXTBOOKS IS A THREE-LETTER WORD

Many students do not learn effectively from textbooks even though they are very bright and are fluid readers of stories (Estes & Vaughan, 1985). As a result, frustrated students sometimes use four-letter words to describe learning from textbooks. We will argue that a three-letter word is more appropriate. That word is *ACE*, which stands for *A*nticipate, *C*ompare, and *E*nrich. We will describe these processes along with the features of the book that will help you use them.

This book is designed to help students by including aids and instructions that improve how well a text is learned and remembered. This design is a practical application of recent basic cognitive research that is described in chapters on perception, learning, and memory. A preview is presented here so that you can start using the aids and instructions now. They will not only help you get textbook information in your head, but they will also help you get it out when you need it on tests, in other courses, and in everyday life.

Psychologists provided a springboard for the development of modern learning aids and instructions on how to learn from textbooks. Traditional aids and instructions were based on a five-step study method called SQ3R (*S*urvey, *Q*uestion, *R*ead, *R*ecite, and *R*eview; Robinson, 1941). Psychologists still recommend these five steps. As described in Chapter 7, however, psychologists now are also able to recommend additional methods that go beyond SQ3R in explaining how each step should be done. These new methods are emerging as products of two interwoven branches of research. One branch concentrates on the textbook (Armbruster & Anderson, 1984; Crismore, 1984;

Kantor, 1983; Shebilske & Rotondo, 1981); the other focusses on the reader (Fisher & Peters, 1981; Rayner, 1983; Shebilske, 1984; Van Rossum & Schenk, 1984).

Schema theory, which is discussed in Chapters 4, 7, and 8, guides both lines of research. According to this theory, both authors and readers play an active role in the communication process. Authors write ideas in a particular structured sequence that can be represented by an outline. Readers construct an internal representation of text that can also be represented by an outline. Cognitive psychologists have learned a great deal about the reading and learning processes by using schema theory. They specify the structure of the text, the structure of the readers' internal representation, and the relationship between these two structures (see Chapter 7). Superior readers quickly develop an internal representation that matches the structure of the text.

Some superior readers survey the material first, ask questions about it, read it, recite it, and review it. But this SQ3R procedure alone is not what makes them successful. They succeed largely because they constantly monitor their knowledge. They ask, "Do I know what the author is saying? What can I do about it if I don't?" (Vaughan & Estes, 1985). This monitoring takes place during every part of studying, from the initial survey to the final review. The monitoring can be done by *a*nticipating what the author's main points are; *c*omparing your understanding of these points with what actually is written, and *e*nriching your understanding with aids that will put important information at your fingertips. These are the steps you need to ACE the text.

Our goal was to include qualities

in this text that would help you with these ACE procedures. The following are qualities and suggestions for how you might best take advantage of them to optimize how well you learn and remember the material:

1. We begin each chapter with a story based on real people in history or current events, and we refer back to the story throughout the chapter. Our purpose is to grab your attention and focus it effectively as you read. We hope that you will enjoy the stories and that they will put you in the mood for reading the chapters. We also hope they will help you ACE the text as follows:

Anticipate how the story will relate to the chapter. You should get some hints about the chapter by reading the outline that appears before the story and by previewing topic headings. But you should get much richer clues in the stories. The Hondo Crouch story is chock-full of them. Can you think of one that might have enabled you to anticipate this discussion of learning from textbooks? The best way to detect them is to ask yourself questions as you read. For example, when the story mentioned that Hondo learned to swim by reading a book you might have asked how one can learn swimming or anything else from a book. You could note this question in your text simply by writing the word "how" in the margin next to the passage on the swimming instruction.

A transition section after each story will help you create expectations about what is to come. The one for this chapter directs you toward wondering about the "hows and whys" of learning, talking, goal setting, emotions, and other behaviors. It focused your attention on individual differences as well as on things that people have in common. If you haven't already done so, you might want to reread the story with an eye out for clues about these topics. Write short notes in the margin when you find one. You should have little trouble finding passages where it would be appropriate to write:

How are people similar and different? What can psychologists tell us about raising children? Why do emotions change? What causes mental illness? How are people special?

Raising such questions in advance will make you a more active reader. The trick will be to learn to raise similar questions in advance when you read the remaining stories for the first time. Mastering this skill will help you anticipate what the chapter will be about.

These anticipations will help you get more out of what you read. The difference between reading with and without expectations is like the difference between being a driver or a passenger in a car. Drivers actively read signs to answer questions about speed and directions. As a result, they can usually tell you much more about speed limits and street names than can a passenger who passively looks at the same signs for no particular purpose. In the same way, you will remember more about chapters if you read actively to answer questions that come to mind while reading the introductory stories.

Compare your understanding and memory with what is said as you read the chapter. The expectations you created while reading the story will be your first state of understanding. Compare this with what is actually written. Did the text say more, less, or

something different from what you thought it would? Note important differences in the margin. You might observe, for example, that the chapter does not directly answer the question of how people are similar and different. It does, however, explain methods used to answer this question and it tells what branch of psychology studies personalities and other kinds of similarities and differences.

A good way to compare your understanding with what is said is to close the book and try to tell the material in your own words. Pay special attention to distortions or omissions.

Enrich your memory in a way that will help you recall the text. One way to improve your memory is to use the story as a framework for organizing the chapter material (see Chapter 7). You might recall behaviorism and humanistic psychology better if you relate the first to Hondo's technique for getting his kids to drink milk and relate the second to his sign "Everybody's Somebody in Luchenbach." Similarly, in the chapter on learning you can use the story about Helen Keller to help you remember the difference between classical and operant conditioning. Students sometimes confuse these two kinds of conditioning. You will avoid this confusion if you remember that the two kinds are related to different parts of the story. If you get an idea for using the story to help you organize your memory, write a reminder in the margin so you won't forget to use it when you review.

2. Other aspects of the text are also designed to help you improve your memory. For instance, the relationships between ideas is clearly signalled by the way the text is physically structured and by labels. In addition, topic sentences and summaries appear before and after main ideas throughout the text. And

finally, many aids such as concrete examples, thought questions, armchair experiments, and applications are included in the text. These features will work best if you deliberately use them to organize your memory as you work through the ACE process.

Anticipate the relationship between main and subordinate ideas by scanning the headings, which are organized in three levels to reflect these relationships. Topic sentences often introduce sections so that you can anticipate what will be said.

Compare your understanding of the relationships with what is said and update your understanding as you read the text. Keep your eyes open for phrases such as "note that," in contrast," or "leads to." These signals indicate important ideas, contrasts, and cause-effect relationships that you should remember. Summary statements often conclude sections so that you can compare your understanding of the main points with ours.

Enrich you memory by thinking of ways to remember the important relationships and facts. One way is to number ideas of approximately the same importance. We often supply the enumeration in the text itself, but if we do not, you can add it yourself by making notes in the margins or in the text. The wording of topic sentences and summary statements might give you hints about the important ideas to be remembered.

3. Finally, we present instructions in Chapter 4 that could double your reading speed in this and other books. You will save a lot of time by doubling your reading speed but don't expect to cut your study time in half. In fact, it might be better not to cut your study time at all. Instead, plan to study more efficiently by reading faster and by using the additional time to ACE the text.

looks darker in an area covered by a shadow. According to structuralists, in doing this, you would be uncovering the sensory elements used to construct your experience. Psychologists stopped relying on analytic introspection because the method could only be used with trained observers, who were usually the psychologists themselves. Furthermore, it gave different results in different laboratories, depending on how observers were trained. But many researchers today carry on the goal of discovering the sensory elements of experiences, using new methods.

Psychologists have developed many new research approaches since the founding of the first psychological laboratory. Some evolved in a very different direction from structuralism. Others were motivated by the desire to study aspects of behavior for which structuralism was not well suited. Let's review some of these other approaches.

Functionalism

While structuralists' publications were still "hot off the press," an American psychologist, William James, proposed a different program of research. His new approach was called **functionalism** because it concerned the way in which mental processes (such as thinking) function to fill needs. While structuralists were asking "What is thinking?" functionalists asked "What is it for?" Emphasis on the function of thought led functionalists to pursue important applications in education. John Dewey, a leading functionalist, strengthened public education in America and was the founder of school psychology, which has become a major subfield. Other functionalists applied their work to a great many pressing problems. For instance, they served as advisers to the United States armed services, they developed tests of personality, and they contributed to the development of child psychology.

Gestalt Psychology

In the 1920s, while Hondo Crouch was in grammar school, a group of German psychologists, Max Wertheimer, Kurt Koffka, and Wolfgang Köhler, established still another approach to psychology. They believed that there are experiences that cannot be broken down into separate elements. They therefore argued that structuralist "elements," or units of analysis, were unnatural. They maintained that some things have to be experienced as wholes—that they cannot be broken down any further. Thus the units of choice in the earlier example would be trees, house, and sky. These psychologists were so committed to analyzing these "whole" units that they named their approach **Gestalt**, which is a German word meaning "whole." Gestalt psychologists argued that it is the organization of elements, rather than the elements themselves, that is important. In order to understand their point of view, think of your favorite tune. Clearly, the tune is made up of musical notes, but it is not the notes themselves that give it melody. Instead, it is the *arrangement* of the notes that is important. We could take those same notes and make a different melody (or maybe just noise) if we organized them differently. In Chapter 4 we will review Gestalt laws of organization and discuss modern attempts to refine those laws.

Wolfgang Köhler was one of the founders of Gestalt psychology.

Behaviorism

When Hondo's children refused to drink their milk, Hondo found that he could quickly change their behavior by dropping a nickel into the bottom of the glass. They then quickly gulped the milk down to get the nickel. In order to understand and predict their behavior, Hondo did not have

B. F. Skinner, a well-known advocate of the behaviorist approach, is shown in the laboratory with the basic experimental apparatus named after him, the Skinner box.

to worry about what his children were thinking or feeling; it was easy to see that "nickel in glass" resulted in "drinking the milk."

This view is characteristic of the **behaviorist approach** that developed in the 1920s. John Watson, one of the first behaviorists, argued that the science of psychology must concern itself only with *observable* events. Watson pointed out that we cannot observe events such as thinking or feeling, nor can we directly observe "the mind." He believed, therefore, that psychologists should not try to explain behavior in terms of something that cannot be observed. Further, he argued that we do not need these "fuzzy" concepts to predict behavior. In the example of Hondo's children we saw that an event could be described by referring only to what could be observed: a stimulus (nickel in the glass) and a response (drinking the milk). Watson argued that we can describe human behavior in the same way, by focussing only on the observable stimulus and response.

In Chapter 6 we will discuss a famous experiment that helped Watson show the power of his behaviorist approach (Watson & Rayner, 1920). In that experiment he was able to predict and control an infant's responses, such as crying, by systematically manipulating observable aspects of the infant's environment.

The behaviorist approach was well received by many psychologists because it represented an approach to understanding behavior that could be directly tested and applied in many settings. One of the well-known advocates of this approach was B. F. Skinner, who is still an active researcher and writer. Skinner has applied the behavioristic approach in a number of different areas, from child-rearing to teaching pigeons to guide missiles (Skinner, 1960; see also Chapter 6).

While the behaviorist approach had many strong points, critics argued that it did not fully take into account the richness of human experience. After all, even though we cannot see a thought or a feeling, we know that people do think and experience emotions. Since these are important parts of the human experience, they should also be material for psychological investigations.

Psychoanalytic Psychology

While many would criticize behaviorism for being too simplistic, few would accuse psychoanalytic theory of the same thing. As behaviorism was being introduced in the United States, a Viennese physician named Sigmund Freud put the European scientific world in an uproar with his unorthodox views of human behavior. Freud, the founder of the **psychoanalytic approach** to psychology, not only suggested that much of human behavior is the result of thoughts, fears, and wishes, he also suggested that people are often unaware of these motivating forces, even though they have a strong effect on their behavior. Freud argued that many, if not most, of these thoughts and wishes result from our experiences during infancy and early childhood. He caused the greatest outcry of criticism when he suggested that infants have sexual fantasies about their parents.

Freud's ideas had a tremendous influence on psychology. Since his early work was aimed at explaining emotional disorders, psychoanalytic theory has played a central role in understanding and treating psychological disorders. We will see this influence in Chapters 13 and 14. Psychoanalytic theory has also been used to explain differences between people. In this role, as we will see in Chapter 12, psychoanalytic theory has been the basis for important advances in understanding personality.

While people no longer express shock and dismay at Freud's ideas, there is still a great deal of controversy about psychoanalytic theory. One of the criticisms of the approach has been that it takes a very dim view of human nature. According to Freud, the unconscious impulses that influence

behavior are often destructive and antisocial. Psychoanalytic theory paints a bleak picture of the individual as being caught in a struggle to control these destructive impulses.

Humanistic Approach

If Hondo had felt inclined to adopt a school of psychology, there is little doubt he would have been comfortable with the humanistic tradition. He strongly believed in the goodness of human nature. He often said that all people need is "half a chance" and they will "do good." In Luckenbach everyone could have their "half a chance." The ragged sign over the general store proclaimed this: "Everybody's Somebody in Luckenbach."

A number of psychologists objected to Freud's view that human beings are basically destructive beasts who are constantly fighting their negative impulses. In the 1950s the *humanistic* movement began. The main theme of the **humanistic approach** is that people are basically good. Instead of being driven by unconscious desires to destroy, people have free will, and, given the proper environment, they will strive to achieve positive social goals. As we will see in Chapter 12, the humanistic psychologists argued that each person is unique, and that psychologists should examine this individuality rather than lumping people into categories. The humanists also reject the behaviorist view that psychologists should only study observable stimuli and responses. Rather, they argue, it is their thoughts, desires, and feelings that make people unique.

SUBFIELDS OF PSYCHOLOGY

By the 1950s psychology had established itself as a major area for scientific study. The field had a rich history; it had developed methods for studying behavior; and it had a rapidly growing library of theory and research. Along with age came a wisdom that only experience can supply. Psychologists began to realize that the study of behavior was so broad that no single approach could be relied on to give the necessary answers to all the questions that were being raised. Each approach had merit, but it would take all of them to solve the puzzle of behavior. For this reason many psychologists stopped identifying with one school or approach to psychology and instead began to define areas where many approaches could be used. As a result, the branches of the psychology family tree took on a new look. They no longer bore the names of approaches to psychology in general; they took on the names of subfields of psychology (see Figure 1–1). The Directory of the American Psychological Association lists 350 subfields, and there are presently 40 divisions or societies (see Table 1–1) in the Association. Let us examine some of these areas to get a better understanding of the field of psychology and anticipate its future directions.

Physiological and Experimental Psychology

Hondo Crouch was a great swimmer during his college days. As a young boy he spent a great deal of time teaching himself to swim. How was he able to do this and achieve such splendid results? Swimming, like many other complex behaviors, involves many steps. Swimmers must learn the best way to move their arms and legs; they must develop their muscles; they must deal with their fear of the water; and they must be able to sense where their body is in relation to the water and to the direction

Figure 1–1
This psychology family tree shows the various subfields of psychology as they are reflected in course titles in most psychology departments. If you decide to pursue your interest in psychology after the introductory course, you will have many of these courses to choose from.

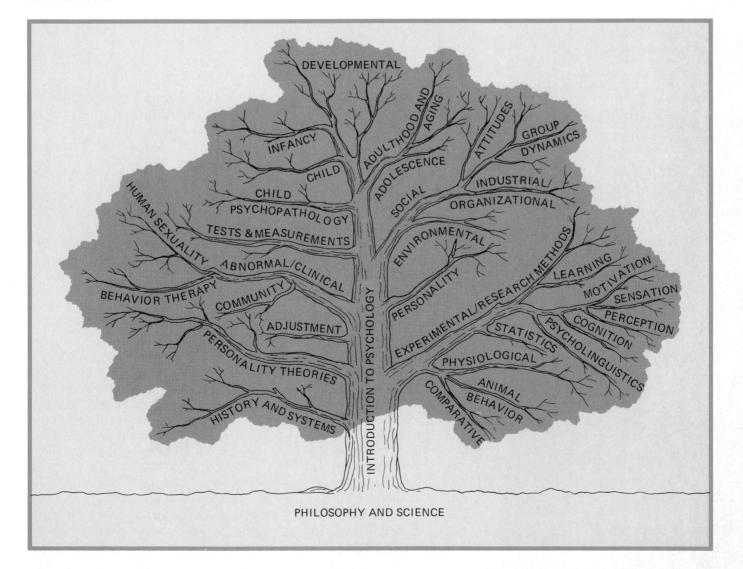

Table 1–1
Divisions of the American
Psychological Association*

Division Number	Division Name
1	Division of General Psychology
2	Division on the Teaching of Psychology
3	Division of Experimental Psychology
5	Division on Evaluation and Measurement
6	Division on Physiological and Comparative Psychology
7	Division on Developmental Psychology
8	The Society of Personality and Social Psychology—A Division of the APA
9	The Society for the Psychological Study of Social Issues—A Division of the APA
10	Division of Psychology and the Arts
12	Division of Clinical Psychology
13	Division of Consulting Psychology
14	The Society for Industrial and Organizational Psychology, Inc.—A Division of the APA
15	Division of Educational Psychology
16	Division of School Psychology
17	Division of Counseling Psychology
18	Division of Psychologists in Public Service
19	Division of Military Psychology
20	Division of Adult Development and Aging
21	The Society of Engineering Psychologists—A Division of the APA
22	Division of Rehabilitation Psychology
23	Division of Consumer Psychology
24	Division of Theoretical and Philosophical Psychology
25	Division for the Experimental Analysis of Behavior
26	Division of the History of Psychology
27	Division of Community Psychology
28	Division of Psychopharmacology
29	Division of Psychotherapy
30	Division of Psychological Hypnosis
31	Division of State Psychological Association Affairs
32	Division of Humanistic Psychology
33	Division on Mental Retardation
34	Division of Population and Environmental Psychology
35	Division of Psychology of Women
36	Psychologists Interested in Religious Issues (PIRI)—A Division of the APA
37	Division of Child, Youth, and Family Services
38	Division of Health Psychology
39	Division of Psychoanalysis
40	Division of Clinical Neuropsychology
41	Division of Psychology and Law
42	Division of Psychologists in Independent Practice

* There are no divisions 4 and 11.
Source: Reprinted by permission of the American Psychological Association.

If Hondo had adopted a school of psychology, there is little doubt he would have been comfortable with the humanistic tradition. The sign over Luckenbach's general store proclaims this: "Everybody's Somebody in Luckenbach."

they wish to move in. In short, swimming involves learning, memory, perception, motivation, and emotion. The subfields of physiological and experimental psychology are concerned with the scientific examination of these areas.

Physiological psychologists examine these areas by studying the neurobiological events that underlie them. They study the eyes, ears, and other organs that we use to sense our environment. They also investigate muscles and other structures that we use to respond to our environment. Another major concern is the brain, which coordinates information coming from sense organs and going to muscles. They carefully map the brain to determine the function of various parts. In addition, physiological psychologists probe the pathways that carry information to and from the brain.

Experimental psychology examines the behaviors and cognitions (thoughts) that are related to learning, memory, perception, motivation, and emotion. The name of this subfield is more a historical accident than an identifying characteristic of the field; as you will see, all the subfields of psychology are experimental in that each uses experimental methods

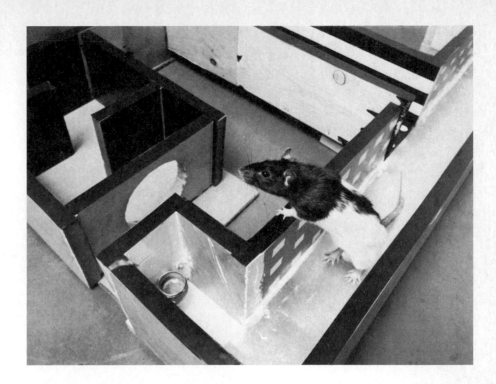

to investigate questions. However, experimental studies of perception and learning were some of the first in psychology, and therefore the subfield was called experimental psychology.

The areas studied by experimental psychologists are amazingly varied, as are the subjects used in these studies. Investigations examine the basic questions of how we see, hear, and feel pain. They study how people learn everything from simple tasks such as sitting upright to more complex things such as emotions and language. Experimental psychologists study both humans and animals. It is the experimental psychologists who brought to psychology the white rat, sometimes referred to as the mascot of the field. Experimental psychologists use animals to investigate a variety of issues, especially those involving learning, memory, and motivation. The use of animals in research allows psychologists to learn about animal behaviors that are important in their own right and to test new directions for human research.

The use of powerful manipulations and fine controls are two advantages of experimenting with animals even when the ultimate goal is to learn about human behavior. Psychologists can use animals to test drugs and other manipulations that might not be safe for humans. They can also control an animal's ancestry and its environment. These advantages are accompanied by the disadvantage best expressed in the question: Do the results hold true for humans? Ideally, this important question is answered in follow-up experiments on humans. In later chapters we will review many examples of animal research that have paved the way for new discoveries about human behavior.

During the heyday of behaviorism experimental psychologists concentrated almost exclusively on behavior. Today, however, they study cognitions as well as behaviors. In fact, a subgroup of experimental psychologists refer to themselves as **cognitive psychologists.** They are concerned with the mental events that intervene between stimuli and responses. Their goals are best understood by comparison with those of physiological psychology. Suppose physiological psychologists analyzed an Atari game of Space Invaders in the same way that they analyze humans. The photo on page 14 shows a home version of this popular video game. Its major components are (1) buttons, which send information into the system; (2) a TV,

Cognitive psychologists are concerned with mental events that intervene between stimuli and responses. In the Atari games, different programs cause different responses—for example, in the Space Invaders game, the program causes a cannon to shoot when a button is pressed. In the same way, we can make up our minds, or "program" our brains, to respond differently to the same stimuli.

which makes responses; (3) a computer, which coordinates information coming from the buttons and going to the TV; and (4) a Space Invaders program cartridge, which is one of many program cartridges used with the Atari system. Physiological psychologists would study the electronic components and the pathways between them.

In contrast, cognitive psychologists would analyze the computer events that took place between button pushes and TV responses. Different programs result in different events, so cognitive psychologists would concentrate on the programs. For example, the Space Invaders program causes a cannon to shoot when one button is pressed, while the Football program causes a football player to pass a ball when the same button is pressed. Cognitive psychologists would try to focus on how the programs caused the different responses. Similarly, we can make up our minds, or "program our brains," to respond differently to the same stimuli. We could make many different responses to this page of print, for example. Often we represent information in many forms during the course of making a response. For example, we might first represent this text as letters, then as words, and finally as a complete train of thought. Cognitive psychologists try to follow this flow and transformation of information that occurs between stimuli and responses.

As you can see, the subfields of physiological and experimental psychology are very large. Most psychologists in these areas are engaged in research at universities and colleges. Recently, however, more and more have been entering applied settings, where they use their knowledge to help solve a wide range of problems. As we will see later in this book, they have

Developmental psychologists study the
function of age on behavior.

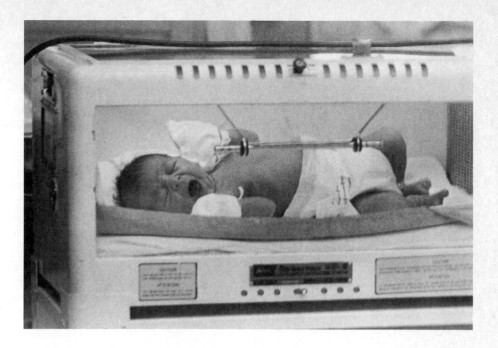

been involved in projects to restore sight to the partially blind and hearing
to the partially deaf; they have worked on finding the best methods for
teaching; and they are discovering new drugs and treatments to help people
with psychological disorders.

Developmental Psychology

One common gift that parents receive at baby showers is the Baby Book.
In this book they can record when their child first smiles, babbles, crawls,
talks, and walks. Many an anxious parent has worried, "Why isn't Johnny
smiling? Helen's baby smiled at 6 weeks." The subfield of **developmental
psychology** examines the function of age on behavior. Developmental psychologists are not only concerned with identifying the age at which people
should be performing various behaviors; they are also interested in how
events that occur at various ages affect behavior. For example, they study
the effects on later development of being born prematurely. They examine
how family changes (such as births of siblings, divorce, or death) influence
the child's development. As we will see in Chapter 9, developmental psychologists are also interested in the changes that take place in middle-
aged and elderly adults. Most developmental psychologists work in universities and colleges, although many are employed in hospitals, schools, and
day-care centers.

Social and Personality Psychology

In many respects Hondo was like all of us, and in other ways he was
different from any of us. Hondo loved the outdoors; he enjoyed being
the center of attention; he had strong attitudes about the way children
should be raised; and he was always willing to help someone in distress.
Most people liked Hondo, but some were irritated by his clowning.

As we examine the story of Hondo's life, many of us can picture ourselves
in similar situations and having similar feelings. In a sense, social psychology is concerned with similarities in people's behavior as they interact
with one another. **Social psychology** is the study of the way people are
affected by social situations. The field examines questions such as how
people form and change attitudes; how they form impressions about them-

selves and each other; why they are attracted to some people and repelled by others; and how being in a group affects their behaviors and beliefs. Social psychologists develop theories that explain why people in general behave as they do in various situations. Although most social psychologists work in university settings, there are many in industry, advertising agencies, political organizations, and hospitals. The research findings from social psychology have been used by lawyers to help in choosing sympathetic juries; by advertisers to plan advertising campaigns; by politicians to design political campaigns; and by negotiators involved in planning bargaining strategies in industry as well as internationally.

While social psychology is concerned with how most people act most of the time, investigators of **personality** are interested in individual differences. Personality psychologists focus on explaining and predicting the unique ways that people respond to their environment. They would, for example, be interested in why Hondo was always joking, while Shatzie, his wife, was serious most of the time. Personality psychologists have designed tests to measure and describe personalities, and they have developed theories to explain why people are different. Their work has been applied in business and the military to help channel the right people into the right jobs.

CAREERS IN PSYCHOLOGY

You can feel at home in a psychology class or be comfortable as a psychology major even if you are not planning to become a psychologist. Psychology classes and psychology majors consist of a good many students who have not yet decided on their career goals. Of those who have fixed goals, many have chosen careers in medicine, law, business, and education, as well as in psychology. Students with a B.A. in psychology find themselves well received in law schools, medical schools, and business schools. Harvard Business School, for example, accepts more psychology majors than students with any other single major, including undergraduate business majors. The diversity of interests served by psychology classes is reflected in the popularity of psychology. It is one of the most popular college majors in America, with about 75,000 psychology majors receiving B.A. degrees in the 1983–1984 school year.

Psychologists seeking jobs in colleges and universities already outnumber the available academic positions. In fact, colleges and universities employ only about 40 percent of people with advanced degrees in psychology (Stapp & Fulcher, 1983). But psychologists have many other job options, and the overall job opportunities in psychology appear very good (Cantrell, 1983). Woods (1976) did a survey for the American Psychological Association that looked into where psychologists are employed outside academia. The following are some excerpts from his list of job descriptions of psychologists in innovative roles:

Consultant to a Public Defender's Office

Employer description. I serve as a full-time consultant to the investigators and lawyers in the Public Defender's Office on matters relating to their clients. . . .

Job description. I am employed by the Community Mental Health Center and am placed in the Public Defender's Office. . . . My activities, which are diagnostic, evaluative, and consultative, are not innovative, but the setting in which I provide my services is a relatively new one for clinical psychologists.

Training. I have found my training in psychological diagnostics to be essential in performing my duties. Of course, training and experience in interviewing have also been essential.

Employment prospects. It seems to me that any large Public Defender's Office could provide more efficient service and enhance the services to defendants if a behavioral scientist with clinical training and experience were added to the staff. . . .

Psychologist in Accident Research

Employer description. The organization gathers and disseminates technical safety information on a nationwide basis.

Job description. The purpose of my job is to review accident literature, to design and execute original research, and to systematically evaluate accident countermeasure programs.

Training. The "traditional" degree is helpful, but I believe more of a "co-op" approach to graduate education is needed, that is, a program in which work in the real world

Clinical Psychology

When people find that you are taking courses in psychology, their first response is often, "Analyze me." Some may begin bringing their personal problems to you and asking for advice. Many people believe that all psychologists analyze and treat psychological disorders, and indeed, the subfield of clinical psychology has more psychologists than any other subfield.

Clinical psychology is dedicated to the diagnosis and treatment of emotional and behavioral disorders. Clinical psychologists are not medical doctors, but some of them work closely with *psychiatrists,* who are medical doctors specializing in psychological problems. Clinical psychologists who work closely with psychiatrists are often in private practice, in mental hospitals, or in mental health clinics. It is highly probable, for example, that clinical psychologists worked with Hondo's son, Kerry, after he was hospitalized. Clinical psychologists are also employed by probation offices, prisons, and institutions for the mentally retarded and physically handicapped. Clinical psychologists apply psychological principles, especially those related to motivation, emotions, and personality. Chapters 10, 11, and 12 will therefore set the stage for a sound introduction to clinical psychology in Chapters 13 (Abnormal Psychology) and 14 (Therapy).

is mixed with academic coursework.

Employment prospects.
There is definitely a job market for as many as 1,000 psychologists. They could be employed by indicating the cost benefit to employers of studying and reducing the tremendous losses caused by accidents, both on and off the job.

Communication Work Between People and Computers

Employer description. We are trying to identify design criteria to aid communication between a com-

puter and a layperson. . . . The Office of Naval Research has partially funded our efforts, but my major employer is the research center of a large computer manufacturer.

Job description. We are trying to find ways of making it easy for people in business to tell their problems to a computer and receive some help. We do experiments to investigate features of programming languages, to study how people specify procedures in natural English, and eventually to test our ideas about how a certain set of natural-language mechanisms could be used to provide an exciting, powerful system.

Training. A person should have training in "artificial intelligence," linguistics, and computer sciences in addition to the traditional degree.

Employment prospects. This field is certainly a potentially expandable job market for psychologists. Since costs in using computers are primarily labor costs, that is, labor for translating a user's problems into computer-compatible form, we can save tremendous sums of money by solving these problems. I suggest contacting in-

dustrial companies for funding or cooperative work.

All of these jobs are held by people with a Ph.D. in psychology. That doesn't mean, however, that you need a Ph.D. to get a good job. People holding bachelor's or master's degrees are hired at salaries comparable to other jobs at entry levels. They get jobs in many settings, including hospitals, mental health clinics, businesses, and government agencies. Their duties range from record keeping to direct-contact activities such as testing and training employees, patients, or clients.

Many people panicked when the academic job market for psychologists started to dry up. Thanks to the diversity and versatility of the field, however, people are beginning to find alternative careers in psychology. Employment opportunity is not the only reason for choosing any major, of course. But if you find that you love psychology, you will be happy to know that the chances of being gainfully employed as a psychologist are excellent.

Counseling and School Psychology

Counseling and school psychology are dedicated to helping people with social, educational, and job or career adjustments. Although most counseling psychologists work in schools, some assist with social and job adjustments in other settings, such as social work offices. Many psychological problems reveal themselves first in schools and homes. School psychologists work with parents and teachers to help individual students before their problems become serious. Another important part of their job is administering and interpreting intelligence, achievement, and vocational tests. Seeing a school psychologist is not necessarily a sign of a problem. Many of the best college students take full advantage of school psychologists for help with vocational planning. Students who are thinking about careers in counseling and school psychology will be especially interested in the clinical and developmental chapters of this book.

Engineering and Industrial Psychology

Hondo's world was a rather simple one. He ran his ranch on horseback or from his beloved pickup truck. He employed a ranch foreman and a few ranchmen, but each man often spent days working alone. The world in which most people live is not so simple. Many workers operate complicated machines that perform delicate and sometimes dangerous tasks. Most people work with groups, and each day they must deal with other workers and supervisors. The workplace can be a place of great stress and strain. Over the last two decades psychologists have entered business and industry to help reduce many of the problems that workers face.

Engineering psychology is concerned with making human interactions with tools and machines as comfortable and error-free as possible. In other words, they work on designing machines that will "fit" people. Engineering psychologists probably played an important role in designing the car you drive; they may have even designed the chair in which you are sitting. The space program employs many engineering psychologists to help design spacesuits, space capsules, and other equipment used by astronauts. Atomic power plants hire engineering psychologists to help design the best control panels for people who operate those plants. The atomic accident at Three

Engineering psychologists are concerned with making human interactions with tools and machines as comfortable and as error-free as possible.

Mile Island was caused in part because operators did not respond effectively when the problem first started. Engineering psychologists have been called in to reduce the chance of this happening again and to lower the overall probability of human error in power plants.

Industrial psychologists are concerned with selecting, training, and managing employees. People have come to expect not only good-paying jobs but also fulfilling ones. Matching people to jobs that they will learn well and enjoy doing is not only good for people, it is also good for business. Industrial psychologists know what Hondo proclaimed: Everyone is special in some way. An important part of an industrial psychologist's job is to make sure that a person's special talents are put to good use. Today psychologists have more knowledge to offer personnel offices than ever before, thanks to intensive investigations of people across the life span.

Other Subfields

The psychology family tree continues to grow. As our world changes and new problems arise, psychologists expand their focus of study to meet these challenges. This is definitely an exciting aspect of psychology; it is a dynamic science that is able to respond to the changing issues and demands of our modern world. **Environmental psychology** analyzes how behavior is influenced by environmental factors such as architecture, weather, space, crowding, noise, and pollution. The close relationship between environment and behavior can be appreciated by trying to imagine how Hondo's life would have differed had he lived outside the Texas ranch country. **Forensic psychology** concerns behaviors that relate to our legal system. Forensic psychologists work with judges and lawyers who are trying to improve the reliability of witnesses and of jury decisions. They consult also on the mental competency of accused people and on the possibilities for rehabilitation of convicted criminals. **Health psychology** is concerned with the influence of psychological variables on physical health. The subfield not only examines issues such as how stress affects the possibility of developing cancer or heart disease, but also concentrates on issues such as

Health psychology is concerned with the influence of psychological variables on physical health.

Figure 1–2

As can be seen here, most psychologists are engaged in research at universities and colleges, but recently more and more have been entering applied settings, where they use their knowledge to help solve a wide range of problems.

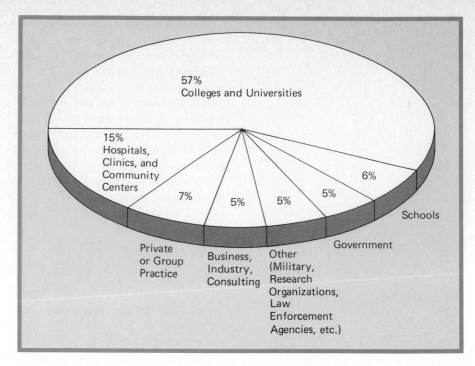

57%
Colleges and Universities

15%
Hospitals, Clinics, and Community Centers

7%

5%

5%

5%

6%

Schools

Private or Group Practice

Business, Industry, Consulting

Other (Military, Research Organizations, Law Enforcement Agencies, etc.)

Government

the factors that enhance the effectiveness of the physician-patient relationship. **Psychology of minorities** examines the behavior of people in minority groups. This subfield has emerged in response to such questions as: How important is it for minority children to have minority schoolteachers for role models? What hiring criteria will give minorities equal opportunities in the business world? What can we do to give minorities equal opportunities in the public school system? **Community psychology** is dedicated to promoting mental health at the community level. Community psychologists prevent and treat psychological problems by working to evaluate and improve community organizations. They get involved in public programs aimed at such problems as employing the handicapped, rehabilitating juvenile delinquents, and caring for the elderly. Investigators interested in **law and psychology** focus on the factors that influence jury verdicts, the way in which people determine what is just and unjust, and how the procedural aspects of a trial affect its outcome. These are just some of the

Figure 1–3

This figure shows a breakdown of the percent of psychologists engaged in work in each of the major subfields mentioned in the text.

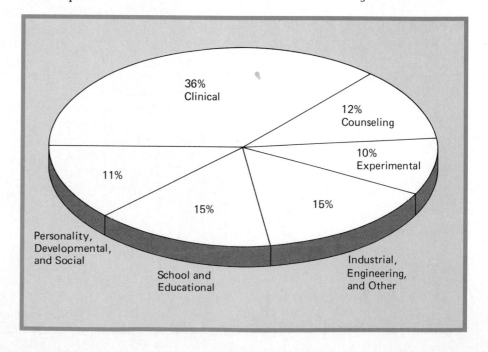

36%
Clinical

12%
Counseling

10%
Experimental

11%

15%

15%

Personality, Developmental, and Social

School and Educational

Industrial, Engineering, and Other

new branches on the psychology family tree. We will introduce others later in the book.

As you can see, there are many areas of psychology. Just because they are set off in subfields, you may get the impression that they are independent of one another. This is far from the case. In fact, the different areas of psychology are very closely related. Research and theory in any one area is important to psychologists in all the other areas. For example, an industrial psychologist must know how people learn (experimental psychology), what workers of different ages are capable of doing (developmental psychology), and the effects of job stress on an employee's emotions and behaviors (clinical psychology). Thus, in order to be a specialist, the psychologist must first acquire a general background in psychology.

RESEARCH METHODS IN PSYCHOLOGY

As you might expect, a field that is concerned with such a dazzling variety of issues has developed an equally diverse array of methods to study these issues. In general, the methods of psychology have been developed to help researchers determine what is happening and why it is happening. No single method can be crowned as the "best method"; each has its strengths and weaknesses. As we will see throughout this book, many methods may be employed to study the same problem.

There is nothing magical or mysterious about the methods of psychology. In a sense, all of us are psychologists. We watch other people, guess what they are thinking, and then test out our guesses. Hondo Crouch followed this procedure each time he went on stage. He reports looking over his audience before each show and deciding which jokes they would like. He would then test the correctness of his decisions by watching the audience's reactions to his chosen jokes.

Psychologists follow much the same procedure. They make guesses or **hypotheses** about how people will behave in certain situations. They might hypothesize, for instance, that people will remember notes in a melody better than notes in isolation. Such hypotheses are generally based on a theory. **Theories** are explanations about *why* behaviors occur. The example of remembering a melody better than isolated notes, for instance, could be based on the Gestalt theory that people respond to whole, organized patterns better than to separate elements. Psychologists test hypotheses in experiments. As we will see, there are many kinds of experiments that can be used to examine hypotheses or, in some cases, to help psychologists develop hypotheses.

In order to see how this process works, let us take an example that was important to Hondo and is still an issue today. Hondo believed that the best way to raise children was to give them a lot of freedom to make their own decisions. However, he was concerned about the effects that television had on his children and he did everything he could to discourage them from watching it. Today the effect of television on behavior, especially aggressive behavior, is an issue of hot debate. Many people believe that watching violence on television causes people to engage in aggressive actions. Some parents' organizations have called for boycotts of the products of companies that sponsor violent programs on television. On the other hand, there are many people who argue that TV violence does not cause people to act violently. Who is correct? How can psychologists find evidence to resolve this debate?

In Chapter 10 we will discuss in detail the research on this issue. In this chapter, therefore, we will not be concerned as much with the question of who is right; instead, we will simply examine the ways in which the answer can be found.

Case History

One way to look at this question might be to examine newspaper accounts and stories about the lives of some violent criminals. We would want to determine when they started committing violent acts and what television programs they watched. If this information were not available in written sources, we might want to interview people who knew these individuals to get the information. In this way, we could learn whether these people began acting violently at the same time they began watching many violent TV programs. A different approach would be to examine people's behaviors before and after a violent program was shown. For example, we might know that a very violent movie was going to be shown on nationwide television on the night of December 14. We could examine national crime statistics for the week before and the week after that date to see if there was an increase in violent crime. Both of these approaches are examples of the **case history.**

This method involves studying in depth a few individuals (sometimes only one) or the effects of a single event. The aim is to discover how a certain event affects behavior. The case history method has a number of strong points. It is a relatively easy way to collect a great deal of information in a short time. It examines people's behaviors in their natural surroundings. However, would you be convinced that watching television violence causes people to act aggressively if the case history studies described above reported a relationship between the two events?

Most people would not be convinced. Because the method uses only a few cases, we would not know whether the findings could be applied to everyone. For example, in the first study we looked at only a few violent criminals. The family and economic backgrounds of these people may have been very different from those of most other people. If this is the case, two conclusions are possible. First, TV violence may only affect people with these backgrounds. Second, these people's violent behavior may have been due to their backgrounds and may have had nothing to do with the TV programs they watched. In the second example, it is possible that the violent TV programs caused police to become more concerned about violent crime, which, in turn, caused them to detect and report more crimes. As you can see, it is very difficult to determine the relationship between events using the case history method. Therefore this method is generally used to help psychologists develop theories and hypotheses, while other methods are used to make clear tests of the hypotheses.

The Survey

One disadvantage of the case history method is that it focusses on only a few people; we learn a lot about a few people, but are unable to easily apply the results to a large population. One way around this problem is to design a questionnaire and give it to a large sample of people. In this way we can choose a sample that includes people from many different family and economic backgrounds. This is the **survey** method.

If we use this method to look at the effects of television violence, we could develop questions that ask people to describe how they behaved after seeing violent TV programs. Then we could have people from all over the country respond to our questionnaire. There are many advantages to surveys. First, we can collect a great deal of information from a large number of people. As we pointed out, we can use people from a number of different backgrounds and ages in our sample. Second, the survey allows

In the survey method, a questionnaire is designed and given to a large sample of people. Using this method it is possible to interview people from a number of different backgrounds and ages.

for flexibility, so that we can examine a number of questions at the same time. For example, in our questionnaire, besides asking people how they *behaved* after viewing violent TV programs, we might also ask questions about how they felt and what they thought after seeing these programs. Thus, in addition to finding out how they behaved, we could determine if bad feelings or hostile thoughts were associated with violent programs.

One problem with surveys is that people often do not remember their behavior in earlier settings. For example, could you tell someone what you did after lunch last Monday? Another problem is that people may slant their answers in order to make themselves look good. In the case of our survey, people might not want to admit that they acted aggressively. A related problem is that people may be responding to the **demand characteristics.** In many cases, people want to be "good" subjects and give experimenters the "right" answers. From the subject's point of view, the right answer is the one that the experimenter is looking for. Therefore the subject may watch the experimenter for cues to the "right" answer. For example, you might express very different attitudes toward violence on television to an experimenter from the "Committee to Ban Television Violence" than you would to an experimenter from the "Let's Put Murder Back in Television Committee."

In spite of these problems, surveys have important applications. For instance, Francis Worchel (1985) developed a survey questionnaire that has shed light on how counselors can help families cope with the stresses of having a child who is dying from cancer.

Naturalistic Observation

There is an old saying that goes, "If you want to know how many teeth are in a horse's mouth, count them." If we were to apply this saying to our question about television, the words might be changed to, "If we want to know how television affects people, go out and observe people after they have seen violent programs. **Naturalistic observation** is the research

Naturalistic observation involves studying people's reactions to naturally occurring events in natural settings. Here a psychologist observes parents and children interacting in a classroom.

method that involves studying people's reactions to naturally occurring events in natural settings. In order to use this method to study the effects of television, we could place hidden cameras to observe children at home and in school settings to see if they aggress after watching violent TV programs.

There are a number of advantages to this method of research. First, the data involve firsthand observations and do not rely on people's memories of events. Second, since people do not know they are being studied, there are few problems with people wanting to be "good" subjects and somehow doing what they believe the observer wants or expects them to do. Third, since people are being observed in their natural environment, we may feel confident that this is really the way they behave.

Despite these strong points, naturalistic observation has a number of drawbacks:

1. Results are difficult to verify because natural events seldom recur in exactly the same way.
2. Naturalistic observations are difficult to analyze precisely because *the amount or degree of a variable such as TV violence may vary considerably in one example.* The same program, for instance, might have parts ranging from moderately violent to very violent.
3. Naturalistic observations cannot establish cause-and-effect relationships. They can only establish **correlations,** which are measures of the extent to which variables change together. If two variables increase and decrease at the same time, they are *positively correlated.* Watching TV violence and behaving aggressively would be positively correlated if aggressive behavior increased after people watched more TV violence. Measures are *negatively correlated* when one increases while the other decreases. Watching TV violence and behaving aggressively would be negatively correlated if aggressive behavior decreased after people watched more TV violence.

The existence of a correlation does not necessarily indicate a cause-and-effect relationship. If researchers observed a positive correlation between watching TV violence and behaving aggressively, for example, they would be faced with three possible cause-and-effect relationships: (1) TV violence causes aggression; (2) aggressive behavior causes people to watch TV programs that have many violent sequences; and (3) neither factor causes the other, but rather, an additional factor, such as grumpiness, could be causing both. That is, grumpiness could cause people to act aggressively *and* to watch more TV violence. These three possibilities are always present when one observes correlations. Despite its drawbacks, however, naturalistic observation is an important research method, especially for coming up with ideas that can be tested in experiments.

The Experiment

When we originally posed our question, we wanted to know whether or not television violence *causes* people to act aggressively. The methods that we have discussed so far may give us clues about the cause-and-effect relationship between these two variables, but we have seen that they cannot definitely establish the cause. In order to determine what events actually cause certain behaviors, psychologists have used experiments.

An **experiment** is an investigation in which a researcher directly manipulates one variable while measuring the effects on some other variable. The manipulated variable is called the **independent variable;** the measured variable is called the **dependent variable.** In one experiment Liebert and Baron (1972) used TV aggression as an independent variable and play aggression as a dependent variable. Their goal was to test whether or not violent TV programs cause aggressive behavior. The subjects were boys and girls between the ages of 5 and 9 years. The experimenters assigned half the children to an experimental group in which children watched 3½ minutes of violence on TV (shooting and fighting). They assigned the other half to a control group in which children watched 3½ minutes of nonviolence on television (racing and high jumping). (A **control group** is made up of subjects who are treated exactly the same as the experimental group except that they are not exposed to the independent variable and thus serve as the basis for comparison.) The experimenters used special procedures to ensure that the two groups were equivalent before they were exposed to the TV programs. After watching TV, both groups had an opportunity to "help" or "hurt" a child playing in another room. The other child was actually an actor who was aiding the experimenters. The actor played a game that required turning a handle. Children in the experiment could "help" by pressing one button that supposedly made the handle

Exposure to violent television episodes, such as the scene from a cartoon shown here, may have behavioral consequences in children and adults.

easier to turn. They could "hurt" by pressing another button that supposedly made the handle hot and difficult to turn. The actor pretended to be helped or hurt, and the experimenter recorded the length of time that children in the experiment held down each button. Children who had watched violence on TV held down the "hurt" button more and the "help" button less than children who had watched nonviolence. These results suggest that violent TV programs *caused* experimental subjects to act more aggressively than control subjects.

Experimental reports rarely go into detail about how an experiment can test cause-and-effect relationships. The same reasoning would be given repeatedly if they did. Once you know the logic, however, you can read it "between the lines" in every experimental report. The argument can be spelled out for Liebert and Baron's experiment as follows:

The experimental and control conditions were identical except that one group watched violent TV programs and the other watched nonviolent ones. Since there was only one difference, this difference must have caused the greater aggression in the experimental group. In general terms, the argument is: Since the independent variable is the only difference, it must have caused any effects that were observed in the dependent measure.

Do you agree that Liebert and Baron's experimental and control conditions were identical except for the independent variable? Did the experimenters overlook any other variables that might have differed? Let's examine what Liebert and Baron did, or could have done, to control other variables.

Subject Differences and Randomization. One thing that can differ between experimental and control conditions is the subjects. They can differ in sex, personality, intelligence, and many other variables. Liebert and Baron controlled such subject differences by using random assignments of subjects to groups. This procedure, called **randomization,** ensures that each person has an equal chance of being assigned to each group. This procedure makes it highly probable that subject differences will be equally distributed between groups. One way to make random assignments is to draw names from a list. Put all subject names in a hat; mix them up; draw them blindly, one by one; assign the first draw and all odd-numbered draws to the experimental condition; and finally, assign the second draw and all even-numbered draws to the control condition. Randomization gave Liebert and Baron a basis for saying that their two groups were the same with respect to subject differences. Randomization sometimes fails to equate subjects, which is one reason why it is important to repeat experiments. It is very unlikely that experimental subjects will respond more aggressively in replications of this experiment if the original results were caused by a failure of randomization.

Subject Expectations and Placebos. We mentioned in our previous discussion of demand characteristics that people's expectations influence their behavior. Perhaps Liebert and Baron's experimental subjects thought that they were expected to be violent, for instance. The experimenters tried to equate such expectations. They did not tell subjects what they were testing until after the experiment. They gave all subjects the same instructions, and they involved all subjects in similar activities before the critical test. Still, one might argue that experimental subjects thought that they were expected to be violent since they had just viewed so much violence. A better control for demand characteristics is possible in drug studies. Experimenters can give both groups pills that look and taste the same. That way both groups can think that they are getting the same drug, when in fact only the experimental group gets a real drug. The control group gets a **placebo,** which is a look-alike drug substitute made from inactive materials.

Experimenter Bias and Double-Blind Control.   Rosenthal (1966) showed that an experimenter's bias can influence the outcome of an experiment. **Experimenter bias** is the expectation on the part of an experimenter that a subject will behave in a certain way. Perhaps Liebert and Baron were biased toward expecting experimental subjects to be more violent. Such a bias would be especially dangerous if the dependent measure had been experimenter ratings of violent behavior. Liebert and Baron reduced this danger by having a machine time the "hurt" and "help" responses. One might argue that some danger remained. The experimenters could have unconsciously communicated their expectations to subjects. They might have done this, for example, with facial expressions, gestures, and word selection.

Experimenter bias is controlled best when the experimenter does not know a subject's group assignment until after the experiment. This could have been done in Liebert and Baron's experiment. One experimenter could have controlled the films while another worked with the subjects. In this way, the one working with the subjects would not have to know which film was shown. Ideally, an experimenter should use a **double-blind control,** which is a procedure in which neither subject nor experimenter is aware of how the independent variable is being manipulated.

Strengths and Weaknesses of Experiments.   Liebert and Baron's experiment reveals advantages and disadvantages of experiments. Several strong points are as follows:

1. Experiments can establish cause-and-effect relationships, as we already mentioned. To do so, however, researchers must be sure that they vary only one thing at a time. They must guard against subject differences, subject expectations, and experimenter bias and other hidden differences between experimental and control conditions.
2. Experiments can be repeated by anyone who may wish to verify and extend them. You could get enough information from Liebert and Baron's original report, for instance, to replicate the experiment in detail.
3. Experiments can be used to analyze variables precisely because researchers can control the variables. They could, for instance, make all the TV programs in one experiment moderately violent and all the programs in another experiment very violent.

Experiments also have several weak points:

1. Subjects know that they are being studied, so they may put on a false front. They may, for instance, reduce aggression when they know that they are being observed.
2. Experimental controls sometimes make independent variables unrealistic. Liebert and Baron's experiment suffers from this problem, since 3½-minute segments might not represent normal TV programming or viewing time.
3. Experimental controls can also make dependent variables unrealistic. Critics of Liebert and Baron's study might wonder if pushing a "hurt" button really represents aggressive behavior. We are on solid ground if we conclude that watching violent sequences on television causes children to hold down a "hurt" button longer. We are on thin ice if we try to generalize beyond the experiment to say that violence in normal TV programming causes children to be more aggressive.

Some of these weaknesses can be overcome by moving experiments from laboratories to more natural settings. Liebert and Baron's study is an example of a **laboratory experiment,** which is done in a controlled environment

ETHICAL ISSUES IN RESEARCH

As we examine the exciting issues addressed by psychology and the methods used, it is easy to overlook an important participant in the effort to understand behavior: the subject in the experiments. Whether we use observational research or laboratory or field experimentation, a common element of these methods is that all involve observing subjects and most involve manipulating the conditions under which the subjects behave. Some research involves simply watching people interact under normal conditions such as in the grocery store. Other research involves making rather harmless manipulations such as the type of television program subjects watch. Still other research may entail more drastic manipulations that cause subjects to experience stress and fear. No research project should be undertaken unless the investigator determines that the issue being studied is important for advancing our understanding of behavior.

However, even if it has been determined that the issue is of importance and the results from the study will be of potential value, no investigator can ignore the rights and safety of the subjects involved in the study. The issue of ethics has long been a concern of psychologists. It is not confined to laboratory studies; it involves all methods. In 1973, and again in 1982, the American Psychological Association published ethical guidelines for psychological research. All research that is supported by U.S. government grants must be examined by a panel of qualified experts to ensure that the investigators follow ethical guidelines. In most universities and colleges investigators must submit their research proposals to "ethics committees" before conducting their studies. These committees evaluate the risk of the research and the safeguards, and may suggest alternative procedures. The question of ethics is clearly a difficult one. The ethical standards for research have become more strict over the last decade and researchers are continuing to develop new safeguards for their subjects. As you read about the studies presented in this book, you may wish to examine them in light of our discussion on ethics.

Numerous ethical issues have been identified and efforts have been instituted to deal with them. One of these issues is *invasion of privacy*. Whether we are merely observing people in their normal daily routine or taking controlled physiological measures in the laboratory, we are learning something about the subject; we are invading the privacy of that individual. In some cases, such as observing shoppers' behaviors, the invasion is mild and the behaviors that we examine are not sensitive ones. In other cases, however, we may be dealing with more sensitive issues (sexual behavior, prejudice) or even illegal behavior (stealing, gambling). But regardless of the content, we are intruding into areas that the individual may wish to remain private.

Given that research involves the gathering of information, how can we protect people's rights to privacy? In most studies, subjects' responses are kept *anonymous*; that is, their names or identity are not associated with their data. A second safeguard is that the data collected in studies are *not made public*. While a summary of the results of a study may be published, the public is not given access to individual responses. Finally, a policy of *informed consent* is followed in most cases. Subjects are not forced to answer any question, and they may withdraw from the experiment at any time. Whenever possible, subjects are told about the procedures to be used in the study before they volunteer. When the subjects are children or people in institutions, the study procedures are explained to a parent or guardian, who must give consent before the subject can take part in the study.

A second ethical issue involves *deception*. In some cases, it would destroy the value of the data if subjects knew *exactly* what the experimenter was studying or what events would occur in the study. For example, if Liebert and Baron (1972) had told subjects that they were interested in studying aggressive behavior, the subjects might have changed their behavior. In this case, the subjects might have become concerned about their own aggression and tried to change their behavior to "look good" to the experimenter. If this had happened, the experiment would not have yielded valid data about the effects of TV violence on behavior. However, the point remains that the experimenter was not truthful with the subjects.

The ethical rules of psychological research dictate that if deception must be used in research, the experimenter must explain this to the subject after the study is over. During this follow-up session, the experimenter reveals the true nature of the study, what issues were being investigated, and why deception was used. After subjects learn about

created for the experiment. In contrast, a **field experiment** is done in a more natural setting. Chapter 10 will discuss a field experiment on TV violence. Experimenters manipulated TV programming in a juvenile home setting, and they measured aggressive behavior in the same setting. Direct

the study, they are given the chance to demand that their data be destroyed and not be used by the experimenter.

A third ethical problem concerns the possible *harmful consequences* that people may suffer as a result of a study. In some psychological experiments people may be exposed to very stressful procedures. If we are interested in studying the effects of fear on helping behavior, we must develop severe enough experimental conditions to make subjects afraid. If our interest is to examine how well people perform under painfully noisy conditions, we must create this type of environment. In another area, we are learning today that the United States military conducted studies over 20 years ago in which soldiers were exposed to radiation. In cases like this, severe physical problems may result.

The issue of harmful consequences is a very difficult one to deal with. In some cases, other procedures that do not involve risk can be used. However, risk may sometimes be necessary in order to investigate the problem at hand. When such a situation arises, the first question to be asked is whether or not the potential benefits of the study are more important than the risks the subjects are exposed to. This is clearly a hard question to answer in some cases. There is no easy formula by which to frame an answer. If the decision is made to proceed with the study despite the risks, at least two steps must be followed. First, subjects must be informed of the risks *before* they volunteer to be in the study. Second, the experimenters must "follow up" and examine subjects for some time after the study to see if they are suffering harmful consequences.

Another ethical problem arises from the fact that subjects may learn something about themselves in the study. For example, subjects in the Liebert and Baron study may have discovered that their behavior is influenced by TV programs. We might argue that this is a valuable lesson for them to learn. However, we must also remember that the subjects did not enter the study wishing to learn about themselves; they may not want to know this information about themselves. And some subjects may be distressed by what they learn about themselves. There is no easy way to deal with this problem. It is important that experimenters be aware of this ethical issue and evaluate their procedures with it in mind.

As we wrestle with these difficult issues, we might be tempted to solve our dilemma by turning to a different population of subjects. Why not use animals rather than people when the experiment calls for particularly severe procedures that may involve pain, stress, or surgery? For some of the issues that psychologists wish to study, such as the solving of complex reasoning problems, the use of animals in place of humans is clearly not possible. However, in other cases, it may be possible and even necessary to use animals. But imply switching from humans to animals will not solve all our ethical problems.

Recently, there has been increasing concern about the treatment of animals used in research (Cunningham, 1983; Miller, 1984). This concern has centered on ensuring that the animals are housed in reasonably decent conditions and are not subjected to any unnecessary or prolonged pain or suffering. Just as committees have been set up to protect the rights of human subjects, so have they been established in many universities to oversee animal research. These committees, which often include a veterinarian, carefully review the housing and feeding of animals and the experimental procedures to be used in research. Most investigators have welcomed these committees. As one put it, "I don't believe that any of the animal rights activism has resulted in a change of investigators' attitudes towards animals because all the investigators I know are sensitive to the welfare of animals—that just makes good research sense" (Ross, 1984). As this investigator and others have pointed out, it is in the best interests of scientists to work with healthy, pain-free animals. Thus most committees established to protect animals have worked in cooperation with investigators. Besides focussing on the specifics of animal care, this increasing concern with animal rights has helped raise people's awareness of the ethical issues involved in the use of animals in experimentation.

Clearly, there are some tough ethical questions that must be addressed, whether the proposed research involves humans or animals as subjects. Concern for the rights of subjects is an ongoing issue that has had an important impact on research. In some cases, methods that were used 20 years ago are not allowed today. In addition, investigators are constantly searching for new ways to guard the rights and safety of their subjects.

manipulations of TV programming gave more control than one gets in naturalistic observations. Doing the experiment in an everyday setting made the independent and dependent variables more realistic. Such field experiments are becoming increasingly popular.

Research Methods: A Final Comment

As you can see, psychologists have developed a number of ways to study behavior. Each one has its strengths and its weaknesses. The experiment is the most widely used method because it allows for the greatest amount of control and enables investigators to determine cause-and-effect relationships. However, just as a carpenter cannot build a house with only one tool, neither can psychologists build an understanding of human behavior with only one method of research. Therefore all research methods are used, often to study the same issue. Imagine what a strong case for the effects of television researchers could make if they found the same results in a case history, a naturalistic observation, and an experiment. Thus the different research methods are often used to increase the credibility of results. Variety of method is also important because there are some events that can only be studied with certain methods. For example, you couldn't study reactions to natural disasters in the laboratory; you would have to use one of the other methods.

Thus no one method is perfect. There is a time and place for each one. The use of many different methods to study the same problem enables the investigator to build a convincing case.

We have concentrated on methods for collecting results. The Appendix to this book discusses closely related methods for analyzing results. It also gives suggested readings on collecting and analyzing behavioral data.

SUMMARY

1. **Psychology** is the scientific study of behavior and the applications gained from that knowledge. Its main goals are to clearly describe, predict, and explain behavior.

2. The most cited date for the birth of psychology is 1879, which is when Wundt set up the first psychological laboratory in Leipzig, Germany. Wundt and Titchener are credited with developing **structuralism,** which is concerned with identifying the elements of human experience and finding out how those elements combine to form thoughts and feelings.

3. **Functionalism** is concerned with the function of mental processes. This emphasis led to important applications in education and to the founding of educational psychology.

4. **Gestalt psychology** was based on the assumption that many experiences cannot be broken down into separate elements—they must be experienced as wholes, or *gestalts.* Gestalt psychologists worked at identifying these and other organizational laws of perception.

5. Watson claimed that we did not need such unobservable events as thinking or feeling to explain behavior. He said that behavior could be explained and predicted by focussing only on observable stimuli and responses, which is the basis of the **behaviorist approach** to psychology.

6. Sigmund Freud is the founder of the **psychoanalytic approach** to psychology, which focusses on unconscious motivations that control human behavior. Freud thought that many of these unconscious thoughts and wishes are the result of our experiences during infancy and early childhood.

7. The **humanistic approach** to psychology is based on the idea that people are basically good and, given the proper environment, will strive to achieve positive social goals.

8. By the 1950s psychology had established itself as a major area for scientific study. Since that time a number of subfields of psychology have developed, in which many of the approaches we have discussed are used. These subfields include the following: **physiological, experimental, cognitive, developmental, social, personality, clinical, counseling and school, engineering,** and **industrial psychology.** Some of the most recent subfields to develop are **environmental, forensic, health,** and **community psychology,** and **psychology of minorities.**

9. In psychological research scientists make **hypotheses** about how people will behave in certain situations. These hypotheses, which can be tested experimentally, are based on **theories,** which are explanations about *why* behaviors occur. A number of different re-

search methods were discussed, including **case history, survey, naturalistic observation,** and **experiment.**

10. An **experiment** is an investigation in which a researcher directly manipulates one variable while measuring the effects on some other variable. The manipulated variable is the **independent variable.** The **dependent variable** is measured to see the effects on it of the manipulation of the independent variable.

11. There are a number of other elements or variables in an experiment that must be carefully controlled. For example, **randomization** assures that subject differences will be equally distributed between the control group and the experimental group, and **double-blind controls** assure that **experimenter bias** cannot affect subjects or the researcher's perceptions of what occurs in the experiment.

Key Terms

analytic introspection
behaviorist approach
case history
clinical psychology
cognitive psychologists
community psychology
control group
correlations
demand characteristics
dependent variable
developmental psychology
double-blind control
engineering psychology
environmental psychology
experiment
experimental psychology
experimenter bias
field experiment
forensic psychology
functionalism

Gestalt
health psychology
humanistic approach
hypotheses
independent variable
industrial psychologists
laboratory experiment
law and psychology
naturalistic observations
personality
physiological psychologists
placebo
psychoanalytic approach
psychology of minorities
randomization
social psychology
structuralism
survey
theories

Suggested Readings

The following book is about Hondo Crouch:
PATTERSON, B. C. *Hondo, my father*. Austin, Tex.: Shoal Creek Publishers, 1979.

American Psychological Association. *A career in psychology*. This booklet outlines career opportunities and the training required in subfields of psychology. It can be obtained by writing the American Psychological Association, 1200 Seventeenth Street N.W., Washington, D.C. 20036.
Annual Review of Psychology. A separate book each year reviews recent literature in about twenty different areas of psychology. An excellent starting point for those who wish to get into the technical literature of psychology.
BRENNAN J. F. *History and systems of psychology*. Englewood Cliffs, N.J.: Prentice-Hall, 1982. Provides a solid foundation for understanding psychology's present and future by tracing its history and development.
MARX, M. H., & HILLIX, W. A. *Systems and theories in psychology*. New York: McGraw-Hill, 1979. Introduces students to classical and contemporary approaches to the science of psychology.
WATSON, R. I. *The great psychologists: From Aristotle to Freud*. Philadelphia: Lippincott, 1978. Traces the history of psychology through the works of those who shaped the field. Interesting reading for those who enjoy biographies.
WEGENER, B. (Ed.). *Social attitudes and psychophysical measurement*. Hillsdale, N.J: Erlbaum, 1982. Individual chapters by authorities not only give a solid foundation in psychological measurement procedures, but also relate those procedures to social applications.

TWO

BIOLOGY AND BEHAVIOR

gnes de Mille had been a believer and a fighter for more than sixty years. She had believed in her own talents as a ballet dancer and choreographer. She had believed in the traditional American form of ballet and the Agnes de Mille Heritage Dance Theater, which she had founded to promote that form. More recently she had believed that she would win the fight for financial support of her theater. She was prepared for a decisive battle in that fight on May 15, 1975: A lecture-dance concert was scheduled in which she, the lecturer, and a host of supporting cast members would determine whether her theater would live or die.

That evening, however, de Mille found herself in a more critical life-or-death battle. At 5:50 P.M., or perhaps shortly before that moment, a blood vessel in her brain gave way and blood gushed forth, tearing and compressing vital centers as it penetrated her brain's soft tissues. From then on, she was engaged in a battle for her own life.

What astonished de Mille most about her stroke was that it occurred without pain or any sensation that something had happened in her brain. She became aware of her unsuspected catastrophe when she tried to sign a contract for a new member of the cast and discovered that she couldn't write. "I can't write," she said quietly. "My hand won't work." She was encouraged to sit down, which she did. Her reports became more alarming. "I have no feeling in my right leg. I can't feel on the right side. Maybe we'd better have a doctor. This is very interesting.

This is curious. I'm cold." It was warm in the theater, and yet she was shivering. Someone told her that she was moving her hand and foot. "But I can't feel," she said. "Am I talking funny? I seem to be talking funny." A friend recalls that she did not panic. She seemed ready to deal with this as she had dealt with other crises in her life.

Fortunately, Dr. George Gorham arrived within minutes. De Mille said, "Please do something fast because I've got to be on the stage in one hour delivering a very difficult lecture, and I've never been late for anything in the theater in my life. Also, I must be bright."

He looked at her gently and said, "You won't be on the stage and you will be late." He then arranged for her to be carried to a waiting ambulance. De Mille had lost her battle for the dance theater, and she was in severe danger of losing the battle for her life. Her principal backers were no longer dancers and concert pianists. Now her supporting cast was her immediate family, close friends, and one of the world's finest medical teams, which included Dr. Gorham, who had responded so promptly to her emergency; Dr. Fred Plum, the neurologist-in-chief, who took charge of the case; and Dr. Caroline McCagg, a specialist in rehabilitation medicine.

De Mille was lucky to have arrived at New York Hospital quickly. She was lucky, too, because it was one of the three hospitals in the world that had computerized axial tomography, popularly called the CAT scanner. The availability of this X-ray device was good news because it would greatly improve the diagnosis of the extent of her stroke. But the pictures the CAT scanner produced were far from "good news." The blood that had been released took over an area as large as a walnut, and it was steadily growing. The doctors murmured, "This is speech, possibly sight." As the blot increased they said, "That is all speech and mobility." After seeing the pictures, the doctors prepared her husband, Walter Prude, for the worst: "There is blood in the spinal fluid, and that is usually fatal."

Her husband was not prepared for this. Fortunately, neither was she. "I will" became the instinctive force of her every moment. She never became discouraged during the difficult days following the stroke, even though her right side was paralyzed and she could neither see nor speak clearly. She simply blocked out doubt as she had learned to do in her work. This will to live gave the doctors the edge they needed to perform a modern "medical miracle." Over the next several months, teams of doctors and rehabilitation therapists worked to help her survive several smaller strokes and delicate surgery performed to remove a blood clot in a critical artery in her neck.

Her speech and sight improved quickly, but her sense of touch never returned to normal. It was as though a line had been drawn down the middle of her body and feeling had been cut off on the right side. Agnes de Mille described this condition as follows:

> We always know, in normal life, where our hands and feet are. We don't think about them consciously, but we know because there is an unceasing radar playback from every part of the body telling us, "This is there," "This is near," "This is not within reach," "This is painful," "This is comfortable," "This is hot!" "This is soft." We don't have to look and we don't have to be aware, we just know. Now I was without those signals, and I didn't know.
>
> I could feel motor impulses, and in a couple of weeks I learned how to know when I was opening and shutting my hand because I could differentiate the effort and I was generally right in my surmises. But if somebody took my hand and moved it for me and my eyes were shut, I had no idea where it was or if it had been touched at all. (de Mille, 1982, p. 57)

De Mille's physical therapy began in the hospital and continued after she returned home. As a dancer, she was accustomed to physical discipline. She was therefore able to handle the strenuous therapy. She worked especially hard after one therapist said that she would never again rise on her toes to do rélévés onto full point (a ballet step). Two months later she was doing four rélévés and in six months she was doing eight.

At her husband's urging, Agnes tried very hard to adjust her mind to a slower pace. It was impossible for her to lie idle, however, and she instead accepted a professional job. Lucia Chase and Oliver Smith of the American Ballet Theatre organized a gala in her honor, which was held at Lincoln Center in New York and featured an entire evening of her works. She conducted rehearsals with the verve for which she was famous, and the gala was a hit. She received many invitations during the months that followed.

One invitation she could not refuse was from President Gerald Ford to attend the ceremonies at which Martha Graham would receive the Medal of Freedom.

She watched proudly as her fellow dancer received the award. But that night, following the ceremonies, she awoke because she was not feeling well. A hotel doctor assured her that it was nothing more than indigestion. Agnes, who had been careful about what she ate and drank, believed that her condition was more serious. Still she decided to return to New York. By 5 P.M. the next day she was on the phone to Dr. Gorham. He met her at the New York Hospital emergency ward and took a cardiogram.

"Wow!" he said. "You're having a coronary. You're going into intensive care this minute.''

Instruments sensed each heartbeat and breath for the next four days. She recovered with great speed, however, and seventeen days after the incident had occurred, she went home.

In the meantime, she missed the final rehearsals and the performance of her ballet *Rodeo* by the Robert Joffrey Company. The performance was well received, which greatly pleased her. In fact, this triumph gave her an idea. She approached Robert Joffrey about doing her *Conversations about the Dance*, the lecture-dance concert that had been interrupted by the original stroke. He agreed.

Her husband was understandably con-cerned about the medical risks of going on stage. De Mille proceeded cautiously, and she consulted with her physicians. Both Gorham and Plum gave their approval as long as she felt up to it. De Mille wanted very much to do this, and she decided to go ahead with her plans for the performance.

The performance was a success. At the end, de Mille threw out both hands, extended and open, to the audience. Caroline McCagg, her rehabilitation therapist, burst into tears, for she knew that Agnes had never used her right arm since the stroke. Dr. Plum, who also attended this performance, later spoke of the example set by Agnes de Mille: "Those who can learn from and follow it will enrich their own lives as Agnes de Mille has enriched hers and, by the radiance of her spirit, mine.''

BEHAVIORAL NEUROSCIENCE

Agnes de Mille's struggle for life raises important questions: How did the doctors know that her stroke threatened her speech, sight, and mobility? Why did it destroy her sense of touch only on her right side? Such questions are the concern of *behavioral neuroscientists*, who study the biological underpinnings of behavior. We will address these questions in the second half of this chapter. In the first half we will examine the brain's basic properties. The brain is part of a pervasive system, the *nervous system*, which monitors our outside world, controls our movements, learns, remembers, and generally controls all of our behavior.

The nervous system works in harmony with the *endocrine system*, which controls body chemistry. Some of de Mille's symptoms may have been related to chemical changes. In our discussion of the endocrine system, we will consider the possibility that her stroke triggered a chain reaction of events in her body's chemistry.

De Mille's struggle brings to mind the many ways that each of us depends on our body. Even a healthy body can impose limitations: A 5 foot, 7 inch male who weighs 147 pounds will probably not be a professional football player, for example. The last section of this chapter discusses how we inherited our body from our parents. That is, it reviews *genetics*, which is the study of how traits are passed on from parent to child.

The first section will discuss the brain in the context of a general overview of the nervous system. Without necessarily denying differences between brains and machines (see Koestler, 1967), neuroscientists analyze brains the way engineers analyze machines. *Neuroanatomists* describe structural elements of the brain and how they are arranged. *Neurophysiologists* study how the parts function. We will describe both structure and function of the nervous system's specialized cells and of the nervous system's major anatomical subdivisions.

NEURONS: BASIC UNITS OF THE NERVOUS SYSTEM

After her triumphant lecture-dance concert, de Mille willfully extended her right arm to the audience, something she previously had been unable to do. How did her brain initiate and control this miraculous movement? We begin our search for an explanation by exploring the brain's basic components, **neurons,** which are cells that are specialized to send and receive information.

Our brain contains between 100 and 200 billion neurons. As shown in Figure 2–1, they are similar to all other cells in that they have a *cell nucleus* within a *cell body*, surrounded by a *cell membrane*. Unlike other cells, however, neurons have tiny fibers extending out from their bodies that allow them to communicate with other cells. Many short branches called **dendrites** receive messages from surrounding cells and carry them to the cell bodies. A single long extension called an **axon** carries messages away from the cell bodies toward terminal branches that reach out to many other cells. Most axons are one or two inches long, but some are much shorter or longer. For example, many axons in the brain are only a fraction of an inch. In contrast, some are several feet long, such as the axon that reaches from the spinal cord to the toe in the giraffe. Some axons have a fatty covering called a **myelin sheath,** which is pinched in at intervals. Neural messages travel faster on myelinated axons because the messages skip from

Figure 2-1
Drawing and photographs of some typical neurons.

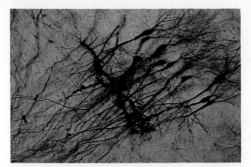

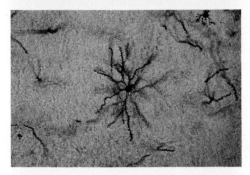

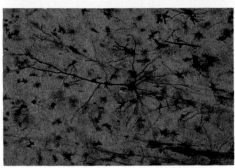

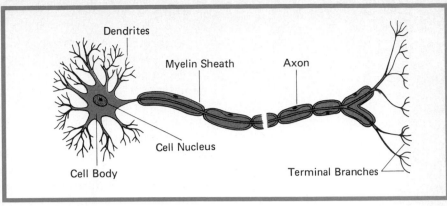

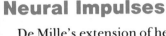

Dendrites

Myelin Sheath   Axon

Cell Nucleus

Cell Body   Terminal Branches

one pinched spot to the next. Let's look first at what neural messages are, and then discuss the way they are transmitted.

Neural Impulses

De Mille's extension of her right arm depended on a complex communication system operating inside her nervous system. The arm movement began with activity in one or more neurons in the form of a neural impulse or message, spread methodically through a network of neurons, and ended with well-coordinated muscle movements. Understanding neural impulses is the key to understanding the language used within the nervous system.

Neurons "speak" a simple language, consisting of an "off-on" code. A neuron is "off" at all times, except during neural impulses. During the "off" or *resting state*, a neuron has an electric tension, or **membrane potential,** existing between the cell's inside and outside environments. The potential is caused by an attraction that exists between negatively and positively charged particles, or *ions*. During the resting state, there are more positively charged ions outside the cell, and more negatively charged ions inside the cell. This resting state of tension is sometimes called a state of **polarization.**

Correspondingly, the "on" state, or neural impulse, is called **depolarization.** It happens when the cell membrane momentarily opens to positive sodium ions, causing the charge inside the cell to go from negative to positive relative to the outside. When the charge reaches the critical value shown in Figure 2–2, the membrane closes to sodium ions, and positive potassium ions are pumped out, bringing the charge back to the resting level.

As soon as the firing process ends in one spot on a neuron, it starts at a neighboring spot, spreading the impulse down the entire length of the neuron. In cells with large myelinated axons, the neural impulses travel

Figure 2-2
Neural impulses occur when a cell membrane momentarily changes. The inside of the neuron goes from negative to positive with respect to the outside when the membrane changes. The graph above shows the magnitude and duration of the voltage changes. (Adapted from Restak, 1984, p. 39)

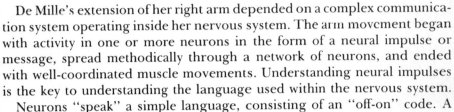

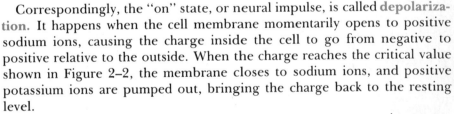

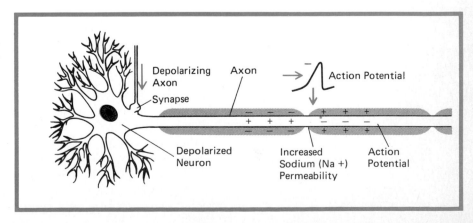

Depolarizing Axon   Axon   Action Potential

Synapse

Depolarized Neuron   Increased Sodium (Na +) Permeability   Action Potential

at speeds of nearly 400 feet per second. Small axons without myelin sheaths carry impulses as slowly as 3 feet per second. When neural impulses reach the end of an axon, they are sent on to other neurons.

This off-on firing process can happen spontaneously, but it is usually triggered by impulses from other neurons. The interaction is what spreads neural messages through the nervous system. Sending messages from one neuron to another depends on both the state of the receiving cell and the strength of the incoming message or stimulation.

Cells are not always responsive. When a cell fires once, it cannot fire again for about 1 millisecond. After this **absolute refractory period,** a cell enters a **relative refractory period** for a few milliseconds, during which time it fires only in response to a very strong impulse.

An incoming impulse must be above a minimum level or threshold of intensity or else a cell will not fire. If the intensity is too low, the membrane will not open up to sodium. Cell thresholds are sometimes compared to triggers on a gun. You must pull a trigger hard enough or a gun won't fire. If you pull a trigger even harder, however, the bullet will not travel any faster or any farther. In the same way, cell firing is an all-or-none action. No response occurs for stimuli below the threshold level; a full response occurs for stimuli at or above the cell threshold as long as the receiving cell is ready to fire. A neuron sends different messages, not by changing the strength of its response, but by changing the *rate* of its response. Stronger stimuli are indicated by faster firing rates.

Synaptic Transmission

We have seen how an impulse moves down an axon of one cell; this is called axonal transmission. **Synaptic transmission** occurs as the impulse moves from one neuron to another. It is called synaptic because a junction between two neurons is called a **synapse.** As de Mille spoke her concluding lines and extended both arms to the audience, she created messages in her nervous system that darted through millions of synapses. Let's look at just one of them to see how it works.

Each synapse has five parts: (1) the **axon terminal,** a tiny knob at the end of an axon's terminal branch; (2) the dendrite of the receiving cell; (3) the **synaptic space,** a very small gap between the axon terminal of one cell and the dendrite of the next cell; (4) the **synaptic vesicles,** tiny oval sacs on the axon terminal filled with a chemical transmitter substance; and (5) the **receptor sites** on the dendrite that receive the chemical transmitter. In most neurons, when an impulse reaches an axon terminal, the synaptic vesicles release a chemical that travels across the synaptic space to a dendrite on a receiving neuron (see Figure 2–3).

Chemical Transmitters. Scientists have learned within the last sixty years that the nervous system contains many kinds of **chemical transmitters.** All carry messages between neurons, but different kinds of chemical transmitters carry different messages. Some excite neurons (that is, they cause the receiving neuron to fire); others inhibit neurons (that is, they keep the receiving neuron from firing). Some transmitters shout loudly and call for a fast response; others speak softly and influence neurons slowly but surely.

The most common transmitter is **acetylcholine (ACh).** Synapses using ACh usually transmit strong, fast-acting, excitatory messages. After ACh delivers its message, it is broken down so that it is prevented from activating the receiving neuron again. ACh components are then transported back to the axon terminal, reassembled, and stored again in the synaptic vesicles.

Research on ACh has led to important applications, including a better understanding of such diseases as myasthenia gravis, a deadly disease in which synaptic transmission fatigues rapidly, preventing normal movement

Figure 2-3
Synaptic transmission occurs when a neurotransmitter carries a neural impulse from the axon of one neuron to the dendrites of another. (Adapted from Restak, 1984, p. 37)

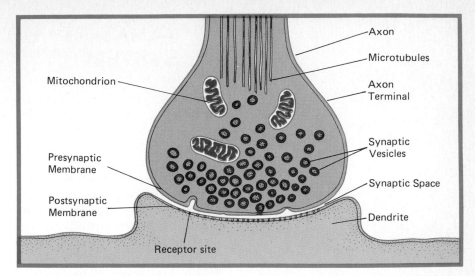

and breathing. Botulism, another deadly disease, works by blocking the release of ACh, which results in paralysis. On the other hand, if too much ACh builds up in the synaptic space, which is the effect of certain poisons (such as the venom of the black widow spider), the neuron can no longer respond to it, again causing paralysis and, in extreme cases, death.

Another important kind of transmitter is a class of substances known as **catecholamines.** Synapsis using catecholamines typically transmits slow-acting, inhibitory messages. Unlike ACh, catecholamines are not broken down after they deliver their message. They are cleared out through a powerful transport system that returns them to synaptic vesicles. This process keeps the catecholamines from activating the receiving neuron again after their message is delivered.

Research on catecholamines has led to important applications, including a better understanding of mental disorders and of commonly used drugs. We now know, for example, that cocaine works by blocking the reabsorption process of catecholamines. Cocaine is used medically to render a local area insensitive to pain. It is also misused by some as a recreational drug. Unsupervised use of cocaine can be dangerous because it can have toxic effects, including dizziness, convulsions, and drastic drops in blood pressure. Popular amphetamines or "pep pills" (such as Benzedrine and Dexedrine) not only block the reabsorption of catecholamines, they also produce an additional chemical response leading to a general state of arousal. Their unsupervised usage is also quite dangerous, especially for people with high blood pressure or women in the early stages of pregnancy.

Still another type of transmitter has a chemical structure similar to opium and its derivatives, morphine and heroin. Transmitters with this property are known as **endorphins,** a word meaning "endogenous morphine." There is a variety of this kind of transmitter including the frequently studied **enkephalins** (Hughes, 1975). This name comes from a Greek word meaning "in the head." Researchers had hoped that endorphins would be useful as nonaddictive painkillers. Although research did not support this hypothesis, it did increase our understanding of both pain perception and addiction (Restak, 1984). This very active area of research also promises to enhance our understanding of emotions, since neurons containing endorphins are concentrated in the areas known to influence emotions (Bloom, Lagerson, & Hofstadter, 1985).

Individual neurons never operate in isolation. Neurons are subsystems whose actions are integrated to form larger subsystems, which in turn are coordinated to form still larger and more complex systems.

In the next section, we will consider some of the major anatomical subdivisions of the nervous system, a major coordinating system in the body.

ANATOMY OF THE NERVOUS SYSTEM

Have you ever tried to place a long distance call on a holiday only to find the lines jammed for hours on end? Telephone operators cannot avoid telephone traffic jams on holidays, even with the help of computers. Yet the brain avoids neural traffic jams, even though "traffic" is much heavier in the nervous system than it is in the Bell System. Consider the neural activity taking place when de Mille threw out both hands to the audience at the end of her performance in *Conversations about the Dance*. Let's compare a single message sent between two neurons at that moment with a single phone call between two houses. De Mille's simple gesture produced more "traffic" than does the telephone system on the busiest holidays. The nervous system is more efficient because of its highly organized structure. In this section we will discuss that structure by analyzing major components of the nervous system.

We will necessarily introduce many new terms. The best way to learn them is not as a random list, but as an organized set of interrelated parts. Since the interrelationships can be hard to keep track of at first, Table 2–1 presents an overview of the contrasts between major components. It gives both structural and functional characteristics, because it is useful to learn how these two aspects correspond to each other. For the same reason, both structure and function are discussed in this and the next section. We will begin our discussion with the brain, the master controller.

The Brain

Dr. Plum knew what patterns to expect when he looked at the CAT scan taken following de Mille's stroke because he knew the relationship between brain structures and functions. Most of us will not treat stroke patients in the near future, so we don't need to learn brain anatomy in detail. Many of you will continue to study psychology, however, and you will find a basic understanding of brain structures invaluable in your studies.

The human brain is about three pounds of soft, spongy, pinkish-gray nerve tissue, made up of billions of neurons. In this section we will discuss divisions and subdivisions of groups of these neurons and the ways in which they are connected. Divisions can be identified on the basis of both structure and function. Here we will focus on structural divisions. It is easiest to see structural divisions in a developing human embryo, where the neural tube is divided into three cores arranged in a row, with one near the bottom (the hindbrain), one in the middle (the midbrain), and one near the top (the forebrain).

Hindbrain. The part of the brain that develops from the bottom core in the embryonic neural tube is called the **hindbrain.** It is shown in Figure 2–4 (p. 42) along with its three main components:

1. The lowest part of the hindbrain is the **medulla,** a slender tube no larger than your finger. It houses nerve centers that control breathing, heartbeat, and posture. For this reason, even slight damage to the medulla could be fatal.
2. Above the medulla is the **pons,** a broader tube formed by a massive cable of nerve fibers. It connects the medulla to the midbrain. If this cable were damaged, you might develop a sleep disorder similar to the "restless-leg" syndrome, which would result in thrashing about during sleep to the point where you would repeatedly wake yourself. This effect on movement makes sense when you consider the third

The human brain is about 3 pounds of soft, spongy, pinkish-gray nerve tissue, made up of billions of neurons.

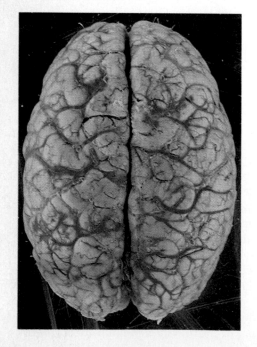

Table 2–1
Overview of Endocrine and Nervous Systems

Contrasts between Subdivisions	Structural or Anatomical Characteristics	Functional or Physiological Characteristics
Endocrine System **vs.**	A system of internal organs or glands that secrete chemical messengers directly into the bloodsteam	Has slow-acting, long-duration effects on the integration and regulation of body activity
Nervous System	A highly organized system of nerve tissue that transmits electrochemical messengers between cells	Integrates and regulates body activity
Central Nervous System **vs.**	Nerve tissue within the brain and spinal cord	Collects sensory information about our environment and controls body activity
Peripheral Nervous System	Nerve tissue outside the brain and spinal cord that connects those structures with sense organs, muscles, and glands	Provides pathways for incoming sensory information about the environment and for outgoing commands that control bodily activities
Sensory Portion of Nervous System **vs.**	Central and peripheral nerve tissue involved in collecting and analyzing information from specialized receptors such as eyes and ears	Reports and analyzes the nature of conditions around our body
Motor Portion of Nervous System	Central and peripheral nerve tissue involved in controlling muscles	Maintains body posture and makes the body move effectively as a whole
Voluntary Portion of Motor Subdivision **vs.**	Central and peripheral nerve tissue connected with skeletal muscles	Controls body posture and movement, often (but not always) with voluntary control
Autonomic Nervous System or Involuntary Portion of Motor Subdivision	Central and peripheral nerve tissue connected with muscles of internal organs and with glands	Controls internal organs and glands, often (but not always) without voluntary control
Sympathetic Division of Autonomic Nervous System **vs.**	Contains chiefly fibers that activate their targets to use energy	Prepares our body for action
Parasympathetic Division of Autonomic Nervous System	Contains chiefly fibers that cause their targets to burn less energy	Opposes and compensates for sympathetic effects allowing body to relax

hindbrain component, which is one of the units tied into the massive pons cells.

3. The third part of the hindbrain is the **cerebellum,** which looks like two wrinkled hemispheres strapped onto the back of the pons. It coordinates the force, range, and rate of body movements. If your cerebellum were injured or even destroyed, you would still enjoy all the sensations of the world around you (such as sights, sounds, and smells), but you would lose muscular tone, strength, and coordination.

Midbrain. Above the pons and cerebellum is a still wider tube, the **midbrain,** which develops from the middle core of the embryo brain. So many vital nerve tracts run up and down it that you would face unconsciousness, if not death, if your midbrain were damaged. The core of the midbrain

Figure 2-4
Hindbrain, midbrain, and forebrain.

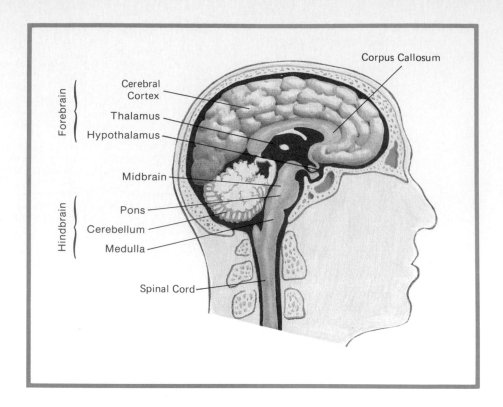

Forebrain

Corpus Callosum

Cerebral Cortex

Thalamus

Hypothalamus

Midbrain

Pons

Cerebellum

Medulla

Hindbrain

Spinal Cord

contains the *reticular formation*, which seems to regulate the strength of responses in surrounding brain areas. The midbrain and hindbrain are together referred to as the **brainstem.**

Forebrain. The rest of the brain develops from the top core of the embryo brain and is called the **forebrain.** In Figure 2–4 the three main components of the forebrain are highlighted.

1. Directly over the brainstem, in the central core of the forebrain, lies the **hypothalamus.** It includes several centers, some of which control body temperature and the rate at which you burn fat and carbohydrates. Since the hypothalamus influences these and other body maintenance functions, injury could be disastrous. Damage to your hypothalamus could hinder your bowel movements, urinary output, sweating, alertness, and reaction to pleasure and pain. The role of the hypothalamus in eating is described in more detail in Chapter 10.

2. Above the hypothalamus are two egg-shaped structures called the **thalamus.** It is often called a relay station, because sensory pathways from all over the body pass through it. Brain relay stations, including the thalamus, modify incoming information by integrating it with information coming from other parts of the body. Injury to the thalamus would distort your sensations of the world around you.

3. Mushrooming out from the brainstem are two wrinkled hemispheres called the **cerebral cortex,** or **cerebrum.** This is the crown jewel of our brain, accounting for about 80 percent of the brain's weight. Among other functions, it governs our most advanced human capabilities, including abstract reasoning and speech. It is more highly developed in humans than in other animals, as shown in Figure 2–5. The effects of injury to the cerebrum depend on which area is injured. De Mille's stroke affected areas related to speech. We will examine those effects shortly when we examine the speech center and other areas in more detail. But first let's point out some landmarks for our discussion.

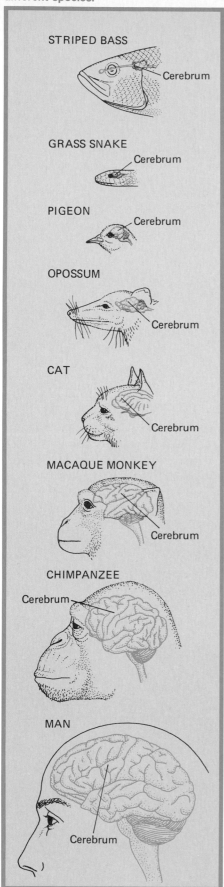

STRIPED BASS
— Cerebrum

GRASS SNAKE
— Cerebrum

PIGEON
— Cerebrum

OPOSSUM
— Cerebrum

CAT
— Cerebrum

MACAQUE MONKEY
— Cerebrum

CHIMPANZEE
Cerebrum —

MAN
— Cerebrum

The cerebrum is divided into left and right *cerebral hemispheres* which are connected by a large cable of nerve fibers called the **corpus callosum.** Figure 2–6 shows a side view of the cerebral hemispheres. Three deep grooves, or *fissures*, are labeled, as are four well-defined areas called *lobes*. The fissures are: (1) the **longitudinal fissure,** which separates the two hemispheres; (2) the *lateral fissure*, or **fissure of Sylvius,** which, if you view the figure as a boxing glove, defines the thumb of the glove; and (3) the *central fissure*, or **fissure of Rolando,** which runs across the knuckle area of our imaginary boxing glove.

These fissures separate each hemisphere into four lobes. The cortex in front of the central fissure and above the lateral fissure makes up the **frontal lobe.** It receives sensory impulses after they have been processed by other lobes, and it sends out commands to muscles to make voluntary movements. The **occipital lobe** is the hindmost lobe. This lobe receives visual impulses from the eyes. The **parietal lobe** extends back from the central fissure to the occipital lobe and responds to touch, pain, and temperature. Finally, the **temporal lobe** is below the lateral fissure and in front of the occipital lobe. (It is the thumb of our imaginary boxing glove.) The temporal lobe receives sound and smell impulses and has centers that control speech.

There is a band of cerebral cortex at the top of the head, on either side of the central fissure, that controls sensory and motor responses. The **motor cortex,** which is directly in front of the central fissure, controls motor responses of the body. The **somatosensory cortex,** which is directly behind the central fissure, controls sensory responses of the body.

We owe much of what we know about the motor and somatosensory cortexes to the research of Wilder Penfield, a Canadian neurosurgeon (Penfield & Rasmussen, 1950). He determined which parts of these cortexes affect which parts of the body. Penfield did his research while surgically treating epilepsy. His technique allowed the patient to remain awake and alert during the operation. Penfield then was able to "map" areas of the cortex by stimulating a certain part and recording the patient's response.

Figure 2–6

Side view of a cerebral hemisphere, showing the various lobes and fissures.

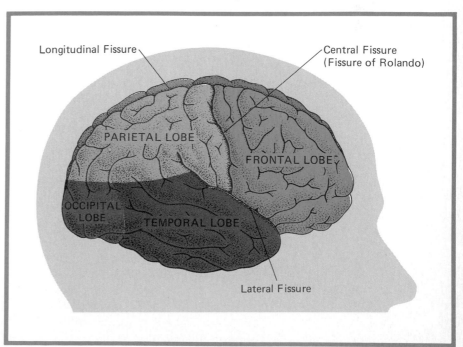

Longitudinal Fissure

Central Fissure
(Fissure of Rolando)

PARIETAL LOBE

FRONTAL LOBE

OCCIPITAL LOBE

TEMPORAL LOBE

Lateral Fissure

CLOSE-UP ON NOBEL PRIZE-WINNING RESEARCH

Roger Sperry, 68, of the California Institute of Technology, won half of the 1981 Nobel Prize in Medicine for his pioneering brain research, which revealed the separate functions of the left and right hemispheres of the cerebrum. These two halves of the brain usually share information across the *corpus callosum*, a network of millions of nerve fibers. This sharing makes it difficult to determine what each half does. Sperry began his research some thirty years ago by cutting the link between the two hemispheres in test animals. His most revealing experiments came later when humans received the same surgery to reduce epileptic seizures, which can spread across the corpus callosum. After this operation, patients are said to have a *split brain*, and they function well in their everyday lives. Sperry discovered with special tests, however, that split-brain patients often function with each hemisphere unaware of what the other is doing. Sperry therefore studied split-brain patients to find out the way each hemisphere functions on its own (Sperry, 1970).

Sperry's experiments took advantage of the fact that each side of the brain services the opposite side of the body. The right hemisphere, for example, receives touch sensations from the left hand and it moves the left hand. Only the right hemisphere receives information, therefore, when objects are placed in the left hand of split-brain patients who are blindfolded. The results were fascinating when Sperry did this experiment with a comb, toothbrush, key case, and other familiar objects. The patients showed how the objects are used by gesturing with their left hand. But they could not *say* how the objects are used and they had no idea of what their left hand was doing. The

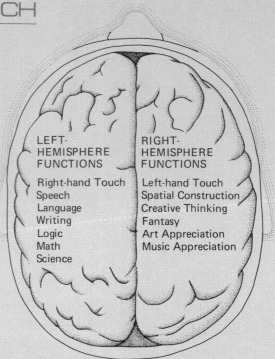

LEFT-HEMISPHERE FUNCTIONS	RIGHT-HEMISPHERE FUNCTIONS
Right-hand Touch	Left-hand Touch
Speech	Spatial Construction
Language	Creative Thinking
Writing	Fantasy
Logic	Art Appreciation
Math	Music Appreciation
Science	

The left and right brain hemispheres specialize in different functions. Split-brain research suggests that functions are divided as indicated in the figure. Electrical recordings (EEG) support the different functions of the hemispheres in normal subjects. (Ornstein, 1977)

right hemisphere can apparently recognize objects, but it cannot speak. When the patients touched the same objects with their right hand, information was sent to the left hemisphere. In that case, they immediately said what the objects were, which indicated that the left hemisphere can speak.

Sperry did similar experiments with visible words and objects. He took advantage of the fact that the two hemispheres see different sides of the world. When a person looks at a point, the right hemisphere sees everything to the left of that point, and the left hemisphere sees everything to the right. Split-brain patients usually move their eyes around in order to send information to both hemispheres. Sperry prevented this strategy in his experiments, however. He flashed a stimulus on one side and then removed it before the eyes could move. Thus, only one hemisphere saw the stimulus.

Sperry found that the left hemisphere understands abstract language, enables people to speak, and performs complicated mathematical computations (see the accompanying figure). The right hemisphere understands only simple nouns and phrases. It can, for example, read the word "nut" and find a nut with the left hand in a pile of unseen objects. It can also find a match when it reads "used for lighting fires." It cannot understand abstract words, it cannot speak, and its mathematical abilities do not go beyond adding two-digit numbers. The right hemisphere is superior to the left in a number of ways, however, such as drawing, assembling blocks to match designs, and recognizing emotions in facial expressions.

Sperry's research formed a foundation for much modern brain research, which in turn guided the development of life-saving techniques of brain surgery.

When he stimulated the motor cortex, muscles would move; when he stimulated the somatosensory areas, people felt sensations in various parts of their body, which they would report to him. Figure 2–7 shows the specific connections that Penfield discovered; note how much of the cortex is devoted to certain areas of the body (e.g., fingers) and how little to other areas (e.g., toes).

The effects of injury to the cerebrum depend upon which area is injured. De Mille's stroke injured parts on her *left* motor and somatosensory cortexes, yet these injuries caused her to lose movement control and feeling on her *right* side. Why is this so? Because the left cerebral hemisphere primarily controls the right side of the body, and the right cerebral hemisphere primarily controls the left side of the body. Roger Sperry, a colleague of Wilder Penfield's, also made a number of discoveries while treating epilepsy through surgery; his pioneering work in split-brain research has provided much information about the differences between the left and right hemispheres (see "Highlight: Close-up on Nobel Prize-Winning Research").

The Spinal Cord

The structure that connects the brain with the rest of the body is the **spinal cord,** a cable of long nerve fibers running from the brainstem down through the backbone to the lower back. Fibers on the outside of the

Figure 2–7
Motor and somatosensory cortexes have regions that are associated with specific body parts. The relationships are shown by drawing body parts over the corresponding brain areas. The body parts are drawn smaller or larger to reflect the amount of brain surface devoted to each.

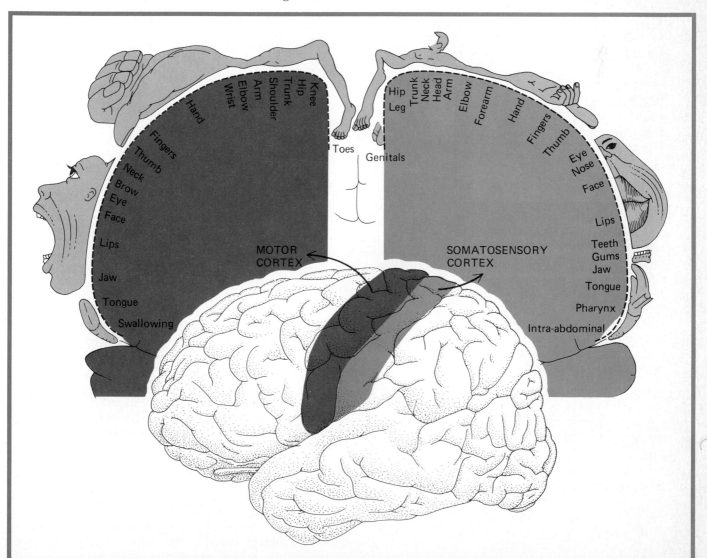

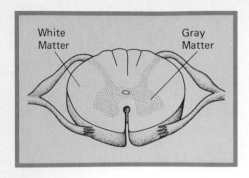

White Matter   Gray Matter

Figure 2–8
Cross-section of the spinal cord.

cord have myelin sheaths, which give this area a whitish color. (As we mentioned earlier, neural impulses travel faster on neurons covered with a myelin sheath.) Fibers on the inside of the cord are unmyelinated, so the color is grayish. The gray area is shaped like a bent *H* (as shown in Figure 2–8).

Nerve tissue in the brain and spinal cord is called the **central nervous system.** All other nerve tissue is called the **peripheral nervous system.** These two systems work together. At the start of a race, for example, runners listen for the starting gun. Peripheral nerves in their ears respond and send impulses to the central nervous system. The brain interprets the impulses as the waited-for "go" signal, and it sends commands to peripheral nerves in muscles that launch the runner down the track.

Sometimes the spinal cord triggers responses without waiting for commands from the brain. Such responses are called **reflexes,** or automatic actions that require no conscious effort on our part. There are a number of different kinds of spinal reflexes. The gray inner area of the spinal cord plays an important role in all of them, as illustrated in Figure 2–9. The stretch reflex, for example, extends your arms and legs, bringing them toward a straight position. Doctors test this reflex when they tap your knee to make your leg straighten out from a crossed position. Another kind of reflex bends your arms and legs to pull them away from painful stimulation, as when you step on a tack and jerk your leg up. When your leg jerks away from that tack, you do not fall down, because still another type of reflex extends or stiffens your other leg, supporting your weight on it.

The white outer spinal area carries impulses up and down the spinal cord. **Ascending nerves** carry sensory information up to specific areas of the brain; **descending nerves** carry commands to move muscles. Diseases and injuries that damage descending nerves can cause paralysis. Polio, for example, is a viral disease that attacks descending nerves, causing paralysis of leg and other muscles. Since Dr. Jonas E. Salk developed an effective vaccine against polio, the disease is less common than it was in the 1950s, when it reached epidemic levels. Injury is also a common cause of paralysis. If the lower spinal cord is severed, the legs are paralyzed. If the upper spinal cord is severed, paralysis occurs in the arms and legs and in breathing. As of yet, no cure has been developed for paralysis related to these unfortunate injuries.

While an intact spinal cord is necessary for normal muscle control, it's not enough on its own. De Mille's spinal cord was in perfect condition, yet she lost a great deal of motor control after her stroke. In the next section we will learn why de Mille's brain injury affected some muscle movements and not others.

FUNCTIONAL SUBDIVISIONS OF THE NERVOUS SYSTEM

De Mille's abilities and disabilities after surgery involve coordinated efforts of many anatomical subdivisions. Parts of her forebrain, midbrain, and hindbrain work together, for example, when she performs on stage. It is useful, therefore, to consider *functional subdivisions*, which are interconnected structures that work together in carrying out certain functions in the body. An everyday example of the distinction between subdivisions can be seen in a bicycle. "Anatomical" subdivisions would include the front section (handlebars, brake controls, front brake, fork, and front wheel); midsection (seat, frame, and peddles); and hind section (rear wheel, rear brake, and chain assembly). A functional subdivision that includes parts from each anatomical section is the braking system. It includes brake

Figure 2–9
Spinal cord reflexes: (left) stretch reflex,
(right) flexor reflex, and (below) flexor-
cross-extensor reflex.

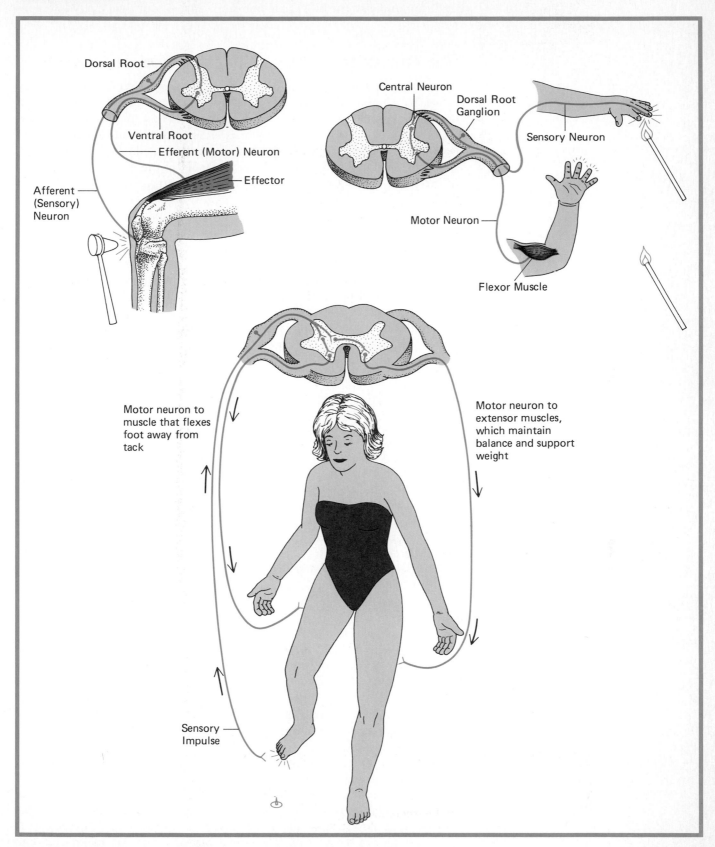

Dorsal Root

Central Neuron

Dorsal Root
Ganglion

Ventral Root

Sensory Neuron

Efferent (Motor) Neuron

Effector

Afferent
(Sensory)
Neuron

Motor Neuron

Flexor Muscle

Motor neuron to
muscle that flexes
foot away from
tack

Motor neuron to
extensor muscles,
which maintain
balance and support
weight

Sensory
Impulse

Figure 2–10
The reticular activating system (RAS).

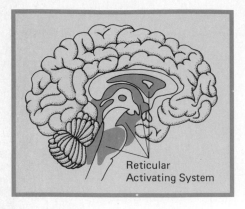

controls, peddles, and the chain assembly, as well as front and rear brakes. In the remainder of this chapter we will discuss functional subdivisions of the nervous system. We will learn the reasons for some of de Mille's handicaps and also the biological underpinnings of our own everyday experiences.

The Reticular Activating System

On the morning of her operation, de Mille was awakened at about six o'clock by a nurse who gave her an injection. She remembers going into the operating room; she remembers nothing after that. As far as she knows, she suddenly fell into a completely dreamless void beyond time and sensation. This place was created for her by a drug that blocked her **reticular activating system (RAS)**. The RAS activates all of the regions of the brain for incoming sensory impulses; when it is blocked, no sensations register at all.

Figure 2–10 shows that the RAS ignores the anatomical divisions that we introduced earlier. The system joins the reticular formation with other parts of the brain to perform the function of making the brain alert. A person is awake only when the RAS is operating. Another function of the RAS is *selective* attention. When two or more messages arrive at the same time, the RAS seems to decide which is most urgent. The system then blocks, or tones down, the irrelevant messages and prepares the upper areas of the brain to respond vigorously to the relevant message. (In Chapter 5 we will further explore general arousal, sleep, and ways to concentrate attention.)

The Limbic System

A functional subdivision of the brain that played a key role in de Mille's struggle to keep her spirits up was the limbic system. This system of brain structures, which plays a role in emotions, memories, and goal-directed behavior, includes the structures shown in Figure 2–11. Limbic system interconnections are clearly defined, and each part seems to depend on all the other parts.

Limbic system functions are less clearly defined, however; the system does so many things that it is hard to characterize any one function. One way to do this is to observe the behavior of people whose limbic system is disturbed by frontal cortex injuries. One patient laughed at sad things and cried at funny things; another was unable to plan a meal because she kept forgetting how to cook; still another urinated in public while dressed in evening clothes (Cotman & McGaugh, 1980). The ill-timed urination is one of many examples of inappropriate actions that seem to result from an inability to deal with two conflicting goals at the same time (one goal was to enjoy social interactions with companions; another was to urinate). Normally we cope with conflicting demands by responding at the right time and place. People with disturbed limbic systems often cannot deal with conflicting goals. From this set of bizarre symptoms, we get the impression that the limbic system controls emotions, memories, and goal-directed behavior.

Another way to study the limbic system is to record cell activity in animals that are performing a task. For example, researchers have recorded cells in the hippocampus of rats while they explored for food in a radial maze. (The hippocampus is known to play an important role in memory.) This kind of maze has spokes that radiate from a hub in eight directions. A food container at the end of each spoke can be either full or empty. The researchers discovered that some cells in the hippocampus fired maximally only when the rats entered a particular spoke and fired at a slower rate

Figure 2–11
The limbic system.

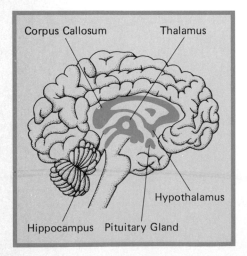

when the rats were anywhere else. They also noted that different cells fired maximally to different spokes. These results suggest that the hippocampus might provide rats with a spatial map of where they are and where they have been (Best & Ranck, 1982).

The Autonomic Nervous System

Have you ever become enraged suddenly, only to calm down after a few minutes? Such responses are governed by our autonomic nervous system, which regulates glands and organs. Rage is triggered by the sympathetic division of the autonomic system. This division prepares the body for action. The calm that follows is controlled by the parasympathetic division, which allows the body to relax. These two divisions, with their effects on the body, may be seen in Figure 2–12.

Sympathetic Division. Sympathetic pathways work all the time to keep our body functions stable. They are especially busy, however, during stressful situations. De Mille reported a stressful episode that took place during the dress rehearsal for the New York gala she was involved in following her stroke. At one point, the dancers became confused. De Mille was frustrated because she was unable to be on stage to demonstrate, and she couldn't get anyone's attention in order to help her. After a second unsuccessful attempt by the dancers, she lost her temper and yelled, "Will nobody help a cripple?!" Her complaint aroused immediate attention and the problem was solved. It wasn't long before de Mille herself was able to laugh at her comment.

Let's look at some of the body changes triggered by de Mille's sympathetic division when she lost her temper:

1. Her heart worked faster and harder to pump more blood to the muscles.
2. Her breathing rate increased, and her air passage opened to carry more air to her lungs.
3. Her sweat glands produced more sweat to help maintain normal body temperature.
4. Her digestion stopped to save energy for the other functions that were speeded up.

All of these responses prepared de Mille for action. Together they are called the *fight-or-flight* responses, because in emergencies they prepare us either to fight or to flee. Sympathetic responses are very helpful in emergencies, but they can be harmful when they are repeatedly used for minor crises. Students who have fight-or-flight reactions every time they think about exams, for example, put undue stress on their bodies. We will discuss this again in Chapter 11.

Parasympathetic Division. Parasympathetic fibers go to all the same glands and organs as the sympathetic division, but they carry the opposite message, as if to say, "Relax." This *relaxation response* was traditionally regarded as being beyond voluntary control, as were all autonomic responses. For this reason, the autonomic nervous system is sometimes called the involuntary nervous system. Recent studies, however, show that we can voluntarily control our autonomic nervous system, as we will discuss in Chapter 6. Even when we learn to control our organs voluntarily, however, we never achieve the same sort of precise control that we have over our skeletal muscles.

Control of Skeletal Muscles

De Mille's mobility was restricted because her ability to control her muscles was reduced. The bones of our skeleton are rigid, but without the

Special x-ray techniques aid the examination of anatomical and functional subdivisions. The top photo shows a *cerebral angiogram.* This x-ray was taken after a dye was injected into cerebral blood vessels. The angiogram indicates the positions of the vessels. Deviations from normal positions can indicate a tumor. The bottom photo shows a computerized axial tomography scan, which is better known as a *CAT-SCAN.* This "picture" was taken without injecting dyes and without presenting special risks or discomforts to the patient. An x-ray beam scanned the brain while a computer recorded how much of the beam was absorbed. The computer then projected the "picture" to indicate in a color code its interpretation of varying densities of tissues, fluids, and bone.

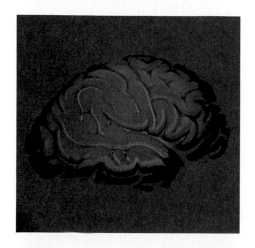

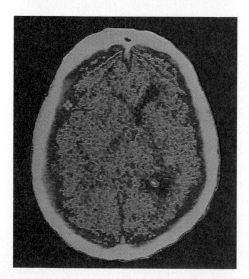

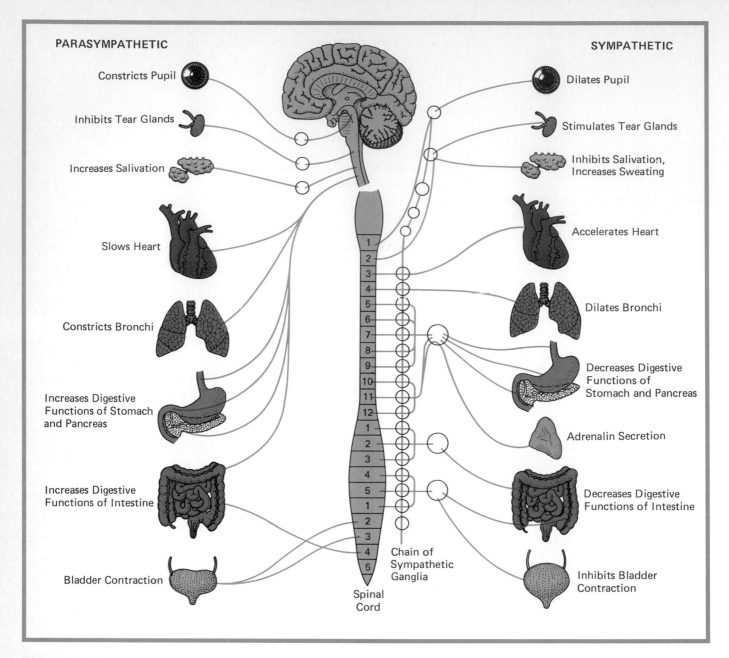

PARASYMPATHETIC

Constricts Pupil

Inhibits Tear Glands

Increases Salivation

Slows Heart

Constricts Bronchi

Increases Digestive
Functions of Stomach
and Pancreas

Increases Digestive
Functions of Intestine

Bladder Contraction

SYMPATHETIC

Dilates Pupil

Stimulates Tear Glands

Inhibits Salivation,
Increases Sweating

Accelerates Heart

Dilates Bronchi

Decreases Digestive
Functions of
Stomach and Pancreas

Adrenalin Secretion

Decreases Digestive
Functions of Intestine

Inhibits Bladder
Contraction

Chain of
Sympathetic
Ganglia

Spinal
Cord

Figure 2–12
The sympathetic and parasympathetic
subdivisions of the nervous system serve
many of the same organs, but they affect
them differently.

muscles that move and support them we would collapse in a heap. Spinal
cord reflexes control most of the work our skeletal muscles do in maintaining our posture against the pull of gravity. We continually control our
skeletal muscles, therefore, without being aware of it. At the same time
we control the same muscles deliberately and purposefully, as when de
Mille performed on stage. In this section we will examine the neural processes that underlie such voluntary muscle control.

The part of the nervous system that controls muscle movements is called
the **motor system.** We have already discussed the spinal reflexes, which
are part of the motor system. Here we will consider three higher centers:

1. **Basal ganglia** are four masses of gray matter located deep in the
   forebrain. They have a number of functions, which are not well understood. One function is to control "background" muscle tone. When
   we write, for instance, our basal ganglia first tenses muscles in the
   upper part of our arm to prepare for the hand movement. In general,
   basal ganglia perform large, general muscle movements to set the
   stage for more detailed, controlled movements.

Shown here are two basic types of muscle movements. The weaver is using pyramidal cells to control precise hand movements. The javelin thrower is using basal ganglia to control general muscle tone.

2. The **cerebellum** participates in controlling fine-grain muscle movements. It "puts a brake" on motor impulses to make them smoother and more coordinated.
3. The **motor cortex,** which is in the frontal lobe (see Figure 2–7), is the place where motor impulses originate. The motor cortex contains giant cells, called **pyramidal cells,** which send a long axon through the brain down to neurons in the spinal cord. From there motor impulses go directly to muscles. Most pyramidal cells in the left hemisphere send their impulses to muscles on the right side of the body, and vice versa. They tend to control precise movements such as those of hand movements and speech. A large part of the motor cortex controls a small number of muscles that we often use in precise movements.

Language Control Centers

Most of us speak, write, listen, and read with such ease that we do not appreciate the work our brain does. But de Mille's stroke made her keenly aware of her brain's role in language. Her stroke temporarily caused aphasia, which is difficulty in producing and understanding language. Her case illustrates two well-known types of aphasia:

1. **Broca's aphasia,** which is characterized by speech that is slow, labored, and slightly distorted. It is caused by injury to *Broca's area*, which is a part of the cortex, shown in Figure 2–13.
2. **Wernicke's aphasia,** which is characterized by speech that sounds normal until one pays attention to the meaning. The speech includes the wrong words and nonsense words, and the message seems to shift from topic to topic. Wernicke's aphasia is caused by injury to the upper area of the left temporal lobe (Figure 2–13).

De Mille's speech was halting and distorted, which is characteristic of Broca's aphasia. Also, she used wrong words and nonsense words when she spoke, which is common with Wernicke's aphasia. The day after her stroke, de Mille spoke mostly gibberish. Here is an example of an exchange with her husband: "Wa listen. Wa I groopes? Ye rideargo sutino? Rev." Her husband pretended he understood her and replied, "Yes, dear—yes. Of course I'll do it."

Two days later, it was easier to understand de Mille, but she still used words incorrectly. For instance, a close friend, Mary Green, related this conversation that she had with de Mille during this period.

Figure 2–13
Broca's area and *Wernicke's area* of the brain.

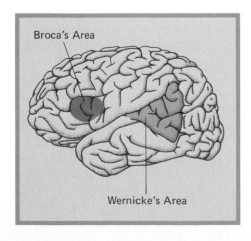

Broca's Area

Wernicke's Area

De Mille:	Mary, the next time bring the Mary Janes with you.
Green:	Are they in your closet, Agnes? [Green thinks she means shoes.]
De Mille:	Of course not in my closet. My God!
Green:	Is it a person?
De Mille:	*Of course.*
Green:	Do I know her?
De Mille:	Of course you know her!
Green:	Is she a member of our company?
De Mille:	Oh, Mary!
Green:	[Now it was a game.] Is it Jane? [Nod] Jane Gilman, our lawyer?
De Mille:	Of course. I *said* Jane.
Green:	I'll have her call you, Agnes.

We have concentrated so far on the direct effects of de Mille's brain damage on her language and other abilities. We will now turn to the possible indirect effects of brain damage on her body chemistry.

THE ENDOCRINE SYSTEM

De Mille's stroke injured her temporal lobe, and such injuries can influence appetites and emotional aspects of behavior (Cotman & McGaugh, 1980). These effects occur indirectly as a result of an imbalance of the endocrine system, a major coordinating system that regulates body chemistry. Let's examine the structure and function of this important system.

Structure

The endocrine system is made up of internal organs called endocrine glands. Located throughout the body (Figure 2–14), they touch almost every aspect of our lives. The glands release hormones (chemical messengers) directly into the bloodstream, and the bloodstream carries the hormones to other body tissues. When hormones reach their target, they either directly change it or they cause it to release other hormones that change tissues elsewhere in the body.

Function

It's easiest to understand the endocrine system's function if we go over each individual gland.

Thyroid Glands.   The thyroid gland is a large butterfly-shaped gland in the front and sides of the throat. It produces thyroxin, a hormone that determines the rate at which you transform your food into energy. This rate, called the metabolic rate, determines how hungry you feel, how energetic you are, and how fast you gain weight.

If your thyroxin level is too high, you will burn food fast, which makes you hungry, gives you lots of energy, and keeps you thin. It also speeds up and intensifies your reactions to stress.

You burn your food too slowly when your thyroxin level is low. Much of your food consequently turns to fat, and you feel sleepy and sluggish. In Chapter 10 we will discuss other factors that influence why we gain or lose weight. Children with extremely low thyroxin levels suffer from *cretinism*, which is characterized by arrested physical and mental development. If untreated with thyroid extract, they will become dwarfed, mentally retarded, and sterile.

Figure 2-14
Glands of the endocrine system release
hormones (chemical messengers) directly
into the bloodstream.

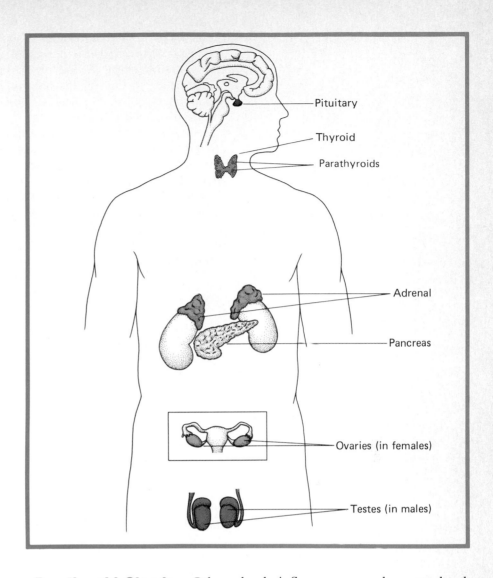

Pituitary

Thyroid

Parathyroids

Adrenal

Pancreas

Ovaries (in females)

Testes (in males)

Parathyroid Glands.   Other glands influence general energy level. One of them is a set of four pea-shaped glands next to the thyroid, called the **parathyroid glands.** The parathyroid hormone causes lethargy when its level is too high, and muscle spasms when its level is too low.

Pancreas.   Another gland that affects general energy level is the **pancreas,** a large gland located behind the stomach. It controls the level of sugar in the blood by secreting two hormones, *insulin* and *glucagon.* Too little sugar in the blood causes chronic fatigue, and too much sugar poisons the blood, causing *diabetes.* A person who has diabetes needs a specially controlled diet and daily injections of insulin to avoid serious complications, which include heart damage, nerve damage, and blindness.

Pituitary Gland.   Another important part of the endocrine system is the **pituitary gland,** which has the widest-ranging effects of all the endocrine glands. This master gland is only the size of a pea. It, like all the endocrine glands, is influenced by the brain. Its location makes that influence especially easy to see. It lies in a small recess at the base of the brain and is connected to the hypothalamus, which controls it. The pituitary gland secretes many different kinds of hormones. One is the **growth hormone,** which controls development of the skeleton. Too little of it causes dwarfism and too much causes giantism. Other pituitary hormones influence reproductive organs and sexual behavior, often indirectly by regulating another endocrine gland, the **gonads.**

Gonads.   In females gonads are called *ovaries,* and in males they are called *testes.* Hormones produced by the gonads are called *sex hormones.*

Ovaries produce two hormones, *estrogen* and *progesterone*; they control ovulation, pregnancy, and the menstrual cycle. Testes manufacture *testosterone*, which stimulates production of sperm. Gonads also regulate *secondary sex characteristics*, such as the distribution of body hair, development of breasts, and pitch of voice. The whole subject of hormones and sexual behavior will be discussed in Chapter 10.

De Mille's sudden clash with death and her amazing recovery are both related to the organization of her body's two coordinating systems, the nervous system and the endocrine system. On the one hand, her stroke affected her in many ways, because parts of her nervous system and endocrine system depend upon one another. When one part breaks down, other dependent parts can fail in a disastrous chain reaction. On the other hand, de Mille's recovery indicates an advantage of this organization. Apparently, when one part fails, other parts can sometimes take over. In other words, within limits, parts of these systems are flexible in their ability to take on duties (Cotman & McCaugh, 1980).

GENETICS

Whether we focus on the negative side of de Mille's illness or on the positive side of her recovery, we can hardly help being reminded of our dependence on our own bodies. Some of us have strong, healthy bodies that give us great freedom. Others of us have disabilities that limit what we can do. In this next section we will consider the origin of our bodies and the factors that determined the specific bodies that each of us inherited.

Genetics is the study of how traits are inherited, or passed on, from parent to child. The cells from which we started contain **genes,** which are the basic units of heredity. They determine our sequence of growth into a human baby instead of into a turtle, rabbit, or some other animal. Genes determine our blood type, coloration, and many other traits. In general, genes determine the resemblance between newborns and parents. People often observe that a baby "has his mother's eyes" or "has her father's chin," and so on. The resemblance becomes even more striking later on as genes continue to influence development.

The Biochemistry of Genes

Genes are located in the nucleus of every cell in the body. They are composed of **deoxyribonucleic acid (DNA),** which contains blueprints for life. Living organisms are made of protein, and DNA controls the way in which protein chains are built. Material for constructing protein surrounds cells and DNA sends out messenger molecules, **ribonucleic acid (RNA),** to control how the material is fashioned into specific kinds of protein chains. James Watson and Francis Crick (1953) made a significant breakthrough in deciphering the chemical "language" in which these genetic blueprints are written (see Figure 2–15).

Every living cell contains between 20,000 and 125,000 genes grouped together in clusters of a thousand or more. They are arranged in threadlike chains called **chromosomes.**

The Structure and Function of Chromosomes

Every plant and animal has a specific number of chromosomes, which are grouped in pairs. Garden peas have 7 pairs, fruit flies have 4 pairs, frogs have 13 pairs, chickens have 39 pairs, chimpanzees have 24 pairs, and humans have 23 pairs. The cells in your body have 46 chromosomes,

Figure 2–15
DNA molecules are shaped like a spiral staircase or double helix. The steps of the staircase contain a genetic code. Four chemical bases make up the steps: Adenine (A), Thymine (T), Cytosine (C), and Guanine (G). Each step contains two bases, A and T or C and G. A single gene might contain as many as 2,000 steps. The specific order of A-T and C-G pairs determines a gene's special character.

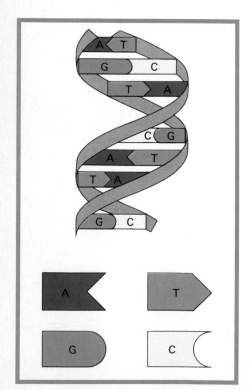

arranged in 23 pairs. You inherited one member of each pair from your mother and the other from your father. If you have children, you will pass along 23 of your chromosomes to each child; the other 23 will come from your partner.

Genes are transmitted from generation to generation by means of sex cells, which are called **gametes.** A female gamete is called an *ovum*, and a male gamete is called a *sperm*. Your gametes have 23 chromosomes each, only half the number of your other cells. Each gamete is formed by randomly choosing one member from each of your 23 pairs of chromosomes. With 23 pairs to choose from, your body can generate an incredible number of unique gametes.

Ovum and sperm combine their chromosomes when they unite to form one cell called a **zygote.** Thus, zygotes have 46 chromosomes, half from the mother and half from the father. Each of us started from the union of one sperm and one ovum. The resulting zygote contained 46 chromosomes, which determined our **genotype,** or genetic inheritance, for the rest of our lives.

Figure 2–16 shows 23 chromosome pairs for a normal human female (left) and male (right). Scientists have classified chromosomes according to size and shape, and they have identified some pairs that carry (and pass on) specific traits. Pair 23 determines sex, for example. Notice that the male has one large X-shaped chromosome and one small, upside down, Y-shaped chromosome in pair 23. The female has two large X-shaped chromosomes in that pair. One of the important consequences of this discovery was the realization that men alone determine the sex of offspring. A female body always contributes an X chromosome to pair 23. A male body can generate gametes with *either* an X or a Y chromosome. Thus, a female is conceived when a sperm carrying an X chromosome unites with an ovum, and a male is conceived when a sperm carrying a Y chromosome does so.

Mutations. Errors are made occasionally in transmitting genes from one generation to the next. As a result, children are sometimes born with abnormal chromosome structures, which are called **mutations.** Scientists have observed mutations of pair 23, as follows:

1. *Two Xs and a Y.* People with an XXY mutation often have characteristics of both sexes. They might have developed breasts and small testicles,

Figure 2–16

Human chromosomes grouped into 23 pairs, with female chromosomes on the left and male chromosomes on the right.

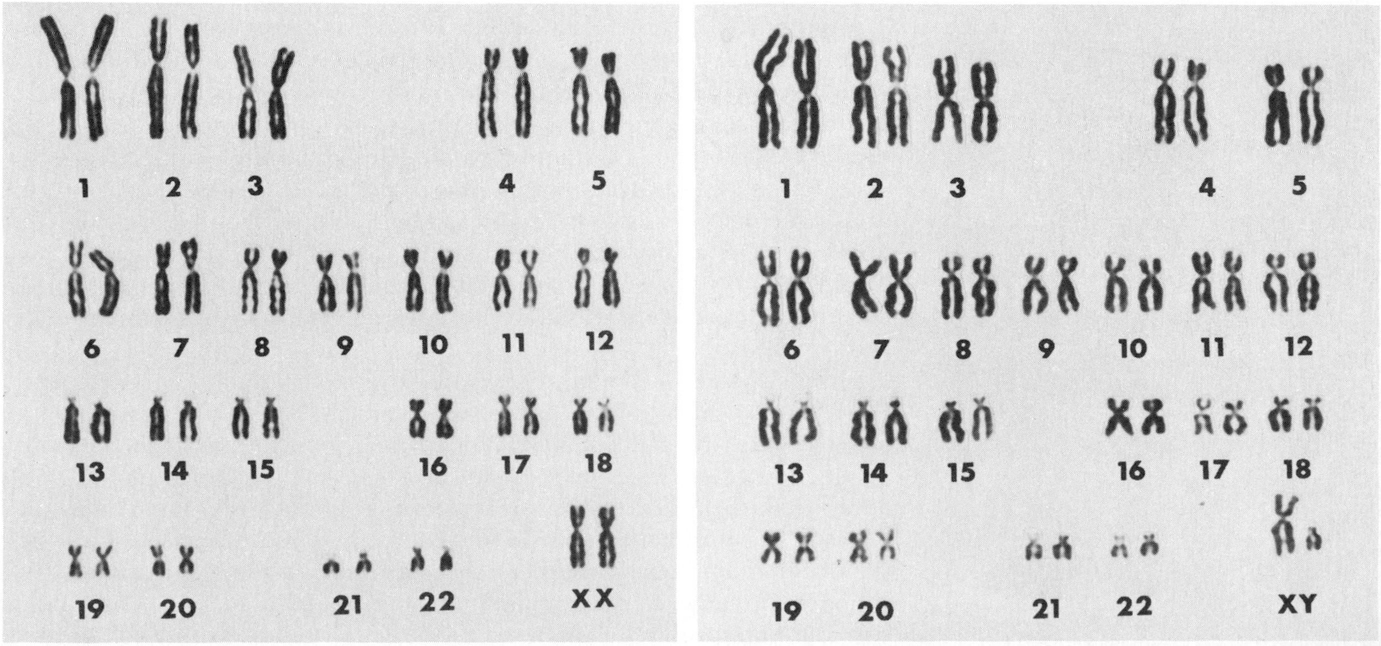

This is a Down's syndrome child, shown taking part in a special education class.

for example. Some superior female Russian athletes have had XXY chromosome structures.

2. *Two Ys and an X*. Males with an extra Y chromosome (XYY) are often taller than other males. Some evidence suggests that they might also be more aggressive, but the evidence is mixed. On the one hand, XYY males are more likely than normal males to be inmates of prisons or mental hospitals. On the other hand, XYY males in the general population (about 1 in every 1,000 births) are no more aggressive than normal males (Hook, 1973; Owen, 1972).

Another kind of genetic mutation is one in which a person has 47 chromosomes because of an extra one added to pair 21. Children with this chromosome abnormality suffer from **Down's syndrome,** a disorder characterized by mental retardation and a unique physical appearance, including folds on the eyelid corners, a round face, a head with a flattened back, a short neck, and a small nose. Before modern medicine, Down's syndrome children often died during or before their teens because they were very susceptible to leukemia (blood cancer), heart disorders, and respiratory infections. Today, Down's syndrome babies live longer because of better treatments for these diseases. Down's syndrome children are usually affectionate, calm, and cheerful.

Down's syndrome can be detected before birth through **amniocentesis,** a process in which fluid is taken from a mother's womb. A fetus sloughs off cells into the fluid, enabling doctors to examine an unborn child's genetic structure, which is recorded in each cell. This procedure is only done when there is a reason for concern. A mother who has already had a Down's syndrome child is about three times more likely to have one again, for example, and mothers over age thirty-five are more likely than younger mothers to have a child with this disorder. Such mothers might consider amniocentesis, which is best done in the sixteenth week of pregnancy. Unfortunately, Down's syndrome cannot be treated, so the only choice when amniocentesis indicates Down's syndrome is whether or not to induce an abortion.

The causes of mutations are not well understood and are of great concern to modern geneticists. They have identified three causes:

1. Some people carry *mutator genes* that increases the rate of mutations in other genes.
2. High temperatures can increase mutation rate. Males generate sperm in their scrotum, a sac that is usually cooler than the rest of the body in mammals. Research has indicated that wearing tight trousers can raise scrotal temperature to a point that could almost double mutation rate (Lerner & Libby, 1976).
3. Radiation has been linked to mutation rate. X-rays are one source of radiation and pregnant mothers are advised to avoid them. Radiation before pregnancy may also increase mutation rate. Recent evidence suggests that more exposure to radiation may explain the increased risk of having Down's syndrome babies for older mothers.

Continuing research on mutations will hopefully allow geneticists to understand and treat the more than 2,000 genetic disorders that are known today.

Genetic Laws of Inheritance

Gregor Mendel started modern genetics by formulating laws of how characteristics or traits are inherited. He based his laws on years of systematic breeding of garden peas. He noticed that peas, like humans, inherit traits from both parents, and he noticed a pattern in the way these traits are passed along.

Single-Gene Traits. Modern geneticists now realize that Mendel studied a special case, known as **single-gene traits**. Some genes single-handedly determine specific traits like eye color in fruit flies. Such genes occur in pairs, with each member located in the same position on paired chromosomes and with each parent contributing one member to each gene pair. A single gene may occur in one of several different forms called *alleles*, which geneticists represent by means of letters. Some alleles, called *dominant*, rule over others, which are called *recessive*. Dominant alleles are respresented by capital letters and recessive alleles are represented by small letters. Allele *E*, for example, produces red eyes in fruit flies, and it dominates over allele *e*, which produces white eyes. Fruit flies therefore have red eyes if one member of its gene pair is *E* and the other is *e*, or if both members are *E*. Fruit flies have white eyes only if both members of its gene pair are *e* (see Figure 2–17).

Sex-Linked Traits. A complication occurs when the gene for a trait is located on the chromosome that determines one's sex. A human gene is *sex-linked* if it is located on the X chromosome in pair 23. The gene for color vision is an example. Allele *C* produces normal color vision, allele *c* produces colorblindness. Either allele occurs in X chromosomes; neither one occurs in Y. Males have only one X chromosome, which comes of course from their mother and which completely determines their color vision. A male will therefore have normal vision if he inherits *C* from his mother, and he will be colorblind if he inherits *c*. A female, on the other hand, has two X chromosomes and therefore has two chances for normal color vision. She will have normal color vision if either one of her X chromosomes is *C*, because the *C* allele is the dominant allele. She will be colorblind only in the unlikely event that she inherits a *c* from *both* her father *and* her mother.

Figure 2–17
Dominant and recessive genes control eye color in fruit flies. The gene for red eyes (*E*) dominates the gene for white eyes (*e*). Offspring get one gene from each parent. An offspring will have white eyes only if it gets an *e* from each parent, forming an *ee* pair.

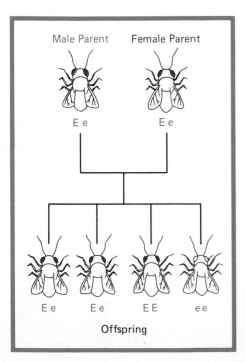

GENETIC ENGINEERING

On January 4, 1982, Judith and Roger Carr took their daughter, Elizabeth Jordan Carr, home from Norfolk General Hospital, where she was born a week earlier. This seemingly ordinary event was in the news because Elizabeth Carr was America's first "test-tube" baby. That is, she was conceived outside her mother's body. An egg, or ovum, was removed from her mother, placed in a test tube, and fertilized with her father's sperm. The united egg and sperm cells were then placed back in the mother, where Elizabeth developed normally.

Elizabeth Carr is the world's nineteenth test-tube baby. Dr. Daniel Petrucci was the first to successfully combine an ovum and sperm in a test tube in 1959. The first test-tube baby, Louise Brown, was born in 1978 at a clinic in England operated by Dr. Patrick Steptoe and Robert Edwards. None of the parents of test-tube babies could have conceived any other way. They and many parents in the future will forever be grateful to **genetic engineering,** the science of applied genetics. The study of how traits are passed on from parent to child led to a basic understanding of how eggs and sperm unite.

Genetic engineers are also credited with at least three other breakthroughs:

1. Dr. H. Gobind Khorana headed a team that achieved the first chemical synthesis of a gene in 1970 at the University of Wisconsin. This work opened the door for creating any gene in a test tube. A Harvard research team recently constructed genes that produce insulin, an important hormone discussed earlier in this chapter (Gilbert & Villa-Komaroff, 1980).
2. An Oxford team of scientists in 1971 changed the structure of defective cells in mice. They injected healthy chick chromosomes into defective mice cells. The cells used the new material to correct their own defect and to reproduce healthy cells. This research was a first step toward correcting defective human genes (see Anderson & Diacomakos, 1981).
3. J. B. Gurdon produced a frog without fertilizing an ovum with sperm. He destroyed the genes in a frog ovum and replaced them with a full set of genes from an intestinal cell of another frog. The ovum then had a full set of genes and it started to reproduce. This process, which is called *cloning*, resulted in a tadpole that was genetically identical to the frog that donated the intestine cell. The tadpole is called a *clone*, which is an "identical twin" to one of its parents because of the cloning processes by which it is produced. Some researchers speculate that a day will come when scientists will be able to produce human clones.

Genetic engineering has risks. Scientists must exercise extreme caution to avoid creating a "doomsday bug," a bacteria that causes mass infections for which there is no cure. Genetic engineering also raises ethical questions. For example, who could be cloned? Despite the dangers and ethical questions, genetic engineering could obviously be a tremendous benefit to society. It will surely be in the news for a long time to come.

Judith Carr with her newborn daughter, Elizabeth Jordan Carr, who is America's first "test-tube" baby.

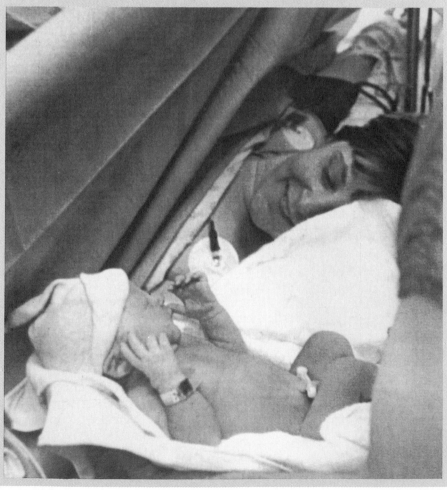

Polygenic Traits. Another complication occurs when traits are **polygenic,** which means that they are determined by the action of more than one gene pair. Most human traits are polygenic. Each human parent contributes a *set of genes*, rather than a single gene, to each chromosome pair to determine specific traits. Rules governing dominant and recessive alleles still apply for polygenic traits. As the number of genes determining a single trait increases, the task of specifying the relationship between genes and traits gets even more complicated.

Today's geneticists cannot even say how many genes go into determining complex traits like intelligence, so they are far from being able to link specific genes to intelligence. Scientists do have evidence, however, that genes influence intelligence. In one experiment, rats were separated into a "bright" group, who were good maze runners, and a "dull" group, who were poor maze runners (Tryon, 1940). "Bright" rats mated together and "dull" rats mated together for eight generations. Tryon continued to use maze-running ability as his critical measure. He found that almost every offspring of the "bright" rats was better than the average of the first generation, and almost all of the offspring of the "dull" rats were poorer maze runners than the original group. The results suggest that genetic inheritance influences intelligence, assuming, of course, that we accept maze running as a measure of rat "intelligence."

While Tryon's experiment and others like it justify further investigations into genetic influences on intelligence, other studies suggest that environment also influences intelligence. For instance, Cooper and Zubek (1958) controlled for genetic background and found that raising rats in an enriched, or challenging, environment also increases "intelligence." Traits that interest psychologists, such as intelligence, personality, and emotions, are generally influenced by both heredity and environment. Genetics sets the theoretical limits, while environment determines how an animal functions within those limits. We will therefore keep track of both factors when we follow the course of human development in Chapters 8 and 9.

SUMMARY

1. Behavioral neuroscientists study both the structure and function of body parts that influence our behavior.
2. **Neurons** are cells specialized to receive and transmit information. They look like other cells except that they have tiny fiber projections that allow them to communicate with other cells.
3. Neurons "speak" a simple language consisting of an "off-on" code. They go off and on at different rates to send messages that can go from neuron to neuron throughout the body.
4. Short branches, called **dendrites,** receive messages from surrounding cells; a single long extension called an **axon** carries messages away from the cell body. **Synaptic transmission** occurs as the impulse moves from one neuron to another.
5. The brain's anatomical subdivisions include the **hindbrain, midbrain,** and **forebrain.**
6. The **cerebrum** is part of the forebrain, and it governs our most advanced human capabilities, including abstract reasoning and speech. The cerebrum is divided into left and right hemispheres, which are further separated into four lobes.
7. The **spinal cord** connects the brain with the rest of the body. It also controls important automatic responses called **reflexes.**
8. The brain's functional subdivisions include the **reticular activating system (RAS),** which

controls waking and sleeping; the **limbic system,** which controls emotions; the **autonomic nervous system,** which keeps our body functions stable; the **motor system,** which controls muscles; and the **language control centers,** which allow us to produce and understand language.

9. The **endocrine system** consists of glands that regulate body chemistry. The glands send **hormones,** chemical messengers, through the bloodstream.

10. Cells contain **genes,** which determine traits that people inherit from their parents. **Genet-** ics is the study of how traits are inherited.

11. Scientists are beginning to understand "blueprints for life," which are contained in the chemical structure of genes.

12. Genes group together in structures called **chromosomes,** which are key units in the study of reproduction and in the study of errors in transmitting genes from one generation to the next.

13. Geneticists have formulated laws of how traits are inherited. These laws or principles have led to important applications in a new field called **genetic engineering.**

Key Terms

absolute refractory period
acetylcholine (ACh)
amniocentesis
ascending nerves
autonomic nervous system
axon
axon terminal
basal ganglia
brainstem
Broca's aphasia
catecholamines
central nervous system
cerebellum
cerebral cortex (cerebrum)
chemical transmitters
chromosomes
corpus callosum
dendrites
deoxyribonucleic acid (DNA)
depolarization
descending nerves
Down's syndrome
endocrine system
endorphins
enkephalins
fissure of Rolando
fissure of Sylvius
forebrain
frontal lobe
gametes
genes
genetic engineering
genetics
genotype
gonads
growth hormone
hindbrain
hormones
hypothalamus

longitudinal fissure
medulla
membrane potential
metabolic rate
midbrain
motor cortex
motor system
mutations
myelin sheath
neurons
occipital lobe
pancreas
parasympathetic division
parathyroid glands
parietal lobe
peripheral nervous system
pituitary gland
polarization
polygenic traits
pons
pyramidal cells
receptor sites
reflexes
relative refractory period
ribonucleic acid (RNA)
single-gene traits
somatosensory cortex
spinal cord
sympathetic division
synapse
synaptic space
synaptic transmission
synaptic vesicles
temporal lobe
thalamus
thyroid gland
thyroxin
Wernicke's aphasia
zygote

Suggested Readings

Agnes de Mille has written several books about her life and career in dance. Our introductory story is based on *Reprieve* (New York: New American Library, 1982), which deals with her stroke and its aftermath. Her other two volumes of autobiography are *Dance to the Piper* and *And Promenade Home* (both published by Da Capo Press, New York, 1951 and 1956).

COTMAN, C. W., & MCGAUGH, J. L. *Behavioral neuroscience: An introduction*. New York: Academic Press, 1980. This book takes students step by step through the process of using biology, chemistry, physiology, and psychology in the study of behavior.

FULLER, J. L., & THOMPSON, W. R. *Foundations of behavior genetics*. St. Louis, Mo.: Mosby, 1978. A comprehensive survey of how genetics influences behavior.

LUBOR, J. F., & DEERING, W. M. *Behavioral approaches to neurology*. New York: Academic Press, 1981. Explores the application of biofeedback and other behavioral medicine techniques to areas for which traditional medical approaches have not been completely satisfactory.

ORBACH, J. *Neuropsychology after Lashley: Fifty years since the publication of brain mechanisms and intelligence*. Hillsdale, N.J.: Erlbaum, 1982. Traces the development and current state of the art in neuropsychology through individual chapters presented by Lashley's students.

THOMPSON, R. F. *Introduction to physiological psychology*. New York: Harper & Row, 1975. A wide-ranging introduction to theories and data of physiological psychology.

WHITAKER, H. A. (Ed.). *Brain and cognition*. A new journal presenting research papers, clinical case histories, and reviews on brain structure and function. Topics include visual processes, memory, emotions, sex differences, hemispheric differences, and cognitive processes.

THREE

SENSATION

Farley Mowat stood alone in the middle of an ice-covered arctic lake surrounded by a mountain of supplies. The decrepit ski-equipped plane that had brought him and his supplies was now climbing reluctantly into the clouds. He reached for his revolver as distant howling sounds brought to mind the hordes of bloodthirsty wolves he had been sent to study.

The Canadian Wildlife Service had sent Mowat to investigate reports that wolves were slaughtering thousands of Arctic caribou. The trappers Farley interviewed informed him that each wolf killed thousands of caribou a year just out of blood lust. Farley didn't believe all that he heard from the trappers of course, but as the howling came closer, he found himself fervently wishing he were somewhere else.

He retreated under his canoe. The sound seemed deafening as the howling animals rushed toward him.

Farley then heard a loud roar followed by silence. In a state of total confusion, he peeked out from under the canoe. At first he could see only wolf feet, but then he fixed his gaze on the most welcome pair of feet he had ever seen. He poked his head out and looked upward into the apprehensive face of a young Eskimo clad in caribou furs. The man stood next to a dog sled and team of 14 Huskies. There wasn't a wolf in sight.

Farley's arbitrarily chosen landing place had been incredibly lucky. It was only several miles from the sole cabin within 70 miles, and he had been seen by one of a handful of human inhabitants in an area of about 10,000 square miles. His 18-year-old rescuer, Mike, was a trapper of mixed Eskimo and white parentage. Mike made room in his cabin for both Farley and his supplies.

After the spring thaw several weeks later, Farley pitched a tent on a hill directly overlooking a den of wolves. This ideal arrangement for observing the study species would have been impossible if wolves were as bloodthirsty as Farley had been led to believe. Farley had found, however, not a den of killers, but a playful, friendly family of skillful providers. The family consisted of four pups, their father and mother, and another male who appeared to be their uncle. Farley named their home "Wolf House Bay," and he named each of the adults. The father, George, was about 8 feet long; the mother, Angeline, was about a third smaller; and the third adult, "Uncle Albert," was smaller than George.

George and Albert hunted every night over a 100-square-mile territory. Angeline stayed in the den with the pups at night, and she entertained them on a playground area near the den during the day. Sometimes when she needed a break, Uncle Albert took over the daytime babysitting duties. Although the adults never seemed to quarrel, they often played rough games of tag or king on the mountain among themselves. The adults played similar games with the pups, who never seemed to tire of roughhousing.

Farley had trouble believing that these playful, loving animals were the killer beasts he had been sent to study. The only bloodthirsty beasts in Wolf House Bay seemed to be the mosquitoes.

But Farley had not had a chance to observe the wolves hunting, and, worse yet, he had no idea what they were eating. Since the caribou had migrated to some 200 or 300 miles north of Wolf House Bay, and since George and Albert never seemed to bring anything back from their hunts, the wolves appeared to be living on air and water. This mystery weighed heavily on Farley's mind, not only because it was central to his mission, but also because he appeared to be the only suitable prey for wolves in the area.

Not that the wolves ever gave Farley reason to fear for his life. They ignored him so long as he respected the boundaries that they marked in a way that might be guessed by anyone who has observed a dog leaving his personal mark on every post in his neighborhood. They didn't even attack when they caught Farley inside their territory trying to sneak a peek inside their den. They were satisfied to stand their ground and watch Farley set a world's record for cross-country retreat. Yet Farley could not easily shake his preconception of the wolves as vicious killers, so he continued to worry about becoming a wolf snack.

This preoccupation greatly delayed his efforts to solve the mystery of the wolves' diet. The solution was under his nose all the while, but he didn't see it because he was only looking for prey worthy of the wolves' reputation. One day Angeline provided an unmistakable clue; she stood in full view of Farley's powerful telescope with the hind legs and tail of a mouse dangling from her mouth. At first Farley thought he was witnessing a between-meal snack, but when Angeline proceeded to catch and gobble 22 more mice, he realized that she had consumed a fair-sized meal. Could the Arctic's most feared carnivores be living on a diet of mice? If the answer was yes, Farley realized that he would have a hard time persuading his superiors. He therefore designed a three-phase test. In the first phase, he did a survey of the small rodent population and determined that it was sufficiently numerous to support the wolves. Farley knew his superiors would remain skeptical, however, because sufficiency in number does not necessarily mean sufficiency in nutritional value. Farley therefore began the second phase of the test, which must have been easier for his superiors to swallow than for him.

For the next several weeks he ate little else besides mice! He ate the whole mouse except the skin. To prepare a meal, he marinated one dozen fat mice for 2 hours in ethyl alcohol, rolled them in a mixture of flour, salt, pepper, and cloves, fried them about 5 minutes in a greased pan, and simmered them slowly for 15 minutes in alcohol. He suffered no ill effects from this diet and remained vigorous, which suggested that mice had a sufficient nutritional value to support him and, by inference, a wolf.

Farley really detested the third phase of his study: gathering and examining several months' worth of excrement from the wolf family. He found that 48 percent of the samples contained rodent remains. Other identifiable food items were fragments of caribou bones, caribou hair, and a few bird feathers. Clearly mice constituted a substantial proportion of the wolves' diet.

Only one puzzle remained. Farley had

never seen George and Albert transport mice back to the pups after a night of hunting and he couldn't imagine how they did it. This puzzle wasn't solved until Mike brought around one of his relatives, Ootek, an elderly Eskimo medicine man. Ootek explained that wolves carry mice in their bellies and regurgitate them, providing a partially digested meal for their pups. After hearing about it, Farley witnessed this procedure several times for himself.

Ootek also told Farley an Eskimo legend about the caribou and the wolf being one because "the caribou feeds the wolf, but it is the wolf who keeps the caribou strong" (Mowat, 1963, p. 85). According to the legend, weak caribou started to outnumber strong ones because people killed the fat and the strong. Kaila, the god of the sky, therefore told wolves to "eat the sick, weak, and small caribou, so that the land will be left for the fat and the good ones" (Mowat, 1963, p. 85).

Farley was stunned to hear the theory of natural selection related in an ancient Eskimo legend. He was also skeptical because he had seen so many skeletons of what appeared to be big and healthy caribou scat-

tered all over the tundra. He asked Mike to have Ootek explain that.

"Don't need to ask him that," Mike replied with unabashed candor. "It was me killed those deer. I got fourteen dogs to feed and it takes maybe two, three caribou a week for that. I got to feed myself, too. It's no use for me to shoot skinny caribou. What I got to have is the big fat ones" (Mowat, 1963, pp. 85–86).

Mike went on to say that he killed about 300 caribou a year and that all trappers did the same. Farley was stunned to find that by this estimate over 100,000 caribou were killed by trappers per year.

Farley knew that his superiors would doubt Mike's story because every trapper interviewed in official surveys had denied killing more than one or two caribou a year. The trappers had also insisted that it was wolves who were slaughtering the deer by the thousands, so Farley's superiors would also be reluctant to believe that wolves helped strengthen caribou herds by selectively killing only the sick and weak ones.

With the help of Mike and Ootek, Farley observed both trappers and wolves kill caribou. He saw for himself that trappers aimed for the biggest, fattest, and strongest, while the wolves selectively hunted the small, sick, and weak. The wolves' selection mechanism was quite simple. They pursued and killed only those they could easily catch.

Farley reported his findings in meticulous detail, pitting his first-hand scientific observations against long-established beliefs based primarily on hearsay. But his efforts were to little avail. The Canadian Wildlife Service continued its policy of wolf control, using ski-equipped aircraft to set out poison-bait stations. One of these "wolf-getters" was set up near Wolf House Bay. The officer who set it ascertained that the den was occupied when he set the trap but was unable to return to check the results because of an early onset of the spring thaw.

It is not known what the results were.

MEASURING SENSATIONS

Farley Mowat became keenly attuned to his senses as weeks passed during his vigil on the arctic tundra. Stars seemed brighter, birds louder, food more tasty, flowers more fragrant, and the sun warmer. This chapter is about these sensations of sight, hearing, taste, smell, and touch. For each one, we will study the sensor, the physical stimulus that excites the sensor, and some of the conditions that can influence sensitivity. We will begin by examining methods for measuring sensations.

Let's imagine that we take a time machine back to join Farley at Wolf House Bay. We are experimental psychologists fully equipped to measure his senses. We find Farley lying comfortably on his back enjoying the billions of stars he can see from his dark camp. He explains how much more sensitive his senses have become, and he is eager to let us study his sensory sensitivity. We agree on a good first question: What is the dimmest star that Farley can see from Wolf House Bay?

This is a psychophysical question.

Psychophysics studies the relationship between physical energies and psychological experiences. In this example, the physical energy is light from a star, and the psychological experience or sensation is seeing the star. Psychophysical questions can be grouped into three categories:

1. What is the absolute threshold, or the least amount of a certain stimulus energy, that can be detected? Our question about the dimmest star is an example.
2. What is the difference threshold, or the smallest difference in intensity, that can be noticed between two stimuli? For example, how bright must a star be in order to appear just noticeably brighter than another star?
3. How do the intensity and other qualities of a stimulus relate to the intensity and other qualities of our sensations and perceptions?

We could measure Farley Mowat's absolute threshold for seeing stars in a variety of ways. In this section we will consider some of the methods that have played a major role not only in the study of sensations but also in the study of psychology in general. We will assume that we are equipped to project artificial stars and that we can vary the intensity of the artificial stars by means of either of two separate control panels.

The Method of Adjustment

In the method of adjustment we would allow Farley to adjust the intensity of the light. We would begin half the trials with the light off, and Farley would increase the intensity of the light until he could just barely see it. The other half of the trials would begin with a visible light. Farley would then decrease the intensity until he could no longer see it. We would run at least 2 trials and probably not more than 10. Each trial would end with the light set to some intensity. The average of these settings would define the absolute threshold.

The Method of Limits

In the method of limits an experimenter would control the light's intensity. Table 3–1 illustrates the procedure that we would follow. Half the trials would begin with the light too dim to be seen. We would ask Farley, "Do you see the light?" He would say, "No, I don't see it." Then we

Table 3-1

The method shown here was used to record responses in a hypothetical experiment on the absolute threshold for seeing a star. On an ascending series the observer first was given a light too dim to see, and reported, "No, I don't see it." The brightness was then gradually increased in equal steps until the observer reported, "Yes, I see it."

On a descending series the observer first was given a light bright enough to see, and reported, "Yes, I see it." The brightness was then gradually decreased in equal steps until the observer reported, "No, I don't see it."

Star Intensity (in quanta)	Alternating Ascending and Descending Series (Yes = "I see it"; No = "I don't see it")					
120						
118						
116		Start				
114		Yes				Start
112		Yes		Start		Yes
110		Yes		Yes		Yes
108		Yes		Yes		Yes
106		Yes		Yes		No
104		Yes		Yes		
102		No		Yes		
100			Yes	No		
98			No		Yes	
96			No		No	
94	Yes		No		No	
92	No		No		No	
90	No		Start		No	
88	No				No	
86	No				No	
84	Start				No	
82					No	
80					Start	
78						
76						
Absolute threshold on each series	93	103	99	101	97	107

Average Absolute Threshold: 100

would increase the intensity slightly and ask again. This would continue until Farley said, "Yes, I do see it." The other half of the trials would start with a very bright light. We would ask Farley, "Do you see the light?" He would say, "Yes, I do see it." Then we would slightly decrease the intensity and repeat the question, proceeding until he answered, "No, I don't see it." Each trial would end with the light at some intensity. The average of these intensities would define the absolute threshold for seeing the star.

The Method of Constant Stimuli

The method of constant stimuli is sometimes used to overcome a problem presented by the other two methods. The problem is that subjects know too much about the sequencing of the intensities. Either they are controlling it themselves, or they know that the intensity is getting slightly more or slightly less on each trial. Despite this problem, the methods of adjustment and limits are often used. But when knowledge of sequencing is a major concern, the method of constant stimuli can be used instead. We would first choose an intensity that is almost always seen and one that is almost never seen. Then we would choose seven or eight equally spaced intensities between the two extremes. On the first trial we would select one of the intensities at random, present it, and record whether or not Farley sees the light. On the next trial we would do the same thing for another intensity. This would continue until all intensities were presented 50 times (more or less, depending on the desired accuracy). Because the sequence is completely random, subjects cannot predict what intensity will be shown; thus the method of constant stimuli eliminates knowledge of sequencing. To calculate the absolute threshold, we would compute the percentage of times that the subject saw each stimulus. This percentage is found by dividing the total number of times the subject said "yes" by 50, which is the total number of times that each stimulus was presented. The data are then

Figure 3-1
Typical threshold data obtained by the method of constant stimuli. The curve crosses the 50 percent *yes* point at a stimulus intensity of 3.7, which is thus considered the threshold for these data.

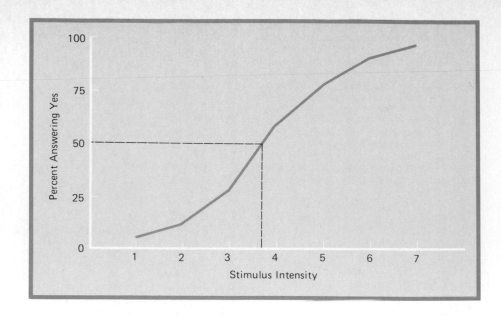

plotted on a graph, which is used to estimate the threshold, as shown in Figure 3–1. The absolute threshold is assumed to be the intensity that is seen 50 percent of the time.

Signal-Detection Theory

Although classical methods of measuring sensory sensitivity have served psychologists well, they have a serious limitation. The problem is that their results can be badly distorted by response biases caused by expectations and other nonsensory factors. Signal-detection theory was developed to isolate separate measures of sensory sensitivity and response bias. The response bias problem can be illustrated in our hypothetical experiments at Wolf House Bay. In those experiments the signal, or the stimulus presented to the observer, was a flash of light. We tried to measure the observer's sensitivity for detecting signals.

Consider how easy it would have been for biases to distort results with the three classical measures. Let's suppose that Farley was honest, but wanted to be judged to be as sensitive as possible. A problem with response bias would arise for three reasons: First, every sensory system has noise, which is spontaneous background activity that can be experienced as sensations. You can see visual noise by closing your eyes in a dark room. Most people see what appear to be flashes of light even though the room contains no stimulus light. These apparent sensations of light are caused by spontaneous neural activity in your visual system (see Chapter 5). Second, threshold experiments use low stimulus intensities that produce weak sensations. The sensations can be so weak in fact that an observer can have a difficult time deciding whether they were caused by signal or by noise. Third, a desire to detect as many signals as possible could bias one in favor of saying "Yes, I see it," when a weak sensation was in fact caused by noise.

Response biases could have distorted our hypothetical experiments with all three procedures. In the method of adjustment Farley could have set the light intensity so low that the only sensations were produced by visual noise. Similarly, in the other two methods, the observers could have said, "Yes, I see it," when they were actually seeing only visual noise. The additional "yes" responses produced in this way would have made the observers appear to be more sensitive under both the method of limits and the method of constant stimuli.

John A. Swets (1964) developed a better way to measure observer sensitivity. According to his **signal-detection theory,** detection of any stimulus depends upon both *sensory sensitivity* and *decisions*, which must be measured separately. Farley could have detected many or few signals in our hypothetical experiments, depending on the decision criterion he adopted. With a very lax criterion he would have said, "Yes, I see it," for every weak sensation, even those caused by noise. With a very strict criterion, he would have said, "Yes, I see it," only for very strong, clear sensations, and consequently would have missed some weak sensations that were actually caused by a signal. Because of different criteria, therefore, the classical methods would mistakenly indicate different sensitivities. In contrast, signal-detection theory enables one to compute both a d' score, which measures sensitivity, and a β score, which measures strictness of a decision criterion. Thus two observers who have the same sensitivity will get the same d' score even if their decision criteria are different. In addition, they will get different β scores to indicate exactly how different their decision criteria are.

Swets got his impetus for developing signal-detection theory from the need for better tests of sensitivity in radar operators. After using the theory to test radar operators, Green and Swets (1966) promoted its use in basic research. Their book is an excellent example of how an attempt to solve a practical problem can result in important theoretical advances.

Methods for Measuring Psychophysical Functions

Up to this point we have been discussing several different methods for measuring the least amount of stimulus energy that can be detected. For any given physical stimulus, the minimal sensitivity represents only one point on the **psychophysical function**. The whole function specifies the relationship between physical energies and psychological experiences over a wide range of physical magnitudes. To determine Farley's psychophysical function for brightness, we would ask him to behave like a measuring instrument. In other words, we would ask him to make responses that could be translated into numbers that represent the relationship between physical energies and psychological experiences. We might show him two lights, for instance, and ask him how bright these lights appeared in comparison to one another. A problem with such an open-ended question is that different people might give different kinds of answers. Thus psychologists have developed special methods to constrain how people respond to questions about psychophysical relationships.

Three of these methods are as follows:

1. One method is *magnitude estimation*, a procedure in which subjects are asked to assign any number they wish to match their psychological experience. In one study on estimating brightness subjects were told:

   Your task is to assign a number proportional to the brightness as you see it. Use any number you find necessary—fraction, whole number or decimal—but try to keep the numbers proportional to brightness. If one stimulus looks twice as bright as another, the number you assign to one should be twice as large as the number you assign to the other (Stevens & Galanter, 1957, p. 392)

2. Another method is *category judgment*, a procedure in which subjects are asked to match their experiences to a small set of numbers. In a study on brightness the instructions might be:

   Tell me how bright each of these lights is on a scale of 1 (very dim) to 10 (very bright).

3. A third technique is *cross-modality matching*, a procedure in which subjects are asked to match one sensory quality with some other sensory quality. A typical instruction might be:

   Indicate how bright each of these lights is by adjusting the loudness of this tone to match the brightness of each light.

All three methods have yielded systematic data, as we will see in the next section.

Weber's Law

Scientists seek general principles to account for their observations. This pursuit takes them back and forth between observations and principles. Observations suggest general principles, and the principles in turn predict new observations. These predictions are either confirmed or disconfirmed. When a prediction is confirmed, scientists begin to test other predictions until one is discomfirmed. Then they refine the principle and start the process all over again. One of the first to propose a general psychological principle was Ernst H. Weber, a German psychophysicist who in 1846 stated the law that now bears his name.

The problem Weber worked on can be illustrated with a simple example. Suppose we held a 1-ounce weight. How much weight would have to be added before we noticed an increase in heaviness? The answer according to Teghtsoonian (1971) is that .02 ounce would have to be added. Now suppose we held a 100-ounce weight. How much would have to be added before we noticed an increase in weight? Would we notice if .02 ounce was added? That would be similar to adding a paper clip to the weight of this book. No, much more weight would have to be added: In fact, we would have to add 2 ounces or about 100 paper clips. It is also true for other kinds of stimuli that smaller changes can more easily be detected when stimulus intensities are low than when they are high. For example, if your reading light is good, you probably would not notice if someone added a 4-watt light. But you would notice if the same light was added to your bedroom at night.

Weber found that a simple relationship exists between an original intensity, which he called I, and the amount that must be added to I before

Table 3–2
Weber Fractions for Various Senses

Sense	Weber Fraction
Electric shock	.013
Saturation, red	.019
Heaviness	.020
Finger span	.022
Length	.029
Vibration, 60 Hz	.036
Loudness	.048
Brightness	.079
Taste, NaCl	.083

Source: Teghtsoonian, 1971.

the intensity is just-noticeably different. He called the amount that must be added ΔI (pronounced "delta I"). Today the amount that must be added is often called a just-noticeable difference (jnd). **Weber's Law** states that for a specified stimulus, when one divides ΔI by I, one always gets the same number, which he referred to as a constant value, K. Weber's Law often appears in the form

$$\frac{\Delta I}{I} = K$$

Teghtsoonian (1971) reported that K is equal to about .02 for heaviness, .08 for brightness, and .03 for length. Knowing these values, we can use Weber's Law to make very precise predictions. For example, suppose the only light in Farley's cabin came from 100 candles. How many more candles would we have to light before the room would become just-noticeably brighter? In this problem I equals 100 candles and K equals .08. To obtain ΔI, simply multiply I times K. The answer is 8 candles. This means that 8 more candles would have to be lit before the room would appear brighter. Now, suppose the original amount of light came from 200 candles. How many more candles would we have to light before the cabin would appear brighter? Here, I equals 200, and, of course, K is still .08 because we are still talking about brightness. The answer is 16 candles. With the room twice as bright to begin with, twice as many candles must be added before the room will appear brighter.

Weber's Law, or principle, stimulated a great deal of research. Scientists have found that it holds up well in all sensory modalities. The value of K is different for different modalities, as shown in Table 3–2. However, within any given modality, the value of K is constant over most stimulus intensities, except that it rises slightly for extremely high or extremely low stimulus intensities.

This discussion of general methods and principles sets the stage for studying specific senses. We will begin with seeing, which is perhaps our most highly developed sense.

Seeing

Farley Mowat had excellent vision, which served him well in his study of wolves and in many other adventures. Millions of people throughout the world have "seen" the Arctic through his eyes in his 25 books, which have been published in over 20 languages. Many of you also enjoy good vision, but many of you do not. Some of you see poorly without corrective lenses, and some do not see at all. The main causes of visual problems and blindness are in the eyes themselves. We will briefly study the eyes and the physiology of the visual system. We will then turn to psychophysical facts that explain some of the things that Farley saw at Wolf House Bay.

The Eyes

Figure 3–2 shows the human eye, which includes the following structures:
1. The **cornea** is the window of the eye. A healthy cornea is transparent and shaped like the side of a crystal ball. The **sclera** is the white, opaque, outer wall of the eye. The cornea is attached to the sclera. Two diseases of the cornea occur when the cornea becomes pointed, like the end of a football, or becomes cloudy. These diseases rarely cause blindness, however, because they can be corrected by corneal transplants.

Figure 3-2

This cross-section drawing shows the basic structures of the human eye: the cornea, iris, pupil, lens, vitreous humor, retina, fovea, and optic nerve.

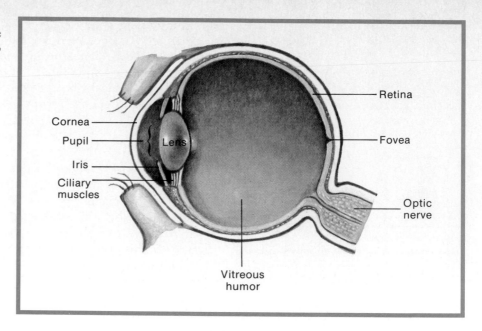

2. The **aqueous humor** is a clear fluid that carries nourishment to the cornea. Have you ever seen spots hovering in front of your eyes? They can be caused by impurities floating in the aqueous humor. The "spots" can disappear and reappear because the aqueous humor is completely recycled every 4 hours. The most common cause of blindness is a problem with the recycling system, which causes pressure to build up inside the eye. The pressure can destroy the eye's critical structures. In America this disease, called **glaucoma**, threatens more than 1.5 million people with blindness. It can be treated with special eye drops and other methods. Early treatment is important, so it is wise to get periodic checkups.

3. When you are asked the color of your eyes, you are really being asked the color of your **iris**, which is a flat, doughnut-shaped network of muscles behind the aqueous humor. What appears to be a black spot in the center of the iris is actually an opening called the **pupil**.

Eye doctors examine the eye's internal structures with an **ophthalmoscope**, which uses mirrors or prisms to direct light through the pupil. This important instrument allows doctors to detect eye diseases and other diseases such as high blood pressure.

4. The **lens** is directly behind the pupil. It helps the cornea focus light onto the back of the eye. The lens does the critical fine adjustments or **accommodations** required to focus objects at various distances. It accommodates by changing its shape; it gets rounder for near objects and flatter for far ones.

The **near point of accommodation** is the nearest point at which print can be read distinctly. As we get older, we all lose some of our ability to accommodate. As a result, the near point of accommodation gets farther and farther away, until reading requires bifocals (or an extra-long arm!).

The most widespread disease affecting vision is **cataracts**, a condition characterized by cloudy lenses. Blindness results if the lenses become too cloudy, but fortunately surgical procedures provide a very effective treatment.

5. The **vitreous humor** is a semiliquid gel that fills the eye's main chamber and gives it a spherical shape. **Nearsightedness** results when an eye is elongated like a horizontal egg. Nearsighted people see near objects well, but see far objects poorly. **Farsightedness** is caused by an eye that is flattened, like a vertical egg (Figure 3–3). Farsighted people see far

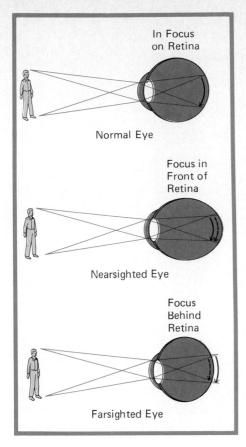

Figure 3–3
Nearsightedness and farsightedness are caused by abnormal eye shapes. For clear vision, light must be focussed directly on the eye's back wall, as it is in the normal eye. The nearsighted eye is too long, so light focusses in front of the back wall; the farsighted eye is too short, so it focusses behind the back wall.

Figure 3–4
To locate your blind spot, close your left eye and stare at the X. Slowly move the book toward you and away from you at a distance of about a foot until the dot disappears.

objects well, but see near objects poorly. Both of these problems are easily corrected by wearing glasses.

6. The **retina** is tissue covering most of the eye's interior wall. It contains receptors that respond to light, blood vessels, and a network of neurons that transmit information to the brain. One area of the retina is blind. This **blind spot** contains no light receptors, which are needed to see. You can find your blind spot with the simple test shown in Figure 3–4. There are no light receptors in this area because the space is taken up by the **optic nerve,** which is a bundle of nerve fibers that carry neural signals to the brain. In contrast to the blind spot, another retinal area, called the **fovea,** is especially sensitive. Most blood vessels and nerve fibers are routed around this sensitive area. In addition, the fovea has special light receptors, called *rods* and *cones*, which we will discuss in detail in the next section.

Light Receptors: Rods and Cones

The retina has two kinds of receptors: (1) **cones,** which are located mostly in the fovea and which are best for seeing details; and (2) **rods,** which are located mostly on the sides or periphery of the retina, and which are best for seeing in dim light.

Cones enable us to see sharp details. When you want to look at something, you move your eyes so that the image of the object you want to see is focussed on your fovea, where most of your cones are. If you want to know what the world would be like without a fovea, look at a flashbulb when someone takes your picture. Almost all you will see with your fovea for the next several minutes is a bright silver spot. You will see the rest of the world only from the periphery or sides of your retina, where details are hard to make out. Try reading while you are still experiencing this and you will find out how hard it is to see details from the sides of the retina. Rods are best suited to seeing in dim light—indeed, they are the only receptors that function at night. When you are using only your rods you cannot see color, which is why you see shades of black and white, but not color, in dim light and at night. Rods are located on the periphery or sides of the retina. As a result, you can see best at night if you look at something to your left or right rather than straight on. This is called **peripheral vision,** because you use the receptors on the periphery of the retina. Pilots who fly at night are trained to use their peripheral vision by looking at the sides or edges of what they want to see. You can use a TV set to demonstrate that peripheral vision is better than central vision for seeing dim lights. Watch the TV set for about 10 minutes in a room with all the lights out. Then turn off the set. The screen's glow will gradually fade. Soon it will be too dim to see when you look directly at it, but it will still be bright enough to see out of the side of your eyes when you look to either side.

Why are cones best for seeing details, while rods are best for seeing dim light? The answer is found in the neural pathways between these receptors and the brain.

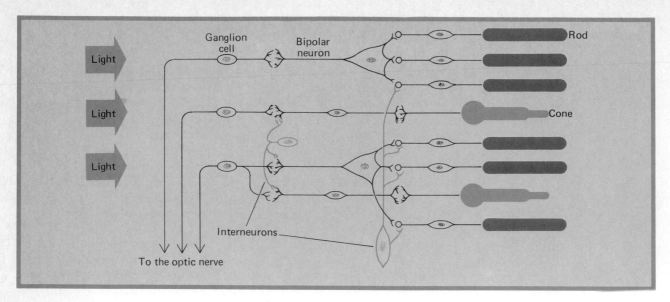

To the optic nerve

Figure 3-5
The visual pathways go from the retina to other brain structures. Messages first go from receptor cells to bipolar cells. Each cone sends a message to a separate bipolar cell. Many rods send messages to the same bipolar cell. Messages go from bipolar cells to ganglion cells, and then exit from the retina as part of the optic nerve.

Pathways to the Brain

The visual pathways connect the eyes with the brain's cortex, which we discussed in Chapter 2. But these pathways are more than passive cables; they contain cells that actively participate in the process of coding or interpreting the information contained in light. This coding process begins in the retina. Here all cones and rods are connected to bipolar cells, which are in turn connected to ganglion cells that send signals out of the retina to the brain (see Figures 3–5 and 3–6).

Cones and rods have different functions, in part because they are connected to bipolar cells differently. Cones are best for seeing detail because almost every cone in the fovea has its own bipolar cell. The one-to-one connections give each cone a way to report to a bipolar cell. Two cones can thus report different messages when the light falling on them is in any way different. The separate messages enable us to discern small differ-

Figure 3-6
Messages from the left visual field travel to the right occipital lobe; messages from the right visual field of each eye go to the left occipital lobe. The place where they cross is called the optic chiasma.

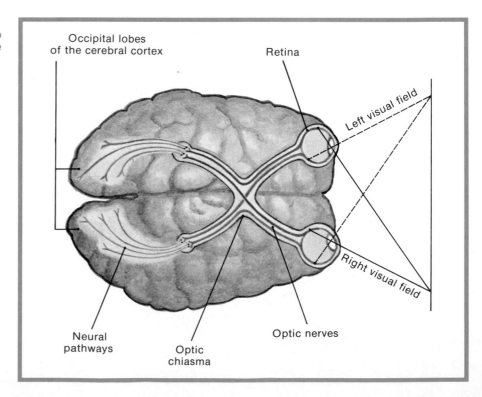

Occipital lobes of the cerebral cortex

Retina

Left visual field

Right visual field

Neural pathways

Optic chiasma

Optic nerves

Figure 3-7
Can you tell whose portrait this is? Block portraits have two parts: a blurred picture of a famous person and a set of sharp edges outlining the blocks. A glance will tell you that this is poor optical information. Your visual system can clear up the information, however, with a little help. Have someone jiggle the picture slightly at a viewing distance of about 8 feet while you squint your eyes to blur your vision.

ences or details in what we see. Cones do not function in dim light because each cone's message gets too weak for bipolar cells to receive it.

Whereas each cone has its own bipolar cell, many rods share the same bipolar cell. These many-to-one connections allow rods to add their messages together to make a signal strong enough for a bipolar cell to receive. For this reason, rods do much better than cones in dim light. The many-to-one connection also means, however, that each rod does not really send a separate message. Rods are therefore poor at discerning details, because of the way they are connected to bipolar cells.

Most cells in the visual pathways to the brain receive messages from many other cells and send messages to many other cells. Information is thereby added and subtracted, coded and recoded, in a series of processes that determine vision. These processes somehow turn poor optical information into clear perceptions. Optical information is poor because the eye's lens creates distorted images like those you see through a cheap magnifying glass. To make matters worse, light must pass through blood vessels and nerve fibers before reaching light receptors. Cells in the visual pathway and cortex work together to "clean up" the information (Campbell, 1974; Pollen & Ronner, 1982). Figure 3-7 illustrates what your visual system can do with poor optical information. Scientists are only beginning to understand how cells in the visual pathways and in the cortex join forces to determine what we see (see Highlight, "The Eye Is Not a Camera").

Light and Dark Adaptation

Farley Mowat saw dim stars that sent very little light into his eyes; and he saw, without pain, bright sunlight reflected from snow. In the same way, we see dimly lit faces in a movie theater and brightly lit faces on a sunny beach. But this large range of sensitivity is never available at any one moment. When we walk from sunlight into a dark theater, for example, we are almost blinded until our eyes adjust. We are again almost blinded until our eyes adjust when we leave the dark theater to go back out into the sunlight.

When the eyes are exposed to light, their sensitivity continually changes. If the amount of light remains fairly constant for about 15 minutes, the eyes will become most sensitive to that amount of light and will be unable to see lights that are about 100 times brighter or 100 times dimmer. Thus, while the overall range of sensitivity is enormous, the range *at any one moment* is relatively narrow. When we enter a movie theater on a sunny afternoon, we encounter more than a hundredfold decrease in light, far outside our momentary range of sensitivity, so we cannot see well. An adjustment in sensitivity starts immediately and continues for about 15 minutes until our eyes become as sensitive as possible to the level of light in the theater. This adjustment of sensitivity is called **dark adaptation.** The adjustment that takes place when we go from the dark theater into sunlight is called **light adaptation.**

Farley saw more stars from Wolf House Bay than he did from the city because the background level of light was lower. The dark background caused an advantageous adjustment in his momentary range of sensitivity.

Color Vision

The night-time arctic sky often treated Farley not only to billions of stars but also to a dazzling display of the many-colored, flashing northern lights. The beauty of this display and many others would be greatly reduced for people who are *colorblind*; **colorblindness** is the inability to distinguish between colors. Imagine walking through a grocery store and seeing yellow beefsteaks and hams, yellow cabbage, yellow radishes, and yellow spinach.

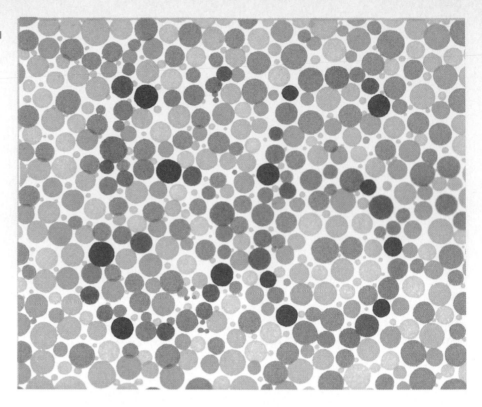

These Northern lights (Aurora Borealis) are one of many feasts for the eyes that nature provides.

Now you leave the store on a bright summer day, walk across a well-manicured yellow lawn and past tall yellow pine trees, and approach a traffic signal containing three vertically arranged yellow lights. This is how the world looks to about 2 out of every 100 males and to about 2 out of every 10,000 females who have red-green colorblindness. (We would have no idea how the world looks to colorblind people if it were not for a few people who had red-green blindness in one eye and normal vision in the other. Things that look red and green to the normal eye look light yellow to the colorblind eye.) There are other, less common kinds of colorblindness. For example, some people have yellow-blue blindness; that is, they can't tell the difference between yellows and blues. Others have total colorblindness. We are not sure how their world looks, but it might be like watching black-and-white TV. Some people do not realize they are colorblind until they are tested with the pictures shown in Figure 3–8.

The high value placed on color is illustrated by the popularity of color television. Today Americans buy more color than black-and-white televisions, even though color sets cost quite a bit more. In this section we will discuss some of the research that led to the development of color television.

The first major breakthrough was Isaac Newton's (1642–1727) discovery that white light from the sun is a compound of all colors. We now know that light travels in waves, with different wavelengths for each color. Figure 3–9 shows the **electromagnetic spectrum** forming the entire range of wavelengths of electromagnetic radiation. The wavelengths corresponding to visible colors cover only a small part of the whole spectrum. For example, we do not see X-rays, which are much shorter in wavelength than light waves, and we do not see radio waves, which are much longer. Objects have particular colors because they absorb some wavelengths and reflect others. We see the reflected wavelengths; a red apple, for example, reflects red wavelengths.

The next major breakthrough occurred when Thomas Young (1773–1829) tackled the problem of how the nervous system responds to different

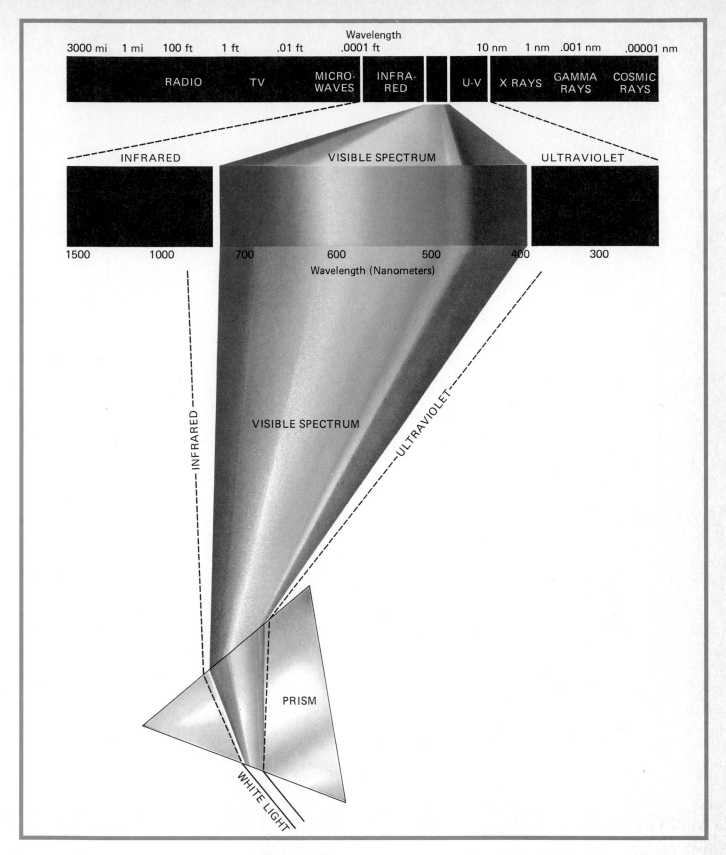

Figure 3–9

Sunlight, or white light, contains all the colors that we can see. A prism separates white light into its component colors. Each color in this visible spectrum corresponds to a specific wavelength. Light travels in waves, and wavelength is the distance between wave crests. The visible spectrum is only a small part of the electromagnetic spectrum which consists of energy traveling in wavelengths that are shorter or longer than the visible spectrum.

THE EYE IS NOT A CAMERA

Scientists used to think that our eyes worked like a camera. Cameras produce images of objects by recording light intensities at each point. If you enlarged a photograph many times, you would see that it is made up of dots ranging in brightness from light to dark. Until fairly recently scientists compared the dots in such pictures with the response of each retinal receptor in the eye; thus they thought that eyes send dotlike pictures to the brain, where they are interpreted.

In the 1950s researchers in a number of different laboratories tried to find out exactly what the frog's eye tells the frog's brain. The answer electrified the scientific community. One kind of cell in the retina responded best when a small black disk was moved about in front of a frog's eye. When this was done, frogs jumped and snapped at it as if they were trying to catch a bug. This class of retinal cell was called a "bug detector." The point was that this response was cued by a cell in the retina—not in the brain.

Those who had been thinking about eyes as cameras suddenly realized that the retina did much more than they thought. It does not just project a picture for the brain to recognize and interpret—it does some of the recognizing and interpreting itself.

David Hubel and Thorsten Wiesel won half of the 1981 Nobel prize for medicine for their research in this field. They found cells that might be called feature detectors because they respond to specific aspects or features of a visual stimulus (just as the frog's bug detector responded to the buglike aspects of certain stimuli). Hubel and Wiesel (1970) gained special recognition by investigating the development and organization of feature detectors.

They discovered that feature detectors develop shortly after birth, and that their development depends upon visual experience. Detectors are permanently altered if kittens get distorted visual experience during critical early stages of life (see Chapter 8). Such studies of altered development depended upon years of research on the normal organization of feature detectors. Hubel and Wiesel (1965) had found, for instance, that detectors of different complexities are neatly organized in the brain (as shown in the figure here). One layer of cells near the brain's surface has *simple cells*, which respond only if a line of a specific orientation falls on a specific retinal location. A deeper layer has *complex cells*, which respond to a line of a specific orientation no matter where it falls on the retina. A still deeper layer has *hypercomplex cells*, which detect angles and other features. One of Hubel and Wiesel's greatest contributions was a model of how such detectors might work together. The accompanying figure shows how cells might be connected, for example. Such models provided the foundation not only for Hubel and Weisel's subsequent research, but also for the work of many modern researchers in vision and development.

Organization of feature detectors.

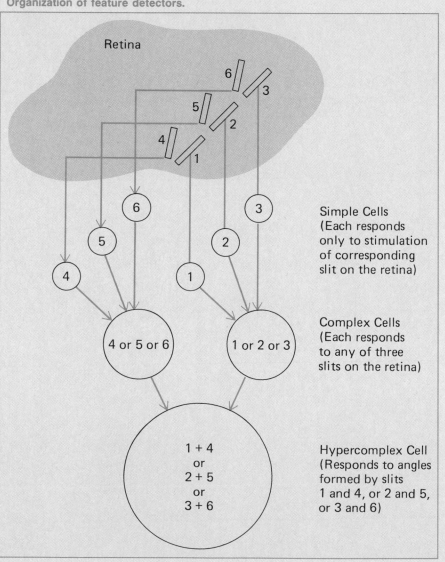

Retina

Simple Cells
(Each responds only to stimulation of corresponding slit on the retina)

Complex Cells
(Each responds to any of three slits on the retina)

4 or 5 or 6

1 or 2 or 3

1 + 4
or
2 + 5
or
3 + 6

Hypercomplex Cell
(Responds to angles formed by slits 1 and 4, or 2 and 5, or 3 and 6)

Figure 3-10

Color mixture of three lights is shown here—red, green, and violet; they are widely spaced on the spectrum. Any color on the spectrum can be produced in the overlapping areas by adjusting the intensities of the three lights. Here we see yellow where green and red mix, and we see white where all three mix.

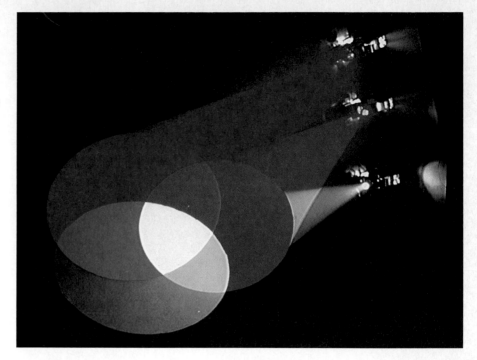

Figure 3-11

This green, black, and yellow flag will turn red, white, and blue in an afterimage. You can make an afterimage by staring at the lower right-hand star for about 45 seconds. You will then see the afterimage when you shift your gaze to a bright white piece of paper.

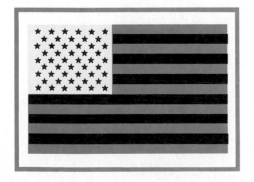

wavelengths. He began with experiments on color mixture, which are illustrated in Figure 3-10. Three colored lights (violet, red, and green) are projected onto a screen in an otherwise dark room. The resulting pattern reminds one of an insignia on a color TV. This is no accident—experiments on color mixing led to the development of color TV. The most unusual aspect of Figure 3-10 is that white is seen where all three colors overlap and yellow is seen where red and green overlap. Young could produce every color of the visible spectrum in the overlapping areas by varying the intensity of the lights. He theorized that the retina contains three kinds of color receptors and that the signals from these merge to produce our sensations of color. With further developments by Hermann von Helmholtz (1821–1894), this theory, called the *trichromatic receptor theory*, led physiologists to verify that the retina does indeed have three kinds of color receptors. Each kind responds differently to colors. One responds most to blue-violet, another responds most to green, and another favors yellow-red (Brown & Wald, 1964; Marks, Dobelle, & MacNichol, 1964).

This is an important fact, but it doesn't explain all aspects of color vision. For example, it does not explain what you see in Figure 3-11. If you stare at the picture for about 45 seconds and then shift your gaze to a white surface, you will see red where green had been, white where black had been, and blue where yellow had been. What you see is an afterimage. It occurs because some activity continues in the retina after you look away from the picture. The trichromatic receptor theory does not account for the colors of afterimages.

To explain this and other observations, Hering (1877) offered the *opponent-process theory*, which states that receptor cells are joined in opposing pairs. The color we see depends on whether a pair responds positively or negatively. For example, blue is seen when a blue-yellow pair responds negatively; yellow is seen when it responds positively. This explains why afterimages appear blue when yellow is in the original. When we look at yellow, the receptor that is sensitive to yellow gets *fatigued*; that is, it responds less to the same stimulus. When cells are not fatigued, light from a white surface stimulates the blue-yellow pair equally so that neither color is seen. But when the yellow side is fatigued, it does not respond as strongly, upsetting the balance in favor of blue. As a result, we see blue. The theory also proposes the existence of a red-green opponent pair and a black-white pair, which explains the other colors we see in the afterimage (Hurvich & Jameson, 1974).

 # HEARING

Although Farley's hearing might have improved during his stay at Wolf House Bay, it never became as sensitive as Ootek's or the wolves', as indicated in the following incident:

> Ootek suddenly cupped his hands to his ears and began to listen intently.
>
> I could hear nothing, and I had no idea what had caught his attention until he said: "Listen, the wolves are talking!" and pointed toward a range of hills some five miles to the north of us.
>
> I listened, but if a wolf was broadcasting from those hills he was not on my wavelength. I heard nothing except the baleful buzzing of mosquitoes; but George, who had been sleeping on the crest of the esker, suddenly sat up, cocked his ears forward and pointed his long muzzle toward the north. After a minute or two he threw back his head and howled; a long, quavering howl which started low and ended on the highest note my ears would register.
>
> Ootek grabbed my arm and broke into a delighted grin.
>
> "Caribou are coming; the wolf says so!"
>
> (Mowat, 1963, p. 89)

This incident raises many interesting questions: How does sound travel for miles over the tundra? Why do people sometimes cup their hands around their ears? Why do animals turn their ears toward sounds? Do sounds really travel on different wavelengths? What is the highest note the human ear can register? This section will answer these and other questions about hearing. (You might also be wondering whether or not wolves can actually send messages about caribou coming. This section will not address this question, but Farley Mowat devotes a whole chapter to it. If you are interested, you can read his rather intriguing evidence that wolves do indeed send complex messages.)

The Ears

Sound travels through air as waves travel through water. A stone dropped in a pond sends out ripples in all directions. Similarly, when objects vibrate in air, they create waves in air. To understand hearing we must learn how these sound waves affect the ears.

The word *ears* brings to mind flaps on the sides of the head. But, as Figure 3–12 shows, these flaps are just one of three basic subdivisions of ears:

1. The *external ear* captures sound traveling through the air. The **pinna** is the elastic flap we usually are referring to when we talk about the ear. The **ear canal** is a tubelike passage that funnels sound. The **eardrum** is a fine membrane stretched over the inner end of the ear canal; it vibrates when sound waves strike it. As you might have guessed from the behavior of Ootek and George, cupping the hands around the ears and turning toward a sound source helps to funnel sound waves into the ears.

Figure 3–12

As can be seen in this diagram, the ear has three parts: the external ear or pinna, which includes the ear canal and the eardrum; the middle ear, which contains the hammer, the anvil, and the stirrup; and the inner ear, which contains the oval window and the cochlea.

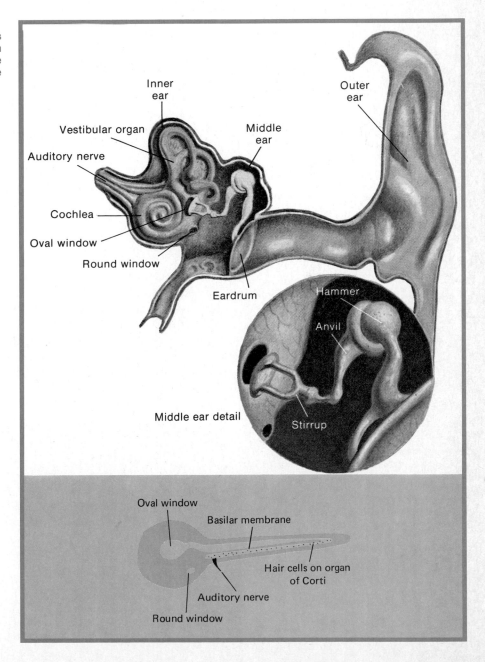

2. The *middle ear* is a small air cavity containing three small bones: the **hammer,** the **anvil,** and the **stirrup.** This delicate chain of bones transmits sounds from the eardrum to the inner ear.

3. The *inner ear* is the part of the ear that transforms sound vibrations into neural impulses, which we discussed in Chapter 2. It receives sounds through the **oval window,** which is a membrane stretched over the opening of the inner ear. Attached to the oval window is a structure that looks like a snail. It is called the **cochlea,** which is the Latin word for snail. It is a coiled tube that makes about three turns, like a spiral around a central core. Inside the cochlea is a flexible membrane, called the **basilar membrane.** It is attached to the oval window at one end and to the tip of the cochlea at the other end. Vibrations in the oval window cause hair cells on the basilar membrane to vibrate. When the hair cells are bent, they send nerve impulses along the acoustic nerve to the brain.

To sum up, the external ear collects and focuses sound, causing the eardrum to vibrate. Three delicate bones carry these vibrations to the oval window, which vibrates receptors in the cochlea, triggering nerve impulses to the brain.

Bone conduction is another way that sound is transmitted. When you speak, your jaw bones conduct vibrations to the cochlea. Thus you hear your voice through bone-conducted sounds and air-conducted sounds. Others hear your voice only through air-conducted sounds. Your tape-recorded voice sounds strange to you because you are not used to hearing only your air-conducted sound, which is the way everyone else hears your voice. Some hearing aids use bone conduction when the middle ear cannot conduct sound. Other hearing aids simply amplify air-conducted sound.

Characteristics of Sound

Sound waves are easier to study when they are converted to visible waves. Figure 3–13 shows a way to do this with an **oscilloscope,** which is similar to a television. We can learn relationships between psychological and physical characteristics of hearing by listening to a sound while watching it on an oscilloscope. Let's imagine taking an oscilloscope to a concert.

Frequency and Pitch. We have all delighted in the mellow low notes of a bass singer and the trilling high notes of a soprano. But have you ever wondered how we hear the difference between low and high notes? Such differences are referred to as differences in **pitch.** In Figure 3–14 we see that changes in pitch correspond to changes in **frequency** of sound waves, which is the number of wave crests that occur in a second. The distance between two wave crests is called a *wavelength* or a *cycle*, so fre-

Figure 3–13
The device shown here, an oscilloscope, makes pictures out of sound waves. A tuning fork makes a sound wave, which, as shown here, consists of compressions and expansions of air molecules. A microphone makes an electrical response to these compressions and expansions. The oscilloscope changes the electrical response into a moving picture on a screen similar to a TV screen. The picture is a wave with high points and low points. A high point on the picture represents a compression of air molecules; a low point represents an expansion of air molecules.

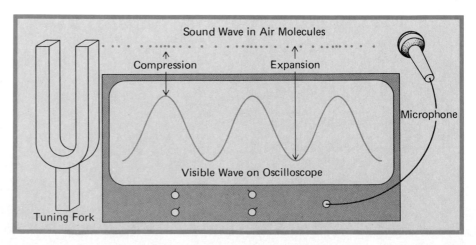

Figure 3-14

Each oscilloscope shows 1/100 of a second (.01 second) from two sound waves: (A) a low-pitched sound, with 600 cycles per second, and a higher-pitched sound, with 1,200 cycles per second; (B) a soft note and a loud note; (C) a note played on a trumpet and on a clarinet.

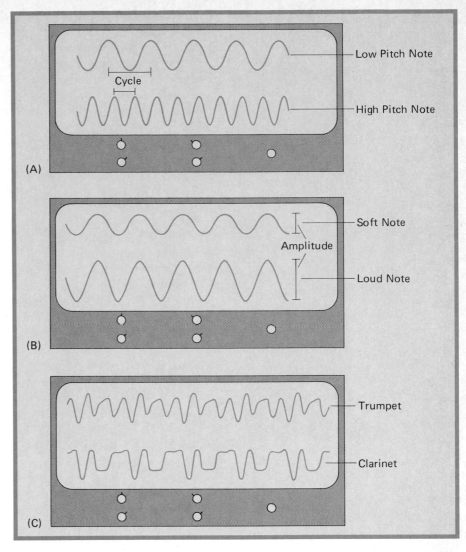

quency is measured in cycles per second. One cycle per second is called a *hertz* (Hz). As most stereo buffs know, frequency is often reported in hertz. A piano plays frequencies ranging from 27.5 Hz (low note) to 4,186 Hz (high note). A bass singer sings notes as low as 82.4 Hz, and a soprano sings notes as high as 1,046.5 Hz. You might want to consider this before buying stereo speakers. Today a good pair of speakers capable of reproducing sounds as low as 35 Hz costs about $100; a good pair of speakers capable of reproducing sounds down to about 25 Hz costs about $1500. That's an expensive 10 Hz—especially when you consider that there is very little music written in that range!

Humans hear sounds ranging from 20 to 20,000 Hz. This means that the ears somehow give different neural responses for different frequencies within this range. Scientists are debating two rival theories of how this is done. According to the *place theory*, one hears different pitches because different frequencies stimulate different places on the basilar membrane. According to the *frequency theory*, one hears different pitches because receptors send pulses up the auditory nerve at the same frequency as the sound wave.

Nobel laureate George von Békésy used a powerful microscope to show that different frequencies vibrate different parts of the basilar membrane. His work convinced most scientists that the place theory explains how people hear frequencies above 3,000 Hz. On the other hand, almost everyone agrees that the frequency theory explains how we hear frequencies below 50 Hz. Thus the debate concerns how we hear frequencies between

People were able to enjoy this tuba concert at Rockefeller Center in part because the center was designed in accordance with principles of how sound waves affect our hearing.

50 and 3,000 Hz. The major proponent of the frequency theory in this range is E. G. Wever. He realized that single nerve fibers cannot respond faster than 1,000 times per second, so he advocated the *volley principle*, which states that the combined response of different fibers corresponds to the frequency of sound waves. In other words, cells take turns firing, similar to the way Revolutionary War soldiers alternated so that one group fired a round, or a volley, while another group reloaded. With the help of the volley principle, the frequency theory could explain hearing up to 3,000 Hz. But no one knows for sure whether or not it does in fact explain it. In the 50 to 3,000 Hz range, the place theory, the frequency theory, or some as yet unspecified theory may be correct. Most speech sounds are in this range, so settling this theoretical issue will have practical consequences for helping the deaf.

Amplitude and Loudness. There is another change in sound waves that occurs as volume is increased. Figure 3–14 shows this change for the same note played softly and loudly. Notice that the frequency is the same, but the amplitude of the waves differs. The amplitude, which can be measured as the distance between a wave's top and bottom, gets larger as sounds get louder. The scientist's unit for measuring loudness is called the *bel*, after Alexander Graham Bell. Often scientists prefer to use a unit one-tenth as large as a bel. They call this a decibel. Each tenfold increase in sound level adds 10 decibels.

From what has been said so far, we would expect to hear the same pitch when we listened to the sound waves illustrated in Figure 3–14. After all, they have the same frequency. Unfortunately hearing is not that simple. A wave's amplitude also influences the brain's interpretation of pitch. As a tone gets louder, its pitch sounds lower. Thus the higher-amplitude wave in Figure 3–14 would seem to have a slightly lower pitch than the other wave, even though the frequencies are the same. When buying a stereo system, you might ask whether or not the system electronically compensates for this distortion; better systems do.

Loud sounds can be irritating and even damaging. For example, riveters and others who work in extremely noisy environments often suffer from boilermaker's deafness. This is a partial hearing loss caused by spending long periods of time amid loud noises. Experts warn that no worker should be exposed to a continuous sound level of 85 decibels (about the loudness of a vacuum cleaner) for more than 5 hours a day without using protective devices. Loud rock bands produce sound levels between 125 and 135 decibels. Thus it is not surprising that college students who frequently listen to loud rock bands suffer some hearing loss (Lipscomb, 1969). Similarly, it is not surprising that Farley, who spent several years in the noisy battles of World War II, could not hear as well as Ootek, who spent his whole life in a quiet environment. Figure 3–15 shows familiar noises that are part of our environment and how they are measured in decibels. We will discuss sound and noise (and noise pollution) in more detail in Chapter 17.

Waveform and Tone Quality. If we watched our oscilloscope during a trumpet solo and then during a clarinet solo, we might notice another way that sound waves change. Figure 3–14 illustrates this change for a trumpet and a clarinet playing the same note at the same sound level. Notice that the frequencies and amplitudes are the same, but the shapes are different. It is this difference in shape, or waveform, that allows us to distinguish between the two sounds.

Waveforms differ because most sounds contain more than one frequency. While it is possible to generate pure tones containing a single frequency, most musical instruments generate complex tones containing many frequencies. The higher ones are called *overtone frequencies*. A trumpet and clarinet sound different because they have different overtone frequencies.

Figure 3-15
A decibel scale for several common sounds.
Prolonged exposure to sounds above 85
decibels can cause permanent damage to
the ears.

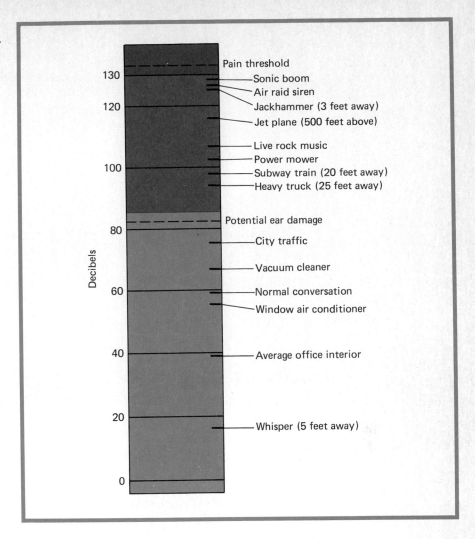

The different frequencies within each complex get combined into a single wave. But, as we see in Figure 3–14, the resulting waves have different shapes when the sounds have different overtones. Both of these waveforms sound quite pleasant. However, sometimes waves combine to create unpleasant sounds. This can happen, for example, in a poorly designed auditorium.

Locating Sounds

When Angeline hunted for mice, she listened for the rodents to reveal their location. Then she pounced on them with one swift lunge. Thus her meals depended upon her ability to localize sound. The ability to tell where a sound is coming from can also be a matter of life or death. How many times do you think our ancestors were saved, for example, by hearing a twig cracked by the foot of a stalking beast? How many lives have been saved on today's highways because a driver was able to tell where a blasting automobile horn was coming from? One way to study this important ability is by taking a mental trip to an imaginary racetrack. If you close your eyes at the racetrack, you will notice that you can locate the cars simply by listening to them. How?

If you listen carefully, you might notice that *loudness* plays a role in hearing a car's distance. In general, you hear louder sounds as being closer than softer ones. You might also notice that moving sounds provide more information. As the race cars roar toward you, their engines have a high-pitched,

A Doppler shift in sound is demonstrated by race cars. The high-pitched whining sound of an approaching car drops to a low pitch when the car zooms by.

whining sound. When the cars zoom by, their engines' sounds drop sharply to a lower pitch. This is called the **Doppler shift.** It happens because sound waves bunch up as the cars approach and spread out as the cars speed away. The bunched-up waves have a shorter distance between their wave crests (higher frequency); the spread-out waves have a longer distance between their wave crests (lower frequency). You can hear both the loudness changes and the frequency changes without special instruments. But you would need to bring special equipment to the racetrack if you hoped to study the other ways you can localize sounds, for they depend on tiny sound differences between the two ears.

When a sound is straight ahead, it reaches both ears at the same time, it sounds equally loud in both ears, and it has the same waveform in both ears. When a sound comes from one side, all three of these things change because the sound is farther from one ear: (1) the sound arrives *later* at the farther ear; (2) the sound is *softer* in the farther ear; and (3) the *phase* is slightly different in the farther ear. That is, the wave is closer to its highest point when it strikes one ear. Researchers have found that we are extremely sensitive to differences in time, loudness, and phase. When you close your eyes at a racetrack and localize the cars by sound, you are using these three sources of information, even though you are not aware of it. Humans apparently have this ability from the moment they are born (Castillo & Butterworth, 1981).

THER SENSES

Earlier we mentioned that Farley tuned into all his senses. In this section we will briefly go over some of his experiences involving the senses of taste, smell, touch, and body orientation.

Individual differences in taste preferences are a major problem not only for parents trying to please a whole family, but also for industries trying to serve millions. The latter are hiring psychophysicists to help them make their food taste good to as many people as possible.

Taste

The typical arctic diet contrasts sharply with our food. Eskimos mostly eat raw or only partially cooked meat. Even as a baby, Ootek ate raw caribou meat prechewed by his mother. Although Farley always insisted on cooking his meat, he did learn to eat plenty of wild game, including venison, caribou tongues, and, as we already mentioned, mice, fresh from the fields. These eating habits often required spending a good part of the day hunting and preparing food. Our ancestors' diets were similar. Today, however, dinners are prepared for us in advance and then frozen, or else all the ingredients are boxed for us in the exact quantities needed. We simply heat and eat, or stir and serve. Whether we like it or not, food preparation has become a big business. As a result, shrewd executives are hiring psychologists to make sure that the company's food tastes good to as many customers as possible. In this section we will examine some of the factors that determine taste.

The primary sense organ for taste is the tongue. As shown in Figure 3–16, the tongue has small elevations called **papillae.** Our taste sensors are called **taste buds.** They are located inside of papillae, away from direct contact with food. We taste solid foods by first dissolving them in saliva. The liquid solution runs down pits in the papillae and stimulates sensory cells in the taste buds. The sensory cells then send messages to the brain, giving rise to our sensation of taste. Taste cells die and are replaced about every 11 days. As people age, when their taste cells die, they are not replaced, which is why the elderly lose some of their taste sensitivity.

There are four primary tastes: sweet, sour, salty, and bitter. Different parts of the tongue are sensitive to different tastes, as shown in Figure 3–16. Our sensitivity to all of these is greatest when the food or drink temperature is between 22° and 32°C. (about 71° to 89°F.). Since the temperature of a substance changes your sensitivity to it, it is important

Figure 3–16
The tongue's taste receptors are called taste buds, which are located inside small elevations or papillae on the surface of the tongue. Different locations on the tongue are most sensitive to the four basic taste qualities: sweet, sour, salty, and bitter.

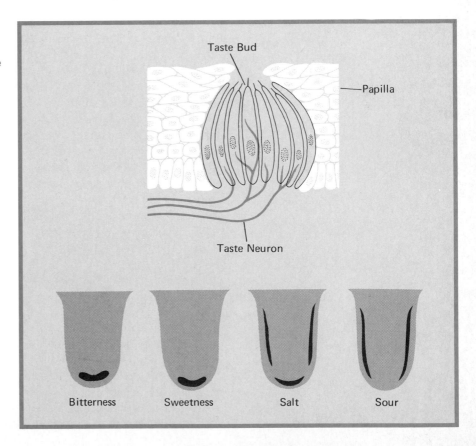

The fragrance of a flower can make us appreciate our sense of smell, about which scientists still have much to learn.

to season food at the temperature at which you intend to eat it. For example, soup salted at room temperature may need more salt when it is warmed up, and lemonade sweetened at room temperature may taste sour when it is chilled (see McBurney & Collings, 1977).

Smell

Can you imagine being brave enough to sample one of Farley's mice meals? You might try to make the experience more tolerable by holding your nose the way children do while taking distasteful medicine. This strategy helps because smell is important to taste. That's why food tastes strange (or seems to have no taste at all) when you have a head cold. Also, some foods taste different to the elderly because of changes in their ability to smell. As people age, they lose olfactory cells, which reduces not only their ability to smell but also their ability to taste. For example, the elderly often lose their fondness for chocolate. Taste receptors register chocolate as very bitter, while smell receptors register chocolate as sweet. For this reason, chocolate has an unpleasant, bitter taste to the elderly with a reduced sense of smell.

The passageway between the nose and the throat contains the odor-sensitive cells called **olfactory cells.** Gases we breathe are dissolved in a fluid covering the receptors, causing the cells to send messages to the brain. We rapidly detect a new odor, but we lose our ability to smell it after several minutes because olfactory cells respond rapidly and fatigue rapidly. We have more to learn about the sense of smell than about any of the other senses.

Touch

Our skin responds to pain, temperature, and pressure. Farley experienced all of these one day as he ran naked over rough ground in pursuit of wolves who had interrupted his nude sunbathing. In this section we will review research developments on each kind of skin sensation and point out how this research has led to important theoretical and practical advances.

A better understanding of pain is being sought in order to find better ways to relieve those who have chronic pain, and to find better ways to restore pain perception to those who have lost it. You might think, "Who needs it?" But pain perception is actually quite important. Diseases that reduce or eliminate pain perception have caused people to inflict injuries inadvertently upon themselves, including serious cuts and burns; one woman, for example, even chewed off the tip of her tongue (Cohen et al., 1955). Most of us use "painkilling" drugs from time to time, but we may depend upon them less in the future because medical doctors are finding new ways to control pain without drugs, which we will discuss in Chapters 5 and 14.

The skin may contain specialized pain receptors, but physiologists have not identified any yet. An alternative theory is that pain results from over-stimulation of the skin's temperature and pressure receptors. However, many facts argue against this. For instance, some drugs reduce pain sensations in the skin without reducing temperature or pressure sensation (Candland, 1968).

Imagine that you are sunbathing at the beach and decide to go swimming. You approach the water with confidence because it is filled with swimmers who seem to be enjoying the water as much as you were enjoying the sun. You touch the water with one toe just to make sure—*Brrr*, how can they stand it! Moments later, after much hesitation, a little coaxing, and many goose bumps, you are enjoying the water as much as the others are. Thanks to our skin's ability to adjust, we can be comfortable over a wide range of temperatures. To date, no one physiological theory can explain all the known facts about temperature perception.

One popular theory is the *vascular theory*, which states that thermal receptors are actually sensory nerves that detect the contraction and dilation of blood vessels. This is a clever theory, because blood vessels contract when the skin is cooled and they dilate when the skin is warmed. However, according to the vascular theory we should be able to experience hot and cold on all regions of our body. This is a problem for the theory, because only hot is felt in some areas, called **warm spots,** and only cold is felt in other areas, called **cold spots.** The average square centimeter of skin has

Our skin can feel comfortable in the hot sun or in a cool lake because of its ability to adjust its range of sensitivity.

OTHER SENSES HELP THE BLIND "SEE"

Technological advances have led to exciting applications of sensory research, including attempts to restore sight to the blind. In a visual substitution system planned by Dr. Dobelle at Columbia University in New York, a subminiature television camera will be mounted in a glass eye. The artificial eye will be attached to eye muscles so that a blind person will point the camera as easily as we point our eyes. The camera will send optical information to the brain via a tiny computer mounted in a pair of eyeglasses. The computer will translate the information into a pattern of stimulation that will be experienced as a black-and-white picture when it is sent to the brain. Microelectrodes mounted on the surface of the visual cortex will stimulate the brain. The best Dr. Dobelle expects in the foreseeable future are low-resolution, slow-scan, black-and-white images that are like the early television transmissions sent by astronauts from the moon (Dobelle, 1977).

Another new device, the Tactile Visual Substitution System (TVSS), which was developed by Bach-Y-Rita (1982) and his colleagues at the Smith-Kettlewell Institute of Visual Science in San Francisco. A miniature television camera is mounted on spectacle frames, allowing the camera to be pointed by head movements. The camera's picture is analyzed into 400 dark or light dots, such that each dot represents a small area of the camera's field of view. Each dot's brightness depends upon the amount of light falling on the corresponding part of the visual

field. Once the brightness of the dots is determined, they are translated to frequencies of vibrations on a matrix of 400 tiny skin vibrators mounted on the abdomen. When the corresponding dot is dark, the vibrator is off; when the dot is gray, the vibrator oscillates at a low frequency; and when the dot is bright, the vibrator oscillates at a high frequency. At first, it takes 5 to 8 minutes to recognize common objects such as telephones, cups, and chairs, but after only 1 hour of training, blind people can identify 25 common objects in about 5 to 20 seconds each. After several weeks of training, blind people learn to negotiate hallways, open doors, and locate and pick up small objects with TVSS.

One of the most promising sensory substitution systems is the Sonicguide, a device developed by Professor Lesley Kay, an imaginative electrical engineer, at

the University of Canterbury, New Zealand (see Strelow, Kay, & Kay, 1978). The Sonicguide shown in the photos here emits high-frequency sounds beyond the human hearing range. These hit objects in the environment and reflect back to the Sonicguide. Here they are converted to audible slashings, "wheeps," and rushing sounds. A user of the Sonicguide must learn to interpret this futuristic electronic "music." The sound's pitch indicates the distance of an object; it goes lower as an object moves farther away. Loudness indicates size; larger objects make louder sounds. Clarity indicates texture; when the "music" sounds like a poorly tuned radio, the object is rough; when it sounds like a well-tuned radio, the object is smooth. The time of arrival of the sounds in the two ears indicates location; objects to the right are heard first by the right ear and objects to the

about six cold spots and one or two warm spots. When a warm object stimulates a cold spot, it feels cold. This is called **paradoxical cold.**

Such results lead to another popular theory, the *specific receptor theory*. According to this theory, distinct receptors exist for the sensation of hot and cold. The problem with this theory is that both hot and cold are experienced on skin areas that have few or none of one kind of receptor. For example, cold can be felt on hairy skin, where there are few if any

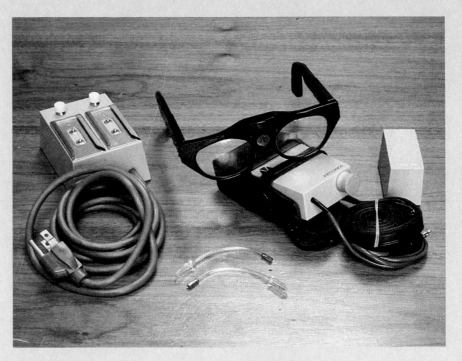

left are heard first by the left ear.

Even infants who are blind can learn to interpret this code. During his first session with a Sonicguide, a 16-week-old baby boy learned to reach out and grab a small object waved in front of his face. Dr. Tom Bower (1977) swung an object by a thread toward the baby until it tapped his nose. After the third presentation, the baby moved both eyes toward his nose as the object approached, and moved both eyes away from his nose as the object receded. On the seventh presentation, the baby blocked the object by putting his hand in front of his face. The object was then moved from right to left. The baby tracked it with his head and eyes and he swiped at it with his hands, hitting it four times. The baby also learned to enjoy a game with his mother. Standing on her knee, he turned his head, bringing her in and out of the Sonicguide's sound field. The baby's smiles and giggles suggested that he enjoyed this game as much as most babies enjoy the "peek-a-boo" game.

The baby's development after the initial session was similar to a sighted baby's. He was able to identify favorite toys without touching them, and he reached for them with both hands when he was about 6 months of age. By 8 months he searched for objects that were hidden, and by 9 months of age he reached out his hand when lowered toward a surface.

The Sonicguide is also used in the United States. For example, in Pennsylvania, James Newcomer (1977) is using the Sonicguide with blind children in public school. Under his direction, Dana, a 5-year-old kindergarten student, is using the device to find her way around school. Already she can locate water fountains and doorways, and she knows when to stop to reach out for objects. Gerry, an 8-year-old second-grader, uses the Sonicguide to maneuver between a maze of poles in a room without touching them. He can also find a person "hiding" in the room between the poles. Fourteen-year-old Wally is the first high-school student to own his own Sonicguide. He has learned to thread his way through congested corridors with few collisions, and he can follow other students at a distance if he chooses.

Looking into the future is always dangerous, so no predictions will be made about the course of psychological research on the senses. But after such an encouraging start, it will certainly be disappointing if in the 1980s a major effort is not made to continue basic and applied research on sensory substitution systems.

In May 1961 President John F. Kennedy declared, "I believe that this nation should commit itself to achieving the goal, before this decade is out, of landing a man on the moon and returning him safely to earth. . . ." On July 24, 1969, that mission was accomplished. And with that success came the "new frontiers in science, commerce, and cooperation" that Kennedy promised in his 1962 State of the Union message. What would happen if an equally strong commitment were made now to rescue the blind and deaf from their prisons of sightlessness and soundlessness before this decade is out?

cold receptors. Thus, for now, we have no satisfactory theory of how we experience temperature on the skin.

The blind depend heavily upon their sense of touch, and psychologists have teamed up with engineers to help the blind capitalize as much as possible on this important sense. Psychologists laid the foundation for helping the blind by doing basic research on the sense of touch. For example, they mapped the skin's sensitivity to slight amounts of pressure. They found, among other things, that the face is the most sensitive, and that females are more sensitive than males to the pressure of touch. Scientists also noticed that two objects touching the skin produce two distinct sensations of pressure if the objects are far enough apart. However, if the objects are too close, they produce a single sensation of pressure. The least distance between two stimuli that can be perceived as separate is called the **two-point threshold.** You can see this for yourself through the following experiment.

Push two pins into a cork 1 centimeter apart. Push one pin into another cork. Blindfold a friend and touch his or her fingertip lightly with either cork. Have your friend say whether or not two distinct sensations of touch are felt. Repeat the experiment on the palm and the forearm. You should observe no mistakes on the fingertips, some mistakes on the palm, and many mistakes on the forearm. Such results provided important information used to develop sensory substitution systems for the blind (see the Highlight, "Other Senses Help the Blind 'See' ").

Body Orientation

How do we know where we are in relation to the world around us? Basically two kinds of senses are involved here: **equilibrium,** our sense of overall body orientation (for example, the difference between standing upright or tilting backward), and **proprioception,** our sense of the position and motion of body parts.

Equilibrium. Equilibrium is based on the body's reaction to gravity. The space program inspired a lot of research in this area, because astronauts wanted to know what to expect in outer space, where they would be free from earth's gravitational pull. In space, **vision** plays an important part in equilibrium; on earth, vision and gravity usually work together. Gravity affects equilibrium through the **vestibular system,** which is an inner-ear structure that detects body orientation and changes in body orientation. Figure 3–17 shows the vestibular system. The three arching structures are the **semicircular canals,** which detect changes in the position of the head. Fluids move in the canals when the head rotates in any direction. The fluid motion causes neural messages about head movements to be sent to the brain.

Semicircular canals stop responding shortly after the head stops moving. Other gravity detectors continue to report head position. They are the **otolith structures,** which are organs that signal head orientation with respect to gravity. The otolith apparatus consists of two sacs located near

Figure 3–17
The semicircular canals of the vestibular system are located in the inner ear. Fluids move in the canals when the head rotates in any direction, sending neural messages to the brain.

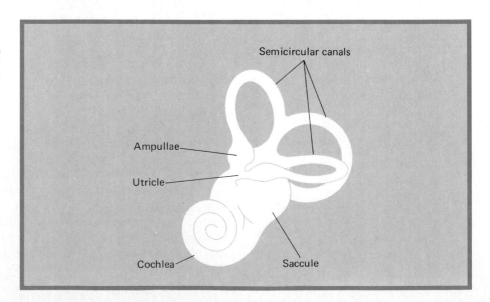

Semicircular canals

Ampullae

Utricle

Cochlea

Saccule

Figure 3-18
This is the apparatus used in the Rock and Harris experiment.

the junction of the semicircular canals. The inside of one of those sacs contains hair cells and a tissue that holds tiny stones over the hair cells. The stones change position when the head changes position. The semicircular canals and the otolith apparatus are idle in outer space, but they are continually active on earth.

Proprioception. Equilibrium is only part of body orientation. We also need **proprioception,** the sense of where our body parts are. Proprioception is determined by sense organs in joints, muscles, and tendons, which connect muscles with bones (Matin, 1981). An experiment by Rock and Harris (1967) illustrates proprioception. It also illustrates people's ability to adjust to an altered environment.

In this experiment subjects held their arm under a glass table top and pointed at targets that were slightly above the table (see Figure 3-18). The experiment had three parts:

1. On pretests, subjects pointed at targets with the glass covered. They pointed accurately with both arms, even though they could not see their arm or hand under the table. Proprioception is indicated by the fact that people knew where their arms were even though they could not see them.

2. During an exposure condition subjects wore goggles that displaced vision. The goggles made targets seem to be about 4 inches to the right of where they actually were. The cover was then removed from the glass table. Subjects practiced pointing at targets with one arm while they rested the other arm. They pointed off to the right at first. Within a few minutes, however, they saw and corrected their mistake.

3. The goggles were removed for posttests. The procedures for these final tests were identical to pretest procedures. Subjects pointed accurately when they used their rested arm. This result suggests that subjects still saw the targets in the correct places. It also suggests that they still knew where their rested arm was without looking at it. They pointed off to the left, however, when they pointed with their practiced hand. This result suggests that subjects had adjusted their arm's proprioception; that is, the goggle exposure caused them to feel that their arm was in a different place than it actually was. When the goggles were on, this adjustment in proprioception helped them coordinate their pointing with the displaced vision. When the goggles were removed, however, the adjustment caused errors until subjects had a chance to readjust to normal vision.

Recent investigations show that people can adjust to a distorted world in many ways (Ebenholtz, 1981; Shebilske, 1981; Welch, 1978). Scientists are not sure why we have this ability, but astronauts are glad that we do because it helped them adapt to outer space.

The ability of sensory systems to adapt also helped Farley Mowat adjust to life at Wolf House Bay. We probably would have verified that Farley's senses were more sensitive if we had actually taken the measurements that we considered at the beginning of this chapter. Furthermore, we probably would have had little trouble explaining this effect in terms of normal sensory adaptation. Farley's night vision adjusted to a more sensitive range because background levels of light were lower than what Farley experienced in city environments. Similarly, his auditory sensitivity increased because background levels of noise decreased.

This comparison of sensory adaptation in space and in the wild is an appropriate transition into the next chapter. There we will examine how modern astronauts and aviators have made good use of the precise sensory and motor skills that they inherited from ancestors who depended upon those skills for survival in the wild.

Summary

1. The study of sensation and perception raises many **psychophysical** questions, that is, questions about relationships between physical energies and psychological experiences. These relationships can be measured by various methods, each of which has advantages and disadvantages. One important psychophysical law is Weber's Law, which states that a just-noticeable change in a stimulus magnitude is proportional to the original stimulus magnitude.

2. The eyes convert light energy into neural responses that we experience as sight. The actual conversion is done by two kinds of receptor cells in the **retina: rods** and **cones.** They send neural messages through visual pathways to other brain structures. The pathways contain cells that participate in the interpretation of these messages.

3. The eyes can adjust their sensitivity to light. They become more sensitive in dim light through a process of **dark adaptation.** They become less sensitive in bright light through a process of **light adaptation.**

4. Light receptors are specialized so that they are more sensitive to some colors than to others. Cells in the visual pathways also participate in the coding of colors.

5. The ears convert sound waves into neural responses that we experience as hearing. The external ear collects and focuses sound, causing the **eardrum** to vibrate. Three delicate bones carry these vibrations to the **oval window,** which vibrates receptors in the **cochlea,** triggering nerve impulses to the brain.

6. **Pitch** (high notes versus low notes) is determined by the **frequency** of sound waves. **Loudness** is determined by the **amplitude** of sound waves. Tone quality is determined by how sound waves combine. We hear the location of sounds in part because we are sensitive to tiny sound differences between the two ears.

7. Our tongue has **taste buds** that convert chemical stimulation into neural responses, which we experience as taste. Different regions of the tongue are sensitive to the four primary tastes: sweet, sour, salty, and bitter.

8. The throat and nasal passages contain **olfactory cells,** which convert the gases we breathe into neural responses that we experience as smell. Olfactory cells also influence taste.

9. The skin responds to pain, temperature, and pressure. Scientists have not yet identified all the receptor cells that underlie these sensations. The understanding that they have gained so far, however, has already helped to relieve pain for many people, and it has helped the blind to ''see'' with their skin.

10. There are two types of body orientation senses: equilibrium and proprioception. **Equilibrium** is our sense of overall body orientation; it is affected by gravity through the **vestibular system,** which consists of the **semicircular canals** and the **otolith** structures. **Proprioception** is the sense of where our other body parts are. It is determined by sense organs in joints, muscles, and tendons.

Key Terms

absolute threshold
accommodations
afterimage
amplitude
anvil
aqueous humor
basilar membrane
blind spot
boilermaker's deafness
bone conduction
cochlea
cold spots
colorblindness
complex tones
cones
cornea
dark adaptation

decibel
difference threshold
Doppler shift
ear canal
eardrum
electromagnetic spectrum
equilibrium
farsightedness
fovea
frequency
glaucoma
hammer
iris
lens
light adaptation
loudness
near point of accommodation

nearsightedness
olfactory cells
optic nerve
opthalmoscope
oscilloscope
otolith structures
oval window
papillae
paradoxical cold
peripheral vision
pinna
pitch
proprioception
psychophysical function
psychophysics
pupil

pure tones
retina
rods
sclera
semicircular canals
signal
signal-detection theory
stirrup
taste buds
two-point threshold
vestibular system
vision
vitreous humor
warm spots
waveform
Weber's Law

Suggested Readings

The following book contains Farley Mowat's account of his study of arctic wolves:

MOWAT, F. *Never cry wolf*. New York: Bantam Books, 1963.

GREGORY, R. L. *Eye and brain*. New York: McGraw-Hill, 1977. This book is interesting reading and very informative; perhaps the most popular book available on the psychology of seeing.

HOCHBERG, J. E. *Perception*. Englewood Cliffs, N.J.: Prentice-Hall, 1978. This book capitalizes on the power of pictorial displays to illustrate principles of perception. Figures and their captions are an integral part of this text on "why things look as they do."

MCBURNEY, D. H., & COLLINGS, V. B. *Introduction to sensation/perception*. Englewood Cliffs, N.J.: Prentice-Hall, 1977. Uses everyday examples to awaken one's curiosity about the sensory world. The structure and function of all the senses are covered.

PERCEPTION AND COGNITION

At 9:08 Central Standard Time on the night of Monday, April 13, 1970, an oxygen tank exploded, tearing away one side of the Apollo 13 service module. John L. Swigert, strapped to his pilot's seat in the command module, felt a shudder. Fred W. Haise, pilot of the lunar module (LM, pronounced "lem"), was in the tunnel connecting the LM and the command module when the whole tunnel violently shook up and down. Captain James A. Lovell, the commander, felt nothing—he was floating, weightless, in front of his seat. He heard a strange noise, but it didn't sound like an explosion—he thought Haise might have dropped something in the LM. Lovell's first clue to the emergency came when the master alarm sounded and Haise scrambled from the LM tunnel, slamming the hatch behind him. All three astronauts knew by then that something was fundamentally wrong, but it would be 15 minutes before they would get a rough idea of what had happened, and about an hour beyond that before they would realize that the odds were now against their ever returning to earth.

Several engineers at the Manned Spacecraft Center near Houston, Texas, 205,000 miles below, saw a tiny flare of light that looked like a distant star exploding, but they did not connect the glow with Apollo 13. They were not the only ones to ignore signs of the disaster. Next door, in the Mission Control Center, other signs were missed. For example, the column of numbers on a television screen that monitored oxygen pressure increased rapidly when the oxygen tank ruptured. The controller looking at the screen didn't notice this because his eyes were directed 3 inches to the right, on the readings from the hydrogen tanks.

The delay in realizing the danger was costly, because during it Apollo 13 passed the point where the spacecraft could easily have returned directly to earth, a trip of about 1½ days. Now it would be necessary to circle the moon before returning, a trip that would take 3 or 4 days. The flight controllers began frantically calculating whether or not the astronauts could possibly last that long. The astronauts had to abandon the command module because it would lose all of its power except for the power in its three reentry batteries. Every bit of that energy would be needed if the astronauts were to return. Before they hit the earth's atmosphere, they would have to get rid of the LM and the service module, because only the command module had the heat shield needed for reentry. Until then, the astronauts could use the LM as a lifeboat because it had power and controls that could maneuver the whole spacecraft. But the LM was designed to support only two men for about a 2-day trip from the command module to the moon. Could the fuel, water, and oxygen be stretched to last three men for a 4-day trip around the moon and back to earth? The answer was "maybe"—a more definite answer could not be given until the very end.

As the ground crew made their calculations, the astronauts climbed inside the LM to fly their crippled spacecraft. Their world seemed to turn over as they entered because the floor of the command module was in the position of the ceiling in the LM. Swigert, who

knew the least about the LM, was worried most. As he watched the world fall away behind him, he had some very depressing thoughts about never returning to the dust of his planet. Lovell and Haise had less time for worrying because they had to follow a perpetual stream of instructions from mission control. They stood for hours grasping the pistol-grip hand controls of the thruster rockets. Their main job was to continuously change the spacecraft's attitude with respect to the sun, or else one side of their vessel would burn while the other froze. About 24 hours after the accident had occurred, the ground crew finally found a way for the LM's computer to do this rotation for the astronauts.

The astronauts then tried to sleep in the dead command module. Relaxing was difficult, even though they had been awake for 48 hours. Their sleeping area looked as if it were being lit by a slow motion disco strobe until Lovell pulled the shades. After the shades were pulled, however, the temperature dropped into the low 40s. The astronauts slept restlessly for the remainder of the trip,

because their clothes and bedding couldn't keep them warm.

By Tuesday afternoon, the moon, which had looked like a small white disc at the time of the accident, now filled the spacecraft's windows. The constant chatter from mission control stopped when the astronauts circled around the moon's dark side and lost contact with earth for about 25 minutes.

As it rounded the moon, Apollo 13 was on a path that would swing it back toward earth, missing it by some 40,000 miles. To return safely, the astronauts would have to correct their course with their manual controls, and they would have to guide their spacecraft through a narrow reentry corridor. If they went outside this narrow path, they would bounce off into space without enough power to return. Their predicament was like that of a sailor using the stars as a guide for steering a floundering vessel. Ironically, however, even though they were in the heavens, they had trouble seeing the stars. Gases coming from the spacecraft clouded their view of the sky, making it almost impossible to hold a sextant on a star long enough to get their bearings. The astronauts thus had to settle for less precise targets to steer by—the sun, the moon, and even the earth itself—which would work until they were close to the earth. Before entering the earth's atmosphere, however, they would somehow have to get a fix on a star. To further complicate matters, controlling Apollo 13 now often called for the efforts of all three astronauts—it was like driving a car with one person working the brake, another the accelerator, and the third controlling the steering wheel.

Although the fate of the astronauts depended on their own visual abilities and their own motor coordination, they were not alone. Dozens of mission controllers, most of them in their 20s or 30s, were making heroic efforts to bring Apollo 13 home safely. They tested Apollo's equipment, trying to get it to do things for which it was never designed, and in 3 days they came up with a plan for reentry that would have otherwise taken 3 months to prepare. One of the most demanding jobs fell to 27-year-old mission controller John Aaron. He had to find a way to stretch the remaining power in the command module over several hours, even though it was designed to last only 45 minutes. The problem was that Aaron's final plan did not give the astronauts enough power to signal their location if they landed off target. The spacecraft would sink shortly after it landed in the ocean; what was the use of coming down safely if the spacecraft sank before it could be found? Aaron was concerned, but he had run out of options. They would have to hope for a direct hit.

When the earth finally loomed in the spacecraft's windows, it was time for one last try at a star check. One of the flight controllers suggested that Swigert try to locate Altair or Vega, two stars on the side of the spacecraft facing away from the sun, where its shadow could cut the glare. When Swigert tried this, he couldn't see anything until a flight controller told him to turn off a nearby light. Meanwhile, Lovell, who could see that they were approaching the earth at an alarming rate, shouted to Swigert to hurry up; unless the adjustments in position were made quickly, they would be too late. With the light out, Swigert found Altair easily. Moments later, the comptuer compared the actual position with the estimated position of Apollo 13. The astronauts could not believe their bleary eyes. There was no error! Somehow, Haise's and Lovell's rough alignment with the sun and moon had turned out to be perfect. The test

was quickly repeated on Vega, and Swigert's results were the same. Suddenly the astronauts, who had been behind schedule, were now slightly ahead. They had 5 minutes to disconnect the LM from the rest of the spacecraft.

With the LM gone, the command module was flying alone. Earlier, when the service module was jettisoned, the astronauts got their only chance to see and photograph the damaged vessel. Lovell, the first to spot it, said, "O.K., I've got her. . . . And there's one whole side of that spacecraft missing." This raised questions in everyone's minds about whether or not the ceramic heat shield on the command module, which had been near the ruptured oxygen tank, was damaged. If it was, the astronauts would burn up during reentry.

This horrible thought returned when radio contact was lost during reentry. The astronauts should have reestablished radio contact 3 minutes and 30 seconds after hitting the atmosphere, but they didn't. Everyone waited anxiously. One minute and forty seconds later, Houston called the spacecraft. There was no answer. Then, 5 seconds later, Swigert called in, "O.K., Joe."

The astronauts splashed down safely near a recovery ship at 12:07 P.M., Houston time, on Friday, April 17. It was an unsuccessful mission, but it was perhaps Apollo's greatest success story.

Figure 4-1
This device, called a "visual cliff," is used for studying depth perception in infants.

PERCEPTION, COGNITION, AND ACTION

It took advanced technology to send the Apollo 13 astronauts to the moon, but it took their perceptual, cognitive, and motor skills to get them back to earth. The manual flying of their spacecraft required a precise coordination among perception, cognition, and action. They had to perceive the location of stars and other objects around them; they had to understand verbal and printed commands; and they had to guide their spacecraft accordingly. In this chapter we will study perception and cognition, and their special function of guiding behavior. We will address many questions about the perceptual and cognitive skills that enabled the astronauts to fly home safely: To what extent are these skills inborn? And to what extent are they learned? How are perceptions organized? How do perceptions remain constant and stable? Can we always believe our eyes? Or, more generally, how reliable are perceptions? How do we perceive and understand spoken and written language?

PERCEPTUAL DEVELOPMENT

It would be naive to ask whether the astronauts inherited or learned their perceptual skills. As we shall see in Chapter 8, most aspects of development are influenced by both heredity and experience. Better questions are: What perceptual skills are present during early childhood? And how are these skills modified by experience? This section will address these questions with respect to seeing depth and size.

Visual Cliff Experiments

Walk and Gibson (1961) designed a clever device for studying infant depth perception. Their apparatus, which is called a **visual cliff**, consists of a special table divided into three parts (Figure 4-1). A mother places her baby on a solid board in the center and then encourages the infant to crawl to one side or the other. The "visual cliff" side has a solid surface covered with a checkered pattern about 4 feet below the center board. It also has a strong glass surface about 1 inch below the board. The other side has a solid surface covered with a checkered pattern about 1 inch below the center board.

Infants between the ages of 6 and 12 months refuse to cross the visual cliff despite their mothers' encouragement. In contrast, they eagerly cross the other side. Apparently infants see depth, but a warning is in order. Parents should not place infants who can crawl on high beds or other high surfaces. Visual cliff experiments show that babies try to avoid a drop-off, but the same experiments show that they are very clumsy—many of the 36 babies that Walk and Gibson tested would have fallen over the cliff if glass hadn't been there. A common mistake was to back off of the "cliff" while looking in the other direction.

Walk and Gibson showed that chicks and lambs avoid the visual side of the cliff 1 day after birth. Experimenters cannot give humans the visual cliff test at such a young age because babies do not crawl until they are at least 4 months old, and usually older. Researchers, however, figured out a way to test younger humans. Campos, Langer, and Krowitz (1970) placed 1½-month-old babies over each side of the cliff and measured their

Modern technology is being used to determine how a baby's brain responds to visual patterns. The procedure is painless and harmless, requiring only that small electrodes be taped to the surface of the head.

heart rates. They found changes in heart rates when babies were placed over the visual cliff, suggesting that babies see depth long before they learn to crawl.

Reaching Experiments

Researchers also observe reaching behavior to study the perceptual world of infants. In one experiment, Bruner and Koslowski (1972) observed reaching to study infant size perception.

If you were asked to grasp a tennis ball held 4 or 5 inches in front of your eyes, you would extend your hands, bringing them closer together and closing them around the ball. If a large beach ball were held in the same position, you would extend your arms, bringing them farther apart and wrapping them around the ball. Before you would begin either movement, you would see that one ball was small and the other large, and you would know what movements were needed to grasp them. What do babies do in this situation? In one study, infants (between 10 and 22 weeks old) looked at a small ball or a large ball placed within arm's reach (Bruner & Koslowski, 1972). The main finding was that babies who had not yet learned to reach and to manipulate objects nevertheless showed size discrimination. They brought their hands to the center and moved them while they were at the center, doing so more often when they saw the small ball. They made more forward sweeps with their arms spread apart when they saw the large ball. Apparently, then, they could see that one ball was small and the other large, and were responding to this.

The babies seemed uncoordinated because they did not order their movements in the proper sequence; they often brought their hands to center and closed them before they extended their arms, for instance. This lack of coordination caused some theorists to argue that babies are confused by what they see. They cannot see size, they argued, until they add to visual information the knowledge they gain from manipulating objects (see Hochberg, 1978). Bruner and Koslowski's experiment contradicts this theory because it suggests that babies see size *before* they learn to manipulate objects. They are uncoordinated *not* because they are visually confused, but because they do not yet know how to control the order of their arm movements.

Babies do not learn successful reaching until about four or five months. Psychologists have shown that unsuccessful reaching before that is not caused by visual confusion but by an inability to coordinate arm movements.

THE BABY AS INTERIOR DECORATOR

What would infants ask for if they could choose decorations for their room? Would pastel blues and pinks remain in vogue for nurseries if infants could choose for themselves? What about the mobiles that are found in most nurseries? Would they go or stay? Research into the perceptual world of infants suggests answers to these questions.

"Looking Box" Experiments
Infants cannot directly answer our questions about their experiences. As a result, their perceptual world remained a mystery until the mid-1950s, when Robert L. Fantz showed that psychologists can coax even newborns into answering questions about what they see (Fantz, 1963).

Fantz used a "looking box" to peek into the perceptual world of infants. The photo below shows a looking box in which an infant is placed on its back. Pads beside the head keep the eyes directed upward

toward two pictures on the ceiling of the box. The pictures are 2 or 3 feet from the infant. An experimenter can determine which picture the infant is looking at by peering through a peephole in the top of the box. Whatever the baby looks at is reflected in the center of its pupil.

Fantz used a looking box to establish that babies have definite preferences in what they choose to look at. His results and those from other laboratories indicate the following looking preferences:

1. Infants as young as 1 week old prefer patterned pictures over unpatterned ones (Greenber & O'Donnell, 1972).
2. Infants as young as 2 months prefer curved lines over straight ones (Ruff & Birch, 1974).
3. Infants as young as 2 months prefer bright colors to pastels (Haith & Campos, 1977; Schaller, 1975).
4. Infants as young as 4 days old prefer a human face over an

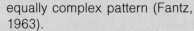

equally complex pattern (Fantz, 1963).
5. Newborns and older infants prefer things that move over things that don't (Carpenter, 1974; Gregg, Clifton, & Haith, 1976).

What do these looking preferences tell us about babies' decor preferences? They suggest that we might see some changes in the nursery if babies could pick their own decorations. The popular pastels would be replaced by bright colors, and pictures of faces would be all the rage. Some popular decorations would remain, however. Mobiles, for instance, would probably stay, because infants enjoy moving objects. Furthermore, since infants enjoy brightly colored curved lines, the increasing popularity of rainbow decorations would be cheered.

Parents need not wait for their own children to speak up. Representative infants have been allowed to choose in carefully controlled experiments. Although silent, the infants cast their votes decidely with their eyes. This is one research result to which parents might want to attend before their own children are old enough to speak for themselves.

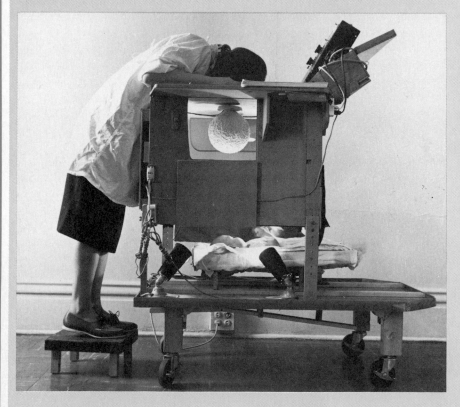

In earlier decades limited response capabilities in infants led many to assume that babies see a "blooming, buzzing confusion." Today opinions are changing. Modern experiments suggest that babies see more than we had previously realized. Parents can directly apply research findings on the perceptual world of infants, as indicated in the accompanying Highlight, The Baby as Interior Decorator.

THE ROLE OF ORGANIZATION IN PERCEPTION

The astronauts saw familiar groupings of stars that guided their search of the heavens for specific navigational guides. Many of us might take for granted their ability to see these groupings because we, too, see the Big Dipper and other familiar constellations. We might think, therefore, that it would be trivial to ask how we organize the separate sensations of stars into groups. In the 1920s, however, a group of German psychologists,

Gestalt psychologists studied our ability to group stars and other discrete points into familiar patterns. Their studies shed light on how we organize everything we see.

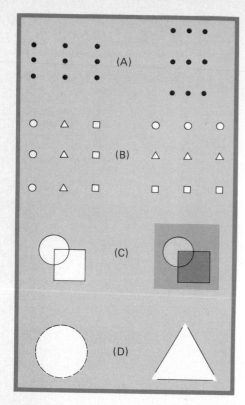

Figure 4-2
These drawings illustrate four Gestalt laws of organization: (A) *The law of proximity*. We group together elements that are close together. (B) *The law of similarity*. We group together elements that are alike. (C) *The law of good continuation*. We group together line segments that form straight or smoothly curving lines (thus you will see a circle and a square in the left figure rather than the two objects shown in the right figure). (D) *The law of closure*. We tend to fill in gaps in straight lines or smooth curves.

Figure 4-3
The reversible goblet can be seen as a white cup against a blue background or as two blue faces against a white background.

called the Gestalt school, argued that this question is far from trivial. You might understand their argument better if you think for a moment about the flood of light rushing into your eyes when you stand at a window and see a house, trees, and sky. Millions of receptors are stimulated by the light stream, which contains many different wavelengths, colors, and intensities. Receptors register these separately, but you do not see separate patches of colors and brightnesses. Somehow separate sensations are organized into wholes so that you see a house, trees, and sky. You would have a hard time seeing other groupings of these stimuli. For example, you could not easily see the trees as part of the house, because you unconsciously follow a set of rules for organizing sensations.

Gestalt Laws of Organization

The Gestalt psychologists attempted to describe the rules by which we organize sensations. *Gestalt* means a structure that forms a unit or a whole, and the Gestalt laws of organization describe the way in which we tend to group objects or stimuli according to certain characteristics that they have. For example, one such law, the **law of nearness or proximity,** says that we group elements that are close together. In Figure 4–2 we see three vertical columns of dots when the vertical dots are closer together than the horizontal ones. When the horizontal dots are closer, then we see three horizontal rows of dots.

Another law is the **law of similarity,** which states that we group elements that are similar, or look alike. In Figure 4–2 we see three vertical columns of figures when the vertical elements are similar, and three horizontal rows when the horizontal elements are similar. Other Gestalt laws of organization are illustrated and briefly described in Figure 4–2.

It was also the Gestalt school that pointed out our basic tendency to divide what we see into **figure** (an object) and **ground** (the background or surroundings of the object). But what happens when figure and ground suddenly reverse, as they do in Figure 4–3? When you look at this figure, you see a goblet at one moment and a pair of silhouetted faces the next. This phenomenon is called **figure-ground reversal** or **multistable perception,** since you perceive more than one image in the same figure (Attneave, 1976).

The fact that figure and ground seem to reverse in this way points up something that we often overlook: *We* impose organization on objects, we do not just passively take in what's there. How else could we see two different pictures in Figure 4–3? The basic drawing, the sensory input, remains the same. It is our perception that changes.

Organization of Moving Patterns

We also actively impose organization on moving objects. As shown in Figure 4–4A, when people view a light on the rim of a rolling wheel in an otherwise dark room, the light appears to hop along, making a series of arches. The same physical motion path looks quite different, however, if a light is added to the opposite side of the rim of the wheel. Both lights then appear to roll smoothly along, spinning around an invisible hub. The same physical motion looks different when the other light is added because viewers impose different organizations on it. Scientists are learning the rules that we use to impose organization on wheel motions, and these same rules explain how we organize more complicated motions as well, such as those made by a walking person or a waving hand, as shown in Figure 4–4B (Johansson, 1976; Proffitt & Cutting, 1980; Cutting & Proffitt, 1981).

We create moving patterns of light whenever we move through our environment. According to the **ecological theory of perception,** these moving

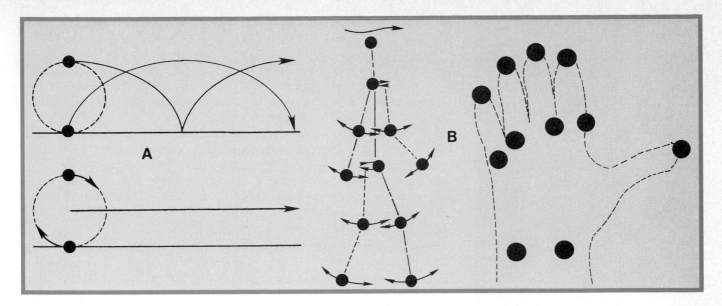

Figure 4-4
This figure shows the various ways that we actively impose organization on moving objects, such as a rolling wheel, a person walking, or a hand waving.

Figure 4-5
When people and other terrestrial animals move through their environment, they encounter "problems." The "solutions" depend on how the light is changed by the animal's movements. According to the ecological theory of perception, the relationship between a moving animal and its environment is such that moving patterns of light uniquely determine our perception of substances, places, objects, and events.

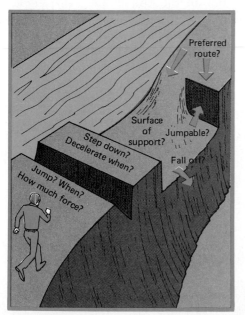

patterns are lawfully generated such that invariant aspects of them specify important aspects of our environment, as shown in Figure 4–5.

In the next chapter we will follow up on the theme of our active contribution to perception. There we will discuss dreams and other experiences in which we seem to construct perceptions out of nothing.

THE ROLE OF CONSTANCIES IN PERCEPTION

If figure-ground reversals make you dizzy, you may find relief in the stability, or constancy, of our perceptual world. We depend on this constancy even to recognize a friend. For example, we may look at a friend from a number of different angles, close up and far away, in bright light or in dim light, and still recognize him or her as the same person under all these different conditions. In the same way, Apollo 13 astronauts depended on constancy as they circled the moon. They identified important land formations even though they saw them under continually changing conditions. This seems simple enough, but there really is nothing simple about it—in fact, scientists still do not understand how it is done. How can perceptions remain constant when optical information changes? Let's look at what scientists have discovered about size, shape, and other perceptual constancies.

Size Constancies

Look at the twins in Figure 4–6. The twin on the right was 4 feet away when the picture was taken, and the one on the left was 8 feet away. Their picture illustrates the **law of size constancy,** which states that we see an object's size as constant even if the object's distance from us changes.

Figure 4–7 explains how **retinal image** sizes change. Light reflects off the twins into the observer's eye. The critical light rays for this discussion are those coming from the feet and the top of the head. They are represented by two lines that cross over inside the eye's lens. The angle between these lines is called the **visual angle.** It gets smaller as an object moves farther away. When the visual angle gets smaller, the retinal image also gets smaller. The closer twin's visual angle is twice as big, and therefore her retinal image is twice as big as the farther twin.

So why do we perceive the twins as being the same size? Scientists don't really know. We might suppose that the perceived size remains constant because we *know* the approximate true size. (For example, we know the twins in Figure 4–6 are the same size.) However, this explanation can be ruled out for two reasons. First, size would be perceived as constant even if unfamiliar objects, such as boards, were seen in place of the twins. Second, if a picture contains misleading information about distance, we will be fooled, even if we know the true size of the objects. For example, the Ames Room (see Figure 4–8) is designed to provide misleading information about distance. As can be seen in the diagram in Figure 4–8, the left corner of the room is actually much farther away than the right corner, yet the corners appear equally far away. People in the far corner of an Ames Room look like dwarfs, while those in the close corner look like giants. Obviously, seeing objects of familiar sizes does not guarantee accurate size perception.

There are two opposing theories of size constancy: the unconscious inference theory (Epstein, 1973; Rock, 1977), and the ecological theory (Gibson, 1979). **Unconscious inference theory** states that we unconsciously make accurate inferences about object size when we have accurate information about retinal image size and object distance. It follows that perceived size should be consistent with perceived distance. In the Ames Room we saw distorted sizes *because* we saw distorted distances. Specifically, the person on the left has a smaller image and she looks just as close as the person on the right; therefore we unconsciously infer that she is smaller.

In contrast, the ecological theory states that we see a constant size because we see some aspect of the visual scene that remains unchanged when distance changes. For example, the twins are the same size with respect to the walls near both of them. If we respond to such relationships, we would be fooled by Ames's trick room because basic relationships are distorted. Notice, for example, the size of the people with respect to the sizes of doors and windows. Accordingly, the trick room misleads us by distorting relationships that are critical for constancy.

Other Constancies

The issues raised about size perception also apply to other constancies. The **law of shape constancy** states that we see an object's shape as constant when the object's slant changes, or when we view it from a different angle. Figure 4–9 (p. 108) shows how this might occur. The checkers are round and the board is square in the view from the top; the checkers are shaped like footballs and the board's side edges are shorter in the side view. Because of shape constancy, however, the checkers look round and the board looks square in both views and the number 9 is recognizable from different angles in the bottom photos.

Figure 4–6
The identical twins, Evangeline and Jacqueline Motely, look the same size in this picture, even though the image of the farther one is only half as large as that of the closer one. This illustrates the law of size constancy.

Figure 4–7
Retinal image size is determined by the visual angle, which is defined at the eye's lens by the angle between light rays coming from the top and bottom of an object. As an object gets closer, its visual angle and its retinal image size get larger.

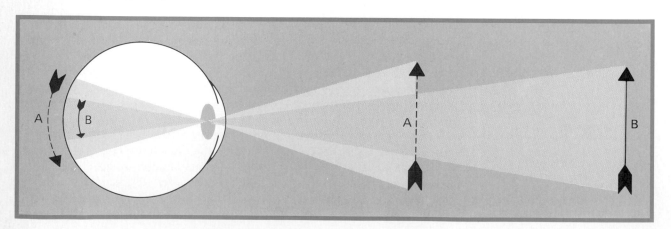

Figure 4–8
The Ames Room, shown here, distorts the apparent size of the woman. Your eye is fooled in this picture because the room looks square, but actually is not. The diagram illustrates the actual shape of the room, which causes the woman to seem to be a different size.

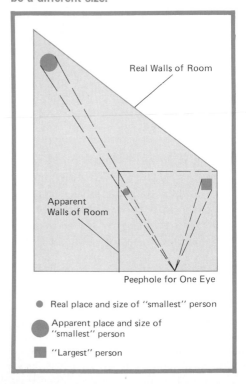

Real Walls of Room

Apparent Walls of Room

Peephole for One Eye

● Real place and size of "smallest" person

● Apparent place and size of "smallest" person

■ "Largest" person

Unconscious inference theory says that we unconsciously infer the correct shapes when we see the correct slants. Ecological theory states that we see a constant shape because we see some aspect of the visual scene that stays the same when the slant changes. For example, the same number of squares run along the left and right edges of the checkerboard whether it is slanted or not.

The **law of brightness constancy** states that we see an object's brightness as constant when the amount of light striking it changes. For example, you see the ink on this page as black and the paper as white in dim light or in bright light. The ink reflects about 5 percent of the light that strikes it; the paper reflects about 80 percent. Thus when 100 units of light strike the page, the ink reflects 5 units and the paper reflects 80 units. When 10,000 units of light strike the page, the ink reflects 500 units and the paper reflects 8,000 units. Hans Wallach (1948) showed that the appearance of black and white remains constant because our perceptual system responds to the *ratio* of the light from an object divided by the light from what surrounds it. In our example, this ratio is the same in dim light, $5/80 = .0625$, and bright light, $500/8,000 = .0625$.

How do our two theories explain this? The ecological theory says that we perceive a constant because some aspect of the visual scene remains constant (in this case, the ratio of light reflected remains constant, even though the light itself may change). Unconscious inference theorists, however, argue that unconscious inferences must also play a role (Gilchrist, 1975). They note that changes in brightness do not always affect objects and backgrounds equally. When the sun comes out from behind a cloud, for instance, more light might shine on the ground than on a tree trunk growing out of the ground. We take into account such differences in lighting, according to unconscious inference theory.

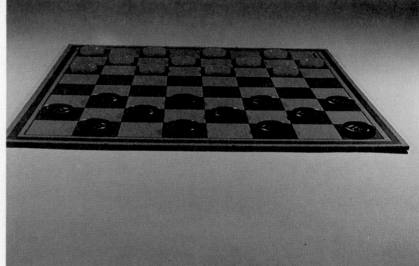

Figure 4–9
The photograph on the top right here shows a quite distorted view of the same checkerboard shown on the left, but, because of shape constancy, the checkers are perceived as round and the board as square in both photographs. Similarly, the lower photos illustrate how shape constancy makes the number 9 recognizable from different angles.

DEPTH PERCEPTION

As Lovell, Swigert, and Haise rounded the back side of the moon, they were presented with a breathtaking sight. For them this was the most important part of their flight. It gave them a chance to bring back scientific data that would, in some minds, justify the expense of the mission. In order to recognize the hills and craters they were looking for, the astronauts had to be able to see the relative depth between the tops and bottoms of the land formations. Figure 4–10 shows how difficult this can be. At first glance, the craters and hills are readily distinguishable. But turn the book upside down and look again. Now what you had identified as craters are seen as hills, and vice versa. This depth reversal is related to shading cues. While shadows have a powerful effect on depth perception, they are by no means the only source of depth information available to us.

We will discuss three kinds of depth information in this section: binocular, monocular, and kinetic. Binocular information is available through the use

Figure 4-10
Can you trust your eyes to distinguish craters from hills in the area indicated on this photograph? Turn the book upside down and try again. Many people see a depth reversal in the two ways of looking at the photo. That is, they see hills where they had seen craters, and vice versa.

Figure 4-11
The left eye view of the man and woman is different from the right eye view. The brain uses this difference or disparity as a depth cue, in this case an indication of how far away these people are from the viewer.

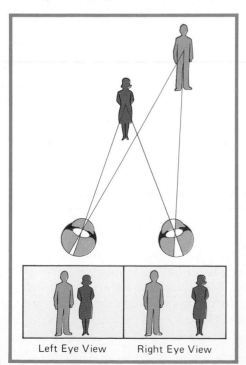

Left Eye View   Right Eye View

of both eyes. Monocular information is available even when we use only one eye. And kinetic information is available only when we move or when the environment moves.

Seeing Depth with Two Eyes

Because our eyes are separated by several centimeters, we get a different view of the world from each eye. This difference is called **binocular disparity.** You can see disparity for yourself by closing one eye while holding your right index finger about 12 inches in front of your nose, and your left index finger about 6 inches in front of your nose. Look at the far finger first with one eye and then the other. Your near finger will appear to be in different places as you look with each eye. Now look with both eyes—you will see a double image of the near finger.

When you look at distant objects, binocular disparity (the different view from each eye) is so small that you usually are not aware of it (see Figure 4–11). Even though you see a single image, however, you notice the disparity at an unconscious level. When disparity is very large, people see double images. When disparity is small, the brain fuses or integrates the images, using the disparity as a source of information about depth. The brain can use even small disparities as a depth cue. In fact, most of us are very sensitive to disparity, and we use it to help us see depth.

Seeing Depth with One Eye

You can get a feeling for **monocular** cues for depth by looking around you with your hand over one eye. You can still see depth, but you are using different cues than you would be if you were using both eyes. Monocular cues are used not only to see depth (the relative distance between objects), but also to see how far away objects are from you. A number of the most common monocular cues are shown in Figure 4–12: clearness, linear perspective, and texture.

One monocular cue is *clearness*. We look at objects on earth through air filled with tiny particles, which causes far objects to look blurry. This cue wouldn't have helped the astronauts on the moon, however, because in that environment there is no air or suspended particles. As a result, far objects look as sharp as near ones on the moon.

One of the most important monocular cues is **linear perspective.** Artists use linear perspective to create the impression of depth in their paintings. Notice, for example, how railroad tracks in Figure 4–12B seem to converge or come together in the distance. We often use linear perspective unconsciously to see depth in our environment.

Generally linear perspective is used in close conjunction with *texture*. Some surfaces, such as plastics and metals, have very little texture—their surfaces are smooth. But most surfaces have noticeable elements, or texture; for example, carpets, lawns, and foliage have texture, and certainly the moon's surface has texture. As we look at something with texture, the nearer elements are spaced farther apart than the more distant elements, forming what is known as a **texture gradient.** Some natural examples of texture gradient are shown in Figure 4–12C.

Seeing Depth through Motion

As the astronauts flew over the moon, their viewpoint changed continuously, giving them a powerful source of depth information. We learned earlier that the brain can determine depth from the two views of the world it gets from each eye. The brain also detects depth by using different views it gets when a person moves. You can see the power of motion or

Figure 4–12
Monocular cues: (A) clearness, (B) linear perspective, and (C) texture gradient.

kinetic depth information while looking at a bush. You will not be able to tell which branches are in front of which when you look with only one eye and with your head held still. But as soon as you swing your head back and forth, you will notice the depth of the bush. James Gibson and Hans Wallach did important experiments on motion and depth (Gibson, 1957; Wallach & O'Connell, 1953).

VISUAL ILLUSIONS

The human sensory and perceptual abilities are reliable enough to bring astronauts back from the moon, but they are far from perfect. They are, in fact, very undependable in some situations. An example of this is **illusions,** which are perceptual distortions. Illusions not only endanger astronauts, they also threaten airplane pilots. Kraft and Elworth (1969) found evidence, for example, that visual illusions cause about 16 percent of all airplane accidents.

Boeing officials had sought scientific help after four Boeing 727s crashed within a 4-month period, without any apparent mechanical cause. Dr. Conrad Kraft, chief scientist for the Personnel Subsystem of Boeing's Commercial Aircraft Division, combined a thorough knowledge of aviation with the data and methods of experimental psychology. In their experiments Kraft and Elworth built a device to simulate night visual approaches. The simulator included a stationary cockpit and a model airport that moved in response to the cockpit controls. The device simulated distances from 34 to 4.5 miles and altitudes from 16,000 feet to *minus* 2,500 feet. Kraft asked 12 experienced pilots to make simulated visual approaches. The simulator reproduced the visual conditions faced by the pilots who had crashed in the four Boeing 727s. Had the simulated flights been real, all but one of the 12 pilots tested would have crashed short of the runway. The one successful pilot was an ex-Navy pilot who had gained his early experience landing on aircraft carriers. Kraft did not explain exactly what kind of illusion caused the others to "crash," but he did explain how the angle of approach distorted important visual information, increasing the pilots' susceptibility to visual illusions.

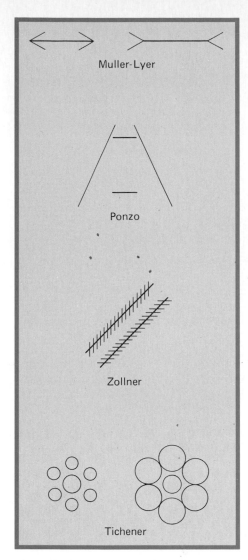

Figure 4-13
These drawings show several geometrical illusions, which cause a disagreement between what you see and what you can measure with a ruler.

Psychologists studied visual illusions long before they knew that these could bring down an airplane. Let's look at some of their findings.

Geometrical Illusions

The illusions shown in Figure 4-13 are line drawings that produce perceptual errors. Look at them and then measure them. In contrast to what the drawings look like, your ruler will tell you the following: the two horizontal lines are the same length in both the Müller-Lyer illusion and the Ponzo illusion; the oblique lines are parallel in the Zollner illusion; and the inner circles are the same size in the Titchener illusion. Scientists have studied such illusions for over 100 years in an attempt to gain a better understanding of perception (Gillam, 1980). In one important experiment Schiller and Wiener (1962) found that illusions are almost full strength when their parts are presented to each eye separately, indicating that the distortions are in the brain and not in the eye. Psychologists study illusions in the hope of better understanding the perceptual system. Whether or not illusions fulfill this hope, they do teach an important lesson. Those who maintain that "seeing is believing" are putting their eggs in the wrong basket. Sometimes "seeing is deceiving" (Coren & Girgus, 1978).

UFOs and Illusions: The Autokinetic Effect

The **autokinetic effect** is the tendency for a stationary light viewed against darkness to look as if it's moving. The light seems to glide, jerk, and swoop through space. The autokinetic effect could be responsible for some reports of unidentified flying objects (UFOs). Word spreads fast about UFO sightings, causing people's imaginations to run wild. This could set the stage for the autokinetic swooping of some distant house light to become a UFO in the mind of some well-intentioned witness (Geldard, 1972).

The autokinetic effect is extremely dangerous for aviators. Planes flying in formation at night have collided because pilots saw autokinetic movement of another plane's wing light. Pilots have also crashed while trying to fly next to what appeared to be another plane but what turned out to be a street light or marker buoy.

You can demonstrate the autokinetic effect by setting a dim penlight on a table edge in an otherwise dark room. This demonstration is fun, especially in a group. If each of you draws the motion path you see, without talking about it, you will all draw different paths. If one of you reports the light's apparent motion out loud, though, most of the rest of the group will tend to see the same path (Sherif, 1936). This shows the power of suggestion and group pressure on the illusion, which we will discuss in more detail in Chapter 16.

Psychologists have debated the cause of the autokinetic effect for over 100 years. The most popular explanation is that eye movements somehow cause the illusion. When we look at a light, our eyes seem motionless, but they actually move about randomly over a tiny area. As a result, the image of the light moves slightly over the retina. Matin and MacKinnon (1964) tested for the autokinetic effect when these small image movements were stopped by a special device. This device greatly reduced the autokinetic effect, suggesting that eye movements do play a part in the illusion. It has been suggested that eye movements produce autokinetic motion of a light because the brain fails to keep track of eye movements unless the light has a fixed relationship to other objects (Worchel & Burnham, 1967).

Psychologists have also attempted to find practical ways to reduce the autokinetic effect. One way is to replace single lights with a cluster of

PERCEPTION OF ART

Illusions underlie a twentieth-century art movement called Op (for optical illusion). Arnold Schmidt, for example, created an optical illusion of pulsing light in his untitled 1965 painting shown here. Op art emphasizes that observers participate in determining what is seen. Bridget Riley provides an example in her work, "Tremor." At first, the painting looks like a slightly modified checkerboard hardly worth a second glance. But look again. You will see the elements merge to form large overlapping triangles; you will see small circles around pinwheels; you will see a grate slanted backward in depth. Once you see the grate, you will see it change its orientation. How did Bridget Riley get so much mileage from one painting? She provided us with ambiguous information and let our minds do the rest.

Another master of the kind of art that appears to change before our eyes was Maurits C. Escher, a Dutch artist. In "Fish and Fowl," for instance, we see a school of fish at one moment and a flock of birds the next. When the fish are in view, the birds lose their identity as they merge into the background. When the birds are in view, the fish merge into the background. Escher's prints were deliberately created to exemplify principles of Gestalt psychology. They illustrate that we contribute to our perceptions.

Artists were aware of the observers' active contribution long before the advent of Op art. The active role of the perceiver seems to be the message of Rene Magritte in his painting "Les Promenades d'Euclide." The canvas has on it two similar triangles. Despite their physical similarity, we see them quite differently: We see the one on the left as a cone-shaped tower, and the one on the right as a street receding into the distance.

Magritte knew full well that we would use all the information surrounding the triangles to impose quite different organizations on each.

It might seem less obvious, but you are imposing organization right now, as you are reading. You also do so when you listen to someone speak, as explained in the text.

Arnold Schmidt. *Untitled* 1965. Synthetic polymer paint on canvas $4'\frac{1}{8}'' \times 8'\frac{1}{8}''$. The Museum of Modern Art, New York (gift of Mr. and Mrs. Herbert Bernard).

Bridget Riley, "Tremor." 1962. 48 × 48 inches. Courtesy of Mr. David M. Winton.

© M. C. Escher Heirs c/o Cordon Art–Baarn–
Holland.

Rene Magritte, ''Les Promenades d'Euclide.'' Courtesy of The Mineapolis
Institute of Arts.

Understanding visual illusions is an important part of making modern air travel safe.

several lights (Royce, Stayton, & Kinkade, 1962). Another way is to flash the light source. A group of researchers showed that autokinetic motion is greatly reduced for lights flashing between 4 and 10 times per second (Page, Elfner, & Jarnison, 1966). No one completely understands why the clusters and flashes work, but the results have practical value. Today lights on towers and aircraft blink. Undoubtably, this has saved many pilots who would otherwise have fallen victim to the autokinetic illusion.

SPEECH PERCEPTION

Illusions are caused in part by the tendency to impose organization on sensory information (see Highlight, Perception of Art). This tendency, which can be disastrous for pilots, can also play a highly beneficial role in perception. For example, the astronauts' ability to understand commands from mission control depended heavily on their active organizational processes. These processes are called **active synthesizing processes.** To synthesize means to combine diverse parts to form a unified whole. The unified whole for the active synthesizing processes is perception, which is constructed out of bits of sensory and memory information. These processes play an important role in speech perception by (1) compensating for distorted speech production, (2) opening gaps where they should be, or (3) closing gaps where they should not be.

Compensation for Distorted Speech

Active synthesizing processes compensate for errors in speech production. This function is critical because slight errors in production produce

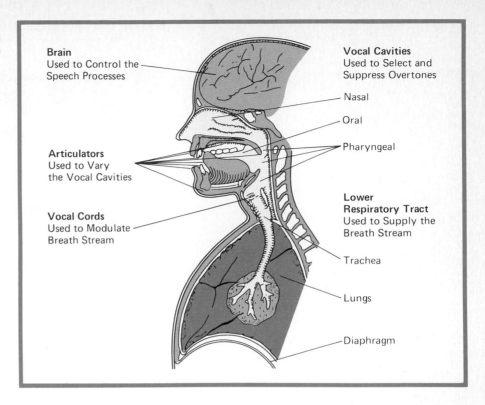

Brain
Used to Control the
Speech Processes

Vocal Cavities
Used to Select and
Suppress Overtones

Nasal

Oral

Pharyngeal

Articulators
Used to Vary
the Vocal Cavities

Vocal Cords
Used to Modulate
Breath Stream

Lower
Respiratory Tract
Used to Supply the
Breath Stream

Trachea

Lungs

Diaphragm

major distortions of sound waves. To appreciate this function, let's consider how a speaker's actions affect speech sounds (Wilde, 1975).

Speech organs produce speech sounds as shown in Figure 4–14. The **lungs** are the source of energy for the production of sounds. This energy is a stream of breath that creates sound by vibrating **vocal cords** in the throat. The role of vocal cords in speech is similar to that of strings on a guitar. We continually change the tension on our vocal cords to alter the pitch of our voice, as when we sing low notes and high notes (see Chapter 3). The pitch is low for low tension and high for high tension. We modify sound from the vibrating vocal cords with the **pharynx, oral cavity,** and **nasal cavity.** These structures function as resonance chambers, like the body of a guitar. Unlike the guitar, though, speech resonance chambers can be altered by the process of **articulation.** We articulate vowels, for example, by changing the location of the highest part of our tongue. The highest part can be in the front, center, or back as in saying the vowels in "eve," "up," and "boot." Figure 4–15 shows these tongue positions. It also shows that different vowels can be created by changing the highest point of the tongue at each position, as in "eve—at," "up—word," and "boot—father."

Visible representations of speech are called **sound spectrograms** (see Figure 4–16). The horizontal axis represents time. The vertical axis repre-

Figure 4–15
We articulate vowels by changing the position of the tongue. The highest part of the tongue can be in the front, center, or back of the mouth and will produce different vowel sounds in each location.

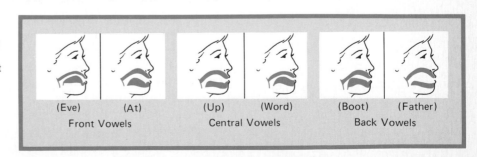

(Eve)   (At)
Front Vowels

(Up)   (Word)
Central Vowels

(Boot)   (Father)
Back Vowels

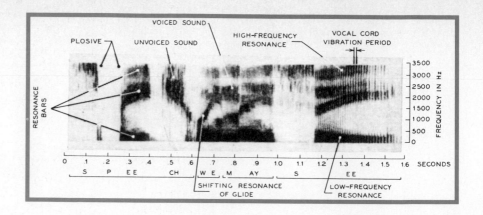

sents the frequency of the sound wave in number of cycles per second (which is referred to as number of "hertz," abbreviated Hz; see Chapter 3). The shade of darkness of the spectrogram lines represents the intensity of the sound. Notice the dramatic difference between the spectrograms in comparison to the relatively slight difference in the articulatory movements required to produce these vowels. Similarly, when we make slight errors of articulation, we produce major changes in the sound waves.

Cole (1973) supported the idea that we use contextual information to compensate for poor articulation. Subjects listened to a passage read from Lewis Carroll's *Through the Looking Glass* and were instructed to push a button whenever they heard a mispronunciation. One mispronunciation was "gunfusion" for "confusion." Only 30 percent of the subjects noticed. In another group all heard the same mispronounced syllable clearly when it was presented out of context. We cannot be sure that the subjects actually *heard* "confusion" instead of "gunfusion," but the results suggest that the active synthesizing processes use contextual information to compensate for mispronunciations.

Opening Gaps. Active synthesizing processes also cause us to hear gaps between words when no gap exists in the speech sound. Figure 4–16 shows a sound spectrogram for the utterance "speech we may see." Notice that no gap exists in the sound between the words "we" and "may." In fact, the sound was quite intense at several frequencies during the entire interval between .7 and .8 seconds. Yet if we were to listen to a tape of the very same speech sounds that produced the spectrogram, we would "hear" a gap between the words "we" and "may." Someone who did not understand English, however, would not hear the gap. Active synthesizing processes use our knowledge of language to construct perception of discrete words even when no break between words exists in the speech sound.

Filling Gaps. Often when we listen to someone talk other sounds drown out parts of the conversation. For example, at a dinner party clinking glasses, loud laughs, and our own munching might muffle parts of our conversation. Warren and Warren (1976), a husband and wife team at the University of Marquette, demonstrated our incredible ability to fill in such gaps. In their experiments they used doctored tape-recorded messages. The original tape said "the state governors met with their respective legislatures convening in the capital city." The doctored tapes omitted the syllable "gis" in "legislatures" and replaced it with a cough, buzz, or tone of the same duration. When people listened to the modified tapes, they heard the missing "gis" as clearly as if it were actually on tape. The important thing here is that people actually *heard* the missing sound.

This effect must be experienced to be appreciated. You can make your own tapes for this purpose. Practice saying something like "Roses are red, violets are blue, sugar is sweet, and so are you." Have an assistant cough at the moment you are saying the "v" in "violets" so that the sound of the letter is not heard on the tape. Not only will others listening to the tape hear the "v," but you will probably hear it too even though you *know* it is not there. How can this happen? The content of the well-known verse creates an expectation for the word "violets." Active synthesizing processes act on the basis of this expectation to manufacture the missing sound. To be sure it's not there, you might want to say "iolets" instead of "violets"; you will still hear the "v."

We can be reasonably sure that the astronauts' active synthesizing processes played an important role in their perception of verbal messages from mission control. They also played a role in reading written messages, as we will see in the next section.

READING

Two characteristics of vision combine to make active synthesizing processes important in reading: (1) We have a narrow range of clear vision; and (2) we move our eyes in a special way to compensate for this narrow range.

The first characteristic was illustrated by an incident during the flight of Apollo 13. You might recall that a mission controller missed a sudden change in oxygen pressure readings because he was looking 3 inches to the right of the critical numbers. You will immediately see the reason for this failure if you try to identify letters that are about 45 letter positions to the right of where you are looking in this text. It's impossible because we see clearly only a short distance from where we are looking at any given moment. Bouma (1973) showed, for example, that when people look at a letter in an unpronounceable letter string, they recognize all other letters that are within about 1 or 2 letter positions. But they recognize only 75 percent of the letters that are 3 or 4 positions away, and only 50 percent of the letters that are 5 or 6 positions away.

We compensate for this narrow range of clear vision with eye movements. When we read, our eyes jerk from one fixation point to the next in a series of eye movements called **saccades.** You can easily detect saccades by watching someone's eyes while that person is reading. These jerky eye movements create gaps in sensory input because the eyes are functionally blind during the saccadic movements. Active synthesizing processes fill in these gaps so well that you may have trouble believing they are there at all. To convince yourself, try the following experiment (see Shebilske, 1977; Woodsworth, 1938):

Fold a 5-by-5-inch card in half and cut a narrow slit out of the center of the fold. Open the card part way to form a wedge. Close one eye and hold the slit close to your other eye by resting it on your face. With the slit this close to your eye, you will be able to see through it when you look straight ahead, but not when you hold your gaze off to the left or right. When you move your eye from one side to the other, your line of sight is momentarily directed through the slit. If you can see while your eye is moving, you should be able to see through the slit as your line of sight goes past it. To find out, have an assistant hold up a large letter that you can easily identify when looking through the slit (see Figure 4–17, p. 119). Hold your direction of gaze off to one side (at this point you should not be able to see the letter because of the wedge). Have your assistant hold up a different large letter. Now move your eye in a single

SPEED READING—
SAVE TIME AND MONEY

This highlight can save you thousands of hours and hundreds of dollars. You can save the time by pushing your reading speed to the upper limit for actual reading of about 500 to 600 words per minute or by learning to skim at even faster rates (Hochberg, 1970). This increase will yield a substantial time saving if you are now reading at 250 to 300 words per minute, which is the average rate for college students. You can save money because you can increase your reading speed without taking courses that often cost hundreds of dollars. We have taught many students to double their reading rate by using the procedures outlined in this highlight. You will have more confidence in these procedures if you first understand why they work.

The key to faster reading is putting your active synthesizing processes to work for you (see text for definition). These processes reduce the amount of visual information you use to read because they take advantage of information from memory. They use three kinds of information from memory:

1. *Orthographic* information about how letters are combined in words
2. *Syntactic* information about how words are combined in sentences
3. *Semantic* information about the meaning of the passage.

To illustrate these, suppose we see all the visual information in the following sentence except for that in the two underlined positions: "Poncho hit the | |." In the first underlined position, the tall vertical line indicates that the letter is a consonant. In the second underlined position, we see no visual

information. In this situation, orthographic rules would provide a great deal of information. Since three of the four letters are consonants, we know the unidentified letter in the second position must be a vowel. Orthographic information thereby reduces the possible alternatives from 26 to 6. Syntactic rules also provide information. They dictate that the unidentified letter must be a noun, eliminating possibilities such as *fill*, *full*, *tall*, and *tell*. In this limited context, the meaning of the sentence (semantics) provides little useful information. Poncho could have hit just about anything: a *ball*, *bell*, *bull*, *bill*, or *till*. In a richer context, semantics could help a great deal. For example, you will probably have no trouble reducing the choices to a single word in the following sentences:

> To save his friend from being gored, Poncho hit the | | with a well-aimed rock.

> With bases loaded in the bottom of the ninth, Poncho hit the | | out of the park.

This sample merely illustrates the meaning of the three kinds of information; it does not show how the sentence might actually be recognized. All the sources of information might be used simultaneously, or in a different order than suggested here.

Doing the following exercise for 15 minutes everyday for a semester should activate your synthesizing processes and increase your speed. Set a timer for three minutes and read at your normal speed from a section of a newspaper or magazine. When the timer sounds, stop reading and count the number

of lines you've read. Multiply this by 1.20 to get the number of lines you should try to read in the next three-minute period. The goal number of lines will be 20 percent more than you read the first time; therefore, you will have to read 20 percent faster than you normally read. It may take a little practice to reach your goal in three minutes but force yourself to read faster until you accomplish it. The required reading speed will be uncomfortable until your active synthesizing processes improve to meet the challenge. When you first speed up, you will not recognize all the words or understand everything you read. After your active synthesizing processes are adjusted to utilize contextual information efficiently, you will be able to read faster with no loss of comprehension. Do not expect to comprehend words that you do not "see." Once your active synthesizing processes are working to their full capacity, you will not process all the visual information, but you will "see" all the words because the processes actually construct perceptions. As soon as you become comfortable at a speed increase your speed by another 20 percent. Continue increasing speed until you reach about 500 words per minute. We hope that many of you will enjoy reading your assignment in half the time that it is now taking you. We also hope that faster reading will lead to higher grades. Studying involves much more than reading. Faster reading can raise your grades, however, by allowing more time for other important study processes (see Chapter 1 Highlight, Learning from Textbooks is a Three-Letter Word).

Figure 4–17
This experiment, described in detail in the text, illustrates the fact that our eye movements or saccades create gaps in sensory input. We're not usually aware of these gaps because of our active synthesizing processes.

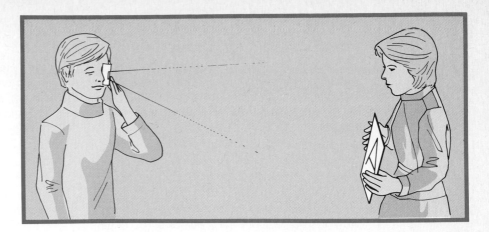

movement to the other side. Can you identify the letter? Most people cannot even see the assistant, let alone the letter. If you see the letter, have your assistant watch your eyes. You are probably stopping briefly to look through the slit.

If you do this experiment correctly, it should convince you that saccades create gaps in the sensory input. McConkie (1978) conducted an experiment that might remove any remaining doubts. He used a computer to show text to people only during their saccadic eye movements. When the eyes fixated between saccades, all the letters were replaced by *X's*. Under this condition, people could not read the text, which suggests that we are functionally blind during saccadic movements. We fill in these blind intervals just as we fill in missing speech sounds during listening.

Active synthesizing processes can also supplement information that is not seen clearly. How much this clarification function of active synthesis is needed depends on how we space fixations. According to Bouma's results, which were reviewed earlier, we see all the visual information clearly if we look at every fourth or fifth letter. For example, if we look at all the underlined letters in this sentence, we see all the letters clearly because they all fall within 1 or 2 letter positions of where we look. If, however, we look at every ninth or tenth letter, we will not see all the letters clearly.

How many letters do you usually look at? Shebilske (1975) suggested that you look at every fourth or fifth letter if you are an average college reader; that is, you read between 250 and 300 words per minute. If you are a highly skilled college reader, you space your looks much farther apart, sometimes as much as every ninth or tenth letter. You are able to space your fixations farther apart because you allow your active synthesizing processes to supplement the visual information. This allows you to read much faster (see Highlight: Speed Reading—Save Time and Money).

We often fail to see the mysteries in our ability to read; recognize a familiar grouping of stars; see the correct size, shape, distance, and slant of this book; or understand a lecture. In contrast, scientists realize that these are amazing abilities that are only partially understood. Scientific studies have not only increased our understanding of these abilities but have also yielded practical knowledge. This information has resulted in safer aviation and space travel, spectacular art, and many other applications. One insight gained is that we sometimes create perceptions by imposing organization on information. We will see in the next chapter that an extension of this insight has gone a long way toward explaining the mysteries of dreams during sleep and experiences during other states of consciousness, such as drug-induced states.

SUMMARY

1. Infants see depth and size and they coordinate their movements with what they see, even though their muscle control is poor. Babies also have strong preferences in what they like to watch.

2. We actively impose organization on what we see, according to various rules. The **Gestalt laws of organization** attempt to describe some of those rules. Our active contribution is clear when appearances alternate back and forth in **multistable perceptions.** Scientists are beginning to understand the rules according to which we organize perceptions of moving objects.

3. We have perceptual **constancies;** that is, perceptions remain constant when visual information changes. For instance, apparent size remains constant when we move further from an object, even though movement shrinks the retinal image of the object. **Unconscious inference theory** and **ecological theory** offer opposing explanations of constancies.

4. We respond to many sources of information about depth. **Binocular** information is available through the use of both eyes. **Monocular** information is available even when we use only one eye. **Kinetic** information is available when we move or when the environment moves.

5. Sometimes, as is the case with illusions, seeing is deceiving. In geometric illusions (such as the Müller-Lyer, Ponzo, Zollner, and Titchener illusions) our eyes tell us one thing, but a ruler tells us something different. Other illusions, such as the **autokinetic effect,** are more serious—the study of such illusions is helping to reduce the number of airplane accidents caused by them.

6. **Active synthesizing processes** construct perceptions out of sensory and memory information. These processes compensate for distorted speech, open gaps between words, and close gaps created by extraneous noises.

7. We have a narrow range of clear vision that forces us to move our eyes when we read. Our eyes jerk from one fixation point to the next in a series of eye movements called **saccades.** The eyes are functionally blind during saccades, but we "see" because the gaps are filled by synthesizing processes. These processes also supplement information that is seen clearly, and enable us to read faster.

Key Terms

active synthesizing processes
articulation
autokinetic effect
binocular disparity
constancies
ecological theory of perception
figure
figure-ground reversal
Gestalt laws of organization
illusions
kinetic depth
law of brightness constancy
law of constancy
law of nearness or proximity
law of shape constancy
law of similarity

linear perspective
lungs
monocular
multistable perception
nasal cavity
oral cavity
pharynx
retinal image
saccades
sound spectrograms
texture gradient
unconscious inference theory
visual angle
visual cliff
vocal cords

Suggested Readings

The following books are about the Apollo 13 mission:

COOPER, H. S. F., JR. *Thirteen: The flight that failed*. New York: Dial, 1973.

LEWIS, R. S. *The voyages of Apollo: The exploration of the moon*. New York: Quadrangle, 1974.

COREN, S., PORAC, C., & WARD, L. M. *Sensation and perception*, 2nd ed. New York: Academic Press, 1984. Uses everyday examples to awaken one's curiosity about the sensory world. The structure and function of all senses are covered.

KUBOVY, M., & POMERANTZ, J. R. (Eds.). *Perceptual organization*. Hillsdale, N.J.: Erlbaum, 1981. Chapters by authorities on theory, history, philosophy, methodology, and recent discoveries in sensation, perception, and cognition. Many illustrations and auditory phenomena are demonstrated on an optional cassette tape.

MICHAELS, C. F., & CARELLO, C. *Direct perception*. Englewood Cliffs, N.J.: Prentice-Hall, 1981. Provides a clear statement of recent theoretical and empirical developments in the theory of direct perception.

PRINZ, W., & SANDERS, A. F. (Eds.). *Cognition and motor processes*. Berlin, Heidelberg: Springer-Verlag, 1984. A collection of papers on how perception and cognition guide actions. Topics include perception of space, development of motor control, action planning, speech perception, and reading.

REED, E., & JONES, R. (Eds.). *Reasons for realism: Selected essays of James J. Gibson*. Hillsdale, N.J.: Erlbaum, 1982. Explores James J. Gibson's revolutionary theory of how we see the world.

WALLACH, H. *On perception*. New York: Quadrangle, 1976. One of the outstanding visual scientists of our day reviews his research, which has contributed significantly to our understanding of perception.

ALTERNATE STATES OF CONSCIOUSNESS

Holding his alarm clock near the hospital night light, Private George Ritchie saw that he could start his long-awaited trip home in one hour—if the Army nurse did not take his temperature again. His condition had gotten much worse during the night. About 2½ hours earlier, at midnight, he had started to cough up bright red blood. Now his chest, throat, and head ached, his legs trembled, his heart pounded, and his body was covered with sweat. But he was going to try to slip out of the hospital unnoticed; he didn't want to pass up the chance of a lifetime because of a stupid cold.

George Ritchie had come to Camp Barkeley, Texas, for basic training in September, 1943. He was 20 years old, tall, slender, and ready to whip the Nazis, but he was less prepared to fight the cold, rainy Texas weather. Then, shortly after Thanksgiving, he got the break of his life—he was offered a chance to start classes in the Army Specialized Training Program on December 22, at the Medical College of Virginia.

Now it was 2:20 A.M. on December 20, and he was determined to catch the last possible train that could get him to Richmond on time. Quietly, he dressed. "Just what is my temperature?" he wondered, as he felt his clothes become soaked with sweat. He walked down to the supply room and asked the night ward boy for a thermometer, which he then tried to read in the light from the supply room doorway. He couldn't make sense of it. The silver mercury seemed to go past the numbers. The night ward boy came up behind him and slipped the thermometer out of his hand, checked the temperature reading, and raced down the hallway to find a nurse.

Within the next few minutes both a doctor and a nurse were examining Private Ritchie. The doctor listened to his chest while the nurse repeated the temperature reading. They quickly sent him by ambulance to another wing of the hospital for X-rays. While standing in front of the X-ray machine, he collapsed. He was taken to a small isolation room where his condition was diagnosed as double lobar pneumonia.

Twenty-four hours later, he sat up in bed with a start. "The train—I must catch the train," he thought. He jumped out of bed and looked for his clothes. Suddenly he froze, realizing that someone was lying in the bed he had just gotten out of. That puzzled him for a moment, but then he decided it was too strange to think about. Besides, he had to hurry. Perhaps the ward boy had his clothes. Running out into the hallway, he was relieved to find a sergeant coming toward him carrying a cloth-covered instrument tray.

"Excuse me, Sergeant," he said. "You haven't seen the ward boy for this unit, have you?"

The sergeant didn't seem to hear or see him—he kept walking toward Ritchie.

"Look out!" Ritchie yelled, jumping out of the way.

This too was strange, but he had no time to figure it out now. He had his mind on one thing: getting to Richmond.

Before he knew what was happening, he found himself outside of the hospital on his way to Richmond, not traveling by train as originally planned, but speeding over the dark, frozen desert a hundred times faster than any train could carry him. He was flying—not in a plane or any other vehicle—he was just flying. Soon he was beyond the desert, passing over snow-covered wooded areas and an occasional town.

Suddenly he slowed down and found himself hovering about fifty feet over a red-roofed, one-story building. A blue neon "Cafe" sign was over the building's door and a "Pabst Blue Ribbon Beer" sign was propped up in the front window. The next thing he knew, he was on the sidewalk in front of the cafe, walking next to a middle-aged man wearing a topcoat.

"Can you tell me, please, what city this is?" Ritchie asked. Then he shouted, "Please sir! I'm a stranger here and I'd appreciate it if . . ." He stopped; the man obviously had heard nothing.

In desperation Ritchie tried to grab the man's shoulder, but he felt nothing, as if the man were only a mirage. Now Ritchie began to think about all of the strange things that were happening to him. He remembered the young man he had seen in the hospital bed. Could it have been the material, concrete part of himself lying there? He had to find out.

In a flash, he was flying again, this time back toward Texas. Before long he was standing next to the bed from which he had started his bizarre journey, but now the person lying in the bed was covered with a sheet from head to toe. Only the arms and hands were exposed. On the left hand was a ring containing a gold owl on an oval, black onyx and the words, "University of Richmond." Ritchie fixed his eyes on the ring. Could this

be *his* ring? How could it be? This man was obviously dead. Ritchie asked himself, "How could I be dead and still be awake?"

Suddenly the room glowed with a light that seemed too bright for mortal eyes, radiating from a man who appeared to be made of light. The man seemed to put thoughts directly into Ritchie's head. "Stand up! You are in the presence of the Son of God." Ritchie stood up and became filled with a mysterious inner certainty that this all-powerful person loved him. At the same time the room filled with a giant, three-dimensional, moving mural showing every episode in his life. It normally would have taken weeks to see so many events, but Private Ritchie seemed to be beyond any ordinary time frame.

A question filled Ritchie's head: "What have you done with your life to show me?" Ritchie knew that the all-loving being in his presence was asking, "How much have you loved with your life? Have you loved others as I am loving you?" For Ritchie, having to answer this question was like having to take a final exam for a course he had never taken. "If that is what life is all about, why didn't someone tell me?" he protested. The man who seemed to be made of light answered that he had tried to tell Ritchie and that he would show him more. With that they started to move toward a distant pinpoint of light that rapidly grew into a large city. It could have been any of several cities in the United States. The streets were crowded with living humans and many substanceless beings that were similar to Ritchie.

These nonphysical beings were unable to perform any physical acts, yet were completely and futilely absorbed in some worldly activity. One spirit constantly begged for cigarettes, while another begged for beer. Another spirit tried to manage a business as he had once done, and still another followed her middle-aged son, nagging constantly without being heard.

Ritchie realized that this was hell—a place where people were powerless to obtain those things for which they had a burning desire.

Suddenly Ritchie and the spirit guiding him were in an immense void traveling toward a seemingly endless city where everything and everyone seemed to be made of light. As he approached, Ritchie thought he might be entering heaven, the home of beings who had incorporated the man made of light and his love into their lives to such an extent that they had been transformed into his very likeness.

But a glimpse is all Ritchie got, because in a flash he was back in the room with his sheet-covered body. The man of light explained that Ritchie had to return to his body.

As Ritchie pleaded to stay with this man, his mind blurred. He was now aware of nothing except his burning throat and aching chest. He tried to move his arms, but only his hands would move. He felt his ring and began to twist it around his finger.

Just then the ward boy, preparing Ritchie for the morgue, noticed Ritchie's hands. He ran to get the doctor who had pronounced Ritchie dead about ten minutes earlier. Doctor Francy repeated his exam and again pronounced him dead.

The ward boy refused to accept this diagnosis and pleaded with the doctor to inject adrenalin directly into the heart muscle, which he did.

Today, George Ritchie is a psychiatrist at the University of Virginia Medical School. Dr. Ritchie has told many about his close encounter with death (Ritchie, 1978). Skeptics assume that he was dreaming or hallucinat-

ing. But even skeptics recognize that his experience profoundly affected his life. He is characterized by a remarkable depth of kindness, understanding, and loving concern for others.

STUDYING THE MIND

George Ritchie believes that he died for about 10 minutes and that his mental activities continued to exist after his body died. That is, he continued to have sensations, mental images, thoughts, desires, emotions, and wishes. Without a body, however, his mind could not contact physical things. Is it possible for a mind to exist without a body? Clearly, in the fourteenth century B.C., ancient Egyptians thought so when they filled the tomb of their dead boy-king, Tutankhamen (King Tut), with food, water, furniture, jewelry, and tools. Egyptians sought eternal life beyond all else, and they believed that King Tut's spirit would enjoy his entombed treasures forever. Hippocrates, the "Father of Scientific Medicine," also thought the mind could continue to exist after death. In the fifth century B.C., on the Greek island of Cos, he taught that the brain and mind are separate entities and that careful observations of people would clarify the relationship existing between mind and body. In this chapter we will: (1) review the debate of modern scientists on the nature of the conscious mind; (2) examine scientific observations of physiological and subjective patterns during different mental states; (3) critically evaluate claims that we might have hidden mental powers, such as the ability to project our minds out of our bodies; (4) review evidence that others have had near-death experiences similar to Ritchie's experience; and (5) discuss whether or not common patterns run through all mental states including near-death experiences.

WHAT IS CONSCIOUSNESS?

Is it possible that what you are experiencing right now is just a dream? Will you soon wake up and find that you have been dreaming instead of reading? Charles Tart (1977) asks similar questions at the beginning of his lectures on consciousness, but his students rarely answer yes. Sometimes dreams seem real, but we hardly ever mistake waking states for dreaming states. We distinguish between mental states easily, even though we would be hard pressed to say how we do it. Researchers studying consciousness start with people's intuitions about mental states and then study the basis for them. In so doing, they hope to precisely define the nature of consciousness.

Alternate States of Consciousness Defined

John Locke (1960) defined **consciousness** as "the perception of what passes in a man's own mind" (p. 138). Locke's definition is fine for everyday usage, but it's not precise enough for our purposes, because it does not distinguish between different kinds of consciousness, such as waking states and dreaming states. Scientists refer to different mental states as **alternate states of consciousness** (Zinberg, 1977), which they define as "a specific pattern of physiological and subjective responses" (Shapiro, 1977, p. 152). By *physiological pattern*, Shapiro means such things as brain activity, eye movement, heart rate, blood pressure, and oxygen consumption. By *subjective pattern*, Shapiro means sensations, thoughts, and emotions. Table 5–1 is a questionnaire that may help you identify patterns in your own experiences. You might enjoy answering the questions to describe your most recent dream, and then answering the same questions with respect to your present state of consciousness. Notice that questions 1, 6, and 7 refer to aspects of sensations; questions 2, 4, 5, and 8 analyze thoughts; and question 3 is about emotions. Zinberg (1977) used an extended version of this questionnaire to help his subjects scan the contents and qualities of their experiences. He found unique response patterns associated with waking states, dreaming states, and other alternate states of consciousness, such as drug-induced states. As we discuss various states of consciousness

Table 5-1
Alternate States of Consciousness Questionnaire

		None	Barely Detectable							Very Vivid
1. How vivid are each of the following kinds of sensations?	Sight	0	1	2	3	4	5	6	7	8	9
	Sound	0	1	2	3	4	5	6	7	8	9
	Taste	0	1	2	3	4	5	6	7	8	9
	Smell	0	1	2	3	4	5	6	7	8	9
	Touch	0	1	2	3	4	5	6	7	8	9

	Absolutely Convinced I Am Not							Absolutely Convinced I Am
2. How sure are you that you are in an ordinary waking state of consciousness?	1	2	3	4	5	6	7	8	9

		None	Barely Detectable							Strong Feeling
3. How much are you feeling the following emotions?	Joy	0	1	2	3	4	5	6	7	8	9
	Rage	0	1	2	3	4	5	6	7	8	9
	Surprise	0	1	2	3	4	5	6	7	8	9
	Interest	0	1	2	3	4	5	6	7	8	9
	Sadness	0	1	2	3	4	5	6	7	8	9

	Events Passing by without My Control							I Am in Complete Control
4. How much are you in control of your experiences?	1	2	3	4	5	6	7	8	9

	Experiences in a Seemingly Random Order							Experiences in a Very Logical Order
5. To what extent are your experiences ordered logically?	1	2	3	4	5	6	7	8	9

	Many Strange Sensations							All Ordinary Sensations
6. To what extent are you experiencing unusual sensations?	1	2	3	4	5	6	7	8	9

	Absolutely Sure That My Experiences Are in My Mind Only							Absolutely Sure That My Experiences Are Being Caused by Something outside of Myself
7. To what extent do you believe that your experiences are being caused by something located outside of yourself?	1	2	3	4	5	6	7	8	9

	I Am Not Thinking about the Fact That I Am Experiencing Things							I Am Thinking a Great Deal about the Fact That I Am Experiencing Things
8. To what extent are you aware of your awareness?	1	2	3	4	5	6	7	8	9

Source: Zinberg (1977).

in this chapter, we will focus on both physiological and subjective patterns for each.

Philosophies and Theories of Mind

Ritchie never doubted for a moment that he actually walked with God. He believes there exists a reality beyond what we can see—another dimension in which our spirits will live on after our bodies die. For centuries people have held similar beliefs. Let's look at some modern theories.

Monism vs. Dualism.   Recently, Wilder Penfield (1975), who carefully observed for more than forty years the connection between the brain and behavior in epileptic patients (see Chapter 2), echoed Hippocrates's claim that brain and mind are separate entities. Penfield took into consideration two philosophies: **monism,** which states that the mind and brain are one organic whole; and **dualism,** which describes the mind and brain as separate things. Monism rules out the possibility that Ritchie's mind continued to exist after his brain stopped functioning. Monists hold that brain functions completely account for mental functions. When the brain dies, the mind dies. Dualism, on the other hand, allows for the possibility that Ritchie's mind existed outside of his body. Dualists believe that brain and mind draw upon different energy sources (neither of which is understood). Thus, when the brain dies, the mind could in principle continue to function, but dualists are not committed to the view that it does.

Penfield favored dualism, knowing full well that scientific evidence does not provide proof on the issue. Some neurobiologists, such as Nobel prize winner Sir John Eccles (1973) and Karl Pribram (1977), realize that they cannot explain all that the mind does on the basis of what is currently known about brain functions, and they favor Penfield's dualistic view. Other scientists, such as Rose (1973), favor monism, believing that someday brain research will explain all mental experiences. Despite their inability to offer firm answers, Penfield and other scientists are optimistic that at some future time science will be able to conclusively answer the age-old question about the relationship between mind and brain.

Mysticism vs. Perceptual Release.   We might be less optimistic about being able to scientifically test *mystical theories*. These theories suggest that alternate state experiences are caused by special external stimulation. The stimulation is from an external reality that is not apparent to our usual senses of hearing, sight, taste, touch, and smell. Egyptian, Roman, and Greek mystics believed, for instance, that we receive messages from God while we dream. Toward the end of the Middle Ages, science dismissed dreams as being unreal. Scientists never really disproved the mystical theory, however, and maybe they never will (Cohen, 1976).

While scientists have little or nothing to say about the possible mystical nature of sleep and dreams, they know a great deal about the physiological and subjective activities that accompany them. Scientists also offer an alternative to mystical theories. The alternative is the *perceptual release theory*, which holds that actions and reactions in our brain cause alternate state experiences. Accordingly, when we sleep our senses dim and we respond to our *internal* brain activity, which we experience as dreams. We might compare this theory to a man looking out a window at dusk. A burning fireplace goes unnoticed as the man attends to things outside. The outside world gradually dims and is replaced by a reflection of the fire and the room it illuminates. The fire and room then appear to be located outside the window. Similarly, external stimuli fade during alternate states of consciousness, and perceptions originating in the brain seem to come from outside.

You are invited to form your own opinion on monism versus dualism and on mystical theories versus perceptual release theories as we review data on consciousness.

SCIENTIFIC OBSERVATIONS OF ALTERNATE STATES OF CONSCIOUSNESS

Dr. Ritchie's book, *Return from Tomorrow*, in which he describes his out-of-body experience, is not a scientific document, nor was it intended to be. Experiences similar to Ritchie's have been studied scientifically, however, and we will analyze existing data after briefly summarizing standard methods of studying alternate states of consciousness.

Methods for Studying States of Consciousness

In the beginning of *Return from Tomorrow*, Ritchie relates a case of a dying patient who is unprepared to face death. The reader learns about Ritchie's experience as it is told to the patient, who is at first skeptical, but who is later inspired, as are many readers. *Return from Tomorrow* goes to one's heart, as Ritchie intended. If Ritchie had chosen instead to objectively examine his experience in order to determine its nature, he could have used his encounter with death as a basis for a scientific inquiry. Such an investigation would be labeled the self-experience approach, the first of three methods used to study subjective patterns in various states of consciousness.

Self-Experience. Andrew T. Wiel, a Harvard researcher, and many other scientists believe that the best way to experiment with alternate states of consciousness is for investigators to experience the states themselves. In one interesting self-experience experiment, Wiel analyzed states of consciousness induced by religious ceremonies inside a Sioux Indian Sweat Lodge. Wiel participated in this ritual several times. He found that "on coming out of sweat lodges I have felt high in many of the same ways I have felt while using some psychedelic drugs. . . . Increased awareness of one's own strength and a sense of well-being may persist for a long time" (Wiel, 1977, p. 45). He also commented on why he didn't get burned by temperatures that reached almost 212°F.: "Curiously enough, one's mental state seems to be the most important determinant of the fate of one's skin. Burning occurs only when you lose contact with the psychic energy of the group" (Wiel, 1977, p. 45). Wiel's suggestion that he was in touch with the psychic energy of the group implies the existence of a distinct source of mental energy.

Some have applied the self-experience approach to the investigation of conscious-altering drugs. They include Havelock Ellis (1902), Aldous Huxley (1952), and Carlos Castaneda (1972). Although such drug research has made important contributions, it has been extremely dangerous even for well-prepared scientists such as Timothy Leary, whose famous research on LSD resulted in tragedy (Cohen, 1976).

In this chapter we will encourage you to use the self-experience approach, but only for safe conscious states, such as sleep and deep relaxation. These states can be accompanied by rich and attractive experiences. In fact, we will introduce the argument that people who learn to enjoy such natural "highs" might have an advantage. Specifically, they might have less need to experiment with artificially induced states of consciousness. We will also encourage you to use questionnaires and interviews, as discussed in the next section.

Questionnaires and Interviews. We have already seen and used a questionnaire earlier in this chapter. Similar questions could be asked in an interview. You can control exact wording better in a questionnaire, but you can often learn more in an interview by following up on a person's interesting comments.

Timing is important in this method. For example, say you want to interview people about their dreams. There are three ways to do this. First, you can ask people to describe the dreams they can remember having during the past week. Second, you can ask them ahead of time to pay special attention to the dreams they have during the next week, because you plan to ask them to describe the dreams. Warning them ahead of time has an advantage—they are not as likely to forget their dreams if they make a conscious attempt to remember them in order to report them. But this kind of ahead-of-time warning also has a drawback. Suppose we told you to report every time you think about pink elephants for the rest of the day. Would your reports reflect how much you usually think about pink elephants? The third way is to administer the questionnaire or interview during or immediately after an experience. An advantage is that the experience is easier to remember. A disadvantage is that the experience usually must take place with the experimenter on hand, often in an artificial laboratory setting. Can people have normal dreams when they know scientists are observing them?

Laboratory Experiments. Despite the fact that they may seem artificial, laboratory experiments are valuable for studying alternate states of consciousness. In one experiment, Hilgard (1969) induced pain by briefly submerging a person's arm in cold water. The water was held at constant temperatures of 0°C, 5°C, 10°C, or 15°C. The pain was real enough, but its consequences were different from those of the chronic pain that is treated in clinics, where patients face the prospect of life-long debilitating pain. Hilgard's subjects knew, in contrast, that their pain would terminate before the end of the experiment. Despite the contrived situation, however, Hilgard was able to validate subjective pain scales by comparing them with objective physiological correlates. The subjective and objective measures increased and decreased together as water temperature varied. Today, subjective pain scales are widely used in laboratories and clinics (Burrows & Dennerstein, 1980). In another laboratory experiment, Hilgard (1967) carefully selected a group from which he could precisely compare different levels of susceptibility to hypnosis, a state induced by the words and actions of a hypnotist whose suggestions are readily accepted. He found that pain relief from hypnosis is related to susceptibility. Hilgard's experiments illustrate three important advantages of laboratory experiments: (1) They can manipulate and control factors such as water temperature and other factors that might influence states of consciousness; (2) they can supplement subjective reports with objective measures such as physiological correlates; and (3) they can carefully select subjects in order to control or study individual differences.

Clinical Methods. Wain (1980) conducted a clinical investigation of hypnotic pain treatment. (Hypnosis is defined and discussed later in this chapter.) In this study, a 58-year-old patient at Walter Reed Army Medical Center responded positively to the suggestion that he could control his severe headaches (Wain, 1980). He had a number of physical pathologies, including high blood pressure and a disorder of the blood vessels serving the brain. The reduction of pain following the first session lasted about six hours. The patient later learned how to hypnotize himself, which he did every three hours during the days that followed. By the time he was released from the hospital, his headaches were less severe and his blood pressure had dropped, both without medication. A six-month follow-up examination revealed that he no longer suffered with severe headaches and that his blood pressure was under control. Many other patients at Walter Reed Army Medical Center and at other clinics have also been able to control their pain through hypnosis (Burrows & Dennerstein, 1980; Erickson, 1980).

An advantage of this and other clinical investigations is that the patients are highly motivated because they are being treated for real problems. A disadvantage is the difficulty of generalizing—the results might only be relevant for people with special conditions. This problem is minimized when investigators treat many patients, report both successes and failures, and describe cases in detail. The problem is magnified when only successes are reported and when no attempt is made to characterize those for whom the treatment succeeds or fails.

Another disadvantage is that the investigator cannot always be sure that symptoms would not have gone away without treatment. A nontreatment control group could solve this problem in principle, but this solution is often unacceptable in clinical situations. One approach to establishing the extent of effectiveness is to analyze abrupt changes in symptoms when treatment is administered. Researchers can apply this strategy by taking quantitative measures of symptoms over a period of time both before and after treatment. If symptoms have remained stable for a long time, abrupt changes after treatment will signal a treatment effect. Another approach is to vary the level of treatment. Researchers can measure different levels of hypnotic susceptibility, for example, using standard scales (e.g., Hilgard & Hilgard, 1975, 1979). A treatment effect is suggested if the degree of symptom change is related to the level of treatment. Thus, although many obstacles stand in the way of definitive clinical studies, a careful researcher can overcome them.

Scientific investigations using all four methods (self-experience, questionnaires and interviews, laboratory experiments, and clinical methods) have greatly increased our understanding of alternate states of consciousness. However, important questions remain unanswered. Scientists are still debating, for example, whether hypnosis should be classified as a special state or as part of the waking state. In the remainder of this chapter, we will review data on physiological and subjective patterns in alternate states of consciousness. You are encouraged to look for patterns that cut across several states and to consider how these common patterns might help you to classify hypnosis and other states.

SLEEP AND DREAMS

Ritchie regained waking consciousness three days after the doctor injected adrenalin into his heart. Is it possible that Ritchie was mistaken in thinking that his experience took place before the doctors injected the adrenalin? Was his tour of hell and his glimpse of heaven only a dream occurring sometime during the three days after he was revived? Let's consider this question in light of the literature on sleep and dreaming. **Sleep** is defined as a period of rest for the body and mind during which bodily functions are partially suspended and sensitivity to external stimuli is diminished but readily or easily regained. **Dreams** are series of images, thoughts, and emotions occurring during sleep. Was Ritchie *only* dreaming? The question's emphasis shows a current attitude that dreams do not reflect a person's direct contact with the supernatural. But dreams were not always regarded as being so "down to earth."

Scientists are beginning to understand why we need to sleep.

Egyptians, Romans, and Greeks believed that we receive messages from God during dreams. Throughout the Middle Ages as well, Greeks slept in churches in order to contact God. Toward the end of the Middle Ages, however, most religions took an official stand against dreams as a means of contacting God. At the same time, science dismissed dreams as unreal or worthless because they could not be studied "objectively" (Cohen, 1976). As a result, the ancient theory was never disproved—it was merely displaced. An objective scientist is free to accept or reject the possibility that Ritchie walked with God *during a dream*. There is no proof one way or the other and perhaps there never will be.

While scientists have little or nothing to say about the possible mystical nature of sleep and dreams, they know a great deal about the physiological and subjective activities that accompany these important states. Two separate research programs sparked scientific interest in sleep and dreams. First, Sigmund Freud (1900) used special interview procedures to record dreams. The contents of the dreams were varied and often bizarre. Freud, however, felt that dreams must have some function for the individual. After intensive study of dream reports, he concluded that there were two levels in dreams. The first, which he called **manifest content,** is the part that the dreamer remembers. For example, a patient might report that she dreamed of being chased by a big snake with a face much like her father's face. There is also a hidden or **latent content** in dreams. The latent content of the dream is determined by impulses of which the individual has no awareness. For example, the latent content in the dream presented above may have been the patient's wish to have a sexual relationship with her father. Freud felt that the latent content generally involved an unacceptable desire that would create pain or anxiety if it were expressed directly. It would probably be very threatening to our dreamer if she dreamed that she was having a sexual relationship with her father. The unacceptable impulse is, therefore, disguised in the dream. Thus, Freud felt that dreams were vehicles through which individuals could express their unacceptable impulses in disguised or acceptable forms. Freud's work contradicted the notion that dreams are worthless.

Second, Eugene Aserinsky and Nathaniel Kleitman, using laboratory techniques to measure physiological responses, demonstrated that sleep is accompanied by a complex and ever-changing pattern of physiological activity (see Kleitman, 1963). In addition, they discovered physiological patterns that occur when a person is dreaming. This means that when such patterns occur, researchers can awaken subjects to get immediate and usually vivid recall of dreams. Aserinsky and Kleitman helped undermine the view that sleep and dreams cannot be studied objectively. Since then scientists have measured physiological patterns and recorded dreams of thousands of people (Webb, 1973). Let's look at some of the patterns that emerged.

Physiological Patterns during Sleep

In "sleep and dream laboratories" (see Figure 5–1) volunteers sleep with electrodes attached to their heads and bodies, which provide data on brain waves, eye movements, muscle tension, heart rate, and respiration. Figure 5–2 shows the pattern of brain waves and other bodily functions during conscious resting and during the five stages of sleep. Resting has an interesting effect on brain waves. When we relax with our eyes closed, the brain emits *alpha* rhythms, which are low-voltage, medium-frequency brain waves. Similarly, various stages of sleep can be characterized by changes in brain waves and other physiological responses.

The beginning of stage-1 sleep is indicated by the appearance of low-voltage, low-frequency brain waves called *theta waves*. In addition, the eyes often begin slow, side-to-side rolling during this stage. Stage 2 is marked by the onset of **sleep spindles,** which are medium-voltage, medium-frequency brain waves. Sleep spindles diminish in stage 3 and are replaced in stage 4 by **delta waves,** high-voltage and extremely low-frequency brain waves. During the first four stages, heart rate, respiration, and muscle tension steadily decline. After completing stage 4, people go back through stages 3 and 2 before entering stage 5. The fifth stage is marked by the onset of rapid eye movements (REM, pronounced "rem") and is referred to as **REM sleep.** During REM sleep, muscles can twitch in the face and limbs, and sometimes the whole body moves. However, general muscle

Figure 5–1
This experimenter in a sleep laboratory is monitoring a number of bodily functions as a subject sleeps, as shown in Figure 5–2.

Figure 5–2
Brain waves, eye movements, muscle tension, heart rate, and breath rate are shown here for the waking state and for the five stages of sleep. (Sterman, 1972)

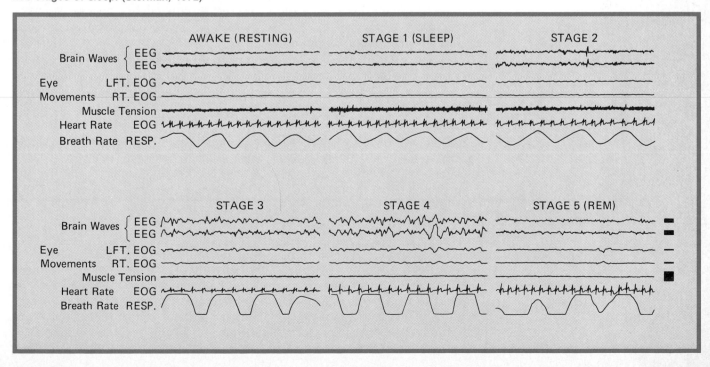

Figure 5–3
This graph shows the typical progression
through the five stages of sleep. Note how
REM intervals become longer and stages 2
through 4 become shorter toward morning.
(Dement, 1974, p. 114)

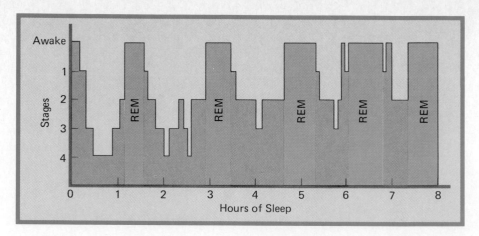

relaxation is characteristic of this stage. Brain waves show increased alpha rhythms, and there is an increase in heart rate and respiration. If people are awakened during REM sleep, they almost always say they have been dreaming, and they are able to recall their dreams in vivid detail. When people are awakened during stages 2 through 4, they rarely claim to have been dreaming and they never remember many details.

We pass repeatedly through these various stages of sleep during the night (Figure 5–3). As we approach sleep, we enter stage 1, the transition stage. Within 90 minutes after falling asleep, we pass through stages 2 through 4, and back through 2 again. Then we begin REM sleep. We enter REM sleep for 10-to-20-minute periods throughout the night, alternating with stages 2 through 4. REM intervals become longer and stages 2 through 4 become shorter toward morning. When we were infants we required 16 to 20 hours of sleep. As adults most of us need between 6 and 9 hours, 25 percent of which is spent in REM sleep.

When we go without sleep for long periods, the pattern of stages that occurs when we finally do sleep changes. In one case, a young man went without sleep for 264 hours in order to qualify for the *Guinness Book of Records*. When he finally gave up his quest, he went to sleep in a sleep and dream laboratory. Scientists observed that on the first night he spent much more time in stage 4, at the expense of stage 2. On the second recovery night, his REM sleep increased sharply at the expense of stages 2 through 4. The phenomenon of increased REM sleep after sleep deprivation is called **REM rebound.**

Total sleep deprivation leads to irritability, fatigue, poor concentration, memory failure, and reduced muscle coordination. Some people behave in bizarre ways associated with mental illness, but usually these symptoms do not last after a person sleeps through a recovery period. The ill effects of total sleep deprivation can also be created in sleep and dream laboratories, where it is possible to deprive a subject only of stage 4 and REM sleep. The selective recovery of stage 4 and REM sleep along with the ill effects of such selective deprivation suggest that these stages are especially significant. It remains to be seen whether or not dreams are what make REM sleep so important.

Subjective Patterns during Dreams

As most of us know, dreaming can be an intense experience, accompanied by unusual images and extreme emotional responses such as joy and fear. If dreams in sleep and dream laboratories are representative of our usual dreaming behavior, however, such intense dreams are the exception rather than the rule. The hundreds of thousands of dreams recorded immediately after subjects are awakened from REM sleep suggest that we dream four

SLEEP DISORDERS

The Association for the Psychophysiological Study of Sleep may be your salvation if you are one of the millions of people who suffers from a serious sleep disorder. The association's researchers have established research laboratories and clinics and have both improved the basic understanding of sleep and developed important clinical applications. Their clinical contributions include spelling out dangers associated with the most common medical treatment, sleeping pills, and advancing more effective therapies. These applications grew directly out of research aimed at distinguishing the many different kinds of sleep disorders. Two broad categories can be identified: *insomnia*, which is abnormal wakefulness, and *hypersomnia*, which is abnormal sleepiness. A sleep clinic may be your best bet if you are one of the 15 percent of all Americans who fall into one, or both, of these categories (Mayer, 1975).

The estimate of 15 percent includes only those who have serious and persistent sleep disorders. You should not count yourself among them if you cannot sleep as long as your roommates, for example. One woman went to a sleep clinic after being treated unsuccessfully with sleeping pills. She took the pills in an effort to get a full nine hours of sleep a night like her husband. It turned out that she only needed six hours, which she could get without pills. It is not unusual for one person to require six hours of sleep while another requires nine. In the same way, you need not worry if you occasionally have sleeping problems associated with specific events. You might have had trouble sleeping, for instance,

on the night before an exciting trip. You might also experience extreme sleepiness during temporary periods of depression. These experiences are common, and they do not indicate that you should tag yourself as one of the 15 percent with sleep disorders.

One serious form of insomnia is *apnea*, an inability to breath properly during sleep. This can eventually lead to heart damage. When breathing is interrupted, the person usually makes loud snoring sounds and wakes up momentarily. A researcher can identify this problem simply by listening to a tape recording of a person's snoring. It might be useful to educate the public about the sound of snores that indicate interrupted breathing, because people who suffer from this problem are often unaware of it. Frequently they complain of being unable to get a restful night's sleep without knowing why. A spouse or friend trained at sizing up snores might be able to warn the afflicted person. Such warnings could signal medical doctors to avoid prescribing sleeping pills, which would only worsen this breathing problem.

A serious form of hypersomnia is *narcolepsy*, recurrent attacks of an uncontrollable desire for sleep. This condition is indicated in the following case report of a 40-year-old businessman:

I began to experience a sudden drop of my head and my upper arms when I laughed or was under stress. . . . Recently, I had two very frightening experiences. I took my car to go back home near 4 P.M. I remember driving out and turning on the freeway. Then I had a complete amnesia. I found myself

70 minutes later somewhere in Oakland. . . . A similar episode occurred recently . . . and when I "came back" I was once again lost, with a complete feeling of disorientation. (Guilleminault & Dement, 1977, p. 444)

Guilleminault and Dement have studied some eighty patients with similar conditions. The patients seem to have a malfunction in the brain mechanisms that control sleep. It is hoped that understanding those mechanisms will lead to a cure. Many experts believe that the problem involves chemicals (neurotransmitters) that increase or decrease the transmission of nerve impulses (see Chapter 2).

Sleep experts are identifying and treating many kinds of insomnia and hypersomnia (Cotman & McGaugh, 1980). Some specialists are working toward safer and more effective drug treatment, while others are developing new approaches. One new therapy involves teaching people to control what are ordinarily involuntary bodily actions. Some researchers are trying to train people to make their brain waves resemble those of normal sleepers. They teach with **biofeedback,** which is a procedure that uses instruments to inform people about the effects of their efforts to control body functions. Such applications are emerging from research that was originally aimed at understanding the psychophysiological processes that underlie sleep. The work of sleep experts is therefore a prime example of how research on basic principles can lead to applications that might benefit you personally.

or five times every night, and that most of our dreams are rather ordinary. We dream about playing ball, riding buses, taking exams, and other every-day activities. Scientists have also recorded some exotic dreams, as well as some terrifying nightmares. Despite all of this, no dream as exotic as

Ritchie's experiences has ever been recorded in a sleep and dream laboratory.

Failure to record similar dreams does not rule out the possibility that Ritchie was dreaming. As mentioned earlier, Freud maintained that dreams reflect memories and feelings. Accordingly, we would expect Ritchie's dreams to be unusual since his prior experiences were unusual. For instance, he had a great desire to go to Richmond—he was even willing to jeopardize his health. His dreams could have been influenced by these wishes that existed before sleep. Many students are quite familiar with daily events influencing dreams, since they often dream about exams during finals week.

Ritchie was in a strange environment and was being prepared for the morgue during the time that he might have been dreaming. These conditions could have influenced his dreams because we are not cut off from external stimuli during sleep. In one famous series of experiments, Alfred Maury arranged for an assistant to stimulate him while he slept. When the assistant tickled his lips and nose, Maury dreamed he was being tortured. When the assistant waved perfume in the air, he dreamed he was in a bazaar in Cairo. When part of the bed accidentally fell on the back of Maury's neck, he dreamed he was being beheaded (Cohen, 1976). Ritchie's experience has themes consistent with what we might expect for a dream under his unusual circumstances.

The profound effect of Ritchie's experience on the rest of his life is also consistent with the possibility that he was dreaming. Many people claim to have had their lives changed by dreams. In fact, Fritz Perls, a pioneer in Gestalt psychotherapy (see Chapter 14), tried to get his patients to use their dreams to discover ways to change their lives. Dreams also can solve problems that we are unable to solve in our waking hours. A classic illustration is Friedrich August Kakule's dream of a snake eating its tail. Kakule, a German chemist, had been unsuccessfully pondering the structures of benzene. His dream suggested a ring structure that provided the correct solution. Many others have tried to utilize the creative potential of dreams, but without much success.

An objective scientist is free to accept or reject the possibility that Ritchie walked with God during a dream. Scientists have not *disproved* this mystical explanation, and perhaps they never will. They have, however, made a strong case for a perceptual release theory, which, as mentioned earlier, is a logical alternative to a mystical theory. Hobson and McCarley (1977) maintain, for instance, that dreams are caused by brain activity during REM sleep. Specifically, they argue that dreams are caused by the firing of giant cells, which are large nerve cells in the brainstem (see Chapter 2). The firing of giant cells is associated with all the physiological patterns that are characteristic of sleep. In addition, giant cells activate parts of the brain that are associated with vision and emotions. This activation could explain the things we "see" and "feel" during our dreams, according to Hobson and McCarley. We might say that giant cells "release" perceptions that we experience as dreams. This theory is consistent with the fact that direct electrical stimulation of the brain by means of electrodes causes people to "see" and "feel" things (see the discussion of Penfield's work in Chapter 2). Studying the biological correlates of sleep and dreams has led to a better understanding of sleep disorders (see Highlight: "Sleep Disorders"). The theory needs further development and testing, however, because it does not yet explain *subjective* patterns in detail. It does not explain, for example, why dreams correspond to memories and to daily events. Perhaps future research will show exactly why it is that the firing of giant cells causes memories to be "released" and to be experienced as dreams.

George Ritchie may have been dreaming, but that doesn't reduce the importance of his experience. Dreams are much more important and far richer than many of us realize. We don't have to solve problems or have psychic powers to benefit from them. Simply by paying attention to them, we take a giant step toward understanding other forms of consciousness. In the next section we will discuss another state of consciousness that is quite common and also safe to explore.

 # VISIONS DURING DROWSINESS

During the drowsy interval before sleep (stage-1 sleep), we sometimes see visions, hear voices, or feel ourselves falling without any apparent external stimuli to support these sensations. Such sensations are **hallucinations,** or false sensory perceptions in the absence of an actual external stimulus. Hallucinations may be caused by emotional factors, drugs, alcohol, or stress, and may occur in any of the senses. Hallucinations that occur during the drowsy interval before sleep are called **hypnagogic images.** (*Hypnagogic* comes from the Greek words *hypnos*, which means sleep, and *agogos*, which means causing.) We will briefly summarize the physiological patterns of stage-1 sleep and then look at its interesting cognitive patterns.

Physiological Patterns

Transition from waking to sleeping is gradual, with no sharp break between the two states. There is, however, an identifiable transition stage (stage 1) between waking and sleeping. Hypnagogic images occur during this drowsy transition interval, which begins with the onset of theta waves and ends with the onset of sleep spindles in EEG patterns. The interval is also characterized by the occurrence of slow, side-to-side eye movements, which are quite different from the rapid eye movements associated with REM sleep.

Subjective Patterns

Hypnagogic images occur in all senses, including smell. For example, one student smelled bacon frying before she fell asleep. When she got up to investigate, she found that she was the only one awake in her apartment. Furthermore, the smell that seemed so strong only moments earlier was gone. She had hallucinated the smell. The most common hypnagogic images, however, are those that we seem to see, hear, or feel.

Visual hypnagogic images occur in a consistent sequence of stages. In the first, we see flashes of color and light; in the second, we see geometric patterns; faces and static objects appear in the third. Finally, landscapes and more complex, prolonged scenes appear in the fourth stage (cf. Schacter, 1976). Stages 3 and 4 are the most interesting. Dreamlike faces occurring in stage 3 are notorious for their vividness, detail, and novelty. Hypnagogic faces usually are not familiar, and they often take on unusual and even grotesque qualities. Stage 3 hypnagogic images may be responsible for the popularity of night lights among children (cf. Schacter, 1976). Presleep visions of landscapes occurring in stage 4 are often beautiful and frequently contain a great deal of activity and movement. Sometimes the landscape appears as if it were being viewed from a moving car or train.

Visual images are sometimes combined with auditory hypnagogic images. We might hear imaginary faces speak or hear road noises associated with visual hypnagogic landscapes. Auditory images also occur by themselves. We might hear our name called or hear music, which can be unfamiliar and bizarre (perhaps similar to the music George Ritchie heard during his experience), or it can be familiar. In one case, a woman tried to turn off her radio after listening to several popular songs. She was amazed to discover it was already off. The music she "heard" was an auditory hypnagogic image.

The feelings of being touched and of being in motion are other possible presleep images. A rich image of riding a horse might include the sight of the landscape passing by, the sound of hooves, and the touch sensations of the reins and saddle. More typical is the sensation of falling with no associated visual or auditory images, sometimes accompanied by several involuntary jerks of the body.

If you have never experienced a hypnagogic image, it may be because you pass through stage 1 too quickly. Some people go through the transition between waking and sleeping much faster than others. You might consider using procedures developed in sleep and dream laboratories to prolong the drowsy interval before sleep. You could, for example, set a "snooze alarm" on a modern alarm clock to go off every five minutes unless you push a button to stop it. Also, you might position a clock so that you must hold your forearm up to hold a button or else the alarm will go off. Either procedure will keep you awake and, if you are tired, you should slip into stage-1 sleep long enough to experience hypnagogic images.

You need not go to such extremes to experience the stage of consciousness discussed in the next section. In fact, some of you may be in it right now.

DAYDREAMS

Imagine going to an emergency clinic with a wound on your right forearm. As the doctor sews up the cut, you wonder what she is thinking about. Most of us would like to believe that her mind is fixed on the stitches she is putting in our skin; more than likely, however, she is daydreaming. One researcher (Csikszentmihalyi, 1974) found that fourteen out of twenty-one surgeons interviewed in his study reported daydreaming during routine aspects of surgery. Their daydreams were about music, food, wine, and the opposite sex, among other things. Daydreams can be defined as "thoughts that divert attention away from an immediately demanding task" (Singer, 1975). We all daydream, and scientists are beginning to carefully study this important aspect of our mental life.

Physiological Patterns

Unlike night dreams, daydreams are not characterized by unique physiological patterns. Physiological responses during daydreams are not very different from those of ordinary waking consciousness. One physiological response that is characteristic of daydreaming is a blank (or unfocused) stare of the eyes, but many daydreams occur without this characteristic "staring off into space." Surely the surgeons in the study reported earlier exhibited no such blank stares. Thus, physiological responses are not useful in distinguishing daydreams from ordinary waking states.

The lack of unique physiological patterns supports Jerome Singer's claim that daydreams are an aspect of ordinary waking consciousness.

We all daydream sometimes. One characteristic of a person who is daydreaming is a rather blank or unfocused stare of the eyes, as can be seen in the photo here.

Subjective Patterns

Singer (1975) believes that daydreams are an extremely important part of our private mental life. He found that daydreams can be divided into three categories: *unhappy*, *uncontrollable*, and *happy*. The first category includes fantasies involving guilt, aggressive wishes, and fear of failure. The second includes fleeting, anxiety-laden fantasies that make it hard to concentrate and to hold attention on outside events. Finally, happy daydreams are characterized by vivid visual and auditory imagery, and by fantasies used for planning future activity. In one study of happy daydreams, Singer (1975) reported that many women daydream during sexual intercourse. These fantasies promote arousal during the sex act, are not associated with sexual conflict, and are characteristic of women who are generally given to happy daydreaming. Each of us might engage in all three kinds of daydreams, but we are likely to experience one kind more often.

An intriguing relationship between daydreaming patterns and alcohol abuse has been observed (Singer, 1975). People prone to unhappy daydreams are more likely to drink excessively. This correlation does not mean that unhappy daydreams cause alcohol abuse (see Chapter 13). Singer speculates, however, that happy daydreams may help *prevent* it. Alcohol and other drugs induce intense, novel sensations, but they are not necessary for experiencing rich, attractive stimulation. Singer maintains, for instance, that someone practiced at attending to his or her "inner" experiences can achieve a "high" while listening to music without the use of drugs. People who learn to enjoy such natural "highs" may have no need to seek artificial ones.

RUG-INDUCED STATES

Drugs that produce subjective effects are called **psychoactive drugs.** The most widely used psychoactive drugs in America are caffeine, which is in coffee and many soft drinks; alcohol; and nicotine, which is in tobacco.

Americans use these drugs for such subjective effects as pepping up, reducing inhibitions, and relaxing. Even though the dangers of smoking are well known, many Americans continue to light up. Some also continue to abuse alcohol and caffeine even though the dangers of excessive use of these drugs are widely publicized. Why?

The Drug Abuse Council, which was established by the Ford Foundation in 1972, addressed this question along with questions about the use of illegal drugs. They did not answer the questions, and we cannot do so here either. They did suggest in their final report, however, that illegal drug use must be considered in the context of the use and misuse of *legal* psychoactive drugs (Drug Abuse Council, 1980). One recent book providing this broad view is *Chocolate to Morphine* (Weil & Rosen, 1983). It offers a straightforward discussion of the widespread use and abuse of legal and illegal psychoactive drugs. Our discussion is necessarily much shorter. We will go over physiological and subjective responses associated with some legal and illegal psychoactive drugs. In later sections, we will show that similar effects can be achieved without the use of dangerous drugs.

This section should give students a chance to exercise the critical thinking required to avoid oversimplifications. Specifically, any statement about drugs must take into consideration dosage, an individual's tolerance for the drug, and the situation in which it is used. For example, we have already said that alcohol and caffeine can be dangerous, depending upon the amount ingested. This does not mean, however, that these are "bad" drugs. In fact, low doses may be beneficial in some situations (Drug Abuse Council, 1980). The problem is complicated further by the fact that what is an "excess" for one person might not be for another. Furthermore, subjective responses are difficult to predict because they are affected by nondrug factors. Cross-cultural comparisons illustrate this point. Psychoactive drugs are used recreationally at social events in our culture, and some of them have gained a reputation for producing heightened enjoyment from food and sex. In contrast, other cultures use psychoactive drugs during religious ceremonies. Ancient Hindus used a hallucinogen called *soma* to feel at one with God, and Aztecs "became one with the Great Spirit of the Universe" by chewing the dried tips of peyote cactus (a source of a hallucinogen). Hallucinogens are associated with reduced sexual appetite and self-denial in these religious contexts. The same drug can increase or decrease sexual activity depending upon the culture in which it is taken, because culture influences the expectations and desires of people using drugs.

Personality also influences subjective responses. Some people have pleasant drug-induced experiences, knowing that their unusual mental state is caused by drugs. Others have terrifying experiences during which they act like they are mentally ill. They might, for example, be unable to distinguish between reality and drug-induced hallucinations. In the worst cases, mentally ill behavior persists after the drug effects have worn off. One generally cannot predict drug responses unless many factors are carefully controlled. We can nevertheless characterize typical responses. Psychoactive drugs fall into three categories: (1) **depressants,** which slow body functions or calm nervous excitement; (2) **stimulants,** which excite body functions; and (3) **hallucinogens,** which cause hallucinations. Let's take a closer look at each category.

Depressants

Three common depressants are *alcohol*, *nicotine*, and *heroin*. You might be surprised to see alcohol listed as a depressant. This classification seems inconsistent with the use of alcoholic drinks to "liven up" a party. The

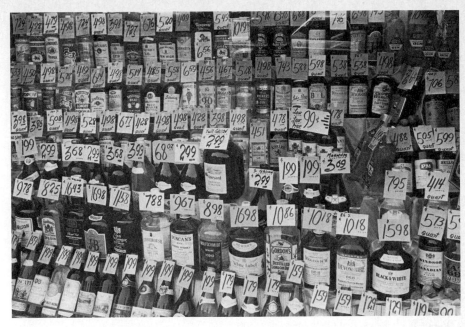

reason for the classification is clear, however, when we consider physiological patterns associated with alcohol consumption.

Physiological Patterns. Alcohol, nicotine, and heroin depress body functions. Alcohol is consumed in beer, wine, and liquor. The alcohol in three beers is enough to dilate the pupils, to slow response time, and to impair motor functions. Extreme doses can cause death. Nicotine is very poisonous, but the amount inhaled while smoking tobacco is too little to cause death. Excessive smoking, however, can cause a weak, rapid pulse, a sense of exhaustion, and a poor appetite. Nicotine is often classified as a stimulant because it initially stimulates the nervous system. We classify it as a depressant, however, because it ultimately depresses the central and autonomic nervous systems. Smoking is also associated with heart disease and lung cancer. Heroin comes from the juice of the opium poppy. It is sold illegally in the United States to users who either sniff or inject it. Heroin reduces sensitivity to pain and it depresses respiration. An overdose can cause death. Alcohol, nicotine, and heroin are all *physiologically addictive*, which means that body functions can become dependent upon the drug's effects and that the body can require increasingly larger doses to obtain the desired effects.

Subjective Patterns. Depressants have highly variable subjective effects. One of alcohol's main effects is to make one feel uninhibited in social situations. This release from social inhibitions explains the party effect mentioned earlier. Large doses can cause anger and aggression in some individuals, and it can cause depression and drowsiness in others. Nicotine's subjective effect is slight in comparison with other drugs. It is characterized by a subtle relaxing response. Heroin, on the other hand, has dramatic subjective effects. In some people it produces a "rush," which is an intensely pleasurable response. It causes some people to forget their troubles. They also feel no hunger, pain, or sexual urge and they often get drowsy. Heroin's dominant effect is a feeling of well-being, which is part of the lure that attracts people to this highly addictive and very dangerous drug.

Stimulants

Stimulants are quite popular in America. A common one is *caffeine*, which is available without prescription, as mentioned earlier. *Amphetamines* stimulate the central nervous system and are available in pill form by prescription

Cocaine is an illegal drug that stimulates the central nervous system and is physiologically addictive. Produced from the coca plant, it is believed to be the strongest natural stimulant known. Most users inhale cocaine, but it can also be injected.

under such trade names as Methedrine, Dexedrine, and Benzedrine. These pills are also sold illegally as "speed," "uppers," or "bennies." *Cocaine* is another stimulant that is sold illegally.

Physiological Patterns. Caffeine, amphetamines, and cocaine all stimulate body functions. Caffeine increases heart rate, and causes restlessness and sometimes tremors. Amphetamines increase blood pressure and breath rate. They also act as an appetite suppressant and can cause rapid and irregular heartbeats, tremors, and dryness of mouth. Cocaine also stimulates the central nervous system. It can cause dizziness, low blood pressure, and even convulsions. All three are physiologically addictive.

Subjective Patterns. Subjective effects are highly variable in stimulants, as they are in other drugs. The main effect for all stimulants is a feeling of energy, which is often accompanied by a feeling of restlessness. Caffeine can also cause irritability. The possible subjective side effects of amphetamine and cocaine use are much worse. They can cause a pleasant "rush," followed by irritability. The stimulating effect can end with a "crash," which is sleep followed by a period of fatigue and depression. Finally, both amphetamines and cocaine can cause behaviors that are indistinguishable from certain kinds of mental illness.

Hallucinogens

Four common hallucinogenic drugs are *marijuana*, *mescaline*, *psilocybin*, and *LSD*. Hallucinogenic drugs are sometimes called *psychedelic*, which means "mind-manifesting." The nature of psychedelic experiences is illustrated in the following quote, which shows a partial transcript of a person who took 20 milligrams of psilocybin.

> It looks like several different whirlpools, with lots of spirals divided up into checks. It's pretty black. There's purple and green glowing areas in the middle of the spirals, kind of clouds around. There are lines going from top to bottom, kind of a grid, but the lines squiggle around. There's odd shapes, but still lots of right angles in them. Seems really bright. . . . There's like an explosion, yellow in the middle, like a volcano gushing out lava, yellow, glowing. There's a black square with yellow light coming behind it. There's a regular pattern superimposed on everything, lots of curlicues, with dots in the middle. Lots of little paisley things that fill up the spaces between the patterns of triangles, squares, or crown-shaped things. And there's a little white star that floats around the picture and sometimes goes behind what's on the screen and illuminates from behind.
>
> Now there's a kind of landscape. Very flat, flat country. The picture is very narrow. In the middle part a tree at the left and then flat with green grass and blue sky above. There are orange dots, oranges hanging all over, in the sky, on the tree, on the ground. A bicycle! Oh, my! It's headed down, not horizontal, like someone's holding it up on end. . . . There's a checkerboard superimposed on everything like the flags they wave at the races.
>
> I can see the street out there. . . . Well, it's old-golly-interesting! It's like in the forties, I guess, or maybe the fifties. . . . And there are people riding their bicycles, and there are, like, boys, in plaid vests and those funny kind of hats. . . . I was at the side walking on the sidewalk, so it wasn't like I was in the middle of the street and [laughter] you can't laugh very long in the middle of the street in the city, so that image kind of went away [laughter]. (Siegel, 1977, p. 139)

Not all drug-induced sensations are as pleasant. Sometimes people imagine that their limbs are distorting and their flesh is decaying, or they see sickly greens or ugly dark reds and experience gloom and isolation. Despite the variability of drug-induced experiences, consistent patterns are present, some of which share characteristics with George Ritchie's experience, even though his was not caused by hallucinogenic drugs.

Physiological Patterns. Marijuana is the least potent of the four hallucinogenic drugs mentioned above. After ingesting marijuana, a person's EEG shows a higher percentage of alpha brain waves, heart rate increases, eyes redden, and the mouth goes dry, while blood pressure and respiration remain unaffected. LSD is the most potent hallucinogen. Brain waves and other physiological responses during LSD intoxication indicate intense activity similar to physiological response patterns during REM sleep. However, the most interesting effects of hallucinogenic drugs are subjective responses.

Subjective Patterns. When we suggested that Ritchie's experience may have been influenced by his background and his immediate situation, we introduced a theme that is especially important in drug research. We cannot yet predict the course of psychedelic experiences because we do not understand all the factors influencing them.

Figure 5–4 shows a model used to help analyze drug-induced states (Tart, 1977). According to this model, we must know what drug a person has taken, how much of the drug was taken, and how the drug was taken, if we want to predict responses to the drug. Even more importantly, we must know many nondrug factors.

Tart's model suggests, first, that a person's mood, expectations, and desires are important short-term or immediate factors influencing drug-induced states. People who are afraid of drugs, for example, will probably have a more anxiety-laden experience than people who are comfortable with them. In addition, the context in which the drug was taken also plays a role. People taking drugs in an unfamiliar environment surrounded by strangers are more likely to be afraid, and their fear response itself can modify the situation by making others around them more anxious. Second, Tart's model suggests that culture, personality, physiology, and learned drug-use skills are long-term factors influencing drug-induced states.

Despite these factors, however, it has been found that drug-induced hallu-

Figure 5–4
This model shows the many variables that should be taken into account in analyzing drug-induced states. (Zinberg, 1977, p. 200)

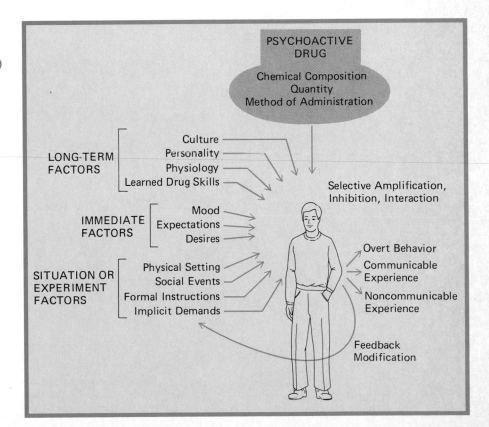

Figure 5–5
In the second stage of drug-induced hallucinations, the color red dominates, along with the appearance of a spiral-shaped tunnel covered with a graph paper design.

Figure 5–6 (Below, left)
In this stage images are sometimes superimposed on the spiral-shaped tunnel that is shown in Figure 5–5.

Figure 5–7 (Below, right)
Images in the third stage often include unusual vantage points, such as this one, showing a view from the bottom of a swimming pool.

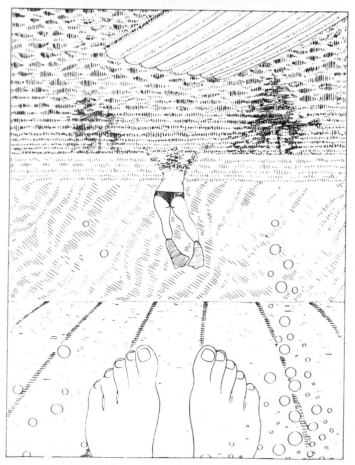

cinations have four stages in a carefully controlled laboratory setting (Siegel, 1977). The first stage is characterized by vague black-and-white forms moving about in one's visual field. You can probably see the same thing by simply closing your eyes, or by gently rubbing your closed eyelids. What you see then are **phosphenes,** visual sensations arising from spontaneous discharges of light-sensitive neurons in your eyes. Apparently, drugs make people more aware of phosphenes.

The second stage begins with the appearance of geometric forms. Siegel created a special keyboard to help people report on second-stage images. He divided the keyboard into three sections (corresponding to form, color, and movement), and put eight keys into each section. The keys offered the following options: form (random, line, curve, web, graph paper, tunnel, spiral, and kaleidoscope); color (black, violet, blue, green, yellow, orange, red, and white); and movement (aimless, vertical, horizontal, oblique, explosive, concentric, rotational, and pulsating). People who were trained on the keyboard reported new images twenty times per minute. Untrained observers could only report five times per minute. Both trained and untrained subjects indicated that second-stage images are colored geometric forms that usually pulsate or rotate. All colors occur, but blue is the most frequent at first. Later, red dominates, and with the shift to red comes the appearance of a spiral-shaped tunnel covered with a graph paper design (Figure 5–5). Often a bright light seems to pulsate in the tunnel's center. The third stage usually begins after the appearance of the tunnel.

The third stage is characterized by meaningful images that sometimes appear superimposed on a spiral tunnel, as in Figure 5–6, and sometimes seem to be images drawn from memory. One student saw the backyard in which she played as a child. Images in this stage often include unusual vantage points, such as George Ritchie's view from about fifty feet directly above a cafe (Figure 5–7). If Ritchie's visual experiences can be identified by any stage, however, it would be the fourth.

Stage-4 images seem more like moving pictures than snapshots—that is, they are more like dreams. Sometimes fourth-stage hallucinations share with Ritchie's experience a feeling that one is part of the imagery and a feeling of being dissociated from one's body.

The four stages of drug intoxication seem to be consistent across cultures. Siegel noted, for instance, that Hindu religious symbols are similar to commonly hallucinated geometric patterns. Furthermore, Huichol Indians show hallucinated patterns in their art and weaving (Figure 5–8). They also report patterns of hallucinations almost identical to those of Americans, even though Huichol Indians have been relatively isolated in Mexico since the Aztec era.

One could argue from a mystical or psychological point of view that drug-induced experiences and near-death experiences are closely related. People who use a drug in religious ceremonies, as Huichols do, obviously believe that it puts them in touch with a sacred external reality, presumably the same reality that Ritchie claimed to have experienced. The similarities between drug experiences and near-death episodes do not rule out the perceptual release theory. A perceptual release theorist would try to explain the similar experiences in terms of similar brain reactions. It remains for future research to determine what the common brain responses might be. A good starting point for this future research would be to replicate and extend Siegel's experiments on stages of hallucinations. Such experiments could answer important questions. For example, will scientists verify Siegel's stages and show corresponding stages of responses in brain chemistry? Scientists are already beginning to understand how hallucinogens affect brain chemistry (Cotman & McGaugh, 1980). Hallucinogens could create an imbalance of chemicals that serve as central neurotransmitters. Such

Figure 5–8
Huichol Indians show hallucinated patterns such as these in their art and weaving, and report other patterns of hallucinations similar to those of Americans.

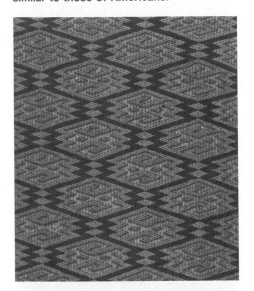

imbalances, according to the perceptual release hypothesis, could cause brain reactions that are experienced as hallucinations.

Hypnosis

George Ritchie took a chance with his professional reputation when he comforted his dying patient with a personal report about life after death. In the same way, Oscar N. Lucas (1975), a dentist, went out on a limb to help his hemophiliac patients, who have a tendency to bleed uncontrollably when they have a tooth pulled. At the risk of appearing unprofessional, Lucas tried to control bleeding with hypnosis, which is a state of consciousness induced by the words and actions of a hypnotist whose suggestions are readily accepted by the subject. Lucas suggested during hypnosis that his patients' mouths were filled with ice that would control bleeding. The effect was astonishing. When hemophiliacs have teeth pulled, they usually receive five pints of blood, spend six days in the hospital, and do not heal for about two weeks. With hypnosis, Lucas's patients received no blood, were not hospitalized, and healed in about four days. Such results are slowly swinging the professional community in favor of hypnosis in some situations.

Successful control of pain has been influential in the acceptance of hypnosis as a professional tool. In the mid-nineteenth century, England's medical society rejected as a hoax claims that hypnosis can control pain during surgery. Today, medical doctors recognize many well-documented cases of pain control by means of hypnosis. Many hypnotized patients who could not use drugs as pain killers have felt little or no pain when having a tooth pulled, after being severely burned, during childbirth, and during the final stages of terminal cancer. Hypnosis has also been used to speed the recovery of heart-attack patients, to cure skin diseases, and to eliminate allergies. We have already cited some important examples of such applications in the earlier section on clinical methods.

Although hypnosis is being used more, it remains controversial as an issue. The controversy has shifted emphasis, however. Originally, it was about what hypnosis can and cannot do. Now it is about how hypnosis works. The debate is fueled by data on physiological patterns; it is calmed by data on subjective patterns.

Physiological Patterns

No consistent physiological patterns accompany hypnosis. Blood pressure, heart rate, and breathing can vary with the suggestions of the hypnotist. In some cases, EEG patterns resemble REM sleep patterns, but they are often indistinguishable from normal waking consciousness.

The lack of distinct physiological patterns raises two possibilities. One is that hypnosis does not induce an alternate state of consciousness. Barber (1970) maintains, for instance, that hypnosis leaves people in a waking state, but it highly motivates them to cooperate with the hypnotist's suggestions. Accordingly, anything people can do under hypnosis, they can also do in a normal waking state, as long as they are highly motivated. Another possibility is that distinct physiological patterns do exist, but scientists have not yet found them. Those who favor the view that hypnosis induces an alternate state of consciousness point to the distinctive abilities that are possible under hypnosis, such as reduction of bleeding and severe pain (Orne, 1972).

Subjective Patterns

Although scientists do not agree about how hypnosis works, they do agree about basic subjective and behavioral patterns associated with it. Even those who deny that hypnosis induces an alternate state of consciousness accept that hypnotists can cause the following changes:

1. Hypnosis influences judgment and suggestibility. A hypnotized subject will disregard his or her own judgment and accept a hypnotist's suggestions. A hypnotist can give suggestions to be followed during or after a hypnotic session. During a session, a subject might disregard sensory information that a paper is white and accept a suggestion that it is another color. The subject does not merely act as if the paper is another color (Orne, 1980). In fact, after accepting the suggestion, subjects will see a negative afterimage (see Chapter 3, Figure 3–11) when they look at a second sheet of white paper (Erickson, 1980). After a session, subjects might follow a **posthypnotic suggestion.** A hypnotist might suggest to a hypnotized subject that she will scratch her ear when she hears a bell ring after hypnosis has ended. A susceptible subject will scratch her ear when she hears the bell. If questioned about it, she will probably say that her ear itched.

   People vary in degree of susceptibility to hypnosis. **Hypnotic susceptibility tests** are therefore used to predict the extent to which people are willing to yield to hypnotic suggestions (Barber & Glass, 1962; Horne & Powlett, 1980; Shor & Orne, 1962; Weitzenhoffer & Hilgard, 1962). These tests are particularly useful when determining whether or not to use hypnosis for medical treatments. Wallace (1979) maintains that most of us could be hypnotized to some extent, particularly if we were trained to do so. He estimates, however, that only 10 percent of us could follow a hypnotist's suggestions well enough to undergo surgery without using drugs as pain killers.

   Wallace also notes that even the most susceptible subjects retain their value judgments. Subjects will not accept a hypnotist's suggestions if doing so would require a behavior that goes against their values (Erickson, 1981).

   A solution for those worried about control is **self-hypnosis.** In this procedure people learn to hypnotize themselves so that they can more readily follow their own suggestions. Following one's own suggestions is simple sometimes, but not always. You might find it easy to follow your own suggestion to stop studying right now. You might not find it so easy to follow your own suggestion to relax on the day of your next big exam. We have already seen in an earlier section on clinical methods that some patients have learned to control severe headaches and high blood pressure with self-hypnosis (Wain, 1980).

2. Hypnotism influences relaxation. Light hypnosis can be induced by procedures that resemble relaxation techniques. A hypnotist might instruct subjects to tighten and then to relax muscle groups such as hands or facial muscles. Various relaxation techniques are used, for instance, in hypnotic reduction of labor pains during childbirth. In one procedure, subjects are put into a state of light relaxation. The hypnotist then gives the following instruction: "If you become uncomfortable, you may drift into a more relaxed state so that you are a bit less aware, more relaxed and with more capacity to remain free of any discomfort" (Hilgard & Hilgard, 1976). While relaxation is often associated with hypnosis, it is not necessary to the hypnotic state. Some hypnotic procedures increase tension and alertness.

3. Hypnotism influences attention. Many hypnotic procedures focus attention on some target, such as a small light or the hypnotist's voice. In addition to attention focusing, hypnotism can influence division

HYPNOSIS AND LAW ENFORCEMENT

Hypnosis is becoming an important law enforcement tool for refreshing the memory of witnesses and victims. Two projects illustrate the value of investigative hypnosis. One of these projects was conducted in the Los Angeles Police Department (Reiser & Nielson, 1980). The department asked Reiser to set up a program after he had helped solve several cases. One case involved a 19-year-old woman who was kidnapped, beaten, and sexually abused by three men. She was unable to recall important details until she was hypnotized. With the aid of hypnosis, she remembered an automobile license plate number and names mentioned during the episode. She also helped the police construct accurate composite drawings. An investigation followed, and three suspects were arrested and sentenced.

An investigative hypnosis program was established for the Los Angeles Police Department in 1975. During the first phase, eleven lieutenants and two captains were trained to conduct hypnotic sessions. The trainees performed supervised practice sessions during the second phase. During the third phase, they worked on their own. Between 1975 and 1979, hundreds of volunteer witnesses and victims were interviewed by the investigators. During that time, 31.3 percent of the cases were solved, with hypnosis being valuable in 65 percent of these cases. The program is now an ongoing service within the police department.

The second project was conducted by the Federal Bureau of Investigation (Kroger & Douce, 1980). Hypnotic investigations were conducted by a consultant in hypnosis and a special agent for the F.B.I. Independent investigations worked to confirm all evidence obtained under hypnosis. This method proved valuable in more than 60 percent of the cases investigated.

One of the cases was the Chowchilla kidnapping case. Three masked men abducted twenty-six school children and their bus driver at gunpoint. They herded them into vans, drove them to a quarry, and sealed them in an underground chamber. Luckily, the bus driver and two boys managed to dig out so that everyone could escape. The driver had seen the license plate numbers on one of the vans, but he could not remember it. Under hypnosis, the driver was induced to imagine himself watching the events on television. Suddenly, he called out two license plate numbers, and one of them was correct except for one digit. This information led to the arrest of the kidnappers, who were convicted and sentenced to life imprisonment.

Another case involved the kidnapping of two San Francisco area girls, ages seven and fifteen. The older girl was repeatedly raped. When the kidnapper released the girls, he warned them that he would kill their parents if they told anyone what had happened. The girls cooperated in an investigation, however, and they agreed to be hypnotized. The older girl responded to the suggestion that she would remain detached while watching the events of the kidnapping on a screen in her imagination. She recalled many details about the car and about a transaction at a gas station. In fact, she remembered that the kidnapper used a credit card to pay for repairs, and she described those in detail. This information led to a quick arrest of the kidnapper.

As a result of these and other cases, the F.B.I. regards hypnosis as a valuable investigative tool. However, the F.B.I. knows that hypnosis can produce memory distortions (e.g., Laurence & Perry, 1983). Hypnosis is therefore used only to gain leads on important facts of an investigation. These leads are then accepted or rejected based on independent evidence.

Frank Ray, the driver of the school bus in the Chowchilla kidnapping case, was at first unable to remember details that would aid police. Under hypnosis, however, he was able to recall the kidnappers' license plate, which led to their eventual arrest.

of attention between two tasks. In one study, subjects performed two tasks: button pushing in a repetitive pattern and color naming. Without hypnosis, the two tasks interfered with each other; with hypnosis, they did not. This result suggests that hypnosis can help subjects divide attention between tasks (Knox, Crutchfield, & Hilgard, 1975).

4. Hypnotism influences memory. It can decrease or increase one's ability to recall facts. **Posthypnotic amnesia** is an example of how hypnosis can decrease recall. A hypnotist suggests that a hypnotized subject will not be able to recall certain experiences until an appropriate cue is given. When tested, some subjects fail to recall anything that happened during the hypnotic sessions. Others recall events, but they distort their sequence. Still others recall facts, but they do not remember that they learned the facts during the hypnotic session. (Orne, 1980).

   Hypermesia is increased recall that can result from hypnosis. One procedure for inducing it is to suggest to subjects that they have great control over their memory. They can project their memories onto a screen. The actions on the screen can be made to go forward or backward, and they can be slowed or stopped (Kroger & Douce, 1980). Hypnosis has been used, for example, to improve the recall of witnesses of aircraft accidents (Hiland & Dzieszkowski, 1984). Hypnotically induced hypermesia has also been a valuable tool in many criminal investigations (see Highlight: "Hypnosis and Law Enforcement"). Another procedure for improving memory through hypnosis may be to put a person into the same emotional state he or she experienced when the memory was acquired. In one experiment, Gordon Bower (1981) used hypnosis to induce bad moods or happy moods, theorizing that people would recall a word list better when they were in the same mood they had been in when they learned the list. The results of his experiment seemed to substantiate this, but these results have not been replicated in subsequent experiments.

While the debate goes on concerning the mechanisms that underlie hypnosis, new applications are being found. Applications in addition to those already mentioned include: treating irrational fears and other behavioral problems; improving athletic skills; and controlling overeating and other bad habits. Interest in hypnosis is expected to increase as potential applications increase.

MEDITATION

Meditation involves a series of mental and physical acts aimed at achieving an alternate state of consciousness. Some meditators encounter many of the experiences reported by George Ritchie. They feel united with God; sometimes their minds seem to leave their bodies; and they believe that they see into the future and into the past with unusual clarity. After one two-hour meditation session, Aldous Huxley reported a fantasy that brings to mind the part of Ritchie's experience in which his life "passed before his eyes." During meditation, 26-year-old Aldous Huxley found himself on a hill with 6-year-old Aldous Huxley. During the confrontation, the adult Huxley experienced in vivid detail the child's growth. As day after day passed, Huxley felt the anguish, relief, and elation of the growing boy. Huxley called his meditation procedure *deep relaxation*, which is an apt term, given recent evidence that meditation is an effective way to cope with fatigue, anxiety, and stress.

We will discuss physiological and psychological patterns associated with meditation. These patterns have been studied in the laboratory.

Eastern forms of meditation are the source of most other procedures. Zen Buddhist monks in Japan practice *Zen* meditation, in which enlightenment is obtained by thinking about paradoxical or nonlogical things such as the "sound of one hand clapping." In India, *yoga* is practiced as part of ancient Hindu efforts to give people control over their minds. Many forms of yoga exist. One emphasizes complete relaxation, another uses strenuous exercise, and still another concentrates on controlling body functions such as breathing. Yoga requires extensive training and is not easily grasped by westerners. **Transcendental meditation (TM)** is a simplified yoga technique that allows people to meditate after a short training course. The technique is simple. An instructor gives you a secret word, sound, or phrase that is called your **mantra.** You can mentally repeat your mantra over and over again while sitting in a comfortable position. If distracting thoughts enter your mind, you disregard them and return your thoughts to your mantra. You are advised to meditate for twenty minutes before breakfast and twenty minutes before dinner. TM was developed by Maharishi Mehesh Yogi, an Indian guru. In the 1960s, TM gained popularity, and over two million people now practice it.

Herbert Benson (1975), Associate Professor of Medicine at the Harvard Medical School and Director of the Hypertension Section of Boston's Beth Israel Hospital, westernized TM even further. Instead of concentrating on your own secret mantra, in Benson's procedure you are asked to keep your thoughts on the word "one." Benson's procedure has six steps:

1. Sit quietly in a comfortable position.
2. Close your eyes.
3. Deeply relax all your muscles, beginning at your feet and progressing up to your face. Keep them relaxed.
4. Breathe through your nose. Become aware of your breathing. As you breathe out, say the word "one" silently to yourself. Breathe easily and naturally.
5. Continue for ten to twenty minutes. You may open your eyes to check the time, but do not use an alarm. When you finish, sit quietly for several minutes, at first with your eyes closed and later with your eyes opened. Do not stand up for a few minutes.
6. Do not worry about whether you are successful in achieving a deep level of relaxation. Maintain a passive attitude and permit relaxation to occur at its own pace. When distracting thoughts occur, try to

Meditation is an effective way to cope with fatigue, anxiety, and stress. There are several different types of meditation, including Zen, yoga, and transcendental meditation, which is a simplified form of yoga.

ignore them and return to repeating "one." With practice, the response should come with little effort. Practice the technique once or twice daily, but not within two hours after any meal, since the digestive processes seem to interfere with elicitation of the relaxation response. (Benson, 1975, pp. 114–115)

Physiological Patterns

Herbert Benson (1975) uses the phrase **relaxation response** to refer to the physiological patterns observed during meditation. The relaxation response decreases oxygen consumption, respiratory rate, heart rate, blood pressure, and muscle tension. At the same time, it increases alpha waves to levels observed during other alternate states, including REM sleep. The relaxation response is the opposite of the **fight-or-flight response** (Cannon, 1914), which involves increased oxygen consumption, respiratory rate, heart rate, blood pressure, and muscle tension (see Chapter 2). Fight-or-flight responses seem to have evolved to prepare animals for emergencies. Perceived danger automatically triggers the response, preparing an animal to run or fight. In humans, stressful situations trigger the response, often needlessly, as when you panic before an exam. Frequent inappropriate responses may be a fundamental cause of strokes, heart attacks, and other stress-related diseases, as we discuss in Chapter 2 and Chapter 11.

Benson's book, *The Relaxation Response*, makes a strong case for our ability to improve our physiological and psychological well-being by learning to elicit the relaxation response through meditation.

Tomio Hirai (1978) has also made significant contributions to our understanding of physiological patterns during meditation. He found, for instance, that Zen meditators achieve various levels of meditation. These levels are reflected in the EEG patterns of subjects. Shallow levels are accompanied by alpha waves, which supports Benson's findings. Deeper levels are characterized by the disappearance of alpha rhythms and the appearance of theta waves (see p. 133).

Subjective Patterns

You could encounter out-of-body experiences, hallucinations, and other psychic phenomena through meditation. You probably will not do so, however, if you limit your meditation to two twenty-minute sessions per day. Cognitive patterns obtained with moderate use of the relaxation response are illustrated in the following quote, which shows a report of a woman who used Benson's procedure to treat her high blood pressure.

The Relaxation Response has contributed to many changes in my life. Not only has it made me more relaxed physically and mentally, but it has also contributed to changes in my personality and way of life. I seem to have become calmer, and more open and receptive, especially to ideas which either have been unknown to me or are very different from my past way of life.

Intellectually and spiritually, good things happen to me during the Relaxation Response. Sometimes I get insights into situations or problems which have been with me for a long time and about which I am not consciously thinking. Creative ideas come to me either during or as a direct result of the Relaxation Response. I look forward to the Relaxation Response twice and sometimes three times a day. I am hooked on it and love my addiction. (Benson, 1975, p. 119)

Swami Muktanda, and others who share his Eastern traditions, agree with Hirai's idea that deep meditation is more than relaxation. Muktanda (1980, p. 24) maintains that "we do not meditate to relax a little and experience some peace; we meditate to unfold our inner being." The goal and ultimate achievement of meditation, according to Muktanda, is to understand and honor oneself.

▌SENSORY DEPRIVATION

The apparent psychological benefits of meditation are consistent with Peter Suedfeld's suggestion that isolation can have positive effects (Suedfeld, 1981). Meditators isolate themselves by focusing on a word or process to block out other sensory stimulation. Suedfeld studies another kind of isolation called **sensory deprivation,** which is a condition in which sensory stimulation is drastically reduced in quantity and intensity. Experimenters induce sensory deprivation in various ways. Some submerge people in a dark, silent tank of water that is at body temperature. The subject's only connection with stimulation outside of the tank is through an air hose (Lilly, 1956). Other experimenters use less extreme procedures, as shown in Figure 5–9. They cover people's eyes with translucent goggles, which let them see constant but formless light. They cover the ears with earphones that play a constant buzzing sound. Finally, they cover the hands and arms with padding to reduce touch stimulation (Heron, 1961). Research done during the early 1960s associated sensory deprivation with negative reactions such as high anxiety. These negative effects are extreme when a person is isolated for a long time. Michel Siffre remained in an isolated cave for six months as part of an experiment. Afterwards he said that he would not repeat the experiment for a million dollars. Obviously, negative reactions to sensory deprivation can be quite real. They can be avoided, however, and replaced by positive reactions. Suedfeld maintains that negative reactions occur because subjects are not properly oriented to the conditions. He finds that with appropriate orientation, sensory deprivation for short periods can induce relaxation and calm. He has used sensory deprivation to treat drug addiction, hypertension, and alcoholism. Let's examine

Figure 5–9
This shows a sensory deprivation chamber, in which goggles, earphones, and padding to cover hands and arms eliminate almost all sensory stimuli. (Heron, 1961, p. 9)

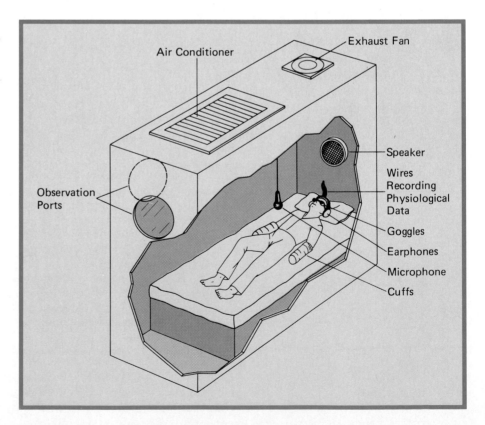

the physiological and subjective responses associated with sensory deprivation.

Physiological Patterns

Researchers have recorded many physiological responses during sensory deprivation. Their measures include breath rate, heart rate, blood pressure, brain waves, eye movements, and muscle tension. Their results suggest conclusions similar to those drawn for hypnosis. Sensory deprivation causes changes in physiological patterns, including changes in brain waves. But the changes do not establish a distinct pattern that can be used to identify a unique state of consciousness. Sensory-deprived subjects alternate between states of being alert, drowsy, and asleep. Physiological measures keep track of these changes.

Subjective Patterns

One of the most publicized results of sensory deprivation research is that alert subjects experience hallucinations and dreamlike episodes. Suedfeld (1975) acknowledges these effects, noting that some subjects think they see tiny spaceships buzzing around and shooting at them. Suedfeld thinks that it is regrettable, however, that these and other negative effects have been sensationalized, while positive effects have been ignored. He presents a more balanced review that includes negative and positive effects. We can group the results into perceptual, cognitive, and suggestibility effects that appear temporarily after sensory deprivation:

1. Certain aspects of perception are distorted. People are off in their perception of colors and spatial orientation, for instance. But they do better in a wide variety of perceptual tasks. They estimate weights better, hear softer sounds, and see more detail.
2. Some cognitive abilities are dulled, but others are sharpened. People do worse on arithmetic and concept formation tasks, but they learn word lists faster and they score higher on IQ tests.
3. People are more open to suggestions. On the negative side, some fear that sensory deprivation could be used to "brainwash" subjects. In one experiment, sensory-deprived subjects were more influenced than control subjects by messages about humans having hidden mental powers, including abilities to read minds and to "see" into the future. On the positive side, people are more susceptible to suggestions to make changes that they want to make. In one experiment, sensory deprivation helped people who were eager to quit smoking. They listened to antismoking messages after sensory deprivation. Over the next two years, these people were more successful than a group who heard the same message without experiencing deprivation (Figure 5–10).

Sensory deprivation procedures not only reduce sensations, they also confine subjects and eliminate social contacts. Therefore, sensory reduction, confinement, and social isolation can all contribute to effects of the procedure. Research is underway to separate the influences of these three variables (Zubek, Bayer, & Shepard, 1969; Zuckerman, 1969). Research is also being done with sensory deprivation to test theories of motivation, personality, and social psychology.

Earlier, we mentioned attempts to "brainwash" people about reading minds and "seeing" into the future; in the next section we will consider such abilities. We do not want to wash any brains or even twist any arms one way or the other.

Figure 5–10
Sensory deprivation has been shown to have positive effects in some cases. In one experiment, subjects who were trying to stop smoking cigarettes were able to reduce their intake more after sensory deprivation than those subjects who had not experienced sensory deprivation.

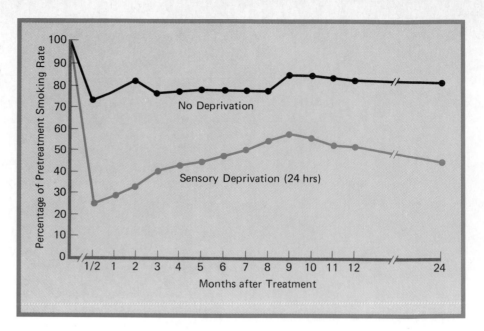

HIDDEN MENTAL POWERS

By virtue of being born human, we have a wide variety of behaviors and experiences available to us. Many of us have the potential for running a four-minute mile, using advanced calculus, and enjoying Beethoven's symphonies. We develop only a fraction of our human potentialities, however. Most of us never run a four-minute mile, and many of us never get beyond basic calculus. Our ability to do more remains hidden inside of us.

What are our hidden abilities and how can we discover them? It has been suggested that we might have to enter alternate states of consciousness to find some of them (Tart, 1977). Many of us discover, for instance, that we can create bizarre images and weird stories in our dreams that are beyond our waking imagination. If we are highly motivated, we may also find in our waking consciousness hidden abilities such as being able to control severe pain (Barber, 1970; Olshan, 1980). We will conclude this chapter with some tests that are designed to test two kinds of mental powers. One type of test is for **extrasensory perception (ESP)**, which is the reception of information by means other than our usual senses of hearing, sight, taste, touch, and smell. The other type of test is for **psychokinesis (PK)**, which is direct mental influence over physical objects or processes. A person with PK could supposedly "will" dice to come to rest at desired numbers, for instance.

Extrasensory Perception

Scientists who study ESP and PK are called *parapsychologists*. They test ESP using a deck of Zener cards. This deck consists of twenty-five cards, five each of the five patterns shown in Figure 5–11. Imagine trying to guess what was on each of the cards: You would expect to get some correct by chance. In fact, less than ten correct guesses would happen often by chance. For example, wild guesses will give five correct answers about half of the time. A better test of ESP versus chance can be done by going through the deck many times. Such procedures are used to test three different kinds of ESP:

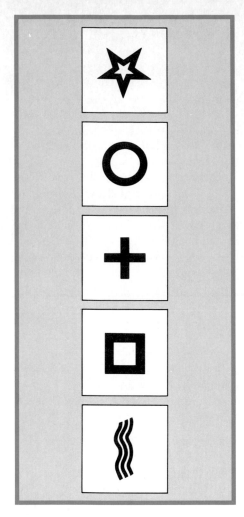

Figure 5–11
Zener cards, which are used to test various kinds of ESP, consist of 25 cards, 5 each of the patterns shown here.

1. A *test of precognition* is a test of one's ability or inability to perceive future thoughts, events, or actions. For example, a person might try to predict the order in which Zener cards will appear when the deck is shuffled and presented one at a time.
2. A *test of clairvoyance* is a test of one's ability or inability to perceive an object, action, or event by means of ESP. For instance, a person might try to indicate the figure on each Zener card without looking. In this test, the deck would have already been shuffled.
3. A *test of telepathy* is a test of one's ability or inability to perceive another's mental state or emotion by means of ESP. Two people are required for this test. One looks at each card and tries to "send" a mental image of it. The other person tries to "receive" this message and indicate what is on the card.

Most people fail these tests. But positive results are obtained occasionally. Soal and Bateman (1954), for example, reviewed a study in which a woman got a total of 707 correct answers after 2,600 times through a deck. This was 187 more than would have been expected by chance.

Psychokinesis

Some people claim to have psychokinetic powers. Unfortunately, we must be on the lookout for frauds when we investigate such claims. Some masters of illusion enjoy perpetrating a hoax; time after time careful investigators have exposed people who are alleged to have used psychic powers to move tables and other objects as frauds (Cohen, 1976).

Some research has supported ESP and PK, as noted earlier. Yet many scientists remain skeptical (Diaconis, 1978; Hansel, 1980; Hyman, 1977). The skepticism stems from two sources. First, many ESP and PK experiments cannot be consistently replicated. Too often, scientists get different results when they attempt to repeat their own experiments or those of others. Second, the likelihood of getting ESP and PK effects goes down when experimental controls improve. The opposite is true in most areas of research: Better controls usually yield larger and more reliable effects. Thus, scientists suspect that results were not influenced by ESP or PK in the first place if better controls reduce the effects.

NEAR-DEATH EXPERIENCES

We are now prepared to cast an analytical eye on George Ritchie's near-death experience. We can employ the same kind of analysis that we applied to other mental states and alleged mental powers. Raymond Moody (1975) interviewed George Ritchie and hundreds of other people who had had similar near-death experiences. Moody presented his results in his book *Life After Life*. Besides being catchy, his title skirts the question of whether or not his subjects had actually died. Moody plays down this issue and emphasizes instead the fact that his subjects are experts on what we all are likely to experience when we encounter death.

Physiological Patterns

Ritchie was pronounced dead because he lost his vital signs: His eyes dilated, his body temperature steadily dropped, his blood pressure became undetectable, and his heartbeat and breathing stopped for an extended period of time. Today, doctors have added a new standard by which to judge death, the absence of electrical activity in the brain as determined by EEG records. Doctors still cannot be certain, however, whether or not a person can be brought back to life in any given case. People have shown no vital signs for about a half-hour and yet have been brought back to life without any evident brain damage. Moody, a physician, suspects that some as yet unmeasurable biological activity continues to supply the brain with oxygen and nourishment for some time after vital signs are gone. He acknowledges that this hypothesis leaves open the possibility that such residual brain activity may also account for near-death experiences. Until we learn to measure this residual function, we will know little about physiological patterns that accompany near-death experiences.

In the meantime, Moody encourages us to think about the possibility that minds are released from bodies at death and that they continue to exist and to experience. Accordingly, Ritchie's mind and those of Moody's other subjects may have been released before their bodies reached the point of no return and rejoined when their bodies recovered. According to Moody's mystical speculation, we would not expect future research to reveal any correspondence between physiological and subjective patterns during near-death experiences, since they would be entirely *separate* during these experiences.

Subjective Patterns

Various reports of near-death experiences are so similar that Moody was able to identify fifteen elements that turn up again and again. None of Moody's subjects reported all fifteen elements, but every element was reported frequently. The elements are as follows:

1. The experience seems beyond words, leading to the feeling that descriptions are inadequate. One woman said, "That's as close as I can get it, but it's not really adequate. I can't really give you a complete picture."
2. People often hear their doctors pronounce them dead.
3. Pain and anxiety are relieved, creating a very pleasant feeling during the early part of the experience.
4. Many subjects reported hearing sounds ranging from extremely unpleasant buzzing noises to very beautiful music.
5. Upon seeming to leave their bodies, people often feel as if they are pulled through a dark space of some kind, often described as a well, a trough, an enclosure, a tunnel, a funnel, a vacuum, a void, a sewer, a valley, or a cylinder.
6. After a rapid passage through the dark tunnel, people find themselves viewing their own physical body, seeing everything going on in the room as if they were watching it from above.
7. Quite a few subjects told Moody that they saw dead friends and relatives during their experience.
8. Many also saw the being of light reported by Ritchie. Not everyone thought the being was the "Son of God," as Ritchie did, but all thought that the being was loving.
9. The being of light presents people with a panoramic review of their lives.
10. Some people report approaching a border of some kind near the end of their experience. Ritchie approached a city made of light; others have reported approaching a body of water, a gray mist, a door, a fence across a field, and a line.
11. All Moody's subjects "came back," of course. Many people resist the return and long to stay with the being of light.
12. People feel certain that their near-death experiences were real, but they are reluctant to tell others about them.

13. Their visions left Moody's subjects with new moral goals and a determination to pursue them, but with no feelings of instant or moral infallibility. Like Ritchie, many developed a deep caring for others.
14. Most of Moody's subjects were no longer afraid of death after their experience.
15. Many people have accurately reported events that occurred while they were supposedly dead. One girl believes that she went out of her body and found her sister in another room of the hospital crying. Later she told her sister where she had been sitting and exactly what she had been saying: "Oh, Kathy, please don't die, please don't die." (Moody, 1975, p. 99)

Moody's data are important and fascinating, but are not proof of mystical theories. Mystics argue that people have similar near-death experiences because they contact the same mysterious external reality. Theorists might argue, however, that people have similar near-death experiences because they have similar brains, and that these brains remain at least minimally active for a certain amount of time after "death." Whether we prefer mystical or psychological explanations, we are faced with deciding how to categorize near-death experiences. Moody argues that they are a novel phenomenon, but we also should consider the possibility that they are closely related to other experiences. You might have noticed, for example, that many of the fifteen elements identified by Moody also characterize other alternate states of consciousness.

 # A FINAL COMMENT

Did you see similarities among the various conditions of consciousness that were reviewed? A number of subjective patterns seem to cut across several states. Time distortions or feeling outside of time occur during many of the conditions that we reviewed. Several of the conditions—drug-induced states, near-death experiences, and meditation—were accompanied by a feeling of being united with the universe. Two conditions, drowsiness and drug-induced states, were characterized by hallucinations that develop in four stages. Ideally, common physiological and subjective patterns would suggest a basis for classifying alternate states of consciousness. Classification, however, is highly debatable at the present time. Scientists do not agree, for instance, about whether hypnosis is part of waking consciousness or whether it is a separate state. Unless you see some pattern that others have missed, we must conclude that the present data do not suggest a clear-cut classification system.

Similarly, the present data do not prove or disprove any one theory of alternate states. According to mysticism, alternate state experiences are caused by stimulation that originates in an external reality that is not apparent to our usual senses. According to perceptual release theory, excitations that originate in the central nervous system cause alternate state experiences when sensory input is reduced. The following generalization may have been instrumental in the development of perceptual release theory: *Whenever sensory sensitivity is extremely reduced, people experience perceptual distortions, hallucinations, or dreams*. This generalization holds when sensory sensitivity is reduced by sleep, drowsiness, drugs, meditation, sensory deprivation, near-death experiences, or hypnosis. Research aimed at articulating perceptual release theory may never disprove mystical theories, but the research has already led to important applications.

Research on perceptual release theory also may contribute to our understanding of everyday perception, learning, and memory. In the preceding chapter, we reviewed arguments that the mind plays an active role in constructing perceptions. In the next two chapters, we will consider the widely held view that the mind also plays an important role in learning and memory.

SUMMARY

1. **Consciousness** is perception of what is in a person's own mind. Some psychologists attempt to distinguish **alternate states of consciousness** in terms of specific patterns of physiological and subjective responses that are brought on by sleep, drugs, meditation, and other causes.

2. **Monism** is the theory that the mind and brain are one unitary organic whole. **Dualism** is the theory that the mind and brain are separate entities.

3. Mystical theories suggest that experiences occurring during alternate states of consciousness are subjective responses to an external reality that is hidden from us during normal waking consciousness. Perceptual release theory holds that visions and other experiences during alternate states of consciousness are subjective responses to internal *brain activity*.

4. Methods for studying consciousness include self-experience, questionnaires and interviews, laboratory experiments, and clinical methods.

5. **Sleep** has five stages that are distinguished by distinct patterns of brain waves and other physiological responses. An increased understanding of sleep is leading to better treatment of sleep disorders.

6. Sleep has distinct subjective patterns that include **dreams** and visions that occur during drowsiness.

7. Daydreams do not have physiological patterns that distinguish them from waking consciousness, but they have subjective patterns that may make an important contribution to our lives.

8. Drugs that produce subjective effects are called **psychoactive drugs.** Three kinds are **depressants, stimulants,** and **hallucinogens.** Each kind produces unique physiological responses. They also produce distinct subjective patterns that can be analyzed in experiments that control the many nondrug factors that ordinarily make subjective responses highly variable.

9. Hypnotists can control both physiological and subjective responses in susceptible subjects. Physiological measures do not distinguish hypnosis from waking consciousness, which leaves room for debate about whether or not hypnosis induces an alternate state of consciousness. While scientists debate this, they agree that hypnotists can influence judgment, suggestibility, relaxation, attention, and memory, both during and after hypnosis. Important applications include the reduction of pain.

10. **Meditation** is a process combining mental and physical acts to achieve an alternate state of consciousness. This process reduces oxygen consumption, respiratory rate, heart rate, blood pressure, and muscle tension. It also induces subjective responses characterized by feelings of calm and well-being.

11. **Sensory deprivation** changes physiological responses, but not in a way that distinguishes a unique state of consciousness. Subjective effects include positive and negative influences on perception, cognition, and suggestibility. Important applications include helping people stop smoking.

12. You can objectively test the possibility that you have hidden mental powers. You can test for **extrasensory perception (ESP),** which is the reception of information by means other than our usual senses of hearing, sight, taste, touch, and smell. You can also test for **psychokinesis (PK),** which is direct mental influence over physical objects or processes. Evidence of such powers does not meet usual scientific standards, but many are continuing to seek better evidence.

13. Many people have lost all measurable vital signs and then have been revived. Some of them report having subjective responses while they were supposedly dead. Near-death experiences are very similar, and many aspects turn up repeatedly.

Key Terms

alternate states of consciousness
biofeedback
consciousness
daydreams
delta waves
depressants
dreams
dualism
extrasensory perception (ESP)
fight-or-flight response
hallucinations
hallucinogens
hypermesia
hypnagogic images
hypnosis
hypnotic susceptibility tests
latent content

mantra
meditation
monism
phosphenes
posthypnotic amnesia
posthypnotic suggestion
psychoactive drugs
psychokinesis (PK)
relaxation response
REM rebound
REM sleep
self-hypnosis
sensory deprivation
sleep
sleep spindles
stimulants
transcendental meditation

Suggested Readings

The following book is about George Ritchie:
RITCHIE, G. G. (with Elizabeth Sherrill). *Return from to-morrow*. Waco, Tex.: Chosen Books, 1978.

BENSON, H. *The relaxation response*. New York: William Morrow, 1975. Reviews the psychological and medical research that led to the development of a simple meditative technique that helps people relax. It also describes the technique in detail.
DEMENT, W. C. *Some must watch while some must sleep*. San Francisco: San Francisco Book Company, 1976. This book introduces the diagnosis and treatment of sleep disorders. It is intended primarily for students who have no prior background in sleep and dream research.
Drug Abuse Council. *The fact about "drug abuse."* New York: Free Press, 1980. A comprehensive final report of the Drug Abuse Council of Washington, D.C., analyzes the illegal use of drugs in the context of the uses and misuses of legal drugs.

HARTH, E. *Windows on the mind*: *Reflections on the physical basis of consciousness*. New York: William Morrow, 1982.
PENFIELD, W. *The mystery of the mind*. Princeton, N.J.: Princeton University Press, 1975. A leading neurosurgeon and scientist gives a clearly written analysis of the extent to which the current state of knowledge about the brain can explain the actions of the mind.
RESTAK, R. *The brain*. New York: Bantam Books, 1984.
ROSSI, E. L. (Ed.). *The nature of hypnosis and suggestion*. New York: Irvington Publishers, 1980.
WEIL, A. & ROSEN, W. *Chocolate to morphine*: *Understanding mind-active drugs*. Boston: Houghton Mifflin, 1983.
ZINDBERG, N. E. (Ed.). *Alternate states of consciousness*. New York: Free Press, 1977. Experts from diverse fields present multiple perspectives on the study of consciousness. The book includes many fascinating reports of experiences during alternate states of consciousness.

SIX

LEARNING AND INTELLIGENCE

On April 5, 1887, nineteen-year-old Anne Sullivan made a dramatic breakthrough in the education of her seven-year-old deaf and blind pupil, Helen Keller. Sullivan described the event in a letter:

> We went out to the pump-house, and I made Helen hold her mug under the spout while I pumped. As the cold water gushed forth, filling the mug, I spelled "w-a-t-e-r" in Helen's free hand. The word coming so close upon the sensation of cold water rushing over her hand seemed to startle her. She dropped the mug and stood as one transfixed. A new light came into her face. She spelled "water" several times. Then she dropped on the ground and asked for its name and pointed to the pump and the trellis, and suddenly turning round she asked for my name. I spelled "teacher" . . . in a few hours she had added thirty new words to her vocabulary. (Lash, 1980, p. 56)

In a moment of insight, Helen learned that the manual alphabet used to spell words in her hand was the key to release her mind from what she later called her "prison-house" of darkness and silence. This was a landmark event in what became a lifelong dedication to teaching and learning.

Helen had not always lived in her "prison-house." Born June 27, 1880, in Alabama, she was a bright child, walking at the age of 1 and beginning to speak fairly early. At the age of 19 months she was struck by a high fever that almost killed her, and she was left deaf and blind. She had been a very lively baby, gay and affectionate; now there was a sad unresponsiveness of tone and look.

Helplessly the family watched her baffled attempts to deal with her world, the things she could touch, but which meant nothing to her. Nothing was a part of anything, and frequently there blazed up in her fierce anger. Helen did whatever she wanted, and the family went along with her, for though she raged and stormed, she was also a loving and lovable child. As she grew older, however, her thwarted passion to communicate produced increasingly violent tantrums, and some members of the family said she should be put in an institution. Luckily, her parents sought advice from Dr. Alexander Graham Bell, inventor of the telephone, who was deeply concerned with teaching the deaf. He suggested they contact Dr. Samuel Gridley Howe, who was director of the Perkins Institute for the Deaf and Blind.

Until the end of the eighteenth century, no special education programs existed for the deaf and blind. Most people avoided the handicapped because they were thought to have been (justly) punished by God. About 100 years before Helen Keller's birth, schools for the deaf and blind were started in France. Dr. Howe promoted this idea in America in 1831 when he became director of the Perkins Institute. Laura Bridgman, who lost her sight and hearing through scarlet fever at the age of 2, was his most famous student, but she only obtained a language ability equivalent to that of a 6-year-old child. Dr. Howe concluded after 20 years of study that the blind as a class are inferior to other persons in mental power and ability.

Anne Sullivan, a pupil at the Perkins Institute, disagreed with this conclusion. She herself had been nearly blind until she was 15, when eye surgery was performed, restoring most of her sight. Before her surgery, she was a student at the Perkins Institute, and she had learned the manual alphabet from some of the deaf students there. Sullivan doubted that young Laura Bridgman and other blind people were mentally inferior. She believed, instead, that the blind simply faced far greater obstacles, which interfered with learning.

After she graduated from the Institute, Anne Sullivan agreed to go to Alabama to work with Helen Keller. This is her first impression of the child: "I remember how disappointed I was when the untamed little creature stubbornly refused to kiss me, and struggled to free herself from my embrace" (Lash, 1980, p. 50). In later years, Helen Keller always celebrated March 3, the day Anne Sullivan had arrived, as her "soul's birthday."

But things did not go smoothly between teacher and student. Although Helen quickly imitated the signs that Sullivan spelled into her hand, she made no connection between them and the objects they symbolized. Finger spelling was just a game that she soon tired of, since she couldn't see the point of it. To make matters worse, she was entirely undisciplined because of her family's indulgence of her slightest whim. Her father sided with Helen in any battle against Sullivan. Battles soon became the rule and cooperation the exception. No progress was being made because of this, and so Sullivan persuaded the Kellers to allow her and Helen to live by themselves for awhile, in a little garden house a quarter of a mile away. Here Sullivan hoped to get her student to trust and obey her, so that she could focus her attention on learning instead of fighting. It worked: "The little wild creature of two weeks ago has been transformed into a gentle child" (Lash, 1980, p.

54). Unfortunately, her parents were unhappy with the separation, and within a month teacher and student had moved back to the Kellers' house. There the battles began again, because Helen soon found that her family would still let her do just as she wished.

All this time Sullivan practiced finger spelling with the young girl, constantly placing articles in Helen's hand and then spelling the names of the objects into her hand. She continued doing this even though Helen showed no sign of understanding that there was a connection between an object and the name that was immediately spelled into her hand.

Then, 2 weeks after they moved back to the main house, the landmark breakthrough happened. They went for a walk by the well-house. Someone was pumping water. Sullivan placed one of Helen's hands under the spout and spelled "water" in the other hand, as she had done with so many other names. But this time was different. Keller remembers it this way:

As the cool stream gushed over one hand, she (Annie) spelled into the other the word water, first slowly, then rapidly. I stood still, my whole attention fixed upon the motions of her fingers. Suddenly I felt a misty consciousness as of something forgotten—a thrill of returning thought; and somehow the mystery of language was revealed to me. I knew then that W A T E R meant the wonderful cool something that was flowing over my hand. . . . I left the well-house eager to learn. Everything had a name, and each name gave birth to a new thought. As we returned to the house every object which I touched seemed to quiver with life. (Lash, 1980, p. 55)

This was the beginning of the remarkable education of Helen Keller, who was the first blind and deaf person to ever attain the full use of her faculties and to pursue a higher education. She went to the Perkins Institute and learned Braille, always accompanied and taught by Anne Sullivan. Next she prepared for and entered Radcliffe College, where she carried a full course load.

Keller attended lectures, with Sullivan by her side. Sullivan spelled the lectures into Keller's hand. Others tried to substitute for this most valuable companion, but no one else could translate lectures as effectively. Others knew the manual alphabet as well as Sullivan, but no one knew as much about how Keller thought. Sullivan knew exactly how to edit lectures in order to make them as clear as possible. At the end of the day, Keller wrote notes on what she remembered of the day's lectures. After finishing her notes, she read whatever assignments had been copied in Braille for her. Most of her assignments were not available in Braille, however, so Sullivan read to her, usually 4 or 5 hours a day.

Helen Keller's academic schedule would have been challenging even for students with no handicaps. But somehow, working against all odds, she and Sullivan not only finished the schoolwork, but they also published a book, *The Story of My Life*, one of five books that this amazing woman published in her lifetime.

Keller received recognition from many sectors. Mark Twain said that "the two most interesting characters of the nineteenth century are Napoleon and Helen Keller." Keller and Sullivan were both awarded the degree of the Doctor of Humane Letters on Founder's Day at Temple University, and Keller received the degree of Doctor of Laws at the University of Glasgow in Scotland. The Glasgow *Herald* reported:

> Yesterday will long be remembered as Helen Keller's day . . . [an] occasion on which honour was paid to one who, partly by her own magnificent character, partly by the help of loving friends, has achieved what is little short of a miracle.

If everyone had viewed her accomplishments as a miracle, the impact of her life would have been diminished. Fortunately, Alexander Graham Bell and others were able to persuade educators that, with the proper teaching methods, they, too, could produce similar results in other deaf and blind children. In *The Silent Educator*, June 1892, Bell wrote:

> It is, then, a question of instruction we have to consider, and not a case of supernatural acquirement. Among the thousands of children in our schools for the deaf . . . there are some who are intellectually as capable of mastering the intricacies of the English language as Helen herself.

Helen Keller strongly agreed with this point of view. She did not consider herself a genius. She credited her accomplishments to the availability of education and to her willingness to take advantage of it. She expressed this best, perhaps, when she spoke to the alumnae shortly before her graduation from Radcliffe. She said: "College has breathed new life into my mind and given me new views of things, a perception of new truths and of new aspects of the old ones. I grow stronger in the conviction that there is nothing good or right which we cannot accomplish if we have the will to strive" (Lash, 1980, p. 315).

LEARNING: WHAT IS IT?

Learning is what released Helen Keller's mind from a "prison-house" of darkness and silence. The transformation that took place in her as a result of her learning experiences inspired our definition of learning. We define **learning** as the process by which experience or practice results in a relatively permanent change in what one is capable of doing. Many books define learning in terms of permanent changes in behavior. The problem with such definitions is that they ignore differences between what we are capable of doing and what we in fact do. If we define learning in terms of what we do, that is, in terms of our performance, we have trouble accounting for learning that is not immediately shown in behavior. Ask yourself, for example, whether or not you learned anything in the last 10 minutes of reading. You might have learned some new things about Helen Keller, but this learning probably has not changed your behavior yet. It changed what you are capable of doing, such as answering test questions, but it probably has not changed anything that you have done so far. It might not change your behavior for weeks, or even months, and probably not until you are asked about Helen Keller, or until you act upon your knowledge for some other reason. Tolman and Honzik (1930), who were leaders in the learning field, introduced the term *latent learning* to describe learning that is not manifested until some later time. The concept of latent learning recognizes the difference between *learning* and *performance*. Our definition of learning itself makes a clear distinction between the two.

Growth of Keller's human potential inspired our definition, but it applied equally to our own learning. Keller's learning process was not unique; it was only more obvious because of the handicaps she had to overcome before she was able to learn. We learn from the time we are born until we die. We learn what we can and cannot eat and what we can and cannot touch. We learn to walk, talk, ride bicycles, and play games. We learn how to relate to parents, brothers, sisters, friends, and teachers. We learn how to read and write, and how to think and reason. Some of what we learn is useless, such as the infectious mannerism of saying "you know" after every sentence. Some of what we learn is even harmful, such as racial prejudice. But for the most part, learning expands our potential as human beings every bit as much as learning expanded Keller's potential.

In this chapter we will learn about learning. We will study basic theories of learning, and we will see how these theories apply in our everyday lives. We will find that no one theory explains every kind of learning—in fact, much remains to be learned about learning.

Ideally, one theory would explain every kind of learning. Although some theorists have tried this, all have failed. Some theories account well for many important kinds of learning, but no one theory explains every important type. Therefore, we will break down our discussion of theories into separate sections on different types of learning. The first section is on a simple kind of learning that sets the stage for more advanced learning.

CLASSICAL CONDITIONING

In 1904, the year that Keller graduated from Radcliffe, Ivan Pavlov won the Nobel prize for his research on digestion. In some of his experiments, Pavlov (1927) measured the amount of saliva that flows when food is placed in a dog's mouth. This automatic, or *reflexive*, response to food was not surprising. But Pavlov also noticed that saliva often flowed before food was presented. It flowed at the sight of food, for example, and even at the sound of Pavlov's footsteps. Shortly after winning his Nobel prize, Pavlov turned to the question of why dogs salivated in response to sights and sounds. The work that followed revolutionized the study of learning.

Pavlov studied a kind of learning that now is called **classical conditioning,** the process by which an originally neutral stimulus (such as footsteps) comes to elicit a response (such as salivating) that was originally given to another stimulus (such as food). This learning process takes place when the neutral stimulus (footsteps) is repeatedly paired with the other stimulus (food). Classical conditioning is only one kind of learning that we will study. But it is such an important kind that we must consider it in detail.

Pavlov's Learning Experiments

Pavlov knew that a dog's mouth waters automatically in response to food. A dog doesn't have to learn this response. Pavlov figured, however, that dogs salivate in response to other stimuli because they learn to do so. He assumed, for example, that his dogs learned to respond to the sight of food and to the sound of footsteps. He decided to investigate this learning process by training dogs to salivate to some stimulus that ordinarily does not cause a dog's mouth to water. He found that a bell served his purpose. Before training, dogs did not salivate to the sound of a bell; after training, they did. Figure 6–1 shows the apparatus that he used to test this.

His experiment included the four basic elements of the training procedure known as classical conditioning:

1. Food causes salivation without conditioning, so it is called the **unconditioned stimulus (US).** Food automatically or reflexively causes a dog's mouth to water.
2. The salivation response to food also happens without conditioning, so it is called the **unconditioned response (UR).** It happens automatically or reflexively in response to food, or the US.
3. The bell does not cause salivation until after conditioning, so it is called the **conditioned stimulus (CS).** It is a stimulus to which an animal learns to respond.

Figure 6–1
Pavlov's basic training apparatus.

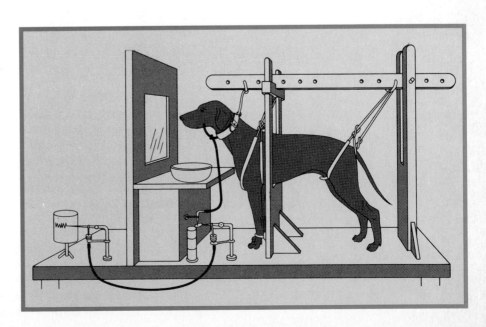

APPLYING CLASSICAL CONDITIONING

Psychologists have used classical conditioning techniques to improve the well-being of their patients. In one case, classical conditioning was used to treat alcoholism (Davidson, 1974). Davidson paired the sight, taste, and smell of alcohol (CS) with a drug (US) that caused vomiting (UR). After many such pairings, Davidson's patients developed a nausea response (CR) to alcohol itself. This treatment is called *aversion therapy*, and it can help break a bad habit when used in combination with other treatments (Cannon & Backer, 1981).

In another case, classical conditioning was used to treat irrational fear, such as the fear of harmless bugs (Wolpe, 1962). Wolpe assumed that bugs were a CS and that fear was a CR. Working from that assumption, he experimentally extinguished the undesirable CR. He first asked patients to think about bugs. This produced a mild fear response. But the response soon extinguished, because it was never paired with a bite or any other US. After the response was extinguished, Wolpe introduced pictures of bugs, which again elicited mild fear. This fear, too, was extinguished. Wolpe gradually extinguished one CR after another, until finally patients could even touch bugs without being

afraid. Wolpe's procedure is called *systematic desensitization therapy*, and it has helped many patients overcome irrational fears.

Classical conditioning research has also helped save wild coyotes, and endangered species. Ranchers wanted to destroy coyotes because they prey on lamb and other livestock. Environmentalists, who wanted to save coyotes, realized that they somehow had to force coyotes to leave livestock alone. A solution emerged from classical conditioning laboratories. In one laboratory, John Garcia found that rats learned to avoid food that made them sick. In another laboratory setting, it was learned that the

"Garcia effect" could be used to solve the coyote problem (Gustavson et al., 1974). The experimenters fed coyotes either poisoned lamb meat or poisoned rabbit meat. The poison (US) made the coyotes sick (UR), but it did not kill them. Afterwards, the coyotes developed an aversion (CR) to the kind of food that had been poisoned (CS). They would eat rabbit meat if lamb had been poisoned, or lamb if rabbit had been poisoned, but they would not touch the kind of meat that had made them sick. The same procedure worked in the wild, forcing coyotes to return to their natural prey and leave livestock alone.

4. The response to a CS, such as Pavlov's bell, is not identical to an unconditioned response. It is therefore called a **conditioned response (CR),** to distinguish it from a UR. One way that a CR often differs from a UR is in the strength of the response. In Pavlov's experiment, for instance, the CR contained fewer drops of saliva than the UR. That is, after conditioning, a dog's mouth watered less in response to a bell than it did in response to food.

Figure 6–2 summarizes Pavlov's conditioning procedure. Before classical conditioning, the CS (bell) did not cause salivation. But the US (food) did cause a UR (salivation). During the conditioning, the CS and US were paired. That is, Pavlov rang the bell and then, shortly afterwards, gave food. After conditioning, the CS (bell) was presented alone and Pavlov's dogs salivated (CR). By pairing the food and the bell, Pavlov established in the dogs a salivation response to the bell.

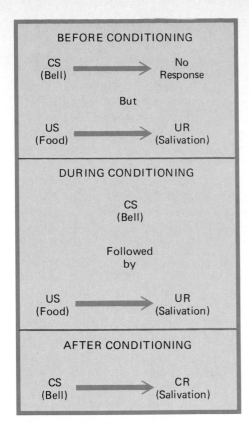

BEFORE CONDITIONING

CS
(Bell) ⟶ No
Response

But

US
(Food) ⟶ UR
(Salivation)

DURING CONDITIONING

CS
(Bell)

Followed
by

US
(Food) ⟶ UR
(Salivation)

AFTER CONDITIONING

CS
(Bell) ⟶ CR
(Salivation)

Figure 6–2
This is a diagram of what occurred in
Pavlov's conditioning procedure.

Classical conditioning is a simple kind of learning that has many important applications in its own right (see "Highlight: Applying Classical Conditioning"). In addition, it may at times provide a temporary stepping stone for more complicated learning processes, which will be discussed later in this chapter. To illustrate this, let's consider the possibility that classical conditioning paved the way for Keller's famous insight about finger spelling of the word *water*.

Recall Sullivan's description of the events leading to her student's insight: "As the cold water gushed forth, filling the mug, I spelled 'w-a-t-e-r' in Helen's free hand. The word coming so close upon the sensation of cold water rushing over her hand seemed to startle her. She dropped the mug and stood as one transfixed. A new light came into her face." Perhaps it was a coincidence that Keller's insight came at that moment. But perhaps there was something special about the pairing of cool water and finger spelling.

To relate this learning experience to conditioning, we might call water the US and finger spelling the CS. Before conditioning, the US (the water) led to a UR, which was a set of automatic responses, such as shivering. The CS (the finger spelling) led to no response. During conditioning the US and CS were paired. After conditioning the CS led to a CR, a response similar to the UR. That is, we might speculate that after the water and finger spelling were paired, finger spelling caused Keller to shiver and make other responses that she had previously made to the cold water. This new stimulus-response connection might have provided a building block for her realization that the finger spelling stood for water. After having made the connection, she repeated the finger spelling, which now had a new meaning for her. We are only speculating, of course, because we cannot be sure that classical conditioning was part of Keller's learning process. One way to evaluate our speculation is to analyze factors that are necessary for establishing and losing classically conditioned responses.

Important Factors in Classical Conditioning

Pavlov's work established many of the factors that are important for establishing and losing classically conditioned responses.

Establishing a Response. The likelihood of establishing a conditioned response depends on five factors:

1. The CS must be *strong and distinctive*. Pavlov's dogs heard his bell easily and were readily conditioned to it. Pavlov probably would have failed, however, if he had tried to condition his dogs to salivate whenever he lightly touched their back. Helen Keller's learning experience passes this criterion, for finger spelling is strong and distinctive.

2. The *order* in which the CS and US are presented makes a difference. Conditioning is best when the CS comes slightly before the US. Pavlov, for instance, rang the bell before giving food. Conditioning is less effective when the CS and US are presented at the same time, and conditioning is weakest if the CS is presented after the US (backward conditioning). Sullivan presented water and finger spelling at the same time, which is not the most effective pairing, but it doesn't rule out classical conditioning.

3. Classical conditioning also depends on the time lapse between the CS and US. Usually, conditioning is best if the interval is between a fraction of a second and a few seconds. Pavlov's dogs did not learn to respond to his bell when Pavlov waited too long to give them food after the bell. Keller's interval was zero, which is acceptable, but not the best.

4. Most classical conditioning requires *repeated pairings* of the CS and US. Pavlov paired the bell and food several times before his dogs

salivated at the sound of the bell. Once salivation occurs in response to a bell, one can measure the strength of the CR by recording the drops of saliva; the more drops the higher the strength. One finds that strength of the CR grows gradually with each presentation, until the CR is almost as strong as the UR. Sullivan noticed a sudden response to finger spelling, but we cannot rule out the possibility that weaker responses built up gradually before that. If we want to argue that classical conditioning was involved, we must assume that a CR strengthened gradually until Sullivan noticed what only appeared to be the first response.

5. The rate at which a classically conditioned response strengthens depends upon how the experimenter *spaces* the pairings of the CS and US. Conditioning will be slower if pairings follow each other too quickly or too far apart. This factor does not help us categorize Keller's experience.

Losing a Response. Classically conditioned responses need not last forever. Going back to Pavlov's dogs, we find that the dogs stopped salivating to the sound of a bell when the bell was rung many times without food being given. Figure 6–3 shows that the strength of a CR gradually decreases to no response at all if the CS is repeatedly presented alone. This falling off is called **extinction**. Once a response has been extinguished it can reappear again without any further pairing of the CS and US. Pavlov called this **spontaneous recovery**. He conditioned dogs to salivate when they heard a bell, and then he extinguished the response so that his dogs' mouths did not water when they heard the bell. Several days later, Pavlov tested his dogs again. As soon as the dogs heard the bell, their mouths began to water. The response reappeared without any retraining. Figure 6–3 shows that spontaneous recovery does not bring a response back to its full strength and the response extinguishes again if the CS is repeatedly presented alone.

After the first pairing of finger spelling the water, finger spelling was undoubtedly presented alone many, many times. Thus, if conditioning played a part in Keller's learning, it was only a temporary role. Because of conditioning, Keller might have shivered in response to finger spelling, and this might have helped her learn the connection between it and water. But this was only a stepping stone to other types of learning, which supplemented and built upon the original conditioning that had taken place.

Figure 6–3
The strength of a CR gradually decreases if the CS is always repeated alone. This is called extinction. Spontaneous recovery occurs if the response reappears again without any further pairings of CS and US; but the response will eventually extinguish again if the CS is repeatedly presented alone.

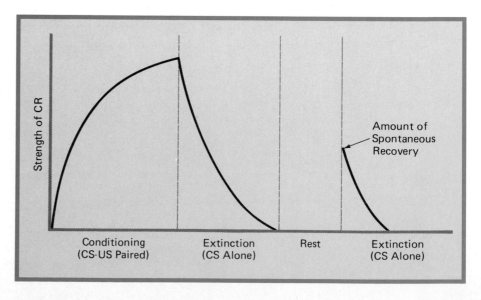

Generalizing Conditioned Responses

Staying with the idea that conditioning might have set the stage for Keller's learning, we can ask other questions about the conditioning. For example, would she have shivered only in response to Sullivan's finger spelling, or would a similar stimulus also have elicited the conditioned response? Pavlov's experiment provided an answer. After Pavlov's dogs had been conditioned to salivate to the sound of a bell, their mouths also watered when they heard a buzzer and a metronome. This reaction to similar stimuli is called **stimulus generalization.** Conditioned responses are elicited not only by the conditioned stimulus, but also by similar stimuli.

John Watson demonstrated stimulus generalization in an experiment that surely would not be allowed today (Watson & Rayner, 1920). Before the experiment, Albert, an 11-month-old boy, was not afraid of white rats. When he saw one, he crawled toward it and wanted to play with it. During conditioning, Watson and Rayner presented the white rat (CS), waited for Albert to approach, and then made a loud noise by clanging steel bars behind him (US). The earsplitting sound made Albert cry (UR). After several such pairings of the rat and noise, Albert developed a conditioned fear of the rat. When he saw it, even if there was no noise, he immediately started to cry, and he tried to crawl away. The experimenters then showed Albert a white rabbit, a fur coat, and a Santa Claus mask. All of these things terrified him; he had generalized from the white rat to the rabbit and other white furry objects.

Discrimination

If stimulus generalization were carried too far, conditioning would not be a useful building block for learning. In finger spelling, for instance, it is necessary to discriminate between different patterns. Pavlov showed that his conditioned dogs could make **discriminations.** Pavlov presented one sound followed by food and a similar sound without food. The dogs learned to salivate to the sound that had been followed by the food, and they learned not to salivate to the other sound. In this way, they learned to discriminate between the stimuli.

Higher-Order Conditioning

Animals and humans often base new learning on old learning—for example, Keller learned new finger spellings based on old ones. If conditioning is a building block for learning, then we should expect Pavlov's dogs to be able to base new conditioned responses upon old ones. What happens is that a well-established conditioned stimulus (CS) comes to act like a US in establishing a *second* conditioned stimulus (CS). Thus a dog or a person learns conditioned responses without getting food or any other US.

In testing this, Pavlov first conditioned his dogs to salivate in response to a bell (CS). He then paired a black square (CS) with the bell. He presented the square and then the bell over and over again, occasionally pairing the bell with food. The dogs learned to salivate in response to the black square, even though *it* was never paired with food. Pavlov called this a second-order conditioned response, and he went on to establish a third-order conditioned response (Kehoe et al., 1981). Pavlov speculated that all learning might be nothing more than long chains of conditioned responses.

Modern psychologists reject the notion that classical conditioning explains all learning. Instead, they see classical conditioning as one of several kinds of learning (Rescorla & Holland, 1982). They would go beyond classical conditioning, for instance, to explain all of Keller's learning. In the next section we will see, in fact, that another kind of conditioning played an important role in changing Keller's behavior. Interest in classical conditioning has remained high, however, despite the discovery of other kinds of learning. As we discussed, modern researchers are developing important applications. They are also exploring biochemical changes in neurons that mediate conditioned responses (e.g., Alkon, 1983).

OPERANT CONDITIONING

A major limitation of Pavlov's work on classical conditioning is that his dogs were restrained and made to respond reflexively to external stimuli. His dogs learned to transfer responses from a stimulus that naturally elicited it to other stimuli that previously did not. When all is said and done, Pavlov's dogs were only making passive responses to stimuli that came from outside them. This limitation is serious, because many of our behaviors are internally motivated active responses. We search for food, seek companions, and ask questions. Psychologists call these actions *operant behaviors* because they actively *operate* on the environment.

Edward L. Thorndike (1913, 1932) began research on operant behaviors in cats at about the same time that Pavlov began his classical conditioning research with dogs. Figure 6–4 shows Thorndike's apparatus, which he called a "puzzle box." The idea was to escape from the box; the puzzle was to find out how to do it. Thorndike made sure that a cat was hungry, then he put it in the puzzle box with a small dish of food on the outside in open view. The cat could not get the food unless it could somehow get free. Thorndike rigged the box so that it opened when a cat brushed up against a string. When the cat escaped and ate the food, Thorndike put the cat back in the box and filled the dish again. Since the dish was small, the cat was still hungry, so it tried to break out again. Each time the cat solved the puzzle, Thorndike set it up again. Gradually, the cat took less and less time to open the box and escape.

Thorndike interpreted the decrease in escape time as evidence of learning. He noticed that a cat usually tried a number of actions that didn't work, such as clawing at the sides of the box before brushing up against the string. Thorndike explained his observations by proposing that animals learn according to the **law of effect.** This law states that animals tend to repeat behaviors that are followed by "good effects" and they tend to stop behaviors that are not followed by desirable results.

About 20 years later, B. F. Skinner (1938) expanded upon Thorndike's observations and he translated the law of effect into the theory of **operant conditioning.** This theory states that operant behaviors are learned when desired responses are reinforced and undesired responses are either ignored or punished. Notice that Skinner replaced the idea of "good effects" with the notion of reinforcement, which has a special meaning in the theory of operant conditioning. An event is a **reinforcement** if its occurrence just after the response increases the likelihood that the response will be repeated. The theory of operant conditioning allowed Skinner to study learning without speculating about whether an animal considered an event to be "good" or "bad." As we discussed in Chapter 1, Skinner was a follower of John Watson's school of behaviorism. Skinner thought, therefore, that he should stick to the observable facts—stimuli and responses made to the stimuli.

Keller's education provides many examples of operant conditioning. Sullivan devoted her life to Keller's education long before psychologists formalized principles of operant conditioning, yet her ingenious instincts

Figure 6–4
Thorndike's experimental apparatus, which he called a "puzzle box," is shown here. In order to escape from the box, a cat had to brush against the string inside the box, which in turn opened the door so that it could get out.

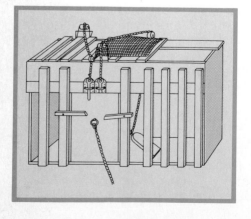

guided her toward operant conditioning methods. In fact, she could not have followed them any better even if she had studied modern teacher's manuals, which are loaded with operant conditioning techniques. We will therefore find many illustrations of operant conditioning in Keller's education.

Acquisition of Operant Behaviors

Skinner (1938, 1966) studied operant behaviors with a procedure that was similar to Thorndike's. Skinner placed a hungry rat in a small cage that contained a food cup with a bar over it (Figure 6–5). The cup was empty until the rat pushed the bar, which made a small pellet of food drop into the cup. This apparatus became known as a *Skinner box*. A cat in a puzzle box had to learn to break out in order to get food; a rat in a Skinner box had to learn how to bring food into the box.

The learning process for Thorndike's cats and Skinner's rats was similar. At first Skinner's rats explored the cage, making a number of ineffective responses until they happened to press the bar. The rat then ate the food pellet that was delivered and continued to explore until it again hit the bar and brought in more food. After two or three bar presses, the rat stopped most of its ineffective responses and started to push the bar repeatedly.

About 30 years earlier Sullivan had used a similar procedure to teach Keller. Teacher and student sat at a table containing familiar objects such as a cup and a doll. Sullivan placed an object in one of Keller's hands and spelled its name in the other. She then guided Keller's fingers to spell the same name. As soon as Keller finished spelling a name correctly, Sullivan gave her a small bit of cake. If the girl made a mistake, she got no cake. Gradually, Keller stopped making mistakes and started making spelling responses quickly and correctly. The parallels between Sullivan's procedure and Skinner's procedure are amazing. Skinner's rats and Keller both stopped making responses that were not reinforced and continued making responses that were.

Positive and Negative Reinforcement. There are several different kinds of reinforcement. The basic definition we gave of reinforcement is an event that increases the likelihood that a response will be repeated.

Figure 6–5
Skinner's experimental apparatus, which became known as a Skinner box, is shown here. In order to get food, the rat had to press the bar inside the box, and a food pellet was delivered into a cup in the box.

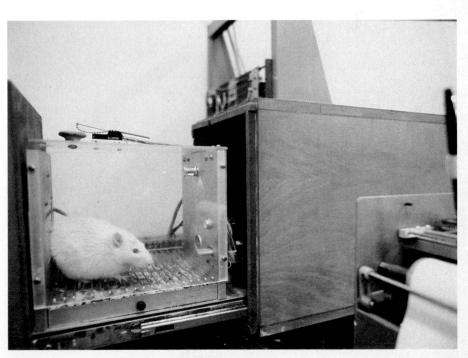

In this context, psychologists distinguish between "positive" and "negative" events. A *positive event* occurs when a stimulus is added to an environment. A *negative event* occurs when a stimulus is taken away. When a positive event serves as a reinforcer, it is called **positive reinforcement**. The rat's food pellets and Keller's cake are examples of positive reinforcement. When a negative event serves as a reinforcer, it is called **negative reinforcement**.

Skinner demonstrated negative reinforcement by using an electric shock grid on the bottom of his Skinner box. He turned on the grid and put a rat in the cage. The rat received a mild shock continuously until it pushed a bar that turned off the grid. After a short time the shock grid went on again until the rat again pushed the bar. The rat soon learned to press the bar to turn off the shock. Turning *off* a shock is a negative event, because it *takes away* a stimulus. It is a reinforcing event because its occurrence increases the likelihood that a rat will push the bar. Thus, it is a negative reinforcer.

Skinner used negative reinforcement in two kinds of training programs. The rat that learned to press a bar to turn off electric shock participated in **escape training**. Skinner also used **avoidance training**, in which a negative reinforcer can be avoided altogether. He placed a rat in a Skinner box, sounded a buzzer, and then turned on a shock a few seconds later. The shock did not go on if the rat pressed the bar after the buzzer sounded and before the shock started. Pressing the bar after the shock started did no good. The shock stayed on for a fixed time, and then it went off until a few seconds after the buzzer sounded again. Gradually, rats learned to press the bar to avoid being shocked.

Learned Helplessness. An avoidance training procedure was used to demonstrate another important learning phenomenon, **learned helplessness**. This type of learning occurs when exposure to unavoidable, unpleasant events leads to an impairment of the ability to avoid the unpleasant event even when avoidance is possible. Maier, Seligman, and Solomon (1969) performed a classic experiment on learned helplessness. Dogs were paired and then randomly divided into two groups. Dogs in both groups were strapped into harnesses that prevented foot movements. Then, at random intervals, shocks were delivered to the feet. Dogs in one group could turn off the shock by pushing a panel that was in front of their nose. Dogs in the other group could not control the shocks. Both dogs in a pair received the very same shocks. The only difference was that one dog could control the shocks while the other could not.

The next day, the dogs who had been able to control the shocks followed the typical avoidance training pattern. Each dog was placed in a box that was divided by a hurdle. At the beginning of each trial, a 10-second warning light flashed. Then the floor of the box was electrified for 50 seconds. At first the dogs received a shock and then jumped the hurdle to escape it—the other side of the box was not wired. Soon, however, they learned to avoid the shock by jumping the hurdle during the warning signal.

Performance on the same avoidance learning task was strikingly different for the dogs who had not been able to control the shocks they received during the first part of the experiment. They neither avoided nor escaped the shocks during ten consecutive trials (Figure 6–6). The day before they could not control their shock. They were truly helpless. During avoidance training, however, they could have helped themselves, but they did not try. They had learned to be helpless.

Jay Weiss (1980) performed a similar experiment with rats, taking it one step further. He explored biochemical changes that correspond with learned helplessness. One group of rats was helpless—they were not given an opportunity to escape or avoid shocks in the experimental situation. In a second situation these rats did not even try to avoid shocks when they were given an opportunity to do so. Another group could control

Figure 6–6
Learned Helplessness

The curves show the time it took two groups of dogs to escape a shock by jumping over a barrier. On each trial, one compartment of a cage became electrified after a 10-second warning signal. A trial ended if a dog did not jump the barrier to escape the shock after 60 seconds. The bottom curve is for a group of dogs who were in a similar experiment the day before. They learned to escape the shock very quickly. The upper curve is for a group of dogs who had also been in a similar experiment the day before. The difference was that they could not escape the shocks the day before. As a result, they learned to be helpless and they failed to help themselves the next day by escaping when they could have. (After Maier, Seligman, & Solomon, 1969)

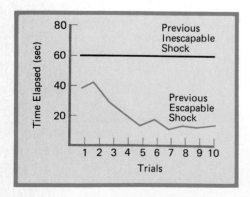

shocks in one situation, and they learned to avoid shocks in another situation. Weiss found that the rats who were in control had normal levels of the neural transmitter norepinephrine in their brains (see Chapter 2). In contrast, the helpless rats had lower levels of norepinephrine in their brains. Weiss concluded that a temporary decrease of norepinephrine is responsible for the inability to learn to avoid unpleasant stimuli. This hypothesis is consistent with other research suggesting that neural transmitters are important in learning and memory (see Chapter 7).

Learned helplessness has also been studied in human social situations (see the discussion of Seligman's work in Chapter 11). In these situations it is related to depression. It is hoped that biochemical research on learned helplessness will lead to more effective treatment of depression (Blood, Lagerson, & Hofstedter, 1985).

Primary and Secondary Reinforcers. Besides positive and negative reinforcers, psychologists distinguish between **primary reinforcers,** which are reinforcing in and of themselves, and **secondary reinforcers,** which are reinforcing only after they have been paired with other primary reinforcers. All the examples that we considered so far (rat pellets, cake, and electric shock) are primary reinforcers. An electric shock is an effective negative reinforcer, for example, even for rats who never experienced it before. In contrast, secondary reinforcers work only after they are associated with other reinforcers. Skinner found that a rat who has had no experience in a Skinner box will not learn to press a bar if the bar turns on a light and nothing more. That is, a light is not a primary reinforcer. Skinner showed that a light can become a secondary reinforcer, however. He rigged his Skinner box to deliver food and turn on a light every time a bar was pressed. After many pairings of the food and the light, Skinner discontinued the food and continued to turn on the light whenever the rat pushed the bar. The rat continued to push the bar because the light had become a secondary reinforcer.

As a child, Keller spelled for cake, a primary reinforcer. But she probably would not have responded as well for money, because it didn't mean anything to her. Later, after money was associated with food and other rewards, Keller worked for money. In fact, she wrote her autobiography, *The Story of My Life*, primarily to earn money for her college education. Money is an effective secondary reinforcer for most of us.

Schedules of Reinforcement. Considering money as a reinforcer brings to mind the fact that we usually are not reinforced every time we do something. We work a certain time interval (a week or a month), and then we get our paycheck. Or we finish a fixed amount of work (mowing the lawn) and then we get paid. When Keller received cake for every correct spelling, she was on a **continuous reinforcement schedule.** Later, when she received royalty checks from the sale of her book (these came twice a year), she was on a **partial reinforcement schedule.**

Psychologists have studied schedules that are based upon time (weekly paychecks) and schedules that are based upon the amount of work done (mowing the lawn). They have also studied schedules that are fixed (e.g., a weekly allowance) and schedules that are variable (e.g., an allowance given whenever parents see fit). The following are four common schedules:

1. **Fixed-interval schedules** reinforce the first response after a constant time interval. Skinner observed a rat responding to a fixed-interval schedule. He trained the rat to press a bar for food. Then he rigged his Skinner box so that it would deliver food after a bar press, wait 5 minutes, deliver food to the next bar press, wait another 5 minutes, and so on. During the 5-minute waiting intervals, bar presses were useless; they did not deliver food. After being on this schedule for a short time, rats stopped responding immediately after food was

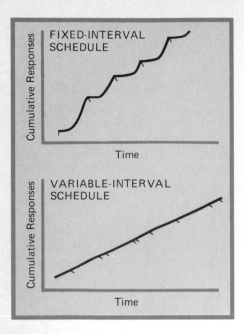

Figure 6–7
These two graphs show the rate of responding under fixed-interval and variable-interval schedules of reinforcement.

delivered and then they resumed the response pattern at a high rate as the end of the 5-minute interval approached (Figure 6–7, top). This response pattern is similar to what students do when exams are given at fixed intervals. They rarely study immediately after exams, but they often cram like mad right before the next exam.

2. **Variable-interval schedules** reinforce the first response after varying time intervals. The first time interval might be 9 minutes, the second one 2 minutes, the third one 4 minutes, and then 3 minutes, 3 minutes, 7 minutes, 5 minutes, and so on. Skinner found that rats give a slow, steady rate of response when they are reinforced on a variable-interval schedule (Figure 6–7, bottom). This pattern is similar to students' study habits in a course in which "pop quizzes" are given at unpredictable times. They study at a steady rate because they have to be prepared for a quiz at any time.

3. **Fixed-ratio schedules** reinforce the first response after a certain number of responses have been made. A fixed ratio of 1 in 10 would reinforce every tenth response. Rats on fixed-ratio schedules respond at a fast, steady rate. They have to push a bar many times to get one reinforcer, and they find that the faster they push, the more reinforcers they get. Factories sometimes pay workers on a fixed-ratio schedule. Knitting mills, for example, may pay workers for every 100 mittens finished. The more mittens workers finish, the more money they get, so they usually work at an incredibly fast rate. A job with a fixed-ratio schedule is called *piecework*; it can work out well for both the employer and the employee.

4. **Variable-ratio schedules** reinforce the first response after a varying number of responses. A variable-ratio schedule might reinforce the tenth response, then the fourth response after that, then the seventh response after that, and so on. Rats on this kind of schedule respond at a very fast, steady rate, as do people. Slot machines are a good example of a variable-ratio schedule. They are set to pay off after varying numbers of attempts. Gamblers might win two in a row, or they might have to play a hundred times before winning. What seems to be important is that the next time *could* always bring the jackpot; one never knows. Gamblers seem to treat each attempt as if it will be the one to pay off. They respond rapidly with hardly any pause, and they continue to respond over and over again for a long time.

Kenny Rogers, in his song "The Gambler," warns us that we "have to know when to walk away and when to run." The best time to run away from slot machines may be before you deposit a single coin. That way you can avoid getting caught up in its captivating reinforcement schedule. Knowing this, some gambling casinos give customers a few complimentary coins to get them started (and hooked). This ploy is one solution to the general problem we will discuss next: How do you get someone to make that first operant response so that the behavior can be brought under the control of a reinforcement schedule?

Encouraging a First Operant Response

Once Keller started finger spelling, her teacher could reinforce her with cake. But how did Sullivan get the young girl started? Indeed, how does any parent or teacher get children to perform desirable behavior the first time? Let's look at some ways this can be done.

Hurry-Up-and-Wait. Some responses occur without special coaxing. To bring such behaviors under the control of operant conditioning, teachers are faced with a hurry-up-and-wait routine. They must hurry up and

Gambling is a good example of a variable-ratio schedule of reinforcement. The best way to avoid being hooked by gambling, as Kenny Rogers warns in his song "The Gambler," may be to know when to walk away.

reward a response when it occurs; then they must wait patiently for the next time it occurs. If a response is ignored, it will stop; if it is reinforced, it will recur over and over again.

Sullivan used a hurry-up-and-wait procedure to teach Keller to ask questions. Sullivan believed that "Why?" would be the door through which her student would enter the world of reason and reflection. She therefore waited watchfully for Keller to ask questions and she immediately greeted every question with warm encouragement as well as with answers. Soon Keller was asking questions all day long. "Who put chickens in eggs?" "Can flies know not to bite?" "Why is Viney black?" Her questions were not all as intelligent as these. In fact, Sullivan always insisted that Keller's mind was not superior to that of others. All children seem to crack open the "Why?" door. Parents and teachers have the power through operant conditioning either to slam the door by ignoring questions or to aid its opening by reinforcing them.

Increasing Motivation. Another way to encourage a first response is to increase the motivation to make the response. Sullivan did this with Keller. She had been refusing to use her napkin, and Sullivan anticipated another protest. She therefore cut down on Keller's snacks, making sure that the girl was hungry before dinner. Keller's hunger increased her motivation for food, which had been paired with proper use of a napkin in earlier battles. That night Keller used her napkin properly, and she was immediately reinforced with a delicious dinner.

Verbal Instructions and Modeling. There is, however, a limit to what one can do by increasing motivation. Even if Keller had been craving cake, she would not have started finger spelling out of the blue if Sullivan had not been "talking" to her constantly. They went for long walks during which Sullivan described in finger spelling everything that they encountered. These walks not only provided instructions in how to form sentences, they also provided a model of the desired behavior. Parents and teachers often must describe and demonstrate operant behaviors in order to get them started in children.

Increasing Restraints on Other Possible Behaviors. Sullivan was every bit as strong willed as Keller, but the child's parents eventually gave Keller her way if she misbehaved long enough. She would grab food from her parent's plate, throw her napkin on the floor, and kick the table until she got exactly what she wanted. Sullivan figured that her war over

This photograph shows a scene from the movie "The Miracle Worker," which is the story of Helen Keller and Anne Sullivan. Here Ann and Helen are engaged in one of their frequent early battles at the table. Once Helen learned that her tantrums were to no avail, she started to learn rapidly in response to positive reinforcement.

table manners was being drawn out because Keller had too many options and too many distractions. Sullivan therefore insisted that she be allowed to spend time alone with the girl in a nearby guest house. It was in this more controlled environment that Sullivan finally gained control over Keller. At first she "kicked and screamed herself into a sort of stupor" everytime she disagreed with a command (Lash, 1980, p. 51). But when Sullivan demanded a certain behavior she allowed Keller no other choice, even if it meant physically restraining her. One night they struggled for 2 hours before Keller finally stayed in bed. Eventually she realized that her tantrums were to no avail, and she started to learn rapidly in response to positive reinforcement.

Decreasing Restraints. Sullivan was strong-willed when she had to be, but she was a flexible person by nature. She disagreed with the rigid methods used to teach language to deaf children in schools. She believed that

> the schoolroom is not the place to teach any young child language, least of all the deaf child. He must be kept as unconscious as the hearing child of the fact that he is learning words, and he should be allowed to prattle on his fingers, or with his pencil, in monosyllables if he chooses, until such time as his growing intelligence demands the sentence. Language should not be associated in mind with endless hours in school, with puzzling questions in grammar, or with anything that is an enemy to joy. (Lash, 1980, pp. 201–202)

Once Keller learned basic obedience, Sullivan removed any restraints that might have stood in the way of learning. She did not require Keller to use complete sentences or proper grammar. At first she reinforced her for using single words to express sentences. For example, she praised Keller for using "milk" to express "Give me more milk." Later she reinforced her for using poorly constructed word strings. Once Keller was trying to express "Baby cannot eat because she has no teeth." Sullivan praised her for spelling "Baby teeth-no, baby eat-no." A school teacher might not have praised this poorly constructed word string. But by allowing Keller more freedom than deaf children generally had in schools, Sullivan started her student down a learning path that led to much greater ease with language than any deaf child had ever had before.

Shaping. Gradually, as Keller's language skill increased, Sullivan became more discriminating with her reinforcement. Looking back, we can see that she used a procedure that is now called **shaping**. That is, she reinforced each part of a behavior that eventually led to the whole behavior. She realized that the child had to go through intermediate steps before she would master the whole of forming sentences, so she shaped the whole by reinforcing the intermediate steps.

Skinner (1938) used shaping to teach a bird to walk in a figure eight. He first reinforced the bird for turning its head in the right direction. When the bird learned that, Skinner withheld reinforcement until the bird stepped in the right direction. Gradually, Skinner demanded more and more before he gave rewards. The pigeon had to take several steps in the right direction. Next, it had to do that and also make the appropriate turn. After doing those two things, the pigeon then had to take a few more steps. Skinner continued with this procedure until the bird was making a figure eight to get its reward.

Benji, a lovable dog who starred in several children's movies, learned his tricks with the help of shaping. In one episode, he climbed a stack of boxes, walked a narrow plank to a roof, climbed the roof, and finally jumped through an open window into a house. Benji's trainer taught the trick by first shaping the last feat of the series, jumping through the window. He then shaped the second to last part, using the window as a secondary reinforcer. That is, Benji had to run across the roof in order to get to the window, which had already been paired with a reward. Benji's trainer

kept working backwards through the steps. Soon Benji could perform the whole behavior chain to the delight of his young audience.

Loss of Operant Behaviors

So far, we have examined operant conditioning when it was being used to establish certain desired responses or behaviors. It can also establish undesirable behaviors. These must then be extinguished. Sullivan's war with Keller over manners was difficult, because the girl's obnoxious behavior had been firmly established by operant conditioning. Her father was the inadvertent trainer. He couldn't stand to see his daughter unhappy, so he gave her what she wanted. When she threw her napkin on the floor, he let her eat anyway. When she grabbed food from his plate, he let her have it. When she resisted going to bed, he let her stay up, and he gave her a little treat to quiet her down. Each time, he provided an immediate reward, thereby reinforcing her behavior. We can examine some of Sullivan's battles with Keller in more detail to learn general principles of wiping out or extinguishing operant behaviors.

Extinction. Operant behaviors are extinguished by withholding reinforcement. But they do not decrease immediately when reinforcement is withheld. In fact, they increase and become more forceful for a brief period after reinforcement stops. The first few times that Sullivan failed to reward Keller's tantrums, the girl unleashed fits of rage that lasted for up to 2 hours. Sullivan made sure that Keller received no rewards for such frenzies. Gradually the outbursts stopped.

Four factors affect how difficult it is to extinguish operant behaviors. Keller's behaviors made extinction difficult on all four counts:

1. The stronger the original learning, the harder it is to extinguish. Keller's tantrums had been stamped in by years of inadvertent, but effective, conditioning.
2. Behaviors are harder to extinguish when they are learned in a variety of settings. Keller's tantrums had worked for her at bedtime, mealtime,

and playtime. They had worked inside or outside the house, in public or in private. In fact, they had worked at any time and in any place.

3. Complex behaviors are more difficult to extinguish. Keller's tantrums consisted of many actions that had to be stopped. She cried, kicked, screamed, hit, scratched, and pinched. Each of these actions had to be extinguished.

4. Behaviors learned by partial reinforcement are harder to extinguish. Keller's father had unintentionally put her on a variable ratio schedule. Sometimes he rewarded her first action; sometimes he held out until she went through 10 or more actions. The girl learned not to expect a reward for every action. She learned to continue to respond until she eventually was rewarded. As a result, when Sullivan permanently withdrew rewards, Keller continued to respond for a long time.

With the deck stacked against her, Sullivan made no attempt to tiptoe around Keller's behavior. She rapidly issued one command after another, forcing the girl to comply each time. We can now see that Sullivan's instincts had taken her in the right direction again. Many experiments with animals have shown that extinction is easier when nonreinforced behaviors occur in rapid succession. Modern studies also show that responses are weaker and easier to extinguish in a new environment. Sullivan's move to the garden house was therefore another factor working in her favor.

Even though she was able to even the odds to some extent, she was not able to eliminate Keller's tantrums simply by withholding rewards. She was forced to use punishment.

Punishment.   A punishment is a stimulus that *decreases* the likelihood of a response when it is added to an environment. Spankings and scoldings are common punishments. Parents may be wise to use these when a dangerous behavior, such as running out into traffic, must be eliminated fast.

Skinner (1938) demonstrated the effectiveness of punishments in experiments on rats who had learned to press a bar for food. Bar pressing was extinguished when Skinner withheld food, but it was eliminated much faster when he shocked rats every time they pushed the bar. Again, notice that electric shock used as a punishment is quite different from electric shock used as a negative reinforcer. Punishments are imposed to eliminate responses; negative reinforcers are stopped to increase responses.

Sullivan used punishment wisely. Every time Keller hit her, she immediately slapped her hand. Studies with animals have shown that both immediacy and consistency are important. Animal studies have also shown that punishments are much more effective when they are not accompanied by rewards. Sullivan's instincts served her well with respect to this variable also. She never followed punishments with rewards. Some parents make the mistake of hugging and kissing their children immediately after a spanking. Sullivan was wise enough to avoid such mixed messages.

Thanks to her superior teaching skills, Sullivan was able to punish Keller without terrifying her. Less skilled teachers disrupt learning by frightening children with punishment. The key to Sullivan's success was her ability to provide Keller with acceptable, alternative behaviors. Keller soon learned that her teacher was as quick to reward her good behaviors as she was to punish her bad ones. Sullivan's unfailing responsiveness to Keller paid off in extremely rapid learning. Less than 2 weeks elapsed between Keller's 2-hour tantrum at bedtime and her finger spelling breakthrough at the pump house.

Spontaneous Recovery.   Keller moved back to the main house shortly after she started to learn names. She explored everything around her with such enthusiasm that she seemed to have no time for tantrums. One might have thought that they were extinguished for good. But when dinnertime came, she refused to use her napkin and threw it to the floor. This mild outburst was an example of *spontaneous recovery*. It occurs in animals as well as humans. Skinner extinguished bar pressing responses in rats and then he tested them again after a delay. The rats pressed the bar again with no retraining.

The spontaneous recovery of Keller's tantrums did not last long. For the most part, she left her spoiled behavior in her "prison-house." With keys provided by her teacher, she emerged from her prison of isolation a new person eager to explore every facet of her new-found world.

Implications for Parents and Teachers. Let's review what we have just discussed by looking at the implications for parents and teachers of the following operant conditioning principles:

1. *Avoid reinforcing undesirable behaviors*. Few parents reward tantrums to the extent that Mr. Keller did, but some parents inadvertently condition tantrums in public. Parents who would not dream of giving in to a tantrum at home do so in public to avoid an embarrassing scene. Such parents are soon asking why their child is an angel at home and a devil in public. The best way to avoid this Jekyll-and-Hyde behavior is to ignore or punish public tantrums right from the start. One or two uncomfortable situations in the beginning will avoid many more later on.

2. *Immediately reward desirable behaviors*. Children love attention, so a smile or a hug is often reward enough. Sullivan used lots of this kind of attention to reinforce her student. In the same way, alert parents can direct most of their attention toward positive reinforcers, which greatly reduce the need for punishment.

3. *Supplement punishments with rewards of desirable responses*. Never reward and punish the *same* behavior by giving hugs and kisses immediately after a punishment, but do watch for good behaviors to reward. If Sullivan had not rewarded good behaviors, her punishments might have terrified Keller. In the same way, children may become too afraid to learn if teachers do not praise correct responses as often as they criticize wrong ones. Today, teachers' manuals include these and other principles of operant conditioning. As a result, formal applications of operant principles have found their way into the classroom.

Generalization

About 1½ months after Keller started to learn names, she demonstrated an interesting example of **stimulus generalization,** which means giving the same response to similar stimuli. One day, shortly after learning to call her little sister "baby," she ran up to Sullivan and spelled "dog-baby" over and over. She also pointed to her five fingers one after another and she sucked them. Sullivan's first thought was that a dog had bitten Keller's sister, but the girl seemed too delighted to be carrying bad news. Sullivan followed Keller to the pump-house where she found that the Keller's setter had given birth to five adorable puppies. Helen had generalized the response "baby" to include the puppies. Sullivan taught Keller the word "puppies," which she used correctly after that. Stimulus generalization is common in children and Keller's example is typical.

Children also demonstrate **response generalization,** which is giving different, but similar, responses to the same stimulus. A child who is reinforced for saying "bye-bye" may also say "gye-gye" "or pye-pye." Parents can eliminate such inappropriate response generalizations by reinforcing only the correct responses.

Discrimination

The opposite of stimulus generalization is **stimulus discrimination,** which means making different responses to different stimuli. Keller demonstrated discrimination when she gave the response "baby" to her sister and the response "puppies" to her new pets.

You are discriminating whenever you stop for a red traffic light and go for a green one. Skinner (1938) showed that even pigeons can learn simple red-green discriminations. He taught pigeons to peck at a white disc and then he presented two discs, one red and one green. He gave food every time the pigeon pecked the green disc, and he gave nothing when the pigeon pecked the red one. Soon the pigeon pecked only the green disc. Skinner's procedure is valuable for parents to remember. When children first learn the word "mama" they often apply it to all women. Mothers can teach the appropriate discrimination by ignoring incorrect applications and by reinforcing the correct one.

In a recent book on animal cognition (Roitblat, Bover, & Terrance, 1984), evidence was reviewed that pigeons can also make much more difficult

APPLYING OPERANT CONDITIONING

One specific application of operant conditioning is a **token economy,** in which children are given play money or plastic chips for good performance. Once a week or so, children turn in their tokens for candy and other primary reinforcers. Token economies are effective at producing short-term changes in behavior. They provide immediate rewards and children learn quickly what is expected of them. Once initial learning is established, however, teachers must substitute rewards that spring from the learning situation itself. The reward for learning how to read new words, for example, might be the ability to read something enjoyable. Children who read to get tokens may stop reading when the tokens stop. But children who enjoy what they read will continue to read even when they get no tokens. Token economies for adults will be discussed in Chapter 14.

Another classroom application of operant conditioning is *programmed instruction*, which is a set of materials specially arranged to be easily mastered. B. F. Skinner used operant principles to produce programmed instruction sequences in the 1950s. The program leads

students to make correct responses and then immediately reinforces those responses. Such programs are often presented in *programmed textbooks*, which present one frame at a time. A frame contains a statement and a fill-in-the-blank question. Answers to the questions are in the margin. Students cover the answers with a slider, answer a question, and then move the slider down to uncover the correct answer and next frame. Skinner also developed *teaching machines* to

present his programs. Students turn a knob to expose a frame, write their answer, and then turn the knob again to expose the correct answer and the next frame.

Modern technology is replacing Skinner's teaching machines with *computerized interactive display systems*. The photo here shows a system that presents an instructional program on a TV screen. Students respond by operating a typewriter keyboard or by touching an electronic pencil to a screen. A large

discriminations. We will delay our discussion of that evidence, however, until we introduce basic concepts of cognitive learning in the next section.

SOCIAL LEARNING THEORY

Conditioning theories are limited to learning by experience. Nobody would deny the importance of their own experiences, but people do not learn everything that way. In fact, learning by experience is sometimes called learning the hard way. Keller learned the hard way, for example, that her temper tantrums were to no avail in the garden house. Often, instead of learning directly through experience, however, it is much easier to learn indirectly, by observing others. Children learn many things by imitating their parents, for instance, and Keller learned many things by imitating Sullivan. Albert Bandura (1962, 1977) proposed social learning theory to account for such learning. Chapter 12 presents social learning theory

computer can teach several hundred topics at once to several thousand students, each of whom learn at their own pace. Skinner's teaching machines were limited to *linear programs*, which move students through the same sequence of frames no matter how they answer questions. Computers, on the other hand, teach with *branching programs*, which give students different frames depending on their answers. Computerized systems give remedial lessons to students who are doing poorly, or they give advanced lessons to students who are doing well. Armed with branching programs, computers provide students with learning tasks that are adjusted to individual interests and abilities.

Earlier in this book (Chapter 4) we discussed Dr. Benson's *relaxation response*, which may be the most important application of operant conditioning research for college students. Dr. Benson's procedure has helped many students cope with the stresses of college life (Benson, 1975). Although Benson's procedure resembles techniques that have been used in Eastern cultures for centuries, it found its way into Western culture through

operant conditioning laboratories.

In earlier discussions of our autonomic nervous system (Chapter 2), we learned that our bodies automatically prepare for emergencies by means of a fight-or-flight response. Our heart rate and breathing rate increase along with other changes, giving us more energy to meet emergencies. The relaxation response works in the opposite direction, allowing our bodies to relax after we are out of danger. A problem is that fight-or-flight responses often occur when people are in no real danger, as when they panic before an exam. The repeated occurrence of such inappropriate responses leads to high blood pressure and heart damage. Benson showed that we can avoid this unnecessary wear and tear on our bodies by learning to control relaxation responses.

Benson based his work on the operant conditioning research of Miller and DiCara (1967) and others (e.g., Schwartz, 1975). Miller and DiCara reinforced rats whenever they spontaneously decreased their heart rates. Soon the rats learned how to decrease their heart rate voluntarily. Other rats learned how to increase their heart rate when

they were reinforced for doing so. Schwartz showed that humans can also learn to control heart rate voluntarily. Schwartz flashed a light and played a tone at every heartbeat to give subjects immediate information about their heart rate. Such immediate information about biological responses is called *biofeedback*. Schwartz rewarded subjects for either increasing or decreasing the light and tone on/off rate, and his subjects learned to control their heartbeat accordingly. Schwartz also reviewed other biofeedback experiments in which people learned to control skin temperature, blood pressure, electrical activity of the brain, and muscle tension. We will discuss the uses of biofeedback again in Chapter 14, Therapy.

Benson carried this line of research forward another step by showing that we can learn to relax at will without the aid of flashing lights or beeping tones. Scientists have a long way to go in explaining the psychobiological mechanisms that underlie self-regulation. In the meantime, we can all enjoy a more relaxed life thanks to this important application of basic research on operant conditioning.

in detail, so we will not discuss it further here. We will return instead to our consideration of various kinds of direct learning.

COGNITIVE LEARNING THEORY

Conditioning and extinction result in learning by gradually strengthening and weakening responses. But we often learn things suddenly and irreversibly. Keller's learning experiences provide many examples. We have already considered her sudden understanding of finger spelling. Another example happened one day when Sullivan saw Keller trying to correct an error that she had made while trying to string beads. Noticing her concentration, Sullivan spelled "t-h-i-n-k" on Keller's forehead. In a flash, Keller realized that the word was the name of the process that was going on in her head. Her insight came suddenly, on Sullivan's first attempt to teach this abstract concept, and Keller never forgot what she learned in that moment.

Conditioning theories try to explain learning without taking into account unobservable mental processes. Yet, as Keller's insights reveal, unobservable thought processes often play an important role in learning. We therefore need to supplement conditioning theories with a theory about thought processes. **Cognitive learning theory** fills the bill. It attempts to explain the function of thought processes in learning. As mentioned in Chapter 1, cognitive theories did not become a dominant force in psychology until the 1960s. But its roots go back much farther than that. Consider, for example, the early work on insights.

Insight

Wolfgang Köhler (1925), a founder of Gestalt psychology, was among the first to demonstrate the importance of insight in problem solving. An **insight** is the discovery of relationships that leads to the solution of a problem. In Köhler's experiments, chimpanzees had to solve the problem of getting bananas that were hung out of reach of the chimps. The relationship between three boxes that were also in the room was essential to the problem's solution. No one box was high enough, but all three together allowed the chimp to climb up and reach the bananas (Figure 6–8).

In another experiment the bananas were placed out of reach outside the chimp's cage. In this case it was the relationship between two sticks that formed the solution. One stick, inside the cage, was too short to reach the bananas, but it was long enough to reach a second stick outside the cage, which in turn was long enough to reach the bananas. Köhler described the behavior of one of his chimps, Sultan, in this situation:

> Sultan tries to reach the fruit with the smaller of the two sticks. Not succeeding, he tears at a piece of wire that projects from the netting of his cage, but that, too, is in vain. Then he gazes about him (there are always in the course of these tests some long pauses, during which the animals scrutinize the whole visible area). He suddenly picks up the little stick once more, goes up to the bars directly opposite to the long stick, scratches it towards him with the "auxiliary," seizes it, and goes with it to the point opposite the objective (the fruit), which he secures. From the moment that his eyes fall upon the long stick, his procedure forms one consecutive whole. . . ." (pp. 174–175)

Köhler set the two-stick problem up again after that and Sultan solved it immediately.

Unlike Thorndike's cats, who *gradually*, through trial and error, learned to solve the puzzle-box problem, Köhler's chimpanzees suddenly learned how to solve the two-stick problem all at once and irreversibly. Köhler

Figure 6–8
In one insight experiment, a chimp had to pile three boxes on top of one another in order to reach some bananas that were hung out of reach from the ceiling.

explained that his chimpanzees had learned by insight, and that Thorndike's cats were denied the possibility of doing so. Köhler's chimps saw the relationship between the sticks, and once they did, the insight guided their behavior. Thorndike's cats could not see the relationship between the string and the door to their puzzle box, because the relationship was complex and hidden. Without the benefit of insight, the cats slowly decreased the time needed to solve their problem through many attempts. With the benefit of insight, the chimps learned to solve their problem quickly, without hesitation, time after time. The same thing happened with Keller. Once she understood what finger spelling meant, she never looked back—it was an instantaneous and irreversible insight.

Insights are common in human learning. We have all experienced the sudden emergence of solutions after the pieces of a problem fall into place in our minds. Such moments of insight are so pleasurable that they are often accompanied by an "Aha!" Cognitive psychologists consequently refer to human insights as "aha" experiences.

Latent Learning and Cognitive Maps

While cognitive psychologists have made their major contributions in analyses of complex human behaviors, such as learning to speak sentences (Chapter 8) and learning from textbooks (Chapter 7), the cognitive approach is not limited to human behaviors. In fact, animal learning experiments laid the basic foundation for cognitive psychology.

Edward C. Tolman and his associates led the way in showing the importance of cognitive factors in animal learning. Figure 6–9 illustrates the apparatus that Tolman used in a classic experiment on the role of cognitive structures in animal learning (Tolman & Honzik, 1930). He placed a hungry rat in a start box and the rat had to find its way through a maze to an end box. He recorded an error every time the rat entered a blind alley in the maze. Tolman and Honzik ran three groups of rats in their experiment.

1. Group 1 ran the maze only to find an empty end box day after day for 16 days. They made about nine errors on the first day and reduced that only slightly to about seven errors by the sixteenth day.

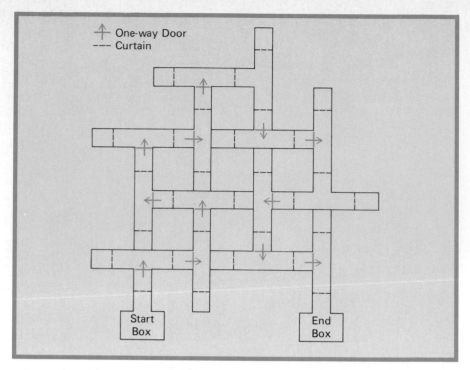

2. Group 2 ran the maze and ate food that was provided in the end box each day for 16 days. They also made about nine errors on the first day, but they greatly reduced errors to about two per day by the sixteenth day.

3. Group 3 started out like Group 1. They received no food reward for the first 10 days. Then they were treated like Group 2 rats, with food provided in the end box, for the last 6 days. They started with about ten errors per day and reduced that only slightly to about seven errors by the tenth day. Tolman and Honzik observed their critical result on the twelfth day. The number of errors dropped sharply to about two and stayed at that level until the end of the experiment. A single reinforcement on day 11 had a powerful effect. It reduced errors to about the same number that were made by rats in Group 2, who had been reinforced every day.

Tolman and Honzik argued that conditioning theories could not explain their results. Conditioning theories hold that performance errors indicate learning strength, and that learning strength increases gradually with reinforcement. Accordingly, learning strength was very low after rats in Groups 1 and 3 ran a maze for 10 days without reinforcement. In other words, their performance suggested that rats in Groups 1 and 3 had *not* learned their way around the maze after 10 days. If that's true, why did Group 3 rats do so well on the twelfth day after receiving only a single reinforcement? Operant conditioning theory provides no satisfactory answer. Tolman and Honzik therefore broke ranks with operant conditioning theorists.

Tolman and Honzik proposed that performance does not necessarily reflect learning strength. As mentioned earlier, they introduced the term **latent learning** to refer to learning that does not show itself immediately in performance. While latent learning makes an important distinction between learning and performance, it leaves open a question: What *is* learned, if it is not *observable* responses? Tolman and Honzik answered this question with the proposal that cognitive structures are learned. Specifically, they suggested that Group 3 rats had learned a **cognitive map,** or mental picture, of the maze. When the rats found food in the end box on the eleventh day, they used their cognitive maps to run the maze almost without error on the twelfth day.

Tolman and Honzik's experiment suggested a need for psychologists to turn away from conditioning theories and toward cognitive learning theories. The proposal of cognitive maps was out of step with conditioning theories not only because cognitive maps are unobservable mental events, but also because they are learned without reinforcement. But psychologists were slow to give up what they hoped would be a general learning theory. Almost 3 decades passed before a significant number of psychologists broke ranks with operant conditioning theory and turned toward cognitive learning theory. Today, cognitive maps make good sense to cognitive psychologists, who assume that we constantly explore and store information about our world. In fact, modern psychologists have even made progress exploring the neural changes that underlie cognitive maps (Chapter 2).

Learning Sets

Sullivan taught Keller at home, which may have made it easier for her to compare the girl's learning to that of other children who learn language at home. Most teachers of deaf children work in school, where it is natural to compare deaf children with other school children. Cognitive psychologists would say that the different experiences may cause different **mental sets.** A mental set is a readiness to view a problem in a particular way—a readiness to see certain relationships. Research shows that past experience affects readiness to solve problems (Harlow, 1949). Harlow gave monkeys the problem of finding food under one of two covers, a square one and a round one. He always placed food under the square cover, and the monkeys gradually learned to look under the square cover whether it was on the right or left side. Harlow then did his critical manipulation. He changed to different covers, such as a red triangle and a green triangle. The monkeys again learned that food was always under one of the covers, but this time they learned faster. After solving hundreds of problems with different covers, the monkeys learned to solve them in one trial. They looked under one cover; if food was there they kept looking under that cover, never bothering to lift the other one. If food was not under the first cover, they looked under the other one on the next trial, and then they stayed with that one. The monkeys had established a mental set, or what Harlow called a **learning set.** Their previous experience made them ready to solve a particular kind of problem.

Sometimes a mental set puts us on the wrong track. When it does, it is called a **negative set,** which is one that reduces our chance of learning a new relationship. Luchin's water jar problem is an example. Table 6–1 illustrates the problem. To solve the problems, you first fill a jar that contains more than the required amount. You then empty the excess using

Table 6–1
Luchins's Water Jar Problems

How do you measure out the right amount of water using any or all Jars A, B, and C?

Problem Number	Jars Available for Use			Required Amount
	A	B	C	
1	27	3	2	2
2	21	127	3	100
3	14	163	25	110
4	18	43	10	5
5	9	42	6	21
6	20	59	4	31
7	23	49	3	20
8	15	39	3	18
9	28	76	3	25

Source: Luchins (1942).

Figure 6-10

Luchins conducted an experiment in which subjects were asked to measure water using any or all of three jars. All of the first problems could be solved by filling the largest jar and then pouring from that jar into the smaller ones as indicated in the upper drawing. The water remaining in the largest jar was the correct amount. This solution also worked for later problems but so did the simpler solution indicated in the lower drawings. The discovery of the simple solution was greatly delayed for people who had experience with the other solution.

smaller jars to measure the amount you need to dump. The first five problems have four steps:

1. Fill the largest jar
2. Fill the next largest jar with water from the largest jar
3. Fill the smallest jar with water from the largest jar
4. Fill the smallest jar again with water from the largest jar

The water remaining in the large jar is the required amount.

The next two problems can be solved in the same way or they can be solved much more easily with two steps:

1. Fill the second largest jar
2. Fill the smallest jar with water from the second largest jar

The water remaining in the second largest jar is the required amount. This simple two-step solution is the only one that works for the last problem (Figure 6-10).

We would solve the last three problems easily if we had not worked on the others. We would have trouble, however, if we had worked on the first five. People who solve the first five problems tend to use the harder four-step solution on the next two problems and they get stuck on the last one. The first five problems establish a negative set that blinds them to the simple solution for the last three problems.

Dunker (1945), a latter-day Gestalt psychologist, looked into a fascinating kind of negative set called **functional fixedness.** This form of mental set reduces our ability to learn new uses of something that has served a specific function in the past. One researcher set up a problem that is useful in demonstrating functional fixedness (Maier, 1931). The problem is to tie together two strings that hang from a ceiling. When the strings hang straight down, you cannot reach both of them at the same time. When you grab one and walk toward the other, you still cannot reach both at once. Can you think of solution? (*Hint*: there are tools in the room such as pliers, a screw driver, and a hammer.) The solution is to tie a tool to one of the strings and swing it. Grab the other string and walk as close as possible to the swinging string. When it swings toward you, grab it and tie the two strings together. If this problem were actually set up for you, you would have a harder time solving it if an experimenter had you build something with the tools first. Your experience with tools in their normal function reduces your chance of seeing them as weights. Figure 6-11 gives you a chance to try other problems that have been used to study mental sets.

Teachers at schools for deaf children may have been victims of functional fixedness. They had always used schools to teach language in a certain way. Their past experience with language lessons in school always involved drills on vocabulary and grammar. Their experience with a school's usual function reduced their chance of seeing schools as a place where children could be stimulated to acquire language naturally. Sullivan's first teaching job was in the Keller home. Ironically, Sullivan's lack of teaching experience may have contributed to her teaching effectiveness with Keller.

Preparedness

In our previous examples, cats learned to brush up against a string, rats learned to press bars, pigeons learned to peck, and children learned names. Does it matter which animals learn which responses? Traditional theorists would have said that operant conditioning can link any stimulus with any response, and that will hold true for all animals. Modern theorists say that **preparedness** is also involved here—that animals are more pre-

Figure 6-11
Typical problems used to study problem-solving behavior.

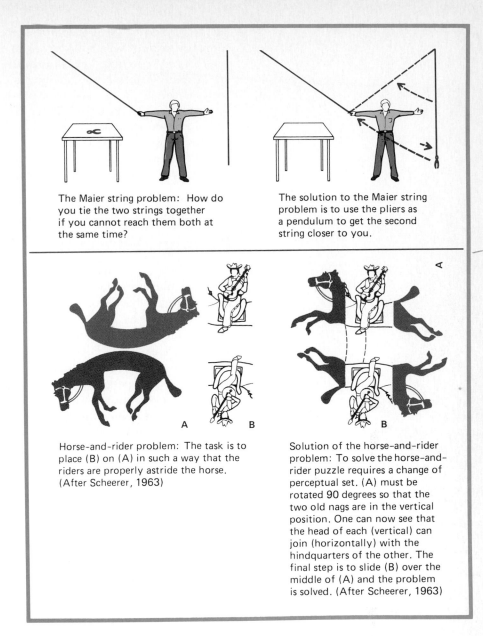

The Maier string problem: How do you tie the two strings together if you cannot reach them both at the same time?

The solution to the Maier string problem is to use the pliers as a pendulum to get the second string closer to you.

Horse-and-rider problem: The task is to place (B) on (A) in such a way that the riders are properly astride the horse. (After Scheerer, 1963)

Solution of the horse-and-rider problem: To solve the horse-and-rider puzzle requires a change of perceptual set. (A) must be rotated 90 degrees so that the two old nags are in the vertical position. One can now see that the head of each (vertical) can join (horizontally) with the hindquarters of the other. The final step is to slide (B) over the middle of (A) and the problem is solved. (After Scheerer, 1963)

pared to make certain responses than others, and may find other responses more difficult to make (Timberlake, Wahl, & King, 1982).

Evidence favors preparedness. Rats learn to jump to avoid foot shocks faster than they learn to press a bar to avoid the same stimulus. This may be because rats are biologically prepared to jump when they are frightened. Pigeons learn to peck a disc for food faster than rats learn to press a bar for food. One might argue that pigeons are smarter. But this explanation seems ruled out by another fact. It takes pigeons longer to learn *not* to peck than it takes rats to learn *not* to press a bar. Apparently, pigeons are more biologically prepared to peck for food than rats are prepared to press a bar for food. These and other results support the theory of preparedness (Wickelgren, 1977).

Preparedness also applies to humans. We are, of course, prepared to learn speech and other behaviors that animals never learn. We are also prepared to learn different things at different times in our lives, as we will discuss in Chapter 8. Sullivan noticed, for instance, that at 15 months Keller's baby cousin could obey verbal commands such as "Go to papa," "Shut the door," and "Give me the biscuit." At the same time, the baby was not producing sentences. When she gave a command of her own, she combined single words and gestures. "Go" with a gesture meant "I want to go outside." Sullivan assumed that Keller would also be able to understand sentences long before she could produce them. Therefore she spent many hours a day spelling complete sentences into Keller's hand without requiring the girl to reproduce them. In this way, Sullivan took advantage of the fact that Keller could understand sentences before she was prepared to produce them. Today the investigation of differences in preparedness as a function of age is part of an active area of research called cognitive development. We will review this topic in Chapter 8 when we compare changes in cognitive capabilities with other aspects of development.

Concept Formation

A concept is a mental grouping of objects (such as minerals), events (such as playing), states (such as cold), or ideas (such as justice). Such groupings are based on similarity. We seem to have a natural ability to form concepts by grouping similar things together into categories. The study of this ability is another line of research that has led toward a cognitive learning theory.

Theories of conditioning have been applied to concept formation. Conditioning theorists suggest that concepts are gradually learned on the basis of repeated encounters with instances of the concept. They focus on three aspects of these encounters. First, certain responses identify concepts. For instance, the response "square" identifies the concept of a plane figure having four equal sides and four right angles. Second, all positive instances of a concept have common elements. All squares, for example, have four equal sides and four right angles. Third, responses to the positive instances are reinforced and responses to the negative ones are not. In other words, the response "square" is reinforced when it is correctly used to identify actual squares and is not reinforced when it is wrongly used to identify other figures. As a result, the responses that identify the concept become conditioned to the common element (Bourne & Restle, 1959).

Jerome Bruner and his colleagues proposed an alternative to conditioning theories (Bruner, Goodnow, & Austin, 1956). Their alternative has been called a cognitive learning theory because it focuses on mental strategies that people use to form concepts. Accordingly, when people encounter instances of a concept, they form a *best guess*, or hypothesis, about what the concept might be. On later encounters they test this hypothesis and form a new one if it is wrong. Evidence favors the cognitive learning theory.

Figure 6–12 illustrates the type of material and concepts used in early investigations of concepts. The dimensions in the stimulus set are size, color, and shape. The values in these dimensions are large or small, blue or red, and square or circle. Six concepts are possible in a single attribute identification task. They are large forms, small forms, blue forms, red forms, square forms, and circular forms. Each concept would have four positive instances and four negative instances, as illustrated in Figure 6–12.

In a typical experiment you would be told the names of stimulus dimensions (size, color, shape) and the attribute values (large/small, blue/red, square/circular) of those dimensions. You would then be shown one of the eight forms for each concept, and you would be asked if it was a positive instance of the correct concept. After you responded "yes" or "no" the experimenter would tell you if you were right or wrong. This procedure would continue until you could verbalize the concept or until you reached some criterion of consecutive correct response.

Figure 6–12 shows a hypothetical sequence of trials. In this sequence, you are shown a large, red circle on the first trial. You hypothesize that

Figure 6–12
The concept of a concept formation experiment can seem quite difficult until you work through a simple concrete example. Try it.

MATERIALS

Dimensions	Attribute Values							
Size	Large				Small			
Color	Blue		Red		Blue		Red	
Shape	Square	Circle	Square	Circle	Square	Circle	Square	Circle
Stimulus Cards	■	●	■	●	■	●	■	●

CONCEPTS

Possible concepts in single attribute identification	Positive incidents of the concept	Negative incidents of the concept
Large Forms	■ ● ■ ●	■ ● ■ ●
Small Forms	■ ● ■ ●	■ ● ■ ●
Blue Forms	■ ● ■ ●	■ ● ■ ●
Red Forms	■ ● ■ ●	■ ● ■ ●
Square Forms	■ ■ ■ ■	● ● ● ●
Circular Forms	● ● ● ●	■ ■ ■ ■

HYPOTHETICAL SEQUENCE OF TRIALS

Trial number	Form presented	Hypothesis	Subject response	Feedback
1	●	Circle	yes	wrong
2	■	Square	yes	right
3	●	"	no	right
4	■	"	yes	right
5	■	"	yes	wrong
6	●	Blue	yes	right
7	■	"	no	right
8	●	"	yes	right

the concept might be a circle so you say "yes." The experimenter informs you that you are wrong. You therefore shift your hypothesis. This time you try square as your best guess. Since the large, blue square on the second trial fits this hypothesis, you say "yes." The experimenter indicates that you are correct so you stay with your hypothesis. You also stay with it on trials 3 and 4 because you are correct. However, your hypothesis of square forms leads to a mistake on trial 5, so you shift to a new hypothesis—blue forms. This hypothesis leads to correct responses on the next three trials and you decide that blue forms is the correct concept.

This hypothetical experiment is simplified, but it does illustrate a strategy that people use in actual experiments with more dimensions and more attribute values. That is, people generate hypotheses and they follow a "win-stay, lose-shift" strategy. As long as a hypothesis generates correct responses, they stay with it. As soon as the hypothesis leads to an incorrect response they shift to a new hypothesis (Bower & Trabasso, 1964; Levine, 1975; Restle, 1962).

Many cognitive psychologists who study categorization have focused on data from human subjects (Rosch & Loyd, 1978; Smith & Medin, 1981). There is, however, a growing interest in animal cognition (Roitblat et al., 1984). Many studies have shown that animals can categorize simple geometric forms and more complicated stimuli (Herrnstein, 1984). In one experiment, pigeons showed evidence of making a discrimination when they pecked for food more often for one group of slides as compared to another (Herrnstein, 1979).

Similar studies show that pigeons can make other interesting discriminations. They can discriminate:

1. Fish from other sea creatures such as turtles (Herrnstein & de Villiers, 1980)

ARE HUMAN LANGUAGE ABILITIES UNIQUE?

We can raise two questions about the uniqueness of human language: (1) Do any naturally occurring nonhuman communication systems have the properties of human language?, and (2) Can scientists teach human language to nonhuman animals? Let's take up each of these questions in turn.

Nonhuman animals communicate in nature. But even the more complex communication systems are simple in comparison to human language. Honey bees do a dance, for example, to tell other bees in the hive the distance and direction of nectar that they have just found (von Frisch, 1974). Their dance is quite involved, but it lacks important properties of human language. Humans use relatively few symbols to express endless ideas. How do humans get so much meaning from so few symbols? A key is a powerful grammar, which is a set of rules for combining symbols. For instance, all human languages have word order rules. They can be used to

change meaning (for example, The Dodgers beat the Yankees, versus The Yankees beat the Dodgers). Honey bees have symbols, but they can only be used to indicate the direction and distance of nectar. They do not have a powerful grammar. As a result, their use of symbols is limited. They cannot, for instance, vary symbol order to change meaning. Thus, human language is superior to the honey bee dance. In fact, human language has properties that set it above all other animal communication systems found in nature so far. The answer to the first question is, therefore, "no." Naturally occurring nonhuman communication systems do not have the powerful properties of human language.

What about the second question? Can scientists teach human language to animals? Early attempts clearly failed. For example, Keith Hayes and Cathy Hayes (1951) tried, without success, to teach a chimpanzee to speak English. The

results of later attempts are far more interesting.

Researchers suggested that chimps might lack human vocal abilities without lacking human language abilities (Gardner & Gardner, 1975). To test their idea, they tried to teach a chimp, Washoe, the American Sign Language, which is a human language used by many deaf people. It is based on hand gestures, which Washoe was able to learn. Once she learned the gestures, Washoe used them in a way that resembled human language. She answered questions with simple statements like "Me Washoe." She made requests such as "Gimme flowers," and she commented on her feelings ("Washoe sorry").

Other scientists have achieved similar results with chimps. In one project, Ann Premack and David Premack (1972) taught Sarah, a female chimp, to read and write using plastic symbols. Other researchers taught Lana, another female chimp, to read and write on a special plastic keyboard (Rumbaugh, 1977).

2. White oak leaves from other tree leaves (Cerella, 1979)
3. Charlie Brown from other Peanuts characters (Cerella, 1982)
4. The letter "A" from the numeral "2," each one being presented in many different type faces (Blough, 1982; Morgan, Fitch, Holman, & Lea, 1976).

A challenge for future research will be to understand the processes underlying concept formation in pigeons (Cerella, 1982).

Despite these impressive performances by pigeons, the real stars of animal cognition are chimpanzees and other higher primates. In fact, classification by chimps has been so outstanding that it has sparked a debate about whether or not chimpanzees and other primates are capable of language (see Highlight: Are Human Language Abilities Unique?). We will now turn our attention away from these differences between species and toward differences within the human species.

INTELLIGENCE: THE CAPACITY TO LEARN

Up until now we have been considering general principles of learning. Now we will consider individual differences in **intelligence,** which may be defined as the capacity to learn. People differ widely in intelligence.

More recently, gorillas have gotten into the act. Francine Patterson (1978) taught Koko, a female gorilla, to use a sign language based on hand gestures. Koko now seems to construct original sentences. For instance, one day she broke a sink by jumping on it. When asked about it, she seemed to blame the damage on a researcher (Kate). She signed, ''Kate there bad.''

What do the chimp and gorilla results say about our second question? Can scientists teach human language to nonhuman animals? The results suggest a qualified ''yes.'' The qualification is that chimps and gorillas can learn only *parts* of human language; they can learn words, but they may not be able to generate sentences by combining those words in different ways, a basic property of human language (Limber, 1977; Terrace et al., 1979). The present results, therefore, provide only a partial answer. They also raise new questions: Are the language skills of specially trained animals too undeveloped to qualify as ''human language''? If they are, will they remain so? Research aimed at these questions will give us not only a better understanding of animals, but also a better understanding of ourselves.

The Gardners taught their chimp Washoe to use American sign Language. Washoe is shown here using two of the over 30 different signs she eventually learned.

At one extreme are people who are totally dependent on others for basic care. At the other extreme are people who are highly successful in college and in professional careers. They seem able to learn whatever society can teach, and they usually add to what society can offer. Most of us fall between the extremes, but it is difficult to pinpoint just where.

The task of specifying the capacity to learn would be relatively easy if we all had an equal opportunity to learn. Differences in accomplishments would then directly reflect differences in capacity. Unfortunately, people do differ in their opportunities to learn. As a result, different achievements can indicate either different capacities or different opportunities. And to make matters worse, opportunities themselves are hard to evaluate. Take Helen Keller, for example. Her accomplishments were outstanding indeed. But does that mean that she had an outstanding *capacity* to learn or an outstanding *opportunity* to learn? Surely her opportunity was reduced by her blindness and deafness, but just as surely it was increased by the constant attention of a highly responsive and insightful teacher, Anne Sullivan. Keller would not have graduated from college if she had not had a high capacity to learn. But, how high was it compared to other deaf and blind people who did not have the advantage of Sullivan's wise tutorship? How high was it compared to all other college graduates? Such questions may never be answered, because it is so difficult to evaluate Keller's opportunity to learn. In general, whenever it is difficult to compare opportunities to learn, it is difficult to compare intelligence.

Psychologists formally recognize the problem of different opportunities by distinguishing between two kinds of tests: (1) **achievement tests,** which are designed to measure a person's current knowledge and skills, and (2) **aptitude tests,** which try to predict capacity for future performance. Some achievement tests are **standardized**; that is, they have been given to many people so that one person's score can be evaluated with respect to a large population. Many achievement tests are not standardized, however. Examples are the tests and quizzes used in most college courses. They enable teachers to evaluate a class, but they do not enable comparisons with a general population.

Most aptitude tests are standardized. You may take standardized aptitude tests on many specific skills, including artistic, musical, mechanical, physical, foreign language, and mathematical skills. Your score in each case would be compared with those of people who are successful in that specific area. You may also take standardized aptitude tests to measure a broad range of aptitudes. An example is the General Aptitude Test Battery (GATB), which measures 10 aptitudes, including verbal, numerical, clerical, and motor speed. Finally, you may take, and probably have taken, intelligence tests, which are broad-range aptitude tests that are designed to predict capacity for future school performance. Let's look at the history of intelligence tests.

The History of Intelligence Testing

Sir Francis Galton developed the first intelligence tests. He administered them to 9,000 people in London in 1884, 4 years after Helen Keller was born. Many of his tests were invalid, since they did not do what they were designed to do. Specifically, they did not distinguish eminent British scientists from ordinary citizens on the basis of their intelligence. In 1905, Alfred Binet, a French psychologist, published the first useful intelligence test. He based his test on the idea that mental ability increases with age. He tested many children on mentally demanding tasks, recording each child's **chronological age** (the age in years and months) and then defining **mental age** as the average performance of children at a specific chronological age. A mental age of 10, for example, is the *average* performance of 10-year-olds. He converted each child's performance score into a mental age. Average children received a mental age that was the same as their chronological age. Below-average children received lower mental ages, and above-average children received higher mental ages. Binet recommended that children should get special educational attention when their mental age was 2 years below their chronological age.

Lewis Terman introduced in the United States in 1916 a modified version of Binet's test under the name of the Stanford-Binet test. Terman also popularized the concept of **intelligence quotient,** or **IQ,** which is determined by a formula that divides mental age by chronological age and then multiplies the resulting sum by 100. For example, a child with a mental age of 12 and a chronological age of 10 would have an IQ of 120:

$$IQ = \frac{\text{Mental Age}}{\text{Chronological Age}} \times 100 = \frac{12}{10} \times 100 = 120$$

Binet assumed that his test measured general intelligence, which he defined as the ability to judge, to comprehend, and to reason. Charles Spearman (1927) also argued that intelligence test items measure general mental capacity, which he called *g*. But he said that test items also measure some specific ability, *s*, although these specific influences cancel out when many items are combined. Later on, Louis Thurstone (1946) concluded that intelligence test items measure seven independent factors. The seven were: verbal comprehension, word fluency, number, space, memory, perceptual

Tests of intelligence quotient, or IQ, are used to predict school performance.

speed, and reasoning. J. P. Guilford (1967) stated more recently that intelligence includes at least 120 separate abilities. Despite these efforts to identify separate mental skills, however, the most popular tests remain those that yield a general IQ score. Such tests predict school performance as well or better than tests yielding multiple scores. See Table 6–2 for sample questions from modern IQ tests.

IQ and Age

Binet introduced the concept of mental age because his research showed that mental abilities increase with age. His investigations were limited to children, however. Modern researchers are only beginning to understand what happens to intelligence in adulthood and old age. Early studies used *cross-sectional* designs that measured different people at different ages; for example, one group at age 15, another at age 30, another at age 60, etc. (Jones & Conrad, 1933). These studies were contaminated by the fact that different age groups had different educational experiences, and thus researchers could not say whether differences between groups were due to differences in age or to differences in education. Later studies used *longitudinal* designs, which measured the same people as they grew older. Overall IQ scores showed gain to age 32, little or no change until age 60, and significant decline thereafter. The decline after age 60 did not include declines in important subtests such as verbal meaning and reasoning (Schaie & Labouvie-Vief, 1974).

Recently, the use of one overall IQ score to represent intellectual changes with age has been criticized (Horn, 1978). Horn argues that the declining scores observed after age 40 represent only one aspect of intelligence. He calls this aspect **fluid intelligence,** which we can roughly define as general mental skills, such as the ability to make inferences. Horn and Donaldson (1980) state that fluid intelligence declines with age mainly

Table 6–2
Sample Questions from a Modern
IQ Test

Verbal Scale	
Information	What is steam made of? What is pepper?
Comprehension	Why is copper often used in electrical wires? Why do some people save sales receipts?
Arithmetic	It takes three people nine days to paint a house. How many people would it take to do it in three days? An automobile goes 25 miles in 45 minutes. How far would it go in 20 minutes?
Digit Repetition	Repeat the following numbers in order: 1,3,7,2,5,4 Repeat the following numbers in reverse order: 5,8,2,4,9,6
Similarities	In what way are a circle and a triangle alike? In what way are an egg and a seed alike?
Vocabulary	What is a hippopotamus? What does ''resemble'' mean?
Performance Scale	
Picture Arrangement	A story is told in three or more cartoon panels placed in the incorrect order; put them together to tell the story.
Picture Completion	Point out what's missing from each picture.
Block Design	After looking at a pattern or design, try to arrange small cubes in the same pattern.
Object Assembly	Given pieces with part of a picture on each, put them together to form such objects as a hand or a profile.
Digit Symbol	Learn a different symbol for each number and then fill in the blank under the number with the correct symbol. (This test is timed.)

Source: Sample questions from Wechsler Adult Intelligence Scale.

because of a decline in physical and neurological functioning. They also feel that part of the decline is due to reduced practice of certain mental skills. Horn's main point, however, is that there is another aspect of intelligence that steadily increases with age. He calls this ever-improving aspect **crystallized intelligence,** which we can define as specific mental skills, such as one's vocabulary, or the ability to define words. Figure 6–13 helps clarify the distinction between general and specific skills by showing test questions that tap either fluid or crystallized intelligence. Crystallized knowledge is specific, in the sense that it depends upon exposure to a specific environment. People in different cultures would learn to define different words, for instance. Horn and Donaldson (1980) imply that such culturally specific knowledge "crystallizes in the mind," so that it is less affected by physical

Figure 6–13
These are sample test items used to measure fluid intelligence and crystallized intelligence. Answers to the items are given below. (Educational Testing Service, 1962, 1976)

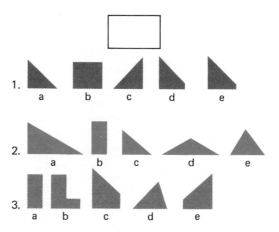

SAMPLE TEST ITEM: FLUID INTELLIGENCE

Below is a geometric figure. Beneath the figure are several problems. Each problem consists of a row of five shaded pieces. Your task is to decide which of the five shaded pieces will make the complete figure when put together. Any number of shaded pieces from two to five may be used to make the complete figure. Each piece may be turned around to any position, but it cannot be turned over.

1.   a   b   c   d   e
2.   a   b   c   d   e
3.   a   b   c   d   e

SAMPLE TEST ITEM: CRYSTALLIZED INTELLIGENCE

Choose one of the four words in the right-hand box which has the same meaning as the word in the left-hand box.

1.	bizarre	market imaginative	conventional odd
2.	pecuniary	involving money trifling	esthetic unusual
3.	germane	microbe relevant	contagious different

Answer:
Fluid intelligence item: (1) a, c, d, e; (2) a, d, e; (3) b, c, e

Crystallized intelligence item: (1) odd; (2) involving money; (3) relevent

Figure 6-14
The graph shows how fluid intelligence first
increases and then decreases with age,
while crystallized intelligence steadily
increases. (Horn & Donaldson, 1980)

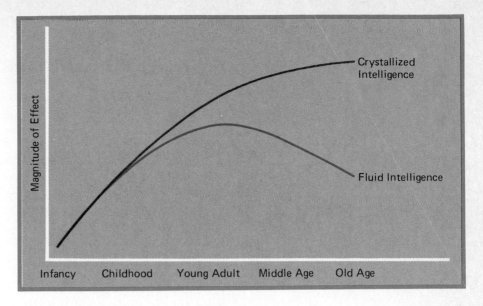

and neurological deterioration. People thus retain culturally based knowledge through the years, and they continually learn new specific facts. Figure 6–14 shows the end result. While fluid intelligence first increases and then decreases with age, crystallized intelligence steadily increases.

IQ: The Extremes

Intelligence tests have been most successful at identifying the extremes of intelligence (Isaacson, 1970). At one extreme, people with IQs below 30 are the totally dependent, to whom we referred earlier. About 1 out of every 1,000 people fall in this category. Those with IQs between 30 and 50 are trainable; that is, they can learn to take care of their daily needs in a sheltered environment. About 3 out of every 1,000 people are in this category. People with IQs between 50 and 70 are educable; that is, with special training, they can learn to support themselves in the community (Zucker & Altman, 1973).

At the other extreme, people with IQs of 140 or above are classified as mentally gifted. In 1921, Terman and his associates started a longitudinal study that followed mentally gifted people from early childhood through adulthood (see Sears, 1977; Sears & Barbee, 1977). The results supported two conclusions. On the one hand, high IQ scores are associated with good health, outstanding school performance, and leadership. On the other hand, a high IQ is not a perfect predictor of success, because other factors are also important. Some of the mentally gifted people in the study, for example, failed in college and in their careers. Many factors are important in determining differences between the least and most successful mentally gifted individuals, including motivation, perseverance, and creativity (Crockenburg, 1972).

IQs: The Controversies

Classifying people at the low and high extremes of intelligence is an important contribution, for it helps educators provide programs that are best suited for individual needs. Few would deny that people and society are well served when educable individuals and mentally gifted individuals receive different education programs. Nevertheless, grouping people for different programs is a sensitive issue, as indicated by several recent controversies. One major public concern is whether or not IQ tests are fair to minority groups. Let's consider this controversy.

Culture Fairness. Those who question the validity of IQ tests for minorities argue that the tests are not fair to blacks, poor whites, and other cultural subgroups. As mentioned earlier, differences in performance on IQ tests could be caused by differences in opportunity to learn the tested material, or by differences in capacity to learn. If everyone has the same opportunity, then differences can safely be attributed to capacity. If, however, a cultural subgroup has had less of an opportunity to learn the tested material, then the IQ test is an invalid test of capacity for that group.

Test-makers have tried to develop "culture-fair" tests. Most often this has meant cutting down on the use of verbal materials, since there are obvious language differences between subcultures. Nonverbal tests usually involve geometric relationships of some kind. The tasks on such tests include fitting pegs into holes, judging relationships between geometric forms, making designs with blocks, and completing drawings (Cattell, 1949; Raven, 1947). Unfortunately, test-makers have too little data to back up their assumption that everyone has an equal opportunity to learn even the skills required for these tasks. Developmental psychologists are only beginning to understand the effects of experience on cognitive development. What they have learned so far suggests that environments during infancy and childhood do make a difference, but many questions remain unanswered: At what age do children learn aspects of geometric relationships? What elements of the environment are essential for providing an opportunity to learn geometry and other skills that are examined on IQ tests? If there are critical environmental factors, how are they influenced by the complex and subtle differences between subcultures? Until these and other questions about opportunities to learn are answered, it will be impossible to establish the validity of even culture-fair IQ tests for cultural subgroups. A closely related controversy concerns the role of heredity and environment in determining IQ.

Nature and Nurture Issue and IQ. What is the relative contribution of heredity and environment to IQ? In the study of genetics one estimates the heritability of traits in plants and animals by controlling environment while manipulating the proportion of genes held in common. Such experiments cannot be done with humans, of course. Although human families vary systematically in the extent to which they share genetic makeup, they also differ systematically in their environments. Specifically, those who have similar genes (parents and children) also have similar environments. Those who have less similar genes (grandparents and grandchildren) also, for the most part, have less similar environments. Some authorities argue, in fact, that genetic similarity is so interwoven with environmental similarity that scientists cannot make meaningful heritability estimates for humans (Feldman & Lewontin, 1975).

Many investigators have nevertheless studied genetic relatedness in humans. They use three procedures:

1. *Studies of identical twins who are raised apart.* These have often failed to separate effects of heredity from effects of environment (e.g., Shields, 1962). The twins were reared in separate but similar environments and often had contact with each other. One study that claimed to avoid this problem (Burt, 1966) is now regarded as fraudulent. Burt apparently invented much of this data (Kamin, 1973).
2. *Studies comparing identical and fraternal twins.* As we discussed in Chapter 2, identical twins come from the same egg, and thus their genes are exactly the same. Fraternal twins, on the other hand, come from two separate eggs, and thus their genetic makeup differs. If correlations of IQs were higher with identical twins than with fraternal twins, this would say something about the heritability of IQ. Such tests, however,

are also inconclusive. Correlations between IQs are higher for identical twins (Erlenmeyer-Kimling & Jarvik, 1963), but this result has two interpretations. The higher correlations could be due to heredity, or to the fact that identical twins are more likely than fraternal twins to share a similar environment—to play together and to have the same friends and teachers (Loehlin & Nichols, 1976).

3. *Studies of adopted children, which compare their IQs to those of both their biological parents and their adopted parents.* Such studies suggest that IQ heritability is low to moderate (Horn et al., 1979; Scarr & Weinberg, 1977). This conclusion is supported by the fact that the IQ correlation between parent and biological child is not consistently higher than that between parent and adopted child. Furthermore, IQ correlation between genetically related brothers and sisters is not consistently higher than that between brothers and sisters who are only related by adoption.

The controversy is far from settled. Jensen (1969) reviewed the literature on genetic relatedness and concluded that heredity is about four times as important as environment in determining IQ. More recent reviews maintain that heredity is no more important than environment, or that it is perhaps not even as important as environment (Kamin, 1979; Plomin & DeFries, 1980).

Race and IQ. The most heated debate about intelligence concerns the fact that in the United States black people average 10 to 15 points lower on IQ tests than white people. A number of researchers (Eysenck, 1971; Herrnstein, 1973; Jensen, 1969, 1973; Shockley, 1972) have used this and other selected results to argue that blacks are innately less intelligent than whites. Other scientists (Kagan, 1973; Kamin, 1976, 1979; Scarr-Salapatek, 1971) rebut this conclusion with one or more of the following arguments:

1. Even if IQ has a hereditary element, that refers only to heredity within the group being studied—it does not say anything about differences *between* groups, such as blacks and whites.
2. IQ tests are biased against black people and other minorities.
3. Average IQ differences can be attributed entirely to environmental differences.
4. Differences in heredity and environment are so interwoven that IQ differences cannot be attributed to one or the other at this time.

IQ and You

You probably know your IQ or your scores on scholastic aptitude tests (SAT), which also are used to predict school performance. You are advised to interpret this information cautiously. On the one hand, don't let a high IQ score give you a false sense of security. Remember that a number of Terman's mentally gifted subjects failed in college. On the other hand, don't give up if you have a modest IQ score. Standard IQ scores predict school performance, but not perfectly.

Some school counselors advise students against a college career unless they have an IQ of 120. This advice amounts to a prediction that people with lower IQs will not succeed as scholars. The uncertainty of this prediction is illustrated by the case of Nobel prize winner James Watson. After having his IQ measured as 115, he not only succeeded in college, he also discovered the structure of DNA (as we discussed in Chapter 2), which is one of the major scientific breakthroughs in modern history. Watson's success brings to mind Helen Keller's earlier quoted graduation speech: "There is nothing good or right which we cannot accomplish if we have the will to strive."

SUMMARY

1. **Learning** is a process by which experience or practice results in a relatively permanent change in what one is capable of doing.

2. **Classical conditioning** occurs when an originally neutral stimulus comes to elicit a response that was originally given to another stimulus. It takes place when the neutral stimulus (CS) is repeatedly paired with the other stimulus (US).

3. A number of factors help in establishing conditioned responses. The CS must be strong and distinctive; the CS should be presented shortly before the US; the time lapse between the CS and the US should be brief; there should be many pairings of CS and US; and the pairings of CS and US must be spaced properly.

4. **Extinction** occurs if the CS is repeatedly presented alone, without the US. But in **spontaneous recovery,** the conditioning effect appears again without any further pairings of CS and US.

5. **Stimulus generalization** occurs when responses are made to stimuli that are similar to, but not the same as, the original CS. **Discrimination,** on the other hand, occurs when subjects learn to respond only to certain stimuli, but not to other, similar stimuli.

6. **Operant conditioning** is a type of learning that occurs when desired responses are rewarded or reinforced and undesired responses are ignored or punished. **Reinforcement** is an event whose occurrence just after a response increases the likelihood that the response will be repeated; **positive reinforcement** is the presentation of a stimulus, **negative reinforcement** is the removal of a stimulus.

7. A subject who learns to make a response to remove a stimulus, through the use of negative reinforcement, has participated in **escape training.** In **avoidance training,** a negative reinforcer can be avoided altogether. **Learned helplessness** occurs when exposure to unavoidable, unpleasant events leads to an inability to avoid the unpleasant event even when it is possible.

8. Schedules of reinforcement can be either continuous (rewarding every response) or partial (rewarding only some responses), based on reinforcement of a certain *number* of responses or reinforcement after a certain *interval of time.* There are four basic schedules: **fixed interval, variable-interval, fixed ratio,** and **variable ratio** schedules of rein-

forcement. Each type affects the rate of responding in different ways.

9. **Extinction** and **spontaneous recovery** occur in operant as well as in classical conditioning (extinction in operant conditioning occurs through the withholding of reinforcement). **Generalization** and **discrimination** also occur in operant as well as classical conditioning. **Punishment** is a stimulus that decreases the likelihood of a response when it is added to an environment.

10. **Shaping** is a procedure used in operant conditioning in which each part of a behavior is reinforced, eventually leading to the whole behavior that is desired.

11. **Social learning theory,** or learning indirectly through observing others, occurs through imitation. It is discussed in detail in Chapter 12.

12. Cognitive learning theory attempts to explain the function of thought processes in learning. It includes such concepts as **insight learning, latent learning, cognitive maps, learning sets, functional fixedness,** and the formation of **concepts.**

13. **Intelligence** has been defined as the capacity to learn. It is difficult to measure intelligence as a capacity, however, since people differ greatly in their opportunities to learn, and it is not easy to see whether test scores reflect capacity or opportunity.

14. **Achievement tests** are designed to measure a person's current knowledge and skills, reflecting past learning. **Aptitude tests** try to predict the capacity for future performance. Many tests are **standardized,** that is, they have been given to many people so that one person's score can be evaluated with respect to a large population.

15. **Intelligence quotient,** or **IQ,** is *mental age* divided by *chronological age* and then multiplied by 100. It is a concept that was popularized through the introduction of the Stanford-Binet test early in this century.

16. It is difficult to estimate the effects of aging on IQ, because it depends on whether one is talking about **fluid intelligence** (general mental skills) or **crystallized intelligence** (specific mental skills). Fluid intelligence first increases and then decreases with age; crystallized intelligence steadily increases.

17. Several controversies of IQ and IQ testing were discussed. They included culture-fair testing, the question of whether heredity or environment is more important in its effect on IQ, and race and IQ.

Key Terms

achievement tests
aptitude tests
avoidance training
chronological age
classical conditioning
cognitive learning theory
cognitive map
concept
conditioned response (CR)
conditioned stimulus (CS)
continuous reinforcement schedule
crystallized intelligence
discrimination
escape training
extinction
fixed-interval schedules
fixed-ratio schedules
fluid intelligence
functional fixedness
generalization
insight
intelligence
intelligence quotient (IQ)
latent learning
law of effect
learned helplessness

learning
learning set
mental age
mental sets
negative reinforcement
negative set
operant conditioning
partial reinforcement schedule
positive reinforcement
preparedness
primary reinforcers
punishment
response generalization
reinforcement
secondary reinforcers
shaping
social learning theory
spontaneous recovery
standardized achievement tests
stimulus discrimination
stimulus generalization
token economy
unconditioned response (UR)
unconditioned stimulus (US)
variable-interval schedules
variable-ratio schedules

Suggested Readings

The following books are about Helen Keller and Anne Sullivan:

KELLER, H. *Story of my life.* Garden City, N.Y.: Doubleday, 1954.

LASH, JOSEPH, P. *Helen and teacher: The story of Helen Keller and Anne Sullivan Macy.* New York: Dell, 1980.

AMSEL, A., & RASHOTTE, M. E. *Mechanisms of adaptive behavior.* New York: Columbia University Press, 1984. This book reviews the work of Clark L. Hull, one of the leading theorists on learning. It is a valuable collection of his theoretical papers with commentary.

ANDERSON, J. R., & KOSSLYN, S. M. (Eds.). *Tutorials in learning and memory: Essays in honor of Gordon Bower.* San Francisco: Freeman, 1984. This is a state-of-the-art tutorial on a variety of important topics in the area of learning and memory. Topics include mental representation, schema theory, mental models in problem solving, and remembering stories.

BRODY, E. B., & BRODY, N. *Intelligence: Nature, determinants, and consequences.* New York: Academic Press, 1976. A balanced coverage of the nature-nurture controversy and related controversies is given in this thorough review.

ESTES, W. K. (Ed.). *Handbook of learning and cognitive processes* (Vols. 1–6). Potomac, Md.: Erlbaum Associates, 1976. This series covers all aspects of learning and cognition at an advanced level.

HILGARD, E. R., & BOWER, G. H. *Theories of learning.* Englewood Cliffs, N.J.: Prentice-Hall, 1975. Presents principal points of view toward learning in their historical settings and summarizes typical experiments to which each theory has led.

TIGHE, T. J. *Modern learning theory: Foundations and fundamental issues.* New York: Oxford University Press, 1982. This book provides a historical context in which to evaluate the new developments in animal learning theory.

UNDERWOOD, B. J. *Studies in learning and memory.* New York: Praeger Press, 1982. This series of selected papers by Benton J. Underwood traces the historical development of the author's work, which had a major impact on our understanding of verbal learning, concept learning, and thinking.

MEMORY AND COGNITION

On December 24, 1919, three bandits attacked a payroll truck in broad daylight, firing at it as it skidded down an icy street in Bridgewater, Massachusetts. The bandits, unsuccessful in their robbery attempt, drove off in a getaway car. No one was injured.

Several months later, there was a similar crime in the neighboring town of South Braintree. At about 3 o'clock on the afternoon of April 15, 1920, armed robbers ambushed and shot two guards in a truck that was carrying the payroll of a local shoe company. The gunmen grabbed the cash box containing $15,000 from the dying guards and jumped into a car that had pulled up while the shooting was going on. Two days later the getaway car was found abandoned in some nearby woods, with the tracks of a smaller car leading away from it. During the investigation that followed, the police theorized that the tracks of the smaller car might have been made by the vehicle used in the earlier crime at Bridgewater. This theory would later form the net that snared Sacco and Vanzetti.

To understand how these two rather ordinary men (one a factory worker, the other a fish peddler) came to the center of national and international attention and why they were ultimately electrocuted in 1927, one must consider the social backdrop as well as the details of the case itself.

The two crimes and the Sacco-Vanzetti trial took place during a period of acute social unrest and upheaval in America. Labor strikes had shocked the nation in 1919, and prominent figures in government and business were targets of radical assassination attempts. Americans blamed their troubles on the strangers (the immigrants) in their midst. Partly for this reason, Congress established in the late 1920s a quota system to drastically cut down on immigration, especially limiting the influx of people from southern and eastern Europe. More than other groups, they were viewed as a main source of America's troubles.

Faced with charges of robbery and murder, Sacco and Vanzetti found themselves doubly handicapped. Both were Italian immigrants; both were anarchists. (The term "anarchist" in those days was used very loosely. It did not necessarily mean that one was a member of an efficient, ruthless organization bent on the overthrow of government. Sacco and Vanzetti's rebellion against authority was a general, poorly organized expression of dissatisfaction with the lot of immigrant industrial laborers.) Neither man had a background of crime or violence.

Eyewitnesses at both the Bridgewater and South Braintree crimes said that the bandits were foreigners. This was enough to convince Bridgewater's chief of police that the crimes had been the work of "Reds and Bolshevists." At the time of the Braintree murders, he was working under the assumption that the culprits were Italians who owned a car in a nearby town. He located an Italian-owned car that was in a nearby garage for repairs and theorized that whoever came for the car must be involved in the two crimes.

On the night of May 5, 1920, Sacco and Vanzetti arrived at the garage. They roughly fit the description of the bandits, and they were carrying guns, so they were arrested. Only Sacco had an alibi for the day of the unsuccessful Bridgewater holdup. Neither Sacco nor Vanzetti had an airtight alibi for the day of the Braintree murders. Thus Vanzetti was charged with the Bridgewater attempt, and both men were charged with the killings in Braintree.

Vanzetti stood trial from June until August of 1920, charged with assault as one of the gunmen who shot at the payroll truck in Bridgewater. The testimony of witnesses for the prosecution was riddled with contradictions and inconsistencies. The district attorney relied heavily upon the testimony of three witnesses to establish the identity of Vanzetti as one of the gunmen. Two of these men had been passengers in the payroll truck and therefore the targets of the shooting. The third man was a bystander, also close to the action and in danger of being shot. The actual exchange of gunfire—the moment when the

men in the truck had the best opportunity to see the robbers—lasted only for a matter of seconds and was viewed at a speed of about 20 miles an hour. Afraid of being shot, the driver had hunched so low in the seat that he lost control of the truck. The other passengers scrambled for the steering wheel, and, in the confusion, ran the truck into a telephone pole. Thus the attention of the passengers in the truck was divided between the gunmen and keeping control of the truck.

The three witnesses gave three reports of the incident: the first on the day of the crime (December 24); the second at a preliminary hearing on May 18; and a third at the trial in late June. The first reports were as follows:

1. Alfred Cox (a passenger in the payroll truck):
"The man with the shotgun was a Russian, Pole or Austrian, 5'8", 150 lbs., dark complexion, 40 years of age, was without a hat and wore a long, dark overcoat with the collar up. He had a closely cropped moustache which might have been slightly gray."
2. Benjamin Bowles (an armed guard who returned the fire from the truck):
"I can positively identify two of the bandits. The man with the shotgun was 5'7", 35 or 36 years, 150 lbs., had a black, closely cropped moustache, red cheeks, slim face, black hair and was an Italian or Portuguese. He had no hat on and had a black overcoat with collar up."
3. Frank Harding (a bystander):
"The man with the shotgun was slim, 5'10", wore a long black overcoat and derby hat. I did not get much of a look at his face but I think he was a Pole."

Vanzetti, who was accused of being the shotgun bandit at Bridgewater, had a distinctively full, long, and droopy mustache, and he had always worn it so. The moustache originally seen on the shotgun bandit was apparently smaller than Vanzetti's, but as time passed and the witnesses had the chance to see Vanzetti, the moustache "grew to fit the man." Other details changed also. For example, Cox changed his description from "dark" complexion to "medium" complexion—closer to Vanzetti's coloring. Bowles added at the trial that the gunman had a "high forehead," moving closer to a description of Vanzetti.

Other confusions were apparent. Under cross-examination, Bowles (the armed guard) revealed that he was unsure of whom he shot at, and was therefore unsure of whom he got a "good look" at. He also was unsure about which of the gunmen had fired first. Inconsistencies in his testimony suggested that he had altered his story (possibly unconsciously) to please his questioners. Adding to the confusion, the district attorney called other witnesses who gave questionable testimonies—for example, that of a 14-year-old newsboy: "By the way he ran I could tell he was a foreigner; I could tell by the way he ran." Despite its defects, the testimony persuaded the jury, for they found Vanzetti guilty. Ruthless news coverage of the conviction added another strike against Sacco and Vanzetti. Because of this, Sacco requested a separate trial, which was denied.

The joint trial of Sacco and Vanzetti began a year later, on May 31, 1921, in Dedham, Massachusetts. It lasted nearly 7 weeks. Only one question was relevant: Were Sacco and Vanzetti the assailants of the two men at Braintree? There was a mass of conflicting evidence regarding this question. The discord in the testimony was summed up by Francis Russell (1962) in his book *Tragedy in Dedham*:

> Scarcely a minute had elapsed from the first shot until the getaway car vanished, but with its disappearance the actuality faded and the myth took over. All in all there were more than fifty witnesses of the holdup in its various stages, yet each impression now began to work in the yeast of individual preconceptions. The car was black, it was green, it was shiny, it was mud-streaked. There were two cars. The

men who did the shooting were dark, were pale, and had blue suits, had gray suits, wore caps, were bareheaded. Only one had a gun, both had guns. The third man had been behind the brick pile with a shotgun all the time. Anywhere between eight and thirty shots had been fired. (pp. 41–42)

Apparently, the witnesses at Braintree could do no better than those at Bridgewater. But again it was good enough for the jury. On July 14, 1921, Sacco and Vanzetti were found guilty of murder in the first degree.

Many who studied the trial carefully were unconvinced. Because of the inconsistencies in the testimony and other irregularities, many thought (and many still think) that Sacco and Vanzetti did not get a fair trial. Six long years passed, taken up with appeals for a new trial. All this was to no avail, however—on August 22, 1927, Sacco and Vanzetti were executed.

Memory is far from perfect even over short intervals. For example, test your own memory by trying to recall the license plate number on the car next to the policeman. See the text for a discussion of the types of memory in this task.

203

HOW MEMORY IS STUDIED

Memory is a system that allows people to retain information over time. Human memory is far from perfect, as we have seen: Why did the Sacco and Vanzetti witnesses remember some facts and forget others? Why do you remember some answers on tests and not others? This chapter will examine the cognitive processes that underlie memory successes and failures. It will test your memory several times by asking what you read earlier in the chapter, so stay alert! The first test will show how good your memory can be; some of the others will probably reveal weaknesses in memory. We will end the chapter with suggestions for improving memory.

Test Yourself

The best way to analyze the relationship between memory research and eyewitness testimony is to take part in a memory experiment. We will test your memory in several different ways. We will then compare these tests with school tests and with interrogations of witnesses in the Sacco and Vanzetti case. Miller, Galanter, and Pribram (1960) outlined an experiment that is fun to experience firsthand. You must first learn the following verse: "One is a bun, two is a shoe, three is a tree, four is a door, five is a hive, six are sticks, seven is heaven, eight is a gate, nine is a line, and ten is a hen." This verse will provide a mental framework for learning a study list. Psychologists call such mental frameworks *schemata* (Thorndyke, 1984). Study the following list of numbers and words, using the verse to help you learn which word goes with each number. You already know that "bun" goes with the number 1. Now you must learn that "ashtray'" goes with 1. Try learning this new relationship by forming a bizarre image in your mind of a bun with an ashtray—you might imagine a pipe spilling ashes into a bun, for example. Follow the same procedure for every number until you have formed an image relating the right verse word to every word on the study list.

Study List	
	1 ashtray
	2 firewood
	3 picture
	4 cigarette
	5 table
	6 matchbook
	7 glass
	8 lamp
	9 shoe
	10 phonograph

When you finish going through the list once, take the following test. Next to each number write the word that was next to it on the study list.

3 _____
8 _____
6 _____
4 _____
9 _____
1 _____
7 _____
2 _____
10 _____
5 _____

How many did you get correct? People often get all the words correct after one time through the list (Miller et al., 1960).

Methods of Testing Memory

You can assume from your performance that you remember all, or nearly all, of the study list. But it is not always safe to assume that performance reflects memory exactly or completely. We have all taken tests in school that have either overestimated or underestimated what we remember. The relationship between performance and memory is a theme that weaves its way through the research on memory. We will follow this important theme better if we understand the different kinds of performance that psychologists often use to measure memory.

Recall Tests. Recall tests measure a person's ability to reproduce material. The test you just took gave a number as a cue, and you had to reproduce the rest of the number word pair. When part of an item is provided as a cue for the other part, the test is called *cued recall*. Teachers use cued recall tests when they ask fill-in-the-blank questions, such as "Mental frameworks are also called _____."

Another kind of recall test is *free recall*, in which no cues are provided and any order of recall is allowed. A teacher might say, "List three technical terms used in last night's homework assignment." Similarly, police asked Cox, Bowles, and Harding to give free recalls of what they had witnessed during the attempted payroll robbery at Bridgewater.

Recognition Tests. Recognition tests measure a person's ability to pick the correct answer when several answers are given. Teachers use recognition tests in the form of multiple-choice questions, such as "Mental frameworks are also called: (a) conditioned stimuli, (b) schemata, (c) operant responses, or (d) primary reinforcers." Recognition is usually, but not always, easier than recall (Hulse, Deese, & Egath, 1975). The difficulty depends on the answers you have to choose from (Hall, 1983). You might have had more trouble, for example, if the answers had been: "(a) schematics, (b) schemata, (c) schemes, or (d) schemas."

You would be taking a recognition test if you tried to select the word that goes with 7 on the earlier study list: Is it firewood, lamp, glass, or table? Witnesses at the Slater and Morrill holdup took recognition tests when they tried to identify the shotgun bandit from a number of pictures of suspects.

Savings Tests. Savings tests measure people's ability to take advantage of what they have learned before in order to relearn material faster. You rely on savings every time final exams roll around. By the time you get to the end of a course you have probably forgotten some of the facts you learned in the beginning, so you must relearn them for the final exam. You might not recall the name of one of the founders of structuralism, for example, even though you learned it in Chapter 1 of this book. You might not even recognize the correct name from the following list: Skinner, Watson, Wundt, James. But if you learned it earlier, you will probably learn very quickly that Wundt is the correct answer. The fact that you relearn old material faster than you learned it the first time shows that you remember something about it even if you cannot recall or recognize the information. To measure your savings in the earlier list you would have to record how long it took you to learn the list the first time and how long it took you to relearn the list at a later time. The difference between your original learning time and your relearning time is your **savings.** (If you waited long enough, you would probably find a time at which you could neither recall nor recognize the list, but you would still show savings.)

Notice that all three tests—recall, recognition, and savings—measure memory indirectly, through performance. Inferring memory from performance is no simple matter. Lawyers know full well that performance is not a perfect indicator of memory. A good question will often bring forth key evidence that a witness failed to produce on earlier occasions. Students also know that tests do not always reflect what they learned in a course. As our analysis of memory research unfolds in this chapter, we will learn many reasons why performance does not perfectly reflect memory.

TYPES OF MEMORY

There are basically two different theories about memory. One theory, called the *multiple memory theory* (Atkinson & Shiffrin, 1971, 1977), states that there are three types of memory (see Figure 7–1): sensory memory, which holds sensory impressions for only 1 or 2 seconds; short-term memory, which holds information for less than 30 seconds; and long-term memory, which holds information for long periods of time (perhaps permanently).

Another theory, the *levels of processing theory*, agrees about the existence of sensory memory. But, beyond that, these theorists argue that we have only *one* kind of memory, which holds different kinds of information. We get the different kinds of information by processing what is stored in memory at different levels (Craik & Lockhart, 1972). According to this theory, we recode information into more and more abstract forms as we process it at deeper levels. At a surface level, we code visual properties when we read. At a deeper level, we recode visual properties of letters and words into word meanings. At a still more abstract level we recode word meanings into concepts expressed by sentences. With these deeper levels of processing, we get different kinds of information, but every kind is retained in the same unified memory.

We'll come back to these two theories as we discuss different kinds of memory and different ways of processing it. First let's look at what the multiple memory theorists call sensory, short-term, and long-term memory. All three types of memory would have come into play if you had been a witness at the Sacco and Vanzetti trial. Let's see how the three types would have operated, for example, if you had had a very brief glimpse of the license plate on the getaway car during the Braintree armed robbery. Suppose you saw the plate for a fraction of a second and then you closed your eyes to concentrate on what you saw.

Sensory Memory

Sensory memory holds visual sensations for up to 1 or 2 seconds, allowing enough time for the recognition processes to operate. Sensory memory would have held the visual sensation of the license plate about 1 or 2

Figure 7–1
Multiple memory models include sensory memory, short-term memory, and long-term memory. The arrows show the flow of information among these three types of memory.

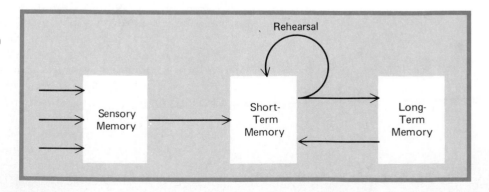

Figure 7–2
A pencil that is wiggled in the hand and waved as shown will appear to bend. Sensory memory helps to create this rubbery appearance by holding an image of the pencil after it has moved to another position.

seconds after you closed your eyes in our hypothetical example. Your recognition processes would have been able to recognize the license number. We often continue to look at a stimulus until we recognize it, but sometimes our view is disrupted by blinks and other disturbances. Sensory memory holds visual information *through* these disruptions so that recognition processes can operate without interruption. You can see evidence of your sensory memory by waving a pencil in front of your eyes (Figure 7–2). The shadowy image that trails behind the pencil means that your sensory representation of the pencil in one position stays on after the pencil moves to a new position. This information fades or decays from sensory memory within 1 or 2 seconds.

Sperling (1960) used an interesting method to study visual sensory memory. In this experiment, he presented 12 letters in three rows with 4 letters in each row (Figure 7–3). He flashed the letters for 50 msec., then asked subjects to name as many letters as they could. They were able to name only 4 or 5 letters, even though they claimed that they had seen more than that. From this Sperling formed the following hypothesis: Subjects did not see all the letters, because the flash was too brief. They saw more letters than they could report, however, because they forget some before they could say them.

Sperling ran a second experiment to test his hypothesis. This time he directed his subjects to view only a portion of the 12-letter display. He did this by using various tones as stimuli, sounding the tones after the letters were presented: A high-pitched tone meant that they should name the letters in the top row; a medium tone cued the middle row; and a low tone indicated that the subjects should concentrate on the bottom row. Sperling called this a *partial report procedure*, because subjects only report part of the display that is shown to them. The procedure is based on the same logic that teachers use to determine course grades. Teachers

Figure 7–3
Sperling's partial report technique is shown in the upper part of the figure. Below it is a graph of the results: The number of letters recalled decreases as the signal to report is delayed. (Sperling, 1960)

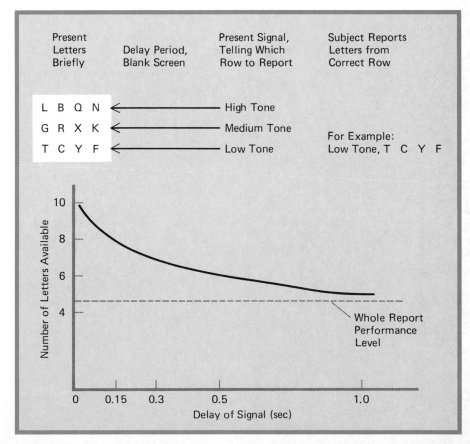

sample only part of a course's material on exams. They then use the percentage correct on the exam to estimate what percentage you know of all the material in the course. If you get 90 percent correct on the exam, the teacher assumes that you know 90 percent of all the material. Sperling found that subjects knew 75 percent of the letters in his display (3 out of 4) when they were cued immediately after the display went off. This suggested that they saw 9 of the 12 letters that were briefly flashed.

In other conditions, Sperling delayed the cue 150 msec., 300 msec., or 1,000 msec. after the letters were presented. This forced subjects to remember all the letters until they got the cue. The percent correct gradually dropped (Figure 7–3). With a 1,000 msec. delay, the cue was useless, since subjects did no better than when they received no cue at all. From this Sperling concluded that sensory memory held visual information for a short time after the display went off, and that the memory gradually faded.

Sperling determined these important properties of sensory memory in related experiments:

1. Visual properties of a stimulus, such as brightness, determine the length of sensory memory. The brighter the stimulus, the longer sensory memory lasts. Usually sensory memory lasts less than 1 or 2 seconds.
2. Sensory memory for one stimulus is wiped out when another stimulus is presented after the first one is out of sight. The ability of a stimulus to wipe out the sensory memory of a preceding stimulus is called **backward masking.**
3. Sensory memory contains visual information that has not yet been recognized or named. Based on physiological evidence reviewed in Chapter 2, we can assume that sensory memory contains information represented in terms of visual features such as angles, curves, and straight lines.

Massaro (1970) showed that auditory sensory memory has similar properties.

Short-Term Memory

Short-term memory holds information that has been transferred out of sensory memory. Information will last only about 30 seconds in short-term memory if it is not repeated. Suppose the license plate number on the getaway car had been SMT–253, and you only had time to recognize the letters. The numbers would have been lost, in addition to many other details that you did not have time to identify. The part you did recognize, however, would be saved. Specifically, it would be transferred to short-term memory for further processing. As this example illustrates, transfer to short-term memory usually involves a considerable loss of information. The process of repeating information in order to retain it in short-term memory is a process called **rehearsal.** If we do not rehearse the information, the memory decays or fades rapidly. A good example of this is the way you repeat or rehearse a phone number that you have just looked up. If you do not repeat it, or if someone interrupts you before you can make the call, you will probably forget the number almost immediately.

Peterson and Peterson (1959) developed a way to measure how long information is held in short-term memory when it is not rehearsed. They divided their procedure into three intervals: presentation, retention, and recall. During presentation, subjects looked at a three-letter unit called a trigram, such as XNT. During retention, subjects did a math problem that was designed to keep them from rehearsing the trigram. During recall, subjects simply attempted to say the trigram that had been presented. Figure 7–4 shows the results. Subjects recalled trigrams correctly about

Figure 7–4
Research has shown that people rapidly forget isolated facts if they do not rehearse them. In the graph here we see a rapid decline in the amount of correct recall of trigrams. (Peterson & Peterson, 1959)

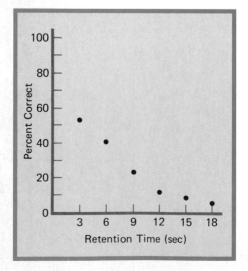

50 percent of the time after 3 seconds, about 25 percent of the time after 9 seconds, and about 8 percent of the time after 18 seconds. This and many other experiments show that we forget new, isolated facts (such as trigrams) in less than 30 seconds if we do not rehearse them.

Any acceptable memory theory would have to explain Peterson and Peterson's results. Multiple memory theory says that we retain isolated facts in short-term memory until we transfer them to long-term memory. Transfer is impossible without rehearsal, so we quickly forget facts that we do not rehearse. Levels-of-processing theorists offer a different explanation for the same results. They assume that facts are remembered longer when they are processed more deeply, not because they are transferred to a different type of memory. Peterson and Peterson's subjects only had time to do surface-level processing of trigrams, so they forgot them quickly. Both multiple memory theories and levels-of-processing theories pass the test of being able to explain the Peterson and Peterson results. We will have to consider other ways to distinguish the two theories.

Long-Term Memory

Long-term memory holds information that is transferred from short-term memory through rehearsal or some other process. As you repeated the letters you had just seen on the license plate of the getaway car, you might have tried to think of ways to remember them. You might have noticed, for instance, that they are the first letters of the first three days of the week. Repetition and additional processing would transfer the information to long-term memory. The longer information stays in short-term memory, the more likely it is to be transferred to long-term memory. Some researchers assume that our long-term memory is virtually permanent— that is, we lose nothing from long-term memory, although we may sometimes fail to retrieve information from it (Atkinson & Shiffrin, 1971, 1977).

Types of Long-Term Memory.   We store concrete information about sensory aspects of our experiences in long-term memory. We remember the sound of voices over long periods, as when an old friend calls and we immediately recognize his or her voice. We remember body movements. If you drive a car with a bright-light switch on the floor, for instance, you will probably hit the switch rapidly on your first try, even if you haven't used it for some time. Keele and Ells (1972) showed that we remember both the switch's position and how far we have to reach to step on it.

We also remember smells extremely well. In one experiment, people recognized smells as accurately after 30 days as they did after 30 seconds, and they forgot very few smells over a period of one full year (Engen, 1980).

Evidence of long-lasting memories does not necessarily prove that the multiple memory theory is right, however. As mentioned earlier, levels of processing can also explain long-term retention. Let's look at some support for the levels-of-processing theory.

Deeper Processing Means Longer Memory.   Many experiments show that memory depends upon levels of processing—the deeper the level, the better the memory (cf. Wickelgren, 1979). There is one experiment that is of particular interest with respect to eyewitness testimony (Bower & Karlin, 1974). The experimenters showed pictures of faces and they manipulated the levels of processing that people engaged in while looking at the pictures. Sometimes subjects used surface levels of processing to make judgments about simple things, such as the sex of the pictured person. Other times subjects used deeper levels of processing to make more difficult judgments, such as likeableness or honesty. Subjects recognized pictures better on a later test when they had processed the pictures more deeply, even though they looked at all pictures for the *same* amount of time. This and other experiments suggest that theories of memory must take into account levels of processing.

We will continue to review evidence for multiple memory theory and levels-of-processing theory as we go on to discuss the processes of encoding, retention, and retrieval in short-term and long-term memory.

ENCODING

Video and audio tape recorders passively take in everything that is bright enough or loud enough to record. A lawyer's job would be much easier if human witnesses did the same. But, of course, people don't; they decide what to take in and how to represent it. For instance, you used a special plan to **encode,** or represent, the study list at the beginning of this chapter. Similarly, Frank Harding may have used a special encoding strategy when he observed the ambush of the payroll truck that caused him to remember a derby hat that wasn't worn by either gunman. Cognitive psychologists include analyses of encoding as a major part of their research on memory. They find that encoding comes into play in sensory memory, short-term memory, and long-term memory. Let's discuss each of these in turn.

Encoding in Short-Term Memory

We have already said that much information is lost between sensory memory and short-term memory. Let's take a closer look at the selective way in which most of us encode information.

Attention. Put yourself in the place of Benjamin Bowles on Christmas Eve in 1919. You are riding shotgun in a payroll truck when suddenly it comes under fire. Your first instinct is to hit the floor, but you have committed yourself to defending the money, so you return the fire. Moments

In traffic, our senses are often flooded with more information than our minds can handle at one time. We manage in this sort of situation because we pay attention only to important stimuli, which, in the case here, might be the speed limit sign.

later the truck swerves out of control and hits a telephone pole. Think about the rush of stimuli you would encounter—the gunmen, the smoke from their guns, the smoke from your gun, bystanders running, the background spinning by, the smell of the truck's heater and of rubber burning, the bumps against your body as you and the other passengers are bounced around, the bangs, the squeals of tires, the shouts. You would not experience all of these to the same extent. Your mind would zero in on some and ignore others. Just by imagining the situation you probably have a good idea about which stimuli would get your attention.

The process by which we notice important stimuli and ignore irrelevant stimuli is called **attention.** Without it, our minds would surely drown in a churning, muddled ocean of stimuli. In traffic, on disco floors, at cocktail parties, and even on a tranquil stroll through the woods our senses are flooded with more information than our minds can handle at one time. We manage in these situations because we attend selectively to important information.

Figure 7–5 illustrates one of the artificial laboratory settings used to study attention. Each earphone carries a separate message. The subject is asked to ignore one message and to *shadow* the other, that is, to repeat it aloud as it is heard, staying as "close behind" the speaker as possible. This procedure allows the experimenter to examine two questions: What happens to the message that the subject is asked to ignore? When does this irrelevant message interfere with perception of the relevant one?

Before looking at the answers, try to guess. What do you think happened to the irrelevant smells, sounds, and bumps rushing in on Bowles when his truck was attacked? Do you think they were ever noticed in the first place? Surely the irrelevant stimuli excited his sensory receptors, but perhaps the signals from the receptors were filtered out before his brain recorded them. If they did reach the brain, and if they were noticed, perhaps they were remembered for only a very short time.

One way to find out is to give subjects a surprise test on their ability to recall the irrelevant message in a shadowing experiment. Research has shown that 30 seconds after the material is presented, the content of the irrelevant message is forgotten (Moray, 1959). In some experiments the irrelevant message was alternately presented in English and an unfamiliar foreign language, or in English and gibberish; 30 seconds later subjects had no recollection of these changes.

In contrast, the physical characteristics of the irrelevant message are remembered. For example, people remember whether it was a man's voice or a woman's voice, whether or not it stopped completely, and whether or not it was replaced by some other sound. Apparently people attend to an irrelevant message enough to determine its physical characteristics, but not enough to determine its meaning, or at least not enough to remember the meaning 30 seconds later.

Figure 7–5
This is the apparatus used in a typical shadowing experiment. Separate messages are played to each ear of a subject, who tries to ignore one message and to repeat the other.

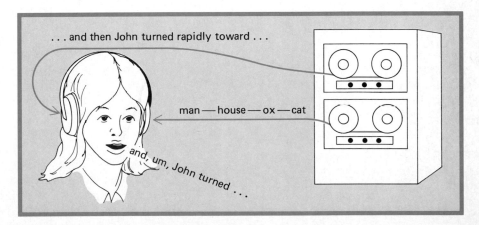

. . . and then John turned rapidly toward . . .

man — house — ox — cat

and, um, John turned . . .

The second question also deserves some thought before we look at the answers regarding the shadowing experiment. We all know that irrelevant stimuli sometimes interfere. For example, try listening to a lecture while someone next to you cracks his or her knuckles. Sometimes, however, irrelevant stimuli don't seem to matter. The background hum of an air conditioner, for instance, probably does not take your mind away from a lecture.

As you might have guessed, the content, or meaning, of an irrelevant message can make a difference. For example, if a subject's name is mentioned, shadowing of the attended message is disrupted. This is similar to losing track of your own conversation when hearing your name mentioned in a nearby discussion. Hearing one's name mentioned is distracting because people are somehow predisposed to hear their names. A researcher found that other words also become distracting when we are inclined to hear them (Treisman, 1960). For example, one sentence in the attended message started with the words "Poor Aunt. . . ." Consequently, subjects expected to hear a woman's name. A woman's name (Jane) was then played in the unattended message and something else was played in the attended message. Subjects suddenly started shadowing the unattended message and said "Jane." This mistake was often noticed and subjects stopped to apologize. These subjects had a hard time ignoring the distracting message when they were predisposed to hear it.

Encoding, of course, is more than selecting certain information; it is also representing it in a certain form. If you had seen the license plate number on the getaway car at the Braintree armed robbery, would you have tried to form a mental picture of the license plate, using a visual code, or would you have repeated the number to yourself? How would you have tried to remember the bandit's face? Would you have repeated facial features to yourself—black hair, red cheeks, slim face—or would you have formed a mental picture of it? Evidence suggests that you would have used both kinds of codes.

Verbal Codes.   Many experiments have shown that we prefer to use verbal codes for verbal materials such as digits, letters, and words. In one study, Conrad (1964) found evidence for verbal codes in the errors that people make. He briefly exposed six consonants and then asked people to write down all six letters in order. When people made mistakes, the incorrect letters were usually ones that *sounded* like the correct ones. For the list R L T K S J, a subject might substitute a B for a T, recalling R L B K S J. It is hard to imagine why subjects would have made this mistake if they had remembered the letters by means of a visual image. After all, a B does not *look* like a T. The mistake makes good sense however, if people are using verbal codes, because B does *sound* like T. Such mistakes, therefore, support people's claims that they remember strings of letters by repeating the letter names to themselves. If we tried to remember a license plate number on a getaway car, we would probably repeat it to ourselves several times until we had a chance to write it down.

Visual Codes.   While we *prefer* verbal codes for verbal material, we don't always use them. For example, we used visual codes to memorize the words in the study list at the beginning of this chapter. Furthermore, we seem to prefer visual codes for memorizing stimuli that are difficult to describe. Kosslyn, Ball, and Reiser (1978) found evidence suggesting that people use visual codes when they are asked to memorize maps. After subjects memorized a map similar to the one in Figure 7–6, they seemed to have a mental image of it. They could use their image to visualize a dot moving from one object (the hut) to another (the pond). The farther the dot had to move, the longer it took to visualize the movement, suggesting that subjects "saw" the dot move across remembered image of the map. This and other evidence (Kosslyn, 1981, 1984; Wickelgren, 1977)

Figure 7–6

People can use visual images to memorize maps. They can also imagine a dot moving from one object to another on the map's image. The reaction time from the beginning to the end of the imagined movement increases as objects on the map are shown farther apart. (Kosslyn et al., 1978)

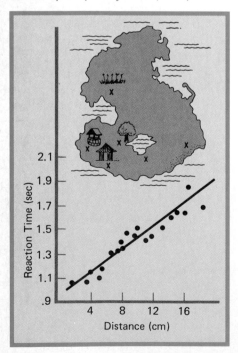

suggest that we use visual codes. We would certainly use them to remember a robber's face if we happened to witness a crime.

Our choice of codes depends to some extent on how long we must remember something. So far we have only talked about experiments on memory for short intervals. Experiments on memory over longer intervals suggest that we *re*code information for long-term memory.

Encoding in Long-Term Memory

Which of the following sentences was the first sentence in this section on encoding?

1. Video and audio tape recorders actively decide what bright or loud information should be recorded.
2. Audio and video tape recorders automatically record everything that is bright enough or loud enough to take in.
3. Video and audio tape recorders passively take in everything that is bright enough or loud enough to record.

Sentence 1 is easy to eliminate because its meaning is different from the first sentence in this section. You may have had more trouble, however, deciding between sentences 2 and 3. Sachs (1967) read sentences to subjects such as "The author sent a long letter to the committee." Two minutes later subjects remembered sentence meanings, but they did not remember exact words. They could not choose between the actual sentence and a different one that had the same meaning: "A letter that was long was sent to the committee by the author." In the same way, you may be representing the meaning of sentences that you are reading here, but you probably are not representing the exact words in long-term memory. Will you remember the meaning at test time? That will depend on many factors that are discussed in the next section.

 # RETAINING AND RECODING

Retention in tape recorders is uninteresting. Tape recorders retain whatever information they pick up, and they play it back in the same form in which they have recorded it. Retention in humans is quite another matter. Humans alter some memories and forget others during retention. Testimonies by Cox, Harding, and Bowles during the Vanzetti trial illustrated the changeable nature of human memory. Over time their descriptions of the bandit changed in many ways; they altered their statements about characteristics such as moustache length, complexion color, and forehead shape. Here we will review experiments that shed light on what might have caused these changes.

We have already discussed the kind of coding that takes place when information is transferred from sensory memory to short-term memory. In this section, we will more closely follow the path of information to explore how it is *retained* after it is encoded in short-term memory and long-term memory.

Capacity of Short-Term Memory

Memory theorists try to distinguish short-term and long-term memory on the basis of how much each holds or *retains*. Try to dial the following number without looking back at it: 924–3401–5732–816. Most of us can't do it. We're used to handling 7 digits without much trouble, but we find

14 almost impossible. Why? Multiple memory theorists say that we have trouble dialing 14 digits because our short-term memory has a limited capacity, or a limit to how much information it can hold. While long-term memory can hold almost any amount, short-term memory can only hold a limited number of digits. Fourteen is well beyond that limit.

Our **memory span** is the number of items that we can read through one time and then recall in sequence with no mistakes. Experiments have shown that seven-digit numbers seem to mark the limit of our memory span. Ebbinghaus (1885) was one of the first to estimate his memory span at seven items. Many years later, Miller (1956) saw the estimate of seven coming up so often in experiments that he wrote a paper entitled "The Magical Number Seven, Plus or Minus Two." While people differ greatly in their ability to remember facts for exams or lines for plays, virtually all normal adults have a memory span that falls between 5 and 9 items.

Multiple memory theorists explain this "magical number" with the assumption that short-term memory has a limited storage capacity of 7 ± 2 items. It is as if short-term memory is a small filing box with only 7 ± 2 slots. When all the slots are filled the only way we can get new information into short-term memory is by displacing some item that is already there (see Waugh & Norman, 1965).

Levels-of-processing theorists explain limited memory span not in terms of *limited storage capacity*, but in terms of *limited processing capacity*. They assume that we are limited in the rate at which we can perform the processes of holding items and of repeating them. Since storage limitations and processing limitations are both plausible, the existence of memory span limitations does not help us choose between multiple memory theories and levels-of-processing theories.

Chunking. We can say that memory span is limited to 7 ± 2 items, but what exactly is an item? Experiments have shown that our memory span can correspond to 7 ± 2 digits, letters, syllables, words, or even sentences. The letter string NOTTER UOL YRAM is well beyond our memory span, but the same string in reverse order, MARY LOU RETTON, is well within our span. In fact, we could manage five or six more names. When we process information, we group elements together to form units that function as wholes. We group visual features into letters, letters into words, and words into sentences. This process is called **chunking.** Miller (1956) labeled the units *chunks* and concluded that memory span corresponds to 7 ± 2 chunks. We can appreciate the economy of chunking

information when we compare memory span for different kinds of items. Our memory span is about seven letters when we try to memorize letter strings that are unpronounceable and meaningless. It is 7 ± 2 sentences, which corresponds to about 80 letters, when we try to memorize sentences (Craik & Lockhart, 1972).

Sometimes we try to memorize information for very short intervals, as when we dial a new telephone number. Most of the time, however, we try to remember things for longer periods, as when we study for exams. Let's look now at the special characteristics of retention in long-term memory.

Retention in Long-Term Memory

The eyewitness testimony at Sacco and Vanzetti's trial illustrates two principles of retention in long-term memory: organization and reconstruction. People organize the information that they store in long-term memory, and they continue to work on or reconstruct that organization as time passes. Initial organization is revealed in reports by Cox, Bowles, and Harding to police at Bridgewater. These descriptions of the "shotgun bandit," which we quoted earlier, depended upon long-term memory, because the police did not arrive immediately. The reports were highly organized. Specifically, all three witnesses used organizations that grouped together facts into four categories: body build, facial features, clothing, and nationality. As time passed, all three witnesses changed their testimony in a way that might have indicated a reconstruction of their original memory. Let's take up this example in more detail and relate it to research on principles of organization and reconstruction.

Organization in Long-Term Memory.   People store a wealth of general knowledge, and they use this background knowledge to organize memories for episodes that they witness. Cox, Bowles, and Harding, for instance, already knew the categories that they used to organize their memories of the "shotgun bandit." Tulving (1972) formalized the distinction between the long-term retention of background knowledge and specific episodes as follows:

1. **Semantic memory** refers to a person's general background knowledge about words, symbols, concepts, and rules.
2. **Episodic memory** refers to a person's memories about events, including the time and place they occurred.

We will use this distinction in the following discussion, even though researchers are still debating its value for theories of memory (McCloskey & Santee, 1981).

The extent to which semantic memory can impose itself on episodic memory is illustrated by Harding's testimony. He did well, remembering details such as a black overcoat, but he got one fact wrong. He reported that the "shotgun bandit" wore a derby hat, when he actually wore no hat at all. Overcoats and derby hats were probably closely associated in Harding's semantic memory, and he may have mixed up his semantic memory with his episodic memory of the event he witnessed. We are, of course, just speculating about the reason for Harding's error. For better evidence of the interaction between semantic and episodic memories, we should turn to the research in this area.

Galton (1879) studied semantic memory with a **free association test,** which is a procedure in which a person looks at, or listens to, a target word and then reports other words that come to mind. Deese (1959) combined free association tests with free recall tests to show that we use seman-

All three witnesses in the Sacco and Vanzetti case changed their testimony from the time they first talked to the police to the time they actually testified at the trial. Their memories of the body build, facial features, clothing, and even nationality of the "bandits" may have been affected by the process of reconstruction in long-term memory.

tic memory to organize episodic memory. Free association tests measure semantic memory, because they reflect the way our general knowledge about words is organized. Free recall tests measure episodic memory in that they reflect the organization of memory for a list learned at a specific time and place. Deese first measured free associations in one group. He then gave a list of words in random order to another group. The second group was allowed to recall the words in any order. The subjects recalled the list not in its original order, but in an order that grouped together things that were related in earlier associations. Apparently, associations that were present in semantic memory imposed themselves on episodic memory.

Other researchers used a clever procedure to study semantic memory (Collins & Quillian, 1969). They measured how long it took people to answer simple true-false questions. Consider one of their questions: A canary can fly, true or false? The question asks about general knowledge; it doesn't ask about a specific piece of information (that is, you can answer it without saying when or where you saw a canary fly, or without ever having seen a canary fly). They used such questions to test a model of how people organize semantic memory. Figure 7–7 shows an example of their model. Information about canaries is stored in different places, according to the model. Some is stored under a high-level category, "animal"; some is under a lower level or subordinate category, "bird"; and some is under a still lower category, "canary." This organization, which is called a **hierarchy,** arranges information into levels of categories and subordinate categories. Collins and Quillian assumed that it would take time to move between categories. They found, in agreement with this prediction, that it takes longer to decide "A canary can fly" than it does to decide "A canary can sing." It takes even longer to decide "A canary has skin." Today many models of semantic structure include similar hierarchical structures (Anderson & Bower, 1973). In addition, other studies show that we use our knowledge of categories and hierarchies to organize and, thereby, to improve our episodic memory (Bower et al., 1969; Horton & Turnage, 1976).

Our semantic memories contain, in addition to associations and categories, rules for structuring stories. The sentences in Table 7–1 can help demonstrate your knowledge of such rules. The sentences can be unscrambled to form a short story about a farmer and a donkey. Try it, and your story will probably be almost identical to the original. How did you know the correct order? You knew because of your semantic memory, which

Figure 7–7
This is a model of semantic memory. This type of organization of ideas is called a hierarchy. (Collins & Quillian, 1969)

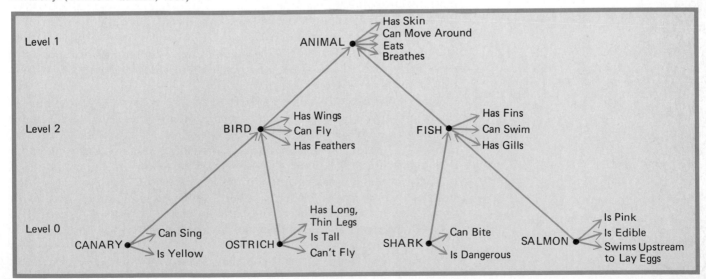

Table 7-1
Scrambled Sentences Test

Unscramble these sentences and put them in the proper order to form a story about a farmer and a donkey.

But the cat replied, "I would gladly scratch the dog if only you would get me some milk."
Thus, the farmer went to the haystack and got some hay.
The barking so frightened the donkey that it jumped immediately into its shed.
So, then, the farmer asked his cat to scratch the dog so the dog would bark loudly and thereby frighten the donkey into the shed.
Then the farmer pushed the donkey, but still the donkey wouldn't move.
As soon as he gave the hay to the cow, the cow gave the farmer some milk.
As soon as the cat got the milk, it began to scratch the dog.
But the cow replied, "I would gladly give you some milk if only you would give me some hay."
Finally, the farmer asked his dog to bark loudly at the donkey and thereby frighten him into the shed.
But the dog refused.
First, the farmer pulled the donkey, but the donkey wouldn't move.
So the farmer went to his cow and asked for some milk to give to the cat.
There once was an old farmer who owned a very stubborn donkey.
As soon as the cat scratched the dog, the dog began to bark loudly.
Then the farmer went to the cat and gave the milk to the cat.
One evening the farmer was trying to put his donkey into its shed.

contains rules for structuring stories (Black, 1984). Most of us started learning these rules as young children by listening to stories our parents told. We can use those rules to make a story out of a scrambled list of sentences (Kintsch, Mandel, & Koziminsky, 1977; Shebilske & Reid, 1979).

Researchers have developed formal grammars for diagramming text structures (Anderson & Bower, 1973; Deese, 1980, 1984; Freder, 1975; Grimes, 1972; Halliday, 1973; Norman & Rumellhart, 1975; Kintsch, 1974; Kintsch & Van Dijk, 1983; Schank & Abelson, 1972; Shebilske, 1980). When diagrammed, these grammars resemble a hierarchical tree structure, with general ideas near the top and specific details near the bottom. These same tree structures are used when people try to summarize a story from memory. Psychologists generate tree structures and predict rank orders according to specific rules. The fact that recalls fit the predicted rank orders suggests that we unconsciously follow similar rules for remembering stories.

We follow unconscious rules when we read textbooks. The rules are different than those we use for stories, because textbooks are different. But the rules are similar in the sense that they distinguish between important and unimportant ideas. Most college students tend to study and to remember important information, while they ignore and forget unimportant material. In contrast, many high school students study textbooks as if all material is of equal importance, or, worse yet, they tend to remember only unimportant information (Deese, 1980; Estes & Shebilske, 1980; Shebilske, 1980). Efforts are being made to help students who cannot learn well from textbooks. A goal is to teach them rules that will assist them in effectively organizing their memory.

Reconstruction in Long-Term Memory. We start organizing material when we first encounter it, and we continue to organize and reorganize as time passes. We are often unaware of our efforts to reorganize, or recode, material in long-term memory, Such unconscious reconstruction of memory is a major source of unreliability in witness testimony.

After witnesses saw Vanzetti during his trial, their description of the shotgun bandit moved closer to a representation of Vanzetti. We might think that the witnesses were deliberately trying to frame Vanzetti. But research suggests another possibility: Witnesses may have unconsciously distorted their memories.

In one experiment, Loftus found that exposure to new information can distort a witness's memory (Loftus, 1975, 1981; Loftus & Palmer, 1974).

Subjects were shown a film of a traffic accident, and they then answered one of five questionnaires. The questionnaires were all the same except for the wording of a question about speed. One questionnaire asked, "About how fast were the cars going when they smashed into each other?" The other questionnaires substituted the verbs "collided, bumped, contacted, or hit" in place of "smashed." Loftus had two ways to measure how much influence the verbs had. One measure, the estimate of speed, showed that the verb "smashed" drew higher speed estimates than the other verbs. A second measure came a week later, when Loftus asked, "Did you see any broken glass?" Subjects who had the questionnaire with the verb "smashed" in it were more likely to say yes, even though there had been no broken glass. Apparently, memory was altered to include details that did not actually exist, but which were consistent with an accident at higher speeds.

In courtrooms, questions that "lead" a witness to a particular answer are called "leading questions," and there are rules against them. However, the rules may be inadequate. Leading questions asked well in advance of a trial seem to alter memory for an event. Consequently, answers to "fair questions" during the trial might be unreliable.

What exactly is a leading question? To get at a precise, unambiguous definition, researchers must show exactly how and when people can be led by questions. Loftus has begun to explore the kinds of questions that cause memory distortions. For instance, she conducted an experiment similar to the one above, except she used a different leading question. Immediately after showing a film of a fast-moving event, she asked a question that presupposed the existence of an object that was not in the film. For example, in a film showing no barns, the leading question was "How fast was the white sports car going when it passed the barn while traveling along the country road?" One week later, nearly one-fifth of the students who heard this question "remembered" a barn being in the film. In a later study, Bekerian and Bowers (1983) suggested that people can recall their original memories better if they have good retrieval cues. Specifically, subjects do poorly when test questions are given in a random order. But they do much better when the question sequence matches the order of

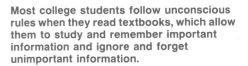

Most college students follow unconscious rules when they read textbooks, which allow them to study and remember important information and ignore and forget unimportant information.

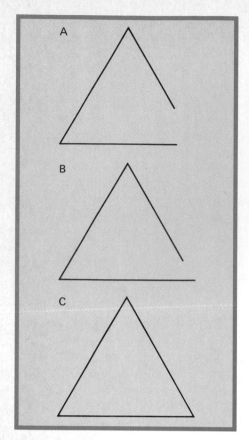

Figure 7–8
People reconstruct their memories to fill in details. Subjects who were shown A and were later asked to draw what they had seen, reproduced drawings B and C after 1 and 3 months, respectively. (Allport, 1958)

the original event. Thus, good retrieval cues might help offset the effects of leading questions.

Even without leading questions, memory changes in predictable ways. For example, memory tends to have standardized representations. Gordon W. Allport (1958) demonstrated this by showing students a roughly triangular drawing (Figure 7–8). He then varied the time at which he asked students to draw what they had seen. Those who were asked immediately after they were shown the picture drew very good reproductions; those who were asked 1 month later produced drawings like Figure 7–8; and those who were asked 3 months after the original viewing produced drawings like Figure 7–8. With time, the student's memories tended to leave out the details that made the original drawing unique. In the end, memory contained a standardized representation of a triangle.

Memory standardization affects witness testimony as well. To test this, one researcher staged an assault on a college campus (Buckhout, 1974). A student "attacked" a professor in front of 141 witnesses, and sworn statements were then obtained from each witness. Buckhout found that witnesses tend to give standardized estimates. For example, heights and weights are overestimated for short or thin people and underestimated for tall or heavy people because memory tends toward the average.

RETRIEVAL

Push a button and mechanical recorders play back all the information that they have recorded. Human **retrieval,** the process of getting information out of memory, is not as reliable. We sometimes fail to retrieve, or get back, information that is stored in our memory. You might be unable to recall a date on a history exam, for example, but then it comes to mind right after the exam. This suggests that the date was in your memory all along, but you failed to retrieve it during the exam. In the same way, witnesses sometimes fail to recall details until a hypnotist helps them remember (see Chapter 5). Such retrieval failures increase unreliability stemming from inattentiveness during encoding and from memory loss during retention.

Memory researchers would have a fairly easy time studying retrieval if all of our retrieval efforts were open to conscious inspection, but they are not. We often search through our memory without being aware of it, which makes memory research both more difficult and more interesting. Let's turn to some of the special techniques used to study conscious and unconscious retrieval processes.

Retrieval from Short-Term Memory

Sternberg (1966) conducted an experiment that shed light on retrieval from short-term memory. You can get a feeling for his experiment easily enough with the following test. Memorize the numbers 2, 3, and 8, and then cover them. Now, ask yourself whether or not the following numbers were on the list: 3, 7, 1, 2, 9, and 8. The answers "yes, no, no, yes, no, yes" come to mind so quickly and effortlessly that it is hard to realize that we have to search our short-term memory at all. Sternberg found evidence, however, that we do, in fact, search our short-term memory for such information.

He recorded how long it takes people to respond "yes" or "no" in a task like the one that you just tried. He had subjects memorize numbers, ranging from one to six items on a list. He tested a list only once, then

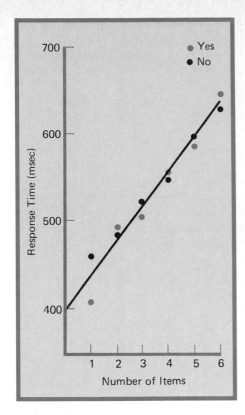

Figure 7–9
The time it takes to decide if an item is in one's memory increases as the number of items in short-term memory increases. This result shows that it takes time to search through items in short-term memory. (Sternberg, 1966)

asked subjects to memorize another list. On each test he presented a digit, and subjects pushed a "yes" button if the digit was on the memorized list and a "no" button if it was not.

Sternberg found that response time depends on the length of the original list (Figure 7–9). It takes about 440 msec. with one item, about 480 msec. with two items, about 520 msec. with three items, and so on, with each additional item taking about 40 additional msec. Sternberg concluded that we retrieve the test digits one at a time, with each comparison taking about 40 msec.

Retrieval is not open to conscious inspection in Sternberg's experiment. Yet he was able to make a strong case that retrieval from short-term memory involves a search process. His experiment and those of others (Glass, 1984) go beyond our intuitions about retrieval from short-term memory. Similarly, cognitive psychologists have been able to go beyond what introspection reveals about retrieval from long-term memory.

Retrieval from Long-Term Memory

We are often unaware of our efforts to search long-term memory (Raaijmakers & Shiffrin, 1981). Sometimes, however, we are aware of our attempts to retrieve information from long-term memory and we deliberately control our search (see Norman, 1973). For instance, Sacco and Vanzetti had to search long-term memory when they were asked to account for their whereabouts during the Bridgewater and Braintree crimes. In more recent cases, people have been mistakenly identified by witnesses (Loftus, 1984). For example, William Jackson spent 5 years in prison, convicted of a rape. In fact, he had not committed any crime. He was released in 1982 after police arrested the real rapist, a man whom Jackson strongly resembled (Figure 7–10).

Suppose you are questioned in connection with a crime because it was committed by someone fitting your description. All you have to do to put a end to this unfortunate case of mistaken identity is account for your whereabouts any time between 3:00 and 5:00 P.M. on the first day of last month. Can you do it? If you try, you will probably find yourself consciously reconstructing the events of that day. You might say to yourself, "I get paid on the first of the month and I usually deposit my check shortly before the bank closes. Oh, yes, I remember now. I deposited my check at about 4:30 on the first of last month. In fact, that was the day I complained to the service manager about an unexplained service charge on my account.

The wrong man: William Jackson, right, was imprisoned for five years for two rapes actually committed by Dr. Edward Jackson, Jr., left.

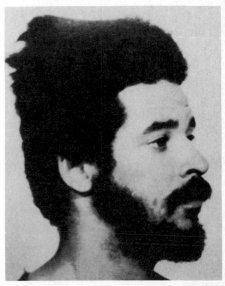

I hope she has a record specifying the time of my complaint." But maybe you are not so lucky. Perhaps you can remember classes you attended in the morning and the play you saw that night, but you cannot remember what your did that afternoon. The point is that you are sometimes aware of your efforts to search your memory.

We are not always aware of our retrieval processes, however. Researchers, therefore, cannot rely entirely on people's direct reports of efforts to search memory. One way that researchers investigate retrieval processes that are not always open to consciousness is by manipulating cues that are designed to aid retrieval.

Organization and Retrieval Cues. Tulving and Pearlstone (1966) argue that we can take advantage of organization when we retrieve information from episodic memory (see also Masson & McDaniel, 1981). They showed subjects long lists containing words from common categories such as animals, colors, and professions. The words were presented in random order, and then subjects attempted to recall the lists. Half the subjects were told the category names at the time of recall; the other half were not. Subjects who were given category names did much better than the other subjects. Both groups were given category names in a later test, and they both recalled the same number of words. Both groups must have had the words in memory, but subjects could not retrieve as many without the help of category names. The category names served as aids to retrieval, or what psychologists call retrieval cues. We apparently use retrieval cues to organize our search through memory.

Tip-of-the-Tongue Phenomenon. We reveal other aspects of our retrieval processes when we come close to information in our memory without actually finding it. Try to recall the words corresponding to the definitions shown in Table 7–2. You will know some immediately; you will not know some of all; and you will hopefully think you know some without being able to recall them right away. This uncomfortable state of being on the verge of recalling something is called the tip-of-the-tongue (TOT) state. Brown and McNeill (1966) produced over 200 TOT states in students who tried to recall words for definitions similar to those in Table 7–2. When students indicated that a word was on the tip of their tongue, Brown and McNeill asked them questions about the word. Students knew the number of syllables in the word over 60 percent of the time; they knew the word's first letter over 50 percent of the time; and they could give words that sounded like the words being defined (for example, *secant* instead of *sextant*). Brown and McNeill suggested that we retrieve information by sound as well as by meaning.

Table 7–2
Definitions Used to Produce a Tip-of-the-Tongue State

1. A fanatical partisan; one who is carried away in his pursuit of a cause or object.
2. Lying on one's back, with the face upward.
3. Selecting, choosing doctrines or methods from various sources, systems, etc.
4. A conciliatory bribe, gift, advance, etc.
5. An instrument having 30 to 40 strings over a shallow, horizontal sounding box and played with picks and fingers.
6. A hiding place used by explorers for concealing or preserving provisions or implements.
7. To clear from alleged fault or guilt; to absolve, vindicate, acquit, or exonerate.

Words corresponding to definitions.

1. Zealot   5. Zither
2. Supine   6. Cache
3. Eclectic   7. Exculpate
4. Sop

Source: Brown & McNeill (1966).

Anxiety and Retrieval. Most of us have panicked on an exam at one time or another. Panic is especially likely when there is a lot at stake. Consider a particularly crucial exam that you have taken. Passing means that you finally reach a long sought after goal; failure prevents you from getting something you really want. Suddenly you become overwhelmed by a fear of failure, even though you know the material. Your anxiety level rises as each difficult question is reviewed until finally you are so panicked that you cannot remember a thing. Anxiety does not wipe out your memory. Things you couldn't remember during the exam often start coming to mind when you calm down after the exam.

Holmes (1974) argues that anxiety does not in itself prevent retrieval. Anxiety produces extraneous thoughts, such as, "I'll never be able to face my dad," or "This is unfair because I've worked so hard." Holmes argues that these thoughts are what stand in the way of retrieving answers to exam questions. You might try to control such distracting thoughts, or you might try to control your anxiety level directly. Chapter 5 outlines procedures that you can use to relax before taking exams. Chapter 5 also reviews evidence that to most easily recall memories, you should be in the same state during study and test periods. Therefore, maintaining lower anxiety levels during both study periods *and* tests may improve your performance.

Decision Factors. Tape recorders report everything that they retrieve. With human retrieval, however, we *decide* what we want to say before we report anything. This intermediate decision allows us time to edit what we report.

Imagine yourself on a television game show. You are asked to name the children in the Walton's television family. How would you answer? That would depend upon the *cost* of wrong answers and the *rewards* for correct answers. If you had everything to gain for correct answers and nothing to lose for errors, you would probably include some guesses. You might say "John Boy, Jim Bob, Mary Ellen, I think there was a Jason, maybe an Aaron, how about a Beth?" If, on the other hand, your winnings were taken away for each error, you might be more cautious. For example, you might say, "John Boy, Jim Bob, and Mary Ellen—that's all I can remember."

Costs and rewards also influence the testimony of witnesses in a trial. The cost in such a situation might be guilt associated with identifying the wrong person; the reward might be the satisfaction of seeing justice done. Buckhout (1974) maintains that two witnesses with the same memory might decide to say quite different things, and he developed a test to identify good witnesses. He based his test on signal detection theory, which makes it possible to measure memory and decision factors separately (Green & Swets, 1966). To give the test he shows a film of a staged "crime" and then presents 20 true statements about the incident and 20 false statements. Witnesses score a *hit* whenever they say "yes" to a true statement, and they score a *false alarm* whenever they say "yes" to a false statement. The percentage of hits and false alarms are used to calculate the witnesses' measure of sensitivity. If witnesses say "yes" as many times to true statements as they do to false statements, they obviously have no sensitivity about the truth of the statements, and their score is 0. If, on the other hand, witnesses almost always say "yes" to true statements and almost never say "yes" to false statements, they are very sensitive and they get a high score. Generally, observers who score high on Buckhout's test prove to be the best witnesses in other situations. For example, they do better at picking suspects from a lineup. For about 80 years, psychologists have warned about the unreliability of witness testimony. Now they are taking positive steps toward identifying reliable witnesses.

FORGETTING

Forgetting is defined as an inability to remember. You probably remember what it is like to forget, but in case you don't, let's probe for some reminders. What was the name of your third-grade teacher? Can you name five students who were in your fourth-grade class? What is the formula for figuring the area of a circle? What is your social security number? Can you name five glands in the endocrine system along with the hormones they secrete (see Chapter 2)?

If you answered all these questions correctly, you should be pleased. If you answered some of these questions wrong, you might ask yourself why your memory failed you. If you knew why, you might be able to improve your memory. With that in mind, let's review the possibilities.

Trace Decay

When we memorize something, we produce a change within our nervous system. The nature of that change is highly debatable. Some argue that the change is confined to some specific location in the brain; others claim that it is dispersed throughout the nervous system (cf. Wickelgren, 1977). Either way, we can use the term **memory trace** to refer to the change that occurs as a result of memorizing. One of the earliest theories of forgetting, **trace decay theory,** holds that memory traces fade away in time. The theory's appeal to early theorists is apparent. Memories are natural, and things of nature change. Trees grow leaves only to lose them again; grass turns green only to fade back to a tawny brown; the sun rises and sets; we wake up fresh only to get tired again.

In the same way, according to trace decay theory, memory traces start out strong, and their strength is maintained through use. But traces gradually weaken and fade away if they are not used. Trace decay theory would explain a failure to recall the name of your third-grade teacher as follows: You once had a strong memory trace for the name and you refreshed the trace regularly by using it. Your trace gradually lost strength, however, when you stopped using it, and it became so weak that you could no longer recall the name.

Wickelgren (1977) argues that trace decay may contribute to forgetting, but other factors are also involved. For example, you learned many names since the third grade, and these may have interfered with your ability to remember your third-grade teacher's name. The next section presents an interference theory of forgetting.

Interference

When we learn different things, we create the possibility that learning one thing will hinder our memory of something else. A popular theory of forgetting, **interference theory,** holds that we forget information because other information gets in the way. Two kinds of interference are as follows:

1. **Proactive inhibition** is interference of previous learning with memory for new learning. Suppose historians suddenly discovered that Columbus really discovered America in 1534. Our previous memory of Columbus discovering America in 1492 would hinder our learning of

Table 7-3
Proactive Inhibition

	Experimental Group	Control Group
Step 1	Learn List A	Rest or engage in unrelated activity
Step 2	Learn List B	Learn List B
Step 3	Recall List B	Recall List B

Table 7-4
Retroactive Inhibition

	Experimental Group	Control Group
Step 1	Learn List A	Learn List A
Step 2	Learn List B	Rest or engage in unrelated activity
Step 3	Recall List B	Recall List A

the new date. The hindrance would be proactive interference. Researchers study proactive interference with experiments similar to the one illustrated in Table 7–3. The experiment has three steps and two groups of subjects.

In the first step, the experimental group learns a list of words, List A; the control group does some unrelated activity. In step two, both groups learn a list, List B. In the third step, both groups recall List B. Proactive inhibition is shown by lower recall of List B for the experimental group, who had previously learned List A.

2. **Retroactive inhibition** is interference of new learning with memory for previous learning. Suppose you went away for 6 months and you did not use your phone number during that time. You might have trouble recalling your number, but you would probably have even more trouble if you had acquired a new phone number during that time. The interference of the new number with your memory for the old one would be retroactive inhibition. An experiment for studying retroactive inhibition is outlined in Table 7–4. It has three steps and two groups.

In the first step, both groups learn List A. In the second step, the experimental group learns List B, and the control group does some unrelated activity. In the third step, both groups recall List A. Retroactive inhibition is shown by lower recall of List A by the experimental group, who learned List B after learning List A.

Old and new material do not always interfere with each other in our memory, of course (see Shebilske & Ebenholtz, 1971). Sometimes old memories help us learn new material, as in the "one is a bun" experiment cited in the beginning of this chapter. Similarly, new learning sometimes helps us remember things that gave us trouble in the past. Isolated dates in history are often difficult to remember until we learn enough facts about a period to provide a frame of reference. Determining when memories will help or hinder the recall of other memories is one of the major challenges facing memory researchers today.

Another challenge is explaining how one memory interferes with another. Some theorists argue that a memory can be erased or dissolved by other memories. Other theorists claim that interfering memories do not destroy other memories, they only make them harder to locate during recall.

In the next section we will discuss the rapidly developing work of neuroscientists. They have taken up the difficult task of specifying the neurobiological basis of learning and memory.

THE NEUROBIOLOGICAL BASIS OF LEARNING AND MEMORY

We have seen that a brief glimpse at a getaway car can trigger a complex sequence of learning and memory processes. We can assume that all of these processes have a neurobiological basis (see Chapter 2). Similarly, as you are reading at this very moment, billions of neurobiological changes are taking place in your brain (see Chapter 4). These physical changes will ultimately determine whether or not you will recall this material at test time. They are the basis of all our cognitive operations—they determine selective encoding, retention, and retrieval processes operating over short-term and long-term periods. Scientists are therefore eager to understand the neurobiological basis of learning and memory.

We will briefly review three approaches used in this important area of investigation:

1. Determining whether damage to specific brain structures produces loss of retention of learned responses
2. Examining changes in the brain that correlate with learning
3. Stimulating brain structures electrically or chemically in order to increase or decrease memories

Effects of Brain Damage on Retention

Researchers have sought the location of memory traces by observing the effects of brain damage on retention (Herbert, 1983; Weingartner, Grafman, Boutelle, Kaye, & Martin, 1983). In Chapter 2 we discussed the possibility that the hippocampus plays an important role in learning and memory. This idea has been supported in animal laboratory experiments in which researchers damage the hippocampus before or after learning (Olton, Becker, & Handelmann, 1980). The importance of the hippocampus is also suggested by clinical research on human patients (see "Highlight: Memory Disorders: A Case Study").

Neurobiological Correlates of Memory

Learning and memory produce many neurobiological changes. For example, learning produces alterations in the following:

1. EEG activity (Landfield, 1976)
2. Firing pattern of single cells (Olds, 1973)
3. RNA and protein synthesis (Glassman, 1974; Shashoua, 1967)
4. Biochemical excitability of cell membranes (Alkon, 1983)
5. The number of connections between neurons (Greenough, 1984)

Greenough (1984) compared and contrasted the neurobiological changes that underlie short-term and long-term effects of learning and memory. Both kinds of learning and memory change the firing pattern of cells. Any given stimulus will cause some cells to "turn on" and others to "turn off." After learning and memory, the pattern of these "on" and "off" responses changes. One way to change firing patterns is to change the excitability of cell membranes in existing pathways between cells. The cell membrane acts as a gate. Thus, a message might not go from one cell to another even though the cells are physically connected. The higher the excitability of cell membranes, the more likely it is that messages will go between cells (see Chapter 2). Another way to change firing patterns is to change the physical links between cells. That is, cells can grow new

MEMORY DISORDERS: A CASE STUDY

In 1957, a 28-year-old man had part of his brain removed in an attempt to ease his violent epileptic seizures. The patient, who is referred to as H.M., developed a severe memory disorder following the removal of the hippocampus and related structures (see Chapter 2). As a result, this procedure has never been repeated. A clinical report describes some of his problems as follows:

Ten months after the operation, the family moved to a new house which was situated only a few blocks from their old one, on the same street. When examined . . . nearly a year later, H.M. had not yet learned the new address, nor could he be trusted to find his way home alone, because he would go to the old house. Six years ago, the family moved again, and H.M. is still unsure of his present address, although he does seem to know that he has moved. [He] will do the same jigsaw puzzles day after day without showing any practice effect, and read the same magazines over and over again without finding their contents familiar.

On one occasion, he was asked to remember the number 584 and was then allowed to sit quietly with no interruption for 15 minutes, at which point he was able to recall the number correctly without hesitation. When asked how he had been able to do this, he replied, "It's easy. You just remember 8. You see 5, 8, and 4 add to 17. You remember 8, subtract it from 17 and it leaves 9. Divide 9 in half and you get 5 and 4, and there you are: 584. Easy."

In spite of H.M.'s elaborate . . . scheme he was unable, a minute or so later, to remember either the number 584 or any of the associated complex train of thought; in fact, he did not know that he had been given a number to remember. . .

One gets some idea of what such [a] . . . state must be like from H.M.'s own comments. . . . Between tests, he would suddenly look up and say, rather anxiously, "Right now, I'm wondering. Have I done or said anything amiss? You see, at this moment everything looks clear to me, but what happened just before? That's what worries me. It's like waking from a dream. I just don't remember" (Milner, 1970).

Such loss of memory is called **amnesia.** It can occur because of physical injury, as in the case of H.M., or because of psychological reasons, which are discussed in Chapter 13. One kind is **retrograde amnesia,** which is loss of memory for events that occurred before the injury. Although H.M. had some retrograde amnesia for events occurring 1 to 3 years before his surgery, he had good recall of his earlier life. He generally experienced **antrograde amnesia,** which is difficulty in remembering events that happen after an injury.

We can get some clue as to the role the hippocampus plays in memory by considering H.M.'s history. First, since he had good recall of his earlier life, we know that the hippocampus does not play a critical role in maintaining or recalling "old" long-term memories. Second, since H.M. had a severe impairment in his ability to form new memories, the hippocampus must be essential for developing "new" long-term memories. In other words, the hippocampus seems to be essential for the *formation* of enduring memories.

branches to reach more cells (see Chapter 2). Greenough (1984) hypothesized that (1) the basis for short-term effects is change in the excitability of cell membranes, and (2) the basis for long-term effects is the establishment of new connections between neurons. Testing this hypothesis will be an exciting task for future researchers.

Electrical and Chemical Regulators of Memory

Scientists have discovered neurobiological manipulations that alter memories. Electronic stimulation of the brain can either increase or decrease memory depending upon a variety of conditions (Gold & McGaugh, 1975). Similarly, many chemicals influence memory and some can either improve or impair memory depending on the dose (Gold & McGaugh, 1977). The chemicals that have been shown to influence memory include the neural transmitters discussed in Chapter 2 and the stimulants discussed in Chapter 5. The effects of both electrical and chemical stimulation are greatest if it occurs shortly before or after training. This time period is when one would expect memory storage processes to be operating. This suggests that electrical and chemical stimulation might affect memory storage.

Will this line of research lead to improved memory through an electronic thinking cap or a memory pill? Probably not in the near future. Although progress has been made, neuroscientists have a long way to go. Their goal is to understand and to control the neurobiological basis of memory. They still have much to learn about the relationship between cognitive processes and neurobiological changes before they will be able to exercise precise control. Therefore, the best way to improve your memory at this time is to concentrate on learning, review, and recall procedures, as described in the next section.

IMPROVING YOUR MEMORY

"You can remember all the things that make the vital difference in your everyday existence, eliminating the unnecessary loss of so much knowledge and information that should be yours to keep and use forever" (Lorayne & Lucas, 1975, p. 1). So begins *The Memory Book*, which is filled with ways to improve your memory for things you do in school, such as giving speeches and taking exams. It also helps you remember people's names, shopping lists, playing cards, and important numbers such as telephone numbers. The book promotes a general understanding of how memory works and it gives hints on how to apply this insight to your own memorizing. We have already discussed how our memory operates. Now let's see how we can make that understanding work to our advantage in our everyday lives.

You can take steps to improve your memory when you first encounter new material, when you review and rehearse, and when you try to recall. These three actions correspond to the three basic processes of memory: encoding, retention, and retrieval.

Encoding Efficiently

A key to encoding is attention. You must pay attention to important material if you want to remember it. We have all had experiences that help drive home the importance of attention. Perhaps you have failed to pay attention during a social introduction. Then you realized immediately afterwards that you did not catch the name of the person to whom you were introduced. Or perhaps you have found yourself at the bottom of a page without any idea of what you have just read. You can take steps to overcome these common problems of not paying attention.

You can ask yourself two questions during an introduction that will heighten your attention:

1. Is there anything unusual about the name?
2. Does the name go with the face?

The first question is easy to answer for some names that have obvious peculiarities, such as Mr. Katz Meow. Finding unusual aspects will be harder for other names. What's unusual about the name Shebilske? Different people will notice different things, of course. Did you notice, for example, that if you allow for misspelling, the name can be broken down into three common words—*she*, *bill*, and *ski*? With practice you will get good at finding something unique about any name. The second question is also easy to

Good study habits can help you get the most out of what you read. A simple, but important, habit is to study in a quiet location without many distractions.

answer for some names. Mr. Katz Meow might have a moustache that looks like cat whiskers. You will have to be more imaginative to link other names with faces. You might notice, when being introduced to Mr. Shebilske, that his "bill" (nose) looks like a ski slope. Get in the habit of asking yourself these questions during every introduction. They will sharpen your attention to details, even if you don't have time to answer them right away.

You might also get in the habit of using the person's name immediately after hearing it. "It's a pleasure to meet you, Mr. Shebilske." You will force yourself to pay attention if you hold yourself responsible for saying the name. Be careful not to get these two habits mixed up. You don't want to find yourself saying, "It's a pleasure to meet you, Mr. Ski Face."

You can also develop special study habits that will help you overcome inattentiveness during reading. First of all, admit that you do not have a will of iron. Certain things are going to capture your attention despite your best efforts to ignore them. You will be distracted by radios, televisions, and nearby conversations when you read. You may do well at first if you try to read in the presence of these distractors. Sooner or later, however, something will capture your attention, and your mind will be taken away from your reading. You will improve your memory if you get in the habit of reading in a quiet place.

The next step is to develop the habit of focusing your attention on important parts of your reading. Your memory will increase significantly if you identify important ideas and concentrate on them (Shebilski & Rotondo, 1981).

There are certain steps that will help you put your attention in the right places. These steps are as follows:

1. Survey material before reading it carefully. You can determine important ideas better after you see a whole passage. You should therefore go over a passage quickly, keeping an eye out for the main ideas. Topic headings often identify main points. Summaries are also helpful. Read them before you read whole passages, even if summaries are placed at the end of chapters, as they are in this book.

2. Ask yourself, "What are the main points?" Come up with a temporary list that can be refined as you read more carefully. Also, ask yourself questions that you think the text will answer.
3. Read the text carefully, noting the main points and answering your self-generated questions.
4. Recite the text in your own words after you finish reading. Note the main points that you do and do not know.
5. Review, firming up what you do know and learning main points that you may have missed the first time.

Organization is another key to efficient encoding. You find information better in an organized memory, just as you find things better in an organized home. Disorganized people spend more time looking through their homes for things they have misplaced than organized people spend returning things to their proper places after each use. In the same way, organizing your memory will take time during encoding, but it will save time during retrieval. It will also save time because you won't need to relearn forgotten material.

The trick in organizing is to relate new material to things that you already know. You can organize shopping lists, for example, according to familiar categories. Consider this shopping list: milk, bananas, spinach, oranges, cheese, lettuce, radishes, apples, and butter. You will have an easier time remembering it if you reorganize it according to categories: milk, cheese, butter, bananas, oranges, apples, spinach, lettuce, radishes (see Bower et al., 1969).

You can reduce organization time by using one of many preestablished systems. Memory-aiding systems are called **mnemonic systems.** The "one is a bun" experiment at the beginning of this chapter taught you an effective mnemonic system. You can use the whole system to learn other lists, or you might simply use the image-forming part of the system. To remember that B. F. Skinner did experiments on operant conditioning, for example, you might visualize a hunter skinning wild game on top of a rat cage. Wallace, Turner, and Perkins (1957) found that people can learn to form images for most word pairs in less than 5 seconds and they can remember about 95 percent of 700 pairs after a single exposure to each. Obviously, imagery can be a quick and effective organizing system.

Imagery is used in the **key-word method** of learning foreign vocabulary. Let's use this method to learn that *muleta* means *crutch* in Spanish. We first look for part of the foreign word that sounds like an English word. "Mule" is an obvious choice, so it becomes our key word. We then form an image between the key word and the English equivalent of muleta. We might visualize a mule hobbling along with its front leg propped up on a crutch. Figure 7–11 illustrates this image. You should find that the key-word method will help you with any foreign language you try to learn (Atkinson, 1975).

Many medical students have learned the twelve cranial nerves by remembering, "On old Olympus' towering top, a fat armed German viewed some hops." The first letter of each word reminds them of the first letter in each nerve: olfactory, optic, oculomotor, trochlear, trigeminal, abducens, facial, auditory vestibular, glossopharyngeal, vagus, spinal accessory, hypoglossal. Similarly, students have learned the Great Lakes by remembering HOMES: Huron, Ontario, Michigan, Erie, Superior. These students are using a memory-aid called *verbal mediation*. They relate new material to **verbal mediators,** which are words that have easy-to-remember structures.

Mediators are extremely powerful. In one study, Bower and Clark (1969) asked 84 subjects to use mediators to learn 12 lists of 10 words each. Subjects made up 12 short stories to connect the words in each list. Afterwards they recalled 90 percent of the words. You can make up your own mediators to improve your memory for facts.

Figure 7–11
Imagery is used in the key-word method of learning foreign vocabulary. Forming an image like the one shown here will help you remember that *muleta* means *crutch* in Spanish, or *pato* means *duck*.

Spanish	Key Word	English
Muleta	Mule	Crutch

Spanish	Key Word	English
Pato	Pot	Duck

Many other easy-to-use memory aids have been described in the literature on memory (e.g., Bellezza, 1983). In addition, try making up your own memory aids. Anything you do to organize your memory at the time of encoding will be to your benefit. No matter how good your encoding procedures are, however, you will often find it necessary to review. It is therefore also important to learn special review procedures.

Better Retention through Better Review

How do you review for exams? Reviewing for some people is characterized by repetition. They reread material, paying special attention to parts that they highlighted or underlined the first time. Such selective rereadings are better than no review at all. But if your reviewing tends to be selective repetition, you are not getting as much out of your reviewing hours as you could be. Effective reviewing is characterized by *organization* and *depth of processing*. You should approach your reviewing with a two-part plan.

The first part of your review plan should serve to improve upon the organization you started during encoding. But it is not essential to finish all your organizing during your first study session. You can use review time to put lists in order, to form verbal mediators, and so on. The techniques used during reviews are identical to those used during encoding, except that you can spend more time on them.

The second part of your review plan should serve to increase your depth of processing. Earlier we learned that the more deeply we process material, the better we remember it. You can increase your depth of processing of textbooks in three ways:

1. First, list all the main topics (for example, theories, encoding, retention, retrieval, forgetting, applications). Under each topic, write as many subheadings as you can remember. If you don't remember some, look them up. Under each subheading write as many facts as you can remember. Again, look up facts you don't remember. Make sure you see how the facts, subheadings, and main topics relate to one another.

2. After you know what is in a passage, think up good test questions for the material and then write out answers. Your questions should cover the material as thoroughly as possible. Your answers should be short notes on key ideas related to each question. You will be processing more deeply because you will be forcing yourself to think about relationships existing in the material.

3. Another way to think about relationships is to criticize the text. Do you think it makes sense to compare human memory with computer memory? What are the strengths and weaknesses of this approach? Does it make sense to distinguish between multiple memory theories and levels-of-processing theories? Can you think of an experiment that would test the two theories? Does the text contain gaps? Have you learned things in other books that fill in gaps in the present text? Perhaps this chapter failed to mention your favorite memory-aid system. How does your favorite memory aid relate to the ones reviewed here? Critical thinking of this sort will increase your depth of processing and thereby improve your retention.

Reviewing is important outside of school as well. You might be introduced to several people at once during your first day on a new job. You would do well to review their names before going to work the next morning. If you memorized a shopping list, you would do well to review it on the way to the store. Follow the same principles outlined above. Your review should improve your organization and your depth of processing. If, for some reason, you don't have time to organize or to process deeply during encoding and retention intervals, don't panic. There are things you can do during retrieval to improve your memory.

Retrieving Information Effectively

We learned earlier that retrieval cues aid recall. People remember lists better, for example, when they are given category names during retrieval. We set up retrieval cues in advance when we form images, key words, and mediators during encoding. The payoff for the extra work comes during retrieval, when all we have to do is use our preestablished memory aids. Planning is recommended but you still can use retrieval cues even if you did not develop memory aids in advance.

What do you do when a memory demand catches you completely off guard? This might happen, for example, if you lost a shopping list which you had not committed to memory. There are two things that would improve your recall in this situation.

1. First, search your memory systematically. Try to think of categories. If you recall one vegetable, try to think of others.
2. Second, try to reestablish the context in which you wrote the list. Lawyers sometimes return witnesses to the scene of a crime because the original context helps them remember details (see Norman, 1973). You might mentally retrace the steps you made when you searched your cupboard to see what you needed.

You can follow these two procedures on exams, too. If a question seems to come out of the blue, search your memory systematically and try to remember the context in which you might have studied the relevant information. Suppose you draw a blank when you are asked to define *mnemonics*. You should try to figure out which main section might have included this word. If you can correctly place it in the section on improving your memory, you will greatly increase your chance of coming up with the definition. Try to remember as much as you can about the session in which you studied the material. What was the first thing you reviewed? What questions

Has your memory ever failed you during a social introduction? You realize immediately afterwards that you do not remember the person's name. The text explains how you can overcome this problem.

COMPUTERS IMPROVE EYEWITNESS MEMORY

Police photograph all convicted criminals and keep their "mug shots" on file. Eyewitnesses are often asked to look at hundreds of such mug shots, and sometimes they correctly identify the culprit. Unfortunately, they too often pick out the wrong person. Computers can reduce these errors. For example, an interactive display system has been developed in which a witness and a computer exchange information.

To test his system, Harmon (1973) set up a mug-shot file containing photos of 256 white males between the ages of 20 and 50 (the photos shown here are the most and least similar of those in the set). For each photo, subjects rated 21 basic facial features, such as hair texture (straight, wavy, curly); chin profile (receding, straight, jutting); or forehead (receding, vertical, or bulging). The computer used the average of these ratings as its "official" description. Armed with this information, the computer was ready to help witnesses.

The computer starts the dialogue by asking the witness to describe the suspect, and the witness chooses one feature to start with—for example, eyebrows. The computer gives a range of numbers that stand for thin, medium, or bushy eyebrows, and the witness selects "1" for "thin." The computer prints the numbers of the five pictures that best fit the description of thin eyebrow weight. The witness then selects the next feature that comes to mind, ear length, and the dialogue continues until the witness cannot remember additional conspicuous features.

At this point, the witness calls for "automatic feature selection," which allows the computer to select features for the witness to rate. The computer selects only those features that discriminate between photos that fit the description given

so far. The computer allows the witness to ask 21 questions, but a dialogue may end much sooner than that, because a certain photo turns out to be the only one that comes close to fitting the description.

This system puts the target picture among the top 10 suspects 99

percent of the time and picks the target picture as the number one suspect 70 percent of the time, which is far better than witnesses do on their own. Computers cannot completely overcome witness fallibility, but they provide valuable assistance.

Most similar and least similar pairs of faces as determined by computer comparison of facial features.

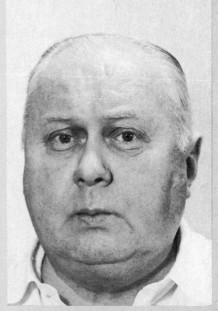

did you ask? You still might not remember, but you will at least be improving your chances.

Based on the overwhelming success of *The Memory Book*, we can assume that it has helped people. Hopefully, this is one application that you will be able to put to use immediately. Someday you may be able to strengthen your memory further with the help of computers. Computerized memory aids are already available on a limited basis. The Highlight here ("Computers Improve Eyewitness Memory") discusses one example that might have changed the outcome of the Sacco and Vanzetti trial, for it uses computers to improve eyewitness memories.

Summary

1. **Memory,** a system that allows people to retain information over time, is measured with three tests: recall, recognition, and savings.

2. Multiple memory theorists distinguish three kinds of memory: sensory memory, which lasts 1 or 2 seconds; short-term memory, which lasts less than 30 seconds; and long-term memory, which may be permanent. Levels-of-processing theorists reject the distinction between short- and long-term memories as separate memories. They believe that all abstractions are held in the same memory no matter how deep the level of abstraction.

3. **Sensory memory** represents, or **encodes,** information in a form, or code, that is similar to sensations. **Short-term memory** uses verbal codes and other abstract codes to represent only a small part of the original information. **Long-term memory** uses even more abstract codes to represent meaning.

4. People recode, or change the representation of, memories during retention intervals. They group or chunk information in short-term memory. They organize long-term memories according to preexisting categories. They sometimes reconstruct these organizations, including new things that were not part of the original memory.

5. People sometimes fail to recall, or to **retrieve,** information that is present in memory. Retrieval from short-term memory involves a search that takes additional time for each item in memory. Retrieval from long-term memory also involves a search that is often very organized. **Retrieval cues** aid in this organization.

6. **Forgetting,** the inability to remember, may be caused by trace decay and/or by interference. There are two kinds of interference: **proactive,** the interference of things learned earlier; and **retroactive,** the interference of things learned later.

7. You can improve your memory by improving your **attention** and organization when you first encounter new material. You will remember textbook material better, for example, if you identify important ideas and concentrate on them when you read. You should also organize new material by relating it to things you already know.

8. You can improve your memory through effective reviewing. Do not just repeat what you have learned—organize it, test yourself, and criticize it.

9. Memory also can be improved during retrieval. At this stage it is important to search your memory systematically, and also to try to recall the context in which something was learned.

Key Terms

amnesia
antrograde amnesia
attention
backward masking
chunking
encode
episodic memory
forgetting
free association test
hierarchy

interference theory
key-word method
long-term memory
memory
memory span
memory trace
mnemonic systems
proactive inhibition
recall tests
recognition tests

rehearsal
retrieval
retrieval cues
retroactive inhibition
retrograde amnesia
savings
savings tests

semantic memory
sensory memory
short-term memory
signal detection theory
tip-of-the-tongue (TOT) phenomenon
trace decay theory
verbal mediation

Suggested Readings

The following books are about the Sacco and Vanzetti case:

FEUERLICHT, R. S. *Justice crucified: The story of Sacco and Vanzetti*. New York: McGraw-Hill, 1977.

FRANKFURTER, F. *The case of Sacco and Vanzetti: A critical analysis of lawyers and laymen*. Boston: Little, Brown, 1927.

LOUIS, J. G., and MORGAN, E. *The legacy of Sacco and Vanzetti*. New York: Harcourt Brace Jovanovich, 1948.

BOURNE, L. E., DOMINOWSKI, R. L. & LOFTUS, E. F. *Cognitive processes* 2nd ed. Englewood Cliffs, N.J.: Prentice-Hall, 1986. The organization of this book is especially compatible with the present chapter. It has separate chapters on encoding, retention, and retrieval, and also relates these basic processes to topics of language, text comprehension, concept formation, problem solving, and reasoning.

CERMAK, L. S. (Ed.). *Human memory and amnesia*. Hillsdale, N.J.: Erlbaum, 1982. This book bridges the gap between those who study normal memory and those who study amnesia. Investigators in both areas discuss common themes, such as the question of whether long-term memory and short-term memory are different storage systems or points on a continuum in a single system.

LOFTUS, E. *Eyewitness testimony*. Boston: Harvard University Press, 1980. Loftus outlines a theoretical framework for research on perception and memory. She also relates that framework to applications in the legal process.

LORAYNE, H., & LUCAS, J. *The memory book*. New York: Ballantine, 1974. Based on results and principles that have emerged from research laboratories, this is primarily a practical book that outlines many techniques for improving one's memory.

NEISSER, U. *Cognition and reality: Principles and implications of cognitive psychology*. Neisser clearly presents modern theories of schemata and attention. He also makes a strong case for relating principles to applications.

NORMAN, D. A. *Learning and memory*. San Francisco: Freeman, 1982. This captivating discussion of memory storage, processing, semantic networks, and schemas is accessible to undergraduates who vary widely in background and motivation.

TULVING, E. *Elements of episodic memory*. New York: Oxford University Press, 1983. The author of this book is the originator of the distinction between episodic and semantic memory. Here he provides a theoretical framework for studying episodic memory and reviews 10 years of research on it.

YNILLE, J. C. (Ed.). *Imagery, memory, and cognition: Essays in honor of Allan Paivio*. Hillsdale, N.J.: Erlbaum, 1983. These proceedings of a state-of-the-art conference on imagery will satisfy students who want to learn more about the powerful effects of imagery on memory.

INFANCY AND CHILDHOOD

A perfect specimen," the nurse said, as newborn Raun Kahlil Kaufman began to breathe and cry at the same time. Raun's parents, Suzi and Barry Kaufman, experienced the birth of their third child and first son with pride and joy. The nurse's initial evaluation of Raun's condition was supported by a physical examination and by a standardized test for alertness and reflexes.

But during Raun's first month at home, Suzi Kaufman sensed that something was wrong. Raun cried much of the time and seemed unresponsive to being held and fed. The doctors found nothing wrong, but when the infant was 4 weeks old he developed a severe ear infection. Instead of improving in response to antibiotics, Raun's condition became worse. He became so dehydrated that he was put in a plastic isolette in a pediatric intensive care unit. His parents visited twice a day but could not hold and comfort their son. This crisis ended after 5 days, when the doctors announced that Raun would survive, but he might be deaf or partially deaf.

The second beginning at home was far more delightful than the first. Raun smiled continually, he enjoyed eating, and he was alert and responsive. He soon won the hearts of his older sisters. Bryn, the oldest, happily attended to him instead of her dolls. Thea, on the other hand, needed some help adjusting to her new role as a middle child. She soon readjusted, however, because her parents supplied the extra attention she needed.

At 1 year, Raun seemed on track for normal and healthy development. The only exception was that he did not put out his arms to be picked up. This peculiarity was of only minor concern until he started to show other signs of aloofness during his second year. Raun became less responsive to his name, even though he would sometimes attend to a soft and distant sound. When his sisters or parents tried to hold or hug him, he often pushed their hands away, and when someone picked him up, he let his arms dangle at his side. Although his family wanted desperately to play with him, he preferred to sit alone and to stare blankly into space. As an experienced and sensitive father, Barry Kaufman knew that these behaviors were unusual. As a former graduate student in psychology, he also knew that many of his son's abnormal behaviors fit a dreaded pattern that defined infantile autism. This subcategory of childhood schizophrenia is the most irreversible condition of profoundly disturbed children.

Besides the aloofness and blank stares, other behaviors fit the pattern. For example, Raun spent long periods rocking back and forth while sitting on the floor. Sometimes he would sit on the floor and spin plates, seeming to be completely absorbed with the spinning objects. However, Raun was unlike autistic children in that he seemed at peace. Autistic children often engage in violent, self-destructive behaviors—for example, some will bang their heads against walls. Raun never did these things. But Raun's parents knew that something was seriously wrong.

They consulted with experts in New York, Philadelphia, and California. When

Raun was 17 months old, he was examined and the results were analyzed. Signs of autism are usually not recognized before the ages of 2½ or 3 years. At first, doctors were reluctant to assign a label. They confirmed, however, that Raun was definitely autistic. They also expressed the widely held belief that autism is irreversible and incurable. Although some treatment programs existed, they were aimed at older children. The Kaufmans were therefore urged to wait until Raun was 9 to 12 months older before starting any type of treatment.

But waiting was impossible; they could not stand by and watch their son slip farther and farther away. After reading everything that they could find about autism and carefully observing Raun, they devised a plan based upon three beliefs about Raun:

1. They believed that Raun's processing of perceptions and utilization of memories were disorganized. A "hidden cookie test" helped reveal this problem. Raun would look at a cookie and follow it as one parent moved it in the boy's field of vision. The parent would then hide the cookie behind a sheet of paper. Raun would then stare and turn away. The average 8-month-old has the ability to retain the hidden object in his or her mind and to look for it, but Raun, at 20 months, could not. For him, out of sight seemed to be out of mind. Similarily, each time his own hands came into view he acted as if he were seeing them for the first time. From these observations, the Kaufmans decided to simplify events as much as possible for Raun. For example, the task of inserting a puzzle piece was divided into four parts. They first taught him to pick up the piece, then to move the piece to the puzzle, to find the right place, and finally to insert the piece.
2. The Kaufmans believed that Raun needed extra motivation because his perceptual and memory problems made interactions very difficult for him. They tried to show Raun that the extra effort was worth it because the outside world is beautiful and exciting.
3. They strongly believed that their son deserved their acceptance and approval. They tried to motivate him to accept attractive alternative behaviors but did not disapprove of his preferred behaviors. They did not try to stop him from rocking or from spinning plates. Instead, they joined in these activities with him. Most importantly, no matter how much time they spent, they were willing to accept no progress. They considered any contact with Raun its own reward.

Since the program called for long, one-on-one sessions in an environment with few distractions, Suzi spent many hours alone with Raun on a bathroom floor in their home. At first, 9 hour sessions were planned. But gradually the time increased until Suzi was spending 75 hours per week working with her son. In addition, Barry spent whatever time he could on evenings and weekends. This schedule continued for 8 weeks. Two volunteers, trained by the Kaufmans, assisted Suzi so she could have more breaks while Raun could continue one-on-one sessions for about 75 hours per week. By the end of 8 weeks, Suzi noted the following changes:

Much less rocking movement
Real eye contact established when playing certain games
More facial expression
Attentive to being called, although most often will not come on request
Making less motion with fingers against lips
Hardly ever pushes away his mother
Has started to indicate wants by crying—first time definite communications effort
Starting to mimic words
Reacts to some spoken words when being addressed—car, cup, bottle, come, up, water
For the first time expressed anger in a game environment—when we tried to remove something he did not want to give up
For the first time he did make an anticipatory arm gesture when about to be picked up
Has begun to drink out of a glass
Cried twice when someone he was playing with left the room
Has started to feed himself with his fingers (Kaufman, 1976, pp. 103–104).

The whole family was deeply involved in the program by the end of the tenth week. In the eleventh week, Barry received a special treat when he returned from work. Raun gave him his typical casual look. But then he raised his arm as if he were taking an oath of office and he flopped his fingers against his palm. He was waving hello.

Feeling so elated because of Raun's response, Barry decided to give Raun the cookie test. With Suzi at his side, he presented a cookie as he had done on each previous night of the program. On previous nights Raun had seemed interested at first, but not after the cookie disappeared behind a paper. This night was different. It was Raun's night for triumph. He pushed the paper aside, grabbed the cookie, and ate it. Barry and Suzi repeated the test again and again. Each time, Raun snatched the cookie with more enthusiasm than the time before. The cookie test had been conquered.

Suzi called Barry at work the next day to tell him about Raun's progress.

This morning when I gave him the puzzle, mixed up all the pieces and scrambled everything, he worked it out. Completely. Without any help or guidance. It's like he can retain more, use more. He's switched on like a thousand-watt bulb!

The whole family celebrated as Raun joined in their activities over the next 4 months. He started talking, using a small vocabulary: "wa" (water), "down," "more," "ba" (bottle), "Mommy," "Da-da," and "hot." He also started to play with them. One morning he joined his mother at the piano. He soon learned to mimic the notes of "Three Blind Mice." Mother and child were equally pleased, smiling repeatedly at each other.

The family went to the beach on another day, and Raun played enthusiastically with his sisters as they built sand castles. But after returning from the beach, Raun started regressing, adopting his unresponsive behaviors again. And 8 days later, he seemed to be back to where he was 4 months earlier.

Then, suddenly, he snapped back and surged forward. His vocabulary expanded in one week from 7 to 75 words. He started using small phrases and sentences, and he learned to sing songs such as "Three Blind Mice," "Over There, Over There," " 'A'-

You're Adorable," and "Splish Splash." Raun developed a morning ritual that contrasted sharply with his earlier withdrawal activities. When he was greeted at his crib, he would clap and shout "Mommy" and "Daddy." Then he would turn toward each and request a big "Hugga Hugga."

Suzi and Barry took Raun to an outpatient clinic for a developmental work-up at the age of 20 months and again at 24 months. Raun's language and socialization at 20 months were on a level appropriate for an 8-month-old. At 24 months, the same tests showed that Raun was functioning at or above his age level in every way. Raun's level on over half of the tests was 30 to 36 months. In four months, he had made an incredible developmental surge of 16 to 26 months.

Raun continued to soar at the age of two-and-a-half when his father recorded the successful effort to reach an "unreachable" child in a book, *Son-Rise*. It ends not with the usual phrase, "The End," but with a more appropriate one, "The Beginning."

At age 12 (1985), Raun has developed into an extroverted, extraordinarily articulate, loving, and playful youngster who demonstrates a near genius IQ and maintains a straight "A" scholastic average at a neighborhood school. He also works with other children with developmental difficulties in programs designed by the Kaufmans for other families.

STUDYING DEVELOPMENT

Human development is a process by which the genes that we inherit from our parents come to be expressed as specific physical and behavioral characteristics. Development is controlled by a continuous interaction between *heredity* and *environment*. The relative influence of these two factors varies from characteristic to characteristic. Heredity alone determined the color of Raun's hair and eyes. But heredity and environment both influenced Raun's learning development. He inherited genes that gave him the potential to learn music, for example, but his mother helped him realize that potential by providing an environment that included lessons and encouragement. Today, heredity and environment continue to work together to determine his development.

Methods of Studying Development

The doctors who observed Raun's rapid developmental surge were both surprised and impressed. They videotaped one of Suzi's sessions with Raun, hoping to gain insights that would help them with other children. They were cautious, however, about generalizing from observations of one person. Surely there are problems with doing so, especially when circumstances are as unusual as Raun's. But are any methods used to study development completely trustworthy?

Longitudinal versus Cross-Sectional Research. In **longitudinal research** investigators periodically test the same person or group of people over a period of time. In **cross-sectional research** investigators compare the responses of different people of different ages. Each method has both advantages and disadvantages:

1. *Measuring stability of behavior* is a main advantage of longitudinal research. Kagan and Moss (1962) studied the same people from birth to the twenties. They found, for example, that children who were passive and dependent at age 6 were also that way as adults. Cross-sectional research cannot examine stability, because it does not measure the same people at different ages.

2. *Cultural and historical experiences* are better controlled by longitudinal research, because investigators can keep track of many aspects of a person's experience. Cross-sectional studies compare people who may have had very different experiences. Suppose you did a cross-sectional study in 1960 to compare thriftiness of 10-, 20-, and 30-year-olds. These people grew up in the 1950s, 1940s, and 1930s, respectively. You would wonder, therefore, if differences between groups existed because of different ages or because of different early experiences. Being raised during the economic depression of the 1930s was surely very different from being raised during the booming economy of the 1950s.

3. *Lack of practicality* is a major disadvantage of longitudinal designs. It takes 20 years to do a longitudinal study on people from birth to 20 years old, and keeping track of people for that long is very expensive. You could do a cross-sectional study on the same age range in about a month for much less money.

4. *Loss of subjects* is another disadvantage of longitudinal designs. People die, move away, or quit because they are tired of the experiment. Such losses can greatly restrict your ability to generalize from the results. Cross-sectional studies reduce this problem by collecting data over a short period.

5. *Flexibility* is another consideration that weighs against longitudinal research, since it must use the same tests over many years in order to provide comparable measures between ages. If improved tests are developed, you cannot go back in time to give the new test to your subjects at earlier years. You would have to continue to use the old test with which you took original measures, or else you would lose the ability to compare different ages. Cross-sectional research allows you to try various measures until an appropriate one is found, and you are always free to use the most up-to-date tests.

No single design is best for every purpose; researchers must select the right design for studying the problem at hand. Ideally, researchers strive to apply both longitudinal and cross-sectional designs to the same problems. They can be more certain that they are on the right track when results from both designs agree. Both designs have been valuable in testing theories of development, which we will discuss in the next section.

Theories of Development

We suggested earlier that Raun's development was influenced by heredity and environment. In the seventeenth and eighteenth centuries, this conclusion would have been at odds with two extreme theories of development. One theory, called *nativism*, emphasizes the role of heredity in the development of mind and behavior. Nativism says that infants are born with innate capacities to experience the world pretty much as adults do. Extreme nativism holds that development is nothing more than **maturation,** which is the unfolding of genetically determined abilities. Another theory, called *empiricism*, holds that experience is the source of all knowledge. This theory states that newborns experience the world as very confusing until they learn to perceive as adults do. Extreme empiricism holds that all development is determined by learning through experience.

Neither extreme theory can explain a phenomenon called a **critical period,** which is a stage of development during which an organism must have certain experiences or else it will not develop normally. Researchers demonstrated critical periods experimentally by carefully suturing closed the eyelids of kittens to deprive them of visual stimulation (Hubel & Wiesel, 1970). They varied the age of the kittens at the beginning of deprivation and they manipulated the length of deprivation. The kittens learned to get along quite well while they were deprived. But, depending on the timing, deprivation sometimes caused permanent damage to the kitten's visual system. Hubel and Wiesel tested development of the visual cortex after deprivation by placing tiny electrodes in cells of anesthetized kittens (see Chapter 2). Deprivation damaged cortical cells only if it came between the fourth and twelfth week of life. Deprivation in kittens younger than 4 weeks caused no noticeable damage, nor did deprivation in kittens older than 12 weeks, even if it lasted for months. In contrast, 3 to 4 days of deprivation during the fourth and fifth week of life caused irreversible damage. Weeks 4 through 12 bound a critical period during which kittens must have visual experience or else their visual system will not develop normally.

We cannot explain critical periods without assuming that heredity (maturation) and environment (learning) interact. Genes regulate a timetable that determines the critical period for developing cortical cells. The environment must then provide certain experiences or development will be knocked off track. Traits that interest psychologists, such as intelligence, personality, and emotions, are generally influenced by both heredity and environment. We will therefore pay attention to both factors when we follow the course of human development in this and the next chapter.

PRENATAL DEVELOPMENT

Prenatal refers to the 9-month period of development before birth. Mothers carry the developing organism in a hollow muscular organ called the uterus or womb. In this section we will outline stages of normal prenatal development and discuss environment forces that affect that development.

Stages of Prenatal Development

We can assume from Raun's healthy condition at birth that his prenatal development was normal. He grew from a microscopic cell through a naturally determined sequence into a beautiful baby. Let's look at some of the highlights of this stage of development.

Period of the Ovum. An ovum is a mature female sex cell which after fertilization develops into an offspring (see Chapter 2). The first two-week period of development after fertilization is called the period of the ovum. A fertilized ovum immediately divides, forming new cells that cluster together in a ball. The cell ball grows to about the size of a poppie seed and implants itself in the wall of the womb.

Period of the Embryo. From the third week through the eighth week the organism is called an embryo. This period is characterized by extremely rapid growth, in which the embryo grows to a weight of about 1 ounce and is about 1 inch long. By that time, the embryo is dependent on the placenta, which is a special filter that allows for the exchange of food and waste with the mother. The embryo develops internal organs, limbs with separate fingers and toes, a face with a prominent nose, and external sex organs (although it is difficult to distinguish males from females at the end of the second month).

Period of the Fetus. From the third month through birth the organism is called a fetus. The following is a breakdown of this period, month by month:

1. By the end of the third month, a heart starts pumping blood through the fetus, and its beat can be heard by a stethoscope. Teeth begin to develop, and males can be distinguished from females.
2. A mother often feels fetal movement during the fourth month. Weight increases to nearly half a pound, and the fetus is about 8 inches long. He or she develops eyebrows, eyelashes, fingerprints, and footprints.
3. During the fifth month the fetus gains about half a pound and grows about 4 inches longer; sucking, swallowing, and hiccoughing reflexes develop.
4. The sixth month adds 1 additional pound and about 2 inches in length. The skin is wrinkled with the first evidence of fat beginning just beneath the skin. Eyes are well developed and they open and close.
5. After 7 months, the fetus reaches the *age of viability*, a time at which the fetus might survive if born prematurely. At this important point, the fetus is about 16 inches long and weighs about 3 pounds, with more fat under his or her skin.
6. Fat continues to develop during the eighth month and the skin loses some of its wrinkles. The fetus gains about 2 pounds and grows another 2 inches longer. The arms and legs move about strenuously, often kicking, or punching the uterine wall. Mothers feel this movement inside them, and others can feel it by placing a hand over the uterus. The fetus will probably survive if it is born after the eighth month.
7. The fetus is fully prepared for birth after the ninth month.

These photos show a fertilized ovum (top, left); an embryo at 4 weeks (top, right), 6 weeks (middle, left), and 8 weeks (middle, right), and a fetus at 4½ months (bottom).

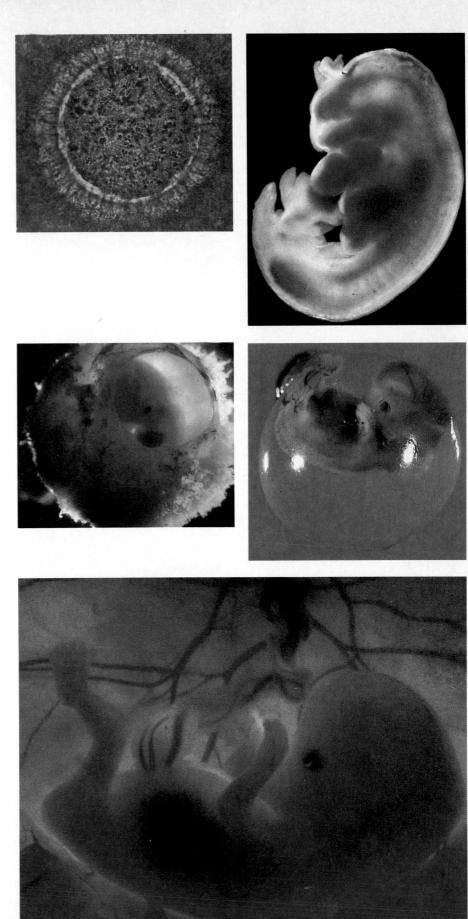

Average birth weight is about 7 pounds, and average length is about 20 inches. Genes determine birth size, for the most part. Mothers who eat more because they are "eating for two" find that the extra food is not used by the baby, but is stored in the mother's body as fat. Mothers do have to be careful about what they eat and drink, however, as we shall see in the next section.

Prenatal Environmental Influences

Heredity and environment start interacting long before birth. A host of environmental influences can prevent an unborn infant from achieving its full inherited potential. Mothers who take the time to learn some fundamental precautions can provide an optimal prenatal environment for their baby. Let's go over some of the major environmental influences.

Nutrition. A good diet is essential for healthy fetal development, including brain development. A baby's brain can be 60 percent smaller than normal at birth if he or she is seriously malnourished (Wyden, 1971). Doctors emphasize adequate amounts of protein in a pregnant woman's diet and they prescribe iron and vitamin supplements.

Diseases. Many diseases, including heart disease, diabetes, and hypertension, have a bad effect on fetal development. Mothers are warned to avoid exposure to German measles during early pregnancy; it can cause many birth defects, including impaired vision and hearing, heart malformation, and mental retardation. *Venereal diseases*, which are contagious diseases that are transmitted by sexual intercourse, also have tragic effects. One venereal disease, *syphilis*, can infect the fetus carried by a woman with the disease, usually causing both physical and mental defects. Fetal infection can be prevented, however, if the mother's infection is successfully treated by the fifth month of pregnancy.

Drugs. Drugs taken by the mother during pregnancy can have disastrous effects on fetal development. A well-known example is the use of *thalidomide*, a drug that had been prescribed to calm nervousness (it has been taken off the market). Its use during pregnancy caused serious developmental deformities of the baby's limbs. Many other drugs are dangerous during pregnancy—even aspirin in high doses can cause fetal blood disorders. Nicotine and alcohol also harm fetal development. Both lead to higher rates of abortions, premature births, and low birthweight. Researchers have also found abnormal behavior patterns in the offspring of moderate drinkers (Landesman-Dwyar, Keller, & Streissguth, 1977).

Delivery Complications. Most births (over 90 percent) occur without serious complications, but sometimes infants get injured during the birth process. The most serious injuries involve too much pressure on the brain and too little oxygen being supplied to the brain. These disorders occur during abnormal deliveries, when the head is squeezed too hard or when the baby is cut off from the placenta's nourishment too soon. Both of these factors can cause neurological damage leading to mental deficiencies (Pasamanick & Lilienfeld, 1955). Such injuries can be detected shortly after birth. Many hospitals assess the condition of newborns with the **Apgar scoring system,** which is shown and described in Table 8–1. Low Apgar scores indicate possible neurological damage. Raun had a high Apgar score, suggesting that he did not suffer neurological damage during birth.

This discussion of environmental factors can create a misleading impression that the odds are against a normal birth. In fact, the odds are overwhelmingly in its favor. Our species would not have survived if we were unlikely to produce healthy offspring, so the odds have been in our favor for some time. The odds are even greater today, because doctors are continually improving their ability to prevent, detect, and correct prenatal prob-

Table 8–1
The Apgar Scoring Method

Sign	0	1	2
Heart Rate	Absent	Below 100	Over 100
Respiratory Effort	Absent	Minimal; Weak Cry	Good; Strong Cry
Muscle Tone	Limp	Some Flexion of Extremities	Active Motion; Extremities Well Flexed
Reflex Irritability (response to stimulation on sole of foot)	No Response	Grimace	Cry
Color	Blue or Pale	Body Pink; Extremities Blue	Pink

Source: Apgar (1953).

lems. Most parents who enter hospitals to have babies leave for home several days later to assume full care of a healthy infant. Let's examine some of the many developmental changes that take place during the first year of the infant's life.

BIRTH TO 1 YEAR

Raun started withdrawing shortly after his first birthday. What was unusual about his first year? What factors contributed to his condition? We will analyze normal patterns of development in detail in order to establish a standard for comparison with Raun. We will also discuss the extent to which heredity and environment influence each aspect of development.

Physical Growth

Was Raun's condition related to abnormalities in his physical growth? This question is not easy to answer. We do know that his rate of growth was normal for his age. That is, it followed two simple rules:

1. An infant grows about 1 inch per month in the first 6 months and about ½ inch per month for the rest of the year.
2. An infant should gain about 5 to 7 ounces a week during the first 6 months and 3 to 5 ounces a week during the second 6 months.

Pediatricians and parents routinely measure gains in height and weight because abnormal growth rates can warn of health problems. On the other hand, some aspects of physical growth cannot be detected during a routine observation. Consider the development of the nervous system, for example.

The physical growth of the nervous system follows a more complex pattern. Infants are born with an incomplete nervous system. It develops rapidly after birth, slowing down between the second and fourth year. Therefore, the first years are vital to normal neural development. The nervous system at birth is "unfinished" in three ways:

1. Parts of the brain that are present at birth are smaller than they will be later in life. The brain is much nearer to its final size, however, than are muscles and other structures.
2. A newborn's cortex is very underdeveloped. During the first year, new cortical cells are formed, cells become larger, and new interconnections are formed between cells. Parts of the cortex develop at different rates. Areas controlling hearing and seeing develop within 6 months, as do areas controlling movement of the head, upper trunk,

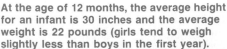

At the age of 12 months, the average height for an infant is 30 inches and the average weight is 22 pounds (girls tend to weigh slightly less than boys in the first year).

arms, and hands. Areas controlling movement of the lower trunk and legs develop slowly over almost a 2 year period. Rosenzweig (1966) found that raising rats in enriched environments (with "toys"—wheels, ladders, platforms, and so on) greatly increases cortical development.

3. Newborns lack some important nerve coverings called *myelin sheaths*, which we discussed in Chapter 2. Development of myelin sheaths, a process called **myelinization,** determines control over body parts. For instance, a child has poor control over lower body parts until spinal cord myelinization reaches a critical stage at about 2 years of age.

The nervous system is most vulnerable to diseases, malnutrition, and other environmental influences while it is developing. Thus, we might wonder whether the development of Raun's nervous system was disturbed, perhaps by the severe dehydration he experienced in early infancy. We cannot, however, rule out other possibilities. For example, Raun might have inherited his condition. Instead of speculating about causal factors, let's continue to compare Raun's condition with normal trends.

Motor Development

Motor development refers to a baby's growing ability to control muscles in order to move around and to manipulate objects. Raun's motor development did not follow normal patterns. He began on schedule, but he fell behind in areas such as controlling his jaw and tongue. Let's examine the normal pattern and the meaning of deviations from it.

Reflexive Movements. Infants are born with many reflexes, which are movements that are made automatically in response to a stimulus (Sheppard & Mysak, 1984). The presence or absence of reflexes can indicate normal or abnormal development. Raun's later abnormal development, however, could not have been anticipated by his early reflexive movements, which were normal.

Some reflexes are protective, such as *coughing* and *sneezing*, which clear the respiratory tract. Other reflexes are involved with eating. The **rooting reflex** causes infants to turn their head toward anything that touches their cheeks. It helps in feeding because it moves the mouth closer to a nipple. The **sucking reflex** causes sucking when anything touches the lips. It is, of course, essential for getting milk from a breast or bottle. Four other common reflexes are:

1. The **grasp reflex,** which causes infants to close their fingers tightly around an object that touches their palm (thumbs do not respond in this reflex). An infant's grip is so strong that you can insert your index fingers into a newborn's palms and then lift the baby into a standing position. The reflex is present at birth, but disappears at about 6 months after conscious control takes over grasping.

2. The **dancing reflex,** which causes babies to prance with their legs in a "tip-toe" stepping motion when they are held upright with feet touching a surface. (Perhaps there is some truth to the saying that we are "born to boogie.") This reflex is usually no longer seen by the seventh or eighth month.

3. The **Moro reflex** or **startle reflex,** which causes a motor reaction of infants' legs, arms, and trunk in response to a sudden loud noise or loss of support. You can observe it best by suddenly slapping a baby's mattress. The newborn will draw up his or her legs with the soles of the feet turned toward each other. The arms will stretch out into an embracing position, and the back will arch. This reflex disappears by the fifth month.

4. The **tonic neck reflex,** which causes infants who are on their back to move their arms and legs into a "fencing" position when the head

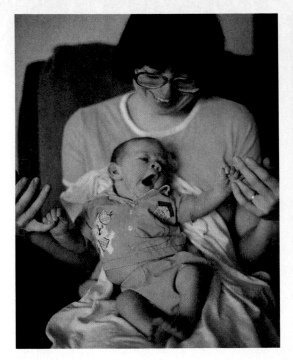

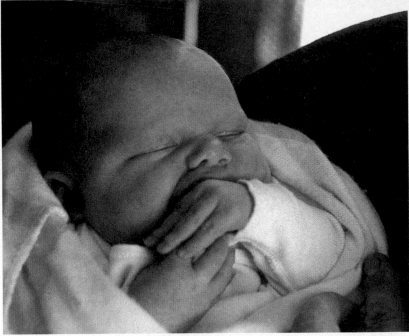

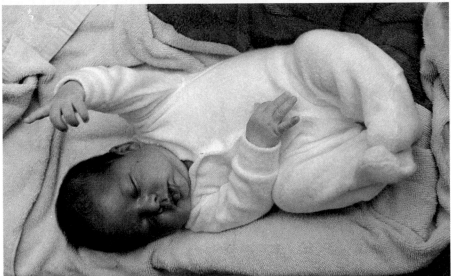

(Top, left) The grasp reflex causes infants to close their fingers tightly around anything that touches their palm.
(Top, right) The sucking reflex causes the baby to suck when anything touches the lips.
(Bottom) In the tonic neck reflex, when the head is turned to one side, infants who are lying on their back move their arms and legs into a "fencing" position.

is turned to one side. Newborns extend the arm and leg on the side that they are facing and draw up the other arm and leg into a flexed position. This reflex disappears by the fourth month.

The lack of any of these reflexes at birth can mean that there is an abnormality in the nervous system. Continuation of these reflexes for too long after they should have disappeared can also be a sign of abnormal neural development.

Voluntary Movements. A major accomplishment in the first year of life is the replacement of motor reflexes with voluntary motor control. This achievement greatly increases an infant's ability to explore its environment. A baby begins to successfully reach for and grasp objects at about 4 or 5 months of age. As noted, 1-year-olds like to feed themselves with their fingers, and they are able to scribble with a crayon.

Figure 8–1 summarizes landmark achievements in infant mobility. Some infants reach each stage ahead of others, as can be seen in the figure. Most babies learn to roll over sometime between the second and fifth

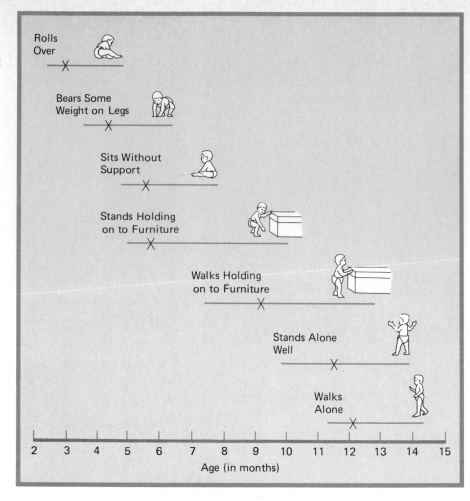

month, and many walk alone by the end of their first year. Raun showed no significant deviations from this schedule.

A baby's first year is also important for perceptual development, which was discussed in Chapter 4, and cognitive development which will be discussed in the next section on childhood.

CHILDHOOD

The rapid growth rate of the first year continues through the second year. It slows down until the end of childhood, when it increases again. Children usually grow about 3 inches and gain about 5 pounds per year between their third birthday and the beginning of adolescence. In addition to growing physically, children between the ages of 2 and 13 make important gains in cognitive and language development, as well as in social and personality development. We will consider normal development in these areas and then examine Raun's patterns.

Cognitive Development

Cognitive development involves changes in how children understand and think about their world as they grow older. This section will review evidence that children understand and think about their world in qualitatively different ways as they pass through various stages of cognitive development. The data on normal development provide a frame of reference for evaluating abnormalities. Recent studies have found, for instance, that a delay in mastering cognitive skills, such as Raun experienced, is characteristic of autistic children (e.g., Waterhouse & Fein, 1983).

Historical Overview.   As we discussed in Chapter 1, American behaviorists in the early years limited their research to discovering relationships between stimulus and observable responses. Their theories held that learning at all ages can be explained without considering what goes on in a person's mind. In contrast, Jean Piaget, a Swiss scientist, made observations precisely in order to figure out what goes on in a child's mind. He argued that: (1) we cannot understand learning without understanding thinking, and (2) that children think differently from adults. We will cover his methods and theories in detail, because they had a tremendous impact on modern psychology.

Piaget's Approach.   Piaget used open questioning sessions with his own three children and with other children to find out how they interpreted objects and events in the world around them. He concluded that children of the same age make similar incorrect responses, which are different from errors made by both older and younger children. This pattern of errors suggested that children develop qualitatively different ways of organizing and responding to experiences. He used the term **schema** to refer to a mental structure that organizes responses to experiences. He proposed that newborns inherit *schemata* (plural of *schema*), which are simple reaction patterns and reflexes, such as a sucking schema and a grasping schema. Gradually, these independent schema become integrated through the process of *organization*, an inherited predisposition to organize simple schema into higher-order ones. A higher-order schema would control a response pattern for grasping a bottle, bringing it to the mouth, and drinking it, for example.

A child also inherits two other processes: (1) **assimilation,** which is the process of responding in a way that fits existing schema; and (2) **accommodation,** which is the process of adjusting a schema to fit environmental demands. Consider a baby with a schema to control bringing a bottle to his or her mouth. Suppose a bottle was placed behind a plexiglass barrier. The barrier allowed the baby to see the bottle, but did not allow the baby to reach the bottle directly. Assimilation would be shown if the baby responded according to its existing schema, that is, if the baby tried to reach directly for the bottle. Accommodation would be shown if the baby changed its schema by reaching around the barrier.

Piaget (1960) is perhaps most famous for his assertion that the sequence of cognitive development is divided into a series of stages. He assumed that stages are organized around a dominant theme and that each stage contains qualitatively different behaviors. He did not claim that all children go through stages at exactly the same ages, but he did state that all children go through the same stages in the same *order*, and he identified four stages.

1. The **sensorimotor stage** extends from birth to about 2 years. Its main theme is discovering relationships between sensations and motor behavior. As we mentioned earlier, children replace reflexes with voluntary actions during the first 2 years. At first, reflexes supply the means for infants to gain nourishment by sucking. Later they learn that they can grasp a bottle and bring it to their mouth at will. They learn that they can cause other sensations as well, such as making noise by shaking a rattle.

    You could easily modify the cookie test devised by Raun's father to use with an infant who is in the first 4 months of the sensorimotor stage. Simply place a favorite toy in front of the infant. He or she will express interest by looking, moving both arms, and so on. Now, drop a screen in front of the toy, hiding it from view. The infant will act as if the toy no longer exists! He or she will not search for

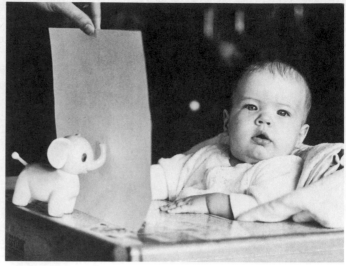

If a screen is put in front of a toy, blocking it from view, infants in the first 4 months will act as if the toy no longer exists, and will not try to find it behind the screen. Piaget says infants do this because they do not yet have the concept of object permanence.

it visually or manually (out of sight, out of mind). Piaget claims that infants act this way because they lack the concept of *object permanence*, which is knowledge that objects continue to exist even when they can no longer be experienced. Object permanence is developed during the sensorimotor stage. Infants usually start searching for concealed objects somewhere between 8 and 12 months of age. In contrast, Raun did not start reaching for a hidden cookie until he was about 21½ months old. Apparently his development of object permanence was delayed until then.

2. The **preoperational stage** extends from about 2 to 7 years of age. Its dominant theme is discovering *operations*, which are plans, strategies, and rules for solving problems and for classifying information. Preoperational children have the basic mental abilities for doing mental operations: They can form mental images and they can represent things symbolically with words. But preoperational children are only beginning to discover the logical mental operations that will characterize their later thinking.

Their immature thinking leads to unique responses, which you might observe during an interview. Striking up a conversation about the sun might reveal two characteristics of preoperational thought: *animism*, which is the tendency to attribute life to inanimate objects, and *egocentrism*, which is the belief that everything is centered around one's self. The following conversation between Piaget and a child illustrates both characteristics (Piaget, 1960, p. 215):

Piaget: Does the sun move?
Child: Yes, when one walks it follows. When one turns around it turns around too. Doesn't it ever follow you too?
Piaget: Why does it move?
Child: Because when one walks, it goes too.
Piaget: Why does it go?
Child: To hear what we say.
Piaget: Is it alive?
Child: Of course, otherwise it wouldn't follow us, it couldn't shine.

One characteristic of preoperational thought is lack of conservation—a lack of the understanding that amounts do not change when shapes change. To test this, Piaget poured water from a short wide glass into a tall narrow glass and asked if the amount of water was the same. Preoperational children tend to say that there is more water in the taller glass.

Another characteristic of preoperational thought is lack of conservation—a lack of the understanding that amounts do not change when shapes change. For example, if you rolled out a ball of clay into a log shape, the preoperational child would say that the log has more clay than the ball. If you spread out a row of five chocolate candies next to a bunched-up row of five pieces, this same child would say that the longer row had more candy, and he or she would be much happier to get it as a prize (Halford & Boyle, 1985). If you poured orange juice from a short wide glass into a tall, narrow one, the child would say that the taller glass has more juice in it. Again, he or she would be much happier to have the taller glass, even after watching you pour the liquid from one glass to the other without adding a drop.

3. The **concrete operational stage** extends from about ages 7 to 12. Its main theme is extending mental operations from concrete objects to purely symbolic terms. Concrete operational children have learned most of the principles of conservation, which means that they correctly use mental operations about concrete objects. They also use operations to form mental maps of their environment. Although preoperational children can find their way to a friend's house by learning a specific place to turn, they do not have an overall picture of their surroundings. Concrete operational children, on the other hand, can draw maps of their environment. They are only beginning to form operations about abstract concepts, however, so their reasoning process differs from those of older children and adults.

    For example, concrete operational children would have much more trouble than an adult with the following problem:

    Andy, Bob, Charles, and Doug are close friends. How many groups of two, three, or four of these friends can be formed with Andy in each group? In a few minutes, you would be able to figure out that the answer is 7, as follows:

    1. Andy, Bob
    2. Andy, Charles
    3. Andy, Doug
    4. Andy, Bob, Charles
    5. Andy, Bob, Doug
    6. Andy, Charles, Doug
    7. Andy, Bob, Charles, Doug

    Preoperational children would probably find this problem to be very difficult for two reasons. First, they have trouble thinking about hypothetical examples. They might wonder why Andy gets to be in every group, for instance, even though that is irrelevant to solving the problem. Second, they have trouble thinking of all the possible combinations of things. The ability to consider many possibilities readily doesn't come until the last stage of development.

4. The **formal operational stage,** Piaget's last stage, extends from about 13 years of age on into adulthood. Its main theme is the ability to consider many possible solutions to a problem and the ability to systematically test those possibilities. Formal operations are required to understand many of the concepts introduced in this text.

Language Development

Children move in a few years from absence of speech to exhibiting an amazing mastery of language. Before starting school at the age of 5, children understand and say thousands of words. They also can combine words to express thoughts in well-formed sentences. Some landmarks in language development are as follows:

1. About 2 months old: Children make cooing sounds, which are pleasant sounds made in response to pleasant stimuli. During their second month many babies also start to express happy feelings by smiling.

Table 8–2
Two-Word Sentences in Children's Speech

Function	Two-Word Sentence
Locate, Name	there book that car see doggie
Demand, Desire	more milk give candy want gum
Negate	no wet no wash no hungry allgone milk
Describe Event or Situation	Bambi go mail come hit ball block fall baby highchair
Show Possession	my shoe mama dress
Modify, Qualify	pretty dress big boat
Question	where ball

Source: Slobin (1971).

2. About 6 months old: Children start making babbling sounds, which are nonsense sounds containing many different speech sounds. At first, babbling contains speech sounds from many languages that babies have not heard as part of their environment (for example, they will make the French "eu" sound, or the German "ü," even though their parents or those around them have never made those sounds). Within several months, however, babbling includes mostly sounds from only those languages that babies hear spoken.

3. About 10 months old: Children distinguish between a few adult words. They might, for instance, give different responses to the words "cookie" and "bed." Thus, comprehension of words seems to start before production of words. The ability to understand speech stays far ahead of the ability to produce it throughout a child's development.

4. About 12 months old: Children utter single words to name people and objects around them. They might, for example, say "dada" and "block." In contrast, Raun did not acquire this ability until he was slightly more than 22 months old.

5. About 15 months old: Single words begin to be used in a new way. They are used in what is called **holophrastic speech,** which is the use of single words to express whole phrases. For example, a child might say "out," meaning "I want to go outside."

6. About 24 months old: Children combine words into two-word statements. Table 8–2 gives examples of some two-word statements and their function.

7. During second year: Children rapidly learn to expand two-word statements into longer, grammatically correct sentences. To illustrate, Limber (1973) reported the following sentence spoken by a 34-month-old child: "When I was a little girl I could go 'geek-geek,' like that; but now I can go, 'This is a chair.'"

Although Raun fell behind initially in language development, he seemed to catch up. By the age of 30 months he spoke in sentences of up to 14 words. Thus, he learned not only the words, but also rules for combining words into sentences. We will consider these rules in the next section, as we review theories of language development.

Theories of Language Development. How do children learn to speak sentences? Psychologists have considered three possible answers. First, social-learning theory suggests that children might learn to speak by imitating adults. Indeed, some children do learn some *words* by imitating elders (Bloom, Hood, & Lightbown, 1974). However, children apparently do not learn *sentences* by imitating. If they did, they would say word combinations that are similar to sentences used by adults. But children constantly say things that adults never say. Table 8–2 gives examples of primitive sentences uttered by 2-year-olds. These observations seem contrary to the idea that children learn sentences by imitating adult utterances.

Second, operant conditioning suggests that parents might teach children to speak by reinforcing correct utterances and by ignoring or punishing incorrect ones. B. F. Skinner (1957), in his book, *Verbal Behavior*, tried to explain language acquisition strictly in terms of such stimuli and response patterns, without reference to cognitive representations. Skinner argued that science has no room for speculations about mental processes, because scientists cannot actually observe them. Most psychologists agreed with Skinner at that time. Gradually, however, evidence was gathered in opposition to this view. Scientists found, for example, that parents rarely pay attention to grammar when children are learning to form sentences (Brown, Cazden, & Bellugi, 1969). Parents do not ignore or punish grammatically incorrect statements. Yet incorrect sentences usually stop anyway, and they are replaced by correct ones.

Interaction with parents is of course important in language learning, but psychologists do not agree on exactly how children learn to speak sentences.

Third, Chomsky, who was a leading critic of Skinner's views, and an advocate of cognitive theories, had his own views regarding language development (Chomsky, 1975). He pointed out that operant conditioning cannot explain the fact that we speak and understand sentences that are novel in the sense that we have had no prior experience with them (Chomsky, 1975). He argued further that scientists must postulate cognitive representations to explain language acquisition. He proposed that children learn cognitive representations that include units of thought and rules for combining those units. For instance, one rule is that "-ed" is added to verbs to change them from present tense to past tense (look-looked). Children give evidence of having formed a rule when they overgeneralize it, producing utterances that they have never seen or heard. They might say, "I goed outside," or "I taked the cookie." Later on, they learn that irregular verbs are exceptions to the rule, and they learn the correct past tense form of these verbs. Cognitive psychologists must observe children's speech to infer the rules that children learn (Bates, MacWhinney, Caselli, Devescovi, Natale, & Venza, 1984). It does no good to ask children what rules they use, because they cannot say. Children learn to verbalize the rule about "-ed" endings, for example, only after the rule is taught in grammar school. By that time, of course, children have been using it for years.

Lenneberg (1967) proposed that human brain development passes through a critical period between 2 years and about 13 years. During this period children learn language "from mere exposure" to it. The "critical period" theory has two versions. One version suggests that people cannot acquire language from mere exposure before or after the critical period;

GENIE, A MODERN "WOLF" CHILD

Children raised with little or no contact with other humans are sometimes called "wolf" children. The name was used first with children who had been lost or abandoned in a forest and supposedly reared by wolves (Brown, 1958). It is now also used to describe children raised by humans under extremely deprived conditions. Genie fits into this second category.

In the winter of 1970 Genie was admitted to a hospital suffering from extreme malnutrition. At the age of 13 years, 7 months, she weighed 59 pounds and was 54 inches long. She could not straighten her arms or legs and she could not walk more than about 10 feet. She could not chew and she swallowed with difficulty. She could not control her feces or urine. She would look at people with interest, but she would not speak. In fact, she suppressed almost all vocalizations.

Genie was a victim of child abuse. At the age of 20 months, her father confined her to a small room. He harnessed her to an infant's potty seat during the day. At night, when he didn't forget, he would put her in a sleeping bag in a crib. He beat her whenever she was noisy, and he never spoke to her. Instead, he barked and growled at her like a dog. He fed her cereals, baby food, and an occasional soft-boiled egg. When Genie was almost 14 years old, her mother finally took action and escaped with her.

After regaining her strength in the hospital, Genie was transferred to a rehabilitation center, where she had greater opportunity to interact with a warm, loving staff. She developed affectionate relationships with several adults, including her mother, who visited her twice a week, and Dr. James Kent, who supervised her activities. Gradually, Genie internalized the caring she experienced from others. On one occasion, a teacher asked a child how many balloons he had.

Although the boy held only two balloons, he answered, "Three." Genie looked startled and quickly gave him one of her balloons. This act of sharing revealed not only her social development, but also her language development.

Genie learned to understand sentences long before she produced them. When she did finally string words together, she produced grammatically primitive and ill-formed strings. Here are some examples, recorded when she was between the ages of 14 and 16 years: "Cow tongue meat," meaning "A cow's tongue is meat"; and "Graduation to buy presents," meaning "At my graduation, people will buy me presents." On the one hand, Genie's progress in language acquisition suggests that people can learn a language from mere exposure after the age of 13. On the other hand, Genie's unusual language habits suggest that people might not be able to acquire *normal* language after that age.

Genie's language is marked by characteristics that are found in people with brain damage. She rarely makes use of rules that she knows, such as forming plurals. And she never learned certain aspects of language, such as asking WH-questions (who, what, where, etc.). Genie may never speak normally, because her brain may have matured past a critical period for normal language development (see Renneberg, 1967).

Genie's cognitive development was also quite abnormal. Standard tests suggested that 20-year-old Genie was in Piaget's concrete operational stage, which usually extends from about 7 to 12 years of age. Genie did make progress, however, after she was free to experience the world. In 1977, Susan Curtiss summarized the progress as follows: "My work with Genie continues, and Genie continues to change, becoming a fuller person, realizing more of her human potential. . . . [My hope is] that I will not be able to keep up with her, that she will have the last word" (Curtiss, 1977, p. 42).

the second version states that people cannot acquire *normal* language from mere exposure before or after the critical period. Evidence is contrary to the first version and supports the second. Some evidence comes from the case of a girl who was locked away and deprived of exposure to language through most of her childhood (see "Highlight, Genie: A Modern 'Wolf' Child").

Personality and Social Development

Language skills influence our personality, which is our unique way of reacting and adjusting to our environment (see Chapter 12). These skills are also an important part of how we develop socially (see Chapter 15). Raun's withdrawal demonstrated, however, that personality and social development include many other behaviors such as smiling and hugging. We will discuss some of these other behaviors in this section.

Smiling: An Early Social Response.   Both heredity and environment influence smiling, an often studied social response. Evidence suggests that genetic factors influence the age at which infants start social smiles. Not all smiles are social responses. Infants sometimes smile, for instance, as a reflex when someone strokes their lips (Gewirtz, 1965). Smiles are not considered to be social responses until they are elicited by social stimuli, such as faces and voices. Social smiles start between 3 and 8 weeks of age. Fraternal twins, who have different genotypes, start smiling at different ages; identical twins, however, who have the same genotype, start smiling at similar ages. The higher correlation of starting age for identical twins suggests that genes influence the onset of social responses. Environmental conditions also influence early social responses. Institutionalized infants decrease their smiling rate when they receive little social stimulation. They smile more again when caregivers play with them regularly (Brackbill, 1958; Dennis, 1973).

Attachment.   Heredity and environment also interact to determine other social behaviors. An important one is **attachment,** which is the tendency of youngsters to seek closeness to certain people. Animal research suggests that this might be a critical period for the development of attachments. Hess (1958) showed, for example, that ducklings are most likely to form attachments during their first 14 hours of life; after 2 days, attachment will probably not occur. A critical period in the formation of human

Ducklings are most likely to form attachments during their first 14 hours of life.

attachment is not easy to identify, if it exists at all (Stendler, 1952). Human attachments normally develop in a series of three steps during the first 6 months of life: (1) infants first begin to show a preference for any human over any object; (2) they then show a preference for familiar people over unfamiliar ones; and (3) finally, they become attached to certain people, usually their mother or other primary caregiver. These attachments provide a foundation for social and personality development. Raun's development in this area was disrupted when he withdrew into his own world. At that point, his parents turned to the psychological literature to determine how to reach him. We will review some of these important works on attachment.

Determining Factors. The three-step pattern of developing attachments is found not only in Western society (Schaffer & Emerson, 1964), but also in cultures with greatly different child-rearing practices, such as Uganda (Ainsworth, 1963) and a Hopi Indian reservation (Dennis, 1940). This developmental consistency across different cultures suggests that genes play a role in developing attachments (Bowlby, 1973). Environmental factors are also important, especially in determining the choice of attachment figures and the quality of attachment.

Early theories on attachment held that a mother's presence becomes satisfying because it is associated with food. Accordingly, attachments should develop only to those who provide nourishment. This prediction was challenged in famous experiments on attachment in monkeys. Harlow and Zimmerman (1959) raised monkeys in the presence of two artificial mothers. One substitute "mother" had a bare wire body and the other had a cuddly terrycloth body. Either one could supply milk from a bottle attached to the "chest." No matter which one provided food, infant monkeys became attached to the terrycloth "mother." They clung to the cloth substitute, for example, in strange environments or in other stressful situations. Harlow and Suomi (1970) showed that infant monkeys also prefer artifical mothers that rock over ones that don't move, and they prefer

In Harlow's study, infant monkeys became attached to the terrycloth "mother" and their typical response when frightened was to cling to it. This occurred even if they had only been fed by the wire "mother."

warm substitute mothers over cold ones. The fact that the mother provides food is neither necessary nor enough to establish attachment.

This conclusion also applies to human infants. Although attachments usually form between infants and their primary caregiver, it is not the giving of routine care, as such, that determines choice of attachment figures. A father who responds appropriately to his child in play is more likely to be an attachment figure than a mother who limits her interactions to mechanical feeding and cleaning (Schaffer & Emerson, 1964). You are more likely to become an infant's attachment figure if you provide appropriate visual, auditory, and tactual stimulation, and if you are responsive to smiles and to other social signals (Gewirtz, 1965).

Mary Ainsworth and her colleagues emphasize the importance of responsiveness of the mother to the infant's needs. Ainsworth (1973) analyzed mothers' responsiveness to their babies in several situations, including face-to-face play and feeding. Responsive mothers continually adjust their actions to maintain their baby's attention in play. They also respond to their baby's hunger, allowing the baby to influence when feeding begins, its pacing, and when it ends. One study periodically observed the same infants from birth to about one year old (Ainsworth et al., 1967). The experiment used a method called the *strange situation procedure*, in which researchers unobtrusively observe an infant in the presence or absence of several combinations of the child, mother, and a stranger. This procedure has played a central role in studies of infant-caregiver relationships (Sroufe, 1985). In the original study, attachments were divided into two categories:

1. Some infants were characterized as *securely attached*. They sought closeness and contact with their mother, but they did not whine and cling. They were not too disturbed by brief separations, and they enthusiastically greeted their mother's return with hugs and affection.
2. Other infants were characterized as *anxiously attached*. If they had any interest in contact with their mother at all, it was often ambivalent: They would seek her contact, and then reject and push her away, especially after she returned from a brief separation. These babies were often upset in the presence of a stranger, whether their mother was present or not.

The infants were observed for a year, during which time it was clearly indicated that responsive mothers tend to have securely attached infants, and unresponsive mothers tend to have anxiously attached babies. A more recent study suggests that intermediate levels of responsiveness are best. Over- or understimulation can lead to less secure attachments (Belsky, Rovine, & Taylor, 1984).

Early attachments influence a child's later development (Contes & Lewis, 1984). Sroufe (1978) argues that "securely attached" infants are more likely to enjoy problem solving at the age of 2 and 3 years: They get more involved in problems and they work on them longer. Lieberman (1977) found that "secure" mother-infant attachments are associated with better relationships with other children. Securely attached children show more sharing or giving and less crying or fighting in social relationships with other children at the age of 3 years. Apparently, a healthy attachment to parents encourages both curiosity in problem solving and generosity in social relationships with others.

Caregivers who provide stimulation and responsiveness become attachment figures and they can influence later development. Raun's parents carefully controlled the stimulation that Raun received and their responsiveness to him. This approach helped them to reestablish attachments before his second birthday. The parents also significantly influenced Raun's development in other areas by reestablishing other processes as well. We will now discuss some of these other processes.

Preschool children often imitate their parents and other family members, as well as TV characters; once they enter school they find other important models in their friends and teachers.

Identification, Imitation, and Reinforcement. Identification is the process of acquiring personality and social behaviors by taking on characteristics of others. Sigmund Freud felt that identification involves more than just copying. He proposed that when children identify with their parents they unconsciously respond as if they *were* their parents. You might, for example, remember feeling proud when your father or mother received an award, as if you yourself had been honored.

Modern psychologists recognize the importance of copying the behavior of others, but they do not necessarily agree with all that the term "identification" stands for in the Freudian sense. They therefore often use the term **imitation** to refer to the process of copying other people's behavior (Hays et al., 1985). Preschool children in our society often imitate their parents and other family members. They also imitate TV characters. Once children enter school, at the age of 5 or 6, they find other important models in their friends and teachers. A child's tendency to imitate is often reflected in games, as when children dress up in their parents' clothes. Raun's older sister Bryn took the game a step further. She often delighted and amused others by acting out expert imitations of family and friends. Psychologists agree that infants have the capacity to imitate no later than about the end of the first year. Some have claimed that the capacity develops much earlier, but more research is needed to verify this claim (Abravanel & Sigafoos, 1984).

Family members, friends, and teachers influence children not only by modeling behaviors, but also by *reinforcing* them. Praise is often an effective reinforcer. If you praise children for a job well done, you will increase the probability that they will repeat their efforts. **Reinforcement,** then, is

Mothers and fathers influence almost every aspect of their children's personality and social development.

another important mechanism for shaping personality and social development.

Now that we know the processes by which people influence development, let's look at some of the important effects they have on children.

Parents. Mothers and fathers influence almost every aspect of their children's personality and social development. Children adopt their parents' values and standards and try to live up to them even when their parents aren't watching. One area of parental influence that has received much attention lately concerns the development of **sex roles,** which are a society's approved ways for men and women to behave (see Chapter 9). Societies assign distinctive roles to males and females. Traditionally, American men were expected to be self-sufficient, powerful, and tough, while American women were supposed to be dependent, weak, and tender. Those expectations are changing. Today, for example, more and more women are becoming equal wage earners in families, and, in general, men and women are exchanging or sharing many responsibilities. Behavior standards still differ for males and females, however, and parents help transmit those standards.

Parents treat boys and girls differently long before the children realize the difference between sexes. Most children cannot use the labels "boy" and "girl" correctly until about the age of 3 years. The labels are first used on the basis of external differences in dress and hair styles. Children are usually 5 or 6 before they relate their concept of boys and girls to genital differences. Parents, however, start treating boys and girls differently at birth. They describe newborn daughters as *delicate*, *beautiful*, and *weak*. But they describe newborn sons of the same height and weight as *robust*, *coordinated*, and *strong* (Rubin et al., 1974). The descriptions apparently reflect parents' expectations. Parents express their expectancies in other ways as their children grow. Mothers and fathers handle their sons more roughly, protect them less from physical harm, and punish them physically more than they do their daughters (Maccoby & Jacklin, 1974). Parents also model sex roles, of course, and by the age of 6 years children prefer to imitate the parent of the same sex. Parents therefore transmit sex roles both through differential treatment of their sons and daughters and through modeling (Perry, White, & Perry, 1984).

Teachers. Personality and social development are also shaped by teachers who transmit personal attitudes and beliefs in addition to academic lessons (Walter & Ashton, 1980). Teachers shape development both through modeling and through reinforcement (Ringness, 1975). In fact, the roles of reinforcer and model seem to be interrelated. In one study, Portuges and Feshbach (1972) demonstrated that children are more likely to imitate teachers that reward successes as opposed to teachers that punish failures. Both reinforcement and modeling may be responsible for the fact that students of warm and friendly teachers tend to be less aggressive, and to be more conscientious in their attitudes toward school (Cronbach & Snow, 1977). Because it is easier for students to imitate teachers who are similar to them, many think that having more black teachers will cause black students to develop a more positive attitude toward school.

Peers. In the normal course of development between the ages of 1 and 11 years, children steadily decrease their contact with adults and increase their contact with other children, as shown in Figure 8–2 (Wright, 1967). They prefer friends of the same sex, especially between the ages of 8 and 11. "Fitting in" with their friends becomes very important. Children want to conform to the trends established by their peers. They try to be as similar as possible in dress, hair styles, language, and mannerisms. Peers gradually take over more and more both as models and reinforcers.

Suzi Kaufman caught a glimpse of what might have been the start of this process in Raun. Some time after passing the cookie test, Raun hugged

WORKING MOTHERS, DAY CARE, AND CHILD DEVELOPMENT

Today, about half of the nation's mothers who have young children work outside the home while their children stay with substitute caregivers. Many of these children stay in day-care centers in which groups of children are cared for by groups of caregivers.

It is important that we determine what effects substitute caregivers will have on our children. Recent literature suggests answers to several important questions.

1. Does day-care experience damage the basic trust and security engendered by the attachment bond between mother and child?

   A few studies have suggested that day-care experience can reduce the quality of the mother-child relationship. Most studies, however, have found no reduction in quality (Clark-Stewart & Koch, 1983). For example, one group of researchers compared infants enrolled in day-care centers with infants reared at home (Kagan, Kearsley, & Zelanzo, 1977). They found that day-care did not weaken attachments to mothers. Similarly, Farron and Ramey (1977) observed that although children prefer their day-care teachers over strangers, they still prefer their mothers over their teachers.

2. How do multiple attachments to day-care staff and mother affect social development?

   On the one hand, some researchers have suggested that children in day-care may be less cooperative with adults (e.g., Schwartz, Strickland, & Krolick, 1974). However, other researchers have found that infants with day-care experience play more with other children and adapt more quickly to new environments (Kagan et al., 1977). It seems to be the quality, not the number, of attachments that makes the difference. Furthermore, a study by Moore (1975) suggests that the positive influence of day-care on peer relationships carries over to the teen years.

3. How does day-care experience influence cognitive development?

   A recent review of studies on child care has addressed this question (Scarr, 1984). It seems that its effect is determined by a child's background. Children from advantaged backgrounds perform well in school whether they are reared at home or in day-care centers. Children from disadvantaged backgrounds, however, seem to do better in school if they have had experience in day-care centers that provide structured educational programs.

4. What features of day-care will optimize healthy child development?

   Most of the research on day care has evaluated high quality day-care centers associated with universities. Little is known about day-care programs in under privileged areas, and still less is known about the effects of leaving children with sitters, which is a popular alternative to day-care. Available data, however, suggest that children left with sitters do not do as well as children enrolled in day-care programs. In fact, a study in England found that one-third of the children who spend their day in a sitter's home become withdrawn and passive (Bruner, 1980).

Such results raise the question of how to optimize the day-care experience. Psychologists have offered a number of suggestions: (1) To avoid severe separation distress, children should be enrolled in day-care either between 1 and 7 months of age or after they are about 18 months old; (2) each caregiver should be responsible for no more than three infants or toddlers; (3) class sizes for older preschoolers should not exceed 12 for 2- and 3-year-olds or 16 for 3- to 6-year-olds; (4) teachers should be trained in early childhood education; (5) the physical space should be safe and attractive, indoors and out; (6) a variety of play materials should be available; and (7) the children enrolled in the program should be happy and involved (Kagan et al., 1977; Ruopp et al., 1979).

Figure 8–2
The graph shows how, between the ages of 1 and 11, children have more and more contact with other children, and less and less contact with adults. (Wright, 1967)

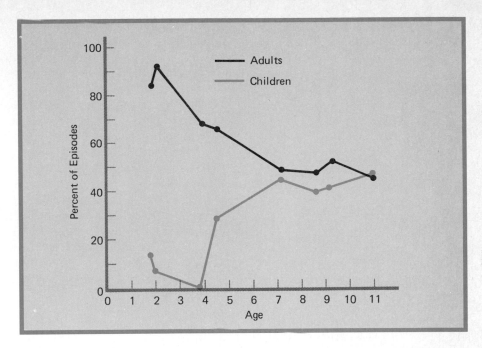

a little boy that he met in a park. The boy was startled and cried. Raun mimicked the boy's sad face, and waited for him to stop crying. Raun then reached out and softly stroked the little boy's arm. At about the same time, Raun started playing with his sisters again, as he had done during his first year. These interactions with his sisters also influenced his personality and social development, as we will discuss in the next section.

Brothers and Sisters. Effects of birth order on personality and social behavior suggest that brothers and sisters (*siblings*) influence development. Firstborn children or only children tend to be more cooperative, conscientious, and cautious than later-born children (Altus, 1966). They also score higher on intelligence tests, go farther in school, and obtain more honors. The sex of older siblings seems to make a difference: For example, boys with older sisters tend to be less aggressive than boys with older brothers (Longstreth et al., 1975). Direct interactions between children probably cause some of the effects. Younger siblings, for example, are notorious for being pests to older brothers and sisters. Older children often control their younger siblings through acts of aggression. The aggressive acts reduce an annoyance and are therefore reinforced (Patterson, 1979).

Parents also contribute to birth-order effects by treating siblings differently. In one study, researchers found that parents spend more time with firstborn infants and talk to them more (Thoman et al., 1972). Parents

Between the ages of 8 and 11, children prefer friends of the same sex—girls tend to play with girls, and boys with boys.

also exert more pressure on firstborn children to achieve (Rothbart, 1971). Birth order does not affect everyone in the same way, of course. Family situations are different, as are individuals. Consequently, children with older brothers and sisters often have qualities that are associated with firstborns, and many later-born children have achieved great accomplishments. One example is Georgia O'Keeffe, a famous American artist, whose life story will be told in the next chapter.

Raun may prove to be another exception. Most later-born children spend less time with their parents; Raun spent much more. Many later-born children are controlled by acts of aggression by older brothers and sisters. Raun's older sisters, however, were very sensitive to his needs and acts of aggression would not have been common. We cannot see into the future, so we cannot know how Raun's unusual early experiences will influence his later development. Since Raun's development at about the age of 2 was at or beyond his age level, however, we can be optimistic.

SUMMARY

1. **Human development** is a process by which the genes that we inherit from our parents come to be expressed as specific physical and behavioral characteristics.

2. *Nativism* emphasizes the role of heredity in the development of mind and behavior. *Empiricism* holds that learning through experience is the source of development. Neither theory, however, can explain the existence of a **critical period,** which is a stage of development during which an organism must have certain experiences or it will not develop normally. Both heredity and environment are necessary to explain this phenomenon, and, indeed, it is through the interaction of these two elements that most development occurs.

3. Prenatal development refers to the approximately 9-month period of development that precedes birth. The stages of prenatal development are divided into the periods of the **ovum,** the **embryo,** and the **fetus.** A number of factors can influence development in this stage, including nutrition, disease, drug use by the mother, and delivery complications.

4. The next stage of development, from birth to 1 year, is marked by the development of the nervous system, including **myelinization,** which determines control over body parts. Motor development is marked by the disappearance of various **reflexes** that the baby is born with, and the development of voluntary movement, such as sitting up, crawling, and standing.

5. Childhood is most notably marked by increases in cognitive development. Piaget studied two processes in children that account for much of this development: **assimilation** and **accommodation.** As a result of his years of observation and research on children, he divided cognitive development into a series of stages: **sensorimotor** (birth to 2 years), **preoperational** (2 to 7 years), **concrete operational** (7 to 12 years), and **formal operational** (13 years and older).

6. Language development is an important element of cognitive development. It progresses in the first 2 years of life from cooing and babbling, through **holophrastic speech,** which is the use of single words to express whole phrases, to two-word statements. During the second year children rapidly learn to expand two-word statements into longer, grammatically correct sentences.

7. There are three basic theories of how language development occurs: social-learning theory, which suggests that children learn to speak by imitating adults; operant conditioning theory, which states that parents teach children to speak by reinforcement; and Noam Chomsky's view, which is that children learn units of thought and rules for combining them as the basis of speech.

8. An important part of personality and social development in infancy is **attachment,** the tendency to seek closeness to certain people. Attachment normally develops in a series of three steps during the first 6 months of life; the quality of attachment, usually between infant and mother, affects later personality and social development in children.

9. Another important element in personality and social development in childhood is **identification,** which is the process of acquiring personality and social behaviors by imitating those around them.

10. Parents transmit **sex roles** to their children both by treating boys and girls differently from an early age, and by modeling different behaviors for each sex.

Key Terms

accommodation
Apgar scoring system
assimilation
attachment
concrete operational stage
critical period
cross-sectional research
dancing reflex
embryo
fetus
formal operational stage
grasp reflex
holophrastic speech
human development
identification
imitation

longitudinal research
maturation
Moro reflex (startle reflex)
myelinization
ovum
placenta
preoperational stage
reinforcement
rooting reflex
schema
sensorimotor stage
sex roles
sucking reflex
tonic neck reflex
uterus (womb)

Suggested Readings

The following book is about Raun:

KAUFMAN, BARRY. *Son-Rise*. New York: Warner Books, 1976.

FLAVELL, J. H. *Cognitive development* (2nd ed.). Englewood Cliffs, N.J.: Prentice-Hall, 1985. An easy-to-understand presentation of Piaget's research and theories.

HETHERINGTON, E. M., & PARKE, R. D. *Contemporary readings in child psychology*. New York: McGraw-Hill, 1981. A collection of readings organized to complement Hetherington and Parke's *Child Psychology: A contemporary viewpoint*. Together these books provide a springboard for those who are preparing to take the plunge into the depths of research on chid psychology. A refreshing style makes the books enjoyable as well as informative.

MASTERS, J. C., & YARKIN-LEVIN, K. (Eds.). *Boundary areas in social and developmental psychology*. New York: Academic Press, 1984. A collection of articles by authors known for their work in areas of social and developmental psychology. Each article attempts to enhance appreciation of the conceptual and methodological interface between these two subdisciplines of psychology. Topics include children's peer

relationships and the influence of group discussions on children's moral decisions.

MORRISON, F. J., & LORD, C. (Eds.). *Applied developmental psychology*. New York: Academic Press, 1984. This collection of articles strikes a healthy balance of basic and applied science. Insights from basic research are brought to bear on complex applied problems, and implications from the applied domain enrich basic research issues related to education, TV viewing, peer relations, and stress in children.

SUGARMAN, S. *Children's early thought: Developments in classification*. New York: Cambridge University Press, 1983. This book describes changes in the way children classify simple sets of objects during the period in which they learn to talk; it also compares developments in thinking with developments in language skills.

SOPHIAN, C. (Ed.). *Origins of cognitive skills: The eighteenth annual Carnegie Symposium on cognition*. Hillsdale, N.J.: Erlbaum, 1984. This collection of articles is structured around three topics: spatial development, number development, and development of categorization. The discussions of each topic include both infancy research and research on later cognitive development.

ADOLESCENCE, ADULTHOOD, AND AGING

On November 15, 1887, in Sun Prairie, Wisconsin, Ida and Francis O'Keeffe gave birth to their second child and their first daughter. Ida named the baby Georgia Totto after Count George Totto, Ida's father, a political refugee who had escaped from Hungary after fighting in a hopeless Hungarian uprising against Austrian rule. Ida and Francis had no way of knowing that their daughter, who looked more like her Irish father than her Hungarian grandfather, was to become one of the world's outstanding artists. Nobody would have guessed that for many years—nobody, that is, except Georgia herself. At the age of 12, after less than a year of private art lessons, she announced to a friend that she was going to be an artist. In 1976, Georgia reflected back on that statement and wrote in her autobiography that it was inspired in part by a small illustration of a beautiful Grecian maiden in one of her mother's books. She wrote, "I believe that picture started something moving in me that kept on going and has had to do with the everlasting urge that makes me keep on painting."

Georgia spent much of her childhood freely roaming the family farm and could often be found at the side of her jovial father, who kept his pockets full of sweets and played Irish melodies on his fiddle. Georgia never lost her rural roots; whenever she counted her blessings, she put at the top of her list having been born a farmer's daughter.

Ida and Francis had three more daughters after Georgia. As Francis worked his dairy farm, Ida tended to the education of her five children. She read to them constantly, and every Saturday she took her daughters by horse and buggy to attend private art lessons. Shortly before Georgia turned 14, Ida entered her in an exclusive convent boarding school.

Georgia, who was eager to please her dignified mother, excelled in school. The following year, Ida sent Georgia and her brother Francis to live with their aunt in Madison, where they could attend Madison High School. One day, as she passed an art classroom, Georgia stopped to watch a teacher who was instructing the class to observe the unusual shapes and subtle shades of a jack-in-the-pulpit plant; she realized for the first time that one could paint living things rather than just copy pictures.

In March, 1903, while Georgia was attending Madison High School, Ida and Francis sold their Wisconsin farm and moved to Williamsburg, Virginia. Georgia went to Chatham Episcopal Institute, a girl's boarding school about 200 miles from Williamsburg. There she was lucky to have a sensitive art teacher, Elizabeth May Willis, who let Georgia work at her own pace. Sometimes Georgia worked intensely; at other times she refused to work for days. When others complained about Georgia not working, Willis would reply, "When the spirit moves Georgia, she can do more in a day than you can do in a week" (Lisle, 1980, p. 34).

During the next few years Georgia attended various art schools, and then, when her parents could no longer afford the tuition, she began to earn her own living. She worked first as a freelance illustrator in Chicago (one of the images she created, a bonneted Dutch girl chasing dirt with an upraised broom, is still used today to sell a cleanser); later she taught art in several public schools in Texas.

In 1914, at the age of 27, Georgia O'Keeffe resumed her academic career in New York at Columbia Teacher's College. After one year at Columbia, she accepted a teaching position at a teachers' college for women in South Carolina. She taught four classes a week and spent many hours each day painting. Throughout the year O'Keeffe corresponded with Anita Pollitzer, a friend she had made at Columbia. In one letter she described her frustration with having taken on the painting styles of her teachers. She wrote, "I feel disgusted with it all and am glad I'm disgusted" (Lisle, 1980, p. 82). O'Keeffe decided to start learning all over again, so she put away all colors and worked only in black and white. She committed herself to stay with those two colors until she had exhausted all their possibilities. During the weeks that followed, O'Keeffe created charcoal drawings unlike anything she had been taught. She saw abstract shapes in her mind that were an integral part of her imagination; she had always seen them, but she had not paid attention to them before. She mailed some of her drawings to Pollitzer, who later recalled, "[I] was struck by their aliveness. They were different. Here were charcoals on the same kind of paper that all art students were using, and through no trick, no superiority of tools, these drawings were saying something that had not yet been said."

Pollitzer took the drawings to a little art gallery run by photographer Alfred Stieglitz, who was famous for showing unconventional art. O'Keeffe had visited Stieglitz's "291" gallery many times while she was a student in New York. She had written to Pollitzer in an earlier letter that she "would rather have Stieglitz like something—anything I had done—than anyone else I know of—I have always felt that—if I ever make anything that satisfies me even ever so little—I am going to show it to him to find out if it is any good" (Lisle, 1980, p. 81). Pollitzer found Stieglitz alone in his gallery, and she unrolled the charcoals for him. He looked at each sheet closely, saying nothing. Then he looked at Pollitzer and declared, "At last, a woman on paper!" (Lisle, 1980, p. 85).

When O'Keeffe heard the news she wrote Stieglitz a letter, the first of more than 3,400 letters and telegrams that they would exchange. They met a month later in New York. He told her that her drawings were so wonderful that he simply had to show them, which he did, creating the sensation that he had predicted.

O'Keeffe and Stieglitz corresponded, often exchanging paintings, photographs, and ideas. Although Stieglitz was about 25 years older, it became apparent that the two had much in common. They valued candor and genuineness, they burned to express themselves in art, and they shared a passion for excellence. O'Keeffe joined Stieglitz in New York in the spring of 1917. During the long romance that followed, O'Keeffe became the favorite subject for Stieglitz's photographs. Many critics recognize his photographs of O'Keeffe as the height of his artistic achievement (Lisle, 1980). The couple married on December 11, 1924.

Several years later, at the age of 41, O'Keeffe returned to the West to seek inspiration. She found what she was looking for in Taos, New Mexico. She returned to New York after a few months with enough paintings to put on an exhibition in February, 1930. O'Keeffe returned to New Mexico during the next two summers, each time returning with paintings that amazed New York art critics. They were especially fascinated by paintings of white animal skeletons. Friends worried that the paintings indicated depression and a morbid concern with death. Their concerns proved valid, for O'Keeffe suffered a nervous breakdown and was admitted to a hospital on February 1, 1933, at the age of 45.

She left the hospital 7 weeks later, spent a quiet winter with Stieglitz, and then once again headed West. Gradually, O'Keeffe started painting again. Although friends saw in her work signs of a triumphant convalescence, she suffered a brief relapse in 1939. Some attributed her rapid recovery after that to Stieglitz's unwavering support and to the fact that she was now widely recognized as

America's most successful female painter.

A combination of factors slowed O'Keeffe down considerably in the 1950s. First, Stieglitz died in 1946 at the age of 82. Even though O'Keeffe had spent many months away from her husband each year, she missed him intensely after his death. Furthermore, his passing put new demands on her time. She put long hours into settling his estate, and she took on the business end of selling her paintings, which Stieglitz had always handled for her.

O'Keeffe made an incredible comeback in the 1960s after taking an around-the-world trip. Her paintings of this period captured her fascination with the extraordinary spectacle of earth and clouds from jet airplanes. At the age of 77 she completed the largest painting of her life, *Sky Above Clouds IV*, a 24' × 8' "chunk of heaven" depicting clouds viewed from above floating off into infinity. She exhibited her new painting in 1966 along with 96 other paintings at the biggest exhibition of her lifetime in Fort Worth. The reviews of her exhibition indicated that, at the age of 78, O'Keeffe had captured the hearts and imaginations of yet another generation of Americans.

O'Keeffe's productivity was slowed once again late in 1971 when she lost her central vision because of an irreversible degenerative eye disease found among the elderly. Her blurred vision stopped her from painting between the ages of 84 and 88. But by 1976, at the age of 89, she again started painting. She proudly stated that her shadowy vision gave her an interesting new way of seeing light and it gave her new painting ideas. By 1980 her paintings were back in the news.

For years O'Keeffe predicted that she would live to be 100. Now that she is in her nineties she has changed that prediction to 125.

A LIFE-SPAN APPROACH TO DEVELOPMENT

Georgia O'Keeffe's career as an artist puzzles those who attempt to classify artists and their works. She joked that critics had tried to place her "in every movement that came along—expressionism, precisionism, regionalism, surrealism, and all the rest—until pop art came along, and then they gave up" (Lisle, 1980, p. 392). She fits no ready niche. In the same way, her incredibly fluid and dynamic life clashes with traditional development theories, which assume that development moves in one direction until maturity, at which point a person remains basically the same until old age causes a decline (Harris, 1957). Such theories do not seem to explain O'Keeffe's life very well. They offer little or no framework for explaining her adaptive responses to life in places as varied as New York City and the desert of New Mexico. They have little to say about the adjustments she made to her husband's death, or about the comeback she made in her career late in life.

A defender of traditional developmental theories might argue that O'Keeffe's life is too exceptional to be captured by theories about ordinary people. It is indeed unusual to find so much dynamism in one lifetime. But when we observe people throughout their life span, we find that change is the rule, not the exception. Thus a developmental framework is needed to integrate changes that occur within an individual over time and the differences in such changes between individuals. That need may be met by a **life-span developmental approach,** which is concerned with the description and explanation of changes in behavior within an individual and differences between individuals from conception to death (Hultsch & Deutsch, 1981, p. 15).

This chapter adopts the life-span approach to development in adolescence, young adulthood, middle age, and old age. If you do not already identify with Georgia O'Keeffe, you may come to feel a bond with her by virtue of being a developing individual. In fact, the life-span perspective on physical, social, and cognitive changes may show you the common themes as well as individual differences running through the lives of all people.

ADOLESCENCE

Adolescence, which extends from about age 12 to the late teens, is a time of passage from childhood to adulthood. Georgia's favorite childhood toy was a dollhouse, but she set it aside at about the age of 12. She announced her desire to be an artist at about the same time, marking the beginning of her transition from a dollhouse world to the real world beyond her home. Let's follow some of the many significant events that happened to Georgia during this period and that happen to each of us during adolescence.

Physical Changes

At 12 O'Keeffe looked like a little girl. By the time she was 16, however, she was the very image of herself as a woman. Such a rapid physical transformation is characteristic of adolescence.

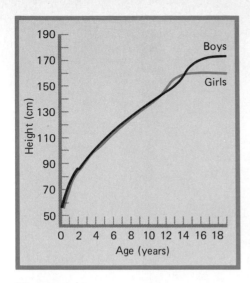

Figure 9-1
The graph here shows average heights and weights for girls and boys from birth to 17 years. Note that on the average the adolescent growth spurt occurs earlier for girls than for boys. (Tanner, 1978)

The timing of the adolescent growth spurt, as well as the onset of puberty, varies considerably among individuals.

Height and Weight. The accelerated growth rate during adolescence (often referred to as a "growth spurt") is apparent in Figure 9-1, which shows average heights and weights for girls and boys from birth to 17 years of age. Girls increase their growth rate earlier than boys, so that most girls are larger than boys between the ages of 11 and 13. Once boys start their growth spurt, however, they rapidly overtake girls. By the age of 17, boys are, on the average, about 4 inches taller and about 17 pounds heavier than girls. Boys and girls also differ in the extent to which their muscles and strength change during adolescence. At the age of 10, girls and boys are generally of equal strength. But, while girls stay about the same strength, boys almost double their strength during their teen years. At the end of the "adolescent growth spurt," adolescents have adult body proportions.

Puberty and Sexual Characteristics. Adolescence is also associated with **puberty**, the time when sexual reproduction is possible. Development occurs in all **primary sexual characteristics**, which are traits directly concerned with reproduction. For instance, girls begin to produce ova and boys start manufacturing sperm. Puberty starts between 11 and 13 for most girls and between 13 and 15 for most boys. The timing varies considerably among individuals, however. The development of secondary sexual characteristics provides external signs of the approach of puberty. **Secondary sexual characteristics** are those traits typical of a sex, but not directly concerned with reproduction.

The first visible sign for girls is usually breast development, followed by the appearance of pubic hair. The onset of puberty is often assumed to be **menarche,** the beginning of *menstruation*, which is the periodic discharge of blood and tissue from a nonpregnant uterus. Using menarche as a dividing line is only an approximation, however, since the ability to reproduce is often not present for 1 or 2 years after menarche.

The first external indicator for boys is growth of the scrotum and appearance of pubic hair. Beard growth is another sign, but this is often delayed for several years. Growth rate and muscular development is the most obvious visible evidence of puberty in boys.

Complex changes in hormones (see Chapter 2) cause both the adolescent growth spurt and the development of sexual characteristics. They also cause behavioral changes, such as interest in the opposite sex. In addition to behavioral changes, there are important psychological and social changes that take place during adolescence.

Moral Development

Moral development refers to development that is related to principles of right and wrong in behavior. Societies have rules about the rightness and wrongness of behaviors, and various authorities enforce a society's rules through rewards and punishments. Parents rely heavily on such external controls to maintain appropriate behaviors in children. Teenagers require less supervision because part of their moral development involves **internalization,** which is the process of bringing behavior under the control of inner, personal standards that make people obey rules even if there are no external restraints. The development of moral reasoning and moral behavior is the focus of research that we will review in this section.

Moral Reasoning. Jean Piaget (1932) and Lawrence Kohlberg (1963, 1969, 1978) have done a great deal of research on the development of internalization and moral reasoning. Both investigators asked children to comment on stories containing moral dilemmas; both proposed theories that related moral development to cognitive development. Here we will concentrate on Kohlberg's more recent, and more refined, theory.

One of Kohlberg's stories was about a man, Heinz, who stole drugs in order to save his wife's life.

Kohlberg asked children of various ages, "Should Heinz have done that? Was it actually wrong or right? Why?" Answers to these questions suggested three levels in the development of moral reasoning, with two stages in each level (Table 9–1). A typical answer in the first level (preconventional) might be, "The man was wrong because he could be sent to jail for stealing." Or it might be, "The man was right because he would get in trouble for letting his wife die." Both answers characterize the preconventional level, because right or wrong is decided in terms of possible punishment. Children often give this kind of answer, but teenagers rarely do. A typical answer in the second level (conventional) might be, "The man was wrong because people don't like thieves." Or it might be, "The man was right because his friends wouldn't like him if he let his wife die." Both answers characterize

Level I	Preconventional morality
Stage 1	Obedience and punishment orientation
Stage 2	Naive hedonistic and instrumental orientation
Level II	Conventional level: Morality of conventional rules and conformity
Stage 3	"Good boy/Good girl" morality
Stage 4	Authority and social order morality
Level·III	Postconventional level: Morality of self-accepted moral principles
Stage 5	Morality of contract, individual rights, and democratically accepted law
Stage 6	Morality of individual principles and conscience

the conventional level, because right or wrong is decided in terms of being liked or disliked for one's actions. Teenagers often give this kind of response. A typical answer in the third level (postconventional) might be, "The man was wrong according to social law, but he was right according to divine law, which holds that human life is sacred." This answer characterizes Kohlberg's highest level, because it is based upon abstract principles. Exposure to other cultures and value systems encourages the development of this level, which few people reach before their twenties (Keniston, 1969; Stevens-Long & Cobb, 1983).

Kohlberg's theory has been criticized for several reasons:

1. The reliability of Kohlberg's scale has been questioned. Poor reliability is indicated because people often disagree when they use Kohlberg's original scoring method. In response to this criticism, Kohlberg and his associates (1978) developed a more objective and easier-to-use scoring method.

2. The predictive validity of Kohlberg's measure has also been questioned. That is, psychologists have questioned whether Kohlberg's scale can be used to predict how individuals will act. A person who knows it is wrong to cheat might still do so. Podd (1972), for instance, found little relationship between moral reasoning and moral behavior.

3. Some investigators have suggested that Kohlberg's scale reflects several kinds of bias (Gilligan, 1976; Harkness, 1980; Hoffman, 1979; Kurtines & Grief, 1974; Simpson, 1974). First, one could argue that the scale is politically biased because the lower levels seem to display political conservation. Second, the scale may be culturally biased. Kohlberg compared people in different cultures, but these comparisons might not have been fair. This criticism stems from the fact that the theory focuses on American values. The classification of levels might not be appropriate, therefore, in cultures with different values. Third, the scale might be biased according to sex because females do not show the expected pattern of movement through the stages (Gilligan, 1977).

4. A final criticism concerns the distinction between moral issues and social conventions. Kohlberg's theory states that people do not make this distinction until they reach the postconventional reasoning level. Accordingly, children would rarely make the distinction. But Turiel (1978) found that most children distinguish between moral rules, such as "Do not steal," and game rules, such as "Do not pass go."

Researchers will have to devise other ways of testing moral reasoning and moral behavior to determine the validity of these criticisms.

Now that we have considered the moral development of adolescents, let's review some highlights of the many psychological and social changes that take place during the teenage years.

Personality Development

As we will discuss in detail in Chapter 12, personality influences the unique way that we adjust and respond to our environment. This section will deal with questions about the development of personality: Does personality develop throughout the life-span? Does it ever stop developing?

O'Keeffe's nonconforming nature illustrates that some personality traits can remain stable throughout a person's lifetime, as evidenced in her childhood: "From the time I was a little girl, if my sisters wore their hair braided, I wouldn't wear mine braided. If they wore ribbons, I wouldn't. I'd think they'd look better without it, too" (Lisle, 1980, p. 11). As an adult, Georgia O'Keefe continued to be a nonconformist. This strong personality trait may have been responsible for launching her career, since she achieved her first widely acclaimed work by consciously breaking with the traditions in which she had been trained. Her popularity survived the coming and going of many different trends in the art world, perhaps because she always had a style of her own. The survival of one personality trait in one person does not mean, of course, that our personality remains the same throughout life, or even that certain traits will stay with us throughout life. In fact, modern theories assume that our personalities continue to develop and change as long as we live. Let's turn to one such theory.

Erik Erikson's Theory. As we will discuss in Chapter 12, Freud and his followers argued that our personality is determined by the time we are 6 or 7 years old; the rest of life is spent following the script written during these "formative years." Erik Erikson, who studied with Freud, acknowledged that early childhood is an important period for personality development. However, he believed that our personality continues to grow and change throughout our lifetime. Erikson, again like Freud, suggested that people go through stages when certain issues or events are critical, but, unlike Freud, he did not believe that these issues are always sexual in nature. He also felt that many of these stages occur well after childhood. According to Erikson, the way in which each crisis is resolved not only shapes the personality, but also influences how the person will approach and resolve the crisis at the next stage.

As you can see in Table 9–2, Erikson listed eight stages of life; the first four correspond to those suggested by Freud, and the other four stages occur after puberty. The first, and probably most critical, crisis involves issues of trust and mistrust. The way in which this crisis is resolved will determine whether a person approaches the world in a trusting, open way or with a suspicious, cautious outlook. According to Erikson, it is the mother who determines whether people will have a predominantly trusting or mistrusting personality. Social trust will develop to the degree that infants have an inner sense of security that their mother will love and take care of their basic needs.

An important stage in Erikson's theory is the **identity crisis,** which occurs during puberty. Identity is an understanding of one's uniqueness and an appreciation of what one has in common with others (Marcia, 1980). The search for an identity is particularly difficult in our complex Western culture.

Table 9–2
Stages of Erikson's Psychosocial Personality Theory

Age	Stage
First year of life	Trust vs. mistrust
1–3 years	Autonomy vs. doubt
3–5 years	Initiative vs. guilt
6–12 years	Industry vs. inferiority
Adolescence	Identity vs. role confusion
Young adulthood	Intimacy vs. isolation
Middle adulthood	Generativity vs. self-absorption
Late adulthood	Integrity vs. despair

The sheer number of choices facing the adolescent is bewildering, and, to complicate matters even further, there are few guides to help someone make these choices. During adolescence, people begin to confront issues concerning career, education, marriage, and place of residence. The decision about each of these issues will influence how people view themselves. In earlier, more traditional societies, the search for an identity was not so difficult. People rarely moved away from the area in which they were raised; male children were generally expected to adopt the occupation of their fathers; and females "naturally" got married, raised a family, and kept house. The difficulty of the identity crisis in our present-day society is reflected in the fact that this period is characterized by a great deal of trying out and testing of different roles as adolescents struggle to "discover" themselves. College students may change their major a number of times as they attempt to discover "their niche." Even by graduation, many college students have not settled on an identity, and an increasing number of them choose to "take a year off" to travel, work at different jobs, and learn about themselves.

Thus, Erikson argues that our personality changes throughout our lifetime. Erikson's theory also includes a certain amount of continuity in personality, however, since the way one crisis is resolved affects later stages. We will return to Erikson's theory and compare it with other theories as we come to other stages of adult life. Here we want to emphasize the identity crisis that must be resolved by adolescents. We will end our discussion of the developing teenage personality by considering how physical changes affect the identity crisis.

Influence of Physical Changes. A teenager's search for identity is influenced by the adolescent growth spurt, which we discussed earlier. Late maturing boys and girls have an especially difficult time. Researchers found that boys who mature late often feel inadequate, and this feeling persists into adulthood (Mussen & Jones, 1957). Early maturers take over as leaders, especially in sports, because of their greater strength. Later maturers try to compensate with immature, attention-seeking behaviors such as bossiness. Reactions of others to these annoying behaviors tend to reinforce the low self-image of the late maturers. These researchers also found that late-maturing girls face similar adjustment problems, but to a lesser extent. High-school girls who are physically mature early on tend to be leaders among girls. Late-maturing girls tend to be less self-confident and less relaxed in social relationships. These effects carry over into adulthood, but they are small in comparison to the influence of late maturing on boys.

One effect these physical changes have is on the way parents, teachers, and friends treat teenagers. The less teenagers *look* like adults, the less they are treated like adults, which could contribute to low self-esteem in late maturers. In addition, many other social variables change dramatically during adolescence.

Social Changes

Think back to the interpersonal, or social, relationships that you had as a 12-year-old. In all likelihood you lived at home, and your parents kept a fairly close eye on your activities. If you got into trouble at school, they found out almost immediately; they decided when, where, and with whom you could date; and they were close at hand when you needed encouragement. Contrast that to your social situation at the age of 19. Many 19-year-olds move away from home and enter college or begin working. Most make their own decisions about school, dating, and careers. Parents care as much as ever, but their involvement is generally limited. O'Keeffe followed this pattern, assuming more freedom and responsibility

Peer-group structures of teenagers seem to develop through several stages. In an early stage, separate cliques of boys and girls start interacting as groups.

during adolescence. At the age of 12 she lived in a sheltered home environment, but by the time she was 19 she was living alone while attending the Art Students League in New York City. Much research has been done on various aspects of the movement toward independence during adolescence.

Peer Groups. As children approach their teen years, contact with other children, that is, their peers, becomes more and more important. Adolescent peer groups often take on highly organized structure. Dunphy (1963) observed, for instance, that peer-group structures of urban teenagers develop through five stages. Boys and girls remain separate in the first stage; they form small groups with members of their own sex. These groups, which are called *cliques*, contain members that share common interests and emotional attachments. Boy and girl cliques start interacting as groups in the second stage. Dating starts in the third stage, causing boy and girl cliques to merge. The isolated sex groups often maintain their identity as well during this stage. The fourth stage is characterized by larger groups, called *crowds*, which are made up of several merged boy-girl cliques closely interacting. These crowds dissolve in the fifth stage, and fully mixed boy-girl cliques reappear. The cliques during this last stage consist of loosely associated couples.

Sexual Behavior. Intimacy during dating includes sexual behaviors ranging from light embracing to sexual intercourse. Almost all American teenagers experience light embracing and slightly more than 50 percent experience sexual intercourse (Gordon & Scales, 1977). One nationwide survey of 13- to 19-year-olds found that 59 percent of the males and 45 percent of the females reported having had sexual intercourse (Sarensen, 1973). In the same survey, 37 percent reported having experienced intercourse before they were 16 years old. When these figures are compared with earlier surveys, one sees a trend of increasing sexual activity at younger ages (Fox, 1979). Adolescent sexual activity seems to be restricted when parents provide sex education, but 85 to 95 percent of today's parents do not discuss sexual behavior with their children, according to a recent survey (Fox, 1979; *Time*, 1978).

Some of the statistics about adolescent sexual behavior in the United States are alarming. For instance, there has been a dramatic increase in *venereal disease* (*VD*), which is any infectious disease transmitted by sexual intercourse. The common cold is the only infectious disease that occurs more frequently today. About 11 percent of females and 12 percent of males contract VD before they are 19 years old (Katchadourian, 1977). Venereal diseases can be cured if they are treated early; if not, they can lead to blindness, sterility, brain damage, heart disease, and death.

Teenage pregnancy is another current problem in the United States, which has the fourth highest teenage pregnancy rate in the world. According to a Planned Parenthood (1976) report, girls under the age of 15 give birth to about 30,000 babies a year. Approximately 1 million girls between the ages of 15 and 19 become pregnant annually. Almost 60 percent of these give birth; nearly 40 percent have abortions. Two-thirds of teen pregnancies are accidental and only about one-third of all teenage mothers are married when they deliver (Castleman, 1977). Those who do get married often get divorced later on (Presser, 1977). Not only do teenage pregnancies cause considerable emotional trauma, they also increase the risk of physical complications for both mother and child (Moore, 1978).

Cox (1974) argues that mass media is seducing teens into earlier sexual activity. Mass media does probably contribute to what Gordon and Scales (1977) call the "myth of the normal outlet." This myth causes some teenagers to wonder if they are "normal" if they delay sexual activity. The reality is that going steady and being sexually active in the early teen years is associated with less maturity (Helms & Turner, 1981).

YOUNG ADULTHOOD

O'Keeffe's life is a valuable reminder that adults do not necessarily experience the same life events in the same order. Many adults marry and have a first child between the ages of 20 and 25. O'Keeffe's parents followed this pattern, but O'Keeffe herself did not marry until she was 37, and she never had children. She did, however, dedicate herself at about this time to what became her lifework, her career in art. This became the most important commitment of her life.

Lowenthal (1977) provided a valuable framework for investigating development during young adulthood. She proposed that researchers could unify various aspects of development by studying commitments. She suggests that young adults make three particularly important commitments: moral, interpersonal, and mastery. *Moral commitments* relate to development in Kohlberg's highest stage of moral development, the postconventional stage, which we discussed earlier. *Interpersonal commitments* relate to Erikson's sixth stage of development, "intimacy versus isolation." Most young adults at this point commit themselves to intimate relationships that are characterized by deep caring and mutual respect. Avoiding this type of commitment may lead to a deep sense of isolation from other people. To illustrate this stage we will discuss marriage and child rearing, which are the most common ways for adults to develop intimate relationships. *Mastery commitments* refer to occupational commitments, such as the one O'Keeffe made to her career in art.

Family Commitments

O'Keeffe's mother, Ida, moved away from her parent's home at the age of 20. She married and had her first child within the next 2 years, and her last of five children was born before she was 30. Much of her young adulthood was therefore committed to starting and raising her own family. About 93 percent of today's women make the same commitment during young adulthood, although recent trends suggest an increase in alternative life styles (see Hultsch & Deutsch, 1981). For example, an unmarried man and woman may live together in a relationship that is very similar to that of a married couple; this is called **cohabitation** (Stafford, Backman, & Dibona, 1977). Communes offer another alternative in which members try to live as one large family (Stinnett & Walters, 1977). Despite the increasing popularity of these alternatives, we will concentrate on marriage, because it affects the vast majority of young adults.

Marriage and the Family Cycle.   Marriage and child rearing create a *family cycle*, which is a sequence of family events that repeat themselves generation after generation. Major events in the family cycle are: (1) leave parental home; (2) marry; (3) have first child; (4) bear last child; (5) first child leaves home; (6) last child leaves home; (7) children marry; (8) grandchildren are born. These events are among the important influences that interact to produce unique patterns of adult development. Researchers therefore observe the timing, duration, and clustering of family-cycle events.

You can compare your family history with those of friends to see that there is considerable variability in the age at which family events occur. Psychologists have nevertheless found interesting trends by observing average ages for these events. Figure 9–2 shows the results of one study that compared averages for women of different social classes (Olsen, 1969).

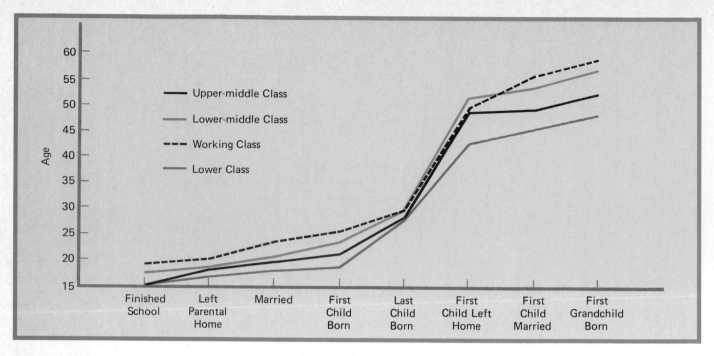

Figure 9-2
These are the results of a study that compared the average age at which certain family events had occurred in the lives of women of different social classes. (Olsen, 1969)

Upper-middle-class women were 4 to 8 years older than lower-class women for each event, with lower-middle-class and working-class women falling in between. A notable difference between groups was the time span between first and last child. The average age for upper-middle-class mothers at the time their first child was born was 26, and it was 29 for the last. The comparable averages for lower-class mothers were 18 and 27. Beyond those differences, the sequencing of events was similar between classes. The average woman left her parents' home 1 to 2 years after finishing her formal education; she got married 1 to 3 years later; and she had her first child 1 to 3 years after that.

Some evidence suggests that timing of family events may be related to marital and parental satisfaction. For instance, middle-class women who marry between 20 and 30 years of age report happier marriages than those who marry earlier or later (Nydegger & Mitteness, 1979). Being "off-schedule" is not always associated with dissatisfaction, however. Most men become fathers before they are 40, but those who wait longer tend to be happier with their parental role. Nydegger and Mitteness suggested that men who wait to have children may experience less conflict between family life and career demands. His explanation is consistent with the existence of heavy career demands during young adulthood, as we shall see in the next section.

Occupational Commitments

O'Keeffe launched her career as an artist with her first showing in Stieglitz's gallery at the age of 28. By the time she reached middle age she was recognized as "the greatest woman painter in America" (Lisle, 1980). Not everyone becomes the greatest in their field, of course, but many young adults achieve high levels in their chosen occupation before they enter middle age. Young adults usually dedicate themselves to the mastery of knowledge and skills, which they achieve through occupational commitments. Typical life events include not only getting married and having children, but also trying several jobs and advancing in a chosen occupation.

Mastery of specific knowledge and job-related skills is not the only developmental change necessary for a successful career commitment. White

SEX ROLES: WHEN ROLES CAN BE HARMFUL

Our society has developed traditional stereotypes of men and women. Men are viewed as being logical, competitive, aggressive, ambitious, and domineering. Women, on the other hand, are viewed as being the "weaker sex"—sensitive, emotional, dependent, and talkative. The traditional view of women is also that they have little business sense (Frieze et al., 1978). These stereotypes are held by both men and women (Broverman et al., 1972) and are often used as the basis for assigning roles to people in various groups. In families, for example, the "logical, competitive, aggressive" male has traditionally been given the role of providing financial security for his family. As such, it is he who must work outside the home. In addition, the "domineering" male is expected to be head of the family: "A *man's* home is his castle." The woman is given the role of managing the household and supporting her husband. If she does seek work outside the household, she is expected to take on more "feminine" occupations such as secretary, nurse, or sales clerk. Further, if she does seek employment, she is not expected to, nor is she usually given the opportunity to, compete with her male counterparts for high salaries.

Children are taught these stereotypes in a variety of ways and places. Parents teach their children how to be a boy or girl. These lessons include allowing children to play only sex-appropriate games, giving instructions about who can express what emotions, and supplying the correct models for sex-related behavior. In school, children read stories in their textbooks that show males as strong, active, and adventurous, while females are shown as gentle and dependent (Wirtenburg & Nakamura, 1976). Even on television, children are shown that the "typical" woman is a housewife with a bunch of kids, while the "typical" man works, fights, plays, and rules the world outside the home.

This assignment of sex roles is not only based on stereotypes about the personality and temperament of men and women, it also *reinforces* those stereotypes. The male who is placed in a competitive job situation must become competitive, domineering, and aggressive if he is to survive in this position. Similarly, the female who is forced into the dependent role cannot function if she seems aggressive and ambitious. Thus a cycle of self-fulfilling prophecy results from the assignment of roles based on stereotypes of males and females (see Chapter 15).

The underlying problem in this situation is that males are not necessarily domineering, logical, ambitious, and businesslike. And all females are not necessarily gentle, sensitive, and not mechanically inclined. The assignment of roles based on these rigid stereotypes has had bad consequences from both the individual's and the group's point of view. For individuals, it has meant that they are often forced to try to fulfill a role that is distasteful and not suited to their abilities. This has been particularly unfortunate for women, who are stereotyped in a more negative light than men

(Deaux, 1976) and who have, consequently, been offered the less attractive alternatives. For the group, whether it is the family or work group, this misguided procedure for assigning roles has often limited effective performance by the group.

Assigning people to roles because of their sex makes no more sense than assigning them to play positions on a baseball team based on their shoe size. There has recently been an increased awareness of the unfairness and negative impact of traditional sex roles. Stereotypes about women are becoming less negative (Der-Karabetran & Smith, 1977). The number of women taking jobs outside the home has increased so that now 52 percent of all women over 16 years of age hold jobs (Bureau of Labor Statistics, *Employment and Earnings*, January 1981).

These changes are viewed with alarm by some people. It is argued that the destruction of traditional sex roles will lead to a state of confusion and chaos that is avoided when everyone knows his or her place. The individual, both male and female, is now faced with a wider variety of alternative roles, occupations, and life styles to choose from. For some, this variety is overwhelming, and being forced to make a personal decision is frightening. However, despite these problems, the ultimate result of this change will be to allow people to adopt roles that are more suited to their personal abilities and preferences. And, consequently, groups will function more smoothly and effectively.

(1975) outlines four aspects of personality and social development that are also associated with careers. Young adults must learn to: (1) respond to people warmly and respectfully without anxiety; (2) base decisions upon their own beliefs; (3) respect cultural values; and (4) care about society

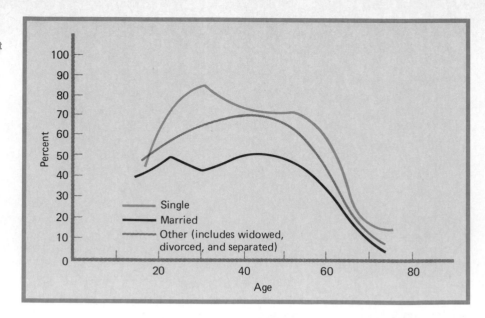

and the people in it. Accordingly, career commitments depend upon cognitive, social, and personality development during young adulthood. As mentioned earlier, Lowenthal (1977) maintains that the commitment to mastery in an occupation is a very important aspect of development in young adults.

Career Women.   An increasing number of women in America are lining up for their paychecks. Women constituted 25 percent of the labor force in 1940 and 50.7 percent in 1980 (U.S. Department of Labor, 1981). Married women account for most of the increase. Their rate of working, however, is still behind that of single women. The difference is especially great during young adulthood, as indicated in Figure 9–3, which shows working rate by age for single and married women. The figure also reflects the tendency for married women to have two entry points into the work force. Their rate of working peaks in their twenties and again in their fifties. The double peaks correspond to women working before their children are born, taking a break while rearing children, and working again when their children leave home. This interruption partially explains why women receive 20 to 25 percent less pay than men in the same occupations. It is only a partial explanation for the pay difference, however. The discrepancy also exists because the American economic system discriminates against women, although this discrimination is decreasing (Hoffman & Nye, 1974; Kreps, 1976; Treiman & Hostmann, 1981).

Housewives versus Career Women.   Who is happier—the full-time homemaker or the career woman? This question is most meaningful when asked about career women with multiple roles of worker, wife, and mother. The answer may surprise you in light of portrayals in modern media. Magazines, television, and movies suggest that careers for women are enriching, liberating, and satisfying. In contrast, the role of homemaker is often pictured as boring, lonely, and demeaning. Accordingly, career women should be happier. In fact, there is no difference! Two separate and extensive studies showed no difference in general life satisfaction or in self-esteem (Baruch & Barnett, 1980; Wright, 1978). This important finding dramatizes a pervasive theme in life-span psychology—there is no single path to happiness.

Profile of a Successful Career Woman.   Henning and Jardin (1976) identified characteristics of 25 women who had established themselves as successful executives by the end of young adulthood. These women tended to be first born in their families and they tended to excel in college. Their fathers were extremely supportive of their careers, encouraged them to

develop their abilities, reinforced them for breaking away from sex-role stereotypes, and financially assisted the launching of their careers. The women accepted assistance from senior male executives in the beginning, but they became independent by the time they reached middle-management positions. This profile of the successful career woman is adequate, but it is sketchy in comparison to the more detailed observations that are available on the successful career man.

Becoming One's Own Man. Daniel J. Levinson (1978) and four colleagues at Yale University conducted one of the most comprehensive studies of development in young male adults. The research team studied 140 men who were either executives, biologists, novelists, or hourly wage earners. The team interviewed the men for a total of 10 to 20 hours, in sessions that were spread over about 1½ years. All men were between 35 and 40 years of age at the first interview; 2 years later the team conducted follow-up interviews. During the sessions the men were asked to recall the events of their young adulthood. The results suggested that males go through three periods during young adulthood:

1. Men go through a phase Levinson called *entering the adult world* between their early and late twenties. In this phase they seek a balance between keeping options open and establishing a stable life structure. A good balance results in a wide exploration of alternatives, followed by strong commitments. As part of this phase, most men get married, have children, and choose an occupation.
2. Most men experience an *age 30 transition* within several years of their thirtieth birthday. They think then that it will soon be too late to make changes, so they carefully evaluate their commitments. Some men make a smooth transition, reaffirming their earlier decisions; others face a severe crisis accompanied by divorce and occupational change.
3. Between the early thirties and about age 40, men go through an important period that Levinson called *settling down*. They emphasize stability and security now, often fixing on some key goal, such as a promotion. The end phase of *settling down* is called *becoming one's own man*. As men grow out of early adulthood, they urgently strive to advance as far as possible in their careers, to gain greater authority, and to be independent. Most men advance within a stable life structure. Changes in residence, job, or life style usually represent advancements rather than basic changes in their established life structure.

According to Levinson, most men experience an age-30 transition, during which they carefully evaluate their lives and their careers. For some this may be a smooth transition; for others, it may be a crisis, leading to divorce or career change.

Some men, however, experience a severe crisis during this phase. Like those who went through a crisis at age 30, men in crisis at this point try to drastically alter their existing life structure through divorce or career changes. The phase of becoming one's own man, whether smooth or rocky, usually ends at about 40 years of age, as new developmental demands usher in middle age.

MIDDLE ADULTHOOD

The adage "Life begins at 40" seems to miss the mark with respect to a person as dynamic as O'Keeffe. She seemed to "begin" over and over again throughout her life. The adage is not entirely inaccurate in her case, however, since one of her fresh starts came at about the age of 40. "Having abandoned the idea of having a child, and approaching her fortieth birthday, Georgia began planning precisely every detail of her daily existence to eliminate anything unnecessary to art. . . . She set new goals for herself and became absorbed in solving various technical problems after the critics had given her high praise for her technical virtuosity" (Lisle, 1980, pp. 182–184). Her experiences between 40 and 60 years of age provide an interesting frame of reference for our discussion of middle adulthood.

Sequence of Development in Middle Years

Erikson's Generativity versus Stagnation.
Erikson (1959, 1963) maintains that one of two feelings dominates at this age: (1) *generativity*, a sense of producing and contributing to the world, or (2) *stagnation*, a sense of not fulfilling expectations. A sense of generativity can be gained through family, job, or community involvement. O'Keeffe clearly gained

Middle years can be dominated by a sense of producing and contributing to the world. This sense can be gained through family, job, or community involvement.

a sense of generativity through her career; her mother gained it by rearing children. People who feel no sense of worthwhile accomplishment form an impression of being bogged down in a life without meaning. People can get beyond this sense of stagnation, however, and doing so can make them more compassionate about the weaknesses and suffering of others.

Levinson's Periods of Middle Adulthood. Levinson (1978) proposed a universal sequence of periods during middle adulthood. They are as follows:

1. Men experience a *midlife transition* between the ages of 40 and 45. This is the period of the so-called midlife crisis, a time of conflict and stress.
2. Forty-five- to fifty-year-old men settle into a new life structure during a period called *entering middle adulthood*. Those who created a satisfactory structure during the previous transitional period enjoy one of the happiest times of their lives. (Levinson's conclusions about life after 45 is more speculative because it is based on biographies instead of interviews.)
3. Another transitional period, *age 50 transition*, occurs between 50 and 55. It is analogous to the *age 30 transition*, in which men reevaluate previous commitments.
4. A stable period, *culmination of middle adulthood*, is enjoyed between 55 and 60. Levinson has very little data on this period, but he suspects it is similar to the settling down period discussed earlier.

Levinson is the first to acknowledge that it is too early to tell if he is correct in postulating a universal sequence. You might judge the appropriateness of his periods for yourself as we consider physical, family, and occupational events during middle adulthood.

Studies of these patterns have practical applications. They might guide employers in the selection of people who will be dependable, for example, and they might help clinicians work with people having adjustment problems.

Physical Changes

O'Keeffe's appearance during the middle years portrayed years of joy, laughter, pain, and sorrow, which, together with the harsh southwestern sun, etched character into her face. Physical alterations in middle age call attention to the aging process. Changes that affect appearance (e.g., baldness, wrinkles, and weight gain) are accompanied by reduced physiological capacities. As indicated in Figure 9–4, muscle strength, lung capacity, cardiac output, and other functions decline (de Vries, 1970; Maranto, 1984). There is also a slight increase in the time it takes to make simple responses, such as braking a car in an emergency (Hodgkins, 1962). People who are middle-aged also start noticing visual loss caused by changes in the eye (Sekuler, Kline, & Dismukes, 1982). The lens becomes yellower, cloudier, and less able to focus light for close work such as reading (Fozard et al., 1977). All these biological changes remind people that their life span is limited (Levinson, 1978).

Physical decline causes professional athletes and others with physically demanding jobs to make radical career adjustments during middle age. Biological changes have little effect, however, on the everyday lives of most middle-agers. Yet, most middle-aged adults, especially men, express considerable concern about their decreased physical efficiency (Neugarten, 1968).

Some changes must be accepted, of course, but currently many more middle-aged men and women are taking steps to stay in shape than in previous years. Exercise programs including calisthenics, running, and

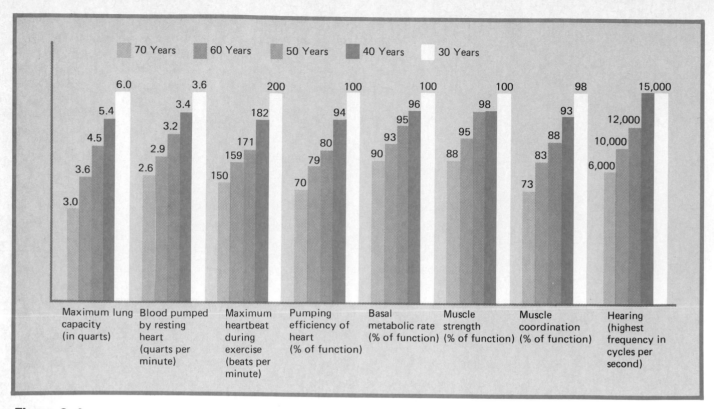

Figure 9-4
Lung capacity, cardiac output, muscle strength, and other functions decline with age.

swimming can be very effective (de Vries, 1970). Physicians highly recommend such rigorous programs for those who can pass a careful physical examination (de Vries, 1975; Woodruff, 1977). Less strenuous programs also help. People can, for instance, take short brisk walks that will help them stay in good physical condition.

Family Commitments

O'Keeffe's family commitments were unusual, as mentioned before. She had only been married 8 years on her forty-fifth birthday, and she had no children. Most middle-aged people have about 20 years of marriage behind them at this age, and they find themselves sandwiched between the needs of two generations. Their children, generally teenagers, have special needs as they seek greater independence, while their aging parents have special needs as they become more dependent.

Many middle-aged people have a special relationship with their own parents. Much as parents value independence, aging parents gradually become more and more dependent upon their offspring (Blenker, 1965). People meet their aging parents' needs in many ways. They visit, do household tasks, run errands, and give physical care (Sussman & Burchinal, 1962). Some even take their parents into their homes (Spark & Brody, 1970). Research has indicated that 80 to 90 percent of parents studied have children living within an hour's driving distance. Of these, 80 percent had seen their children within the past week (Riley, Johnson, & Foner, 1972). Such interactions are best when elderly parents are allowed to preserve their personal dignity and when middle-aged sons and daughters are allowed to pursue their other commitments (Blenker, 1965).

Occupational Commitments

O'Keeffe made stronger commitments to her career, and she became more successful during her middle years. Many people follow this pattern. An increasing number, however, change careers at this age. Clopton (1973)

People at this age are truly the "middle" generation—they are parents themselves, and they usually have their own parents living within visiting distance. As their children grow and become independent, their aging parents often begin to become more dependent.

calls those who stay with the same career *persisters*, and he calls those who change careers *shifters*. Let's look at the developmental patterns of men and women who fall into these two categories.

Career Men. Evidence indicates that there is a strong positive side to midlife career shifts. Researchers found, for instance, that such shifts can be satisfying, productive, and orderly (Murray, Powers, & Havighurst, 1971). This positive pattern is more likely in white-collar workers than in blue-collar workers (Schein, 1975). It is also associated with certain personality and situational factors, as shown in Table 9–3.

Males who persist in a career are not always highly successful. In one study, Bray and Howard (1980) found considerable variability in success of managers who had stayed with the Bell Telephone System for over 20 years. The successful managers were more intelligent, more motivated, and more aggressive than less successful ones. They were also happier with their jobs, but they were not necessarily happier in their overall life situations. The most and the least successful managers found happiness through different life patterns.

Table 9–3
Effects of Personality and Situation on Occupation

Personality Factors	Situational Pressures	Stability or Change in Occupation
Low self-direction	Little pressure to change	Routine career; advancement follows seniority
High self-direction	Little pressure to change	Flexible career; initiative for change and type of work assumed by person
Low self-direction	Much pressure to change	Disjointed career; technologically oriented reasons for unemployment (e.g., blue-collar workers), no skill or experience (e.g., widow)
High self-direction	Much pressure to change	Orderly, sequential career; well-planned effort in making changes by person

Source: Murray et al. (1971).

3
8

16
21

Career Women. We have already identified various career patterns: women who stay with the same company through young adulthood and middle adulthood, women who remain full-time homemakers, and women who interrupt their outside-the-home careers to raise children. We might call the first two groups *persisters* and the third one *shifters*.

The shifters are especially interesting. Many of these women return to school during their middle years for a wide range of reasons. At one extreme, some women merely brush up on previously held skills before resuming a career. At the other extreme, some women complete graduate degrees in order to become full-time professionals. Middle-aged women tend to enter graduate school with fire in their eyes. Their confidence often diminishes midway through the program, as both school and family pressures mount. The original determination usually wins out, however, and the women emerge with increased self-esteem and assertiveness (Lefevre, 1972). These shifters tend to be happy despite unfortunate discrimination against them in wages and job opportunities (Blau, 1975; Ritzer, 1977). In fact, shifters seem to be as happy as persisters, which is consistent with an important theme that emerges from life-span research: There are many ways to be happy.

26
29

25
30
47

LATE ADULTHOOD

The Census Bureau predicts a drastic increase in the number of senior citizens in this country (Ubell, 1984). In 1900, 1 American in 25 was over 65; today, it's 1 in 9. The prediction for the middle of the next century is that 1 American in 4 will be 65 years of age or older. This dramatic increase in the elderly is expected to include a sixfold increase in those over the age of 85. Adjusting to old age is sometimes difficult. O'Keeffe provides a marvelous example of how satisfying these later years can be.

O'Keeffe's ability to survive a trying struggle was shown again in late adulthood when her husband died. She virtually retired from her career during her first 10 years of widowhood; then she made an incredible comeback. The spirit that enabled her to rekindle her career is catching on today with more and more elderly adults. That spirit is symbolized in one of O'Keeffe's adventures: In 1961, at the age of 74, she took a 10-day, 185-mile raft trip down the Colorado River. She handled her own equipment, helped with the rowing, and remained cheerful through very hot days, freezing nights, and drenching thunderstorms. Her keen insights heightened the experience for her companions. She didn't have time to paint on the first trip, but she returned many times after that, trying to capture on canvas the beauty she had seen.

O'Keeffe's elderly years, like her earlier ones, are typical in some respects and unusual in others. Having to face the death of a spouse is typical. Having a zest for life is also prevalent. Her mental and physical agility, however, are uncommon, as is her persistence in the same career. In this section, we will examine current trends in aging and we will try to predict future ones. As we progress, you might ask yourself whether O'Keeffe's river trip was something that only she would do at that age, or whether it forecasts the adventures that could well be ours in late adulthood.

Physical and Mental Abilities

O'Keeffe has always taken an active part in maintaining her good health. She has an organic garden that forms the basis of her carefully planned diet. A typical day begins with a big breakfast that includes beef butchered to her specification, a morning snack of homemade yogurt, a lunch consisting of an organic salad, and a light dinner of little more than fruit and cheese. She especially loves the strong flavors of garlic, raw onion, and chili peppers. She maintains her weight at 127 pounds, and she is very healthy for her age.

We all understand the qualifier, "for her age," to some extent because of our experiences with grandparents and other older adults. We know that our health will decline. Physical changes will eventually touch nearly every aspect of our lives, including our mental abilities. We may have to give up things that we now enjoy; we may have to slow down. But we can follow O'Keeffe's example in taking steps to maximize our health as we age. We can stack the deck in our favor by knowing what to expect and by planning for it.

Biological Theories of Aging.
Not everyone accepts aging as a natural and inevitable process. Bjorksten (1968), for example, argues that aging is a disease. He maintains that humans might live for 800 years or more in good health if that disease could be cured. Few researchers express such optimism. Many believe, however, that the maximum life span, which is now about 110 to 120 years, will increase as researchers discover the basic mechanisms of the aging process (Medvedev, 1975). Cell malfunctions

51

53

Although we all age, we do not all do so at the same rate. Some people, such as the woman shown in the photos on these two pages, go through life with great energy and enthusiasm, as much in their fifth decade as in their first.

Georgia O'Keeffe is shown here at age 75, shortly after her rigorous raft trip down the Colorado River. When this photograph was taken, she had just been elected a member of the American Academy of Arts and Letters, the nation's highest honor society of the arts.

in elderly people are caused in part by mutations that damage genes, according to Sinex (1974). (See the discussion of genetics in Chapter 2.) Abnormal cell functioning interferes with the normal operation of physiological systems such as the endocrine system. This in turn leads to the physical changes we know as aging. Knowing the physical changes associated with aging can be valuable if you ever care for an elderly person (see the Highlight, "Sensory Changes and Caring for the Elderly").

Cognitive Changes. Elderly people are often the first to admit a decline in their cognitive abilities. Those who work with the elderly also notice declining mental abilities in their patients. Experimenters, however, have had trouble analyzing cognitive changes because of certain methodological pitfalls.

A study by Jerome (1959) illustrates some of the snags. He tested problem-solving abilities with a logical analysis device. People had to gather information piece by piece and then integrate it to solve problems. A group of subjects who were about 66 years old did much worse than a group of subjects who were about 23 years old. The older people tended to ask for the same information over and over again. Jerome tried to cut down on the need to remember information by allowing subjects to write notes. Younger people made good use of the notes, but older people did not. Jerome's experiment left no doubt that the older subjects had greater difficulty solving problems because they approached the problems haphazardly, but its meaning is nevertheless uncertain. This is because we cannot be sure that age caused the difference that was observed between young and old subjects. The two groups might have differed in motivation. Perhaps older people considered the problems meaningless and irrelevant and therefore may have exerted themselves less. Furthermore, the two groups might have had different educational experiences. Schools for the younger subjects may have put greater emphasis on problem solving. As a result, the younger subjects may have been better problem solvers than the older people were at *any* point in their lives. For these reasons, Jerome's experiment does not prove that age causes a decline in problem-solving ability.

Whenever researchers compare different age groups, age is not the only difference. Motivation and education are two other factors that often differ. Researchers do not agree on how to define motivation or on how to measure it. Until they agree on these issues, there will be little hope of controlling motivation in studies of aging (Botwinick, 1977). Motivational changes could cause changes in performance even when researchers study the same people at different ages. Education is also difficult to control for because the educational system keeps changing. Despite these methodological problems, however, researchers have gathered important data on cognitive changes.

Botwinick (1977) suggests six cognitive changes that occur with age and aids to counteract them:

1. Older people need more time to respond in learning situations (Canestrari, 1963). The pacing of learning tasks should be slowed to allow for this.
2. Older people are prone to have high anxiety, which limits responses in learning tasks (Eisdorfer, 1968). Researchers should take steps to reduce anxiety as much as possible in learning and testing situations.
3. Elderly people tend to resist learning things that seem to them to be irrelevant and meaningless (Hulicka & Grossman, 1967). It's a good idea to make sure an elderly person wants to learn something or understands why it is important before teaching is begun.
4. The elderly often fail to take advantage of organizational strategies that could help them learn. We learned in Chapter 7, for instance,

that list learning is easier when similar items are grouped together. Elderly learners do not try such groupings on their own (Denny, 1974). They may improve considerably if they are helped to organize in this way (Hultsch, 1971).

5. Elderly people tend to be insecure. They will therefore respond much better if they are praised rather than criticized.

6. Elderly people's short-term memory (Chapter 7) is better for things they hear than it is for things they see (Arenberg, 1967). If you want

SENSORY CHANGES AND CARING FOR THE ELDERLY

Stephen Cohen (1981) has described sensory changes in the elderly, and he has also outlined procedures that will help if you ever care for an elderly relative or some other elderly person. Some of his main points are as follow:

1. Vision is impaired in the elderly because of structural changes in the aging eye (which we discussed in Chapter 3). When you assist an elderly person, you should be aware that there are reductions in abilities to see depth (for example, distance of floor from bed), to see objects located off to the side, and to see detail. Old eyes also take longer to adjust when going from dark to dim places. The elderly have trouble seeing blues, greens, and violets; they have an easier time seeing reds, oranges, and yellows. You should, therefore, select lighting, positioning, and coloring of objects carefully, especially critical objects such as stairs, handrails, doorknobs, and light switches.

2. Aging also causes hearing problems. One reason for this is a decrease in the number of nerve fibers that carry sound information (see Chapter 3). Hearing loss especially affects the ability to hear high-pitched sounds, such as high notes on a piano. Thus elderly people hear low-pitched sounds better than high-pitched sounds. You can help an aging person hear important sounds such as

doorbells, smoke alarms, and telephone bells not only by increasing the volume, but also by lowering the pitch. You can help an aging person understand speech by teaching yourself and others how to modify your voice. You should speak loudly, but do not shout. Shouting conceals high-pitched speech sounds that the elderly person already finds difficult to hear. You should slow down, to space your sounds as far apart as possible. Finally, you should lower the pitch of your voice as much as possible. A deep male voice is easiest for a hard-of-hearing person to understand.

3. Other sensory impairments must be overcome. The sense of smell and taste are reduced, so that foods with intense aromas and

flavors will be appreciated by the elderly. Avoid piping hot food, however, because an elderly person's ability to detect heat is dangerously reduced. For the same reason, protect the aging from hot surfaces such as faucets, radiators, pots, and pans. The sense of touch and of pain is reduced to the point where the elderly might not realize that they are cutting off blood circulation. They should be encouraged, therefore, to wear loose clothing and to change positions every so often when they are lying or sitting for long periods.

Cohen convincingly demonstrates that knowing the nature of sensory changes can make life safer for elderly people.

to help an aging person remember a phone number long enough for a single dialing, say it for them.

Most of you will not personally experience sensory or cognitive declines for many years. You may, however, be able to help aging relatives counteract such sensory and cognitive changes. We mentioned earlier, for instance, that aging parents often depend upon support from their sons and daughters (Spark & Brody, 1970). In the next section, we will reexamine this important phase of the family cycle from the aging parents' perspective.

Family Commitments

O'Keeffe's decision not to have children meant that she had few family commitments during late adulthood, especially after her husband died. She made up for this, however, by becoming a "foster grandparent" to children in her village. These children visited her regularly. They ate with her, colored with crayons in her studio, and sometimes they even helped her prepare canvases. She took some of her favorites camping with her, and she sent several to private schools. She supplied a Little League team with uniforms, balls, and bats. She provided funds to bring educational programs to local television stations, and she supported the construction of a local recreational center with a donation of about $60,000. She may have been motivated by the fond memories she had of her own grandmothers. Psychologists are only beginning to gather data on grandparenting. They are finding that this important role enriches the lives of grandchildren *and* grandparents.

Being a Grandparent.   Clavan (1978) called grandparenting a "roleless role" because its rights and responsibilities are not clearly defined in our society. Grandparents and grandchildren mutually enrich each others' lives. Ninety-two percent of grandchildren in one study thought that grandparents contribute much to growing up (Robertson, 1976). Children like doing things with their grandparents, and they value the love and gifts they receive from them (Kahana & Kahana, 1971). In return, they give their grandparents great satisfaction. The majority derived pleasure from a feeling of renewal, from meaningful companionship, and from being able to contribute to the development of their grandchildren. Grandparents also enjoy seeing their grandchildren accomplish things that neither the grandparent nor their own children were able to do. Grandparenting can become especially important when death of a spouse deprives an elderly person of one of his or her most important sources of life satisfaction.

Elderly Husbands and Wives.   Marital satisfaction is very high for elderly couples. In fact, it may reach its highest level during late adulthood (Miller, 1976). Older husbands and wives find happiness in companionship, mutual expression of true feelings, and economic security, among other things (Stinnett, Carter, & Montgomery, 1972). Contrary to common belief, they also enjoy sexual relations to the age of 80 years and beyond (Rubin, 1966). Reduced occupational commitments enable elderly couples to spend more time together. In the best situations, husbands help more around the house and women become more loving and understanding (Troll, 1971). Such adjustments increase marital satisfaction for those who had happy relationships during younger years (Peterson & Payne, 1975).

Occupational Commitments

O'Keeffe widely exhibited new paintings as she advanced in years through her eighties and into her nineties. She remained in the mainstream of art when others her age had long since retired. Many people cannot stay engaged in their careers as she did. But most people can make up for

Grandparents and grandchildren mutually enrich each others' lives.

career retirement by increasing involvement in other activities (Neugarten & Hagestad, 1976). Retirement, from this point of view, can be as fulfilling as O'Keeffe's late-life career. In this section, we will consider how people plan for retirement, how they adjust to it, and how satisfied they are with it.

Planning for Retirement.   Retirement in the United States is usually mandatory at the age of 65 or 70 years. The mandatory versus voluntary retirement issue will probably be debated for some time to come. On the one hand, mandatory retirement seems to discriminate against older people who are ready and able to continue to work. On the other hand, Botwinick (1977) argues in favor of mandatory retirement on several grounds, one of which is that a fixed age limit will better enable people to plan for retirement.

To what extent do people actually plan under the present mandatory system? There is no simple answer, because many variables influence the extent of planning. A tendency for men to plan is positively associated with high socioeconomic status, leisure-time interests, financial security, and good health (McPherson & Guppy, 1979). These same variables are associated with a positive attitude toward an upcoming retirement in men. The variables of socioeconomic status and financial security affect women

Most people plan to make up for retirement by increasing their involvement in other activities, such as playing sports or attending school.

differently. Women with high-status jobs and high income do *not* want to retire (Streif & Schneider, 1971). This sex difference is ironic, because women often adjust more easily than men when they do retire.

Adjusting to Retirement. Lowenthal (1972) suggests that the trick to a successful retirement is substituting activities for the time previously spent on an occupation. Career women are often better prepared to make this adjustment because the role of homemaker is a traditionally acceptable substitution. Men also adjust better when they share in household tasks. Some men, however, especially working-class men, consider "women's work" demeaning. As a result, adjusting to retirement can be more problematic for this group (Troll, 1971). A second popular substitution is another job. Streif and Schneider (1971) observed that 73 percent of people who consider work to be a major source of satisfaction find another job after retirement. A third substitution is well-planned leisure activity, which can be especially fulfilling for those who have a history of sharing recreational interests with their spouses. Whatever the substitution is, a redistribution of energy seems to be basic to a satisfying adjustment.

Retirement and Life Satisfaction. The impact of retirement is often not as negative as people anticipated, according to Streif and Schneider (1971). They measured attitudes of 4,000 people before and after retirement. Their sample included people from many walks of life, ranging from unskilled laborers to professionals. The results indicated that about 33 percent found retirement to be better than they had anticipated. Only about 5 percent found it to be worse. Most people in the sample adjusted well to retirement and were satisfied with life.

Streib and Schneider's study raises the question of why so many people are overly pessimistic about retirement. One reason may be that some of the negative feelings are not actually related to retirement itself. A worker inevitably associates retirement with old age, and that may be associated with death. Older people have had a chance to come to grips with aging and they are less fearful of death (Kalish & Reynolds, 1976). After retirement we would therefore expect a reduction in some of the pessimism that was associated with the fear of aging and death.

DEATH AND DYING

O'Keeffe was almost 60 when her husband died. Many friends and relatives also died as she advanced through her sixties. These deaths forced her to realize that she must make plans for her estate in the event of her own death. She assigned some paintings to be left to several museums and universities. She wants most of her art to be displayed, however, in an O'Keeffe art museum in New Mexico. In terms of Erikson's (1963) theory, O'Keeffe faced the last stage of development, the crisis of *integrity versus despair*. Resolution of this crisis determines whether one faces the end of life with a feeling that a full and meaningful life has been led or with a feeling that life has been wasted. O'Keeffe emerged with wisdom that is related to integrity. She achieved the wisdom to be pleased with her accomplishments and to be accepting of her death. We will conclude our life-span investigation with a brief discussion of the processes of accepting the deaths of others and accepting one's own death.

Adjusting to the Death of Loved Ones

O'Keeffe grieved over the deaths of her parents, other relatives, and friends. But the death of her husband seemed to be most devastating. Death of a spouse requires more than an emotional adjustment. It also requires the adoption of new roles and responsibilities. Life-satisfaction ratings of widows and widowers correlate highly with having skills necessary for making these adaptations (Rux, 1976). Another important factor is the extent of involvement in a spouse's life. Lopata (1973a, b, c) observed, for instance, that widows report more life disruption when they identified strongly with their husband's activities. Widows and widowers experience severe loneliness and grief, however, whether or not they are forced to make drastic life-style changes.

Psychologists are only beginning to learn about the grief process (e.g., Parkes & Brown, 1972). Glick, Weiss, and Parkes (1974) outlined distinct phases of grieving:

1. The *initial response* is a phase characterized first by shock and then by an overwhelming sorrow.
2. The second phase, *coping with anxiety and fear*, is characterized by worry of a nervous breakdown. Some people depend upon tranquilizers during this period.
3. The third phase, the *intermediate* phase, consists of obsessional review of how the death might have been prevented and a review of old memories of times with the loved one.
4. *Recovery* is the last phase, which usually begins after one year. People become proud that they survived an extreme trauma, and they begin to develop a positive outlook once again.

Accepting One's Own Death

How often do you think about your own death? Can you face it without fear or despair? Your answers probably depend upon your age. Young people think about death much less than old people, and they are more fearful of it (Kalish & Reynolds, 1976). The question of accepting one's own death becomes especially relevant to those who are told that they have a terminal illness. In her book, *On Death and Dying*, Elisabeth Kübler-Ross (1969) summarized results of interviews with over 200 people in this situation. She identified five stages in the adjustment process:

1. *Denial and isolation* is first. A common initial statement is "No, not me, it cannot be true." Some denials are long lasting and are accompanied by conviction that the doctors are wrong. Other denials are soon replaced by isolation, which is the ability to talk about one's own death as if it were happening to someone else.
2. The second stage is *anger*, which typically stems from resentment and from concern about being cast aside. One patient reported wondering, "Why couldn't it have been old George instead of me?" An-

other patient cried out "I am alive, don't forget that. You can hear my voice, I am not dead yet!"

3. Anger is often replaced by *bargaining*. This third stage usually involves private promises with God. For "a little more time," patients promise "a life dedicated to God" or "a life in the service of the church."

4. Most people move quickly from bargaining to *depression*, the fourth stage. Kübler-Ross distinguishes two kinds of depression: *Reactive depression* is feeling downcast because of people and things that need to be taken care of. A mother will be depressed, for instance, until she knows the kind of care that will be provided for her children. *Preparatory depression* is a sense of impending loss of everything and everybody one loves. Patients at this time are grateful to those who can sit with them in silence.

5. People who work through their depression reach the final stage, *acceptance*. It is not a happy stage, but it is a time of peace. Most patients in the Kübler-Ross study died in this stage without fear or despair.

Kübler-Ross (1974) warns that her "stages" are not invariant or universal. She was not trying to prescribe a "best way" to prepare for death. She is disturbed that some health caretakers are trying to manipulate patients through her stages. It is far better to accept an individual's response pattern.

If you were told that you had a terminal disease and had 6 months to live, how would you want to spend your time? One study obtained answers to this question from people in three age groups: 20 to 39 years old, 40 to 59 years old, and over 60 years old (Kalish & Reynolds, 1976). More younger respondents thought that they would change their life styles, and more older people thought that they would reflect on spiritual needs. Such reflection may be adaptive since people with strong religious beliefs have less fear of death (Nelson & Nelson, 1973; Templar, 1972).

Georgia O'Keeffe revealed that she reflects on spiritual beliefs. In fact one wonders if her desire to display her art in New Mexico is related to a view she once expressed about death: "When I think of death, I only regret that I will not be able to see this beautiful country [the New Mexico countryside] anymore, unless the Indians are right and my spirit will walk here after I'm gone" (Lisle, 1980).

Summary

1. The **life-span developmental approach** deals with changes that occur within an individual over time as well as the differences in such changes among individuals.

2. In **adolescence** the physical changes include the adolescent "growth spurt," **puberty,** and the development of **primary** and **secondary sex characteristics.** Morally, teenagers generally progress through Kohlberg's conventional level of moral reasoning. According to Erikson, an important stage in the personality development of the adolescent is the **identity crisis,** which occurs during puberty. Peer groups become very important and early sexual activity seems to be becoming more common.

3. One way of looking at development in young adulthood is in terms of commitments that are made at this time: moral commitments (Kohlberg's postconventional stage is usually reached at this point); interpersonal commitments (Erikson's stage of intimacy versus isolation, in which marriage and family commitments are a major theme); and mastery commitments (the establishment of and mastery in a career or occupation).

4. Levinson's framework for development in young adulthood includes several stages, including a transition stage at about age 30, and a *settling down* stage, in which in terms of occupation the person seeks a certain amount of independence.

5. Middle age is concerned first with Erikson's generativity versus stagnation stage, in which one's involvement in family, job, or community work can either be fulfilling or leave one with a sense of being meaningless. In the same way, Levinson's framework at this age includes a kind of midlife transition (often called a *midlife crisis*, but not necessarily so). In terms of family commitments, this is a time when children begin leaving the home, while, at the same time, middle-aged people often become more involved in caring for their elderly parents.

6. Late adulthood involves many physical changes, which affect sensory abilities as well as general health and mobility. There are also changes at this age in cognitive abilities, but only of a certain type. Family commitments at this point include being a grandparent, and there is often an increase in marital satisfaction for elderly couples. In terms of occupation, one of the major themes is planning for and adjusting to retirement. The elderly face Erikson's final crisis, the stage of integrity versus despair, which determines one's final outlook on life.

7. Just as there are stages that we go through adjusting to life, there seems to be stages in adjusting to death—the death of those close to us and our own death. Kübler-Ross has outlined what seem to be five distinct stages in this adjustment process: denial and isolation, anger, bargaining, depression, and, finally, acceptance.

Key Terms

adolescence
cohabitation
identity crisis
internalization
life-span development approach

menarche
primary sexual characteristics
puberty
secondary sexual characteristics

Suggested Readings

The following book is about Georgia O'Keeffe:

LISLE, L. *Portrait of an artist: A biography of Georgia O'Keeffe*. New York: Washington Square Press, 1980.

ERIKSON, E. E. (Ed.). *Adulthood*. New York: Norton, 1978. Various authorities have written separate chapters on adults in contemporary society. The writers take many perspectives, including cultural, historical, and medical.

KÜBLER-ROSS, E. *Living with death and dying*. New York: Macmillan, 1981. A warm, sophisticated, and sensitive sequel to Kübler-Ross's *On death and dying*, which is reviewed in this chapter.

MCKENZIE, S. C. *Aging and old age*. Glenview, III.: Scott, Foresman, 1980. This text is an integrated, multidisciplinary analysis of psychological, social, and biological aspects of aging.

POON, L. W. *Aging in the 1980s*. Washington, D.C.: American Psychological Association, 1980. This collection of articles by leaders in the field of aging identifies what we know and what we need to know in areas such as stress and coping, interpersonal relations, and cognition.

SCHAIE, K. W. (Ed.). *Longitudinal studies of adult psychological development*. New York: The Guilford Press, 1983. This volume contains clearly written and authoritative chapters on the major longitudinal studies that have been done on adult development.

STEVENS-LONG, J. *Adult life*. Palo Alto, Calif.: Mayfield, 1979. A chronologically organized analysis of developmental processes from young adulthood through old age. The book reviews both basic and applied research on adult development in modern society.

MOTIVATION

As dawn broke, the airport in Uruguay was filled with the excited chatter of the forty passengers who waited to board the plane for the four-hour trip to Santiago, Chile. Fifteen of the passengers, ages eighteen to twenty-six, were members of the Old Christians Club rugby team, which had organized the trip and chartered the airplane. They were going to Chile to play a number of rugby matches with the tough Chilean national teams. At 8:05 A.M., on October 12, 1972, the plane taxied down the runway and took off for the 900-mile trip. The flight plan took them through Argentina and over the snow-covered peaks of the Andes.

The plane bounced savagely in the light air as it tried to climb above the clouds. Among the passengers there was a holiday atmosphere as the young men joked at each lurch of their tiny aircraft. The atmosphere in the cockpit, however, was not so jovial; the pilot fought to maintain control of the plane and searched for landmarks.

Suddenly the plane swooped out of the clouds just in time for everyone to see a massive rock not more than ten feet from the wing tip. The wing slammed into the mountain, ripped off, and sliced into the tail section. The torn body of the plane hurtled down the snowy mountainside like a toboggan. Finally it came to rest in a snowbank. For a moment, there was utter silence, and then the moans of the injured filled the air. One by one, those who were not hurt climbed out of the plane and sat bewildered in the snow.

Soon the survivors began a gruesome survey of what was left of the plane. Five people, including the pilot and copilot, were dead, and many of the others were so badly injured it was clear that they, too, would soon die. Mustering all of their strength, they untangled the injured and dead from the wreckage; the dead were dragged out of the plane and the injured were carefully laid inside.

The subzero cold of the Andes quickly made the survivors realize that their first task must be to clear an area inside the wreck for shelter. Seats were dragged out and a makeshift wall was built over the gaping hole in the tail area. No one was prepared for the cold; many of the passengers wore only short-sleeved shirts. As the sun began to set, they huddled together inside the shelter.

By morning, more of the injured had died, leaving twenty-eight survivors to share the twenty-foot section of the plane. The morning also brought another problem; many of the survivors began to complain of thirst. This problem was especially acute for those who had lost a lot of blood. A careful search was made and an odd assortment of food and drink was discovered, including some bottles of wine, brandy, whiskey, and creme de menthe; eight bars of chocolate; three jars of jam; and two cans of mussels. With all the snow around, they felt that water would not be a problem, but they were wrong. They soon found that it was hard to melt the snow, and eating snow did little to quench their thirst. Finally they found they could get water by putting a little snow in some pans and placing the pans in the sun.

The survivors organized themselves into three teams. Some of the men were in charge of melting ice to provide water. A second team, which included three medical students, was responsible for the injured. A third team had the duty of clearing more space in the wrecked plane. It was impossible to stretch out in the area they had—each time someone moved, he intruded on the others around him. One of the men found a transistor radio; on

it they were excited to hear that search parties had been sent out to find them. But no help came that day, and the survivors trudged into the plane as night came and temperatures again plunged below zero.

The expected rescue did not come the next day, or the day after that. As time wore on, many of the survivors became more and more irritable; the slightest frustration was met with a stream of curses, and conflicts between survivors led to violent confrontations. During the day, they could not stray far from the plane because the snow was soft and they would sink into it over their waists. They spent the time exploring the area immediately around the plane and talking about their families.

The days passed and they began to realize that no help was coming. By the ninth day, another realization began to sink in, one that was even more frightening than the diminished prospects for a speedy rescue. As the survivors looked at one another they became aware of wrinkled skin, protruding bones, and sunken eyes; they were all slowly starving to death. Their meager food supply was nearly gone. The strength of even the strongest survivors had dwindled to the point where a walk around the plane left them panting and exhausted. A few of the men at this point cautiously mentioned the possibility of eating the dead whose bodies had been preserved in the frozen snow outside the plane.

At first this idea was met with shock and disgust. But by the ninth day their situation was desperate, and a meeting of the twenty-eight survivors was called. Most of them realized that eating human flesh was the only way they could survive, however much they might dislike the thought of it. One of the rugby players argued, "I know that if my dead body could help you stay alive, then I would want you to use it. In fact, if I do die and you don't eat me, then I'll come back from wherever I am and give you a good kick in the ass" (Read, 1974, p. 84). Another of the men argued that it was like Holy Communion: "When Christ died he gave his body to us so we could have spiritual life. My friend has given us his body so that we can have physical life" (Read, 1974, p. 91).

One of the medical students walked to a body that was sticking through the snow and cut a number of slices of frozen flesh. He thawed these on the outside of the plane and forced some meat into his mouth. One by one, over the next few days, the starved survivors forced themselves to eat human flesh. Finally, only an older couple refused to eat it. Their strength slowly ebbed and finally on the sixteenth day they too gave in and ate the flesh. A group was chosen to find the rest of the bodies and prepare the meat and fat for eating.

Then another disaster struck: Without warning, a wall of snow broke through the barrier at the back and swept through the plane. The buried survivors began frantically clawing their way out as the snow pressed down on them. As each person found a way out of the white tomb, he began digging furiously to help others get out. Tears filled their eyes as they uncovered the dead bodies of their companions. Nine people died in the avalanche, leaving a grieved group of nineteen survivors.

Slowly they regrouped and all agreed that they could not wait for rescue; they must send out their own search party. A new group was formed for this purpose, made up of the four most physically able young men. In the weeks that followed the avalanche, this group began to explore the area around the plane in order to find a way out of the mountains.

On the fifty-sixth day after the crash, the survivors saw their first signs of outside life; two giant birds circled lazily over the wreck. That same day a bee flew into the plane. These signs brought the realization that the snow was melting as summer came to the Andes. The melting snow meant that the bodies of the dead would thaw and rot, and the only source of life for the survivors would then be gone. The search party would have to go for help now, or it would soon be too late.

Three of them, dressed in many layers of clothing and carrying socks full of meat, began their journey. After three days of walking they found that the trip would be more difficult than expected, and one of them was sent back to the plane so that the other two could use his food. After struggling through the mountains for nine days, they saw a peasant tending his cattle. The young men screamed and wept with joy; they had been saved.

The other survivors were soon picked up and taken to Santiago. The world buzzed with excitement as news spread that the young men had survived for seventy days in the subzero temperatures of the Andes. The excitement, however, gave way to horror when pictures of human bones scattered around the wreckage were published, and it became known that the survivors were forced to eat the flesh of their dead friends to stay alive. Their survival was truly remarkable, but the moral questions raised by their methods of survival were debated for many years afterward.

MOTIVATION: THE ENERGIZER AND DIRECTOR OF BEHAVIOR

As you read the story of the survivors, you are likely to find yourself asking: "What would I do in their situation? Would I eat human flesh rather than starve to death? Would I be the person to encourage the group about the hope of survival, or, as some of the survivors did, would I give up?" Each of us has the ability and knowledge to behave in any of these ways. But given a particular set of circumstances, how would we actually behave?

It is on this question of how people behave and why that we now focus our attention. We have already examined the human being much as we would a machine. In Chapter 2 we discussed the physical makeup of the human machine. In Chapter 3 we looked at how these parts work together, and in other chapters we have seen how humans learn to behave. Now we will examine what energizes this wonderful machine and guides its actions.

As an analogy, we might consider a jukebox. It has the necessary parts to play music and it has a wide selection of tunes. The biological and physiological components of the individual are like the physical parts of the jukebox; they define the capacity of the machine (the human) to act. A jukebox does not have the physical components that would enable it to think, and the human body is not endowed with the components necessary for flying. Learning, along with a limited range of innate behaviors, determines the specific behaviors that can occur at any time. These learned behaviors are similar to the records in the jukebox. Together, the biological structure and learning form the enduring capability of the individual to perform certain behaviors. In order for the jukebox to play, someone has to plug it in (that is, give it energy) and select a tune. In a similar way, the human machine has a wonderful variety of behaviors it can perform, but it needs energy and some selection device to determine which behaviors it will perform in a particular situation. The energy source temporarily translates the capabilities into actions; it is temporary in the sense that it determines why the individual acted in a specific way at a specific time, given the wide range of capabilities that existed.

Psychologists have used the term **motive** to describe the condition that energizes and directs the behavior of organisms. **Motivation** explains why an organism acts in a certain way at a certain time—it provides the bridge between learning and performance. For example, we may ask why, on the ninth day, did some of the survivors turn to eating human flesh? The bodies of the dead were there right after the crash, and those who survived could have eaten them at any time. To answer this question we talk about motivation; the survivors were driven to this act by the motive of hunger.

The concept of motivation is widely used in our everyday world. In courts of law, lawyers argue about the motive behind criminal acts, and penalties for crimes may vary according to the motive behind the crime. For example, murder performed in self-defense or for humanitarian reasons (mercy killing) may go unpunished, while murder motivated by the desire for personal gain will be severely punished. The victim has been killed in both cases; it is the intent or motivation of the murderer that is different.

Even our own behavior toward others is strongly influenced by our evaluation of their motives. We will be attracted to people who do something nice for us if we feel that they are truly interested in our well-being. However, the same behavior may bring repulsion if we feel that they have been motivated solely by self-interest. As we will see in Chapter 15, we spend a great deal of time and energy trying to determine the motives behind the behavior of others.

When we speak of motives, we can loosely place them in one of two groups. On one hand, we have **primary motives,** which concern our biological needs. These motives are usually unlearned, common to all animals, and vital for the survival of the organism. Motives such as hunger, thirst, the need for air and rest, and sexual desire fall in this category. The second type of motive is the **social motive.** These motives come from learning and social interaction and include affiliation, aggression, and achievement. We will see, however, that almost all motives are influenced to some extent by our environment and learning. Before looking at specific motives, let us take a quick look at some of the theories that explain how and why we have motives.

THEORIES OF MOTIVATION

Possibly no question about the human being has raised such violent disagreement as the issue of motivation. Since the time of the early Greeks, debates have been flavored with religion, philosophy, and science (Geen, Beatty, & Arkin, 1984). Gods, demons, and even tiny creatures (homunculi) have been said to guide and energize human behavior. People have been burned, poked, stabbed, whipped, and otherwise tortured to rid them of these influences on their behavior and to "change their motivation." The nature of the human organism has been questioned and debated. According to the doctrine of *determinism*, the human is like a machine. An extreme view of this doctrine holds that humans, like any other living creatures, react automatically to internal and external forces; there is no planning or control exercised over behavior. The doctrine of *rationalism* or *free will* holds that people make free choices about how they will behave; in other words, their actions are controlled by reasoning and planning. Implicit in some of the debates was the desire to distinguish humans from animals. Some rather distinct theoretical views about the motivation of behavior have developed from these debates.

Instinct Theory

During the seventy days after the crash, the survivors did many different things. In addition to eating, drinking, and breathing, they spent a lot of time together talking about home, fighting and arguing, exploring the plane and the area around it, and even hoarding bits and pieces of objects they found. Where did the motives come from for each of these behaviors?

A view that was popular at the turn of the century would have suggested that the survivors acted as they did because they had the instincts to do so. **Instincts** are innate or inborn predispositions to act in specific ways. According to these early views, "nature" supplied organisms with a pattern of behavior *and* the energy to perform these actions. Thus, the conditions inside the organism push it to action as these instinctive behaviors seek an outlet.

However, the idea of instinct began to fade by the late 1920s. A major reason for the decline of instinct theories for humans was the great diversity found in human behavior. If a certain instinct exists in a species, then we should find similar behavior in all members of that species. However, this is not true with humans; for example, we can find some societies where a behavior such as aggression is very common, while in other societies the behavior is almost nonexistent. Even within a society, there are wide differences in behaviors.

A second problem is that it is difficult, if not impossible, to clearly identify

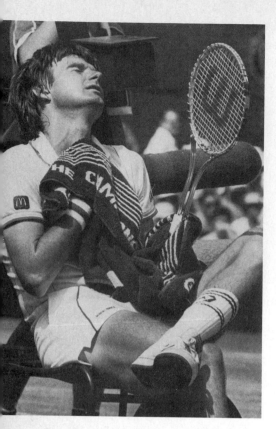

Drive theory states that the needs of our bodies motivate behavior. According to this position, the motivation to drink results when our bodies lose liquids.

specific instincts. In other words, how do we prove that a certain behavior is caused by an instinct? Holt (1931) showed this problem by saying:

> Man is impelled to action, it is said, by his instincts. If he goes with his fellows, it is the "herd" instinct which activates him; if he walks alone, it is the "antisocial instinct"; . . . if he twiddles his thumbs, it is the "thumb-twiddling instinct"; if he does not twiddle his thumbs it is the "thumb-not-twiddling instinct." (p. 4)

Drive Theory

In a room filled with photographers and reporters, one of the survivors told of the dreadful ordeal in the Andes. He described the physical pains caused by the intense cold and the mental torment he experienced as he watched his best friend die. He also told of how hunger gnawed at his body and drove him to eat the flesh of the dead passengers.

The idea that the living organism is driven to actions by the needs of its body has served as the basis for many theories of motivation. This point of view suggests that *needs* result when the body has gone without something for a period of time and is thus in a state of deprivation. The need creates a tension or *drive* that compels the organism to satisfy the need. Once the need is satisfied, the drive is reduced, and the organism is no longer motivated to act. Looking at the plight of the survivors, we can see that the nine days of starvation created a need for food. This need created a tension and drove them to find food. When a food source had been found and their hunger had been satisfied, the survivors were no longer motivated to search for food.

The basis of drive theory is the principle of **homeostasis**. According to this principle, the body tries to keep a constant internal state. When changes occur, the homeostatic mechanism stimulates the organism to act in ways that will return the internal state to what it was. This mechanism works much like the thermostat in your home. The thermostat is set to maintain a certain temperature. When the temperature in the home goes too high, the thermostat will turn on the air conditioner; when it drops too low, the thermostat will turn on the heater. In this way, the temperature in your house can be kept at a certain level. The human body works in a similar fashion. When your body temperature drops, the homeostatic mechanism may cause your body to shiver and constrict your blood vessels. If these actions do not make you warm enough, you may be motivated to seek shelter. On the other hand, if you become too hot, the homeostatic mechanism may stimulate your body to sweat, which causes cooling. If this fails to reduce your body temperature, you may find yourself seeking out a cool swimming pool.

As we can see, drive-reduction theories view deprivation as the source of motivation and do not presume that organisms are born with patterned behaviors (instincts) to reduce their drives. They readily admit that learning can influence the way an organism reduces drives.

Incentive Theory

If we look at many of the survivors' actions, we will find that much of their behavior cannot be explained easily by drive-reduction theories. For example, there were many cases where, after the survivors had eaten and were fairly warm inside of the plane, one or another of them spent time looking into small nooks of the plane that clearly could not hold objects useful for survival. These behaviors were adopted to increase stimulation rather than to reduce it. There are many everyday examples of our own behavior aimed at increasing arousal. Some of us engage in dangerous sports such as mountain climbing or sky diving; others spend money on movies guaranteed to scare or sexually arouse.

Incentive theory suggests that external events (or objects) can motivate our behavior. In this case, it could have been the availability of the ice cream or seeing others eating that motivated these people to eat.

In addition to finding that drive reduction is not the aim of every motive, investigators have also realized that not all motives are aroused solely by internal states. For example, we sometimes eat when we are not hungry, simply because food is there. Strange objects or novel events often motivate people to explore. Sir Edmund Hillary, a famous explorer and mountain climber, was asked why he climbed mountains. To this question he responded, "Because they are there." In each of these cases, it is not an internal bodily need that motivates behavior. Rather, it is an *incentive* outside of the organism that motivates it to act. Thus, we can view drive theories as "push" theories; they argue that internal states push the organism to act. On the other hand, incentive theories are "pull" theories, since they suggest that external stimuli pull behaviors from the organism. Incentives can be either positive or negative. In either case, the incentive motivates the organism to move toward or away from a situation. Motivation then can be the result of either internal drive states or external incentives.

We have now examined the general nature and theories of motives. With this background in mind, let us turn our attention to specific motives. We will begin by looking at hunger and thirst, which are physiological and drive-reducing motives. Next we will examine the sex motive, which, although it is largely physiological, has a very strong incentive element. We will then briefly turn to the exploration and manipulation motives, which are even more clearly activated by incentives. Finally, we will focus on three psychological or social motives—affiliation, aggression, and the need to achieve.

HUNGER

As time passed and hunger gripped the survivors, they began to look for food. Their first efforts turned up a meager assortment of candies, jam, and some tins of canned fish. Soon, however, this supply began running out, and their search intensified. By the ninth day, the once stout and husky rugby players became aware of their deteriorating physical conditions (one of them lost eighty pounds during the ordeal). Their gnawing hunger made them decide to eat the flesh of their dead companions.

Clearly, hunger was the motivating force behind many of the survivors' behaviors. Much of our own behavior is also aimed at satisfying our desire for food. In order to prove this, make a note of the amount of time you spend in food-related activities: eating, shopping for food, talking about food, worrying about your weight, and so on. *Hunger,* then, is a motive common to us all.

The Experience of Hunger

The Gut Reaction. When most of us think about hunger we think of cramping and pangs coming from an empty stomach. This was, in fact, the position accepted over 200 years ago when one scientist wrote that hunger arises when "the naked villi of nerves on one side (of the stomach) grate against those on the other (side) . . ." (Cofer & Apley, 1964). Cannon and Washburn (1912) set out to demonstrate that contractions of the stomach cause people to feel hungry. Washburn swallowed a balloon, which, when it reached his stomach, was inflated and hooked to an amplifying device (see Figure 10–1) to record the contractions of his stomach. He sat with this balloon in his stomach and pressed a key each time he felt hungry. The results showed that feelings of hunger often occurred at the same time as strong contractions of the stomach.

This experiment seemed strong support for the internal cause of hunger. However, later experiments cast doubt on this theory. For example, researchers (Penick et al., 1963; Tsang, 1938) found that rats whose stomachs had been removed and whose esophagi were connected to their small intestines searched for food and ate as much as those with normal stomachs. The only difference was that the former group of rats ate less food; however, they ate more often. In the same way, human patients whose stomachs have been removed report feeling hungry (Janowitz, 1967).

The most recent conclusion is that while stomach contractions may play some role in signaling our hunger, the role is probably a minor one. However, while our stomachs may not motivate us to start eating, there is evidence that a full stomach plays a large part in getting us to stop eating.

Blood-Sugar Level. If we can't blame our stomachs for making us eat, what can we blame? One answer may be the glucose (blood-sugar) level in the blood. When we eat, enzymes in the saliva, stomach, and small intestine break down the food into sugars, amino acids, and fats (Petri, 1981). The first two products are absorbed into the bloodstream, where they travel to the liver and later to the brain. Investigators began to focus on the role of glucose when it was found that a hungry animal (one that

Figure 10–1
In this experiment, Washburn swallowed a balloon, which was inflated once it reached his stomach. The balloon was attached to an amplifying device to record contractions. Washburn pressed a key every time he felt hungry. The results showed that Washburn's feelings of hunger often occurred at the same time as strong contractions of the stomach. (Cannon & Washburn, 1912)

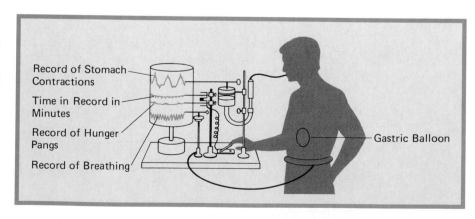

Record of Stomach Contractions

Time in Record in Minutes

Record of Hunger Pangs

Record of Breathing

Gastric Balloon

had not eaten for a period of time) would not eat at all or would eat less food when it was injected with the blood of another animal that had been well fed (Davis et al., 1967, 1971).

But how is the glucose level monitored? A simple theory would be that the *hypothalamus,* an area of the brain that is rich in blood vessels, has receptors (called **glucoreceptors**) that detect the level of glucose in the blood. When the blood is low in glucose, it is a sign that the animal is hungry and the hypothalamus signals that it is time to start eating. Hunger, like life, proved not to be this simple.

Other research (Mayer, 1955) reported that diabetics who have high levels of glucose in their blood tend to eat more, rather than less, than healthy people. This suggested that the glucoreceptors cannot monitor only the absolute levels of glucose in the blood. Instead, Mayer suggested that the glucoreceptors monitor the *difference* in glucose levels of blood in the arteries (carrying blood from the heart) and veins (carrying blood to the heart). A small difference would signal hunger, while a large difference would indicate that a person is full.

Two types of experiments have shown the important role of the hypothalamus in eating. In one type, areas of the hypothalamus are stimulated with electrical current. When these "eating centers" are stimulated, even an animal that has been well fed starts to eat (Hoebel & Teitelbaum, 1962). Such studies have also shown that there are areas of the hypothalamus that, when stimulated, will cause the animal to stop eating, even if it is hungry. The other type of experiment involves destroying cells in the hypothalamus. Results from these studies have shown that destruction of certain areas will cause the animal to refuse food. Destruction of other areas will result in the animal eating continuously. In some cases the animal will eat until it has doubled or even tripled its body weight. In other words, we may have different "on" and "off" centers that monitor the level of glucose in our blood and regulate our eating.

The hypothalamus is not the only place where blood-sugar levels are monitored. The liver is also sensitive to the content of the blood and the liver regulates eating behaviors (Russek, 1971). In fact, the liver may supply us with the first signals of hunger or satiation. After food is broken down in our stomachs and small intestines, nutrients are absorbed into the blood. The blood then flows to the liver before going to other parts of our body, including the brain. Thus, the liver is the first organ to examine the content of the blood. Research has shown that there are indeed centers in the liver that monitor the blood-sugar level of the blood and transmit signals to the brain (Nijima, 1969).

The Role of Taste. The evidence for the role of glucoreceptors in eating is strong. There are, however, some nagging loose ends that suggest that this may not be the whole story. Recall that on the ninth day after the crash, some, but not all, of the survivors ate the flesh of the dead. Some of those who did not eat actually put the flesh to their mouths, only to become violently sick. Their eating behavior was not simply determined by the level of glucose in their blood. On the other hand, you might recall a time when you went to a party shortly after eating a large meal. You were stuffed, but when the host or hostess placed a tantalizing tidbit in your hand, you quickly devoured it and spent much of the night munching away. Again, this behavior was probably not motivated by the level of glucose in your blood. One possible reason for the above behaviors is learning; we learn what (and what not) to eat and when to eat. We will soon examine the role of learning on eating.

Another explanation for why and what we eat centers on taste. Indeed, if the glucoreceptor mechanism completely controlled our eating, we would expect organisms to eat the same amount of food whether they took food through the mouth or directly into the stomach. One investigator compared the eating behavior of rats who ate normally with those who pressed a bar to have food delivered directly to their stomachs through a tube (Snowden, 1969). There were some interesting differences. First, although rats fed through a tube maintained their original body weight, they did not grow as fast as rats normally do. Second, while it is generally easy to teach rats to press a bar to get food that can be eaten, it is difficult to teach them to press a bar to get food delivered directly into their stomachs.

Other studies have shown that taste is also important for the cessation of eating behavior. For example, the esophagi of rats have been cut so that when they eat, the food never reaches their stomachs. If blood sugar levels regulate eating, we might expect these rats to eat continuously because food never gets into their stomach or bloodstream. However, the rats do not eat continuously; although they eat larger than normal meals, they do pause for some time before eating again (Janowitz & Grossman, 1949).

Body Weight and Long-Term Eating. Thus far we have focused on short-term mechanisms of hunger; they are short-term in the sense that they control our behavior from meal to meal. There is another interesting phenomenon of eating behavior, however, that cannot easily be explained by these short-term mechanisms. Most animals, including humans, tend to keep a stable body weight for long periods of time even though the availability of food may change over this time. If you think about your own weight, you will probably find that it varies by less than 5 percent annually. You may also notice how difficult it is to gain or lose weight. Few people can sustain weight loss for one year, regardless of the weight loss program they follow (Grinker, 1982).

Our bodies require a certain energy level to keep going. The exact amount of energy (measured in the form of **calories**) varies from one person to another and is dependent on such factors as size, level of activity, and metabolism. When we take in more calories than our bodies need, these calories are converted to fat and the fat is stored in our body tissues.

These fat deposits or fat cells play a role in determining our weight and our long-term eating behavior. According to **set-point theory** (see p. 308), the number of fat cells in the body is established during early childhood. Receptors, probably located in the hypothalamus, monitor the condition and size of these cells. Based on the information it receives from these cells, the hypothalamus regulates eating and body metabolism to maintain the body's weight in a normal range (Keesey et al., 1976; Nisbett, 1982).

The important issue here is that there may be two general mechanisms controlling our eating behavior. The short-term mechanism seems to center on the nutritional requirements of the body, while the long-term mechanism seems most sensitive to body weight.

What We Eat: The Role of Learning

Thus far we have been discussing why we eat. Our focus has mainly been on how deprivation causes us to become hungry and to search for food. It is also believed that the types of foods we choose to eat are, to some degree, controlled by our needs. In support of this position, Davis (1928) allowed newly weaned infants to choose their diet over a period of months from a cafeteria-like selection of foods. On any given day the infants might choose a "bad diet," but over a long period of time they selected foods that met their nutritional needs. In one case, a child who had rickets chose foods that had high concentrations of cod-liver oil and in doing so helped cure the rickets. In another study, rats were fed a diet that did not provide enough calcium (Rozin & Kalat, 1971). When

The differences in food preferences among cultures show the impact of learning on eating behavior. What we like to eat is influenced by what we have learned to enjoy.

these rats were later given a choice of things to eat, they chose high-calcium foods. The survivors of the plane crash also seemed to select what to eat according to their needs. At first they ate only the flesh of the dead victims. After a time, however, many of the survivors began eating kidneys and liver, which were high in necessary vitamin and mineral content, even though the high-protein flesh was still available.

It seems logical to conclude that people eat because they are hungry and that they eat the foods needed to nourish their bodies. Unfortunately, this is not always the case; animals and humans, even at early ages, learn to prefer certain foods, and they even learn when to be hungry. Often these learned preferences go against the body's needs. For example, Harriman (1955) found that rats learned to prefer sugar over salt. Even when these rats had their adrenal glands removed and needed to eat salt to survive, they continued choosing the sugar diet. Some of them died as a result of this choice. Thus, when we eat and what we eat are influenced by our bodily state *and* by our learned habits and preferences. And in many cases learning can override our physiological needs.

Obesity

While our bodies may have natural selection processes that help ensure our nourishment, those of us who have struggled with diets know that our eating patterns can present major problems for our body weight.

Incidences of obesity have reached epidemic proportions in the Western world; over half the people in the United States can be classified as being significantly overweight. In humans, **obesity** is defined as more than 15 percent over the "ideal" weight, given a person's height and overall body build. Obesity is a major factor in many physical and psychological disorders. It has been found to increase the likelihood of cardiovascular disease and diabetes (Geen et al., 1984). In addition, obesity reduces job advancement opportunities (Jeffrey & Fatz, 1977) and feelings of self-esteem (Leon & Roth, 1977).

In some cases the causes of obesity can be traced to physical, hormonal, or emotional disorders. But in most cases the problem is overeating; that is, taking in more calories than are used or needed by the body. The important task is, then, to identify why obese people have such a difficult time controlling their food intake.

EATING DISORDERS: ANOREXIA NERVOSA AND BULIMIA

An alarming number of people are starving themselves, and not because food is unavailable. In most cases, these people come from middle and upper-middle-class families. **Anorexia nervosa** is a condition in which a person loses his or her appetite, eats little, and slowly "wastes away." A weight loss of 25 percent is one of the main criteria for diagnosing anorexics. Bachrach, Erwin, and Mohr (1965) report a case where their patient's weight fell from 118 to 47 pounds. At first, anorexia was thought to be relatively uncommon, but more recent estimates suggest that between .5 to 15 percent of adolescent females suffer the disorder (Crisp et al., 1978; Nagelberg et al., 1983). The condition is most commonly found in white adolescent females, although males in early adolescence make up about 10 percent of the cases. For unknown reasons, anorexia is very rare in black women (Kalat, 1984). It has

been reported that about 15 percent of the cases actually end in death (Van Buskirk, 1977). In February 1983, popular singer Karen Carpenter died of a heart attack related to anorexia. At the time of her death, she had brought her weight up from 82 to 108 pounds. But doctors learned that the greatest strain on a person's heart comes when they begin regaining their weight.

Anorexics starve because they are unhappy with their physical appearance. Casper and Davis (1977) identified three phases of anorexia. In the first phase, people develop a low self-esteem and an increasing concern for their physical appearance. The second phase is characterized by an intense fear that eating will make them very fat. They adopt a very restricted diet and begin to lose weight. When hunger pains occur, anorexics exhaust themselves through strenuous exercise. The severe loss of weight is accompanied by constipation,

Karen Carpenter, a popular singer, died of a heart attack related to anorexia. Her weight had dropped to 82 pounds, but she was slowly gaining weight when the heart attack occurred.

The Role of External Cues.   If we ate only when our bodies signaled the need for food, few of us would ever have to worry about being overweight. Unfortunately, many people, especially obese people, do not eat only when their bodies command. Rather, their eating behavior may be triggered by external cues such as the sight or smell of food. Researchers have speculated that obese people do not know when they are hungry but, instead, eat whenever they are stimulated by external cues (Rodin, 1975, 1977).

For example, Schachter and Gross (1968) suggested that obese people are more likely than normal-weight people to "eat by the clock"; that is, obese people will eat because the clock says it's dinner time. In order to show this, the investigators had normal-weight and overweight subjects arrive at the laboratory at 5:00 P.M. The subjects were told that their physiological responses would be measured while they worked on tasks. Their watches were removed and electrodes were strapped on their arms; then the experimenter left the room so that they could work. There was a large clock in front of the subjects, which, unknown to them, was controlled by the experimenter. The experimenter returned to the room thirty minutes later (5:30) eating crackers. However, in some cases, the clock in front of the subjects had been slowed to read only 5:20, while in other cases it had been moved forward to read 6:05. The experimenter asked the subjects to complete questionnaires and left the box of crackers with them

cessation of menstruation, and a slowing of the pulse and respiration. Interestingly enough, no matter how thin they are, they still feel fat (Gomez & Dally, 1980). In the third phase, anorexics admit that they have a problem and they increase food intake. However, at the first sign of weight gain, they begin to fear that they will become fat, and the slow starvation process may begin again.

A related eating disorder is known as **bulimia**. It is most common among females in their late teens and early twenties (Herzog, 1982). Like the anorexic, a person suffering from bulimia also has a distorted image of her body and is obsessed with weight. However, the bulimic person is generally not grossly underweight like the anorexic (Schlesier-Stropp, 1984). The bulimic goes through cycles where she will diet for a period of time and then gorge herself with food, which is referred to as binging. At the time of binging, the bulimic may

consume over 20,000 calories (Russell, 1979)! After binging, the bulimic will purge the food by vomiting, or by using laxatives or diuretics (Fairburn & Cooper, 1982). One study reported that vomiting occurred more often during the cycle than did binge eating; 56 percent of the sample reported vomiting at least once a day. The average duration of the bulimic symptoms is over six years (Herzog, 1982). In December 1984, actress Jane Fonda shocked her fans by revealing that she had suffered from bulimia from the age of twelve to thirty-five. She reported that she often vomited fifteen to twenty times a day. She stated, ''It's an addiction like drugs or alcohol.''

There are many theories about the causes of anorexia and bulimia. Some focus on the possibility that the cause may be a hormone disorder or a malfunctioning of the hypothalamus. Women with anorexia have abnormally low levels of reproductive hormones released

by the hypothalamus and the pituitary (Beumont et al., 1982). Other researchers (e.g., Minuchin, Rosman, & Baker, 1978) suggest that the problem may be the result of family conflict. Many anorexics report feeling intense pressure from their parents to attain high goals, including standards involving their physical appearance. Their cessation of eating may be an attempt to rebel against these demands; they adopt the ''I'll show you'' attitude. An interesting finding is that almost half of the bulimics in one study (Herzog, 1982) reported alcoholism and weight problems among family members.

Other researchers argue that anorexia and bulimia result as a means of coping with depression and feelings of helplessness (Sugarman et al., 1981). According to this point of view, anorexics and bulimics attempt to demonstrate control over the environment by showing that they have mastered their own bodies.

so that they could munch while they worked. The number of crackers eaten by the subjects was counted. As can be seen in Table 10–1, obese subjects ate more crackers than did normal-weight subjects when the clock read 6:05 (dinner time), but they ate fewer crackers than the others when the clock read 5:20.

There are a number of other external cues that affect the eating behaviors of obese people. Nisbett (1968) found that obese subjects ate more than thin subjects if the food tasted good, but less than the thin subjects if it had an unpleasant taste. Overweight subjects will also increase their food intake if the food looks attractive (Hashim & Van Itallie, 1965) and is easily available (Schachter & Friedman, 1974). Obese people will actually eat less than normal-weight subjects if they have to work in order to get their food.

While this theory is an interesting one, it has been criticized. There are many situations in which normal-weight people are not less sensitive than obese people to external cues such as time (Nail et al., 1981; Rodin, 1981). In addition, losing weight does not result in a decrease in sensitivity to external cues. Thus, the role of sensitivity to external cues in obesity is still unclear.

Arousal and Eating. What red-blooded American can resist the lure of popcorn and other munchies while watching an exciting movie? In an interesting study, White (1977) had normal-weight and obese subjects

Table 10–1

Amount eaten by obese and normal subjects in each of two conditions: slow (when the clock has been slowed to read 5:20 P.M.) and fast (when the clock has been speeded up to read 6:05 P.M.).

Subjects	Amount Eaten	
	Slow	Fast
Obese	19.9	37.6
Normal	41.5	16.0

Source: Schachter & Gross (1968).

watch four different movies; three of the movies were arousing and one was a nonarousing travelogue. After each session, the subjects were allowed to sample crackers under the guise of consumer-preference research. While normal-weight individuals ate about the same amount no matter which film they had seen, obese subjects ate a lot more after seeing the arousing films than after the travelogue.

These results suggest that obese people are not insensitive to their internal cues. Rather, they may have a hard time figuring out or understanding the cues their bodies are sending them (McKenna, 1972). In the experiment just mentioned as well as in others, obese subjects respond to most types of arousal by eating. In a sense, they may be misinterpreting the arousal as hunger rather than as anxiety, fear, or anger. This type of misinterpretation is not as common in thin or normal-weight people.

Set-Point and Obesity. For dieters who work and sweat to lose a few pounds, the tendency to regain lost weight is a curse. The ease with which weight is regained, along with the fact that obesity tends to run in families, has led investigators to look for a physiological basis for many cases of obesity.

The set-point theory, introduced on page 304, provides such a link. Nisbett (1972) points out that weight is a function of the *number* and *size* of fat cells. The size of these fat cells is determined by daily food intake. Thus, it is possible to control the size of your fat cells by controlling your diet. However, the *number* of fat cells is not affected by your daily diet. The number of fat cells that you have is partly an inherited trait and partly determined by your diet during the first two years of life (Knittle, 1975). Eating a great deal as a youngster, then, may increase a person's number of fat cells; what one eats as an adult will not affect this number.

Björntorp (1972) found that obese people have more than double the number of fat cells compared to normal-weight people. Thus, regardless of how they try to starve themselves, obese people will not be able to reduce the number of fat cells in their body. On the other hand, thin people will have a very difficult time gaining weight no matter how much they eat; these people do not have a large number of cells for storing fat.

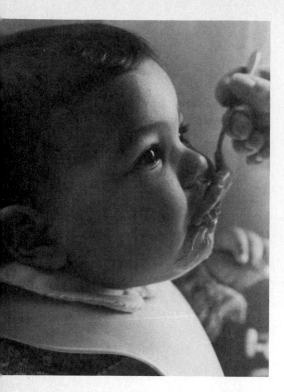

According to set-point theory, the number of fat cells that you have is partly an inherited trait and partly determined by diet during the first two years of life.

THIRST

The morning after the crash, the dazed survivors were awakened by the cries of the injured begging for water. Those who had lost blood made the most agonizing appeals. In a short time, the survivors realized that they may be able to live for days on very little food, but that they had to have a supply of drinking water. Why do people become thirsty? This may sound like a silly question; an immediate response might be that thirst results from a lack of water. But how do we know when our bodies require fluids?

Early researchers argued that thirst results when our mouths feel dry (Cannon, 1929). However, other studies have shown that this is not the case (Fitzsimmons, 1973). People who experience frequent dryness of the mouth (common with the use of certain drugs or because of other physical conditions) may drink more often, but they do not drink more than those not suffering from excessive dryness. As with hunger, our search for the cause of thirst will take us to many regions of the body.

In order to understand thirst, we must first understand the distribution

Thirst results when either intracellular or extracellular fluid is decreased. Thirst not only motivates drinking behavior but it also initiates internal activities (e.g., the kidneys reabsorb water) to conserve fluids.

of water in our bodies. Two-thirds of the water is located within our cells (*intracellular*), and about 26 percent of the water is located in the spaces around these cells (*extracellular*). The remaining 7 percent of the water is contained in the blood. The water within and outside our cells is not pure; it normally contains .9 percent salt (sodium chloride). While water can pass in and out of the cells by a process called **osmosis,** the salt cannot. We will now use this information to examine how the body experiences thirst.

Osmometric Thirst.   If the concentration of salt in the extracellular fluid increases, water seeps out of the cells to restore the original concentration. Water moving from the cells puts the extracellular fluid in proper balance, but the intracellular water level becomes depleted. Investigators believe that there are cells called **osmoreceptors** in the hypothalamus that are sensitive to the intracellular water levels (Bass, 1968). When they detect that water is being depleted from the cells, they send "thirst" signals to other areas of the brain and motivate the person to drink liquids. Thus, drinking motivated by **osmometric thirst** restores intracellular fluid levels.

The hypothalamus also stimulates the pituitary gland to release the antidiuretic hormone (*ADH*), which causes the kidneys to reabsorb more water. Normally our kidneys filter about forty-five gallons of water a day. Most of this water is reabsorbed back into the system, but some of it is excreted in the form of urine. The increase in ADH causes the kidneys to reabsorb more water than usual to combat the decrease in intracellular water level.

Volumetric Thirst.   Why were the injured survivors so thirsty? They did not have an increased concentration of salt in their extracellular fluid. Similarly, people who have diarrhea or vomiting generally experience thirst, but the salt content of their extracellular fluid does not change either. In these cases, fluid is lost directly from the extracellular areas while intracellular fluid is not depleted. What mechanism is at work, then?

When the volume of extracellular fluid decreases, there is an accompanying decrease in blood pressure. As a result, the blood supply to the kidneys and heart is reduced. Investigators have suggested that there are volumetric receptors in both these locations that detect this drop in blood pressure (Carlson, 1980). When this change is detected, these receptors stimulate thirst (called **volumetric thirst**) and trigger the pituitary gland to release ADH. As in the case of osmometric thirst, the ADH and other hormones secreted by the kidneys cause the kidneys to reabsorb more water than usual. The intake of additional fluids restores the extracellular fluid level.

As you can see, the thirst mechanisms are wonderfully adaptive. They motivate drinking behavior by signaling thirst *and* they start immediate adjustments within our bodies to conserve the liquids that are available.

The Effect of Eating on Drinking.   An interesting feature of drinking that is often overlooked is its relationship to eating. If we consider our own behavior, we will find that much, if not most, of our drinking occurs during mealtimes. Similarly, normal drinking in other mammals occurs at mealtimes; for example, rats take 70 to 90 percent of their liquids between ten minutes before meals to thirty minutes after eating (Kissileff, 1969). This observation has prompted many investigators to suggest a link between eating and drinking. One theory is that predigested food stimulates cells in the mucus membranes of our mouths and esophogi to release a substance (histamine). This substance stimulates other receptors which motivate drinking (Kraly, 1984). Another theory is that the predigested food stimulates the release of insulin in the digestive tract, which in turn motivates drinking (Kraly et al., 1983). While these theories must await further testing, they do point out the importance of examining drinking behavior in light of other related behaviors and encourage people to study naturally occuring patterns of drinking.

SEXUAL BEHAVIOR

As you can see, hunger and thirst are powerful drives. Sex, too, can be a powerful motivator. However, unlike hunger and thirst, sex is not necessary for the survival of the individual. In addition, deprivation is only one of the motivators of sexual behavior; as we will see, hormone levels and external stimuli are more important. And, sexual behavior uses up energy, whereas eating and drinking restore energy.

Another interesting difference that sets sex apart from most other motives involves its history of study. Motives such as hunger and thirst have been carefully studied in both animals and humans and have been widely discussed in textbooks for nearly a century. The study of sexual behavior, however, was avoided for years. Until the late 1940s few investigators dared study the topic.

The Biological Basis of Sex

It may seem like a simple question to ask if biological changes regulate sexual behavior. However, an examination of research in the area shows this to be an exceedingly complex issue; the answer depends on whether we are interested in the sexual behavior of animals or humans (and other primates), and whether we are interested in males or females. There are some general statements that should be made before we begin our discussion. First, sexual behavior in animals is often *controlled* by the levels of certain hormones in the blood; human sexual behavior is not. Second, although sexual behavior is evident in young animals and children, the strongest sex drive occurs when the organism reaches sexual maturity. In humans, **puberty** is the period when this sexual maturity begins. Interestingly enough, the age at which puberty occurs has been decreasing over the last 150 years. As Figure 10–2 shows, in 1840 the average age at which women reached puberty (signaled by the onset of menstruation) was about seventeen years, while in 1960 it was twelve and a half (Tanner, 1962). Investigators have suggested that improved diet and health may be the reason for this dramatic change (Schulz, 1984). With these points in mind, let us briefly examine the biological bases for male and female sexual behavior.

When the male reaches sexual maturity, the *pituitary gland* (as discussed in Chapter 2) located at the base of the brain stimulates the *testes* (the male reproductive gland) to secrete **androgens** into the bloodstream. These androgens, or male sex hormones, increase the sex drive in men. In humans, androgens also influence the development of **secondary sex characteristics,** such as the growth of pubic hair and the deepening of the voice. Androgens are found in their highest concentration shortly after the male has reached sexual maturity. While the concentration of androgens may vary slightly over long periods of time, androgen concentration over a shorter time span is fairly constant. In other words, there are no definite biological cycles for male sexual behavior; given the proper stimuli, sexual behavior from both animal and human males can be elicited at almost any time. While androgens are necessary for the development of sexual behavior, they do not control the sex drive after maturity.

Female sexual behavior has a more complicated biological basis. On reaching sexual maturity, the pituitary gland stimulates the **ovaries,** which are the female reproductive glands, to secrete **estrogen** (the female sex hormone). However, unlike males, the rate of secretion of estrogen rises

Figure 10-2
The graph shows the average age of first menstruation for girls in Western countries in the last 150 years. As can be seen, the average age has gone from 17 years in 1840 to 12½ years in 1960. (Tanner, 1962)

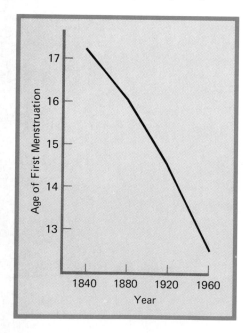

and falls in a cyclical way. The secretion of estrogen is at its highest level during the period of ovulation, the time when the egg is available to be fertilized. In most animals, this time is called being "in heat," and it is only during this time that the female animal is receptive to sexual advances. Therefore, the level of hormones controls the animal's sexual response patterns. Removal of the ovaries eliminates sexual behavior for these animals (Carlson, 1977). This, however, is not the case for humans. Many women who have had their ovaries removed or who have reached menopause still have strong sex drives and are sexually active. Thus, while the level of estrogen determines the onset of menstruation and the period of fertility, it does not control the human female's sex drive. The human female may engage in sex at any time; as we will see, human sexual behavior (both male and female) is more influenced by learning and external stimuli than by hormone levels. Despite these facts, we cannot completely disregard the influence of hormones on female sexual behavior in humans. There is presently a controversy as to whether the female human's sex drive is influenced by hormonal levels (Moos & Lunde, 1968; Bancroft, 1984). There is some evidence that females are more likely to engage in sexual behavior at some times during their cycle, but there is disagreement about what these times are and whether they are influenced directly by hormones.

The Importance of External Cues. Even with lower animals, it takes more than hormones to elicit sexual behavior. The existence of sex hormones only primes the animal or places it in a state of readiness for sexual behavior. In order for sexual behavior to occur, some added stimulation is necessary. In animals, this comes from the partner. One of the most common forms of external stimulation for males involves cues of smell. Receptive females in many species discharge a vaginal substance that has a particular odor; when the male catches scent of this odor, he becomes sexually aroused. However, despite advertisements insisting that Brand X perfume or Brand Y cologne will drive your mate wild, there is no evidence that human sexual behavior is innately influenced by odors (Doty, 1975).

On the other hand, humans certainly have plenty of other external cues that are capable of sexually arousing them. Almost any object that people have learned to associate with sex is capable of arousing them. These objects can include anything from high-heeled shoes and black leather pants to a particular song. The principle, however, is the same; even with the proper amount of hormones flowing in the veins, external cues are needed to initiate sexual behavior.

The Human Sexual Response

The Role of Learning. In much of the discussion thus far regarding sexual behavior, we have had to qualify statements by saying "except with humans."

Human sexual behavior is neither as dependent on hormones nor as stereotyped as animal sexual behavior. Because of this, humans have to learn the "when and how" of sexual behavior. This seemingly simple fact of life has many important consequences. One consequence is that human sexual behavior is widely varied, being limited only by a person's imagination and physical capabilities rather than a predetermined plan set by nature. A second consequence, as we have pointed out, is that humans can learn to be sexually aroused by an almost inconceivable range of stimuli.

While these points add to the excitement and variety of human sexual behavior, the important role of learning adds a third consequence that is anything but exciting. That is, if the proper learning situations do not occur, normal sexual behavior will fail to develop. Much of this learning takes place through social interaction and play with peers during childhood. It has also been reported that early childhood experiences in humans influence the development of later sexual behavior (Rosen & Rosen, 1981).

Four Phases of Sexual Response. In the early 1920s, the well-known behaviorist John B. Watson decided to investigate the physical effects of sexual behavior on the human body. He placed electrodes on his own body and that of his partner and recorded their responses during various stages of intimacy. His valiant effort was met with dismay and disgust by his colleagues and little attention was given to his data.

It was not until the late 1950s, when the team of William Masters and Virginia Johnson began their studies, that much of the mystery of the human sexual response was lifted. Masters and Johnson carefully monitored the responses of a large number of subjects engaged in both intercourse and masturbation. They found that male and female sexual responses were alike in a number of ways.

These researchers found that it was possible to roughly categorize the human (male or female) response into four phases (Masters & Johnson, 1966, 1975). The first phase is the *excitement phase,* which may last anywhere from a few minutes to several hours. During this phase, arousal increases and the genital areas become engorged with blood. The *plateau phase,* the second stage, is characterized by increased body tension, heart rate, and blood pressure. In males there is an erection of the penis, and in females the glands in the vagina secrete lubricating fluid. The *orgasm phase* is accompanied by rhythmic contractions in the genitals of both sexes and by ejaculation in the males. These contractions occur every eight-tenths of a second and last for varying lengths of time. The orgasm is experienced as a pleasurable sudden release of sexual tension. Masters and Johnson exploded some earlier myths by finding that women were not only capable of having orgasms, but that these orgasms were pleasurable experiences.

The final phase is the *resolution phase,* during which the body gradually returns to its normal state. One major difference between men and women is that women are capable of having multiple orgasms in quick succession. We should note that females exhibit a range of responses—while some enjoy multiple orgasms, others do not experience orgasm during sexual stimulation (Hite, 1976). Males usually are not multiorgasmic; instead they enter a *refractory phase,* which may last from a few minutes to several hours. During this time males are incapable of sexual arousal or orgasm.

Comparing Male and Female Sexual Response. There are many other similarities between the phases of male and female sexual responses. Both males and females show similar changes in breathing, muscle tension, and heart rate during the phases. Enlargement of *genitals* occurs in both sexes (Maier, 1984). Further there is an indication that males and females experience orgasm in a similar way. In one study, investigators asked male and female subjects to write descriptions of their orgasms (Vance & Wagner, 1976). These descriptions were then shown to a group of judges (clinical psychologists, medical students, and gynecologists) who were asked to decide which descriptions were written by males and which by females. The results showed that these judges could not correctly match the description with the sex of the author.

While there are many similarities in the sexual responses of males and females, there are also some important differences. While males generally have only one orgasm, females show more variability. Some women have no orgasm while others experience multiple orgasms during intercourse. A second difference is that males generally become sexually aroused more quickly than females (Hite, 1976). Finally, women report considerable variation in the strength and duration of orgasm from one intercourse experience to the next. The orgasm for the male is generally very similar on these dimensions across sexual encounters.

Human Sexual Behaviors

Throughout much of time, many parents resorted to the "ultimate threat" to control their child's sexual behavior: "Nice girls (boys) don't do that (e.g., masturbate or engage in premarital sexual intercourse)." This type of statement could hardly be challenged before 1948 because we had little idea of the type or frequency of sexual activities of humans in general, let alone that of "nice girls and boys." However, attitudes began to change in the late 1940s when Kinsey and his colleagues (1948, 1953) interviewed a large sample of American males and females on a wide range of topics regarding their sexual habits. Because of this study and those that followed we now have a clearer picture of the nature of human sexual activities (Hite, 1976; Hunt, 1974).

Autosexual Behavior. The first and most common sexual experience for most people is **masturbation,** or autosexual behavior, the self-manipulation of one's genitals. Masturbation is common among both children and adults; Kinsey found that more than 90 percent of males and more than 60 percent of females masturbate. A later survey supported these findings (Hunt, 1974). Hunt also found that 72 percent of married men over age thirty and 68 percent of married women over age thirty masturbate.

For a long time, masturbation was not only thought to be a shameful practice, it was also seen as dangerous. Some physicians suggested that masturbation caused such maladies as feeble-mindedness and nervousness (Kellogg, 1902). Children have been told that masturbation leads to blindness and, for males, the eventual separation of the penis from the body. Kinsey (1948) summed up early feelings about masturbation: "Every conceivable ill, from pimples to insanity, including stooped shoulders, loss of weight, fatigue, insomnia, general weakness, neurasthenia, loss of manly-mindedness, genital cancer, and the rest, was ascribed to masturbation" (p. 513). In the early part of the century, the U.S. Patent Office issued a patent for a device that would ring a bell in the parent's room if the child's bed moved in a pattern suggesting masturbation (LoPiccolo & Heiman, 1977)! Today we know that masturbation is not physically harmful; in fact, the most damaging results come from the emotional trauma and guilt instilled in children to prevent masturbation. In some cases, masturbation is recommended by therapists treating sexual disorders (McMullen & Rosen, 1979).

Heterosexual Behavior. The Kinsey report also shed light on heterosexual behavior, the sexual desire for people of the opposite sex. Despite religious and social taboos and the fear of pregnancy, 27 percent of college-educated women and 49 percent of college-educated men said that they had engaged in premarital sex. This was considered by many to be a high figure for those times. The last two decades have seen vast changes in social attitudes toward premarital sexual behavior. In addition to these changing attitudes, there has been the introduction of "the Pill" and other safe and easy means of birth control. These changes have also been accompanied by changes in sexual practice. Surveys done in the 1970s found that between 60 and 85 percent of the males interviewed and 43 to 80 percent of the females had engaged in premarital sexual intercourse. In one study, an investigator interviewed married people and found that of those under age twenty-five, 95 percent of the males and 81 percent of the females had engaged in premarital intercourse (Hunt, 1974).

Simply looking at the numbers gives the impression that the sexual experience of males and females is becoming a great deal more alike than was the case twenty years ago. To a degree this is true; however, there are some important differences in the way in which males and females regard sexual behavior. Women who engage in premarital sexual intercourse tend to do so with more emotional involvement and with fewer partners than do men; Hunt reports that the average number of premarital partners for men was six, while it was two for women. Further, male and female attitudes toward sex are different. Females tend to voice concerns about pleasing their partner, while males are often more concerned about their own pleasure in a sexual relationship (Bardwick, 1971, Tavris & Offir, 1977). However, just as similarity in the sexual practice of males and females has increased over the last few years, it is likely that in the next decade there will be a greater similarity in attitudes and beliefs about sex held by males and females.

In addition to studying when people engage in sexual intercourse, investigators have examined how often people engage in it. The median frequency of sexual intercourse for married males in the United States was three times a week; median frequency means that half of all married males had sex more often than this and half had less often than this (Hunt, 1974). In this same survey, Hunt found that some people reported having intercourse more than once a day, while others reported averaging less than once a year.

Also, as can be seen in Table 10–2, frequency of sexual intercourse declines as people get older. However, although the frequency of sexual activity in older people declines, reports indicate that men and women continue to enjoy active sex lives. While older men require longer periods of stimulation to achieve an erection, they are typically able to maintain an erection longer than younger men (Schulz, 1984). Women experience **menopause,** the cessation of menstruation, in their late forties or early fifties. Menopause marks the end of a woman's ability to bear children and is accompanied by physical and hormonal changes. This period does not signal the end of a woman's sexual drive, however, and hormone treatments can inhibit or reverse many of the physical changes associated with menopause (Geer, Heiman, & Leitenberg, 1984). Clearly, then, heterosexual behavior has changed over time and varies widely between individuals.

Homosexual Behavior. In recent years, the Gay Rights movement has focused national attention on **homosexuality,** the sexual desire for those of the same sex as oneself. For years homosexuality was treated as a mental or physical disorder. In many states homosexual behavior is still considered a "crime against nature," and jail sentences can be given to people convicted of the "crime" even when it occurs between consenting adults.

In terms of percentages, the number of people who engage exclusively in homosexual behavior is rather low; it has been estimated that about 4 percent of men and slightly over 2 percent of women in the United States are exclusively homosexual (Gebhard, 1972). However, Kinsey and others have estimated that possibly as high as 45 percent of all people in the United States have had some homosexual encounter during their lives, often during childhood. Further, most people who are labeled homosexuals are not exclusively homosexual; rather, they are bisexual and are attracted to members of both sexes.

Table 10–2
Weekly Frequency of Marital Coitus in the United States, 1938–1949 and 1972

1938–1949		1972	
Age	Median	Age	Median
16–25	2.45	18–24	3.25
26–35	1.95	25–34	2.55
36–45	1.40	35–44	2.00
46–55	0.85	45–54	1.00
56–60	0.50	55 and over	1.00

Source: Hunt (1974), p. 196.

There is still not a clear understanding of why some people engage in homosexual behavior. In some cases it is possible to point to a hormonal imbalance. For example, researchers found lower levels of the male sex hormone in males who were exclusively homosexual than in males who practiced only heterosexual behavior (Kolodny et al., 1971). However, they were quick to point out that this finding does not demonstrate that the level of hormones *causes* homosexual behavior. It is possible, too, that the stress and anxiety associated with a homosexual life-style causes the reduction in hormone level. Also, other researchers have reported no notable differences in hormone levels when comparing homosexuals and heterosexuals (Sayler et al., 1978).

Some investigators have suggested a link between early family experiences and homosexuality. For example, Bieber (1976) found that the homosexuals he counseled tended to have dominant mothers and passive fathers. Other research shows that **lesbians,** female homosexuals, often had lost one or both parents before the age of ten or had poor relations with their mothers (Saghir & Robins, 1973). However, these results have not been confirmed (Siegelman, 1974). In addition, these studies rely on people's memories of their family relationships, and it is possible that memories may be distorted.

Another theory links physiological changes and social development with homosexuality (Storms, 1981). According to this theory, a homosexual orientation may develop if an individual's sex drive develops during a period when most friends are of the same sex. This period is generally during childhood and before adolescence. Thus, Storms argues that the sex drive in homosexuals may have developed at an earlier age than that of heterosexuals.

While the causes of homosexuality still remain a mystery, it has become clear that homosexuality is not a mental disease or disorder and does not demand treatment. In fact, Masters and Johnson (1979) reported that homosexuals have no inadequacy in sexual functioning and, in some cases, achieve greater satisfaction for themselves and their partners than do heterosexual couples.

STIMULUS-SEEKING MOTIVES

After dealing with the immediate perils of the crash, many of the survivors began to get restless; they wanted something to do while they waited for rescue. As a result, despite the bitter cold, some of them spent their daytime hours searching the area around the plane, and several set out to explore the larger area around the crash site. Others spent time wandering through the plane. When a new object was found, such as a broken piece of radio, the discoverer spent hours examining and fingering it.

Many animals have this same desire to explore and manipulate new objects, which is also referred to as a **stimulus-seeking motive**. When rats, cats, or dogs are put in a new environment, their immediate response is to explore the area. Dember (1965) found that rats will choose a new environment when given the choice between a familiar area and a new one. It also has been observed that monkeys will spend hours opening and closing locks and other mechanical devices (Harlow et al., 1950).

Anyone who has been around young children has seen the stimulus-seeking motive in action. A walk through a home in which a young child lives will show that almost every moveable object has been carefully placed on high shelves out of the child's reach and inviting but dangerous passageways are barricaded. An awareness of children's curiosity and what it can lead to was acknowledged by the Food and Drug Administration when it ordered the use of "child-proof" caps on bottles containing dangerous drugs.

What is behind this common and seemingly insatiable behavior? Two important elements are novelty and complexity. Researchers have found that infants spend more time looking at complex figures than at simpler figures (Berlyne et al., 1957, 1958, 1966). Adults also focus their attention more quickly and for a longer period of time on complex and novel pictures (see Figure 10–3).

The motive to explore and manipulate is an important one for our survival. It is through searching new areas and feeling, touching, and manipu-

The motive to explore is found in animals and humans. Harlow observed that monkeys will spend long periods opening and closing locks in their cages. Exploring behavior seems to be an end in itself.

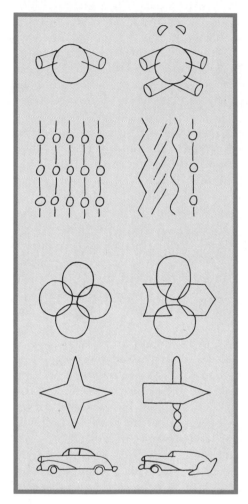

lating objects that we learn about our environment and how it works. In addition, exploration and manipulation help us learn how to control our environment. The motives to explore and manipulate do not easily fit the drive-reduction models of motivation. First, they do not seem to be caused by some internal state or lack. Rather, it is new and complex stimuli that elicit these responses. Second, the aim of these motives is to increase arousal or tension, not to reduce it. Seeking out new objects or areas to explore excites people.

Similarly, some investigators have suggested that there may be a motive for arousal, or a **sensation-seeking motive** (Franklin, 1982). We can name a long list of examples where people take risks or perform behaviors designed to arouse them. Some people are actively drawn to horror movies and scary amusement park rides, for example, while others find thrills in parachuting from an airplane. Once a task is mastered, people often are quick to search out one of even greater risk. For example, the rugby players on the team chose to go to Chile to find stiffer competition; they were able to beat the teams in Uruguay, and the Chilean teams represented a greater challenge.

These sensation-seeking behaviors, like the stimulus-seeking behaviors, do not fit the drive-reduction model. For this reason, they have captured attention and many arousal theories have been advanced to explain them. One position is that people seek high levels of arousal because the reduction of these high arousal levels is more rewarding than the reduction of lower arousal levels. This position tends to stretch the limits of credibility; it suggests that we might seek out painful experiences because the elimination of pain is so satisfying. Further, this theory does not explain why people increase their level of risk over time. A second position suggests that high arousal releases a drug called norepinephrine into our systems (Zuckerman, 1979). According to this theory we seek arousal so our bodies will release norepinephrine into our systems; the drug makes us feel good. Risk-taking is kept within reason, however, because there are negative costs associated with higher risks.

SOCIAL MOTIVES

Affiliation

The crash caused many drastic changes in the lives of the survivors. No longer were they faced with a familiar environment and a routine daily schedule. Their lives were filled with fear: fear of the cold, fear of going hungry, fear that they would never be found, and fear that each day might be their last. Their response to this situation was to seek comfort in one another. The survivors sat together, talked together, slept together, ate together, and even went outside together to go to the bathroom.

The **affiliation motive,** the desire to be with others, does not only occur in the cold isolation of the Andes. If you look around your own environment, most of the people you see will be in pairs, trios, or other small groups. And if you talk to those people, you are likely to find that most of them spend a great deal of their time with other people.

While it may seem that humans have a natural drive to affiliate, research suggests that learning and early experiences strongly affect our desire to be with others. Harry Harlow (1971) studied infant monkeys who were raised in social isolation. Although they were well fed, they lacked the comfort of a mother and the opportunity to play with peers. When these isolated monkeys were one year old, Harlow placed them in a cage with other young monkeys who had been raised in a normal environment. Instead of joining the others in play, the isolated monkeys avoided social contact and cringed in a corner of the cage. If one of the other monkeys approached, the isolated monkey would react viciously. Thus, it seems that without the early experience of social comfort and interaction, the desire to affiliate does not develop.

Taking another approach, a number of experiments were performed to show that fear often leads to the desire to affiliate (Schachter, 1959). Imagine yourself in the following situation. You and some other subjects report for an experiment and are met by a very serious-looking man dressed in a white laboratory coat with a stethoscope hanging from his pocket. He introduces himself as Dr. Gregory Zilstein, and as he points to a ghastly array of electrical equipment, he informs you that you are in a study concerning the effects of electrical shock. He says that you will have electrodes placed on your hand and will be given a series of electrical shocks so that your reactions can be studied. In a very somber manner he confesses: "Again, I do want to be honest with you and tell you that these shocks will be quite painful, but, of course, they will do no permanent damage" (Schachter, 1959, p. 13). These were the instructions you would have received if you had been assigned to the high-fear group.

If, on the other hand, you had been randomly placed in the low-fear group, you would have been met by a friendly Dr. Zilstein wearing sports clothes. Electrical equipment would not have been present in the room. After greeting you, Dr. Zilstein would tell you that the experiment concerned the effects of electrical shock. However, he would quickly add: "We would like to give each of you a series of very mild electric shocks. . . . It will resemble more a tickle than anything unpleasant" (Schachter, 1959, pp. 13–14).

After manipulating fear in this way, Dr. Zilstein told the subjects that there would be a ten-minute delay before the experiment would begin. He then gave the subjects (all women) the option of waiting alone, waiting with others, or stating no preference. What would be your desire in the two conditions? As shown in Table 10–3, subjects in the high-fear group had a much greater desire to be with others than did low-fear subjects. Thus, Schachter demonstrated that fear leads people to affiliate.

There were two other interesting findings from Schachter's research. First, he found that the subjects preferred to wait with other people who were in the same situation as opposed to others who were not waiting to be in the fear-arousing situation. In other words, misery loves miserable company. Second, the fear-affiliation relationship was found only for subjects who were firstborn or only children. Fear did not motivate later-born subjects to affiliate with others.

Schachter suggested that the fearful situation was rather ambiguous for subjects; they didn't know what to expect or what they should be feeling. Their desire to be with others resulted because they wanted to reduce the ambiguity. They could observe the response of others, especially others who were in the same situation, and adjust their own actions and feelings

Table 10–3
Effect of Fear on Affiliation

Group	Number Choosing		
	Waiting Together	Didn't Care	Waiting Alone
High fear	20	9	3
Low fear	10	18	2
Source: Adapted from Schachter (1959).			

accordingly. Firstborn and only children had learned to use the response of others to help determine their own feelings.

According to Schachter, firstborns learn to seek out companionship when they are fearful. Later-born children do not receive the same degree of attention from their mothers as firstborns do and thus do not learn to seek companionship to deal with fearful situations.

While Schachter's theory is an interesting one, another explanation has been suggested recently to explain affiliation (Rofe, 1984). According to the *utility affiliation theory*, people will seek out others who they think can help them reduce anxiety or fear. Further, they will avoid people who may increase fear or anxiety. In support of this position, one study found that severely ill patients (suffering from cancer, diabetes, and hypertension) preferred to be with healthy people rather than other patients with similar diseases (Rofe & Lewin, 1983). Further, they preferred to talk about topics other than their disease.

As we can see, both Schachter's position and the utility affiliation theory could explain the behavior of the plane-crash survivors. The survivors may have wished to be together in order to gain information about their situation and compare their feelings. On the other hand, they may also have wanted to be with others as a way of reducing their fears and reassuring each other that things would be all right. It is likely that there is no single reason that explains our desire to be with other people; instead our motivation to affiliate may have many causes.

Aggression and Violence

In addition to hunger, thirst, and cold, the plane-crash survivors were forced to deal with one another's reactions to the crisis. From the very beginning there were fights. Many a night's calm was suddenly shattered by angry shouts and fighting. Some of the men fought easily and often, while others rarely, if ever, participated in a fight.

Examples of violence and aggression constantly surround us. Nearly every page of a newspaper carries a story of violence; even the comics are liberally sprinkled with it. As a case in point, count the number of aggressive incidents or stories of aggression that occur around you in one day. It seems, then, that while humans have a desire to affiliate, many of their social encounters are characterized by aggression. The question of why people aggress has long intrigued psychologists.

Instinct Theories. One of the earliest views was that aggression is an instinct. Influenced by the human destructiveness that he witnessed in World War I, Sigmund Freud held that humans have a basic instinct to aggress. To Freud, the motivation to aggress arises within the person.

The instinct position was further developed by those who argued that while an organism may be naturally endowed with the readiness to aggress, an external cue is necessary to release the response. According to these theorists, only certain stimuli are capable of releasing aggression. This external trigger is viewed as a key that opens the door for aggression; just as only the proper key can open a lock, so it is that only certain predetermined stimuli can trigger aggression.

While such theories are of value in explaining aggression in some animals, it is hard to apply them directly to human behavior. Human aggression varies from culture to culture. For example, in Tokyo, a city with a population of 11 million people, there were 213 homicides in 1970, while during that same year in New York City (with a population of 8 million) there were 1,117 murders. Even looking at the experiences of the survivors, we find that in the same situation some of them acted aggressively and others did not. Thus it is difficult to argue that humans are instinctively aggressive.

Biological Theories. It is possible that there are genetic or biological factors that determine our aggression. There have been many different attempts to identify these factors. Some research has focused on hormones (Maccoby & Jacklin, 1980). For example, the male of most species is more aggressive than the female. Therefore, it may be that the male sex hormone, testosterone, is responsible for aggression. Opponents of this position, however, argue that it is learning and not hormones that accounts for this sex difference (Eron, 1980).

Other researchers have attempted to identify "seats of aggression" in the brain. The notion here is that aggression results from stimulation of an area of the brain. For example, one study reported that injecting the hypothalamus of peaceful rats with stimulating drugs made them behave in an aggressive manner (Smith et al., 1969).

While this line of research is interesting, it raises many questions. First, does stimulation of these parts of the brain motivate aggression, or does it cause pain, which leads to increased aggression? It may also be that such stimulation leads to a heightened state of arousal; as we will see, people are often more likely to aggress when they are aroused. Finally, even if we find some physiological basis for aggression, it is clear that no human or animal is constantly aggressive. We must, therefore, identify the conditions that are likely to lead to stimulation of this area.

Frustration-Aggression Theory. Despite attempts to show that the motivation for aggression arises from within the individual, most investigators believe that violence is set off by external events. One of the most widely studied theories was developed by a group of psychologists at Yale. John Dollard and his colleagues (1939) stated, "aggression is always a consequence of frustration," and "frustration always leads to some form of aggression" (p. 1). **Frustration** results when people are blocked from getting what they want when they want it. This **frustration-aggression theory** fits many of the incidents of aggression we discussed that occurred among the survivors in the Andes. A survivor's desire to sleep was clearly thwarted when he was stepped on or kicked in the face by a neighbor. In many cases, the result of this frustration was aggression.

While many of the survivors directly fit the model, there are some who did not. Canessa was one of the strongest of the survivors, and he was also the one who tended to bully the smaller young men. While there were some direct attacks on him, his actions often set off a chain reaction; he attacked one person, who, in turn, took out his anger on another, smaller young man. This behavior has been labeled **displaced aggression.** Dollard and his colleagues argue that when we are frustrated, our first tendency is to attack the person responsible. However, if that person is either unavailable or feared (as in the previously cited example), we will displace our aggression onto another target. In Chapter 16 we will discuss how displaced aggression may be at the root of some cases of prejudice.

Another important but controversial part of the theory deals with reducing the urge to aggress. According to the theory, as we face various frustrations in our daily lives, tension builds up inside us. This tension must be released in some way. One of the quickest ways to do this is through aggression. Dollard and his colleagues suggest that if people behave aggressively they will release the tension and thus be less likely to aggress in the near future. **Catharsis** is the term used to describe this release of tension. This is a very important concept, because it argues that aggressive behavior can have a good effect on people and, in some cases, should be encouraged. However, while catharsis may occur after some acts of aggression, more recent surveys and research indicate that the effect is, at best, limited to a very narrow range of conditions (Geen & Quanty, 1977; Konecni & Doob, 1972). In many cases, the expression of aggression not only fails to reduce future aggression, but actually increases the probability of it.

The frustration-aggression theory has received both support and criticism. It has been generally accepted that frustration often sets off aggression. However, frustration is not the only source of aggression, nor does it always lead to aggression. Further, the theory does not adequately explain the wide variety of human aggressive behavior. For example, why did some of the plane-crash survivors respond aggressively to their frustrations while others did not? Why did some of the young men use physical violence as a response to frustration while others resorted to verbal abuse?

Social-Learning Theory. Despite the wide appeal of frustration-aggression theory, it is clear that not all aggression is the result of frustration. It has been argued that aggression, like most other behaviors, is the result of learning, rather than some natural link with frustration (Bandura, 1973, 1977; Bandura & Walters, 1963). The **social-learning theory** suggests that we learn both when and how to aggress. The theory focuses on two major mechanisms for the learning of aggression: *reinforcement* and *imitation*.

As we have seen in Chapter 6, we tend to repeat behaviors that bring positive rewards. According to Bandura and Walters, children in our society are often rewarded for behaving aggressively; the rewards come in many forms. In one case, the reward may be a direct result of aggression. For example, Johnny may find that no matter how much he begs and pleads, little Billy will not give him any marbles. However, Johnny may quickly find that one sure way to get the marbles is to hit Billy. In another case, rewards may come as an indirect result of aggression. For example, Suzy may find that the teacher never pays attention to her in class; no matter how often she holds up her hand, the teacher fails to notice her. However, the teacher's attention (and even that of the principal) is quickly captured if Suzy pulls the hair of the girl sitting in front of her.

A second important way to learn aggression is through the imitation of models. Many of the successful models available to children achieve success through aggressive behavior. On television, the children see such stars as Magnum P.I. achieve fame through strength and aggression. Even at home, children see their parents use strength and aggression (spankings) to control their offspring. All these models broadcast the lesson that successful people use aggression to achieve their success.

In order to demonstrate the effectiveness of models, Bandura, Ross, and Ross (1961, 1963a) had nursery school children observe an adult model aggressively playing with an inflated doll ("Bobo doll"); the model kicked, hit, and beat the doll with a hammer (see Figure 10–4). When the children were later allowed to play with the doll, they too kicked, hit, and beat the doll with a hammer, just as the model had done. Bandura and his associates (1963b) also found that children imitated an aggressive model even when the model was seen on film or in a cartoon. While learning occurs through imitation, research suggests that people express aggression when they feel they will be rewarded for their behavior (Bandura, 1965).

Social-learning theory helps us understand why different people respond to the same situation in different ways. For example, Canessa may have learned that physical aggression was an effective way for him to deal with people who annoyed him. Thus, when people bothered him or got in his way during the mountain ordeal, his response was a violent one. Other survivors may have had very different experiences and models and, as a result, learned to approach problems with reason and calm.

In addition to explaining why people aggress, social-learning theory can also be used to develop ways to reduce aggression. Bandura and Walters (1963) point out that when parents use physical violence to punish their children, they are providing them with aggressive models. In fact, studies show that children who were severely punished at home for aggression were likely to act aggressively outside the home (Sears et al., 1953). Thus,

Figure 10–4
These photos were taken during Bandura's study of modeling and aggression. After watching an adult model kick and beat up the Bobo doll, boys and girls repeated these actions when they were allowed to play with the doll. (Bandura et al., 1963)

it follows that parents should punish their children by withholding love or other rewards rather than by using aggression. Social-learning theory also argues strongly against the catharsis notion: If people learn aggression, then allowing them to participate in aggressive activities will increase their future aggression, not reduce it, as suggested by the catharsis hypothesis. In the next section, we will see yet another implication of social-learning theory for the control of aggression.

Media Violence and Aggression. It is interesting to examine frustration-aggression theory and social-learning theory in light of a major controversy that still rages today: what are the effects of media violence on aggression? An act of violence is shown on television every fifteen minutes, and a murder occurs every thirty-one minutes. If you grew up in the average family, you probably saw about 13,000 murders on television by the time you were sixteen years old (Waters & Malamud, 1975). Even shows specifically designed for young audiences are filled with examples of aggression: Nine out of ten characters in weekend children's programs are involved in some type of violence (Comstock et al., 1979).

What is the effect of watching such violence? On one hand, the frustration-aggression theory suggests that it may result in a reduction in actual aggression. It could be argued that people who watch television take part in these acts through fantasy—they release their aggressive feelings in this way. On the other hand, social-learning theory suggests that we learn aggression through modeling. According to this theory, we learn to aggress from watching these violent models.

The majority of the evidence supports social-learning theory. Evidence for this relationship comes from studies that show that aggressiveness increases in isolated communities after television is introduced (Nimh, 1982). Other evidence comes from laboratory studies. One group of researchers divided juvenile delinquents in minimum custody units into two groups: One group watched aggressive movies every night for a week, while the other group saw only nonaggressive movies during the week (Parke et al., 1977). The effect of the aggressive movies was to increase aggressive behavior—those who saw the violent films behaved more violently than those who had seen the nonviolent films.

A second study showed that, in addition to affecting our behavior, the regular viewing of aggression on TV also affects our *general* reactions to violence (Thomas et al., 1977). In this study, children watched either an aggressive episode of a TV program or a nonviolent film showing a game of volleyball. After this they were all shown a scene of "real-life" aggression. Those who had seen the aggressive film first were less affected by the "real" violence than those who had seen the nonviolent film. Such results suggest that viewing aggression on TV may make us less sensitive to and less bothered by aggression in our own lives.

In 1969 the National Commission on the Causes and Prevention of Violence stated: "It is reasonable to conclude that a steady diet of violent behavior on television has an adverse effect on human character and attitudes. Violent behavior fosters moral and social values about violence in daily life that are unacceptable in a civilized society." More recent research (Eron, 1982) suggests that not everyone is affected the same by television violence. Overall, boys are more affected by violence than girls. And boys who are low achievers and unpopular at school are more likely to imitate aggression they see on television.

Desire for Control. Among the plane-crash survivors, much of their aggression seemed unprovoked. At times, one of the biggest players would push or threaten one of the smaller players seemingly without reason and without reward. In a sense, vandalism follows a similar script. An individual or group may explode with violence aimed at destruction; it seems senseless because the aggressors get nothing for their actions.

Investigators examined vandalism and proposed a theory to explain it and other types of aggression (Allen & Greenberger, 1980). They argued that some people use violence to demonstrate their control. Being able to destroy an individual or object offers the ultimate sense of control; the act of destruction can give the aggressor a feeling of success and mastery over the environment. These investigators suggested that people who feel that they are losing control over their environment may turn to aggression to demonstrate to themselves that they are still in control.

Hence, seemingly senseless acts of aggression such as vandalism may be aimed at no other purpose than increasing the aggressor's perception of control. Similarly, some of the unprovoked acts of aggression that occurred among the plane-crash survivors may have been aimed at giving them some feelings of control over their very difficult situation.

The Role of Arousal in Aggression. The survivors were in a constant state of tension during their mountain ordeal due to fear and anxiety about keeping alive and about being rescued. Outside of the airplane nearly every step taken was a major ordeal as they sank into snow up to their waists. A walk around the outside of the plane would leave them gasping for breath. Is it possible that these additional sources of arousal increased the aggressiveness of the survivors?

Researchers have suggested that arousal of any type can cause people to act more aggressively when they are frustrated (Zillman, 1983). In one study, Zillman (1971) showed subjects either an aggressive film, a sexually arousing film, or a nonarousing film. The subjects were then either angered or not angered by an experimental confederate. Finally, they were given the chance to shock the confederate under the guise of a learning task. The results showed that subjects who were sexually aroused and later angered were the most aggressive (delivered the highest amount of shock), and subjects who watched the nonarousing film were least aggressive. Researchers also found that watching arousing but displeasing sexual films increased later aggression (Zillman et al., 1981).

Other research has shown that arousing exercise (Zillman et al., 1974), humor (Mueller & Donnerstein, 1977), and noise (Donnerstein & Wilson, 1976) can also increase aggression when subjects are frustrated. There are two possible explanations for this effect. First, the heightened state of arousal may serve to energize people's responses. A second explanation is that people may misinterpret the cause of their arousal, as we shall discuss in Chapter 11. That is, the person who is first sexually aroused and then frustrated may feel that all the arousal is a result of anger.

THE ACHIEVEMENT MOTIVE

Many years ago, Harry Murray (1938) suggested that some people are driven by the motive "to do things as rapidly and/or as well as possible." Later, McClelland (1958) argued that people can be categorized by the strength of their **achievement motive (nAch)**. People with high nAch are driven by the general desire to set and achieve high standards of excellence. These people seek out challenging tasks and do their best to perform well even if the task holds no special interest for them. These people have an internal standard of excellence that they strive to meet.

Atkinson and Birch (1978) suggested that the achievement motive is really the result of two desires: *hope for success* and *fear of failure*. The need for achievement will be highest in people who have a high hope for success and a low fear of failure. People with a high hope for success should seek out tasks that will challenge their abilities yet not be unattainable. On the other hand, people who are dominated by a fear of failure should be attracted to either very easy goals or very difficult ones. They can be certain to achieve the simple goals, while failing to meet a very difficult one cannot be too upsetting because failure would be expected from the start. In an interesting study designed to test this theory, subjects who had been identified as either very hopeful for success or highly fearful of failure were given some practice trials in a ring-toss game (Hamilton, 1974). After seeing their ability in the game, the subjects were given the opportunity to choose their own distance for the next trials in the game. Subjects hoping for success chose distances where the probability of success was moderate (40 percent). However, subjects who were very fearful of failure chose distances where success was very unlikely (10 percent).

Measuring the Achievement Motive. How can we tell if someone has a high need to achieve? One way is simply to ask. However, McClelland felt that the achievement motive is largely an unconscious one, and people are unlikely to know whether or not they have it. In order to measure the strength of this motive, McClelland and his colleagues (1953) adapted the *Thematic Apperception Test* (*TAT*). This approach involves showing people a picture (such as a boy daydreaming) and having them tell a story about what is happening in the picture and what led up to these events (we will discuss this test in more detail in Chapter 12). The subjects' responses are then examined to identify themes involving achievement and success. McClelland felt that people who had a high nAch would tell stories involving themes of achieving and striving to obtain high goals, but that people with a lower nAch would not develop stories around achievement themes. For example, let us assume that a picture of a boy daydreaming was shown to subjects. In this case, we might expect those high in nAch to say that

Horner suggested that traditional training led some women to fear and avoid success. The breaking down of sex roles and stereotypes should reduce sex differences in the need to achieve.

INTRINSIC AND EXTRINSIC MOTIVATION

An important and central question in the study of motivation can be examined by focusing on your present behavior: reading this book. What is it that motivates you to read and learn the material in this book? That may seem like an unnecessary question. Certainly you are reading so you can do well on your tests and earn a good grade in the course. While this answer may reflect reality, it is not the response that we, as textbook writers and teachers, would like to hear. Our hope is that students will be "turned onto" their texts because of the pride and satisfaction they feel in knowing more about themselves and their world. These two answers represent the basic reasons why people work or perform almost any other task. The first response (reading to pass a test) is an example of *extrinsic motivation*. This type of motivation comes from factors external to the individuals; it can be based on a desire for pay, status, grades, promotion, or any similar types of rewards. The second response is an example of *intrinsic motivation*, which involves deriving enjoyment and satisfaction from performing the task itself, not from the rewards expected. There are two bases for intrinsic motivation. The first is the belief that people have a need to see themselves as controlling their own behavior. The second is the belief that people want to see themselves as capable and competent (Deci, 1971). Intrinsic rewards such as intellectual challenge or pride make us feel that we are in control. On the other hand, when we work only for an external reward such as money, it is the reward that is controlling our behavior.

These two concepts give rise to some interesting and important predictions regarding work

behavior. One prediction is that people who are extrinsically motivated will stop working when that reward is no longer available. On the other hand, people who are intrinsically motivated will continue to work regardless of external conditions. In a series of studies, subjects were either paid money (extrinisic motivation) or given no reward to work on puzzles (Calder & Staw, 1975; Deci, 1972). When they completed the experiment, subjects were given free time to engage in a number of activities such as reading magazines or working on more puzzles. The results showed that subjects who had been paid to work on the puzzles spent less free time (and unpaid time) working on the puzzles and reported enjoying the puzzles less than subjects who had never been paid to work on the puzzles. Likewise, if you are reading this book only to pass the course (extrinsic motivation), it is unlikely that you would continue to read it after the course is over.

This does not mean that rewards are always bad. Research indicates that rewards will increase performance on dull and uninteresting tasks (Leeper & Greene, 1978). But, the story is different when we consider tasks that are interesting and can be intrinsically motivating. In this case, giving people a reward for performing a task that they enjoy performing may change their perception of their own behavior; they may see themselves as working only for the reward, and consequently reduce performance when the reward is no longer available. This effect can be seen clearly in the old Jewish fable offered here.

In a little Southern town where the

Klan was riding again, a Jewish tailor had the temerity to open his little shop on the main street. To drive him out of the town the Kleagle of the Klan sent a gang of little ragamuffins to annoy him. Day after day they stood at the entrance of his shop. "Jew! Jew!" they hooted at him. The situation looked serious for the tailor. He took the matter so much to heart that he began to brood and spent sleepless nights over it. Finally out of desperation he evolved a plan.

The following day, when the little hoodlums came to jeer at him, he came to the door and said to them, "From today on anybody who calls me 'Jew' will get a dime from me." Then he put his hand in his pocket and gave each boy a dime.

Delighted with their booty, the boys came back the following day and began to shrill, "Jew! Jew!" The tailor came out smiling. He put his hand in his pocket and gave each of the boys a nickel, saying, "A dime is too much—I can only afford a nickel today." The boys went away satisfied, because, after all, a nickel was money, too.

However, when they returned the next day to hoot at him, the tailor gave them only a penny each.

"Why do we get only a penny today?" they yelled.

"That's all I can afford."

"But two days ago you gave us a dime, and yesterday we got a nickel. It's not fair, mister."

"Take it or leave it. That's all you're going to get!"

"Do you think we're going to call you 'Jew' for one lousy penny?"

"So don't!"

And they didn't.

the boy is thinking about becoming a successful lawyer and winning important cases, or he is thinking about solving a difficult math problem. Those scoring low in nAch, on the other hand, might say that the boy is thinking about what he will have for lunch or about what his girlfriend is doing at that particular moment. The TAT cards have been widely used to tap the achievement motive.

Basis for the Achievement Motive.   Given that everyone does not have equally high motives to achieve, we can ask where his motive comes from. As with so many things in life, it seems that the blame (or praise) rests with our parents. Family characteristics and life style influence the development of the achievement motive. Winterbottom (1953) found that the mothers of those high in nAch raised their children to act independently. The children were allowed to make decisions on their own and were rewarded with affection for independent actions. Other researchers found that both the opportunity for independence and the reward for independent behavior were necessary for developing high nAch (Teevan & McGhee, 1972). Children who are forced to act independently but are not rewarded for these behaviors do not develop high achievement motive; they may learn to act on their own, but they do not strive for excellence. Thus, it is clear that early childhood experiences have a strong influence on the achievement motive.

Characteristics of People Scoring High on Achievement Motive.   For the most part, a strong drive for achievement is a good thing to have. People with high nAch outperform those who are low in achievement motivation, even though the IQ scores of both groups are the same. People with high achievement motive tend to get better grades in school (Raynor, 1970) and be more successful in business (Andrew, 1967) than those who have a low need to achieve.

Research has shown that the strength of a person's motive to achieve is related to the type of occupation he or she chooses. McClelland (1955) found that people scoring low on the need to achieve chose jobs that involved few risks and few opportunities for independent decision making. However, people scoring high in nAch chose entrepreneurial positions such as sales, or were self-employed; in either case they had to make decisions and their salary and success were dependent on their own actions.

The reason for these differences are not entirely clear. However, it seems that people scoring low in nAch tend to be most concerned with either succeeding or having an excuse for not succeeding. To the contrary, those higher in nAch desire a challenge that they can work and succeed at, with success measured by their own ability and work.

While having a high need to achieve has many positive consequences, it does have its drawbacks. Recent evidence suggests that people scoring high in nAch take everything as a challenge. In their drive for perfection, they run the risk of becoming "workaholics." In some cases, they have difficulty "letting go" and relaxing and are prone to getting ulcers (as we will discuss in Chapter 11).

Fear of Success.   The strong desire to achieve and be successful in school and business is encouraged for males, but what about females? Researchers point out that the traditional view of women in our society discourages success and striving for achievement (Frieze et al., 1978). Women are not encouraged to seek independent careers, and, when they do so, they are often the object of social scorn and discrimination. As a result of these values, Horner (1968) argued that women learn to avoid and fear success.

In order to demonstrate this position, Horner asked male and female subjects to write a story about the following situation: "After first-term finals, Anne (John) finds herself (himself) at the top of her (his) medical school class." As can be seen in Table 10–4, when males wrote about

Table 10-4
Sex Differences
and the
Achievement Motive

Sample Male Response
John is a conscientious young man who worked hard. He is pleased with himself. John has always wanted to go into medicine and is very dedicated. His hard work paid off. He is thinking that he must not let up now, but must work even harder than he did before. His good marks have encouraged him. . . . He eventually graduates at the top of his class.

Sample Female Response
Anne has a boy friend in the same class and they are quite serious. Anne met Carl at college and they started dating. . . . Anne is rather upset and so is Carl. She wants him to be higher in school than she is. Anne will deliberately lower her academic standing next term, while she does all she subtly can to help Carl. His grades come up and Anne soon drops out of medical school. They marry and he goes on in school while she raises their family.

Source: Horner (1968).

Figure 10-5
Maslow's Hierarchy of Needs

Maslow believed that motives at each level must be satisfied before motives at the next higher level will direct behavior.

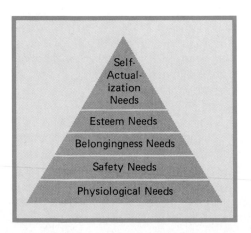

John, they described him in positive terms and predicted that he would have a happy future. However, when females wrote about Anne, their descriptions were far from flattering and they expressed concern about her future.

While Horner's conclusions are provocative, they have been criticized. For example, one study had men write about Anne's outcome and women write about John's outcome (Monahan et al., 1974). The results showed that men wrote less successful outcomes for Anne than women wrote about John. Another study found that women wrote successful outcomes about a female in a more "typically female role" such as nursing (Feather, 1975). Two explanations can be offered for these responses. One is that the stories written about Anne and John simply reflected prevailing expectations and sex stereotypes. In other words, the writers were indicating that Anne might meet social rejection if she succeeded, whereas John would not. A second explanation focuses on the importance of succeeding in a particular task (Eccles, 1983). That is, the situations involved in the stories may have been ones where males felt it was important to succeed while females did not. A similar explanation has been used to explain racial differences in achievement motivation (Banks & McQuater, 1976). Research indicates that on boring tasks, black children do show less desire to achieve and succeed than do white children. However, on interesting tasks, both black and white children express high achievement motivation.

A HIERARCHY OF MOTIVES?

We have examined a number of different motives. Looking back over these motives, we ask whether some are more important or basic than others. We can begin to answer this question by reviewing the behavior of the survivors.

Immediately after the crash, the survivors turned their attention to clearing out what was left of the plane and trying to warm themselves. After doing this, they worried about finding a water supply and seeing what food was available. The survivors seemed to care very little about what others thought of them during these early days. Some openly wept, some reverted to childish behavior, and others performed such socially disapproved behaviors as wetting their pants. After their hunger and thirst had been satisfied, the survivors began organizing themselves into groups. Leaders emerged, and people who broke loosely defined rules were reprimanded. As time passed, some of the young men began thinking about their families and sweethearts, and a few even wrote letters expressing their feelings for their loved ones.

Looking over this sequence of behaviors, we can ask why the survivors did particular things in a certain order. Why did it take them so long to think about their families? Why didn't the survivors organize into effective working groups right after the crash?

It has been suggested that our motives are organized into a hierarchy, like the rungs of a ladder, with the stronger biological motives at the bottom and the more complex psychological motives at the top (Maslow, 1954, 1970). Maslow further believed that the motives at the lower level must first be satisfied before the motives at the next higher level will influence or direct one's behavior. For example, if you look at Maslow's hierarchy (see Figure 10–5), you can see that hunger and thirst must be satisfied before you will begin to direct behavior at satisfying security or social order needs. You might have had your own experiences with this hierarchy of motives if you have ever tried to study when you were hungry. It is likely that this was a difficult, if not hopeless, undertaking. You probably interrupted your studies frequently to search your room for food. If you didn't find any, your mind may have wandered as you stared at the pages of your books while visions of a thick, juicy steak, a steaming baked potato, and chocolate pudding kept flashing in your mind. The behaviors of the survivors fit nicely into Maslow's scheme. Their first actions were aimed at satisfying their physical needs (warmth, liquid, and food), while later actions seemed to be directed by desires for social order, thoughts of their families, and the need for respect from their companions.

Research findings do not support Maslow's theory, however. Much of the research on the hierarchy has been conducted in work settings. For example, in one study managers and other white-collar workers were asked to rank a list of needs in order of importance (Wahba & Bridwell, 1976). These rankings did not fit Maslow's hierarchy. Other investigators (e.g., Alderfer, 1972) have suggested that there are three types of needs: existence (physiological and safety), relatedness (love needs), and growth (esteem and self-actualization). Unlike Maslow's model, this theory suggests that more than one need may be operating at one time. That is, a person may be striving to satisfy both existence and growth needs. This theory does not specify the order in which needs occur. This newer theory seems to more closely fit the results obtained in a variety of settings and may more accurately reflect the way in which our motives are interrelated (Geen et al., 1984).

SUMMARY

1. The study of **motivation** is concerned with how and why people behave as they do—what energizes and directs their behavior.

2. A distinction is made in the chapter between **primary motives** (such as hunger, thirst, the need for air and rest, and sex) and **social motives** (such as affiliation, aggression, and achievement).

3. The basic theories of motivation are instinct theory, drive theory, and incentive theory.

4. **Hunger** is one of the most basic primary motives. In looking for what controls eating and hunger, researchers have studied contractions of the stomach, the level of glucose in the bloodstream (as monitored by the hypothalamus and the liver), the role of taste, and the influence of body-weight.

5. There are a number of factors associated with **obesity** and overeating. The most important of these are an increased sensitivity to external cues to eat, a difficulty in interpreting inner cues of hunger (or lack of hunger), and the sheer number of fat cells in the body.

6. Osmometric thirst is motivated by a reduction of intracellular fluid levels—the hypothalamus is believed to signal the need for fluids when the intracellular fluid levels are changing. Volumetric thirst is a reaction to changes in blood pressure.

7. Unlike hunger, sex is not necessary for the survival of the individual; but it is necessary for the survival of the species. The biological basis of male and female sexual behavior is hormonal (**androgen** in the male, **estrogen** in the female), which also influences the development of secondary sex characteristics. Human sexual behavior is neither as dependent on hormones nor as stereotyped as animal sexual behavior. Because of this, learning and external cues play an important role in human sexual response.

8. Masters and Johnson have categorized the human sexual response into four phases: the excitement phase, the plateau phase, the orgasm phase, and the resolution phase. Males then usually enter a refractory phase, which may last from a few minutes to several hours, during which time they are incapable of sexual arousal or orgasm. Women, on the other hand, are capable of multiple orgasms in quick succession.

9. The desire to explore and manipulate new objects is called a **stimulus-seeking motive.** It is important for our survival, because it causes us to learn about our environment, how it works, and how to control it. The **sensation-seeking motive** is based on the desire to be aroused.

10. The **affiliation motive,** the desire to be with others, is a social motive. As noted in experiments by Schachter, fear often increases one's desire to affiliate with others.

11. The question of why people aggress has long intrigued psychologists. Among the theories considered here are instinct theories, biological theories, frustration-aggression theory, and social-learning theory. Three factors that are thought to influence aggressive behavior are media violence, desire for control, and arousal.

12. The **achievement motive (nAch)** can be defined as the general desire to set and achieve high standards of excellence. McClelland devised the Thematic Apperception Test to measure the strength of this motive.

13. Maslow has suggested that our motives are organized into a hierarchy, like the rungs of a ladder, with the stronger primary motives at the bottom and the more complex social motives at the top. Motives at the lower level must first be satisfied before the motives at the next higher level. Another theory suggests that there are three types of needs, that more than one need may be operating at the same time, and that the order may vary.

Key Terms

achievement motive (nAch)
affiliation motive
androgens
anorexia nervosa
bulimia
calories
catharsis
displaced aggression
drive
estrogen
frustration
frustration-aggression theory
glucoreceptors
homeostasis
homosexuality
instincts
lesbians
masturbation
menopause

motivation
motive
obesity
osmometric thirst
osmoreceptors
osmosis
ovaries
ovulation
primary motives
puberty
secondary sex characteristics
sensation-seeking motive
set-point theory
social learning theory
social motive
stimulus-seeking motive
testes
volumetric thirst

Suggested Readings

The following book is about the Andes survivors:
READ, P. T. Alive: The Story of the Andes Survivors. Philadelphia: Lippincott, 1974.

ARNOLD, W., & LEVINE, D. (Eds.). Nebraska symposium on motivation. Lincoln, Neb.: University of Nebraska Press. Issues are published once a year. They include original articles on a wide range of topics related to motivation. The articles are timely and focus on both theory and research.

BECK, R. Motivation: Theories and principles, 2nd ed. Englewood Cliffs, N.J.: Prentice-Hall, 1983. Discusses the major theories of motivation; also focuses on many specific motivations, such as aggression and achievement.

COFER, C., & APPLEY, M. Motivation: Theory and research. New York: Wiley, 1964. An excellent and complete discussion of a wide range of motivation theories. The volume presents research associated with each theory and examines the strengths and weaknesses of the theories.

DOLLARD, J., DOOB, L., MILLER, N. E., MOWER, O., & SEARS, R. Frustration and aggression. New Haven, Conn.: Yale University Press, 1939. Presents the frustration-aggression theory and discusses applications of it.

MAIER, R. Human sexuality in perspective. Chicago: Nelson Hall, 1984. An up-to-date examination of human sexual behavior. Especially strong section on the development of sexuality.

GEER, J., HEIMAN, J., & LEITENBERG, H. Human sexuality. Englewood Cliffs, N.J.: Prentice-Hall, 1984. Frank discussion of human sexual behavior. Authoritative chapters on sexual dysfunction and treatment, and sex education.

SCHACHTER, S., & RODIN, J. Obese humans and rats. Hillsdale, N.J.: Erlbaum, 1974. Discusses the major theories and research on obesity. The emphasis is on the relationship between obesity, attribution, and eating behavior.

ELEVEN

EMOTIONS AND STRESS

Have you ever wondered what people in the United States did for entertainment before television? During the first part of this century and for much of the last century the circus brought joy and excitement to residents of large cities such as New York and Boston and to small towns such as Cabool, Missouri, and Old Dime Box, Texas. The young and young-at-heart eagerly awaited the arrival of John Robinson's Circus, Howe's Great London Circus, Hagenbeck-Wallace Company, or the Sells-Floto Circus. Some of these circuses were so small that they traveled on makeshift horse-drawn wagons, while others, such as the Ringling Brothers and Barnum & Bailey Circus, needed over a hundred railway cars to transport the show.

Emmett "Tater" Kelly became a part of the circus tradition in the early part of the twentieth century, and his name quickly became a household word. He had a rather usual and uneventful childhood. He was born in Sedan, Kansas, on December 9, 1898. One of his earliest recollections was his first spanking. At the age of five, he climbed a tall telegraph pole and sat surveying the world from the crossbeam. Suddenly the serenity of this world was broken by the shrieking of his terrified mother and neighbors. Seeing their fear caused Emmett to reassess his own situation; his own exhilaration quickly changed to fear.

Kelly, like other children in this Kansas farming community, was fascinated by the circus, and he looked forward to the arrival of the traveling companies. However, his main interest lay in art; he wanted to draw cartoons. While his parents did not understand this desire, they encouraged him and even paid the $25 tuition to enter Kelly in the Landon School of Cartooning correspondence course. Kelly worked hard; he carefully studied people's expressions and learned to draw humorous pictures of people in many different moods.

In 1917 he headed for Kansas City with $20 in his pocket and visions of earning a fortune as an artist. He soon found that realizing his ambitions as an artist would be more difficult than he expected. His first "art job" was painting letters on signs. His next job involved painting faces on plaster kewpie dolls that were given as prizes in circus sideshows. Then he painted horses for circus merry-go-rounds. Kelly's work thus brought him into contact with the circuses that traveled through Kansas City. He became intrigued with the work of the aerial trapeze acts, and he began practicing on the trapeze in his spare time.

The persistent Kelly finally got a job as a trapeze artist with Howe's Great London Circus. He was delighted with his job until he was told that he would also have to do a clown act. He had no desire to be a clown, but he reluctantly acted the part.

The typical clown act of the time was called "whiteface." The clown painted his face white with a mixture of zinc oxide and lard. Next, grease paint was used to outline the eyes and exaggerate the nose and mouth. Kelley's costume included a white wig and comic oversized shoes. The goal of a clown was to capture an emotion such as joy, surprise, or sadness, exaggerate the expression of the emotion, and portray it in situations that made it funny. For example, a favorite act of the time was a sad-faced clown who searched for his dog, who secretly trailed along behind the clown during the search.

Kelly loved the circus and the people in it. He was captivated by their approach to life. "They (circus performers) may die broke or sick or unhappy, but they seldom give up hope. . . . They just can't quite settle for the idea that the deck is stacked, the wheel is fixed, the dice frozen or the whole game rigged against them. Show people are hopeful people" (Kelly, 1954, p. 97).

While Kelly loved the circus and the peo-

ple, he was not happy being a clown. When the chance arose he switched to a new circus, where his only job was on the trapeze. There he met Eva Moore, a tiny, slim blond who excited the circus patrons with her daring acts high above the big top. He proposed to Eva at the top of the Ferris wheel at a carnival, and they were married a few days later.

About this time the Depression began to grip the Western world, forcing a number of circuses to close, including the one Kelly worked for. After searching desperately for a job, Kelly reluctantly accepted an offer to be a clown, but he decided that he would do a different kind of act.

He wanted to do something that would turn people's attention away from their own sadness and depression and cause them to laugh as they watched someone less fortunate deal with hard times. He wanted to show people that there was both humor and hope in their situation. So, "Weary Willie" was born. In Kelly's own words, Willie was "a sad and ragged little guy who is serious about everything he attempts—no matter how futile or how foolish it appears to be" (Kelly, 1954, pp. 125–126). Willie was a tramp with a dirty face, exaggerated frown, and ragged clothes who delighted circus fans when he tried to crack a peanut with a sledgehammer or sweep away light rays with an old broom.

Kelly (or Willie, as he became known throughout the United States) won the hearts of thousands even though he never spoke a word in his act. Kelly clowned around the world. He found that he could get his greatest laughs when he performed after the most dangerous circus acts, such as the lion-taming or trapeze acts. He also found that no matter what language circus patrons spoke, they all understood the silent antics and sad face of Willie.

Emmett Kelly continued his act until the 1960s. He became a featured performer in the world's largest circus. He brought his clown act to Broadway and found his way into the hearts of millions in the movie *The Greatest Show on Earth*. Even in the complicated world of the 1980s, clowns who imitate many of Willie's antics bring laughter and tears of joy to circus audiences.

EMOTIONS

A Search for a Definition

Emmett Kelly spent his life influencing people's emotions. As Willie, the little tramp, Kelly could make the audience feel sad when he smashed his peanut into an inedible pulp with his sledgehammer. And just as quickly, Willie could make the audience feel happy and burst out laughing as he frantically chased the light beams with his frayed old broom. All of us are familiar with emotions; we talk about emotions and we experience them many times a day. We seek out situations that arouse certain emotions and avoid other situations because they will arouse unwanted emotions.

Despite this everyday familiarity, the concept of emotion holds a certain mystery for those studying it. Some investigators argue that emotions are the same as motives (which we discussed in Chapter 10), while others see a clear distinction between the two. Despite these disagreements, **emotions** are generally defined as affective states (or feelings) that are accompanied by physiological changes (Izard, 1977; Strongman, 1973). These changes often influence behavior. The emphasis in the definition is on feeling; emotions, unlike motives, are something that we feel. As Cofer (1974) points out, "We usually say 'I am hungry' or 'I am thirsty,' not that we feel hungry or thirsty" (pp. 56–57). Emotions such as happiness or sadness, on the other hand, are states that we feel.

Another distinctive feature of emotions that tends to separate them from motives is that emotions are usually aroused by events outside us. You are likely to feel happy because you get a good grade in class or a large raise at work. As we pointed out in Chapter 10, motives are often caused by our inner bodily states.

The Physiology of Emotion

As we pointed out in Chapter 2, the sympathetic nervous system is mainly concerned with preparing the body for action and using energy. It increases heart rate and blood pressure, stimulates the adrenal glands to secrete adrenalin, increases breathing rate, and increases perspiration. The parasympathetic nervous system, on the other hand, works to conserve energy. It returns the body to a normal resting state after the sympathetic nervous system has aroused the body for action.

Since most of our emotions, such as anger, fear, joy, and even love, are states that prepare us for action, the physiological effects associated with most emotions are influenced by the sympathetic nervous system. You may recall the exhilaration you felt the first time you fell in love. Or you may remember running faster than you believed possible after you disturbed a bee's nest. Occasionally we read stories of people performing superhuman feats while being gripped by a strong emotion such as fear or anger. In most cases, after the situation that gave rise to the emotion passes, the parasympathetic nervous system takes over to return the body to its normal state.

For the most part this cooperative relationship between the sympathetic and parasympathetic nervous systems is elegantly adaptive. The systems prepare the individual for action and then "close down" when the need for action has passed. Unfortunately the relationship is not a perfect one and, as we will see later, the physiological changes associated with emotions can create problems for the individual.

GETTING THAT FEELING: THEORIES OF EMOTION

On the afternoon of July 6, 1944, Kelly was busy getting into his costume for the first performance of the day in Hartford, Connecticut. The show had started and the big top was packed. Suddenly someone ran past Kelly's tent and shouted "Fire!" Kelly ran outside and saw a column of black smoke billowing from the main tent. His heart quickened its beat and fear gripped him as he ran to the big top. A sickening sight greeted Kelly; hundreds of people ran screaming from the tent, circus animals stampeded in wild panic through the smoke, and the stench of burning flesh settled over all. The disaster was one of the worst in circus history; scores of people were killed and hundreds were seriously injured.

Kelly experienced a wide variety of emotions in a short period of time during that tragic day. He reported feeling fear when he heard about the fire and saw the smoke, hope that the fire was not in the main tent, anger as he grabbed a bucket of water to fight the fire, and sadness as he cried when he saw some charred little shoes and part of a clown doll lying in the smoldering ashes. Why did Kelly experience these particular emotions in this situation? How did Kelly know he was "feeling" fear when he heard the scream of "fire" and saw the smoke?

Psychologists have been investigating how we experience emotions for over a century. Today there is still not complete agreement about how we experience emotions, but there is increasing interest in the study of emotions. Not only are emotions an important part of our everyday lives, but, as we will see, they involve the complete human experience. Emotions represent a combination of our physiological responses, our senses, our cognitions (or thoughts), our behavior, and our environment. While we can identify the components of emotions, the goal of the theories has been to determine how they interact. Let us now examine some of the important theories that attempt to tell us how and why we experience emotions.

James-Lange Theory

Kelly vividly described his feelings of fear and sadness on the day of the Hartford fire. The common-sense view of emotions suggests that the feeling of emotions caused Kelly to react in certain ways. For example, we might argue that when Kelly saw the charred shoes and doll he felt sad, and because of this feeling he began to cry. This sequence of events makes sense to most of us, but it did not to William James, writing in the 1880s. James argued that it is difficult to imagine feeling an emotion without experiencing a bodily change at the same time. He also pointed out that people often feel emotions without knowing exactly what has caused the emotion (James, 1890). For example, you may be suddenly overcome with feelings of sadness while you are sitting quietly in your room. You may not know why you feel sad, but you can clearly identify your feelings.

Because of these and other considerations, James (1884) argued that events cause bodily and behavioral changes in people, and the emotion lies in the *perception* of these physiological and behavioral changes. According to this investigator: "Common sense says that we lose our fortune, are sorry, and weep; . . . (My) hypothesis . . . is that we feel sorry because we cry, angry because we strike, afraid because we tremble . . ." (James, 1890). The Danish psychologist Carl Lange arrived at the same conclusion,

TRUTH IN EMOTIONS: LIE DETECTION

As we have seen, emotions are reflected in physiological arousal. This fact has long intrigued researchers who wanted to find a way to tell when a person is lying. The basic assumption in the search for the perfect lie detector is that people experience a twinge of guilt or stress when they tell a lie. This "twinge" should be reflected in their physiology, which, unlike verbal behavior, is not under their control. Thus, all that is needed to detect lying is some way to measure a person's physiological responses.

Like so many of our "modern" inventions, a search of history reveals that the concept of the lie detector was conceived hundreds of years ago. The ancient Chinese had a suspect chew rice powder while being questioned (Rice, 1978). After the questioning period the wad of powder was carefully examined. If it was found to be dry, the suspect was found guilty. The Chinese reasoned that lying would create tension, which would slow or block the flow of saliva. Thus the dry mouth resulted in dry rice powder, which, in turn, resulted in a guilty verdict. Interestingly enough, the basic theory behind this test was quite sound; strong emotions are associated with less secretion of saliva.

The modern lie detector, called a **polygraph,** does not use rice powder. Instead, it records changes in heart rate, blood pressure, respiration, and **galvanic skin response** (GSR). Suspects are hooked up to the polygraph, and the operator asks them a number of questions (see Figure A). Lies are identified when there is a *change* from the baseline response; there

is no absolute level of physiological response associated with telling a lie. The operator generally avoids asking the "did you do it" question, since this question may cause even innocent suspects to feel stress. Rather, the operator asks questions that are related to the crime but would create stress only in someone who was familiar with the crime. For example, Lykken (1959) had subjects act out a crime that involved stealing an object from an office and hiding it in a locker in the hallway. The subject in each case was then given a polygraph test in which the operator asked questions about where the object was hidden. "Was it (a) in the men's room, (b) on the coat rack, (c) in the office, (d) on the window sill, or (e) in the locker?" (p. 386). The mention of

the locker would have meaning only for someone who was familiar with the crime. Thus, if the suspect showed a change in physiological response at the mention of the locker, the operator could detect his or her guilt.

Unfortunately, determining innocence or guilt is not this simple, and two points should be emphasized concerning the accuracy of the polygraph. First, the polygraph only charts physiological arousal; it does not identify lies. Second, it is the examiner that must read and interpret the charts. With regard to the first question, Kleinmuntz and Szucko (1984) offer the biblical story of King Solomon. In it, two women claimed that an infant was theirs. Solomon decided to cut the infant in half and give each

Figure A

The polygraph records heart rate, blood pressure, respiration, and galvanic skin response (GSR). The basic assumption is that people's physiological functioning changes when they tell a lie. There are still many questions about the accuracy of the polygraph in detecting lies and about the ethics of forcing people to submit to a lie detection test.

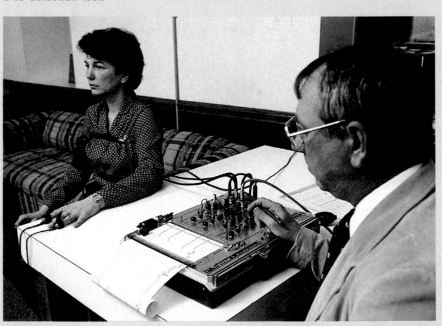

which has become known as the James-Lange theory of emotion (see Figure 11–1). An example of this theory that is familiar to many of us occurs during "near miss" automobile accidents. In such cases, when you are confronted with the possibility of an accident, you respond almost without thinking: you swerve and brake your automobile. After the danger has passed, you notice yourself trembling or sweating. Only then do you feel

woman an equal share. One of the women calmly accepted this decision, but the other woman became emotionally distraught and begged that the baby be spared. Solomon believed that the *calm* woman was lying about being the infant's mother and gave the baby to the woman who was upset about the decision to kill the baby. In this example, it was the lack of arousal that branded the liar. It is important to understand that people respond differently to lying and that the polygraph may not identify these differences. Further, a guilty person may be able to fake responses and "fool" the lie detector. A person may intentionally make him- or herself tense during the neutral questions so that a baseline cannot be established. This might be difficult for many of us, but one investigator reports a case where a prison inmate coached twenty-seven other inmates on how to lie successfully when attached to the polygraph machine (Lykken, 1981). All twenty-seven had admitted their guilt, yet after a 20-minute coaching session, twenty-three of the twenty-seven passed the lie detector test.

The role of the operator is also important because that person must read and interpret the charts. Some studies have shown high agreement (80 to 90 percent) between operators reading the same chart (Hunter & Ash, 1973), yet other studies have found that agreement is not much greater than would occur by chance (Kleinmuntz & Szucko, 1984). Not only may agreement be low between operators, but the accuracy of detecting lies may also be low. In one study, polygraph operators were shown 100 charts—50 from guilty persons and 50 from innocent persons (Kleinmuntz & Szucko, 1984). They were asked to identify the guilty and innocent by analyzing the records. On the average, 37 percent of the innocent people were classified as guilty! This number of incorrect interpretations is frightening, particularly if your freedom, or perhaps your life, is to be based on the results of the test. Clearly there is still a great deal of debate about the reliability and accuracy of lie detectors.

Recently, a new method of lie detection has been introduced. During the Vietnam War, the Army searched for a simpler, more covert way to detect lies, one that could be used during the interrogation of prisoners (Rice, 1978). They turned to voice analysis. The theory behind this method is that the muscles controlling voice tremor are affected by stress. The voice can be recorded and a visual picture of voice tremor can be made on graph paper, as shown in Figure B, by a machine called a **voice stress analyzer.** Subjects can be asked questions similar to those used in the polygraph test. A lie can be detected when the voice stress analyzer indicates tension in the individual's voice (that is, when the voice tremor decreases) in response to the critical questions.

The beauty, and the frightening feature, of this method is that it can be used to analyze any voice that can be recorded. This includes personal conversations, telephone conversations, and even speeches by politicians. And people can have their voices recorded without their knowledge or consent. This raises an important ethical question about the use of lie detection. There is, in fact, considerable study of this issue before the United States Congress, and it is likely that within the next few years laws will be passed concerning the use of these devices. In addition to the question of ethics, there is also the question of how accurate the voice stress analyzer method is. There have only been a few carefully controlled studies and the results are often contradictory.

Figure B
The voice stress analyzer measures voice tremor. It has been found that the arousal produced by telling a lie changes the voice tremors. The graph on top is the voice tremor of a relaxed speaker. The graph on the bottom shows the voice tremor of a speaker under stress. (After Holden, 1975)

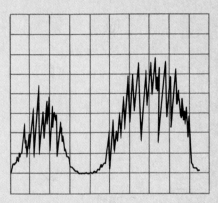

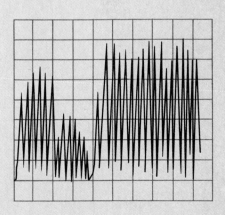

overcome with fear. It was not the emotion that guided your actions or affected your physiological responses. It was your perception of these responses (physiological and behavioral) that cause you to feel fear. One assumption of the James-Lange theory is that we have different physiological arousal patterns for each emotion. Supposedly the perception of these arousal patterns "tells" us what emotion we are feeling.

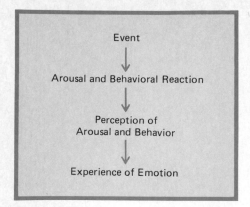

Figure 11-1
James-Lange Theory of Emotion

According to the James-Lange theory, emotion is the result of perceiving our arousal and behavior.

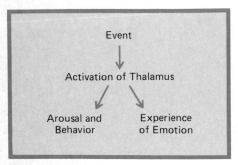

Figure 11-2
Cannon-Bard Theory of Emotion

The Cannon-Bard theory states that events activate the thalamus, which in turn leads to simultaneous arousal of organs and the experience of emotion.

Figure 11-3
Schachter-Singer Cognitive Theory of Emotion

According to Schachter and Singer, unexplained arousal leads people to search their environment to find a label for the arousal. The interpretation of the arousal leads to a specific emotion.

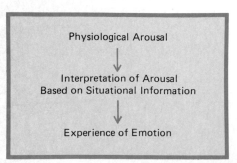

Cannon-Bard Theory

It was this focus on physiological changes that led Walter B. Cannon (1929) to criticize the James-Lange theory and offer another point of view. Cannon argued that physiological changes in bodily organs occur too slowly to be the basis of emotions. He further pointed out that such organs are relatively insensitive, and people are not normally aware of changes in them, such as contractions or relaxations of stomach muscles, the intestines, or other organs. Cannon performed experiments in which he severed the sympathetic nervous system tract in cats. As a result of this operation, heart rate did not increase, body hairs could not be erected, and the liver was unable to release sugar into the blood. However, Cannon found that these animals continued to show typical behavioral reactions of fear, anger, and pleasure in the appropriate situations. Given these criticisms, Cannon argued that emotions could not be simply the perception of physiological changes.

Cannon proposed a theory (see Figure 11–2) that was later extended by Bard (1938). According to this theory, events activate the thalamus (see Chapter 2), which sends messages to the cerebral cortex and to organs such as the heart and the stomach. The stimulation of the cerebral cortex leads to the emotional experience, while the excitation of the organ leads to the accompanying physiological arousal. Thus, Cannon argued that emotional experience and arousal occur at the same time, rather than one after the other, as proposed by James.

More recent research has shown that Cannon's theory was not entirely correct (Plutchik, 1980). The hypothalamus and limbic system, and not the thalamus, play central roles in the experience of emotion. Also, emotions are not simply events that we experience only for the moment; emotions can last long after the event has passed. Thus, while Cannon was correct in pointing out the complexity of the process involved in emotions, there were problems with his theory.

Cognitive Theories

As can be seen from the discussion so far, most of the early theories of emotion focused on the specific role and timing of physiological arousal. Many investigators over the last three decades have turned their attention to the role of cognitions or interpretations in the experience of emotion. While they have still been concerned with the raw materials of emotions such as physiological arousal and behavior, they have also been interested in how the mind processes these data to yield a specific emotion. Although these cognitive theories have much in common, their different emphases show the rich diversity in the study of emotion. Let us examine three cognitive theories to illustrate this point: the Schachter and Singer theory, the appraisal theory, and the somatic theory.

Schachter and Singer Theory. Schachter and Singer (1962) agreed with James's position that emotions occur after physiological arousal. But they argued that specific arousal patterns are not associated with specific emotions. They suggested that the arousal accompanying emotions is diffuse and that the same pattern of arousal could be found with many emotions. According to Schachter and Singer, people became aware that they are aroused and then they seek the reason for this unexplained arousal (see Figure 11–3). The interpretation of this arousal serves as the basis for labeling a specific emotion. People may use their actions, the actions of others, and/or events occurring in the environment to explain their arousal and label their emotion.

In order to illustrate this theory, let us take the example of Emmett Kelly at the circus fire. Kelly fought the fire and helped people and animals escape from the burning tent. Surely all these activities caused a heightened arousal state. Kelly was probably not completely aware of how aroused he was until it was over and he had time to look back on the situation. At this point Kelly saw the charred shoes and the doll. According to the Schachter and Singer theory, Kelly may have used the sight of these pitiful remains to label his emotional state as sadness. If, on the other hand, Kelly had seen a happy scene such as a little girl being reunited with her family, he might have interpreted his arousal state to be happiness or relief.

In an effort to support their theory, Schachter and Singer (1962) conducted a fascinating study. Subjects who volunteered for the study were told that the research was aimed at examining the effects of a vitamin supplement. The subjects were then given an injection that they believed was the vitamin supplement being studied. Unknown to them, some of the subjects were actually injected with epinephrine, a hormone that increases heart rate, raises blood pressure, and increases breathing rate. Subjects were then given one of the following explanations:

1. Informed: These subjects were accurately informed; they were told that the injection would increase arousal.
2. Misinformed: These subjects were given incorrect information; they were told that the injection would cause some numbness, itching, and headaches.
3. No information: This group was told nothing about the effects of the injection.

A final group—the control group—was given an injection of a saline solution that did not have any physiological side effects, and they were told nothing about the injection.

After the injections, subjects were led to a waiting room. In the room was another subject, who was actually working for the experimenter. When the experimenter left the room, this confederate began to act either happy and euphoric or angry. In the former case, he danced around the room, threw wads of paper at a wastebasket, and twirled a hula hoop. The angry confederate tore up a questionnaire on which he had been working and spoke angrily about the experiment. At this point, the experimenter reentered the room and asked subjects to complete a questionnaire describing how they felt.

Schachter and Singer believed that subjects in the no information and misinformed conditions would have unexplained arousal. This arousal should cause them to search the environment for a label. Those paired with the euphoric confederate would use his happy behavior to label their own state as happiness, while those paired with the angry confederate would label their arousal as anger. Subjects who were informed already had a reason for their arousal and, hence, their emotional state should not be influenced by the confederate's behavior. Finally, subjects who were in the control group would not experience arousal and would not be concerned with the confederate's behavior.

The results of the experiment generally supported the Schachter and Singer hypotheses. One of the most interesting results was that subjects in the no information and misinformation conditions labeled their emotions in line with the confederate's behavior. That is, subjects with the happy confederate reported that they felt happy and subjects with the angry confederate labeled themselves as being angry. This difference in emotional label occurred despite the fact that both groups of subjects had received the same injection and should have been experiencing the same arousal.

The Schachter and Singer theory of emotions generated a great deal of interest and research. Many investigators extended and modified the theory. For example, Mandler (1982, 1984) focused on the conditions that cause arousal. He suggested that arousal results when people's behaviors or plans are interrupted. For example, a person who is trying to study is likely to become aroused if his or her roommate turns on a radio. Mandler added that the degree of arousal determines the intensity of our emotion, while our interpretation of the arousal determines its quality.

Criticisms of the Schachter-Singer Cognitive Theory. As we have seen, the Schachter and Singer approach suggests an exciting way to view emotions. However, some important criticisms have been raised. One serious problem is that some researchers have not been able to replicate the Schachter and Singer findings (Hogan & Schroeder, 1981; Rogers & Decker, 1975). Second, another investigator found that unexplained arousal caused subjects to feel uncomfortable and negative; they did not simply search the environment for an explanation, as suggested by Schachter and Singer (Maslach, 1979).

Finally, a different relationship between emotional label and arousal is possible. People may first give their feelings a label and then look for evidence to support that label. In order to test this idea, Pennebaker and Skelton (1981) told subjects that they would listen to an ultrasonic noise and then be asked questions about it. Some subjects were told that earlier research had shown that ultrasonic noise caused increased skin temperature, while other subjects were told that the noise might lower skin temperature. A control group was told nothing about the effects of the noise. The subjects then listened to a noise while the experimenter recorded their skin temperature. As predicted, those subjects who expected the noise to increase their skin temperature reported being warmer during the study than those who expected the noise to lower their skin temperature. While the self-reports were not related to actual skin temperature, they were related to changes in temperature. That is, subjects who expected the noise to increase temperature interpreted any change in temperature as an increase. On the other hand, subjects who expected to have decreased temperature believed that the same changes represented a decrease in temperature.

While the Schachter and Singer theory may not describe how we feel all emotions, it has played an important role in shaping the way investigators examine emotions. The theory has focused attention on the role of cognitive process and environmental cues in the experience of emotion. Clearly, our emotions are determined not only by body cues but also by environmental cues.

The Role of Appraisal

Imagine how Emmett Kelly felt when he saw smoke coming from the big top. Probably his heart rate increased tremendously, his muscles tensed, and he may have felt like running from the scene as the fear of fire and the thoughts of the potential tragedy gripped him. However, would Kelly's emotions and his actions have been the same if he had known that this was all part of another clown's act (for example, a clown performing an act that involved a little dog jumping out of a smoking house into a firefighter's net)? If he had thought this, it is unlikely that he would have become tense and fearful when he saw the smoke and heard a few screams. He may even have been amused by the screams as he imagined the success of the act in thrilling the spectators.

This example shows that the way we evaluate a situation affects not only our response but also our emotions related to it. It has been suggested that the first step in experiencing emotions is appraising (judging or interpreting) the situation (Arnold, 1960; Lazarus, 1968, 1981). The appraisal takes place immediately after the event is perceived, and it is intuitive

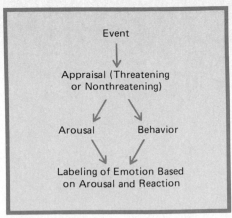

Figure 11–4
The Appraisal Theory

This theory suggests that people automatically appraise events as threatening or nonthreatening. This appraisal influences arousal and behavior. The experience of emotion is the result of interpreting the arousal and reactions. In some cases, behavior may follow the labeling of emotion.

Figure 11–5
In this experiment, all subjects saw the same film, but were divided into groups that heard one of four different sound tracks to accompany the film. As measured by their GSR, arousal was higher in the group that heard the sound tract emphasizing the pain of what was being seen in the film. (Speisman et al., 1964)

and automatic. It determines whether we view the situation as threatening or nonthreatening, and it also determines our reponse to the situation. Our emotion surfaces as we examine both our appraisal of the situation and our responses to it. Sometimes, the emotional label may guide our behavior. Figure 11–4 illustrates the appraisal theory.

In an effort to demonstrate this effect, Speisman and his colleagues (1964) showed subjects a film of the gory and painful circumcision rites practiced by an aboriginal Australian tribe to initiate boys into adulthood. While all subjects saw the film, Speisman varied the sound track that went with the picture. In one track (stress), the narration emphasized the pain associated with the rites. In the second (intellectual), the ceremony was described in a detached, clinical manner. A third track (denial) glossed over the pain and focused on the boy's happiness at becoming a man. Finally, in a control condition, subjects saw the film with no sound track. The experimenters recorded subjects' arousal (heart rate and GSR, or galvanic skin response) while they watched the film. As can be seen in Figure 11–5, subjects who watched the film with the sound track emphasizing pain were significantly more aroused than the other subjects. The investigators reasoned that the sound track influenced the subjects' judgment of the event, and so influenced their emotional response to it. The appraisal theory may explain the popular saying, "If you expect something to make you feel bad, chances are it will."

Somatic Theory of Emotions

Kelly made an interesting observation about his own feelings that leads us to another theory of emotions. He reported that no matter how he

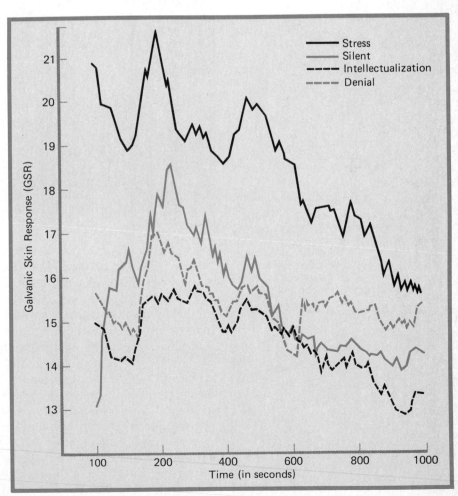

When we experience emotions, our facial expressions are usually dramatically altered. Somatic theory argues that these changes in expression help us determine and label our own emotions.

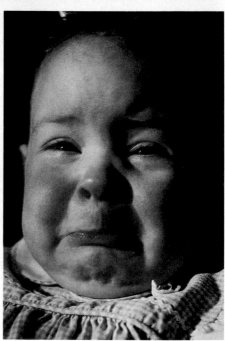

Figure 11–6
Somatic Theory of Emotions

The Somatic theory argues that events lead to reactions of the facial muscles and possibly behavior. The emotion label is the result of interpreting these reactions. The theory also holds that the autonomic nervous system can respond either before or after the labeling of emotion.

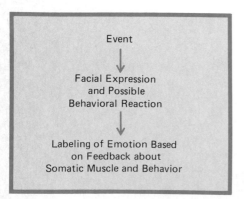

Event
↓
Facial Expression
and Possible
Behavioral Reaction
↓
Labeling of Emotion Based
on Feedback about
Somatic Muscle and Behavior

felt before a show, his feelings changed when he painted on the face of "Willie" and did his act. When he acted sad, he felt sad; when he acted and looked embarrassed, he felt embarrassed.

The other theories we have discussed focus on how arousal (such as rapid heartbeat, sweating, or fluttering stomach) affects emotions. This type of arousal involves the autonomic nervous system (see Chapter 2). Some investigators have argued that another nervous system plays a central role in the experience of emotion; this system is the *somatic nervous system* (Izard, 1977, 1982). The somatic nervous system controls many of our muscles, including the muscles of our face. These muscles not only receive messages about when and how to respond, they also feed messages back to the brain when they are activated.

According to the somatic theory, it is this feedback that is vital to our emotional experience (see Figure 11–6). The theory argues that there are distinct facial expressions that accompany a number of emotions including fear, excitement, joy, surprise, anger, scorn, and sadness. When an event occurs our facial muscles react with an emotional expression. The message of how the face is responding is transmitted to the brain, which uses this information to label a specific emotional state (Leventhal, 1982). Thus, our emotions are the result of our interpretation of our responses, especially those of our face. This theory allows that autonomic arousal may occur either before or after the labeling of an emotion. If the arousal occurs before, it may be incorporated in the label, influencing the interpretation about the magnitude of the emotion.

There is some support for this position. For example, one study found that subjects reported feeling happier after they were instructed to smile (Kleinke & Walton, 1982). In another study, subjects rated cartoons as more aggressive if they were asked to frown before they gave the ratings (Laird, 1974). Finally, research has found that reports of emotion and physiological arousal can be reduced if people are told not to change their facial expressions during arousing events, such as watching a funny movie or experiencing pain (Lanzetta et al., 1982; Oll & Lanzetta, 1984).

Theories of Emotion: An Overview

It may seem odd that while performers such as Emmett Kelly can so easily cause people to feel certain emotions, it is very difficult to explain why people experience those emotions. However, if we take another look at the theories we can see how this happens. The differences in the theories are important because they indicate the true complexity of emotions. But there are also important similarities in the theories.

All the theories show that events do not automatically lead to specific emotions. They also propose that no single factor is responsible for emotions. Instead, a picture emerges that shows emotions to be a combination of arousal, facial expressions, behavior, environmental events, and cognitive interpretation. Changes in any of these factors may alter the emotion that is experienced. Thus, while there is some question as to what components are most central and how these components are combined, we can see that emotions represent a unique combination of the mind and body.

 # NONVERBAL COMMUNICATION OF EMOTIONS

After Kelly joined the Ringling Brothers and Barnum & Bailey Circus, he had the opportunity to take his clown act to Cuba. He wondered whether they would be able to understand his act; would they recognize sadness in Willie's drooping eyes and turned-down mouth? Since Willie never spoke a word, it was very important that the audience respond to his actions and facial expression. On opening night Kelly bravely walked into the ring and began sweeping at the little white puddle that the spotlight threw at his feet. He heard some laughs and his spirits rose. Soon he heard the crowd hissing and waving him away. Kelly turned and ran off the stage, feeling that for the first time in his life he had found a group of people he couldn't communicate with (or who didn't like his act).

Once off the stage, Kelly sought out a clown that spoke Spanish and told him what had happened. The other clown laughed and explained, "In Cuba, that waving means they want you to come closer." He also told Kelly, "That isn't hissing as we know it in America; that's part of the handwaving—to get your attention, just as we do when we yell Hey" (p. 238).

The face shows others the emotion we are feeling, and may also help us to determine our own emotions.

Kelly's adventures in Cuba tell us two things about nonverbal communication. First, that it is possible to communicate without words and to communicate across national boundaries—the Cuban audience understood immediately what Willie was all about. The second thing is that the style of nonverbal communication used in some cultures may be misunderstood in others. How much of nonverbal communication is universal and how much is learned as part of one's culture?

The Face

The most important part of a clown costume is the face. Kelly would spend hours getting his face ready for a show; he worked on accentuating his mouth and eyes, building up his nose, and emphasizing the wrinkles in his brow. Research indicates that this concern with the face may be well placed.

In an interesting study, researchers cut photographs of faces into three partial pictures: brow-forehead, eyes, and mouth (Boucher & Ekman, 1975). These partial photos were then shown to judges who were asked to guess which of six emotions (surprise, anger, fear, disgust, sadness, or happiness) were being illustrated. The researchers discovered that different parts of the face are important for communicating different emotions. For example, the eyes are most important in communicating sadness, while the mouth best communicates happiness and disgust, and the forehead sends signals of surprise. All three parts of the face, however, are necessary to clearly communicate anger. In another study, Ekman and his colleagues were able to determine which of two films their subjects preferred simply by examining the subjects' facial expressions (Ekman, Friesen, & Ancoli, 1980). According to these investigators, we can accurately determine what other people are feeling if we can learn the "language of the face." However, this may not be an easy task—Ekman reports that there are over 7,000 different combinations of muscle movements in the face!

In an earlier study, Tomkins and McCarter (1964) tried to map out how the face communicates primary or basic emotions. As can be seen in Table 11–1, they found that each emotion has a characteristic facial pattern. It is interesting to note that their description of distress involves just those features that were drawn on Willie's face.

Body Language

Not only does our face speak, but according to one researcher, our bodies are also expressive (Birdwhistell, 1967). Birdwhistell used the term **kinesis** to mean the study of body language. He argued that no body

Table 11–1
Characteristic Facial Patterns for Eight Primary Emotions

Emotion	Facial Pattern
Interest–Excitement	Eyebrows down, eyes track, look, listen
Enjoyment–Joy	Smile, lips widened up and out, smiling eyes (circular wrinkles)
Surprise–Startle	Eyebrows up, eyes blink
Distress–Anguish	Cry, arched eyebrows, mouth down, tears, rhythmic sobbing
Fear–Terror	Eyes frozen open; pale, cold, sweaty, face; trembling; hair erect
Shame–Humiliation	Eyes down, head up
Contempt–Disgust	Sneer, upper lip up
Anger–Rage	Frown, clenched jaw, eyes narrowed, red face

Source: Tomkins & McCarter (1964).

After giving her speech, First Lady Nancy Reagan suddenly remembered that she had forgotten to introduce the president. This picture shows how clearly emotions can be communicated nonverbally.

movement is accidental or meaningless and that something is communicated in even the slightest movement. For example, Beier (1974) studied fifty newly-wed couples and found that conflict and insecurity were expressed by frequent self-touching, sitting with arms and legs crossed, and avoiding eye contact.

Physical distance also sends emotional messages (see Chapter 17 for a more complete discussion). One anthropologist found that people feel a sense of ownership of the space that directly surrounds them (Hall, 1966). They attempt to protect their personal space by "keeping their distance" from other people, and they feel uncomfortable if someone moves into this space. People will attempt to restore the proper space, the size of which is largely a function of the type of interaction and attraction involved. People allow friends to come closer than strangers. Thus, one way in which we communicate attraction is to get physically close to others.

An interesting feature of body language is that we are often unaware of it. We usually do not consciously decide that we will smile, dilate our pupils, and move closer to someone to show our attraction. Because of this lack of awareness, people may give themselves away through nonverbal cues when they are lying. Mehrabian (1971) asked subjects to tell a lie while he studied their body language. He found that people who are telling a lie show less frequent body movement, smile more, keep a greater distance from the listener, and lean backwards more than people telling the truth.

What does body language communicate? Efforts to decode specific messages from body movements have met with only moderate success. After reviewing the literature and observing many communicators, Mortensen (1972) suggested that our bodies may not communicate specific emotions. Rather, he suggested that the body indicates the *strength* of emotion, while the face expresses the *quality* of emotion being experienced. This is an interesting possibility that has not yet been fully explored.

Emotional Expression: Innate or Learned?

Clearly, we all use our face and bodies to express our emotions. But an interesting question is whether this expression is a natural innate tendency or whether it is learned. Almost 100 years before Kelly's experience in Cuba, Charles Darwin studied how humans express emotions. Darwin believed that the human expression of emotion is inborn and has definite survival value. He pointed out that many animals bare their teeth and the hair on their neck becomes erect when they are angry and ready to attack. This has survival value because other animals of the same species can readily interpret it and avoid the angered animal. Darwin pointed out, too, that humans also grit their teeth and the hair on their neck becomes erect when they are angry.

At the base of Darwin's evolutionary theory of emotion is the hypothesis that some, but not all, of the ways in which humans express emotions are inborn. In order to support this position Darwin needed to show two things: (1) Emotions are expressed the same way by all people regardless of their background, and (2) people inherit rather than learn the tendency to express emotions in these patterned ways.

Darwin made careful observations of the people he met on his voyages around the world. He found many similarities in the way people from different cultures expressed specific emotions. For example, he reported that Australian aborigines, African Kafirs, Malays, "Hindoos," and South American Guaranies frown when they are puzzled, and they express grief using similar facial signs. Darwin's observations were supported by Ekman, Sorenson, and Friesen (1969), who showed pictures of faces expressing various emotions to subjects in the United States, Brazil, Japan, New Guinea, and Borneo. The subjects were asked to identify the emotion expressed in each photo, and there was relatively high agreement in their judgments of the pictures. In a follow-up study, Ekman and Friesen (1971) found that even members of the Fore tribe, a preliterate group who led an isolated, almost Stone Age existence in New Guinea, were able to judge the facial expressions correctly. The high degree of agreement found in these studies suggests that there is some universality in the way people in different cultures express emotions. However, none of the cross-cultural studies found complete agreement, which suggests that culture and background also influence the way emotions are expressed. Kelly learned this painful lesson when he interpreted the waving hands of the Cuban audience to be signs of anger or disapproval.

While these cross-cultural studies demonstrate some degree of universality in emotional expression, they do not prove that this expression is inborn. It is possible that people in the various societies simply learn to express themselves in similar ways. How would you go about demonstrating that the nonverbal expression of emotions is innate rather than learned? Darwin answered this question by observing children who had been blind from birth. He reasoned that it would be impossible for these children to have learned the intricacies of nonverbal expression of emotions, since they could not observe others. His observations and those that followed showed that the emotional expression of both blind and blind-and-deaf children was similar to that of sighted children for a number of emotions (Eibl-

Members of the Fore tribe of New Guinea were asked to show on their faces the appropriate expression for each of several emotion stories. From the left, the emotion stories were: "Your friend has come and you are happy"; "Your child has died"; and "You are angry and about to fight."

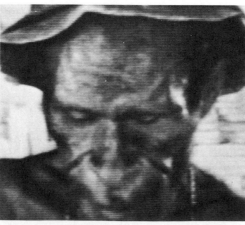

Eibesfeldt, 1973; Thompson, 1941). For example, the blind children cried when unhappy, laughed and smiled when happy, frowned and stamped their feet in defiance, and shook their heads as a gesture of refusal. These observations strongly support Darwin's position, but they cannot be taken as absolute proof; it is still possible that the children learned some of their responses by receiving rewards for "proper" expressions. These rewards could have been in the form of touching or hugging.

While many of our expressions are innate, learning and experience also play a role. Indirect evidence supporting this position comes from a number of studies examining people's ability to recognize emotions in others. This research shows that children become better at recognizing emotional expressions as they get older (Rosenthal et al., 1979) and that women are better than men at interpreting nonverbal cues (Hall, 1979). These differences cannot be due to genetic make-up and must, therefore, be the result of learning.

THE INFLUENCE OF EMOTIONS

We have now examined how people experience and express emotions. It is clear that emotions influence how we feel; happiness and joy make us feel good, while sadness and anger are associated with bad feelings. Recent research has shown, however, that the experience of emotion has a much wider effect on our lives.

Persuasibility

Spend an evening watching television commercials or leaf through a magazine and note the many advertisements. You will quickly become aware of the commercials or ads that are designed to arouse an emotion in you. Some will be aimed at getting you sexually aroused; others will try to get you excited by portraying an exciting sports game; still others will try to make you happy by picturing a cuddly kitten or a happy event. These attempts to arouse you are not accidents—research has found that people are more easily persuaded when they are emotionally aroused. This effect has been found for both positive emotions (Biggers & Pryor, 1982) and mildly negative emotional states such as fear (Leventhal & Niles, 1965).

Judgment

There is evidence that our emotions affect our judgment and memory (Bower & Cohen, 1982). In one study, subjects who were either happy, angry, or sad were asked to describe what was happening in a rather ambiguous picture (Clark, 1982). Subjects described the pictures to fit their own emotions; happy people saw happy events, sad people described sad events, and so on. Leventhal (1982) found that emotions affect how people respond to illness. For example, depressed cancer patients focused on their pain and the futility of life, while angry patients focused on coping and ways to combat their illness. Summing up these effects, one investigator noted that "when we are feeling good, the evidence indicates that we tend to view others more positively, to give more favorable reports about products we have purchased, to rate ambiguous slides more pleasant, to have more positive expectations about the future, and to give more positive associations to situations in which we imagine ourselves" (Clark, 1982, p. 264). Still another interesting finding is that men who were romantically aroused perceived a female who had expressed very different attitudes as being

People's attention becomes more narrow and restricted when they are emotionally aroused. The people in this audience are only paying attention to the performer while ignoring other events.

more similar to themselves than did men who were not aroused (Gold et al., 1984).

Perceptions

Favorite hangouts for pickpockets are sporting events and rock concerts. This is because people who are in an intense state of arousal tend to focus only on the event that is arousing them, and not on other events. Thus, it is often easy for a thief to steal wallets or purses from excited people who are intently focused on a sporting contest or musical event. An interesting effect of this attentive state is that it may intensify an emotional experience (Worchel & Cooper, 1983). For example, at a sporting event you may be aroused by the closeness of the crowd, the cheerleaders, the loud noise, and the sporting activity. However, because your attention is focused on the sports activity, you may attribute all arousal as resulting from the sporting event alone. Hence, you probably will judge the event as being more exciting than if you had watched it on television, alone.

SPECIFIC EMOTIONS

We have examined the basic theories of emotions and learned how people express emotions. Now we will illustrate these points by examining some specific emotions. Rather than making comments on an endless list of emotions, we will look at two: fear and love. These two emotions represent extremes on many levels. Fear is considered to be negative, while love is viewed as positive, and many of us will go to great lengths to experience this positive emotion. Also, fear has been studied a great deal, while love has, until recently, been seen as the domain of only poets and playwrights.

Fear and Anxiety

Fear is one of the most carefully studied emotions, along with the related concept of anxiety. Sigmund Freud built much of his psychoanalytic theory around the concept of anxiety (Freud, 1933). He believed that there are three types of anxiety: reality anxiety, neurotic anxiety, and moral anxiety.

Reality anxiety is the response to a specific danger in the environment. In other words, people know (or think they know) what is causing the anxiety. Reality anxiety is more popularly referred to as **fear,** which is a reaction to a specific object or event. On the other hand, Freud viewed **neurotic anxiety** as resulting from unconscious conflict within the person. Because the person is unaware of the roots of the anxiety, it is experienced as a general state of apprehension or dread with no definable object. **Moral anxiety** occurs because people fear they will do something contrary to their moral code; in this sense it is similar to guilt. Here, as with neurotic anxiety, the source is within the person. While we may distinguish between fear and anxiety based on the causes of each, the feelings and the physiological responses associated with the two states are very similar. Because of this, many investigators use the terms fear and anxiety interchangeably, and we will follow this practice in this text.

While we can develop new fears at almost any time in our lives, some fears are age-related. For example, infants between 6 and 9 months of age develop a fear of strangers (Sroufe & Waters, 1976). The fear of noises tends to decrease between the ages of 1 to 6 years, while the fear of animals increases until the age of 4 and then levels off. One fear that does seem to increase with age is the fear of imagined situations. An example of this age-related fear can be seen in the reaction of Emmett Kelly's mother upon seeing her 5-year-old son sitting atop the telegraph pole. She was overcome by fear because she imagined the numerous disastrous consequences that could result from the situation. However, the brave 5-year-old showed no fear because his imagery process had not developed to the extent that he could conjure up these consequences.

The Functions of Fear.   Imagine a life without fear. You could go into an exam for which you had not studied feeling confident. You could walk through the most wicked neighborhood on the darkest night feeling secure and safe. Sound nice? As hard as it may be to believe, a life without fear could be far more dangerous than Kelly's trapeze act. Fear is important in our lives; it leads us to avoid objects and situations that are dangerous.

Many fears are age-related. The fear of strangers develops in infants between the ages of 6 and 9 months.

For example, people who cannot swim may fear jumping into deep water. This fear leads them to refrain from this life-threatening activity.

Fear also prepares the body for action. The heart rate increases, muscles tense, digestive functions slow, and epinephrine pours into the bloodstream when we face the object of fear. These physiological changes enable us to act quickly and decisively. In addition, fear often leads to the strengthening or forming of social bonds (Suomi & Harlow, 1976). Children seek out their parents when they are fearful and, as we will see in the next section, fear leads adults to affiliate with others.

Thus, while the experience of anxiety may be unpleasant, it can play a constructive role in our lives. Of course, fear can become destructive. Problems occur when we develop irrational fears of objects that are not real dangers. Fear can also be destructive when we are consumed by it and are unable to direct our behavior to deal with the object of our fear.

Reactions to Fear and Anxiety. Research has shown that fear influences our perceptions, our performance, and our social behavior. With regard to our perceptions, Izard (1977) states that fear is the most limiting emotion. It leads to "tunnel vision," where people block out all stimuli except the object of their fear. Thinking becomes rigid and concentrated on the objects related to fear. This rigidity may lead to tragic results.

Anxiety also affects performance, but not in the way many people might expect. As we have shown, anxiety is accompanied by physiological arousal. According to the **Yerkes-Dodson principle,** the most effective level of arousal for performance depends on the difficulty of the task. Some degree of arousal is necessary to perform well on any task. However, while high levels of arousal will aid work on an easy task, they will hinder work on difficult tasks (see Figure 11-7).

In addition to perception and performance, social interaction is influenced by fear. In Chapter 10 we discussed in some detail an experiment which demonstrated that fear causes people to want to be with others.

A negative aspect of anxiety is that it can lead to symptoms such as insomnia, depression, inactivity, forgetfulness, and dread (Gatchel & Baum, 1983). These problems generally result when people feel helpless and are unable to cope with a situation and their feelings. In extreme cases, the end result can be a severe emotional disorder (see Chapter 13).

Defense Mechanisms

The reactions to anxiety and fear that we have discussed are relatively fleeting responses; fear may affect our performance or social interaction for a short period of time. However, there is another set of reactions to anxiety that people generally learn early in life. These reactions influence

Figure 11-7

The Yerkes-Dodson Principle

The graph shows the relationship between arousal and performance. A certain amount of arousal is necessary to function, but a very high degree of arousal, such as that caused by excess anxiety, makes it difficult to perform at all. The most effective level of arousal for performance depends on the difficulty level of the task. (After Hebb, 1955)

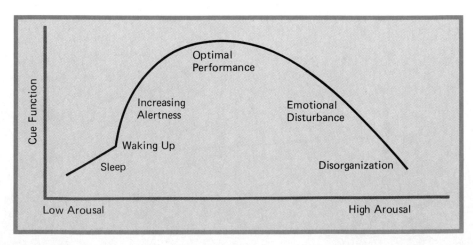

their personality (see Chapter 12) and characterize their reactions to anxiety throughout their lives. In order to demonstrate these reactions, let us examine two incidents from Kelly's life.

One of the incidents involves Kelly as a young boy. He recalls feeling very upset that he could not participate in sports activities with some of the older children. He felt slighted and lonesome, but he used his response in a positive way—he began to draw and paint. The result was that he developed some new skills.

The second incident occurred when Kelly was an adult. Eva and Emmett Kelly lived an event-filled life after they were married. However, the strain of constant travel and concern about finding jobs slowly destroyed their relationship. In 1935 Eva filed for divorce. For Kelly, the divorce was difficult. He experienced periods of melancholy—he felt alone, and he was worried about his future. But eventually Kelly was able to deal with his feelings. He developed new clown routines and worked a great deal. Kelly found new joy in his work and in circus life in general. It might seem odd that a person could react to the anxiety of being excluded by developing new talents, as Kelly did. But most of us would agree that people should respond directly to anxiety. By looking honestly at our feelings, we can learn effective ways to cope with them and to avoid their unpleasant recurrences in the future.

People, however, do not always deal with anxiety or fear in direct ways; the discomfort associated with anxiety makes it difficult to deal directly and constructively with it. Freud became aware of this problem when he observed people struggling with their anxieties. He found that people often distort reality in order to defend themselves against painful conflicts and anxieties. This distortion is done unconsciously to help people cope with unpleasant situations. Such distortions are known as **defense mechanisms,** and they are normal ways of coping with anxiety. However, because they involve self-deception and distortions of reality, they keep us from dealing with the basic causes of anxiety. Let us examine some of these defense mechanisms. Which do you use and what has been the result?

Rationalization. Rationalization means finding logical or desirable reasons for our behavior. In this way, we try to justify our actions by giving good reasons (making excuses) for them. Rationalization reduces anxiety by (1) limiting the person's responsibility or guilt for undesired events, and (2) decreasing the person's disappointment about failing by belittling the goal. A review of your own behavior should demonstrate how common this method is for dealing with anxiety in everyday life. How often have you tried to convince yourself that you are "better off" without the friend you just lost or the job you didn't get? These efforts to reassure ourselves are generally harmless, and they help us get over disappointments. However, too much reliance on rationalization can keep us from dealing with the reasons for failure or from taking helpful steps to avoid future failures.

Repression and Suppression. After their divorce, Emmett and Eva Kelly met occasionally. Kelly reports that their meetings were always cordial and that he had no ill feelings toward his ex-wife. Some of us may question the last statement. Regardless of the reasons for divorce, it is difficult to conceive of one that does not lead to some hurt feelings, a tendency to assign blame, and some hostility. It is possible that Emmett had these feelings but that he repressed them and thus was not aware of them. **Repression** means blocking or keeping unpleasant thoughts or memories from conscious awareness.

Although Freud was convinced that individuals do repress threatening thoughts, others have questioned this concept. They argue that these thoughts are merely suppressed. **Suppression** involves a conscious effort to avoid thinking about events. You have probably told yourself at times, "I don't want to think (or talk) about that." In other words, you'd rather forget "about the whole thing." Suppression is different from true repression, since you are aware of the thoughts and events. As we pointed out, repression occurs when you are unaware of the thoughts hidden in your unconscious. The controversy surrounding repression and suppression has not been resolved, and both concepts are still widely used in the clinical literature.

Displacement.   After the divorce, Kelly went through a period during which he was irritable, and he quarreled with others with little provocation. Some of these actions may have been the result of displacement. **Displacement** involves redirecting feelings from the individual that caused them to a safer or more available target. Thus, Kelly may have felt anger toward his ex-wife, but since she was not with him, he displaced his anger onto the people around him in the circus. Students may use displacement when they are angered by a professor's assignment of an unfair grade. It is somewhat risky to express this anger toward the professor, so students may take it out on their friends. Displacement allows people to work the stress out of their system and, thereby, reduce tension. However, it does not allow a person to deal with the real cause of the stress.

Sublimation.   Kelly threw himself into his work following the divorce. He planned new routines, did extra acts, and was determined to be the best possible clown. This response was similar to his reaction when he took up art after being rejected by his childhood friends. These behaviors may seem strange if we expect the problems associated with disappointment to interfere with our work. In many cases disappointment and depression do interfere with other activities, but sometimes people channel the energy associated with one activity or event into a seemingly unrelated activity. This rechanneling is called **sublimation**. It differs from displacement because it does not merely redirect feeling from one target to another; it involves changing the whole nature of the feeling. It is considered a defense because it keeps the individual from focusing on the earlier stress or unpleasant activity.

Projection.   All of use have qualities or feelings that we would rather not recognize or acknowledge. One way to protect ourselves from focusing on our own shortcomings is to *project* these shortcomings or undesirable traits on other people. **Projection** reduces our anxiety because it helps justify our actions or feelings: "If other people feel that way, it's not so bad for me to feel that way." Thus, people who are filled with hostility often see the people around them as being very hostile—this justifies their own actions and feelings, because it means they are reacting to other people's hostility.

Reaction Formation.   Earlier we pointed out that Kelly's relationship with Eva continued to be friendly after their divorce. This cordiality seemed to be somewhat of a surprise even to Kelly, who expected to respond with tenseness and hostility in his later meetings with her. As we suggested, he may have been suppressing or repressing his hostility and simply not recognizing it. There is, however, another possibility. Kelly's cordiality and even expressed friendliness toward his ex-wife may have been his way of dealing with his guilt and hostility. **Reaction formation** is a defense mechanism used to conceal unacceptable impulses by expressing instead the opposite impulse. For example, a man who fears that he has impulses to sexually molest children may react by voicing strong support for laws to severely punish child molesters. Or a woman who feels guilty about her negative feelings toward her mother may go out of her way to send her mother expensive gifts and cards on her birthday and other holidays. It is important to realize that these actions are not motivated by caring for the mother. Rather, they are attempts to hide negative feelings and reduce the guilt associated with these feelings. Admittedly, it is difficult to determine if an action is influenced by reaction formation or is an expression of true feelings. However, reaction formation is characterized by excessiveness in behavior. Thus the woman might not send her mother just any gift; the gift would probably be expensive to the point of straining her budget.

Defense Mechanisms: A Concluding Note. These are just a few of the defense mechanisms used to deal with uncomfortable feelings or stress. You can probably think of many more. After reading about defense mechanisms you may be shaking your head and thinking that people do funny things. It is, however, important to realize that we live in a complex physical and social environment and that we sometimes face difficulties adjusting to that environment. Pressures may build up slowly or we may be suddenly overwhelmed by a situation. In these cases we may need a temporary safety valve to help us cope with the difficulty. Defense mechanisms are safety valves that we all use. They redirect, reinterpret, or block out difficult situations and anxiety. Some may seem more unusual than others, but the basic purpose of all the defense mechanisms is the same. They can be helpful when used as a temporary crutch to help us stand up to difficult situations.

Because defense mechanisms do cover up much emotional experience, people who rely *solely* on these defenses are doomed to an unhappy life. They must constantly battle to keep their hidden anxiety under control. These people are often described as suffering from psychological disorders called neuroses (which we will discuss in Chapter 13).

Love

In 1923 sisters Eva and Mitzie Moore brought their trapeze act to John Robinson's Circus. Emmett Kelly watched with a pounding heart as Eva Moore hurled her tiny, slim body through the air. This young woman had talent and courage. There was only one problem: She also had a protective father. Mr. Moore did not want his children to get married and break up their circus act. Kelly fell in love, however, and soon he and Eva were arranging secret meetings. The romance progressed quickly despite the interferences, and when the circus set up in Charlottesville, Virginia, the couple sneaked off to the home of a preacher and got married.

While love is a common theme in our history, our literature, and even in our own daily lives, it has generally eluded the careful eye of the scientific researcher. Only recently have investigators begun to study love.

There are at least two reasons for this. One reason has been the popular feeling that love should not be the subject of scientific study. Love seems to have a mysterious and almost holy quality for many people, and there is an undercurrent of feeling that the scientific study of love would remove these qualities.

Another reason why love has not been widely studied is the difficulty encountered in defining love. Investigators are not the only ones who have had trouble with this endeavor. The Random House Dictionary gives 24 definitions of "love," while it only gives 5 of "hate." Unlike fear, shame, or anger, there are many components of love.

For example, one investigator identified four components of love: caring, needing, trusting, and tolerating (Kelley, 1983). Liking, on the other hand, involves evaluations of the other persons as mature or responsible. In one interesting study, people reported that caring was the most important component of love (Steck et al., 1982). Need was the second most important factor, and trust was rated third. While trust was least important in judging love, it was rated as very important in judgments of "friendship."

While we can identify some of the components of love, we have a more difficult time in giving a clear definition to the concept. How would you define love? Investigations suggest that this may be an unfair question.

Romantic love is a state of intense absorption in another. Mature love, on the other hand, involves less emotional intensity and is more controlled than romantic love.

Love may not be a single concept; rather, there are many types of love. One type of love is *romantic love*. This love is a "state of intense absorption in another . . . a state of intense physiological arousal" (Berscheid & Walster, 1978, p. 176). Romantic love is based on strong need. It develops quickly and may last for a relatively short time (Berscheid, 1983). It is accompanied by a high level of fantasy and often jealousy, sexual arousal, and fear of rejection. People report that love intensifies the events of their lives; love relationships have strong impacts on both satisfying and frustrating our needs (Dans, 1985). While romantic love is difficult to maintain, it may provide conditions from which other types of love can grow.

A second type of love is *mature* or *pragmatic love*. Mature love develops more slowly and involves less emotional intensity. A relationship based on mature love is more controlled, as compared to a romantic attachment. There is more a sense of sharing, with equal give-and-take between partners. Mature love is characterized by openness, communication, and the development of trust.

Altruistic love is yet another type of love (Kelley, 1983). It is seen in the relationship between parent and child, where the parent may sacrifice his or her own interests for the welfare of the child. A significant characteristic of altruistic love is that one partner gives without expecting to receive anything in return. It has been suggested that this type of love is very rare, if ever attained, in adult heterosexual relationships.

Learning to Love. Love is an emotion that most of us regard as positive and desirable, and many people spend much of their lives in search of it. An interesting but sad feature of love is the fact that some of these "searchers" have a very difficult time experiencing love. This is not because they do not have the opportunity to form a loving relationship, however. Many researchers believe that people must learn to love (Fromm, 1956, Harlow, 1971). The ability to experience love and form loving relationships is strongly influenced by past experience. Harlow (1971) demonstrated this by removing infant monkeys from their mothers shortly after birth. These monkeys received adequate care and feeding, but because they were reared in isolation they were deprived of maternal love. At 3 months, 6 months, and 2 years of age these monkeys were introduced to other monkeys their own age, and their interactions were observed. The isolated monkeys could not form friendships or play with their own age-mates. Nor were they receptive to sexual advances from other monkeys. Harlow impregnated some of the isolated female monkeys in order to study whether or not they could develop maternal love for their own offspring; the results were startling. The isolated mothers failed to feed or care for their young, and in many cases the mothers treated them so brutally that the infants would have been killed had the experimenter not removed them.

Emmett Kelly recalls "falling in love" with Eva as he watched her flying through the air on the trapeze. His story is reminiscent of romantic cases of "love at first sight." This "instant love" phenomenon, however, seems to be found more frequently in novels and poems than in actual life. In one study, 226 engaged couples were interviewed, with only 8 percent of the men and 5 percent of the women revealing that they felt "strong physical attraction" for their partners during the two days following their first meeting (Wallin, 1953). Thus, love does seem to be an emotion that takes some time to develop.

Effects of Arousal. There are, however, certain conditions that are conducive to falling in love. Berscheid and Walster (1978) suggest that it often follows the same course as any other emotion. That is, people experience arousal when they are together, and they attribute this arousal to love. This hypothesis leads to an interesting prediction that was tested by Dutton and Aron (1974). An attractive female experimenter approached men as they walked across a bridge. In half the cases, subjects walked on an old wooden bridge that swayed above a 230-foot precipice. All other subjects used a solid bridge that crossed a small stream 10 feet below. The experimenter showed the men a picture of a woman covering her face with her hand and asked the subjects to make up a story about the picture. After they finished, she gave the subjects her name and telephone number and said they could call her if they had any questions. Two differences were found in the responses of the two groups. First, the subjects who had just crossed the rickety bridge told more sex-related stories about the picture than subjects who had crossed the sturdy bridge. Second, subjects who had walked across the old wooden bridge were more likely to call the interviewer after the study than were subjects who had used the sturdy bridge. How can we explain these results? Dutton and Aron argued that crossing the swaying bridge aroused subjects. In most circumstances individuals would interpret this arousal as fear. However, when the subjects met the attractive female, they attributed their arousal as attraction or sexual arousal. On the other hand, individuals crossing the sturdy bridge would not be aroused and, hence, they were less likely to experience attraction when met by the female experimenter. While this explanation is consistent with the Schachter and Singer theory of emotion, an alternative explanation is that the attractive female reduced the men's fears on the rickety bridge. As a result of this fear reduction, the men became attracted to the experimenter (Kenrick & Cialdini, 1977).

The possibility that passionate love may result from the misidentity of arousal has some intriguing applications. Often, young lovers are faced with interference and disapproval from their parents. These interferences and frustrations may arouse the lovers, who may misidentify the cause of the arousal as being love. Thus, the attempts by parents to break up a love relationship may unwittingly increase the feelings of love between the thwarted adolescents. Another intriguing possibility derivable from the cognitive theory of passionate love was suggested by the Roman author and philosopher Ovid in his first century Roman handbook on romantic conquest. Ovid suggested that an excellent time to arouse passion in a woman was while she was engrossed in watching gladiators attack each other. The modern interpretation of this advice would be that the exciting gladitorial event arouses the woman, and the task of the amorous-minded male is to have the woman interpret the arousal as love or sexual excitement. It is, in fact, interesting that Kelly's love for Eva bloomed while he watched her perform dangerous and exciting feats on the trapeze.

Certainly, love is a complex emotion. Social scientists are just scratching the surface in understanding the pathways to love. It is, however, important to notice that a familiarity with the basic theories of emotion may help in understanding the more complicated emotions such as love.

STRESS

When Emmett Kelly was 19 years old he decided he had had enough of life on the farm; he wanted the excitement and fortune offered by the city. He packed his bag and off he went to Kansas City. However, life in the city was not what Kelly had imagined it would be. Everything about the city was different from his Kansas farm life, and Kelly spent the first few days exploring his surroundings. His introduction to Kansas City involved changing jobs frequently. He made sign frames, he painted the inside of steel tanks, he tried to drive a lumber truck, and he painted kewpie dolls. Kelly rarely had much money, and at times he went to bed hungry because he couldn't afford to buy food. The fast life of the city and the numerous changes in job and life style most certainly created a great deal of stress for this young man from the farm.

The concept of stress is one that we are all familiar with. Many of us use the term "stress" to describe a feeling or emotion. Stress, however, is not an emotion; rather, it is the process by which the individual responds to environmental and psychological events that are perceived as threatening or challenging (Gatchel & Baum, 1983). The events that give rise to stress are called stressors. Such events are *perceived* as threatening; this emphasis on perception means that an event may be a stressor for one person, but not for another person (Lazarus, 1982). For example, Kelly's move to Kansas City was a stressor because he worried about how he would support himself and whether or not he would make friends. This same move for a person who had ample resources and knew people in the city would not be perceived as threatening. Hans Selye, a Canadian physician, spent years examining the body's response to stressors. He found that the stress response, which he called general adaptation syndrome (Figure 11–8), was very systematic and could be charted in three phases (Selye, 1976). The first phase (the *alarm reaction*) involves the release of adrenal hormones into the bloodstream; heart rate and breathing rate increase. During this stage the body prepares to meet the stressor; in a sense, the body musters its defenses and prepares for action. Because the focus is on preparation, the body's resistance to disease is temporarily lowered. If the stressor continues to be present the body enters the *stage of resistance*. The body's functioning returns to normal levels as it attempts to resist and adapt to the stressor. We should note that while resistance to the specific stressor increases, there is lowered resistance to other stimuli. If the stressor disappears during this stage the person will quickly recover from the stress. On the other hand, if the stress-producing situation continues, the *stage of exhaustion* begins. This is the point where the body begins to wear down, and many of the symptoms of the alarm reaction reappear. If the stress is extreme and the stressor is not removed quickly, the person will die.

Accordingly to Selye, the general adaptation syndrome occurs regardless of the stressor. The stressor may be external (such as a loud noise or adverse climate), internal (such as disease or physical injury), or emotional (such as conflict, fear, or anger).

The Causes of Stress

The range of events that give rise to stress is almost unlimited. While the list of potential stressors is almost inconceivably long, there are certain characteristics that increase the degree of stress arising from a situation. We will quickly examine four of these factors: change, unpredictability, lack of control, and conflict. (In Chapter 17, we examine stress related to environmental variables.)

Figure 11–8
General Adaptation Syndrome (Selye, 1956).

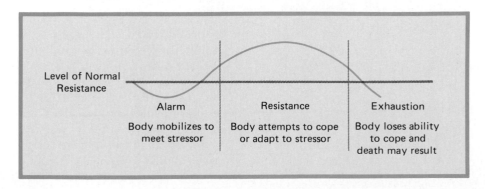

Level of Normal Resistance

Alarm	Resistance	Exhaustion
Body mobilizes to meet stressor	Body attempts to cope or adapt to stressor	Body loses ability to cope and death may result

Change. There are many ways to describe Kelly's life in the city, but it clearly involved a great deal of change. He changed his home, his life style, and his diet; his friends changed; and he changed jobs many times. Kelly enjoyed some of these changes, but some were not as pleasant as others. All of us experience a great deal of change in our lives; we look forward to some of the changes, while we would prefer to avoid others. It may, however, come as somewhat of a surprise to learn that change itself, whether positive or negative, is a stressor.

Thomas Holmes and his colleagues (Holmes & Masuda, 1974; Holmes & Rahe, 1967) studied thousands of medical histories and interviews and then questioned over 400 men and women in an effort to identify stressful events. Based on their research, the investigators developed the Life Events Scale (see Table 11–2), which attempts to give stress values to life events. As can be seen from the list, the common thread is that each event involves some *change* in an individual's life. Although many of the events are negative (death of a spouse, being fired from a job), some are clearly positive changes (outstanding personal achievement, vacation). Holmes argued that stress is directly related to major illness, and he suggested that the scale could be used to predict when an individual is most likely to suffer a severe illness. Specifically, he predicted that individuals who score over 300 points during a 1-year period run a high risk of being struck down by a major illness during the following year.

In general, research supports the position that major life changes create stress (Garrity & Marx, 1979; Rahe, 1975). Three points must be considered, however, when evaluating these findings. First, life change scores rely on people's memory and interpretations of the events. Second, some of the items in the Life Events Scale itself are directly related to health—for example personal injury or illness, change in eating habits, and change in sleeping habits. If we find that these events are related to later illness, we cannot clearly argue that *change* is responsible for illness. It may simply

Table 11–2
Life Event Scale

Life Event	Stress Value	Life Event	Stress Value
Death of spouse	100	Son or daughter leaving home	29
Divorce	73	Trouble with in-laws	29
Marital separation	65	Outstanding personal achievement	28
Jail term	63		
Death of close family member	63	Wife begins or stops work	26
Personal injury or illness	53	Begin or end school	26
Marriage	50	Change in living conditions	25
Fired at work	47	Revision of personal habits	24
Marital reconciliation	45	Trouble with boss	23
Retirement	45	Change in work hours or conditions	20
Change in health of family member	44	Change in residence	20
Pregnancy	40	Change in schools	20
Sex difficulties	39	Change in recreation	19
Gain of new family member	39	Change in church activities	19
Business readjustment	39	Change in social activities	18
Change in financial state	38	Mortgage or loan less than $10,000	17
Death of close friend	37	Change in sleeping habits	16
Change to different line of work	36	Change in number of family get-togethers	15
Change in number of arguments with spouse	35	Change in eating habits	15
Mortgage over $10,000	31	Vacation	13
Foreclosure of mortgage or loan	30	Christmas	12
Change in responsibilities at work	29	Minor violations of the law	11

Source: Holmes & Rahe (1967).

Our discussion thus far has suggested that stressful events exhaust people and lead to illness. The research supports this. Recently, however, investigators have found that some people do not react to stressful events by suffering and becoming ill; some people seem to respond to stress more effectively than others (Ganellen & Blaney, 1984; Kobasa, 1982). Kobasa (1979) studied executives and found that while some experienced illness due to high stress, it did not have this effect on others. She identified a personality—*the hardy personality*—that characterized those who did not experience illness. This personality has three dimensions involving *control*, *commitment*, and *challenge*. The hardy personality types tend to feel that life events can be controlled and

influenced; this belief enables them to avoid feeling helpless when difficult situations arise. The commitment component is reflected in a tendency to become actively involved in events, rather than to be passively influenced by them. The hardy personality types show a sense of purpose and meaning in their lives. Finally, these people view life events as a challenge and an opportunity to develop rather than as a painful ordeal to be endured. They transform threat into a challenge. It seems that hardy people experience stress, but their response to stress diminishes its negative effects.

It is still unclear exactly how these people buffer the effects of stress. It does not seem that they take better care of themselves than do others; for example, there is no relationship

between hardiness and physical exercise (Kobasa et al., 1982). On the other hand, there is a relationship between hardiness and social support (Ganellen & Blaney, 1984). Hardy people seem to get more support from others than people who do not score high on the hardiness scale. Because the data are correlational, we cannot determine whether social support plays a role in the development of a hardy personality, or possessing a hardy personality leads people to seek out and use social support. While more research is needed to clarify these and other points, keep in mind that all people do not react to life events in the same way. Also, the response to the stress of life events is an important factor in determining the likelihood of illness following stress.

be that the presence of illness or other health-related factors (eating and sleeping) are responsible for later illness (Schroeder & Costa, 1984). In order to test the theory that life change is related to future illness we would need to develop a scale that was not contaminated with items concerning present physical health. Finally, it is important to remember that the results suggest only a relationship between life changes and illness; clearly, not everyone who experiences a number of life changes will become ill.

The work on life changes has focused generally on relatively major events that are likely to occur infrequently over a year. Recently Richard Lazarus and his colleagues examined the effects of minor but frequent daily events on illness (Lazarus, 1981; Lazarus & Delongis, 1983). Lazarus identified two types of daily events involving change. On the negative side are *hassles*, which are the "irritating, frustrating, or distressing incidents that occur in our everyday transactions with the environment" (p. 58). Common hassles include misplacing or losing things, having too many things to do, and being concerned about physical appearance. On the positive side are *uplifts*, which include such pleasures as completing a task, visiting or phoning a friend, and feeling healthy.

Lazarus selected a sample of 100 people (48 men, 52 women) who were mainly middle-aged, middle-class, and white. At the beginning and at the end of the year-long study, the subjects filled out the Holmes and Rahe Life Events Scale. Each month during the study the subjects indicated the hassles and the uplifts that had occurred during the month. Lazarus also collected information on the subjects' physical health and mood during the study.

A number of interesting findings came out of this study. First, Lazarus found that hassles "turned out to be much better predictors of psychological

Change, even positive change, leads to stress.

and physical health than life events" (1981, p. 62). People who suffered frequent and intense hassles had the poorest health, while the link between major life events and health was weak. Lazarus also found that uplifts did not offset the negative impact of hassles. In fact, the study found that, for women, uplifts had a temporary negative effect on emotions and mental health.

While this study supports the position that change itself can be stressful and contributes to physical and mental alertness, Lazarus concludes, "It is not the large, dramatic events that make the difference, but what happens day in and day out, whether provoked by major events or not" (1981, p. 62). Clearly, more research needs to be done in this area; and this study suggests that research should focus on the effects of the small hassles in life as well as the more infrequent dramatic life changes.

While this research suggests that change can be a stressor, other research suggests that this statement must be qualified. One qualification is that the effects of change may be determined by the way the individual interprets or appraises the change (Coyne & Lazarus, 1981). For example, two men may learn that they are to be transferred to another city by the company that they work for. One of them may interpret the change as a sign that his boss likes his work, and he may begin to imagine making new friends and having new experiences. The other man may view the transfer as a sign that his boss is unhappy with his work, and he may think sadly about leaving his old friends and about the problems of adjusting to a new position. In this case the change is the same for both men, but the latter one will experience more stress. This point will be raised again when we discuss how to cope with stress.

Finally, before we accept change as a villain, we should realize that a lack of change can also be stressful. We saw in Chapter 5 that sensory deprivation and social isolation, which are characterized by a lack of stimulation, can be very stressful. Similarly, boredom and monotony can distress people. In fact, Kelly writes that he was becoming depressed and restless with his dull life on the farm. It was this boredom that led him to seek change and move to Kansas City. Taking another perspective, one researcher reported that if a person expects change, no change may actually be more stressful than the expected change (Graham, 1974). You can understand this if you have ever spent time preparing for an exam only to find out that it has been postponed, or if you have had an expected vacation cancelled.

Despite these qualifications it is clear that change in many situations can create a great deal of stress. Change, whether positive or negative, requires the individual to make psychological and physical adjustments. These adjustments place certain demands on the body and, hence, each is experienced as stress. Also, change often makes our lives less predictable and reduces our feelings of control. As we will soon see, both of these factors are stressors.

Unpredictability. While all change is stressful, we are able to predict and prepare for some events while others are unpredictable. For example, you know that you will graduate college on a certain date, and if you are planning a wedding, you probably will know many months in advance the date on which you will get married. Many other events, however, happen in a very unpredictable fashion.

Unpredictability is stressful because you cannot plan for these random events—you have to be constantly "on your toes." One of the most vivid examples of unpredictability occurs in the job of air-traffic controllers. Imagine yourself as a controller at Chicago's O'Hare Airport, where an airplane lands or takes off on the average of every 20 seconds. While some of the flights are scheduled, many others are not. Martindale (1976)

compared the medical records of 4,000 air-traffic controllers with those of second-class Air Force airmen who generally have regular and predictable jobs. The controllers were significantly more likely to suffer from high blood pressure, anxiety attacks, peptic ulcers, and depression.

You may wonder exactly how stressful unpredictability really is. The answer seems to be that it is highly stressful. In an experiment, rats were allowed to choose between predictable and unpredictable shock (Badia, Culbertson, & Harsh, 1973). If a rat pushed a button at the start of the study, all the shocks received would be preceded by a warning tone. If the lever was not pushed, no warning tone preceded the shocks. The tone allowed the rat to predict when the shock would come. Not only did the rats prefer the signaled shocks, but they maintained their preference even when the predictable shocks were longer and stronger than the unpredictable shocks.

Lack of Control.   After overcoming his early fears, Kelly loved the city life. He could choose where and what he ate because of the wide variety of restaurants. He could decide what type of entertainment would fill his evenings. He had a wide variety of people from which to choose his friends. And he found that if he became bored with one job, he could always find other types of work. In short, Kelly found that the variety of the city offered him a chance to control his own destiny and life. These opportunities for control may well have reduced the stress that Kelly might otherwise have experienced in the city.

In order to study the effects of control, a group of elderly residents in a nursing home were given more control over their day-to-day lives (Langer & Rodin, 1976). These residents were able to do such things as choose their own meals, care for plants in their rooms, and decide how to arrange the furniture in the rooms. A second group of residents were treated according to the standard nursing home routine where staff members make all decisions on these issues. The results of the study showed that residents given control over their own lives became more alert and more involved in activities than residents who did not have this control. The residents given control also showed significantly greater improvement in their health than residents who did not have control. In fact, during the 18 months of the study, only 15 percent of the patients with control over their daily lives died; 30 percent of the comparison group died.

Many events in our environment may be particularly stressful because they emphasize our vulnerability and lack of control. For example, natural disasters such as earthquakes or nuclear accidents such as Three Mile Island cause stress for many people long after they have passed. Events such as these force people to see that they cannot control their environments. A similar effect is seen in victims of crime (Normoyle & Laurakas, 1984). People who are robbed, raped, or assaulted are not only burdened with the immediate injury; they must also struggle with the fact that these incidents show that they are not in control of their environment and their own bodies. Because of this, the after effects of these acts can be equally or more devastating.

It is not entirely clear why control reduces stress. One view is that having control increases the predictability of events and allows people to feel more prepared to deal with their environment (Pervin, 1963). Whatever the reason, we do know that the degree of control people have over their lives influences the amount of stress that they experience.

Conflict.   Kelly had an important choice to make when he found that he would have to be a clown in the circus: Would he do a white-face act like other clowns, or would he develop a whole new character? While there were strong points in favor of each of the acts, Kelly had to choose one—he couldn't do both. This is an example of **conflict,** which is a state that occurs when a person is motivated to choose between two or more mutually exclusive goals or courses of action. Events are mutually exclusive when choosing one automatically eliminates the other.

Some conflict occurs almost every time you make a choice; the degree of conflict is influenced by the attractiveness of each choice and by how equally they are matched in attractiveness. (For example, there would be little conflict in choosing between a new Rolls-Royce and a broken-down 1962 Ford.) Conflict has been found to be one of the conditions that causes stress for people. While there are many situations in which a person will experience conflict, investigators have identified four major types of categories of conflict (Lewin, 1931; Miller, 1944). In defining these types, they have focused on people's tendencies to either approach or avoid a goal.

1. Approach-Approach Conflict. After Kelly had become famous as the clown Willie, he was offered a chance to act in the movies. This excited him, because it meant that millions of people could see Willie, and it also offered him financial rewards. However, becoming an actor would force Kelly to give up the circus for a certain amount of time. He loved working with circus people and dealing with live audiences. Thus, Kelly was faced with making a choice between two very attractive alternatives.

This is an example of an approach-approach conflict, which involves a choice between two attractive goals. In theory, this conflict should be easy to resolve, because it is a "no lose" situation—either choice brings rewards. However, anyone who has had to make the choice between two good job offers or two attractive dates knows that this type of conflict can be stressful.

2. Avoidance-Avoidance Conflict. This type of conflict results when people must choose between two unattractive goals. Kelly faced this type of conflict when he considered divorcing Eva. He felt that he was unhappy with Eva, but he also knew that he would be unhappy without her. Thus the choice between whether to stay married or get divorced involved two unattractive goals. This type of conflict is difficult to resolve. For this reason, people faced with this situation often try to delay making a decision. They sometimes hope that if they delay long enough, they can either escape the situation or something will happen that will make the decision for them.

3. Approach-Avoidance Conflict. Kelly's first job offer in the circus involved being a clown. This created a great deal of conflict for him. On the positive side, he would be with the circus, and he would be earning a regular salary. On the negative side, however, Kelly knew nothing about clowning

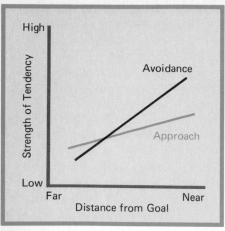

Figure 11–9
The graph shows approach and avoidance tendencies as one nears a goal. Both approach and avoidance curves increase the closer one gets to the goal, but the avoidance curve increases more rapidly than the approach curve.

and he really wanted to be a trapeze artist. The approach-avoidance conflict involves only one goal which has both attractive and unattractive qualities. People's desire to both obtain the goal and avoid it traps them in conflict.

4. Double Approach-Avoidance Conflict. This type of conflict results when a person has to choose between two goals, each of which has both positive and negative qualities. For example, as a teenager, Kelly had to choose between staying on the farm or going to the city. Kelly had many friends (+) and security (+) at home on the farm, but he was bored (−). On the other hand, Kansas City offered excitement (+) and jobs (+), but he had no friends there (−). The double approach-avoidance conflict is the most common of the four types we have discussed, because it is rare that people are faced with goals that are completely positive or negative. In fact, many conflicts that appear to be simple approach-approach conflicts can actually be viewed as double approach-avoidance conflicts, because choosing one goal (+) means giving up the other (−).

As we all know, conflicts can be hard to resolve. An interesting point about most conflicts is that the closer we get to a goal, the stronger the approach and avoidance forces become. Unfortunately, as can be seen in Figure 11–9, the strength of the avoidance tendencies increases at a faster rate than the strength of the approach tendencies. In other words, the closer you get to making a decision, the more you will be disturbed by the negative qualities of the choice. You may have experienced this in choosing what college to go to: When you first learned that you had been accepted at your two top choices, you were very happy and felt the decision would be easy. However, as the decision deadline approached, you found the choice increasingly hard to make. This fact not only increases the stress associated with conflict, but, as we will see in Chapter 15, it increases how hard we must work to justify our final decision.

The Reactions to Stress

All of us experience stress many times each day. In fact, some of us seek out stress-producing situations by engaging in sports such as sky diving or going to scary movies. In most cases, the level of stress is not particularly high, and if it becomes too uncomfortable, we take the necessary steps to reduce the stressor. However, some people are subjected to such high levels of stress or to such long periods of stress that they develop severe physical or psychological symptoms. Let us examine some of these symptoms. First, we will take a quick look at bodily reactions and then examine some behavioral reactions.

Psychophysiological Disorders. Few college students need to be told that stress can make people physically sick. Anyone who has had to prepare for a big exam knows that stress can lead to a loss of appetite, insomnia (the inability to fall asleep), and tension headaches. **Psychophysiological disorders,** often called psychosomatic illnesses, are real physical illnesses in which stress is a contributing factor. The list of psychophysiological disorders is long and includes a surprising range of illnesses.

One of the most common disorders associated with stress is the *peptic ulcer.* Ulcers are lesions or holes that develop in the stomach or upper part of the small intestine. These holes are caused by the oversecretion of stomach acid, which literally eats through the lining of the digestive tract. Ulcers are often referred to as the "executive's disease," and it was once thought that the stress associated with making decisions was responsible for the oversecretion of the acid. However, further research indicates that control and decision-making are not responsible for ulcers (Weiss, 1972). Rather, it is the pressure arising from the need to respond quickly over an extended period of time, and the uncertainty associated with choosing an effective response, that cause ulcers.

Other psychophysiological disorders include asthma, hypertension (high blood pressure), headaches, and heart disease. For example, one group of researchers found that widowed people are more likely than others to die of heart disease; this is especially true within 6 months of the spouse's death (Stroebe & Stroebe, 1983). Stress has even been related to cancer and the rate of tumor growth (Adler, 1981; Sklar & Anisman, 1981).

Stress contributes to getting sick in a number of ways. First, because the body must mobilize to deal with the stress, the resistance to diseases is lowered. Second, people may become so preoccupied with or depressed about the stress that they fail to notice or deal with symptoms of impending illness. We do not know exactly what factors determine the specific psychophysiological illness a person will suffer. That is, why does one person get colds when distressed while another suffers from ulcers? Part of the answer may involve constitutional weakness. That is, people may be born with or develop a weak spot in their stomach. When these people encounter stress, the symptoms find expression in the already weak stomach and an ulcer appears. Other people may have a high susceptibility to colds, and, when stress lowers their immunity, they catch colds. Another factor may be the environment or culture in which we live. Certain bacteria or viruses are more common in some environments than in others, and lowered immunity will allow these more common bacteria to take control of our systems, giving rise to specific diseases associated with particular bacteria or viruses.

Coronary-Prone Behavior Pattern. Stress not only causes changes within our bodies, it also may move us to action. Some people seek to "get away from it all" when they feel the pressure building. These people may take a relaxing drive or engage in a hobby to relieve the pressure. Others may turn to alcohol or drugs when they feel pressured. However, some people may respond to stress by becoming competitive and hostile. These people often feel increasing time pressures to "get the job done" and they feel overwhelmed by external demands. Their desires for achievement increase and their actions and speech patterns become more animated and abrupt. These individuals give the impression of someone running on "nervous energy" with the single goal of achievement (Friedman & Rosenman, 1974; Jenkins, 1976). This constellation of behaviors has been labeled *Type A behavior* or *coronary-prone behavior pattern* because people who behave this way are more likely to become the victims of heart attacks than those who do not respond to stress in this manner. While early research focused on males, more recent research (Matthews & Carra, 1982) has found that Type A women exhibit similar behavior patterns to Type A men. The Type B pattern has been defined as an absence of these behaviors (see Table 11–3). Investigators argue that Type A behavior is a learned response to stress (Glass, 1977). The Type A person seems to be trying to get control over the situation. While this may be adaptive in some cases, it is not possible to be in complete control in all situations. This intense desire for control causes Type A people to be more likely to blame themselves for failure than are Type B people (Musante et al., 1984). When

Table 11–3
Research Findings on the Type A Personality

Type A people are more likely than Type B people to:
1. Be aggressive when frustrated (Strube et al., 1984)
2. Judge that a time period has passed more quickly (Burnam et al., 1975).
3. Show impatience when slowed down in making a decision (Glass et al., 1974).
4. Be motivated to win in conflict situations (Smith & Brehm, 1981).
5. Exaggerate the meaning of information from an opponent in conflict (Smith & Brehm, 1981).
6. Show higher blood pressure when performing a competitive task or when challenged (Goldband, 1980).
7. Suppress fatigue or deny being tired (Carver, Coleman, & Glass, 1977).

talking about the cause of events, Type A people often refer to themselves (Rhodewalt, 1984).

There have been a number of interesting experiments demonstrating the unrelenting drive of these Type A people. Burnam, Pennebaker, and Glass (1973) identified Type A and Type B people. They presented them with 240 simple arithmetic problems ($6 + 9 - 2 = $ ____). Half the subjects were told that they had only 5 minutes to solve as many problems as they could, while the other subjects were given no time deadline. The results indicated that Type A and Type B subjects solved an equal number of problems when working under a time deadline. However, when there was no time deadline, Type A subjects solved significantly more problems than Type B subjects. Thus, Type A subjects worked fast regardless of whether or not there was a deadline. These Type A subjects could not relax; they imposed their own time deadlines when there was no external deadline. In another study, rewards were offered to Type A and Type B subjects if they responded slowly (Glass, Snyder, & Hollis, 1974). They found that the Type B subjects had little difficulty learning to respond slowly. However, the Type A subjects had a great deal of difficulty learning to slow down their response rates.

We have painted a somewhat dismal picture of Type A people. There is, however, another side. Type A people have been found to report greater life satisfaction and higher self-esteem than Type B people (Sporacino et al., 1981). They also feel more involved in their work than do Type B people.

Learned Helplessness. The Type A person is constantly striving to control his or her environment; the greater the difficulty and ambiguity of the situation, the harder this person tries to gain control. There is, however, another response pattern that may result from finding that one's environment cannot be controlled. In this case, people may make repeated attempts to control stressful events in their environment. If they fail to gain control, they may give up, even in situations where control is possible. In a sense, these people have learned to respond as if they were helpless pawns; they have developed a state of **learned helplessness** (Seligman, 1975). Apathy, depression, reduced intellectual abilities, and negative emotions are associated with learned helplessness.

The effects of learned helplessness have been illustrated by one researcher (Hiroto, 1974). In this experiment, subjects in one condition were

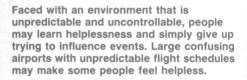

Faced with an environment that is unpredictable and uncontrollable, people may learn helplessness and simply give up trying to influence events. Large confusing airports with unpredictable flight schedules may make some people feel helpless.

forced to listen to noise, and they were unable to escape it. In another condition, the subjects could stop the loud noise by pushing a button, and in a third condition, the subjects were not exposed to any noise. In the next phase of the study, all subjects were given a finger shuttle box. The box was designed so that loud noise was played when the subject's finger was on one side of the box. A subject could stop the noise by moving one finger to the other side of the box. Subjects who had been in the escapable or no noise conditions in the first phase of the study quickly learned to control the noise. However, subjects who could not escape noise in the first phase of the experiment did not learn to control it in the second phase.

An unfortunate aspect of learned helplessness is that it tends to feed upon itself. That is, people who stop trying because they feel they can't control their stressful environment may never learn to exercise control in situations where control is possible. In addition, the learned helplessness response may generalize from one situation to another (see Chapter 17). For example, one group of investigators found that students who were unable to control social interactions in their dormitories showed a pattern of learned helplessness in a laboratory setting (Baum & Valins, 1977).

Delayed Stress Reaction. Of all the stressful events a person can experience, being taken captive must rank as one of the most stressful. After the Vietnam War was over, heart-rending scenes of POWs who had been held prisoner for years were commonplace news items. In 1976, the world was puzzled by the bizarre actions of Patricia Hearst, a wealthy heiress, who had been kidnapped by the Symbionese Liberation Army, an underground political group. In 1979, threats of war filled the air when 52 U.S. State Department employees were taken hostage in Iran. In each of these cases and in many other hostage situations, the change, uncertainty, and lack of control in the situation is extreme. Given the degree of stress, people are amazed to see how fit many captives look after their ordeals.

However, recent observations suggest that surviving captivity may only be the first step on a rocky road to recovery for hostages. These people must undergo a great deal of psychological and social adjustment, which may take months and even years. One problem is the so-called *delayed stress reaction*. This response includes depression, anxiety, an inability to concentrate, insomnia, edginess, and night sweats (Lagone, 1981). What is unusual about this condition is that it may occur months or years after the captivity has ended and after the person seems to have readjusted to his or her environment. Flashbacks of the captive situation may occur for long periods of time after release. There is no way to control or even anticipate when such flashbacks will occur. Along with the flashback come the arousal and emotions that were experienced during the period of captivity.

During captivity many hostages may experience a sense of bewilderment and anger that their country, family, or friends have not come to their rescue. The question "Why don't they do something to get me out of here?" may constantly be in the back of a hostage's mind. However, hostages cannot express their feelings during captivity because the captors will interpret such feelings as signs of weakness. In many cases, immediately after being released the hostage is made the center of attention. The expression of anger at the assumed inactivity of others would at this point be viewed as inappropriate, so these feelings must be repressed. Some ex-hostages have experienced a delayed anger reaction long after their captivity has ended. Because of the time delay, many people cannot understand the reasons for this response, and the anger seems to be without cause.

While this chain of events may explain the response in some cases, it cannot be the whole story because the delayed stress response is not only suffered by victims of captivity; many veterans of the Vietnam War who

Research shows that the effects of captivity may be seen long after freedom is achieved. Delayed stress reaction involves depression, anxiety, anger, insomnia, and an inability to concentrate.

were not captives have suffered such reactions. Psychologists do not completely understand why these delayed reactions occur or what factors bring on the attacks. There is some evidence that suggests that people who were already predisposed to anxiety disorders before the stressful situation are most likely to suffer from delayed stress reaction (Committee of Veterans' Affairs, 1981).

 # COPING EFFECTIVELY WITH STRESS

Emmett Kelly longed to do the trapeze act in the circus. He thought his chance had come when he was offered a job in Howe's Great London Circus. Unfortunately he found that the job involved being a clown, not swinging from the high trapeze. The situation created a great deal of stress for Kelly. How could he cope with the disappointment?

Kelly had many options. Many of the responses we have previously examined are essentially examples of trying to cope with stress; however, most of these are ineffective. For example, Kelly may have responded by becoming tense and anxious, thinking he would never be a trapeze artist. This tension may have given rise to psychophysiological illnesses such as ulcers. Or he could have responded by adopting a pattern of learned helplessness. However, there are other more effective responses to cope with stress. Let us review coping responses according to three categories: cognitive, informational, and behavioral (Taylor et al., 1984).

Cognitive Responses

Reappraisal. Not getting the job that he wanted was disappointing and stressful, but the degree of stress would have increased greatly if Kelly interpreted this failure to mean that he would never do the trapeze act. As we pointed out earlier, the amount of stress experienced is as much a function of the way we interpret the event as it is due to the event itself (Brenner, 1984). Thus Kelly could have reduced his stress by reexamining the situation and identifying the positive aspects of it. For example, he would not be doing a trapeze act, but he would be working with the circus. This would give him the opportunity to watch trapeze artists and perfect his act. Further, being a clown would offer him the chance to be the center of the audience's attention and he could dazzle them in a different way. By viewing his situation in this manner he could turn defeat into a minor victory and reduce the sting of his disappointment. Note that reappraisal does not involve denying the situation or the disappointment; it does involve looking at the good as well as the bad.

The effectiveness of this approach was demonstrated in a study of patients undergoing surgery (Langer et al., 1975). In many cases, patients tend to look at the gloomy side of surgery; they think of the pain, the risks, and the inconvenience of a hospital stay. One group of patients was trained to look at the good and bad aspects of surgery. They acknowledged the pain and risk, but they focused also on how the operation would improve their health and give them the opportunity to participate in new activities. In addition, the patients were trained to consider that the hospital stay would give them the opportunity to rest and get away from daily stress. Patients who were taught this approach experienced less pain and requested less pain medication than patients who did not go through the reappraisal technique.

Belief in Self-Efficacy. As we pointed out, the feeling that one is not in control and cannot handle the situation is very stressful. Bandura

(1982) focused on this aspect of stress and suggested that stress could be reduced by increasing people's *belief in their self-efficacy*, their judgment of their ability to cope with situations (see Chapter 14). Bandura suggests that people's reaction to stressful situations and, indeed, the amount of stress they experience is directly related to their beliefs about the effectiveness of their actions.

According to this theory, we develop beliefs in our self-efficacy through our experiences. Hence, people can be trained to handle situations that were once out of their control. There are many ways that this training can occur. Bandura found that he could reduce people's fear of snakes by having them successfully perform a number of unrelated tasks. Other research suggests that regular exercise may be beneficial in reducing stress (Davidson & Schwartz, 1977). There are a number of possible reasons, both physiological and psychological, for this effect. One possibility is that exercise may allow us to gain mastery over our environment and increase our belief in our self-efficacy.

Informational Responses

Kelly's job offer as a clown was stressful not only because it was not the position he wanted, but also because he knew nothing about being a clown. The uncertainty caused by his lack of information contributed to the stress of the situation. In a similar way, uncertainty may contribute to the stress people experience upon learning that they have a physical ailment such as cancer (Taylor et al., 1984). Imagine that you have just been told that you have cancer; a million thoughts probably run through your mind including the fear that you may soon die and the gruesome stories that you have heard about the treatment of cancer. These thoughts, which may well be based on your ignorance of cancer, will greatly increase your stress and may actually interfere with effective treatment of your condition. One study found that patients who believed their condition was incurable delayed treatment two and a half times longer than people with the same disease who believed it was curable (Safer et al., 1979).

Seeking out information and gaining a better understanding of the stressful situation can be an important step in coping with stress. Seeking out information not only helps people make an accurate appraisal of the situation, but it also can help them develop an effective response to cope with their stress.

Behavioral Responses

Exercise, rest, and good diet are behavioral responses that help the body cope with stressors. In addition to behavioral responses that prepare the body, we can add the broader response of seeking *social support* (see Chapter 14). Social support involves enlisting the aid of other people to help deal with the stressor. The value of social support can be seen in the fact that people often cope better with severe stress associated with a natural disaster, for example, than they do with a series of less severe stressors such as not getting a promotion or having conflicts with a spouse. There are a number of possible reasons for this. One focuses on the availability of social support (Gottlieb, 1983). A natural disaster such as a tornado or flood generally affects a number of people, and these people generally band together. More minor stressors tend to affect only a few people at a time, and therefore the social support is not readily available.

Social support can take many forms including (1) physical assistance; (2) material aid; (3) intimate interactions; (4) guidance or the provision of information; (5) feedback, such as helping one understand problems; and (6) social participation, such as cheering someone up. One individual may offer a number of types of social support, or a person may seek different types of social support from different people. For example, a person may rely on his or her parents for material aid, a doctor for guidance, and a friend for feedback and social participation. Research has found that social support can be very effective in reducing stress and the psychological problems that result from stress (Heiler & Swindle, 1982). In addition, social support can have a positive effect on health.

Given the variety of types of social support, it is not unusual to find that social support can reduce stress in a number of ways. Social support can help people reappraise potential stressors. Second, social support may reduce stress by supplying people with information and guidance about how to deal with stressful situations. In some cases, people may have difficulty interpreting their situations or emotions; seeing how others respond in the setting can provide useful information for interpreting one's own feelings. Third, the presence of other people may have a soothing effect and reduce the intensity of negative emotions (Friedman, 1981). Fourth, having the support of others may serve to distract the person from the stressor; this temporary distraction may reduce the intensity of the stress. For example, a student who is so worried about an exam that he or she cannot study effectively may benefit by having friends provide an atmosphere that is relaxing. Fifth, social support may increase a person's self-esteem; knowing that one has friends who are willing to help can make a person feel better about himself or herself. Finally, social support may be aimed at helping a person directly cope with stress.

SUMMARY

1. **Emotions** are feelings that are accompanied by physiological changes—the changes affect behavior. One method of measuring the arousal associated with emotions, the modern polygraph, uses physiological changes in order to tell if a person is lying.

2. Several viewpoints have contributed to the present theories of emotions. James and Lange argue that external events cause physiological changes in people and that it is the perception of these changes that leads to emotions.

3. Cannon, however, showed that emotions can occur in the absence of physiological responses. Cannon and Bard propose that emotions and physiological changes occur together.

4. Schachter and Singer introduced cognitions as most important in labeling emotions. They suggest that once people are physiologically aroused, they will search for environmental cues to determine the nature of their emotional arousal.

5. Another theory assumes that the way we interpret a situation influences the emotion we experience. In other words, interpretation or appraisal comes before emotion.

6. According to the somatic theory, the somatic nervous system, which controls many of our muscles, sends messages to the brain when muscles respond to an event. Thus, emotions are the result of how we interpret our responses.

7. Emotions can be expressed without words. Facial expressions and body language are effective methods of communicating emotions.

8. Emotions affect how easily persuadable we are. They also affect judgment and memory and they influence perceptions.

9. Two emotions have been examined in this chapter. The first, **fear,** which may be either inborn or learned, serves two important functions. Fear causes us to avoid situations that may be dangerous and, when danger is encountered, prepares the body for action.

10. People often cope with their anxiety by using unconscious **defense mechanisms** such as **rationalization, repression, suppression, displacement, sublimation,** and **projection.** Although these mechanisms may help to temporarily redirect or block out anxieties, they are seldom effective over an extended period.

11. Although **love** has not been as widely studied as fear, it has been suggested that romantic love differs from mature love and that our ability to love may be affected by our past experiences.
12. **Stress** was defined not as an emotion, but as a general response by the body to any demand made on it. **Stressors** are the events that cause stress. Several factors that affect the amount of stress experienced in a situation are change, unpredictability, and lack of control. Change, whether positive or negative, may be stressful; however, the stress is lessened if we are able to predict and control the situation.
13. Another element of stress is **conflict,** which is a state that occurs when a person is motivated to choose between two or more mutually exclusive goals or courses of action. Some of the various types of conflict are approach-approach, avoidance-avoidance, approach-avoidance, and double approach-avoidance.
14. When people are exposed to a great deal of stress, they may develop **psychophysiological disorders,** ranging from insomnia and headaches to ulcers and heart attacks.
15. When people repeatedly find themselves unable to control a stressful situation, they may develop a state of **learned helplessness** in which they become apathetic, depressed, and do not make any effort to control their environment.
16. There are three major categories of coping responses: cognitive, informational, and behavioral.

Key Terms

conflict
defense mechanisms
displacement
emotions
fear
galvanic skin response (GSR)
general adaptation syndrome
kinesis
learned helplessness
love
moral anxiety
neurotic anxiety
polygraph

projection
psychophysiological disorders
rationalization
reaction formation
reality anxiety
repression
stress
stressors
sublimation
suppression
Type A behavior
voice stress analyzer
Yerkes-Dodson principle

Suggested Readings

The following book is about Emmett Kelly:
KELLY, E. *Clown*. Englewood Cliffs, N.J.: Prentice-Hall, 1954.

GATCHEL, R. F., & BAUM, A. *An introduction to health psychology*. Reading, Mass.: Addison-Wesley, 1983. A brief and simple introduction to the area of health psychology. The volume covers topics such as stress, learned helplessness, psychophysiological disorders, pain and pain management, and the effect of the medical setting on patient behavior.
IZARD, C. *Human emotions*. New York: Plenum, 1977. A discussion of the major theories of human emotions. A careful examination is given to the role of nonverbal (especially facial) cues used in determining emotions.
MANDLER, G. *Mind and body: Psychology of emotion and stress*. New York: Norton, 1984. A volume that focuses on the role of cognition and cognitive processes in the experience of emotion. Relates emotion to anxiety, stress, physical illness, and creativity.

PLUTCHIK, R. *Emotion: A psychoevolutionary synthesis*. New York: Harper & Row, 1980. Examines the parallels in emotional development in animals and humans. Draws on material from psychology, biology, ethology, and psychiatry to show how emotions evolve.
SELIGMAN, M. *Helplessness: On depression, development, and death*. San Francisco: Freeman, 1975. Discusses the theory of learned helplessness, showing how a loss of control can lead to depression and contribute to death.
STONE, G., COHEN, F. & ADLER, N. (Eds.). *Health psychology*. San Francisco: Jossey-Bass, 1979. Presents original chapters discussing the role of psychology in health and health care. The chapters discuss topics ranging from how people determine when they are sick to the factors that determine when people will seek and follow medical advice.
WALSTER, E., & WALSTER, G. *A new look at love*. Reading, Mass.: Addison-Wesley, 1978. Discusses the differences in passionate and mature love. Examines the research on love and attraction.

PERSONALITY: THEORIES AND ASSESSMENT

Just as David and Goliath dueled before anxious onlookers on the field, every four years in the United States two or more warriors march out from the ranks of their political parties to fight the battle for the presidency. The candidates typically hurl challenges and charges at each other as they try to convince voters that they are the best choice and that their opponent is unfit for office. This ritual battle took place in 1984 when Ronald Reagan and Walter Mondale sparred to gain the voter's favor. The campaign was like most that had preceded it, with one rather frightening exception. Faintly hidden in many lines of the campaign rhetoric was the portrayal of President Reagan as a man who not only might lead the nation into war, but who might order the use of nuclear weapons. This portrayal came at a time when there was widespread fear that the world was slowly sliding toward its ultimate destruction in a nuclear holocaust; movies graphically showed the terrible destruction that would result from a nuclear blast and new words such as *nuclear winter* were making their way into everyday language. While many voters were concerned about this image of their president, most dismissed it as untrue. Certainly, no civilized person could order the unleashing of this terrible weapon of doom and destruction.

While the voters in the 1984 election reassured themselves about the utter folly of the use of nuclear weapons, they would only have had to turn back the pages of the history book thirty-nine years to find the one person who did order the use of nuclear weapons.

Who was this person who added a terrible note of reality to our present day concern about nuclear war? This man had just sat down to eat lunch with a group of officers on the presidential yacht in 1945 when he was handed a telegram: HIROSHIMA WAS BOMBED VISUALLY WITH ONLY ONE TENTH COVER AT SEVEN FIFTEEN PM WASHINGTON TIME AUGUST FIVE. THERE WAS NO FIGHTER OPPOSITION AND NO FLAK. FIFTEEN MINUTES AFTER DROP CAPTAIN PARSONS REPORTED "CONDITIONS NORMAL IN AIRPLANE FOLLOWING DELIVERY. RESULTS CLEAR CUT SUCCESSFUL IN ALL RESPECTS. VISIBLE EFFECTS GREATER THAN IN ANY TEST." The man nodded in deep thought as he carefully read and reread the telegram. President Harry S. Truman had made the decision to drop the atomic bomb on Hiroshima. And, three days later, he would make the decision to drop a second atomic bomb on Nagasaki. The destruction caused by the two bombs was tremendous; over 100,000 people died immediately, and countless others were afflicted with radiation sickness that would slowly and painfully end their lives.

Was the use of the atomic bomb necessary? This question is still debated today. Truman, however, never took part in these debates. He felt that he had made the best decision possible based on the facts available at the time. He would not labor over a past decision nor become involved in second guessing.

Truman held a similar attitude about the

other decisions he made during his eight years as president. While his other decisions may not seem as momentous as the one involving "the bomb," many of them still play a dramatic role in our lives today. Truman helped develop the Marshall Plan, which rebuilt Western Europe and made it one of the closest allies of the United States. He took part in the Potsdam Conference, which divided Europe into a free Europe and a Communist-controlled group of countries, forming the Iron Curtain around the Soviet Union. During his second term of office, Chinese and North Korean troops invaded South Korea and Truman sent United States troops into battle. Truman also entered the United States as a charter member of the United Nations.

Many historians rate Truman among the greatest presidents of the United States. This praise is particularly striking in light of several facts. First, Truman probably never would have been president except for the death of Franklin D. Roosevelt; Truman was a rather obscure politician before being named Roosevelt's vice president. Second, Truman had one of the most humble and least glamorous backgrounds of all our modern presidents.

In fact, only four years before Truman became president, the banks foreclosed on his mother's farm because there was no money to make the mortgage payments.

Harry S. Truman was born on a small farm outside of Independence, Missouri, in 1876. His parents could not agree on a middle name for their first child, so they simply gave him the initial "S." Harry's father was a farmer with an eye for speculation and he was also a mule trader. He had a reputation of being the most honest man in Jackson County. The elder Truman, a small, neatly dressed man, was a fighter: ". . . he could whip anybody up to two hundred [pounds] if they got in his way" (Miller, 1973, p. 66). Harry's mother was a strong woman who paid close attention to her children's education. She was very strict and insisted on obedience and honesty.

As a child, Truman received a great deal of warmth and affection from his parents. At the age when other boys were becoming interested in sports, Harry developed a fondness for books. He read the Bible twice through before he began school. His choice of the Bible as his reading material was not due to his religious devotion. Rather, Truman states, "I guess I read the Bible because the type was large, but then it developed about the time I was six years old, it was then that we first noticed it, that I had flat eyeballs" (Miller, 1973, p. 52). Harry's eyesight was so bad that he had to be fitted with thick eyeglasses.

The glasses were a major influence on his life. They set him apart from the other kids, and they restricted him. As a result, he became even more absorbed in books. His eye defect also brought him closer to his mother. She encouraged his reading and, later, his interest in the piano. "Harry was a sort of mamma's boy, oddly more like a little old woman than a sissy child. He helped in the kitchen with neither reluctance nor boyish clumsiness" (Daniels, 1950, p. 50).

Although he dreamed of becoming a concert pianist, economic considerations forced him to change his plans. After he graduated from high school, Truman took a job as time keeper for a railroad construction crew. This job presented quite a picture of contrast as the small, owlish-looking young man worked with the burly construction workers. Truman, however, found that his size was no handicap, and he got along well with the construction workers. After working at the railroad, Truman went to Kansas City, where he worked as a bank clerk and joined a field artillery unit. Truman soon became a captain and was sent to France to command Battery D during World War I. The battery, known as "Dizzy D," had already had four commanding officers, none of whom could control the outfit. Truman took charge of the unit and won the trust of his men.

On his return from the war, Truman married his childhood sweetheart, Bess. He had known her since he was 4 years old. Truman had always been painfully shy around women; this shyness, combined with the feeling that Bess deserved more, kept him from proposing until he was 35 years old. Bess was much the opposite of her new husband. She came from a well-to-do family and was outgoing.

After the war, Truman opened a clothing store with a war buddy, but economic times were bad and the business went bankrupt. Soon after the store closed, Mike Pendergast persuaded Truman to run for a county judge post. The Pendergast family headed a strong political machine in Missouri; with the help of the Pendergast machine, Truman was elected county judge.

Truman served in this capacity until 1934. One of his major jobs was overseer of the road system in the county. The previous judges had been corrupt, taken bribes, and given contracts to political friends. Truman attacked the job with a zeal and honesty that surprised even the Pendergasts. While controversy and accusations of graft swirled around the Pendergast machine, Truman remained an impeccably honest man.

In 1934 the Missouri Democratic party, headed by the Pendergasts, ran Truman for United States senator. He won the election and went to Washington, D.C. He thought he was the poorest senator in Congress, and he was very self-conscious about not having a college education. Truman became a champion of the "common man" in Washington. He served on a committee to investigate graft in the nation's railroads, and he gave a stirring criticism of big business on the floor of the Senate in 1937. "One of the difficulties as I see it is that we worship money instead of honor. A billionaire in our estimation is much greater in the eyes of the people than the public servant who works for the public interest. It makes no difference if the billionaire rode to wealth on the sweat of little children and the blood of unpaid labor . . ." (Miller, 1973, p. 152). Truman's work earned him the reputation of being an honest politician. However, he was also a modest man who never boasted of his power and accomplishments. Therefore, Truman was surprised to learn that he had been chosen to be Franklin D. Roosevelt's running mate in 1944. Eighty-two days after Roosevelt was elected to his fourth term, he died, and Truman became the thirty-third president of the United States. It has often been argued that power has a way of corrupting those who hold it, but Truman proved to be an exception to this rule.

The debates about what type of president Truman was will probably rage on for many years to come. Eric Sevareid, however, expressed the opinion of many. "A man's character is his fate, said the ancient Greeks. Chance, in good part, took Harry Truman to the presidency, but it was his character that kept him there and determined his historical fate. He is, without any doubt, destined to live in the books as one of the strongest and most decisive of the American Presidents."

DEFINING PERSONALITY

". . . but it was his *character* that kept him there and determined his historical fate." The concept of character or personality is often used to explain, excuse, or justify people's actions. Eric Sevareid used the concept of character to explain why Truman achieved a great place in history.

What do we mean when we talk about Truman's personality, or our own personality? Most of the work of psychologists is aimed at studying and developing theories about how "people in general" behave. We have already discussed the basic principles of learning, perception, motivation, and emotion. The major aim in each of these areas is to identify the most likely response that people will make to a particular situation, stimulus, or event. In each case, we lump people together and try to find rules to explain how they behave or why they behave in a particular manner.

We know, however, that all people do not act the same, even when faced with the same situation. For example, think of how people behave in a restaurant when the service is very slow. Some wait patiently to be served, others "make a scene" and grumble loudly at the waiter, while still others simply get up and leave. Why do these people act differently when they are all faced with the same bad service and are all unhappy about it?

The study of personality is aimed at answering questions like these. The basic question of personality research is to explain why people act differently in the same setting; in other words, the focus is on *individual differences*. There have been many attempts to define personality. Gordon Allport (1937) suggested the global view, that personality "is what man really is." Most other definitions, however, are not so ambitious. We will define **personality** as the unique set of behaviors (including thoughts and emotions) and enduring qualities that influence the way a person adjusts to his or her environment. In this definition personality is seen as influencing, guiding, and motivating behavior. Presumably, personality is what makes people unique and causes them to act or see situations differently from anyone else. As we will see, personality theories grapple with some basic questions about human nature. One of these questions concerns whether people are inherently evil and must be controlled by their consciences and society, or whether they are basically good and caring. Another question revolves around free will. Are people generally pawns controlled by their instinctive forces or environmental conditions, or do they have the freedom to determine their own behaviors?

The task of explaining why people act differently in situations is clearly a big one. As a result, there are many approaches to and theories about personality. One approach is concerned with identifying and describing different forms of personalities. We will examine this approach when we discuss type and trait theories. A second approach focuses on the structure and dynamics of personality. The emphasis of this approach is to identify forces such as drives, motives, or goals that arise within the individual and to relate these forces to behavior. The psychoanalytic theories of Sigmund Freud and his followers and the humanistic theories are examples of this type of theory. A third approach that we will examine is concerned with the way in which external events influence behavior. Learning theories argue that we can explain many individual differences by focusing on the learning process. According to this approach, each of us has a unique history and this history influences the way we respond to the world.

The similarities and differences of these three approaches will become clearer as we discuss them in the chapter. What is important to remember is that each approach is aimed at explaining why people act differently in similar situations.

A Question of Behavioral Consistency

At the end of his speeches, Truman would hold question-and-answer sessions. During one of these sessions a small, red-haired boy meekly asked him, "Mr. President, was you popular when you was a boy?" Truman smiled and slowly replied, "Why no, I was never popular. The popular boys were the ones who were good at games and had big, tight fists. I was never like that. Without my glasses I was blind as a bat, and to tell the truth, I was kind of a sissy. If there was any danger of getting into a fight, I always ran. I guess that's why I'm here today" (Miller, 1973, p. 32). Truman's answer shows a modesty that characterized him throughout his life. He rarely boasted about his accomplishments. He was always willing to praise others, but slow to take credit himself.

One of the basic assumptions of many personality theories is that individuals behave consistently over time and across many situations. This assumption is based on the belief that personality is a relatively stable part of the person that guides behavior. Thus, if we believe that modesty is a component of Truman's personality, we would expect him to display modest behavior in situations where he was dealing with an audience of children as well as in situations where he interacted with dignitaries or generals.

The issue of consistency has sparked a lively debate that continues to rage today (Conley, 1984; Peake & Mischel, 1984). Clearly, no one would argue that personality is an absolute dictator of behavior regardless of the situation. As we will see in Chapter 13, this type of rigid consistency that does not allow for situational influences is one symptom of a psychological disorder. Similarly, very few investigators would suggest that people show no consistency in their behavior from one setting to the next. The argument, therefore, centers on how much consistency there is; in other words, how much do personal dispositions influence behavior?

One group of investigators has amassed an impressive collection of data suggesting that behavior is largely determined by the situation (Mischel, 1968; Mischel & Peake, 1982). They argue that accurately predicting how a person will act in one situation based on knowledge about his or her behavior in a previous situation is improbable. For example, in a classic study, children's moral behavior was examined in a wide variety of situations

Bernhard Goetz had shown little tendency to act violently until he shot four teenage boys on a subway in New York City. Goetz, however, lived in fear of being mugged and had planned in his mind how he would defend himself. Were Goetz's actions due to the particular situation on the subway or to his personality and long-standing fears?

(Hartshorne & May, 1928). Each child was given the opportunity to commit dishonest behavior (lying or cheating) in a number of settings (home, classroom, party, and athletic contest). If we believe that behavior is consistent across situations, we would predict that a child who acted dishonestly in one setting would do so in other settings. However, the results of the study did not strongly support this position. There was only a slight tendency for children who were dishonest in one setting to be dishonest in other settings.

Other investigators dispute the conclusion that there is little consistency in behavior (Epstein, 1983; Rushton et al., 1983). They argue that the scope of the studies must be broadened. Instead of looking at one situation and trying to predict behavior in another situation, they say that we must examine behaviors across a wide variety of situations to predict future behavior. In other words, we can discover a person's characteristic way of acting by studying his or her behavior in other situations. Their results suggest that when this procedure is followed, behavior does show a moderately high degree of consistency.

Bem and Allen (1974) have taken another approach to the question of situational consistency in behaviors. They argue that certain traits may show more situational consistency than others. Further, they point out that the specific traits in which consistency is evident will be different for different people. For example, modesty may have been an important or central trait of Truman's and, hence, he may have shown this modesty in many situations. On the other hand, while you may consider yourself modest, this may not be of primary importance to you. Therefore, you are unlikely to show strong situational consistency in this trait. In order to demonstrate this position, the investigators asked subjects to rate themselves on a friendly-unfriendly dimension and to indicate how consistent their behavior was on this dimension (Bem & Allen, 1974). The subjects' actual behaviors were then rated by observers across a number of situations. The results indicated that those subjects who rated themselves as being consistently friendly, did, in fact, respond in a friendly manner across a range of situations. However, the subjects who described themselves as variable in friendliness did not respond consistently.

Another factor that determines the relative importance of person and situation is the clarity and intensity of situational cues (Mischel, 1981). When the cues are very clear, the situation rather than the personality will rule behavior. On the other hand, when the situation is unique or the cues are ambiguous, person factors such as traits will play a larger role in guiding behavior. For example, imagine receiving an invitation to attend a party that reads: "Your presence is requested at the home of Dr. and Mrs. Smith. Cocktails will be served at 4:30 P.M. Dress is formal." In this case the demands of the situation are clear, and it is likely that everyone who attends will be present at 4:30 P.M. and will be wearing formal attire. On the other hand, imagine an invitation that reads: "You are invited to a party at John and Melinda Smith's house. Come any time between 4:30 and 11 P.M. Hope to see you there!" In this case the rules of the party are less clear, and people's preference and personality will be more likely to influence when they arrive and what they wear.

While the exact magnitude of behavioral consistency may be debated, most investigators agree that both person and situational factors influence behavior. As we will see, the various personality theories place different emphasis on these two factors. In addition, a surprisingly wide variety of person variables have been suggested as the basis for influencing behavior; these variables range from an unconscious predisposition to act to a learned tendency to perceive and evaluate situations in a particular way. The richness of the theories should challenge you to think and, in some cases, they may test the limits of your imagination.

As the situational cues become more clear, the influence of personality on behavior decreases. For example, a party invitation that states "formal dress required" leaves little room for personal preferences to affect dress.

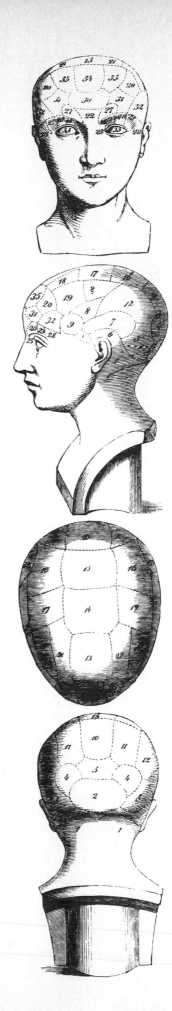

Types and Traits

Types. One of the earliest theories of personality was proposed by the Greek physician Galen in the second century. He suggested that there were four temperaments or personalities (melancholic, choleric, phlegmatic, and sanguine); according to this theory, the temperaments were caused by the balance of body fluids such as blood and bile. The basic idea behind this approach was that people could be one of these types; in other words, you might be the aggressive and violent (choleric) type *or* the happy-go-lucky and cheerful (sanguine) type. Essentially, these types are mutually exclusive boxes or categories in which people could be placed; these categories could then be used to predict the range of a person's behavior.

In the eighteenth century, Franz Joseph Gall introduced the "science" of **phrenology.** Gall believed that it was possible to determine an individual's personality type by examining the bumps and contours on his or her head. Almost a century later, Cesare Lombroso, an Italian psychiatrist and criminologist, suggested that criminals could be identified by the structure of their face. He argued that some people were born with the physical features of primitive man; these features showed that such people were destined to lead a life of crime. Although it offers some interesting possibilities, Lombroso's work has been largely discredited.

While not adopting phrenology or accepting Lombroso's theory, William Sheldon suggested that body build determines behavior (Sheldon, 1942). In order to test his theory, Sheldon photographed thousands of students and developed three dimensions along which body builds could be rated: endomorphic (soft, round, fat); mesomorphic (muscular, hard, rectangular); and ectomorphic (tall, thin, fragile). Sheldon argued that each body could be rated on a seven-point scale according to these three dimensions. Each person could, therefore, be given a three-number rating (for example, 1:2:7 or 6:4:1) that would describe his or her body build or **somatotype** (see Figure 12–1).

Sheldon's next step was to relate somatotype or body build to personality. After observing people with various body types, Sheldon arrived at the following conclusions:

1. Endomorphs love comfort and food; they are relaxed and need social approval and affection.
2. Mesomorphs are assertive, physical, aggressive, and active.
3. Ectomorphs are restrained, socially inhibited, artistic, and oriented toward intellectual activities.

While Sheldon's theory is thought-provoking, it has not stood the test of close scrutiny. For example, investigators point out that the relationship between body build and personality is neither as simple nor as direct as Sheldon suggested (Hall & Lindzey, 1978). Instead, we often have ideas about how people with certain body builds should behave—we expect a strong, muscular man to be an athlete; a fat person to be jolly; a skinny person who wears thick glasses to be an "egghead" who would rather read a good book than play football. These expectations influence the way we respond to others and, consequently, they influence the way others behave. Thus, it is possible that other people's expectations, rather than body build, influence behavior.

Because it offers a rather simple classification, there might be a temptation to embrace the type approach. But there are drawbacks to this theory. A major problem is that people are not generally one type or another. For example, you might consider yourself to be rather relaxed and easygoing. However, you probably know other people whom you would rate as being more easygoing than you and still others who are less tolerant than

Figure 12-1
Sheldon's Somatotypes

Sheldon argued that body type determines personality. According to him, endomorphs love food and comfort and need social approval and affection; mesomorphs are assertive, physical, aggressive, and active; and ectomorphs are restrained, socially inhibited, artistic, and oriented toward intellectual activity.

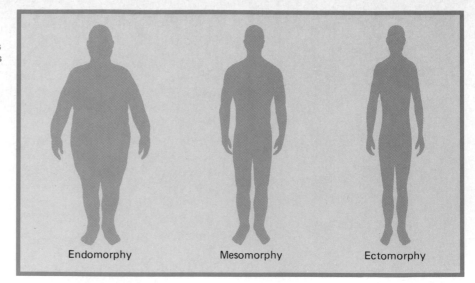

Endomorphy   Mesomorphy   Ectomorphy

you. In other words, people don't simply fall into categories such as easygoing or tense; rather, they vary in the degree to which they possess a certain characteristic. A second problem is that types are often broad classifications that may actually supply little information. For example, Eysenck (1981) has suggested that people can be classified as introverted or extroverted. However, he points out that more information is needed to accurately describe people. For example, in addition to being outgoing, the extrovert may also be aggressive, restless, impulsive, and touchy. This person is clearly different from another extrovert who is sociable and relaxed. Therefore, because types are generally so broad, they are of limited value.

Trait Theories. In order to deal with some of these issues, many theorists have adopted a *trait* approach to describe personality. Gordon Allport (1937), one of the early advocates of the trait approach, stated that traits are "the building blocks of personality." **Traits** represent an organization of a person's experience. We can think of them as a *readiness to think, perceive, or act in a particular way across a variety of different situations*. People possess varying degrees of traits. For example, we might want to rate the presidents of the United States on honesty. Truman might fall farther to the honest side of the scale, while other presidents might be classified along varying degrees of dishonesty.

According to Allport, all traits are not equal; some are more important and more likely to influence behavior than others. The most influential are the *cardinal traits*. These are traits around which an individual's life will revolve. For example, we could conceive of someone whose life was guided by blind ambition and the desire for power. Everything that person did would be aimed at gaining more power. Fortunately, Allport suggested that few people are dominated by cardinal traits. More common are *central traits*, which play a major role in guiding a person's behavior, but the person is not consumed by them. In examining the life of Truman, we might conclude that honesty and modesty were central traits for him. *Secondary traits* are the least influential characteristics; they involve specific situations or events. We might consider these traits as preferences or attitudes. For example, Truman preferred small towns over large cities. What makes people unique is the degree to which they possess traits, and which of those traits are central to them.

One of the major issues faced by trait theorists is the identification of traits. Researchers have pointed out the size of this problem by drawing up a list of 17,953 English words that could be used to indicate personal traits (Allport & Odbert, 1936). Imagine having to describe Truman by showing where he falls on 17,953 dimensions! Raymond Cattell (1973)

Figure 12–2

Cattell's 16-Factor Questionnaire

Shown here are scores from three quite different groups: Olympic athletes, clergymen, and sales representatives. Cattell tried to identify the 16 basic traits that describe personality. (Cattell, 1965, pp. 242, 347)

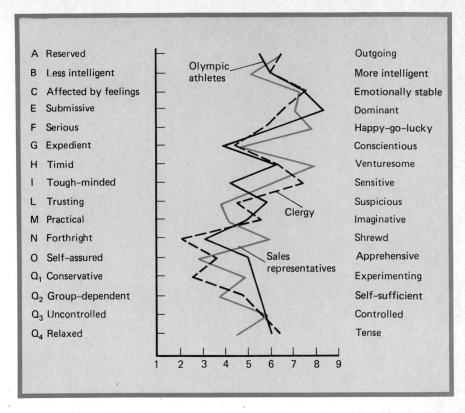

set out to reduce this unmanageable number and to identify the "basic traits." He spent a number of years collecting data on the personality and behavior of thousands of subjects. Cattell identified 16 basic traits that could be used to describe people. He also developed a questionnaire, the "Sixteen Personality Factor Questionnaire," to find out where an individual was located on these 16 dimensions (see Figure 12–2). Despite Cattell's work, there is still a great deal of disagreement about the nature and number of the basic traits.

The Trait Approach: An Evaluation

The trait approach became popular for a number of reasons. First, it suggests that personality can be measured. Indeed, a number of scales have been developed to measure specific traits. Second, the view that behavior is caused by an individual's personality traits and that a person can be described with these traits seems logical. In our everyday interactions, all of us use traits to describe other people. Your roommate is friendly, kind, and studious; your professor is absent-minded, humorous, and indecisive; your local politician is smooth-talking, suspicious, and tense. In fact, investigators found that we tend to view other people's behavior as being caused by their personality traits (Jones & Nisbett, 1972; Nisbett & Ross, 1980) (see Chapter 15).

Despite the appealing nature of the trait approach, there have been some important criticisms. First, the use of traits to explain behavior can lead to circular reasoning. Traits are not something that we can see or directly measure. Rather, we must infer them from behavior or answers to personality tests. Thus, we may infer that Bill is aggressive because we see him hit other people or verbally abuse them. This may, indeed, be a reasonable conclusion to draw from his behavior. However, we then get into trouble if we conclude that Bill acted aggressively because he is an aggressive person. In essence, we would be saying that Bill is aggressive because he acts aggressively and he acts aggressively because he is aggressive.

A second problem is that many trait theories do not pay enough attention to the influence of the situation on behavior. For example, we might conclude that Truman was a shy and modest person. However, in 1948, Truman was in danger of losing his bid for reelection. He chartered a train and went across the country giving speeches about his accomplishments and shaking hands with thousands of people. In these situations he acted neither shy nor modest. Clearly, then, situations play a large role in determining behavior.

Finally, trait theories are criticized because they are designed to identify traits and measure them, but they are not involved with how personality develops or changes. In this sense, they are not really theories of personality; instead, they are models. Despite these problems, the identification and measuring of traits represents an active and important area of personality psychology.

PSYCHOANALYTIC THEORY

Trait theories are criticized because they take too simple a view of personality and because they generally avoid the issue of how personality develops. **Psychoanalytic theory** certainly avoids these criticisms; it is not simple, and its major focus is on the development of personality. In fact, psychoanalytic theory is one of the most comprehensive and ambitious theories in psychology, but it is also one of the most controversial. The man who first proposed the theory spent much of his life in the center of controversy, emerging as the best-known figure in psychology.

Sigmund Freud

Sigmund Freud was born in 1856 in Freiburg, Moravia (Czechoslovakia). He studied medicine at the University of Vienna. He was interested in the scientific approach used to study medical problems, and while attending the university, he worked as a laboratory assistant examining the nervous system of animals.

Freud would have been content to continue research in the laboratory, but his plans to marry demanded that he find a position that offered financial security. He therefore began a private medical practice. Two years later, however, he was awarded a fellowship to study the treatment of nervous disorders with the famous French neurologist, Jean Charcot. This proved to be a turning point in Freud's career. Charcot used hypnosis to treat patients classified as hysterics. These patients suffered from paralysis of limbs or from partial or total loss of sight or hearing. The cause of these symptoms was not physical; the paralysis was the result of psychological stress. Charcot discovered that he could relieve the physical symptoms through hypnotic suggestion.

Freud became dissatisfied with hypnosis as a tool because not everyone could be hypnotized. He found, however, that he could uncover the events that were related to the hysterical symptoms by having patients express every thought (no matter how unimportant or irrelevant) that came into their minds during the therapy session. Freud used this method of **free association** to discover the traumatic (painful, emotional, shocking) events that were the root of his patients' problems.

Most of Freud's patients were women from middle- and upper-class Victorian society. As Freud listened to them talk, he noticed a striking similarity in their stories. Many of his patients talked about upsetting events related to sexual experiences in early childhood. The patients talked about strong

Sigmund Freud, founder of psychoanalytic theory.

sexual urges and fantasies that they had experienced as children. This was especially surprising because the people of Freud's time believed that children did not have sexual urges or fantasies.

His discussions with patients led Freud to draw two conclusions. First, early childhood is a critical time for the formation of personality. Second, children, indeed even infants, have sexual urges, and much of their behavior is motivated by these urges. This second idea shocked people, and Freud was viewed as "a dirty old man."

The Unconscious. In addition to having patients free-associate, Freud also had them report their **dreams** (Jones, 1957). In fact, he conducted self-analysis by interpreting his own dreams. The contents of the dreams were varied and often bizarre. Freud, however, felt that dreams must have some function for the individual. He believed that dreams represented thoughts and feelings of which people were unaware. Thus, Freud felt that dreams were vehicles through which people could express their unacceptable impulses in disguised or acceptable forms.

This conclusion reinforced Freud's feeling that much of our behavior is the result of unconscious desires. He divided the personality into three parts or processes. The **conscious** includes what the person is perceiving or thinking at the moment. The **preconscious** is essentially one's memory; it includes thoughts that people may not be aware of but can retrieve from memory. Finally, the **unconscious** is the "storehouse of unacceptable images, including past events, current impulses, and desires of which one is not aware" (Byrne & Kelley, 1981). The unconscious makes up the largest part of our personality. Impulses are "filed" in the unconscious because people find them painful or threatening. Examples of these impulses might be the sexual desire to possess one's mother or an intense hatred of one's brother or sister. Once these images are *repressed*, or forced into the unconscious, they are removed from our awareness. However, the fact that we are not aware of these images and desires does not mean that they do not influence our behavior. According to Freud, these desires "push" for expression, but because of their threatening nature they are expressed only in disguised form.

As we discussed earlier, one of these disguises is dreams. Unconscious impulses can also find expression through "Freudian slips" or humor. Accidents are still another way in which unconscious impulses are expressed. According to Freud, there is likely to be a "hidden message" when your roommate "accidentally" spills coffee on your psychology term paper, or when your neighbor "unintentionally" loses control of his 1962 Ford station wagon and dents your new Porsche.

"Freudian slips" are one way that people express unconscious feelings.

The Structure of Personality

Freud believed that the individual's personality is the scene of a never-ending battle: On one hand there are primitive and unacceptable drives striving for expression, while on the other hand there are forces trying to deny or disguise these impulses. Freud not only viewed the personality as a battlefield, but he also identified the participants in this battle: the id, the ego, and the superego (see Figure 12–3).

The Id. Freud believed that each of us has a savage quality at the root of our personality. He labeled this part of the personality the **id.** According to Freud, people are born with two instinctual drives that serve as the basic motivation for all behavior. One, called *Eros*, is the drive for survival. Included in this drive are the needs to eat and drink, to be warm, and above all, to engage in sexual activity. The energy force that propels the person to satisfy these drives is called **libido.** The second innate drive, *Thanatos*, is a destructive drive. The aim is to destroy others, but there is also a self-destructive aspect to it. In fact, Freud took the grim position that "the aim of all life is death." This self-destructive impulse is seen not only in suicide, but in the harmful excesses in which so many people engage, such as drinking alcohol, smoking, and overeating. According to Freud, it is the unconscious desire for self-destruction that motivates people to drive an automobile at dangerously fast speeds, to get drunk at parties, and to smoke cigarettes, which have been proven to be harmful.

The id, like the savage, wants to satisfy these primitive drives in the most direct and immediate way. It is not concerned with reality, logic, or manners. It functions on the **pleasure principle,** which dictates the immediate satisfaction of drives. We are not aware of these drives because the id operates at the unconscious level of our personality.

The Ego. While each of us may have these primitive desires, it is clear that we could not function long in our social world if we gave free expression to the savage within ourselves. Thus, Freud suggested that at around the age of 6 months the **ego** develops to control the impulses of the id. The ego is the person's view of physical and social reality. It tries to satisfy the id impulses by taking into account the possibilities of reward and punishment that exist in a situation. In other words, it works on the **reality principle.** For example, suppose you are very thirsty and see a nice, cold beer sitting on a table in a restaurant. Your id impulses would tell you to grab

Figure 12–3

Freud divided the personality into three parts—the conscious, preconscious, and unconscious. As shown here, the unconscious is the largest of the three, because Freud believed that much of our behavior is the result of unconscious desires. Personality is also divided into three dimensions—the id, ego, and superego. The id is made up entirely of unconscious motives and impulses, while both the ego and superego are more evenly divided among the conscious, preconscious, and unconscious.

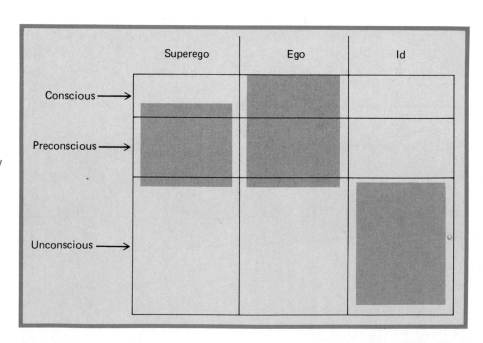

the beer and drink it. The ego, however, would calculate the possible results of this action, the worst thing being that the 200-pound man at the table will punch you and the bartender will call the police. Thus, the ego would direct you to order and pay for your own beer. It is important to understand that the ego is only concerned about the consequences of actions; it does not ask such moral questions as, "Is this the right thing to do? Is it ethical?"

The job of the ego is a tough one. Sometimes the id impulses come dangerously close to taking control of a person. In these cases the person will experience anxiety, and the ego will have to use defense mechanisms to redirect behavior and protect the person. As we pointed out in Chapter 11, there are a number of these defenses, such as projection, rationalization, reaction formation, and identification. The defense mechanisms used by the person become a part of his or her personality. For example, you may have a friend who always tries to rationalize when things go wrong.

The Superego. We can view the id as operating on the signal "I want it now." The ego answers this demand by saying, "Let's be realistic and get it in a way that won't cause trouble." These two forces, however, must also deal with the **superego,** which says, "Think. Is it right to want it?" The superego represents our conscience. It includes the moral values of right and wrong that are largely instilled in us by our parents. The superego makes us feel guilty when we have done the wrong thing. As you might imagine, people who are dominated by the superego will be very up-tight and self-conscious; they must constantly ask themselves, "Is it right to feel or act this way?" It is also the superego that motivates us to better ourselves and to live up to our ideals. As can be seen in Figure 12–3, the superego operates in both the conscious and unconscious regions of our personalities.

The Emergence of Personality

We have set the stage (unconscious, preconscious, and conscious) and introduced the cast of characters (id, ego, and superego). Now we must turn our attention to the play itself. What determines the specific type of personality that someone will have? Freud believed that the major "battles" of the personality are fought during childhood. Events that occur during childhood mold and form the personality, which then remains basically stable throughout the rest of the person's life. Freud argued that there are certain critical events during childhood; these events occur in a fixed order and in distinct time periods or stages. The important issue at each of these stages is the expression of the libido, or sexual energy. At each stage, the libido seeks an outlet through a different part of the body. According to Freud, if people suffer a traumatic experience or are overprotected in a particular stage, they may become fixated at that stage. The personality will then take on the characteristics of the stage in which the fixation occurred. The earlier in life the fixation occurs, the stronger the influence on the personality. While most of Freud's specific assumptions about the stages of childhood have been criticized, his suggestion that traumatic events in early childhood can influence personality has received some support. Let us, therefore, examine Freud's view of how the personality develops.

Oral Stage. According to Freud, the infant is born with the general desire for physical pleasure, which quickly becomes focused on the mouth region. This is known as the **oral stage.** The infant satisfies these impulses by eating, sucking, and biting. In addition to satisfying the need for food, these behaviors are also a source of sexual pleasure.

Fixation at this stage can occur in two ways. On one hand, a mother

Orally fixated people orient much of their life around their mouth. They may be heavy smokers, constant eaters, or excessive talkers.

may overindulge her infant's sucking desire, feeding on demand and catering to all his or her wishes. This overindulgence will result in the development of an oral personality characterized by excessive trust, unreasonable optimism, and a strong dependence on others (Blum, 1953). Further, this type of individual will admire strength and leadership, but generally will not take a leadership role (Tribich & Messer, 1974). Fixation can also occur at the oral stage if the mother is underindulgent and abruptly weans the infant. The underindulged infant will develop into an aggressive, sadistic person who exploits others for his or her own benefit. Orally fixated people may also orient much of their later life around the mouth. This can be seen in people who always seem to be eating, smoking, or spending a large amount of time talking (a politician, a professor, a gossip, a lawyer) or singing (a performer).

Anal Stage. During the second and third years, the child enters the anal stage. The main focus of pleasure shifts from the mouth to the anal area. During this period children are faced with the trauma of toilet training. A major battle between the child and parents occurs during this stage; the parents try to force the child to control his or her bowels, and the child resists and strives to be independent. The child takes a negative attitude toward the parents and is determined to do just the opposite of what the parents want. Two types of anal personalities can result from fixation during this stage. The *anal retentive* is compulsively neat, stingy, and orderly. The *anal expulsive* is rebellious and very messy.

Phallic Stage. The phallic stage begins around the age of 4. During this stage the child discovers his or her genital organs and delights in masturbation. The trauma of this stage is different for males than it is for females. According to Freud, boys desire a sexual relationship with their mother. This desire, however, is thwarted by the realization that the father already possesses the mother. The little boy becomes fearful that the father will discover his lust and castrate him as punishment. In order to get rid of these fears, the child identifies with and tries to be like his father. This identification with the father helps form the superego, because the child internalizes the father's values. Freud called events occurring to males during the phallic stage the Oedipus complex, since they reminded Freud of the Greek play, Oedipus Rex, in whch the hero, Oedipus, kills his father and marries his mother.

If you find it difficult to understand the Oedipus complex, Freud's view of the female's conflict during this stage will stretch your powers of imagination even further. According to Freud, during the phallic stage girls discover that they are biologically inferior to males; to their horror, they find out that they lack a penis. While girls were sexually attracted to their mothers, they now blame her for this "anatomical inferiority." They envy their father's penis and become attracted to him. The little girl now begins to fantasize about having a male baby by her father; in this way she can deliver an individual into the world who possesses the desired penis. Freud delivered the crowning blow by concluding that because females never experience castration anxiety, they must have inadequate superegos and, hence, cannot be as morally strong as males. Some of Freud's followers refer to this situation as the **Electra complex** after a story in Greek mythology in which Electra feels love for her father and induces her brother to kill her mother.

An inadequate resolution of the Oedipus complex leads to a personality that is reckless and self-assured. The phallic-type male overvalues his penis and seeks to prove that he is a "real man"; he has a constant need to sexually conquer women. This individual is also likely to be vain and boastful. The female who becomes fixated at this stage will develop the "castrating female" syndrome. She will strive for superiority over males and may seek out "typically male professions." The castrating female will delight in criticizing and dominating males. As we will see later in this chapter, the Oedipus and Electra complexes are among the most criticized and least empirically supported of Freud's ideas.

Latency Period. The **latency period** begins during the child's sixth year and lasts until puberty. Freud felt that the individual's personality is generally determined by this time. During this period children lose interest in sex-related activities and focus their energy on other things, such as schoolwork and hobbies. There is also a tendency for children to confine themselves to all-male or all-female groups at this age.

Genital Stage. The **genital stage** begins at puberty, when sexual tension erupts. If the person has successfully weathered the earlier stages, he or she will seek to marry, raise a family, and join the work force. However,

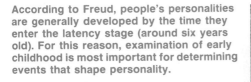

According to Freud, people's personalities are generally developed by the time they enter the latency stage (around six years old). For this reason, examination of early childhood is most important for determining events that shape personality.

people who have become fixated at one of the earlier stages will have a great deal of difficulty adjusting to puberty.

Psychoanalytic Theory: An Evaluation

We have covered a lot of ground with psychoanalytic theory. Before evaluating it, let's quickly review how we might use the theory to better understand Truman. As we've seen, Truman was a modest and very honest man. He was excessively neat and paid close attention to even the smallest detail. He did not like people in authority, especially the military. He described generals and admirals as being "like horses with blinders on. They can't see beyond the ends of their noses, most of them" (Miller, 1973, p. 220). Following psychoanalytic theory, we would examine Truman's early childhood to better understand his personality. We would pay particular attention to his relationship with his parents, noting with interest the indulgence of his mother and the strict discipline of his father. We would also look for traumatic events that might have led him to become fixated in one of the stages. We would explain many of Truman's adult characteristics as the result of unconscious desires and fears that were repressed during childhood. We would also argue that Truman was unaware of many of the forces that influenced his behavior.

Does this approach help us to better understand Truman or give us insights into why he developed his particular personality? More generally, we might ask whether or not psychoanalytic theory is useful in understanding human behavior and personality. The theory is so broad and covers so many areas that a definite answer cannot be given. Psychoanalytic theory has greatly influenced the study of human behavior. In fact, Freud is generally identified as the person who has had the greatest impact on psychology (Phares, 1984). Freud's influence also can be seen in art, in poetry, and in literature. Freud was most influential in the areas of infancy and early childhood concerning the formation of the personality. Freud's emphasis revived the study of early childhood, and in a very real sense, his work served as a foundation for the emergence of developmental psychology (see Chapters 8 and 9). Freud also pointed out that our behavior can be influenced by motives of which we are unaware. While there is still a great deal of disagreement about how the unconscious works, research has shown that hidden motives can influence us.

While Freud is clearly a major figure in the study of modern psychology, his theory has been criticized on a number of levels. The broadest criticism concerns whether or not Freud's work is really a theory in the scientific sense. It is difficult, if not impossible, to test many parts of psychoanalytic theory. For example, could we test a speculation that Truman's dislike of military officers was motivated by his unconscious hatred for his father? A second criticism is that psychoanalytic theory places too much emphasis on early childhood. It largely ignores the effects of events occurring during adulthood, and it de-emphasizes the likelihood of personality change during adulthood. Another broad criticism was raised by some of Freud's very close followers (Alfred Adler, Carl Jung, and Karen Horney). They argued that Freud overemphasized the role of sex in the development of personality. While guilt and conflict about sexual matters may be an issue that influences the formation of personality, there are many issues that have at least as much, if not more, influence.

In addition to the broad criticisms, a number of questions have been raised about specific parts of the psychoanalytic theory. For example, Freud's view that women are biologically inferior to men and, therefore, doomed to have inadequate superegos was first attacked by Karen Horney (1937). She pointed out that Freud's argument was typical of the male point of view. She argued that women may envy the status that society

Karen Horney argued convincingly against the male bias in Freud's theory. Her views laid the early framework for studying sex differences in light of social variables such as status and power rather than biological differences.

has given men, but not the penis that men are born with. She also attacked the position that penis envy is the basis for the "castrating female" personality, saying that the drive for power is at least as common in men as it is in women. Cross-cultural research (Malinowski, 1927; Mead, 1928) has produced results that question Freud's idea that the Oedipus complex is universal and based on sexual dynamics. Finally, research has not found strong support for Freud's identification of specific stages of personality development (Kline, 1972).

Thus, while the psychoanalytic position is creative, radical, and rich in ideas, many of the specific hypotheses have not been supported.

A Change of Focus: Revisions from Psychoanalytic Theory

In 1902 Freud formed the Vienna Psycho-Analytic Society, which consisted of a small group of scholars who met to discuss and advance psychoanalytic theory. However, it was not long before some of the members began to find fault with traditional psychoanalytic theory. In some cases these disagreements gave way to bitter disputes that led to the defections. Some of the scholars who rebelled went on to make notable revisions in psychoanalytic theory and others developed their own theories that represented significant departures from Freud's position. Two of the best-known figures in this latter group were Carl Jung and Alfred Adler.

Carl Jung: Analytical Psychology. Jung broke with Freud over the interpretation of libido. As you will recall, Freud viewed libido as being the sexual energy that directs personality. Jung (1928), on the other hand, felt that the libido was a force resulting from the desire to be creative; it resulted from spiritual needs rather than biological needs. From this foundation, Jung went on to develop a complex, almost mystical theory of personality, generally referred to as **analytical psychology**.

Personality Structure. Jung suggested that the personality has three components (Stein, 1982). The *ego* includes everything that we are conscious of. Its main function is to see that our everyday activities are carried out. In this sense, it is similar to Freud's concept of the ego. The second component is the *personal unconscious*, which is similar to Freud's preconscious. The personal unconscious includes material that was once conscious but has been repressed or forgotten.

The most unusual and controversial component is the *collective unconscious*. According to Jung, this component holds memory traces of experiences from our ancestral past. It includes material not only from human history— it holds experiences from our prehuman and animal ancestors as well. The contents of the collective unconscious are similar for all people since they share roughly the same common history. The ancestral experiences are stored in the collective unconscious in the form of *archetypes*, which are inherited predispositions to respond to certain concepts. For example, throughout history, and specifically in the early cave drawings, there has been a tendency to view the sun with awe and wonder. Other archetypes include such common concepts as God; heroes; sun; moon; fire; water; the wise old man; Mother Earth; and the Shadow, which contains inherited animal instincts such as aggression and unchecked passion. In order to show the existence of these archetypes, Jung studied myths and art throughout human history. He tried to show that there were common themes and symbols that have been expressed throughout time in these mediums.

To Jung, like Freud, the personality was the result of an inner struggle. While Freud viewed this struggle as resulting from the person's efforts to keep unacceptable biological urges in check, Jung saw the struggle resulting from opposite tendencies fighting for expression. Jung believed that for every force, there is a counter-force; the goal in life is to achieve a

Jung was one of the earliest theorists to discuss introversion and extroversion. He suggested that an introvert who is quiet, withdrawn, and interested in ideas rather than people will also have an extroverted side that will struggle for expression.

good balance between these opposing forces. For example, he believed that every person has both a masculine and feminine tendency within their personality. If one tendency is emphasized, it is at the expense of the other. The unexpressed tendency will often occur in the form of dreams or fantasies. Therefore, Jung believed that dreams function to compensate for neglected parts of the personality. A man who overemphasizes the masculine tendencies of his personality may find himself having dreams centering on feminine themes or symbols. Therefore, analyzing dreams is one method of identifying the neglected aspects of one's personality (Hall, 1982).

In addition to the struggle between male and female tendencies, Jung believed there were other pairs of opposites affecting our personalities. One of these opposites concerns our basic relation to our environment: introvert and extrovert. The introvert is quiet, withdrawn, and interested in ideas rather than people. The extrovert is outgoing and socially oriented. Other opposites struggling for expression cited by Jung include the conscious and the unconscious; rational and irrational impulses; and the archetypes involving one's public self and private self. We achieve a healthy personality to the extent that we realize these opposite tendencies within ourselves and can express each.

Jung, in contrast with Freud, held an optimistic view of human nature. Despite the struggles within, Jung believed that people strive to achieve a balanced and integrated personality. This positive view anticipated the humanistic emphasis on personal fulfillment and self-actualization (see pp. 391–394). Also, while Jung acknowledged the importance of childhood on the development of personality, he viewed later life as an important period for the synthesis of personality. Jung felt that we are able to achieve the insight and integration of personality only in our middle and later years.

As you might expect, there have been many criticisms of Jung's theory. Some find his views too mystical, too spiritual, and "too far out" to represent a true theory of personality. His ideas tend to be scattered, unclear, and hard to draw together. Finally, it is difficult to test many of his central concepts such as archetypes.

Alfred Adler: Individual Psychology.   Alfred Adler, like Jung, felt Freud placed too much emphasis on sexual instincts. Instead, Adler believed that we are influenced by our social environments and genetic makeup. However, he did propose that we have the freedom to shape our own personalities. Adler termed his approach **individual psychology** because he believed that each person is unique and adjusts differently to social influences. He stressed the positive nature of humans.

Adler's (1927, 1939) theory evolved over a period of years. The foundation of the theory is that people develop as they strive to overcome or compensate for inferiorities. His first focus was on physical problems or *organ inferiorities*. He noted that people who have a physical ailment or bodily defect often devote much of their life to compensating for this defect (see Highlight, "Organ Inferiority"). In doing so, the weakness becomes a strength.

Adler soon realized that a personality theory could not be based solely on the concept of organ inferiority. He turned his focus to the psychological feelings of inferiority. He argued that all people begin life feeling inferior: Children see themselves as helpless in the face of powerful adults. Just as people attempt to compensate for organ inferiority, Adler felt that the feeling of inferiority leads people to compensate by striving for power and perfection—the *striving for superiority*. An *inferiority complex* results when people are overwhelmed by feelings of inferiority. In this case the inferiority acts as a barrier to positive adjustment.

ORGAN INFERIORITY

An interesting concept developed by Adler was organ inferiority. Adler felt that people who are born with organ defects have feelings of inferiority centering on these deficiencies. He felt that it was likely that they would develop a life style to compensate for these defects.

In fact, the history of sports is filled with athletes who overcame organ inferiorities to become stars. For example, Wilma Rudolph had polio as a child, but she went on to become one of the greatest women runners of all times, winning three gold medals in the 1960 Olympic games. As a young boy, Johnny Weissmuller was frail and sickly. Many childhood diseases sapped him of his strength, and it was feared that he would be bedridden for the

rest of his life, even if he managed to survive childhood. Weissmuller was determined to prove the doctors wrong. This frail boy went on to set 67 world swimming records, and he lead the United States team in the 1924 and 1928 Olympics. After his amazing swimming career, Weissmuller became an actor, and, as the first actor to play Tarzan in the movies, he became a universal symbol of health and strength around the world.

At the age of 8, Walt Davis was stricken with infantile paralysis that left both legs and one arm paralyzed. Learning to walk would have been an unbelievable accomplishment for someone with this condition. Davis not only learned to walk, but he became a world class high jumper, winning a gold medal at the 1952 Olympics and setting five world records. After his career as a high jumper, Davis became a professional basketball player.

The list of famous people who were motivated to overcome organ inferiorities is long. Recently, the media reported the heart-rending story of someone whose accomplishments were equally as great as those found in the history books. Terry Fox was a 22-year-old student in Canada when his right leg was amputated below the knee to stop the spread of bone cancer. After a long recuperation period spent learning how to walk with an artifical leg, Terry learned that his cancer was spreading. At that point, he set out to raise money for cancer research. On April 12, 1977, he dipped his artificial leg in the Atlantic Ocean off Newfoundland and began jogging across Canada. For 4½ months he did what he called his "Fox trot," averaging almost 30 miles a day. Terry ran 3,339 miles before lung cancer made him too

weak to continue and eventually took his life. His heroic efforts raised 20 million dollars for the Canadian Cancer Society.

When Jeff Keith completed his cross-country run across America on February 18, 1985, he said he "wanted to get my message across to the world that I'm not physically handicapped. I was physically challenged."

Stories such as these make Adler's ideas about organ inferiority seem more believable. It must be remembered, however, that there are many other cases in which people become overwhelmed by their defect. It remains an interesting research question: Why do defects motivate some people to strive for accomplishment, while they have the opposite effect on others?

Alfred Adler emphasized the importance of family relationships and other family variables such as birth order and family size for the development of an individual's style of life.

In the final version of his theory, Adler stated that the striving for superiority was aimed not at individual superiority but at building a superior society. He suggested that people have an innate *social interest* that motivates them to seek perfection in their society and interpersonal relationships. Whether or not people have a well-developed social interest is largely dependent on the relationship they have had with their mothers. A positive nurturant relationship will encourage the development of this social interest; an overprotective mother will foster low social interest.

While striving for superiority is the energy behind personality, the *style of life* represents the form of the personality. A person's style of life determines how he or she will solve problems, get along with others, and work for superiority. One's style of life is essentially formed by the age of 5. It is affected by relationships within the family, including such variables as family size, relations between siblings, and birth order.

Adler's view of striving to overcome inferiority has been applied to such historical figures as Napoleon (Singer, 1984); it is suggested that his drive for power may have resulted from his desire to compensate for his short stature. In a similar way, we could suggest that Truman's fascination with reading was influenced by his very poor eyesight—an organ inferiority.

Adler had important impacts in many areas of personality psychology. He stressed the importance of social interaction in influencing the personality. He argued for the role of free will in the forming of the personality. Adler, even more so than Jung, anticipated the position of the humanistic movement (Ellis, 1970). In addition, his theory stimulated some important research in such areas as the effect of birth order on personality and behavior (Schachter, 1959; Zajonc, 1976). But despite these contributions, Adler's theory has been criticized because it lacks precision and integration. Unlike Freud, Adler did not develop a structure of personality; it is unclear, for example, how Adler views the roles of the conscious and unconscious. Overall, the theory lacks the systematic nature characteristic of Freud's psychoanalytic theory.

HUMANISTIC THEORIES

Harry Truman lived during a difficult period in United States history. The country and its people experienced two World Wars, the Korean War, and the Great Depression. It was a time when a person, especially one in politics, had to be tough and fight hard to survive. Truman had these qualities, but biographies of Truman show another side of him; he was also a person who genuinely cared about others and who tried to solve problems in creative ways. During World War I he showed this concern for his men and their families. A soldier who served with Truman said: "He used to get a lot of letters from the old Irish mothers of the boys in the outfit, and most battery commanders, company commanders, wouldn't pay any attention, but not Harry. I don't think he ever went to bed at night before he answered every one of those letters" (Miller, 1973, p. 97).

The fact that so much of human behavior has a positive, caring overtone led a number of personality theorists, such as Abraham Maslow, Carl Rogers, and Rollo May, to form the humanistic movement, which rejected Freud's position that humans are inherently evil savages who must be controlled by society. Instead, the humanists argued that people are basically good and worthy of respect. We saw earlier that Jung and Adler also began to adopt this position in their revisions of psychoanalytic theory. **Humanistic psychology** stresses the creative aspect of people and argues that they are driven by the desire to reach their true potential. Society often serves only to force people to act in a conforming, conventional way and inhibits them from reaching their true potential.

The humanists argue that the study of personality should include human virtues: love, humor, creativity, joy, and personal growth (Maslow, 1968). In light of the gloomy outlook projected by psychoanalytic theories, the humanistic approach stands as an optimistic testimony to human personality. Let us briefly examine two of the more widely known humanistic theories of personality.

Abraham Maslow

Abraham Maslow believed that humans have a natural motivation to be creative and reach their highest potential. Maslow (1970) argued that people cannot begin to achieve their highest potential until their more basic needs have been met. As we pointed out in Chapter 10, Maslow suggested that human needs are arranged in a hierarchy like the rungs on a ladder. The bottom rungs are the basic or lower-order needs, while the top rungs include the growth needs. Once these basic needs are satisfied, a person can focus on the desire to belong to groups and experience love, the wish to be competent and develop a positive self-esteem, and the need to be creative and become self-actualized. The concept of **self-actualization** is a bit fuzzy, but it is conceived of as the process by which people strive to learn, create, and work to the best of their ability.

Maslow believed that to strive for self-actualization is an aspect of human nature. In other words, people have an innate, inborn drive to be good, to be creative, and to grow. Therefore, the role of society should be to create an environment that will encourage these natural tendencies.

If the environmental conditions are right and if people are willing to take the risks to achieve their full potential, personal growth will result. As people move toward self-actualization, they will experience periods of increased insight and feelings of completeness and of being in harmony

Table 12–1
Characteristics of Self-Actualizing People

1. They perceive reality accurately and fully.
2. They demonstrate a greater acceptance of themselves, others, and/or nature in general.
3. They exhibit spontaneity, simplicity, and naturalness.
4. They tend to be concerned with problems rather than with themselves.
5. They have a quality of detachment and a need for privacy.
6. They are autonomous and therefore tend to be independent of their environment and culture.
7. They exhibit a continued freshness of appreciation.
8. They have periodic mystic or peak experiences.
9. They tend to identify with all of mankind.
10. They develop deep interpersonal relations with only a few individuals.
11. They tend to accept democratic values.
12. They have a strong ethical sense.
13. They have a well-developed, unhostile sense of humor.
14. They are creative.
15. They resist enculturation.

Source: Maslow, 1970.

with their surroundings. These feelings, which Maslow called **peak experiences,** are fleeting moments in people's lives when they feel truly spontaneous and unconcerned with time or other physical constraints. You may have had such a peak experience while walking in a peaceful forest or viewing a beautiful picture; the feeling is one of being totally absorbed in the situation, in the moment, without cares from the past or concern for the future.

Maslow, unlike many personality theorists, felt that research in personality should focus on healthy individuals. He criticized theories that were based on studying people with psychological disorders; ". . . the study of crippled, stunted, immature, and unhealthy specimens can yield only a cripple psychology and a cripple philosophy" (Maslow, 1970, p. 80). He identified a group of historical figures whom he considered self-actualized (Maslow, 1954). Included in his list were Abraham Lincoln, Thomas Jefferson, Eleanor Roosevelt, Ludwig von Beethoven, and Albert Einstein. Table 12–1 lists the characteristics that Maslow felt these self-actualized people possessed. He later extended his research to college students and concluded that less than 1 percent of all people are truly self-actualized. Thus, the state of self-actualization is one to which we all aspire, but few of us ever reach it.

Carl Rogers

While Maslow focused on the importance of satisfying needs, Carl Rogers identified another hurdle that had to be overcome before people could reach their full potential. Rogers believed that people had to accept themselves (their feelings and behaviors) first. This may sound simple, but, according to Rogers, most people hide or deny parts of their own personality and behavior. This is because there are rules or norms in society that outline a wide range of behaviors and thoughts that are "permissible." When people do not act "in the right way," they are scorned by those around them. According to Rogers, all of us have a need for *positive regard* from others; that is, we want other people to like and value us. Not only do we try to think and behave in the "correct way," but we also may deny or reject those parts of ourselves that do not conform to the way we think we ought to be.

We develop our self-concept by accepting certain values and behaviors and rejecting others. **Self-concept** consists of our judgments and attitudes about our behavior, ability, and even our appearance; it is our answer to the question, "Who am I?" The self-concept is very important, because it determines how we act and how we perceive our world. Many studies

The humanists stress the importance of accepting ourselves. In order to develop our self-concept, it is important that our self-concept reflect our desires and attitudes rather than living up to a standard set by others.

have shown that people with positive self-concepts also tend to be high in achievement (Green et al., 1975). Because our self-image is so vital to the way we behave, it is crucial that it include an honest representation of our feelings, values, and experiences, not just those that society or the people around us find "acceptable." In fact, Rogers believes that people can become self-actualized only to the extent that they can accept all of their personal experiences as part of their self-concept. A cornerstone in Rogers's approach is the belief that people have the freedom to chart their destiny and determine their self-concept.

Sound complicated? Let's take an example from Truman's life. As a young boy, he enjoyed rather domestic activities, such as reading, cooking, and playing the piano. His father and peers pressured him to engage in more "manly" activities such as sports and farming. These pressures conflicted with Truman's true feelings and experience and could have made him deny his own desires. Fortunately, Truman did receive support from his mother and some other friends, and he was able to include his love for reading, cooking, and playing the piano in his self-concept.

Truman was fortunate compared to many other people. According to Rogers, many people react to similar pressures by denying parts of their experience in an effort to gain positive regard from others. They try instead to adopt the values and attitudes of others and, as a result, they lose touch with themselves. They become defensive, depressed, tense, and unable to form close relationships with others. Rogers believed that this damaging situation could be reversed by getting people to recognize and accept a broader range of their own experience.

In order to do this, a different social environment must be created; this environment must include **unconditional positive regard** from others. People must be made to feel accepted and liked regardless of their behavior. This does not mean that one must be told that everything he or she does is "good." Rather, the message must be, "While we may not like that specific behavior or agree with that attitude, we still like and accept *you*." In this way, the person can learn to accept more of his or her experiences as part of the self-concept and can move closer to or begin to work toward self-actualization.

As you can imagine, it is often difficult to shape our everyday environment into one that includes unconditional positive regard. Rogers, however, felt that the therapy sessions could do this. As we will see in Chapter 14, Rogers developed *person-centered therapy*, in which the therapist offers unconditional acceptance of the client. It is important to see how Rogers, like Maslow, believes that, given an open and accepting environment, people will naturally strive for positive personal growth and self-improvement.

Humanistic Theories: An Evaluation

Compared to the gloomy positions taken by other personality theories such as psychoanalytic theory, the humanistic theories are like a bright light on a dark night. In a broad sense, the humanistic concern with people's integrity and uniqueness has influenced research in many areas. Research on the self has ranged from interest in how self-concept develops (Wegner & Vallicher, 1981) to people's perception and awareness of the self (McGuire, 1984). Some investigators (Buss, 1980; Fenigstein, Scheier, & Buss, 1975) have distinguished between the private self (our thoughts, fantasies, and emotions) and the public self (the way we appear to others). Since the 1940s, well over 2,000 studies on self-concept have been completed (Gergen, 1971). The humanistic values have been adopted in applied settings such as clinical therapy (person-centered therapy) and in the T-group or encounter group movement, which is aimed at providing environments to aid personal growth. We will discuss these in detail in Chapter 14.

There have also been criticisms of the humanistic approach. Some investigators have argued that the humanists have failed to clearly define the important terms of their theories. For example, what is self-actualization and how can we measure it (Hall & Lindzey, 1978)? This kind of vagueness makes their theories difficult to test. A second criticism is that the humanistic approach is mostly concerned with human nature. In doing this, it takes such a broad view that it is impossible to make predictions about behavior in specific situations. Finally, Rykman (1979) argues that humanistic theories rely on too few concepts to explain the complexity of human behavior. The theories fail to take into account situational variables that can affect behavior. Thus, while the humanistic position is appealing, more attention must be given to making the theories more testable and more applicable to specific situations and behaviors.

LEARNING THEORIES

While each of the theories we have discussed so far explains behavior in a different way, they all have one point in common: They start from an internal drive or need. In all of them, people are seen as acting because of a motivation arising from inside of them. As we have pointed out, it is difficult if not impossible to measure these internal forces. We are placed in the position of guessing that these internal drives exist because we see the results in the person's behavior. The learning theory approaches to personality were developed to avoid this problem. Learning theorists not only point out these measurement difficulties, but they also argue that we do not need to assume the existence of these "internal forces" to explain behavior and individual differences. They argue that much, if not all, human behavior can be explained by looking at environmental conditions and examining the rewards or punishments the person receives or expects to receive for certain behaviors.

Behaviorism

It is somewhat ironic for us to examine the work of B. F. Skinner in a section devoted to personality theories. As Phares (1984) suggests, it is like "inviting a wolf to a party of lambs" (p. 308). Skinner rejects personality theories altogether. He argues that we do not need to use such concepts as traits, psychodynamics, or free will to explain human behavior. Behavior for Skinner is not something directed by the individual; behavior is determined by the environment. More directly, behavior is the result of rewards and punishments in the environment. For example, Skinner would propose that Truman acted decisively and honestly because he was rewarded for such behavior. Further, if the reinforcement contingencies (see Chapter 6) changed so that Truman was rewarded by being indecisive and dishonest, his behavior would soon change toward these directions.

With a masterful touch, Skinner (1953, 1974, 1978) presents an intriguing case for explaining behavior in terms of operant conditioning. As you will recall from Chapter 6, the operant principle suggests that behaviors are learned and continue to be displayed when they are positively reinforced or rewarded. Behaviors that are not reinforced or those that are punished are extinguished. Another rule of operant conditioning is that behaviors reinforced on a partial reinforcement schedule will resist extinction longer than behaviors that have been reinforced on a continuous schedule. Complex behaviors can be taught by applying shaping, which involves rewarding

According to behaviorism, our actions are determined by the system of rewards and punishments in our environment. A person will continue to perform a behavior if he or she is rewarded for that behavior.

each small part of the larger behavior. According to the behavioristic approach, we need merely examine a person's past schedule of reinforcement and punishment to predict how he or she will respond in the present situation.

In his book *Walden II*, Skinner (1948) painted the picture of a society based on the principles of behavior modification. Here behavior was skillfully manipulated by careful control of rewards and punishments. While *Walden II* was a fictional society, Skinner's concept of the *token economy*, where rewards or tokens are used to shape behavior, has been incorporated in therapeutic techniques (see Chapter 14) and in the management of institutions such as prisons and mental hospitals.

As you can see, Skinner's model is a radical departure from most personality theories. According to Skinner's view, a person is little more than a lump of clay in the hands of the environment, which can shape and reshape it by varying rewards and punishments. It is hard to decide whether Skinner's view of the person as lacking will or freedom is much more flattering than Freud's view of the individual as driven by primitive instincts of lust and aggression! As you might imagine, Skinner has been strongly criticized by humanists, who attack the position that people have no free will. Skinner's description of a society of people totally controlled by rewards and punishments has also pricked the sensitivity of many who view this possibility as dangerous and as having fascist overtones. However, operant principles have been successfully used to treat a wide range of behavior disorders (see Chapter 14). There can be little argument that reinforcement schedules can influence people's behavior. The real question is whether or not the behaviorist position can explain the rich range of human behaviors, thoughts, and feelings.

Social-Learning Theories

As we have seen, Skinner believes that the environment controls people's behavior, while the psychoanalytic theorists argue that internal forces guide behavior. The social-learning theorists suggest that both these approaches are too narrow (Bandura, 1977; Rotter, 1982). They take a position of *reciprocal interaction*, which states that the person and the environment affect each other. For example, recall how Truman answered each of the letters he received from his men's parents during World War I. This behavior impressed his unruly troops, who became more loyal and willing to obey Truman. This new loyalty may further have motivated Truman to do other things for his men. Hence, Truman's initial behavior affected his environment (his troop's behavior), which, in turn, influenced Truman's behavior.

Social-learning theorists also expand the scope of what can be learned. Skinner focused strictly on behavior because only overt behavior can be observed. The social-learning theorists argue that in addition to behavior, people learn rules, languages, feelings, and expectancies. They form goals and plans, and they adopt internal standards of excellence. In other words, the theory focuses on cognitions as well as behavior. This is important because the cognitions that we learn affect the way we interpret our environment and the stimuli that we accept as rewarding (Rotter, 1954). This expansion also allows people to determine their own behavior, rather than being controlled by their environment.

Learning. The social-learning theorists divide behavior into two processes, learning and performance (Bandura, 1977; Bandura & Walters, 1963). We *acquire* knowledge and behavior in many ways—one of the most important is **imitation.** We learn by watching other people act and by observing what happens to them. We can then copy their behavior. For example, we discussed research in Chapter 10 that showed that children could learn how to aggress by observing a model. When they were given

According to social learning theory, we learn by observing and imitating others. Performance will be determined by the system of reinforcement.

the opportunity, they imitated this behavior. We can also imitate behavior that we read about or that has been explained to us. This type of learning is called **observational learning;** it occurs without external reinforcement or without even performing the behavior.

Reinforcement and Performance. Does this mean that external reinforcement has only a slight effect on human behavior? Obviously not. According to the social-learning approach, reinforcement may not be necessary for learning, but it does determine the actual performance of what has been learned. For example, you certainly know how to yell loudly. It is, however, unlikely that you will demonstrate your talents during a psychology lecture or in the library; you would be punished for yelling in these situations. On the other hand, you would probably yell until you were exhausted if you entered the annual hollerin' contest at Spivy's Corner, North Carolina; your loud yell in this situation could bring you a trophy, fame, and a reward. Bandura (1965) demonstrated this principle under more rigorously controlled conditions. As we discussed in Chapter 10, he had subjects observe an adult model hitting and kicking the Bobo doll. In some conditions the model's behavior was punished, in other conditions it was rewarded, and in a third set of conditions there was no reinforcement. The children were then placed in a room with the Bobo doll and their behavior was observed. The children who had seen the model rewarded acted most aggressively toward the Bobo doll. We might wish to conclude that those children had learned more aggressive behavior than did children who had observed the punished or unrewarded model. This, however, was not the case. When Bandura offered these children rewards for imitating the model's behavior, there was no difference in the aggression displayed by any of the children. Therefore, all the children had learned from the model; whether or not they were reinforced determined whether or not they *performed* the behaviors they had learned.

Person Factors Affecting Performance.   While this research demonstrates that environmental reinforcers will influence whether or not behaviors are performed, the social-learning theorists have identified important person factors that also influence behavior. Rotter (1966, 1978), for example, focused on the role of *expectancies*. An expectancy is a belief that a reinforcement will follow a specific behavior. In other words, people learn to expect that rewards will follow certain behaviors. Further, because people have different experiences, they learn different expectancies. For example, you may hold the expectancy that hard work and careful studying will bring you good grades in school. Your roommate, however, may not have this expectancy; in fact, he or she may believe that good grades are a matter of chance. In this case, your studying behavior will probably differ from that of your roommate.

A second important factor that influences whether or not a behavior will be performed is *self-efficacy* (Bandura, 1982). Self-efficacy involves our beliefs about what we can or cannot do. In general, it is the degree of confidence we have in ourselves. For specific behaviors, it concerns the belief that we can or cannot successfully execute that behavior. People with a high degree of self-efficacy will attempt to do things that people with low self-efficacy will not. For example, a person who believes that he or she could not pass college courses would not choose to enter college. Once again, the degree of self-efficacy a person holds is subjective and not necessarily realistic. Hence, we may have friends that we think are very capable of doing well in college. However, they may be unwilling to go to school because they believe they will fail.

Mischel (1973, 1981) identified five person variables that account for why people in the same situation may act differently.

1. *Competencies.* The individual's social skills, task accomplishments, and abilities. (Self-efficacy involves the person's perceptions of his or her competencies.)
2. *Encoding strategies.* The way the individual categorizes and interprets events and the features of the environment to which the individual attends.
3. *Expectancies.* What the individual expects will happen in different situations and the rewards or punishment he or she will receive for certain behaviors.
4. *Subjective values.* The value or importance the individual attaches to various outcomes.
5. *Self-regulatory systems and plans.* The rules that guide the individual's behavior, his or her goals, and the self-imposed standards for behavior.

Locus of Control.   As you will recall, Rotter believed that people learn to expect certain outcomes from their behaviors. The probability that a certain behavior will occur is determined by what the person expects as a reward for that behavior, and what the reward means to the person. Rotter worked with the premise that our general expectancies lead us to act in consistent ways. (These expectancies are like traits, but they are viewed as *learned*, and thus can be influenced by the environment.) Let us briefly examine one of the more widely researched expectancies, **locus of control,** to see how it can affect our behavior.

When Truman became president, he placed a sign on his desk that read "The Buck Stops Here." One of his favorite sayings was, "Things don't just happen, you have to *make* them happen" (Ferrell, 1980). Truman was a man of action and he believed that his actions had consequences. Truman's attitude is characteristic of an internal locus of control position.

Table 12-2
Sample Items from Rotter's Internal/External (I-E) Scale

> 1A. Many of the unhappy things in people's lives are partly due to bad luck.
> *1B. People's misfortunes result from the mistakes they make.
> 2A. No matter how hard you try, some people just don't like you.
> *2B. People who can't get others to like them don't understand how to get along with others.
> *3A. In the case of the well-prepared student, there is rarely if ever such a thing as an unfair test.
> 3B. Many times exam questions tend to be so unrelated to course work that studying is really useless.
> *4A. Becoming a success is a matter of hard work, luck has little or nothing to do with it.
> 4B. Getting a good job depends mainly on being in the right place at the right time.
> *5A. The average citizen can have an influence in government decisions.
> 5B. This world is run by the few people in power, and there is not much the little guy can do about it.
>
> * These items represent an internal locus of control outlook; the others reflect an external locus of control view.
>
> Source: Rotter (1966), p. 11.

Parents who are warm and supportive and give praise for accomplishments are likely to foster the development of internal locus of control . . . their children.

According to Rotter (1966), individuals learn generalized expectancies to view reinforcing events either as being directly dependent on their own actions or as being beyond their control. In other words, people develop expectancies about the locus of control of reinforcements. At one extreme are *internals* who believe that they control their own fate. Internals feel that they can have an effect on the environment through their actions and they feel responsible for the results of their behavior. To the other extreme are *externals*, who believe that what happens to them is the result of luck and chance; they believe that they can do little to directly influence their own surroundings. Rotter (1966) developed the I–E Scale (see Table 12–2) to measure people's perceptions of locus of control.

Expectancies about locus of control are not inherited, they are learned. One investigator found that internals grew up in families where the parents were warm and supportive and gave praise for accomplishments (Crandall, 1973). This atmosphere encouraged children to learn to accept blame for failure and praise for success. Crandall also found that as these children grew up, the parents became more detached and encouraged their children to become more independent. This withdrawal forced the children to exercise more control over their surroundings and gave them the opportunity to see the behavioral outcomes.

An individual's perception of locus of control not only influences the way he or she interprets situations, it also affects behavior. For example, Seeman and his associates found that internals are more likely to seek out information to help them cope with problems than are externals (Seeman & Evans, 1962). In one study, the investigators found that tuberculosis patients described as internals were more likely than external patients to ask their doctor for information about their disease. This finding was expected because internals believe they can influence their own fate; the information should help them decide on behaviors to further their cure. Externals, on the other hand, believe that their fate is out of their control.

Locus of control also influences the attribution one makes about the reasons for success and failure. It was found that internals believed that their failures were due to their own lack of ability or effort (Phares, 1976). Externals, though, felt that their failures were due to task difficulty or bad luck. As a result of these attribution differences, internals felt more shame for their failures than did the externals. These attribution differences extend beyond explaining the individual's own behavior. Phares (1976) also found that internals felt that other people are in control of their own outcomes. As a result, internals judged others more severely than did externals, and they were more likely to deliver harsh punishment for failures or rule violations.

Learning Theories: An Evaluation

As we suggested, the main strength of Skinner's theory of behaviorism is its clarity. It offers numerous testable hypotheses, and, for the most part, its concepts are precise and clear. It deals with observable behavior and can make a wide range of predictions without resorting to events that may be going on within the person. In a real sense, behaviorism's strength is also its weakness. Because it avoids activities within the individual, it cannot capture the richness of human thought, feelings, and plans. Opponents argue that behaviorism cannot explain the complex and complicated nature of human behaviors. Nor does behaviorism adequately account for the wide range of individual differences characteristic of human action.

Social-learning theory, on the other hand, stresses the importance of language, information processing, and planning. The theory attempts to integrate environmental variables with cognitive functioning to explain human behavior. Social-learning theory emphasizes the importance of the present and the future for predicting behavior. Like behaviorism, the theory suggests that behavior can change as present environmental factors change; it does not accept the psychoanalytic position that personality is largely determined by the time a person is 5 or 6 years old. By focusing on the present and future, social-learning theory offers an optimistic outlook for humans. The theory suggests that even some of the most dysfunctional behavior patterns can be changed through observational learning and the proper reinforcements in the environment. Finally, social-learning theory, like behaviorism, has initiated a tremendous amount of research, and, as we will see in Chapter 14, the theory has served as the foundation for some very successful therapy techniques.

Social-learning theory has been criticized because it lacks the integration found in psychoanalytic theory. Social-learning theory is constantly changing, and it stands as a number of interesting concepts and observations without neat ribbons to tie it all together. It lacks the unity we would like to see in such theory. A second criticism is that the theory fails to take into account the importance of developmental change in personality formation. As children grow, they experience dramatic physical, biological, and psychological changes that should affect their behavior and perceptions of their environment. While much of the social-learning research involves children, the theory does not address how maturational changes influence behavior. Finally, some critics feel that learning theories are theories of specific behaviors, not of people. In other words, we might be able to explain why a person behaves in a certain way in a certain situation, but we do not get a picture of the person as a whole; we cannot see how all these behaviors "fit together" to make up the total personality.

PERSONALITY THEORIES: A CONCLUDING REMARK

This brief introduction to personality theories may have left your head spinning, wondering which one is right. There is no one theory that explains personality. As we have pointed out, each of the theories has its strengths and weaknesses. The answer to the question of what makes people act differently is found in all the theories together and in none of them on its own. Research is even now going on to define and redefine the theories. Few investigators are willing to adopt one theory and exclude the others.

Theory and Major Figures	Important Period(s)	View of Basic Human Nature	Guiding Force of Personality	Important Concepts
Psychoanalytic Freud	early childhood	evil	internal (libido)	id, ego, super-ego, conscious, preconscious, unconscious
Analytical Psychology Jung	early childhood, middle years, and later years	positive—strive to achieve balance among opposites	internal	ego, personal conscious, collective unconscious, archetypes, opposites
Individual Psychology Adler	childhood	positive	internal, but influenced by social environment	social interest, organization in family, inferiority complex, style of life
Humanistic Theory Rogers, Maslow	childhood, later adulthood	very positive	internal—needs and striving for self-actualization	needs, self-actualization, self-concept, unconditional positive regard
Behaviorism Skinner	present	no reference to human nature	external environment	operant behavior, schedules of reinforcement, shaping
Social-Learning Theory Bandura, Rotter, Mischel	present (past and future experiences also influential)	no reference to human nature	external and person factors—reciprocal interaction	response, observational learning, expectancies, self-efficacy

Table 12–3
Theories of Personality

The human personality is wonderfully complex and the various theories offer different perspectives to follow in the effort to understand it. Psychoanalytic theory suggests that we can best understand human behavior by identifying internal forces that are set into action during infancy and childhood. Humanistic theories argue that we can understand personality by looking at the "good side" of people and examining how the desire for self-fulfillment guides behavior. Learning theories add that our quest to understand personality must take into account external events; these theories also suggest that personality changes throughout life, as well as present situations, are at least as important as past events in directing behavior.

These different theories influence the direction of research. For example, an investigator guided by psychoanalytic theory will focus his or her attention on early childhood experiences, while a researcher who adopts a learning perspective will study external variables that occur in the person's present environment. While the different methods of study uncover different characteristics of the personality, we cannot conclude that one method is more correct than the others; each has a purpose and helps us understand personality. And, as we will see in the next two chapters, each theory offers insight into the nature of psychological disorders and helps chart treatment programs for those disorders.

PERSONALITY ASSESSMENT

We began this chapter asking the question, "What was Harry Truman really like?" How was he different from other people and why was he different? Our discussion of personality theories focused on the *why* issues. We used the various theories to explain why Truman chose to enter politics or why he became a modest, studious individual. We will now turn our attention away from the issue of *why* Truman was the way he was and focus on identifying what Truman was like.

Personality assessment is the description and measurement of individual characteristics. We all make personality assessments, almost every day. On the first day of class, for example, you might anxiously assess the personality of your professor. Is she rigid and a tough grader, or is she a rather easygoing, vague type who will generally assign good grades? There are many ways you can make your assessment. You can concentrate on what the professor says: "There will be no curves, and I am willing to fail half the class." Or, you can review the professor's behavior: Last semester she failed 72 percent of the class. A third way of learning about the professor is to see how she interprets some rather ambiguous information about grading at your university or college. For example, does she think that grading has become too easy because last semester over half the students at the school had an A average? If so, you had better plan on spending a lot of time preparing for the course.

Each of these methods (looking at behavior, examining verbal or written responses, and studying the interpretations given to ambiguous information) is used to assess personality. The method a researcher will use often depends on the particular theory or approach to personality that he or she holds. Also, just as there are strengths and weaknesses associated with each theory, the different personality tests, too, have strengths and weaknesses.

Before discussing the specific methods of assessment, let us look at some requirements for any test, whether it is measuring personality characteristics or what you learned in class last week.

Requirements of a Test

Any test that measures stable dimensions, whether it be personality or one's academic abilities, must have two qualities before it can be considered a good test. First, the test must be **reliable**—it must yield consistent results. There are many types of consistency that a test must have. There must be *inter-rater reliability* so that a test scored by one person yields the same results as when the test is scored by another rater. There must also be *test-retest reliability* so that the results on the test are similar each time the same person takes the test. Consider this example. You took the college entrance examination twice in a 2-month period. The first time you took it, you scored 1200, the second time you scored 650. Since it is unlikely that your ability to do college work changed that much over time, you could rightfully argue that the test was not reliable. In this case, the test-retest reliability was low.

On the other hand, suppose you took the test and scored 640 the first time and 650 the second time. In this case, you could not criticize the test's reliability. However, before you decide not to go to college, you could evaluate the test—what is the test estimating? Does it really measure one's ability to do well in college? In other words, is the test **valid**—does it measure what it is designed to measure? One of the most popular ways to determine the validity of a test is to see if it is a good predictor of the behaviors it was designed to test. Consider the college entrance examination. We could examine the college performance of students who had scored high or low on the test. If we found that the high scorers did better in college than the low scorers, we could argue that our entrance examination was a valid test; it proved to have predictive validity. In the same way, if we design a personality test to measure aggressiveness, we could determine validity by examining the behaviors of people who had received different scores on the test.

A useful measure of personality must be both reliable and valid. The test must give consistent scores and it must measure what it is designed to measure.

Behavioral Assessment

Since one of the aims of personality tests is to predict behavior, a number of investigators have examined an individual's present behavior to predict future actions, which is known as **behavioral assessment.** Behavioral assessment can also be used to assign traits to individuals. There are a number of techniques of behavioral assessment. One involves observing an individual's behavior in natural settings. For example, if we wanted to determine how modest or friendly Harry Truman was, we could carefully watch him in a number of settings. We could note his verbal behavior (how often he talked about himself, praised others, asked for help) and his nonverbal behavior (how often he smiled, touched other people, moved away from crowds). It is important that we make our observations in a number of different settings to ensure that we are not simply seeing how Truman is affected by one specific situation.

This *natural observation* method has many advantages. It is unobtrusive in the sense that people do not know they are being studied. There is a great deal of research showing that people are likely to change their behavior if they are aware that they are being studied (Orne, 1962). The natural observation method may also offer a high degree of predictive validity because it offers a sample of behavior in a number of real settings.

Despite these important strengths, there are also problems with the natural observation method (Kent & Foster, 1977). First, it takes a great deal of time. In many cases, the researcher may have to observe a single individual for many days in many settings. Second, it may be hard to get a high degree of interjudge reliability. For example, the acts that one judge rates as "friendly" may not be rated the same by another judge. One might categorize a person's behavior as friendly when he or she smiles and says hello to a professor; another person might score this behavior as manipulative.

The Interview

There is an old story about two philosophers who wanted to know how many teeth were in a horse's mouth. These two learned individuals spent days arguing about such issues as how many teeth the horse needed, the optimal arrangement of teeth in the horse's mouth, and the probable size of the horse's teeth. In the middle of their heated argument, a small child walked up to the horse, forced its mouth open, and counted the teeth. This solution was so simple that it had not occurred to the two philosophers. We might apply the same type of reasoning to the measurement of personality; if we want to know what people are like, why not ask them? Psychologists do use the "asking" method, in the form of the **interview.** Two main types of interviews have been used.

In the *unstructured interview*, the interviewer has a particular area in which he or she is interested, and the interview begins with some planned questions. However, the later questions are determined by the subject's responses. The unstructured interview is often used in clinical settings or in other situations where the interviewer is interested in getting a broad picture of what the person is like.

In the *structured interview*, the interviewer asks specific questions following a set plan. This type of interview is aimed at getting specific information from someone. Employers often use this method when they are interviewing prospective employees. Some personality tests are also conducted in the

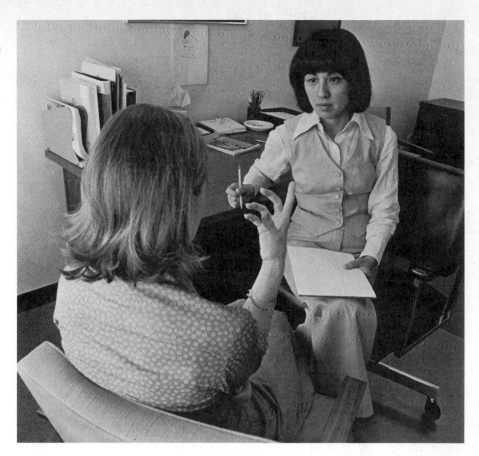

Interviews are used to assess personality. In the unstructured interview, the examiner's questions are influenced by the subjects' responses. In the structured interview, the examiner has a set of predetermined questions that the subject answers.

form of structured interviews. The advantage of asking all the people the same questions is that responses can then be directly compared.

The interview is a direct method of obtaining information and is very useful. It does, however, have drawbacks. In some cases it may have little validity because respondents are reluctant to present themselves in a bad light. For example, imagine how you might respond if an interviewer asked you to discuss your sex life. Reliability may also be low, because people's responses can be affected by their feelings about the interviewer. An interviewer who seems cold and critical may get very different responses than would a warm and understanding interviewer. Finally, interviews are very time-consuming. Generally only one person can be interviewed at a time, and someone must spend time reviewing and scoring the responses.

Thus, assessing personality is not as simple as counting the teeth in a horse's mouth; the most direct method may not always give us the most useful information. However, valuable information can be obtained from an interview. The interview can also be used to make someone feel more at ease before taking some other personality test. Because of this, interviews, like behavioral assessments, are often used along with other tests.

The Questionnaire. In order to get around some of the problems associated with behavioral assessment and interviews, many personality tests in the form of questionnaires have been developed. The **questionnaire** involves a standard set of questions; often people respond by indicating their answers on computer forms. The questions are often true/false or multiple choice. The strengths of the questionnaire are: (1) They can be given to many people at one time; (2) all people answer the same questions under the same conditions; and (3) the tests usually can be scored quickly. A number of questionnaires have been administered and scored by computer (Butcher & Owen, 1978; Korchin & Shuldberg, 1981). In some cases, a person can read the questions on a monitor and type a response on the computer keyboard. The computer can then immediately score the test.

There are, however, potential problems with questionnaires. The first problem concerns understanding. Because people may fill out the questionnaire either alone or in groups, we can't be sure that they understand each question or even interpret the questions in the same way. A second problem is that we can only assume that people answer honestly. In some cases, people may be motivated to give the answer that makes them look good or the answer that they feel the examiner wants. It would be difficult for some people to answer "true" to the following question, even if it honestly reflected their feelings: "Sometimes I feel intense hatred toward my mother." The third problem of this test is *response bias*. Some people have a tendency to agree to almost any position presented.

Let us examine one questionnaire.

Minnesota Multiphasic Personality Inventory (MMPI). One of the most popular personality questionnaires used by clinicians in diagnosis is the **Minnesota Multiphasic Personality Inventory (MMPI)** (Hathaway & McKinley, 1942, 1943). The MMPI was designed to identify specific psychological disorders. Hathaway and McKinley developed the scale by preparing a number of one line statements to which the individual could respond "true," "false," or "cannot say." The items concerned a wide range of issues such as attitudes, past experiences, emotions, and psychological symptoms. For example, the following statements were offered to people: "I tire easily," "I believe there is a God," "My mother often made me obey even when I thought it was unreasonable." The investigators then presented these items to patients in mental hospitals who had been diagnosed as suffering from specific psychological disorders (e.g., depression, hysteria, paranoia). They also had a control group of nonpatients answer the questions. Their next step was to choose the items that distinguished patients from nonpatients. For example, they would look for an item that most depressed patients answered in the same way, but that was answered differently by the control group. This item would be included in the test as one that could identify depression. Using this procedure, Hathaway and McKinley eventually chose 550 questions to be included in the MMPI. The MMPI has sets of items or scales aimed at identifying ten different disorders (e.g., hysteria, depression, or schizophrenia). The investigators also added some items to determine the validity of responses. For example, the Lie Scale included an item, "I do not always tell the truth." It is, indeed, a rare individual who never tells a falsehood; thus, a "false" response to this question would cast some doubt on the validity of the individual's responses to other items in the questionnaire.

The MMPI is most effective in separating those suffering from mild disorders from people suffering from more serious personality disturbances. Subscales of the MMPI have also been developed to predict alcohol and drug abuse (Zager & Megargee, 1981). Because the MMPI was designed to detect psychological disorders, it is of little use for identifying personality traits in a "normal" population. The California Psychological Inventory (CPI) was designed to incorporate many of the strengths of the MMPI in a test that could be used to measure more normal traits such as poise, dominance, self-assurance, sociability, maturity, achievement, and aptitude. The CPI is similar in form to the MMPI; in fact, half of the CPI items are taken from the MMPI. The test has been used widely in personality research.

Projective Tests

As we discussed earlier, Freud believed that people have unconscious drives that motivate their behavior. Some of these drives are very threaten-

MEASURING SELF-CONCEPT

How do you measure what people think of themselves? Self-concept is one of the basic dimensions of the humanistic theories of personality, and people have tried through the years to develop a test or scale of self-concept.

One way is simply to present people with incomplete sentences, each starting with "I am _____," and see how they respond. The first time this was done, in the 1950s,

most responses referred to social status ("I am a student, parent, dancer," etc.). More recently, in the 1970s, most people used traits or other abstract terms to describe themselves ("I am aggressive, shy, outgoing," etc.).

The questionnaire that follows is designed to measure self-concept, but it also asks questions about what people would like to be (their self-ideal). People filling out this

questionnaire are asked to give two answers to each question: "I am" and "I would like to be." The answers show not only a positive or negative self-concept, they also show how close to the "ideal" people perceive themselves to be. This in turn can be used to determine people's general level of frustration: The closer they are to their own self-ideal, the less frustrated they are.

	I am a person who:					II I would like to be a person who:				
	very often	often	sometimes	seldom	never	very often	often	sometimes	seldom	never
1. feels he must win an argument.	1	2	3	4	5	1	2	3	4	5
2. plays up to others in order to advance his position.	1	2	3	4	5	1	2	3	4	5
3. refuses to do things because he is not good at them.	1	2	3	4	5	1	2	3	4	5
4. avoids telling the truth to prevent unpleasant consequences.	1	2	3	4	5	1	2	3	4	5
5. tries hard to impress people with his ability.	1	2	3	4	5	1	2	3	4	5
6. does dangerous things for the thrill of it.	1	2	3	4	5	1	2	3	4	5
7. relies on his parents to help make decisions.	1	2	3	4	5	1	2	3	4	5
8. has periods of great restlessness when he must be on the go.	1	2	3	4	5	1	2	3	4	5
9. seeks out others so they can listen to his troubles.	1	2	3	4	5	1	2	3	4	5
10. gets angry when criticized by his friends.	1	2	3	4	5	1	2	3	4	5
11. feels inferior to his friends.	1	2	3	4	5	1	2	3	4	5
12. is afraid to try something new.	1	2	3	4	5	1	2	3	4	5
13. gets confused when working under pressure.	1	2	3	4	5	1	2	3	4	5
14. worries about his health.	1	2	3	4	5	1	2	3	4	5
15. has difficulty in starting to get down to work.	1	2	3	4	5	1	2	3	4	5
16. is dissatisfied with his sex life.	1	2	3	4	5	1	2	3	4	5
17. bluffs to get ahead.	1	2	3	4	5	1	2	3	4	5
18. goes out of his way to avoid an argument.	1	2	3	4	5	1	2	3	4	5
19. makes quick judgments about other people.	1	2	3	4	5	1	2	3	4	5
20. wonders whether parents will approve of his actions.	1	2	3	4	5	1	2	3	4	5
21. is afraid to disagree with another person.	1	2	3	4	5	1	2	3	4	5
22. ignores the feelings of others.	1	2	3	4	5	1	2	3	4	5
23. feels angry when his parents try to tell him what to do.	1	2	3	4	5	1	2	3	4	5
24. likes to gossip about the misfortunes and embarrassments of his friends.	1	2	3	4	5	1	2	3	4	5
25. takes disappointment so keenly that he can't put it out of his mind.	1	2	3	4	5	1	2	3	4	5

ing and, consequently, they are repressed or disguised. In fact, people may not be aware of these drives even though they affect their behavior. One of the disguised ways in which these drives are expressed is through projection; people see others as having these forbidden drives and desires. According to this position, we might have difficulty learning about an individual's personality by asking direct questions about his or her personal feelings and desires. However, these unconscious drives will be expressed if we ask the individual questions about others or about ambiguous events. In these cases the individual will project these unconscious desires onto the ambiguous and unthreatening stimulus.

This is the reasoning behind **projective tests.** In these projective measures of personality, the individual is asked to discuss an ambiguous or vague stimulus. The individual's responses are analyzed to determine what they tell about him or her. An advantage of projective tests is that there are no correct or incorrect answers. Thus, it is unlikely that a person will give the answer that he or she assumes the examiner wants. And, unlike many of the questionnaires, projective tests can be used with people who do not read or write.

There are, however, problems with projective tests. First, they are often difficult to interpret or score; the same response may be interpreted differently by different judges. Second, responses to projective tests have not proven to be good predictors of specific behaviors. For example, we might find that certain people have a strong unconscious aggressive drive. However, they may rarely act in an aggressive way. Finally, because most projective tests are given individually, the administering and scoring is very time-consuming.

Despite these problems, projective tests are used by many clinicians to aid them in diagnosis. Let us examine two of the most widely used projective techniques.

Rorschach Inkblot Test.   Have you ever become absorbed in watching clouds floating lazily through the sky and suddenly realized that you "saw" pictures in the clouds? In one cloud you might have seen a fat woman sitting on a broken chair, while in another cloud you noted the outline of a lion attacking a small lamb. Yet another person may see completely different scenes in the same formations. These "pictures" are projections that are being made onto ambiguous stimuli.

Hermann Rorschach, a Swiss psychiatrist, was aware that people "see things" in ambiguous stimuli, and he felt that much could be learned about individual personalities from the things that people "saw." In 1911, Rorschach began showing cards containing inkblots to his patients. He asked them to describe what they saw in the blots. After using many different inkblots for over a decade, he chose the 10 blots that brought out the most vivid and emotional responses. These blots make up the **Rorschach inkblot test.**

Each blot has a different shape; some are colored and others are black-and-white (Figure 12–4). The blots are printed on cards and presented to subjects in a set order. The individual is asked to describe what he or she "sees" in the blot.

Controversies about the Rorschach test do not so much center on the gathering of responses as they do on the scoring or interpretation of these responses. There are a number of techniques used for scoring the Rorschach test (Holtzman, 1975). However, regardless of the specific method, the scoring focuses on the same general questions. The scorer examines whether the response was concerned with the whole blot or only part of it; the shape, color, and amount of activity present; and the subject of the response (human figure, animal, plant, or inanimate object). In addition to the responses given to the inkblot, the tester notes the individual's behavior while taking the test. Was the individual nervous? Did he or she take a great deal of time studying the blot before responding? As you might imagine, it takes a great deal of training to interpret the Rorschach test. This test has been used almost exclusively for the diagnosis of personality and emotional disturbances. Recently, investigators have shown that the Rorschach can be used to differentiate between opiate addicts and psychiatric patients (Blutt & Berman, 1984).

Figure 12–4
The Rorschach inkblot test involves subjects stating what they see in ambiguous inkblots. It is assumed that subjects will project their feelings in their responses.

Figure 12–5

Thematic Apperception Test (TAT). While the Rorschach test was developed to identify psychological disorders, the Thematic Apperception Test (TAT) was originally designed to identify people's needs and motives (see Chapter 10). In the test, the subject is shown a picture of an ambiguous scene (see Figure 12–5) and asked to tell a story about it. The subject is asked to discuss what is happening in the scene, what events preceded the situation, what the people in the picture are thinking, and what will happen in the end. The TAT is a projective test because it is assumed that people identify with one of the subjects in the picture and reveal their own concerns about achievement in the story. While the TAT was first used to measure achievement motivation, other scoring techniques have been developed to measure such areas as affiliation and person fears. Variations of the TAT have also been used as research tools in other cultures. As can be seen in Figure 12–5, it may be necessary to redraw the pictures to make them more suitable to the culture being examined.

The TAT suffers from the same problems of reliability and validity found with the Rorschach test; it has proven very difficult to predict specific behaviors from responses on the TAT, and there is not a generally-agreed upon scoring system for the test. Therefore, the TAT, along with most projective tests, is often used as only one of the tools in a whole group of tests aimed at assessing personality.

Choosing an Assessment Technique

As you can see, there are a number of ways to measure an individual's personality. Given this wide range of methods, how do you decide which ones to use? One of the major factors that will determine your decision is the personality theory in which you most strongly believe. For example, if you adopt the psychoanalytic theory, you will be interested in measuring unconscious drives that influence people's behavior. Given this approach, you will most likely choose projective tests as the basis for your assessment. However, if you are a learning theorist, you will use behavorial assessment. As you will recall, learning theories argue against the importance of internal drives; instead they focus on observable events such as behavior. If you adopt the humanistic point of view, one of your main interests will be to identify goals; you will want to learn what type of person the individual desires to be. The most direct way to determine these goals is to ask the person. Therefore, you will use the questionnaire method.

In addition to theoretical considerations, you must also take into account the characteristics of the people who make up your sample. Can they read or write? If they cannot, you will not use a questionnaire.

Clearly there are many factors that will influence your choice of an assessment technique. It should, however, be remembered that in almost all cases, the psychologist will not rely on only one method. Rather, a battery of techniques will be used. This battery will often include an interview, behavioral assessment, and questionnaire or projective test. Just as we pointed out that no single theory can account for the complexity of human personality, no single assessment method can adequately measure personality.

Summary

1. **Personality** is defined as a unique set of behaviors and enduring qualities that influence the way a person adjusts to the environment. The study of personality involves examining individual differences and explaining why people act differently in similar situations.

2. Many personality theories assume that people tend to act the same way in many different situations. Research, however, has shown that situational variables may determine a person's behavior. It therefore seems that personality factors predispose the individual to act in a certain way, but this predisposition may be overridden by situational factors.

3. Some of the earliest theories of personality were type theories, which tried to place people into "either/or" personality categories. A related approach occurs in trait theories. These theorists try to determine the structure of personality by identifying relatively permanent qualities that people may possess.

4. **Psychoanalytic theory** was developed by Sigmund Freud. It focuses on the internal, often unconscious forces that cause people to act in certain ways. Freud described personality as the result of a constant struggle between the **id, ego,** and **superego.** Freud argued that an individual's personality is formed during the first 6 years of life.

5. Some scholars, such as Carl Jung and Alfred Adler, accepted much of Freud's psychoanalytic theory but argued that Freud focused too heavily on sex. They suggested other motives, such as power and the social environment, that influence personality.

6. **Humanistic theories** suggest that people

desire to become **self-actualized** and experience personal growth. Humanists encourage people to learn about and accept themselves rather than try to live up to standards set by others.

7. Learning theorists argue that outside events determine human behavior. According to learning theories, people act only to obtain rewards and avoid punishment. Their personality is dependent on the rewards available in their environment, and because of this personality is formed and changed throughout people's lives.

8. **Social-learning theory** suggests that people learn new behaviors by **imitating** others. One thing that people can learn is a generalized expectancy to perceive events either as being dependent on their own actions or as out of their control. People with an internal **locus of control** believe they control their own fate; those with an external **locus of control** see their fate as determined by chance.

9. **Personality assessment** is the description and measurement of individual characteristics. While there are many techniques used to assess personality, a good measure must be both reliable and valid.

10. One of the most common assessment techniques is **behavioral assessment.** This method involves observing how people act and determining what their actions indicate about their personality.

11. Both structured and unstructured **interviews** are used to obtain information about an individual's personality.

12. A number of **questionnaires** have been de-

veloped to examine specific parts of the personality. For example, the **Minnesota Multiphasic Personality Inventory (MMPI)** includes 550 questions aimed at identifying personality disorders.

13. **Projective tests** are based on the psychoanalytic theory position that unconscious motives influence behavior. These tests attempt to identify these unconscious motives by allowing people to project their feelings onto ambiguous stimuli. For example, the **Rorschach inkblot test** involves having people describe what they see in inkblots. With the **Thematic Apperception Test (TAT),** people tell stories about what is happening in a series of pictures.

14. Most personality assessments involve using many assessment techniques together. However, the main focus of the assessment is often based on the examiner's preference of personality theories and on the characteristics of the subject. For example, an examiner who was strongly influenced by psychoanalytic theory may rely on projective tests, while one who agreed with learning theory would emphasize behavioral assessment.

Key Terms

anal stage
analytical psychology
behavioral assessment
conscious
dreams
ego
Electra complex
free association
humanistic psychology
id
imitation
individual psychology
interview
latency period
libido
locus of control
Minnesota Multiphasic Personality Inventory (MMPI)
observational learning
Oedipus complex
oral stage
peak experiences
personality

personality assessment
phallic stage
phrenology
pleasure principle
preconscious
projective tests
psychoanalytic theory
questionnaire
reality principle
reliable
Rorschach inkblot test
self-actualization
self-concept
social-learning theory
somatotype
superego
Thematic Apperception Test (TAT)
traits
unconditional positive regard
unconscious
valid

Suggested Readings

The following books are about Harry Truman:

DANIELS, J. *The man of Independence*. Philadelphia: Lippincott, 1950.

MILLER, M. *Plain speaking*: An oral biography of Harry S. Truman. New York: Berkley, 1974.

BANDURA, A. *Social learning theory*. Englewood Cliffs, N.J.: Prentice-Hall, 1977. Bandura presents an overview of social-learning theory and applies it to many areas, including the development of personality.

HALL, C. S., & LINDZEY, G. *Theories of personality* (3rd ed.). New York: Wiley, 1978. This book presents a summary of the major theories in personality and some of the important criticisms of each. It is widely used as a reference for personality theories.

ROTTER, J. B. *The development and application of social learning theory*: Selected papers. New York: Praeger, 1982. A collection of papers expanding Rotter's position on social learning theory. Topics include trust, locus of control, and internal-external orientation.

SKINNER, B. F. *Beyond freedom and dignity*. New York: Knopf, 1971. Skinner discusses behaviorism and how it can be applied to many situations.

STEIN, M. (Ed.). *Jungian analysis*. La Salle, Ill.: Open Court Publishing, 1982. An edited volume focusing on the theory of analytical psychology and how the principles can be applied in psychotherapy.

VERNON, P. *Personality assessment*: A critical survey. New York: Wiley, 1964. This volume presents many of the major methods for assessing personality. It shows how these methods relate to the major theories of personality and examines the merits and problems with the methods.

WOLLHEIM, R. *Sigmund Freud*. New York: Viking Press, 1971. This book discusses Freud's life and psychoanalytic theory.

ABNORMAL PSYCHOLOGY

The little man's eyes blazed as he watched the jurors file into the courtroom. Everyone was strangely silent; the longest criminal trial in American history was about to end. The trial had lasted 9½ months, cost over a million dollars, and produced 31,716 pages of transcript. The clerk solemnly accepted the written verdict from the jury foreman. He paused a moment and then read, "We, the jury in the above-entitled action, find the defendant, Charles Manson, guilty of the crime of murder. . . ." It took 38 minutes for the clerk to read all the verdicts; Manson and his three female codefendants were found guilty of murdering seven people, including pregnant actress Sharon Tate.

The trial had uncovered the gruesome details of how four members of the Manson Family had followed Manson's orders to break into two fashionable Beverly Hills homes and murder all the residents. Five people inside one of the homes were beaten, shot, and slashed to death, and the raiders wrote the word "PIG" on the walls of the house with the blood of their victims. Later the Manson Family members entered the house of a wealthy businessman and slaughtered him and his wife and scrawled the words "Helter Skelter" with the victims' blood. Nothing was taken from either house and the murderers did not know their victims; their sole purpose was to kill whomever they found in the houses.

The trial not only revealed the details of the bizarre and shocking deeds of this band of killers, it also sketched a picture of the man who ordered this senseless slaughter. Charles Manson was born "No Name Maddox" on November 12, 1934; he was the illegitimate son of a 16-year-old girl named Kathleen Maddox (Bugliosi & Gentry, 1974). According to Manson, his mother was a prostitute, and he was not sure who his father was. His mother, who lived with a number of men, was, however, married to a William Manson for a short time and for this reason Charles was given the name Manson.

Kathleen was not to be tied down by her child; she would leave her young son with a neighbor "for an hour or so" and then disappear for days or weeks. In 1939, Kathleen and her brother were caught robbing a service station and were sentenced to a state penitentiary. Charles went to live with a very strict aunt who thought that all pleasures were sinful, but who gave him love. Three years later Kathleen reclaimed him, and she spent the next few years dragging him from one rundown rooming house to another. At the age of 12, he was placed in an institution for boys because his mother was unable to care for him. The school records indicate that Manson "had a tendency toward moodiness and a persecution complex. . . ." Ten months later he ran away from the institution and began his life of crime.

Over the next 4 years Manson was arrested eight times for crimes ranging from auto theft to armed robbery. By the age of 16, he was a hardened criminal. His behavior was erratic and unpredictable. For example, less than a month before his parole hearing at one institution, he held a razor blade against the throat of another inmate while he raped him. Prison authorities labeled Manson a dangerous homosexual and he was transferred to the Federal Reformatory at Petersburg, Virginia. Here Manson's behavior suddenly changed. He took an active interest in the work and educational programs, learning to read and to solve simple arithmetic problems. He was granted parole, but in less than a year he was back in the penitentiary for stealing an automobile. At times he was so depressed that he avoided all social contact; at other times he sought out others and tried to impress them.

Manson spent the next several years in and out of prison. During this time he developed three obsessions. One was with mystical religions; he became an avid reader of literature on different religious philosophies such as Buddhism and Scientology. His second obsession was with music. He learned to play the guitar in prison, and he would spend hours each day practicing. His third fascination was with the Beatles, the British singing group that rose to fame in 1964. Manson studied their music, listened to their records over and over, and tried to find the hidden message in the words of their songs.

On March 21, 1967, Charles Manson was released from prison. He was 32 years old and had spent over 17 years in prison. On his release, he begged prison officials to let him remain in prison. He said that it was the only home he knew and he was afraid of the outside world.

The authorities refused Manson's request, and on obtaining his parole, he went to San Francisco. There he found free food, music, drugs, and love; in 1967 the hippie movement was at its peak and San Francisco was the center of the flower culture. Manson was fascinated with the whole scene: ". . .

I started playing my music and people liked my music and people smiled at me and put their arms around me and hugged me—I didn't know how to act. It just took me away (Bugliosi & Gentry, 1974, p. 222). Unfortunately, Manson did not know how to accept the warmth that was offered to him. He did, however, see a way to use the situation. He began playing up to a number of the young women who had "made the scene." Manson charmed these vulnerable flower children with his mystical quotes and soft music. In a very short time he had 18 followers, all of whom he controlled through the use of drugs, sex, and his almost hypnotic personality. He used the women to lure men into his fold, and the Manson Family was born.

Manson was overjoyed with his power over the Family, and his thinking and behavior became increasingly bizarre. He developed the belief that he had lived before, nearly 2,000 years ago, and that he had died on the cross. He reinforced his belief that he was Jesus Christ by highlighting his name, "Man Son." His obsession with the Beatles grew. He believed that they were angels of God who spoke to him through the words of their songs. He was especially fascinated with the Beatles' *White Album* and with the song "Helter Skelter." He was convinced that the song predicted a black revolution, which "would begin with the black man going into white people's homes and ripping off the white people, physically destroying them, until there was open revolution in the streets. . . . Then the black man would assume white man's karma" (Bugliosi, 1974, p. 331). According to Manson, the blacks would destroy all the whites except for the Manson Family, who would be hiding in the desert and multiplying while the revolution was going on. After the revolution, Manson and his Family, which would then number 144,000, would emerge and assume control over the inferior blacks.

Manson's whole life began to revolve around Helter Skelter, the black-white revolution that he had imagined.

He started training the Family for the revolution. One of his favorite tactics was to "creepy-crawly" houses. This involved sneaking into a home while the unsuspecting residents slept, rearranging furniture and other items, and then leaving—all done without waking the residents.

Manson soon decided that he must be the one to start the revolution. Therefore, he ordered his family members to break into two houses on the nights of August 9 and 10, 1969, and murder whoever was in those houses. He further instructed his followers to make the scene look as if black people had committed the crime. According to Manson's thinking, this tactic would serve two purposes. First, it would teach blacks how to revolt. Second, it would cause the white establishment to turn against the blacks and bring the black-white conflict to a head. Charles Manson believed that he could bring about Helter Skelter, a national racial revolution, by murdering seven people in Hollywood.

It was this Charles Manson who sat in court on March 29, 1971, and heard the clerk read, "We, the jury . . . do fix the penalty as death." Because of later changes in the California laws concerning the death penalty, Charles Manson instead remains in a California prison awaiting his next parole hearing. In September 1984 another inmate became upset with Manson and set him afire. Although Manson survived, he was severely burned.

CASES OF PSYCHOLOGICAL DYSFUNCTION: SOME OPENING COMMENTS

Before we begin to explore this fascinating area, some comments about the case of Charles Manson are in order. Throughout this book our aim has been to choose opening cases that demonstrate, as broadly as possible, the area to be examined in the chapter. The life of Charles Manson does this very well; it is a cafeteria of bizarre thinking and behavior. His story shows the challenge and the difficulty of understanding and explaining a wide range of unusual behaviors, emotions, and thoughts.

Charles Manson's hideous crimes terrorized and shocked a nation. His case became a front-page story in the newspapers, and it forced people to consider many legal and ethical issues surrounding disturbed behavior. Sensational cases of people such as Manson, and John Hinckley, who attempted to assassinate President Reagan in 1982, tend to immediately capture our attention.

As tragic and bizarre as these events are, it is important to keep in mind that for each sensational case, there are tens of thousands of others that come to few, if any, people's attention. In its September 1984 report, the National Institute of Mental Health estimated that 20 percent of the population will suffer from some type of psychological disturbance that is severe enough to warrant treatment. There are over 200,000 cases of child abuse reported each year and 200,000 people attempt suicide each year. In the overwhelming number of these cases, people suffer and struggle on their own. There is none of the sensation of the Manson case; there is only personal pain and despair for the individual and those close to him or her. These people are not dangerous or homicidal; they are threatening only in the sense that their behaviors are different and difficult to understand.

Cases such as Charles Manson's are important because they do challenge us to become concerned with the area of psychological dysfunction. However, our attention should not become riveted to the sensational outcomes of a few cases; rather, we should examine the broad range of actions and thoughts that are considered abnormal.

DEFINING ABNORMALITY

The nation was shocked and outraged by the Manson Family crimes; as the trial went on, people around the country were aghast at details of Manson's behavior. Newspapers described Manson as weird, crazy, and subhuman. This man believed he was Jesus Christ and lived by stealing food out of garbage cans; he believed a British rock group spoke to him through their songs; and while he would go into a rage if one of his followers killed a snake or spider, he thought nothing of ordering them to kill people. Few of us would argue with the statement that Manson's behavior was *abnormal*.

However, while we might be comfortable in labeling Manson's behavior abnormal, there are many other cases where labeling is more difficult. Let's take some examples:

1. You may know fellow students who stay up studying all night and sleep during the day. Are they normal?

2. And what about a woman who, on giving birth to twins, proceeds to kill one of the infants? Would we consider her abnormal?

Situations like these call into question the way we define the word **abnormal.**

One of the definitions of the word in the Random House Dictionary is "not average, typical, or usual." This is a *statistical definition*, describing as normal what most people do, and as abnormal any deviation from the average. According to this position, college students who sleep during the day and study all night are abnormal, because most people do not follow this pattern. At first glance, you may accept the statistical definition of abnormality. However, you may begin to feel uneasy when you find yourself having to label Christopher Columbus abnormal because he believed the earth was round when others "knew" that it was flat. The uneasiness may persist when you find that the abnormal "night-owl" students we mentioned are earning straight A's. If we use statistics to define normality, then any behavior that is outstanding or different is abnormal—this will be the case even if the behavior is outstandingly good.

A second way to define abnormality is in light of what the *culture* defines as acceptable and normal behavior. Under this kind of definition, an act that is abnormal in one culture may not be abnormal in another. For example, if we examine the Zhun/twa culture of Zambia, we find that killing a twin is standard practice. It is not done out of cruelty; on the contrary, it is done as a humanitarian act. Practice has taught the Zhun/twa people that there is not enough food to keep two newborns alive. Thus while killing a twin would be abnormal in our culture, it would not be considered so in the Zhun/twa culture.

Another way to define abnormality is to examine whether the individual's action or thoughts enable him or her to successfully adapt to the situation. Under this definition, abnormality is equated with *maladjustment*. Manson's belief that he was Jesus made it difficult for him to fit into society. Because of this belief, Manson felt that he could do no wrong; everything belonged to him and all people should obey him. Thus his beliefs and his actions were not only unusual, they caused distress to others and made it difficult for him to adjust to his environment as well. On this basis, we can label Manson's beliefs and behavior abnormal. On the other hand, students who study all night and sleep in the day seem to have adjusted to the demands of academic life, and their behavior does not bother others. Therefore their behavior may be unusual, but we would not generally consider it abnormal. As you can see, there are many ways to define abnormality, and psychologists take into account all of these when examining behavior.

 # CLASSIFYING PSYCHOLOGICAL DISORDERS

The list of Manson's bizarre behaviors is certainly quite long. Included in such a list would be the multiple murders, which he either ordered or directly participated in; his inability to form close relationships with others; his moodiness and erratic behavior; his belief that he was Jesus; and his obsession with Helter Skelter. If someone were to ask you to describe Charles Manson, it would be inconvenient to recite such a long list of his specific actions. It would be a great deal simpler if you could use a single word or phrase to classify his behavior; this classification would serve as a shorthand summary of a number of behaviors or traits.

Almost every field of science and even our own everyday language make use of classification systems. If someone asks you how you are feeling, it

is unlikely that you will reply that you have been sneezing, your nose has been "running," you have a slight fever, and your head feels stuffy. You are more likely to reply that you have a cold. The classification *cold* is a short way to summarize your symptoms.

Modern attempts to classify psychological disorders date back a hundred years to the German psychiatrist Emil Kraepelin. Although he believed that psychological disorders could be traced to specific organic causes, Kraepelin's focus on symptoms is still used in today's classification systems. The most commonly employed system is the *Diagnostic and Statistical Manual* (*DSM*), which was developed by the American Psychiatric Association. Psychologists and psychiatrists are continually refining the classification system and shaping it to bring it into line with current views and research on psychological disorders. The third edition of the manual (DSM III) was published in 1980.

DSM III focuses on describing the symptoms of disorders rather than interpreting them or speculating about their causes. Rather than placing people in a single category, it classifies them along five axes or dimensions. The first axis is *current clinical syndromes*, such as major depression or schizophrenia. Axis II lists *personality disorders*; these are generally considered to be long-standing behavior tendencies such as an antisocial personality. Axis III is concerned with *physical and medical disorders* that may be relevant to the psychological problem. The fourth axis focuses on *psychosocial stressors*, such as divorce, that may be contributing to the person's condition. On Axis V, the individual is rated on the *highest level of adaptive functioning* during the past year. Taking the whole system together, we might see a classification of alcohol dependence (Axis I), antisocial personality (Axis II), diabetes (Axis III), widowed (Axis IV), good level of functioning (Axis V).

DSM III is a complex and involved classification system. Its complexity is both a curse and a blessing. On the negative side, the system is difficult to grasp and much training is necessary to use it correctly. In addition, DSM III says little about the causes of disorders. On the positive side, because of its complexity, DSM III allows professionals to achieve greater validity in their diagnoses. As we will see, psychological disorders are composed of a number of symptoms; it is difficult to capture this variability under a single classification. Also, more precision can be gained by using the multiple axes.

Because it is new, the verdict is still out on the value of DSM III (Schecht, 1985). It is likely that it will undergo many changes as practitioners identify its weaknesses.

There are several points to remember about classification. First, a classification system is only an attempt to arrive at a shorthand method for communicating and keeping records on psychological disorders; it does not dictate the treatment of these disorders. Another point to keep in mind is that people often suffer from symptoms associated with a number of disorders.

Insanity is a legal term, not a psychological one. In order to prove insanity, it is necessary to show that the person did not know right from wrong at the time of the crime. Because of the bizarre motives behind John W. Hinckley's assassination attempt on President Reagan, the jury found him not guilty by reason of insanity. Despite the outcome of the case, insanity is very difficult to prove and rarely used as a defense.

There are few "pure" obsessive-compulsives or paranoid schizophrenics. As we examine Charles Manson's behavior in this chapter, we will see this point very clearly: Manson showed behaviors that could be associated with a number of different disorders. People are placed in the categories that most nearly represent their symptoms. Finally, a useful classification can only be made by carefully considering a great deal of information about the individual. In order to arrive at a classification, clinicians and counselors review the individual's life history, examine test results, interview the individual and his or her acquaintances, and consider the individual's environment.

Insanity: The Legal Label

The bizarreness of Manson's history and behavior prompted his lawyers to suggest that he plead not guilty by reason of insanity. Manson was appalled by this suggestion and refused to consider it; such a plea would cost him the blind obedience of his followers. Others, however, have not been so reluctant to use the insanity defense.

Insanity is a legal term, not a psychological one. It was used in English law as early as the thirteenth century; the prevailing feeling was that a person who was "mad" was not responsible for his or her actions and therefore could not be held accountable. In 1843 Daniel M'Naghten, a Scottish wood turner, was found not guilty by reason of insanity of assassinating the secretary to the prime minister of England. The judges stated that M'Naghten "did not know he was doing what was wrong." The *M'Naghten rule* became the Anglo-American legal standard for defining insanity; it argued that an individual must be able to determine right from wrong at the time of the crime before he or she can be judged responsible and therefore guilty.

There have been numerous revisions of the M'Naghten rule. The present standard used in the United States courts is the Brawner rule, which states that a person is not responsible for an act committed if, "as a result of a mental disease or defect, he lacks substantial capacity to appreciate the wrongfulness of his conduct to the requirements of the law." As you might imagine, it is exceedingly difficult to "prove" insanity, and such court trials often result in a battle between the conflicing testimony of experts (psychologists and psychiatrists). Because of this problem, many judges, including the Chief Justice of the Supreme Court, have suggested that the insanity ruling be abolished or drastically restricted. Despite recent publicity, however, the insanity plea is rarely used; in less than 3 percent of homicide trials is the plea invoked (Lunde, 1975).

There are many reasons for not using this plea besides the difficulty of proving insanity. The label "mentally ill" or "insane" often carries a worse social stigma than the ruling "guilty" of a crime. Further, a person who is judged "insane" under the law can be sentenced to a mental institution until he or she has "recovered sanity." In some cases, this sentence keeps a person institutionalized for a longer period than the ordinary prison sentence for the crime. In other cases, the person may be kept in a mental hospital only a short time and then be set free. Both alternatives present dangers to the individual and to society. Finally, an individual who is committed to a mental treatment center will often have fewer facilities and personal rights than one who is put in prison (Brooks, 1974).

The Danger of Labeling

As we have seen, a classification system can be a handy, time-saving device. However, using a label to describe an individual's behavior can also have some rather dire consequences. Imagine that a man living down the block from you was suddenly classified as "violently antisocial." Chances are good that your behavior toward him would change rather dramatically. You would avoid meeting him as much as possible. If you did run into him, you would find it awkward to talk to him and look him in the face, and you would probably warn your kids not to play near his house. Everyone else in your neighborhood would react the same way. Naturally he would notice that people were treating him differently. He might react with hurt and anger to the new situation, perhaps seeking confrontations with his formerly friendly neighbors. This would play into people's expectations and further convince them that the "violently antisocial" label was correct. This type of vicious cycle has been labeled the **self-fulfilling prophecy,** a situation in which one's expectations cause to happen what one expects to happen. (See Chapter 15 for a more complete discussion of self-fulfilling prophecy.)

Another potential problem with labels is that observers may interpret behavior to fit the label. In a controversial study, eight people, including a pediatrician, a psychiatrist, and three psychologists, requested permission to enter psychiatric hospitals (Rosenhan, 1973). Each pseudopatient complained, "I hear voices, unclear voices. I think they say 'empty, how-wow, thud.' " The pseudopatients gave false names and occupations to the hospitals. They were admitted and, in all cases except one, were given the diagnosis of "schizophrenic."

After being admitted, all the pseudopatients stopped faking the symptom of hearing voices and acted normally. Rosenhan states that "Despite their public 'show' of sanity, the pseudopatients were never detected." They stayed in the hospital from 7 to 52 days, with the average stay being 19 days. At discharge, their records carried the label "schizophrenia in remission." It was impossible for the pseudopatients to overcome their label; even their normal behavior was interpreted to support it. For example, one pseudopatient took notes of what happened in the hospital during his stay. A nurse noted on this patient's record that "patient engages in writing behavior." Thus even normal behavior became interpreted as symptomatic.

Rosenhan (1973, 1975) argues that psychologists should avoid labeling their patients. If a label must be used, it should focus only on the specific symptom or symptoms shown by the patient. Not only would this reduce the problem of observers "seeing" normal behaviors as supporting a label, but it could also help in identifying specific problems rather than misidentifying broadly based disorders. Rosenhan's position has been criticized by a number of investigators. Spitzer (1975, 1976) argues that the fact that Rosenhan's pseudopatients were able to lie their way into the hospital does not invalidate the system of diagnosis. After all, clinicians do not expect patients to lie about their symptoms, and it is considered important to observe individuals who have the symptoms reported by the pseudopatients. He also points out that the pseudopatients actually had very short hopsital stays for people diagnosed as schizophrenic. Therefore the diagnosis did not interfere with the treatment or the observation of the pseudopatients.

APPROACHES TO PSYCHOLOGICAL DISORDERS

How can we explain Manson's bizarre behavior? What caused his moodiness and erratic behavior? Why was he unable to form close relationships with others? What caused him to plot the gruesome murders of people he didn't even know? Throughout history people who showed unusual and bizarre behavior and beliefs were regarded with curiosity and a mixture of awe and fear. During the sixteenth century in England, people visited the "insane asylums" to watch the antics and ravings of the patients, much as we visit zoos today to look at the animals. In one such institution, St. Mary of Bethlehem (or Bedlam, as it was called), the public watched plays put on by the patients. The plays were so disorganized and chaotic that the word *bedlam* came to be used to describe confused and disorganized situations.

A large part of this fascination with bizarre behavior comes from the difficulty we have explaining why people act this way. Psychological disorders are mysterious and their causes represent intriguing unknowns for many people.

The Early Views

A rather simple explanation for Manson's unusual behavior would be that he was possessed by some supernatural or demonic force. In other words, "the devil made him do it." The view that a supernatural or spiritual force is responsible was one of the earliest explanations for abnormal behavior and it is still held today by some primitive tribes. An interesting feature of the "supernatural explanation" is that some societies believed that the force was godlike and good, while others believed that it was an evil demon. In societies where the spirit was believed to be a good one, the "possessed individual" was given a special position and received good treatment. In some Plains Indian tribes the "touched" person was felt to have special healing powers and he was made the shaman or medicine man. On the other hand, in societies that believed the spirit was evil, the possessed person was subjected to torture to drive out the evil spirit (see Chapter 14).

The Medical Model

Few of us are likely to accept the idea that Charles Manson was possessed by the devil. We may, however, be willing to conclude that Manson was "sick," because only someone with a sick mind could order those senseless murders and truly believe he was Jesus. If we view Manson as mentally *ill*, we are likely to feel a certain amount of pity for him and believe that he might be "cured." This point of view represents the medical approach, which explains mental disorders in somewhat the same way we explain physical disorders. In fact, even the vocabulary has a medical flavor: mental illness, diagnosis, cure, mental hospital.

The medical approach has been accepted by many people. If we were to adopt the medical model, we would look for genetic or biological defects that could cause abnormal behavior. As we will see, there is evidence that heredity and physical abnormalities are related to some psychological disorders. Treatment for psychological disorders often includes drugs, and the search for causes centers on biological and physical bases. There have, however, been criticisms of this model (Bandura, 1977). In many cases, it has proved impossible to identify an organic or biological cause for disorders. Rather, research has shown that personal and social variables are the root of many disorders. Also, the medical definition of "abnormal" behavior is based on social norms, and as Szasz has shown, social norms can change over time (Szasz, 1961, 1970). Finally, Szasz argues that it is demeaning to label someone "mentally sick" because this label implies a great deal more than simply identifying certain abnormal or unusual behaviors.

The Psychoanalytic Model

The psychoanalytic perspective focusses on early childhood and argues that abnormal behavior is the result of unresolved conflicts that occur during infancy and childhood. As we saw in Chapter 12, Sigmund Freud believed that personality is formed in early childhood as an individual attempts to resolve conflicts concerning aggression and sexual behavior. Freud argued that if these conflicts are not successfully resolved during childhood, the person will repress them into the unconscious and not deal with them. Later in life these repressed conflicts will influence the person's behavior because they will try to push their way into consciousness. When this happens, the person experiences anxiety and tries to cope by using defense mechanisms such as rationalization, projection, or reaction formation, as we discussed in Chapter 11. If these efforts are not successful, the anxiety will increase and the individual will develop *neurotic* patterns of behavior. In some cases, the disturbance caused by these unresolved conflicts may become so great that the person can no longer deal with reality; the person then develops his or her own world and behaves in ways that make it difficult to adjust to the real world. This poor contact with reality is called *psychosis.*

As you might imagine, it has proved very difficult to establish clear evidence that specific abnormal behaviors are the result of childhood conflicts. How could we "prove" that Manson developed antisocial behavior because he experienced conflicting feelings of love and hate for his mother during childhood? While proof may be difficult, there are many reports in the scientific literature supporting the position that some cases of abnormal behavior may indeed have their roots in early childhood experience.

The Learning Model

According to the medical and psychoanalytic models, we must find the cause of the illness before we can treat it. This is good medical practice; we would be foolish to continue to treat a persistent headache when that headache could be the signal that something more serious is wrong. While this approach may be effective for medical problems, learning theorists argue that it is not necessarily the best method for treating psychological disorders. The learning model suggests that we learn abnormal behaviors in the same way in which we learn other behaviors. Thus Manson may have learned his antisocial behavior by imitating people in his environment or by being rewarded for this behavior. If we adopt this position, we will not view abnormal behaviors as a symptom of some underlying disease or deep-rooted conflict. Rather, we will see the abnormality as the product of the individual's learning environment.

The Cognitive Model

The cognitive approach also focusses on people in their present setting. According to this view, people's behavior is strongly influenced by their beliefs and attitudes (Beck, 1983). The basis for irrational or bizarre behavior is irrational beliefs or attitudes. Therefore the way to change behavior is first to change the underlying attitudes. Using the cognitive approach, we would argue that Manson's belief in Helter Skelter caused him to develop irrational rules for the Family and led to many of his antisocial actions. Further, we would try to change Manson's behavior by first seeking to change his beliefs. As you can see, the cognitive approach is similar to the learning approach in that both deal with the present and both involve retraining. The difference is that while learning approaches work directly with behavior, the cognitive approach works on teaching the person new attitudes or beliefs in order to change his or her behavior.

The Humanistic Model

As we saw in Chapter 12, the humanists believe that people are basically rational and good. Left to their own devices, they will strive for personal growth and self-actualization. However, problems will arise if people are prevented from satisfying their basic needs or are forced to live up to the expectations of others in their surroundings. When this occurs, people will lose sight of their own goals and develop distorted perceptions of themselves. Then they will feel threatened and insecure and be unable to accept their own feelings and experiences. It is losing touch with one's feelings, goals, and perceptions that forms the basis of psychological disturbance.

The Systems Model

Thus far we have examined theories that explain abnormal behavior by focussing on the individual and his or her weaknesses. The systems approach, as represented by community psychology, regards the individual as part of a social network made up of family members, friends and acquaintances in the community, and various community organizations. The individual plays a role in relation to each of these people and agencies. For most people, the social network supports and maintains their behavior. However, for some people, the social network is filled with stress and conflicting demands, which play a major role in fostering their abnormal and maladaptive behavior. Thus the community approach suggests that abnormal behavior may be caused as much by a "sick" system as by a "sick" person.

Investigators studying social networks have pointed out that certain psychological disorders are often associated with certain socioeconomic groups (Kohn, 1972). For example, schizophrenia is most prevalent in lower socioeconomic areas. Hollingshead and Redlich (1958) argue that it is the stress associated with the substandard housing, high crime rates, and broken families in these areas that causes the high rate of mental illness. Others, however, dispute this position, arguing instead that more psychological disorders are found in these areas simply because people who suffer behavior disorders often drift downward into the lower classes (Dunham, 1965; Levy & Rowitz, 1973). A resolution of this disagreement has still not been reached. However, it does seem reasonable to conclude that the stress associated with lower socioeconomic conditions and certain cultural environments may create maladaptive behavior.

As we will see, the types of psychological disorders are many and varied, and anyone searching for quick or simple answers in the research and theories may become frustrated. While medical research on physical illness has a long history, careful research on psychological disorders is relatively recent. Therefore psychologists cannot give answers to many of the questions about what causes psychological disorders. The present theories serve as guidelines by pointing out ways to examine the disorders. It is unlikely that any single model or approach can explain all disorders. It is more probable that each of the modern perspectives explains certain disorders and that any single maladaptive behavior has many causes. As we examine the disorders, we will give examples of different explanations that have been advanced as the "roots of abnormality."

Identifying the Causes of Psychological Disorders

There are a number of theories about the specific causes of psychological disorders. Some, such as the medical model, locate the causes inside the individual; the causes are due to inherited tendencies or physical abnormali-

Table 13-1
Approaches to Psychological
Disorders

Approach	Critical Period	Importance of Determining Cause	Main Focus
Medical	Past	Very important	Physiological function
Psychoanalytic	Past	Very important	Childhood conflicts
Learning	Present	Not important	Present behavior
Cognitive	Present	Not important	Present behavior and beliefs
Systems	Present	Important	Person's role in social network
Humanistic	Past/present	Mildly important	Conditions preventing person from achieving personal growth

ties. Other theories, such as the psychoanalytic, learning, cognitive, systems, and humanistic, argue that some external event serves as the catalyst for the disorder. How do we go about determining cause? As we will see, the problems and solutions encountered in attempting to answer this question are almost as interesting as the disorders themselves. As a starting point, let us assume that we have diagnosed Charles Manson as an antisocial personality. We now wish to determine whether the cause of his condition is physical (inherited) or environmental.

We might begin with the *case history* method. Using this method, we could compare Manson's background with that of other people with antisocial personalities. If we did this, we would find that Manson, like others suffering from this condition, came from a broken home and had few friends and social contacts. With a gleam in our eye, we might proudly announce this as the cause of his disorder. But our conclusion would be premature for a number of reasons. First, case histories generally rely on people's memories, which can be biased and incomplete. Second, our "cause" might well be the result of the disorder: A child who shows antisocial tendencies may create stress in the family and alienate potential friends.

A second approach would be to search for physiological abnormalities that could be the root of the disorder. Research has in fact found some hormonal and brain-wave abnormalities (Gorenstein, 1982) in people with antisocial personalities. These findings are of interest, but do they demonstrate cause? It may be that people with this disorder experience unusual stress or lead the type of life that could cause these types of physiological patterns. As we saw in Chapter 11, stress can indeed affect a person's physiological functioning. Once again, we are left wondering what is cause and what is result.

While these two methods give us some clues to the cause of the disorder, they leave a number of questions unanswered. Hence some investigators have turned to studies of twins. There are two types of twins. Fraternal twins (*dizygotic*) are formed from the fertilization of two separate ova by two separate sperm cells. The genetic makeup of the two dizygotic individuals will not be the same because they develop from the union of different cells. On the other hand, identical (*monozygotic*) twins are formed from the union of a single sperm and ovum; after fertilization, the cell (zygote) divides into two new cells that develop into two embryos. Because these monozygotic twins come from the same sperm and ovum, their genetic composition is the same.

Since in identical twins we have two individuals with the same genes, we can use them to study the role of heredity on a disorder. If the antisocial personality is inherited, we would expect both monozygotic twins to show the disorder if it is present in either of them. While this looks like the ideal solution, there is one catch: environment. We might also expect two individuals of identical appearance who were born at the same time into the same family to share very similar environments. Indeed, many parents go so far as to always dress their twins alike. Thus the finding that twins share a disorder may be attributed to the environment in which they were raised. In order to avoid this problem, investigators have gone one step further: They have examined the occurrence of disorders in twins who were separated at or shortly after birth (Kallman, 1946). In most of these cases, the twins were adopted into different families. Their procedure allows us to study individuals who share identical genes but who have grown up in different environments. If heredity is the sole cause of a disorder, both twins should suffer it if it is present in either of them. But if environment is the sole cause of the disorder, the likelihood of identical twins suffering the same disorder should be no greater than the probability of two unrelated individuals having the same disorder.

This discussion should make you appreciate the exciting challenge of identifying the causes of psychological disturbances. This type of exacting research plays a vital role in our understanding of disorders and our attempts to prevent or treat them. A different treatment procedure would be followed for dealing with a disorder that was the result of heredity than with one that was the result of environmental factors. As we will see in our discussion of the specific disorders, the research suggests that many disorders are caused by a combination of heredity and environment.

THE MEDICAL STUDENT SYNDROME

Before examining specific psychological disorders, there is one point we should address. As the symptoms of the various disorders are reviewed, you may find yourself growing increasingly uneasy. Some of these symptoms are depression, difficulty in falling asleep, loss of appetite, headaches, and sexual dysfunction. As you read about them, you may recall that you have periodically felt depressed, suffered headaches, lost your appetite, been unable to sleep, and not functioned sexually according to your expectations. These realizations may cause you to leap to the conclusion, "I've got it!" In a near panic you may decide that you are schizophrenic, or that you have an affective disorder, or that you suffer from a psychosexual disorder.

The "I've got it" conclusion is often found among medical students as they study different diseases. They remember times when they felt dizzy and had no appetite, and conclude that they are suffering from cancer; or they recall a time when they had a burning sensation when they urinated, and conclude that they have venereal disease; or they remember when their heart beat wildly and they were short of breath, and decide that they have heart disease. They rush to the emergency room in a state of panic, fearing the worst, only to find out they are in fine physical shape.

It is important to remember that most of us have at some time displayed some of the states associated with the psychological disorders, just as we have had some symptoms of severe medical ailments. However, in most of us, these psychological symptoms are not intense and do not occur with any great frequency. Occasionally experiencing symptoms of this kind is normal and does not suggest mental illness or psychological disorder. The symptoms associated with the psychological disorders are generally intense and enduring, and they interfere with people's adjustment to their physical and social worlds. With this thought in mind, let us examine some specific psychological disorders.

Childhood Disorders

Psychologists have identified a wide variety of severe psychological disorders that occur during childhood. While the nature of these disorders varies, they tend to show an interesting pattern: The childhood disorders occur with greatest frequency during two rather distinct age periods (Rutter, 1974). The first period is between 6 months and 3 years of age, and the second is during early adolescence (12–14 years of age). These two "high-risk" periods are not confined to American children; research done in Great Britain, Japan, and the U.S.S.R. has also found a strong tendency for childhood disorders to begin during these two periods.

The diagnosis of childhood disorders can be very difficult because of natural differences in the maturation process (Gibbs, 1982). However, the proper and early diagnosis of such disorders is very important for two reasons. First, early diagnosis can lead to early treatment, which will improve the child's chances of making a satisfactory adjustment (Ollendrick & Hersen, 1983). Second, an incorrect diagnosis can have long-term consequences for the child. In many cases, the diagnosis influences how people react to the child, and these reactions, in turn, encourage certain patterns of behavior from the child.

While there are many childhood disorders, we will examine one that occurs during early childhood and generally has severe consequences.

Infantile Autism

In 1943, Leo Kanner, a child psychiatrist, observed that some very young infants seemed to live in a world of their own. These infants were suffering from **infantile autism.** They showed no interest in social stimulation. They would not hold eye contact with others and showed no reaction to noise or to the speech of others. By the age of 18 months or 2' years, when most children begin increasing their vocabulary and interacting with others, these autistic children would not talk and became preoccupied with inanimate objects. They were particularly fascinated with spinning objects and formed attachments to them much as normal children form attachments to other people. These autistic children spent hours on end touching objects or engaging in other motor activities such as rocking back and forth. They developed very rigid schedules and showed strong resistance to change; they refused new foods and new activities.

One of the most serious symptoms of this disorder is self-destructive behavior: Autistic children will often bang their heads on floors and walls with such force that they suffer severe concussions. Because of their failure to develop speech, these children have often been diagnosed as mentally retarded. However, it has been found that while autistic children do show retardation on some skills, they generally do not have subnormal intelligence (DeMeyer, 1976). As can be seen, a number of disturbances are involved in autism. Because of this, there has been some disagreement as to the type of disturbance that is most central. Most investigators believe that perceptual or cognitive disturbances make up the core of autism (Wicks-Nelson & Israel, 1984).

Autism usually begins during the first year, and certainly by age 3. It is relatively rare, occurring in about 4.5 per 10,000 children. It is four times more likely to be found in boys than in girls, and it is most common in firstborn children. The parents of autistic children are generally in the higher social classes and have above-average intelligence.

The prognosis for autistic children is not good. No specific treatment

Autistic children live in a world of their own. They are not responsive to other people and they will often spend hours on end engaged in various actions, such as rocking back and forth. One of the most serious symptoms is self-destructive behavior such as banging one's head into a wall.

has been found effective in dealing with autism. Drugs have been used with some success, and behavior-modification programs have been applied to increase the child's language and social skills. However, the autistic child rarely improves enough to be placed in regular schools. In fact, Stafford-Clark and Smith (1978) report that most autistic children stay in institutions, with only about 10 percent making some social adjustment to life outside the institution.

What could cause such an unfortunate condition in infants? Most current theories focus on damage to the central nervous system (see Chapter 2 and Cohen & Shaywitz, 1982). Organic diseases that can cause damage to the central nervous system have been associated with autism. For example, a child who has encephalitis or meningitis during infancy is more likely to become autistic than a child who has not had these diseases. Other research has found that women who have rubella during their first trimester of pregnancy have a greater chance of giving birth to an autistic child than women who do not contract this illness (Chess, 1971). Present research efforts are aimed at identifying exactly what nervous system damage leads to autism and determining how the social environment influences the probability of autism.

NEUROTIC BEHAVIOR

Charles Manson spent a great deal of his life in prison. Prison gave him some security that he did not get in the outside world; in prison he lived by a schedule, had a roof over his head, was fed, and had a group of associates (other inmates) with whom he could interact. It was also a world of rules he understood and could live with. The outside world was filled with conflict and uncertainty. On several occasions Manson admitted fearing freedom, but he also said he wanted freedom "more than anything." The conflict about freedom led him to develop some bizarre behavior patterns that kept him in prison. He tried to escape a short time before each of his parole hearings; in most cases, he was caught, denied parole, and sent back to prison. When he did win his freedom, he would quickly violate the law—not just any law, but federal laws that carried long prison sentences.

Manson's seemingly bizarre behavior pattern had a purpose: It helped reduce his anxiety about entering the outside world by keeping him in prison. However, it was maladaptive in that it increased his conflict about freedom, and he was forced to experience the anxiety all over again each time a new parole hearing came up. **Neurosis** is the term that has been used to describe maladaptive behaviors aimed at dealing with anxiety and stress. The behaviors are maladaptive because they do not completely succeed in controlling the anxiety and they keep the person from developing more effective ways of reducing the anxiety. They often take the form of exaggerated versions of normal defenses, which we discussed in Chapter 11. In most cases, people realize that they are having difficulty adjusting, but may feel helpless to do anything about it.

While the term *neurosis* has been used by psychologists for a number of years, it has proved to be rather vague and confusing in some situations. Because of this, DSM III has dropped the term as a diagnostic category. Instead, DSM III uses separate categories to identify the wide variety of "neurotic disorders." These categories include anxiety, somatoform, dissociative, affective, and sexual disorders. We will look at a number of disorders from each of these categories.

Anxiety Disorders

We have all experienced anxiety. Remember how you felt when you were in your first school play, went out on your first date, or had an important job interview. You probably had trouble falling asleep the night before each of these events. And as the time for the event approached, you probably felt tense and were afraid to open your mouth for fear that the butterflies in your stomach would escape. While you may have been troubled by anxiety, you probably found a way to control it and were able to complete the task at hand.

Unfortunately, some people experience anxiety that is far out of proportion to the situations they are in, and their responses to these anxiety-arousing situations are exaggerated and interfere with normal daily functioning. These characteristics are common to a group of conditions classified as **anxiety disorders.** It has been estimated that 2 to 4 percent of the population suffers from anxiety disorders. There are a number of behavior patterns classified as anxiety disorders; the common thread, however, is that each is a maladaptive reaction to excessive anxiety.

General Anxiety Disorder. As can be seen in the case study highlighted, **general anxiety disorders** keep people in a constant state of agitation and dread. People suffering from this disorder have trouble falling asleep, experience a loss of appetite, feel tense and keyed up, and may have increased heart rate and faintness. They also have trouble concentrating, and consequently their work suffers. At times, this general anxiety may turn into panic, at which point victims are overwhelmed by fear; their heart races and they become short of breath. They may think that they are going to die or that they are going crazy. These panic attacks can

CASE STUDY
OF A GENERALIZED ANXIETY DISORDER

At the time of onset, Miss M. had been doing secretarial work in a large business office, a position in which she took dictation from a number of salesmen and minor executives. Although intellectually competent and physically very attractive, the patient had always been extremely shy in any personal situation involving a man. She led a restricted social life and very seldom went out on dates. She functioned adequately, however, in most business and other group settings. While working for the firm, Miss M. secretly developed a romantic interest in one of the young executives, an interest that she scarcely acknowledged even to herself. She managed to banish it from her (conscious) thoughts entirely when she learned, in casual office conversation, that he was married.

The company offices were on an upper floor of a large downtown office building equipped with automatic elevators. One morning, arriving at work an unaccustomed few minutes late, Miss M. found herself alone in an elevator with the young executive. The man made a complimentary but slightly suggestive remark about the patient's dress. Miss M. blushed and became highly embarrassed, tense, and anxious. By dint of considerable effort, she managed to get through the day's work. The next morning, as she was about to enter the elevator, she experienced an attack of anxiety so severe as to verge upon panic. She left the building, walked about for nearly an hour, and then was able to return. This time she climbed six flights of stairs to the office.

During succeeding days the patient made several efforts to use the elevator, but she invariably found herself becoming too anxious to do so. She continued to use the stairs, and for several months was able to continue work in reasonable comfort, having taken this precaution. Eventually, the use of the stairs became as disturbing as that of the elevator. At this point, the patient was compelled to ask for a leave of absence, and she had not returned to work at the time of consultation.

At no point did the patient consciously associate her attacks of anxiety with the young executive. In fact, as she told the psychiatrist, she "no longer thought of him at all." Miss M. had no doubt that she was ill, but she considered the nature of her illness to be inexplicable.

Source: C. K. Hofling, *Textbook of Psychiatry for Medical Practice,* 1975, p. 326.

---

last anywhere from a few seconds to many hours. The most disturbing aspect of the general anxiety disorder is that those suffering from it cannot identify the cause.

We do not know the reasons why some people suffer anxiety disorders. We do know that they are twice as common in females as in males and that they run in families. Research on this last point suggests that people learn to experience these attacks by imitating other family members. On the other hand, psychoanalytic theorists suggest that the cause may be repressed feelings or conflicts that threaten to surface. The anxiety that this causes makes people repress the feelings rather than let them surface, which would force them to deal with these feelings.

Phobia. Phobia occurs when people have an irrational fear of an object or event. The name is derived from Phobos, who was the Greek god of fear, and most phobias have Greek names (see Table 13–2). Phobics know what causes their fear; it is attached to a specific, identifiable object. They can control their anxiety by avoiding that object or situation. While this may seem to be a simple solution to anxiety, many phobias can be very disruptive. For example, people suffering from agoraphobia (fear of open or unfamiliar places) may be so overwhelmed by their fear that they will not leave their home. People who suffer a fear of crowds may be unable to go to parties, the movies, the library, class, an office, or other places where crowds may be found. As can be seen from the representative list in Table 13–2, phobias can involve a wide range of objects. In most cases, phobics recognize the irrationality of their fear, but they are powerless to do anything about it. This realization only makes the phobia more troublesome.

Table 13–2
Familiar and Rare Phobias

Acrophobia	Fear of heights
Agoraphobia	Fear of open spaces
Haphephobia	Fear of touching or being touched
Hematophobia	Fear of blood
Melanophobia	Fear of bees
Ophidiophobia	Fear of snakes
Panophobia	Fear of everything
Phonophobia	Fear of speaking aloud
Scopophobia	Fear of being stared at

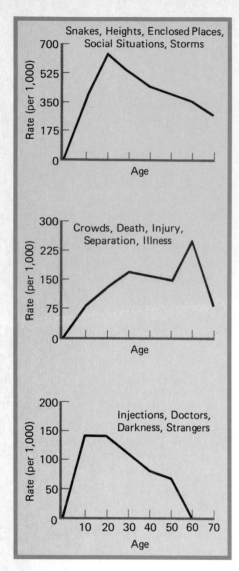

Figure 13-1
Specific phobias tend to occur at certain ages.

There are some striking statistics regarding phobias. Women are more likely to suffer from phobias than men. For example, it has been estimated that 95 percent of all zoophobics (people who fear animals) are women (Davison & Neale, 1978). Also, phobics tend to be of average or above-average intelligence, and many of them show few signs of any disorder except the phobia. While phobias occur most often around the age of 50, specific phobias tend to have very distinct age peaks (see Figure 13–1).

Freud was one of the first people to carefully study phobias. He believed that the phobic object is chosen to symbolize the real source of fear or conflict. For example, a woman may harbor a deep resentment and fear of her father. Since these feelings are very threatening to her and make her feel guilty, she may displace them onto some other object, such as an animal, a color, or a situation that can be avoided more easily. The chosen object may be only remotely associated with the real, feared object. However, she can now control the anxiety by avoiding the new, substitute object.

Other theorists believe that phobias, like other behaviors, are learned (e.g., Bandura, 1969). Some phobias may result from classical conditioning (see Chapter 6). For example, a boy wakes up one dark, stormy night fearing that his parents have left him. After a frantic search of the house, he finds his parents, but the trauma of the experience leaves him with a fear of the dark or of lightning. Phobias can also be learned by watching other people showing fear of certain objects or situations (Hygge & Ohman, 1978), or by hearing people express their fear of objects (Bootzin & Max, 1981).

While the learning approach offers an important explanation for phobias, an interesting question can be raised: Why do phobias focus on some objects and not on others? For example, consider our story of the child who wakes up on a stormy night and cannot immediately find his parents. As we pointed out, he might develop a phobia involving darkness or lightning. While this process is understandable, we might ask why the boy doesn't also become afraid of his room or the red blanket that is present when he cannot find his parents. One suggestion is that human beings are *prepared* to develop aversions to certain objects but not to others (Eysenck, 1979). Those objects that we are prepared (or preprogrammed) to fear are ones that actually represented some danger for us at some time in our history. Thus phobias may focus on heights, snakes, darkness, open spaces, or blood because these objects were once real threats to humans. On the other hand, phobias will not center on doors, bed sheets, or chairs because these objects historically never represented any danger to people.

Obsessive-Compulsive Disorders. One of the most bizarre points brought out in Manson's trial was that he had ordered the killing of seven innocent people on the belief that it would start a black revolution. Thoughts of this revolution, which he called Helter Skelter, were never out of Manson's mind. Manson planned his whole life around the coming revolution; in short, he was obsessed with Helter Skelter. In psychological terms, an **obsession** is a recurring, irrational thought that cannot be controlled or banished from one's mind. Some obsessions are quite harmless. For example, you may have had the experience of hearing a catchy tune on the radio that you then hummed for the next few days. No matter where you went or what you did, you couldn't seem to get it out of your mind. While this type of obsession is at worst annoying, other obsessions can cause a great deal of stress. Imagine constantly having thoughts of murdering your brother or being obsessed with the belief that your house is going to burn down. Not only is the content of these thoughts disturbing, but their constant occurrence keeps you from concentrating on anything

CASE STUDY
OF AN OBSESSIVE-COMPULSIVE DISORDER

A department store clerk quickly lost her job because of complaints from customers over her slowness in making change and her eccentric behavior. She was obsessed with the number seven. If the number appeared in the cents column, she found herself unable to stop repeating the figure over and over. If the number appeared in the dollars column or in any other circumstance, she felt a strong urge to omit it. She could not take the seventh step on a stairway in stride but always managed to do a little skip. Rather than getting off the elevator on the seventh floor of any building, she preferred the inconvenience of going to a higher or lower floor and walking the rest of the way. She changed her residence several times in order to live in a district where the telephone was given an area code without a seven. When asked about the inconveniences, she commented: "You think it would be easy to stop this thing with numbers altogether; actually it's worse if I don't count. Then I start to feel like something bad is going to happen. And pretty soon I feel this ball inside me, growing like a cancer, a tension that's going to explode . . . and I can't concentrate, until I count my seven's again. Now I'm comfortable again, and I feel safe, really safe."

The patient had been raised by her divorced mother. Throughout her life she heard endless accounts of the cruelties of life and the necessity of being so self-reliant and competent that she would never have to rely on anyone else. Her mother used every waking moment to instruct her daughter by continuously evaluating her performance on trivial as well as important matters. The mother died after an agonizing battle with cancer. She died on the seventh day of July. (Suinn, 1984, p. 141)

Suinn, Richard M. *Fundamentals of abnormal psychology.* Nelson-Hall, 1984, p. 141.

else. You might realize that your fears are irrational, but no matter what you do, you cannot control them or block them out. A related problem involves **compulsions,** which are irrational behaviors or rituals that people cannot control. They have a recurring compulsion to perform an act but cannot determine why they feel this desire. Generally, people who have obsessions also suffer compulsions (Rachman & Hodgson, 1980). Children often become caught up with harmless compulsive actions such as not stepping on the cracks in the sidewalk: "Step on a crack and break your mother's back." Shakespeare's Lady Macbeth experienced a hand-washing compulsion; she continually washed her hands in an effort to cleanse the guilt she felt for taking part in a murder. Davison and Neale (1978) report the case of a woman who washed her hands over 500 times a day. Another common compulsive behavior involves neatness and orderliness; people suffering from this compulsion may spend every day cleaning their room and putting things away. Such behavior not only interferes with the obsessive-compulsive's own life, it also makes life miserable for others who have to associate with that person.

The last point may be one reason why surveys have shown that almost half of all people suffering from obsessive-compulsive disorders remain unmarried. It has also been reported that obsessive-compulsive behaviors are most commonly found in people of high intelligence and socioeconomic status. Further, unlike many other anxiety reactions, this disorder occurs about equally in men and women.

Some explanations for obsessive-compulsive disorders are based on psychoanalytic theory. One view is that people try to keep unwanted thoughts or feelings from entering their consciousness by performing compulsive acts or engaging in obsessive thinking. By constantly engaging in such activities, these people do not allow themselves the chance to focus on threatening thoughts. It has been suggested that guilt underlies obsessive-compulsive disorders (Rosen, 1975). People may experience guilt over actions they did or thought about doing; they then adopt an obsession or a compulsive behavior as a form of self-punishment.

More recently, cognitive theorists have suggested that the irrational anxiety that underlies this disorder may be the result of faulty judgments that people make about objects or situations. They may overestimate and then become obsessed with the danger in a certain situation. Their obsessive thoughts may be warnings they are giving themselves about the possible dangers in the situation, and their compulsive behaviors may be aimed at avoiding these dangers.

Somatoform Disorders

Anxiety often leads to the bizarre changes in behavior that we discussed in the previous section. There is, however, another class of disorders, called **somatoform disorders,** in which anxiety affects the person's physical well-being. Most of us have felt sick and experienced stomach problems before an important event such as a final exam or a singing debut. We might look to others for sympathy, only to be told that our problem is "psychological." In Chapter 11 we examined psychophysiological disorders, in which a person suffers actual physical damage such as an ulcer or a migraine headache as the result of stress and anxiety. In somatoform disorders people feel ill or show other physical symptoms such as blindness or paralysis, even though there is no evident organic damage. For example, stress may cause an ulcer; if we examine the person's stomach, we will actually see a hole in the stomach wall. But when stress results in a somatoform disorder such as paralysis of a hand, close inspection of the hand will show no physical damage. There are a number of types of somatoform disorders. Here we will examine two of the most distinctive.

Somatization Disorder. This condition is characterized by a number of vague but dramatic complaints. People with **somatization disorder** may experience headaches, nausea, vomiting, stomach pains, tiredness, and menstrual problems. These people really believe that they are sick, and their belief may cause them to feel depressed and threaten suicide. They may make frequent trips to the doctor and even demand surgery, though the physician can find no organic cause for their complaint. The fact that there is no organic problem does not mean that these people do not feel bad. Quite the contrary, stress is making them feel sick. Still, there is simply no physical problem on which the doctor can work. As you might expect, people with somatization disorders have long medical histories, and they are some of the most difficult patients a medical doctor has to deal with. Somatization disorders are more common in women than in men; it has been estimated that almost 1 percent of all women suffer from this disorder to some degree. It generally begins in young adulthood, with peak complaints occurring in the 20s (Suinn, 1984).

Conversion Disorder. While the somatization disorder involves a number of vague problems, the **conversion disorder** almost always concerns one specific symptom. The most common symptoms are paralysis of a limb, loss of sensation in a part of the body, blindness, or deafness. There are some distinct factors that make conversion disorders rather easy to diagnose. First, as with other somatoform disorders, there is no organic damage: A patient may be unable to move her left arm, but there is no physical reason for this immobility. Second, the disorder often appears shortly after some stressful event and has a sudden onset; as can be seen in the case study highlighted, Sam's symptoms occurred after the minor traffic accident and after the arguments with his family. Third, the symptoms do not make anatomical sense. For example, people with glove anesthesia report losing sensation in a hand, although they have normal feelings in that arm (see Figure 13–2). Given the connecting system of nerves in the hand and arm, the loss of sensation in a hand is impossible without loss of sensation in parts of that arm as well. Fourth, the symptoms (paralysis,

Figure 13–2
The symptoms involved in a conversion disorder do not make anatomical sense. On the left is shown the loss of feeling complained of by people with glove anesthesia; on the right is shown the loss of feeling that would occur if there were actual nerve damage.

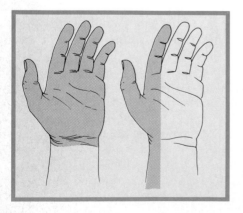

CASE STUDY OF A CONVERSION DISORDER

Sam B., a college student, was involved in a minor traffic accident on his way home from classes. Although he was slightly bruised, medical examination showed no serious physical involvement, and the patient was discharged from the hospital. "I woke up the next morning and couldn't feel my legs, they were numb. . . . I supposed they had gone to sleep on me, but then I tried to move them, and my legs wouldn't move. . . . I couldn't walk anymore." Sam was returned by ambulance to the hospital for extensive neurological and X-ray examinations with negative results. Throughout, he seemed bemused by the procedures, intrigued by the machinery, and taken by the nurses. The diagnosis: conversion disorder.

When Sam was interviewed by a psychologist, the following facts came to light. Just prior to the accident, he had another of many arguments with his family over his education. He wanted to get a job in order to make some money. His parents, both from immigrant backgrounds, had forced him to continue his schooling in spite of constant bickering. He was on an allowance on the condition that he remain in school. Money had always been a problem, since the patient tended to squander it on social activities, girl friends, and his motorbike:

I was on my bike going home and thinking about the exams coming up the next day. I had the bad luck of having three exams on the same day, and it's tough getting up for them all, you know how it is with teachers, they give you a bundle of stuff to read at the last moment. . . . Anyway, I had to really ace the finals because things hadn't gone so good on the quizzes I took . . . the way grades were determined, if I didn't get three As on these three finals, I could wind up with two Fs and one D.

So I guess I was distracted going home, I knew there was no way I could cram, I tried that before and look at what it got me. My big worry was the draft, I could be called up if I lost my student deferment. . . . They already took some of my friends.

The accident itself came as a surprise since Sam had always been reasonably cautious on his motorbike. Yet, he had been driving in a carefree and even reckless fashion when the accident occurred. When he was first released from the hospital, he felt "kinda lucky that I wasn't killed, but kinda sorry I wasn't scraped up more than I was." The impression was that a disabling injury would have been painful but useful. (Suinn, 1984, p. 219)

Suinn, Richard M. *Fundamentals of abnormal psychology.* Nelson-Hall, 1984, p. 219.

---

deafness, or blindness) disappear when people are asleep or hypnotized. It has also been found that the symptoms may disappear when people are in an emergency situation. Thus "deaf" people will hear the scream "Fire!" if they are in a burning building. The fifth factor that distinguishes conversion disorders from real physical problems is that those who have them often show little concern or anxiety about the disabling symptoms. Imagine your own reaction if you suddenly found that your legs were paralyzed. In the highlighted case, we can see that Sam was more interested in the machinery and nurses than in his paralysis.

At this point you may be thinking that people with conversion disorders are simply faking it. This is not true, however. The paralyzed person actually cannot move the affected limb. With people who have lost sensation in a particular area, it is possible to stick pins in that area without getting a response. This proves the person is truly experiencing the symptom and has no control over it, even though there is no organic cause for the problem.

Many theories about the causes of conversion disorders have been proposed. Freud believed that the symptoms were a way of controlling threatening impulses. For example, people who have been taught that masturbation is wrong may develop arm paralysis to control their urges to masturbate. The paralysis solves the problem by making it physically impossible for them to masturbate. Learning theorists argue that conversion disorders are the result of reinforcement patterns. People may find that they can gain attention from others (positive reinforcement) by having these conversion symptoms. Sometimes they receive more direct rewards because of this disorder—for example, they can escape family or job pressures, and get sympathy and attention at the same time.

Dissociative Disorders

All of us have experienced especially difficult times in our lives—a heated argument with a loved one, being fired from a job or failing a course, wrecking the family Mercedes. When something like this happens, we may secretly wish that we could remove ourselves (physically or psychologically) from the situation, pretend it never happened, and just start over. There is a set of particularly fascinating disorders where these secret wishes almost become reality.

Dissociative disorders are characterized by "tuning out" or dissociating a part of oneself from the situation at hand. It is almost as if part of the person has split off and taken on its own identity.

Most people who suffer dissociative disorders do not have control over the onset of the disorder; the symptoms tend to occur after a stressful period or a traumatic event. The most common explanation for dissociative disorders is that they result from repression of unwanted thoughts or urges. People try to control these threatening urges by psychologically separating off the stressed parts of their personality. It is almost as if they tie a number of unwanted thoughts or feelings in a package and store it in one part of their personality. This solution enables them to avoid dealing with these unwanted thoughts or feelings—most of the time. However, the price for this solution is that this "package" of unwanted thoughts may suddenly open up and take control. Or, if the unwanted feelings do not actually take control, they may threaten the individual to such an extent that he or she blocks out *all* thoughts, feelings, or memories. Dissociative disorders are quite rare but let us briefly examine some of them.

Psychogenic Amnesia. A classic movie theme involves a character who suddenly forgets who he or she is and spends the rest of the movie trying to recover his or her true identity. **Amnesia** is a selective forgetting of past events. Interestingly enough, the memory loss is often limited to certain events or time periods. For example, a man may forget who he is or where he lives, but remember how to perform acts such as driving an automobile. Some forms of amnesia (organic) are caused by physical injuries, such as a blow to the head. However, the term *psychogenic* indicates that the cause of the memory loss is stress rather than physical injury.

There are some interesting differences between psychogenic amnesia and organic amnesia (Rosenhan & Seligman, 1984). First, psychogenic amnesia is characterized by memory loss of both the recent and the remote past; the individual cannot remember what he ate before the attack began nor the name of his hometown. A person with organic amnesia can remember the distant past very well; it is just recent events that elude him. Second, psychogenic amnesiacs can recall events that occurred after their amnesia began, but they cannot remember events surrounding the stressful situation that initiated their amnesia. People with organic amnesia often cannot remember events that occurred after the physical damage that precipitated their attack. For example, they cannot remember how they got to the hospital. Finally, psychogenic amnesia often ends quickly (in a few hours or days), and when memory returns, all events, including the stressful one, are generally recalled. In organic amnesia, memory returns gradually, and memory of the trauma may never return.

Psychogenic Fugue. On September 13, 1980, a park ranger patrolling a wooded area in Birch State Park in Florida found a naked, half-starved young woman lying in the brush. The woman could not remember her name or events about her past. She was also unable to remember how she got to the park. Authorities named her "Jane Doe" and an exhaus-

When "Jane Doe" was found in a state park, she could not remember her name or how she got to the park. She was suffering from fugue which involves memory loss and physical flight.

tive search was launched to discover her true identity. With the help of a sedative and hypnosis, Jane Doe began to recall details of her childhood. She had lost her memory and wandered away from her home after having some difficulty with her boyfriend. This is an example of a **fugue** (from the Latin word meaning "to flee"), which involves not only the loss of memory, but also phsyical flight. The person may leave home for a matter of hours or for years. Often the person will suddenly "come to" and remember his or her past. What is interesting is that once the person has "snapped out" of the fugue, he or she will not remember events that occurred during it (Cameron, 1963)—it's like trading one memory loss for another.

Multiple Personality Disorder. The most bizarre of all the dissociative disorders is the **multiple personality disorder.** We open the next chapter with a description of Chris Sizemore, who suffered this disorder. Multiple personality is rare and is most often found in women. The person develops two or more personalities that are displayed at different times; in a sense, she *is* different people at different times. Each personality is self-contained and independent of the other personalities (Bliss, 1980). In fact, some degree of amnesia is generally present, so that while some of the personalities may be aware that the others exist, other personalities remain unaware of the existence or character of the others. The personalities generally show radical differences in attitudes, morals, age, learning ability, and speech patterns. This difference often extends into the physical realm, so that the personalities have different heart rates and blood pressure. In some cases, women with this disorder report that they menstruate much of the month because each personality has a different menstrual cycle (Jens & Evans, 1983). The personalities may differ in physical health, with the dominant personality often being the healthiest. When the personalities are aware of the existence of others, they may go as far as to communicate through letters and notes. In one case, investigators report that one personality wrote the other to give it medical advice (Taylor & Martin, 1944)!

There is an interesting pattern in the way many multiple personality disorders develop. First, between the ages of 4 and 6, the person faces a serious emotional problem; in the case of Chris (p. 459), the event was the arrival of her twin sisters. The child copes with the problem by creating another personality to deal with the situation. Second, Bliss (1980) reports that people with multiple personality disorders are very adept at inducing self-hypnosis; this ability enables them to form and embrace the new personality. The third step seems to be that the person finds out that retreating into the new personality helps resolve the emotional crisis. This sets the stage for developing new personalities whenever stressful events occur later in life.

Affective Disorders

As we have seen, Charles Manson displayed a wide array of unusual behaviors that would lead us to believe he was psychologically disturbed. As a young man, Manson showed another symptom that is often the signal of psychological disorders. This symptom involved his mood. At times Manson was depressed and sullen. During these periods he showed an almost pathetic sadness and became withdrawn; he would eat very little and remained in one place for hours on end. At other times he was happy and became wildly elated. These shifts in mood were noted by his caseworker, who indicated that Manson should receive counseling to deal with them.

Affective disorders represent a major category of psychological disorders involving problems with emotions and moods. While we all have periods when we feel down or up, some people are consumed by their moods and have trouble functioning because of them. It is these people who are classified as suffering from an affective disorder.

Depression.　Think about the last time you felt depressed. How did you feel and act? For most people, **depression** affects their mood, thoughts, motivation, and physical appearance. Looking first at *mood*, we find that depressed people feel sad, irritable, and hopeless; they find little joy in living. They are often consumed by their sadness. Their *thoughts* are filled with self-pity; they see themselves as useless, incompetent, and inferior. They think that their future is hopeless. Given these emotions and thoughts, it is little wonder that these depressed people feel little *motivation* to do anything. They often lose their appetite; they lose interest in sex. Even their movements and actions slow down; to an observer, they appear to be moving and talking in slow motion. All of these effects conspire to affect the *physical appearance* of the depressed person. Because these people often have trouble sleeping and pay little attention to their physical appearance, they may look gaunt, ragged, almost ghostlike.

Depression is a normal reaction to a sad event such as the loss of a job, the end of a relationship, or the death of a friend. In most cases, the depression—even if it is very deep—soon passes and the person begins to cope with the world. However, some people are unable to shake their depression; instead, they sink deeper into it. When the depression lasts an unusually long time and interferes with the person's functioning, it can be considered a disorder. In some cases, it can reach psychotic proportions (see p. 442) and hospitalization may be necessary.

Depression is the most common psychological disorder; it has been referred to as the "common cold of mental illness" (Rosenbaum & Seligman, 1984). In any single year 15 percent of all adults may suffer from a depression disorder, and at any one time 2 to 4 percent of the population has impaired functioning due to depression (Secunda et al., 1973). Depressive disorders tend to reappear; a person who has had one episode has a 50 percent chance of suffering another one at some time in his or her life. While the average length of a depressive episode is 3 to 6 months, many people suffer depression for periods of 2 years or more (Keller, 1981). There is also evidence that some people spend their lives in a chronic state of low-level depression; traumatic events only increase the depth of their depression. At one time it was believed that older people were most likely to have depressive episodes. However, more recent evidence shows that depression is also common among younger people, especially college

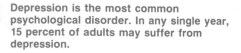

Depression is the most common psychological disorder. In any single year, 15 percent of adults may suffer from depression.

SUICIDE

Our examination of depression leads us into another area: suicide. The old saying that nobody ever died from feeling depressed is not exactly true. It has been estimated that depression plays a major role in almost 80 percent of suicide attempts. The act of suicide is tragic in any case, but it is especially upsetting when it is committed by young people. It is difficult to pick up a daily newspaper without reading about a suicide; in fact, there have been numerous stories of multiple suicides involving high school friends. In some cities, special teams of psychologists have been called in to counsel students and their parents in an attempt to stem what appears to be an adolescent "suicide epidemic."

A look at the figures on suicide shows the magnitude of the problem. It has been estimated that there is an attempted suicide every 30 minutes in the United States (Suinn, 1984). The most conservative estimate is that 25,000 people kill themselves every year; a more correct number is probably between 50,000 and 100,000. The rate of suicide has jumped fourfold during the last 30 years. Women attempt suicide three times more frequently than men, but men are three times more likely to be successful in attempts to kill themselves. Rates for blacks and

"Lethality Checklist" for Evaluating Suicide Risk

"Yes" answers to the following questions indicate a higher risk of suicide:

- Does the individual communicate an intent to commit suicide? Is the person highly specific about the details of the suicide plan? (For instance, "I know how many pills it will take for my body weight; my will is folded under the telephone; I will end it at sunset looking out my window; I will be wearing . . .")
- Does the person have no family or other social support system?
- Is the person facing a concrete life stress?
- Is the individual suffering from a serious illness?
- Has the person suffered from symptoms such as insomnia, depression, or alcoholism?
- Is the individual a male?

SOURCE: Los Angeles Suicide Prevention Center

American Indians are two to five times higher than suicide rates for whites. Religion does not seem to be a factor in determining who will commit suicide; rates are roughly the same for Catholics, Protestants, Jews, and nonreligious persons. The rate of suicide tends to increase with age, with the highest rates occurring in old age. However, the last few years have witnessed a dramatic rise in the suicide rates for adolescents and young adults. Today suicide is the second most frequent cause of death among college students.

Two major motivations for suicide have been identified (Beck et al., 1976). The main reason (56 percent of suicides) is simply the desire to end life. These individuals are generally depressed, lonely, and feel hopeless. They view suicide as a way to end their problems and stop their suffering. The second

motivation is manipulation of others. These people attempt suicide to "teach others a lesson," make them feel guilty, have the final word in an argument, or draw others to them. In many manipulative suicides, the individual intends to remain alive; he or she attempts suicide using less lethal means than do people who are using suicide as a means of ending their problems. Depression is not as evident in manipulative suicides.

"Hotlines" have been set up in many cities to identify people at risk and offer help. These lines are staffed by professionals and paraprofessionals who offer understanding, information, and hope to people contemplating suicide. At one center in Los Angeles, volunteers are provided with a "lethality checklist" to identify the high risk cases, as shown in the table here.

students. Researchers report that 46 percent of college students will seek professional help for depression during their college years (Beck & Young, 1978). Depression is more common among women than among men; in fact, two-thirds of those who suffer a depression disorder are women. In addition to the problems of life adjustment created by depression, another concern is suicide (see box on this page). People who are depressed often get the feeling that nothing will ever go right for them and there is little point in going on with life. As a result of these feelings, they may contemplate suicide. Research has found that the best indication that people will attempt suicide is that they talk about it; few people attempt suicide without first talking about it (Stafford-Clark & Smith, 1978). The greatest time of risk is not when people are in the grips of a depressive episode, but rather when they are pulling out of such an episode.

Suicide is the ninth most common cause of death in the United States. Although women are more likely to attempt suicide, males are more likely to succeed at it. Depression is evident in 80 percent of suicide attempts.

Theories of Depression.   Because it is such a common and destructive disorder, there have been many attempts to identify the causes of depression.

1. One of the earliest explanations was based on *psychoanalytic theory*. According to this theory, people may suffer the loss of a loved one or the loss of self-esteem during childhood, but instead of expressing their natural feelings of grief and anger, they inhibit them or turn them on the self (Newman & Hirt, 1983). Then, later in life, they may suffer a loss that reminds them of the earlier loss; in other words, the recent loss symbolizes the earlier event and brings up those repressed feelings of guilt and sadness. These people now respond to the current event—which may be the death of a pet or the loss of a job—not only with the feelings aroused by it, but also with the repressed feelings that surrounded the childhood loss. In addition to intense feelings, these people have developed the pattern of turning their anger upon themselves. Turning anger inward results in low self-esteem and, in extreme cases, suicide. In an interesting

study researchers found that women who had lost their mothers before the age of 11 were more likely to suffer adult depressive disorders than women who had not experienced such a loss (Brown et al., 1977).

2. *Learning theories* identity reinforcement schedules as the cause of depression. Some investigators argue that people become depressed because they find few positive rewards in their environment (Lewinsohn, 1974; Lewinsohn et al., 1980). Life loses its zip and excitement because they feel there is little to be happy about. As a result, they become sad, irritable, and self-pitying. By itself, this depression would certainly make them uncomfortable, but it is only the beginning of a vicious cycle. As they become depressed, other people avoid them; few of us enjoy being around people who are sullen and depressed. As friends retreat, they become even more depressed and develop feelings of worthlessness. Research has indeed shown that people who are depressed cause others to feel hostile and anxious (Coyne, 1976).

Hammen and Peters (1977) suggest a somewhat different relationship between reinforcement and depression. They argue that the reason that fewer men than women show depressed behavior is that male depression is more negatively reinforced than female depression. That is, a depressed female may receive attention and sympathy, while a depressed male is treated with indifference or a lecture to the effect that it is "unmanly" to be inactive and sulk. Males therefore find other ways to respond to stress and anxiety.

3. According to learning theory, people learn to behave in depressed ways and feel depressed because of their reinforcement schedules. *Cognitive theories* take this explanation one extra step: They propose that people learn negative views of the world and of themselves, and it is these negative views that lead to depression (Beck, 1983).

The negative views that serve as the foundation for depression form a *cognitive triad*—that is, they involve negative thoughts about the self, the world, and the future. Coupled with these negative views are illogical interpretations of events. For example, there is a tendency to magnify the importance of minor negative events and minimize the importance of major positive events. Thus a woman may dwell on the fact that she spilled coffee on an old shirt, while dismissing as insignificant a major job promotion. Finally, depression-prone people tend to overgeneralize from failures and focus on their negative characteristics. They become overwhelmed with a sense of worthlessness or personal failure and this leads to depression.

4. Other investigators combine learning and cognitive theories to explain depression (Seligman, 1974, 1975). In Chapter 11 we discussed a study in which dogs were placed in a situation where they could not escape electric shocks (Seligman et al., 1968). The dogs first responded by yelping and trying to find a way out. After a time, however, they "gave up" and no longer sought to escape. Later, when they were put into a situation where escape from the shock was possible, they remained passive and did not try to get away. In short, they learned to be helpless. This **learned helplessness model** has been applied to explaining the cause of depression (Peterson & Seligman, 1984).

According to this approach, people must make three choices when explaining uncontrollable bad events that happen to them. First, they must decide whether the event was due to their own actions (internal) or to the situation or circumstances (external). Second, they must determine whether the cause is due to a factor that will persist across time (stable) or one that is momentary and fleeting (unstable). Finally, they must decide whether the cause affects a variety of outcomes (global) or is limited to this single event (specific). As can be seen from Table 13–3, the consequences of these decisions may be very different. The model suggests

Table 13-3

Examples of Causal Explanations for the Event "My Checking Account Is Overdrawn"

Style	Explanation	
	Internal	External
Stable		
Global	"I'm incapable of doing anything right"	"All institutions chronically make mistakes"
Specific	"I always have trouble figuring my balance"	"This bank has always used antiquated techniques"
Unstable		
Global	"I've had the flu for a few weeks, and I've let everything slide"	"Holiday shopping demands that one throw oneself into it"
Specific	"The one time I didn't enter a check is the one time my account gets overdrawn"	"I'm surprised—my bank has never made an error before"

Source: Abramson et al., 1979.

that believing that one cannot control outcomes or events in the future sets the stage for depression. Explaining bad events as reflections of internal, stable, and global dimensions of the self will initiate a loss of self-esteem and a long-lasting depression. Therefore the explanatory style that people develop helps determine whether or not they will become a strong risk to suffer depression.

5. Another set of theories focusses on the possibility that *physiological conditions* can cause depression. Depression runs in families; people who have a depression disorder are likely to have relatives who have also suffered from depression (Rosenthal, 1970). Recently a number of investigators have uncovered evidence that depression is linked to an unusual structure in the genes (Crow, 1983). This structure is inherited and is therefore likely to be found in many members of certain families. The researchers, however, emphasize that this gene abnormality does not cause depression. Rather, it predisposes the person to suffer from a depressive disorder under certain environmental conditions. This finding is exciting because it offers the possibility that doctors can identify and treat depression-prone people before they experience a depressive episode.

It is still somewhat of a mystery how the gene structure can make a person prone to depression. A number of theories have focussed on the neurotransmitters. In Chapter 2 we discussed how neurons transmit messages. As you will remember, neurons do not touch one another. Rather, there is a very small gap between the end of one neuron and the beginning of the next. Electrical impulses are passed between this gap by a chemical substance called a neurotransmitter. Many substances serve as neurotransmitters, but the two associated with depression are norepinephrine and serotonin. One biological view is that depression is the result of a lack of these neurotransmitters (Berger, 1978). Another theory argues that depression is the result of too much sodium, which slows the transmission of nerve impulses (Depue & Evans, 1976). It has been found that exercise reduces the level of sodium in the blood, and some clinicians suggest that jogging and other physical exercise may reduce depression.

This is, indeed, a long list of explanations for depression. It might make a neat package if we could conclude by saying that this theory or that one is the "correct" answer. We cannot do this, however, as each theory offers some insight into depression but no single theory holds the key. It may well be that many roads lead to depression. The theories play many key roles; not only do they help us understand the many characteristics

CASE STUDY OF A MANIC DISORDER

As seen on the ward the morning after admission, Mrs. L. J., aged 38, presented a striking picture. She had been too excited to eat breakfast, but after gulping a cup of coffee she had taken several daisies from the centerpiece on the table and entwined them in her hair. She paced briskly up and down the hallways singing snatches of popular songs, and she paused briefly from time to time attempting to get other patients and personnel to join in the singing. . . .

Mrs. J. took the initiative in greeting everyone she encountered, patting the women on the back in a familiar manner and putting her arms around the men. It was, however, almost impossible for personnel to maintain a conversation with her. She responded with smiles and laughter to most remarks addressed to her and often talked volubly, but she was too distractible to give attention to any one subject for more than a moment. If an effort was made to detain her or to hold her attention, she would break away with a transient flash of anger.

A brief excerpt from the patient's stream of talk was as follows: "How do I feel? I feel with my hands. How do you feel? No, seriously, everything's wonderful. Couldn't be better. Going 'From Bed to Worse,' Benchley said." (Laughs.) "Really, honey, this is a marvelous place you've got here, mar-ve-lous. 'Marvelous Vel.' I really must shampoo my hair.". . .

In the course of the diagnostic evaluation and subsequent treatment of Mrs. J., a full background history was obtained, of which two features may be mentioned here. (1) The present illness had begun about ten days prior to admission upon the patient's having received the information that an ambitious volunteer-service project she chaired had failed to gain the approval of the community agency on which it depended. (2) Her initial response had been one of low spirits and irritability, lasting two or three days and then giving way to a mood of unusual cheerfulness, accompanied by various erratic activities and gaining in intensity until it reached the reckless and irrational gaiety shown on admission. On the previous day, the patient had stopped at a travel agency where, despite her confusion, she had arranged passage for five on a luxury cruise at a cost which was wildly beyond the family's means.

Source: C. K. Hofling, *Textbook of Psychiatry for Medical Practice*, 1975, pp. 351–352.

of depression, but they also help us plan ways to prevent and treat the disorder.

Mania and Bipolar Disorders. While depressives seem to drag themselves around and have no interest in becoming involved in any project, people in a state of mania have the opposite problem. Manics are a fountain of energy who feel ready to take on the world; they have very positive self-images. Unfortunately, they often fail to stay with a project until it is completed, but rather jump from one thing to another. They are easily distracted; they may begin a sentence and fail to finish it because they start another sentence on a new topic. People in a manic state often have an increased sex drive and seem to need less sleep than usual. These manic periods may last for days or even weeks. Pure cases of mania are relatively rare. In most cases, people suffer from a bipolar disorder, which means they alternate between manic and depressive stages. People with this bipolar disorder generally behave normally in the periods between the extreme affective states. In many of them the extreme mood states appear for only a short time.

Recent research suggests that heredity plays a strong role in the cause of bipolar disorders. Evidence has been discovered linking the bipolar disorders to the X chromosome (Cadoret & Winokur, 1975). As we discussed in Chapter 2, females have two X chromosomes and males have only one. This situation would lead us to expect that more females than males have the bipolar disorder and that transmission of the disorder must be from an affected mother. Research has generally supported these predictions. It has, however, proved difficult to pinpoint exactly what is inherited. Bunney and his colleagues (1972) have suggested that the inherited feature is a condition at the nerve endings that allows for a buildup of norepinephrine. During the buildup phase, little of this neurotransmitter passes between the neurons, causing vulnerability to depression. However, at some point the level of norepinephrine reaches a concentration at which a stressful event causes the neuron to "dump" the neurotransmitter, resulting in a high level of neuron activity and mania.

Psychosexual Disorders

The history of Manson's sexual behavior falls somewhere between an X-rated movie and a horror story. As an adolescent inmate, Manson repeatedly engaged in homosexual behavior—he sometimes found willing partners, but he forced others by threatening them with a knife. Outside prison, Manson engaged in heterosexual behavior, married twice, and fathered two children before he formed the Family. Sex in these relationships was not an intimate union based on love. Instead, Manson used sexual behavior to dominate his partners; he forced his second wife to become a prostitute to support him. Manson continued to use sex to lure young women into the Family. Once a woman joined the Family, Manson insisted that she participate in group sex and engage in sex while pretending to be an animal; he felt that these activities would rid her of her middle-class sexual hang-ups (Sanders, 1974).

Should we consider Manson's sexual activities clinically abnormal or simply deviant? The definition of normal sexual behavior is very difficult to determine. For one thing, we have very little data on current sexual practices. As we pointed out in Chapter 10, it was not until the work of Ellis and Kinsey in the late 1940s that investigators began to collect information on sexual behavior.

A second factor complicating the issue is that social views of "normal" and "abnormal" sexual behavior are constantly changing. This change has been reflected in the classification of systems. For example, DSM II classified homosexuality as a maladaptive sexual behavior; homosexuality is not considered a disorder of any kind in DSM III. This difference in the two classification systems is largely the result of greater social acceptance of homosexuality today compared to just a few years ago.

The most common position is that sexual behavior is maladaptive only if people are disturbed by their activities or if other people are hurt by them. Admittedly, this definition is not so precise as we might like, but it can serve as a guideline in many cases. The list of psychosexual disorders is long and includes some rather unusual practices. Let us briefly examine some of these disorders.

Gender Identity Disorders. Imagine parents' reaction as their rugged young son strides into the living room sporting a dress and hugging a doll. Equally upsetting to some parents is a little daughter who insists on dressing like a cowboy and beating up the little boy next door. We discussed the development of sex roles in Chapters 8 and 9 and pointed out that at a certain age these cross-gender behaviors are indeed normal. In fact, it is now recognized that sex-typing children and forcing rigid sex-role behavior on them is inadvisable. But while a rigid view of the role prescribed for one's sex may have undesired consequences, the problems created when people rigidly adopt the role of the opposite sex are even greater. This relatively rare childhood gender identity disorder is more often found in males than in females. Boys who suffer this disorder often shun playing with other boys, develop female gestures, and engage solely in female play activities. Girls with a gender disorder join male groups and engage in male play activities. While it is often difficult to distinguish between a gender disorder and a healthy ability to avoid stereotyped sex-role behavior, the gender disorder is characterized by an exclusive or near-exclusive attraction for the opposite-sex role.

People who have a gender disorder are likely to be ridiculed and rejected by their peers and punished by their parents. These responses often lower their self-esteem and create a great deal of unhappiness. There is disagreement about the cause of the disorder. Some investigators believe that hormone disturbance is responsible. Others argue that the root of the problem lies in the family. Boys who develop the disorder often have mothers who are overly protective, and fathers who are absent or very submissive. In this case, the boy identifies with the mother and begins to model her behaviors. Girls with gender disturbances come from families in which the mother is either absent or cold. Their fathers, on the other hand, are affectionate and serve as their role model. It is likely that future research may show that the disorder results from a combination of hormonal disturbances and family patterns. This would explain why every child who lacks the right role model does not develop a gender disorder. As we have seen, Charles Manson, who from birth did not have a father, did not show signs of gender disorder.

Transsexualism. Gender identity disorders often disappear at an early age. However, in some cases, the disorder persists into adulthood and becomes stronger. These people progress from wanting to play and dress like members of the opposite sex to actually wanting to be a member of the opposite sex (**transsexualism**). This longing may lead them to seek a sex-change operation that alters their anatomical features so that they are like those of the desired sex. Transsexuals may also take the necessary legal steps to become members of the opposite sex.

Transsexualism is a relatively rare condition, affecting fewer than 1 out of every 100,000 people. Most transsexuals have suffered from a gender disorder as children. The condition persists and they begin experiencing feelings of self-doubt and depression; they "feel" like the member of one gender but have been "born into" the body of the opposite gender. There have been few studies of transsexuals, but there is some evidence suggesting that a positive adjustment often follows the sex-change operation (Pierce et al., 1978). Others, however, argue that psychiatric counseling rather than surgery is the best treatment for transsexuals (Restak, 1979). Because of uncertainty about the best way to treat transsexuals, many clinics have stopped performing transsexual operations.

The lack of much research on transsexuals makes it difficult to determine the cause of the disorder. Many professionals believe that genetic or hormonal disturbances are at its base. Others, however, argue that learning plays a major role. A third explanation is that it is a fear of homosexuality that motivates people to seek sex-change operations. According to this position, these people are repulsed by their own homosexual tendencies (Leitenberg & Slavin, 1983). This fear, along with the view that society is more accepting of transsexuality than homosexuality, leads them to desire a sex-change operation.

Sadomasochism. One of the features that characterized Manson's sexual relationships was the cruelty and pain he inflicted on his partners. He seemed to delight in their pain. The term *sadomasochism* refers to sexual arousal that results from giving or receiving physical pain (Geer et al., 1984). Actually, there are two forms of sadomasochism. One is **sadism,** which involves deriving sexual pleasure from inflicting pain on others. The other is **masochism,** which involves becoming sexually aroused from having pain inflicted on oneself. In one survey slightly less than 5 percent of male and 2 percent of female respondents reported having experienced sexual arousal from receiving or inflicting pain (Hunt, 1974). Of this group, more males reported pleasure from inflicting pain than receiving pain; the reverse relationship was found among females. The likelihood of sadomasochism was greater among young people than old, and much greater among single males than married males.

Physical pain is inflicted through biting, whipping, slapping, or pinching. In addition, psychological humiliation is often inflicted through threatening, belittling, or bullying tactics. These acts do not occur in random ways. Rather, there is often an elaborate script whereby one partner plays the dominant role, such as acting like a master or jailer, while the other person plays the submissive role of a slave or a misbehaving student. Elaborate props such as whips, chains, masks, and leather clothing may be employed to enhance the drama. As you might imagine, the sadist and masochist often seek each other out.

There have been a number of attempts to explain sadomasochistic behavior. One of the main explanations suggests that the pattern results from the effort to relieve guilt over sexual behavior. The masochist may be able to accept sexual experience only by rationalizing that he or she was helpless throughout it. Other explanations suggest that these behaviors may be learned through modeling. Finally, it has been proposed that sadism is the result of a deep-seated dislike of the opposite sex or of people in general (Maier, 1984).

Sexual Dysfunctions. The most common group of sexual disorders falls under the category of sexual dysfunctions. For males, these dysfunctions include **erectile dysfunction** (the inability to have an erection or maintain one long enough for ejaculation), **premature ejaculation,** and *retarded ejaculation* (the inability to ejaculate during intercourse). For females, the most common disorders are the *inability to achieve orgasm*, **dyspareunia** (the experiencing of pain during intercourse), and **vaginismus** (the involuntary tightening of the vagina so that intercourse is impossible). Most of these dysfunctions are disorders of degree rather than kind. That is, many people have temporary dysfunctions in sexual behavior. For example, it has been estimated that half the male population has experienced periodic impotence, and dysfunctions in both sexes may occur during periods of stress, tiredness, or drunkenness (Kaplan, 1974). While these dysfunctions are troublesome, they quickly pass and there is little reason to be overly concerned about them. Some people, however, experience a dysfunction for an extended period of time; their problem is distressing and inhibits normal adjustment. In some cases, the root of the dysfunction may be physiological, such as diabetes or a hormone imbalance. Most of the time, however, the dysfunction has a psychological cause. LoPiccolo (1978) found that many of the psychological roots of sexual dysfunction are in childhood experiences or teaching. For example, someone may have been taught that premarital intercourse is evil and morally wrong; this lesson may conflict with present desires and result in impotence. An early sexual trauma, such as being the victim of rape or molestation in childhood, may also interfere with satisfying sexual experiences in adulthood.

PSYCHOSIS

The disorders we have described so far involve interference with people's basic adjustment to their world. In most cases, people realize they are acting or feeling "abnormally" and are distressed by this realization. They try to deal with reality and the social world in spite of their disorder.

People suffering from **psychosis,** on the other hand, have lost touch with reality. They no longer attempt to adjust to the world as others see it. Instead, they create their own world, different and apart from others, and they respond only to their own reality. Their bizarre behavior and perceptions severely impair their functioning. Most psychotics can no longer care for themselves, and they usually must be hospitalized.

Some investigators believe that psychosis is simply a severe form of the neurotic disorders we just discussed (Mayer-Gross, Slater, & Roth, 1960). Indeed, some neurotic disorders do have their psychotic counterpart. For example, there is a manic-depressive psychotic disorder in which people become so overwhelmed by their moods that they lose touch with reality, cannot function, and must be hospitalized. There are, however, psychotic disorders—including the most common one, schizophrenia—whose symptoms do not resemble those of the less severe, neurotic disturbances. Further, many people who suffer from psychosis never show signs of neurotic behavior. These points have led many researchers to conclude that psychosis really is a different type of disorder and not just the extreme end of a continuum going from normal to neurotic to psychotic.

Here we will examine the most common psychosis, schizophrenia. As you read, compare this disorder with the neurotic disorders we discussed and determine for yourself whether psychosis is a distinct category of psychological disturbances.

Schizophrenia

A study of Charles Manson's life reveals bizarreness in almost every aspect of his personality. The most pronounced area is his thinking. We have already pointed out that Manson believed he was Jesus Christ and felt that the Beatles were angels of God who spoke to him through their songs. Manson also had some unusual perceptions. At times he heard the voice of God giving him instructions to prepare for Helter Skelter. Manson's emotions showed such wide variation that it was impossible to predict how he would act next. During his trial he would sometimes sit for hours smiling at the most damaging testimony; this calmness might then be shattered by a wild outburst as he leapt on top of the table and angrily denounced the court, the witness, and the world.

Many of Manson's bizarre feelings, thoughts, and behaviors are considered symptoms of the psychotic disorder known as schizophrenia. Schizophrenia is actually a group of disorders characterized by disorganization in (1) thoughts, (2) perceptions, (3) communication, (4) emotions, and (5) motor activity. The term **schizophrenia** was first used by the Swiss psychiatrist Bleuler. It literally means "split mind." Bleuler used this term because he observed that in some patients certain mental functions seemed to be separated or split off from others—that is, their thoughts seemed unrelated to their emotions or perceptions. This does not mean, however, that schizophrenics have multiple personalities.

Schizophrenia is the most common severe psychological disorder. Over half the beds in all psychiatric hospitals are occupied by people who have been diagnosed as schizophrenic (Kramer, 1976). It has been estimated that 1 percent of the population will suffer from schizophrenia at some time during their lives (DSM III, 1980). The peak onset period is between the ages of 20 and 35. Men are at highest risk before the age of 25, while women's highest risk period is after age 25 (Lewine, 1981). Schizophrenia is most commonly found in people from the lower socioeconomic classes. Unlike some of the psychological disorders we have examined, it is not a product of our modern stressful society; there is evidence that it has occurred throughout history, and today it is found in simple primitive societies as well as in more modern industrial countries.

Table 13–4 lists the most common subtypes of schizophrenia with their most common symptoms. People may show all or only a few of the symptoms for a type. Whatever the array of symptoms or the subtype of disorder, schizophrenia is a disabling condition that often requires long periods of hospitalization. Let us briefly examine some of the most common symptoms.

Table 13–4
Major Types
of Schizophrenia

Type	Description
1. Disorganized (hebephrenic)	This type is characterized by many delusions, hallucinations, and inappropriate emotions. People may laugh and giggle for no apparent reason. They become childlike, urinate and defecate on the floor, and refuse to wear clothing.
2. Catatonic	The major characteristic of this type is disturbance of motor activity. People may remain in one position for long periods of time without moving, their body almost waxy; if someone moves them, they will remain in the new position. In agitated cases, they will show wild, constant movement, often becoming violent and destructive.
3. Paranoid	The major problem in this type is cognitions or thoughts. People believe that others are trying to destroy or control them (delusions of persecution), and they trust no one. They will not let others get close to them for fear that these others will harm them. In some cases, there may be delusions of grandeur in which people believe that they are a famous person or a powerful figure who controls the world. These people may have difficulty functioning because they are concentrating on the "sinister" acts of others.
4. Undifferentiated	This type involves delusions, hallucinations, and disorganized emotions. This is really a "catchall" category for cases that are characterized by extreme disorganization but do not fit any of the other types.

Symptoms of Schizophrenia

Disorganization of Thought. One of the most common symptoms or schizophrenia is **delusions**—irrational beliefs that are held in spite of the existence of contrary evidence. There are many types of delusions. One is the delusion of grandeur, which is the belief that the person is special or different from other people. Manson's belief that he was Jesus and that the Beatles were sending special messages to him through their music are examples of delusions of grandeur. Those with delusions of persecution believe that people are "out to get" them and that such people are controlling their thoughts or behaviors. Examples of this type of delusion are Manson's belief that all blacks were plotting a revolt and that society itself was against Manson. During one of his court appearances, Manson passionately spoke of this persecution: ". . . I have done my best to get along in your world and now you want to kill me, and I look at you, and then I say to myself, You want to kill me? Ha!" (Bugliosi & Gentry, 1974, p. 526). People with delusions of persecution are called **paranoid**; they mistrust others and interpret their actions as plotting.

Disorganization of Perception. When you look at a tree, what do you see? Probably you see some green leaves clinging to some branches and a large trunk supporting this structure. This is the way most of us view a tree. Now imagine looking at that tree in much greater detail. Look at every leaf. Is the leaf dark green or light green? Look at each branch. Is the branch thick or thin, long or short, bent or straight, brown or gray? Now examine the trunk closely. At this point you may be throwing up your hands and exclaiming that this is crazy, that at this rate you could spend the whole afternoon looking at just one tree, and anyway, why examine a tree with such care? You are correct, of course, but this is an example of the perceptual process used by some schizophrenics. They become engrossed in minute details and are unable to block out irrelevant stimuli. They can spend hours looking at a simple object. They may pay this same

CASE STUDY OF PARANOIA

A prosperous builder aged forty-four was refused a very substantial overdraft from a local bank against the collateral of his firm and property. This was his first serious business reverse in sixteen years of independent building; and he became morose and disturbed about it.

After some months he suddenly expressed the conviction that people were talking about him because the loan had been refused; and that the basis of its refusal was the fact that he had syphilis, and had passed it on to his wife and children. He then went about demanding legal action against the Bank Manager, and various other people, and accusing his General Practitioner of having falsified and then published medical reports about him. He was admitted to the hospital, having refused to see any doctors, after a suicidal attempt in which he had tried to hang himself; leaving a note saying that no one man could stand up to the devilish and calculated campaign of mind reading, calumny, and persecution to which he had been submitted.

During the course of treatment in the hospital he disclosed that his mind was still being read by an electronic machine, in which his thoughts were transcribed into a formula for a new and more terrible atomic bomb. He made a partial remission in response to treatment, and returned to take control of his firm and property; seen for outpatient follow-up and assessment he remains deluded, but can discuss and accept support and reassurance about his general predicament while remaining a competent builder and manager of his business.

Source: From D. Stafford-Clark, & A. C. Smith (1978), *Psychiatry for Students*, 5th ed.

deep attention to noises. They hear each and every noise in their environment. The schizophrenic may become engrossed in his or her own body, listening to each heartbeat and feeling each surge of blood through the veins. In each of these cases, the schizophrenic pays attention to the smallest detail of stimuli or events without trying to organize them into larger, meaningful wholes.

Another perceptual phenomenon experienced by some schizophrenics is **hallucination,** which, as we discussed in Chapter 5, involves having a sensory experience without the external stimuli. Hallucinations can involve

The words of the schizophrenic person who did this painting underline the misery caused by this disorder: "The painting really symbolizes a silent scream. . . . [describing], my life or much of it at that time."

BOBBY'S STORY

My brother, Bobby Hirsch, shot and killed himself Friday night. Close friends of the family have heard the whole story, but there are others who knew Bobby and might want to understand why he did what he did.

Bobby fought a severe mental illness for many years. Bobby's problems were caused by a chemical imbalance in his brain that caused him to perceive his world in bizarre ways and to make him interpret his perceptions in equally bizarre ways. Gradually, through the use of medication, Bobby was correcting many of these problems. In recent months he had come to understand the truth about his world and himself, and to understand the cause of his old perceptions and beliefs—and the solutions to his problems.

Bobby was well on the road to recovery and only two obstacles remained in the way of his becoming a nearly-normal taxpaying citizen. One was controlling the side effects of the medication, which made him very sleepy and lethargic. The other was controlling what he called "panic attacks." Sometimes even medication could not control irrational, unspecific emotions of fear, horror and dread, which would last a couple of hours and then go away.

It was during a "panic attack" on Friday that Bobby took his life. In that moment he did not understand the consequences of the sudden impulse. He did not leave a note.

Bobby died from his illness in the same way someone with heart disease can die from a heart attack or someone with diabetes can die from an insulin crisis.

Mental illness is not well understood and often carries a social stigma not attached to other illnesses. For years the family has tried to "keep it quiet" to protect Bobby, so that when he was ready to rejoin the world, the world wouldn't be prejudiced against him. But now that Bobby has all his answers, it is better that people know the whole story.

Mary Hirsch
Houston

Bryan-College Station Eagle, January 28, 1985, p. 6A

vision, hearing, taste, touch, or smell. The most common types are auditory: People "hear" voices that are not there. Manson stated that God actually talked to him in the desert. Many times the voices accuse the hearer of doing or thinking bad things. Visual hallucinations can involve seeing people, even those who died many years earlier, or seeing monsters that have come to punish the person.

Clearly, the schizophrenic's perceptions are strange and troubled. But there is an intriguing side to their disorganization. Some investigators have found that people who have a genetic predisposition for schizophrenia tend to display highly creative tendencies (Karlsson, 1972; Magaro, 1981). In fact, a number of the most creative people in music, literature, physics, and art have developed psychological disorders. Hence, hidden deep within the bizarre perceptions of the schizophrenic may lurk the seeds of creativity. However, the other factors associated with the disorder may prevent this creativity from developing or being appreciated.

Disturbances in Communication. Talking to a schizophrenic is often like communicating with someone who is talking in his or her sleep. The schizophrenic talks in a dreamy tone of voice and does not seem to be paying attention to anything anyone says. For example, if you asked a schizophrenic how he or she is feeling, you might get the following response:

Yesterday I was fine. The fine head of a pin can fit into a very small hole. The whole group of birds landed in the field and ate corn.

In this case, the schizophrenic's speech follows no train of thought. Instead, each sentence follows from an association with a word in the previous sentence. The schizophrenic may also give completely irrelevant replies to questions or may launch into a highly intellectual and complex reply to a very simple question. In the latter instance, the schizophrenic, when asked how he is feeling, may discuss the distinction between being physically healthy and feeling well. Needless to say, communication with a schizophrenic is often difficult and forces people to stretch their imagination.

Inappropriate Emotions. Schizophrenics may giggle and laugh when talking about the death of a close friend or relative. On the other hand, they may sob uncontrollably when talking about matter-of-fact issues. Overall, it is difficult to predict what emotions they will show, because their feelings seem to have little connection with the situation or what is happening to them. Another rather common emotional pattern of schizophrenics is apathy. No matter what is happening, they show almost no emotion or feeling. Some do not even move when pricked with a sharp object or when burned.

Unusual Motor Activities. A wide variety of unusual motor activities is associated with schizophrenia. In some cases, people move in slow motion, as if every movement is achieved only with the greatest effort. They may slowly move their head and stare around the room with an almost vacant glance. In the most extreme instances, they may spend hours without moving. If they move their arms, they let them remain in the new position; they are like molding wax, since they exercise no control over how their body is manipulated. Others may repeat the same motor activity for hours on end. For example, one schizophrenic spent four hours touching first the end of her nose and then her ear. Whatever the particular motor activity, the major characteristic is that it has no connection with the physical reality of the situation and is not aimed at achieving any identifiable goal.

Theories of Schizophrenia

Schizophrenia is one of the most studied of all the psychological disorders. There are at least two reasons for this. The first is the seriousness of the disorder. Second, schizophrenia is very widespread. As we pointed out, schizophrenia is found in almost every culture and is the most common diagnosis for patients hospitalized for a mental disorder. Despite the large amount of research, investigators have not reached agreement as to the cause of schizophrenia. There are many theories about its cause; it is likely, in fact, that there are many causes of schizophrenia.

Biological Theories. The story of attempts to show a biological cause of schizophrenia reads much like a Sherlock Holmes mystery. When we talk about biological cause, we focus on the issue of inheritance. Each of us has many clearly visible traits inherited from our parents. For example, your blue eyes, curly hair, bushy eyebrows, large chest, and bony knees are features you received through a combination of your parent's genes. It is rather easy to show that there is a biological cause—inheritance—rather than an environmental one. It is unlikely that your eyes turned blue because you moved to Texas as an infant or that your hair became curly because you spent many cold winters in Kansas. But how can we prove that a psychological disorder like schizophrenia is inherited in the same way as these physical features?

Some evidence for a biological cause comes from studies of identical twins (see pp. 422–423). Research has found that if one twin has schizophrenia, the other twin has almost a 60 percent chance of developing the disorder (Ban, 1973; Gottesman & Shields, 1972). While this may be strong evidence that schizophrenia is inherited, it can be argued that besides their identical genetic structure, monogygotic twins also share a very similar childhood environment. Thus learning and other environmental factors could still be responsible for the disorder.

In an effort to counter this environmental argument, investigators examined the development of schizophrenia in people who were born to schizophrenic parents but were adopted as infants by nonschizophrenic parents (Kety et al., 1968; Rosenthal, 1973). The researchers found that these people were more likely to develop schizophrenia than adopted children who did not have schizophrenic parents. These studies, combined with

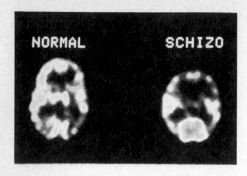

PET (positron emission tomography) scans show the rates at which glucose is consumed in the brain. There has been some research that links chemical imbalances in the brain with schizophrenia. In the PET scan shown here, the normal brain in the left photo shows moderate rates of consumption; the scan on the right is of someone diagnosed as schizophrenic and shows increased levels of consumption, indicated by the light area at the base of the scan.

the twin studies mentioned above, suggest that genetic factors can be one cause of schizophrenia. We must emphasize, however, that genetics can only be one of the causes, since schizophrenia does not always occur in both identical twins when one has the disorder, and not all, or even most, adopted children whose natural parents were schizophrenic became schizophrenic themselves.

Given that schizophrenia can be inherited, our next question concerns how the disorder is passed on. More directly, what does the defective gene do to people that causes them to develop schizophrenia? One study focusses on a neurotransmitter called *dopamine* (Davis, 1974). This research suggests that schizophrenics have too much dopamine and that this dopamine overstimulates their brains, causing schizophrenic behavior (Crow, 1983). Another set of theories focusses on chemicals in the blood. Early research produced some excitement by showing that tadpoles died when placed in the blood serum of schizophrenics (Lazell & Prince, 1929) and that spiders injected with a schizophrenic's blood built inadequate and bizarre webs (Bercel, 1960). While these results have been disproved, Wagemaker and Cade (1977) reported a recent discovery that has revived interest in the blood chemistry theories. These investigators treated a schizophrenic woman for a physical disorder by filtering her blood through a dialysis machine. To their surprise, her schizophrenic symptoms almost disappeared after this treatment. When dialysis was tried on three other schizophrenics, their symptoms were also reduced after a short period of time. The investigators argued that the filtering may have removed some substance from the blood that is responsible for schizophrenia. Research in this area is still continuing.

Learning Theories. Schizophrenics have been described as living in a world of their own. Learning theorists have suggested that schizophrenics may have learned that being in their own world is more rewarding and less stressful than living in the real world. They argue that schizophrenics are rewarded for escaping into their own world and acting in bizarre ways. One type of reward is attention. If you were to sit in the corner of your room for a long period of time, it is likely that your roommate would soon approach you and ask, "What's wrong?" If you continued with this behavior, other people might be called in to do something about you. It has been reported that the bizarre behavior of schizophrenics diminished when they were ignored by hospital personnel (Agras, 1967).

Cognitive Theories. As we have pointed out, one of the main characteristics of schizophrenics is the way they perceive and think about the world. They often spend large amounts of time focussing on small details and cannot "block out" irrelevant stimuli. One researcher suggests that one cause of schizophrenia may be that people develop faulty ways of perceiving the world; they learn a certain set of expectations that causes them to focus on unimportant parts of their environment (Shakow, 1977). Their adjustment is therefore retarded because they are responding to a world that is different from the one that you and I perceive. Treatment should, therefore, focus on changing the way schizophrenics perceive situations.

Maher (1970) offers another interesting view. He suggests that schizophrenics suffer from a biochemical disturbance that causes them to experience distorted sensations that are different from those experienced by other people. Their seemingly bizarre behavior and beliefs are their efforts to deal with this unusual stimulation. Hence there may be nothing wrong with schizophrenics' reasoning or belief systems. They may be simply using logical processes to deal with the unusual sensory stimulation that they experience.

Family Approach. If we return to the example of Charles Manson, we can see that his early childhood was filled with family stress. His mother

The double bind.

fought very hard with his aunt and the courts to regain custody of her son. However, once she had custody of Manson, she left him with neighbors and friends for days at a time. Did she love her son or dislike him?

Research on families suggests that certain types of stress can lead to schizophrenia. A **double-bind conflict** results when children receive contradictory messages from their parents. These messages create a "no-win" situation for the child. The example of Manson's mother fighting for him and then giving him away created a double-bind. The following is another example:

> A young man who had fairly well recovered from an acute schizophrenic episode was visited in the hospital by his mother. He was glad to see her and impulsively put his arm around her shoulders, whereupon she stiffened. He withdrew his arm and she asked, "Don't you love me anymore?" He then blushed and she said, "Dear, you must not be so easily embarrassed and afraid of your feelings." The patient was able to stay with her only a few minutes more and following her departure he assaulted an aide. . . . (Bateson et al., 1956, p. 144)

Children faced with a double-bind situation will begin to withdraw and cease trying to form close relationships with people. The family situation teaches them that dealing with others is confusing because people's words and actions are often very different. Therefore they often retreat into a world of their own.

Finally, other research has examined the characteristics of the parents of schizophrenics (Lewis et al., 1981; Shapiro, 1981). The mothers of schizophrenics tend to present a picture of inconsistency and unpredictability. For instance, they may remain aloof and avoid intimacy, yet insist on sharing their child's every activity. The fathers of schizophrenics are often passive, rigid, and detached. While their actions are more consistent than those of the mothers just described, they present poor models of adjustment.

Taken as a whole, the family theories argue that stress and conflict present in family situations can cause people to develop a distorted view of reality and force them to retreat into a private world. The question that is still unanswered is why some people faced with this type of conflict develop schizophrenia while others do not.

Schizophrenia: Normal Adjustment to an Abnormal World?

The usual reaction to schizophrenic behavior is, "These people are really crazy." Certainly people have to be crazy to believe they are Jesus, to hear voices coming out of light sockets, to repeat the same word five times in each sentence, and to spend hours touching their navel. R. D. Laing, a humanistic psychologist, presents an alternate view. Maybe schizophrenics are not so crazy; they are simply trying to adjust to a crazy family situation and social environment (Laing, 1964). Laing argues that schizophrenic behavior may actually be a reasonable response to a bizarre environment. He believes that we can understand schizophrenics by examining the environment they are responding to. According to Laing, we need to try to perceive schizophrenics' environment in the same way that they perceive it. By doing this, we will understand schizophrenic behavior. In short, Laing suggests that it is the world, not the schizophrenic, that is crazy.

There are certainly times when many of us would agree with this last statement. It does not, however, explain why certain people develop schizophrenia and others do not, even when they face similar environments. Despite this problem, Laing's radical view has forced investigators to examine more closely schizophrenics' environment in an effort to find out how schizophrenics interpret that environment.

PERSONALITY DISORDERS

We have used Manson's behavior to illustrate symptoms related to many disorders. As we pointed out at the beginning of this chapter, we do not have enough information to definitely categorize Manson as suffering from one of the disorders we have discussed. Considering the amount of time he spent in prison, Manson had surprisingly little contact with psychologists and other counselors. The lack of a professional perspective on Manson further complicates any efforts to determine his psychological problems. However, a review of the records that do exist shows that the clinicians and counselors who had contact with Manson described him as having an antisocial personality disorder.

Personality disorders are rigid and maladaptive ways of dealing with the environment. They are characterized not so much by a specific behavior as by a general approach to dealing with events. They usually become evident during adolescence and remain with people throughout their life. Unlike many of the disorders we have discussed, most personality disorders are not characterized by wild or bizarre behaviors. In fact, most people with a personality disorder can function and seldom require hospitalization. However, their behavior is strange enough that other people avoid interacting with them or are distressed by the interactions. The most noticeable characteristic of the personality disorder is that people tend to react to stress in a patterned way. This response is seldom affected by the requirements of the situation. For example, if someone intentionally stepped on your toe, you would most likely shout and make your anger known. But if that someone happened to be a 280-pound, 6'7" male, chances are your shouts would not be so loud. People with an antisocial personality disorder, however, would probably respond to this intimidating person in the same way they would respond to someone of more manageable size.

There are a number of types of personality disorders; in fact, DSM III lists 12. Here we will examine only one, the antisocial personality. This is the type most characteristic of Manson, and it is the type most commonly found in Western society.

Antisocial Personality

Vincent Bugliosi, the prosecuting attorney, reported being most surprised at two of Manson's characteristics. The first was that Manson never seemed to learn from his mistakes. He continued to violate federal laws even though this resulted in long prison sentences. The second characteristic was Manson's total disregard for anyone other than himself. Manson felt no remorse or guilt in ordering the murders of at least seven people whom he did not know. And during the trial he showed that he felt nothing for his three female codefendants, who had killed for him. He told Bugliosi that he was more than willing to let the girls go to prison if it would save him.

These characteristics are common in people with antisocial personalities (often referred to as psychopaths or sociopaths). Research shows that people with antisocial personality disorders perform violent and hurtful acts without experiencing the least bit of guilt or remorse (Cleckley, 1976). They are incapable of forming close relationships with others, and they are manipulative and insincere. They also seem to be incapable of learning from their mistakes. Many antisocial people serve prison terms, but once released, they continue with the same kind of behavior that got them into trouble in the first place. One of the more frightening aspects of this disorder is that antisocial people are often very intelligent and use their intelligence to "get away with" their behavior. It is very revealing that Manson was not the one who actually murdered Tate and the others; he manipulated the devoted members of the Family to do the killing.

Antisocial personality is a relatively common disorder. It has been estimated that 3 percent of American men and 1 percent of American women have this type of personality. In fact, this estimate may be low, since antisocial people seldom seek professional help, and many of the statistics must be based on cases that have come to the attention of law enforcement officials (Widom, 1978). Clearly, not all people who take part in crimes or antisocial behavior are suffering from antisocial personality disorders. The disorder can be identified if the person has a long history of antisocial behavior that began by adolescence and continued into adulthood. In addition, people with antisocial personality disorders do not limit their activities to one crime or behavior; rather, they engage in a wide variety of behaviors such as lying, stealing, irresponsible parenting, dealing drugs, and writing bad checks. The behavior of people with antisocial personality disorders seems irrational and not aimed at personal gain. An example is Manson's "creepy-crawly" activities, where he broke into houses and rearranged furniture, but took nothing of value for himself.

What causes people to treat others with such indifference? There is some evidence that an antisocial personality may be inherited. One investigator found that children of antisocial parents who were adopted at birth were more likely to show antisocial behavior than adopted children who did not have antisocial parents (Cadoret, 1978). However, other research has not found a strong link to genetics (Farber, 1981). Another line of research has found that many sociopaths have abnormal brain-wave patterns (Hare, 1978). It has been suggested that these abnormal patterns keep the person from experiencing fear, and hence free him or her to act in antisocial ways. Turning away from biological explanations, some investigators have focussed on early-childhood conditions. Many people with antisocial personality disorders came from broken homes. It was not the absence of a parent that was associated with the disorder, however. Rather, it was the specific atmosphere surrounding the divorce that was the contributing factor. This included violent arguments, instability, parental neglect, and lack of affection (McCord, 1979).

SUBSTANCE USE DISORDERS: ALCOHOL AND OTHER DRUGS

The prosecuting attorney told the court that Manson controlled the minds of his followers by his almost hypnotic words and he controlled their bodies through the use of drugs. Manson was portrayed as the typical "hippie" of the time. During the 1960s and early 1970s hippies served as the symbol of drug abuse to many people. As that era faded, however, society realized that the problem of drug and alcohol abuse was not confined to a handful of hippies. Abuse occurred in the old as well as the young, the rich as well as the poor, whites as well as blacks, females as well as males. It also became clear that the range of abused substances was far wider than just "hard drugs."

As we examine substance use and abuse, there are some important points to keep in mind. The first is that the legal issues must be separated from the clinical considerations. For example, a person who smokes marijuana at a party may be breaking the law, but he or she would not necessarily be classified as a drug abuser in the clinical sense. The second point is

Because substance abuse involves tolerance and withdrawal, abusers must often be treated in a special program. Elizabeth Taylor went through such a program to deal with her drug dependence.

that there are actually two categories of **substance use disorders** (see Table 13–5), and that use of drugs does not necessarily indicate either of these disorders. The first category is **substance abuse,** which results when (1) there is pathological use of the drug, (2) there is a reduction in social or occupational functioning because of the drug, and (3) there is at least one month's duration of disturbance. Thus a person who has a few drinks at lunch would not be classified as suffering from drug abuse. However, if that person were to feel that he or she had to have a couple of drinks to get through the day, and the drinking resulted in poorer work performance, the classification of substance abuse would be appropriate. In addition to substance abuse, DSM III (1980) lists the category **substance dependence** (addiction), which includes the presence of tolerance or withdrawal. **Tolerance** means the need to increase the amount of the drug to achieve the same effects. Withdrawal means the presence of physical symptoms such as pain or nausea when use of the substance is discontinued.

Alcoholism

Addiction to alcohol (alcoholism) is the most common addiction in today's society. Most of us use alcohol on occasion; in fact, two-thirds of adult Americans drink alcohol at times. In low or moderate doses, alcohol may have a relaxing effect, help in sleeping, lower pulse rate, and aid in social interaction. There is evidence that small doses of alcohol may reduce the risk of heart attack, and nursing mothers may be encouraged to drink a glass of beer or wine to help their milk flow (Turner, 1981).

Table 13–5
Substance Use Disorders

Substance Abuse
1. Pathological use of drug, *and*   2. social or occupational impairment as a result of drug use, *and*   3. duration of at least one month.
Substance Dependence
1. Tolerance—need to increase dose of drug to achieve similar effects over time; *or*   2. withdrawal—presence of physical symptoms such as pain or nausea when use of drug is discontinued.

It may seem hard to believe that a drug that has these positive effects could have so many negative ones when taken in large doses. Large amounts of alcohol lead to impaired judgment, slowed reflexes, nausea, fainting, and possibly death. Extended use of large quantities of alcohol results in liver damage, hypertension, and malnutrition. Coleman (1980) states that alcohol is associated with over half of all deaths and major injuries in automobile accidents, 50 percent of all murders, and 30 percent of all suicides. He also points out that nearly one-third of all arrests in the United States are the result of alcohol abuse. Highway accidents in which alcohol is a contributing factor are the greatest cause of death for young people. Because of this, many states have recently raised the legal drinking age from 18 to 21 years old.

When we talk about alcohol abuse, we are really talking about two categories of people. The larger category is the **problem drinker** or alcohol abuser. This includes people who often drink too much and whose drinking has undesirable effects. Problem drinkers may be people who have learned to deal with stressful situations by drinking, or they may be people who enjoy drinking or getting drunk. A small number of these problem drinkers fall into the category of alcoholic. **Alcoholics** are dependent on alcohol. They have an uncontrollable urge to drink, and because of an increasing tolerance, they must continue to increase the dosage of alcohol. Since they consume such large amounts of alcohol, alcoholics are often in poor physical health and their social relationships suffer.

The number of problem drinkers in the United States is surprisingly high; 10 percent of adult males and 3 percent of adult females are problem drinkers. Less than half of these problem drinkers are alcoholics. With these large figures, it is surprising to learn that the United States ranks only fifteenth in amount of alcohol consumed; France ranks first. Although today much attention and concern is focussed on "hard drugs," the problem of alcohol abuse is increasing. For example, in England and Wales the number of individuals admitted to hospitals for alcoholism is 20 times greater today than 25 years ago. It has been estimated that alcoholism costs industry $10 billion a year in the United States (Jaffe et al., 1980).

Why would some people become addicted to alcohol and develop an uncontrollable urge to drink when others neither become addicted nor feel a need to drink? As with most other disorders, there are many theories. One view is that alcoholism is inherited. For example, Goodwin (1979) found that sons of alcoholic parents are four times more likely to become

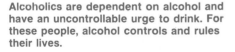

Alcoholics are dependent on alcohol and have an uncontrollable urge to drink. For these people, alcohol controls and rules their lives.

alcoholics than sons of nonalcoholic parents. This figure holds true even if the children are not reared by their natural parents. Interestingly enough, daughters of alcoholic parents do not run a greater risk than daughters of nonalcoholic parents of becoming alcoholic. While there is evidence that alcoholism is inherited, we are still unsure of how it works. It may be that individuals inherit an allergy-like response to alcohol. Other theories adopt the position that alcoholism is learned. The individual finds that alcohol reduces stress and therefore "turns to the bottle" whenever stressful situations arise. Still other theories take the psychoanalytic approach, arguing that alcoholism is the result of childhood trauma during the oral stage (from birth to 2 years old). According to this theory, people fixated at the oral stage focus on their mouth area; they try to satisfy their oral need by putting things into their mouth. In some cases, they smoke a great deal; in other cases, they are compulsive gum chewers; and in still other cases, they turn to alcohol.

Drug Addiction

The term *drug* has become a catchword in today's society. Making the statement that "drugs" were used heavily by members of the Manson Family could have many meanings. On the one hand, we might be referring to **narcotics** (morphine, heroine, opium). Narcotics are drugs that in small doses reduce pain, cause drowsiness, and give the individual a feeling of happiness and well-being. The term drug might also be used to refer to *amphetamines* (speed and pep pills) or *cocaine*, which are **stimulants** causing the individual to feel excited and full of energy. Another category of drugs is the **hallucinogens** (LSD, STP, mescaline, peyote—see Chapter 5), which cause the individual to feel happy and see visions and illusions. *Barbiturates* and *tranquilizers* are **depressants** that slow the body functions, reduce anxiety, and have a relaxing effect.

The use of drugs seems to be almost as old as civilization itself. There is reference to the use of marijuana in China in 2737 B.C. and to the use of opium in the Middle East before the eighth century B.C. In most cases, the substances that we call "drugs" have medical importance when used in small doses in prescribed ways. Narcotics, for example, reduce pain, and marijuana has been used to treat glaucoma (a disease of the eye). However, taken in large doses, most of the drugs that we listed can cause serious physical and psychological impairment and even lead to death.

Although addiction is possible with most of the drugs, it seems to have different characteristics depending on the specific substance being used. For example, the body builds up a tolerance for each of certain drugs. This means that people must increase the dose to get the desired effect from the drug. However, research suggests that while a physical dependence develops for narcotics, amphetamines, barbiturates, and nicotine, there is no physical dependence on hallucinogens. Thus withdrawal from the former set of drugs will be *physically* painful. This finding seems to argue that we need to have little concern about addiction to hallucinogens because withdrawal will not be physically painful. However, closer examination of the issue reveals that there are actually two types of dependence that can develop. The first, *physical dependence*, means the body develops a need for the drug. The second, *psychological dependence*, means that people feel they must have the drug; in other words, the dependence is in the mind. In the latter case, withdrawal may not cause physical pain, but will result in the psychologically painful symptoms of anxiety, depression, and uneasiness. These symptoms are often as difficult to cope with as physical withdrawal symptoms. Psychological dependence develops to each of the drugs we have discussed.

Today a great deal of controversy surrounds the drug called *cannabis*,

David Kennedy died of a drug overdose. He seemed to have everything to live for, coming from a wealthy family and being educated at the best schools. Drug addiction is a rapidly growing problem that often has tragic consequences.

which is found in marijuana. Cannabis can be smoked, eaten, or drunk in tea. It generally causes people to feel relaxed and happy, and reduces inhibitions. The majority of research (Stafford-Clark & Smith, 1978) suggests that people do not develop a physical dependence on cannabis. However, psychological dependence can result from prolonged use.

Drug addiction has physical, social, and psychological effects. The physical effects include the possibilities of malnutrition, infection, and other physical diseases such as hepatitis. There are two categories of psychological problems. The first concerns the direct effect of the drug. It has been aruged that marijuana causes people to lose motivation, become apathetic, and reduce striving for future goals. Hallucinogens can cause people to experience psychotic episodes in which they lose touch with reality and cannot function. These episodes may last a long time, and later flashbacks can occur in which the symptoms of an earlier episode suddenly return and overwhelm the person without warning and without that person's having taken the drug again. Another issue here involves the long-term effects of drugs. Because concern about many drugs is a fairly recent issue, there is little research aimed at examining how the use of drugs for a period of years may affect people. The issue of long-term effects has become especially important with marijuana; some people have argued that its use should be legalized, while others demand stiffer prison sentences for users.

The second category of psychological problems includes the depression and feelings of helplessness that people who are addicted may experience. In essence, their dependence eliminates their freedom to control their lives and makes them a slave to the drug.

The social effects are many also. On the one hand, there are the loss of productivity, high absenteeism, and impaired performance that may be caused by the drug. Social relationships may suffer as people retreat into the world of drugs. Another problem is legal. Because most of these drugs are illegal, the cost of supporting a habit may run well over $200 a day. Most people do not have this amount of spending money and must turn to crime to pay for their drugs. The Manson Family, in fact, participated in many burglaries to pay for the drugs they used. Our jails and prisons have become overcrowded as a result of the large number of people serving time for drug or drug-related offenses.

Drug addiction is widespread in our society and is not confined to individuals in any particular class, race, or sex.

A great deal of research is being conducted to identify factors that determine addiction and the effects of addiction. This research is complicated by the legal, social, and moral issues surrounding drug use. It will probably take many years to completely understand the effects of drugs on people. Even with this information, the controversy surrounding the legalization of drugs may continue. This is because the research is unlikely to paint a completely negative or positive picture of these substances. While some drugs may be shown to be less harmful than others, the exact effects of a substance will be influenced by the characteristics of the person using it. As we have seen, this is the case with alcohol. Overuse has negative consequences for everybody, but even moderate use causes some people to suffer negative effects while others do not.

SUMMARY

1. A behavior is labeled **abnormal** when it causes distress to others and hinders people from adapting to their environment. The most commonly used system of classifying psycho- logical disorders today is the **Diagnostic and Statistical Manual (DSM III).**

2. Six approaches for explaining deviant behav- ior were discussed in this chapter: the medi-

cal, psychoanalytic, learning, cognitive, systems, and humanistic models.

3. Childhood disorders are most likely to occur either between 6 months and 3 years of age or during early adolescence. **Infantile autism** is characterized by social withdrawal, the failure to develop language and communication skills, and a rigid use of schedules.

4. **Neurotic behaviors** are attempts to cope with anxiety. **Anxiety disorders** occur when people experience fear that is out of proportion to the situation they are in. In **general anxiety disorders,** the person does not know what is causing the anxiety; he or she simply feels overwhelmed with anxiety. **Phobias** are irrational fears of objects or events that not only cause people to psychologically suffer but may also strongly influence their behavior. **Obsessive-compulsive disorders** occur when the person feels an overwhelming need to think a certain thought (obsession) or perform a certain behavior (compulsion).

5. **Somatoform disorders** involve physical symptoms that are caused by stress and have no physiological basis. Included under this category is the **somatization disorder,** in which people have a wide variety of general complaints, such as headaches, nausea, and stomach pains. **Conversion disorders** are characterized by one specific and often dramatic symptom. This may be blindness or paralysis.

6. In **dissociative disorders,** people separate or dissociate part of their personality from the situation. These disorders include **amnesia, fugue,** and **multiple personalities.** In each of these cases, the person tries to escape anxiety by removing part of his or her personality from consciousness. The disorder results when the person must deal with the anxiety because it is pushing into the consciousness.

7. **Affective disorders** are disturbances in mood. The most common affective disorder is **depression.** There are numerous theories about how depression develops, ranging from early childhood experiences to a lack of positive reinforcement in people's present environment. The **learned helplessness**

approach combines learning theory and cognitive theory by arguing that depression occurs when people feel that they have no control over their environment. Finally, there is some evidence that biochemical imbalances either in neurotransmitters or in the blood cause depression.

8. **Bipolar disorders** occur when the person shows wild swings in mood between depression and **mania** (elation). Recent evidence suggests that this disorder is inherited.

9. It is difficult to determine abnormality in sexual behavior because we have little knowledge about people's sexual practices and social views about sexual behavior are continually changing. Sexual dysfunctions are the most common sexual disorders. Included in this group are **impotence** and **premature ejaculation** in males and **dyspareunia** and **vaginismus** in females.

10. **Psychoses** are disorders in which people lose touch with reality and have difficulty functioning in their environment. **Schizophrenia** is the most common psychosis. There are many types of schizophrenia; symptoms include disturbances in thinking, disorganized perceptions, disturbances in communication, inappropriate emotions, and unusual motor activities. Theories of schizophrenia have focussed on biological problems, disturbances in learning, and conflict in the family setting.

11. **Personality disorders** involve rigid and maladaptive ways of dealing with the environment. People with this disorder can function, but they often have problems forming close relationships with others. The **antisocial personality** is characterized by the performance of violent or hurtful acts without experiencing guilt or regret.

12. There are two categories of **substance use disorders.** The first is **substance abuse,** which includes pathological use of the drug and a decrease in functioning for at least one month in duration. The second category is **substance dependence** (addiction), which includes the presence of either tolerance or withdrawal, two different physical reactions to drugs.

Key Terms

abnormal
affective disorders
alcoholics
amnesia
antisocial personality disorders
anxiety disorders

bipolar disorders
compulsions
conversion disorders
delusions
depressants
depression

Diagnostic and Statistical Manual (DSM III)
dissociative disorders
double-bind conflict
dyspareunia
erectile dysfunction
fugue
general anxiety disorders
hallucination
hallucinogens
impotence
infantile autism
learned helplessness model
mania
masochism
multiple personality disorders
narcotics
neurosis
neurotic behaviors
obsession
obsessive-compulsive disorders

paranoid
personality disorders
phobia
premature ejaculation
problem drinker
psychoses
sadism
schizophrenia
self-fulfilling prophecy
somatization disorder
somatoform disorders
stimulants
substance abuse
substance dependence
substance use disorders
tolerance
transsexualism
vaginismus
withdrawal

Suggested Readings

The following book is about Charles Manson:

BUGLIOSI, V., & GENTRY, C. Helter Skelter: The true story of the Manson murders. New York: Norton, 1974.

American Psychiatric Association, Diagnostic and statistical manual of mental disorders (3rd ed.). Washington, D.C.: American Psychiatric Association, 1980. This book presents the latest classification system of psychological disorders.

DAVISON, G., & NEALE, J. Abnormal psychology: An experimental clinical approach. New York: Wiley, 1978. This text takes a learning approach in discussing the causes of maladjusted behavior. It outlines controversies and describes other approaches to studying psychological disorders.

JAFFE, J., PETERSON, R., & HODGSON, R. Addictions. New York: Harper & Row, 1980. An easy-to-read and informative overview of addiction to a wide variety of drugs. In addition to presenting statistics on addictions, the book examines theories of why people become addicted.

ROSENHAN, D. L., & M. E. SELIGMAN. Abnormal psychology. New York: Norton, 1984. Review of abnormal psychology with a strong chapter on depression.

SARASON, I., & SARASON, B. Abnormal psychology (3rd ed.). Englewood Cliffs, N.J.: Prentice-Hall, 1980. This textbook examines the historical approaches to abnormal psychology and also presents a broad coverage of the psychological disorders.

STAFFORD-CLARK, D., & SMITH, A. Psychiatry for students (5th ed.). London: Allen & Unwin, 1978. This text examines the psychological disorders and modern approaches to treatment. The discussions are illustrated with actual case histories.

SUINN, R. M. Fundamentals of abnormal psychology. Chicago: Nelson Hall, 1984. This presents an up-to-date coverage of abnormal psychology with illustrative cases.

SZASZ, T. The myth of mental illness: Foundations of a theory of personal conduct. New York: Harper & Row, 1961. Szasz presents a controversial view of abnormal behavior. In short, he offers the position that in some cases the behavior represents reasonable ways to cope with chaotic environments.

THERAPY

It was with fear and uncertainty that Chris entered Dr. Thigpen's office. According to the country lore on which she had been raised, psychiatrists were doctors for crazy folks; they often locked these crazy people in dark padded rooms and let them scream until they exhausted themselves. Was this going to happen to her? Dr. Thigpen sensed Chris's uneasiness and he greeted her with a smile. "Mrs. White, I work a little differently from other doctors. I don't physically examine my patients. I talk to them, and they talk to me. They tell me things about themselves: what is worrying them, what they feel, what they think" (Sizemore & Pitillo, 1977, p. 288).

During the first few sessions Chris talked about her troubles with her husband. She revealed that she did not like living in her present home, and she talked about her feelings toward her child and her parents. She portrayed herself as a timid woman with little self-confidence who cared little about her appearance. Sometimes she hesitated to discuss a topic; during these periods Dr. Thigpen would hypnotize her and ask her questions, often about her childhood.

An early memory of Chris's was watching with awe as her mother stepped out of the car holding her newborn twin sisters. She was delighted to have not one but two new sisters. But her delight began to fade as her relatives rushed to admire the matched pair; no one was paying any attention to 6-year-old Chris.

Chris's chance for revenge came one day when she was alone in the house with the twins. She walked quietly to the side of the little green bed and peered down at the sleeping girls. She shut her eyes tightly, and when she opened them again, she saw a thin girl with a bony face standing by the bed. The girl looked familiar, but Chris could not recognize her. This other girl threw the bed covers off the twins; she poked her finger into their eyes, grabbed their legs, and fiercely bit their toes. Chris's mother heard the twins shrieking and rushed to the bedroom to find Chris terrorizing the little girls. Her frantic cries snapped Chris out of her daze. Chris looked around, but the terrible little girl who had tortured her sisters had disappeared. "Look what you've done!" Mrs. Costner cried as she wrenched Chris's arm. Chris was astonished; it was not she who had hurt the twins. The other girl had done it. "But, Mother, you saw her, you saw her do it!?" (Sizemore & Pitillo, 1977, p. 118). Her mother's anger increased; not only had Chris hurt her sisters, but now she was lying about it.

This was one of a series of bizarre incidents that were to plague Chris throughout much of her life. When stressful events occurred, Chris would feel faint or suffer a severe headache; then a "different" Chris would appear and respond to the situation. One Chris was often unaware of how the other Chris behaved.

This created quite a problem, because other people did not know that at least two "Chrises" resided in the body of the young girl. They would stare disbelievingly when they observed Chris perform a certain behavior and only a few minutes later heard her deny having behaved that way.

Chris's childhood was a nightmare; she never knew which personality would dominate. Oftentimes the "naughty" Chris emerged to commit some mischievous act and then quickly retreated, leaving the little freckled girl to take the blame and to explain behaviors of which she was unaware. These multiple personalities were an even greater problem when Chris became an adult.

When Chris was 19 she married Ralph White. She soon began having fights with him over his inability to hold a steady job. Then the headaches came; these were of such intensity that Chris often fainted from the pain. The headaches signaled the coming out of a new personality; one that hated Ralph and cursed him. Chris's pain and confusion had become so great that her family decided she should see a psychiatrist, at which point she began her sessions with Dr. Thigpen.

One day Chris abruptly interrupted her therapy session to ask, "Doctor, does hearing voices mean you're going insane?" Dr. Thigpen was surprised by this question and asked Chris to explain more about the voices. Chris said that she often heard a strange voice coming from inside her head. The next few sessions were spent talking about the voice, examining what it said and when it appeared. Dr. Thigpen was intrigued by this strange complaint, but his interest sharply increased a few months later, when Chris revealed another problem.

On that day the session began with Chris discussing her feelings. Suddenly her face tightened, she grabbed her temples, and she began to moan. The pain was terrible and Chris's world began to whirl. Dr. Thigpen was about to comfort her when Chris raised her head. Dr. Thigpen was surprised as Chris sat up in her chair with her eyes glowing; there was an unusual spark of life in this usually drab woman. "Hi, Doc," she chirped as she assumed a sexy slouch in the chair. "Gimme a cigarette," she asked as she winked at Dr. Thigpen. The psychiatrist could hardly contain his surprise as he asked, "Who are you?" As she inched her skirt higher up her leg, Chris answered, "I'm Chris Costner. Chris White is *her*," she said, pointing off into space.

After talking to this new Chris Costner, Dr. Thigpen was convinced that Chris was not faking; she did indeed possess two personalities. One was the dutiful but unhappy Chris White, who struggled to please her unreliable husband. The other was the sexy Chris Costner, who enjoyed flirting, loved expensive clothes, and who truly believed, "I ain't married to that jerk, *she* is." Dr. Thigpen soon found that he could cause Chris to change personalities simply by calling for either Chris White or Chris Costner. He also found that Chris White was unaware that Chris Costner existed, but that Chris Costner was well aware of Chris White. He diagnosed Chris as suffering from the rare psychological disorder called dissociative personality, which we discussed in Chapter 13.

Dr. Thigpen continued to question Chris about her childhood in an effort to determine how the "split personalities" had developed. He made Chris White aware of Chris Costner, and he often served as a negotiator between the two personalities. At times he even had the two personalities write notes to each other. Dr. Thigpen structured therapy sessions so that good behavior by each of the personalities was rewarded.

However, just when it seemed that the two personalities might be united, Chris began to experience headaches and blackouts again. She had entered into another difficult period in her life. Her marriage had broken up and she was trying to make it on her own. Was she now undergoing a psychotic break with reality that would require hospitalization? As Dr. Thigpen's concern for Chris increased, another personality, Jane, emerged as a cultured and self-assured young woman. She was not frivolous like Chris Costner nor weak like Chris White. It was Jane who got a job as a bookkeeper and managed the money. However, even Jane's best-laid plans were sometimes ruined when Chris Costner "came out" to create havoc.

Dr. Thigpen continued to probe Chris to determine how Jane fit in. More tests were given. An EEG (electroencephalogram), which measures brain waves, revealed that

Jane was the most relaxed of the personalities and that Chris Costner did show signs of a psychopathic personality (see Chapter 13).

After 14 months of treatment, Chris was significantly improved. She had fallen in love with Don Sizemore, and after discussing her unusual psychological problem, the couple decided to get married. At this time both Chris White and Chris Costner faded into obscurity, and only Jane was present. Dr. Thigpen and his associate, Hervey Cleckley, wrote a book called *The Three Faces of Eve*, in which they described Chris's unusual case; in an effort to protect her identity, the therapists referred to her personalities as Eve White, Eve Black, and Jane.

But just as it seemed that Chris would be able to lead a normal life, she suffered a setback; other personalities began to appear. In fact, 12 new personalities "emerged" during the next few years.

Don encouraged Chris to see another psychiatrist near their new home. This psychiatrist attempted to show Chris that all her personalities were the same person. He suggested that she reveal herself to her friends and explain what she had been going through. Chris began working on a book, *I'm Eve*, in which she described her life. With the help of her family, her new therapist, and her new project, Chris gained confidence and showed tremendous improvement. At the end of her book, Chris stated, "I am in control of my life, I am comfortable in my world" (Sizemore & Pittillo, 1977). And in a newspaper interview, she reported, "You don't know how wonderful it is to go to bed at night and know that it will be you that wakes up the next day" (*New York Post*, September 15, 1975, p. 4).

WHAT IS THERAPY?

It was clear at an early age that Chris needed special help and guidance to adjust to her surroundings. Even as a young child, she was unhappy and bewildered by her own actions. She had difficulty making friends and interacting with other people. Overall, she was unable to change her behavior; she did not know what to do to make people like her and she could not stop the "other Chris" from emerging and causing problems for herself and others. Chris needed therapy to help her adjust to her environment and have fulfilling interactions with other people.

There are two broad classifications of therapy that are aimed at dealing with psychological disturbances. One is **psychotherapy,** which is the use of psychological techniques by a professionally trained individual to help a client change unwanted behavior and adjust to his or her environment. In short, it is the use of language to make positive changes in the life of another (Davison & Neale, 1978). Dr. Thigpen used psychotherapy to treat Chris; he talked to her about her problems, attempted to show her why her different personalities emerged, and discussed methods that she could use to control her behavior. A second type of therapy is **biotherapy,** which may be used together with psychotherapy. This therapy includes the use of drugs, surgery, or electric shock to induce behavior change.

As we will see, the concept of therapy covers a wide variety of techniques and processes aimed at dealing with psychological disturbances. In fact, one investigator (Corsini, 1981) identified almost 250 therapeutic techniques. All, however, have three basic goals (Millon, 1969). The first goal of the therapist is to be sure that his or her techniques do not bring harm to or intensify the problems of the client. The second goal of the therapist is to seek to reduce the individual's present discomfort. And finally, the therapist should attempt to aid in the development of a healthier and more adjusted individual. This last goal can present an interesting challenge to the therapist. As we saw in Chapter 12, it may be difficult to clearly define "well-adjusted." Hence, in many situations the therapist and client must work together to identify the specific outcomes they desire from therapy (Woolfolk & Richardson, 1984).

Historical Background of Psychotherapy

In order to understand the psychotherapy of today, it is useful to turn back to its beginnings. The treatment of psychological disorders is not a modern invention; throughout time people have been intrigued, bewildered, and often afraid of the strange or different behaviors of others. The treatment prescribed for disordered behaviors was generally based on the "theories" people held about the cause of the disorders. As we pointed out in Chapter 13, the ancient view of psychological disorders was that they were caused by demons who inhabited the person. These demons had to be coaxed out of the person and destroyed. Those who were "possessed" were beaten, burned with hot irons, starved, or had holes chipped in their skull (a process called *trephining*) to allow the demon to escape. In 1500 B.C. the Egyptians used magic potions, which included lizard's blood, crocodile dung, and fly specks, to combat the evil spirits. Although Hippocrates and his followers (about the fifth century B.C.) urged a more humane treatment of the mentally ill, the belief in demons persisted throughout the Middle Ages. In many societies large asylums were built to keep the "possessed" from interacting with and contaminating other

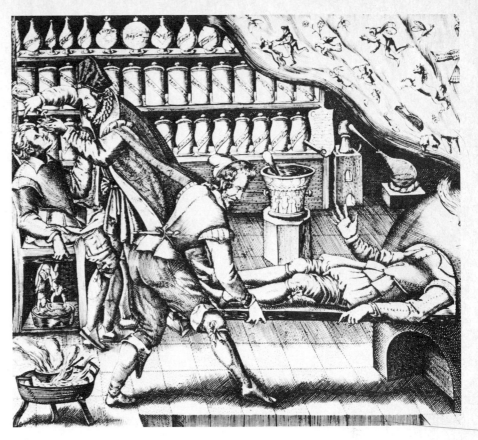

An early view of psychological disorders was that they were caused by demons and evil spirits living inside the person. Treatment focussed on getting rid of these spirits. In trephining, a hole was chipped in the head to allow the demon to escape. The photo on the right shows a sixteenth-century physician's treatment of "fantasy and folly."

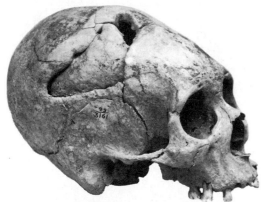

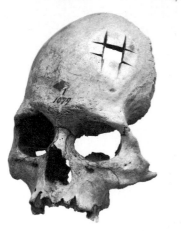

people. These asylums were really prisons characterized by filthy conditions where the mentally ill were often mistreated.

One of the first major changes in the treatment of people suffering from psychological disorders occurred in the late 1700s and early 1800s. These changes were aimed at reforming the asylums. Philippe Pinel in France and Dorothea Dix in the United States campaigned to improve the treatment of disturbed people in institutions. They criticized the inhumane conditions of the asylums and fought hard to eliminate the corruption and torture present in so many of them. Through their efforts and the efforts of others like them, changes were slowly made. In some institutions patients were given sunny, bright rooms; they were allowed more freedom and exercise; their diets were improved; and they were treated with greater kindness and understanding. As a result of these advances, many patients made dramatic recoveries and were able to return to society.

While some important changes were made in the living conditions of institutionalized patients, there was little advance in therapy techniques until late in the nineteenth century. At this time a young Viennese physician named Sigmund Freud began developing his psychodynamic model (see Chapter 12) of personality. Freud believed that many psychological problems were the result of feelings and emotions that had been repressed during childhood. His position was that treatment of these disorders would be best achieved by helping people recognize and deal with their repressed feelings. Freud's psychoanalytic therapy was characterized by treatment techniques that involved a professional working with one patient at a time in the professional's office. While therapists adopted many different styles, the psychotherapy of the early twentieth century consisted mainly of individual therapy involving a single patient.

The early 1900s were also the time of advances in biotherapy. The assumption underlying much of the work in biotherapies was that mental disorders were diseases much like other physical diseases and should be

World War II initiated many changes in therapy. One of the most dramatic was the rapid development of group psychotherapy. The number of soldiers who suffered battle stress and other disorders was so great that there were not enough therapists to treat them on a one-to-one basis.

treated in a similar manner. Since the seat of mental diseases was supposedly in the brain, the focus of biological cures was on techniques involving manipulation of the brain. In 1938 Ugo Cerletti reported therapeutic effects from electric shock therapy. This technique involved administering electric shocks to the patient's brain, causing him or her to experience epileptic-like convulsions. Cerletti believed that the electric shocks brought the patient close to death; as a result, the body's natural defenses were aroused, and these defenses not only fought the effects of the shock but also worked on eliminating the mental disease. This work was the basis for **electroconvulsive therapy (ECT),** which was widely used during the early 1900s and is still used today. During this same period Egas Moniz, a Portuguese psychiatrist, reported the use of a surgical technique known as **prefrontal lobotomy** to treat psychological disorders.

World War II was responsible for the next chapter in the history of therapy. An alarming number of young men received draft deferments for psychological reasons; further, many soldiers suffered stress disorders from combat (Sheras & Worchel, 1979). These two facts led to the realization that psychological difficulties were more common than previously believed. Unfortunately, there was a serious shortage of professionals qualified to treat psychological disorders. The shortage led to a reexamination of the field of clinical psychology and a concentration of resources to train more professionals. **Group therapy** was also developed, in which many individual therapy techniques were adapted for use with groups of people who suffered from similar problems. Not only was there a strong theoretical rationale for this practice, but it also allowed for more economical and widespread use of professional resources.

The World War II era also saw significant advances in biotherapy. Doctors working with patients suffering from hypertension and high blood pressure accidentally discovered two drugs that had a calming effect on people suffering from psychological disorders. These drugs are known as **tranquilizers;** their discovery led to the widespread use of drugs to treat both mild and severe psychological disturbances. In fact, **drug therapy** is so popular today that many professionals have voiced concern that this use of drugs has actually become a misuse.

Starting 20 years ago and continuing today, a new and exciting page in the history of therapy is being written. A policy of **deinstitutionalization** is being embraced (Shadish, 1984). In short, this policy involves treating people in their local environments rather than placing them in large, isolated state institutions. Treatment of even severely disturbed people in local settings has been made feasible by a number of developments. First, dramatic advances in drug therapy have enabled professionals to help people suffering from a wide range of disturbances achieve a functioning relationship with their environment. People who would once have been hospitalized can now stay in their local settings and receive psychotherapy there. A second important development was the passage of the Community Mental Health Centers Act by Congress in 1963; it directed that 600 community-based mental health centers be established. These centers are aimed at supplying outpatient and emergency services. Those working in health centers help people deal with crises and stress before severe and deep-seated disorders develop. Many of these centers have "hot lines" so that people can call in and receive immediate help and advice. Since the centers are located in the community, people needing help can receive it on an outpatient basis without disrupting their lives. A third factor driving community-based treatment is economics; the costs of hospitalizing people are staggering. Finally, there is the realization that in many cases the most effective therapy involves the family and other possible support groups. Removing the individual from the environment in which he or she must

learn to function is disruptive and ignores an important element in the adjustment process (Kiesler et al., 1983).

The emphasis on deinstitutionalization has been accompanied by a focus on *prevention*. As we will see in our discussion of community psychology (pp. 486–489), efforts are being made to identify people who are considered "at risk" for developing psychological disturbances, and then to work to make their environments less stressful. The aim is to promote adjustment rather than treat problems after they arise.

THE THERAPISTS

Once Chris and others realized that she needed professional help in adjusting to her environment, the next decision concerned who could provide this help. If her problem had been a medical one, this decision would have been relatively easy. She would seek help from an orthopedist if her complaint involved bones; she would consult an obstetrician if she were pregnant; she would call a dermatologist if her problem concerned a skin rash. There are, however, a number of professionals who could be consulted for a psychological disorder.

The **psychiatrist** is a medical doctor who has received a degree in medicine and has taken part in a residency program (usually 3 years) for emotional disorders. Psychiatrists may specialize in any of the psychotherapy techniques, and they are the only professionals who can prescribe drugs or conduct psychosurgery. Dr. Thigpen, Chris's first therapist, was a psychiatrist.

The **psychoanalyst** is often a psychiatrist who has had a great deal of training in psychoanalytic techniques. As part of this training, psychoanalysts must themselves undergo psychoanalysis, which involves between 200 to 2,000 sessions. As we will see, psychoanalytic therapy is very time consuming and involves some very specialized techniques.

The **clinical psychologist** has received a Ph.D. or Psy.D. in clinical psychology. The degree program generally takes from 3 to 6 years after graduating from college. The clinical psychologist receives extensive training in therapy techniques, in methods of testing, and in interpretation of psychological tests. Most clinical psychologists also receive training in conducting research. Most practicing clinical psychologists have interned for a year, during which time they worked with a wide range of clients under the close supervision of other clinical psychologists and psychiatrists. Dr. Thigpen consulted a number of clinical psychologists and had them administer psychological tests to Chris in an effort to arrive at a clear identification of her disorder.

The **counseling psychologist** has earned either an M.A. or a Ph.D. Most counseling psychologists take a one-year internship, during which time they work with clients under the direction of a practicing counselor. Generally, counseling psychologists are trained to deal with adjustment problems rather than with psychological disturbances. For example, the counselor may work with adjustment problems in a school or college setting or work situation. The aim of counseling is to help the person adjust to a situation rather than "treat" a specific disorder.

The **psychiatric social worker** has a master's degree in social work and often has served an internship. Social workers have special training in interviewing techniques, and they may visit individuals in their homes to collect information, to interview relatives and friends, and to make assessments. Social workers are often called upon by juvenile courts to make reports about the family environments of delinquents.

The **psychiatric nurse** is a registered nurse who has received special training in dealing with psychological disorders. Psychiatric nurses are employed by institutions, where they are responsible for a wide variety of activities, including caring for patients and making careful observations of patient behavior.

These are the professionals who administer therapy to the 6 million Americans who seek professional help each year. There is, however, an even larger group of people who are called upon to deal with those who are emotionally disturbed. These people include the police officer who must "defuse" a family conflict or calm a distraught victim of crime; the paraprofessional who receives training to handle crisis calls on a "hot line"; the minister, rabbi, or priest who counsels disturbed individuals or families. Even the neighbor or friend who lends a sympathetic ear so that a distressed individual can "talk out" his or her problems plays a vital role in the effort to deal with psychological disorders. Research suggests that the majority of people with mental health problems do not first go to mental health professionals (Gottlieb, 1983). Instead, they turn first to family members, physicians, neighbors, and members of the clergy for help. In fact, Chris credits her understanding husband, Don, and her cousin Elen with helping her cope with some of her biggest crises.

Now that we have given a brief history of therapy and reviewed the cast of professionals who practice it, we can turn our attention to some of the specific types of therapy that are in use today. As we will see, each type is based on a theory of the cause of psychological disturbances. For example, person-centered therapy has its roots in humanistic psychology (see Chapter 12), while psychoanalysis grew out of Freud's psychodynamic theory of personality. Although many therapists have favorite types of therapy with which they are most comfortable, few practice only one type.

Rather, after carefully evaluating a client, they choose the therapy that they feel will be most effective with that person. The chosen therapy usually involves techniques taken from a number of types of therapies, which we will now examine.

BIOTHERAPY

Ancient history is filled with examples of attempts to treat psychological disorders with physical methods. These early methods were based on the assumption that the disorder was caused by some physical or supernatural invader in the individual's body. As medical science developed, the uselessness of these methods was recognized. However, the desire to treat psychological disorders by physical methods remained. In some cases, this desire was based on the medical model, which viewed all psychological disorders as diseases or illnesses whose causes were due to a malfunction of the body. In other cases, the desire for a physical treatment was based on the belief that even problems of a psychological nature could be treated quickly and effectively with drugs.

The quest to find medical cures for psychological disorders, however, did not lead to a careful, concentrated effort to develop these cures. Rather, until recently, the story of biotherapy has been one of *serendipity*, or accidental, lucky discoveries. A procedure or drug that was being used to treat one type of medical illness was accidentally discovered to have therapeutic effects on a psychological disorder. In most of these cases, the discoverers had no idea why the procedure was effective; they only knew that it seemed to work. As we will see, even with the improved techniques and methods of study used today, scientists are still unsure why many drugs are effective.

Biotherapy includes a wide range of techniques that involve some type of physical treatment. Most of these treatments must be administered under the direction of a psychiatrist or other medical doctor. Most individuals who receive biotherapy are also given some type of psychotherapy.

Electroconvulsive Therapy

When Chris first visited Dr. Thigpen, she was very depressed and had considered suicide. After talking to Chris for several sessions, Dr. Thigpen suggested that she undergo electric shock treatment. Chris recoiled in fear—she had visions of jerking in pain on a cold steel table while electric shocks were sent through her head. Because of her extreme fear of the treatment and because she began to recover from her depression, Dr. Thigpen decided against shock therapy in Chris's case.

Chris's fears were somewhat exaggerated. **Electroconvulsive therapy (ECT)** has been developed to the point where it does not cause the patient great discomfort. However, the preparation for the procedure can frighten some patients. Before receiving ECT, patients are given a sedative and a muscle relaxant to reduce the risk of injury. They are then placed on a well-padded mattress, and electrodes are attached to the head. In order to reduce the risk of injury, the electric current is applied to only one side of the head. The current of 70 to 130 volts is given for a period of .1 to .5 second. The shock causes the patient to go into convulsions similar to those suffered in an epileptic seizure. Following the convulsions, most patients remain unconscious for 5 to 30 minutes. ECT generally involves 8 to 20 treatments at the rate of 3 per week. All this may sound terrible, more like something from a horror movie than a humane treatment for psychological disorders! However, people generally awake feeling only a little hazy; they have no memory of the procedure.

While patients are not harmed by the procedure, that alone is not sufficient reason to employ it. The crucial question is: Does it relieve their psychological suffering? Research suggests that electroconvulsive therapy has short-term benefits for those suffering from depressive disorders (Scovern & Kilmann, 1980). In fact, 60 to 90 percent of those who receive this therapy show rapid signs of improvement, as opposed to the 40 to 50 percent recovery rate found in those who are not treated (Fink, 1978). The beneficial effects are the result of the convulsions rather than the shock itself, since convulsions brought on by drugs also yield these short-term benefits.

While the research is encouraging, it also points out the limits of electroconvulsive therapy. First, the procedure has little effect on disorders other than depression. Second, there are few *long-term* benefits from the procedure. In fact, people who receive ECT for depression suffer a relapse (become depressed again) more frequently than those who recover without therapy (Millon, 1969). Finally, some people experience considerable stress and uncomfortable side effects such as headaches, nausea, and memory loss that can last for days or longer.

Clearly, there are pros and cons to electroconvulsive therapy. After reviewing both sides of the issue, the American Psychiatric Association (1979) concluded that this therapy should be regarded as a useful procedure under the right circumstances. Electroconvulsive therapy is given to over 100,000 Americans each year. Often these people are suffering from severe depression, have not responded to drug treatment, and the therapist has concluded that they may attempt suicide if not relieved of their depression. In many cases, patients are placed on drug therapy after ECT, and studies have shown this combination of treatments can be effective (Dietz, 1985).

Psychosurgery

For many decades it has been known that certain parts of the brain control different functions (see Chapter 2). In the early 1930s Egas Moniz, a Portuguese psychiatrist, reasoned that people suffering from emotional disorders might be helped by destroying the connections from the parts of the brain that control emotions. He developed a surgical technique, **psychosurgery,** that became known as the **prefrontal lobotomy,** which involved cutting the connections between the thalamus (emotional center) and the frontal lobes (thought center). Moniz reported that this procedure calmed patients and helped many recover from severe psychological disturbances. Psychosurgery was hailed as a major breakthrough in the treatment of emotional disorders, and Moniz was awarded a Nobel Prize for his work. Thousands of prefrontal lobotomy operations were performed during the 1940s and 1950s. Other psychosurgery techniques were also developed. In one (transorbital lobotomy), for example, a thin surgical instrument is inserted through the eye socket and tissue in the frontal lobe is cut.

However, it was not long before research began to cast doubt on the effectiveness of psychosurgery. It seems that psychosurgery does succeed in reducing the intensity of people's emotions. As such, it can help those suffering from high levels of anxiety or agitated emotions. But the research also showed that many people became human vegetables after the operation; they went through the motions of life without showing any emotional reaction to their environment or expressing any ambition or hopes. This aspect of psychosurgery has received attention in the movies made from the novel *One Flew Over the Cuckoo's Nest* (Kesey, 1962) and the tragic true-life story of Frances Farmer, a well-known actress during the 1940s. Further, the effects of psychosurgery cannot be undone; once the connections are

Movies such as *One Flew Over the Cuckoo's Nest* dramatize the concerns surrounding psychosurgery. The effects of the surgery cannot be undone so misuses of the procedure or an incorrect diagnosis are particularly tragic.

severed, they cannot be reattached. For these reasons, psychosurgery is seldom done today; it has become the procedure of last resort, used only when all other methods have failed.

Chemotherapy

Drug therapy, **chemotherapy,** began in 1952 in a very accidental way. Indian doctors had used reserpine, an extract of *Rauwolfia serpentina* (snakeroot plant), as a general medicine since 1920. As the use of the drug became more widespread, physicians noticed that reserpine had a calming effect on patients. More importantly, this calming effect occurred without making the patient drowsy or reducing alertness. In 1952 reserpine and another drug (chlorpromazine), which had also been used for medical purposes, were introduced as *tranquilizers*, medication for the treatment of emotional disturbances. Chemotherapy was readily embraced by the medical and psychological world as a major advance because it seemed to be a quick and inexpensive way to treat psychological disturbances. The discovery of tranquilizers launched the field of **psychopharmacology,** which is the study of drugs to treat psychological disorders.

Drugs are currently divided into three categories. **Antianxiety drugs** (minor tranquilizers) reduce anxiety and tension without causing drowsiness or a loss of mental alertness. The most popular antianxiety drugs are Valium, Librium, and Miltown. Since almost everyone suffers attacks of anxiety and tension at some time, antianxiety drugs have become the most widely used prescription drugs in the United States; in fact, almost 60 million prescriptions were written for Valium alone in 1975 (Reinhold, 1980). Dr. Thigpen, for example, gave Chris tranquilizers to calm her during her fits of anxiety. These minor tranquilizers are not only prescribed by psychiatrists for people suffering from diagnosed disorders; family physicians and other doctors tend to prescribe them to help people cope with stressful situations. The wide use of tranquilizers has recently been viewed with alarm. There is a fine line that separates wise use from abuse, and people must be careful not to rely on these drugs to solve all their problems. This warning is particularly important because scientists have not yet discovered exactly how these drugs work. There has been some information suggesting that prolonged use can lead to dependence (Baker, 1983). Further, people may use the drugs to treat the symptoms of stress without trying to uncover and deal with the causes of their tension.

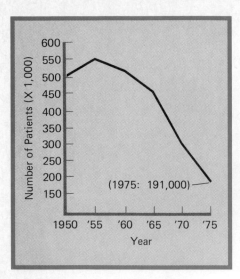

Figure 14–1
Reduction of patients hospitalized for mental disorders, 1950–1975.

A second category of drugs is made up of **antipsychotic drugs.** These drugs, which include Thorazine and Stelazine, are used to calm and relieve the delusions of schizophrenics. They do not "cure" schizophrenia, but they do calm the person so that he or she can be helped or reached by psychotherapy. Further, these drugs reduce the symptoms of some schizophrenics to such a degree that they can leave the hospital and live in a home environment while receiving other treatment (see Figure 14–1). Antipsychotic drugs are so effective that nearly 87 percent of all patients hospitalized for psychological disorders receive some form of such medication (MacDonald & Tobias, 1976).

In spite of the value of the antipsychotic drugs, they are not without their critics (MacDonald, Lidsky, & Kern, 1979). One of the criticisms of drug therapy involves the issue of side effects. Many people who take these drugs suffer from headaches, nausea, blurred vision, drooling, stiff muscles, and fainting. There is even some evidence that prolonged use of the drugs can cause permanent brain damage (MacDonald et al., 1979). Another criticism is that drugs are often used to control patients rather than to treat their disorders. Patients taking antipsychotic drugs become docile and are easily controlled by hospital staff. Thus there is a strong temptation to prescribe drugs when a patient is acting in a disruptive manner (Sobel, 1980). Despite these criticisms, many clinicians agree that the careful use of antipsychotic drugs along with psychotherapy can have very positive effects. Research efforts are now being aimed at developing drugs that do not have undesired side effects and at determining exactly how these antipsychotic drugs work.

Tranquilizers are drugs that bring people "down" from highly anxious or agitated states. **Antidepressant drugs,** such as Tofranil and Elavil, work by lifting the person's spirits and increasing his or her activity level. Generally, the antidepressant drugs are given to people who are suffering from deep states of depression. It is interesting that the antidepressant drugs do not work equally well with all depressed individuals; in some cases, they are very effective, while in others, they have almost no effect (Gelenberg, 1979). Factors such as the person's age, specific symptom pattern, personality, and emotional state influence the effect that the drug will have. Hence there is a certain degree of unpredictability in using these drugs. Unfortunately, there are also a number of unpleasant side effects associated with antidepressant drugs; these include nausea, restlessness, and insomnia.

Another drug, *lithium carbonate,* has been introduced in the last decade. Lithium is used to treat people suffering from bipolar disorders (see Chapter 13), which are characterized by wide swings in mood. If used in the proper dosage, the drug is effective in keeping people from becoming too elated or too depressed. However, lithium is a dangerous drug that can cause death if its concentration in the blood becomes too high. Thus people who receive lithium treatment must take regular blood tests.

The advances in chemotherapy have both exciting and frightening implications. On the positive side, drugs offer the possibility that people suffering from psychological disorders can be treated quickly, efficiently, and inexpensively. Further, there is evidence that drugs can be used to treat people who suffer disorders, such as schizophrenia, which are difficult to treat with psychotherapy. These points suggest that drugs can be invaluable in the treatment of psychological disorders. However, some issues must be considered before adopting chemotherapy. First, drugs generally reduce only the symptoms of the disorder and not its cause. Because patients receive quick relief of unpleasant symptoms, they may be tempted to avoid dealing with the underlying problem. If they take this position, they will lose control over their lives; they will become dependent on drugs to make them feel good. A second problem related to chemotherapy is that the drugs can be used simply to control people's behavior rather than to treat

BIOFEEDBACK: BRIDGING THE TWO TYPES OF THERAPY

The present American generation has often been called the "generation of the pill." For any disorder, physical or psychological, there seem to be at least three pills available to treat it. There is little doubt that drugs can play a very valuable role in therapy when they are used properly; however, one of the problems with using pills is that people often lose control and come to depend on them.

Many drugs work by regulating physiological functions such as heart rate, blood pressure, and body temperature. For many years it was believed that drugs were necessary because people could not control these physiological functions on their own (Ivey & Simek-Downing, 1980). However, more recently investigators have found that people do have some degree of voluntary control over these functions. One interesting example of this control was shown by a yogi practitioner named Swami Rama. When he was carefully studied at the Menninger Foundation, it was found that he could do such things as stop his heart from pumping blood for 17 seconds and change the temperature in two adjacent areas of his palm in different directions.

One of the problems with teaching people how to control their bodies is that most of us are not good at monitoring physiological messages such as our heart rate or muscle tension. For example, it is unlikely that you are aware of how fast your heart beats at different times during the day. **Biofeedback** techniques are designed to help people control their physiological functions without the use of drugs. The technique is based on principles of learning theory (see Chapter 6). The idea is

that people must be given information about the behavior (physiological response) that they wish to change, and positive reinforcement when they make the desired response. In practice, these goals involve connecting the person to a device that will measure the desired physiological response; this may be heart rate, muscle tension, skin temperature, blood pressure, or even brain waves. These devices not only monitor the response, they also give the person information about the state of the response. Sometimes the feedback is in the form of a tone. As the physiological condition changes, the tone changes. The reinforcement for the

Biofeedback is based on principles of learning theories. People are given information about their physiological responses such as heart rate or breathing, and they are given feedback when their responses change.

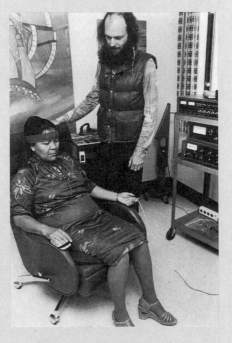

desired change is that the person hears the tone change in the desired direction. In actual practice, the person is given several training sessions on how to relax and control breathing (Miller, 1978).

Biofeedback has been used to treat a wide range of problems including high blood pressure, migraine headaches, asthma, tension, peptic ulcers, and even epilepsy (Williams, 1982). Several years ago the technique was hailed as a major breakthrough and it was even claimed that people could use biofeedback to control their own brain waves.

Recently, however, some important questions have been raised (Miller, 1983). For one thing, some of the earlier claims, such as self-conditioning of brain waves, have not been replicated in later research. A second question concerns the process by which biofeedback works. Specifically, investigators wondered if it was the physiological response itself that was being conditioned, or if people were learning to indirectly control their physiological response by tensing and relaxing various skeletal muscles or through cognitive processes such as imagination. While the answer to this question is not necessarily important to the therapeutic effectiveness of biofeedback, it does raise the issue of whether other less elaborate and expensive techniques could be used to achieve the same ends.

Answers about the scope and process of biofeedback will have to await future research. It is now clear, however, that biofeedback can be successfully used to treat a wide variety of problems, especially psychophysiological disorders related to stress.

their problems. People who work on wards in mental health institutions are often faced with the simultaneous demands of a number of patients. Because they cannot help all of them immediately, they may resort to drugs to quiet disruptive patients and bring peace to the wards. This is clearly a misuse of drugs.

PSYCHOTHERAPY

During her long battle to deal with her problem, Chris went to a number of psychiatrists and psychologists. These interactions were characterized by discussions between Chris and the therapist. In some cases, the therapist reviewed Chris's background to see what was causing the multiple personalities. In other cases, the aim of the session was for Chris to gain insight into her problem and to give her a chance to vent emotions building up inside her. Still other sessions were devoted to showing Chris how she could change her behavior, and she was rewarded for positive changes. All of these techniques are examples of **psychotherapy,** which involves social interaction between a therapist and client aimed at changing the client's behavior.

There are two major categories of psychotherapy. One—**global therapies**—focusses on the individual as a whole; the aim is to help the person gain insight into his or her problems and life (Rosenhan & Seligman, 1984). Global therapies deal with the complete personality, often exploring the person's history to shed light on his or her present state. While these therapies deal with the patient's presenting problem, they view this problem as a sign of a broader disorder. We can include psychoanalysis, humanistic, and Gestalt therapies under this category. The other major category—**specific therapies**—is most concerned with the presenting problem. These therapies do not delve deeply into the person's personality or seek insights. Behavior and cognitive therapies fall into this category. These two categories should be taken only as general orientations; global therapies do not ignore dealing with the presenting problems, and specific therapies do not avoid examining the person as a whole when the situation dictates this approach. Most therapies—both global and specific—are based on themes about the cause of psychological disorders. As you read about the therapies, you may wish to refer back to Chapter 12 to identify the theoretical roots of the techniques.

Psychoanalysis

As we discussed in Chapter 12, Sigmund Freud believed that our personalities are shaped by events in early childhood. According to Freud, as children, each of us go through stages. A traumatic event that occurs at any of these stages can have a lasting effect on us. Many of us witness events, have thoughts, or experience emotions that we have been taught are bad and unacceptable. In response to these teachings, we attempt to defend ourselves against these unacceptable thoughts or feelings by forcing them into our unconscious; in other words, we repress them. These thoughts or emotions fight to enter our consciousness, and we must constantly use energy to keep them locked in the unconscious. Freud believed that anxiety results whenever these unconscious thoughts threaten to break into our consciousness.

To treat these anxiety disorders Freud developed the method of psychoanalysis. According to Freud, people can be helped only when they recognize and deal with (work through) their repressed feelings. Hence the aim of therapy is to help people identify these "hidden emotions," bring them into the open, and deal with them. This may sound like a difficult task for a therapist; after all, these feelings have been repressed since early childhood. How can they be identified?

When Freud initially developed the psychoanalytic technique, he relied heavily on hypnosis. He felt that through hypnosis he could peer into people's unconscious and identify their repressed experiences and feelings. However, it soon became apparent that hypnosis was not effective with everyone. Also, Freud found other gates into the unconscious. As psychoanalysis evolved, he relied on two techniques to unlock the unconscious. One was **free association.** This method involves having clients talk about whatever thoughts come into their mind. Clients are told to reveal every thought that comes to mind without worrying about how much sense it makes or its structure. While this may sound easy, it is often rather difficult, especially when the thoughts are embarrassing or sensitive. Sometimes clients resist expressing certain thoughts or associations. This resistance may be shown by "forgetting" to attend sessions or by simply refusing to talk. Freud believed that resistance indicated that the client was close to revealing the repressed emotions and was using delaying tactic to avoid doing so. The psychoanalyst listens to the client's free associations, observes the resistance, and attempts to interpret their meaning. These interpretations are the basis for identifying the repressed emotions.

The second method used to uncover repressed feelings is *dream interpretation.* Freud believed that during sleep our defenses are relaxed and repressed feelings come close to the level of consciousness. However, because our defenses are not completely lifted, the repressed emotions are expressed in a disguised form in dreams. Thus the therapist must look beyond the expressed content (manifest content) to determine the true meaning

Free association is one technique used in psychoanalysis. This method involves having clients talk about whatever thoughts come into their mind.

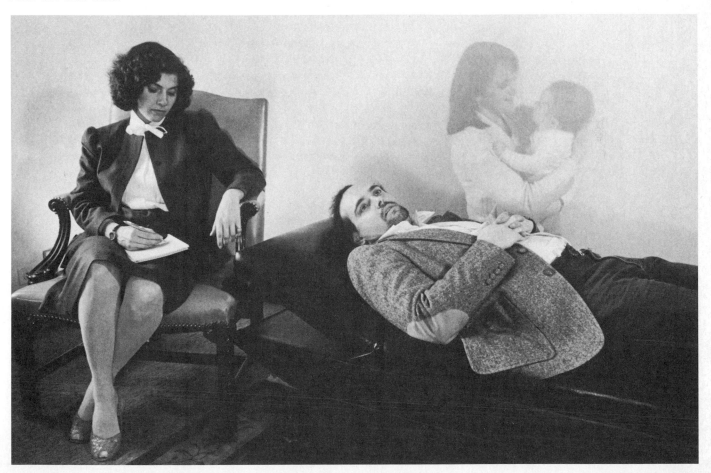

(latent content) of the dream (as we discussed in Chapter 5). For example, a man might report dreaming that he stands by helplessly as a young boy burns in a fire (manifest content). The therapist might interpret this dream as an expression of the client's resentment of his younger brother (latent content).

As psychoanalysis progresses, people reveal many intimate and usually secret details about their life to the therapist. In a sense, the therapist learns as much, if not more, about clients than their parents ever knew. Because of this, clients develop strong feelings about their therapist; some of these feelings may be positive, while others are very negative. Freud believed that clients transfer to the therapist feelings that were originally aimed at their parents or other authority figures; in this way clients "relive" these early relationships. *Transference* is a very important part of therapy. It gives people the chance to voice emotions that may have been repressed during childhood. According to psychoanalytic theory, these repressed emotions are the cause of anxiety. The expression of these repressed feelings allows the therapist to help clients deal with them in a constructive way. When these feelings are brought from the unconscious to the conscious and worked through with the therapist, they will no longer cause anxiety attacks.

The underlying aim of these activities (free association, dream interpretation, and transference) is to allow the person to gain *insight* into the foundation of his or her personality and behavior (Gilliland et al., 1984). By examining and reexperiencing these early events, the person can see how unresolved conflicts have shaped his or her life. This insight releases the tension and frees the person from the invisible grasp of those long-repressed feelings.

The practice of classical psychoanalysis has an almost mystical quality to it. The client is given a comfortable couch to recline upon and the lights of the therapy room are usually dimmed. The therapist sits in a chair out of the line of sight of the client. These conditions are designed to relax the client and promote free recall. The therapist takes a neutral role, becoming involved only to encourage the client to talk, or to offer an interpretation of a dream or recalled materials. The client meets with the therapist four or five times a week over a period of time that ranges from one to several years. Needless to say, classical psychoanalysis is a very expensive procedure that may cost over $15,000 a year. It is also apparent that the procedure is designed for the relatively well educated who can express themselves well in free recall and in reporting dreams (Luborsky & Spence, 1978). Finally, psychoanalysis seems to be a therapy best suited to treating disorders involving anxiety rather than more severe cases such as schizophrenia.

While classical psychoanalysis is still practiced today, some therapists have modified the technique. Many psychoanalysts have their patients sit in chairs facing them. The number of sessions is shortened, so that clients attend therapy only once or twice a week. The therapist may also take a more active role, with greater emphasis on interpreting and directing (Zaiden, 1982). In addition to these modifications of classical psychoanalytic therapy, numerous therapies have been developed that are based on psychoanalytic theory but represent more radical departures in technique. Some of these therapies are based on positions that place less emphasis on sexual themes and the id, and more emphasis on the social relations and the ego. Other approaches such as short-term psychodynamic therapy (Davenloo, 1978) replace free association in favor of active confrontation of the client's defenses until unconscious desires and feelings "break through."

In our example at the beginning of the chapter, Dr. Thigpen's approach was basically a psychoanalytic one. He had Chris talk about her childhood and her feelings toward her parents for hours. He attempted to interpret her dreams as they related to her childhood experiences. Through therapy Dr. Thigpen discovered that as a young child, Chris had seen a number of people die in various accidents. She became terrified of death and viewed herself as responsible for the deaths of these people. Was anxiety and guilt about these early deaths responsible for her multiple personalities? While we cannot be sure, it is evident from her book that Chris believed that repressed feelings about death influenced her condition.

Person-Centered Therapy

As we have seen, psychoanalysis focusses on "reconstructing" people's childhood and interpreting their problems in light of this. Carl Rogers (1942, 1951, 1980) and other humanistic psychologists also believe that the root of many disorders is in childhood. However, their approach is very different from that of psychoanalysis. The humanists argue that we naturally strive to reach our potential and lead a fulfilling life. However, as children we often learn that other people have expectations about how we should behave. We also learn that the way to get rewards is to live up to others' expectations. If we follow these lessons, however, we may lose touch with own own desires and feelings. When this happens, we become unhappy and experience anxiety.

According to Rogers, given the proper conditions, people will become more self-aware and happy, and they will strive to meet their own goals. In short, Rogers suggests that people will reduce their own anxiety and mature by their own efforts if they are given the right opportunities. Therefore the aim of therapy is to provide the proper setting for this self-growth to occur. The proper setting is one in which people do not fear social rejection for expressing themselves. In order to achieve this climate, three conditions are necessary. First, the therapist must give clients *unconditional positive regard;* that is, accept and care for them no matter what feelings or behaviors they reveal in the sessions. Second, the therapist must be *genuine* or real. He or she must be open enough to express feelings, whether positive or negative. This may seem to go against the first condition— unconditional positive regard—but it does not. For example, a therapist can show that he or she is very accepting of a client even though certain of the client's behaviors bore or even anger the therapist. It is important for the therapist to express these feelings so that they will not continue to intrude on the client-therapist relationship. Also, the therapist can demonstrate to the client that it is possible to be accepting while still having negative feelings. The final important condition is *empathy* (Rogers, 1977). The therapist comes to sense the feelings and meaning experienced by the client and communicates this understanding to the client. Under these conditions, clients will gain enough confidence to begin the self-exploration process and strive toward personal fulfillment.

The emphasis in person-centered therapy is on the person rather than on the therapist. The person determines what will be discussed during therapy. The therapist does not attempt to diagnose or interpret the client's condition. According to the humanists, a diagnosis serves no purpose and only places the client in a dehumanized category. Instead, the therapist responds to the person as a unique individual and attempts to experience the world from the client's perspective. In doing this, the therapist mirrors and rephrases what he or she hears the client saying. Unlike most other therapies, person-centered therapy has no specific "techniques."

In contrast to psychoanalysis, person-centered therapy focusses on the here-and-now. While difficulties may have begun in childhood, people must deal with them in the present. According to the humanistic position, there is little value in spending time tracing problems to the client's past. The

Carl Rogers, founder of person-centered therapy, believes that the therapist must create an atmosphere of unconditional positive regard during the session. The therapist should be genuine in the expression of feeling and experience empathy for the client.

cause of present difficulties is not as important as how the person is responding to these difficulties now. Thus the therapist helps the client focus on present feelings. But person-centered therapy does share with psychoanalytic therapy a concern for the global personality. It is not simply aimed at dealing with a single behavior problem.

If Chris had seen a person-centered therapist, her therapy sessions would have gone very differently. Unlike Dr. Thigpen, the therapist would have spent little, if any, time discussing her early childhood. Instead, he or she would have supported Chris as she examined her present feelings and attempted to deal with her multiple personalities. The therapist would not have tried to diagnose Chris or probe for the hidden meaning in what she said. He or she would have treated Chris as a unique individual and not just a patient who had come to be cured.

We cannot determine if this type of therapy would have been successful in Chris's case. There is, however, a mounting body of research (Mitchell, Bozarth, & Krauft, 1977; Truax & Mitchell, 1971) that indicates that therapist characteristics have a strong effect on the progress of therapy: Therapy is most successful when the therapist is perceived as genuine, warm, and caring. Research has also shown that person-centered therapy leads to improvement in the client's self-concept and better interpersonal relationships outside the therapy setting (Rogers & Dymond, 1954; Rubin, 1967).

Gestalt Therapy

While it may seem that the theories behind psychoanalysis and person-centered therapies are very different, Gestalt therapy borrows ideas from both theories. It has been argued that our actions are often influenced by emotions and thoughts of which we are unaware (Perls, 1969). These unconscious motivations can lead to unsatisfying social interactions. For example, you might find yourself becoming very angry as you wait a long time for a waitress to take your order. You believe that your anger is the result of the waitress's incompetent actions (*figure*, in Gestalt terminology). However, much of your emotion may actually be the anger aroused by a professor who criticized your work earlier that day. That anger, which was repressed at the time, serves as the *background* for your feelings in the restaurant. Perls agrees with the psychoanalytic position that we need to become aware of the unconscious influences on our behavior. Putting it in Gestalt terms, people need to bring together awareness of both figure and background in order to become "whole" and reduce their anxiety.

While he accepts these psychodynamic positions, Perls also adopts many humanistic principles. He believes, for instance, that we can take responsibility for our own actions. Like Carl Rogers, Perls argues that we become sidetracked from personal growth and self-awareness when we try to live up to the expectations of others rather than following our own desires. Perls (1969) makes this position explicit in the following statement:

> I do my own thing and you do your thing. I am not in this world to live up to your expectations. And you are not in this world to live up to mine. You are you and I am I. And if by chance we find each other, it's beautiful. If not, then not.

Finally, Perls argues that while the past may shape our feelings, we can only live and experience in the present. "The past is no more and the future not yet. Only the now exists" (Perls, 1970, p. 14). A person who is preoccupied with the past or too concerned with the future cannot function well in the present.

Awareness is the central concept in Gestalt therapy (Frankel, 1984). Clients must be aware of their feelings, behaviors, and even body sensations. Gestalt therapy also forces the person to accept responsibility for these emotions rather than trying to excuse them. In other words, *why* someone feels angry is of less importance; what is more important is that the individual *be aware* that he or she is angry and *express* this anger.

Gestalt therapy uses a number of interesting techniques to help people develop greater self-awareness and responsibility. For example, there is heavy emphasis on using *first-person pronouns*. A person might say, "It really makes you mad when people don't do the things they promise." The therapist in this situation would then challenge the person by asking, "Who does it make mad?" The person must then "claim" his or her emotion by replying, "I really get mad when . . ." In this way, people are forced to take responsibility for their feelings.

Role playing is often used to clarify a feeling. For example, the therapist might take the role of the client's mother and encourage the client to act out his or her feelings toward the mother. This exercise can make the client more aware of these feelings and demonstrate how they are affecting his or her present interactions with the mother. Another interesting technique is the **empty chair technique,** in which clients place different parts of their personality in chairs and act each of these parts. For example, a client may feel conflict about being aggressive. "Aggression" is put in one chair and "passiveness" is placed in another chair. The individual alternates sitting in the two chairs and taking the role prescribed for that chair. He or she acts aggressively and talks to the passive part of the personality when sitting in the aggression chair. This technique allows clients to become more aware of the conflict between these two parts of their personality. It also makes them actually experience both emotions. Gestalt therapy is often conducted in a group setting, but the focus of attention is aimed at one individual at a time.

Unfortunately, little research has been done on Gestalt therapy, though the goals of being aware of one's emotions and being more expressive are assumed to be positive. Gestalt therapy techniques have been used in a number of different types of therapy. There are, however, still many questions about the effectiveness of the therapy and the conditions under which it is best used.

In the "empty chair" exercise, the client places a part of her personality in the empty chair and attempts to explore it and deal with it.

Cognitive Therapies: Changing Thoughts, Beliefs, and Attitudes

Had Chris undergone either psychoanalytic or humanistic therapies, strong emphasis would have been placed on exploring and dealing with her feelings. However, if she had gone to a therapist who used a cognitive approach, the course of therapy would have been different. Cognitive therapists (Beck, 1976; Meichenbaum, 1977) argue that behavior is guided by mental events such as attitudes, beliefs, expectations, and appraisals. Therefore behavior and feelings that are out of touch with reality are signals that the person is operating with faulty attitudes, expectations, or evaluations of situations. The aim of cognitive therapy is to identify and change these faulty thoughts on the presumption that changes in thought will lead to changes in behavior and feelings. There are a large number of cognitive therapies. In order to appreciate how these therapies work, let us focus on one type: rational emotive therapy.

Rational Emotive Therapy (RET). Albert Ellis, the developer of **rational emotive therapy (RET)** (Ellis, 1962; Ellis & Grieger, 1977), believes that our problems are not the result of how we feel; rather, he suggests that how we *think* and *believe* determines how well we will adjust to our environment. In fact, Ellis argues that the way we feel depends on the way we interpret events rather than on the events themselves. For example, imagine that a friend turns down your invitation to go to the movies. According to Ellis, this refusal by itself will not make you too

He: "Want to go to the movies tonight?"
She: "I'm sorry, I'm afraid I can't make it."

Oh, well, maybe next time.

Gee, what's wrong with me, she must not like me.

Ellis believes that the way we feel depends on the way we interpret events rather than on the events themselves. The man shown here can interpret this event in one of two ways, and it is the way that he interprets it, not the event itself, that will determine how he feels.

unhappy. However, if you interpret the refusal as a sign that the friend really does not like you and that you are thus an unlikeable person, you will feel very depressed.

There are a number of irrational and destructive attitudes that can lead to depression. Among the most common are:

1. It is necessary that I be loved by every significant person in my environment.
2. It is absolutely necessary that I be completely competent, adequate, and achieve in all areas or I am worthless.
3. If something is dangerous, I must be constantly concerned about it.
4. It is a terrible disaster if things do not turn out the way I want them to turn out.

We can see from Chris's report of her childhood that she felt that she was a failure if everyone did not always express approval of her. She was always striving to please others because she feared their rejection.

Since it is these attitudes that are the root of anxiety, Ellis argues that therapy should be aimed at restructuring the way people think. In order to do this, therapists must take an active and direct teaching role. They must point out people's irrational beliefs and identify more rational attitudes to hold. For example, a therapist might point out to Chris how her irrational fear of rejection makes her adjustment so difficult. The therapist might challenge her belief, asking, "What's so bad about being rejected by others? What's the worst thing that can happen if someone doesn't like you?" The therapist attempts to substitute or replace the person's beliefs that behaviors or events *must* or *should* occur with beliefs that "it would be nice if they did occur, but all will be well even if they do not happen." The therapist who practices RET acts in a directive and challenging manner and is not too concerned about forming a warm, caring relationship with the client (George & Cristiani, 1981). The therapist may also use techniques like role playing to demonstrate the irrationality of many of the client's beliefs. As you can see, RET focusses on the present; while the irrational attitudes may have been learned in the past, the problem (and its solution) is in the present.

RET is widely practiced with people who suffer from anxiety. This form of therapy has the advantage of working faster than therapies that focus on developing insight and warm relationships between therapist and client. Despite this advantage, RET has been criticized on the grounds that too much insensitivity to the client's feelings on the part of the therapist can be destructive in some cases (George & Cristiani, 1981). In responding to this issue, many therapists have combined techniques of RET with those from other therapies in dealing with their clients.

Behavior Therapies

We might refer to the therapies that we have been discussing as "inside" therapies. They are "inside" in that they attempt to change how the person thinks or feels on the assumption that inner processes are responsible for the person's stress and failure to adjust. Changing these inner processes, then, should result in positive changes in behavior. If Chris had been treated by any of these therapies, many hours would have been spent examining how she felt or thought.

Behavior therapies take a very different approach. These therapies are based on the assumption that maladaptive behavior is learned through the same process by which other behaviors are learned. Given that abnormal behavior is learned, it can also be unlearned and a new, more adaptive behavior substituted in its place. According to behavior therapies, it is a waste of time to focus on internal events like emotions and attitudes. Therapy will be more effective if it concentrates on behavior, an external and observable factor. Behavior therapies can be considered specific therapies because they generally concentrate on changing a clearly identified behavior rather than restructuring the whole personality.

There are a number of therapies based on the principles of learning theories. We will examine four of the most common therapies in an effort to show the broad range of behavior therapies.

Aversive Conditioning. From the moment the twin girls were born, Chris felt that people stopped paying attention to her. The little girls received everything, including Chris's bed. However, on the day that the thin, bony-faced girl appeared and hurt the sleeping girls, Chris got attention from her mother. After that, Chris found that she quickly got others to pay attention to her when a different personality emerged. Thus, despite the problems that resulted in her life, there may have been some pleasure associated with the emergence of a different personality.

According to **aversive conditioning therapy,** the way to handle this type of difficulty is to reverse the process. That is, the person must learn that the presence of a target behavior is associated with an unpleasant event. Thus the therapy is designed so that the person receives unpleasant consequences for undesired behavior.

Aversive conditioning has been used to help people break such undesirable habits as smoking and drinking and to treat sexual deviations. For example, people with a drinking problem may be given a drug that will cause nausea if they drink alcohol. The drug can be taken before the drink (Lemere & Voegtlin, 1950) or mixed with the drink (Nathan, 1976). In this way, drinking alcohol becomes associated with an unpleasant feeling. Your parents may have used a form of aversive conditioning to prevent you from smoking after they found you hiding in a closet taking a few puffs. Their "cure" may have been to force you to smoke the whole cigarette, the result being that you became violently sick. After that, you remembered your "near-death" feeling every time you were tempted to smoke. A similar technique, called *rapid smoking*, has been used to help adults stop smoking (Lichtenstein et al., 1977). The technique involves having people smoke rapidly until they become sick. While it has proved useful in some cases, critics argue that rapid smoking may be dangerous, leading to problems such as nicotine poisoning.

A form of aversive conditioning has been developed where people only *imagine* a negative event being associated with a certain behavior (Cautela, 1977). For example, if you wished to stop eating sweets, you might be asked to imagine that candy is actually sugar-coated worms that will invade your stomach when you bite into it.

There has been a lot of controversy about the effectiveness of aversive conditioning. Some therapists report that the technique is very successful. Others argue that it does not produce lasting results; people return to the undesired habits after the therapy is over (Conway, 1977). There has also been some concern that the technique results in overgeneralization, in which the person stops performing many positive behaviors. For example, if you imagined worms in candy, as we just mentioned, you might not only stop eating candy, you might also give up eating other good foods that remind you of candy. In spite of these criticisms, aversive conditioning is used to help people change undesired behaviors.

Systematic Densensitization. Two-year-old Chris watched in horror as her father and other men pulled the bloated body of the old man from the irrigation ditch. "It's ole man Williams, I think he's dead." At the word *dead*, Chris gasped and felt her body tremble. From that moment, she developed an irrational fear of death that may have been one of the causes of her multiple personalities.

A number of behavioral techniques have been developed to treat phobias (irrational fears) and other anxiety disorders. One of the techniques is known as **systematic desensitization** (Wolpe, 1958, 1974). This technique is based on the assumption that it is impossible to be relaxed and anxious at the same time. The therapist's aim is to make the client relax in the presence of an object or event that used to cause anxiety. Systematic desensitization involves three steps. First, on the basis of interviews and psychological tests, events or objects that cause stress are identified. These events are arranged in a hierarchy according to the amount of anxiety that they cause. Table 14–1 shows a hierarchy that Wolpe (1958) developed from a client's fear of death; a similar hierarchy might have been created if Chris has been involved in systematic desensitization.

The second step involves teaching the client deep muscle relaxation (Jacobson, 1938). This method calls for clients to focus on and relax different parts of their body. The therapist might first have clients tense and then completely relax the muscles in their arms. Next they may practice relaxing leg or stomach muscles. After about four sessions clients should be able to deeply relax their whole body in practice at home.

The third phase pairs relaxation with the events listed in the hierarchy. The therapy starts with the least stressful event. Clients are told to remain relaxed and calm while vividly imagining the event. If they are successful in doing this, the therapist moves on to the next event in the hierarchy. If they show signs of anxiety or tension, the therapist moves back to the next lower event and begins the relaxation process again. After some time, clients are able to relax even when imagining the most stressful event in the hierarchy.

According to Wolpe and others (Denney & Sullivan, 1976), people who can relax while imagining feared events can also relax when they encounter these events in their everyday lives. Other investigators have changed the procedure to include actual contact with the feared objects or events. For example, Moss and Arend (1977) have used *contact densensitization* to treat clients who have a fear of snakes by having them first relax while holding a rope. Later they practice relaxation while watching a live snake in the room, and in the final sessions they use their relaxation techniques while handling a live snake. As you can see, desensitization involves learning a new response to a stimulus that previously aroused fear and stress. It is evolved from classical conditioning principles (Chapter 6) in that its aim

Table 14–1
Systematic Desensitization Hierarchy

This hierarchy was developed by Wolpe from a client's fear of death. Events that cause stress are identified and arranged according to how much anxiety they cause.

a. Seeing first husband in his coffin
b. Attending a burial
c. Seeing a burial assemblage from afar
d. Reading an obituary notice of a young person dying of heart attack
e. Driving past a cemetery
f. Seeing a funeral
g. Passing a funeral home
h. Reading an obituary notice of an old person
i. Being inside a hospital
j. Seeing a hospital
k. Seeing an ambulance

Source: Wolpe (1958)

is to condition a new response to an old stimulus. It is also a technique that focusses only on the present situation; there is no attempt to trace the cause of the anxiety. The technique has been used with a wide range of problems, including phobias, alcoholism, test anxiety, and insomnia (Rimm & Masters, 1979).

Operant Conditioning Therapies. Dr. Thigpen used positive reward to reduce the frequency of Chris's multiple personalities. When he wanted to talk with the "Jane" personality, he would reward Chris with kind words and sweets if she would produce this other personality. If one of the other personalities surfaced, Dr. Thigpen would scold Chris and withhold rewards until Jane reemerged. In this way, Dr. Thigpen was able to call up the personalities at will and keep them for a long time.

The process of rewarding desired behaviors is based on operant conditioning, which we discussed in Chapter 6. As you will remember, this type of learning involves rewarding the desired behavior after it has occurred. People soon learn that they can obtain the reward by performing the "right" behavior. As we saw previously, this technique has been used to condition and shape a wide variety of behaviors. In addition to rewarding desired behaviors, *selective* punishment can also be used to extinguish unwanted behaviors. For example, in one case an autistic child was given a mild shock each time he hit himself (Dorsey et al., 1980). The child quickly associated the shock with his hitting behavior and the self-destruction ceased.

Operant conditioning therapy can be used in an individual therapy setting, as it was with Chris and Dr. Thigpen. It has also been employed in a variety of institutional settings such as mental hospitals and prisons. When used in this type of setting, it involves designing a token economy (Kazdin, 1976). People taking part in a token economy are given rewards such as poker chips for performing certain behaviors. They can use the tokens to purchase things they want, such as candy or cigarettes. One of the authors conducted research in a juvenile prison that was based on a token economy. When a juvenile entered the prison, he lived first on the top floor, in a room that was bare except for a bed and a sink. He was given plastic tokens for performing such duties as cleaning his room. When he had earned a certain amount of tokens, he could "buy" his way to the next lower floor, which had larger rooms with more attractive furnishings. A new set of behaviors was reinforced with tokens; for example, he might receive tokens for reading books. Once again, when the prescribed amount of tokens was collected, he could move to a lower floor that had other attractive features such as curtains on the windows and a television. The token economy continued on each floor, with the ground floor being set up so that the boy could obtain his freedom with the proper number of tokens.

Other token economies have been used in mental hospitals. For example, Ayllon and Azrin (1968) used a similar type of token economy to get schizophrenic patients to perform such behaviors as eating, taking care of their personal hygiene, and doing chores. Another researcher used the technique to get autistic children to talk (Lovaas, 1977). A number of investigators have reported great success using token economies (Goldfried & Davison, 1976).

Other investigators, however, have criticized the technique on a number of grounds. First, it invests a great deal of control in the person who gives out the tokens. This person determines the "desired" behaviors and exercises complete control over all others in the economy. Many humanists view this as a negative situation; they feel that it is wrong for one person to have so much control over others. A second criticism is that the desired behavior sometimes stops when the reward is no longer available. For example, inmates in the juvenile prison that we just discussed perform

This is a token economy program at Camarillo State Hospital. In this program, residents receive token rewards for performing desired behaviors.

behavior for the rewards or tokens. In the outside world no one is going to give them a reward each time they make their bed or clean their room. As a result, the positive behavior may not occur outside the prison. In order to increase the probability that the behaviors will occur outside the token economy, small rewards or self-rewards are often used (Krasner, 1971). These rewards do increase the likelihood that the person will continue performing the desired behavior outside the token economy·setting. A third criticism is that the token economy teaches people to perform behaviors only for rewards; because of this, they may fail to appreciate or value the behavior in its own right. For example, if you are given a reward each time you read a book, you may read simply to obtain the reward and never develop pleasure in reading.

Despite all the criticisms of operant conditioning therapies, it is clear that such therapies can bring about behavioral change. In some cases, this technique may be the only way to change someone's behavior. A therapist who uses it, however, must take into account the ethical and methodological considerations that we have discussed.

Modeling. Clearly people learn new behaviors through reinforcement; they also learn by watching other people and *imitating* their actions. Statements such as "like father, like son" and repeated requests to "set a good example for others" remind us that modeling is an effective teaching technique. The human tendency to imitate has been used as the basis of the therapeutic technique of **modeling,** which is aimed at teaching clients new behaviors or strengthening existing behaviors (Dustin & George, 1977).

Albert Bandura and his associates have used the modeling technique to reduce a wide range of phobic behaviors, such as fear of dogs and snakes (Bandura, 1968; Rosenthal & Bandura, 1978). The procedure generally involves showing clients a series of pictures of a model interacting with the feared object. For example, people who are afraid of snakes may first see the model watching a snake from a distance. In the next picture, the model may move closer to the snake. As the sequence progresses, the model will touch the snake and finally handle it. Research has found that watching these models over a period of time does reduce the strength of clients' phobias (Bandura & Menlove, 1968; Rosenthal & Bandura, 1978).

The modeling technique can also be used to get clients themselves involved by asking them to perform the behavior that is modeled by the therapist or other model. In our snake example, after people watch the model handle the snake, they will be asked to handle a live snake themselves. This participant modeling is effective in reducing fears and teaching new behaviors (Bandura, 1977). Further research has found that modeling is most effective when the model is similar to the client. For example, Kornhaber and Schroeder (1975) found that children were more likely to handle a snake after watching a child model this behavior than after seeing an adult handle the snake.

Modeling offers a number of exciting therapeutic possibilities because the technique is relatively easy to use and almost any behavior can be modeled. There is, however, still some question about why the technique is effective (Sherman, 1979). Does the model teach a new behavior? Does watching the model allow the viewer to imagine performing the behavior? Does the model show the observer that no negative consequences will follow the feared behavior? These questions need to be answered by research so that the most effective modeling techniques can be identified.

Group Therapies

If we examine Chris's life, we find that many of her problems resulted from her attempts to interact with other people. As a child, Chris lived with her parents, grandparents, uncles, aunts, and cousins. She longed for attention and often felt neglected. Her multiple personality problem began at a time when she felt most neglected. As a school-aged youngster, she had difficulties making friends and interacting with her schoolmates. She was poorer than many of the other children and she felt different. Still later in life, Chris had difficulties interacting with her own family, and family stress caused a new personality to emerge. Chris entered psychotherapy with Dr. Thigpen in the late 1940s. Dr. Thigpen used the individual, or one-on-one, therapy method that was widely practiced at that time. This method involved a single patient discussing his or her problems with the therapist in much the same way as you might interact with a physician if you had a medical problem.

However, the late 1940s and early 1950s saw the emergence of a different style of therapy, called **group therapy.** This type of therapy generally involves one therapist and a group of clients (usually 6 to 12). The clients discuss their problems in the group and receive feedback from other group members as well as from the therapist. No single therapy technique characterizes group therapy; in fact, almost all the techniques that we have discussed have been adapted for group settings.

The role of the therapist differs in groups from what it is in individual therapy. In groups, the therapist must focus on creating a good group climate. Group members look to the therapist to define the basic rules of therapy. The therapist must teach by setting examples for other members

Group therapy is not only more economical than one-to-one counseling, but it can be especially helpful in problems arising from social interactions. Since the root of much stress involves interacting with other people, the group is the natural place to deal with these problems.

to follow; in a sense, the therapist must play two roles—that of therapist and that of group member. The relationship of the therapist to group members is important, but so are the relationships among group members. Because of these many demands, some groups are run by two therapists.

As time passes, the therapist works on developing a trusting and cohesive relationship within the group. Cohesiveness is the solidarity and "we-feeling" that binds groups together, as we will discuss in Chapter 16. Members of cohesive groups are more open in their feelings, more committed to group goals, and more likely to attend therapy regularly. One patient recalled, "The most important thing in it [group therapy] was just having a group there, people that I could talk to, that wouldn't walk out on me. There was so much caring and hating and loving in the group and I was part of it" (Yalom, 1975, p. 48).

Group therapy offers a number of advantages over individual therapy (Yalom, 1975). First, as we pointed out earlier, it is more economical. One therapist can work with a number of clients at the same time. Second, since many of the clients' problems involve interpersonal relationships, the group setting is the best place to examine these problems and "practice" interpersonal behaviors. Third, Yalom points out that other group members often serve as a source of hope and encouragement for individual members. Group members encourage one another to deal with their problems and offer hope for improvement. Fourth, the other group members show each individual member that he or she is not alone in having problems. People who suffer psychological disorders often fall into the trap of thinking they are the only ones who ever had this problem. In the group they can see that others have similar problems. Finally, other group members can serve as a source of information. They can point out problems and give helpful feedback. The group members and the therapist can also serve as models of positive social skills. Thus group therapy can have very positive results for both clients and therapist.

After this long list of advantages, you might naturally ask why all therapy is not practiced in groups. Despite the many positive characteristics of group therapy, it has some important limitations. Researchers point out that many clients may need individual therapy before they can function well in a group setting (Shertzer & Stone, 1974). These clients may be too insecure to interact with others. Some people find it difficult to develop trust in a group interaction, and lacking this trust, they are unwilling to discuss their problems and feelings openly. In some groups the therapist's attention may be spread too thin to give each client the help that he or she needs. Finally, the pressure to conform to group rules may limit the therapy process (Corey & Corey, 1977).

Clearly, then, there are advantages and disadvantages to group therapy. While group therapy may be appropriate for many people, individual therapy will be best suited to others. Just as we cannot argue that chemotherapy is always better than psychotherapy, we cannot say that group therapy is always better than individual therapy. The old saying that there is a time and a place for everything applies to therapies as well. In some cases, chemotherapy is most appropriate; in other cases, individual therapy may be called for; and in still other situations, group therapy will be most effective. Let us now examine a specific use of group techniques that aids personal adjustment and changes behavior.

Family Therapy

If Chris has consulted a family therapist, her experience in therapy would have been very different from what it was with Dr. Thigpen. The family or systems approach views the family as a unique organization having roles, rules of behavior, and identifiable communication patterns (Perez, 1979). Although members may be unaware of the family structure, a trained therapist can often identify it by watching family members interact in a therapy setting. The family therapist believes that the family system can create stress and contribute to the development of psychological disorders. While one member of the family may be presenting particular problem behavior, this behavior may simply be a symptom of a problem within the family unit (Levant, 1984). In other words, the family, as well as individuals, need to be treated. In addition to causing psychological disorders, some family structures maintain maladaptive behavior in family members. For

Family therapy involves the therapist working with the family as a unit. The aim is to make the family a more effective group and help family members see the roles and communication patterns that have developed.

example, when Chris began suffering her multiple personalities, she took on the role of "problem child" in her family. Her mother became the "protector" who cared for Chris and tried to explain her behavior to others. Her father took on the role of "concerned parent" who worried about Chris and talked about her problem to other family members. Chris's sisters became "helpers" who had to aid in the daily chores because Chris's problems took up much of their parents' time and energy. As you can see, a system of roles developed in the family around Chris's problem. While the system was designed to help Chris, it could also have contributed to maintaining her behavior by labeling her the "problem child." Further, if therapy was to change Chris's behavior so that she no longer fit the role of "problem child," all the other members of her family would have had to change their roles, too. There would no longer be a need for a "protector" or "concerned parent," or "helper" sisters. The point here is that it makes little sense to create change in one individual and then return that person to a family setting that encourages the old maladaptive behavior.

With these considerations in mind, the family therapist attempts to work with the whole family. The therapist sees all the members of the family together and observes their behavior. He or she attempts to identify the family role structure and communication patterns. In "treating" the family, the therapist will take an active role, requesting family members to behave in certain ways (Haley, 1980). He or she will have the members work on open communication and encourage the expression of repressed emotions. The "rules" of the family will be identified and openly stated. These unwritten rules will then be examined, and the therapist will point out how many of them have outlived their usefulness and exist now only through habit. The therapist may also have family members play different roles so that they can see how they are perceived in the family. Through this process, the family system is changed to encourage more adaptive behavior from its members. The beauty of this approach is that the therapist sets change in motion and observes during the therapy sessions how well this change is working to increase the "health" of the family (Boszormenyi-Nagy & Ulrich, 1981). If additional change is required, these steps can be taken. Thus family therapy allows the therapist to examine how people react in their natural group, the family.

There are many variations of family therapy. Some methods borrow heavily from Gestalt therapy (Guerin & Sherman, 1982), others use psychoanalytic methods (Levant, 1984), and still others are rooted in behavioral therapy (Liberman, 1970). In some cases, the therapist may see only the family; in other cases, the therapist may work with both the family and individual members. Family therapy is often the preferred method when dealing with a child showing poor patterns of adjustment or in treating anorexia nervosa (see Chapter 10); however, it can also be used very effectively when the troubled individual is a parent or an adolescent.

Community Psychology

In the late 1950s and early 1960s, attitudes about the treatment of psychological disturbances began to change in this country. As we pointed out earlier, it was realized that hospitalization was not the best means of treatment for many people, and besides, it was very expensive. It also became clear that traditional individual and small-group therapy efforts would not be sufficient; the demand was outstripping the resources, and traditional therapy was often unavailable to the people who needed it the most, such as the poor and the culturally deprived. Finally, mental health care providers agreed that after-the-fact treatment of problems should not be the only

A veteran discusses his problems with a counselor in a government-sponsored "Vet Center" in Chicago. These community-based programs are aimed at helping veterans adjust and deal with potential problems before they develop into severe disorders.

way of dealing with mental health problems; steps should be taken to prevent many problems from developing in the first place.

These attitudes gave rise to a policy of deinstitutionalization (Shadish, 1984; also see p. 464) and to the development of **community psychology**. There were two cornerstones of community psychology. One was the decision to give attention to the *prevention* as well as the treatment side of mental health problems. In fact, it was thought that prevention should be given priority over treatment (Iscoe, 1982). The second was that mental health programs should be *community based*; that is, training, education, prevention, and treatment programs should be available in local communities where they would be near the people who needed them. In support of this policy, Congress passed the Community Mental Health Centers Act in 1963. The act stated that one mental health center should be developed for every 50,000 people. The centers would be set up in local communities, where they could offer a wide variety of services in a convenient and nondisruptive manner. For example, a person could walk into the center during a lunch break or after work and receive psychotherapy on an outpatient basis. If the person required hospitalization, he or she could be accommodated in the local center, where frequent visits by family members would be possible. Many of the centers would operate "hot lines" so that people suffering a crisis could talk with a professional or trained paraprofessional on the phone. Over 600 of these centers have been established to date.

The concept of prevention is broadly defined by community psychologists. There are, in fact, three levels of prevention.

Primary Prevention. Efforts of primary prevention are aimed at eliminating the cause of mental health problems. In the case of Chris Sizemore, we might ask whether or not steps could have been taken to prevent her from developing multiple personalities. A major thrust of primary prevention programs is education. For example, new parents are often offered child-rearing classes to prepare them to care for their children and anticipate problems that might arise when the new baby is taken home. It is possible that if Chris's parents had received such a program, they may have been able to take steps to lessen Chris's anxiety when they brought home the twins. Other educational programs include classes on drug abuse, prenatal care, and planning nutritional meals. Another part of primary prevention involves identifying groups of people who are likely candidates to experience mental health problems. These "at risk" groups may be people of certain ages (adolescents or the elderly) or socioeconomic positions (poor), or those undergoing particular work stress (workers on strike). Once these groups are identified, efforts are made to take facilities and educational programs to them, rather than simply waiting for them to come to a center (Katoff, 1984). In this sense, prevention efforts are mobile, reaching out to the people who may be in need of them.

Secondary Prevention.   Primary prevention efforts are like medical inoculations; their aim is to prevent people from developing the problem. If this goal cannot be accomplished, the next best alternative is *secondary prevention*, which aims to identify and treat problems early in order to reduce their severity and duration and the suffering associated with them. For example, if Chris had been treated as a child, when her multiple personality symptoms first appeared, she might have been spared years of suffering and her treatment might have progressed much more smoothly. The concept of early identification sounds great, but how can it be achieved? Clearly, we cannot have teams of mental health professionals stalking the community to identify problems! The answer is not to infiltrate the community with additional resources, but rather to train people living in the community to identify problems and know how to refer troubled people to professional help. As we pointed out earlier, when people experience stress and disturbances, they usually first turn to friends, clergy, family members, or physicians. The aim of many secondary prevention efforts is to develop an "early-warning network" by training people in the community to identify psychological problems and help troubled people get in contact with the treatment facilities they need. If Chris's pediatrician or parents had received such training, they might not have passed off her bizarre behavior as simple childish fantasies.

Secondary prevention programs also have *hot lines*, which people can use to talk to a trained paraprofessional about their problems. Hot lines have been set up to aid people contemplating suicide, alcoholics, runaways, and battered women. The trained people who staff these lines give counseling, sympathy, and information about where the person can receive further help. In addition, there are crisis intervention centers where people can receive immediate short-term help to get them through a particularly difficult situation.

Tertiary Prevention.   The third level of prevention is rehabilitation and follow-up treatment of people who have been hospitalized or have been in long-term treatment. The aim here is to help these people reenter society and lead productive lives. Educational activities include job training, family counseling, and social skills training. In addition, *halfway houses* may be established, where people with common problems can live together after they have been discharged from hospitals. They receive training and counseling on everyday issues, from how to shop in a grocery store to how to write out a check. They may also receive psychotherapy. Research (Fairweather et al., 1969) has found that people who have spent time in halfway houses are less likely to require rehospitalization than people who are thrust immediately into their old environmemt. Halfway houses have also been set up for alcoholics, drug addicts, and ex-prisoners.

Community mental health centers also offer a wide range of counseling and consulting services on a sliding-fee scale so that they are affordable to all (Cooper & Hodges, 1983). Thus they offer counseling to many people who would normally be unable to afford it. The centers have also made people more aware of the value of counseling and therapy.

The mental health centers' role in prevention is indeed a valuable one. Nevertheless, there have been a number of criticisms of these centers (Holden, 1972). Often they do not have a large enough staff to meet the problems of the community. Goals may not be clearly stated, so that people are confused about the purpose and types of service offered by a center (Lamb & Zusman, 1979). We need more research to evaluate the effectiveness of community-based programs. While it is clear that the number of admissions to psychiatric hospitals has declined since the community psychology movement started, it is also true that there has been a large increase in the number of patients with psychological disorders admitted to general hospitals (Kiesler et al., 1983). In 1979 there were 1.2 million admissions of this nature. Clearly, the community mental health movement is open to improvement, and efforts should be made to identify the changes that are needed most.

DOES PSYCHOTHERAPY WORK?

We have traveled through the complex and sometimes confusing world of psychotherapy. As we have seen, there are long-term and short-term therapies, global and specific therapies, therapies that focus on the client's emotions and therapies that focus on changing behaviors, therapies that use drugs and therapies that use words. Regardless of the type of therapy, the aim is the same: to help people deal with psychological disorders and change maladaptive behaviors. Now we must ask the basic question: Is psychotherapy effective in treating psychological disturbances?

At first glance, this seems a simple question to answer. All we need to do is give psychotherapy to one group of people suffering from a disorder and withhold it from another group of people suffering the same disorder. At the end of a certain period of time, we can check to see which group has improved the most.

This solution seems so simple that it is hard to believe that there is still so much controversy as to the effectiveness of psychotherapy. However, as is so often the case in scientific investigations, the simple here turns out to be very complex. The first question that is raised deals with the issue of improvement. What does it mean to say someone is improved? For example, after many sessions with Dr. Thigpen, Chris understood her problem of multiple personalities and felt better about herself. However, she continued to suffer the emergence of different personalities. Would we say that Chris was improved because she felt better, or would we say that she showed no improvement because the multiple personalities still existed? It seems possible to make a strong argument for either position. A second issue involves the duration of improvement (Meltzoff & Kornreich, 1970). How are we to compare the effectiveness of a therapy that results in a quick but temporary change in the person's behavior with the effectiveness of a therapy that takes a long time but results in a more permanent change? A third issue concerns who is to determine the success of therapy. The therapist's opinion may be biased because he or she has a strong interest in believing that the therapy is successful. The client's opinion may also be influenced by the expectation and desire to see the therapy as successful. Objective criteria such as test scores or behavioral measures may be the most unbiased, but they are difficult to use on a long-term basis.

A related issue is why therapy works. If we can determine that psychotherapy is successful, we would also like to know why this is so. Does the success of therapy depend on characteristics of the client, characteristics

THE PLACEBO EFFECT: THE IMPORTANCE OF BELIEF

Throughout history, the physician has been one of the most respected people. Stories of miracles worked by physicians are commonplace in every age. But when we look at the history of medicine, it seems amazing that even the hardiest patient could have survived, let alone improved, under early medical techniques. Patients took almost every known organic and inorganic material, including crocodile dung, teeth of swine, powder of precious stones, furs, feathers, human perspiration, oil of ants, blood, and earthworms. They were purged, poisoned, punctured, cut, blistered, bled, leached, heated, frozen, and sweated (Shapiro, 1971). Today we know that most of these treatments had no medical value. Yet there are carefully documented stories of patients improving. How could this have happened?

A number of investigators have suggested that these miraculous recoveries are examples of the placebo effect (Honigfield, 1964; Shapiro, 1971). Simply put, the **placebo effect** describes the situation in which a treatment that has no curative value of its own has a healing effect on the patient because of the patient's belief in its effectiveness. While the placebo effect has been most frequently applied in medicine, some clinicians (Wilkens, 1973) have suggested that it may be one of the reasons that psychotherapy works. According to this position, almost any method of psychotherapy should show positive results if the client believes it will be effective. In other words, it is the client's belief that the method will work that causes the positive results. If this is the case, it is clear that the therapist must convey to the client that the method being used will be successful.

There are a number of possible reasons for the placebo effect. One of the most common explanations focusses on the "self-fulfilling prophecy," which we discussed in Chapter 13. According to this position, people are motivated to interpret events to support their expectancies. In order to illustrate this, let us suppose that we have two people, Bob and Mary, who are in group therapy to overcome shyness. Mary strongly believes that the therapy will be effective, while Bob does not. After two sessions of therapy, Mary and Bob meet a stranger on the bus and strike up a short conversation. For Mary, this becomes a sign that the therapy is working; even though she still found it hard, she would never have been able to talk to a stranger at all before therapy. Her new confidence motivates her to talk to other people. Bob, on the other hand, focusses on the fact that he felt uncomfortable talking to the stranger. For Bob, this is a sign that reinforces his belief that the therapy has not been helping him. His trust in the therapy decreases even further, and he eventually drops out of the group. In this example we can see that the expectancy not only influenced the way Mary and Bob interpreted their behaviors, but it also had future consequences for their efforts in therapy.

A second reason for the placebo effect involves the feelings of control. In Chapter 11 we discussed how a lack of control can cause stress. Many people enter therapy because they believe that they have no control over their feelings or behaviors. Gatchel (1980) suggests that the expectancy that therapy will be effective gives people a feeling of control over their lives. This perceived control reduces their stress and anxiety.

A third explanation for the placebo effect focusses on effort justification. As we will see in Chapter 15, research on cognitive dissonance theory has found that people are motivated to justify their effort; the more effort they choose to expend, the greater their need to justify it. One way to justify effort is to change one's attitudes to believe that the effortful behavior was a positive and valuable experience. Cooper and Axsom (1982) point out that therapy frequently involves a great deal of effort on the part of clients. Not only is it often difficult to talk about one's problems, but clients must also sacrifice their time and money. It would be even more difficult to continue making these sacrifices if they believed that the therapy wasn't helping them. Therefore, in order to justify their sacrifices and efforts, clients may become motivated to believe in the effectiveness of the therapy.

At first glance, it may seem that the placebo effect suggests that therapy is simply a process of self-deception. This is not the case. Rather, both physicians and therapists have known for a long time that a patient's attitudes and beliefs are very important in determining the effectiveness of treatment. Any treatment will be more effective if the patient believes in it and is willing to use it in the proper manner. Research on the placebo effect suggests that the way in which the treatment is presented to the patient or client is one major factor in determining the effectiveness of that treatment.

of the therapist, the specific techniques used in therapy, or simply the expectations of those involved? You can see now why the "simple" question: Does it work? is very complicated.

Given this complexity, it is easier to understand why there are no clear-cut answers about the effectiveness of therapies. In 1952 Hans Eysenck created a furor when he concluded that people receiving psychotherapy showed no more improvement than those receiving no treatment. Eysenck based his conclusion on a review of 24 studies of people suffering moderate psychological disturbances (neuroses). His shocking conclusion led a number of investigators to review his data and to conduct additional research (Bergin, 1971; Smith & Glass, 1977). These more recent reviews of a larger body of research suggest that psychotherapy does have positive effects, although it does not work for everyone (Shapiro & Shapiro, 1983). An examination of a larger number of studies on the outcome of psychotherapy led investigators to conclude that a person receiving psychotherapy is generally better off than 75 percent of those people who receive no treatment (Smith et al., 1980; Glass & Kliegl, 1983). While this is encouraging, there is also an indication that psychotherapy may actually leave a small percentage of clients worse off than they would have been had they received no treatment (Bergin & Lambert, 1978).

Results such as these raise an additional interesting question: What factors determine the effects of psychotherapy? The answers are characteristics of the client, characteristics of the therapist, the nature of the problem, and the type of therapy.

Looking first at *client characteristics*, it has been shown that people who are physically healthy, highly motivated to improve, and of relatively high intelligence are most likely to make rapid progress in therapy. On the other hand, people who have a low tolerance for anxiety, low motivation to improve, and feel that they have been forced into psychotherapy may actually get worse from therapy (Strupp, 1980).

Numerous studies have found that empathy, warmth, and genuineness are important *therapist characteristics* (Rogers & Truax, 1967; Gurman, 1977). Regardless of the type of therapy, an open, trusting relationship between client and therapist is vital to the success of the treatment. Therapists who show empathy, warmth, and genuineness are much more able to establish this type of relationship than are cold, distant therapists. This position was supported in a study that found that male college students suffering from neurotic disorders showed equal improvement when treated by either an experienced therapist or a college professor who was chosen for personal characteristics of warmth and understanding (Strupp & Hadley, 1979).

The *nature of the problem* also influences the success of therapy. Psychotherapy as the sole method of treatment has not proved particularly effective in treating serious disorders such as schizophrenia, alcoholism, certain types of affective disorders, or drug abuse. However, psychotherapy can play an important role in these cases when biological methods such as chemotherapy or ECT are used. On the other hand, high rates of success for psychotherapy have been found for anxiety and psychosexual disorders.

The final factor concerns the *type of therapy*. Is one type of therapy more effective than another? This is a particularly difficult issue to address because the goals of the different therapies are often different. For example, behavior therapy aims to change a specific behavior, while humanistic or psychoanalytic therapies are concerned less with specific behaviors and more with broader changes in personality and emotion. With this very important caution in mind, studies aimed at carefully reviewing research in the area suggest that behavioral therapies and cognitive therapies tend to be somewhat more effective than psychoanalytic or humanistic therapies

PROMOTING MENTAL HEALTH THROUGH PERSONAL GROWTH GROUPS

One of the major thrusts of community psychology is to prevent problems and promote mental health by making the community a less stressful place to live. Techniques that encourage personal growth are also aimed at promoting mental health. The focus of these efforts is on the individual; the goal is to help people lead more fulfilling and satisfying lives by learning to be more sensitive and aware of themselves and others. Personal growth techniques are not forms of psychotherapy; the aim is not to treat people with psychological disturbances. Most people in growth groups have adjusted to their physical and social environments but feel that something is missing in their "normal" lives. They may be dissatisfied with their relationships or feel unfulfilled in their work.

Many different techniques have been developed to help people in their quest for personal growth. They are extremely varied. Some are based on theory and careful research, while others have a dubious grounding. Many in the field are professionals who have received extensive training and are experts in their area. Unfortunately, there are others using personal growth techniques whose training is inadequate. Given this disparity in qualifications, it is important to be careful when choosing a personal growth technique and leader.

Transpersonal psychology is one personal growth approach. It attempts to increase people's awareness of themselves, to expand their experiences, and teach them how to become completely absorbed in experiences. The transpersonal movement is a mixture of psychological theory, religion (including the teachings of Buddha, Lao Tzu, and the Dali Lamas of Tibet), and modern philosophy. Transpersonal psychology operates on the assumption that physical, emotional, intellectual, and spiritual growth are interrelated. The movement argues that intuition, imagination, and altered states of consciousness (dreams, meditation, and drug-related experiences) are all part of human experience and should be examined.

Transpersonal psychologists attempt to develop all parts of the person, including the physical, emotional, mental, intuitive, psychic, and mystical aspects of personality (McWaters, 1975). In order to develop the physical parts, exercises such as jogging, yoga, dance, and massage are used. The aim of these physical exercises is to make people more aware of their bodies and to help them relax. Emotional development is encouraged through the use of

various psychotherapy techniques such as Gestalt therapy and personal expression in music and art. Mental development takes the form of lectures from leaders on topics ranging from philosophy to language and math. The psychic and mystical functions are developed through meditation, biofeedback training, prayer, and astrology.

T-groups have a different goal. The emphasis of these groups is on allowing people to experience how groups develop and to receive feedback about their effectiveness as a group member. These groups are generally made up of 8 to 15 members and 1 or 2 trainers. These trainers are not leaders in the sense that they set group goals or structure the group. Rather, they make observations about the process of the group, focussing on such issues as how decisions are made, how group roles and norms form, and how individual members contribute to the process. The group itself begins with no structure and no assigned task. Because of this, individual members are forced to develop this structure and define the group's goals. This process not only gives the members additional insight into how groups operate, but also gives them information about how they as individuals help or hinder the group process. T-groups have been widely used in industrial

(Andrews & Harvery, 1981; Shapiro & Shapiro, 1982; Smith et al., 1980). In addition, family therapy seems to be the most effective type of group therapy (Epstein & Vlok, 1981).

As you can see, an overall picture of the effectiveness of psychotherapy is difficult to form on the basis of existing research. All we can conclude is that psychotherapy is effective in some cases, and that the degree of effectiveness is influenced by the disorder, the client's characteristics, the personal traits of the therapist, and the type of therapy. Clearly, more research is needed, not only to clear up confusion about the value of current techniques, but also to serve as the basis for developing new and more effective ways of working with psychological disorders.

and educational settings to aid group performance (Heller & Monahan, 1977).

While the aim of the T-group is to help members examine the group process, the aim of the **encounter group** or **sensitivity group** is to expand personal awareness and growth (Brammer & Shostrom, 1977; Shapiro, 1978). Encounter groups provide intense, personal interactions in a setting where self-expression is encouraged. In a sense, encounter groups attempt to rid people of their interpersonal "hang-ups." There are numerous exercises emphasizing nonverbal expression. For example, someone may be asked to express his or her feelings about another person without saying a word. It is from such exercises that encounter groups have gotten the label "touchy-feely" groups. The variations on the encounter group are almost unlimited. In the marathon group, members interact and live together for 2 or 3 days. It is believed that this increases the intensity of interaction and removes many inhibitions about interpersonal communication.

Many people profit from encounter groups by becoming freer in their expression and more sensitive to their own feelings (Dies & Greenberg, 1976; Golembiewski & Blumburg, 1973). However, during the 1960s the encounter group became something of a fad; groups were led by unqualified leaders and variations were tried, not because they served a purpose, but simply because they were unusual. Because of the intensity of interaction, there were "casualties," people who suffered negative effects from the group experience. Sometimes these negative effects caused long-term suffering. It has been estimated that from 9 to 33 percent of the participants in encounter groups had negative experiences (Lieberman, Yalom, & Miks, 1973; Yalom & Lieberman, 1971). Some of these casualties resulted because participants had not been properly selected for the group. Plainly, encounter groups can be misused, so it is important to choose one that has a competent leader.

Encounter or sensitivity groups are aimed at expanding self-awareness and personal growth. Exercises, often nonverbal in nature, are used to emphasize issues and heighten the degree of involvement and experience.

SUMMARY

1. Many methods of therapy have been developed for dealing with psychological disturbances. These methods may be broadly divided into psychotherapy and biotherapy. **Biotherapy** involves some type of physical treatment, including the use of drugs, surgery, and electric shock to induce behavior change. **Psychotherapies** involve a trained professional who uses verbal interactions to bring about behavior change and positive adjustment in an individual or group.

2. There is a wide variety of biotherapies. **Electroconvulsive therapy (ECT)** involves electric shock; it is used most often with severely depressed patients. **Psychosurgery** involves cutting connections between different parts

of the brain; the **prefrontal lobotomy** is the best-known type of psychosurgery. **Chemotherapy** is the use of drugs (antianxiety, antipsychotic, and antidepressant drugs) to treat psychological disorders. **Biofeedback** is a method that teaches people to control their physiological functions by giving them feedback about these functions.

3. Many types of psychotherapy were discussed in this chapter. **Psychoanalysis,** developed by Sigmund Freud, is based on the notion that events in early childhood are important determinants of one's personality. Feelings or events associated with early childhood may be **repressed,** leading to anxiety later on. Freud believed that these repressed feelings enter the person's **unconscious** and can be released through the use of **free association** or **dream interpretation.**

4. Carl Rogers and other humanistic psychologists propose that **person-centered therapy** will help people through a process of self-growth. Person-centered therapy involves creating an atmosphere of **unconditional positive regard** in which the therapist relays warmth and concern for the client. In this setting the client is able to gain the confidence necessary for self-exploration and personal growth.

5. **Gestalt therapy,** developed mainly by Fritz Perls, proposes that unconscious thoughts and emotions (background) may lead to behaviors (figure) that are inappropriate to the situation. In Gestalt therapy people are helped to take responsibility for their actions, while understanding the emotions that are influencing their behaviors.

6. According to **rational emotive therapy (RET),** irrational thoughts are responsible for the way we feel about ourselves and others. RET therapists are concerned only with the present, and use a challenging, directive approach to help clients discover their anxiety-producing irrational thoughts.

7. **Behavior therapies** assume that abnormal behaviors are learned, and thus can be unlearned by changing the events that reinforce maladaptive behaviors. Behavior therapists may use **aversive conditioning** to break undesirable habits, or **systematic densensitization** to help overcome phobias. With **operant conditioning,** positive rewards are used to motivate people to perform desirable behaviors. These rewards often take the form of **token economies.** A fourth method of changing behaviors involves **modeling.** With this type of behavior therapy, the client watches someone else engage in the desired behavior.

8. In psychotherapy, a therapist may see only a single client at a time, or may work with a group of clients. In **group therapy,** clients not only receive feedback from the therapist, but the other group members also contribute. **Family therapy** involves seeing the family unit as a whole during the therapy session. Family therapy assumes that the family system can create stress and contribute to the development of psychological disorders.

9. **Community psychology** attempts to prevent stress by changing the environment. When environmental change is not possible, community psychologists strive to help those people suffering from mild disorders before their disturbances become severe. These goals are often met through the use of self-help groups of community mental health centers.

10. There are a number of techniques used to help people achieve greater personal growth. These methods are not really therapies, since they are not aimed at treating a specific disorder. Included in this category are **transpersonal psychology, T-groups,** and **encounter** and **sensitivity groups.**

Key Terms

antianxiety drugs
antidepressant drugs
antipsychotic drugs
aversive conditioning therapy
behavior therapies
biofeedback
biotherapy
chemotherapy
clinical psychologist
community psychology
counseling psychologist
deinstitutionalization
dream interpretation

drug therapy
electroconvulsive therapy
empty chair technique
encounter group (sensitivity group)
family therapy
free association
Gestalt therapy
global therapies
group therapy
modeling
person-centered therapy
placebo effect
prefrontal lobotomy

psychiatric nurse
psychiatric social worker
psychiatrist
psychoanalysis
psychoanalyst
psychopharmacology
psychosurgery
psychotherapy
rational emotive therapy
repressed (repression)

role playing
specific therapies
systematic desensitization
T-groups
token economy
tranquilizers
transpersonal psychology
unconditional positive regard
unconscious

Suggested Readings

The following books are about Chris Sizemore:

SIZEMORE, C., & PITTILLO, E. S. *I'm Eve*. Garden City, N.Y.: Doubleday, 1977.

THIGPEN, C. H., & CLECKLEY, H. M. *The three faces of Eve*. New York: Popular Library, 1974.

GARFIELD, S., & BERGIN, A. (Eds.). *Handbook of psychotherapy and behavior change: An empirical analysis*. New York: Wiley, 1978. Presents a number of original chapters examining a wide range of types of psychotherapy.

GILLILAND, B. E., JAMES, R. K., ROBERTS, G. T., & BROWN, J. T. *Theories and strategies in counseling and psychotherapy*. Englewood Cliffs, N.J.: Prentice-Hall, 1984. A brief review of most major therapy techniques. Sample cases are provided to illustrate each technique.

KORCHIN, S. *Modern clinical psychology*. New York: Basic Books, 1976. A comprehensive overview of the field of clinical psychology. Korchin focuses on testing, therapy, and community psychology.

LEITENBERG, H. (Ed.). *Handbook of behavior modification and behavior therapy*. Englewood Cliffs, N.J.: Prentice-Hall, 1976. This book is a collaboration of chapters dealing with the use of behavior modification and other learning techniques in therapy.

LEVANT, R. F. *Family therapy: A comprehensive overview*. Englewood Cliffs, N.J.: Prentice-Hall, 1984. Examines the family as a system and its impact on psychopathology. Reviews methods of family therapy from a wide variety of approaches.

SHAPIRO, J. *Methods of group psychotherapy and encounter*. Itasca, Ill.: Peacock Publishers, 1978. An examination of the various methods of group psychotherapy, the book presents cases and exercises for using groups in therapy and for personal growth.

INTERPERSONAL RELATIONS

As I stand before the American people and think of the honor this great convention has bestowed upon me, I recall the words of Dr. Martin Luther King, Jr., who made America stronger by making America more free. He said: "Occasionally in life there are moments which cannot be completely explained by words. Their meaning can only be articulated by the inaudible language of the heart." Tonight is such a moment for me. My heart is filled with pride.

When the speaker finished her speech, the people attending the Democratic convention stood and erupted with wild cheering. Geraldine Anne Ferraro had made history with her acceptance speech; she was the first woman candidate for vice president nominated by one of the major political parties. But even while they were cheering, some of the people were wondering who Geraldine Ferraro was and how she came to be chosen to run for the nation's second-highest office. Their puzzlement was understandable because six years earlier few people outside of Queens, New York, had ever heard of Geraldine Ferraro. While Ferraro's story is not one of those rags-to-riches sagas beloved of certain kinds of novels and movies, it is significant for its revelations about modern-day American life and politics.

Geraldine Ferraro was born into a middle-class family on August 26, 1935. Her father had emigrated from Italy 15 years earlier and her mother was a second-generation Italian-American who had grown up in New York City. The family was devoutly Catholic, and Domonick and Antonetta showered their children with gifts, love, and attention. Geral-dine's wonderland, however, was suddenly shattered when her father died at age 46, leaving his family with few resources.

In order to support her family, Antonetta moved them to the Bronx, where she took a job crocheting beads onto fancy party dresses. Determined to give her daughter the best possible education and religious training, Antonetta spent every spare penny to send Geraldine to private Catholic schools and later to Marymount College.

When she graduated, Geraldine took a job teaching public school and attended Fordham Law School at night. This marked her "coming out" from what had been a very safe and protective home and school environment. At Fordham she got her first taste of sex discrimination. "After a day of second-graders, off I would go to Fordham University to sit in a law class with just one other woman and a string of male professors who sincerely believed I was taking a man's rightful place" (Katz, 1984, p. 51). To make life tough on the women, the professors often called on them to recite rape laws in front of the male students. The ugly head of sex discrimination reared itself once again when Geraldine Ferraro looked for a job in 1960, only to be told by law firms, "You're terrific, but we're not hiring any women this year" (Katz, 1984, p. 53).

The disappointment of these experiences was blunted by Ferraro's marriage to John Zaccaro. John worked in his family's prosperous real estate firm, and it seemed that Geraldine's future was secure. The couple had three children in five years and Geraldine was content to stay home and raise them.

However, once the children were established in school, Geraldine decided that she wanted to reach beyond the bounds of home life. She had made a commitment to her mother that her education would pay off, and she was determined to honor that promise. Her chance came in 1973 when her cousin was elected district attorney in Queens. Geraldine applied for a position as assistant prosecutor. When she started in the D.A.'s office, Geraldine insisted that she be referred to as Geraldine Ferraro rather than Geraldine Zaccaro. This desire was not based on a wish to assert her independence from her husband; rather, she wanted to honor her mother by having her mother's last name appear on her professional stationery.

This job marked the beginning of many changes in this housewife from Forest Hills. Ferraro worked on a number of cases involving abuse of women, children, and the elderly. These represented some of the most hideous crimes imaginable. Ferraro had to gently encourage the victims to talk about and relive these experiences in court, and then she had to convince juries of the defendant's guilt. These cases brought her into daily contact with the underprivileged, and she came to understand their terrible lot in life. At work she saw another example of discrimination: She learned that she was making several thousand dollars less than male attorneys doing the same job. When she confronted her boss, he lightly passed it off, saying, "But, Gerry, you have a husband." These experiences liberalized Ferraro's attitudes and gave her new appreciation of the women's movement.

Work in the district attorney's office whetted her appetite for more active roles. She saw the importance and power of law and she wanted to have a hand in making it. In 1978 the long-time Democratic congressman from her district announced that he would not

seek reelection and Ferraro decided to run. She was relatively unknown but worked hard to get her message to the voters. Through radio and television and in face-to-face meetings, she discussed the issues important to her district: crime, Social Security, housing for the elderly. She borrowed money from her family so she could constantly keep herself in front of the voters. She won the Democratic primary and then went to Washington, D.C., to seek endorsements for her race against the Republican candidate. She persuaded Tip O'Neill, the house speaker, to campaign for her, and President Jimmy Carter sent Miss Lillian, her mother, to make appearances with her. It was a tough campaign. Ferraro's district was largely conservative; in fact, it included the neighborhood where Archie Bunker, the fictional character in the popular television program *All in the Family*, was supposed to live. But the voters were impressed by this bold woman who took strong stands on important issues. In the end Geraldine Ferraro eked out a victory and went to Washington.

True to her character, she worked to repay the many debts she felt she owed. For the people in her district, she turned her attention to such mundane, but locally important, issues as getting new zip codes for the area and having streets paved. For the Democratic leadership who had supported her, she became a loyal party member who voted with the party on almost every bill that came up. For her family, she was determined to avoid letting her new job disrupt their home life. First she tried commuting between New York and Washington every other day, but this proved unworkable. She then developed a schedule that took her home to New York every Thursday and back to Washington on Sunday night.

Geraldine Ferraro won reelection to Congress in 1980 and 1982. By 1984 she had expanded her interests to include topics of national and international importance. Her closest friends were other congresswomen, and together they worked to bring many feminist issues to the forefront. Some inconsistencies came to light that placed Ferraro in the center of controversy. She was an outspoken supporter of equal pay for women and men, yet women on her staff received significantly lower salaries than men doing similar jobs. She was a devout Catholic, yet she created a stir within the Church when she refused to take the antiabortion position.

Despite these controversies, Ferraro was

seen as a tough but fair congresswoman. She had quickly learned the ropes in Congress and knew how to get things done. She was a staunch supporter of the Democratic party and worked hard to bring it together. She had the support and trust of Democratic leaders like Tip O'Neill, and women's groups like the National Organization of Women (NOW) appreciated her outspoken support for women's issues. Ferraro showcased women's concerns not as a rebel but as an effective team member who could quietly garner support for these positions.

As the 1984 presidential election approached, the Democrats knew they were in trouble. The economy was improving; the Republican party was more united than it had been in years; and President Ronald Reagan was seen as a strong leader. The Democrats needed to do something dramatic to capture the imagination of the voters if they hoped to put up a good fight in November. President Reagan appeared most vulnerable on the issue of women's rights. Women's groups had lambasted him for his insensitivity to their concerns and his administration's poor performance in appointing women to important positions. Polls showed a significant "gender gap," in which Reagan's support was considerably lower among women than among men. And women were becoming increasingly more likely to vote.

The time seemed ripe for the Democrats to run a woman for vice president. And the most likely candidate was Geraldine Anne Ferraro. She had recently chaired the important Democratic Platform Committee and her name was becoming nationally recognized. Thus the stage was set for Walter Mondale's historic call to Geraldine Ferraro on July 11, 1984, to offer her the vice presidental position on the Democratic ticket. Though the Democrats lost the election and President Reagan captured a landslide victory, American women and the nation as a whole also won a major victory as one more barrier against sexual equality was scaled.

THE SCOPE OF SOCIAL PSYCHOLOGY

As we read about Geraldine Ferraro's climb into history, it is easy to focus on the glamorous aspects of her life. In fact, we often make our historical figures "bigger than life." Newspaper and television aid us in building these images, with their sensational stories and dramatic news flashes about the lives of our heroes and heroines. However, we're often a bit disappointed to learn that these famous people share many of the problems and foibles of ordinary people. Thus many of us were shocked to learn that President Reagan sometimes falls asleep during long, boring meetings or that Jimmy Carter "lusted in his heart." Revelations such as these make us realize how understanding human behavior in general will help us to better understand the behavior of any single person, whether that person be the first woman candidate for vice president or ourselves.

Social psychology is the branch of psychology that takes this approach to understanding social behavior; its aim is to develop general theories of human behavior. Social psychologists are interested in identifying factors that influence most people most of the time. For example, in this chapter we will review research showing that people are generally attracted to those who are similar to them. This is a general rule of human behavior. It does not mean that you will always be attracted to someone who is similar to you. It does mean, however, that in most cases, most people will be attracted to people who are like them.

Social psychology is a relative newcomer to the family of psychology. It began to develop in the late 1930s with the research and theories of Kurt Lewin, who believed that much of a person's everyday behavior is influenced by other people. In order to develop a deeper understanding and appreciation of human behavior, therefore, we must study how people are affected by their social situations. Lewin also emphasized the need for a systematic and scientific approach to the study of social behavior and stressed the importance of developing theories of behavior and testing them in carefully controlled experiments. Therefore we can define **social psychology** as the scientific study of the way in which people are affected by social situations and social relationships (Worchel & Cooper, 1983).

Let us now look at some of the specific areas of interpersonal behavior that have been investigated by social psychologists.

ATTITUDES

During the 1984 campaign Ferraro attacked the Republican's economic policy, saying she believed it was aimed at helping the rich at the expense of women and the poor. In her debate with Vice President George Bush she bluntly stated that it was difficult to determine what his attitude on economic policy was. She pointed out that he had once characterized the Reagan program as "voodoo economics," but now was supporting it strongly. In her attacks on Bush, Ferraro attempted to show that the differences between the Democrats and the Republicans centered on attitudes about such important issues as defense, treatment of the poor, economics, and abortion.

The concept of attitude is one we often hear discussed. Although there are many definitions, most present **attitudes** as learned, relatively enduring feelings about objects, events, or issues (McGuire, 1968). It is generally agreed that attitudes have three components.

1. The first is *evaluation*; that is, attitudes place a positive or negative meaning on the object or event in question. For example, embedded in Ferraro's attitude that women should receive equal pay for equal work is the position that discrimination in pay on the basis of sex is wrong.
2. Attitudes have a *belief* component. Beliefs are statements that express a relationship between events or objects. Ferraro's attitude on equal pay rests on the belief that a person's salary should be determined by the job that person does.
3. The third component is *action*. Attitudes often describe how people should act toward an object or event. The action implied in Ferraro's attitude is that laws should be passed to protect the rights of women to receive pay equal to their male counterparts.

The Development of Attitudes

Public interest and controversy surrounded Geraldine Ferraro during her bid for the vice presidency. The issue that often appeared at the forefront was her attitude toward abortion. She stated that while she would not have an abortion herself, she felt that the choice whether or not to have one should be left up to the individual. Ferraro's attitude on abortion was surprising given her deep religious convictions and the strong stand against abortion taken by her Church. It raises for us the interesting question about how people develop attitudes.

Clearly people are not born with attitudes. And just as clearly, we all have attitudes toward people and events with which we have had no experience. For example, most of us have attitudes toward the Russians; but few of us have been to Russia or met a single Russian. Where, then, do our attitudes come from?

Parents.   One part of Ferraro's attitude on abortion was that she would never have one. This position was also held by her mother. If you review your own attitudes, it is likely that you, too, will find that many of your beliefs reflect those of your parents. It is likely that you support the same political party as your parents do, that you hold similar religious beliefs, and even that your attitude on abortion is similar to that of your parents.

Parents influence their children's attitudes in two ways. First, they use rewards and punishments. Children who voice the "right" attitudes are likely to get praise and smiles, while children who express the "wrong" attitudes are likely to be greeted with frowns and scolding. Parents are especially powerful sources of influence for young children because they have almost total control over the rewards and punishments in their children's world. Second, parents are able to control the information that reaches their children. Many parents decide which television programs and books their children will watch and read.

Parental influence on attitudes is strong and lasting. There are several reasons for this. One is that children tend to believe their parents; they see them as the best and smartest people in the world. A second reason is that it's much easier to create new attitudes than it is to change old ones. Parents in this sense are in at the start; because they help their children form attitudes to begin with, they don't have to change their preexisting ones. Finally, attitudes formed when young tend to persist because people tend to seek out information that supports their attitudes and ignore information that conflicts with them.

Parents have strong influences on their children's attitudes. They determine the information and the models available to their children.

Peers.   As we discussed in Chapters 8 and 9, from around age 6 through at least the early teen years, children are more and more affected by their peers. When they start school, they begin to spend more time with peers in the classroom, on the playground, and in other formal and informal groups.

These peers supply the child with new information and present different ways to look at issues. This in itself would influence the child's attitudes. There is, however, another way that peers shape attitudes, and that is the threat of rejection. Children quickly learn that the way to be accepted by other children is to act and believe as they do. Rejection is often the penalty for taking a position different from the group's. Thus both children and adults often adopt the attitudes of their peers because they fear rejection if they do not (see Chapter 16).

Personal Experience.   On numerous occasions Ferraro was asked how, given her religion and upbringing, she could take a prochoice attitude on abortion. She replied that her experience in the Queens district attorney's office had influenced her. There she had prosecuted many child abuse, child abandonment, and rape cases. Seeing the sorrow and pain associated with these cases convinced her that abortion was preferable to forcing women to have children they did not want and couldn't or wouldn't care for.

Just as Ferraro, we hold many attitudes as the result of personal experiences. In fact, many of our most strongly held and most difficult to change attitudes result from our personal experiences (Olson & Zanna, 1983). The reason is that we tend to trust knowledge from personal experience more than that gathered from other people. There is, however, a danger in this tendency. Because we are so prone to trust our own experiences, we may be tempted to overgeneralize from them without careful consideration. For example, you might have had a particularly bad experience on your first visit to New York City. You may therefore conclude that New York is a terrible city and that New Yorkers are an unfriendly lot. With this attitude firmly entrenched, it is unlikely that you will visit the city again or question whether your experience was truly representative of that city or its people.

The Media. Geraldine Ferraro was very aware of the influence of the media. When she ran for Congress in 1978, she greatly outspent her opponent, putting much of her campaign money into newspaper ads and radio and television time. She felt this was the best way to reach the greatest number of people in the shortest amount of time. In fact, after examining her loss to the Reagan-Bush ticket, Ferraro, laid some blame on her poor handling of the media: "If I had it to do over, I would've become an immediate expert with the press" (*Good Morning America*, January 1, 1985). The power of the media to influence people has been recognized even in our laws; one federal law guarantees the political parties "equal time" on television to get their positions across to the public.

One reason for the power of the media is their ability to reach so many people. For example, 97 percent of American homes contain at least one television set. This is a higher percentage than the number of homes that have indoor plumbing! By the age of 12, most children in the United States have spent more time watching television than attending school (Gerbner & Gross, 1976).

A second reason for media power is that the media are often the only source of information we have about events. For example, most of us base our attitudes about the Russian invasion of Afghanistan, the Solidarity Union in Poland, and Geraldine Ferraro on information we received from the media. We have no direct experience with any of these events or people, nor do we know anyone who has.

While it is generally accepted that the media do influence us, there has been some disagreement over which media has the greatest influence. Our first response on this question might be that television has the greatest effect because it allows us to both see and hear the communicator. However, a recent review of the research has failed to find that one medium is always

By age 12, most children have spent more time watching television than going to school. Because the media reach so many people and are often the only source of information on topics, they play a major role in attitude formation.

more persuasive than every other medium (Taylor & Thompson, 1982). Rather, it seems that a medium's effectiveness depends on such factors as the audience, the type of message, and the communicator.

Attitude Change

Up to this point, we have focussed on the agents that influence the development of new attitudes. In a sense, we can view these agents as the pioneers of our attitudes; they tread on new territory, trying to get us to accept new information about issues that are often unfamiliar to us.

The focus changes when people are older. Then we are frequently no longer dealing with the formation of new attitudes, but rather with the effort to bring about an **attitude change.** When Ferraro began her campaign for the vice presidency, polls showed that most voters preferred the Republican ticket. Mondale and Ferraro faced the uphill battle of changing existing attitudes, not creating new ones. The task facing those who wish to change our attitudes is somewhat different and more difficult than that faced by those aiming to get us to develop new attitudes. When we change an attitude, we are not only accepting a new position or new information, we are also giving up an old position. We may be reluctant to do this because our existing attitude is part of an interlocking or balanced system (Heider, 1946). If we change it, there is often pressure to change other attitudes. For example, a voter who favored a prochoice position on abortion could comfortably believe that Geraldine Ferraro would make an excellent vice president. However, if that person held a strong antiabortion position, maintaining strong support for Ferraro would be difficult.

Although the issue of attitude change has always been central to social psychology, it received added emphasis during World War II. While a war of bullets and bombs raged in many parts of the world, a war on attitudes was being waged in the United States. In order for the nation to successfully prosecute the war, Americans had to change many of their habits and attitudes. Since the war was being fought in Europe, many Americans felt that it posed little danger to their homeland. A successful war effort required that this attitude be changed. Other attitudes of concern involved people's daily habits. For example, although the war created a shortage of beef, there was no shortage of beef entrails such as kidneys, brains, and sweetbreads. There was a greal deal of nutritional value in these foods, but Americans resisted eating them. Therefore it became important to change attitudes about what foods were edible (Lewin, 1943).

Given this important need, investigators began to carefully study attitude change. Their research focussed on three factors: the communicator, the message, and the audience.

The Communicator.   As we pointed out, the task facing Ferraro was to change the attitudes of her audience to support her positions and the Democratic party. With her lack of broad experience in national and international affairs, Ferraro was hardly a walking dictionary of facts and figures. But she had another weapon: herself. After hearing Ferraro give a speech, a congressman's aide commented, "God, she was terrible. She didn't say anything and her speech was terrible, but everyone loved her. They applauded every line and they were ecstatic about her" (Katz, 1984, p. 156).

These comments demonstrate the importance of the communicator in changing attitudes. *Who* says something is often as, if not more, important than what is said. It seems there are several factors that determine the effect of a communicator. One is *credibility*—how believable the communicator is. For example, Hovland and Weiss (1952) found that an audience was more likely to believe an eminent scientist than the Communist newspaper *Pravda* on the subject of building nuclear submarines. Interestingly

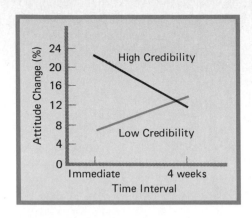

Figure 15-1
The sleeper effect occurs when people separate the source from the message over time. As a result, the influence of communication credibility on attitude change is reduced or eliminated.

enough, this effect disappeared over time (see Figure 15–1). That is, the more credible source had a greater effect on people's attitudes than the less credible source right after the message was given. But the credibility of the communicator made no difference when people were asked their opinion 4 week after hearing the message. This pattern of results has been called the **sleeper effect** (Gruder et al., 1979; Kelman & Hovland, 1953). Although there has been some controversy about how often this effect occurs, it has been explained by suggesting people tend to separate the source from the message as time passes. In other words, they forget who said what, so the early advantage of the more credible communicator is reduced, just as is the disadvantage of the less credible source.

As might be expected, we are also more persuaded by a *trustworthy* communicator than by one whose motives we suspect. In an interesting experiment Eagly, Wood, and Chaiken (1978) found that communicators were seen as more trustworthy and persuasive if they took positions that were unexpected or opposed to their own best interests. This may explain why Ferraro's prochoice position created such an impact; since she was a Catholic, most people expected her to be strongly antiabortion.

There is another factor that affects how persuasive a communicator is: *similarity* to the audience. Imagine that you are interested in buying some paint to redecorate your apartment. You walk into a paint store and choose your paint, and while waiting at the cashier's counter, you meet a salesman who tells you that he recently completed a painting job much like the one you're about to undertake. After noticing the brand of paint you have

Communicators who are seen as similar to the audience are effective in changing attitudes. In this advertisement, the communicator is shown in a situation experienced by many people—drinking bitter-tasting reheated coffee.

chosen, he states that he used another brand and was very happy with it. He suggests that you switch brands. Now imagine yourself in a similar situation, but this time you are met by a paint salesman who informs you that he recently completed a painting job that was not only very different from the one you're planning but also took a lot more paint. He, too, notices your brand of paint and suggests you change to another brand. In which case would you be more likely to buy the brand being pushed by the salesman? Brock (1965) conducted this study in a paint store and found that the salesman who said he had used the different brand of paint for a job similar to the one the customer was planning was more persuasive than the other salesman. Other research has found that similar communicators are more effective when the issue involves evaluations—what is good or bad—rather than facts (Goethals & Nelson, 1973). Along these lines, note that it was Miss Lillian rather than President Carter who campaigned for Geraldine Ferraro in her first bid for Congress; Ferraro's district had a large concentration of elderly voters, who saw themselves as having more in common with Miss Lillian than with Jimmy Carter.

The Message. Moving from the communicator to the message, we find that there are many ways to structure a message to increase its persuasiveness. One of the favorite ploys of media experts is to create an atmosphere that arouses people or makes them feel good (Cialdini, 1984). Political messages are often delivered with a background of peaceful scenes, the American flag, or a cheering crowd. Advertisers attempt to sexually arouse their audience or picture exciting sporting events or funny situations (see the highlight).

Fear can effectively be used to increase persuasion. The research suggests that messages that arouse a moderate degree of fear in the audience *and* then present a way to avoid the fear-arousing situation are often very persuasive (Leventhal & Niles, 1956). During the 1984 campaign both the Democrats and the Republicans used this approach in their political ads. For example, the Republicans ran an advertisement that showed a bear (representing the Russians) stalking in the forest, followed by the message to keep America strong and vote for Reagan. The intent was to imply that the Russians were an immediate danger to the United States (arouse fear) and that voting for Reagan would keep the Russians away from our doorstep.

Messages can also be effective to the extent that they *capture the audience's attention* and *get them involved*. It can be argued that efforts to create a mood (happiness or fear) have this effect. Other ways to increase involvement include asking rhetorical questions and using multiple speakers so the audience will not get bored listening to the same person (Harkins & Petty, 1981). Reagan masterfully used the rhetorical question technique when he asked the voters, "Are you better off today than you were four years ago [when a Democrat was president]?"

The Audience. We find the research in this area much less conclusive than that on the communicator and the message. Few personal characteristics that make people sitting ducks for persuasion attempts have been identified. For example, we might expect people of lower intelligence to be more easily influenced than more intelligent people. However, people of lower intelligence may have difficulty understanding the message and therefore be less affected by it. Overall, it seems that personal characteristics of the audience influence the type of message that will be most persuasive. For example, people who hold a position opposite to that advocated by the communication will be most influenced by a message that is two-sided and draws specific conclusions (Linder & Worchel, 1970). On the other hand, an audience that already agrees with the message's position may be more influenced by a one-sided argument that does not explicitly draw conclusions.

ADVERTISING, THE ULTIMATE IN ATTITUDE CHANGE

The advertising industry can be viewed as the industry of attitude change. Imagine the huge task facing advertisers: They have only a small space in a magazine or a 30-second spot on television to convince the audience to buy their product. Given our discussion of the difficulty of changing attitudes, this would seem to be an impossible task. However, a great deal of money is riding on the possibility that the advertising industry can succeed in its task: More than $55 billion was spent during 1982 for advertising in the United States. Advertisers have developed very sophisticated techniques to convince us to drink Coke when thirsty, eat Big Macs when hungry, and take Alka Seltzer when our stomachs don't agree. And Wells (1975) points out that advertisers are often able to change our attitudes without teaching us anything about their product. How are they able to do this?

When we examine advertising techniques, we find that they use many of the theories that social psychologists have studied.

Communicator similarity is frequently used in advertisements. For example, we often see the "average American family" using brand X soap and proclaiming how clean and refreshed they feel

afterward. Or we find the "typical housewife" exclaiming how clean brand Y laundry powder gets her wash. The message clearly is that if the product works well for these people, it will certainly work well for the majority of us.

The "hidden camera" technique is used to give the impression of a *trustworthy communicator*. In these types of advertisements the audience is led to believe that the communicator does not know that he or she is being taped, and is therefore speaking honestly.

Credible communicators are often created. For instance, we may see a person dressed in a white laboratory coat proclaiming that "three out of four doctors" recommend a certain brand of aspirin. An interesting twist on the expert approach is to use an expert in one field to advertise products in another. We may find a famous baseball player advertising an automobile or a well-known actor or actress advising us to buy a certain breakfast cereal. In each example the aim is to enhance the product by associating it with an "expert" source.

Emotional appeals are often used to sell a product. One favorite ploy is to play a catchy tune while advertising a product. Another plan

is to use a communicator who will sexually arouse the audience. It is common to see a scantily dressed woman or a handsome male recommending a certain automobile, wine, or shave cream. In all these cases, the aim is to have the audience associate the product with a pleasant feeling (sexual arousal).

Conversely, a number of advertisements use *fear appeals* to get their message across. A common ad for wearing seat belts shows a terrible automobile accident and presents the message that injury could have been avoided if the driver had worn a seat belt. As we pointed out, arousing a moderate degree of fear and then presenting a means to reduce that fear is an effective persuasive technique.

Repeated exposure is another common advertising technique. The aim here is simply to have the audience see the product as often as possible. This approach is consistent with research showing that the more people are exposed to an object, the more attractive they find it (Zajonc, 1968).

It is obvious that research in social psychology can help explain the effectiveness of advertising campaigns.

The Relationship between Attitudes and Behavior

Before leaving our discussion of attitudes, we need to address one more issue. When we defined attitudes, we pointed out that they have an action component. In other words, they have a tendency to direct behavior. There is, however, an interesting example in Geraldine Ferraro's background that should cause us to question this relationship. Ferraro was an outspoken supporter of paying men and women equally for doing the same job. Yet it was revealed that in 1983 the average salary for a man on her staff was $28,500 while the average salary for a woman was $22,000 (Katz, 1984). We would not have been able to predict this action on the basis of her stated attitude.

Current research has shown that there are many considerations in trying to predict behavior from attitudes (Zanna et al., 1982). One important consideration is the situation. In many cases, the particular situation may play a larger role than attitudes in determining behavior. Another important factor is how the attitudes were formed. Fazio and Zanna (1981) argue that attitudes formed through direct personal experience are better predictors of behavior than attitudes not based on experience. A third factor is how closely tied to a specific behavior the attitude is. The closer the tie, the better a predictor of behavior the attitude will be (Ajzen & Fishbein, 1977). For example, Ferraro's general attitude toward equal pay did not predict her behavior. A better indicator would have been her attitudes regarding her own office staff. Finally, there is the question of salience. Langer (1978) suggests that we often act in a "mindless" way; that is, we act without thinking about our attitudes. In these instances, our behavior may not be a good reflection of our attitudes. Attitudes are better predictors of our behavior if we are forced to survey our feelings and beliefs before acting. In a series of experiments in which investigators had people behave in front of a camera or mirror, their actions and attitudes were more consistent than when they were not in front of the mirror or camera (Carver & Scheirer, 1981; Duval & Wicklund, 1972). The investigators argued that the mirror or camera caused people to focus their attention on themselves, making them more aware of their attitudes. Thus any situation that causes us to focus on or remember our attitudes will result in a closer link between attitudes and behavior.

WHEN BEHAVING IS BELIEVING

We have seen that attitudes can guide our behavior under some circumstances. There is, however, a flip side to this relationship that has been recognized by social psychologists for years. That is, our behavior may also drive our attitudes.

A Theory of Cognitive Dissonance

One of the first investigators to recognize this behavior-attitude relationship was Leon Festinger. Festinger's theory (1957) was actually rather simple, but it gave rise to a large number of unique predictions and studies. He argued that people strive to have their attitudes, beliefs, and behaviors support one another. When these components (*cognitions*, in Festinger's terminology) come into conflict, a person will become uncomfortable and experience a state of cognitive dissonance. In order to relieve the dissonance, the person will try to change the cognitions so that they will once again be in agreement.

The most interesting cases of cognitive dissonance involve the relationship between attitudes and behaviors (Wicklund & Brehm, 1976). We desire consistency between our attitudes and behaviors, and if we cannot justify our behavior by external factors, we change our attitudes to justify the behavior. When we believe that we have *freely chosen* to perform a particular act, we will become motivated to realign our attitudes to justify that behavior.

Let us now examine some of the interesting predictions that are based on this theory. In each of these cases, notice that the final attitude is a function of the behavior.

Effort Justification. According to dissonance theory, we love those things for which we suffer (effort justification). In other words, suffering

According to dissonance theory, we attempt to justify our effort by inflating the value of effortful tasks. We might anticipate that this runner would rate jogging as an enjoyable and valuable exercise!

leads to liking. As we can see, it would be dissonant to hold the two cognitions that (1) I worked hard for X and (2) X is worthless. Since I cannot change the fact that I have worked hard for X, I can reduce my dissonance by changing my attitude about X; I can come to believe that X is valuable. In one of the early dissonance experiments investigators had subjects perform either a very difficult task, an easy task, or no task at all to get into a group (Aronson & Mills, 1959). The subjects then heard their group discuss a very boring topic. Although all the subjects heard the same discussion, those who had performed the difficult task to gain admission to the group rated the discussion as more interesting than did the other subjects. More recent research found that we are especially likely to justify our actions when we perform an unpleasant task for an unpleasant person (Rosenfeld et al., 1984)! Along these lines, it is interesting to see how highly Ferraro valued her law school training despite the fact that she had to attend night classes and was subjected to sex discrimination in the classroom. Could the hard schedule and difficult circumstances have encouraged her to increase her estimate of the importance of her schooling?

Insufficient Reward. Dissonance theory suggests that the smaller the external reward we receive for completing a task, the more we will value that task. Once again, the cognitions that (1) I performed a dull task and (2) I received very little reward for this work are dissonant. I can reduce this dissonance and justify my work by believing that the tasks were interesting or important.

In a number of studies subjects were enticed to volunteer to perform rather dull tasks for either a small reward or a large reward (Cooper & Worchel, 1970; Festinger & Carlsmith, 1959). Even though the tasks were the same, those performing them for a small reward stated that they enjoyed them more than did the subjects who received a large reward. Since the reward did not justify the behavior in the low-reward condition, it is obvious that the subjects had changed their attitudes about the tasks.

Cialdini (1984) points to one of those secret influences in our everyday lives that nicely combines effort justification and **insufficient reward** to change our attitudes. Recall the contests by makers of products such as breakfast cereals that ask us to write a slogan glorifying Crunchy O's cereal. To entice us to undertake this literary exercise, the company promises that we have a one-in-a-million chance of winning $100,000. And to further emphasize our freedom to choose to do this task or not, the company boldly states that "no purchase is necessary." We may spend hours working, and even risk failing our psychology test because of lost study time, as we strain to author the prize slogan. In the end, however, we cannot really justify our behavior by saying that we truly believed we would win. We have entered 2,211 previous contests without winning, so why should we expect to win this one? One way to justify our behavior is to convince ourselves that we really do like Crunchy O's, and we are only writing what we believe; this, indeed, is the effect the sponsoring companies are betting on.

Just-Barely-Sufficient Threat. Imagine that a young child is told by his mother she will be very upset if he takes a cookie from the cookie jar. The mother leaves the room and the hungry child longingly eyes the scrumptious cookies, but he does not take one. He now has the dissonant cognitions that (1) I am not taking a cookie and (2) the cookie looks wonderfully delicious. How does he resolve this dissonance? If his mother's threat had been severe or drastic ("I'll cut your hands off if you take a cookie!"), the child could justify his actions by believing that he did not take the cookie because of his mother's severe threat. However, he knows that as his mother's threats go, this one was rather mild, so it does not justify his behavior. He can, however, justify his behavior by derogating the cookies: "They're probably stale and taste awful." Adopting this attitude, the child now has the cognitions that (1) he did not choose to eat (2) a terrible-tasting cookie. These cognitions fit nicely together. Thus dissonance theory suggests that we will derogate attractive objects or activities that we chose to forgo without strong external constraints (just-barely-sufficient threats). This effect was demonstrated in a study in which children received either a mild or severe warning not to play with a toy robot (Aronson & Carlsmith, 1963). Those children who did not play with the robot rated it lower in attractiveness in the mild-warning case than in the severe-warning case.

Foot-in-the-Door

Cognitive dissonance theory demonstrates that we often change our attitudes about events or objects to help justify our behavior. There is another line of research that suggests that our behavior may lead us to change our attitudes about ourselves, which, in turn, influences our future behavior. This effect may have helped lay the groundwork for Geraldine Ferraro's rise to prominence. John Zacarro came from a very traditional background and held traditional values when he married Ferraro. He believed that it was his responsibility to support his family and that his wife's responsibility was to raise their children and tend to household matters. During the first few years of their marriage, Geraldine Ferraro was content with this relationship. However, she soon wanted a career of her own. Had she approached her husband with the suggestion that she open up a full-time law practice (or run for Congress), a difficult argument might have resulted. Instead, she proposed to open a small office in their home where she would handle some real estate–related legal matters. Although Zacarro was a bit uneasy with even this action, he helped his wife set up her home office. The next step was Ferraro's job outside the home as assistant district attorney, and not too many years later Zacarro found himself lending his wife $134,000 to run for Congress. Thus the man who believed that women should stay at home ended up helping his wife win a position that would require her to live apart from her family. What would explain this strange chain of events?

One explanation is known as the **foot-in-the-door** phenomenon, which suggests that in order to get people to perform a large or difficult task, we should first get them to perform a small, related task. By committing themselves to this small task, people will change their attitude about themselves; they will see themselves as people who get involved or support causes (Rittle, 1981). This new self-image then makes it easier to get these people to commit themselves to a larger task. Thus Zaccaro's agreement to support his wife's part-time practice may have changed his self-image to that of a man willing to help his wife's career. With this new self-image, his future help for larger advances in her career was more easily forthcoming.

In a study demonstrating this effect investigators approached some residents of Palo Alto, California, and asked them to either place a small sign that read "Be a safe driver" in their window or sign a petition for safe driving (Freedman & Fraser, 1966). Two weeks later a second experimenter approached these same residents and another group of residents who had not been asked to comply with the small request. This second experimenter asked both groups if they would allow a large "Drive carefully" sign to be placed in their front yard. While 55.7 percent of the residents who had gone along with the earlier small request allowed the sign to be placed in their yard, only 16.7 percent of those who had not received the earlier request allowed the sign. The investigators reasoned that by agreeing to the small request, residents had come to view themselves as action-oriented and were therefore more willing to comply with the

People often get us to agree to large commitments by first getting us to engage in smaller ones.

second request. After reviewing research showing the power of this effect, one author commented, "It scares me enough that I am rarely willing to sign a petition anymore, even for a position I support" (Cialdini, 1984, p. 80).

Door-in-the-Face. The opposite approach, the **door-in-the-face** technique, also works. Researchers have found that people who at first refuse a large request will be more likely to go along with a smaller request than those not given the chance to refuse the large request (Cialdini et al., 1975). This effect may be because people feel a bit guilty about turning down the first request; they therefore go along the second time in order to reduce their guilt. It is also possible that, compared to the large first request, the second request seems quite reasonable.

PERCEIVING AND EVALUATING OTHERS

Throughout our discussion of attitudes, we often stated that how we act toward other people and how effective they are in influencing us are affected by the way we evaluate them. We suggested that those we view as similar to us, trustworthy, and credible will be effective communicators in changing our attitude. Geraldine Ferraro went to great lengths to have the voters see her as possessing these traits. She stressed her religious and ethnic background; she emphasized her concerns as a woman and a mother; she referred to her experience in the district attorney's office; and to suggest her knowledge of foreign affairs, she showed pictures of her recent trip to Central America.

Underlying Ferraro's approach was the idea that people use the information they have and the behaviors they observe to form impressions of others. They go on from specific and often limited information to form broader pictures of the individual. This means that we can influence people's general impression of us by carefully controlling the specific information they receive. In Ferraro's case, it meant the planning of a careful campaign to emphasize certain points and deemphasize others. Pictures of Ferraro talking to farmers in Iowa were aimed at giving the impression that she understood and was sympathetic to farmers; pictures of her going to church with her family were designed to promote the picture of her as profamily and proreligion.

The rules that people follow and the mistakes they make in forming these impressions constitute a fascinating area of study. Understanding these rules and biases not only helps us see how we get to know others, but also shows how people decide what we are like.

In attempting to bring the work on impression formation together, we should keep in mind two models of the way people process information about their world. One model (attribution theories) views people as scientists who take observable events and attempt to determine the causes behind them. The second model (social cognition) sees people as having preconceived notions and expectations that they attempt to support. Let us examine the attribution process and the biases associated with it before we turn to the social cognition model.

The Attribution Process

The **attribution model** suggests that we act like scientists in our everyday world. We observe behaviors and attempt to determine whether they are caused by the actor or the environment. If we decide that the actor was

The voters had only a limited view of Ferraro. However, based on this information they had to attribute traits and attitudes and determine what type of vice president she would make. Person perception involves inferring traits from observable behavior.

responsible, we ask what the behavior tells us about that actor. In taking this final step we often attribute traits or characteristics to the actor. For example, let us assume that we met Ferraro during her campaign. She smiled at us and shook our hand. From these actions we would begin the attribution process of trying to determine why she did this (internal or external causes) and what these behaviors indicated about her.

Internal versus External Causes.   One of the first objectives in getting to know people is to figure out what causes their actions. For example, did they act because of some inner need, attitude, or ability? Or did outside events or situations cause their behavior? If we think there is an internal cause, then we learn something about that particular person. However, if we decide that there is an external cause, then we learn about the situation the person is in, but not about the person's characteristics.

Harold Kelley (1967) uses the example of seeing a woman, Mary, laugh while watching a movie. We have two choices in deciding what caused Mary's laughter: (1) it could be caused by Mary herself (she has a good sense of humor, she laughs at anything and everything); or (2) it could result from the situation Mary is in (the movie is so funny that anyone who saw it would laugh).

According to Kelley (Kelley, 1973; Kelley & Michele, 1980), we can make our decision on the basis of answers to the following three questions:

1. How distinctive is the behavior? Does Mary respond this way to all such situations (all movies) or only to this particular situation (this movie)? If Mary laughs only at this movie, it is a funny movie. If Mary laughs at most movies, however, we are more likely to decide that the behavior is caused by a personal characteristic of Mary's.
2. How do other people respond to the same situation? If everyone responds in the same way to an event, we assume that the behavior is caused by the event. But if Mary is the only person responding this way to this particular event, we assume her behavior is caused by something in her.
3. How consistent is the person's behavior? Does Mary laugh every time she sees this movie? If there is no consistency in her behavior, then we can't really infer anything about her from this behavior.

Making Specific Inferences.   Determining that an action is internally caused is only half the battle in making an attribution. We also have to decide what the particular action tells us about the person. For example, imagine that we hear Geraldine Ferraro give a speech strongly supporting the Equal Rights Amendment. As voters, we are not in a position to know whether she truly believes this position or has taken it for some other reason. We are in a position only to observe the action (the speech) and its effects (wild cheering by some members of the audience and heckling by others). From these observations we must now make inferences about Ferraro's internal belief. How do we do this?

According to Jones and Davis (1965), we must first ask ourselves which of the effects Ferraro *knew* would follow her speech and whether or not she had the *ability* to create these effects. On the basis of these decisions we must decide what effects she *intended* to follow her action. And finally we attribute some underlying trait or disposition to her.

Although this sounds rather involved, it is really a straightforward process that we can demonstrate by focussing back on Ferraro. Let us assume that we decide Ferraro knew only that cheering and support would follow her speech. This puts us in a quandary: We must now decide either that she intended this effect or that she intended to state her true position on the issue. If we assume that she intended only to elicit the cheering, we cannot make any inference about her true attitude on the issue. This is a situation that often arises in political campaigns. We believe that candidates are only taking a certain position to get votes, and therefore we cannot make an attribution about their internal beliefs.

On the other hand, let's assume that we decide that Ferraro knew she would be heckled and lose some support because of her position. We would not decide that her intention was to be the target of heckling. Rather, we would decide that she intended to express her opinion on the issue despite the expected reaction of part of the audience. Once we assume this intention, we can make the attribution that Ferraro truly does support the Equal Rights Amendment.

As we pointed out, the ultimate aim of the attribution process is to explain other people's behavior. Once we can do this, we can also begin to predict their future actions (Shaver, 1973). Therefore, assigning a trait or disposition to a person not only explains his or her present behavior but also predicts future behavior. Once we decide that Ferraro supports the ERA, we would expect her to work to get this amendment passed if she were to become vice president.

Tendencies and Biases in Attribution

The attribution model is very rational. If we were to build a robot to make attributions, we would program it to follow exactly these principles. But while the result might be a machine that spits out very logical inferences, it would not duplicate the attributions made by people. And though we might like to consider ourselves as rational, logical human beings, we know that we are not always completely rational and unemotional. Just as our feelings and biases affect how we act, they also influence how we make attributions about other people. Since these biases are very interesting and revealing, let us quickly examine how some of them affect our attributions.

Hedonic Relevance. Consider this situation: You observe a young man break into the front of a long line of people waiting to purchase the few remaining tickets to a Prince concert. If you were merely passing by, you might see this action as somewhat rude, but you might also try to explain it by saying that other people in the line were "saving his space." However, if you were one of the people in line, your attribution would probably not be so kind; you would probably see this man as terribly rude and uncaring. The difference in the two cases is that in the first situation the behavior did not directly affect you, whereas in the second situation it did. **Hedonic relevance** refers to the degree to which a person's behavior is rewarding or costly to the observer.

Hedonic relevance influences attributions in two ways. First, it increases the likelihood that a person's behavior will be seen as representing an underlying trait or disposition. In our previous example this means that the person waiting in line would be more likely to attribute a trait to the line-breaker than would the passerby. The second consequence of hedonic relevance is that it increases the extremity of the evaluation. While the passerby may see the line-breaker as somewhat rude, the person waiting in line would see this same man as very rude. The important point to remember in this example is that the behavior of the person is exactly the same in both cases. Therefore a completely rational attribution would not take into account whether or not the observer was affected by it.

Overemphasizing Behavior/Underemphasizing Context. Suppose that your professor designates you to argue in a debate the position that the tuition in your school should be raised so high that only the rich can afford it. Wanting to do well in the course, you comply with the assignment. At a later time you may be surprised to find that a number of your classmates believe you truly feel that higher education should be available only to the rich. In this case, your classmates are attributing an attitude to you solely on the basis of your behavior; they have failed to give sufficient weight to the situation in which your behavior occurred. A truly accurate attributor would carefully review both the behavior and the context in which it took place. Unfortunately, research (Jellison & Green, 1981; Jones, 1979) has shown that the tendency to overemphasize behavior and underemphasize context occurs in a wide variety of situations.

Actor and Observer Differences. During the Ferraro-Bush debate Geraldine Ferraro blasted the Republican administration for taking the role of aggressor in Central America. She felt that Reagan and Bush were creating a dangerous situation in the area that could eventually lead to widespread war. George Bush responded that their approach was a defensive one. He argued that they were only responding to the situation: Russian- and Cuban-backed troops had moved into the area, forcing the United States to defend its interests. Both Ferraro and Bush were addressing the same situation. But Ferraro attributed U.S. actions to the aggressive character of the Reagan-Bush administration, while Bush attributed these same actions to the situation itself. While we will not question here the validity of these attributions, Jones and Nisbett (1972) report that there is a general tendency for people to view the behavior of others as being caused by internal traits, while they see their own behavior as being determined by the situation they are in. Two possible reasons have been suggested to explain this interesting bias.

One reason is that people have more information about themselves than they do about others (Monson & Snyder, 1977). In other words, we know that we tend to behave differently in different situations. However, since we do not know the history of other people, we may assume that their behavior is less varied than our own and therefore caused by their personal traits.

Another reason has to do with the *salience* of information. (What is salient in a situation would be what is outstanding or what we focus on.) When we observe other people acting, our attention is focussed on them and they become the most central piece of information. However, when we act, our attention is focussed on the environment. There is a great deal of evidence that we base our attributions on the most salient information in a setting. In one study experimenters told subjects to focus their attention on one member of a pair during a conversation (Taylor & Fiske, 1975). Subjects rated the member on whom they had focussed as being the person who directed the flow of conversation. Taking another approach, investigators found that when actors were forced to focus their attention on themselves (acting in front of a mirror), they made attributions more like an observer's (Duval & Hensley, 1976). Hence salience of the stimulus influences the attributions we will make.

The Order of Information. When we sat down to write about the life of Geraldine Ferraro, we were faced with an interesting dilemma: How should we present her story to the readers? We were clear about the points we wanted to emphasize—her strong religious beliefs, her devotion to her family, her liberal position on abortion and the Equal Rights Amendment, her loyalty to the Democratic Party, her strong drive and efficiency, and her nomination as the first woman vice presidential candidate of a major party. Given this agreement on the information, you may question what caused our hesitation. Our dilemma centered on how to present the information: In what order should we give the facts? Should we begin with Ferraro's present political career and then discuss her family and religious

First impressions are very important in influencing attributions. Later information is often interpreted to fit first impressions.

orientation, or should we use the reverse order? Would the order in which we presented the information affect your impression of Ferraro? As we will see, the answer to this question supports the Chinese proverb that cautions a storyteller to be less concerned with the details of the story than with the way in which those details are presented.

If we followed strictly logical rules in making attributions, the order in which we receive information would make no difference in our final impression. However, once again, the research suggests that we do not follow the rules of logic when making attributions. In general, the first information we receive has greater influence than later information; in other words, there is a **primacy effect** influencing our attributions. In order to demonstrate this effect, consider the following two descriptions:

Person A	Person B
intelligent	envious
industrious	stubborn
impulsive	critical
critical	impulsive
stubborn	industrious
envious	intelligent

What is the general impression you get of these two people? Solomon Asch (1946) gave these descriptions to subjects and asked them to give their impression of the person described. Despite the fact that the information is the same in both lists, people gave Person A a more positive rating than Person B. As you can see, the only difference in the two lists is that the positive traits come first in Person A's description, while they come last in the list for Person B.

In addition to general impressions of personality, there is also evidence for a primacy effect in impressions of intelligence. A group of researchers had subjects observe a person answering 30 multiple-choice questions (Jones et al., 1968). In all conditions, the person answered 15 questions correctly. However, in one condition, the person started off very well but missed a number of questions toward the end. In the other case, the person began slowly but did very well at the end. After observing the person, subjects were asked to rate his or her intelligence and predict how well he or she would do on the next series of problems. The person who did well in the beginning was rated as more intelligent and more likely to succeed in the future than the person who did poorly in the beginning.

In general, primacy effects are strongest when we are judging stable characteristics such as personality or intelligence. Clearly the message here is that if you want someone to form a good impression of you, it is most important that your first encounter be the best. The first information people receive about you will have the strongest influence on their overall impression.

There are a number of explanations for the primacy effect (Asch & Zukier, 1984). One suggests that we form an impression on the basis of the first information we receive and then interpret later information to fit this impression. For example, if we decide that a person is intelligent, we may interpret "critical" as meaning thoughtful or thorough. However, if we decide the person is envious, we may interpret "critical" to mean nasty or negative. Looking at performance, if a person does well on an early test and we decide he or she is intelligent, we may explain away later poor performance as being due to the person's temporary state (a sleepless night before the test) or to the environment (the test was not a good one). Similarly, if we decide that a person is unintelligent on the basis of early performance, later good performance can be explained as being due to luck. In each of these cases, we can maintain our first impressions by the way we interpret later information.

The Social Cognition Model

As we have seen, the attribution model presents a picture of people carefully sifting through information (although often using biased rules) before arriving at a position (attribution). The **social cognition model** takes a different position (Fiske & Taylor, 1984). It argues that people have **schemas**, or preconceived notions about how their social world works. These schemas can be about events such as going to the circus, roles or occupations such as politician or professor, or specific people such as your roommate or yourself. They influence the way we interpret events and even the information we remember. Once a schema is formed, we tend to process information in a way that supports the schema (Cantor & Mischel, 1979). According to the social cognition position, this process is automatic. That is, we don't recall a schema and then intentionally try to support it. Rather, schemas are always present in our minds, guiding the way we deal with our world.

In order to show how schemas influence our interpretation of events and people, investigators had students rate the facial expression of "Kurt Walden" (Rothbart & Birrell, 1977). Some students were told that Walden was a Nazi Gestapo leader who carried out cruel experiments during World War II. Others were told he was a leader of the anti-Nazi underground movement and that he saved thousands of Jews. Subjects who believed

Walden was a Nazi rated his facial expression as hard, cruel, and frowning, whereas students who believed he had saved lives rated his face as warm and kindly. Thus students' preconceived notions about a Nazi leader and an anti-Nazi leader affected how they viewed his picture.

Schemas also influence how we recall past information. In one study students saw a film of a traffic accident (Loftus & Palmer, 1973). They were then asked to report how fast the cars were going "when they *smashed* into each other" or "when they *hit* each other." Subjects who were asked the question containing the word *smashed* gave higher estimates of speed than subjects who were asked the question containing the word *hit*. Further, when they were asked a week later whether they recalled seeing broken glass in the film, twice as many subjects who had been asked the *smashed* question reported seeing broken glass compared with the *hit* group. Actually, the film showed no broken glass; the students' preconception about the effect of cars "smashing into each other" influenced what they remembered seeing.

The attribution and social cognition models suggest two of the ways in which we process information and form impressions of others. Both models are useful in helping us understand this complex process and both identify some interesting biases and tendencies in the way we perceive our world. The models raise some points that are important to remember. First, we do not intentionally misrepresent our world or the people in it. We call it as we see it, but the way we see it may not be completely accurate. Second, we generally believe that our perceptions reflect reality. We rarely take into account a possible bias in our own perceptions, though we have little trouble believing that people whose perceptions do not agree with ours are biased. Finally, despite the problems associated with these processes, they are necessary if we are to function in our world. We are bombarded with too much information every day to remember and store it all. We must organize it and choose what is important. The assignment of traits or dispositions and the development of schemas help us in this necessary task.

Consequences of Forming Impressions: The Self-Fulfilling Prophecy

We may feel it is unfortunate that people form impressions on the basis of so little information. On the other hand, we may argue that impressions are a personal thing and that no one is hurt by an impression. We may also believe that first impressions should be easy to change as more information is provided. This is far from true, however. First impressions often prove difficult to change because they set in motion a chain of events known as the self-fulfilling prophecy.

The self-fulfilling prophecy follows this pattern:

1. Person A develops a first impression of Person B.
2. Person A then acts toward Person B in a way consistent with the first impression.
3. Person B responds to Person A's behavior in a way that confirms the first impression.
4. Person A's first impression becomes more rigid in light of Person B's behavior.

Rosenthal and Jacobson (1968) present a dramatic example of how this process may intrude into the classroom. These investigators told elementary-school teachers that tests had indicated that some of their students could be expected to out-perform other students. These "high achievers"

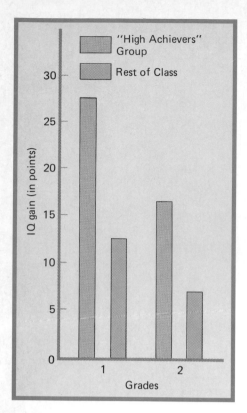

Figure 15-2
In this study, the teacher's expectations about students' ability created a self-fulfilling prophecy and led to the "high achievers" performing better.

were clearly identified to the teachers. In fact, no tests had been given; these "high achievers" had simply been chosen at random. At the end of the school year, the students' IQs were measured. As can be seen from Figure 15–2, the "high achievers" dramatically outperformed the other students in the classroom—despite the fact that there were no real differences in the ability of any of these students. The only difference was the expectations of the teachers.

The teachers could have fulfilled their expectations in a number of ways. They may have smiled at and given more reinforcement to the "bright" students. Because of this reinforcement, the "bright" students may have begun to try harder than students who did not receive this support. The teachers may have assigned more challenging and difficult tasks to the "bright" students. In this way, the students were encouraged to use their abilities to the fullest. Finally, the teachers may have given more feedback and spent more time with the "bright" students. Each of these efforts would have helped the students perform better and thereby reinforced the teachers' first impression. The interesting point in this and similar research is that the teachers were totally unaware that they were responding more favorably toward some students. Thus the self-fulfilling prophecy occurs without the awareness of the parties involved.

The self-fulfilling prophecy is found in a wide range of situations and can involve either positive or negative expectations (Crano & Mellon, 1978). As you can see, these events help cement first impressions and give importance to the study of how people make attributions from minimal information.

INTERPERSONAL ATTRACTION

As we have seen, we make attributions about and form impressions of people every day. In reading about Geraldine Ferraro, for instance, we attempt to determine what she is like on the basis of the information we have. In our interpersonal relations an equally common process involves our decision about whether we like or dislike someone. In the proper sense, **attraction** can be defined as a positive attitude we have about another person (Hendrick & Hendrick, 1983). Like the other attitudes we discussed earlier in this chapter, attraction often influences our behavior with specific other people; we move toward those people to whom we are attracted and away from those to whom we are not attracted. And, as we saw with attribution and impression formation, we often make decisions about how attracted we are to another person without being aware of the factors affecting our attitude. For this reason it is interesting to examine the reasons we are attracted to others; some of these will seem only common sense, while others may surprise you. We will also see that there is no foolproof way to curry attraction; each method has its exceptions.

In order to understand the reasons behind the "ties that bind," we will focus on some of the relationships in Ferraro's life and speculate about their foundation.

Reward

When Geraldine Ferraro began her quest for Congress in 1978, she asked Tip O'Neill to appear in the district on her behalf. O'Neill consented, and this began a close friendship between the pair that was to pave Ferraro's way to the vice presidential nomination. After Ferraro won her race, she became a loyal supporter of O'Neill in the House. She helped organize an effort to restore some of the speaker's power that had been stripped away in previous years. O'Neill responded by placing Ferraro on the committees she wanted and eventually suggesting her for the vice presidential nomination.

While this trading-of-favors view of the Ferraro-O'Neill friendship may seem rather crass, many investigators have suggested that we do view our relationships as economic transactions (Homans, 1974; Lindskold, 1982). We weigh the rewards and costs and are attracted to those poeple who provide the greatest profit for us. The rewards and costs include many items, such as emotions, materials, power, security, or, as in the O'Neill-Ferraro case, political advancement. According to this position, social relationships are similar to business transactions: We are attracted to people who reward us and are repelled by those who are a burden to us.

There is considerable evidence supporting the view that we like people who reward us, and there have been many interesting extensions of the reward hypothesis. One extension is that we like not only the people who directly reward us but also those who are around us when good things happen to us—even if they had nothing to do with the positive event. For example, Veitch and Griffit (1976) found that a stranger who appeared in a room after a subject heard good news was liked better than one who appeared after the subject heard bad news.

The strategy we use to give rewards also influences attraction. Investigators had subjects hold a conversation with another person (who was actually an experimental accomplice) (Aronson & Linder, 1965). The subjects then "overheard" the accomplice on a number of occasions making evaluative statements about them. Some subjects heard the accomplice make only positive and rewarding statements (positive-positive). Other subjects heard the accomplice making only negative comments (negative-negative). In the negative-positive condition, the accomplice began by making negative statements about the subjects, but the evaluations became increasingly positive as the conversations continued. The final group of subjects (positive-negative) heard the accomplice begin with positive evaluations, but the remarks became increasingly negative.

Afterward the subjects were asked to rate how much they liked the accomplice. In which condition do you think attraction was highest? As can be seen in Table 15–1, subjects were most attracted to the other person when she began her evaluation of them by making derogatory comments but

Table 15–1
The Gain-Loss Effect on Ratings in the Aronson and Linder Study

Experimental Condition	Mean
Negative-positive	+7.67
Positive-positive	+6.42
Negative-negative	+2.52
Positive-negative	+0.87

Source: Aronson and Linder (1965).

We generally like people who reward and validate our attitudes and decisions.

later switched to positive, rewarding comments. Interestingly, the number of rewarding statements was lower in this condition than in the positive-positive condition—rated the second most attractive condition. The results indicate that subjects were least attracted to the accomplice when she began with positive comments, but later switched to negative evaluations—a phenomenon referred to as the gain-loss effect. One explanation for these results is that a need for positive reward was created when the accomplice began by making negative statements, and her later positive comments satisfied this need. In the positive-positive condition, the subject did not have as strong a need for positive reward.

Despite the strong pull of rewards, there is one case in which they can turn us off a relationship. That is when we think the other person is rewarding us simply to curry favor (Jones & Wortman, 1973). People in positions of power or high status constantly have to decide whether others are giving them rewards and compliments because they genuinely believe they deserve them or because they want something in return. For example, Tip O'Neill was impressed by Geraldine Ferraro's honest approach: She directly asked him to campaign on her behalf. His reaction might have been very different if Ferraro had set the stage for this request by telling O'Neill that he was the greatest leader she had ever seen or by sending him expensive gifts. When we do receive rewards, we must engage in the attribution process to determine the sincerity and intent of the giver.

Birds of a Feather . . . Similarity

During her years in the Queens district attorney's office, Ferraro's closest relationship was with Pat Flynn, her secretary. Flynn had children about the same age as Ferraro's, and she, too, had gone to work after spending time at home raising a family. When Ferraro moved to Washington to begin serving in the House of Representatives, her earliest friendships were with other congresswomen. They often went out together in the evenings and discussed topics ranging from women's political issues to clothes to where their kids might find summer jobs. In both instances, Ferraro was attracted to people who shared many things in common with her.

There has been a large amount of research showing that similarity is one of the strongest predictors of attraction (Byrne, 1971). The similarity can be on almost any dimension, including attitudes, ability, intelligence, economic condition, race, height, physical attractiveness, and sometimes personality. As with most rules, there are also some exceptions to the similarity-attraction relationship. It seems that we are not attracted to people who have a characteristic that we do not admire in ourselves (Goldman & Olczak, 1976). For example, if you are unhappy with the fact that you weigh 345 pounds, you will not necessarily be attracted to another person who weighs 345 pounds. There is also evidence that having certain opposite personal needs and motives may lead to attraction. If you have a strong need to be dominant, for example, you may be attracted to a submissive person. In this relationship your needs will not be in conflict with your partner's needs.

There are several possible reasons for this similarity-attraction effect. First, similar others tend to validate our own opinions and actions, and this validation is rewarding. For example, if you have just purchased a new jeep, it is gratifying to find someone else who has just bought a jeep. Seeing that others have done the same thing makes you feel that your own action was not unusual or incorrect. A second reason for the similarity-attraction relationship is that we often expect to have a positive interaction with similar others. For example, if you were raised on a farm, you would have a great deal to discuss with another person raised on a farm. You might have a somewhat more difficult time engaging in conversation with

Ferraro attempted to establish her similarity with the groups to whom she spoke. In this group of women, she emphasized her sex. Research shows that people are attracted to others they view as similar.

someone who was raised in a large city and has very different opinions and interests. A third reason is that we expect similar others to like us. Since we enjoy being liked, we are attracted to those similar others. Thus there are a number of reasons why "birds of a feather flock together" (and like each other).

To Be Near You . . . Proximity

As her fame and responsibilities grew, Geraldine Ferraro became increasingly uneasy about the lack of time she was spending with her family. She placed great importance on the family spending time together. During the early years of her marriage she chose to forego a law career in order to be with her growing family. As a prosecuter, she sometimes annoyed her colleagues by refusing to work long hours of overtime at the office. She insisted that her job not keep her apart from her family. She faced an interesting dilemma when she was elected to Congress: How could she work in Washington and still have the time she wanted with her family? She devised a plan whereby she would fly to Washington on Monday morning, stay overnight, and fly home the next evening. She would then return to Washington on Wednesday morning, stay overnight, and fly home again on Friday for the weekend. In this way she would only be apart from her family for two nights a week. Her aides took to calling the Eastern shuttle between Washington and New York the "Ferraro Shuttle." This arrangement soon proved unworkable, but Ferraro continued to find ways to spend as much time as possible with her family. Was this concern about her family worth all the trouble? If you examine your own relationships, do you find yourself choosing friends from among the people you see most often?

As far back as 1932, Bossard noticed a relationship between physical closeness (**proximity**) and attraction. In examining the application for marriage licenses in Philadelphia, he found that an overwhelming number of the engaged people tended to live close to their partners-to-be (Bossard, 1932). Clearly these results could occur for two reasons: It is possible that people who like each other choose to live close together. Or it is possible that simply being close together leads people to like each other.

In order to test the latter possibility, Festinger, Schachter, and Back (1950) studied friendships in a married-student housing project. Couples in this project were randomly assigned to apartments so that there was no chance that previous attraction would influence where they lived. During the course of the year the residents were asked to indicate whom they were most friendly with. The results showed that 44 percent of the couples were most friendly with their next-door neighbor, while only 10 percent were most friendly with people who lived down the hall. The fact that proximity leads to liking has been found in dormitories, intercity housing projects, and surveys of residential neighborhoods.

There are many reasons why proximity leads to liking. Simple familiarity is one. There is a great deal of research showing that the more we are exposed to a person, name, or song, the more we come to like it (Moreland & Zajonc, 1982; Zajonc, 1970). This may be one of the reasons politicians are so determined to get the most media coverage possible. They will often go to great lengths just to be seen by the public. Another reason for the proximity effect is that people who are physically close are more likely to reward each other than people who are physically distant. Finally, since it is a fact that people must interact with those who are physically close to them, it is certainly more comfortable to like these people than to dislike them (Berscheid & Walster, 1978).

Proximity does not always lead to liking, however. FBI statistics show that muggings, murders, robberies, and assaults are most likely to be committed by people in the victims' family or neighborhood (Berscheid & Walster, 1978).

The Way You Look . . . Physical Attractiveness

Voters were attracted to Ferraro for a number of reasons. She captured their imagination with her strength, wit, and grasp of the issues. Another possible reason was her appearance. California Representative Tony Coelho said that Ferraro had just the right appearance. "She's a beautiful person, but she's not glamorous. She has a very nice physique, but it's not a Miss America bathing suit contest physique" (Katz, 1984, p. 156). The issue of physical appearance became a central topic in the 1984 campaign after the first Reagan-Mondale debate. When the media reported that Reagan looked old and tired, Reagan replied that, unlike his opponent, he hadn't been wearing makeup during the debate. It seems that physical appearance not only influences whom we choose as friends, but also whom we choose as leaders.

We pointed out earlier that we often use physical appearance as the basis for our attributions about people's personality and intelligence (see Highlight on p. 524). Research has shown that our attraction to others is also affected by their physical appearance. Several studies have found that physically attractive people are liked better and judged to be more pleasant than less attractive people (Kleck & Rubenstein, 1975; Walster et al., 1966). For example, Walster and her colleagues arranged dates at a dance for subjects. Before the dance a panel of judges rated the physical attractiveness of each subject. During an intermission at the dance subjects were asked how much they liked their partners. The results indicated that liking was directly related to the partner's physical attractiveness: Attractive partners were liked more than unattractive partners.

Results such as these might suggest that a person of average or less than average attractiveness is doomed to a life of loneliness. This, however, is not the case. While research shows that we are usually attracted to the most physically attractive people, other research shows that we tend to become romantically involved with people whose physical attractiveness is about equal to our own (Murstein, 1972). This "matching rule" probably results because we fear rejection by someone who is "out of our league" in terms of physical attractiveness. Thus, while we may desire the most attractive person around, we are most likely to wind up with someone who is about as attractive as we are.

The Many Roads to Attraction

It should be very clear by now that there are many reasons for interpersonal attraction. This explains why a single individual may have a variety of friends. He or she may be attracted to some of them because they live close by; others may be friends because they have similar attitudes or backgrounds; still others may be included in the circle of friends because of their ability to give rewards. Table 15–2 lists eight reasons why we are attracted to others. A review of your own history may give you additional reasons.

Table 15–2
Gateways to Friendship

We like people who:
1. reward us
2. like us
3. are similar to use
4. live close to us
5. are physically attractive
6. are around us when good things happen
7. like the same people and things we like
8. satisfy our needs

While we may desire the most attractive person around, we are most likely to become romantically involved with someone of comparable attractiveness to ourselves.

JUDGING PEOPLE BY THEIR COVERS

Of all the biases in attribution, the tendency to use physical appearance to determine traits is one of the strongest. Throughout our lives we are cautioned against judging people by their looks: "Don't judge a book by its cover." General George Patton is said to have bought his daughter the ugliest dog he could find in order to teach her that ugly things can be loveable. Despite the wisdom in these cautions, research shows that people make a number of attributions on the basis of physical appearance. As we will see, almost any physical trait can be used as the basis for attributions.

Beauty
Being physically attractive may elicit a wide range of positive attributions from others. Attractiveness is often associated with intelligence. For example, fifth-grade teachers were shown a number of report cards (Clifford & Walster, 1973). Although all carried the same information, a

picture of an attractive boy or girl was attached to some cards, and a picture of an unattractive student was attached to other cards. Teachers rated the attractive students as more intelligent and more likely to do good work than the unattractive students. In addition to being thought intelligent, research has found that physically attractive people are seen as being happier, more pleasant, more sensitive, kinder, more poised, and more outgoing than unattractive people (Adams & Huston, 1975). Remember that the raters in this research never met or interacted with the people; they made these attributions solely on the basis of pictures.

Another somewhat startling effect is that physically attractive people are often seen as being less guilty of committing a crime than are unattractive people. Efran (1974) asked subjects to decide the fate of a defendant in a college cheating case. The facts of the case were

held constant, but in some conditions the defendant was attractive, while in others the defendant was unattractive. Physically attractive defendants were better liked, judged less guilty, and received milder punishments than unattractive defendants. One exception to this finding is that attractive people are seen as guiltier and deserving of stronger sentences when the crime involves taking advantage of one's attractiveness, such as a confidence game or swindle (Sigall & Ostrove, 1975).

Another exception to the attractiveness-good relationship is found in people's perception of business executives. Research suggests that while attractiveness is an asset to males throughout their careers, it may actually hinder women as they move into higher levels of management (Heilman & Stopeck, 1985). People tended to attribute the success of attractive female managers more to social

HELPING BEHAVIOR

When Ferraro first ran for Congress, she was in danger of losing. Her opponent was better known to the voters and had a strong organization behind him. Ferraro appealed to tip O'Neill and President Carter for help. She was pleasantly surprised when O'Neill came in person to speak for her and President Carter sent Miss Lillian. Neither O'Neill nor Carter knew Ferraro, but both came to her aid and helped her win the election.

We might find it odd that such simple acts of **helping behavior** could be viewed as so unusual; surely people go out of their way to help each other many times a day. Unfortunately, a look at any newspaper will provide us with many examples of situations where desperately needed help was not given. One of the more publicized cases involved a young woman named Kitty Genovese.

At 3:20 A.M. on March 13, 1964, Kitty Genovese got off the subway in the borough of Queens in New York City and began walking home. A man brandishing a knife came out of the dark, grabbed her, and began beating her. Kitty screamed for help, broke away, and ran down the street. The man followed her and stabbed her. Again the young woman escaped, screaming, "He stabbed me! Please help me!" Lights went on in apartments

graces than to competence or ability. Attractive female managers were judged to be less capable than unattractive female managers, even though the actual performance of the two managers was found to be the same.

Eyeglasses

For many people, wearing eyeglasses is inconvenient and annoying. However, for observers, eyeglasses serve as the basis for attributing intelligence. In one study, subjects were shown a videotape of a person sitting at a desk (Argyle & McHenry, 1971). In some cases, the person was wearing eyeglasses, while in others he was not. Subjects rated the person wearing glasses as more intelligent than the one not wearing glasses.

Body and Facial Hair

The amount and color of hair can trigger a number of attributions. Verinis and Roll (1970) found that college students felt that men with a lot of body hair were more virile, active, and potent than men with less body hair. Bearded men are seen as more masculine, dominant, liberal, and courageous than men with cleanshaven faces (Pellegrini, 1973). An old advertisement for hair coloring proclaimed that "blondes have more fun." Apparently, most of us agree. Research shows that people perceive blond women as being more warm, beautiful, and entertaining than brunettes. On the other hand, brunettes are seen as being more intelligent than blonds. Interestingly, dark-haired men are seen as being more masculine, ambitious, and rugged than blond or red-haired men (Lawson, 1971).

Dress

In an interesting study Darley and Cooper (1972) set up two tables for political candidates at a shopping center. The tables contained no information about the positions of the candidates. However, three well-dressed college students sat at one table, and three long-haired students dressed in jeans and work shirts sat at the other. When passersby were questioned about the positions of the candidates, they saw the candidate supported by the long-haired group of students as being more liberal with regard to gun control, legalization of marijuana, and the Asian policy of the United States than the candidate supported by the well-dressed students.

This research shows that while our physical appearance may be only skin deep, it serves as the basis for attributions made about characteristics deep inside us: intelligence, personality, and attitudes. These attributions are made despite the fact that people have little control over whether or not they are blond or brunette, wear glasses, have a great deal of body hair, or are physically attractive.

Does the young man need help? In cases when it is difficult to determine the needs of the victim, helping is unlikely to take place.

overlooking the scene. The attacker again caught up with Kitty, and this time his attack was fatal; Kitty Genovese lay dead on the sidewalk. It was estimated that the incident lasted almost 45 minutes and at least 38 people heard the young woman's screams for help, yet not a single person came to her aid or even lifted the telephone to call the police. Had one person given some type of help, it is likely that Kitty Genovese would have been saved.

More recently (February 1982) newspapers carried the story of a 62-year-old grandmother who was beaten and tied to a chair. She managed to inch her way out of the office where the attack took place and into the middle of a busy street. There she sat in disbelief as numerous cars passed her by. It was 2 hours before anyone stopped to help her.

Stories such as these give us reason to wonder: Are humans really as uncaring and insensitive as these examples suggest? Certainly helping someone in need seems a simple behavior that should occur almost automatically. If this is so, why don't people help others in need?

Why Do People Help . . . Or Not Help

Using our two examples, Geraldine Ferraro's campaign and Kitty Genovese's murder, we can ask why people helped Ferraro but not Genovese. There are obviously a number of differences in the two cases, but let's use them to speculate about the reasons for helping.

Rewards. It would be nice to believe that people are basically good and that they help others out of the goodness of their hearts. No so, argue many scholars who have studied helping behavior (Bar-Tal, 1984; Blau, 1964). They suggest that people make decisions about helping in the same way they decide about many of their other behaviors; that is, they consider the cost of the behavior and the rewards that will follow. If the rewards will be greater than the costs, they help. However, if the costs will exceed the rewards, they do not help. We could therefore argue that O'Neill and Carter helped Ferraro because they believed that if she won, she would pay them back by supporting their positions in Congress. However, the situation of the people who heard Kitty Genovese screaming was very different. If they tried to help, they could suffer grave personal injury or death, and there would be little payoff for them even if their efforts were successful.

This seems to be a terribly cold way to view human behavior. We can counter this cold view by pointing out that people give to charities designed to aid others they don't even know. For example, why did Americans give so much food and other aid to people starving in Ethiopia in 1984 and 1985? The Ethiopians could give the donors nothing in return; they didn't even know the names of the people who contributed. However, the reward theory can be used to explain these charitable acts. It has been argued that helping others can lead us to feel powerful (Worchel, 1984) and reduce our unpleasant feelings such as guilt for or empathy with the unfortunate (Hoffman, 1984). In order to illustrate this point, recall how you felt on seeing pictures of starving Ethiopian children; these pictures probably caused you to suffer as you experienced some of the pain these innocent victims were feeling. One way for you to reduce your own discomfort would be to send food or money to the victims. If you did so, you were helping others to help yourself. Research also shows that we will help someone even if we have been made to feel guilty in a situation completely unconnected with that person (Regan et al., 1972). Thus helping may be motivated by a desire to make ourselves feel good; the silver lining here is that we do feel bad when we see others suffer.

Norms. Norms are general rules of behavior that apply to everyone (see Chapter 16). There are, in fact, many norms that guide our helping behavior. For example, the *norm of social responsibility* states that we should help people in need without concern for future exchanges (Berkowitz, 1972; Schwartz & Howard, 1984). In addition, there is the Golden Rule, which says that we should "Do unto others what we would have them do unto us." In support of these norms, research has found that people are more willing to help others who are dependent on them than people who are not (Berkowitz & Connor, 1966).

There is, however, another side to the norm story. We also live by a norm that dictates that we should respect other people's privacy; in other words, "mind your own business." This norm may make us reluctant to become involved with people for fear of invading their privacy. For example, some of the people who overheard Kitty Genovese's screams may have thought she was simply having a fight with her boyfriend. They may not have become involved for fear of embarrassing both her and themselves.

The Decision to Help

Up to this point we have been talking about helping behavior as if it involved one simple decision to help or not to help. A closer look, however, reveals that the situation is more complex than that.

Latané and Darley (1970) suggest that the decision to help involves a number of steps. If any one of these steps is not taken, the individual will not help. First, the individual must *notice* the person in distress. Second, he or she must *interpret* the situation as an emergency and decide that the person does indeed need help. Next, the individual must *decide* that he or she has a responsibility to help. Fourth, the individual must have the *ability* to supply the appropriate form of assistance. For example, if you see someone having a heart attack, you may be reluctant to help because you do not know how to aid the victim. Finally, the individual who has gone through each of these steps must decide to implement the decision to help.

Each of these steps is necessary before an individual will help. Let us examine them in turn.

Noticing the Victim.   In order for bystanders to help, they must notice the victim. This seems so obvious, yet it is a point often overlooked. The more salient or noticeable the victim is, the more likely it is that the victim will receive help. In an interesting study a confederate was placed on a subway (Piliavin et al., 1969). At one point during the ride the confederate collapsed on the floor, either because he was drunk (he smelled of alcohol) or because he was ill (he carried a black cane). A number of results from the study are of interest. The one most relevant to this discussion is that passengers seated near the victim were more likely to offer help than those seated farther away. In fact, in some cases, passengers who did not offer help moved farther away from the victim. Thus when the victim was clearly visible to the passengers, he was more likely to receive help. Bystanders who wanted to avoid helping moved so that the victim would be less salient to them.

Interpreting the Situation as an Emergency.   Not only must people see the victim, they must also know that the person needs help. For example, assume you notice a man and a woman fighting on a street corner. Is this a simple family squabble, or does the woman (or man) need rescuing? If the situation is the former and you decide to help, you may be embarrassed. Researchers set up just such a situation in which a woman was attacked by a man (Shotland & Straw, 1976). In one condition, she yelled, "I don't know you," in the middle of the fight; in the other, she made no reference to her relationship to the attacker. In the first case, 65 percent of the male bystanders intervened to help, while in the latter case, only 19 percent helped. When the assailant was unknown to the woman, it was clear that this was not a "lovers' quarrel" and she needed help.

Investigators attempted to identify the types of situations people interpreted as emergencies by having them rate a large number of theoretical situations (Shotland & Huston, 1979). As can be seen from Table 15–3, people generally agreed that emergencies were accidents where harm to the victim was evident or very likely. Least likely to be seen as an emergency were everyday problems where no harm to the victim was likely.

Assuming Responsibility: Is There Safety in Numbers?   Assume you knew that at 3 P.M. on a given day you were going to faint and that you would need the help of others to revive you. As the fateful time approached, would you rush to a busy street corner where there were many passersby, or would you choose a less popular side street where fewer people passed? Most of us would probably choose the busy street, thinking that in a crowd there would be at least one person who would stop to help us. Research, however, indicates that the majority choice may not be a wise one (Bar-Tal, 1976; Latané & Darley, 1970). In fact, indications are that when there are fewer people present, there is a greater chance of an individual receiving help.

In order to illustrate this phenomenon, Darley and Latané (1968) asked college students to participate in a discussion about their problems in adjusting to college life. When the subject arrived, he or she was told that in order to prevent embarrassment, subjects would communicate with each other from private booths over a sound system. There would be no face-to-face interaction. The subject was then led into a booth. In some

Table 15–3

Classification of Events
as Emergencies
or Nonemergencies

Event	Category
Definite emergency	
Cut artery, profuse bleeding	Accident
House ablaze, people screaming for help	Accident
Child poisoned	Accident
Child swallowed razor blade	Accident
Person in shock, lying on ground	Accident
Heart attack	Illness, disease
Airplane crash, some passengers still alive	Accident
Rape in progress	Act of violence
Car accident, driver motionless on ground	Accident
Drug overdose	Accident
Not sure	
Terminal cancer, 3 mos. to live	Illness, disease
Lost person in woods shouting for help	Miscellaneous
Car broken down on side of road	Everyday problem
Emergency landing by airplane, passengers shaken but unhurt	Accident
Burning leaves, no one attending, windy day	Accident
Rock stars in danger of being trampled by fans	Miscellaneous
Mildly intoxicated friend wants to drive home	Everyday problem
Blackout in neighborhood	Miscellaneous
Man on first date with woman he likes, no money	Everyday problem
Friend states he is miserable and depressed	Psychological and emotional problems
Probably not an emergency	
Car door chips other car's paint	Everyday problem
Telethon wants to get $20 million for muscular dystrophy	Miscellaneous
Car parked by fire hydrant	Everyday problem
Scraped knee	Everyday problem
Tramp panhandling	Everyday problem
Tray of hors d'oeuvres drops at party	Everyday problem
Child holds breath in protest	Everyday problem
Person loses dime in pay phone	Everyday problem
Cat is stuck in a tree	Everyday problem
Someone has cigar, no match	Everyday problem

Source: Shotland & Huston (1979).

cases, the subject believed that there would be only two people in the group. In other cases, the subject thought that there would be three people in the group. In the third condition, the subject believed that six people would participate in the discussion. Actually, there was only one subject in the study. The voices of other discussants were tape-recorded.

In the discussion one tape-recorded voice, designated as the "future victim," spoke first. He talked about some of his difficulties and then mentioned that he was prone to seizures in times of stress. After the other subjects spoke, the "victim" began to speak again. Suddenly he seemed to be having a seizure and said, "I-er-um-I think I-I need-er-if-if-could-er somebody er-er-er-er-er-er give me a little-er give me a little-er give me a little help here because I-er-I'm . . ." (chokes, then quiet) (Darley & Latané, 1968, p. 379). The experimenter, sitting outside the booth, recorded the amount of time it took the subject to search for help for the victim. As can be seen from Figure 15–3, the larger the group, the less likely the subjects were to help. In fact, 85 percent of the subjects helped if they believed that no one else knew of the victim's plight, while only 31 percent helped if they felt that four others (in the six-person group) knew of the victim's need.

How can we explain such an effect? One possible explanation is based on the notion of responsibility. When the subjects believed that they were

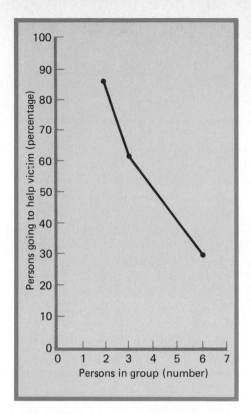

Figure 15–3
The research shows that the more people that are present in an emergency, the less likely it is that an observer will offer help.

the only ones who knew of the problem, they were likely to feel responsible for helping the victim. However, when there were other people present, the subject was not as likely to feel responsible for helping the victim. It was easy for the subject to think that "others must be doing something." How many times have you passed an accident on the road and said to yourself, "Someone must have already called the police?" Another possible reason for the effect involves the interpretation of the problem. In the large group the subject may have felt that the victim did not really need help because he or she did not hear anyone else making an effort to aid the victim. In this case, the subject used the response of the others to determine the extent of the emergency. When the subject was alone, however, he or she had to make a decision about the urgency of the situation based solely on a personal interpretation of the victim's plight.

Thus simply having a number of people present does not increase the likelihood of helping behavior. In such cases, bystanders may *diffuse* responsibility for helping.

Knowing How to Help. Imagine finding an unconscious woman on the sidewalk who is bleeding from the mouth and ears. You can see clearly that she needs help and that no one else is available. What do you do in this case? For most of us, this would be a very threatening situation. We have heard that it is dangerous to move an unconscious person. But do we leave the woman lying on the sidewalk and go search for medical help? Or do we stay with her, hoping someone else will come along? This type of dilemma may cause people to feel so helpless and that they take no action (Bar-Tal, 1976). In order to be of assistance, people must decide that they can take some action that will help the victim. Since many people do not have specific training in how to help in emergencies, they may decide that there is nothing they can do.

Taking Action. Even after going through all the earlier steps, the bystander must finally decide to take action. There are a number of variables that determine whether or not a person will actually decide to help. One involves his or her belief as to whether the victim actually deserves to be helped. In one study that was discussed earlier, subway riders were more likely to help the ill victim than the drunk victim (Piliavin et al., 1969). Presumably they felt that the ill person was deserving of help, while the drunk person was responsible for his plight and therefore did not deserve help. Another factor involves the costs of helping (see p. 526). Finally, even the mood of the individual influences whether he or she will offer help. For example, in one study subjects leaving a theater were asked to donate money to the Muscular Dystrophy Foundation (Underwood et al., 1977). The researchers found that moviegoers were more likely to donate if they had seen a happy movie than a sad one.

These studies give us a greater understanding of why people do not rush to help victims in situations such as the Genovese attack. Clearly helping behavior is complex and involves many decisions on the part of the helper. The social psychological research has identified many of the factors that influence helping behavior, and this research can serve as the basis for creating situations in which people will offer help.

Recipient Reactions to Helping

Our attention thus far has been focussed on the helper. We have been asking questions about why people help or do not help, and we have assumed that the victim wants help and will be glad to receive it. This may be the case in dire emergencies such as the Genovese example. But most situations of helping do not involve such immediate danger. You may offer to assist your roommate with his homework, for example, or to help a stranded stranger change a tire. Even though your offer of aid is made with the best of intentions, you may be surprised at the response you get. Instead of a friendly acceptance, the other person may tell you that your help is not needed, or may accept it only reluctantly. Social psychologists have begun to uncover the reasons behind such puzzling responses.

In order to understand this situation, we must view helping in the broader context of social interaction. Greenberg (1980) points out that accepting help often obligates the person to reciprocate at some later time: "One good deed deserves another." Therefore if someone does something nice for you, it is likely that you will feel indebted to that person. The feeling of indebtedness will create a tension that will not be reduced until you have returned the favor. Looking at helping in this way, we can see that some people will be reluctant to accept aid because they do not wish to feel obligated to reciprocate in the future.

Another consequence of helping is that it demonstrates a difference in power and competency between the helper and the recipient. In the helping relationship the helper indicates that he or she knows what should be done and how it should be done. On the other hand, the recipient may be admitting that he or she is incompetent to perform the task alone. In support of this position, research has shown that people like others with whom they can cooperate on an equal basis better than they like people who give them help (Worchel, 1984). Other investigators have argued that receiving help may lower one's self esteem (Nadler & Fisher, 1984; Rosen, 1984). They suggest that one of the motives for reciprocation is to regain status and self-esteem.

These findings increase our understanding of how people react to help, and they also offer another reason why people may be reluctant to give help. That is, people may not help because they fear that the recipient may feel uncomfortable or resent their aid. As you can see, helping can be a complex social interaction that involves many decisions and has many implications for social relationships.

Summary

1. **Social psychology** is the scientific study of the way in which people are affected by social situations and social relationships. Social psychologists attempt to develop theories to explain factors that influence most people most of the time.

2. **Attitudes** are learned, relatively enduring feelings about objects, events, or issues. They have three components: evaluation, belief, and action. Parents, peers, personal experience, and the media all play a role in the development of attitudes.

3. Attitude change involves substituting new attitudes for old ones. Research in this area has focussed on the communicator, the message, and the audience.

4. **Cognitive dissonance** theory is based on the assumption that people strive to have their attitudes, beliefs, and behaviors support one another. Dissonance theory suggests that changing behavior often causes people to change their attitudes. Both **foot-in-the-door**

and **door-in-the-face approaches** have also been found to change attitudes. These approaches are aimed at changing the way people feel about themselves.

5. **Attribution** involves inferring personal characteristics from observable behavior. In order to determine that an act tells us something about a person, we must decide what the person intended to achieve by a behavior. Intentions are determined by deciding both whether the actor knew the effects of a behavior and whether the actor had the ability to achieve these effects.

6. There are many biases in the attribution process. People make stronger attributions when the behavior affects them; there is also a bias toward giving more weight to the behavior than to the situational context it occurred in.

7. According to the **social cognition model,** people make attributions guided by schemas or preconceived notions about the world. These schemas influence our interpretations

of events and people; they even influence how we recall past information.

8. As a part of the attribution process, first impressions are difficult to change because they set in motion the **self-fulfilling prophecy.**

9. We are attracted to people who reward us directly or who are present when good things happen to us. We like people who are similar to us in any one of a number of ways. There is also a tendency to like people who are physically close to us, although proximity can also lead to disliking. Whereas we may be most attracted to physically attractive others, we often choose to become romantically involved with people whose physical attractiveness is about equal to our own.

10. The decision to help is only the end result in a complex chain of events. Before helping will occur, people need to notice the person in distress, interpret the situation as an emergency, feel responsible to help, know the appropriate way to help, and decide to offer aid. Research has shown that an individual is less likely to help in a group situation because responsibility is diffused.

11. Oftentimes recipients are unwilling to accept help. By accepting help, they may feel indebted to the helper. Further, helping often distinguishes the helper as powerful and competent and shows the recipient to be incompetent in the particular situation.

Key Terms

attitude change
attitudes
attribution model
cognitive dissonance
door-in-the-face
effort justification
foot-in-the-door
hedonic relevance
helping behavior
insufficient reward

just-barely-sufficient threat
norms
primacy effect
proximity
schema
self-fulfilling prophecy
sleeper effect
social cognition model
social psychology

Suggested Readings

The following book is about Geraldine Ferraro:
KATZ, L. M. *My name is Geraldine Ferraro*. New York: Signet, 1984. A short review of Geraldine Ferraro's life and rise to fame.

BERKOWITZ, L. (Ed.) *Advances in experimental social psychology*. New York: Academic Press. A new edition of this series is published each year. It includes contributed chapters on areas of social psychology that are timely. It includes chapters on new theories, revisions of older theories, new areas of study, and reviews of research in focused areas.

CIALDINI, R. B. *Influence: How and why people agree to things*. New York: William Morrow, 1984. A very readable application of social psychology to the area of influence. Examines advertising, sales techniques, and variables affecting attitude change.

FELDMAN, R. S. *Social psychology: Themes, research and applications*. New York: McGraw-Hill, 1985. An up-to-date review of social psychology that includes applications to law, environment, and the workplace.

LINDZEY, G., & ARONSON, E. (Eds.) *Handbook of social psychology*, 2nd ed. Reading, Mass.: Addison-Wesley, 1969. These five volumes offer an indepth examination of the areas of social psychology, its research, and the methods used in this research. Each volume focuses on a specific topic such as methods, groups, and applied social psychology. (A third edition is scheduled for publication in 1985.)

SHAW, M., & COSTANZO, P. *Theories of social psychology*, 2nd ed. New York: McGraw-Hill, 1982. This book discusses the development of theory in social psychology and examines each of the major theories. It is up-to-date and complete.

WORCHEL, S., & COOPER, J. *Understanding social psychology*, 3rd ed. Homewood, Ill.: Dorsey Press, 1983. This textbook discusses the major theories and research in social psychology and applies this work to understanding everyday events. It introduces the major topics with stories from classical literature and current events and shows how social psychology can be applied to these situations.

In the Asch studies on conformity, one naive subject (Subject #6 in the photos here) was placed in a group of experimental confederates. The subjects were asked to make simple judgments in turn. In the top photo, Subject #6 listens in surprise as the confederates give the incorrect answer. When it is his turn, he must decide whether to give the correct answer or follow the example of the other group members. The results of the research showed that subjects would conform to the group and give an incorrect answer over one-third of the time.

would be able to exert less pressure on you than nine unrelated individuals would. This is because you would view the players as a unit and respond to them as a unit rather than as separate individuals.

The Task. As might be expected, conformity is greater when the task is difficult or ambiguous. This, however, does not mean that there isn't considerable conformity on simple tests that have clearly correct answers. We saw an example of the latter type of conformity in the original Asch study.

Obedience to Authority

There was another pressure besides peer pressure that influenced Josh's behavior and that of his teammates. This was the orders of Oscar Charleston, the manager of the team. It was up to Charleston to blend the talents

A STUDY OF OBEDIENCE: HOW WOULD YOU RESPOND?

In an effort to determine the power of orders, Stanley Milgram (1963) developed a situation where he could control the nature of the orders given and observe people's responses to those orders. He recruited subjects in the New Haven, Connecticut, area through newspaper advertisements. Imagine yourself as one of these subjects. How would you respond to the following situation?

Upon arriving at the experimental room, you sit down and begin talking to a middle-aged man who is also waiting for the experiment to begin. Soon the experimenter, dressed in a white laboratory coat, enters and explains that he is studying the effects of punishment on learning. He further explains that one of you two subjects will be the "teacher," who will ask the other, the "learner," questions and deliver electrical shocks whenever the learner gives incorrect answers. You become a little concerned at the mention of electric shock as you remember the jolt you once received when touching a bare wire. The other subject is also concerned and voices his fear of shock. The experimenter reassures him that the shock will not be dangerous. At this point you draw lots to determine who will be the teacher and who the learner; it is with some relief that you find you will be the teacher.

The other subject is led to an enclosed booth where the experimenter straps him into a chair and attaches electrodes to his wrists. The experimenter returns and shows you the "teaching machine." The machine contains a row of levers and under each lever is a shock level. The first level reads 15 volts, and each level thereafter increases by 15 volts, with the last lever being marked 450 volts. The lower levels are marked "Slight Shock," while the upper levels are labeled "Danger: Severe Shock." The 450-volt switch carries the ominous sign "XXX." The experimenter explains that you are to read a prepared list of questions and wait for the learner's answer. If he answers incorrectly, you are to give him a shock and call out the correct answer. You should then go to the next question. Each shock you deliver to the learner must be 15 volts higher than the previous shock; the first shock will be 15 volts, the second will be 30 volts, and so on. In principle, the procedure seems quite simple and you inform the experimenter that you are ready to start.

Before the test begins, the experimenter gives you a sample shock from the lower end of the scale. Even this level hurts and you become increasingly thankful that you are the teacher rather than the learner. Now the experiment begins. You begin reading the questions and waiting for the learner's answers. He gives an incorrect answer and you deliver the 15-volt shock. After each incorrect answer you increase the shock level as instructed. When you deliver the 90-volt shock, the learner gives a cry of pain. At 150 volts the learner screams and asks to be let out of the booth. You look to the experimenter, who calmly instructs you to "proceed to the next question." At 180 volts there is another cry of pain and the subject begs to stop the study. Your concern for the learner increases and you ask the experimenter to check on him. The experimenter instructs you to continue, and despite your uneasiness, you go on to the next question. When you deliver the 300-volt shock, the learner cries that he is getting sick and refuses to answer any additional questions. From this point on, there is no response from the booth; both your questions and

---

of the players into a team; a baseball club could have a great deal of talent, but it would not be a winner if the players did not play together as a team. When necessary, Charleston was a strict and demanding coach, and there was no question but that he was in charge.

Obedience involves the following of direct and explicit orders given by someone who is in a position of authority. Sometimes the result of obedience is positive. The Craws were a better team because they followed the directions of Oscar Charleston. You can probably point to examples where you followed the orders of an authority figure with positive results.

Because it is possible to point to so many examples where obedience to orders has positive results, many people become all too willing to follow the demands of authority figures. Unfortunately, blind obedience can have disastrous consequences. Six million innocent men, women, and children were tortured and killed during World War II by Nazis who confessed they were only following the orders of their superiors. In November 1978 over 900 members of the Peoples Temple committed suicide by drinking

shocks are answered only with silence.

Would you continue to follow the orders of the experimenter and deliver shocks to the maximum 450-volt XXX, or would you refuse to continue and disobey the experimenter? What percentage of "average, normal" subjects recruited for this study do you think would continue to the maximum shock level? These were the questions that Milgram sought to answer.

He ran the first study at Yale University, using male subjects between the ages of 20 and 50. The subjects came from a variety of backgrounds and occupations; 40 percent held unskilled jobs, 40 percent had white-collar sales jobs, and 20 percent were professionals. As can be seen from the table here, 26 of the 40 subjects (65 percent) went all the way and gave the maximum shock; not a single subject stopped before the level of *intense shock*.

In actuality, the "learner" in the study was an experimental confederate who was trained to play a role. He did not actually receive any shocks; he merely recorded the level of shocks that the subjects

Maximum Shock Levels in Milgram's Obedience Study

Verbal Designation and Voltage Indication	Number of Subjects for Whom This Was Maximum Shock	Verbal Designation and Voltage Indication	Number of Subjects for Whom This Was Maximum Shock
Slight shock		Intense shock	
15	0	255	0
30	0	270	0
45	0	285	0
60	0	300	5
Moderate shock		Extreme-intensity shock	
75	0	315	4
90	0	330	2
105	0	345	1
120	0	360	1
Strong shock		Danger—severe shock	
135	0	375	1
150	0	390	0
165	0	405	0
180	0	420	0
Very strong shock		XXX	
195	0	435	0
210	0	450	26
225	0		
240	0		

Source: Milgram (1963).

administered. It is, however, important to note that the subjects did not know of this trickery; they believed they were shocking the innocent learner. Though many of the subjects expressed concern about the learner, they still followed orders to shock him.

In a later study Milgram moved his experiment to a rundown office building in Brockport, Connecticut. The experimenter did not wear the white laboratory coat and subjects were not told of any affiliation with Yale University. Even in this unimpressive setting, Milgram found that 48 percent of the subjects obeyed the order to give the maximum shock.

Kool-Aid laced with cyanide; they were following the orders of their leader, Jim Jones. When most of us read about such events, we comfort ourselves by saying it could never happen to us—"those other people" were either stupid or under a great deal of stress. A "normal" person in "normal" times would not follow orders that would directly harm innocent people.

Unfortunately, Stanley Milgram (1963; 1965) found that "normal" people in "normal" times often will blindly follow orders even if it hurts innocent people. He set up a situation (described in the Highlight on these pages) in which subjects were ordered to inflict what they thought was a painful shock to a protesting victim. Sixty-five percent of the subjects in his studies dutifully followed the orders, despite their belief that they might be injuring their victim. Most of us would claim that we would never do such a thing. In fact, Milgram asked a group of senior psychology students at Yale University and a group of psychiatrists to predict how many subjects would follow orders to inflict the maximum level of pain. They predicted that less than 2 percent would obey the order to give the 450-volt shock. Yet the results suggest that two out of three people did indeed follow orders till the end!

In a very different setting, Hofling and his colleagues (1966) studied whether nurses in a hospital would follow orders to violate hospital rules and deliver a potentially harmful dosage of a drug to a patient. Nurses on duty received a phone call from a doctor they did not know. He ordered them to administer 20 milligrams of a drug for which the maximum stated dosage was 10 milligrams a day. This order not only was higher than the maximum safe dosage, but it violated hospital policy that no nurse was to a give a patient drugs without the doctor being physically present. Despite these violations, 21 of the 22 nurses who were telephoned followed the doctor's orders.

These studies demonstrate the power of orders. People seem to be willing to follow the orders of an authority figure even when their behavior brings harm to others. These and other studies suggest that this willingness occurs because people do not accept responsibility for actions they perform under orders. They feel that the person giving the orders has taken the responsibility for the results of their actions (Kilham & Mann, 1974; Milgram, 1977). This sentiment was clearly echoed at the Nüremburg trials after World War II when many of the Nazi war criminals stated that they believed their actions were wrong but did not feel responsible for them, because they were merely following orders. Findings such as these should cause us to pause and question our actions. How often do we justify our behavior by convincing ourselves that we are not responsible because we are only doing what we are told to do.

Another factor that influences whether or not we follow orders is the *role* we are filling. Roles often include rules that we follow the orders of certain others. In the Milgram study people were in the role of "subject"; it is expected that someone in this role will follow the commands of the experimenter. In the Hofling study the role of "nurse" includes following the orders of doctors. In a study demonstrating the power of roles one investigator sets up a mock prison in the basement of Stanford University (Zimbardo, 1971). College students were recruited and assigned the role of guard or prisoner. To emphasize these roles, both groups were given appropriate uniforms and the prisoners were placed in cells.

The results of this experiment were shocking. Zimbardo reports that the situation "undid (temporarily) a lifetime of learning; human values were suspended, self-concepts were challenged, and the ugliest, most base, pathological side of human nature surfaced." Many of the guards became tyrannical and brutalized the prisoners. The prisoners were allowed little sleep and sometimes the guards withheld their food. The inmates, on the other hand, became "servile, dehumanized robots" who thought only of their own comforts. They obeyed the guards' orders even though it caused them great discomfort and suffering. In a sense, they became prisoners of the role. The role dictated that they obey, so they obeyed, forgetting that they could stop the study anytime simply by demanding to be allowed to go home. Conditions became so bad that Zimbardo ended the experiment after only 6 days rather than the planned 2 weeks. The frightening point here is that we may blindly adopt a role without thinking to question its value or how reasonable its requirements are.

A Question of Ethics. The research on obedience is eye-opening for a number of reasons. Not only are the results quite startling, but the methods used to obtain them also give us reason for reflection. Was it fair and ethical to place unsuspecting people in such an uncomfortable position? Subjects in the Milgram study suffered a great deal of psychological stress. Even though they continued to give the ordered shocks, Milgram reports that many of his subjects sweated profusely, fidgeted incessantly, fell into uncontrollable fits of nervous giggling, and showed other signs

These phots were taken during the Zimbardo "mock prison" study (1971) at Stanford University.

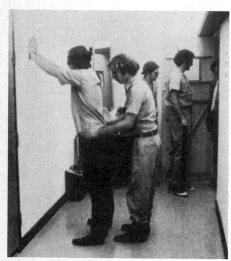

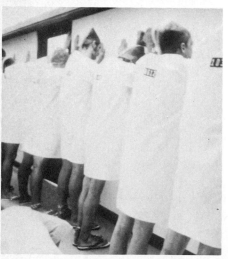

of discomfort and stress. Another disturbing by-product of the Milgram study is that the subjects were forced to learn about an unpleasant aspect of themselves—namely, that they would follow orders to hurt an innocent person. They left the experiment with the unpleasant realization that they had given shocks in the belief that they were hurting the learner. Most of us can comfort ourselves by saying that we would not hurt another person simply because we were ordered to do so. The subjects in the Milgram studies could not protect their self-image with such thoughts, for they had just learned that they would do exactly this.

While there are a number of reasons to question the procedures used in the obedience studies, there were some positive outcomes. In a follow-up questionnaire sent to subjects who had been in the Milgram study, 84 percent reported that they were glad they had participated. Also, the results obtained from the studies on obedience have furthered our understanding of human behavior. We now know the power of orders and we have a greater comprehension of why people act as they do. The impact of the results would have been considerably less if Milgram and others had used a less powerful task, such as ordering subjects to write down random numbers or compose uncomplementary stories about another person.

The issue of ethics is difficult to address in regard to designs such as those used in the obedience studies. On the one hand, psychologists need to use designs that have a strong impact on subjects if they wish to obtain valid results. On the other hand, they need to constantly keep in mind their responsibility as researchers to protect the rights and welfare of subjects. Today most psychologists submit the design of their studies to ethics committees for review to ensure that subjects' rights are protected. Committees suggest different procedures if they think greater protection is necessary. Guidelines for the ethical conduct of research have been devised by the American Psychological Association, and there are now federal and state laws protecting human experimental subjects. The effort to guarantee the rights and safety of human subjects is a continuing one, and, with the wholehearted cooperation of researchers, experimental designs that are sensitive to the subjects' welfare have become the rule, as we discussed in Chapter 1.

LEADERSHIP

The discussion of obedience demonstrated how readily people will follow the orders of leaders. Because leaders can have such a strong influence on group members' behaviors, it is important to understand how someone becomes a group leader and what factors play a part in making a person an effective leader.

A **leader** can be defined as the person who has the greatest influence on the activities of the group (Shaw, 1981). The use of this definition has given rise to two interesting observations. As far back as 1904, Terman pointed out that each member of a society is both a leader and a follower. It is unusual to find a group where the same person is always the leader; different people at different times are able to influence the group's activities. Some people may lead more often than others, but, depending on the time and circumstances, we are all leaders and we are all followers.

A second point is that at any one time there are often two leaders in a group. One of these leaders (the *task specialist*) is generally concerned with solving the tasks facing the group; he or she is most involved with getting the job done and presenting the group with guidance on solving problems.

A leader is the person who has the greatest influence on the activities of the group. Some leaders tend to focus on solving the immediate task facing the group, while others get the job done by showing concern for the feelings and welfare of group members.

The other person who has a strong influence on the group is concerned with person-oriented activities. This person is usually most involved with seeing that other group members are happy and that they are allowed to contribute to the group. This *socioemotional* leader may be the clown in the group, since he or she often reduces group tension, diffuses interpersonal conflicts, and influences the emotional tone of the group.

It is interesting to find that the Craws' pattern of leadership fit this scheme. Oscar Charleston, the player-manager, was clearly the task specialist. He was older and more experienced than the other players, and even had he not held the title of manager, his main concern would have been to get the Craws to play a good "brand" of baseball. He set the rules for the team, instructed the players about hitting techniques, and advised them about how to play their positions. But Charleston, because of his age and focus, was not the person who set the emotional tone of the team. Players like Josh and Jimmie Crutchfield were the social/emotional leaders. They kept the team members from becoming too depressed when they were playing badly, and they thought up jokes to reduce tensions when personal conflicts threatened the team spirit. These two types of leadership helped the team function more smoothly.

Theories of Leadership

Once we understand the concept of leadership, we can ask why some people have more influence on groups than others. Why did Josh Gibson, Oscar Charleston, and Jimmie Crutchfield occupy the leadership roles on the Craws? On a more global level, why have such people as John F. Kennedy, Martin Luther King, Jr., Golda Meir, Abraham Lincoln, and Ayatollah Khomeini emerged as leaders?

The Great Person Theory. Some of the earliest theories argued that leaders have certain traits that propel them into positions of influence (Terman, 1904). Literally hundreds of studies found only weak relationships between specific traits and leadership (Forsyth, 1983). For example, leaders tend to be somewhat more intelligent than other group members, but they are often not the most intelligent member (Shaw, 1981). A somewhat surprising finding is that taller people often exert more influence than shorter ones. An interesting aside to this is a study that compared the average salaries of 17,000 Air Force cadets in 1943 and 1968 (Keyes, 1980). As can be seen from Table 16–1, although the cadets had roughly equal salaries in 1943, the salaries attained by these men 25 years later were

Table 16-1
Relationship between
Height and Salary,
1943–1968

Height	Mean 1943 Salary	Mean 1968 Salary
5'3"–5'5"	$3,500	$14,750
5'6"–5'7"	3,750	16,500
5'8"–5'9"	3,900	17,000
5'10"–5'11"	3,900	17,500
6'0"–6'1"	4,100	19,000
6'2"–6'3"	4,000	18,500
6'4"–6'6"	3,700	19,500

Source: Adapted from Keyes (1980).

related to their height. The taller men had higher incomes; in fact, every inch over 5'3" was worth about $370 in annual income. Short people, however, should not despair because some of the most famous and infamous world leaders (Napoleon, Hitler, Meir, King) were short in stature.

Another unusual variable related to leadership is talkativeness—leaders talk more than the average group member. Some studies suggest that any group member who monopolizes group discussions can rise to the position of leader (Ginter & Lindskold, 1975; Sorrentino & Boutillier, 1956). This "blabbermouth rule" seems to hold even when the quality of the person's conversation and suggestions is low!

Although we can point to certain traits that may be related to leadership, the research has not identified any traits that clearly set leaders apart from followers. It is now generally agreed that we cannot identify who will emerge as a leader by looking at personal traits (McGrath, 1984).

Despite this failure to find specific leadership traits or qualities, the search goes on. Many businesses and military organizations use tests to help identify those with leadership potential. And many of us still believe that there is something special that sets leaders apart. Napier and Gershenfeld (1981) argue that the reason for this is that people have a need to believe that their leaders possess some special traits. We seem to find comfort in thinking that our leaders are unusual or superhuman.

Situational Theory. The failure to find traits that identify leaders led psychologists to examine how the group situation influences who becomes a leader. The *situational theory* assumes that the needs of the group change from time to time, and as a result, the type of person who leads the group also changes. Thus it is situational factors that determine who will lead and for how long. For example, one researcher suggests that it was prevailing conditions in the United States that determined when John Kennedy and Lyndon Johnson would be accepted as leaders (Toynbee, 1965). At the time of Kennedy's election there was a need for a president who could deal with questions regarding an international nuclear test ban and mounting problems in Cuba. However, the situation changed when Johnson was running for election; at that time there was a need for a tactician who could manipulate the Congress to pass important civil rights legislation. In each case, a person whose qualifications fit the needs of the situation emerged as leader. Toynbee points out, "It is one of the ironies of history that President Johnson had been more successful than Kennedy himself in getting the Kennedy Program enacted. If Kennedy had lived to be reelected it seems probable that a good deal less of his program would be on the statute books by now."

There has been some research showing that situations do affect who will emerge as leader. For example, several studies have found that the person seated at the head of the table often becomes the leader because he or she can maintain eye contact with most of the other group members (Howells & Becker, 1962; Lecuyer, 1976). It is interesting to note that

The situational theory of leadership states that conditions rather than personal traits determine who will emerge as the leader. Research has shown that the person seated at the head of a table often becomes the group leader.

Josh Gibson, who played the position of catcher, became a leader of the Craws. Catcher is the head position on the team; it is the one position where a player can see all the other team members and all can see him.

Looking at another issue, it seems that the specific requirements of the task facing the group will influence who emerges as the leader (Shaw, 1981). The individual who has the skills needed for the task at hand will often become the leader. Finally, groups are more likely to accept a leader and reject a deviant when there is an external threat or crisis (Lauderdale et al., 1984). In fact, leaders may invent threats or invite crises to consolidate their power (Du Brin, 1982).

This discussion leaves us wondering which theory is right, the great man theory or the situational theory. The answer is that neither theory alone seems correct. More recent approaches to the question of leadership have focussed on combining these theories. For example, Hollander (1978) argues that it is a combination of the characteristics of the leader, the followers, and the situation that determines who will emerge as the leader.

The Effective Leader

Overall, the research suggests that we cannot rely only on traits or only on situational variables to predict who will be a leader. More recently Fiedler has taken a somewhat different approach to the study of leadership (Fiedler, 1973, 1978). Instead of asking who will emerge as a leader, he has concentrated on determining who will be an effective leader. The *contingency model of leadership* says that the answer to this question is a function of both individual traits and situational factors (Chemers, 1983).

According to the contingency model, there are two styles of leadership. One focusses on task considerations. Leaders with this style attempt to get group members to concentrate on working and solving any problem related to the task. The second style of leadership stresses relationships. Leaders who take this approach try to get the job done by emphasizing the feelings of group members and trying to develop a good working relationship with their group. Thus while both types of leaders have the same goal—solving problems so a certain task can be accomplished—they take different approaches to achieve this goal. Leadership style can be measured by a questionnaire asking people to rate their least preferred co-worker (LPC) on a number of dimensions.

Identifying leadership style is only half the battle in determining who will be an effective leader; both types of leader can be effective, depending on the situation. The model suggests that some group conditions are very positive for the leader, while others are very negative. For example, a positive situation exists when leader-member relations are good, when the group's task is clear, and when the leader's position is well defined. A negative situation exists when the leader and group members do not get along well, the task is very unclear, and the leader's position is not well defined.

After examining leaders in many groups, including sports teams, fire departments, and tank crews, Fiedler concluded that task-oriented leaders are most effective when the group climate is either very favorable or very unfavorable. On the other hand, relationship-motivated leaders are most effective when the group climate is scored as moderate. Thus both situational and personal factors determine who will be an effective leader.

The contingency model has some important implications for choosing a leader. Many organizations spend a great deal of time and money trying to train people to be leaders. Fiedler argues that this may be a waste of resources. Instead, organizations should carefully examine the situation and then choose a person whose style of leadership is right for the particular conditions. There is still disagreement about how accurate Fiedler's theory is, but his work does show how personality and situation interact to determine leadership effectiveness (Graen et al., 1970).

RESISTING INFLUENCE

From our review of the research on conformity and discussion of the power of leaders and groups, you may find it hard to believe that our social world is not filled with robots waiting to be guided. Clearly this is not the case. We do not always conform nor do we always do what others tell us. For example, research has found that fewer than 50 percent of

The contingency theory of leadership suggests that the most effective leader is a function of the situation and the personality of the individual.

patients comply with their doctor's orders to take their medication (Ley, 1977). Therefore let us briefly examine the flip side of the influence coin and ask what factors lead us to resist pressures from other individuals and groups.

Status

If we examine conformity on the Craws, we find that it was the older, more established players like Satchel Paige and Oscar Charleston who went their own way and seemed immune to the pressures of their teammates. If we move from the baseball field to the business organization, we find that those employees who are "working their way up the corporate ladder" follow company policy as if it were law. Top executives are less likely to abide by company policy; they come and go with more freedom and often wear what they please rather than dressing to fit the group norm. It has been suggested that as members of groups we accumulate "idiosyncrasy credits" by following group norms and helping the group achieve its goals (Hollander, 1958). Just as we bank our money, we can save our credits. Whenever we deviate or break rules, we lose some of our credits, but as long as we have enough left to "pay for" our deviation, the group will continue to accept us. However, we will be punished or rejected if we have not accumulated enough credits to balance out our deviation. In most cases, high-status people have earned a lot of idiosyncrasy credits by contributing to the group, and therefore they can afford to deviate. Thus having credits or status helps insulate us from group pressure and allows us to deviate to a certain degree. In Satchel Paige's case, for example, he was the most famous player on the team and he earned his credits by drawing fans to the ball park.

Presenting an Image

Most of us have an idea of the way we would like other people to see us (Schlenker, 1985). We mold our behavior, dress, and social interactions to present the desired image. But while we may feel the need to appear reasonable and sociable, many of us also see ourselves as unique and independent. We want to stand out from the crowd, but we also want to appear to be charting our own course in life. One way to demonstrate our independence and uniqueness is to resist the pressures of groups to conform and instead act differently from others (Santee & Maslach, 1982). Not only does deviating from group norms demonstrate our independence, but it is also an effective way to capture the attention of other people. For example, which of the people in Figure 16–1 grabs your attention?

Figure 16–1
Deviating from the group is one way to establish independence and become the focus of attention.

Restoring Our Freedom

On their long bus trips between games, the Craws would often pass the time playing jokes on one another. All the players were eventually the target of these antics, but on one trip Tincan Kincannon decided he had had enough. To punctuate his position, he placed a gun in his lap and ordered the others to keep their distance. While this might seem like an airtight strategy to ensure peace and quiet, it had the exact opposite effect. During the whole trip the players schemed to make Tincan the butt of their joke; as we pointed out in the introduction, they succeeded.

This example demonstrates an important point about social pressure. Pressure aimed at making us act or think in a certain way often creates a counterpressure within us to take the opposite course of action. It has been argued that all of us feel that we have the freedom to engage in a wide range of behaviors or hold a variety of attitudes (Brehm & Brehm, 1981). Pressure to adopt certain positions threatens our freedom. When this happens, we experience a psychological state (**reactance**) that motivates us to regain our freedom by resisting the pressure. One way to demonstrate our freedom to ourselves and others is to adopt an attitudinal position opposite that demanded of us or to engage in a behavior that has been forbidden. For example, Tincan's threat to shoot anyone who made him the butt of a joke threatened the freedom of the players to carry out this activity. Although there was clearly pressure (the loaded gun) to leave Tincan alone, there was also the opposite pressure to regain freedom. Researchers have found that threats to freedom lead to an increase in the attractiveness of the threatened freedom and a stronger desire to engage in the threatened behavior. Many a parent has successfully employed the reactance effect to get a child to drink his milk (go to bed, brush his teeth, etc.) by announcing, "Johnny, you *cannot* drink your milk (go to bed, brush your teeth) tonight." Thus reactance may be one of the factors that leads us to resist pressure.

Lack of Identifiability

When he was on the field or in a town where people recognized him, Josh felt that he had to live up to his image and act the way people expected him to. In these cases, if he made a mistake or did something wrong, people would know about it. However, he reported feeling free when he played his first season in Puerto Rico. There he was just another face in the crowd; people didn't know him and he didn't have to be so careful about how he acted.

As far back as 1903, the sociologist Le Bon realized that groups often change people into "primitive beings," causing them to do things they would not think of doing on their own. A number of years later Zimbardo (1970) examined the reasons why groups have such an effect on people. He suggested that in some groups people tend to lose their personal identity and assume the identity of the group; in more psychological terms this is referred to as **deindividuation.** Because they no longer seem to have a personal identity, group members lose the feeling of responsibility for their own actions, and they no longer feel the same restraints against socially disapproved behavior. People's behavior in such a situation is generally emotional, impulsive, and intense. Deindividuated people show little concern for the results of their actions because they feel that they cannot be personally identified and that the group will assume responsibility for whatever they do. Further, people in the deindividuation condition are less aware of their feelings and behavior and less concerned about social evaluation (Prentice-Dunn & Rogers, 1980).

A number of factors are likely to make people in groups feel deindividuated. The first is anonymity: When people feel they cannot be personally identified, they are most likely to feel deindividuated. Anonymity can often be achieved by having everyone in a group dress alike so that no one person stands out. A second factor is group size: The larger the group, the more likely it is that people will feel deindividuated. A third factor is emotional: Deindividuation is more likely to result when people are aroused and in a new or unstructured situation.

The feeling of not being responsible for one's behavior can have many effects on people. For our present purposes, we will focus on one study (Singer et al., 1965). It found that deindividuated subjects were less likely to conform to group opinions than were subjects who were more identifiable. It seems that the reduced concern about social evaluation freed people to express their own opinions rather than conform to group pressure. Sometimes people find being deindividuated an exhilarating experience that frees them to act more spontaneously. For example, we often find the meekest person screaming and shouting during a football or basketball game where he or she is an anonymous face in the crowd. This person would never dream of behaving in this way when alone or in a small group. In some cases, then, deindividuation can be fun and have positive results.

However, there is a darker side to deindividuation. People who live in large cities often feel deindividuated (Milgram, 1977). As a result, they interact in an impersonal way, and this type of interaction can lead them to feel lonely and alienated. Since they are uncomfortable with the loss of personal identity associated with deindividuation, many people will try to regain their uniqueness by wearing clothing that separate them from the crowd, by putting their name on their automobile license plate, or by decorating their home in an unusual way.

GROUP DECISION MAKING

In previous sections we focussed on the general structure of groups and the types of pressures they can place on individuals. The points we raised apply to any group of people regardless of the purpose they have for coming together. Let us now narrow our focus a bit and look at specific activities. If we examine our own groups, we will be able to identify two rather common activities. One is decision making; in many, if not most, groups decisions must be made on a variety of topics ranging from who will lead to how the group will solve problems. In fact, the sole purpose of some groups such as juries is to make decisions. The other common activity of groups is to perform tasks; the task may range from playing baseball to building a house. In this section we will examine the decision-making process, and in the next we will focus on task performance.

To begin our study of decision making let's look once again at the Craws. An important dilemma faced by many of the Craws at the end of the 1932 season was whether or not to play winter baseball in Latin America. Josh didn't know what to do. He loved playing baseball and he needed extra money; playing winter baseball would satisfy both of these desires. On the other hand, he had heard stories about the political unrest in many Latin American countries and about the rowdy fans whose wild enthusiasm sometimes resulted in serious injury to the players. Many of the other players felt the same way, so they came together to discuss the situation and make a decision about their future. Given the diversity of opinions, it was somewhat surprising that after a discussion of the risks, Josh's whole circle of friends decided to play winter baseball. This example raises a number of important questions. How are group decisions made? What factors in a group influence the decisions it will make? Do groups generally make wiser decisions than individuals acting alone?

Group Polarization

One of the interesting aspects of the Craws' decision to play winter ball was its rather drastic nature. The players knew little about Latin America, the league, or the conditions under which they would be playing. Given this uncertainty, the wise decision might have been to take the cautious route of having a few go to the winter league for the first year, and the remainder follow the next year if the experience proved positive. However, the Craws threw caution to the wind and decided to drastically alter all their lives on the basis of very little information.

This decision seems odd, especially in view of early theories about groups that held that people are less bold in groups than when acting alone. For example, William Whyte (1956) speculated that people in organizations and business bureaucracies were less creative and less risk-oriented because they feared being ridiculed for taking extreme positions. A graduate student in the School of Industrial Management at MIT decided to show the conservative effect of groups. He wrote up some cases about people facing problems or dilemmas and asked groups to discuss these cases and arrive at a solution (Stoner, 1961). To his surprise, he found that the group solutions were more risky and extreme than the solutions individuals suggested when working on their own.

Wallach, Kagan, and Bem (1962) developed additional case problems and had people suggest solutions by themselves. After deciding on these individual solutions, the subjects met in groups of five to discuss the cases and arrive at group decisions. Later the subjects were again asked to give individual solutions to the dilemmas. Two interesting results emerged from this study. First, the group decisions were more extreme and risky than the average individual decisions. Second, when the subjects made individual decisions after the group discussion, their solutions were more risky than the individual solutions they made before the group discussion. Thus not only did the groups make more risky decisions, but participating in group discussions also made the subjects take more risks when they later acted on their own. In another study on a different problem, researchers found that groups made riskier bets in a blackjack game than did individuals (Blaskovitch, Ginsburg, & Howe, 1975).

For a number of years, therefore, investigators believed that groups free their members to make more risky decisions, and this area of research was referred to as the "risky shift." However, more recent research has found that people do not always become more risk-oriented when placed in groups. This research showed that groups tended to polarize people and move them to believe more strongly in the position they initially held (Moscovici & Zavalloni, 1969). For example, if someone is inclined to make a risky decision on a particular issue, discussing the issue in a group will probably push him or her to take an even riskier position. However, if the person prefers a conservative position, the group discussion will push him or her to take an even more conservative position. Further, the research showed that the **group polarization effect** occurs in a wide range of areas, including attitudes, interpersonal impressions, and judgments about the importance of values. For example, Paicheler (1976) measured groups of French students' attitudes toward equal rights for women and found them moderately favorable on the issue. She then had them discuss the topic in groups and remeasured their attitudes. The results indicated that as a result of the discussion the student groups reported being more in favor of equal rights for women. Given this new evidence, we can argue that the team discussion resulted in a decision for the Craws to play baseball in Latin America because most of the individual members were already leaning in this direction. If most of the players had had serious reservations, the group discussion would have strengthened these reservations and the players would have decided not to go to Latin America.

There are a number of possible reasons for this polarization effect. One explanation suggests that because the group rather than the individual will be held responsible for the decision—the diffusion of responsibility theory—people feel more free to adopt extreme opinions as group members. For example, if winter baseball had turned out to be a disaster, no single Craws player could be held responsible for getting the others to go to Latin America. A second explanation suggests that individual group members compare their viewpoints to the positions held by others in the group (Baron, 1984). When they find that their position is not as extreme as that of some other members, they change their position to be more extreme. We want to be at least as extreme as others in our group (Myers, 1982). According to this *social comparison approach*, the positions held by the other group members is the most important information influencing the decision making of an individual group member.

However, a third approach takes a rather different view (Burnstein, 1984). The *persuasive argument hypothesis* argues that it is the information about *why* people hold certain positions that is most important. People examine the arguments that others use to support their positions, and they change their position in the direction of the most persuasive arguments. One study found that increasing information about *why* people adopted a certain position led to greater polarization than simply increasing information about the position of other people (Burnstein, Vinokur, & Trope, 1973). As is the case with many social behaviors, it is probable that all these factors (diffusion of responsibility, social comparison, and persuasive arguments) influence the polarization of attitudes in groups.

Groupthink

We have seen that groups often make more extreme decisions than people acting on their own. This finding leads us to ask another question regarding such decision making: Are the decisions made by groups of better or worse *quality* than those made by one person? Offhand, we might expect to find that groups make better decisions than individuals. Groups are usually made up of people who have different information and who may present different ways of looking at a problem. This diversity should allow them to consider the many aspects of a problem and arrive at the best alternative. This seemed to happen when the Craws considered the possibility of playing winter baseball in Latin America. Each of the players had heard different stories about the pros and cons of baseball "south of the border," and through an exchange of information the players were able to make a decision. In this case, it was a wise decision, since most of them enjoyed the experience and returned to play on Latin American teams for many years after.

Unfortunately, groups do not always make the best use of the information available to them. The results of an unfortunate group decision were seen on April 17, 1961. On that date 1,400 Cuban exiles landed at the Bay of Pigs in Cuba. They planned to set up a beachhead there, and unite with Cuban rebels in the Escambray Mountains to overthrow Premier Fidel Castro. They felt that their plan could not possibly fail. Their mission had been devised by one of the best intelligence organizations in the world, the United States Central Intelligence Agency (CIA), and the plan had been approved by President John F. Kennedy and his personal advisers.

However, the impossible happened. Nothing went as planned; instead of being greeted by friendly rebels, the exiles were met by a well-prepared

Groupthink occurred in Kennedy's group of advisors who planned the Bay of Pigs invasion. The group had a strong leader in President Kennedy, and many members were afraid of voicing disagreement.

Groupthink occurred in Kennedy's group of advisors who planned the Bay of Pigs invasion. The group had a strong leader in President Kennedy, and many members were afraid of voicing disagreement.

Cuban Army that quickly killed or captured the whole group. The United States suffered a severe political setback, and the world wondered how such a respected group of men as Kennedy and his advisers could have decided on such a foolish plan.

Irving Janis (1982) carefully analyzed the Bay of Pigs fiasco and concluded that the decision-making process was responsible for the poor decision. Janis suggested that the Kennedy group, like many other decision-making groups, was a victim of groupthink. **Groupthink** occurs when group members become so concerned with reaching agreement among all members of the group that they fail to critically evaluate their ideas. Because they are so worried about keeping a happy group atmosphere, they fail to make good use of the information available to them. Groupthink is most likely to occur in close-knit groups in which group members like one another and are proud to belong to the group. Thus an illusion of agreement exists in the group; because no one is openly expressing disagreement, group members feel that everyone must be feeling the same way. The group also develops the illusion that it can do no wrong. A strong and respected leader reinforces groupthink, since group members are unwilling to "buck" his or her authority and have a false confidence that their leader cannot be wrong.

Can groupthink be avoided? Janis says yes. He cites many examples, including one involving Kennedy and his advisers, where groupthink did not occur. Just over a year after the Bay of Pigs incident, Kennedy learned that the Russians were positioning nuclear missiles with atomic warheads in Cuba. He called a series of meetings with his advisers, many of whom had been involved in the Bay of Pigs decision. However, Kennedy was determined to avoid the pitfalls of that earlier decision so this time he encouraged his advisers to consider numerous alternative plans and to critically evaluate each one. Persons outside the group were called in to give advice. Kennedy himself did not take an early stand and even stayed away from several meetings. As a result of these actions, groupthink was avoided and the advisers settled on an effective and successful plan of action.

How can groupthink be avoided? Janis has the following suggestions:

1. Group members should be encouraged to carefully consider each alternative and to play the role of devil's advocate.
2. The leader should refrain from stating a preference and encourage group discussion.

3. Outsiders should be invited to give their opinions on the issues.
4. Several meetings should be called to reassess new information and review the most preferred decision.
5. From time to time the group can be subdivided into smaller groups, each to consider the problem independently.

Who Influences the Decision?

If we knew that seven of the Craws players wanted to play winter baseball and two did not, we would not be surprised to find that the decision of the team was to play winter baseball. Both our own experience and research results show that the majority opinion generally rules the group's decision (Davis, 1980; McGrath, 1984). What may surprise you, though, is that the minority can sometimes win the day. In a series of studies using mock injuries and problem-solving groups, investigators examined the steps that minorities can take to maximize their influence (Moscovici & Personnaz, 1980; Nemeth, 1985).

The most important feature of minority influence is *consistency*. The minority members must stick with the position they adopt and not appear willing to compromise or give in to the pressures of the majority. Second, the minority position must be *clear*; the other group members must be able to identify the minority's stand on the issue. For example, if only two Craws did not want to play winter baseball, they would not be effective in swaying group opinion if they stated, "We think that maybe we shouldn't play ball this winter unless some things change." Finally, the minority must appear *self-confident* and certain of their position. They will be less effective if they look hesitant and unsure of themselves.

It is rather easy to understand the power of the majority. As we pointed out, the majority often has the power to eject members from the group if they deviate from the norms. Thus, in addition to informational pressure, the majority exerts its influence through normative social pressure. The minority, on the other hand, has no normative power. They must rely on informational pressure. By adopting a consistent and confident stand even in the face of group pressures, the minority may cause other group members to question the majority position. They may begin to think that the minority position may be correct, given the risk and discomfort the steadfast minority are willing to suffer for it.

Before rushing out to trumpet minority positions in groups, we must recall two points. First, in most cases, the majority determines group deci-

Although majorities usually rule in groups, people in the minority can be effective if they take a clear, consistent stand and show their confidence in the position.

THE JURY IS OUT

The work on group dynamics can be applied to many areas of our lives. Recently psychologists have begun to apply the research on group decision making to explain how juries reach their verdicts (Monahan & Loftus, 1982). For centuries the traditional jury in England, Canada, and the United States has consisted of 12 people who must arrive at a unanimous decision of guilt before a defendant can be convicted of a crime. What factors are important in determining the jury's decision and how does this group come to a decision?

One factor is the size of juries. Is it necessary to have 12 people, or would a smaller number arrive at the same decision? Also, is it important for the jury to arrive at a *unanimous* decision, or would a simple majority rule give the same results? Researchers examined these questions using mock juries of college students (Davis, Bray, & Holt, 1977). In these studies the juries listened to a staged trial and then were asked to decide the guilt or innocence of the defendant. Davis compared the verdicts from 12- and 6-person juries, and also the verdicts reached by juries who were told that a unanimous decision was necessary as opposed to juries who were told that a two-thirds majority could convict the defendant.

The results indicated that 6-person and 12-person juries generally arrive at the same verdict. Further, the verdicts reached by the juries who had to make a unanimous decision were generally the same as those reached by juries who only had to have a two-thirds majority agreement. Davis et al. did find, however, that the unanimous juries took a longer time to reach their verdict than did the two-thirds majority juries. These results seem to suggest that the court system could be run more cheaply and

efficiently with smaller juries who did not have to reach unanimous decisions. Davis cautions, however, that most of the juries had a two-thirds majority on the first poll of votes; if juries were allowed to submit a verdict at this point, discussion of a case would be greatly reduced and many important issues might be overlooked.

In many cases, defendants are charged with multiple crimes relating to the same incident. For example, in late 1984 and early 1985 there were a number of tragic incidents in which a student shot teachers and other students in the classroom. In these cases, the students were often charged with multiple felonies, including murder, attempted murder, malicious wounding, discharging a firearm in a public place, and trespassing. Legally, each of these is a separate crime and decisions about guilt on any one charge should be made independently of considerations of the other charges. However, in order to save time and because the evidence relating to each charge is roughly the same, a single trial may be held; the same jury must decide guilt or innocence on each charge. Despite being instructed to consider each charge separately, research

shows that a guilty verdict is more likely to be returned for a specific charge if it is considered with other charges than if it is considered alone (Tanford & Penrod, 1982). Further, the order in which the charges are considered also affects judgment. One study found that a guilty verdict was more likely on a charge if the preceding charge was more serious than if it was less serious (Davis et al., 1984). For example, a guilty charge for attempted murder was more likely if the jury was asked to decide on the charges in descending order (murder, attempted murder, discharging a firearm) than in ascending order (discharging a firearm, attempted murder, murder).

There have been some other interesting findings about juries. For instance, what do jurors talk about when they are deciding a case? James (1959) found that at least half of their discussion is devoted to personal experience, while only about 15 percent is about the actual testimony presented during the trial. Other researchers have found that high-status members of a jury participate more and are more influential than low-status members (Strodbeck & Mann, 1956).

According to social facilitation theory, performance of well-learned behaviors is enhanced by an audience. Josh hit his longest homeruns when he was in front of large crowds of screaming fans.

sions. Second, being in the minority can be a lonely and difficult position. Research has found that deviants may be rejected from the group and that other group members may cease communicating with them (Schachter, 1951). This is especially true in very cohesive groups when group decisions are important to the group members.

GROUP PERFORMANCE

We now turn our attention to task performance in groups. There are a number of interesting questions concerning the work of groups. One of the oldest is whether groups are more effective than individuals. In other words, if you have a job to do, should you do it on your own or enlist the aid of other group members? At first glance the answer may seem simple. Certainly groups should be more effective because the more people you can enlist, the greater the variety of talents you will have to draw on. Also, group members bring different backgrounds and perspectives to a problem. Then, too, groups permit the division of tasks so that individuals have a chance to become experts in a single area. All these factors argue in favor of using a group, and clearly there are certain tasks that can only be performed by a group. However, before embracing the group as the ideal solution to all situations, we must consider other issues.

There is an age-old warning: If you want something done right, do it yourself. Anyone who has sat through seemingly endless committee meetings knows painfully well that groups can get sidetracked on unimportant issues as different members press for influence and control. Investigators have identified two general types of problems that can plague groups and reduce their effectiveness (Steiner, 1976). The first is *coordination loss*; groups lose effectiveness to the extent that they cannot identify and coordinate the talents of their members. For example, a baseball team may have players with tremendous ability, but the team will only function well if these talents are identified and the players are assigned to the appropriate positions.

A second potential problem for groups is *motivation loss*, which takes place when members do not utilize their talents and give their maximum effort to the task. This loss often occurs when group members become discouraged because they feel their efforts are going unrecognized. They will then withdraw and stop contributing to the group. In professional sports one sign of loss of motivation is when players demand to be traded because they are not being recognized or given enough playing time.

There is no simple answer to the question of whether groups are better at task performance than individuals acting alone. The answer depends on the type of task, the talents of the group's members, and how well the group can solve the problems of coordination and motivation loss.

Thus far we have been comparing individual to group performance. There is an equally interesting comparison to be made between the performance of individuals working alone and the performance of people working in or in front of groups. In other words, how does the group affect individual performance?

Social Facilitation

Whether we are athletes or students in a class, some of our most agonizing moments come when we are called on to perform in front of other people. All eyes are riveted on us as our moment of reckoning arrives. Is the audience our friend or foe? Does its presence help us perform better or destroy our best-laid plans? A related question is how can we best prepare for these times. If we know we will be performing in front of an audience, should we practice under similar conditions or should we seek isolation to prepare? Questions such as these have intrigued psychologists for decades, and the answers they have discovered have stimulated some interesting theories.

In order to place these questions in a clearer light, we begin by examining the approach of the Craws. Like many other athletes, the Craws players felt that they could best prepare if they were not distracted by their attentive fans. Each year they gathered in Hot Springs, Arkansas, for spring training. Here the players could practice their hitting and fielding without the hordes of fans that would be present during their regular games. Josh Gibson enjoyed spring training, but he was always anxious for the season to start. He usually hit his longest homeruns and made his best defensive plays when he was in front of large crowds of screaming fans. In fact, Josh hit his longest homerun in Yankee Stadium in front of a nearly packed house; it is said to be the longest ball ever hit in Yankee Stadium (Brashler, 1978).

A number of early studies showed that people work faster when in the presence of others than when alone (Allport, 1924; Travis, 1925). Investigators found that this effect even transcends human beings. Chen (1937) studied ants digging tunnels and building nests. In some cases, he had the ants work alone, while in other cases, the subject ant worked with one or two other ants. Chen examined the balls of dirt excavated by the ant to determine the speed of work. He found that the ant worked harder (removed more dirt balls) when other ants were present. In addition to supplying such practical information as to how to get lazy ants to work, these early studies suggested that working in the presence of others increased individual performance.

Other studies, however, show that sometimes groups are bad for people's performance. For example, Pessin (1933) found that the presence of an audience inhibited the learning of a maze task and a nonsense-syllable task. However, Pessin made another interesting discovery: After subjects had learned the tasks on their own, their performance increased when they were placed in front of a group.

Robert Zajonc (1965) attempted to make sense out of these contradictory results. He suggested that the presence of others tends to arouse and excite people. This arousal creates an additional pool of energy that aids the performance of well-learned behaviors. We call this social facilitation. However, this additional arousal hinders the learning of new and complex

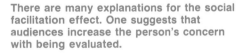

There are many explanations for the social facilitation effect. One suggests that audiences increase the person's concern with being evaluated.

responses. We call this social inhibition. Thus the presence of others leads to social facilitation of well-learned responses, but leads to social inhibition for learning new and complex behaviors.

While Zajonc's reasoning explains some of the social facilitation results, it does not explain others. For example, Martens and Landers (1972) found that audiences were most likely to cause social facilitation when the actor felt that he or she was being evaluated. This prompted Cottrell (1972) to suggest that social facilitation is caused by the concerns about evaluation rather than by the simple presence of the audience. Still a third explanation suggests that audiences are distracting (Sanders, 1981). The conflict between paying attention to the audience and concentrating on the task at hand increases the performer's arousal. This, in turn, energizes the performance of simple and well-learned tasks, but inhibits the performance of new tasks. Regardless of the reason, however, the implication of the research on social facilitation is that people should learn new responses while they are alone and then perform these responses in front of a group.

Social Loafing

In most of the research on social facilitation, subjects work on a task where their individual performance is visible and measurable. This is similar to the situation faced by a baseball player; although he is a member of a team, people can easily determine how well he is playing. The research shows that in situations like these the group often has a positive effect on the person's performance. However, what happens when the person performs in a group where his or her contribution is not easily observable? In this type of situation the group has a very different effect.

In one experiment groups of one to eight people were instructed to pull on a rope, and then the total force was measured (Ringelmann, as reported in Moede, 1927). When Ringelmann looked at the average force exerted by each member, he found that as the group size increased, the force supplied by each individual member decreased. More than 50 years later Latané, Williams, and Harkins (1979) had people cheer as loudly as they could. Sometime after this the cheerers were placed in groups ranging in size from two to six members. They were then asked to cheer as loudly as they could. Again, the results showed that while more noise was produced by groups, each individual cheered less loudly in the groups than when alone. The larger the group, the less loudly each person cheered.

It has been argued that people's motivation to work decreases when they are in groups where their individual performance cannot be observed (Kerr & Bruun, 1981; Latané, Williams, & Harkins, 1979). Being in a group allows people to reduce their efforts without being detected. Also, the larger the group, the less likely that people will pay attention to any individual's performance. This general effect has been called social loafing. Kerr and Bruun argue that the social-loafing effect would be reduced if group members felt that others could identify their contribution to the group. From the research, then, it is clear that, depending on the nature of the task, groups may either increase an individual's performance or decrease it.

 # PREJUDICE AND DISCRIMINATION

As we have seen, groups are wondrously complex and affect our lives in many ways. On the positive side, they help us establish our identity; they enhance order in our world; they offer us protection and comfort; and they can increase our performance on tasks. These advantages are, however, achieved at a price. Being in a group often means that we must conform to group rules, and in doing so, we may lose a bit of our uniqueness. But this cost is minor compared to another effect that often accompanies the formation of groups; that cost is prejudice and discrimination.

Josh Gibson was well acquainted with prejudice and discrimination; his life was greatly influenced by these social phenomena. Because of the racial prejudice that existed during his lifetime, he could only play baseball on black teams in the United States. In order to have the opportunity to play with white players, he was forced to go to South America. Racial prejudice determined the restaurants where Josh could eat, the dressing rooms where he could change his clothes, and the hotels where he could sleep. Racial prejudice meant that Josh had to fear for his life and safety in the same towns where he entertained baseball fans.

Before examining prejudice more closely, there are a few points that must be made. Although the terms *prejudice* and *discrimination* are often used interchangeably, this usage is incorrect. **Prejudice** is an unjustified negative *attitude* toward an individual based solely on that person's membership in a group (Brewer & Kramer, 1985). Our prejudices are generally supported by *stereotypes* about the group in question. **Stereotypes** are oversimplified generalizations about the characteristics of a group (Miller, 1982). They influence our memory and interpretation of events involving members of the group. For example, research suggests that we will interpret ambiguous events to fit our stereotypes (Wilder, 1985). Further, we are less likely to distinguish between members of a stereotyped group than we are to make distinctions between members of our own group (Brigham, 1985). **Discrimination,** on the other hand, is negative, often aggressive *behavior* aimed at the target of prejudice. Exclusion from social clubs, neighborhoods, or jobs are examples of discrimination. Everyone who holds prejudicial attitudes does not practice discrimination. However, such attitudes do make discrimination more likely.

Prejudice and discrimination have a number of characteristics that make them more difficult to understand than many other attitudes and behaviors. First, prejudice is baseless. These attitudes are not formed from facts or personal experience—it is not unusual to find someone who is racially prejudiced despite having limited interaction with blacks. Second, discrimination is often practiced even when it hurts the person practicing it. For example, employers may hire a less qualified white male even when they have applications from more qualified blacks or females. Finally, the person who is the target of prejudice often takes on these prejudicial attitudes. For example, Goldberg (1968) asked female students to evaluate a manuscript. Half the students were told that the article was written by a man and half were told that it was written by a woman. Despite the fact that the articles were the same, even women rated the manuscript higher if they thought it was written by a man.

The Roots of Prejudice

How do people develop prejudicial attitudes? There are a number of theories about the roots of prejudice. Some of the earlier theories tried to lay the blame for prejudice on the individual's personality (Adorno et al., 1950). These investigators had some success in identifying certain personality traits that made people more likely to develop prejudicial attitudes. However, all people with these traits do not hold prejudicial attitudes, and many people without these traits are prejudiced. Thus we cannot blame prejudice on personal characteristics. As a result, most theories of prejudice are aimed at identifying situational causes of prejudice.

Discrimination is often practiced even when it hurts the person practicing it. Employers may hire a less qualified white male even when they have applications from more qualified blacks or females.

Group Formation and Discrimination

At the start of this section we hinted at the possibility that prejudice was somehow related to the formation of groups. This may seem like an odd suggestion, but investigators have suggested that prejudice and discrimination may be one of the products of group formation (Tajfel & Turner, 1985). These investigators suggest that we often gain our own identity through the groups we belong to. Because of this, we are motivated to present our own group in the best light possible, while presenting other groups in the worst light. This makes our own group seem better, and consequently helps give us a more positive identity.

A number of studies have found that simply placing people in groups leads them to discriminate against those in other groups. This occurs even when people are randomly assigned to groups, and when they have never before met the members of their own group or of the out-group. For example, Tajfel (1970) assigned subjects to two groups on the basis of their judgment of some paintings. He then gave the subjects the opportunity to award money to members of their own group and members of the out-group. He found that subjects gave more money to in-group members than to out-group members. This effect occurred even when subjects did not anticipate meeting members of either group (Turner, 1981).

Recently researchers found that group formation affects the way people perceive members of their own group as well as of the out-group (Jones et al., 1981). In a series of studies these investigators found that people tend to see out-group members as being relatively similar, while they see greater variability in members of their own group. In other words, people tend to believe that their own group is made up of people with many different traits, while members of the out-group are all the same. These biased perceptions lead people to draw another conclusion: that one can generally determine what all the out-group members are like by observing the behavior of only a few (Quattrone, 1985). In other words, the formation of groups not only leads members to conclude that the out-group members are all alike, but also to adopt the position of "seen one, seen them all."

The simple formation of groups may sow the seeds of prejudice. There does seem to be a strong tendency to prefer members of one's own group over members of the out-group. However, while this research suggests one of the bases for prejudice, it does not describe why certain groups become the object of prejudice and others do not. As we have seen, people belong to many different groups at any one time. Why is it that only certain groups become the object of prejudice?

Learning. In Chapter 15 we examined how parents influence their children's attitudes through their control of rewards and information. Just as parents can teach other attitudes to children, so, too, can they teach their children to be prejudiced against specific groups. The child who hears his or her parents criticize a particular group of people may mimic this position. In some cases, the parents will even directly reward their children for expressing prejudicial attitudes. But more often the prejudice is transmitted in a less direct way. For example, a child may hear his or her father characterize women as being poor drivers. Even though the father may have done so in jest, the child may not distinguish the humor. He or she may consequenlty adopt the position that women are poor drivers. The strong influence of parents is seen in the fact that prejudicial attitudes are observable in many children as young as 3 years old (Milner, 1981).

Prejudicial attitudes are also reinforced by the media, which present certain groups in a negative way. Many times the negative portrayal is done indirectly. This occurred some years ago when the news media habitually reported the race of a criminal if he or she was black, but made no mention of race when the criminal was white. Newspaper readers might easily have gotten the impression that most criminals were black.

Thus, like many other attitudes, prejudice may be taught. The prejudicial attitude will be very difficult to change if it is further supported by peer groups. For instance, children who see that most of their friends have a negative attitude toward blacks or Hispanics will express similar attitudes. In doing this, they are accepted by the group; to do otherwise would lead to rejection. It will be extremely difficult to change their prejudice so long as they continue to associate with that peer group.

One way to reduce prejudice is to have people work for a common goal with those they may be prejudiced against.

Scapegoat Theory. Aronson (1976) relates an interesting story about the origin of the term **scapegoat**. During the Hebrew days of atonement in ancient times, a rabbi would place his hands on the head of a goat while reciting the sins of his congregation. The intent was to symbolically transfer the sins from the people to the goat. The goat was then chased into the wilderness, taking the sins of the congregation with him. This animal became known as the scapegoat.

One of the earliest theories of prejudice suggested that prejudice and discrimination are the result of scapegoating (Dollard et al., 1939). In Chapter 10 we discussed frustration-aggression theory—the view that frustration motivates aggression. Once frustrated, people will aggress *unless* the cause of the frustration is beyond reach or too powerful to attack. In these cases, the frustrated person may displace his or her aggression onto a safer target, even if this target (like the goat of the ancient Hebrews) is not directly responsible for the frustration. According to this theory, then, a minority group may be singled out as the target or scapegoat for aggression and hostility because it is safe to attack and it often has highly visible characteristics (color, accent, name, etc.) that separate it from the more powerful majority (Konečni, 1979). These highly visible characteristics are also important because they make the group salient (Worchel, 1985). Salience focusses our attention on the group and allows us to establish its boundaries. For example, because of physical features it is easier for us to quickly determine who fits into our category of blacks or women than it is for us to identify Germans and Lutherans.

Researchers have found some support for this scapegoat theory. For example, Miller and Bugelski (1948) frustrated workers at a civilian work camp by not allowing them to attend a movie. They then measured the workers' attitudes toward Mexicans and Japanese and found them more hostile toward these minority groups after being frustrated than before. It seems that the workers displaced their anger onto these minority groups. It is interesting to note that the greatest violence against the Jews in Russia occurred during times of economic hardship.

Reducing Prejudice and Discrimination

It is one thing to know what causes prejudice and quite another to know how to reduce or combat it. This point is painfully clear from the history of the United States. Although many theories exposed the roots of prejudice before 1950, significant steps toward reducing racial discrimination were not taken until the late 1950s, after the Supreme Court ruled that "separate but equal" schools for blacks and whites were inherently unequal and unfair. It took the passage of the Voting Rights Act in 1965 to ensure equal access to one of the basic freedoms (voting) in the United States. And even today statistics demonstrate that discrimination still exists in the work world, and social research indicates that antiblack attitudes and behavior are still with us (Crosby et al., 1980). These points demonstrate the importance of developing an understanding of how prejudice can be reduced.

Equal-Status Contact. One of the earliest suggestions on how to reduce prejudice was to increase contact between the members of different groups (Allport, 1954). Supposedly contact would allow members of the different groups to learn about each other and see that their stereotypes were invalid. Arguments such as this played a role in the Supreme Court's decision to mandate integration of public schools. Despite enthusiastic predictions that desegregation would reduce prejudice, the results of research have been disappointing (Amir & Sharan, 1984; Stephan, 1978). Studies showed that an *increase* in prejudice often followed desegregation. Further, the self-esteem of black children did not increase, and in some cases actually decreased, when they entered integrated schools. The only bright spot in this largely dismal picture was that achievement by black children tended to increase in the integrated setting.

These results may seem surprising and discouraging. However, to put them in proper perspective, imagine that tomorrow you were suddenly enrolled in a fourth-year medical school anatomy class. Obviously you would not be on an equal footing with the other students. At first you would probably be perceived by the other students as rather dumb and your self-esteem would suffer as you compared yourself to them. Over time, however, your performance would improve and your self-image would be restored.

This example makes two points about the value of contact. First, contact in itself will not necessarily reduce prejudice. In order to be effective, the contact must be between people of equal status so that neither party is inherently disadvantaged by the situation. Equal-status contact has been found to reduce prejudice and intergroup stereotypes (Brewer & Miller, 1984). Second, we must distinguish between the immediate and long-term effects of the contact. While equal-status contact may not immediately reduce prejudice, the longer-term effects may well be positive.

Cooperation. The integration of baseball could have taken place in two ways. One method would have been to have the black and white teams play each other. This would have allowed contact between a team of black players and a team of white players. Or integration could have been (and was) achieved by having whites and blacks play together on the same team. This procedure would also have resulted in contact between members of the two racial groups. Which method would we expect to be more successful?

The research strongly suggests that the latter method would be the more successful method of integration by far because it would bring people from the two racial groups together to work toward a common goal (winning) rather than competing against each other.

In a classic study Sherif and his colleagues created hostility between two groups of children at a summer camp (Sherif et al., 1961). The groups competed against each other on a series of tasks and soon they were openly fighting against each other. Sherif then decided to find out if simple contact between the two groups would reduce intergroup hostility. Accordingly, the two groups were brought together in a number of situations that did not involve competition: for example, eating together in the dining hall. This did not, however, lead to less hostility—it just gave them an additional chance to fight, and insults as well as food were hurled between them.

The researchers then had the two groups come together in situations where their combined efforts were needed to solve problems that involved both groups. For example, the groups went on a camping trip together, and the truck bringing their food became stuck. In order to move the truck, members from both groups had to push together. After a series of such events where the groups had to work on a common problem, the hostility between the two groups decreased markedly. Further research found that cooperative efforts aimed at a common goal reduce intergroup hostility only when those efforts succeed in obtaining the goal (Worchel, et al., 1978).

This research suggests that prejudice can be reduced if people can be placed in situations where they must work with the people or groups they are prejudiced against. This reasoning served as the basis for the *jigsaw method* that has been successfully used to reduce prejudice in the classroom (Aronson et al., 1979). Students are divided into ethnically mixed groups and given a problem to solve. Each member of the group receives only one part of the answer; in order for the group to solve the problem, all members have to contribute their part. A weak group member will hurt the whole group. Thus group members must help one another in order for their group to be successful.

It has been suggested that intergroup cooperation works because it causes people to redefine their groups (Worchel, 1985). In such situations it is no longer blacks against whites; the group contains both white and black members. In this way the salience of racial distinction is reduced.

Experiencing Prejudice. Young white middle-class individuals in the United States rarely, if ever, experience what it is like to be the object of prejudice. They don't know what it is like to be told they cannot play on a team because of their skin color or be refused a job because they are "too old." In a fascinating demonstration a third-grade schoolteacher in Riceville, Iowa, decided to turn the tables (Elliot, 1971). One day she announced to her class that "The blue-eyed people are smarter than the brown-eyed people. . . . Blue-eyed people are cleaner than brown-eyed people. They are more civilized." She let the blue-eyed students sit in front of the room and forced the brown-eyed children to sit in the back. The blue-eyed children were also given extra privileges. Almost immediately the blue-eyed children adopted this prejudice and began to tease and ridicule the brown-eyed students. They refused to associate with them and a fight even broke out because one boy called another "Brown-eyes."

The next morning the teacher told the class that she had lied and that the brown-eyed children were actually the better and brighter group. With the situation reversed, the brown-eyed children began to tease and taunt the blue-eyed children.

On the third day the teacher and children talked about the experience and how it felt to be the object of prejudice and discrimination. The teacher pointed out that they had only had this experience for one day, but that some children have to face prejudice every day of their lives. The children talked about how bad prejudice was and decided they didn't like themselves when they discriminated against others.

This method has been used by other investigators in school settings (Weiner & Wright, 1973). They have found that children who personally experienced prejudice and discrimination were less likely to adopt these attitudes and behaviors toward others. Other investigators have found that students were more likely to adopt a positive attitude toward old people if they were given lessons on what it is like to be old (Glass & Trent, 1981). These studies suggest that the more we learn about prejudice and its devastating effects on its victims, the less likely we will be to adopt prejudiced attitudes.

Summary

1. People belong to **groups** for many reasons. In some cases, they get rewards such as money, prestige, and security. In other cases, they join groups in order to evaluate their attitudes, values, and abilities. A third reason is that groups may be necessary for a person to obtain his or her goals.

2. Almost all groups develop **norms,** which are rules that apply to all members. Norms define what must be done and when. **Roles** are norms that apply only to people occupying a specific position in the group. While norms and roles can help a group run smoothly by making the behavior of members predictable, they can sometimes be harmful. For example, people who follow rigid sex roles may not be able to use their own creativity or behave in a way that is most comfortable for them.

3. **Conformity** occurs when people change their attitudes or behaviors as a result of real or imagined group pressure, despite personal feelings to the contrary. Conformity may involve only a change in behavior, or it may include changing both public behavior and private attitudes.

4. **Obedience** involves following the direct and explicit orders of a leader. Research conducted by Stanley Milgram showed that a surprising number of people would follow the orders of an authority figure even when they were ordered to hurt someone.

5. The **leader** is the person who has the greatest amount of influence in the group. Both personal and situational factors influence who will become the leader of a group. The contingency model of leadership suggests that leaders who are task oriented will be most effective when the group climate is either very positive or very negative. Leaders who are concerned with social relationships will be most effective in moderate group climates.

6. **Deindividuation** occurs when the person becomes submerged in the group and loses his or her individual identity. Deindividuation is most likely to result in large groups where uniforms are worn and members are anonymous. As a result of deindividuation, people may not feel responsible for their behavior.

7. Being in a group leads people to take stronger stands on issues than they would outside the group. This effect has been referred to as **group polarization.** It has been argued that this effect occurs because information is exchanged in group discussion and because people in groups do not feel personally responsible for their attitudes or behaviors. It also seems that people in groups compare their attitudes and behaviors, and since no one wants to be seen as the most undecided, each group member tries to adopt a position that is at least as strong as that of the other group members.

8. **Groupthink** results when people are more concerned about arriving at a group consensus than in making the best decision. In order to avoid groupthink, group members must be

encouraged to express their opinions even if they disagree with the position of the other group members. The group also needs to seek outside information and opinions.

9. A person's performance is also influenced by the group. Research has shown that while people can learn new and complex tasks better if they are alone, their performance of well-learned tasks is aided by being in front of a group. However, **social loafing** may result if people perform tasks as part of a group effort and if their individual input on the task is not identifiable.

10. **Prejudice** is an unjustified negative attitude toward an individual based solely on that person's membership in a group. **Discrimina-**tion is negative, often aggressive, behavior aimed at the target of prejudice. There are a number of theories about why prejudice and discrimination develop: one places the blame on the formation of a group; another suggests that people learn how to be prejudiced and against whom they should direct their prejudice; a third argues that prejudice and discrimination are the result of displaced aggression.

11. It is very difficult to change prejudice. In order to change biased attitudes, it is important to have people work together to achieve common goals. The effects of cooperation are most positive when the combined effort is successful in obtaining the desired goal.

Key Terms

conformity
discrimination
deindividuation
group
group polarization effect
groupthink
informational pressure
leader
normative social pressure
norms

obedience
prejudice
reactance
roles
scapegoat
social comparison theory
social facilitation
social loafing
social reality
stereotype

Suggested Readings

The following book is about Josh Gibson:
BRASHLER, W. *Josh Gibson: A Life in the Negro Leagues*. New York: Harper & Row, 1978.

FORSYTH, D. *An introduction to group dynamics*. Monterey, Calif.: Brooks/Cole, 1983. A comprehensive review of research and theory on group behavior. Includes discussion of groups in work, educational, legal, athletic, and clinical settings.

SHAW, M. *Group dynamics: The psychology of small group behavior*, 3rd ed. New York: McGraw-Hill, 1981. Presents an up-to-date review of theory and research on small group behavior. Topics of discussion include leadership, social facilitation, group performance, the group environment, and methods for studying group behavior.

TURNER, S., & GILES, H. (Eds.). *Intergroup behavior*. Chicago: University of Chicago Press, 1981. This is an edited volume of papers by British psychologists working in the area of intergroup relations. It is up to date and presents a broad view of the field.

WHEELER, J., DECI, E., REIS, H., & ZUCKERMAN, M. *Interpersonal influence*, 2nd ed. Boston: Allyn & Bacon, 1978. A short but informative discussion of social influence. The book focuses on theories, examining such topics as conformity, group polarization, obedience, power, and social comparison.

WORCHEL, S., & AUSTIN, W. *The psychology of intergroup relations*. Chicago, Ill.: Wilson Hall, 1985. This is a volume of original papers in the area of intergroup conflict. The chapters focus on causes, effects, and ways to reduce intergroup conflict.

ENVIRONMENT, BEHAVIOR, AND HEALTH

On the day Robert Stroud was born in 1890, Seattle, Washington, was slowly being rebuilt. The city of 20,000 had burned to the ground a few months earlier, and its inhabitants were determined to rebuild a well-ordered city of brick and mortar that would never again fall victim to fire. However, within a few years these careful plans were shelved and the city struggled to deal with a new role and a flood of humanity. Gold was discovered in Alaska, and Seattle became the crossroads for miners from all over the world who dreamed of making their fortune in the frozen hills of the Yukon. As a young boy, Robert was fascinated by the hustle and bustle of the city. He quit school after the third grade and spent his time on the docks listening to the miners' stories.

With an alcoholic father and a domineering mother, Stroud's home was not a happy one. When he turned 17, he could stand the situation no longer; he headed for Alaska. There, instead of a fortune, he found cold and isolation. But the shy young man also found Kitty O'Brien, a dance-hall girl who was twice his age. Robert and Kitty made an odd pair, but Stroud worked the railroad and even sold popcorn to support his first and only love.

Stroud's world abruptly changed when he came home one night and found that Kitty had been beaten by a bartender. In a fit of rage he tracked the man down and killed him. Stroud, now 19, was sentenced to 12 years in prison for his crime.

He was placed in McNeil Prison, a dirty, crowded institution with a strict warden. Stroud quickly hardened himself to institutional life; his trip from the freedom of Alaska to the confines of prison had been difficult, but he was determined to survive. In an effort to gain control over his depressing surroundings, Stroud began to break prison rules. He fought with other inmates, and in one case buried a paring knife in the shoulder of a fellow prisoner who had snitched on him. This act lost him all chance of parole.

By 1912 the overcrowding in federal prisons had become an open scandal. An enormous new prison covering 16 acres, with 40-foot walls, was built in Leavenworth, Kansas. It was designed for maximum security and hard-core troublemakers from other prisons were packed in there. Stroud was one of the first to be transferred from McNeil. At Leavenworth he was placed in a cell with one other person. Stroud and his cell mate, Eddie, tried to make their small room as comfortable as possible. They became close friends and Eddie encouraged Stroud to take some correspondence classes. To everyone's surprise, Stroud excelled in these efforts, first teaching himself to read and then sailing through courses in mathematics, astronomy, and structural engineering. But while Stroud's mind improved, his attitude did not. He hated his captivity and his captors. Leavenworth had 1,200 inmates at this time and privacy was impossible. Some of the guards delighted in demonstrating their control over the inmates.

The hatred that seethed in Stroud came to a head one day when a guard taunted him in the dining hall. Stroud leaped at the guard and plunged a knife through his heart. Robert

Stroud was sentenced to death for this murder, but 8 days before his scheduled execution President Wilson commuted his sentence to life. This good news, however, was tempered by the warden's announcement that Stroud would be kept in a segregated cell for the duration of his sentence. He would be allowed a half hour each day for exercise in the courtyard and his only visitors would be members of his immediate family.

On April 15, 1920, Robert Stroud was moved into his new home: a 6-by-12-foot cell with gray walls, a bed, washbasin, lavatory, and a single 25-watt light bulb. There were 18 cells in the Isolation Unit. Here Stroud faced endless days, months, and years without hope of freedom. His only human contacts were the guard who brought him food each day and the other faceless inmates in the unit, who could shout at, but rarely see, one another.

Throughout his ordeal Stroud's mother had been his constant support. She had hired lawyers to defend him and written dozens of letters on his behalf; by now she had exhausted her meager savings. In the confines of his tiny cell Stroud decided to try to repay her. With a stolen razor blade, watercolors, and pencils, he began making Christmas and birthday cards which he gave to his mother to sell. To his surprise, his efforts met with some success and his mother was able to supplement her income by selling these cards.

Stroud slowly adjusted to his solitary existence but looked forward to his half hour in the open sunlight each day. One day he watched a mighty storm rumble in. Among the leaves and branches that rained on his tiny yard he saw the scattered remnants of a bird's nest. On closer examination he discovered four fledgling sparrows that looked more like tiny mice than birds; three were moving and one was still. He quickly picked up the three tiny creatures, placed them in his handkerchief, and hurried back to his cell. There Stroud built a small nest and carefully collected every scrap of food he could find. To his joy, the birds wolfed down these small morsels and greedily begged for more. Stroud now had a purpose in life. The tower guards were amused to see his lanky frame in the courtyard each day chasing grasshoppers and flies to feed "his family." He taught his birds tricks such as flying into his pocket and rolling over and playing dead. After putting on his show for the warden, he was delighted to receive a present of two canaries.

The birds absorbed Stroud's attention. He spent hours studying their every move, making detailed drawings of them and teaching them new tricks. He begged and bartered for food, and with the aid of a rusty razor blade, he built a magnificent cage for his friends. To his delight, he discovered four tiny eggs in the canary nest, and before long his family grew in size. He decided to raise canaries for his mother to sell.

Soon carefully crafted cages covered his cell. Stroud read every bird book and magazine he could get his hands on. He began a journal detailing the birds' activities, feeding habits, and diseases. Stroud was the only bird expert in the world who spent 24 hours a day with birds. He wrote, "I want to go on record against that very popular and very stupid abomination, the round canary cage. . . . Birds like corners for the same reason you like them; they give a sense of protection" (Gaddis, 1955, p. 150). Stroud was soon writing articles for the *Roller Canary Journal*. Thousands of bird lovers throughout the world benefited from his skillful observations.

When a bird died, Stroud painfully dissected it and studied every organ. Through friends in the prison hospital, he was able to obtain chemicals to mix for medicines. At one point his bird colony numbered 300, all packed into his tiny cell. This unusual man with a third-grade education had become a leading world expert on birds. He discovered medicines to cure illnesses that before were fatal to birds. People all over the world wrote to him for advice; at one point he was receiving an average of 12 letters a day. Stroud answered each one with care and concern. His written work numbered over 1,000 pages when he decided to bring it together as a book. Through the efforts of bird lovers and his family, he found a publisher for one of the world's most authoritative books on birds, *Stroud's Digest of the Diseases of Birds*.

While Stroud worked feverishly in his cell, conditions at Leavenworth deteriorated. Politics led to several changes in prison personnel, and the prison population had grown to 3,770 by 1929. During that summer Leavenworth "sucked heat like a rock stove." All of these problems exploded in a riot that left several people dead and scores more injured. In its wake prison officials decided to clamp down on prisoners and enforce the rules. They threatened to take Stroud's birds away from him. In a last-ditch effort to save his colony, Stroud smuggled out letters to bird fanciers who had written him in the past. The reply was tremendous; a petition with over 50,000 names was delivered to the congressmen from Kansas demanding that Stroud be allowed to continue his work.

Stroud was permitted to go on with his work, but he was now labeled a "troublemaker" by prison authorities. As the years and decades rolled by, all of his appeals for parole were turned down and he remained in isolation. Still, he continued to fight the system each time it threatened to take away his birds.

This solitary figure toiled in isolation through two world wars and the Great Depression. He was a constant thorn in the side of Leavenworth officials; he began to read law books so he would know how to fight legally to protect his birds. In 1942 the Leavenworth officials decided they would tolerate him no longer and he was moved to a newly refurbished prison on a small island in San Francisco Bay: Alcatraz. Now a stooped old man, Stroud was again placed in isolation. His birds were confiscated by the officials,

his spirit was broken, and his health was failing. He survived the bloodiest riot in federal prison history on the Rock, as Alcatraz was known. After a decade in Alcatraz and 32 years of living in isolation, Stroud carefully assembled a cache of pills. In December 1951 he attempted his only escape from the cells that had been his home since he was 19: He swallowed his pills and lay down to die.

But the system would not let Stroud go. He was accidentally discovered by a guard, who rushed him to the hospital. After weeks of treatment he recovered and was taken back to his isolation cell. The Bird Man of Alcatraz, as he was known, could only look forward to pardon or death. The birds that had once been his cheerful companions in solitude were now only small dead ghosts in his memory. In 1959 Robert Stroud was transferred to the Medical Center for Prisoners in Springfield, Missouri. This ended his solitary confinement of 39 years, the longest endured by any United States prisoner in history. But only death in 1963 ended his captivity.

UNDERSTANDING OUR PARTNERSHIP WITH THE ENVIRONMENT

As we trace Robert Stroud's life, we can see that despite spending over 50 years in prison, Stroud experienced a wide variety of environmental settings. As an infant, he lived in a crowded tent city while Seattle was being rebuilt. As a child, he lived in a home in an orderly new city. His next stop was the frigid, barren slopes of the Alaskan Territory. His first prison experience was in McNeil Prison, an old, crowded institution where he spent a great deal of time in an open dormitory area. Leavenworth presented Stroud with a new set of living conditions. Here he lived first in a small cell with one other man, then in a solitary 6-by-12-foot isolation cell. The Kansas weather swung from blistering summers to very cold winters. The Rock challenged Stroud with still a different physical setting and weather conditions.

When we think about human behavior, we often focus on social influences. More recently psychologists have begun to realize that our physical environment also affects our behavior, our social relationships, and even our physical health. In addition, it is equally clear that people influence their physical environments; we change the course of our rivers, create lakes, build cities, and even flatten mountains. The field of **environmental psychology** was developed to study the interrelationship between the physical environment and human behavior and experience (Holahan, 1982). Although environmental psychology is a relative newcomer to the family of psychology, we have already learned of some important characteristics of the human-environment interaction.

When most of us think about how the environment affects our behavior, we focus on specific factors such as loud noises, extreme heat, or high density. As we will see in our examination of environmental psychology, while the extremity or absolute level of a variable is important, some of the most striking effects are created by more subtle dimensions. For example, the degree of *predictability* and the amount of *control* a person has over the environment are often more important than the physical intensity of the environment. We will see that people can adjust to a very harsh environment if they feel that they have control over that environment. Another important factor involves the *meaning* that people place on environmental variables. For example, a low level of noise can be very stressful and disruptive if a person believes that it signals an impending danger.

Stroud's last prison was Alcatraz, or the Rock as it became known. The prison environment presented a constant challenge of survival to the inmates.

ENERGY CONSERVATION: SAVING OUR ENVIRONMENT TO SAVE OURSELVES

In the last decade we have witnessed almost inconceivable changes in our world. Robots have begun to replace people in factories; computers send us bills, guide our airplanes, and monitor our automobiles. Dreaded diseases like smallpox have vanished. But of all the changes, one of the most dramatic has been people's concern with energy. Before 1973 gasoline sold for around 29 cents a gallon in the United States; many cars got less than 10 miles to a gallon of gasoline; monthly electric bills of under $15 were not unusual. In 1973 all this changed. This was the year of the Arab embargo on oil shipments to the West. The energy crisis was upon us. Along with these skyrocketing prices came the realization that conservation of energy was necessary if we wished to keep our comfortable life style.

While some people immediately adopted conservation measures, many others did not; energy conservation was a painfully slow process in the United States during the mid-1970s. Recently a number of psychologists have pointed out some of the reasons for this reaction.

Becker and Seligman (1981)

argue that people feel they have little control over their own energy usage and even less over the bigger problem of worldwide energy conservation. People believe that the energy problem is so large that it will not be helped by their saving a few gallons of gasoline. Brechner and Linder (1981) identify another reason by viewing the energy question as a social trap. Social traps arise when behaviors that help the individual hurt the group. For example, driving your automobile three blocks to the grocery store may be convenient for you, but it reduces the amount of gasoline that will be available for others. In many cases, energy conservation forces people to decide whether or not they will sacrifice their own comfort and convenience for the good of the larger group.

Other researchers have outlined steps to aid energy conservation. One of the more novel approaches has involved giving people feedback on how their behavior saves energy. In many cases, people are unaware of how much they can save by turning off the lights in their home or reducing the temperature of their hot water. Most people receive a utility bill only once

a month, so they have no immediate information on how much savings these behaviors produce. In order to show the importance of immediate feedback, Seligman and Darley (1977) recorded the amount of electricity used by a sample group of residents. Half of the residents then received a letter telling them that air conditioning uses the greatest amount of energy in the summer. This group was also told that each day they would receive information on how much electricity they had used the day before. A control group received the same letter but was not told about and did not receive daily information about their energy use. Over the next month the group receiving daily feedback used less electricity than the group that did not receive daily feedback. The information not only allowed people to see how much energy they were using but also showed them that they did have control over their energy consumption.

This research does show that effective programs can be developed and the use of psychological knowledge can help in the fight to conserve our environment's resources.

Therefore when we study the environment we must be concerned with the psychological properties as well as the physical properties of stimuli. This point applies to almost any quality of the environment, including density, heat, noise, and the design of buildings.

PHYSICAL SPACE AND BEHAVIOR

One of the most basic elements of our environment is physical space. Whether our focus is on the small area that directly surrounds our bodies, the larger space on which our homes are built, or the far more immense area of our country, our own lives are very much affected by the way we and others treat physical space. Many people spend their lives working so that they can afford to buy a piece of land they can call their own. Countless other people have lost their lives in wars and disputes over territory.

Territoriality

When we speak of "physical space," most of us think about a room, a house, or a building lot. As far back as 1920, Eliot Howard noted that birds often lay claim to a certain area and will fiercely protect it against other members of the same species. Stroud observed this when he took his new canaries into his cell, which was already occupied by his sparrows. The sparrows darted at the intruders to keep them from their territory on the water pipes in the cell. The bird songs that gladden our ears are often a bird's way of announcing "ownership" of a certain area. **Territoriality** involves the claiming of control or ownership of areas or objects (Porteous, 1977). Once the claim is made, the territory will be defended against other members of the same species.

In order to stake out their territory, both humans and animals set out identifiable markers. Dogs, for example, use scent; they urinate around the boundary of their area so that intruding dogs will be able to smell when they are entering another's territory. Humans put up fences around their land, plant hedges, or place signs to warn that a territory has been claimed.

Humans, unlike animals, retain ownership of their territory even when they are not occupying it. If we own a beach house, for example, we expect others to keep out of it even though we occupy the house for only a few months each year. We even feel that we should have the right to determine who can occupy our territory after we die! Animals, on the other hand, control an area only when they are in actual residence (Ittleson et al., 1974). Another difference is that territory for humans involves more than space. Out territory includes objects such as boats, cars, furniture, books, and tennis rackets. It was not so long ago that human territory also included other humans.

An interesting feature of human territorial behavior is that all territory is not equal; in other words, there are different categories or types of territory, and each evokes a different behavior from us (Altman, 1975). **Primary territories** are owned and controlled by people and are central to their lives. Uninvited trespassing into primary territories is likely to meet with aggression. For example, your home is your primary territory, and an unwanted intruder is likely to provoke a strong response from you. Stroud's tiny cell was his primary territory. Humans also have **secondary territories,** which are not as central to their lives and which are not "owned" by them. However, people often become emotionally attached to these areas and try to control them. Secondary territories may be a private country club or social club or a neighborhood street. If you have a regular seat in a classroom, you can understand the meaning of secondary territories. You are likely to feel that this is your space even though you don't own it, and you may feel upset if someone "steals" your space in class. Finally, humans have **public territories,** which do not involve feelings of ownership, but people do feel that they control these areas while they are occupying them. For example, when you are at a table in a restaurant in the United States, you will feel that it is your territory, and you will react with surprise and possibly anger if a stranger walks over and sits down in an empty chair at your table. Western Europeans, on the other hand, have a very different concept of public territory in a restaurant, and Americans in Europe may be shocked to find strangers invading "their" table.

People, unlike animals, feel ownership of territory even when they are not occupying it. People use signs, fences, and other markers to protect their territory from intrusion.

Public territory is space that people do not own but control while they occupy it. A spot on the beach is an example of public territory—as can be seen, people mark their public territory in many ways to show that they are occupying it.

The Functions of Territoriality. One important function of territoriality is *survival*. Territory is a place where an individual or group can carry on the basic functions of survival: raising food and reproducing. Any one area will only be able to sustain a limited number of people or animals. Thus allowing outsiders into one's territory can result in a direct threat to survival.

Related to survival is the *protective function* of territory. Knowing the characteristics of an area can give an individual or group an advantage if it must hide from or fight an intruder. In the battle of athletic teams we refer to this as the "home court advantage." Many sports fans swear that the outcome of a game is determined more by where it's played than by the skill of either team involved. For this reason, professional gamblers generally figure the odds to reflect an advantage to the "home team." The belief in the home court advantage is supported by Schwartz and Barsky (1977), who found that such an advantage does exist in professional basketball, football, and baseball. However, before rushing out to bet your last dollar on the home team, be advised of recent research that found that home teams tend to lose decisive championship games (Baumeister,

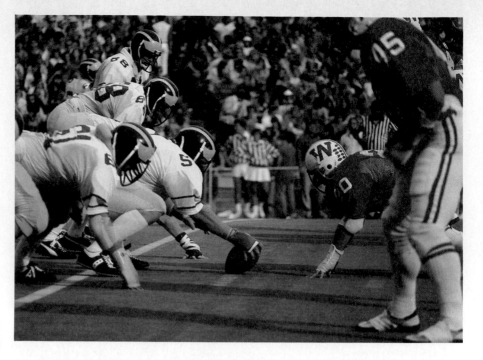

Because people are more familiar with their own territory, they have an advantage over intruders. Statistics show that the home team is more likely to win a sports contest than the visiting team, except when that contest is a decisive championship game.

1985; Baumeister and Steinhiber, 1984). The investigators argue that the presence of a supportive audience in those critical situations increases the cost of not winning. The added pressure may cause players to become more self-conscious and inhibit their performance. Another example of the protective function was found in research examining the characteristics of homes that are targets for burglary (Brown, 1979). Investigators found that a home was less likely to be burglarized if it had clear signs of territorial markings such as a fence around the yard, a nameplate and address sign, and indications of occupancy (see Figure 17–1).

Territorial behavior may *increase social order* and ensure privacy (Edney, 1975). If people have clearly staked out their own territories, they are less likely to fight over questions of ownership. The poet Robert Frost stated this position when he wrote, "Good fences make good neighbors." In an interesting study Rosenblatt and Budd (1977) found that married couples tended to be more territorial than did unmarried people who were living together. For example, married couples were more likely to have clear understandings about who sleeps on what side of the bed and who sits at a particular spot at the dining table. Presumably married couples realize that they will most likely be together for a long time and wish to take steps to avoid future conflict in their relationships. Similarly, when Stroud first arrived at Leavenworth, he shared a tiny cell with Eddie. The cell mates quickly developed a routine for using the space and the facilities in their cell. Because the two men had to live together 24 hours a day, conflict over territory would have been disastrous.

Figure 17–1
The appearance of a home can influence its chances of being burglarized (left, nonburglarized; right, burglarized).

It has been suggested that territory is also used by people to *identify* themselves and establish their uniqueness (Altman & Chemers, 1980). In a way, a person's territory becomes a representation of that individual. A walk through a dormitory or office building will highlight this function. For example, the person who loves to ski will have skiing pictures and posters of snow-covered mountains on his or her wall. The country music fan may have posters showing Waylon Jennings, Johnny Cash, and Dolly Parton. In this way, people use their territory to set themselves apart from others and to present attitudes, traits, or values that are important to them.

Personal Space

When we speak of territoriality, we refer to the use of fixed or tangible pieces of property that remain even when the person goes away. A number of years ago another type of territorial behavior was identified in humans (Hall, 1959, 1966). After observing people in many cultures, Hall reported that people act as if they "own" the space that directly surrounds them. Hall found that no matter where they are, people maneuver to keep others from trespassing on the area directly surrounding their bodies. This area, or **personal space,** is like a bubble surrounding the person wherever he or she goes. Even though we are generally unaware of our spatial behavior, we tend to follow very regular and predictable rules concerning it. The term **proxemics** was coined to describe the study of this personal space.

Hall was most interested in our use of space when we are with other people. He watched people from a number of different cultures interacting in various situations, and concluded that humans use basically four different interaction distances. As can be seen from Table 17–1, the chosen distance is affected by the type of interaction and the relationship between the people involved.

The Functions of Interpersonal Distance. It's not hard to see why we claim fixed pieces of property. But why do we need to have a bubble of space around us?

The fact that most interaction distances (except for the intimate distance) are large enough to keep people out of one another's reach led Evans and Howard (1973) to suggest that personal space plays the important function of controlling aggression. Keeping a "neutral zone" between people may inhibit physical violence by keeping people apart. For example, Kinzel (1970) found that violent inmates had larger personal spaces than did nonviolent inmates. The violent prisoners did not trust others, and their large personal space zone served as a buffer of protection. It has also been reported that people keep greater distances when they are angry (O'Neal et al., 1980).

The distance at which we interact determines the way we communicate. In order to see this, talk with a friend at the intimate distance (about 12 inches away). What do you see and hear at this distance? In addition to

Table 17–1
Types of Interpersonal Relationships and Activities and Interpersonal Space

	Appropriate Relationships and Activities
Intimate distance (0 to 1½ feet)	Intimate contacts (e.g., making love, comforting) and physical sports (e.g., wrestling)
Personal distance (1½ to 4 feet)	Contacts between close friends, as well as everyday interactions with acquaintances
Social distance (4 to 12 feet)	Impersonal and businesslike contacts
Public distance (more than 12 feet)	Formal contacts between an individual (e.g., actor, politician) and the public
Source: Based on Hall, 1963.	

the person's voice, you can also hear his or her breathing. You can see facial details, such as wrinkles and muscle twitches, observe the focus of your friend's eyes, and even spot drops of sweat on his or her forehead. Each of these channels may be used to communicate a message. While you get greater clarity from some channels, at the intimate distance you cannot observe your friend's hands, feet, or body posture. Thus, while the intimate distance opens some channels, it closes others. Now try talking at the social distance (5 or 6 feet). At this distance hand and body movements are easily observed, but eye contact is more difficult and you cannot observe small changes in muscle tone.

Also, we often show the degree of intimacy we feel toward another by how close we get to that person; we stand closer to people we like than to people we dislike (Argyle & Dean, 1965). You can verify this by putting a larger-than-normal interaction space between you and a very close friend. The friend's first response may be to "close the gap" between the two of you. However, if you continue to back off, he or she will probably ask, "What's the matter with you—are you angry at me?"

What Affects Interaction Distances?   What determines how close you get to other people? In some cases, such as in a crowded subway, you have little choice about your distance. However, in most cases, you do determine the space that separates you from others. The nature of the relationship, mood, age, sex, culture, and physical surroundings influence the distance people keep between themselves and others. Let's look at how two variables, culture and sex, influence our personal space.

Cultural Background.   In his early research into personal space Hall studied people from many cultures. He found that Latin Americans, Arabs, Greeks, and French people interact at closer distances than Americans, Germans, and English people. This information may seem to be only a bit of trivia, but there is an amusing story, often called the "Latin Waltz," that shows why such cultural differences can be important. The story involves two men, one from Mexico and one from the United States, who met at a party. As their conversation progressed, the Mexican moved closer to his new acquaintance in order to establish a "comfortable" interaction distance. The American, however, quickly felt uneasy with this close distance, and moved backward to establish a spacing that was comfortable for him. This backward movement brought the Mexican charging in to close the gap between them. Like two dancers in perfect step, the conversationalists waltzed around the room. Neither was trying to be impolite and neither was even conscious of his behavior. Each was simply trying to establish a distance that was comfortable for him.

It's funny to imagine two men dancing around the room, but cultural differences in spatial behavior can have important consequences. In many large cities people from different cultural backgrounds interact on a daily basis. Differences in language and customs can sometimes make these meetings difficult or stressful (Worchel & Cooper, 1983). There is additional discomfort if people must silently battle for comfortable interaction distances. Further, since most people are unaware of their spatial behavior, they are likely to have a difficult time realizing the real source of stress in these cross-cultural encounters.

Sex.   It seems that somewhere in our early learning of how to be a boy or girl, there is a lesson on spatial behavior, and that lesson appears to be different for each sex. The most generally observed sex difference is that females have a smaller personal space than do males (Aiello & Aiello, 1974; Heckel & Hiers, 1977). Also, mixed-sex pairs interact at closer distances than do same-sex pairs (see Figure 17–2). There is one interesting exception to this rule: When women start an interaction with a stranger, they keep a greater distance from a man than from a woman (Dosey & Meisels, 1969). As we have seen, intimacy can be communicated by spacing,

Figure 17–2
Personal space zones tend to be egg-shaped rather than neat round bubbles. (Horwitz et al., 1964)

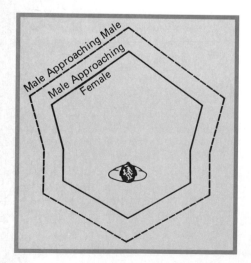

People go to great lengths to protect their personal space from intrusion. In libraries people may build a barricade of books and personal belongings to keep others at a distance. Men generally are most concerned with protecting the frontal space, while women guard the space to their sides.

and it is likely that women are especially careful not to communicate nonexistent feelings of attraction to a strange man. A similar line of reasoning has been used to explain why men have greater interaction distances in same-sex dyads than do women. Hall (1966) points out that in Western societies taboos against male homosexuality are strongly stressed, and as a result men are particularly sensitive about "keeping their distance" when interacting with other men.

In addition to distance, there seems to be another page in the lesson book on sex and spatial behavior. Imagine yourself seated at an uncrowded library table, minding your own business, when suddenly a stranger takes a seat too close to you. The stranger invades your personal space by taking either the seat next to you or the seat opposite you. Which type of invasion would make you more uncomfortable? Byrne and his colleagues (1971) found that men reacted more negatively to frontal invasions, while women were most upset by invasions from the side. In an interesting observation related to this finding, Fisher and Byrne (1975) found that when men sat down at a library table they most often placed their personal belongings on the table in front of them. This acted as a barrier against frontal invasions. Women, on the other hand, placed their belongings in adjacent chairs, thus ensuring against invasions from the side.

Responses to Invasion of Personal Space. You may want to try the following experiment—it won't win friends, but it will show something about what it means to violate someone's personal space. During a conversation slowly move closer to your companion; if the other person retreats, continue your charge. How does the other person respond to this?

The most common response is likely to be stress. The other person will probably feel tense and uncomfortable and you may observe some fidgeting (Worchel & Teddlie, 1976). What you cannot observe is the "internal fidgeting" your attack is likely to set off. Your victim's heart rate and blood pressure will increase and muscles are likely to become taut (McBride et al., 1965).

Another common response is flight: Your victim is likely to move away from you. This reaction was dramatically demonstrated by Sommer (1969)

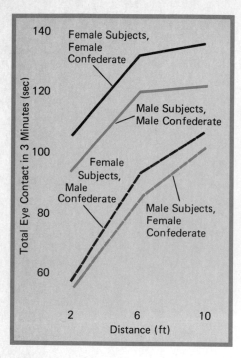

Figure 17–3
When interpersonal distances are violated, people engage in other behaviors, such as avoiding eye contact, to reduce intimacy. (Argyle & Dean, 1965)

in a university library setting. When a female seated alone at a table was spotted, an experimenter approached and took a seat immediately next to the unsuspecting subject. In 70 percent of these cases the subject had left the table within a 30-minute period after the intruder arrived. In a control condition where there was no invasion of the area, only 10 percent of the subjects abandoned their table in the same time period.

If your own victim does not flee or if you're successful enough to maneuver him or her into a corner where flight is impossible, you should begin to see blocking movements. Earlier we discussed the fact that close distance communicates intimacy. Researchers reported that a number of other nonverbal behaviors also communicate intimacy (Argyle & Dean, 1965). For example, you can signal that you like other people by maintaining eye contact with them, leaning toward them, and facing them directly rather than placing your folded arms or shoulders between them and you. According to Argyle and Dean, all of these channels are used together to signal the degree of intimacy you wish to have. In fact, they form an equilibrium system so that too much intimacy in one channel can be compensated for by reducing intimacy in other channels. Thus, if you move into other people's personal space, which signals intimacy, their response might well be to reduce eye contact or turn their bodies away from you ("giving the cold shoulder"). In order to show this, Argyle and Dean had subjects converse with a confederate at distances of 2, 6, or 10 feet. As can be seen in Figure 17–3, the closer the subjects were to the confederate, the less eye contact they maintained (Argyle & Dean, 1965).

Finally, you will probably find that your inappropriate closeness to another person is likely to cause him or her to dislike you. This reaction has been found even in situations where the violation was not deliberate. One exception to this finding occurs when people interpret the violation as a sign of friendliness on the part of the invader (Schneider & Harsuick, 1979).

Density and Crowding

During Stroud's five decades in prison one of the biggest problems faced by the correctional system was the rapidly increasing size of the prison population. Stroud was moved from McNeil to Leavenworth and finally to Alcatraz as the United States built new prisons to keep up with the demand. But population explosion was not only a problem in prisons. While Stroud's life went on in his solitary cell, the world population was expanding at an alarming rate. Paul Ehrlich, who refers to the rapid growth in the world's population as the *population bomb*, pointed out that in the 200 years between 1650 and 1850, the world's population doubled, reaching the 1 billion mark. By 1980 the world's population was over 4 billion, and only 38 years will be needed for it to double again (see Table 17–2). One consequence of this population explosion is that people are living closer together and each person has less space in which to live.

Recently social scientists have begun to identify the consequences of living at increasingly smaller distances from other people. Before we look at this research, it is important to explain the difference between two terms: density and crowding. **Density** is a measure of the space available to people in a given area. For example, you can find the density of your city by dividing its population by its area. In 1973 the density of New York City was about 450 people per acre, while Hong Kong had a density of 2,000 people per acre. **Crowding,** on the other hand, is a psychological state rather than a physical measure (Stokols, 1972). You can *feel* crowded, but you cannot feel density. Density and crowding are often related; but as we will see later, this is not always the case.

Density and Behavior. In 1962 John Calhoun published the results

Table 17–2
Doubling Times of Population under Various Rates of Natural Increase

	Crude Birth Rate (per 1,000)	Crude Death Rate (per 1,000)	Rate of Natural Increase (annual, percent)	Number of Years to Double
World	30	12	1.8	38
Major Regions				
Africa	45	19	2.6	27
Asia	32	12	2.0	35
Europe	15	10	0.4	173
Latin America	36	9	2.7	26
North America	15	9	0.6	116
Oceania	22	9	1.3	53

Source: Population Reference Bureau (1977).

of a study that shocked social scientists and added a new urgency to the study of density and crowding. Calhoun built a rat colony with four "rooms" designed to hold about 48 animals. He let the population grow until it reached 80, however, and then he removed young rats after they had been weaned. The colony dwellers were given enough food, water, and nesting material to maintain a "high standard of living," but problems soon began to develop. Some dominant rats laid claim to two of the rooms, forcing the rest of the animals to live in the remaining two pens. As a result of overcrowding, these two pens became *behavioral sinks*, which "aggravated all forms of pathology that can be found within a group." Females often abandoned their young and failed to build nests. Many of the rats became cannibals and devoured the unattended young. Aggression was frequent, and the pens became smeared with the blood of the injured animals. Abnormal sexual behavior was observed as male rats tried to mate with immature females or engaged in homosexual acts. Females suffered a large number of miscarriages, and many developed cancer of the sex organs and mammary glands.

Is this the fate that awaits humans as their population explosion continues? In order to examine this question, a number of investigators conducted studies comparing the behavior of individuals living in different densities. The results of these studies were largely inconclusive; some found bad effects (high rates of mental illness and juvenile delinquency) associated with high density; others did not. Further, even in the studies that reported negative behaviors related to high density, it was not possible to know for sure that density was the cause of the problems. For example, the highest-density areas are usually found in the inner cities, and residents of these areas are often poorer, less educated, and have less job security than people living in the lower-density suburbs. Any one or all of these differences might be responsible for the physical, mental, and social difficulties found, rather than density alone. The laboratory research found few consistent effects on subjects confined to high-density rooms for short periods (Sundstrom, 1978).

Crowding. This conclusion may cause many of us, especially those living in high-density areas, to breathe a sigh of relief. However, before becoming too complacent, we must examine the research on crowding. As we pointed out earlier, crowding is a feeling or a psychological state that often, but not always, accompanies high density. Investigators have therefore turned their attention to identifying the conditions under which high density leads to crowding, stress, and behavioral effects (Baum et al., 1981; Gatchel & Baum, 1983).

A number of factors have been found to influence the amount of crowding people will experience. First, the focus of our attention determines when we will feel crowded (Worchel & Brown, 1984). When other people who are violating our personal space become the center of our attention, we will attribute our arousal and discomfort to their closeness. This will result in our feeling crowded. However, if our attention is not focussed on other people, we will not experience crowding, even in high-density situations. For example, at an athletic event people's attention is focussed on the competition and not on the other spectators. As a result, they are not likely to experience much crowding. On the other hand, in a busy store crowding will result because people must focus their attention on other shoppers as they make their way to the cashier.

It has also been suggested that high density will lead to crowding when people feel that they have lost control over their environment (Rodin & Baum, 1978; Rodin & Langer, 1977). Again, if you remember your experiences in a packed store, you may recall feelings of utter helplessness; you were unable to get the attention of the salesperson, the dressing rooms were fully occupied, and you didn't dare go against the flow of traffic for fear of being trampled. At the athletic event the need for control is not as important; you only want to be able to see the contest. Further, there is some order to the seating of the crowd, and if you wish to leave, you can walk through the aisles to get out.

Third, crowding is likely to be felt when people cannot achieve the amount of *privacy* they desire (Altman, 1975). Privacy involves being able to choose whether or not to interact with others. Altman believes that when high density forces us to interact with others against our will, we will experience crowding. For example, Stroud felt uncomfortable when he shared a cell with one other inmate even though he had more space there than he had in solitary confinement. However, he never had any privacy in the two-man cell.

Effects of Crowding on Behavior. Earlier we saw that high density does not necessarily lead to negative responses from humans. Unfortunately, the research on crowding presents a different picture; the experience of crowding often has negative effects on our emotions, performance, and interpersonal relations.

One common effect is that we are *less attracted* to people in crowded than in noncrowded conditions. Interestingly enough, this effect has been consistently found for males but not for females (Epstein & Karlin, 1975).

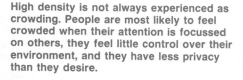

High density is not always experienced as crowding. People are most likely to feel crowded when their attention is focussed on others, they feel little control over their environment, and they have less privacy than they desire.

The difference may be due to the larger personal space zones that males have or to a general tendency of females to act cooperatively while males are more likely to respond to others competitively (Fisher et al., 1984). A related finding is that crowding often increases the likelihood of aggression (Ginsberg et al., 1977). This finding may give us one reason for the high incidence of aggression in prison. The story of Stroud's prison life is studded with fights among inmates, between inmates and guards, and riots. Often the incident that triggered these violent acts was trivial, but its effect was magnified because of the crowded conditions. In addition to tending toward aggression, people are less likely to help others in crowded as opposed to noncrowded environments (Nadler et al., 1982).

Investigators have also observed that as the environment becomes more crowded, some people withdraw from social contact. For example, observations of children on the playground found that some of them tended to play by themselves and interact less with others as the playground became increasingly crowded (Loo, 1972; McGrew, 1970). We have too little information to be able to predict whether people will aggress or withdraw in the face of crowding. However, while withdrawal may be an option in many situations such as the playground, it is not an option in others such as prison.

Given the list of negative effects of crowding that we have already discussed, we might expect that crowded individuals would not perform well. To a certain degree this is true. Research has shown that crowding interferes with performance of complex or detailed tasks (McClelland, 1974) as well as tasks that require social interaction and coordination (Heller et al., 1977). On the other hand, people sometimes perform simple tasks better when they are crowded than when they are not crowded. At first glance, this might seem like a curious pattern of results. However, if you will recall our discussion of social facilitation in Chapter 16, you will remember that the heightened arousal caused by an audience inhibited performance of complicated tasks, but aided work on easy and well-learned tasks. The effect of crowding may be the same: It may arouse individuals to such a degree that they cannot concentrate on details, but the arousal may give them the energy to quickly deal with simple problems. The message of this research is that you should choose an environment that suits the type of problem on which you will be working.

Crowding and Health. Disease, both psychological and physical, raged around Stroud when he was in prison. In fact, his first cell mate began to show such bizzare behavior that he was classified as mentally disturbed and moved to another prison. It began when Eddie complained of hearing voices in the floor. He was soon inspecting the cell very carefully for the Devil. Then one day Eddie set fire to his mattress to chase the devils out.

It is impossible to determine if these illnesses were caused by the congested conditions of the prison. We could easily argue that the men might have gotten sick outside prison. But there is evidence that extreme crowding is stressful and can affect our health. At the most basic level, research has shown that crowding increases physiological arousal (Evans, 1979). This research has found that high density leads to increased blood pressure, higher pulse rate, elevated skin conductance levels (GSR—galvanic skin response), and increased cortisol levels (indication of stress). One study found higher levels of epinephrine in urine samples taken from male passengers on crowded commuter trains (Singer et al., 1978).

There is also evidence suggesting that crowding is related to illness. Records at one student health center showed that visits were more frequent from students living in crowded dormitories than from students living in less crowded dormitories (Baron et al., 1976). Research on prisons has found increases in stress reactions, visits to the infirmary, number of inmates admitted for psychiatric care, and death rate as the population of the prison expanded (Paulus & McCain, 1983). Finally, investigators found a rise in illness as crowding increased aboard naval vessels (Dean et al., 1978).

All these studies indicate that crowding can affect our health. However, as we pointed out earlier, research examining density in neighborhoods has sometimes found that it is related to physical and mental health, but in other cases no relationship has been found. It has therefore been suggested that the relationship between crowding and health is influenced by the way people have learned to cope with crowding, the availability of opportunities to escape the crowded environments for a period of time, and the social organization that exists among the people in the environment (Holahan, 1982).

Reducing Crowding. The distinction between density and crowding has some very important implications for managing our environment. The first implication is that bigger is not necessarily better. This is, simply giving people more space may lower density, but it will not necessarily reduce crowding or the effects of crowding. For example, imagine that you have had a very hectic day and want to spend some time by yourself. In this mood you will probably feel crowded in either a large or a small room if other people are present. In fact, you might prefer to hide in a closet where you have little physical space but a great deal of privacy.

A second implication of the density-crowding distinction is that crowding can be reduced without reducing density. For example, Sherrod (1974) found that people who believed they could leave a tightly packed room felt less crowded than people who did not feel free to leave the room. The density was the same in each case, but the people who could leave felt some control over their environment. Those who could not leave did not have this control. Other research has found that people feel less crowded in high-density environments if they have control. For example, passengers in an elevator reported feeling less crowded if they had access to the control panel than if they did not (Rodin et al., 1977). In another study Worchel and Teddlie (1976) found that people felt less crowded and performed better in a room with pictures on the walls than in a room with no pictures. This effect was found even though the density in the room was the same for both groups. The investigators argued that the pictures made the presence of other people less obvious and thereby reduced crowding.

Hence there are many ways that crowding and its effect can be reduced without increasing space or decreasing the number of people in the environment.

OTHER ENVIRONMENTAL VARIABLES

Noise

One of the features of prison that gave Stroud trouble when he first entered was noise. Noise echoed off the prison walls and he never had a quiet moment. The symphony of noise during the day included the simultaneous voices of hundreds of men, blaring radios, shouting guards, and the sudden slamming of doors. At night inmates could be heard snoring, sobbing, or talking. The solitary cell offered Stroud quiet, broken only by the sound of his own voice and the cheerful song of his canaries.

When we visualize our own town or city, we see busy sidewalks with people hurrying to unknown destinations; cars, buses, trucks, and motorcy-

PUTTING KNOWLEDGE OF THE ENVIRONMENT TO USE

A well-dressed man stands to address the Board of Supervisors in a small Virginia county: "The rock quarry that I propose to build in your county will bring you many benefits. It will add thousands of tax dollars to your revenues. It will create a number of new jobs. People in the county will be able to buy stone at a cheaper price, and that will make building cheaper. Since the state will be able to buy crushed stone cheaper, you will have more and better roads in the county."

The man is jeered by a large group of citizens who have gathered to protest the quarry. One by one they present their case. Evidence is presented that blasting at the quarry will shake houses and rattle windows in homes near the site. Noise, dust, and the traffic of heavy trucks are also given as reasons for not allowing the quarry to be built. Another resident talks about the beauty of the county and how an "ugly pit" will scar it. Tempers rise on both sides as the meeting comes to an end.

Which side is right? If you were a supervisor, would you vote for or against the quarry? How would you weigh the tangible benefits of greater tax income, more jobs, and cheaper stone against the intangible or potential effects of noise, dust, rattling windows, and the scar of an "ugly pit"? It is clearly a difficult decision.

This is a situation where a knowledge of environmental psychology could help the supervisors make an informed decision. Knowing the possible effects of unpredictable noise, pollution, and blasting would help them in weighing these consequences against the monetary gains from the quarry. Unfortunately, this is seldom done, for several reasons. First, it is sometimes hard to put a price tag on the psychological effects of environmental stress. For example, the quarry operator can specify exactly how much tax money and how many jobs his project will create, but it's not easy to translate the stress, discomfort, and possible illness that could result from the quarry into money terms. It can be done, by calculating the cost of reduced job performance, increased sick leave, and more medical expenses, but it's not an easy job. Also, many of the conclusions reached in psychological research are tentative and suggest several, sometimes conflicting, courses of action. Policymakers are often confused by this. Finally, there is often a conflict of interest involved in such decisions—some people may be stressed by an environmental change, others may benefit. The people living close to the quarry would suffer, but those who needed and got a job there would benefit. How do we weigh the suffering of some against the benefits to others?

There are no simple answers here, but knowledge of the effects of the environment on human behavior can help policymakers make wiser decisions (Cone & Hayes, 1980; Dimento, 1981). The interaction between lawmakers, architects, businesspeople, and city planners—those involved in making such decisions—and psychologists can benefit both. It would make the policymakers more aware of research findings in this area, and it would show psychologists the problems and critical questions faced by the decision makers, which would in turn help define new areas for research and training.

---

cles making their way down crowded streets; and occasionally the reflection of a silver airplane in the sky. But no matter how detailed the picture, it would not be complete without the sounds of our civilization: the rumble of engines, the cacophony of honking horns, blaring music from record stores, screaming low-flying jets. The variety (and level) of sound in our environment is astonishing.

The increasing noise in our environment has led scientists to examine the effects noise has on us. As we review this research, you should keep in mind that most of the sounds in our environment are made by humans and their inventions. Thus this is one environmental variable that humans may be able to control.

One of the first steps in the investigation has been to distinguish between sound and noise. As we discussed in Chapter 3, **sound** is a physical property caused by changes in air pressure. We measure sounds in units called decibels (for example, 55 db is the sound of light traffic; 120 db is equal to a jet taking off at 200 feet). **Noise,** on the other hand, is a "psychological concept and is defined as sound that is unwanted by the listener because it is unpleasant, bothersome, interferes with important activities, or is be-lieved to be physiologically harmful" (Cohen & Weinstein, 1981). While extremely loud sounds can cause physical damage, most of the research in this area has concentrated on the effects of noise. As you can see, the sound-noise distinction is similar to the density-crowding distinction. Sound and density are physical properties, while noise and crowding are psycho-logical concepts. With this distinction in mind, let us examine some of the effects of sound and noise.

Effects of Noise on Performance. If you were asked whether noise affects a person's ability to work on tasks, your first response might be a quick "yes." However, after giving this question some thought, you might remember a friend who studies successfully with the stereo blasting.

This pattern of thought parallels the progression of a series of studies done by Glass and Singer (1972) on the effects of short-term noise. Subjects worked on different tasks while noise was played in the room. Sometimes the noise was played loudly, while at other times it was played softly. In some of the studies subjects could predict or control the noise, while in others they could not.

Surprisingly, these studies showed that the noise had little effect on arousal or performance. Subjects reacted to the onset of the noise, but they were able to adapt to it quickly, especially when it was predictable. Even the initial stress responses shown by such physiological measures as increased heart rate and blood pressure were followed by a return to normal levels.

In a further effort to assess the possible effects of noise, the investigators had subjects listen to a loud or soft noise that was either predictable or unpredictable (Glass et al., 1977). Then subjects were asked to perform tasks in a quiet room. This procedure brought to light the effects of noise on performance. The "effects" of noise are really aftereffects; after the subjects had been exposed to noise, especially unpredictable noise, their performance suffered. The investigators suggested that people can adjust to noisy conditions over a short period of time. However, this adaptation requires the use of a great deal of energy, which makes them less able to cope with later environmental or task demands.

Noise may present an even bigger problem for children. In order to find this out, Cohen, Glass, and Singer (1973) examined the reading abilities of children living in a high-rise apartment building built directly over a New York City freeway. The children living on the lower floors were ex-posed to a great deal more highway noise than those on the upper floors. The children on the upper floors had a higher reading ability than those students who lived on the lower floors.

In another important study children whose school was in the flight path of Los Angeles International Airport were observed and examined (Cohen et al., 1981). Compared to children in quiet schools, these pupils had higher blood pressure, were more likely to fail in a puzzle-solving task, and were more inclined to give up when faced with a difficult task. The longer the child had been in the noisy school, the more distractible he or she was. One of the more disturbing factors was that these problems tended to remain even after the children's school had been insulated and the noise level reduced. This suggests that the effects of noise are long-term.

Noise in work settings has been found to interfere with communication and to reduce employee performance (Broadbent & Little, 1960). Interest-ingly enough, one of the most bothersome noises is loud background con-versation (Olszewksi et al., 1976). Apparently the interference effect is so strong because people focus their attention on trying to determine what is being said.

Noise that is unpredictable and uncontrollable is the most damaging type of noise. People who live close to busy airports cannot predict or control the noise in their environment. Research has found that students who live close to the Los Angeles International Airport have higher blood pressure and perform more poorly than students living in a quieter environment.

Effects of Noise on Social Relationships.   Noise also seems to affect our interactions with other people. Appleyard and Lintell (1972) compared the everyday life of people living on a busy, noisy street with that of residents of a quiet block. People who lived on the noisy street rarely interacted with neighbors outside their apartments, and they reported that their street was a lonely place to live. On the other hand, those who lived on the quiet street often sat on their doorsteps chatting with neighbors, and they reported a great deal of contact with other residents of the area. In another study it was found that people are less likely to stop and offer help in a noisy environment than in a quiet area (Mathews & Cannon, 1975). In one set of conditions the investigators had a confederate who was wearing a cast on his arm drop a load of books in front of a subject walking down a sidewalk. In some cases, the area was quiet, while in others, a lawn mower was running close by. Whereas 80 percent of the subjects helped in the quiet environment, only 15 percent helped in the noisy environment. Finally, it has also been found that noise, especially uncontrollable noise, increases the likelihood that an angry person will aggress (Donnerstein & Wilson, 1976). This result is especially applicable to prison settings, which house men who are seething with anger in an environment they have little control over.

Noise and Health.   Much of the work on health has focussed on high-intensity sounds. If you have at times been concerned that your own hearing is not as sensitive as it was when you were younger, your concern may be well founded. In 1972 the Environmental Protection Agency estimated that 3 million Americans suffer hearing loss caused by loud sounds. In hearing tests for high-frequency sounds, the EPA found that 3.8 percent of sixth-graders, 10 percent of ninth- and tenth-graders, and a staggering

61 percent of college freshmen showed hearing impairment. Anspacher (1972) studied the hearing of rock musicians, who are often exposed to noise levels over 125 db. He found that 41 of the 43 musicians studied had permanent hearing loss. In possibly the most revealing study it was reported that 70-year-old tribesmen living in quiet Sudanese villages have hearing sensitivity comparable to that of 20-year-olds in the United States (Rosen et al., 1962). Recent research has found that certain drugs may increase the physical damage caused by noise (Miller, 1982). Some of the drugs identified are antibiotics and, possibly, aspirin (Fisher et al., 1984).

Welsh (1979) reviewed a number of studies that examined the effects of loud industrial sounds on workers' health. He concluded that long-term exposure (3 to 5 years) increased the likelihood of cardiovascular problems. Other research suggests that prolonged exposure to loud sounds increases the possibility of ulcers and other digestive tract problems (Kangelari et al., 1966). Noise is also associated with increased blood pressure, but this effect can be reduced by wearing protective ear plugs. Finally, one study reported higher infant mortality rates among expectant mothers exposed to aircraft noise than among those not exposed to the noise (Ando & Hattori, 1973). Because the concern about the effects of sound on health is relatively recent and the research is often based on after-the-fact observations, we do not yet have enough evidence to draw strong conclusions. However, the results we do have suggest that we need to pay more attention to the problem.

Theories on the Effects of Noise. It is easy enough to understand why deafening sounds decrease performance, hurt the quality of social interactions, and create stress. However, it is more difficult to understand why lower-intensity sounds that are experienced as noise also have these effects. A number of theories have been proposed. Some are relatively straightforward; for example, Isen (1970) suggests that noise puts people in a bad mood, and Poulton (1978, 1979) argues that intermittent noise is distracting. When people are continuously distracted, it is difficult for them to concentrate on tasks or on social interactions.

A number of other investigators suggest that noise causes people to narrow their focus of attention (Broadbent, 1971; Cohen & Weinstein, 1981). They focus their efforts on trying to explain or control the noise and thus pay less attention to other features in the environment, such as other people or task requirements. Noise that is either unpredictable or uncontrollable demands the most attention and therefore is the most disruptive.

Overall, these theories point out that the noise level of our environment can have a great deal of influence over a large part of our lives.

Air Pollution

Robert Stroud never drove an automobile, never flew in an airplane, and never saw a large factory. However, from his cell in Alcatraz he could look across the bay to San Francisco and see an unfortunate by-product of these developments. This man who studied nature so carefully reports noticing a haze that sometimes hung over San Francisco; it was not the famous fog that inspired songs, but rather air pollution. When Stroud died in 1963, people were just becoming aware of the fact that the air they breathed was poisoned.

Pollution is a special type of environmental stressor. Unlike crowding, noise, and temperature, we generally cannot see it, feel it, or hear it. For example, one of the major pollutants is carbon monoxide, which is both odorless and colorless. We sometimes see a haze of dirty air or experience skin or eye irritation, but in most cases, we cannot easily detect air pollution. Another troublesome problem is that the steps we take to control the

environmental problems sometimes increase the pollution of our air. For example, in order to reduce energy consumption, we attempt to make our homes airtight. Yet studies have found that airtight homes may contain two to three times more pollution than the outside air (Guenther, 1982).

For all these reasons it is difficult to arouse people's concern about the quality of their air. Fortunately, government action has been taken to improve air quality. The Clean Air Act established emission standards for automobiles. Factories and power plants have been ordered to reduce the amounts and types of particles they release into the air. Even air pollution by individuals is being reduced by rules prohibiting smoking in certain areas. However, the effort to reduce environmental pollution is often slowed because people do not believe they can exercise any real control over the problem (Evans & Jacobs, 1981).

Pollution and Behavior. Pollution can have a number of far-ranging effects on our behavior. One such effect is on our work performance. In order to demonstrate these effects, investigators collected air from 15 inches (the level of automobile exhaust) above the ground level of a fairly busy English road (Lewis et al., 1970). They had people breathe either this air or pure, unpolluted air. The subjects then performed a number of tasks. Subjects who had breathed the polluted air performed more poorly than subjects who had inhaled the clean air. Thus there may be important short-term as well as long-term effects from breathing polluted air. Another study showed that people who breathed moderate concentrations of carbon monoxide showed impaired performance on judgment tasks.

Pollution may also affect our social interactions. One effect is that people are less likely to engage in recreational activities outside when the air is heavily polluted (Chapko & Solomon, 1976). A second effect is that people tend to become more aggressive when exposed to moderately unpleasant odors in the air compared to odorless air (Rotton et al., 1979). Interestingly enough, aggression decreased somewhat when subjects in the experiment were placed in an environment with very foul smelling air. Foul odors may also reduce our appreciation of our environment. One study found that people rated paintings and photographs lower when exposed to badly-smelling air than when in an odorless environment (Rotton et al., 1978).

Pollution and Health. While we might be somewhat amused at the effects air pollution has on our behavior, there is little to be amused about when we examine its effects on our health. In the United States 140,000 deaths each year are attributed to pollution (Mendelshon & Orcutt, 1979). The President's Council on Environmental Quality (1978) reported that the air is unhealthy in 43 major American citites where half the population lives. Prolonged exposure to carbon monoxide (CO) has been linked to visual and hearing impairment, epilepsy, headaches, and mental retardation (Fisher et al., 1984). Smog, which often contains particles of nitrogen and sulphur, causes eye irritation, respiratory and cardiovascular diseases, and possibly cancer. Physicians have even identified an **air pollution syndrome (APS)** characterized by headache, insomnia, gastrointestinal problems, irritated eyes, and depression (Hart, 1970). Psychiatric admissions are higher during times of high levels of air pollution (Rotton & Frey, 1982).

There is some indication that people can adjust physiologically to some levels of pollution. Pollution seems to affect most strongly those who are newly introduced to it. However, adaptation is not possible when the levels of pollution are high.

Heat

One of the worst prison riots that occurred during Stroud's life erupted in Leavenworth in August 1929. Throughout the hot summer tensions had been mounting. Small frustrations often turned into major conflicts. For example, the inmates began complaining about the food, suggesting that the cooks "seemed unable to serve anything except for Spanish rice." The crowding, which had always been present, seemed more intolerable during this summer. Finally, the tension exploded into a major riot that left a number of inmates dead and scores seriously injured.

As we examine the account of the riot, we can see a number of environmental factors that may have contributed to it. We have already discussed the influence of crowding on behavior. Another feature that stands out is heat; this was an especially hot summer and the prison seemed to soak up the heat. Could the heat have contributed to the tragic events? What other effects might heat have on our own behavior? Researchers have recently become interested in answering these and other questions. Their work is especially important in an age when industrialization and urbanization have created a noticeably warmer environment. For example, the central areas of large cities are actually 10°–20°F. warmer than the surrounding countryside. One investigator calculated that the air conditioners in downtown Houston gave off enough waste heat into the outside air in 8 hours to boil 10 kettles of water the size of the Astrodome (Hurt, 1975)!

When we consider heat, most of us immediately think of the thermometer; as the temperature rises, it becomes hotter. This is definitely true, but if you have ever been in a desert area, you may wonder about the relationship between temperature and the *perception* of heat. A temperature of 110°F. in Sedona, Arizona, may be experienced as "dry heat" and may not feel as hot as 90°F. in Baltimore, Maryland. As Tables 17–3 and 17–4 show, our perceptions of heat and cold depend on many factors, including temperature, humidity, and wind speed.

With these points in mind, let us examine the effects that heat can have on our behavior and health.

Heat and Behavior. Stroud's observation of the possible effect of heat on the rioters was echoed by the United States Riot Commission (1968). The commission noted that of the numerous riots that occurred in United States cities during 1967, all but one began when the temperature was over 80°F. Other research, both in the laboratory and in the field, has also suggested that heat increases the likelihood of aggression (Anderson & Anderson, 1984; Griffith, 1970). This conclusion, however, was disputed by investigators, who reported that at very high temperatures (95°F.),

Table 17-3
Effective Temperature (°F) at 0 Percent Humidity as a Function of Actual Temperature and Humidity

Relative Humidity (%)	Thermometer Reading (°F)					
	41°	50°	59°	68°	77°	86°
	Effective Temperature					
0	41	50	59	68	77	86
20	41	50	60	70	81	91
40	40	51	61	72	83	96
60	40	51	62	73	86	102
80	39	52	63	75	90	111
100	39	52	64	79	96	120

Source: Fisher, Bell, & Baum, 1984.

people seek to withdraw from social interaction rather than aggress. Most of us have known that feeling of simply not wanting to deal with other people on very uncomfortable hot days. As with crowding, however, we can speculate that while withdrawal may be desired, those in a restricted environment do not have the option of getting away from others. Heat, like many of the other environmental variables we have discussed, may increase arousal and frustration, so that events that would normally be passed off as minor annoyances may be experienced as greater provocations.

Looking at task performance, research suggests that temperatures above 90°F impair both physical work and judgment tasks (Bell, 1981). For classroom performance, the picture becomes a bit more unclear. Investigators have found that heat hurts the performance of some students but helps the performance of others (Benson & Ziemon, 1981). As we dig deeper into this issue, we find that heat is most damaging when people are exposed to it for long periods of time and are working on complex tasks. However, task performance may actually be increased with short exposures to heat or when the task is a very simple one. There are at least two explanations for this interesting pattern. First, heat may increase arousal; as we saw in Chapter 16, we perform simple and well-learned tasks better when aroused, but arousal inhibits the performance of complex tasks or the learning of new skills. Second, heat may serve as a stressor that focusses our attention on some feature in the environment. If our attention is directed at the task, we may perform better. However, if our attention is directed at some other feature of our surroundings, our performance will suffer. The type of task, surroundings, and our past experience will affect what event our attention is focussed on (Bell, 1978).

Heat and Health. Our bodies are designed to maintain an internal temperature of 98.6°F. As our temperature increases, the hypothalamus initiates a number of responses designed to combat this effect. Heat is released from the body through sweating, panting, and a dilation of peripheral blood vessels. If these adaptive mechanisms are unable to stem the rising internal temperature, a number of serious disorders can occur. We

Table 17-4
Wind-Chill Index*

Actual Temperature (°F) at 0 mph	Wind Speed			
	5 mph	15 mph	25 mph	35 mph
	Equivalent Temperature (°F)			
32	29	13	3	−1
23	20	−1	−10	−15
14	10	−13	−24	−29
5	1	−25	−38	−43
−4	−9	−37	−50	−52

* Equivalent temperatures (°F) at 0 mph as a function of actual temperature and wind speed.
Source: Fisher, Bell, & Baum, 1984.

may experience **heat exhaustion**, which involves fainting, nausea, vomiting, and headaches. **Heatstroke,** a more serious disorder, results when the body's sweating mechanism completely breaks down. This will be accompanied by headache, staggering, coma, and possibly death. The overheating of the body can cause permanent damage to the brain. Excessive heat may also contribute to *heart attack*. As the blood vessels dilate, the heart must work harder to pump blood throughout the body. The extra work may overtax the heart and cause it to malfunction.

In addition to these direct effects, heat may have an indirect effect on our health. If you compare your behavior in winter and summer, one difference you may notice is that you interact with more people during the warm months. The cold of winter limits us to indoors or short-duration outside activities. However, during the warmer months we participate in a wider range of activities and may have greater social contact. These increased contacts provide the opportunity for the spread of disease (Porteous, 1977). For example, polio outbreaks were most common during the summer months. Investigators found that the disease was often spread through public swimming pools where large crowds congregated and the chemical balance of the pools could not be adequately controlled to destroy the virus.

Cold

Just as our bodies react to heat to keep a constant internal temperature, so, too, do they react to cold to maintain a 98.6°F. internal temperature. As you might expect, the adaptation process is much the reverse of the one we just examined. The body retains heat by constricting peripheral blood vessels to keep the warm blood away from the cold surface. Metabolism increases and shivering occurs as means of staying warm. Hairs on the skin stiffen and "goose bumps" appear; these responses increase the surface of the skin and help keep a layer of insulating air close to the skin.

While cold can affect performance, the negative effects can be reduced if the hands are kept warm.

There has been a great deal less research on the effects of cold than on the effects of heat. People rarely spend much time working in very cold conditions. When they do, they are usually well clothed so that their bodies are warm despite the outside temperature. What research there is suggests that cold reduces performance levels on tasks requiring muscle coordination, quick reaction times, and sensitivity of touch (Poulton, 1970). An interesting finding is that even in very cold temperatures performance does not suffer as much if the hands are kept warm (Fox, 1967). This confirms the wisdom of football players who wear gloves when playing in very cold weather.

The two most common health problems related to cold are frostbite and hypothermia. **Frostbite** results when ice forms in the skin cells. These frozen cells die, and if the affected area is large enough, a finger, toe, or large patch of skin may literally die. **Hypothermia** occurs when the internal body temperature drops below a normal level. As this begins to occur, heart rate and blood pressure increase dramatically. If the temperature does not increase, cardiovascular activity falls off and becomes irregular and death due to heart attack will result.

Other than these effects, cold does not seem to be related to any particular illnesses. For example, Eskimos do not suffer from prolonged illnesses associated with the cold (Fisher et al., 1984). There also seems to be little direct relationship between cold and mental illness. The "cabin fever" and depression and irritability reported by Arctic explorers or people who work at weather stations in frigid areas are the effects of isolation rather than the cold itself.

THE BUILT ENVIRONMENT

Robert Stroud spent the last 54 years of his life in prison. Some of this time he lived in a large dormitory room with a number of inmates. When he first arrived at Leavenworth, he lived in a small cell with one other inmate; the cells were in long rows and were stacked several stories high. When he was placed in solitary confinement, he lived in a 6-foot cell in an area that had 12 other cells. In all these environments the furniture was fixed to the floor and Stroud could do little to arrange his environment. His only control came when he began to construct bird cages; these he could hang around his cell as he pleased within the physical limits.

Stroud was acutely aware that the particular environment one lives in has an effect on behavior. He used this awareness to build more desirable cages for his birds. His cages had no more than three levels and avoided rounded walls.

Stroud's observations that our built environment affects our behavior has been supported by research. Fortunately, we generally have control over our built environment. We can design buildings to fit people's needs and help them adapt; we can arrange the furniture in our rooms to promote the type of social interactions we desire. Because we have control over this part of our environment, it is especially important to understand how it affects our behavior. As we will see, almost every feature of the built environment can influence our behavior and adjustment.

Rooms

Shape. One of the characteristics of a room easiest to describe is its shape. Is it square or rectangular? How many doors and windows does it have? When constructing a dwelling, decisions about the shape of rooms and numbers of windows and doors are often made on the basis of money alone. This, however, may be a mistake, since research has shown that these room variables influence human behavior and perception. For example, Ruys (1971) interviewed 139 female workers in windowless offices and found that 47.5 percent felt that the lack of windows had a bad effect on them. These workers believed they suffered more headaches and physical discomfort and worked more slowly and erratically in this environment. Desor (1972) designed two model rooms of the same overall size but varied the shape (square or rectangular) and the number of doors in the room (two or six). Subjects placed stick figures that represented people in the rooms until they felt the room to be "crowded." The subjects felt that more figures (people) could fit comfortably into the rectangular room than into the square room (even though the space was the same). Further, more people were placed in the two-door room than in the six-door room.

Furniture Arrangement. The placement of furniture in a room can have a marked effect on both the amount and type of social interaction. In an interesting demonstration of this, Sommer and Ross (1958) observed patients in a newly remodeled geriatric ward. Hoping to encourage more interaction among patients, the hospital administration painted and carpeted the dayroom and put in new furniture. Much to their disappointment, however, the patients continued to sit in the dayroom "like strangers in a train station waiting for a train that never came." Sommer and Ross felt that one reason for this lack of social interaction was the arrangement of the furniture: Chairs were lined up in long straight rows so that the patients had to sit side-by-side or back-to-back. The researchers changed this pattern by grouping four chairs around small tables. The result was quite striking. In a few weeks interaction among the patients had nearly doubled, and the dayroom was being used more often. Thus the furniture arrangement affected the social interaction among patients.

The type of interaction that people expect to engage in has also been found to influence their preference for seating arrangements (Sommer, 1969). People involved in casual conversation prefer to be seated either corner-to-corner or face-to-face. If the people plan to cooperate, they want to sit side-by-side. But if they are going to compete, they want to be able to keep an eye on each other and therefore choose a face-to-face arrangement.

Buildings

Living in a High-Rise. Many Americans feel that the ideal living arrangement is a house with a yard with trees and flowers. However, in large cities where land is scarce and people find it expensive and inconvenient to commute, many people rent or buy apartments in high-rise buildings. As the populations of the cities increase, apartment buildings grow higher. For some people the high-rise is an answer to their dreams; no yards to water, no grass to cut, and no cars blocking their driveways. However, for many others high-rise living is full of problems and discomforts.

One of the clearest examples of the problems of high-rise living occurred in St. Louis, Missouri, in the late 1950s. As a result of efforts to improve housing conditions for the poor, 43 11-story apartment buildings were built on a 57-acre tract. The Pruitt-Igoe complex was praised for its beauty, and with much fanfare the 12,000 residents moved into their new homes. There was, however, a great deal less celebration when in April 1972 the last occupants had moved out of the buildings and the city was forced to order the project demolished. The Pruitt-Igoe complex was a good idea turned bad because it had been designed without proper thought for the human problems of high-rise living. Parents were unhappy because they could not supervise their children, who wanted to play in the playground several stories below their apartments. The long hallways in the buildings did not allow the type of interaction that residents had enjoyed on the doorsteps of their houses or small apartment buildings. There were areas such as elevators and stairwells that were unguarded and not well lit; these became prime areas for rape and robbery, and residents became afraid to go out of their own apartments. These problems were not unique to the Pruitt-Igoe complex; Cappon (1971) reports similar problems in many high-rise buildings throughout the world.

In addition, McCarthy and Saegert (1979) found that high-rise residents tend to form fewer relationships with other building residents than do those of low-rise buildings. High-rise residents also seem to be more distrustful of their neighbors and less willing to give help than residents of low-rise buildings (Bickman et al., 1973). These feelings are reflected in statistics showing that the higher the apartment building in which people live, the greater the chance that they will fall victim to a crime (Newman, 1972).

This discussion paints a rather bleak picture of high-rise buildings, but that is no reason to write them off entirely. There have been some suggestions about how to make these buildings safer and more enjoyable for their residents. Newman (1972, 1975), for example, argues that crime can be reduced and social interaction increased by doing away with indefensible spaces in the apartment complex. **Indefensible spaces** are areas that are not open to observation, such as enclosed stairways and alleys, so that it is not clear who controls them. These areas invite intruders and breed

It is especially important to provide defensible spaces in high-rise buildings. These buildings are often threatening because people feel that they have little control over their environment.

Building for beauty rather than for people has reduced the desirability of many buildings. One extreme example of this was the Pruitt-Igoe complex. In spite of the fact that the buildings won a number of design awards, people found them difficult to live in, and the complex had to be destroyed after only a few years.

crime. Newman suggests that stairways and elevators be enclosed in glass so that people can see who is inside them before they enter. Outside the building, hedges or low fences can be used, which allow residents to claim and use certain areas and also make it easy to observe these areas. Common meeting places can be created in certain apartments to get residents to gather and interact socially on a regular basis. Research has shown that such changes may indeed cause residents to feel safer and to enjoy the facilities of their apartment buildings (Kohn et al., 1975). This, then, is an example of using research and theory to *improve* the environment rather than just giving up on it as hopeless.

The Dormitory. A building with which many of us have had some experience is the college or university dormitory. Most of these buildings are built in a corridor design: a long hall with rooms on either side and a communal bathroom somewhere along the corridor. Oftentimes there is a community lounge at the end of the corridor. Recently many institutions have been experimenting with a different type of dormitory. The suite dormitory is built with three or four bedrooms surrounding a common lounge or living-room area, with a bathroom serving all residents of the suite.

While the amount of living space for each resident is often the same in the corridor and suite dormitories, the designs seem to have different effects on residents' behavior. Baum and Valins (1977) questioned residents of the two types of dwellings (see Figure 17–4). They found that suite residents tended to have more friends and to work together as groups more often than did residents of corridor dorms. Corridor residents complained of constantly seeing strangers on the floor; suite residents seldom had this problem. Overall, suite residents felt that they had more control over their lives and environment than did corridor residents. Students living in the corridor rooms reported feeling more crowded and having less privacy than did suite residents.

This, again, is an example of how the architectural design of our environment affects our feelings and actions. We can aid adjustment to our environ-

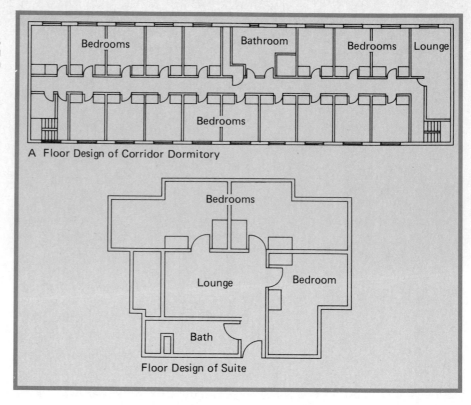

A   Floor Design of Corridor Dormitory

Floor Design of Suite

ment by designing our buildings and rooms to fit our needs. To continue to design our buildings with only cost and architectural beauty in mind is to make our adjustment and enjoyment of our environment more difficult.

The City

In 1889 the city of Seattle burned to the ground. Twenty thousand people were left homeless but determined to rebuild their city. As a small child, Robert Stroud watched this city being rebuilt. Clearly it was an enormous task, but it was also a great opportunity to redesign a city that would meet the needs of its people. Unfortunately, the planners did not have available to them the information that has since been accumulated on how the design of a city affects people's behavior.

The scientific study of urban design is a relatively new field sparked, first, by the rapid influx of people into cities, and then by the realization that many of our inner cities had become decaying relics that were not meeting the needs of their inhabitants. In fact, in 1980 over 70 percent of the people in the United States lived in urban areas (U.S. Bureau of the Census, 1981). This concentration of people has created great density, noise, and air pollution, as well as skyrocketing crime. In an effort to avoid these problems, many middle-class residents have abandoned the city for the suburbs, in some cases traveling many hours from their suburban home to their urban job. This flight to the suburbs has led to increased social problems, since the poor are still trapped in the urban areas and the cities have had a difficult time raising the money to run necessary facilities such as schools, hospitals, police and fire departments, and social services. There are now indications that the flight from the cities may be reversing. The enormous increases in the price of gasoline over the past decade has made it hard for many people to afford the cost of traveling great distances to their place of employment. Thus it is increasingly urgent to understand how the urban environment affects individuals.

The one term that seems to fit almost every city is *diversity*. A walk down a city street will present you with buildings of several architectural styles and a mind-boggling array of noises, smells, and sights. Further, the number and types of people you will see will be enormous. One researcher reports that a person working in midtown Manhattan can meet 220,000 people within a 10-minute radius of his or her office (Milgram, 1970). On the one hand, this diversity can be a huge barrier to human development. Cohen (1977) points out that a person can attend to only a limited amount of stimuli in his or her environment. When there are too many events occurring in the environment, people become **cognitively overloaded**; it becomes impossible for them to respond to each stimulus. An environment that is overloaded with stimuli is a stressful place to live in. In some cases, the response to this overload is a psychological or social breakdown. Incidences of mental illness have been reported to be the highest in the busiest and most crowded parts of the city (Factor & Wildron, 1974). Crime statistics show a similar pattern.

While some people cannot cope with the overstimulation of the city, most residents do take steps to adapt to their environment. Milgram (1970, 1977) examined how people in cities respond to the overstimulation. He reports that they often give less time to each event; they deal with situations more quickly and pay less attention to details. They also filter incoming stimuli and disregard inputs that are unimportant. For example, Milgram had students walk down a street and extend a hand of friendship to people in a city and in a small town (Milgram, 1977). Over two-thirds of those approached in the small town accepted the handshake, while only a third of those in the large city did. A stranger trying to be friendly was probably not a very important stimulus for many of the people in the city, and they simply ignored him or her.

Another response that Milgram noted was that city dwellers tended to depersonalize and deindividuate (see Chapter 16) others in their environment. People are identified with and responded to as roles rather than as people. Thus a person will respond to all strangers in one way, to all police officers in another way, and to all bus drivers in still another way. By placing others into categories and responding to the category, the urban dweller does not respond to everyone in a separate way. While this depersonalization may help reduce the variety of incoming stimuli, it leads to the characterization of the city dweller as cold and unfriendly. Further, the city dweller is less likely to offer help to deindividuated others. In

Cognitive overload occurs when people are bombarded by too much stimulation. The large numbers of people, wide variety of buildings and many different noises of a modern city can cause cognitive overload and make adjustment difficult. In responding to cognitive overload, we often place people and events into categories.

Chapter 15 we discussed the case of Kitty Genovese, who was attacked and killed while 38 people looked on and did nothing to help. In another demonstration of the guardedness of city dwellers, Altman, Levine, and Nadien (1970) had individual students approach apartment residents in Manhattan and in a small town. The students explained that they had lost the address of a friend who lived nearby and asked to use the resident's telephone. Male students were refused entry into 86 percent of the Manhattan apartments but only 50 percent of the small-town apartments. Female students were not allowed into 40 percent of the Manhattan apartments, while only 6 percent of the small-town apartment dwellers refused them entry. We might argue that the city dwellers were doing the proper thing and looking out for their own welfare. Even if this is a wise course of action, the point is that there was significantly less helping in the city.

Clearly the city has both its bitter and sweet aspects. A government commission investigating French cities felt that the bad aspects far outweighed the advantages and recommended that newer cities in France not be allowed to grow beyond 200,000 (Kandell, 1977). This certainly seems a drastic measure. A wiser approach may be to use the knowledge we have gained through environmental research to control and direct the growth of our cities. For example, some cities have created shopping malls in downtown areas and have restricted the amount of automobile traffic in these places. These steps reduce noise and air pollution in the area and give residents a rather quiet place to congregate and interact. Clearly other actions can be taken to reduce the hazards of city living while still preserving the vitality and excitement of urban diversity.

Perceiving Our Cities. Although our cities and other parts of our environment exist in reality, they also exist in our mind. And from the standpoint of our behavior, the environments in our mind are more important. For many years investigators have realized that we mentally represent our environment in the form of **cognitive maps** (Lynch, 1960). These maps are the way we organize and recall our environment. Each of us has a different map, but we generally base these maps on similar components.

If you draw a map of the city in which you live, you will be able to identify many of these components. One component is *paths*, which include streets and walkways. We don't include all the city's streets in our map; rather, we focus on the ones that are important to us or stand out for some other reason. Your map will probably also contain *nodes*, which are the intersections of several paths; in some cities these may be traffic circles or the main square. When we view our city, we often divide it up into *districts* or neighborhoods. For example, you may include the business district, the slum area, the wealthy section of town, and the college area. *Landmarks* are also vital to our maps. These landmarks may be a tall building, hill, or tower; often they serve as the focal points of our maps. Finally our maps will have *edges* that serve as boundaries. Clear edges such as rivers, beaches, walls, or major highways help us define what we consider to be our city.

Cognitive maps are not perfect representations of our environment. We tend to give greater detail to the areas that are important to us and those with which we are familiar (Holahan, 1980). We often distort distances between places and may even add features that are not actually there.

Despite their imperfection, these cognitive maps are very important to us because they boil our environment down to manageable dimensions. (Imagine trying to remember every house and store between your home and your university!) They help us navigate through our city and give us a sense of control over the environment. For this reason, cities that can easily fit into cognitive maps are often easier to adjust to than cities that do not lend themselves to this sort of mapping. For example, regardless

Developing a cognitive map of New York City is easier than developing such a map for Los Angeles. New York City has distinctive landmarks, districts, and edges where Los Angeles has fewer of these important markers.

of where you are in New York, you can see the Empire State Building (on a clear day). This landmark helps you orient yourself in the city and you will rarely feel hopelessly lost. Los Angeles, on the other hand, has few distinct landmarks that can help you locate yourself. This presents problems for the newcomer who is desperately trying to find his or her way around. Finally, cognitive maps help us communicate about our environment to others. You may guide people to your home by saying, "Take a left at the Sears store on Mill Street, go about a mile until you come to the corner with the Gulf station that has a car wash, and then take a left there."

The way people use cognitive maps is important to remember when designing a city or neighborhood. Clear landmarks, nodes, districts, and paths are important features in helping people adjust to their environments. Imagine the difficulty you might have in a city where every store looked the same and every house was built of a similar design. Knowing how people perceive their environment is another example of how we can use an understanding of environment and behavior to design areas to better meet our needs.

SUMMARY

1. **Environmental psychology** examines the relationships between people and their environment. The findings from this field may help show how people can form a harmonious partnership with their environment.

2. **Territoriality** involves claiming control or ownership over a certain area or object. Humans have three types of territory: **primary territories** are owned by them and are central to their lives; **secondary territories** are not owned, but they are the focus of a strong emotional attachment; **public territories** are areas that people control only when they occupy the space.

3. **Personal space** is the area immediately around the person, over which he or she feels ownership. Unlike territory, which involves a fixed piece of property, personal space moves with the individual. The amount of space that people consider personal is af-

fected by the type of interaction they are engaged in, their sex, and their cultural background. Violations of personal space often cause people to feel stressed and anxious.

4. **Density** is a physical measure of the amount of space available to a person in a particular setting. High density does not necessarily have negative effects on humans. **Crowding** is a psychological state that may or may not be associated with high density. Research has found that crowding results in stress, reduced task performance, and hostility. Extreme crowding can affect our health.

5. **Sound** is a physical property caused by changes in air pressure. **Noise,** on the other hand, is a psychological concept that includes sound that is unpleasant, bothersome, and interferes with important activities. Exposure to loud sounds can cause physical damage to people's ears and can increase the risk

of cardiovascular diseases, ulcers, and headaches. Noise that is unpredictable and uncontrollable can have negative effects and after effects on task performance and social interactions.

6. People are often unaware of air pollution because they cannot see or smell some of the most dangerous pollutants. Some studies have shown that people do not perform as well in polluted air as in clean air, and pollution has also been shown to affect our relations with other people. Pollution has a very strong effect on health; physicians have even identified an **air pollution syndrome (APS)** characterized by headache, gastrointestinal problems, and depression.

7. Weather also affects our performance and social behavior. Performance suffers in very hot and very cold conditions. Moderately high temperatures have been linked to increased aggression, although aggression declines in extremely hot conditions. Excessive heat can have serious effects on health, leading to **heat exhaustion, heatstroke,** and even heart attacks. The two most common health problems related to cold are **frostbite** and **hypothermia.**

8. Much of our physical environment has been built with our own hands. Research has found that the design of buildings and rooms can influence peoples' behavior. For example, the shape of rooms and furniture can influence our social behaviors and personal comfort; high-rise buildings that have a lot of **indefensible space** are unpleasant environments for people; and residents feel more control over their lives in suite-type dormitories than in long-corridor dormitories.

9. Cities present a great deal of excitement and diversity. However, in some cases there can be too much stimulation, leading people to experience **cognitive overload.** Cognitive overload may cause people to become less open to social contact, and they may seem unfriendly to strangers.

10. Cities and other parts of our environment also exist in our mind; we mentally represent our environment in the form of **cognitive maps.** Cognitive maps help us navigate through our cities and give us a sense of control over the environment.

Key Terms

air pollution syndrome (APS)
cognitive maps
cognitive overload
crowding
density
environmental psychology
frostbite
heat exhaustion
heatstroke
hypothermia

indefensible spaces
noise
personal space
primary territories
proxemics
public territories
secondary territories
sound
territoriality

Suggested Readings

The following book is about Robert Stroud, the Birdman of Alcatraz:
GADDIS, T. E. *Birdman of Alcatraz*. New York: Random House, 1955.

BAUM, A., & SINGER, J. (Eds.). *Advances in environmental psychology* (Vol. 3); *Energy*: *Psychological perspectives*. Hillsdale, N.J.: Erlbaum Associates, 1981. Presents a series of original chapters discussing the energy problem and how psychology can be used to help people conserve energy.
FISHER, J., BELL, P., & BAUM, A. *Environmental psychology*, 2nd ed. New York: Holt, Rinehart & Winston, 1984. An up-to-date and thorough introduction to research on environmental psychology. Includes theory, research, and application.
GELLER, E. S., WINETT, R., & EVERETT, P. *Preserving the environment*: *New strategies for behavior change*. New York: Pergamon Press, 1982. Emphasizes learning and behavioral approaches for dealing with environmental problems such as litter control, energy conservation, and water conservation.
HOLAHAN, C. *Environmental psychology*. New York: Random House, 1982. A textbook that provides a broad view of the field of environmental psychology. Easy to read and up to date.
Journal of Social Issues, *37* (1), 1981: *Environmental stress*. This issue of the journal is devoted to the topic of environmental stress. It presents some interesting articles on stress resulting from noise, pollution, crowding, and heat.
WICKER, A. *An introduction to ecological psychology*. Monterey, Calif.: Brooks/Cole, 1979. This volume examines the area of ecological psychology, which involves studying people in their natural settings.

APPENDIX
STATISTICAL METHODS

M. ELIZABETH WETMORE

Table A–1

Subject Number	Number of Ideas Recalled
1	37
2	31
3	33
4	36
5	28
6	44
7	43
8	20
9	21
10	37
11	36
12	32
13	35
14	31
15	31
16	40
17	41
18	27
19	25
20	30
21	38
22	30
23	30
24	30
25	41

Students often complain that multiple-choice tests do not fairly measure their knowledge. They feel shortchanged, not only in their classes, but also in the entrance exams that determine whether or not they can go to college in the first place. Such tests always seem to be asking about things that students do not know, while not asking about things that they do know. An alternative is to give an open-ended test. A teacher might, for instance, ask students to write down everything that they remember about a lesson. How would students respond to such open-ended questions? Would performance on multiple-choice entrance exams be similar to performance on open-ended questions? Psychologists are now investigating these and other questions about open-ended exams. In doing so, they take advantage of **statistics,** a branch of mathematics used to describe data and to draw conclusions based on data. You don't have to be an expert in math to understand statistics, but you do have to learn a special vocabulary. To make statistics and their use more interesting and understandable, we will analyze data from an actual experiment on open-ended exams.

Twenty-five students from introductory psychology courses at the University of Virginia took part in an experiment investigating how students learn from textbooks (Wetmore, 1982). The students were asked to read a selection from an introductory biology textbook. This selection contained 54 ideas. The students were told to read the selection at whatever speed they felt comfortable and to do whatever they normally do when reading a homework assignment for the first time. After they were through reading, they were asked to recall in their own words everything they could remember from what they had just read. These lists were then analyzed to see how many of the 54 ideas each student recalled. Table A–1 shows the number of ideas recalled by each student. Statistics can help us understand this data. We will use one branch of statistics to describe the data and then another branch to draw conclusions from the data.

DESCRIPTIVE STATISTICS

Descriptive statistics are tools for summarizing data so that the data can be more easily understood. The data may be any set of measurements taken of a group of objects, people, or events.

Frequency Distributions

A **frequency distribution** is one way of summarizing data; it reduces individual scores into groups of scores. To do this, we simply select a set of intervals and count how many scores fall into each one.

Table A–2

Rank Order of Raw Scores			
20	30	35	40
21	30	36	41
25	31	36	41
27	31	37	43
28	31	37	44
30	32	38	
30	33		

Table A–3

Frequency distribution for scores in Table A–1	
Class Interval	Number of Scores in Each Interval
20–24	2
25–29	3
30–34	9
35–39	6
40–44	5

We can make a frequency distribution for the data presented in Table A–1 in two steps: (1) arrange (or rank order) the scores from lowest to highest as shown in Table A–2; (2) using an interval of 5, list the number of scores in each interval. These two steps produce the frequency distribution shown in Table A–3.

Such a frequency distribution can often be better understood if shown on a graph rather than in a table. The two most commonly used graphs are the frequency histogram and the frequency polygon.

Once a frequency distribution has been made, most of the work of making both a frequency histogram and a frequency polygon has been done. **Histograms** are made by placing the intervals along the horizontal axis and marking the frequencies along the vertical axis. A histogram for the data presented in Table A–3 can be seen in Figure A–1.

Another way of showing frequency distributions in graph form is to use a frequency polygon. **Polygons** are made by connecting a series of points representing the frequency of scores in each interval. A polygon for the data presented in Table A–3 can be seen in Figure A–2.

Figure A–1
A frequency histogram for data in Table A–3. The numbers under each bar indicate an interval of exam scores. The height of the bar indicates the number of scores (frequency) in each interval.

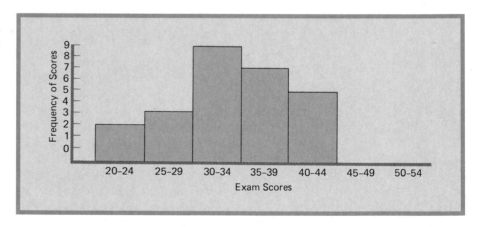

Figure A–2
A frequency polygon for data in Table A–3. The points represent the number of scores in each interval.

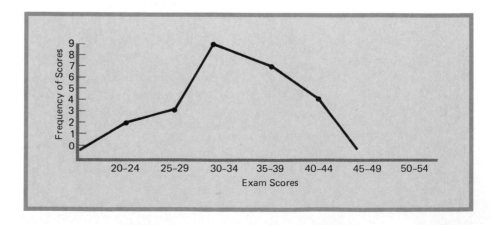

The frequency distribution, histogram, and polygon for the data presented in Table A–1 show at a glance that the scores were well below the highest possible score of 54. They ranged from the low 20s to the mid 40s, with the most frequent scores in the low 30s. Students apparently had trouble recalling all the ideas. But let's look more closely before drawing conclusions.

Measures of Central Tendency

Frequency distributions, histograms, and polygons all summarize whole distributions. Sometimes, however, single numbers are easier to compare. Statisticians therefore summarize properties of distributions with single numbers. An interesting property is a **measure of central tendency,** a score value that represents the mathematical center of a group of scores, or, to put it another way, a score that represents in some sense the "typical" score. Three different statistics are used to describe the central tendency of a distribution: the mean, the median, and the mode.

The **mean** is the most widely used measure of central tendency. It is commonly called the average and is determined by adding all the scores in the sample and dividing by the total number of scores in the sample. The mean number of ideas recalled in Table A–1 is 33.08. It was determined by adding all the students' scores to get 827 and dividing by 25 (the number of students in the sample).

The **median** is the score that divides a distribution in half. Look back at the rank ordering of scores in Table A–2. In this case the median is 32, because there are as many scores ranked above it as ranked below it. In other words, 50 percent of the scores fall above 32 and 50 percent fall below.

The **mode** is commonly called the most typical score. It is simply the score that occurs most often in a sample. You can see in Table A–2 that 30 is the most frequent score for number of ideas recalled. Therefore, 30 is the mode of this data.

Measures of Variation

Measures of central tendency do not always tell us all we need to know about a distribution. They do not tell us, for example, how different the scores are from one another; that is, they do not show variation in scores. Several distributions could have the same mean, but differ in their variation. Table A–4 shows examples for three subsets of data taken from Table A–1.

All three of these subsets have a mean of 33, but they differ greatly in

Table A–4

	Subset 1		Subset 2		Subset 3
Subject Number	**Number of Ideas Recalled**	**Subject Number**	**Number of Ideas Recalled**	**Subject Number**	**Number of Ideas Recalled**
1	37	6	44	11	36
2	31	7	43	12	32
3	33	8	20	13	35
4	36	9	21	14	31
5	28	10	37	15	31
Mean	33.00		33.00		33.00
Range	9.00		24.00		5.00
Variance	10.80		110.00		4.40
Standard Deviation	3.29		10.50		2.10

Figure A–3

Frequency histograms for data presented in Table A–4.

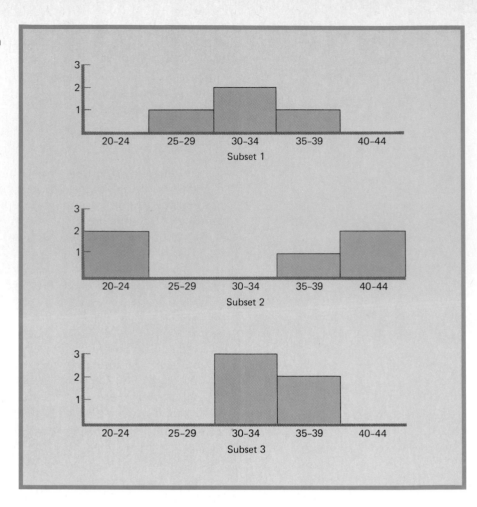

Table A–5

	d (Difference from Mean)	d (Difference squared)
37–33	4	16
31–33	−2	4
33–33	0	0
36–33	3	9
28–33	−5	25
44–33	11	121
40–33	7	49
36–33	3	9
41–33	8	64
37–33	4	16
35–33	2	4
27–33	−6	36
25–33	−8	64
31–33	−2	4
30–33	−3	9
38–33	5	25
31–33	−2	4
30–33	−3	9
43–33	10	100
20–33	−13	169
30–33	−3	9
30–33	−3	9
32–33	−1	1
21–33	−12	144
41–33	8	64
		964
	$\frac{964}{25} = 38.56$	

their variation. The subjects in subset 3 have scores that are relatively close to one another, the subjects in subset 1 have scores that are slightly farther from one another, and the subjects in subset 2 have scores that are quite different from one another. The histograms in Figure A–3 show this more clearly. Three statistics are used most often to describe variation. These are called the range, the variance, and the standard deviation.

The simplest measures of variation is the **range,** the difference between the largest and smallest number in the distribution. The range for the data presented in Table A–1 is 24 ($44 - 20 = 24$).

The range uses only extreme scores. A more common measure, the **variance,** uses every score to compute a single number to summarize the variation. It is the average squared difference of each number in the sample from the mean of all numbers in the sample. To compute the variance for the data in Table A–1, we first subtract the mean of 33 from each score and square the difference. We then find the average or mean of these squared differences; this is the sum of the squared differences divided by the number of squared differences. In this case, variance of the number of ideas recalled $= \dfrac{964}{25} = 38.56$.

The **standard deviation** is simply the square root of the variance. Therefore, the standard deviation for the number of ideas recalled (Table A–5) is $\sqrt{38.56} = 6.21$. The standard deviation is often used to express how far any given score is from the mean of a set of scores. For example, in Table A–1, subjects 8 and 9, with respective scores of 20 and 21, are more than one standard deviation below the mean. Subjects 6 and 7, with respective scores of 44 and 43, are more than one standard deviation above the mean.

Table A-6

Subject Number	SAT Verbal Score
1	530
2	620
3	580
4	640
5	380
6	530
7	760
8	560
9	580
10	690
11	720
12	560
13	660
14	560
15	610
16	690
17	650
18	590
19	560
20	560
21	710
22	780
23	580
24	630
25	630

Mean = 614.4
Standard Deviation = 83.19

INFERENTIAL STATISTICS

Statistics can be used to organize and describe data, but they have another very important use. Psychologists often make educated guesses, or **hypotheses,** about their data. They use inferential statistics to test those hypotheses. We might, for example, try to form an hypothesis to explain why most scores in the present data were well below the total possible score of 54. One hypothesis is that the experiment used poor students. The experiment used a sample of college students, which is a subset of all college students. The hypothesis is that the sample does not represent enough good students from the population of all college students. Table A–6 provides data that allow us to test this hypothesis. The table shows SAT verbal scores for the sample of students who gave the original data in Table A–1. We can compare this sample to the national population by using a special distribution that is discussed in the next section.

Normal Distribution

When we take a large number of measurements of almost any characteristic or event, we come up with a **normal distribution,** which represents the assumption that most measurements taken of a characteristic or event will be close to average, some measurements will be a small distance from average, and few measurements will be very far from average. For example, people's heights are approximately normally distributed; most people have a height close to average, some people have a height slightly above or below average, and very few people have a height greatly above or below average. This is also true of people's weights, their IQs, and many of the behaviors studied by psychologists.

The normal distribution can be plotted as a frequency polygon called the **normal curve,** which is symmetrical and shaped like a bell. The mean, median, and mode of a normal curve have the same value, which corresponds to the highest point on the curve.

We can make a normal curve if we know the mean and standard deviation of a set of scores. The national mean for college-bound students taking the SAT verbal subtest is 424, and the standard deviation is 110. Figure A–4 shows the normal curve for the SAT verbal subtest on the College Boards Entrance Examination.

As shown above, 68 percent of all measurements are between one standard deviation below the mean and one standard deviation above the mean. We can see in Figure A–4 that 68 percent of all college-bound students score between 314 and 534 on the SAT verbal subtest. A more detailed listing of areas under portions of the normal curve can be found in Table A–7.

Now let's compare the scores in Table A–6 with the national scores. The mean score in Table A–6 is 614. We can see in Figure A–4 that this mean is a little over 1.5 standard deviations *above* the national mean score of 424. Table A–7 shows that only .067 of the area under the normal curve lies to the right of 1.5 standard deviations above the mean. This indicates that only 6.7 percent of college-bound students score higher than 1.5 standard deviations above the mean. The results are therefore contrary to our hypothesis. The sample was *not* made up of only poor students. In fact, the students were very good compared to the national population. The high quality of the students is further shown in the next section, which describes a way to compare each individual with the population.

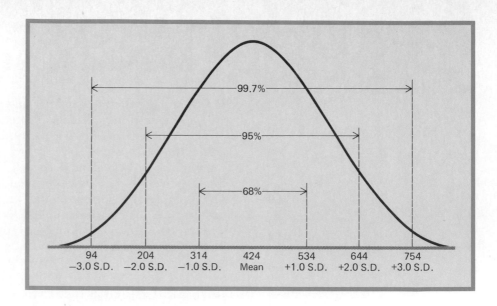

| | Area Under Normal Curve as Proportion of Total Area | | |
Standard Deviation	Area to the Left of This Value Indicates the Proportion of People Who Score *Lower* Than This Score	Area to the Right of This Value Indicates the Proportion of People Who Score *Higher* Than This Score	Area Between This Value and the Mean Indicates the Proportion of People Whose Scores Fell between This Score and the Mean
−3.0	.001	.999	.499
−2.5	.006	.994	.494
−2.0	.023	.977	.477
−1.5	.067	.933	.433
−1.0	.159	.841	.341
−.50	.309	.691	.191
0.0	.500	.500	.000
+.05	.691	.309	.191
+1.0	.841	1.590	.341
+1.5	.933	.067	.433
+2.0	.977	.023	.477
+2.5	.994	.006	.494
+3.0	.999	.001	.499

Standard Scores

Often we want to know how a particular person scores in relation to other people. For example, you may have taken the SAT verbal subtest yourself and may want to know how you performed relative to the average college-bound student. To do this, you could compute your standard score and, using Table A–7, see what percentage of students scored lower and higher than you.

A **standard score** is a single number that expresses where a score lies relative to a population. For example, subject number 17 in Table A–6 got a score of 650 on the SAT verbal subtest. To compute his or her standard score, you simply subtract the mean from his or her score and divide by the standard deviation. (Recall that the national mean was 424 and the standard deviation was 110.)

Standard score for score of 650:

$$= \frac{650 - 424}{110}$$

$$= \frac{226}{110} = 2.05 \text{ standard deviation units from the mean}$$

$$= 2.05 \text{ standard score}$$

Using column one of Table A–7, we see that subject number 17 scored higher than 97.7 percent of all college-bound students. Column two indicates that only 2.3 percent scored higher, and column three indicates that 43 percent of the national population received a score falling between this subject's score and the national mean score.

By contrast, subject number 5 received a score of 380:

$$= \frac{380 - 424}{110}$$

$$= \frac{-44}{110} = -.4 \text{ standard deviations}$$

$$= -.4 \text{ standard score}$$

Using Table A–7 again, we see that subject number 5 scored higher than only 30.9 percent, 69 percent scored higher, and 19 percent of the national population received a score between this score and the national mean score.

You can use standard scores to compare each individual in Table A–6 with the national population. These comparisons will show clearly that we have no basis for saying that good students were underrepresented.

Table A–8

Data from Experimental Group	
Subject Number	Number of Ideas Recalled
26	32
27	41
28	40
29	43
30	35
31	39
32	34
33	36
34	28
35	40
36	37
37	41
38	44
39	37
40	41
41	25
42	30
43	47
44	42
45	39
46	25
47	31
48	27
49	26
50	42

Mean = 36.08
Standard Deviation = 6.33

Statistical Significance

Perhaps students scored low because they did not study enough. From this we could form the hypothesis that extra study will improve performance. Table A–8 provides data for testing this hypothesis. The students who gave the data in Table A–8 read the passage, rated the importance of each idea in the passage, and then read it again before they tried to recall it. Let's call this the *experimental group.* The students who gave the data in Table A–1 read the passage once and then tried to recall it. We will call this group of students the *control group.* Students had an equal chance of being assigned to the experimental group or to the control group, and both groups were treated identically except for the different amounts of study. We can test our hypothesis about studying by comparing the data from the two groups.

One of the descriptive statistics that we discussed earlier provides a good comparison. The mean number of ideas recalled for the experimental group was 36 ideas. The mean for the control group was 33 ideas. It appears that having students study more improves comprehension and memory of ideas. But we cannot accept this without first performing a test of **statistical significance,** which determines whether the difference in the mean performance of these two groups reflects a true difference between the groups or is simply a result of sampling error. The difference would be due to **sampling error** if by chance we happened to get better readers in the experimental group than in the control group, or if we happened to get more students in the experimental group who knew a great deal about biology.

A test of statistical significance gives us a precise way to evaluate an obtained difference between sample means. To test statistical significance, we compute a test statistic that takes into account both the size of the difference in the means and the variation of the means being compared. To compute this statistic we must know not only the difference between the means, but the variation of the mean scores as well.

Standard Error of the Mean. If we draw several samples from the same population and compute the mean of each sample on some characteristic, the means of these samples will be different. Random samples drawn from a population vary simply due to chance. The **standard error of the mean** indicates the variation of a sample mean and tells how likely it is that the sample mean represents the population mean.

To determine the standard error of the mean, we simply divide the standard deviation of a sample by the square root of the number of subjects in the sample. The standard error of the mean for the data in Table A–1 is

$$\frac{6.21}{\sqrt{25}} = \frac{6.21}{5} = 1.24$$

The standard error of the mean for the data in Table A–8 is

$$\frac{6.33}{\sqrt{25}} = \frac{6.33}{5} = 1.27$$

The standard error of the mean will decrease with an increase in sample size. Thus, the mean of a large sample is more likely to be representative of the population mean.

From the standard error of the means, we can compute a **standard error of the difference between two means.** It is computed by finding the square root of the sum of the standard errors. The standard error of the difference between the means in the present experiment is

$$\sqrt{1.24 + 1.27} = \sqrt{2.5} = 1.58$$

Once we know the standard error of the difference between two means, we can compute the test statistic, the ratio of the difference between the means to the standard error of the difference between the means.

$$\text{test statistic} = \frac{\text{difference between means}}{\substack{\text{standard error of the} \\ \text{difference between the means}}}$$

A ratio of 2.0 or more generally indicates a statistically significant difference between means, or a true difference between groups, not simply a sampling error.

A test statistic of 2.0 is selected because a value that large or larger can occur by chance less than 5 in 100 times. We treat the test statistic as a standard score. Looking at column two in Table A–7, we can see that the probability of obtaining a standard score two deviations above the mean is .023, and the chance of obtaining a standard score two standard deviations below the mean is also .023. The total probability, therefore, is .046. This means that, if we get a test statistic of 2.0, we are likely to say there is a difference between the population means (when there really isn't one) only 5 out of 100 times; 95 percent of the time we will be correct.

Recall our hypothesis that having students study more will improve their recall. This hypothesis appears to be correct. The mean of the experimental group was 36 and the mean of the control group was 33. Now, using a test statistic, let's see if this difference is statistically significant.

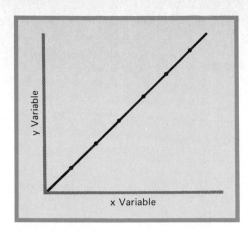

Figure A-5

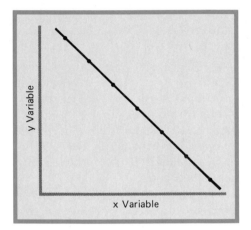

Figure A-6

Figure A-7

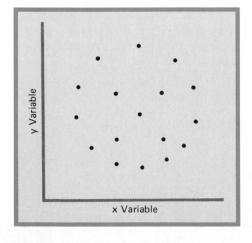

$$\text{test statistic} = \frac{\text{difference between means}}{\substack{\text{standard error of the} \\ \text{difference between the means}}}$$

$$= \frac{36 - 33}{1.58} = \frac{3}{1.58} = 1.90$$

Since this value is less than 2.0, we must conclude that the difference between the means is not statistically significant. We *cannot* say with 95 percent certainty that having college students study the passage more improves their comprehension and recall of those ideas.

A nonsignificant test statistic means that we must withhold conclusion. It means that we must design more sensitive tests if we are still interested in the original hypothesis. For example, we might have another experimental group study even harder. However, in the present comparison, considerably more studying produced only three more ideas on the average. Therefore, it may be better to consider other hypotheses.

One alternative is that scores were low because students left out unimportant ideas. Deese (1981) supported this hypothesis to some extent, but he also showed that students omitted many important ideas. In fact, the data available at the present time suggest that students do not respond extremely well to open-ended questions about lessons. Apparently, they need more structure than that provided by open-ended tests.

Another question that one can ask about open-ended tests is how they relate to multiple-choice tests. We will take up this question in the next section.

Correlation

Correlation is a procedure for describing the relationship between two sets of paired scores. The sets are said to be positively correlated if high scores in one set are paired with high scores in the other set, while low scores are paired with low scores. Height and weight, for example, are positively correlated; tall people tend to weigh more, and short people tend to weigh less. The sets are said to be negatively correlated if high scores in one set are paired with low scores in the other. Reading ability and reading time, for example, are negatively correlated; more able readers require less time to read a passage. The two sets are said to be independent or uncorrelated if there is no such relationship. The number of letters in a person's last name and his or her IQ, for example, are uncorrelated; there is no relationship between these two sets of data.

We can quickly determine if two sets of scores are correlated by drawing a **scatter plot.** We place one variable (height) on the horizontal axis of a graph, and the other (weight) on the vertical axis. Then we plot a person's score on one variable along the horizontal axis and his or her score on the second variable along the vertical axis. We draw a dot where the two scores intersect. Figure A-5 shows a scatter plot of two variables that have a perfect positive correlation. Figure A-6 shows a scatter plot of two variables that have a perfect negative correlation. Figure A-7 shows a scatter plot of two variables that are totally uncorrelated.

Let's examine a scatter plot of the present data to compare SAT scores, which are based upon multiple-choice test results, with open-ended test scores. There is obviously not a perfect correlation between these two variables, but there does appear to be a slight positive correlation. Those students who recalled a larger number of ideas also tend to be those students who received a higher SAT verbal subtest score, and those students who recalled fewer ideas tend to be those students who received a lower SAT verbal subtest score.

Table A-9

Subject Number	Number of Ideas Recalled	Difference from Mean	SAT Verbal Subtest Score	Difference from Mean
1	37	4	530	−84
2	31	−2	620	6
3	33	0	580	−34
4	36	3	640	26
5	28	−5	380	−234
6	44	11	530	−84
7	43	10	760	146
8	20	−13	560	−54
9	21	−12	580	−34
10	37	4	690	76
11	36	3	720	106
12	32	−1	560	−54
13	35	2	660	46
14	31	−2	560	−54
15	31	−2	610	−4
16	40	7	690	76
17	41	8	650	36
18	27	−6	590	−24
19	25	−8	560	−54
20	30	−3	560	−54
21	38	5	710	96
22	30	−3	780	166
23	30	−3	580	−34
24	30	−3	630	16
25	41	8	630	16

Table A-10

Subject Number	Product of the Differences
1	$4 \times -84 = -336$
2	$-2 \times 6 = -12$
3	$0 \times -34 = 0$
4	$3 \times 26 = 78$
5	$-5 \times -234 = 1170$
6	$11 \times -84 = -924$
7	$10 \times 146 = 1460$
8	$-13 \times -54 = 702$
9	$-12 \times -34 = 408$
10	$4 \times 76 = 304$
11	$3 \times 106 = 318$
12	$-1 \times -54 = 54$
13	$2 \times 46 = 92$
14	$-2 \times -54 = 108$
15	$-2 \times -4 = 8$
16	$7 \times 76 = 532$
17	$8 \times 36 = 288$
18	$-6 \times -24 = 144$
19	$-8 \times -54 = 432$
20	$-3 \times -54 = 162$
21	$5 \times 96 = 480$
22	$-3 \times 166 = -498$
23	$-3 \times -34 = 102$
24	$-3 \times 16 = -48$
25	$8 \times 16 = 128$
	5152

To more precisely describe the relationship between two sets of scores, we use a **correlation coefficient,** which ranges from +1.0 to −1.0. A perfect positive correlation receives a +1.0, while a perfect negative correlation receives a −1.0. Most correlation coefficients, however, fall between +1.0 and −1.0 because few things are perfectly correlated. If two sets of scores are uncorrelated, the correlation coefficient will equal 0.

The Product-Moment Correlation. The most widely used index of correlation is called the **product-moment correlation** coefficient. We can compute this coefficient in five steps. Let's compute the coefficient for the present data to see if there is a relationship between number of ideas recalled in a textbook selection and SAT verbal subtest scores (Tables A–1 and A–6). First we must determine the differences of all the scores in each set from their respective means (see Table A–9). Remember that the mean number of ideas recalled was 33 and the mean SAT verbal subtest score was 614. Second, we must determine the sum of the products of the differences. See Table A–10. Third, we compute the standard deviations for both sets of scores. In this case, we have already computed them. Remember that the standard deviation for the number of ideas recalled was 6.21, and the standard deviation for the SAT verbal subtest scores was 83.19. Fourth, we multiply the product of the two standard deviations by the number of subjects in the sample.

$$25(6.21 \times 83.19) =$$
$$25(516.61) = 12915.15$$

Fifth, we divide this number into the sum of the products of the differences.

$$\frac{5152}{12915} = .399$$

As we predicted from the scatter plot in Figure A–8, this is not a perfect correlation, but it is a moderate positive correlation. For the number of

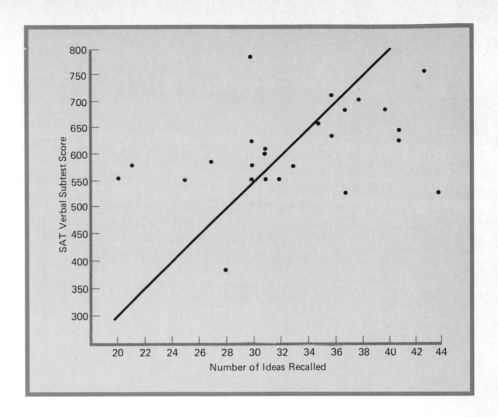

subjects in this sample, it is statistically significant at the .05 level. This means that performance on the SAT verbal subtest score does appear to be similar to performance on open-ended tests, and we are 95 percent certain that this correlation did not occur simply due to sampling error or chance.

Statistics go hand in hand with research designs. Chapter 1, for example, discusses the use of correlations with specific designs, and it goes over the logic of drawing conclusions from correlations. The more you learn about experimental designs, the more you will understand statistics. And the more you learn about statistics, the more you will understand research designs. You will do well, therefore, to refer back to this appendix when you read Chapter 1 and other chapters that take up specific research designs.

In summary, students question the accuracy of highly structured multiple-choice exams. The research reviewed here suggests, however, that going to the opposite extreme of open-ended tests is not the answer. The research suggests further that scores on very structured and very unstructured exams are correlated. Teachers are as eager as students to improve exams—if you have some ideas, speak up. Your ideas could become the bases for future experiments.

SUMMARY

1. **Statistics** is a branch of mathematics used by psychologists to describe data and to draw conclusions based on data.
2. **Descriptive statistics** are tools for summarizing data taken on a group of objects, people, or events.
3. **A frequency distribution** is a useful way of summarizing data. It tells how many scores fall into each of the intervals chosen to describe the data.
4. A **measure of central tendency** is a score value that represents the center of a group

of scores. The **mean,** the **median,** and the **mode** are used to describe the central tendency of a distribution.

5. **Measures of variation** tell us how different the scores in a distribution are from one another. The **range,** the **variance,** and the **standard deviation** are used to describe the variation of a distribution.

6. **Inferential statistics** are used to test hypotheses made by psychologists.

7. The **normal distribution** represents the assumption that most measurements taken on a characteristic or event will be close to average, some measurements will be a small distance from average, and few measurements will be very far from average.

8. **Standard scores** are used when we want to know how a particular person scores in relation to other persons on some characteristic or event. They express the value of a score relative to the mean and the standard deviation of its distribution.

9. A **test of statistical significance** is performed to determine if the difference in the mean performance of two groups reflects a true difference between groups or is simply a result of sampling error.

10. **Correlation** is a procedure for describing the linear relationship between two sets of paired scores. A correlation coefficient tells us whether or not we can predict one measure knowing another, but does not indicate that one variable causes another.

Key Terms

correlation
correlation coefficient
descriptive statistics
frequency distribution
histograms
hypotheses
mean
measure of central tendency
median
mode
normal curve
normal distribution

polygons
product-moment correlation
range
sampling error
scatter plot
standard deviation
standard error of the difference between two means
standard error of the mean
standard score
statistical significance
statistics
variance

Suggested Readings

CALFEE, R. C. *Human experimental psychology.* New York: Holt, Rinehart & Winston, 1975. Calfee teaches students to think like experimental psychologists. He immerses students in problems that force them to combine experimental psychology with statistical design and analysis.

FREEDMAN, D., PISANI, R., and PURVES, R. *Statistics.* New York: W. W. Norton and Co., Inc., 1978. Freedman et al. explain the basic ideas of statistics in nonmathematical terms through the use of real examples.

HAYES, W. L. *Statistics for the social sciences* (2nd ed.). New York: Holt, Rinehart & Winston, 1973. Hays presents a more advanced introduction to probability and statistics. This text goes into more detail than most introductory texts and places greater emphasis on the theoretical than on the computational aspects of statistics.

MOSTELLER, F., ROURKE, R. E. K., and THOMAS, G. B., JR. *Probability with statistical applications* (2nd ed.). Reading, Mass.: Addison-Wesley, 1970. Mosteller et al. explain the theory of probability and apply this theory to statistical theory. Two courses in high-school algebra are required to understand this text.

ROBINSON, P. W. *Fundamentals of experimental psychology: A comparative approach* (2nd ed.). Englewood Cliffs, N.J.: Prentice-Hall, 1981. Robinson emphasizes procedural aspects of psychological investigations. He also provides complete step-by-step examples of how to statistically analyze data from many types of experimental designs.

GLOSSARY

Abnormal behavior. Behavior may be labeled abnormal when it is unusual, causes distress to others, and makes it difficult for a person to adjust to his or her environment.

Absolute refractory period. A period after a cell has fired, during which it will not fire again—it usually lasts for about 1 millisecond.

Absolute threshold. The least amount of a certain stimulus energy that can be detected.

Accommodation. Term used by Piaget to refer to the process of adjusting one's schema to fit environmental demands. Compare with *assimilation.*

Acetylcholine (ACh). A chemical transmitter in neurons that tends to transmit fast-acting, excitatory messages.

Achievement motive (nAch). Motive to do things as rapidly and/or as well as possible.

Achievement tests. Designed to measure a person's current knowledge and skills—reflect what has been learned in the past.

Active synthesizing process. Mental operations that impose organization on sensory information.

Addiction. The physical dependence on a substance, so that the body develops a need for the drug. The body builds up a tolerance for a dose of the drug and needs ever-increasing doses. If the drug is not taken, people experience the painful symptoms of withdrawal, which may include headaches, cramps, nausea, uncontrollable trembling, and restlessness.

Adolescence. Extends from about age 12 to the late teens, is a time of passage from childhood to adulthood.

Affective disorders. A group of disorders involving problems with emotions and mood. People are said to be suffering from an affective disorder when their moods, such as depression, take over and they have trouble functioning because of them.

Affiliation motive. Motive or desire to associate with, be around other people.

Afterimage. Visual experience that continues after the stimulus has ceased; occurs because some activity continues in the retina after seeing the stimulus. The afterimage consists of the opposite color of what was seen in the original stimulus: blue for yellow, red for green, black for white.

Aggression cues. Stimuli that a person has learned to associate with aggression (examples are guns or knives); when these cues are present in the environment they tend to elicit aggression.

Aggression motive. Motive, whether innate or learned, to attack objects or other organisms.

Air pollution syndrome (APS). Physical reactions to pollution characterized by headache, insomnia, gastrointestinal problems, irritated eyes, and depression.

Alcoholics. People who are addicted to alcohol; they have an uncontrollable urge to drink, and, because of increasing tolerance, must continue to increase their consumption of alcohol.

Allele. A single gene may occur in one of several different forms called alleles; alleles may be dominant or recessive.

Alternate states of consciousness. Mental states that differ, as measured by a specific pattern of physiological and subjective responses.

Amnesia. A selective forgetting of past events. Some forms of amnesia are caused by physical injuries, such as a blow to the head. *Psychogenic amnesia* means that the cause of the memory loss is stress rather than physical injury.

Amniocentesis. Process in which fluid is taken from a mother's womb to test for Down's syndrome and other genetic disorders.

Amplitude. Distance between the top and bottom of a sound wave; amplitude increases as sounds get louder.

Anal stage. During second and third years, the main focus of pleasure shifts from the mouth to the anal area. A major battle between child and parents occurs during this stage over the issue of toilet training.

Analytical psychology. Jung's complex, almost mystical theory of personality; includes his belief that the libido was a force resulting from the desire to be creative.

Analytic introspection. Method used in structuralism; a way of isolating the elementary sensations of which experiences are made.

Androgens. Male hormones secreted by the testes that increase male sex drive and influence the development of secondary sex characteristics.

Anorexia nervosa. A condition in which a person loses his or her appetite, eats little, and slowly begins to starve.

Antianxiety drugs. Minor tranquilizers that reduce anxiety and tension without causing drowsiness or a loss of mental alertness. Most popular are Valium, Librium, and Miltown.

Antidepressant drugs. Drugs that work by lifting the person's spirits and increasing his or her activity level. Two examples are Tofranil and Elavil.

Antipsychotic drugs. Major tranquilizers that are used to calm and relieve the delusions of schizophrenics. Two most commonly used are Thorzaine and Stlezine.

Antisocial personality disorder. Disorder in which people perform violent and hurtful acts without the least bit of guilt or regret, are incapable of forming close relationships, and are manipulative and insincere.

Antrograde amnesia. Difficulty in remembering events that happen after an injury.

Anvil. One of three small bones in the middle ear, it transmits sounds from the eardrum to the inner ear.

Anxiety disorders. A group of conditions in which people feel anxiety that is far out of proportion to the situations they are in; their responses interfere with normal daily functioning.

Apgar scoring system. Scale used to assess the condition of newborns; low scores show possible neurological damage.

Aptitude tests. Try to predict capacity for future performance.

Aqueous humor. Clear fluid that carries nourishment to the cornea of the eye.

Ascending nerves. Carry sensory information up the spinal cord to specific areas of the brain.

Assimilation. Term used by Piaget to refer to the process of interpreting events in a way that fits existing ideas (or schema). Compare with *accommodation.*

Attachment. Tendency of youngsters to seek closeness to certain people.

Attention. Paying mind to important stimuli and ignoring irrelevant ones; a selective process in memory.

Attitude change. Accepting a new position or new information while giving up an old position.

Attitudes. Learned, relatively enduring feelings about objects, events, or issues.

Attraction. A positive attitude we have about another person.

Attribution. The process of inferring characteristics of people from their observable behavior; our way of explaining the behavior of others.

Autokinetic effect. The tendency for a stationary light viewed against darkness to look as if it is moving; the light seems to glide, jerk, and swoop through space.

Autonomic nervous system. Functional subdivision of the nervous system; regulates glands and organs. Divided into sympathetic and parasympathetic divisions.

Aversive conditioning. Type of behavior therapy often used to break bad habits such as smoking and drinking; in this type of therapy the person receives unpleasant consequences for undesired behavior. This may mean taking a drug (Antibuse) that will make them sick if they drink, or making them smoke so much and so quickly that they become sick.

Avoidance training. Occurs when a subject learns to make a response to avoid a negative reinforcer.

Axon. Long fiber that carries neural impulses away from the cell body of the neuron to the terminal branches to be passed on to other neurons.

Axon terminal. A tiny knob at the end of an axon's terminal branch.

Backward masking. The ability of a stimulus to wipe out the sensory memory of a preceding stimulus.

Barbiturates. Depressant drugs that slow the body functions, reduce anxiety, and have a relaxing effect.

Basal ganglia. Four masses of gray matter in the brain that control background muscle tone and large, general muscle movements—part of the motor system.

Basilar membrane. Located inside the cochlea in the inner ear, it is attached to the oval window at one end and the tip of the cochlea at the other end. Vibrations in the oval window cause hair cells on the basilar membrane to move. When these hair cells are bent, they send nerve impulses to the brain that are experienced as sound.

Behavioral assessment. Assessment by means of examining a person's present behavior to predict future actions. Can also be used to assign traits to people.

Behavioral medicine. New field in medicine; focus is on the effects of stress and better ways of dealing with it.

Behavioral sinks. Develop as a result of overcrowding; they aggravate all forms of pathology that can be found within a group.

Behaviorism. Approach to psychology, based on the premise that human behavior can be described by focusing only on the observable stimulus and response.

Behavior therapies. Therapies based on the assumption that maladaptive behavior is learned through the same process by which other behaviors are learned and can be unlearned by substituting a more adaptive behavior in its place.

Binocular cues. Cues to depth perception that we use when we are looking with both eyes.

Binocular disparity. This is the experience of seeing a different view from each of our eyes; two views are fused by the brain and produce depth perception.

Biofeedback. Technique that provides people with feedback on their physiological functions (such as heart rate and blood pressure) so that they can learn to control these functions and achieve a more relaxed state.

Biofeedback therapy. A type of therapy designed to help people control their physiological functions without the use of drugs or other biotherapy techniques. Helps people reduce tension and stress, reduce phobic reactions, and control headaches. Has also been combined with other psychotherapies. See also *biofeedback*.

Biotherapy. The use of drugs, surgery, or electric shock, with or without accompanying psychotherapy, to induce behavior change.

Bipolar cells. Cells in the retina, connected to rods and cones; actively participate in the process of coding or interpreting the information contained in light. One-to-one connections to cones; one-to-many connections to rods.

Bipolar disorder. A disorder in which the person alternates between manic and depressive stages. Often the extremes of each mood state appear for only a short time and the person generally behaves normally when between states.

Blind spot. Area in the retina that is blind because it is where the optic nerve exits from the retina.

Body language. Communication through body movement.

Boilermaker's deafness. Partial hearing loss caused by spending long periods of time around loud noises (above 85 decibels).

Bone conduction. Another way that sound is transmitted; when a person speaks, the jaw bones conduct vibrations to the cochlea. We hear our own voice through bone-conducted and air-conducted sounds; we hear others' voices only through air-conducted sounds.

Brainstem. Midbrain and hindbrain combined.

Broca's aphasia. Speech that is slow, labored, and slightly distorted; caused by injury to Broca's area in the cortex.

Bulimia. Eating disorder in which the individual goes through cycles of dieting for a period of time and then gorging with food (binging). After binging, the person will purge the food by vomiting or using laxatives.

Calories. Units of energy produced when food is oxidized or burnt by the body.

Case history. Method used in psychology that looks in depth at a few individuals or at the effects of a single event.

Cataracts. Widespread disease affecting vision; a condition characterized by cloudy lenses; can result in blindness if lenses are not removed surgically.

Catecholamines. Chemical transmitters in neurons that tend to transmit slow-acting, inhibitory messages.

Catharsis. Release of tension through aggression.

Central nervous system. Nerve tissue in the brain and spinal cord.

Cerebellum. Part of the hindbrain; made up of two wrinkled hemispheres. Coordinates the force, range, and rate of body movements.

Cerebral cortex (cerebrum). Two wrinkled hemispheres that are part of the forebrain; governs our most advanced human capabilities, including abstract reasoning and speech.

Chemical transmitters. Chemicals that carry messages between neurons; some are excitatory, some inhibitory.

Chemotherapy. Treatment of disorders through the use of drugs; a form of biotherapy.

Chromosomes. Threadlike chains of genes; humans have 23 pairs of chromosomes.

Chronological age. A person's age in years and months.

Chunking. Process of grouping elements such as letters or words into units (or chunks) that function as wholes. Memory span consists of 7 ± 2 chunks.

Clairvoyance. The perception of an object, action, or event by means of ESP.

Classical conditioning. The process by which an originally neutral stimulus comes to elicit a response that was originally given to another stimulus. It takes place when the neutral stimulus is repeatedly paired with the other stimulus.

Clinical psychology. Subfield of psychology dedicated to the diagnosis and treatment of emotional and behavioral disorders.

Cochlea. Part of the inner ear; a tube coiled in on itself about three turns, like a spiral around a central core. Contains the basilar membrane inside it.

Cognitive dissonance. State that occurs when a person's attitudes, beliefs, and behaviors are in conflict. In order to relieve the dissonance, the person will try to change the cognitions so that they will again be in agreement.

Cognitive learning theory. Attempts to explain the function of thought processes in learning.

Cognitive map. A mental picture. In the Tolman and Honzik experiment described in Chapter 5, the rats had learned a cognitive map of the maze.

Cognitive overload. An inability to respond to stimuli because there are too many events occurring in the environment.

Cognitive psychology. Subfield of psychology concerned with the mental events that intervene between stimuli and responses.

Cohabitation. Relationship between two unmarried people who live together.

Cold spots. Areas on the skin where only cold is felt, even if stimulated by a warm object (when this occurs it is called *paradoxical cold*).

Colorblindness. Inability to see or distinguish between colors. There are several types of color blindness: red-green, blue-yellow, and total color blindness.

Community psychology. Subfield of psychology dedicated to promoting mental health at the community level; seeks to prevent and treat psychological problems by working to evaluate and to improve community organizations.

Complex tones. Sounds containing many frequencies.

Compulsion. Irrational behavior or ritual that people cannot control; often they do not know why they need to do this. See also *obsession*, which involves thought rather than behavior.

Concept. A mental grouping of objects, events, states, or ideas based on similarity.

Concrete operational stage. One of Piaget's stages of cognitive development; lasts from 7 years to 12 years of age. Main theme is extending mental operations from concrete objects to purely symbolic terms.

Conditioned response (CR). A learned response to a conditioned stimulus (CS). Usually a less strong response than an unconditioned response (UR).

Conditioned stimulus (CS). Stimulus to which a subject learns to respond, through repeated pairings with an unconditioned stimulus (US).

Cones. Light receptors in the eye; located mostly in the fovea, are best for seeing details, and are responsible for color vision.

Conflict. A state that occurs when a person is motivated to choose between two or more mutually exclusive goals or courses of action.

Conformity. Occurs when a person changes his or her behavior or attitudes as a result of real or imagined group pressures, despite personal feelings to the contrary.

Conscious element of personality. According to Freud, this includes whatever the person is perceiving or thinking at the moment.

Consciousness. The perception of what passes in a person's own mind (Locke's definition).

Continuous reinforcement schedule. Subject receives a reinforcer for every correct response.

Control group. The group of subjects in an experiment that is treated exactly the same as the experimental group(s) except that the control group is not exposed to the independent variable and thus serves as the basis for comparison.

Conversion disorder. One of the somatoform disorders, usually involving one specific symptom. The most common symptoms are paralysis of a limb, loss of sensation in a part of the body, blindness, and deafness. There is no organic basis to this disorder.

Cornea. Part of the eye, it is transparent, shaped like a crystal ball.

Corpus callosum. Large cable of nerve fibers that connects the two cerebral hemispheres.

Correlation. A measure of the extent to which variables change together. If two variables increase and decrease at the same time, they are positively correlated; if one increases while the other decreases, they are negatively correlated. This does not necessarily indicate a cause-and-effect relationship between the variables, however.

Correlation coefficient. Tells whether or not one can predict one measure knowing another, but does not indicate that one variable *causes* another.

Counseling and school psychology. Subfield of psychology that helps people with social, educational, and job or career adjustments.

Critical period. A stage of development during which the organism must have certain experiences or it will not develop normally.

Cross-sectional research. Research in which people of all different ages are tested in various ways; compare with *longitudinal research*, in which the one group is tested continually over a period of time, at different ages.

Crowding. Feeling or psychological state that often, but not always, accompanies high density.

Crystallized intelligence. Specific mental skills, such as one's vocabulary.

Dancing reflex. Causes infants to prance with their legs in a "tip-toe" stepping motion when they are held upright with feet touching a surface.

Dark adaptation. Downward adjustment of sensitivity to light; occurs in the rods when one enters a dark room, for example.

Daydreams. Thoughts that divert attention away from an immediately demanding task.

Decibel. Unit for measuring loudness; each tenfold increase in sound level adds 10 decibels.

Defense mechanisms. Ways of coping with anxiety; an unconscious distortion of reality in order to defend against anxiety. See *displacement; projection; rationalization; reaction formation; repression; sublimation;* and *suppression.*

Deindividuation. Occurs in groups when people tend to lose their personal identity and assume the identity of the group.

Deinstitutionalization. The policy of treating people with psychological problems in their own local environments rather than placing them in large, isolated institutions.

Delta waves. High voltage, extremely low-frequency brain waves characteristic of stage-4 sleep.

Delusions. Irrational beliefs that are held in spite of contrary evidence, that have no base in reality. For example, the delusion of grandeur is the belief that the person is special or different from other people (one may think one is Napoleon or Joan of Arc, for instance).

Demand characteristics. Elements in a questionnaire or experiment that communicate what behavior is expected from the subjects.

Dendrites. Short fibers extending out from the body of a neuron, which receive impulses from other neurons and carry them to the cell body.

Density. A measure of the number of people in a given area. Not to be confused with crowding, which is a psychological state rather than a physical measure.

Deoxyribonucleic acid (DNA). Controls the way in which protein chains are built, and, thus, contain the basic blueprints for life; genes are made up of DNA.

Dependent variable. The variable that is measured in an experiment.

Depolarization. Occurs when a neuron is sending or receiving a neural impulse.

Depressants. Drugs that slow body functions or calm nervous excitement; examples are alcohol, nicotine, and heroin.

Depression. A disorder in which there is a loss of interest in most activities, including eating or sex; lack of concentration; inability to sleep. May lead to suicide in its extreme forms. See also *bipolar disorder*.

Descending nerves. Carry commands down the spinal cord to move muscles.

Descriptive statistics. Tools for summarizing data taken of a group of objects, people, or events.

Development. A process by which the genes that an organism inherits from its parents come to be expressed as specific physical and behavioral characteristics.

Developmental psychology. Subfield of psychology that examines the function of age on behavior. Examines the age at which people should be performing certain behaviors and how events that occur at various ages affect behavior.

Difference threshold. Smallest difference in intensity that can be noticed between two stimuli.

Discrimination. (1) Occurs when subjects learn to respond only to certain stimuli, but not to other, similar stimuli.

Discrimination. (2) Negative, often aggressive, behavior aimed at the target of prejudice.

Displaced aggression. Taking out one's anger and/or frustration on someone or something other than the actual cause of one's anger.

Displacement. A defense mechanism that involves redirecting an emotion from the person who caused it to another, safer or more available, target.

Dissociative disorders. Characterized by "tuning out" or dissociating a part of the person from the situation at hand. It is almost as if part of the person has split off and taken on its own identity.

Door-in-the-face approach. Persuasive technique based on the fact that people who at first refuse a large request will be more likely after that to comply with a smaller request.

Doppler shift. Occurs as cars zoom by on a racetrack; as they go by, the engine sound drops sharply to a lower pitch. Sound waves bunch up as cars approach on a racetrack and spread out as cars speed away. The bunched-up waves have a shorter distance between their wave crests (higher frequency); the spread-out waves have a longer distance between their wave crests (lower frequency).

Double-bind conflict. Results when children receive contradictory messages from their parents, messages that create a "no-win" situation for them—no matter what they do, they are wrong.

Double-blind control. Procedure used in an experiment in which neither subject nor experimenter is aware of how the independent variable is being manipulated.

Double helix. Model of the structure of DNA molecules, similar to a spiral staircase, the steps of which contain a genetic code.

Down's syndrome. Disorder characterized by mental retardation and altered physical appearance; caused by genetic mutation that adds an extra chromosome to the twenty-first pair, giving the child 47 chromosomes.

Dream interpretation. Part of Freud's technique of psychoanalysis; involves helping clients to understand the latent content of their dreams, which represents the repressed feelings that are being expressed.

Dreams. Series of images, thoughts, and emotions that occur during sleep.

Drive. A tension or state that results when a need is not met; it compels the organism to satisfy the need.

Drug therapy. The use of medications to treat both mild and severe psychological disturbances.

DSM III. Stands for Diagnostic and Statistical Manual, third edition, which was published in 1979. It is one of the most commonly used systems for classifying abnormal behavior, and was developed by the American Psychiatric Association.

Dualism. The theory that the mind and brain are separate entities. See also *monism*.

Dyspareunia. A sexual disorder in which females experience pain during intercourse.

Ear canal. Tube-like passage that funnels sound to the eardrum.

Eardrum. A fine membrane stretched over the inner end of the ear canal; vibrates when sound waves strike it.

Ecological theory of perception. Theory that our own movements change the light entering our eyes in lawful ways such that unchanged aspects of the environment are specified by unchanged aspects of the light.

Effort justification. The attempt to make something we have to work hard for more valuable to make the effort worthwhile.

Ego. According to Freud, a second dimension of personality, which works to control the impulses of the id; tries to satisfy the desires of the id by dealing with the environment.

Electra complex. According to Freud, during the phallic stage, girls discover that they are biologically inferior to boys because they lack a penis. They envy their father's penis and become attracted to him, fantasizing about having a male baby by their father.

Electroconvulsive therapy (ECT). A technique of biotherapy in which electric shock is administered to the patient's brain, causing epileptic-like convulsions. Has been shown to have short-term benefits for those suffering from depressive disorders.

Electromagnetic spectrum. Forms the entire range of wavelengths of electromagnetic radiation; wavelengths corresponding to visible colors cover only a small part of this spectrum.

Embryo. Term for a human organism from the third week through the eighth week in the uterus.

Emotions. Affective stages or feelings, accompanied by physiological changes, that often influence behavior.

Empty chair technique. A therapeutic technique in which clients place different parts of their personality in chairs and act each of these parts.

Encode. To select and represent information in a specific form (verbally, visually) in memory.

Encounter group (also called sensitivity group). Aims at expanding personal awareness and growth rather than treating emotional disorders. Such groups try to rid people of their interpersonal "hang-ups." Variations include marathon groups and nude encounter groups.

Endocrine system. Major coordinating system that regulates body chemistry.

Endorphin and enkephalin. Neural transmitters with chemical structures similar to opium and its derivatives, morphine and heroin.

Engineering psychology. Subfield of psychology that is concerned with making human contact with tools and machines as comfortable and as error free as possible.

Environmental psychology. Subfield of psychology that analyzes how behavior is influenced by environmental factors such as architecture, weather, space, crowding, noise, and pollution.

Episodic memory. A person's memories about events, including the time and place they occurred.

Equilibrium. Sense of overall body orientation (for example, the difference between standing upright or tilting backwards).

Erectile dysfunction. The inability to have an erection or maintain one long enough for ejaculation.

Escape training. Occurs when, through the use of negative reinforcement, a subject learns to make a response to remove a stimulus (such as a shock).

Estrogen. Female sex hormone. The level of estrogen is at its highest during the period of ovulation, and determines the onset of menstruation and the period of fertility. Estrogen also influences the development of secondary sex characteristics.

Ethologists. Scientists who study animal behavior in natural settings.

Experiment. An investigation in which a researcher directly manipulates one variable while measuring the effects on some other variable.

Experimental psychology. Subfield of psychology that examines the behaviors and cognitions (thoughts) that are related to learning, memory, perception, motivation, and emotion.

Experimenter bias. Expectations on the part of the person running an experiment that subjects will behave in a certain way—these behaviors can affect the subjects as well as the perceptions of the experimenter.

Extinction. A gradual falling off or decrease in a response when the conditioned stimulus (CS) is repeatedly presented alone, without the unconditioned stimulus (US). In operant conditioning, a falling off of a response when it is no longer followed by a reinforcer.

Extrasensory perception (ESP). The reception of information by means other than our usual senses of hearing, sight, taste, touch, and smell.

Family therapy. A type of psychotherapy that involves the whole family, rather than just one member of it, since it is often the family system as a whole that can create stress and contribute to the development of psychological disorders.

Farsightedness. Occurs when an eye is flattened in shape, like a vertical egg; farsighted people see far objects well, but see near objects poorly.

Fear. Reaction to a specific danger in the environment.

Fetus. Human organism from the third month through to the time of birth.

Field experiment. An experiment performed in a natural setting rather than in the controlled setting of the laboratory.

Fight-or-flight response. Response of the sympathetic division of the autonomic nervous system, involves increased oxygen consumption, respiratory rate, heart rate, blood pressure, and muscle tension.

Figure. An object standing out against a background or against its surroundings.

Figure-ground reversal (or multistable perception). Occurs when figure and ground in a picture suddenly reverse; what was seen as figure is seen as background, and vice versa.

Fissure of Rolando (central fissure). One of three fissures of the cerebral cortex.

Fissure of Sylvius (lateral fissure). One of three fissures in the cerebral cortex.

Fixed-interval schedule. Reinforces the first response made after a certain time interval (after 5 minutes, or after 2 weeks). Produces a slow rate of responding immediately after a reinforcer is received, building up to a high rate of response as the end of the time interval is reached.

Fixed-ratio schedules. Reinforce the first response after a certain number of responses have been made. Produces a fast, steady rate of responding.

Fluid intelligence. General mental skills, such as the ability to make inferences, or deductive reasoning.

Foot-in-the-door approach. Persuasive technique that gets people to agree first to a small request, then later they are more willing to agree to a second request.

Forebrain. The part of the brain that develops from the top core of the embryo brain; contains the hypothalamus, thalamus, and the cerebrum.

Forensic psychology. Subfield of psychology concerned with behaviors that relate to our legal system—forensic psychologists work with judges and lawyers who are trying to improve the reliability of witnesses and jury decisions; also consulted on the mental competency of accused people.

Forgetting. An inability to remember or retrieve information from memory.

Formal operational stage. One of Piaget's stages of cognitive development; lasts from about 13 years of age through adulthood. Main theme is the ability to consider many possible solutions to a problem and the ability to systematically test those possibilities.

Fovea. Center area of the retina where vision is best; contains most of the cones on the retina.

Free association. Freud's method of having patients express every thought (no matter how unimportant or irrelevant) that came into their mind during the therapy session.

Free association test. Procedure in which a person looks at, or listens to, a target word, and then reports other words that come to mind.

Frequency. Number of wave crests that occur in a second; measured in cycles per second.

Frequency distribution. Tells how many scores fall into each of the intervals chosen to describe the data.

Frequency histogram. Way to show frequency distribution in graph form; intervals are placed along the horizontal axis; frequencies along the vertical axis.

Frequency of sound waves. Number of wave crests that occur in a second. Changes in pitch correspond to changes in frequency.

Frequency polygon. Way to show frequency distribution in graph form; line graph connecting a series of points representing the frequency of scores in each interval.

Frontal lobe. One of four lobes in the cerebral cortex; receives sensory impulses after they have been processed by other lobes and sends out commands to muscles to make voluntary movements.

Frostbite. A result of ice forming in the skin cells; these frozen cells die, and if the affected area is large enough, a finger, toe, or large patch of skin may literally die.

Frustration. Basically, the result of being blocked from getting what you want when you want it.

Frustration-aggression theory. Theory that aggression is always a consequence of frustration and frustration always leads to some form of aggression.

Fugue. Involves loss of memory and also physical flight, in which the person wanders away from his or her home for a matter of an hour or, in some cases, for years.

Functional fixedness. A kind of negative set that reduces our ability to learn new uses of something that has served a specific function in the past.

Functionalism. An approach to psychology that emphasizes the function of thought; led to important applications in education and the founding of educational psychology, a subfield of psychology.

Fundamental attribution error. Attributing an attitude based only on a person's behavior failing to give sufficient weight to the situation in which that behavior occurred.

Galvanic skin response (GSR). The resistance of the skin to electrical current.

Gametes. Sex cells; female gamete is an ovum, male gamete is a sperm. Each gamete has 23 chromosomes; ovum and sperm combine to form a zygote.

Gender identity disorder. A disorder that occurs in childhood, when a child rigidly adopts the role and outlook of the opposite sex.

General adaptation syndrome. Stress response noted by Hans Selye, occurs in three phases—alarm reaction, stage of resistance, and stage of exhaustion.

Generalization. See *response generalization; stimulus generalization.*

Generalized anxiety disorder. A disorder in which people experience overwhelming anxiety, but cannot identify its source.

Genes. The basic units of heredity. Located on the chromosomes.

Genetic engineering. The science of applied genetics.

Genetics. The study of how traits are inherited.

Genital stage. Begins at puberty with the start of sexual tension. Basic goals are to marry, raise a family, and become involved in a life's work.

Genotype. Unique set of genes that we inherit from our parents.

Gestalt psychology. German school of

psychology based on the premise that we experience wholes, or gestalts, rather than separate sensations.

Gestalt therapy. Developed by Fritz Perls, proposes that unconscious thoughts and emotions (background) may lead to behaviors (figure) that are inappropriate to the situation. Encourages people to take responsibility for their actions in the present, while understanding the emotions that are influencing them.

Glaucoma. Eye disease that causes pressure to build up inside the eye; most common cause of blindness.

Global therapies. Therapies that focus on the individual as a whole and aim to help the person gain insight into his or her problems and life.

Glove anesthesia. People with this symptom report losing all sensation in a hand, although they have normal sensation in the arm. This is physically impossible given the system of nerves in the hand and arm; glove anesthesia is a conversion disorder.

Glucoreceptors. Cells in the hypothalamus that monitor the glucose content of the blood. If the blood is low in glucose, the glucoreceptors send out signals that cause hunger and motivate us to eat.

Gonads. Reproductive organs that secrete sex hormones. Called ovaries in females, testes in males. Sex hormones control ovulation, pregnancy, and the menstrual cycle in females, and the production of sperm in males, as well as regulating secondary sex characteristics in both sexes.

Grammar. A set of rules for combining language symbols to form sentences.

Grasp reflex. Causes infants to close their fingers tightly around an object that touches the palm.

Ground. The background or surroundings against which an object stands out.

Group. Two or more persons who are interacting with one another in such a manner that each person influences and is influenced by each other person.

Group polarization effect. Groups tend to polarize people and move them to believe more strongly in the position that they first held.

Group therapy. Involves 1 (sometimes 2) therapists and from 6 to 12 clients; clients receive feedback from others in the group as well as from the therapist. Many different therapeutic techniques may be used in group therapy.

Groupthink. Occurs when group members become so concerned with reaching agreement of all members of the group that they fail to critically evaluate their ideas.

Growth hormone. Secreted by the pituitary gland, controls development of the skeleton; too little causes dwarfism, too much, giantism.

Hallucination. Involves having a sensory experience without the external stimuli that would have caused it. Hallucinations can involve vision, hearing, taste, touch, and smell, but the most common types involve people "hearing" voices that are not there.

Hallucinogens. Drugs such as LSD, STP, mescaline, and peyote, which cause people to see visions and illusions.

Hammer. One of three small bones in the middle ear, transmits sounds from the eardrum to the inner ear.

Heat exhaustion. A reaction to heat which involves fainting, nausea, vomiting, and headaches.

Heatstroke. A serious disorder that results when the body's sweating mechanism completely breaks down; it is accompanied by headache, staggering, coma, and possibly death.

Hedonic relevance. Refers to the degree to which an actor's behavior is rewarding or costly to the observer.

Helping behavior. Coming to the aid of another person.

Hertz. One cycle per second of a sound wave.

Hierarchy. An organization that arranges information into levels of categories and subordinate categories.

Hindbrain. The part of the brain that develops from the bottom core in the embryonic neural tube; contains the medulla, pons, and cerebellum.

Holophrastic speech. Use of single words to express phrases. For example, "out" might mean "I want to go out."

Homeostasis. The attempt by the body to maintain a constant internal state.

Homosexuality. The sexual desire for those of the same sex as oneself.

Hormones. Chemical messengers released by the glands into the bloodstream. Either directly change their target tissue or cause it to release other hormones that change tissues elsewhere in the body.

Humanistic psychology. Movement formed by Carl Rogers, Abraham Maslow, and Rollo May which rejects Freudian view of people; argues that people are basically good and worthy of respect; stresses the creative aspect of people in reaching their true potential.

Hypermesia. Increased recall that can result from hypnosis.

Hypnagogic images. Hallucinations that occur during the drowsy interval before sleep.

Hypnosis. A state of consciousness induced by the words and actions of a hypnotist, whose suggestions are readily accepted by the subject.

Hypnotic susceptibility tests. Tests that are used to predict the extent to which people are willing to yield to hypnotic suggestions.

Hypothalamus. Part of the forebrain; controls body temperature and the rate at which we burn fat and carbohydrates, among other functions.

Hypothermia. Occurs when the internal body temperature drops below a normal level; heart rate and blood pressure increase dramatically and death due to heart attack can result if temperature does not increase.

Hypothesis. An idea that is tested experimentally; an assumption that is based on theory.

Id. According to Freud, part of the personality made up of instinctual drives that serve as the basic motivation for all our behavior.

Identification. Process of acquiring personality and social behaviors by taking on characteristics of others.

Identity crisis. Term used by Erikson to describe what occurs during adolescence; refers to the search at this age for an identity, which involves trying out and testing different roles.

Illusions. Perceptual distortions.

Imitation. Acquisition of knowledge and behavior by watching other people act and then doing the same thing ourselves.

Impotence. A sexual disorder in which males are unable to have an erection or maintain one long enough for ejaculation.

Imprinting. Attachment formed by duckling for almost any moving object that it first sees (usually, of course, its mother); imprinting occurs during a *critical period* of the first 14 hours to 2 days of life.

Indefensible spaces. Areas in an apartment complex that are not open to observation, such as enclosed stairways and alleys; such areas invite intruders and breed crime.

Independent variable. The variable that is manipulated in an experiment.

Individual psychology. Adler's approach to personality development, based on his belief that each person is unique and adjusts differently to social influences.

Industrial psychology. Subfield of psychology concerned with selecting, training, and managing employees.

Infantile autism. Infants who from a very early age are withdrawn, do not react to others, and become attached to inanimate objects rather than to people.

Inferential statistics. Used to test hypotheses made by psychologists.

Informational pressure. A type of influence a group has, based on the group's value as a source of information.

Insanity. A legal term, not a psychological one. Based on the McNaghten rule, which says that a person must be able to determine right from wrong at the time of the crime before he or she can be judged responsible and therefore guilty. Someone who has been judged incapable of determining right from wrong will be found not guilty by reason of insanity.

Insight. The discovery of relationships that lead to the solution of a problem. Insight learning is the sudden and irreversible learning of a solution to a problem.

Instincts. Innate or inborn predispositions to act in specific ways.

Insufficient reward. The aspect of dissonance theory that suggests that the smaller the external reward we receive for completing a task, the more we will value that task.

Intelligence. The capacity to learn.

Intelligence quotient (IQ). Mental age divided by chronological age and multiplied by 100.

Interaction distance. Amount of space between people in various situations; differs with the relationship between people and the kind of interaction they're engaged in.

Interference theory. The theory that we forget information because other information gets in the way. See also *proactive inhibition; retroactive inhibition.*

Internalization. The process of bringing behavior under the control of inner, personal standards that make people obey rules even if there are no external restraints.

Interview. Assessment technique that involves direct questioning of a person. Unstructured interview consists of planned questions to start, but interviewer is free to develop the conversation as he or she wishes. Structured interview consists of a set of specific questions asked according to a set plan.

Iris. Flat, doughnut-shaped network of muscles behind the aqueous humor of the eye.

Just-barely-sufficient threat. The aspect of dissonance theory that suggests that we will derogate attractive objects or activities that we choose to forgo without strong external constraints.

Key-word method. Mnemonic system of using imagery to learn foreign vocabulary; consists of forming an image that will act as a link between the key word and the other word we want to remember.

Kinesis. The study of body language, or communication through body movement.

Kinetic depth. Detection of depth through movement.

Laboratory experiment. An experiment performed in a controlled environment created for the experiment.

Latency stage. Lasts from sixth year to puberty. Children lose interest in sex-related activities and focus energy on schoolwork and hobbies, among other things.

Latent content of dreams. A hidden content determined by unconscious impulses. Freud says the latent content of dreams often involves an unacceptable desire that would create pain or anxiety if it were expressed directly, so it is disguised in a dream.

Latent learning. Refers to learning that does not show itself immediately in performance.

Law of brightness constancy. States that we see an object's brightness as constant when the amount of light striking it changes.

Law of effect. The law that animals tend to repeat behaviors that are followed by "good effects," and they tend to stop behaviors that are not followed by desirable results.

Law of nearness or proximity. One of the Gestalt laws of organization; states that we group elements that are close together.

Law of shape constance. States that we see an object's shape as constant when the object's slant changes, or when we view it from a different angle.

Law of similarity. One of the Gestalt laws of organization; states that we group elements that are similar, or look alike.

Law of size constancy. States that we see an object's size as constant even if the object's distance from us changes.

Leader. The person in a group who has the most amount of influence.

Learned helplessness. A response to prolonged stress; the feeling that one's actions do not affect one's environment or what happens to one. Can lead to apathy and depression.

Learning. The process by which experience or practice results in a relatively permanent change in what one is capable of doing.

Learning set. Occurs when one's previous experience makes one ready to solve a particular type of problem.

Lens. Part of the eye that is located directly behind the pupil; helps the cornea focus light onto the back of the eye.

Lesbians. Female homosexuals.

Libido. Energy force that propels people to satisfy the drive for survival (includes eating, drinking, and sexual activity).

Life-span developmental approach. Concerned with the description and explanation of changes in behavior within an individual and differences between individuals from conception to death.

Light adaptation. Upward adjustment in sensitivity to light; occurs in the cones when one suddenly goes from a dark room into bright sunlight, for example.

Limbic system. Functional subdivision of the nervous system; controls emotions, memories, and goal-directed behavior.

Linear perspective. Monocular cue to depth; artists use it to create the impression of depth in their paintings. See Figure 3-20 for an example.

Locus of control. According to Rotter, people learn general expectancies about whether the source of control of what happens to them is outside them or inside them. Internals believe they control their own fate; externals believe luck and chance control their fate.

Longitudinal fissure. One of three fissures in the cerebral cortex; separates the two cerebral hemispheres.

Longitudinal research. Research in which the same person or group of people is tested over a period of time. An example would be studying the same group of people from their birth until they were in their twenties. Compare with *cross-sectional research,* in which a number of people of different ages are tested at one time.

Long-term memory. Holds information that is transferred from short-term memory; it can last a lifetime.

Loudness. Measurement of sound based on the amplitude of sound waves.

Mania. A disorder in which people feel full of energy, but find it difficult to stay with any one project for long, are easily distracted, have an increased sex drive, and need less sleep than usual. See also *bipolar disorder.*

Manifest content of dreams. The portion of the dream that the person remembers. Contrast with latent content, which is the hidden element determined by impulses of which the person is unaware.

Mantra. A secret word, sound, or phrase used in Transcendental Meditation.

Masochism. Becoming sexually aroused by having pain inflicted on oneself.

Masturbation. The self-manipulation of one's genitals.

Maturation. The unfolding of genetically determined abilities.

Mean. Often called the average; is determined by adding all the scores in a sample and dividing by the total number of scores in the sample.

Measure of central tendency. Score value that represents the mathematical center of a group of scores.

Median. The score that divides a distribution in half—there are as many scores ranked above it as below it.

Meditation. A state of consciousness similar to hypnosis, except that the hypnotist's authority is transferred to the meditators themselves.

Medulla. Lowest part of the hindbrain; slender tube housing nerve centers that control breathing, heartbeat, and posture.

Membrane potential. An electric tension that exists in a neuron between the cell's inside and outside environment. Also called *polarization.*

Memory. A system that allows people to retain information over time.

Memory span. The number of items that we can read through one time and then recall in sequence with no mistakes.

Memory trace. The change that occurs as a result of memorizing.

Menarche. The beginning of menstruation, which marks the onset of puberty for girls.

Menopause. The cessation of menstruation, marking the end of a woman's ability to bear children; accompanied by physical and hormonal changes.

Mental age. Average performance of children at a specific chronological age.

Mental sets. A readiness to view a problem in a particular way—a readiness to see certain relationships.

Metabolic rate. Rate at which food is transformed by the body into energy.

Midbrain. The part of the brain that develops from the middle core of the embryo brain; contains the reticular formation.

Minnesota Multiphasic Personality Inventory (MMPI). One of the most popular personality questionnaires, used by clinicians. Designed to identify specific psychological disorders. Consists of 550 statements to which people can respond true, false, or cannot say. Aimed at identifying 10 different disorders.

Mnemonics. Systems created to aid memory; examples are the key-word method and verbal mediation.

Mode. Often called the most typical scores, it is the score that occurs most often in a sample.

Modeling. Used as a therapeutic technique to teach new behaviors or strengthen existing ones. Also used to reduce a number of phobias, by showing the model interacting with the feared object.

Monism. The theory that the mind and brain are one organic whole. See also *dualism.*

Monocular cues. Cues to depth perception that operate even when only one eye is used.

Moral anxiety. Anxiety that occurs because people fear they will do something contrary to their moral code.

Moro reflex (also called the **startle reflex**). Causes a motor reaction of infant's arms, legs, and trunk in response to a sudden loud noise or loss of support.

Motivation. Why an organism acts in a certain way at a certain time.

Motive. A condition that energizes and directs the behavior of an organism.

Motor cortex. Part of the cerebral cortex; located in front of the central fissure. Controls motor responses of the body.

Motor system. Functional subdivision of the nervous system; includes basal ganglia, cerebellum, and the motor cortex. Controls voluntary muscle movements.

Multiple personalities. A disorder in which one person assumes two or more personalities. Each personality has its complete set of memories, and one is often "unaware" of the existence of the other.

Multistable perceptions (also called **figure-ground reversal**). Occurs when a picture shows alternating appearances; what was seen as figure becomes the background, and vice versa.

Mutation. Abnormal chromosome structure, responsible for such diseases as Down's syndrome.

Myelinization. Development of myelin sheaths during infancy, childhood, and adolescence.

Myelin sheath. A fatty covering of some axons, which allows neural impulses to be conducted faster.

Mysticism. The view that alternate state experiences are a response to an external reality that exists beyond the visible and understandable universe.

Narcotics. Drugs that in small doses reduce pain, cause drowsiness, and give a feeling of happiness and well-being. Examples are morphine, heroine, and opium.

Naturalistic observation. Research method that involves studying people's reactions to naturally occurring events in natural settings.

Near point of accommodation. Nearest point at which print can be read distinctly.

Nearsightedness. Occurs when an eye is elongated like a horizontal egg; nearsighted people see near objects well, but see far objects poorly.

Negative reinforcement. Occurs when a stimulus is taken away or stopped.

Negative set. A mental set that reduces the chance of learning a new relationship.

Neurons. Cells in the nervous system that receive and send impulses.

Neurosis. A broad pattern of psychological disorders characterized by anxiety, fear, and self-defeating behaviors.

Neurotic anxiety. Anxiety resulting from unconscious conflict within an individual.

Neurotic behaviors. Attempts to cope with anxiety.

Noise. A psychological concept; unwanted sound, sound that is unpleasant, bothersome, or actually physiologically harmful.

Nonverbal communication. Communication through facial expression, gesture, body movement, etc.

Normal curve. Symmetrical, bell-shaped curve that occurs when a normal distribution is plotted as a frequency polygon.

Normal distribution. Represents the assumption that most measurements taken will be close to average, some will be a small distance from average, and few will be very far from average. People's height, weight, IQs show this distribution.

Normative social pressure. A type of group pressure based on the desire to belong to the group.

Norms. Rules that govern specific behavior and apply to all members of the group.

Obedience. The following of direct and explicit orders of a person in a position of authority.

Obesity. In humans, being more than 15 percent over the "ideal" weight, given the person's height and overall body build.

Observational learning. Learning by watching other people and observing the consequences of their actions. This type of learning occurs without external reinforcement or without even performing the behavior.

Obsession. Recurring, irrational thought that cannot be controlled or banished from one's mind. See also *compulsion,* which involves behavior rather than thought.

Obsessive-compulsive disorders. Disorders that occur when the person feels an overwhelming need to think a certain thought (obsession) or perform a certain behavior (compulsion).

Occipital lobe. One of four lobes in the cerebral cortex; receives visual impulses from the eyes.

Oedipus complex. According to Freud, boy desires sexual relationship with mother, but is afraid his father will found out and castrate him as punishment. In order to get rid of these fears, boy identifies with and tries to be like his father. Identification with father helps form the superego because boy internalizes the father's values.

Olfactory cells. Odor-sensitive cells contained in the passageway between the nose and the throat.

Operant conditioning. A type of learning that occurs when desired responses are rewarded or reinforced and undesired responses are ignored or punished.

Ophthalmoscope. Uses mirrors or prisms to direct light through the pupil so that eye doctors can examine the eye's internal structures.

Optic nerve. A bundle of nerve fibers that carry neural signals to the brain.

Oral stage. Infant is born with general desire for physical pleasure, which is focused in the mouth region; these impulses are satisfied by eating, sucking, and biting. This is a stage of total dependency on the parents.

Oscilloscope. Device for converting sound waves to visible waves.

Osmometric thirst. Thirst motivated by osmoreceptors in the hypothalamus that detect the depletion of intracellular water levels.

Osmoreceptors. Cells in the hypothalamus that are sensitive to intracellular water levels; they send "thirst" signals to other areas of the brain when they detect that water is being depleted from the cells.

Osmosis. The process whereby substances pass in and out of cells.

Otoliths. Organs that signal head orientation with respect to gravity.

Oval window. A membrane stretched over the opening of the inner ear.

Ovaries. Female reproductive glands, which secrete estrogen into the bloodstream.

Ovulation. In women, the time when the egg is available to be fertilized, and secretion of estrogen is at its highest; occurs once a month.

Ovum. A mature female sex cell which after fertilization develops into an offspring. The first two week period of development after fertilization is called the period of the ovum.

Pancreas. A large gland located behind the stomach; as part of the endocrine system, it controls the level of sugar in the blood by secreting insulin and glucagon.

Papillae. Small elevations on the tongue; contain our taste sensors, called taste buds.

Paradoxical cold. Occurs when a warm object stimulates a cold spot on the skin—cold is felt.

Paradoxical warmth. Occurs when a cold object stimulates a warm spot on the skin—warmth is felt.

Paranoid. People suffering from delusions of persecution are called paranoid; they believe that people are "out to get" them and interpret others' actions as plots against them.

Parapsychologists. Those who study ESP and PK.

Parasympathetic division. Part of the autonomic nervous system; functional subdivision of the nervous system; controls the relaxation responses.

Parathyroid glands. Four pea-shaped glands next to the thyroid in the throat; part of the endocrine system. Produce a hormone that causes lethargy when its level is too high, and muscle spasms when its level is too low.

Parietal lobe. One of four lobes in the cerebral cortex; responds to touch, pain, and temperature.

Partial reinforcement schedule. Subject is reinforced every few responses or every once in awhile, but not for every response.

Peak experiences. Fleeting moments in people's lives where they feel truly spontaneous and unconcerned with time or other physical constraints. A feeling of being totally absorbed in the situation, in the moment, without cares from the past or concern for the future.

Peripheral nervous system. All nerve tissue that is not in the brain and spinal cord.

Peripheral vision. Using the sides of one's eyes (and thus depending on the rods rather than the cones) to see something—usually occurs at night or in dim light.

Personality. The unique set of behaviors (including thoughts and emotions) and enduring qualities that influence the way a person adjusts to the environment.

Personality assessment. The description and measurement of individual characteristics.

Personality disorders. Rigid and maladaptive ways of dealing with the environment, characterized by a general approach to dealing with events rather than by any one specific behavior. The example discussed in the text is the *antisocial personality disorder*, which is the type of personality disorder most often found in Western society.

Personality psychology. Subfield of psychology that focuses on individual differences and on explaining and predicting the unique ways that people respond to their environment.

Personal space. An area directly surrounding one's body that is regarded as one's personal territory.

Person-centered therapy. Created by Carl Rogers, aimed at providing the proper setting for the self-growth of the person. Since the person (rather than the therapist) determines what will be discussed during therapy, it is referred to as person-centered therapy.

Phallic stage. According to psychoanalytic theory begins at the age of four; focus of pleasure is the genital organs. Trauma at this stage is called Oedipus complex for boys, Electra complex for girls.

Phenotype. The way one's genotype (genetic inheritance) is expressed in observable characteristics.

Phobia. A phobia is an irrational fear of an object or event. The fear is attached to a specific, identifiable object; phobics can control their anxiety by avoiding that object or situation.

Phosphenes. Visual sensations arising from spontaneous discharges of light-sensitive neurons in the eyes.

Phrenology. The determination of an individual's personality type by the examination of the bumps and contours on his or her head.

Physiological psychology. Subfield of psychology that examines the areas of learning, memory, perception, motivation, and emotion by studying the neurobiological events that underlie them.

Pinna. The outer flap of the ear.

Pitch. Difference between low and high notes. Changes in pitch correspond to changes in frequency of sound waves.

Pituitary gland. Small gland that lies in a recess at the base of the brain and is connected to the hypothalamus, which controls it. Part of the endocrine system, it is often called the master gland because it has such wide-ranging effects. Secretes many different types of hormones, which control growth and sexual reproduction, among other things.

Placebo. In drug studies, a drug substitute made from inactive materials that is given to the control group in drug research.

Placebo effect. A situation in which a treatment that has no curative value of its own has a healing effect because of the patient's belief in its effectiveness.

Placenta. A special filter used to exchange food and wastes between an embryo and his or her mother.

Pleasure principle. This is what guides the id, the immediate satisfaction of drives without regard to reality, logic, or manners.

Polarization. An electric tension that exists in a neuron between the cell's inside and outside environment. Also called *membrane potential*.

Polygenic traits. Traits that are determined by the action of more than one gene pair. Most human traits are polygenic.

Polygraph. Also called a lie detector. Records changes in heart rate, blood pressure, respiration, and galvanic skin response. Lies are identified when there is a change from baseline responses to neutral questions to a heightened response to questions about critical events.

Pons. Part of the hindbrain; a tube formed by a massive cable of nerve fibers. Connects the medulla to the midbrain.

Positive reinforcement. Occurs when a

positive stimulus is added to the environment.

Posthypnotic amnesia. The inability of a hypnotized subject to recall certain experiences until an appropriate cue is given.

Posthypnotic suggestions. Suggestions made to a subject while hypnotized, which are to be carried out after hypnosis has ended.

Precognition. Perception of future thoughts, events, or actions.

Preconscious element of personality. According to Freud, the preconscious is essentially one's memory, including thoughts that people may not be aware of but that they can retrieve from memory.

Prefrontal lobotomy. Surgical technique for treating extreme psychological disorders. Involves cutting connections between the thalamus and the frontal lobes. Seldom used today, only when all other methods have failed.

Prejudice. An unjustified negative attitude toward an individual based solely on that person's membership in a group.

Premature ejaculation. Ejaculation which occurs too quickly, according to the definition of the male and the couple.

Preoperational stage. One of Piaget's stages of cognitive development; lasts from 2 years to 7 years of age. Main theme is discovering mental operations, which are plans, strategies, and rules for solving problems and for classifying.

Preparedness. The idea that animals are more prepared to make certain responses than others, and may find other responses more difficult to make.

Primacy effect. In impression formation, the fact that people tend to base their impressions on what they hear first.

Primary motives. Motives such as hunger, thirst, and the need for air and rest. These motives are usually unlearned, common to all animals, and vital for the survival of the organism or the species.

Primary reinforcer. Events or objects that are reinforcing in and of themselves (such as food).

Primary sexual characteristics. Traits directly concerned with sexual reproduction; the production of live ovum by girls and live sperm by boys.

Primary territories. Owned and controlled by people; these territories are central to their lives.

Proactive inhibition. Interference of previous learning with memory for new learning.

Problem drinkers. People who often drink too much and whose drinking has undesirable effects on their lives or on others. See also *alcoholics*.

Projection. Defense mechanism that involves seeing our own shortcomings or undesirable traits in other people rather than in ourselves.

Projective tests. Based on Freud's theory that people will project unconscious desires onto ambiguous and nonthreatening stimuli. The stimuli can be an incomplete sentence or a picture. People's responses are analyzed to see what they tell about them.

Proprioception. The sense of where our body parts are; determined by sense organs in joints, muscles, and tendons, which connect muscles with bones.

Proxemics. Study of personal space.

Proximity. Physical closeness.

Psychiatric nurse. A registered nurse who has received special training in dealing with psychological disorders.

Psychiatric social worker. Someone who has an M.A. in social work and has served an internship.

Psychiatrist. A medical doctor who has received an M.D. degree and has taken part in a residency program in emotional disorders; the only type of therapist who can prescribe drugs or conduct psychosurgery.

Psychoactive drugs. Drugs that produce subjective effects: depressants, stimulants, and hallucinogens.

Psychoanalysis. Freud's technique of treating anxiety disorders by helping people recognize and deal with their repressed feelings.

Psychoanalyst. A psychiatrist who has had a great deal of training in psychoanalytic techniques, and has often undergone psychoanalysis him- or herself.

Psychokinesis (PK). Direct mental influence over physical objects or processes.

Psychological test. A test designed to identify individual differences among people; tests have been developed to measure attitudes, abilities, achievement, and personality traits.

Psychology. The scientific study of behavior and the applications gained from that knowledge.

Psychology of minorities. Subfield of psychology that examines behavior of people in minority groups, including women who are minorities in some contexts.

Psychopharmacology. The study of drugs to treat psychological disorders.

Psychophysical function. The relationship between physical energies and psychological experiences over a wide range of physical magnitudes.

Psychophysics. Studies the relationship between physical energies and psychological experiences.

Psychophysiological disorder. Often referred to as psychosomatic illness; an actual physical illness in which stress is a contributing factor. An example is a peptic ulcer.

Psychosis. A disturbance caused by unresolved conflicts that is so great that the person can no longer deal with reality.

Psychosurgery. Various techniques of biotherapy involving surgery to the brain. The best known is the *prefrontal lobotomy*, in which connections are cut between the thalamus and the frontal lobes. Seldom used today, only when all other methods have failed.

Psychotherapy. The use of psychological techniques by a professionally trained person to help a client change unwanted behavior and adjust to his or her environment. In short, the use of language to make positive changes in the life of another.

Puberty. The time in adolescence when sexual reproduction becomes possible.

Public territories. Territories that do not involve feelings of ownership, but people feel that they control them while they are occupying them; an example is a table at a restaurant.

Punishment. A stimulus that decreases the likelihood of a response when it is added to an environment. Compare with *reinforcement*.

Pupil. An opening in the iris of the eye; looks like a black spot in the center of the iris.

Pure tones. Sounds containing a single frequency.

Pyramidal cells. Giant cells of the motor cortex, which send a long axon through the brain down to neurons, in the spinal cord. Control precise movements such as those of hand movements and speech.

Questionnaire. A standard set of questions used to assess behavior that can be given to many people at one time and usually can be scored quickly.

Randomization. Procedure used in an experiment by which subjects are randomly assigned to either the control group or the experimental group(s). It ensures that each person has an equal chance of being assigned to each group, thus making it highly probable that subject differences will be equally distributed between groups.

Range. A measure of variation, the difference between the largest and smallest number in the distribution.

Rational Emotive Therapy (RET). Type of therapy developed by Albert Ellis; focuses on the present and on the client's irrational beliefs. Therapist plays a much more directive and even challenging role than in most other therapies.

Rationalization. A defense mechanism

that involves justifying one's behavior by finding logical or desirable reasons for it.

Reactance. A psychological state that motivates us to regain our freedom by resisting group pressure.

Reaction formation. Defense mechanism that conceals unacceptable impulses by expressing instead the opposite impulse.

Reality anxiety. Response to a specific danger in the environment.

Reality principle. This is what guides the ego; it tries to satisfy the desires of the id by taking into account the possibilities of reward and punishment that exist in the situation.

Recall tests. Measure a person's ability to reproduce material. *Cued recall* is when part of the material is provided as a cue for the rest; *free recall* is when no cues are provided and any order of recall is allowed.

Receptor sites. The areas on the dendrite that receive the chemical transmitter.

Recognition tests. Measure a person's ability to pick the correct answer when several answers are given; often occur in the form of multiple-choice questions on tests.

Reconstruction. The organization and recoding (often done unconsciously) of memory over time; may lead to distortions of memory.

Reflex. Automatic action that requires no conscious effort.

Rehearsal. Process of repeating information in order to retain it in short-term memory or transfer it to long-term memory.

Reinforcement. An event whose occurrence just after a reponse increases the likelihood that the response will be repeated. See *positive, negative reinforcement;* compare with *punishment.*

Relative refractory period. Period during which a cell will only fire in response to an extra-strong impulse; lasts for a few milliseconds.

Relaxation response. Phrase used by Benson to refer to the physiological patterns observed during meditation; a decrease in oxygen consumption; respiratory rate, heart rate, blood pressure, and muscle tension.

Reliability of a test. Means that you get the same results on the test every time you administer it.

REM rebound. Sharp increase of REM sleep after going through a period of sleep deprivation.

REM sleep. Stage of sleep marked by rapid eye movements (REMs) and dreams.

Repression. A defense mechanism that involves blocking or keeping unpleasant thoughts or memories from conscious awareness. Differs from suppression in that it is an unconscious

process, suppression is a conscious process.

Response generalization. Means giving different, but similar, responses to the same stimulus.

Resting state. Occurs whenever a neuron is not sending or receiving neural impulses.

Retention. Process of holding information in memory.

Reticular activating system (RAS). Functional subdivision of the nervous system; activates all regions of the brain for incoming sensory impulses, plays an important part in alertness and selective attention.

Retina. Tissue covering most of the eye's interior wall; contains rods and cones.

Retrieval. Process of getting information out of memory.

Retrieval cues. Aids to retrieval that are often encoded with the information to be remembered; an example would be category names.

Retroactive inhibition. Interference of new learning with memory for previous learning.

Retrograde amnesia. Loss of memory for events that occurred before an injury.

Ribonucleic acid (RNA). Messenger molecules sent out by DNA to control how specific kinds of protein chains are made.

Rods. Light receptors located on the periphery or sides of the retina; they are best for seeing in dim light.

Roles. Group rules that apply only to people in certain positions; roles define the obligations and expectations of that specific position.

Rooting reflex. Causes infants to turn their head toward anything that touches their cheek.

Rorschach inkblot test. A projective test that measures personality by having subjects describe what they see in ten different inkblots.

Saccades. Eye movements from one fixation point to the next as we read.

Sadism. Deriving sexual pleasure from inflicting pain on others.

Savings. The difference between one's original learning time and the relearning time; measured by a savings test.

Savings tests. Measure people's ability to take advantage of what they have learned before in order to relearn material faster.

Scapegoating. Singling out a person or a minority group as the target (scapegoat) for aggression and hostility, when the real target is too powerful to be attacked.

Schema (plural, **schemata**). Term used by Piaget to refer to a mental structure that organizes responses to experiences.

Schizophrenia. A group of disorders

characterized by disorganization in thoughts, perceptions, communication, emotions, and motor activity.

Sclera. The white opaque outer wall of the eye.

Secondary reinforcers. Events or objects that are reinforcing only after they have been paired with other, primary reinforcers. Money is a good example of a secondary reinforcer.

Secondary sexual characteristics. Traits typical of a sex, but not directly concerned with reproduction; for girls, the development of breasts and pubic hair; for boys, growth of the scrotum, pubic hair, and a beard.

Secondary territories. Not "owned by people," and not as central to their lives; examples are the neighborhood street, the social or country club, or even a regular seat in a classroom.

Self-actualization. Process by which a person strives to learn, create, and work to the best of his or her ability.

Self-concept. Consists of our judgments and attitudes about our behavior, abilities, and even our appearance; it is our answer to the question, "Who am I?"

Self-fulfilling prophecy. An expectation that leads one to behave in ways that will cause that expectation to come about.

Self-hypnosis. A procedure in which people learn to hypnotize themselves so that they can more readily follow their own suggestions.

Semantic memory. A person's general background knowledge about words, symbols, concepts, and rules.

Semicircular canals. Three arching structures in the inner ear that detect changes in head position.

Sensation-seeking motive. A motive for arousal.

Sensorimotor stage. One of Piaget's stages of cognitive development, extends from birth to about 2 years of age. Main theme is discovering relationships between sensations and motor behavior.

Sensory deprivation. The absence of almost all sensory stimulation.

Sensory memory. Holds sensations briefly so that they can be identified; lasts from 1 to 2 seconds.

Set-point theory. The theory that the number of fat cells in the body is established during early childhood and does not change later in the life span.

Sex-linked traits. Occur when the gene for a trait is located on the chromosome that determines one's sex (in humans, on the X chromosome in pair 23). Examples are color blindness and hemophilia.

Sex roles. Society's approved ways for men and women to behave.

Shaping. A procedure used in operant conditioning in which each part of a behavior is reinforced that eventually leads to the whole behavior that is desired.

Short-term memory. Holds information that has been transferred out of sensory memory; lasts about 30 seconds unless information is repeated or rehearsed.

Signal detection theory. A theory that attempts to explain people's perceptual judgments by analyzing their sensitivity to sensory stimuli in addition to the criteria they use to make decisions.

Single-gene traits. Some genes determine specific traits all on their own, rather than in combination with other genes. An example is eye color.

Sleep. A period of rest for the body and mind, during which bodily functions are partially suspended and sensitivity to external stimuli is diminished, but readily or easily regained.

Sleeper effect. The fact that over time, the credibility of a communicator makes no difference in people's attitudes; seems to occur because people tend to separate the source from the message as time passes.

Sleep spindles. Medium-voltage, medium-frequency brain waves characteristic of stage-2 sleep.

Social cognition model. Belief that people have schemata, or preconceived notions about how their social world works; these schemata influence the way people interpret events and even the information they remember; once formed, information is processed in a way that tends to support the schema.

Social comparison. Using social reality to evaluate oneself—comparing oneself against the beliefs, attitudes, and behaviors of other people.

Social facilitation. Occurs because the presence of other people tends to arouse people; this arousal creates an additional pool of energy that aids the performance of well-learned behaviors.

Social learning theory. Learning by imitation.

Social loafing. Peoples' motivation to work decreases when they are in groups where their individual performance cannot be observed; the larger the group, the easier to reduce effort without being detected.

Social motives. Motives that come from learning and social interaction rather than based on biological needs (see *primary motives*). These motives include affiliation, aggression, and achievement.

Social psychology. The scientific study of the way in which people are affected by social situations and social relationships; the scientific study of the way most people act most of the time.

Social reality. Beliefs, attitudes, and behaviors of other people.

Social skill training. Aimed at teaching people to exercise control over their social environment and thus avoid a state of learned helplessness.

Somatization disorder. One of the somatoform disorders. Characterized by vague but dramatic complaints such as headaches, nausea, vomiting, stomach pains, and tiredness. There is no organic basis for these problems, although people suffering from this disorder actually do feel sick—they are not pretending.

Somatoform disorders. Group of disorders in which people feel ill or show other symptoms such as blindness or paralysis, but there is no organic damage.

Somatosensory cortex. Part of the cerebral cortex; located behind the central fissure. Controls sensory responses of the body.

Somatotype. A person's body build. Sheldon characterized people as either endomorphic (soft, round, fat), mesomorphic (muscular, hard, rectangular), or ectomorphic (tall, thin, fragile).

Sound. A physical property caused by changes in air pressure; measured in decibels (db.). Contrast with *noise,* which is a psychological concept.

Sound spectrograms. Visible representation of speech.

Specific therapy. Therapy aimed at changing a specific behavior or thought pattern.

Spinal cord. A cable of long nerve fibers running from the brainstem down through the backbone to the lower back, through which ascending nerves carry sensory information up to the brain and descending nerves carry commands down from the brain to move muscles.

Spontaneous recovery. Occurs when a response reappears without any retraining, after having been extinguished.

Standard deviation. Measure of variation, the square root of the *variance;* often used to express how far any given score is from the mean of a set of scores.

Standard error of the difference between two means. Computed by finding the square root of the sum of the standard errors of the means.

Standard error of the mean. Shows the variation of a sample mean and tells how likely it is that the sample mean represents the population mean.

Standardized achievement tests. Tests that have been given to many people so that one person's score can be evaluated with respect to a large population.

Standard score. A single number that expresses where a score lies relative to a population. Expresses the value of a score relative to the mean and the standard deviation of its distribution.

Statistical significance. Means that a difference in scores is a true difference, not a result of sampling error.

Statistics. A branch of mathematics used by psychologists to describe data and to draw conclusions based on data.

Stereotypes. Oversimplified generalizations about the characteristics of a group.

Stimulants. Drugs that excite body functions; examples are caffeine, amphetamines, and cocaine.

Stimulus discrimination. Making different responses to different stimuli.

Stimulus generalization. Occurs when responses are made to stimuli that are similar to, but not the same as, the original conditioned stimulus (CS).

Stimulus-seeking motive. Motive to explore and manipulate new objects, to increase stimulation and arousal.

Stirrup. One of three small bones in the middle ear; transmits sounds from the eardrum to the inner ear.

Stress. General response of the body to any demand made on it.

Stressor. The event that gives rise to stress.

Structuralism. An approach to psychology based on identifying the elements of human experience and finding out how those elements are combined into thoughts and feelings.

Sublimation. Defense mechanism that involves rechanneling the energy associated with one emotion or event into a seemingly unrelated activity.

Substance abuse. The disorder that results from a pathological use of a drug; a reduction in social or occupational functioning because of the drug; and a duration of disturbance of at least one month.

Substance dependence. Addiction including the presence of tolerance or withdrawal.

Substance use disorders. Disorders including the categories of substance abuse and substance dependence.

Sucking reflex. Causing sucking in infants when anything touches the lips.

Superego. According to Freud, the superego represents our conscience, including the moral values of right and wrong instilled in us by our parents.

Suppression. A defense mechanism that involves consciously blocking or avoiding unpleasant thoughts. Differs from repression in that it is a conscious process, repression is unconscious.

Survey. Method used in psychology; uses questionnaires that are given to large samples of people.

Sympathetic division. Part of the autonomic nervous system; functional subdivision of the nervous system; controls the fight-or-flight responses.

Synapse. A junction between two neurons.

Synaptic space. A very small gap between the axon terminal of one cell and the dendrite of the next cell.

Synaptic transmission. Occurs as a neural impulse; moves from one neuron to another.

Synaptic vesicles. Tiny oval sacs on the axon terminal filled with a chemical transmitter substance.

Systematic desensitization. Type of behavior therapy that is based on the assumption that it is impossible to be relaxed and anxious at the same time. Clients are taught deep muscle relaxation; they then pair this with feared or stressful events or objects, with the idea that the relaxation response will overcome the fear reaction. It is often used to treat phobias.

Taste buds. Taste sensors contained in papillae on the tongue.

Telepathy. The perception of another's mental state or emotion by means of ESP.

Temporal lobe. One of four lobes in the cerebral cortex; receives sound and smell impulses and has centers that control speech.

Territoriality. The claiming of control or ownership of areas or objects.

Testes. Male reproductive gland, which secretes androgens into the bloodstream.

Test statistic. Ratio of the difference between the means to the standard error of the difference between the means.

Texture gradient. Monocular cue to depth. As we look at something with texture, the nearer elements are spaced farther apart than the more distant elements. Some examples are shown in Figure 3–20.

T-groups. A type of group therapy that focuses on how people function in groups rather than on emotional disorders. Widely used in industrial and educational settings to aid group performance.

Thalamus. Two egg-shaped structures that are part of the forebrain. Often called a relay station because sensory pathways from all over the body pass through it.

Thematic Apperception Test (TAT). A projective test that measures personality by showing the subject an ambiguous scene and asking him or her to tell a story about it.

Theory. Explanation about why behavior occurs; theories generate hypotheses that can be tested experimentally.

Theta waves. Low-voltage, low-frequency brain waves characteristic of stage-1 sleep.

Thyroid glands. Large, butterfly-shaped gland in the front and sides of the throat; part of the endocrine system. Produces thyroxin, a hormone that determines the rate at which food is transformed in the body into energy.

Thyroxin. Hormone produced by the thyroid glands; determines the rate at which food is transformed in the body into energy.

Tip-of-the-tongue (TOT) phenomenon. A state of being on the verge of recalling something; often subjects say that the word or whatever they are trying to record is "on the tip of the tongue."

Token economy. Operant conditioning technique in which subjects are given tokens for good performance or behavior which they can exchange for treats or other primary reinforcers.

Tolerance. The need to increase the amount of the drug to achieve the same effects.

Tonic neck reflex. Causes infants who are on their back to move their arms and legs into a "fencing" position when the head is turned to one side.

Trace-decay theory. The theory that memory traces fade away in time if their strength is not maintained through use.

Traits. Fairly permanent qualities that people possess to a greater or lesser degree.

Tranquilizers. Depressant drugs that slow the body functions, reduce anxiety, and have a relaxing effect.

Transcendental Meditation (TM). A simplified Yoga technique that allows people to meditate after a short training course.

Transference. Part of Freud's technique of psychoanalysis; occurs when clients transfer to the therapist feelings that were originally aimed at their parents. In this way they are able to work them through on a rational, conscious level.

Transpersonal psychology. Tries to increase people's self-awareness through a mixture of psychological theory, religion, and modern philosophy. Its aim is to increase personal growth in many different ways and on different levels.

Transsexual. A person who has undergone a sex-change operation that changes the anatomical features to be like those of the opposite sex.

Two-point threshold. The least distance between two stimuli that can be perceived as separate on the skin.

Type A behavior. Coronary-prone behavior pattern; a response to stress that involves becoming more active, more competitive, more "driven."

Unconditional positive regard. Part of client-centered therapy, in which the therapist tries to create a condition of unconditional positive regard by accepting and caring for clients no matter what feelings or behaviors are revealed in the session.

Unconditioned response (UR). An automatic or reflexive reaction to a stimulus.

Unconditioned stimulus (US). Something that automatically or reflexively causes a response.

Unconscious. According to Freud, a storehouse of unacceptable images, including past events, current impulses, and desires of which one is not aware.

Unconscious inference theory. Theory that we unconsciously make accurate inferences about object size when we have accurate information about retinal image size and object distance.

Uterus (womb). A hollow, muscular organ in which a mother carries a fetus in the 9 months before birth.

Vaginismus. A sexual disorder in which the involuntary tightening of the vagina makes sexual intercourse impossible.

Validity of a test. Means that the test actually measures what you say it measures; best way to tell this is to see if the results of the test successfully predict the type of behavior in which you are interested.

Variable-interval schedule. Reinforces the first response made after varying time intervals (the first interval might be 5 minutes, then 9 minutes, then 1 minute, etc.). Produces a slow, steady rate of response.

Variable-ratio schedule. Reinforces the first response made after a varying number of responses (the tenth response; the fourth response after that; the twelfth response after the previous response, etc.). Produces a rapid, steady rate of responding.

Variance. Measure of variation, the average squared difference of each number in a sample from the mean of all numbers in the sample.

Verbal mediation. Mnemonic system in which one relates new material to verbal mediators, which are words that are easy to remember.

Vestibular system. An inner-ear structure that detects body orientation and changes in body orientation.

Visual angle. Angle between lines formed by the top and bottom of an object one is looking at. The visual angle gets smaller as an object moves farther away, which means that the retinal image of the object also gets smaller.

Visual cliff. Apparatus used to test depth perception in infants.

Vitreous humor. Semiliquid gel that

fills the eye's main chamber and gives it a spherical shape.

Voice stress analyzer. Records amount of voice tremor, which may be affected by stress. A decrease in voice tremor indicates tension, and, presumably, the fact that the person is lying.

Volumetric thirst. Thirst motivated by a drop in blood pressure caused by a depletion of extracellular fluid.

Warm spots. Areas on the skin where only hot is felt, even if stimulated by a cold object (when this occurs it is called *paradoxical warmth*).

Waveform. Shape of a sound wave; changes in waveform allow us to distinguish between the sound of a piano and a violin, for instance.

Wernicke's aphasia. Speech that includes wrong words and nonsense words, shifting from topic to topic.

Caused by injury to Wernicke's area in the cortex.

Yerkes-Dodson principle. The theory that the most effective level of arousal for performance depends on the difficulty of the task.

Zener cards. Special cards used to test for ESP.

Zygote. A cell formed by the union of an ovum and a sperm.

REFERENCES

Abramson, L., Seligman, M., & Teasdale, J. (1978). Learned helplessness in humans. Critique and reformation. *Journal of Abnormal Psychology, 87*, 49–74.

Abramson, P., Perry, L., Rothblatt, A., Seeley, T., & Seeley, D. (1981). Negative attitudes toward masturbation and pelvic vasocongestion: The thermographic analysis. *Journal of Research in Personality, 15*, 497–509.

Abravanel, E., & Sigafoos, A. P. (1984). Exploring the presence of irritation during early infancy. *Child Development, 55*, 381–392.

Adams, G., & Huston, T. (1975). Social perception of middle-aged persons varying in physical attractiveness. *Developmental Psychology, 11*, 657–658.

Adler, A. (1927). *The practice and theory of individual psychology*. New York: Harcourt, Brace & World.

Adler, A. (1939). *Social interest*. New York: Putnam.

Adorno, T. W., Fenkel-Brunswick, E., Levinson, D. J., & Sanford, R. N. (1950). *The authoritarian personality*. New York: Harper & Row.

Agras, S., Sylvester, D., & Oliveau, D. (1969). The epidemiology of common fears and phobias. *Comprehensive Psychiatry, 10*, 151–156.

Agras, W. S. (1967). Behavior therapy in management of chronic schizophrenia. *American Journal of Psychiatry, 124*, 240–243.

Aiello, J. R., & Aiello, T. (1974). The development of personal space: Proxemic behavior of children 6 through 16. *Human Ecology, 2*(3), 177–189.

Ainsworth, M. D. (1963). The development of infant-mother interactions among the Ganda. In D. M. Foss (Ed.), *Determinants of infant behavior* (Vol. 2). New York: Wiley.

Ainsworth, M. D. (1973). The development of infant-mother attachment. In B. Caldwell & H. Ricciuti (Eds.), *Review of child development research* (Vol. 3). Chicago: University of Chicago Press.

Ainsworth, M. D., Salter, D., & Wittig, B. A. (1967). Attachment and exploratory behavior of one-year-olds in a strange situation. In B. M. Foss (Ed.), *Determinants of infant behavior* (Vol. 4). New York: John Wiley.

Ajzen, I., & Fishbein, M. (1977). Attitude-behavior relations: A theoretical analysis and review of empirical research. *Psychological Bulletin, 84*, 888–918.

Akiskal, H. S., & McKinney, W. T., Jr. (1975). Overview of recent research in depression. *Archives of General Psychiatry, 32*, 285–305.

Alderfer, C. (1972). *Existence, relatedness and growth*. New York: Free Press.

Alkon, D. L. (1983). Learning in a marine snail. *Scientific American, 249*, 70–84.

Allen, V., & Greenberger, D. (1980). Destruction and perceived control. In A. Baum & J. Singer (Eds.), *Advances in environmental psychology* (Vol 2). Hillsdale, NJ: Erlbaum.

Allport, F. H. (1924). *Social psychology*. Cambridge, MA: Riverside Press.

Allport, G. W. (1937). *Personality: A psychological interpretation*. New York: Holt, Rinehart and Winston.

Allport, G. W. (1954). *The nature of prejudice*. Reading, MA: Addison Wesley.

Allport, G. W., & Odbert, H. S. (1936). Trait names: A psycholexical study. *Psychological Monographs, 47* (1, Whole No. 211).

Altman, I. (1975). *The environment and social behavior*. Monterey, CA: Brooks/Cole.

Altman, I., & Chemers, M. (1980). *Culture and environment*. Monterey, CA: Brooks/Cole.

Altman, I., Levine, M., & Nadien, J. (1970). Unpublished results cited in S. Milgram, "The experience of living in cities." *Science, 167*, 1461–1468.

Altman, I., & Vinsel, A. (1977). Personal space: An analysis of E. T. Hall's proxemics framework. In I. Altman & J. Wehwill (Eds.), *Human behavior and environment: Advances in theory and research* (Vol. 1). New York: Plenum.

Altman, I., Vinsel, A., & Brown, B. (1981). Dialectic conceptions in social psychology: An application to social penetration and privacy regulation. In L. Berkowitz (Ed.), *Advances in experimental social psychology* (Vol. 14). New York: Academic Press.

Altus, W. D. (1959). Birth order, intelligence and adjustment. *Psychological Reports, 5*, 502.

Altus, W. D. (1966). Birth order and its sequelae. *Science, 151*, 44–49.

American Psychiatric Association. (1979). *Diagnostic and statistical manual of mental disorders* (3rd ed.). Washington, DC: American Psychiatric Association.

Amir, Y., & Sharan, S. (1984). *School desegregation: Cross-cultural prospectives*. Hillsdale, NJ: Erlbaum.

Amsel, A., & Lashotte, M. E. (1984). *Mechanisms of adaptive behavior*. New York: Columbia University Press.

Anderson, C. A., & Anderson, D. C. (1984). Ambient temperature and violent crime: Tests of the linear and curvilinear hypothesis. *Journal of Personality and Social Psychology, 46*, 91–97.

Anderson, J. R., & Bower, G. H. (1973). *Human associative memory*. Washington, DC: Winston.

Anderson, J. R., & Kosslyn, S. M. (Eds.). (1984). *Tutorials in learning and memory: Essays in honor of Gordon Bower*. San Francisco: Freeman.

Anderson, W. F., & Diacomakos, E. G. (1981). Genetic engineering in mammalian cells. *Scientific American, 245*, 106–121.

Andersson, B., & Larsson, S. (1961). Influence of local temperature changes in the preoptic area and rostral hypothalamus on the regulation of food and water intake. *Acta Physiologica Scandinavica*, 15–89.

Andersson, B., & Larsson, S. (1961). Physiological and pharmacological aspects of the control of hunger and thirst. *Acta Physiologica Scandinavica*, 188–201.

Ando, Y., & Hattori, H. (1973). Statistical studies in the effects of intense noise during human fetal life. *Journal of Sound and Vibration, 27*, 101–110.

Andrew, J. D. W. (1967). The achievement motive and advancement in two types of organizations. *Journal of Personality and Social Psychology, 6*, 163–168.

Andrews, G., & Harvey, R. (1981). Does psychotherapy benefit neurotic patients? *Archives of General Psychiatry, 38*, 1203–1208.

Anspacher, C. (1972). Rock really does deafen. *San Francisco Chronicle*, January 26, p. 1.

Apgar, V. A. (1953). A proposal for a new method of evaluation of the newborn infant. *Current Researches in Anesthesia and Analgesia, 32*, 260–267.

Appleyard, D., & Lintell, M. (1972). The environmental quality of city streets: The residents' point of view. In W. Mitchell (Ed.), *Environmental design: Research and practice*. Los Angeles: University of California/EDRA.

Arenberg, D. (1967). Regression analyses of verbal learning on adult age at two anticipation intervals. *Journal of Gerontology, 22*, 411–414.

Argyle, M. (1967). *The psychology of interpersonal behavior*. Baltimore: Penguin.

Argyle, M., & Dean, J. (1965). Eye-contact, distance and affiliation. *Sociometry, 28*, 289–304.

Argyle, M., & McHenry, R. (1971). Do spectacles really affect judgments of intelligence? *British Journal of Social and Clinical Psychology, 10*, 27–29.

Armbruster, B. B., & Anderson, T. H. (1981). *Content Area Textbooks*, Reading Education Report No. 23 (Center for the Study of Reading), University of Illinois at Urbana-Champaign, Urbana, IL.

Armbruster, B. B., & Anderson, T. H. (1984). Structures of explanation in history textbooks or So What if Governor Stanford Missed the Spike and Hit the Rail? *Journal of Curriculum Studies, 16*, 181–194.

Arnold, M. B. (1960). *Emotion and personality* (2 vols.). New York: Columbia University Press.

Aronson, E. (1976). *The social animal* (2nd ed.). San Francisco: Freeman.

Aronson, E., & Bridgeman, D. (1979). Jigsaw groups and the desegrated classroom: In pursuit of common goals. *Personality and Social Psychology Bulletin, 5*, 438–446.

Aronson, E., & Carlsmith, J. M. (1963). The effect of the severity of threat on the devaluation of forbidden behavior. *Journal of Abnormal and Social Psychology, 66*, 584–588.

Aronson, E., & Linder, D. E. (1965). Gain and loss of esteem as determinants of interpersonal attractiveness. *Journal of Experimental Social Psychology, 1*, 156–171.

Aronson, E., & Mills, J. (1959). The effect of severity of initiation on liking for a group. *Journal of Abnormal and Social Psychology*, *59*, 177–181.

Asch, S. (1946). Forming impressions of personality. *Journal of Abnormal and Social Psychology*, *41*, 258–290.

Asch, S. (1951). Effects of group pressure upon the modification and distortion of judgment. In H. Guetzkow (Ed.), *Groups, leadership and men*. Pittsburgh: Carnegie Press.

Asch, S. (1952). *Social psychology*. Englewood Cliffs, NJ: Prentice-Hall.

Asch, S. (1956). Studies of independence and conformity: I. A minority of one against a unanimous majority. *Psychological Monographs*, *70*, No. 9.

Asch, S. E., & Zukier, H. (1984). Thinking about persons. *Journal of Personality and Social Psychology*, *46*, 1230–1240.

Association of American Publishers. (1983). *How to prepare for and take examinations*. New York.

Atkinson, J., & Birch, D. (1978). *An introduction to motivation*. New York: Van Nostrand.

Atkinson, R. (1957). Motivational determinants of risk-taking behavior. *Psychological Review*, *64*, 359–372.

Atkinson, R. C. (1975). Mnemontechnics in second-language learning. *American Psychologist*, *30*, 821–828.

Atkinson, R. C., & Shiffrin, R. M. (1971). The control of short-term memory. *Scientific American*, *224*, 82–90.

Atkinson, R. C., & Shiffrin, R. M. (1977). Human memory: A proposed system and its control processes. In G. H. Bower (Ed.), *Human memory: Basic processes*. New York: Academic Press.

Attneave, F. (1976). Multistability in perception. In R. Held & W. Richards (Eds.), *Recent progress in perception*. San Francisco: Freeman.

Ayllon, T., & Azrin, N. H. (1968). *The token economy: A motivational system for therapy and rehabilitation*. New York: Appleton-Century-Crofts.

Bach, G., & Wyden, P. (1968). *The intimate enemy: How to fight fair in love and marriage*. New York: Avon.

Bachrach, A. J., Erwin, W., & Mohr, J. P. (1965). The control of eating behavior in an anorexic by operant conditioning techniques. In L. P. Ullman & L. Krasner (Eds.), *Case studies in behavior modification*. New York: Holt, Rinehart and Winston, pp. 153–163.

Bach-Y-Rita, P. (1972). *Brain mechanisms in sensory substitution*. New York: Academic Press.

Bach-Y-Rita, P. (1982). Sensory substitution in rehabilitation. In L. Illis, M. Sedwick, & H. Granville (Eds.), *Rehabilitation of the neurological patient*. Oxford: Blackwell Press, pp. 361–383.

Badiaj, P., Culbertson, S., & Harsh, J. (1973). Choice of longer or stronger signalled shock over short or weaker signalled shock. *Journal of the Experimental Analysis of Behavior*, *19*, 25–32.

Baker, C. (1983). *Physicians desk reference*. Oradell, NJ: Medical Economics.

Bales, R. F., & Slater, P. (1955). Role differentiation in small decision-making groups. In T. Parson & R. F. Bales (Eds.), *Family socialization and interaction processes*. Glencoe, IL: Free Press.

Bancroft, J. (1984). Hormones and human sexual behavior. *Journal of Sex and Marital Therapy*, *10*, 3–21.

Bandura, A. (1962). Social learning through imitation. In M. R. Jones (Ed.), *Nebraska symposium on motivation*. Lincoln, NE: University of Nebraska Press.

Bandura, A. (1965). Behavior modification through modeling procedures. In L. Krosner & L. P. Ullman (Eds.), *Research in behavior modification*. New York: Holt, Rinehart, and Winston.

Bandurn, A. (1965). Influence of models' reinforcement contingencies on the acquisition of imitative responses. *Journal of Personality and Social Psychology*, *1*, 589–595.

Bandura, A. (1968). Social learning interpretation of psychological dysfunctions. In P. London & D. Rosenhan (Eds.), *Foundations of abnormal psychology*. New York: Holt, Rinehart and Winston.

Bandura, A. (1969). Social-learning theory of identificatory processes. In D. A. Goslin (Ed.), *Handbook of socialization theory and research*. Chicago: Rand McNally.

Bandura, A. (1973). *Aggression: A social learning analysis*. New York: Holt, Rinehart and Winston.

Bandura, A. (1977). *A social learning theory*. Englewood Cliffs, NJ: Prentice-Hall.

Bandura, A. (1982). Self-efficacy mechanism in human agency. *American Psychologist*, *37*, 122–147.

Bandura, A., & Menlove, F. L. (1968). Factors determining vicarious extinction of avoidance through symbolic modeling. *Journal of Personality and Social Psychology*, *8*, 99–108.

Bandura, A., Reese, L., & Adams, N. (1982). Microanalysis of action and fear arousal as a function of differential levels of perceived self-efficiency. *Journal of Personality and Social Psychology*, *66*, 3–11.

Bandura, A., Ross, D., & Ross, S. A. (1961). Transmission of aggression through imitation of aggressive models. *Journal of Abnormal and Social Psychology*, *63*, 575–582.

Bandura, A., Ross, D., & Ross, S. A. (1963). Imitation of film-mediated aggressive models. *Journal of Abnormal and Social Psychology*, *66*, 3–11.(a)

Bandura, A., Ross, D., & Ross, S. A. (1963). Vicarious reinforcement and imitative learning. *Journal of Abnormal and Social Psychology*, *67*, 601–607.(b)

Banks, W., & McQuater, G. (1976). Achievement motivation and black children. *IRCD Bulletin*, *11*, 1–8.

Banks, W., McQuater, G., & Hubbard, J. (1977). Task-liking and intrinsic-extrinsic achievement orientations in black adolescents. *Journal of Black Psychology*, *3*, 61–71.

Barber, T. X. (1961). Antisocial and criminal acts induced by hypnosis: A review of experimental and clinical findings. *Archives of General Psychiatry*, *5*, 301–312.

Barber, T. X. (1970). *LSD, marihuana, yoga and hypnosis*. Chicago: Aldine.

Barber, T. X., & Glass, L. B. (1962). Significant factors in hypnotic behavior. *Journal of Abnormal and Social Psychology*, *64*, 222–228.

Bard, P. (1938). Studies in the cortical representation of somatic sensibility. *Harvey Lectures*, *33*, 143–169.

Bardwick, C. (1971). *The psychology of women: A study of bio-cultural conflicts*. New York: Harper & Row.

Barker, M. (1976). Planning for environmental indices: Observer appraisals of air quality. In K. Craik & E. Zube (Eds.), *Perceiving environmental quality*. New York: Plenum Press.

Baron, R. A., & Bell, P. A. (1976). Aggression and heat: The influence of ambient temperature, negative affect, and a cooling drink on physical aggression. *Journal of Personality and Social Psychology*, *33*, 245–255.(a)

Baron, R. A., & Bell, P. A. (1976). Physical distance and helping: Some unexpected benefits of "crowding in" on others. *Journal of Applied Social Psychology*, *6*, 95–104.(b)

Baron, R. A., & Lawton, S. F. (1972). Environmental influences of model effects by high ambient temperatures. *Psychonomic Science*, *26*, 180–182.

Baron, R. M., Mandel, D., Adams, C., & Gaffen, L. (1976). Effects of social density in University residential environments. *Journal of Personality and Social Psychology*, *34*, 434–446.

Baron, R. S. (1984). Group dynamics. In I. A. Kohn (Ed.), *Social psychology*. Dubuque, IA: W. C. Brown.

Bar-Tal, D. (1976). *Prosocial behavior: Theory and research*. Washington, DC: Hemisphere.

Bar-Tal, D. (1984). American study of helping behavior: What? Why? and Where? In E. Staub, D. Bar-Tal, J. Karylowski, & J. Reykowski (Eds.), *Development and maintenance of prosocial behavior*. New York: Plenum.

Bar-Tal, D., & Saxe, L. (1976). Perceptions of similarly and dissimilarly attractive couples and individuals. *Journal of Personality and Social Psychology*, *33*, 772–781.

Baruch, G. K., & Barnett, R. C. (1980). On the well-being of adult women. In L. A. Bond & J. C. Rosen (Eds.), *Competence and coping during adulthood*. Hanover, NH: University Press of New England.

Bates, E., MacWhinney, B., Caselli, C., Devescovi, A., Natale, F., & Venza, V. (1984). A cross-linguistic study of the development of sentence interpretation strategies. *Child Development*, *55*, 341–354.

Bateson, G., Jackson, D. D., Haley, J., & Weakland, J. (1956). Toward a theory of schizophrenia. *Behavioral Science*, *1*, 251–264.

Baum, A., Fisher, J., & Solomon, S. (1981). Type of information, familiarity, and the reduction of crowding stress. *Journal of Personality and Social Psychology*, *40*, 11–23.

Baum, A., & Greenberg, C. (1975). Waiting for a crowd: The behavioral and perceptual effects of anticipated crowding. *Journal of Personality and Social Psychology*, *32*, 667–671.

Baum, A., Singer, J., & Baum, C. (1981). Stress and the environment. *Journal of Social Issues*, *37*, 4–35.

Baum, A., & Valins, S. (1977). *Architecture and social behavior: Psychological studies in social density*. Hillsdale, NJ: Erlbaum.

Baumeister, R. E. (1985, April). The championship choke. *Psychology Today*, pp. 48–53.

Baumeister, R., & Cooper, J. (1981). Can the public expectation of emotion cause that emotion? *Journal of Personality*, *49*, 49–59.

Baumeister, R., & Steinhiber, A. (1984). Paradoxical effects of supportive audiences on performance under pressure: The home field disadvantage in sports championships. *Journal of Personality and Social Psychology*, *47*, 85–93.

Baumrind, D. (1968). Authoritarian vs. authoritative control. *Adolescence*, *3*, 255–272.

Baumrind, D. (1971). Current patterns of parental authority. *Developmental Psychology Monograms*, *1*, 1–103.

Baumrind, D. (1982). Reciprocal rights and responsibilities in parent-child relations. In J. Rubinstein & B. D. Brent (Eds.), *Taking sides: Clashing views on controversial psychological issues*. Guilford, CT: Dushkin.

Beck, A. T. (1967). *Depression: Clinical, experimental and theoretical aspects*. New York: Harper & Row.

Beck, A. T. (1976). *Cognitive therapy and emotional disorders*. New York: International University Press.

Beck, A. T. (1983). Negative cognitions. In E. Levitt, B. Lubin, & J. Brooks (Eds.), *Depression: Concepts, controversies, and some new facts* (2nd ed.). Hillsdale, NJ: Erlbaum.

Beck, A. T., Rush, J. A., Shaw, B. R., & Emery, G. (1978). *Cognitive therapy of depression: A treatment manual*. Copyright A. T. Beck, M.D.

Beck, A. T., & Young, J. E. (1978). College blues. *Psychology Today*, *12*, 80–92.

Beck, R. C. (1978). *Motivation: Theories and principles*. Englewood Cliffs, NJ: Prentice-Hall.

Becker, L., & Seligman, C. (1981). Welcome to the energy crisis. *Journal of Social Issues*, *37*, 1–7.

Bekerian, D. A., & Bowers, J. M. (1983). Eyewitness Testimony: Were we mislead? *Journal of Experimental Psychology: Learning, Memory, and Cognition*, *9*, 139–145.

Bell, A. P., & Weinberg, M. S. (1978). *Homosexualities*. New York: Simon & Schuster, p. 442.

Bell, P. A. (1978). Effects of noise and heat stress on primary and subsidiary task performance. *Human Factors*, *20*, 749–752.

Bell, P. (1981). Physiological, comfort, performance and social effects of heat. *Journal of Social Issues*, *37*, 71–94.

Bellezza, F. S. (1983). Mnemonic-device instruction with adults. In G. M. Pressley, & J. R. Levin (Eds.), *Cognitive strategy research: Psychological foundation*. New York: Springer-Verlag.

Belsky, J., Rovine, M., & Taylor, D. G. (1984). The Pennsylvania infant and family development project, III: The origins of individual differences in infant-mother attachment: maternal and infant contributions. *Child Development*, *55*, 718–728.

Bem, D. J., & Allen, A. (1974). On predicting some of the people some of the time: The search for cross-situational consistencies in behavior. *Psychological Review*, *81*, 506–520.

Benson, G., & Ziemon, G. (1981). The relationship of weather to children's behavior problems. Unpublished manuscript Colorado State University Cited in J. D. Fisher, P. Bell, & A. Baum, *Environmental psychology* (2nd ed.), 1984.

Benson, H. (1975). *The relaxation response*. New York: Morrow.

Bentler, P., & Prince, C. (1970). Psychiatric symptomology in transvestites. *Journal of Clinical Psychology*, *26*, 434–435.

Bercel, N. A. (1960). A study of the influence of schizophrenic serum on the behavior of the spider: Zilla-X-notata. In D. D. Jackson (Ed.), *The etiology of schizophrenia*. New York: Basic Books.

Berger, P. A. (1978). Medical treatment of mental illness. *Science*, *200*, 974–981.

Bergin, A., & Lambert, M. (1978). The evaluation of therapeutic outcomes. In S. Garfield & A. Bergin (Eds.), *Handbook of psychotherapy and behavior change* (2nd ed.). New York: Wiley.

Berkowitz, L. (1962). *Aggression: A social psychology analysis*. New York: McGraw-Hill.

Berkowitz, L. (1965). The concept of aggressive drive: Some additional considerations. In L. Berkowitz (Ed.), *Advances in experimental social psychology* (Vol. 2). New York: Academic Press.

Berkowitz, L. (1972). Social norms, feelings, and other factors affecting helping and altruism. In L. Berkowitz (Ed.), *Advances in experimental social psychology* (Vol. 6). New York: Academic Press.

Berkowitz, L., & Connor, W. H. (1966). Success, failure, and social responsibility. *Journal of Personality and Social Psychology*, *4*, 664–669.

Berlyne, D. E. (1957). Perceptual curiosity, exploratory behavior, and maze learning. *Journal of Comparative and Physiological Psychology*, *50*, 228–232.

Berlyne, D. E. (1958). The influence of complexity and novelty in visual figures on orienting responses. *Journal of Experimental Psychology*, *55*, 289–296.

Berlyne, D. E. (1960). *Conflict, arousal and curiosity*. New York: McGraw Hill.

Berlyne, D. E. (1969). *The justifiability of the concept of curiosity*. Paper delivered at the XIX International Congress of London.

Bernard, P. (1924). *Instinct*. New York: Holt, Rinehart and Winston.

Berrera, M., Sandler, I., & Ramsay, T. (1981). Preliminary development of a scale of social support: Studies on college students. *American Journal of Community Psychology*, *9*, 435–447.

Berscheid, E. (1982). Attraction and emotion in interpersonal relationships. In M. Clark & S. Fiske (Eds.), *Affect and cognition*. Hillsdale, NJ: Erlbaum.

Berscheid, E. (1983). Emotion. In H. Kelley et al. (Eds.), *Close relationships*. New York: Freeman.

Berscheid, E., & Walster, E. (1978). *Interpersonal attraction*. Reading, MA: Addison-Wesley.

Best, P. J., & Ranck, J. B., Jr. (1982). The reliability of the relationship between hippocampal unit activity and sensory-behavioral events in the rat. *Experimental Neurology*, *75*, 652–664.

Bettelheim, B. (1960). *The informed heart*. New York: Harper & Row.

Beumont, P. J., Abraham, S., & Turtle, J. (1980). Paradoxical prolactin response to goradotropin-releasing hormone during weight gain in patients with anorexia nervosa. *Journal of Clinical Endocrinology and Metabolism*, *51*, 1283–1285.

Bickman, L., Teger, A., Gabriele, T., McLaughlin, C., Berger, M., & Sunaday, E. (1973). Dormitory density and helping behavior. *Environment and Behavior*, *5*, 465–490.

Biggers, T., & Pryor, B. (1982). Attitude change: A function of emotion-eliciting qualities of environment. *Personality and Social Psychological Bulletin*, *8*, 94–99.

Bindrim, P. (1968). A report on a nude marathon. The effect of physical nudity upon the practice interaction in the marathon group. *Psychotherapy: Theory, Research and Practice*, *5*, 180–188.

Binet, A., & Simon, T. (1905). New methods for the diagnosis of the intellectual levels of subnormals. *Annals of Psychology*, *11*, 191.

Birdwhistell, R. L. (1967). Some body motion elements accompanying spoken American English. In L. Thayer (Ed.), *Communication: Concepts and perspectives*. Washington, DC: Spartan Books.

Bjorksten, J. (1968). The cross-linkage theory of aging. *Journal of the American Geriatrics Society*, *16*, 408–427.

Björntorp, P. (1972). Disturbances in the regulation of food intake. *Advances in Psychosomatic Medicine*, *7*, 116–127.

Black, J. B. (1984). Understanding and remembering stories. In J. R. Anderson & S. M. Kosslyn (Eds.), *Tutorials in reading and memory*. San Francisco: Freeman.

Blackwell, B. (1981). Biofeedback in a comprehensive behavioral medicine program. *Biofeedback and Self-Regulation*, *6*, 445–472.

Blair, S. M. (1973). Psychiatric diagnosis (letter). *Science*, *180*, 363.

Blaskovitch, J., Ginsburg, G. P., & Howe, R. C. (1975). Blackjack and the risky shift: II. Monetary stakes. *Journal of Experimental Social Psychology*, *11*, 224–232.

Blatt, S., & Berman, W. (1984). A methodology for the use of the Rorschach in clinical research. *Journal of Personality Assessment*, *48*, 226–239.

Blau, F. D. (1975). Women in the labor force: An overview. In J. Freeman (Ed.), *Women: A feminist perspective*, Palo Alto, CA: Mayfield.

Blau, P. M. (1964). *Exchange and power in social life*. New York: Wiley.

Blenker, M. (1965). Social work and family relationships in later life with some thoughts on filial maturity. In E. Shanas & G. Streif (Eds.), *Social structure and the family*. Englewood Cliffs, NJ: Prentice-Hall.

Bliss, E. (1980). Multiple personalities: Report of fourteen cases with implications for schizophrenia and hysteria. *Archives of General Psychiatry*, *37*, 1388–1397.

Bloom, F. E., Lazerson, A., & Hofstadter, L. (1985). *Brain, mind, and behavior*. New York: Freeman.

Bloom, L. M., Hood, L., & Lightbown, P. (1974). Imitation in language development: If, when and why. *Cognitive Psychology*, *6*, 380–420.

Blough, D. S. (1982). Pigeon perception of letters of the alphabet. *Science*, *218*, 397–398.

Blum, B. (1953). *Psychoanalytic theories of personality*. New York: McGraw-Hill.

Bochner, S., & Insko, C. A. (1966). Communicator discrepancy, source credibility, and opinion change. *Journal of Personality and Social Psychology*, *4*, 614–621.

Bondford, L., Giff, T., & Benne, K. (Eds.). (1964). *T-group theory: Laboratory method*. New York: Wiley.

Bootzin, R. R., & Max, D. (1981). Learning and behavioral theories of anxiety and stress. In I. L. Kutash & L. B. Schlesinger

(Eds.), *Pressure point: Perspectives on stress and anxiety*. San Francisco: Josey-Bass.

Borchardt, D. H., & Francis, R. D. (1984). *How to find out in psychology: A guide to the literature and methods of research*. New York: Pergamon Press.

Bossard, J. (1932). Residential propinquity as a factor in marriage selection. *American Journal of Sociology*, *38*, 219–224.

Boszormeny-Nagy, I., & Ulrich, D. (1981). Contextual family therapy. In A. Gorman & A. Kniskern (Eds.), *Handbook of family therapy*. New York: Brunner/Mazel.

Botwinick, J. (1977). Intellectual abilities. In J. E. Birren & K. W. Schaie (Eds.), *Handbook of the psychology of aging*. New York: Van Nostrand.

Boucher, J. D., & Ekman, P. (1975). Facial areas and emotional information. *Journal of Communication*, *25*, 21–29.

Bourne, L. E., & Restle, F. (1959). A mathematical theory of concept identification. *Psychological Review*, *66*, 278–296.

Bower, G. H. (1981, June). Mood and memory. *Psychology Today*.

Bower, G. H., & Clark, M. C. (1969). Narrative stories as mediators for serial learning. *Psychonomic Science*, *14*, 181–182.

Bower, G. H., Clark, M., Winzenz, D., & Lesgold, A. (1969). Hierarchical retrieval schemes in recall of categorized word lists. *Journal of Verbal Learning and Verbal Behavior*, *8*, 323–343.

Bower, G., & Cohen, P. (1982). Emotional influences in memory and thinking: Data and theory. In M. Clark & S. Fisher (Eds.), *Emotions and affect*. Hillsdale, NJ: Erlbaum.

Bower, G. H., & Karlin, M. B. (1974). Depth of processing pictures of faces and recognition memory. *Journal of Experimental Psychology*, *103*, 751–757.

Bower, G. H., & Trabasso, T. (1964). Concept identification. In R. C. Atkinson (Ed.), *Studies in mathematical psychology*. Stanford, CA: Stanford University Press.

Bower, T. (1977, February). Blind babies see with their ears. *New Scientist*, pp. 255–257.

Bowlby, J. (1973). *Attachment and loss* (Vol. 2): *Separation, anxiety and anger*. New York: Basic Books.

Brackbill, Y. (1958). Extinction of the smile response in infants as a function of reinforcement schedule. *Child Development*, *29*, 115–124.

Brady, J. V., Porter, R. W., Conrad, D. G., & Mason, J. W. (1958). Avoidance behavior and the development of gastroduodenal ulcers. *Journal of the Experimental Analysis of Behavior*, *11*, 69–73.

Bramel, D., Jaub, B., & Blum, B. (1968). An observer's reaction to the suffering of his enemy. *Journal of Personality and Social Psychology*, *8*, 384–392.

Brammer, L. M., & Shostrom, E. L. (1977). *Therapeutic psychology: Fundamentals of counseling and psychotherapy* (3rd ed.). Englewood Cliffs, NJ: Prentice-Hall.

Brashler, W. (1978). *Josh Gibson: A life in the Negro Leagues*. New York: Harper & Row.

Bray, D. W., & Howard, A. (1980). Career success and life satisfaction of middle-aged managers. In L. A. Bond & J. C. Rosen (Eds.), *Competence and coping during adulthood*. Hanover, NH: University Press of New England.

Brechner, K., & Linder, D. (1981). A social trap analysis of energy distribution sys-

tems. In A. Baum & J. Singer (Eds.), *Advances in environmental psychology* (Vol. 3). Hillsdale, NJ: Erlbaum.

Brehm, J., & Crocker, J. (1962). An experiment on hunger. In J. Brehm & A. Cohen (Eds.), *Explorations in cognitive dissonance*. New York: Wiley.

Brehm, S. S., & Brehm, J. W. (1981). *Psychological reactance: A theory of freedom and control*. New York: Academic Press.

Brewer, M., & Kramer, R. (1985). The psychology of intergroup attitudes and behavior. In *Annual Review of Psychology*. New York: Annual Reviews Inc.

Brewer, M., & Miller, N. (1984). Beyond the contact hypothesis: Theoretical perspectives on desegregation. In M. Brewer & N. Miller (Eds.), *Groups in contact: The psychology of desegration*. New York: Academic Press.

Brier, E. G. (1974, October). Nonverbal communication: How we send emotional messages. *Psychology Today*, 53–56.

Brigham, J. C. (1985). Race and eyewitness identifications. In S. Worchel & W. Austin, *The psychology of intergroup relations*. Chicago: Nelson Hall.

Brim, O. G., Jr. (1976). Theories of male mid-life crisis. *Counseling Psychologist*, *6*, 2–9.

Broadbeck, J. (1957). Neural control of hunger, appetite and satiety. *Yale Journal of Biological Medicine*, *29*, 565–574.

Broadbent, D. (1971). *Decision and stress*. New York: Academic Press.

Broadbent, D., & Little, E. (1960). Effects of noise reduction in the work situation. *Occupational Psychology*, *34*, 133–140.

Brock, T. (1965). Communicator-recipient similarity and decision change. *Journal of Personality and Social Psychology*, *1*, 650–654.

Brooks, L. (1974). *Law, psychiatry and the mental health system*. Boston: Little, Brown.

Brooks, L. W., & Dansereau, D. F. (1983). Effects of structural schema training and text organization on expository prose processing. *Journal of Educational Psychology*, *75*, 811–820.

Broverman, J. K., Vogel, S. R., Broverman, D. M., Clarkson, F. G., & Rosenkantz, P. S. (1972). Sex-role stereotypes: A current appraisal. *Journal of Social Issues*, *28*, 59–78.

Brown, B. B. (1979, August). Territoriality and residential burglary. Paper presented at American Psychology Association, New York.

Brown, G. W., Harris, T., & Copeland, J. R. (1977). Depression and loss. *British Journal of Psychiatry*, *130*, 1–18.

Brown, P. K., & Walk, G. (1964). Visual pigments in single rods and cones of the human retina. *Science*, *144*, 45–52.

Brown, R. (1965). *Social psychology*. New York: Free Press.

Brown, R., Cazden, C. B., & Bellugi, U. (1969). The child's grammar from I to III. In J. P. Hill (Ed.), *Minnesota symposium on child psychology* (Vol. 2). Minneapolis: University of Minnesota Press.

Brown, R. W., & McNeill, D. (1966). The "tip-of-the-tongue" phenomenon. *Journal of Verbal Learning and Verbal Behavior*, *5*, 325–337.

Brownell, K., & Venditti, B. (1983). The etiology and treatment of obesity In W. Fann et al. (Eds.), *Phenomenology and the treat-

ment of psychophysiologic disorders*. New York: Spectrum.

Bruner, J. S., Goodnow, J. J., & Austin, G. A. (1956). *A study of thinking*. New York: Wiley.

Bruner, J. S., & Koslowski, B. (1972). Visually preadapted constituents of manipulatory action. *Perception*, *1*, 1–122.

Bry, A. (1976). *60 hours that transform your life: est*. New York: Avon Books.

Buck, R. (1980). Nonverbal behavior and the theory of emotions: The facial feedback hypothesis. *Journal of Personality and Social Psychology*, *38*, 811–824.

Buckhout, R. (1974, December). Eyewitness testimony. *Scientific American*, 231(b), 23–31.

Bugliosi, V., & Gentry, C. (1974). *Helter skelter: The true story of the Manson murders*. New York: Norton.

Bunney, W. E., Jr., Goodwin, F. K., Murphy, D. L., & Borge, G. F. (1972). The "switch process" in manic-depressive illness: I and II. *Archives of General Psychiatry*, *27*, 295–302.

Burgess, E., & Wallin, P. (1953). *Engagement and marriage*. Philadelphia: Lippincott.

Burnam, M. A., Pennebaker, J. W., & Glass, D. C. (1975). Time consciousness, achievement striving, and the type A coronary-prone behavior pattern. *Journal of Abnormal Psychology*, *84*, 76–79.

Burnstein, E., Vinokur, A., & Trope, Y. (1973). Interpersonal comparison versus persuasive argumentation: A more direct test of alternative explanations for group-induced shifts in individual choice. *Journal of Experimental Social Psychology*, *9*, 236–245.

Burnstein, S. (1984). Persuasion as argument processing. In M. Brandstatter, J. Davis, & G. Stocker-Kreichgaver (Eds.), *Group decision processes*. London: Academic Press.

Burrows, G. D., & Dennerstein, L. (Eds.). (1980). *Handbook of hypnosis and psychosomatic medicine*. Amsterdam: Elsevier/North Holland.

Burt, C. (1966). The genetic determination of differences in intelligence: A study of monozygotic twins reared together and apart. *British Journal of Psychology*, *57*, 137–153.

Buss, A. H. (1980). *Self-consciousness and social anxiety*. San Francisco: Freeman.

Butcher, J., & Owen, P. (1978). Objective personality inventories: Recent research and some contemporary issues. In B. B. Wolman (Ed.), *Clinical diagnosis of mental disorders: A handbook*. New York: Plenum Press.

Butler, R., & Alexander, H. (1955). Daily patterns of visual exploratory behavior in the monkeys. *Journal of Comparative and Physiological Psychology*, *48*, 249–257.

Byrne, D. (1971). *The attraction paradigm*. New York: Academic Press.

Byrne, D., Baskett, C. D., & Hodges, L. (1971). Behavioral indicators of interpersonal attraction. *Journal of Abnormal and Social Psychology*, *1*, 137–149.

Byrne, D., & Kelley, K. (1981). *An introduction to personality* (3rd ed.). Englewood Cliffs, NJ: Prentice-Hall.

Cadoret, R. J. (1978). Psychopathology in adopted-away off-spring of biological parents with antisocial behavior. *Archives of General Psychiatry*, *35*, 176–184.

Cadoret, R. J., & Winokur, G. (1975).

X-linkage in manic-depressive illness. *Annual Review of Medicine*, *26*, 21–25.

Calder, B., & Staw, B. (1975). Self-perception of intrinsic and extrinsic motivation. *Journal of Personality and Social Psychology*, *31*, 599–605.

Calhoun, J. (1962). Population density and social pathology. *Scientific American*, *206*, 139–148.

Cameron, N. (1963). *Personality development and psychopathology*. Boston: Houghton-Mifflin.

Campbell, F. W. (1974). The transmission of spatial information through the visual system. In F. O. Schmitt & F. G. Worden (Eds.), *The neurosciences: Third study program*. Cambridge, MA: M. I. T. Press.

Campos, J. L., Langer, A., & Krowtiz, A. (1970). Cardiac responses on the visual cliff in prelocomotor human infants. *Science*, *170*, 196–197.

Candland, D. K. (1968). *Psychology: The experimental approach*. New York: McGraw-Hill.

Canestrari, R. E. (1963). Paced and self-paced learning in young and elderly adults. *Journal of Gerontology*, *18*, 165–168.

Cannon, D. S., & Baker, T. B. (1981). Emetic and electric shock alcohol aversion therapy. *Journal of Consulting and Clinical Psychology*, *49*, 20–33.

Cannon, W. B. (1914). The emergency function of the adrenal medulla in pain and the major emotions. *American Journal of Physiology*, *33*, 356–372.

Cannon, W. B. (1929). *Bodily changes in pain, hunger, fear and rage*. New York: Appleton-Century-Crofts.

Cannon, W. B., & Washburn, A. (1912). An explanation of hunger. *American Journal of Physiology*, *29*, 441–454.

Cantor, N., & Mischel, W. (1979). Prototypicality and personality: Effects of free recall and personality impressions. *Journal of Research in Personality*, *13*, 187–205.

Cantrell, D. P. (1983). *Psychology: Strategies for success*. Tempe, AZ: Amoleside Publishers.

Cantril, H. (1965). *The pattern of human concerns*. New Brunswick, NJ: Rutgers University Press.

Cappon, D. (1971). Mental health in the high rise. *Canadian Journal of Public Health*, *62*, 426–431.

Carlsmith, J. M., & Anderson, C. (1979). Ambient temperature and the occurrence of collective violence: A new analysis. *Journal of Personality and Social Psychology*, *37*, 337–344.

Carlsmith, J. M., Ellsworth, P. C., & Aronson, E. (1976). *Methods of research in social psychology*. Reading, MA: Addison-Wesley.

Carlson, V. R. (1977). Instructions and perceptual constancy judgements. In W. Epstein (Ed.), *Stability and constancy in visual perception: Mechanics and processes*. New York: Wiley.

Carpenter, F. (1974). *The Skinner primer*. New York: Free Press.

Carpenter, G. C. (1974). Visual regard of moving and stationary faces in early infancy. *Merrill-Palmer Quarterly*, *20*, 181–194.

Carver, C., & Glass, D. (1978). Coronary-prone behavior pattern and interpersonal aggression. *Journal of Personality and Social Psychology*, *36*, 361–366.

Carver, C., & Scheier, M. F. (1981). *Attention and self-regulation* New York: Springer-Verlag.

Casper, R. C., & Davis, J. M. (1977). On the course of anorexia nervosa. *American Journal of Psychiatry*, *134*, 974–978.

Castaneda, C. (1972). *Journey to Ixtlan: The lessons of Don Juan*. New York: Simon & Schuster.

Castillo, M., & Butterworth, G. (1981). Neonatal localization of a sound in visual space. *Perception*, *10*, 331–338.

Castleman, M. (1977, November 26). Why teenagers get pregnant. *The Nation*, pp. 549–552.

Cattell, R. B. (1949). *The culture free intelligence test*. Champaign, IL: Institute for Personality and Ability Testing.

Cattell, R. B. (1965). *The scientific analysis of personality*. Harmondsworth, England: Penguin Books.

Cattell, R. B. (1973). *Personality and mood by questionnaire*. San Francisco: Jossey-Bass.

Cautela, J. R. (1977). Covert conditioning: Assumptions and procedures. *Journal of Mental Imagery*, *1*, 53–64.

Cavan, S. (1966). *Liquor license*. Chicago: Aldine.

Cerella, J. (1979). Visual classes and natural categories in the pigeon. *Journal of Experimental Psychology: Human Perception and Performance*, *5*, 68–77.

Cerella, J. (1982). Mechanisms of concept formation in the pigeon. In D. J. Ingle et al. (Eds.), *Analysis of visual behavior*. Cambridge, MA: MIT Press.

Chapko, M. K., & Solomon, M. (1976). Air pollution and recreation behavior. *Journal of Social Psychology*, *100*, 149–150.

Chavis, D. M., Stucky, P. E., & Wandersman, A. (1983, April). Returning basic research to the community. *American Psychologist*, pp. 424–434.

Chemers, M. (1983). Leadership theory and research: A systems-process integration. In P. Paulus (Ed.), *Basic group processes*. New York: Springer-Verlag.

Chen, S. C. (1937). Social modifications of the activity of ants in nest building. *Physiological Zoology*, *10*, 420–437.

Chess, S. (1971). Autism in children with congenital rubella. *Journal of Autism and Childhood Schizophrenia*, *1*, 33–47.

Chomsky, N. (1975). *Reflections on language*. New York: Pantheon.

Churchland, P. M. (1984). *Matter and consciousness: A contemporary introduction to the philosophy of mind*. Cambridge, MA: MIT Press.

Cialdini, R. B. (1975). Reciprocal concessions procedure for inducing compliance: The door-in-the-face technique. *Journal of Personality and Social Psychology*, *31*, 206–215.

Cialdini, R. B. (1984). *Influence: How and why people agree to things*. New York: Morrow.

Clapton, W. (1973). Personality and career change. *Industrial Gerontology*, *17*, 9–17.

Clark, K. B., & Clark, M. P. (1947). Racial identification and preferences in Negro children. In T. M. Newcomb & E. L. Hartley (Eds.), *Readings in social psychology*. New York: Holt, Rinehart and Winston, pp. 169–178.

Clark, M. (1982). A role for arousal in the link between feeling states, judgements, and behavior. In M. Clark & S. Fisher, *Emotions and affect*. Hillsdale, NJ: Erlbaum.

Clarke, A. (1952). An examination of the operation of residual propinquity as a factor of mate selection. *American Sociological Review*, *27*, 17–22.

Clavan, S. (1978). The impact of social class and social trends on the role of grandparents. *The Family Coordinator*, *27*, 351–358.

Cleckley, H. (1976). *The mask of sanity* (5th ed.). St. Louis, MO: Mosby.

Clifford, M., & Walster, E. (1973). The effect of physical attractiveness on teacher expectation. *Sociology of Education*, *46*, 248.

Coates, D. L., & Lewis, M. (1984). Early mother-infant interaction and infant cognitive status as predictors of school performance and cognitive behavior in six-year-olds. *Child Development*, *55*, 1219–1230.

Cochise, C. N., & Griffith, A. (1971). *The first 100 years of Nino Cochise*. New York: Abelard-Schuman.

Coe, W. C. (1977). The problem of relevance versus ethics in researching hypnosis and antisocial conduct. *Annals of the New York Academy of Sciences*, *296*, 90–104.

Cofer, C. (1974). *Motivation and emotion*. Glenview, IL: Scott, Foresman.

Cohen, A. (1959). Communication discrepancy and attitude change: A dissonance theory. *Journal of Personality*, *27*, 386–396.

Cohen, D. (1976). *Dreams, visions, and drugs: A search for other realities*. New York: Franklin Watts.

Cohen, D., & Shaywitz, B. (1982). Preface to the special issue on neurobiological research on autism. *Journal of Autism and Developmental Disorders*, *12*, 103–107.

Cohen, L. D., Kipnes, D., Kunkle, E. G., & Kubzansky, P. E. (1955). Observations of a person with congenital insensitivity to pain. *Journal of Abnormal and Social Psychology*, *51*, 333–338.

Cohen, S. (1977). Environmental load and the allocation of attention. In A. Baum & S. Valins (Eds.), *Advances in environmental research*. Hillsdale, NJ: Erlbaum.

Cohen, S. (1981). Sensory changes in the elderly. *American Journal of Nursing*, *81*, 1851–1880.

Cohen, S., Evans, G., Krantz, D., Stokols, D., & Kelly, S. (1981). Aircraft noise and children: Longitudinal and cross-sectional evidence of adaptation to noise and the effectiveness of noise abatement. *Journal of Personality and Social Psychology*, *40*, 331–345.

Cohen, S., Glass, D. C., & Singer, J. E. (1973). Apartment noise, auditory discrimination, and reading ability in children. *Journal of Experimental Social Psychology*, *9*, 407–422.

Cole, C. S., & Coyne, J. C. (1977). Situational specificity of laboratory-induced learned helplessness. *Journal of Abnormal Psychology*, *86*, 615–623.

Coleman, J. C., Butcher, J. N., & Carson, R. C. (1980). *Abnormal psychology in modern life* (6th ed.). Glenview, IL: Scott, Foresman.

Collins, A. M., & Qillian, M. R. (1969). Retrieval time from semantic memory. *Journal of Verbal Learning and Verbal Behavior*, *8*, 240–247.

Collins, B. (1973). *Public and private conformity: Competing explanations by improvisation, cognitive dissonance, and attribution theories*. Andover, MA: Warner Modular Publications.

Committee of Veterans Affairs (1981). *Legacies of Vietnam: Comparative adjustment of veter-*

ans and their peers. Washington, DC: U.S.G.P.O.

Comstock, G., Chaffe, S., Katzman, N., McCombs, M., & Roberts, D. (1979). *Television and human behavior*. New York: Columbia Press.

Cone, J., & Hayes, S. (1980). *Environmental problems and behavioral solutions*. Monterey, CA: Brooks/Cole.

Conley, J. J. (1984). Relation of temporal stability and cross-situational consistency in personality: Comment on the Michel-Epstein debate. *Psychological Review*, *91*, 491–496.

Conrad, R. (1964). Acoustic confusions in immediate memory. *British Journal of Psychology*, *55*, 75–84.

Conroy, J., & Sundstrom, E. (1977). Territorial dominance in dyadic conversation as a function of similarity of opinion. *Journal of Personality and Social Psychology*, *39*, 570–576.

Conway, J. (1977). Behavioral self-control of smoking through aversive conditioning and self-management. *Journal of Consulting and Clinical Psychology*, *45*, 348–357.

Cook, S. W. (1978). Interpersonal and attitudinal outcomes in cooperating interracial groups. *Journal of Research and Development in Education*, *12*.

Cooper, H. (1979). Statistics combining independent studies: A meta-analysis of sex differences in conformity research. *Journal of Personality and Social Psychology*, *37*, 131–146.

Cooper, J., & Axson, D. (1982). Effort justification in psychotherapy. In G. Weary & H. Mirels (Eds.), *Integrations of clinical and social psychology*. New York: Oxford University Press.

Cooper, J., Darley, J. M., & Henderson, J. T. (1974). On the effectiveness of deviant and conventionally appearing communicators: A field experiment. *Journal of Personality and Social Psychology*, *29*, 752–757.

Cooper, J., & Fazio, R. (1979). The formation and persistence of attitudes that support intergroup conflict. In W. Austin & S. Worchel (Eds.), *The social psychology of intergroup relations*. Monterey, CA: Brooks/Cole.

Cooper, J., & Worchel, S. (1970). Role of undesired consequences in arousing cognitive dissonance. *Journal of Personality and Social Psychology*, *16*, 199–206.

Cooper, R., & Zubek, J. (1958). Effects of enriched and restricted early environments on the learning ability of bright and dull rats. *Canadian Journal of Psychology*, *12*, 159–164.

Cooper, S., & Hodges, W. (1983). *The mental health consultation field*. New York: Human Sciences.

Coren, S., & Girgus, J. S. (1978). *Seeing is deceiving*. Hillsdale, NJ: Erlbaum.

Corey, G., & Corey, M. S. (1977). *Groups: Process and practice*. Monterey, CA: Brooks/Cole.

Cornsweet, T. N. (1970). *Visual perception*. New York: Academic Press.

Corsini, R. J. (Ed.). (1981). *Handbook of innovative psychotherapies*. New York: Wiley.

Costa, P. T., Jr., & McCrae, R. R. (1980). Still stable after all these years: Personality as a key to some issues in aging. In P. B. Baltes & O. G. Brim, Jr. (Eds.), *Life-span*

development and behavior (Vol. 3). New York: Academic Press.

Cotman, C. W., & McGaugh, J. L. (1980). *Behavioral neuroscience*. New York: Academic press.

Cottrell, N. (1972). Social facilitation. In C. McClintock (Ed.), *Experimental social psychology*. New York: Holt, Rinehart & Winston.

Cox, F. D. (1974). *Youth, marriage and the seductive society*. Dubuque, IA: William C. Brown.

Coyne, J. (1976). Toward an interactional description of depression. *Psychiatry*, *39*, 14–27.

Coyne, J. (1976). Depression and the response of others. *Journal of Abnormal Psychology*, *85*, 186–193.

Coyne, J., & Lazarus, R. (1981). Cognition, stress, and coping: A transactional perspective. In I. Kutash & L. Schlesinger (Eds.), *Pressure point: Perspective on stress and anxiety*. San Francisco: Jossey-Bass.

Craig, C., & McCann, J. (1980). Developing strategies for influencing residential consumption of electricity. *Journal of Environmental Systems*, *9*, 175–188.

Crandall, V. (1973). Achievement. In H. Stevenson (Ed.), *Child psychology*. Chicago, IL: University of Chicago Press.

Crano, W., & Mellon, P. (1978). Causal inference of teachers' expectations in children's academic performance across logged panel analysis. *Journal of Educational Psychology*, *70*, 39–49.

Crismore, A. (1984). The rhetoric of textbooks: Metadiscourse. *Journal of Curriculum Studies*, *16*, 279–296.

Crisp, A. H., Palmer, R. L., & KaLucy, R. S. (1976). How common is anorexia nervosa? A prevalence study. *British Journal of Psychiatry*, *128*, 549–554.

Crockenburg, S. B. (1972). Creativity tests: A boon or boon-doggle for education? *Review of Educational Research*, *42*, 27–45.

Cronback, L. J., & Snow, R. E. (1977). *Aptitudes and instructional methods*. New York: Irvington.

Crosby, F., Bromley, S., & Saxe, L. (1980). Recent unobtrusive studies of black and white discrimination and prejudices: A literature review. *Psychological Bulletin*, *87*, 546–563.

Crow, T. (1983). *Disorders of neuronumoural transmission*. New York: Academic Press.

Crutchfield, R. S. (1955). Conformity and character. *American Psychologist*, *10*, 191–198.

Csikszentmihalyi, M. (1974). Flow: Studies of enjoyment (Report No. RO1 HM22-883-02). Washington, DC: U.S. Public Health Service.

Cunningham, S. (1983, June). Animal activists rally in streets, urge Congress to tighten laws. *APA Monitor*, pp. 1–27.

Curtiss, S. (1977). *Genie: A psycholinguistic study of a modern-day "wild child."* New York: Academic Press.

Cutting, J. E., & Proffitt, D. R. (1981). Gait perception as an example of how we may perceive events. In R. D. Walk & H. L. Pick, Jr. (Eds.), *Intersensory perception and sensory integration*. New York: Plenum.

Daniels, J. (1950). *The man of independence*. Philadelphia: Lippincott.

Darley, J. M., & Cooper, J. (1972). The "Clean for Gene" phenomenon: Deciding to vote for or against a candidate on the basis of the physical appearance of his sup-

porters. *Journal of Applied Social Psychology*, *2*, 24–33.

Darley, J. M., & Latane, B. (1968). Bystander intervention in emergencies: Diffusion of responsibility. *Journal of Personality and Social Psychology*, *8*, 377–383.

Davenport, Y. B., Adland, M. L., Gold, P. W., & Goodwyn, F. K. (1979). Manic-depressive illness: Psycho-dynamic features of multigenerational families. *American Journal of Orthopsychiatry*, *49*, 24–35.

Davidson, W. S., II (1974). Studies of aversive conditioning for alcoholics: A critical review of theory and research methodology. *Psychological Bulletin*, *81*, 571–581.

Davis, C. M. (1928). Self-selection of diet by newly weaned infants. *American Journal of Diseases of Children*, *36*, 651–679.

Davis, J. A. (1974). A two-factor theory of schizophrenia. *Journal of Psychiatric Research*, *11*, 25–29.

Davis, J. H. (1980). Group decision and procedural justice. In M. Fishbein (Ed.), *Progress in social psychology* (Vol 1). Hillsdale, NJ: Erlbaum.

Davis, K. E. (1985, February). Near and dear: Friendship and love compared. *Psychology Today*, pp. 22–32.

Davis, J., & Lamberth, J. (1974). Affective arousal and energization properties of positive and negative stimuli. *Journal of Experimental Psychology*, *103*, 196–200.

Davis, J., Bray, R., & Holt, R. (1977). The empirical study of decision processes in juries. In J. Tapp & F. Levine (Eds.), *Law, justice and the individual in society: Psychological and legal issues*. New York: Holt, Rinehart & Winston.

Davis, J., Campbell, C., Gallagher, R., & Zukrakov, M. (1971). Disappearance of a humoral satiety factor during food deprivation. *Journal of Comparative and Physiological Psychology*, *75*, 476–482.

Davis, J., Gallagher, R., & Ladove, R. (1967). Food intake controlled by a blood factor. *Science*, *156*, 1247–1248.

Davis, J., Tindale, R., Nagao, D., Hinsz, V., & Robertson, B. (1984). Order effects in multiple decisions by groups: A demonstration with mock juries and trial procedures. *Journal of Personality and Social Psychology*, *47*, 1003–1012.

Davison, G. C., & Neale, J. M. (1978). *Abnormal psychology* (2nd ed.). New York: Wiley.

Dean, L., Pugh, W., & Gunderson, E. (1978). The behavioral effects of crowding. *Environment and Behavior*, *10*, 419–431.

Deaux, K. (1976). *The behavior of women and men*. Belmont, CA: Brooks/Cole.

Deci, E. (1971). Effects of externally mediated rewards on intrinsic motivation. *Journal of Personality and Social Psychology*, *18*, 105–115.

Deci, E. (1972). Intrinsic motivation extrinsic reinforcement and equity. *Journal of Personality and Social Psychology*, *22*, 113–120.

Deese, J. (1959). Influence of inter-item associative strength upon immediate free recall. *Psychological Reports*, *5*, 305–312.

Deese, J. (1965). *The structure of associations in language and thought*. Baltimore, MD: Johns Hopkins University Press.

Deese, J. (1980). Text structure, strategies, and comprehension in learning from textbooks. In J. Robinson (Ed.), *Research in science education: New questions, new directions*. Boulder, CO: BSCS.

Deese, J. (1984). *Thought into speech*. Englewood Cliffs, NJ: Prentice-Hall.

Deiner, E. (1977). Deindividuation: Causes and consequences. *Social Behavior and Personality*, *5*, 143–155.

Deiner, E., Fraser, S. C., Beaman, A. L., & Kelem, R. T. (1976). Effects of deindividuation variables on stealing among Halloween trick-or-treaters. *Journal of Personality and Social Psychology*, *33*, 178–183.

Delgado, J. M. R. (1960). Emotional behavior in animals and humans. *Psychiatric Research Reports*, *12*, 259–266.

Dember, W. (1965). A new look in motivation. *American Scientist*, *53*, 409–427.

Dement, W. C. (1974). *Some must watch while some must sleep*. New York: Norton.

DeMeyer, M. K. (1976). The nature of the neuropsychological disability in autistic children. In E. Shopler & R. J. Reichler (Eds.), *Psychopathology and child development*. New York: Plenum Press, pp. 93–114.

De Mille, A. (1981). *Reprieve: A memoir*. Garden City, NY: Doubleday Co.

Denney, N. W. (1974). Classification abilities in the elderly. *Journal of Gerontology*, *29*, 309–314.

Dennis, W. (1940). Does culture appreciably affect patterns of infant behavior? *Journal of Social Psychology*, *12*, 305–317.

Dennis, W. (1973). *Children of the creche*. Englewood Cliffs, NJ: Prentice-Hall.

Denny, D., & Sullivan, B. (1976). Desensitization and modeling treatments of spider fear using two types of scenes. *Journal of Consulting and Clinical Psychology*, *44*, 573–579.

Depue, R. A., & Evans, R. (1976). The psychobiology of depressive disorders. In B. H. Maher (Ed.), *Progress in experimental personality research* (Vol. 8). New York: Academic Press.

Der-Karabetran, A., & Smith, A. (1977). Sex-role stereotyping in the United States: Is it changing? *Sex Roles*, *3*, 193–198.

Desor, T. (1972). Toward a psychological theory of crowding. *Journal of Personality and Social Psychology*, *21*, 79–83.

Deutsch, J. A. (1983). *The physiological basis of memory*. New York: Academic Press.

De Vries, H. A. (1970). Physiological effects of an exercise training regimen upon men aged 52 to 88. *Journal of Gerontology*, *25*, 325–336.

De Vries, H. A. (1975). Physiology of exercise and aging. In D. S. Woodruff & J. E. Birren (Eds.), *Aging: Scientific perspectives and social issues*. New York: Van Nostrand.

Diaconis, P. (1978). Statistical problems in ESP research. *Science*, *201*, 131–136.

Dies, R., & Greenburg, B. (1976). Effects of physical contact in an encounter group context. *Journal of Consulting and Clinical Psychology*, *44*, 400–405.

Dietz, J. (1985, February 10). Electroshock therapy is making a comeback. *Boston Globe*. (Citing research from National Institute of Mental Health).

DiMento, J. (1981). Making usable information on environmental stressors: Opportunities for the research and policy communities. *Journal of Social Issues*, *37*, 172–205.

Dittes, J., & Kelley, H. H. (1956). Effects on different conditions of acceptance upon conformity to group norms. *Journal of Abnormal and Social Psychology*, *53*, 100–107.

Dobelle, W. H. (1977). Current status of research on providing sight to the blind by electrical stimulation of the brain. *Journal of Visual Impairment and Blindness*, *71*, 290–297.

Dollard, J., Doob, L., Miller, N., Mowrer, O., & Sears, R. (1939). *Frustration and aggression*. New Haven, CT: Yale University Press.

Donnerstein, E., & Wilson, D. W. (1976). Effects of noise and perceived control on ongoing and subsequent aggressive behavior. *Journal of Personality and Social Psychology*, *34* 774–781.

Dorsey, M. F., Iwata, B. A., Ony, P., & McSween, T. (1980). Treatment of self-injurious behavior using a water mist: Initial response suppression and generalization. *Journal of Applied Behavior Analysis*, *13*, 343–353.

Dosey, M. A., & Meisels, M. (1969). Personal space and self-protection. *Journal of Personality and Social Psychology*, *11*, 93–97.

Doty, R. L. (1975). Changes in the intensity and pleasantness of human vaginal odors during the menstrual cycle. *Science*, *190*, 1316–1318.

Draik, F. I. M., & Lockhart, R. S. (1972). Levels of processing: A framework for memory research. *Journal of Verbal Learning and Verbal Behavior*, *11*, 671–684.

Drug Abuse Council, (1980). *The facts about "drug abuse."* New York: The Free Press.

DuBris, A. J. (1982). *Contemporary applied management*. Plano, TX: Business Publications.

Dunham, H. W. (1965). *Community and schizophrenia: An epidemiological analysis*. Detroit: Wayne State University Press.

Dunke, K. (1945). On problem solving. *Psychological Monographs*, *58*, 5 (Whole NO. 270).

Dunphy, D. C. (1963). The social structure of urban adolescent peer groups. *Sociometry*, *26*, 230–246.

Durlak, J. (1979). Comparative effectiveness of paraprofessional and professional helpers. *Psychological Bulletin*, *86*, 80–92.

Dustin, R., & George, R. (1977). *Action counseling for behavior change* (2nd ed.). Cranston, RI: Carroll Press.

Dutton, D. G., & Aron, A. P. (1974). Some evidence for heightened sexual attraction under conditions of high anxiety. *Journal of Personality and Social Psychology*, *30*, 510–517.

Duval, S., & Hensley, V. (1976). Extentions of objective self-awareness theory: The focus of attention causal attribution hypothesis. In J. H. Harvey, W. J. Ickes, & R. F. Kidd (Eds.), *New directions in attribution research* (Vol. 1). Hillsdale, NJ: Erlbaum.

Duval, S., & Wicklund, R. A. (1972). *A theory of objective self-awareness*. New York: Academic Press.

Eagly, A., Wood, W., & Fishbaugh, L. (1981). Sex differences in conformity: Surveillance by the group as a determinant of male conformity. *Journal of Personality and Social Psychology*, *40*, 384–394.

Ebbinghaus, H. (1885). *Memory: A contribution to experimental psychology* (H. A. Ruger & C. E. Bussenius, trans.). New York: Teachers College.

Ebenholtz, S. M. (1981). Hysteresis effects in the vergence control system: Perceptual implications. In D. F. Fisher, R. A. Monty, & J. W. Senders (Eds.), *Eye movements: Cognition and visual perception*. Hillsdale, NJ: Erlbaum.

Ebbenholtz, S. M., & Shebilske, W. L. (1975). The doll reflex: Ocular counterrolling with head-body tilt in median plane. *Vision Research*, *15*, 713–717.

Eccles, J. C. (1973). *The understanding of the brain*. New York: McGraw-Hill.

Eccles, J. C. (1983). Attributional processes as mediators of sex differences in achievement. *Journal of Educational Equality and Leadership*, *3*, 19–27.

Edney, J. J. (1975). Territoriality and control: A field experiment. *Journal of Personality and Social Psychology*, *31*, 1108–1115.

Efran, M. G. (1974). The effect of physical appearance on the judgement of guilt, interpersonal attraction, and severity of recommended punishment in a simulated jury task. *Journal of Research in Personality*, *8*, 45–54.

Ehrlich, P. (1968). *The population bomb*. New York: Ballantine Books.

Eibl-Eibesfeldt, I. (1970). *Ethology: The biology of behavior* (E. Klinghammer, trans.). New York: Holt, Rinehart & Winston.

Eisdorfer, C. (1968). Arousal and performance: Experiments in verbal learning and a tentative theory. In G. A. Talland (Ed.), *Human aging and behavior*. New York: Academic Press.

Ekman, P., & Friesen, W. V. (1971). Constants across cultures in the face and emotion. *Journal of Personality and Social Psychology*, *17*, 124–129.

Ekman, P., Friesen, W., & Ancoli, S. (1980). Facial signs of emotional experience. *Journal of Personality and Social Psychology*, *17*, 1125–1134.

Ekman, P., Sorenson, E. R., & Friesen, W. V. (1969). Pancultural elements in facial displays of emotion. *Science*, *164*, 86–88.

Elkind, D. (1979). Growing up faster. *Psychology Today*, 38–45, February.

Ellis, A. (1962). *Reason and emotion in psychotherapy*. New York: Lyle Stuart.

Ellis, A., & Grieger, R. (1977). *RET: Handbook of rational-emotive therapy*. New York: Springer.

Ellis, H. (1902). Mescal: A study of a divine plant. *Popular Science Monthly*, *41*, 52–71.

Ellsworth, P., & Tourangeau, R. (1981). Our failure to disconfirm what nobody ever said. *Journal of Personality and Social Psychology*, *40*, 363–369.

Engen, T. (1980, May). Why the aroma lingers on. *Psychology Today*, p. 138.

Epstein, N., & Jackson, E. (1978). An outcome study of short-term communication training with married couples. *Journal of Consulting and Clinical Psychology*, *46*, 207–212.

Epstein, N., & Vlok, L. (1981). Research on the results of psychotherapy: A summary of evidence. *American Journal of Psychiatry*, *138*, 1027–1035.

Epstein, S. (1979). The stability of behavior: I. On predicting most people much of the time. *Journal of Personality and Social Psychology*, *37*, 1097–1126.

Epstein, S. (1983). The stability of confusion: A reply to Mischel and Peake. *Psychological Review*, *90*, 179–184.

Epstein, W. (1973). The process of "taking into account" in visual perception. *Perception*, *2*, 267–285.

...ein, Y. (1981). Crowding, stress and human behavior. *Journal of Social Issues*, *37*, 126–145.

Epstein, Y., & Karlin, R. (1975). Effects of acute experimental crowding. *Journal of Applied Social Psychology*, *5*, 34–53.

Erikson, E. H. (1959). Identity and the life cycle: Selected papers. *Psychological Issues*, *1*, 50–100.

Erikson, E. H. (1963). *Childhood and society*. New York: Norton.

Erickson, M. H. (1980). The hypnotic induction of hallucinatory color vision followed by pseudonegative after-images. In E. L. Rossi (Ed.), *The nature of hypnosis and suggestion*. New York: Irvington Publishers.

Erlenmeyer-Kimling, L., & Jarvik, L. F. (1963). Genetics and intelligence: A review. *Science*, *142*, 1477–1479.

Eron, L. (1980). Presumption for reduction of aggression. *American Psychologist*, *35*, 244–252.

Eron, L. (1982). Parent-child interaction, television violence, and aggression of children. *American Psychologist*, *37*, 197–211.

Estes, T. H., & Shebilske, W. L. (1980). Comprehension: Of what the reader sees of what the author says. In M. L. Kamil & S. J. Moe (Eds.), *Twenty-ninth yearbook of the national reading conference*, pp. 99–104.

Estes, T. H., & Vaughan, J. L., Jr. (1985). *Reading and learning in the content classroom: Diagnosis and instructional strategies* (3rd ed.). Boston: Allyn and Bacon.

Evans, G. W. (1979). Behavioral and physiological consequences of crowding in humans. *Journal of Applied Social Psychology*, *9*, 27–46.

Evans, G. W., & Howard, R. B. (1973). Personal space. *Psychological Bulletin*, *80*, 334–344.

Evans, G. W., & Jacobs, S. (1981). Air pollution and human behavior. *Journal of Social Issues*, 95–125.

Exner, J. (1974). *The Rorschach: A comprehensive system*. New York: John Wiley.

Eysenck, H. J. (1952). The effects of psychotherapy: An evaluation. *Journal of Consulting Psychology*, *16*, 319–324.

Eysenck, H. J. (1971). *The I. Q. argument: Race, intelligence, and education*. La Salle, IL: Open Court Publishing Company.

Eysenck, H. J. (1979). The conditioning model of neurosis. *Communications in Behavioral Biology*, *2*, 155–199.

Eysenck, H. J. (1981). *A model for personality*. New York: Springer.

Fairborn, C., & Cooper, P. (1982). Self-induced vomiting and bulimia nervosa: An undetected problem. *British Medical Journal*, *284*, 1153–1155.

Fairweather, G., Sanders, D., Maynard, H., Cresler, D., & Bleck, D. (1969). *Community life for the mentally ill: An alternative to institutional care*. Chicago: Aldine.

Fantz, R. L. (1963). Patterns of vision in newborn infants. *Science*, *140*, 296–297.

Farber, S. (1981). *Identical twins reared apart: A reanalysis*. New York: Basic Books.

Farina, A., Ghlia, D., Boudreau, L. A., Allen, J. G., & Sherman, M. (1971). Mental illness and the impact of believing others know about it. *Journal of Abnormal Psychology*, *77*, 1–5.

Faris, R. E. L., & Dunham, H. W. (1939). *Mental disorders in urban areas: An ecological study of schizophrenia and other psychoses*. Chicago: University of Chicago Press.

Farran, D. C., & Ramey, C. T. (1977). Infant day care and attachment behaviors toward mothers and teachers. *Child Development*, *48*, 1112–1116.

Fazio, R., & Zanna, M. (1981). Direct experience and attitude-behavior consistency. In L. Berkowitz, *Advances in Experimental Social Psychology* (Vol. 14). New York: Academic Press.

Feagin, J. R. (1984). *Racial and ethnic relations* (2nd ed.). Englewood Cliffs, NJ: Prentice-Hall.

Feather, N. T. (1975). Reactions to male and female success and failure in sex-linked occupations: Impressions of personality, causal attributions, and perceived likelihood of different consequences. *Journal of Personality and Social Psychology*, *31*, 20–31.

Feldman, M. W., & Lewontin, R. C. (1975). The heritability hang-up. *Science*, *190*, 1163–1168.

Fenigstein, A. (1984). Self-consciousness and the overperception of self as a target. *Journal of Personality and Social Psychology*, *47*, 860–870.

Fenigstein, A., Scherer, M., & Buss, A. H. (1975). Public and private self-consciousness: Assessment and theory. *Journal of Consulting and Clinical Psychology*, *43*, 522–524.

Ferguson, M. (1973). *The brain revolution: The frontiers of mind research*. New York: Taplinger.

Ferrell, R. (1980). *Off the record*. New York: Harper & Row.

Ferrero, G. (1911). *Criminal man according to the classification of Cesare Lombroso*. New York: Putnam's.

Festinger, L. (1954). A theory of social comparison processes. *Human Relations*, *7*, 117–140.

Festinger, L. (1957). *A theory of cognitive dissonance*. Stanford, CA: Stanford University Press.

Festinger, L., & Carlsmith, M. (1959). Cognitive consequences of forced compliance. *Journal of Abnormal and Social Psychology*, *58*, 203–210.

Festinger, L., Schachter, S., & Back, K. (1950). *Social pressures in informal groups: A study of a housing community*. Stanford: CA: Stanford University Press.

Fiedler, F. E. (1971). *Leadership*. New York: General Learning Press.

Fiedler, F. E. (1973). The trouble with leadership training is that it doesn't train leaders. *Psychology Today*, *6*, 23–30.

Fiedler, F. E. (1978). The contingency model and the dynamics of the leadership process. In L. Berkowitz (Ed.), *Advances in experimental social psychology* (Vol. 2). New York: Academic Press.

Fink, M. (1978). Myths of "shock therapy" *American Journal of Psychiatry*, *134*, 991–996.

Fishbein, M. (1974). Attitudes towards objects as predictions of single and multiple behavioral criteria. *Psychological Review*, *81*, 59–74.

Fishbein, M., & Azjen, I. (1975). *Belief, attitude, intention, and behavior: An introduction to theory and research*. Reading, MA: Addison-Wesley.

Fisher, D. F., & Peters, C. W. (1981). *Comprehension and the competent reader*. New York: Praeger Publishers.

Fisher, J. D., Bell, P., & Baum, A. (1984). *Environmental psychology* (2nd ed.). New York: Holt, Rinehart and Winston.

Fisher, J., & Byrne, D. (1975). Too close for comfort: Sex differences in response to invasions of personal space. *Journal of Personality and Social Psychology*, *32*, 15–21.

Fisher, J., Nadler, A., & Whitcher, S. (1980). Recipient reactions to aid: A conceptual review and a new theoretical framework. Unpublished manuscript. University of Connecticut, Storrs.

Fiske, S., & Taylor, S. (1984). *Social cognition*. Reading, MA: Addison-Wesley.

Fitzsimons, J. (1973). Some historical perspectives in the physiology of thirst. In A. Epstein et al. (Eds.), *The neuropsychology of thirst*. Washington, DC: V. H. Winston.

Flowers, M. L. (1977). A lab test of some implications of Janis' groupthink hypothesis. *Journal of Personality and Social Psychology*, *35*, 888–897.

Forsyth, D. R. (1983). *An introduction to group dynamics*. Montery, CA: Brooks/Cole.

Fox, G. L. (1979, May–June). The family's influence on adolescent sexual behavior. *Children Today*, pp. 21–25.

Fox, W. F. (1967). Human performance in the cold. *Human Factors*, *9*, 203–220.

Fozard, J. L., Wolf, E., Bell, B., McFarland, R. A., & Podolsky, S. (1977). Visual perception and communication. In J. E. Birren & K. W. Schaie (Eds.), *Handbook of the psychology of aging*. New York: Van Nostrand.

Frankel, A. J. (1984). *Four therapies integrated: A behavioral analysis of Gestalt, T. A., and ego psychology*. Englewood Cliffs, NJ: Prentice-Hall.

Frankenburg, W. K., & Dodds, J. B. (1967). The Denver developmental screening test. *Journal of Pediatrics*, *71*, 181–191.

Frankin, R. (1982). *Human motivation*. Monterey, CA: Brooks/Cole.

Fraser, S., Gouge, C., & Billig, M. (1971). Risky shifts, cautious shifts and group polarization. *European Journal of Social Psychology*, *1*, 7–29.

Frederick, C. J. (1978). Current trends in suicidal behavior in the United States. *American Journal of Psychotherapy*, *32*(2), 172–200.

Frederiksen, C. H. (1975). Effects of context-induced processing operations on semantic information acquired from discourse. *Cognitive Psychology*, *1*, 139–166.

Frederiksen, C. H. (1975). Representing logical and semantic structures of knowledge acquired from discourse. *Cognitive Psychology*, *1*, 371–458.

Freedman, J., & Fraser, S. (1966). Compliance without pressure: The foot-in-the-door technique. *Journal of Personality and Social Psychology*, *4*, 195–202.

Freedman, J., Heshka, S., & Levy, A. (1975). Population density and pathology: Is there a relationship? *Journal of Experimental Social Psychology*, *11*, 539–552.

Freedman, J., Klevansky, S., & Ehrlich, P. (1971). The effect of crowding on human task performance. *Journal of Applied Social Psychology*, *1*, 7–25.

Freedman, J. L., & Doob, A. N. (1968). *Deviancy*. New York: Academic Press.

French, E. G. (1958). Effects of interaction of motivation and feedback on task performance. In J. W. Atkinson (Ed.), *Motives in fantasy, action, and society*. New York: Van Nostrand, pp. 400–408.

Freud, S. (1900). *The interpretation of dreams*,

Vols. IV, V. London: Hogarth Press (standard edition, 1953).

Freud, S. (1933). *New introductory lectures on psycho-analysis.* New York: Norton.

Freud, S. (1955). *Beyond the pleasure principle.* The standard edition (Vol. 18). London: Hogarth Press. (Originally published in 1920.)

Frey, D., Irle, M., & Hochgurtel, G. (1979). Performance of an unpleasant task: Effects of over- vs. under-payment on perception of adequacy of rewards and task attractiveness. *Journal of Experimental Social Psychology, 15,* 275–284.

Friedman, L. (1981). How affiliation affects stress in fear and anxiety situations. *Journal of Personality and Social Psychology, 40,* 1102–1117.

Friedman, M., & Rosenman, R. H. (1974). *Type A behavior and your heart.* New York: Knopf.

Frieze, I., Parsons, J. E., Johnson, P. B., Ruble, D. N., & Zellman, G. L. (1978). *Women and sex roles: A social psychological perspective.* New York: Norton.

Fromm, E. (1955). *Man for himself.* New York: Holt, Rinehart & Winston.

Fromm, E. (1956). *The art of loving.* New York: Harper & Row.

Gaddis, T. E. (1955). *Birdman of Alcatraz.* New York: Random House.

Galanter, E. (1962). Contemporary psychophysics. In R. Brown et al. (Eds.), *New directions in psychology.* New York: Holt, Rinehart & Winston, pp. 89–156.

Galizio, M., & Hendrick, C. (1972). Effect of musical accompaniment on attitude: The guitar as a prop for persuasion. *Journal of Applied Social Psychology, 2,* 350–359.

Galton, F. (1879). Psychometric experiments. *Brain, 2,* 149–162.

Ganelley, R., & Blaney, P. (1984). Hardiness and social support as moderators of the effects of life stress. *Journal of Personality and Social Psychology, 47,* 156–163.

Garcia, J., & Koelling, R. A. (1966). Relation of cues to consequences in avoidance learning. *Psychonomic Science, 4,* 123–124.

Gardner, B. T., & Gardner, R. A. (1975). Evidence for sentence constituents in the early utterances of child and chimpanzee. *Journal of Experimental Psychology: General, 104,* 244–267.

Gardner, R. A., & Gardner, B. T. (1969). Teaching sign language to a chimpanzee. *Science, 165,* 664–672.

Garfield, S. L., & Bergin, A. E. (Eds.). (1978). *Handbook of psychotherapy and behavior change* (2nd ed.). New York: Wiley.

Garner, W. (1970). Good patterns have few alternatives. *American Scientist, 58,* 34–42.

Gatchel, R. (1980). Perceived control: A review and evaluation of therapeutic implications. In A. Baum & J. Singer (Eds.), *Advances in environmental psychology.* Hillsdale, NJ: Erlbaum.

Gatchel, R., & Baum, A. (1983). *Introduction to health psychology.* Reading, MA: Addison-Wesley.

Gebhard, A. (1972). Incidence of overt homosexuality in the United States and Western Europe. In J. M. Livingood (Ed.), *National Institute of Mental Health task force on homosexuality: Final report and background papers.* Rockville, MD: National Institute of Mental Health.

Geen, R. G., Beatty, W., & Arkin, R. (1984).

Human motivation: Physiological, behavioral, and social approaches. Boston: Allyn and Bacon.

Geen, R. G., & Quanty, M. (1977). The catharsis of aggression: An evaluation of a hypothesis. In L. Berkowitz (Ed.), *Advances in experimental social psychology* (Vol. 10). New York: Academic Press.

Geer, J., Heiman, J., & Leittenberg, H. (1984). *Human sexuality.* Englewood Cliffs, NJ: Prentice-Hall.

Geldard, F. A. (1972). *The human senses.* New York: Wiley.

Gelenberg, A. J. (1979). The rational use of psychotropic drugs: Prescribing antidepressants. *Drug Therapy, 9,* 95–112.

Geller, S. H., Endler, N. S., & Wiesenthal, D. L. (1973). Conformity as a function of task generalization and relative competence. *European Journal of Social Psychology, 3,* 53–62.

George, R., & Christiani, T. (1981). *Theory, methods, and process of counseling and psychology.* Englewood Cliffs, NJ: Prentice-Hall.

Gerard, H. B., Wilhelmy, R. A., & Connelly, E. S. (1968). Conformity and group size. *Journal of Personality and Social Psychology, 8,* 79–82.

Gerbner, G., & Gross, L. (1976). The scary world of TV's heavy viewer. *Psychology Today, 89,* 41–45.

Gergen, A. E. (1971). The evaluation of therapeutic outcomes. In A. E. Bergin & S. L. Garfield (Eds.), *Handbook of psychotherapy and behavior change: An empirical analysis.* New York: Wiley.

Gergen, K. (1971). *The concept of self.* New York: Holt, Rinehart, & Winston.

Gergen, K., & Gergen, M. (1971). International assistance from a psychological perspective. *Yearbook of world affairs* (Vol. 25). London: Institute of World Affairs.

Geschwind, N. (1979). Specializations of the human brain. *Scientific American, 241,* 180–199.

Gewirtz, J. L. (1965). The course of infant smiling in four child-rearing environments in Israel. In B. M. Foss (Ed.), *Determinants of infant behavior* (Vol. 3). London: Methuen.

Gewirtz, J. L., & Baer, D. M. (1958). The effect of brief social deprivation on behaviors for a social reinforcer. *Journal of Abnormal Social Psychology,* 165–172.

Gibbs, M. (1982). Identification and classification of child psychopathology. In J. Lachenmeger & M. Gibbs (Eds.), *Psychopathology in childhood.* New York: Gardner Press.

Gibson, J. J. (1957). Optical motions and transformation as stimuli for visual perception. *Psychological Review, 64,* 288–295.

Gibson, J. J. (1979). *The ecological approach to visual perception.* Boston: Houghton Mifflin.

Gilbert, W., & Villa-Komaroff, L. (1980). Useful proteins from recombinant bacteria. *Scientific American, 242,* 74–94.

Gilchrist, A. (1975). Perceived achromatic color as a function of ratios within phenomenal planes. Ph.D. thesis, Rutgers University.

Gillam, B. (1980). Geometrical illusions. *Scientific American, 242,* 102–111.

Gilligan, J. (1976). Beyond morality: Psychoanalytic reflections on shame, guilt, and love. In T. Pickona (Ed.), *Moral development*

and behavior theory, research, and social issues. New York: Holt, Rinehart and Winston.

Gilliland, B., James, R., Roberts, G., & Bowman, J. (1984). *Theories and strategies in counseling and psychotherapy.* Englewood Cliffs, NJ: Prentice-Hall.

Gillin, J. D., Kaplan, J., Stillman, R., & Wyatt, R. J. (1976). The psychedelic model of schizophrenia: The case of N,N-dimethyltryptamine. *American Journal of Psychiatry, 133,* 203–208.

Ginsberg, H., Pollman, V., Wausm, M., & Hope, M. (1977). Variation of aggressive interaction among male elementary school children as a function of changes in social density. *Environmental Psychology and Nonverbal Behavior, 2,* 67–75.

Ginter, G., & Lindskold, S. (1975). Rate of participation and expertise as factors influencing leader choice. *Journal of Personality and Social Psychology, 32,* 1085–1089.

Glass, A. L. (1984). Effect of memory set in reaction time. In J. L. Anderson & S. M. Kosslyn (Eds.), *Tutorials in reading and memory.* San Francisco, Freeman.

Glass, D. C. (1977). *Behavior patterns, stress, and coronary disease.* Hillsdale, NJ: Erlbaum.

Glass, D. C., & Singer, J. (1972). *Urban stress: Experiments on noise and social stressors.* New York: Academic Press.

Glass, D. C., Singer, J. E., & Pennebaker, J. (1977). Behavioral and physiological effects of uncontrollable environmental events. In D. Stokols (Ed.), *Perspectives on Environment and Behavior, 5,* 131–149.

Glass, D. C., Snyder, M. L., & Hollis, J. F. (1974). Time urgency and the type A coronary-prone behavior pattern. *Journal of Applied Social Psychology, 4,* 125–140.

Glass, G., & Kliegl, R. (1983). An apology for research integration in the study of psychotherapy. *Journal of Counseling and Clinical Psychology, 51,* 28–41.

Glass, J. C., & Trent, C. (1981, March/April). Changing students' attitudes toward older persons. *The Social Studies,* pp. 72–76.

Glass, L., Kirsch, M., & Parris, F. (1977). Psychiatric disturbance associated with Erhard Seminars Training: I. A report of cases. *American Journal of Psychiatry, 134,* 245–247.

Glassman, E. (1974). Macromolecules and behavior: A commentary. In F. O. Schmitt & F. G. Worden (Eds.), *The neurosciences: Third study program.* Cambridge, MA: MIT Press.

Glenn, M. D. (1975). Psychological well-being in the post-parental stage: Some evidence from national surveys. *Journal of Marriage and the Family, 32,* 105–110.

Glick, I. O., Weiss, R. S., & Parkes, C. M. (1974). *The first year of bereavement.* New York: Wiley.

Goethels, G. R. (1984, August). *Social comparison theory: Psychology from the lost found.* Presented at American Psychology Association, Toronto.

Goethals, G. R., & Darley, J. M. (1977). Social comparison theory: An attributional approach. In J. M. Suls & R. L. Miller (Eds.), *Social comparison processes: Theoretical and empirical perspectives.* Washington, DC: Hemisphere/Halsted.

Goethals, G. R., & Nelson, R. (1973). Similarity in the influence process: The belief-value distinction. *Journal of Personality and Social Psychology, 25,* 117–122.

Goethals, G. R., & Worchel, S. (1981). *Adjustment and human relations*. New York: Knopf.

Goethals, G., & Zanna, M. (1979). The role of social comparison in choice shifts. *Journal of Personality and Social Psychology*, *37*, 1469–1476.

Gold, J., Ryckman, R., & Mosky, N. (1984). Romantic mood induction and attraction to a dissimilar other: Is love blind? *Personality and Social Psychology Bulletin*, *10*, 358–368.

Gold, P. E., & McGaugh, J. L. (1975). A single-trace, two-process view of memory storage processes. In P. Deutsch & J. A. Deutsch (Eds.), *Short-term memory*. New York: Academic Press, pp. 355–378.

Gold, P. E., & McGaugh, J. L. (1977). Hormones and memory. In L. H. Miller, C. A. Sandman, & A. J. Kastin (Eds.), *Neuropeptide influences on the brain and behavior*. New York: Raven, pp. 127–143.

Goldband, S. (1980). Stimulus specificity of physiological response to stress and the Type A coronary-prone behavior pattern. *Journal of Personality and Social Psychology*, *39*, 670–679.

Goldberg, P. A. (1968). Are women prejudiced against women? *Trans-action*, *5*, 28–30.

Goldfried, M. R., & Davison, G. C. (1976). *Clinical behavior therapy*. New York: Holt, Rinehart & Winston.

Goldman, J., & Olczak, P. (1976). Psychosocial maturity and interpersonal attraction. *Journal of Research in Personality*, *10*, 146–154.

Goldman, R., Jaffa, M., & Schachter, S. (1968). Yom Kippur, Air France, dormitory food, and the eating behavior of obese and normal persons. *Journal of Personality and Social Psychology*, *10*, 117–123.

Goldstein, M. J. (1959). The relationship between coping and avoiding behavior and response to fear-arousing propaganda. *Journal of Abnormal and Social Psychology*, *58*, 247–252.

Golimbiewski, R., & Blumburg, A. (1973). *Sensitivity training and the laboratory approach*. Itasca, IL: Peacock Press.

Gomez, J., & Dally, P. (1980). Psychometric ratings in assessment of progress in anorexia nervosa. *British Journal of Psychiatry*, *136*, 290–296.

Goodwin, D. W. Alcoholism and heredity. *Archives of General Psychiatry*, *36*, 57–61.

Gordon, S., & Scales, P. (1977). The myth of the normal sexual outlet. *Journal of Pediatric Psychology*, *2*, 101–103.

Gorenstein, E. (1982). Frontal lobe functions in psychopaths. *Journal of Abnormal Psychology*, *91*, 368–379.

Gottesman, I. I., & Shields, J. (1972). *Schizophrenia and genetics: A twin study vantage point*. New York: Academic Press.

Gottlieb, B. H. (1983). Social support as a focus for integrative research in psychology. *American Psychologist*, *38*, 278–288.

Graen, G., Alvares, K., Orris, J., & Martella, J. (1970). Contingency model of leadership effectiveness: Antecedent and evidential results. *Psychology Bulletin*, *74*, 284–296.

Graham, K. G., & Robinson, H. A. (1984). Study skills handbook: A guide for all teachers. *ERIC Clearinghouse on Reading and Communication Skills*, Urbana, IL: International Reading Association.

Graham, S. (1974). The sociological approach to epidemiology. *American Journal of Public Health*, *64*, 1046–1049.

Gray, J. (1971). *The psychology of fear and stress*. New York: McGraw-Hill.

Green, D., Miller, N., & Gerard, V. (1975). Personality traits and adjustment. In H. Gerard & N. Miller (Eds.), *School desegregation: A long-range study*. New York: Plenum Press.

Greenberg, D. J., & O'Donnell, W. J. (1972). Infancy and the optional level of stimulation. *Child Development*, *43*, 639–645.

Greenberg, M. A. (1980). A theory of indebtedness. In K. Gergen, M. Greenberg, & R. Willis (Eds.), *Social exchange: Advances in theory and research*. New York: Plenum.

Greenough, W. T. (1984). Structural correlates of information storage in the mammalian brain: A review and hypothesis. *Trends in Neurosciences*, *7*, 229–233.

Gregg, C., Clifton, R. K., & Haith, M. M. (1976). A possible explanation for the frequent failure to find cardiac orienting in the newborn infant. *Developmental Psychology*, *12*, 75–76.

Griffith, W. (1970). Environmental effects on interpersonal affective behavior: Ambient effective temperature and attraction. *Journal of Personality and Social Psychology*, *15*, 240–244.

Griffith, W., & Veitch, R. (1971). Hot and crowded: Influence of population density and temperature on interpersonal affective behavior. *Journal of Personality and Social Psychology*, *17*, 92–98.

Grim, R., Kohlberg, L., & White, S. (1968). Some relationships between conscience and attentional processes. *Journal of Personality and Social Psychology*, *8*, 239–253.

Grimes, J. F. (1972). *The thread of discourse*. The Hague: Mouton.

Grinker, J. (1982). Physiological and behavioral basis of human obesity. In D. Pfaff (Ed.), *The physiological mechanisms of motivation*. New York: Springer-Verlag.

Gruder, C. L., Cook, T., Hennigan, K., Flay, B., Allesi, C., & Halamaj, J. (1978). Empirical tests of the absolute sleeper effect predicted from the discounting cue hypothesis. *Journal of Personality and Social Psychology*, *36*, 1061–1074.

Guenther, R. (1982, August 4). Ways are found to minimize pollutants in airtight houses. *Wall Street Journal*, p. 25.

Guerin, P., & Sherman, C. (1982). Review of "Gestalt-system family therapy." *American Journal of Family Therapy*, *10*, 86–87.

Guilford, J. P. (1967). *The nature of human intelligence*. New York: McGraw-Hill.

Guilleminault, C., & Dement, W. C. (1977). Amnesia and disorders of excessive daytime sleepiness. In R. R. Drucher-Colin & J. L. McGaugh (Eds.), *Neurobiology of sleep and memory*. New York: Academic Press.

Gurman, A. S. (1977). Therapist and patient factors influencing the patient's perception of facilitative therapeutic conditions. *Psychiatry*, *40*, 218–231.

Gustavson, C. R., Garcia, J., Hankins, W. G., & Rusiniak, K. W. (1974). Coyote predation control by aversive conditioning. *Science*, *184*, 581–583.

Gynther, M., & Green, S. (1980). Accuracy may make a difference, but does difference make for accuracy? A response to Prichard and Rosenblatt. *Journal of Consulting and Clinical Psychology*, *48*, 268–272.

Haber, R. N. (1969). Eidetic images. *Scientific American*, *220*, 36–55.

Hagestad, G. O. (1980). Role change and socialization in adulthood: The transition to the empty nest. Unpublished manuscript, The Pennsylvania State University.

Haith, M. M., & Campos, J. J. (1977). Human infancy. *Annual Review of Psychology*, *28*, 251–293.

Haley, J. (1980). *Leaving home: The therapy of disturbed young people*. New York: McGraw-Hill.

Halford, G. S., & Boyle, F. M. (1985). Do young children understand conservation of number? *Child Development*, *56*, 165–176.

Hall, C. (1966). *The meaning of dreams*. New York: McGraw-Hill.

Hall, C., & Lindzey, G. (1978). *Theories of personality* (3rd ed.). New York: Wiley.

Hall, E. T. (1959). *The silent language*. New York: Fawcett.

Hall, E. T. (1966). *The hidden dimension*. New York: Doubleday.

Hall, J. A. (1982). The use of dreams and dream interpretation. In M. Stein (Ed.), *Jungian analysis*. LaSalle, IL: Open Court.

Hall, J. F. (1983). Recall versus recognition: A methodological note. *Journal of Experimental Psychology: Learning, Memory, and Cognition*, *9*, 346–349.

Halliday, M. A. K. (1973). *Explorations in the functions of language*. London: Edward Arnold.

Hammen, C. L., & Peters, S. D. (1977). Differential responses to male and female depressive reactions. *Journal of Consulting and Clinical Psychology*, *45*, 994–1001.

Hanes, B., Prawat, R. S., & Grissom, S. (1979). Sex-role perceptions during adolescence. *Journal of Educational Psychology*, *71*, 850–855.

Hansel, C. E. M. (1980). *ESP and parapsychology: A critical re-evaluation*. New York: Prometheus Books.

Harc, R. (1978). Electrodermal and cardiovascular correlates of sociopathy. In R. Harc & D. Schalling (Eds.), *Psychopathic behavior: Approaches to research*. New York: Wiley.

Harkins, S., & Petty, R. E. (1981). Effects of source magnification of cognitive effort in attitudes: An information-processing view. *Journal of Personality and Social Psychology*, *40*, 401–413.

Harlow, H. F. (1949). The formation of learning sets. *Psychological Review*, *56*, 51–65.

Harlow, H. F. (1971). *Learning to love*. San Francisco: Albion.

Harlow, H. F., Harlow, M. K., & Meyer, D. R. (1950). Learning motivated by a manipulation drive. *Journal of Experimental Psychology*, *40*, 228–234.

Harlow, H. F., & Suomi, S. J. (1970). Nature of love simplified. *American Psychologist*, *25*, 161–168.

Harlow, H. F., & Zimmerman, R. R. (1959). Affectional responses in the infant monkey. *Science*, *130*, 421–432.

Harmon, L. D. (1973, November). The recognition of faces. *Scientific American*, pp. 32–38.

Harriman, A. (1955). The effect of preoperative preference for sugar over salt upon compensatory salt selection by adrenalectomized rats. *Journal of Nutrition*, 57, 271–276.

Harris, D. B. (1957). Problems in formulating a scientific concept of development. In D. B. Harris (Ed.), *The concept of development*. Minneapolis: University of Minnesota Press.

Hart, R. (1970). The concept of APS: Air Pollution Syndrome(s). *Journal of South Carolina Medical Association*, 66, 71–73.

Hartshorne, H., & May, M. A. (1928). *Studies in the nature of character* (Vol. 1). *Studies in deceit*. New York: Macmillan.

Hasdorf, A. H., Osgood, D. E., & Ono, Y. (1966). The semantics of facial expressions and the prediction of the meanings of stereoscopically fused facial expressions. *Scandinavian Journal of Psychology*, 7, 179–188.

Hashim, S. A., & Van Itallie, T. B. (1965). Studies in normal and obese subjects with a monitored food dispensary device. *Annals of the New York Academy of Science*, 131, 654–661.

Hatch, O. G. (1982, September). Psychology, society, and politics. *American Psychologist*, pp. 1031–1037.

Hathaway, S. R., & McKinley, J. (1942). A multiphasic personality schedule (Minnesota): III. The measurement of symptomatic depression. *Journal of Psychology*, 14, 73–84.

Hathaway, S. R., & McKinley, J. C. (1943). *MMPI Manual*. New York: Psychological Corporation.

Hay, D. F., Murray, P., Cecire, S., & Nash, A. Social learning of social behavior in early life. *Child Development*, 1985, 56, 43–57.

Hayes, C., & Hayes, K. (1951). *The ape in our house*. New York: Harper & Row.

Hebb, D. O. (1955). Drives and the C. N. S. (conceptual nervous system). *Psychological Review*, 62, 243–254.

Heberlein, T. A., & Black, J. S. (1976). Attitudinal specificity and the prediction of behavior in a field setting. *Journal of Personality and Social Psychology*, 33, 474–479.

Heckel, R. V., & Hiers, J. M. (1977). Social distance and locus of control. *Journal of Clinical Psychology*, 33, 469–471.

Heider, F. (1946). Attitudes and cognitive organization. *Journal of Personality*, 21, 107–112.

Heller, J., Goff, B., & Solomon, S. (1977). Toward an understanding of sounding: The role of physical instruction. *Journal of Personality and Social Psychology*, 35, 183–190.

Heller, K., & Monahan, J. (1977). *Psychology and community change*. Homewood, IL: Dorsey.

Helms, D. B., & Turner, J. S. (1981). *Exploring child behavior*. New York: Holt, Rinehart & Winston.

Hendrick, C., & Hendrick, S. (1983). *Liking, loving and relating*. Monterey, CA: Brooks/Cole.

Henning, M., & Jardin, A. (1976). *The managerial woman*. New York: Doubleday.

Herbert, W. (1983). Remembrance of things partly. *Science News*, 124, 378–381.

Hergenhan, B. (1980). *An introduction to theories of personality*. Englewood Cliffs, NJ: Prentice-Hall.

Heron, W. (1961). Cognitive and physiological effects of perceptual isolation. In P. Solomon et al. (Eds.), *Sensory deprivation*. Cambridge, MA: Harvard University Press.

Herrnstein, R. J. (1973). *IQ in the meritocracy*. Boston: Atlantic Monthly Press.

Herrnstein, R. J. (1979). Acquisition, generalization, and discrimination reversal of a natural concept. *Journal of Experimental Psychology: Animal Behavior Processes*, 5, 116–129.

Herrnstein, R. J. (1984). Objects, categories, and discriminative stimuli. In H. L. Roitblat, T. G. Bever, & H. S. Terrace (Eds.), *Animal cognition*. Hillsdale, NJ: Erlbaum.

Herrnstein, R. J., & DeVilliers, P. A. (1980). Fish as a natural category for people and pigeons. In G. H. Bower (Ed.), *The psychology of learning and motivation* (Vol. 14). New York: Academic Press.

Herzog, D. (1982). Bulimia: The secretive syndrome. *Psychosomatics*, 23, 481–483.

Hess, E. H. (1958). "Imprinting" in animals. *Scientific American*, 286, 81–90.

Hess, E. H. (1965). Attitude and pupil size. *Scientific American*, 212, 46–54.

Hetherington, A., & Ranson, S. (1939). Experimental hypothalamohypapyseal obesity in the rat. *Proceedings for the Society of Experimental Biology and Medicine*, 41, 465–466.

Hetherington, E. M., Cox, M., & Cox, R. (1978). The aftermath of divorce. In J. H. Stevens, Jr. & M. Matthew (Eds.), *Mother-child, father-child relations*. Washington, DC: National Association for the Education of Young Children.

Hiland, D. N., & Dzieszkowski, M. A. (1984). Hypnosis in the investigation of aviation accidents. *Aviation, Space, and Environmental Medicine*, 55, 1136–1142.

Hilgard, E. R. (1965). *Hypnotic susceptibility*. New York: Harcourt, Brace and World, Inc.

Hilgard, E. R. (1967). A quantitative study of pain and its reduction through hypnotic suggestion. *Proceedings of the National Academy of Sciences*, 57, 1581–1586.

Hilgard, E. R. (1967). Individual differences in hypnotizability. In J. E. Gordon (Ed.), *Handbook of clinical and experimental hypnosis*. New York: Macmillan. pp. 391–443.

Hilgard, E. R. (1969). Experimental psychology and hypnosis. In L. Chertok (Ed.), *Psychophysiological mechanisms of hypnosis*. Berlin: Springer-Verlag, 123–138.

Hilgard, E. R. (1969). Pain as a puzzle for psychology and physiology. *American Psychologist*, 24, 103–113.

Hilgard, E. R., & Hilgard, J. R. (1975). *Hypnosis in the relief of pain*. Los Altos, CA: William Kaufman.

Hirai, T. (1978). *Zen and the mind: A scientific approach to Zen practice*. Scranton, PA: Japan Publications, Inc., c/o Harper & Row.

Hiroto, D. S. (1974). Locus of control and learned helplessness. *Journal of Experimental Psychology*, 102, 187–193.

Hirsch, E. D. (1977). *The philosophy of composition*. Chicago: University of Chicago Press.

Hite, S. (1976). *The Hite report*. New York: Macmillan.

Hobson, J. A., & McCarley, R. W. (1977). The brain as a dream state generator: An activation-synthesis hypothesis of the dream process. *American Journal of Psychiatry*, 134, 1335–1348.

Hochberg, J. (1970). Components of literacy: Speculations and exploration research. In H. Levin & J. P. Williams (Eds.), *Basic studies on reading*. New York: Basic Books.

Hochberg, J. E. (1978). *Perception*. Englewood Cliffs, NJ: Prentice-Hall.

Hochreich, D. J., & Rotter, J. B. (1970). Have college students become less trusting? *Journal of Personality and Social Psychology*, 15, 211–214.

Hodgkins, J. (1962). Influence of age on the speed of reaction and movement in females. *Journal of Gerontology*, 17, 385–389.

Hoebel, B. G., & Teitelbaum, P. (1962). Hypothalamic control of feeding and self-stimulation. *Science*, 61, 189–193.

Hoffman, L. W., & Nye, F. I. (1974). *Working mothers*. San Francisco: Jossey-Bass.

Hoffman, M. L. (1979, May/June). Empathy, guilt and social cognition. Paper presented at the Ninth Annual Symposium of the Jean Piaget Society, Philadelphia.

Hoffman, M. L. (1980). Moral development in adolescence. In J. Adelson (Ed.), *Handbook of adolescent psychology*. New York: Wiley.

Hoffman, M. L. (1984). Parent discipline, moral internalization and development of prosocial motivation. In E. Staub et al. (Eds.), *Development and maintenance of prosocial behavior*. New York: Plenum.

Hofling, C. K. (1975). *Textbook of psychiatry for medical practice* (3rd ed.). Philadelphia: Lippincott.

Hofling, C. K., Brotzman, E., Dalrymple, S., Graves, N., & Pierce, C. M. (1966). An experimental study in nurse-physician relationships. *The Journal of Nervous and Mental Disease*, 143(2), 171–180.

Hogan, R., & Schroeder, D. (1981, July). Seven biases in psychology. *Psychology Today*, 15, 8–14.

Hogan, T. P., & Hendrickson, E. (1984). The study habits of adult college students. *Lifelong Learning*, 8, 7–10.

Hokanson, J. E., & Shelters, S. (1961). The effect of overt aggression on physiological arousal level. *Journal of Abnormal and Social Psychology*, 63, 446–448.

Hokanson, J. E., Burgess, M., & Cohen, M. (1963). Effect of displaced aggression on systolic blood pressure. *Journal of Abnormal and Social Psychology*, 67, 214–218.

Holahan, C. J. (1980). Action research in the guilt environment. In R. Price & P. Politser (Eds.), *Evolution and action in the social environment*. New York: Academic Press.

Holahan, C. J. (1982). *Environmental psychology*. New York: Random House.

Holden, C. (1972). Nader on mental health centers: A movement that got bogged down. *Science*, 177, 413–415.

Holden, C. (1975). Lie detectors: PSE gains audience despite critics' doubt. *Science*, 190, 359–362.

Hollander, E. P. (1958). Conformity status and idiosyncrasy credit. *Psychological Review*, 65, 117–127.

Hollander, E. P. (1978). *Leadership dynamics*. New York: Free Press.

Hollander, E. P., & Julian, J. W. (1978). A further look at leader legitimacy, influence, and innovation. In L. Berkowitz (Ed.), *Group process*. New York: Academic Press.

Hollingshead, A. B., & Redlich, F. C. (1958). *Social class and mental illness, a community study*. New York: Wiley.

Holmes, D. S. (1974). Investigations of repression: Differential recall of material experimentally or naturally associated with ego threat. *Psychological Bulletin*, 81, 632–653.

Holmes, D., Frost, R., & Lutz, D. (1981).

Multiple sessions of systolic blood pressure biofeedback: Its effects on ability to control systolic pressure during training, after training, and its effects on pulse rate. *Journal of Research in Personality*, *15*, 30–44.

Holmes, T., & Masuda, M. (1974). Life change and illness susceptibility. In B. Dohrenwend & B. Dohrenwend (Eds.), *Stressful life events: Their nature and effects*. New York: Wiley.

Holmes, T. H., & Rahe, R. H. (1967). The social readjustment rating scale. *Journal of Psychosomatic Research*, *11*, 213–218.

Holt, A. (1931). *Animal drive and the learning process, an essay toward radical empiricism* (Vol. I). New York: Holt, Rinehart & Winston, p. 4.

Holtzman, W. (1975). New developments in Holtzman inkblot techniques. In P. McReynolds (Ed.), *Advances in psychological assessment* (Vol. 3). San Francisco: Jossey-Bass.

Homans, G. (1974). *Social behavior in its elementary forms* (rev. ed.). New York: Harcourt Brace Jovanovich.

Honigfeld, G. (1964). Non-specific factors in treatment. I. Review of placebo reactions and placebo reactors. *Diseases of the Nervous System*, *25*, 145–156.

Hook, E. B. (1973). Behavioral implications of the human XYY genotype. *Science*, *179*, 131–150.

Horn, J. L. (1978). Human ability systems. In P. B. Baltes (Ed.), *Life-span development and behavior* (Vol. 1). New York: Academic Press.

Horn, J. L., & Donaldson, G. (1980). Cognitive development II: Adulthood development of human abilities. In O. G. Brim, Jr. & J. Kagan (Eds.), *Constancy and change in human development: A volume of review essays*. Cambridge, MA: Harvard University Press.

Horn, J. M., Loehlin, J. C., & Willerman, L. (1979). Intellectual resemblance among adoptive and biological relatives: The Texas adoption project. *Behavior Genetics*, *9*, 177–208.

Horner, M. S. (1968). Sex differences in achievement motivation in competitive and non-competitive situations. Doctoral dissertation, University of Michigan.

Horner, M. S. (1970). *Feminine personality and conflict*. Monterey, CA: Brooks/Cole.

Horney, K. (1937). *The neurotic personality of our time*. New York: Norton.

Horowitz, M. J., Duff, D. F., & Stratton, L. O. (1964, December). *Archives of general psychiatry* (Vol. II). Washington, DC: American Medical Association.

Horton, D. L., & Turnage, T. W. (1976). *Human learning*. Englewood Cliffs, NJ: Prentice-Hall.

Horton, R. W. (1973). An empirical investigation of variation in students' premarital sex standards and behavior. *Diss. Ab. Int'l.*, *34*, 1385–1386.

Hovland, C. I., Lumsdaine, A., & Sheffield, F. (1949). *Experiments on mass communication*. Princeton, NJ: Princeton University Press.

Hovland, C. I., & Weiss, W. (1952). The influence of source credibility on communication effectiveness. *The Public Opinion Quarterly*, *15*, 635–650.

Howard, D. (1972). *Territory in bird life*. New York: Dutton.

Howells, L., & Becker, S. (1962). Seating arrangement and leadership emergence. *Journal of Abnormal and Social Psychology*, *64*, 148–150.

Hubel, D. H., & Wiesel, T. N. (1965). Receptive fields and functional architecture in two nonstriate visual areas (18 and 19) of the cat. *Journal of Neurophysiology*, *28*, 229–289.

Hubel, D. H., & Wiesel, T. N. (1970). The period of susceptibility to the physiological effects of unilateral eye closure in kittens. *Journal of Physiology*, *206*, 419–436.

Hughes, J. (1975). Isolation of an endogenous compound from the brain with pharmacological properties similar to morphine. *Brain Research*, *88*, 295–308.

Hughes, J., Smith, T. W., Kosterlitz, H. W., Fothergill, L. A., Morgan, B. A., & Morris, H. R. (1975). Identification of two related pentapeptides from the brain with potent opiate agonist activity. *Nature*, *258*, 577–579.

Hulicka, I. M., & Grossman, J. L. (1967). Age-group comparisons for the use of mediators in paired associate learning. *Journal of Gerontology*, *22*, 46–51.

Hultsch, D. F. (1971). Adult age differences in free classification and free recall. *Developmental Psychology*, *4*, 338–342.

Hultsch, D. F., & Deutsch, F. (1981). *Adult development and aging*. New York: McGraw-Hill.

Hunt, M. (1974). *Sexual behavior in the 1970s*. Chicago: Playboy Press.

Hunter, F., & Ash, P. (1973). The accuracy and consistency of polygraph examiner's diagnoses. *Journal of Police Science and Administration*, *1*, 370–375.

Hurt, H. (1975). The hottest place in the whole U.S.A. *Texans Monthly*, *3*, 50ff.

Hurvich, L. M., & Jameson, D. (1974). Opponent processes as a model of neural organization. *American Psychologist*, *29*, 88–102.

Husband, R. W. (1940). Cooperation versus solitary problem solution. *Journal of Social Psychology*, *11*, 405–409.

Huxley, A. D. (1952). *The doors of perception*. New York: Harper & Row.

Hygge, S., & Ohman, S. (1978). Modeling processes in the acquisition of fears: Vicarious electrodermal conditioning to fear-relevant stimuli. *Journal of Personality and Social Psychology*, *36*, 271–279.

Hyman, R. (1977). The case against parapsychology. *The Humanist*, *37*, 47–49.

Isaacson, R. L. (1970). When brains are damaged. *Psychology Today*, *3*, 38–42.

Iscoe, I. (1982). Toward a viable community health psychology: Caveats from the experiences of the community mental health movement. *American Psychologist*, *37*, 961–965.

Isen, A. (1970). Success, failure, attention, and reaction to others: The warm glow of success. *Journal of Personality and Social Psychology*, *15*, 294–301.

Ising, H., & Melchert, H. (1980). Endocrine and cardiovascular effects of noise. *Proceedings of the Third International Congress*. ASHA Report No. 10.

Ittleson, W. H., Proshansky, H. M., Rivlin, L. G., & Winkel, G. (1974). An introduction to environmental psychology. New York: Holt, Rinehart & Winston.

Ivey, A., & Simek-Downing, L. (1980). *Counseling and psychology*. Englewood Cliffs, NJ: Prentice-Hall.

Izard, C. E. (1977). *Human emotions*. New York: Plenum Press.

Izard, C. E. (1981). Differential emotions theory and the facial feedback hypothesis of emotion activation: Comments in Tourajeau and Ellsworth's "The role of facial response in the experience of emotion." *Journal of Personality and Social Psychology*, *40*, 350–354.

Izard, C. E. (1982). Comments on emotion and cognition: Can there be a working relationship? In M. Clark & S. Fiske (Eds.), *Emotions and cognition*. Hillsdale, NJ: Erlbaum.

Jaffe, J., Patterson, R., & Hodgson, R. (1980). Addictions, issues and answers. Holland: Multimedia Publications.

James, R. (1959). Status and competence of jurors. *American Journal of Sociology*, *64*, 563–570.

James, W. (1884). What is emotion? *Mind*, *19*, 188–205.

James, W. (1890). *The principles of psychology*. New York: Holt, Rinehart & Winston.

James, W. (1967). The varieties of religious experience. New York: Modern Library. (Originally published, 1902)

Janis, I. L. (1971). Groupthink. *Psychology Today*, *5*(6), 43–46ff.

Janis, I. L. (1972). *Victims of groupthink: A psychological study of foreign policy decisions and fiascoes*. Boston: Houghton-Mifflin.

Janis, I. L. (1982). *Groupthink: Psychological studies of policy decisions and fiascoes* (2nd ed.). Boston: Houghton Mifflin.

Janis, I. L., & Feshbach, S. (1953). Effects of fear-arousing communication. *Journal of Abnormal and Social Psychology*, *48*, 78–92.

Janis, I. L., Kaye, D., & Kirschner, P. (1965). Facilitating effects of "eating-while-reading" on responsiveness to persuasive communications. *Journal of Personality and Social Psychology*, *1*, 181–186.

Janowitz, H. D. (1967). Role of gastrointestinal tract in the regulation of food intake. In C. F. Code (Ed.), *Handbook of physiology: Alimentary canal*, *I*. Washington, DC: American Physiological Society, pp. 219–224.

Janowitz, H. D., & Grossman, M. (1949). Some factors affecting the food intake of normal dogs and dogs with esophagostomy and gastric fistula. *American Journal of Physiology*, *159*, 143–148.

Jecker, J., & Landy, D. (1969). Liking a person as a function of doing him a favor. *Human Relations*, *22*, 371–378.

Jeffrey, D., & Katz, R. (1977). *Take it off and keep it off*. Englewood Cliffs, NJ: Prentice-Hall.

Jellison, J. M., & Green, J. (1981). A self-presentational approach to the fundamental attribution error: The horn of internality. *Journal of Personality and Social Psychology*, *40*, 643–649.

Jenkins, C. D. (1976). Recent evidence supporting psychologic and social risk factors for coronary disease. *New England Journal of Medicine*, *294*, 987–994.

Jens, K., & Evans, H. (1983). *The diagnosis and treatment of multiple personality clients*. Snowbird, UT: Rocky Mountain Psychological Association.

Jensen, A. R. (1969). How much can we boost IQ and scholastic achievement? *Harvard Educational Review*, *39*, 1–23.

Jensen, A. R. (1973). *Educability and group differences*. New York: Harper & Row.

Jerome, E. A. (1959). Age and learning-experimental studies. In J. E. Birren (Ed.), *Handbook of aging and the individual*. Chicago: University of Chicago Press.

Jersild, A. T., & Holmes, F. B. (1935). Children's fears. *Child development monograph*, No. 20. New York: Teacher's College, Columbia University.

Johansson, G. (1976). Visual motion perception. In R. Held & W. Richards (Eds.), *Recent progress in perception*. San Francisco: Freeman.

Jones, E. (1957). *The life and work of Sigmund Freud* (Vol. 3). New York: Basic Books.

Jones, E. E. (1979). The rocky road from acts to dispositions. *American Psychologist*, *34*, 107–117.

Jones, E. E., & Davis, K. (1965). From acts to dispositions: The attribution process in person perception. In L. Berkowitz (Ed.), *Advances in experimental social psychology* (Vol. 2). New York: Academic Press.

Jones, E. E., & Harris, V. A. (1967). The attribution of attitudes. *Journal of Experimental Psychology*, *3*, 1–24.

Jones, E. E., & McGillis, D. (1976). Correspondent interferences and the attribution cube: A comparative reappraisal. In J. H. Harvey, W. J. Ickes, & R. F. Kidd (Eds.), *New directions in attribution research* (Vol. I). Hillsdale, NJ: Erlbaum.

Jones, E. E., & Nisbett, R. (1972). The actor and the observer: Divergent perceptions of the causes of behavior. In E. E. Jones, D. Kanouse, H. H. Kelley, R. E. Nisbett, S. Valins, & B. Weiner (Eds.), *Attribution: Perceiving the causes of behavior*. Morristown, NJ: General Learning Press, 79–94.

Jones, E. E., & Wortman, C. (1973). *Ingratiation: An attribution approach*. Morristown, NJ: General Learning Press.

Jones, E., Wood, G., & Quattrone, G. (1981). Perceived variability of personal characteristics in in-groups and out-groups: The role of knowledge and evaluation. *Personality and Social Psychology Bulletin*, *7*, 523–528.

Jones, E., & Wortman, C. (1973). *Ingratiation: An attributional approach*. Morristown, NJ: General Learning Press.

Jones, E., Rock, L., Shaver, K. G., Goethals, G. R., & Ward, L. M. (1968). Pattern of performance and ability attribution: An unexpected primacy effect. *Journal of Personality and Social Psychology*, *10*, 317–340.

Jones, E. E., Worchel, S., Goethals, G. R., & Grumet, J. F. (1971). Prior expectancy and behavioral extremity as determinants of attitude attribution. *Journal of Experimental Social Psychology*, *7*, 59–80.

Jones, H. E., & Conrad, H. S. (1933). The growth and decline of intelligence: A study of a homogeneous group between the ages of ten and sixty. *Genetic Psychology Monographs*, *13*, 223–298.

Jones, R. A., & Brehm, J. W. (1970). Persuasiveness of one and two-sided communications as a function of awareness there are two sides. *Journal of Experimental Social Psychology*, *6*, 47–56.

Julian, J. W., Regulo, C. R., & Hollander, E. P. (1968). Effects of prior agreement from others on task confidence and conformity. *Journal of Personality and Social Psychology*, *9*, 171–178.

Jung, C. G. (1928). *Contributions to analytical psychology*. New York: Harcourt Brace.

Kagan, J. (1973). What is intelligence? *Social Policy*, 88–94.

Kagan, J., & Freeman, M. (1963). Relation of childhood intelligence, maternal behaviors, and social class to behavior during adolescence. *Child Development*, *34*, 899–911.

Kagan, J., & Moss, H. (1962). *Birth to maturity*. New York: Wiley.

Kagan, J., Kearsley, R. B., & Zelanzo, P. R. (1977). The effects of infant day care on psychological development. *Educational Quarterly*, *1*, 109–142.

Kahana, B., & Kahana, E. (1971). Theoretical and research perspectives on grandparenthood. *Aging and Human Development*, *2*, 261–268.

Kalat, J. W. (1984). *Biological psychology* (2nd ed.). Belmont, CA: Wadsworth.

Kalish, R. A., & Reynolds, D. K. (1976). *Death and ethnicity: A psychocultural study*. Los Angeles: University of Southern California Press.

Kallman, F. (1946). The genetic theory of schizophrenia. *American Journal of Psychiatry*, *103*, 309–322.

Kamin, L. J. (1973). IIcredity, intelligence, politics and society. Invited address, Eastern Psychological Association, Washington.

Kamin, L. J. (1976). Heredity, intelligence, politics, and psychology. In N. J. Block & G. Dworkin (Eds.), *The IQ controversy*. New York: Pantheon.

Kamin, L. J. (1979). Psychology as social science: The Jensen affair, ten years after. Presidential address, Eastern Psychological Association, Philadelphia.

Kandell, J. (1977, August 7). French rank crime high on their list of major worries. *The New York Times*, p. 13.

Kangelari, S., Abramovich-Polyakov, D., & Rudenko, V. (1966). The effects of noise and vibration on morbidity rates (Russia). *Gigiena Truda: Professional 'Nye Zabolevaniy*, *6*, 47–49.

Kantor, R. N. (1983). How inconsiderate are children's textbooks? *Journal of Curriculum Studies*, *15*, 61–72.

Kaplan, H. S. (1974). *The new sexual therapy: Active treatment of sexual dysfunctions*. New York: Brunner-Mazel.

Karlins, M., Coffman, J., & Walters, G. (1969). On the fading of social stereotypes: Studies in three generations of college students. *Journal of Personality and Social Psychology*, *13*, 1–16.

Karlsson, J. (1972). An Icelandic family study of schizophrenia. In A. Kaplan (Ed.), *Genetic factors in schizophrenia*. Springfield, IL: Charles C Thomas.

Katchadourian, H. A. (1977). *The biology of adolescence*. San Francisco: Freeman.

Katkoff, L. (Ed.). (1984). *Primary prevention in the work place*. New York: Haworth.

Katz, I. (1967). The socialization of academic motivation in minority group children. In D. Levine (Ed.), *Nebraska symposium on motivation* (Vol. 15). Lincoln, NE: University of Nebraska Press, pp. 133–191.

Katz, L. M. (1984). *My name is Geraldine Ferraro*. New York: Signet.

Kazdin, A. E. (1976). The rich rewards of rewards. *Psychology Today*, *10*(6), 98, 101–102, 105, 114.

Keele, S. W., & Ells, J. G. (1972). Memory characteristics of kinesthetic information. *Journal of Motor Behavior*, *4*, 127–134.

Keesey, R., Boyle, P., Kemnitz, J., & Mitchell, J. (1976). The rule of the lateral hypothalamus in determining the body weight set point. In D. Novin et al. (Eds.), *Hunger: Basic mechanisms and clinical implications*. New York: Raven Press.

Keesey, R. E., & Powley, T. L. (1975). Hypothalamic regulation of body weight. *American Scientist*, *63*, 558–565.

Kehoe, J. E., Feyer, A. M., & Moses, J. L. (1981). Second-order conditioning of the rabbits' nictitating membrane response as a function of the CS2-CS1 and CS-1-VS intervals. *Animal Learning and Behavior*, *9*, 304–315.

Keller, H. (1954). *The story of my life*. New York: Doubleday.

Keller, M. (1981, December 2). Treatment for depression varies. In a series by Dava Sobel, *The New York Times*.

Kelley, H. H. (1952). Two functions of reference groups. In G. E. Swanson, T. M. Newcomb, & E. L. Hartley (Eds.), *Readings in social psychology* (2nd ed.). New York: Holt, Rinehart & Winston.

Kelley, H. H. (1967). Attribution theory in social psychology. In D. Levine (Ed.), *Nebraska Symposium on Motivation*, *15*, 192–238.

Kelley, H. H. (1971). *Attribution in social interaction*. Morristown, NJ: General Learning Press.

Kelley, H. H. (1973). The process of causal attribution. *American Psychologist*, *28*, 107–128.

Kelley, H. H. (1983). Love and commitment. In H. Kelley, E. Berscheid, A. Christensen, J. Harvey, T. Huston, G. Levinger, E. McClintock, L. Peplau, & D. Peterson (Eds.), *Close relationships*. New York: Freeman.

Kelley, H.H., & Michele, S. (1980). Attribution theory and research. *Annual Review of Psychology*, *31*, 457–502.

Kellogg, T. H. (1902). The histrionic element of mental disease. *New York Medical Journal*, *LXXVI*, 107–110.

Kelly, E. (1954). *Clown*. Englewood Cliffs, NJ: Prentice-Hall.

Kelman, H. C., & Hovland, C. I. (1953). "Reinstatement" of the communicator in delayed measurement of opinion change. *Journal of Abnormal and Social Psychology*, *48*, 326–335.

Kenny, W. R., & Grotelueschen, A. D. (1984). Making the case for case study. *Journal of Curriculum Studies*, *16*, 37–51.

Kenrick, D., & Cialdini, R. (1977). Romantic attraction: Misattribution versus reinforcement explanations. *Journal Personality and Social Psychology*, *35*, 381–391.

Kensiton, K. (1969). The uncommitted: Alienated youth in American society. *Youth and Society*, *1*, 110–127.

Kent, R., & Foster, S. (1977). Direct observational procedure: Methodological issues in naturalistic settings. In A. Ciminero, K. Calhoun, & H. Adams (Eds.), *Handbook of behavioral assessment*. New York: Wiley.

Kerr, N., & Bruun, S. (1981). Ringelmann revisited: Alternative explanations for the social loafing effect. *Personality and Social Psychology Bulletin*, *7*, 224–231.

Kesey, K. (1962). *One flew over the cuckoo's nest*. New York: Viking.

Kety, S. S., Rosenthal, D., Wender, P., & Schulsinger, F. (1968). The type and prevalence of mental illness in the biological and adoptive families of adopted schizophrenics. In D. Rosenthal & S. S. Kety (Eds.), *The transmission of schizophrenia*. New York: Pergamon Press.

Keyes, R. (1980). *The height of your life*. Boston: Little, Brown.

Kiesler, C. A., & Kiesler, S. B. (1969). Group pressure and conformity. In J. Mills (Ed.), *Experimental and social psychology*. New York: Macmillan.

Kiesler, C. A., McGuire, T., Mechanic, D., Mosher, L. R., Nelson, S., Newman, F., Rich, R., & Schulberg, H. (1983). Federal mental health policymaking: An assessment of deinstitutionalization. *American Psychologist*, *38*, 1292–1297.

Kiewra, K. A. (1983). The process of review: A levels of processing approach. *Contemporary Educational Psychology*, *8*, 366–374.

Kilham, W., & Mann, L. (1974). Level of destructive obedience as a function of transmitter and executant roles in the Milgram obedience paradigm. *Journal of Personality and Social Psychology*, *29*, 696–702.

Kinsey, A. C., Pomeroy, W. B., & Martin, C. E. (1948). *Sexual behavior in the human male*. Philadelphia: Saunders.

Kinsey, A. C., Pomeroy, W. B., Martin, C. E., & Gebhard, P. H. (1953). *Sexual behavior in the human female*. Philadelphia: Saunders.

Kintsch, W. (1974). *The representation of meaning in memory*. New York: Wiley.

Kintsch, W., Mandel, T. S., & Kozminsky, E. (1977). Summarizing scrambled stories. *Memory and Cognition*, *5*, 547–552.

Kinzel, A. S. (1970). Body buffer zone in violent prisoners. *American Journal of Psychiatry*, *10*, 263–270.

Kissileff, H. R. (1969). Food-associated drinking in the rat. *Journal of Comparative and Physiological Psychology*, *67*, 284–300.

Kleck, R. E., & Rubenstein, C. (1975). Physical attractiveness, perceived attitude similarity, and interpersonal attraction in an opposite-sex encounter. *Journal of Personality and Social Psychology*, *31*, 107–114.

Kleinke, C., & Walton, J. (1982). Influence of reinforced smiling on affective responses in an interview. *Journal of Personality and Social Psychology*, *42*, 557–565.

Kleinmuntz, B., & Szucko, J. (1984). A field study of the fallibility of polygraph lie detection. *Nature*, *308*, 449–450.

Kleinmuntz, B., & Szucko, J. (1984). Lie detection in ancient and modern times. *American Psychologist*, *39*, 766–776.

Kleitman, N. (1963). *Sleep and wakefulness*. Chicago, IL: University of Chicago Press.

Knittle, J. L. (1975). Early influences on development of adipose tissue. In G. A. Bray (Ed.), *Obesity in perspective*. Washington, DC: U.S. Government Printing Office.

Knowles, E. (1982). From individuals to group members: A dialectic for the social sciences. In W. Ickes & E. Knowles (Eds.), *Personality, roles and social behavior*. New York: Springer-Verlag.

Knox, V. J., Crutchfield, L., & Hilgard, E. R. (1975). The nature of task interference in hypnotic dissociation: An investigation of hypnotic behavior. *International Journal of Clinical and Experimental Hypnosis*, *23*, 305–323.

Knox, V. J., Morgan, A. H., & Hilgard, E. R. (1974). Pain and suffering in ischemia:

The paradox of hypnotically suggested anesthesia as contradicted by reports from the "hidden observer." *Archives of General Psychiatry*, *30*, 840–847.

Kobasa, S. (1979). Stressful life events, personality, and health: An inquiry into hardiness. *Journal of Personality and Social Psychology*, *37*, 1–11.

Kobasa, S. (1982). Commitment and coping in stress resistance among lawyers. *Journal of Personality and Social Psychology*, *42*, 707–717.

Kobasa, S., Maddi, S., & Kahn, S. (1982). Hardiness and health: A prospective study. *Journal of Personality and Social Psychology*, *42*, 168–177.

Koestler, A. (1967). *The ghost in the machine*. New York: Macmillan.

Kohlberg, L. (1963). The development of children's orientations toward a moral order. I. Sequence in the development of moral thought. *Vita Humana*, *6*, 11–33.

Kohlberg, L. (1978). Revisions in the theory and practice of moral development. *New Directions for Child Development*, *2*, 83–88.

Kohlberg, L., Colby, A., Gibbs, J., & Speicher-Dubin, B. (1978). *Standard form scoring manual*. Cambridge, MA: Center for Moral Education.

Kohler, W. (1925). *The mentality of apes*. New York: Harcourt Brace Jovanovich.

Kohn, I., Franck, K., & Fox, A. (1975). Defensible space modifications in row-house communities. *National Science Foundation Report*.

Kohn, M. L. (1972). Class, family, and schizophrenia: A reformulation. *Social Forces*, *50*, 295–313.

Kolodny, R., Masters, W., Hendryx, J., & Toro, G. (1971). Plasma testosterone levels and semen analysis in male homosexuals. *New England Journal of Medicine*, *285*, 1170–1174.

Konecni, V. J. (1975). Annoyance, type, and duration of post-annoyance activity and aggression: The "catharsis effect." *Journal of Experimental Psychology: General*, *104*, 76–102.

Konecni, V. J. (1979). The role of aversive events in the development of intergroup conflict. In W. Austin & S. Worchel (Eds.), *The social psychology of intergroup behavior*. Monterey, CA: Brooks/Cole.

Konecni, V. J., & Doob, A. N. (1972). Catharsis through displacement of aggression. *Journal of Personality and Social Psychology*, *23*, 379–387.

Konecni, V. J., Libauser, L., Morton, H., & Ebbesen, E. B. (1975). Effects of a violation of personal space on escape and helping responses. *Journal of Experimental Social Psychology*, *11*, 288–299.

Korchin, S. (1976). *Modern clinical psychology*. New York: Basic Books.

Korchin, S., & Shuldberg, D. (1981). The future of clinical assessment. *American Psychologist*, *36*, 1147–1158.

Korhaber, R., & Schroeder, H. (1975). Importance of model similarity on extinction of avoidance behavior in children. *Journal of Consulting and Clinical Psychology*, *43*, 601–607.

Kosslyn, S. M. (1981). The medium and themessage in mental imagery: A theory. *Psychological Review*, *88*, 46–66.

Kosslyn, S. M. (1984). Mental representations. In J. R. Anderson & S. M. Kosslyn

(Eds.), *Tutorials in reading and memory*. San Francisco, Freeman.

Kosslyn, S. M., Ball, T. M., & Reiser, B. J. (1978). Visual images preserve spatial information: Evidence from studies of image scanning. *Journal of Experimental Psychology: Human Perception and Performance*, *4*, 47–60.

Kraemer, H. C., Becker, H. B., Brodie, H. X. H., Doering, C. H., Moos, R. H., & Hamburg, D. (1976). Orgasmic frequency and plasma testosterone levels in normal human males. *Archives of Sexual Behavior*, *5*, 125–132.

Kraft, C. L., & Elworth, C. L. (1969). Measurement of aircrew performance: The flight deck workload and its relation to pilot performance. (NTIS70-19779/AD699934-DTIC).

Kraly, E. S., Miller, L., & Hecht, E. (1983). Histaminergic mechanisms for drinking by insulin in the rat. *Physiology and Behavior*, *31*, 233–236.

Kraly, E. S. (1984). Physiology of drinking by eating. *Psychological Review*, *91*, 478–490.

Kramer, M. (1977). *Psychiatric services and the changing institution scene, 1952–1985*. National Institute of Mental health (DHEW publication #Adm. 77–433).

Krasner, L. (1971). The operant approach in behavior therapy. In A. Bergin & S. Garfield (Eds.), *Handbook of psychotherapy and behavior change*. New York: Wiley.

Krech, D., Crutchfield, R., & Ballachey, E. (1962). *Individual in society: A textbook of social psychology*. New York: McGraw-Hill.

Kreps, J. M. (Ed.). (1976). *Women and the American economy*. Englewood Cliffs, NJ: Prentice-Hall.

Kroger, W. S., & Douce, R. G. (1980). Forensic uses of hypnosis. *American Journal of Clinical Hypnosis*, *23*, 86–93.

Krupat, E. (1982). *Psychology is social* (2nd ed.). Glenview, IL: Scott, Foresman.

Kübler-Ross, E. (1969). *On death and dying*. New York: Macmillan.

Kübler-Ross, E. (1974). *Questions and answers on death and dying*. New York: Macmillan.

Kuhn, M., & McPhartland, T. (1954). An empirical investigation of self-attitudes. *American Social Review*, *19*, 68–76.

Kurtines, W., & Grief, E. B. (1974). The development of moral thought: Review and evaluation of Kohlberg's approach. *Psychological Bulletin*, *81*, 453–470.

Lackey, E., & Nass, G. A. A. (1969). A comparison of sexual attitudes and behavior in an international sample. *Journal of Marriage and the Family*, *31*, 364–379.

Lagone, J. (1981, March). Healing the hostages. *Discover*. New York: Time, Inc.

Laing, R. D. (1964). Is schizophrenia a disease? *International Journal of Social Psychiatry*, *10*, 184–193.

Laird, J. (1974). Self-attribution of emotion: The effects of expressive behavior on the quality of emotional experience. *Journal of Personality and Social Psychology*, *29*, 475–486.

Lamb, H. R., & Zusman, J. (1979). Primary prevention in perspective. *American Journal of Psychiatry*, *136*, 12–17.

Lamm, H., & Myers, D. (1978). Group-induced polarization of attitudes and behavior. In L. Berkowitz (Ed.), *Advances in Experimental Social Psychology* (Vol. 11). New York: Academic Press.

Landesman-Dwyer, S., Keller, S. L., &

Streissguth, A. P. (1977). Naturalistic observations of newborns: Effects of maternal alcohol intake. Paper presented at the American Psychological Association Annual Meeting, San Francisco.

Landfield, P. W. (1976). Synchronous EEG rhythms: Their nature and their possible functions in memory, information, transmission, and behavior. In W. H. Gispen (Ed.), *Molecular and functional neurobiology*, pp. 389–424. Amsterdam: Elsevier.

Langer, E. (1978). Rethinking the role of thought in social interaction. In J. H. Harvey, W. Ickes, & R. Kidd (Eds.), *New direction in attribution* (Vol. 2). Hillsdale, NJ: Erlbaum.

Langer, E., Janis, I., & Wolfer, J. (1975). Reduction of psychological stress in surgical patients. *Journal of Experimental Social Psychology*, *11*, 155–165.

Langer, E. J., & Rodin, J. (1976). The effects of choice and enhanced personal responsibility for the aged: A field experiment in an institutional setting. *Journal of Personality and Social Psychology*, *34*, 191–198.

Lanzetta, J. T., Biernat, J., & Kleck, R. (1982). Self-focused attention, behavior, autonomic arousal and the experience of emotion. *Motivation and Emotion*, *6*, 49–63.

LaPiere, R. T. (1934). Attitudes vs. actions. *Social Forces*, *13*, 230–237.

Lash, J. P. (1980). *Helen and teacher: The story of Helen Keller and Anne Sullivan Macy*. New York: Dell.

Laska, S. B., & Micklin, M. (1979). The knowledge dimension of occupational socialization: Role models and their social influences. *Youth and Society*, *10*, 360–378.

Lasswell, H. D. (1948). The structure and function of communication in society. In L. Bryson (Ed.), *Communication of ideas*. New York: Harper & Row.

Latane, B., & Darley, J. M. (1970). *The unresponsive bystander: Why doesn't he help?* New York: Appleton-Century-Crofts.

Latane, B., Williams, K., & Harkins, S. (1979). Many hands make light the work: The causes and consequences of social loafing. *Journal of Personality and Social Psychology*, *37*, 822–832.

Lauderdal, P., Smith-Cunnica, P., Parker, J., & Inverarity, J. (1984). External threat and the definition of deviance. *Journal of Personality and Social Psychology*, *46*, 1058–1068.

Laurence, J. R., & Perry, C. (1983). Hypnotically created memory among highly hypnotizable subjects. *Science*, *222*, 523–524.

Lawson, E. (1971). Hair color, personality, and the observer. *Psychological Reports*, *28*, 311–322.

Lazarsfeld, P. F., Berelson, B., & Gaudet, H. J. (1948). *The people's choice* (2nd ed.). New York: Columbia University Press.

Lazarus, R. (1981). A cognitivist's reply to Zajonc on emotion and cognition. *American Psychology*, *36*, 222–223.

Lazarus, R. (1981, July). Little hassles can be hazardous to health. *Psychology Today*, pp. 58–62.

Lazarus, R. (1982). Thoughts on the reduction between emotion and cognition. *American Psychology*, *37*, 1019–1024.

Lazarus, R., Coyne, J., & Folkman, S. (1982). Cognition, emotion, and motivation. The doctoring of Humpty Dumpty.

In R. Newfeld (Ed.), *Psychological stress and psychopathology*. New York: McGraw-Hill.

Lazarus, R., & DeLongis, A. (1983). Psychological stress and coping in aging. *American Psychology*, *38*, 245–254.

Lazarus, R., & Launier, R. (1978). Stress-related transactions between person and environment. In L. Pervin & M. Lewis (Eds.), *Perspectives in interactional psychology*. New York: Plenum Press.

Lazarus, R. S. (1968). Emotions and adaptation: Conceptual and empirical relations. In W. J. Arnold (Ed.), *Nebraska symposium on motivation*. Lincoln, NE: University of Nebraska Press.

Lazell, E. W., & Prince, L. H. (1929). A study of the causative factors of dementia praecox. *U. S. Veterans Bureau Medical Bulletin*, *114*, 241–248.

LeBon, G. (1903). *The crowd* (trans.). London: Allen & Unwin.

Lecuyer, R. (1975). Space dimensions, the climate of discussion and group decisions. *European Journal of Social Psychology*, *5*, 509–514.

Lecuyer, R. (1976). Social organization and spatial organization. *Human Relations*, *19*, 1045–1060.

Lee, T. (1970). Perceived distance as a function of direction in the city. *Environment and Behavior*, *2*, 40–51.

Leeper, M., & Greene, D. (1978). *The hidden costs of reward: New perspectives in the psychology of motivation*. Hillsdale, NJ: Erlbaum.

Lefevre, C. (1972). The mature woman as a graduate student. *School Review*, *80*, 281–297.

Leiberman, A. F. (1977). Preschooler's competence with a peer. Relations with attachment and peer experience. *Child Development*, *48*, 1277–1287.

Leitenberg, H., & Slavin, L. (1983). Comparison of attitudes toward transsexuality and homosexuality. *Archives of Sexual Behavior*, *12*, 337–346.

Lemere, F., & Voegtlin, W. L. (1950). An evaluation of the aversion treatment of alcoholism. *Quarterly Journal of Studies on Alcohol*, *11*, 199–204.

Lenneberg, E. H. (1967). *Biological foundations of language*. New York: Wiley.

Leon, G., & Roth, L. (1977). Obesity: Psychological causes, conditions, and speculations. *Psychology Bulletin*, *84*, 117–139.

Lerner, I. M., & Libby, W. L. (1976). *Heredity, evolution, and society*. San Francisco: Freeman.

Leslie, L. (1980). *Portrait of an artist: A biography of Georgia O'Keeffe*. New York: Washington Square Press.

Levant, R. (1984). *Family therapy: A comprehensive overview*. Englewood Cliffs, NJ: Prentice-Hall.

Leventhal, H. (1982). The integration of emotion and cognition: A view from the perceptual monitor theory of emotion. In M. Clark & S. Feske, *Affect and emotion*. Hillsdale, NJ: Erlbaum.

Leventhal, H., & Niles, P. (1985). (1965). Persistence of influence for varying duration of exposure to threat stimuli. *Psychology Reports*, *16*, 223–233.

Leventhal, H., Singer, R., & Jones, S. (1965). The effects of fear and specificity of recommendation upon attitudes and behavior. *Journal of Personality and Social Psychology*, *2*, 20–29.

Levine, M. (1975). *A cognitive theory of learning*. Hillsdale, NJ: Erlbaum.

Levinson, D. J. (1978). *The seasons of a man's life*. New York: Knopf.

Levinson, P., & Flynn, J. (1965). The objects attacked by cats during stimulation of the hypothalamus. *Animal Behavior*, *13*, 217–220.

Levy, L., & Rowitz, L. (1973). *The ecology of mental disorder*. New York: Behavioral Publications.

Lewin, K. (1931). Environmental forces in child behavior and development. In C. Murchison (Ed.), *A handbook of child psychology*. Worcester, MA: Clark University Press.

Lewin, K., Lippitt, R., & White, R. (1939). Patterns of aggressive behavior in experimentally created social climates. *Journal of Psychology*, *10*, 271–299.

Lewine, R. (1981). Sex differences in schizophrenia: Timing or subtypes. *Psychological Bulletin*, *90*, 432–444.

Lewinsohn, P. H. (1974). A behavioral approach to depression. In R. J. Friedman & M. M. Katz (Eds.), *The psychology of depression: Contemporary theory and research*. Washington, DC: Winston-Wiley.

Lewinsohn, P. M., Mischel, W., Chaplin, W., & Barton, R. (1980). Social competence and depression: The role of illusory self-perceptions. *Journal of Abnormal Psychology*, *89*, 203–212.

Lewis, J., Baddeley, A. D., Bonham, K. G., & Lovett, D. (1970). Traffic pollution and mental efficiency. *Nature*, *225*, 96.

Lewis, R., Rodnick, E., & Goldstein, M. (1981). Interfamilial interactive behavior, parental communication deviance, and risk of schizophrenia. *Journal of Abnormal Psychology*, *90*, 448–457.

Lewis, S., Langan, C., & Hollander, E. P. (1972). Expectations of future interaction and the choice of less desirable alternatives in conformity. *Sociometry*, *35*, 440–447.

Ley, D., & Cybriwsky, R. (1974). Urban graffiti as territorial markers. *Annals of the Association of American Geographers*, *64*, 491–505.

Ley, R. (1977). Encoding specificity and associates in cued recall. *Memory and Cognition*, *5*, 523–525.

Libermann, R. (1970). Behavioral approaches to family and couple therapy. *American Journal of Orthopsychiatry*, *40*, 106–118.

Lichtenstein, E., Harris, D., Birchler, G., Wahl, J., & Schmahl, D. (1973). Comparison of rapid smoking, warm, smoky air, and attention placebo in modification of smoking behavior. *Journal of Consulting and Clinical Psychology*, *40*, 92–98.

Lidz, T. (1968). The family language and the transmission of schizophrenia. In D. Rosenthal & S. Kety (Eds.), *The transmission of schizophrenia*. New York: Pergamon Press.

Lieber, A., & Sherin, C. (1972). Homicides and the lunar cycle: Toward a theory of lunar influence on human emotional disturbance. *American Journal of Psychiatry*, *129*, 69–74.

Lieberman, M. A., Yalom, I. D., & Miles, M. B. (1973). *Encounter groups: First facts*. New York: Basic Books.

Liebert, R. M., & Baron, R. A. (1972). Some immediate effects of televised violence on children's behavior. *Developmental Psychology*, *6*, 469–475.

Liebert, R. M., Neale, J. M., & Davidson, E. S. (1973). *The early window: Effects of television on children and youth*. Elmsford, NY: Pergamon Press.

Liem, J., & Liem, R. (1976). Life events, social supports, and physical and psychological well-being. Paper presented at American Psychological Association meeting, Washington, DC.

Lilly, J. C. (1956). Mental effects of reduction of ordinary levels of physical stimuli on intact healthy persons. *Psychiatric Research Reports*, 5, 1-9.

Limber, J. (1973). The genesis of complex sentences. In T. E. Moore (Ed.), *Cognitive development and the acquisition of language*. New York: Academic Press.

Limber, J. (1977). Language in child and chimp? *American Psychologist*, 32, 280-295.

Linder, D. E., & Worchel, S. (1970). Opinion change as a result of effortfully drawing a counter-attitudinal conclusion. *Journal of Experimental Social Psychology*, 6, 432-448.

Lindskold, S. (1982). *You and me*. Chicago: Nelson Hall.

Lipscomb, D. M. (1969). Ear damage from exposure to rock and roll music. *Archives of Otolaryngology*, 90, 545-555.

Lisle, L. (1980). *Portrait of an artist: A biography of Georgia O'Keefe*. New York: Washington Square Press.

Little, K. B. (1965). Personal space. *Journal of Experimental Social Psychology*, 1, 237-347.

Locke, J. (1959). An essay concerning human understanding (Vol. I). New York: Dover. (Originally published, 1690)

Loehlin, J. C., & Nichols, R. C. (1976). *Heredity, environment and personality*. Austin, TX: University of Texas Press.

Loftus, E. F. (1975). Leading questions and the eyewitness. *Cognitive Psychology*, 1, 560-572.

Loftus, E. F. (1981). *Eyewitness testimony*. Cambridge, MA: Harvard University Press.

Loftus, E. F. (1984, February). Eyewitnesses: Essential but unreliable. *Psychology Today*, pp. 22-26.

Loftus, E. F., & Palmer, J. (1974). Reconstruction of automobile destruction: An example of interaction between language and memory. *Journal of Verbal Learning and Verbal Behavior*, 13, 585-589.

Longstreth, L. E., Longstreth, G. V., Ramirez, C., & Fernandez, G. (1975). The ubiquity of Big Brother. *Child Development*, 46, 769-772.

Loo, C. (1972). The effects of spatial density in the social behavior of children. *Journal of Applied Social Psychology*, 4, 372-381.

Lopata, H. Z. (1973). Self-identity in marriage and widowhood. *Sociological Quarterly*, 14, 407-418. (a)

Lopata, H. Z. (1973). *Widowhood in an American city*. Cambridge, MA: Schenkman. (b)

LoPiccolo, J. (1978). The professionalization of sex therapy: Issues and problems. In J. LoPiccolo & L. LoPiccolo, *Handbook of sex therapy*. New York: Plenum Press, pp. 511-526.

LoPiccolo, J., & Heiman, J. (1977). The role of cultural value in the prevention and treatment of sexual problems. In C. Quills, V. Wincze, & D. Barlow (Eds.), *The prevention of sexual disorders*. New York: Plenum.

LoPiccolo, J., & Lobitz, W. (1972). The role of masturbation in the treatment of orgasmic dysfunctions. *Archives of Sexual Behavior*, 2, 163-172.

Lorayne, H., & Lucas, J. (1974). *The memory book*. New York: Ballantine Books.

Lorenz, K. (1966). *On aggression*. New York: Harcourt Brace Jovanovich.

Lotter, V. (1974). Factors related to outcome in autistic children. *Journal of Autism and Childhood Schizophrenia*, 4, 263-277.

Lovaas, O. I. (1977). *The autistic child*. New York: Halsted.

Lowe, C. A., & Kassin, S. M. (1948). Biased attributions for political messages. The role of involvement. Paper presented at Eastern Psychological Association meeting.

Lowenthal, M. F. (1972). Some potentialities of a life-cycle approach to the study of retirement. In F. M. Carp (Ed.), *Retirement*. New York: Behavioral Publications.

Lowenthal, M. F. (1977). Toward a sociopsychological theory of change in adulthood and old age. In J. E. Birren & K. W. Schaie (Eds.), *Handbook of the psychology of aging*. New York: Van Nostrand.

Lowenthal, M. F., & Chiriboga, D. (1973). Social stress and adaptation: Toward a life-course perspective. In C. Eisdorfer & M. P. Lawton (Eds.), *The psychology of adult development and aging*. Washington, DC: American Psychological Association.

Lowrey, G. H. (1978). *Growth and development of children*. Chicago: Year Book Med. Pub., Inc.

Luborsky, L., & Spence, D. P. (1978). Quantitative research on psychoanalytic therapy. In S. L. Garfield & A. E. Bergin (Eds.), *Handbook of psychotherapy and behavior change: An empirical analysis* (2nd ed.). New York: Wiley.

Lucas, O. N. (1975, January 20). The use of hypnosis in hemophilia dental care. *Annals of the New York Academy of Science*, 240, 263-266.

Lunde, D. (1975). *Murder and madness*. Stanford: Stanford Alumni Association.

Luria, A. R. (1968). *The mind of a mnemonist: A little book about a vast memory* (L. Solotaroff, trans.). New York: Basic Books.

Lykken, D. T. (1959). The GSR in the detection of guilt. *Journal of Applied Psychology*, 43, 385-388.

Lykken, D. T. (1975, March) Guilty knowledge test: The right way to use a lie detector. *Psychology Today*, pp. 56-60.

Lykken, D. T. (1981). *A tremor in the blood: Uses and abuses of the lie detector*. New York: McGraw-Hill.

Lynch, K. (1960). *The image of the city*. Cambridge, MA: MIT Press.

McArthur, L. A. (1976). The lesser influence of concensus than distinctiveness information on causal attributions: A test of the person-thing hypothesis. *Journal of Personality and Social Psychology*, 33, 733-742.

McBride, G., King, M. G., & James, J. W. (1965). Social proximity effects on galvanic skin responses in adult humans. *Journal of Psychology*, 61, 153-157.

McBurney, D. H., & Collings, V. B. (1977). *Introduction to sensation/perception*. Englewood Cliffs, NJ: Prentice-Hall.

McCarthy, D., & Saegert, S. (1978). Residential density, social overload and social withdrawal. *Human Ecology*, 6, 253-272.

McClelland, D. C. (1955). Some social consequences of achievement motivation. In M. R. Jones (Ed.), *Nebraska symposium on motivation*. Lincoln, NE: University of Nebraska Press.

McClelland, D. C., Atkinson, J. W., Clark, R. A., & Lowell, E. I. (1953). *The achievement motive*. New York: Appleton-Century-Crofts.

McClelland, L. A. (1974). *Crowding and social stress*. Unpublished doctoral dissertation, University of Michigan.

McClelland, L. A., & Cook, S. (1980). Promoting energy conservation in master-metered apartments through group financial incentives. *Journal of Applied Social Psychology*, 10, 20-31.

McCloskey, M., & Santee, J. (1981). Are semantic memory and episodic memory distinct systems? *Journal of Experimental Psychology: Human Learning and Memory*, 7, 66-71.

Maccoby, E. E., & Jacklin, C. N. (1974). *The psychology of sex differences*. Stanford, CA: Stanford University Press.

McConkie, G. W. (1978, November). *Where do we read?* Paper presented at the annual meeting of the Psychonomic Society, San Antonio, TX.

McCord, J. (1979). Some child-rearing antecedents of criminal behavior in adult men. *Journal Personality and Social Psychology*, 37, 1477-1486.

MacDonald, M. L., Lidsky, T. I., & Kern, J. M. (1979). Drug-instigated affects. In A. P. Goldstein & F. H. Kanfer (Eds.), *Maximizing treatment gains: Transfer enhancement in psychotherapy*. New York: Academic Press, pp. 429-444.

MacDonald, M. L., & Tobias, L. L. (1976). Withdrawal causes relapse? Our response. *Psychological Bulletin*, 83, 448-451.

McGrath, J. (1984). *Groups: Interaction and performance*. Englewood Cliffs, NJ: Prentice-Hall.

McGrew, P. L. (1970). Social and spatial density effects on spacing behavior in preschool children. *Journal of Child Psychology and Psychiatry*, 11, 197-205.

McGuire, W. (1961). The effectiveness of supportive and refutational defenses in immunization and restoring beliefs against persuasion. *Sociometry*, 24, 184-197.

McGuire, W. (1968). The nature of attitude and attitude change. In G. Lindzey & E. Aronson (Eds.), *The handbook of social psychology* (Vol. 3). Reading, MA: Addison-Wesley.

McGuire, W. (1984). The search for self: Going beyond self-esteem and the reactive self. In R. A. Zucker, J. Arnoff, & A. I. Robin, (Eds.), *Personality and the prediction of behavior*. New York: Academic Press.

McKenna, R. J. (1972). Some effects of anxiety level and food cues on the eating behavior of obese and normal subjects. *Journal of Personality and Social Psychology*, 22, 311-319.

Mackintosh, N. J. (1983). *Conditioning and associative learning*. New York: MIT Press.

Mackworth, N. (1961). Researches on the measurement of human performance. In H. Sinaiko (Ed.), *Selected papers on human factors in the design and use of control systems*. New York: Dover.

McMullen, S., & Rosen, R. (1979). The use of self-administered masturbation training in the treatment of primary dysfunction. *Journal of Consulting and Clinical Psychology*, 47, 912-918.

MacNichol, E. F. (1964). Three-pigment

color vision. *Scientific American*, *211*, 48–56.

McPherson, B., & Guppy, N. (1979). Pre-retirement life-style and the degree of planning for retirement. *Journal of Gerontology*, *34*, 254–263.

McTeer, W. (1972). *The scope of motivation*. Monterey, CA: Brooks/Cole.

McWaters, B. (1975). An outline of transpersonal psychology: Its meaning and relevance for education. In T. Roberts (Ed.), *Four psychologies applied to education*. New York: Schenkman.

Maher, B. (1966). *Principles of psychopathology*. New York: McGraw-Hill.

Maher, B. A. (1970). Delusional thinking and cognitive disorder. Paper presented at annual meeting of the American Psychological Association.

Maier, N. R. F. (1931). Reasoning in humans. II: The solution of a problem and its appearance in consciousness. *Journal of Comparative Psychology*, *12*, 181–194.

Maier, R. (1984). *Human sexuality in perspective*. Chicago: Nelson-Hall.

Maier, S., & Seligman, M. (1976). Learned helplessness: Theory and evidence. *Journal of Experimental Psychology: General*, *105*, 3–46.

Maier, S. F., Seligman, M. E. P., & Solomon, R. L. (1969). Pavlovian fear conditioning and learned helplessness. In B. A. Campbell & R. M. Church (Eds.), *Punishment and aversive behavior*. New York: Appleton-Century-Crofts.

Malamud, W. (1944). The psychoneuroses. In J. McV.Hunt (Ed.), *Personality and the behavior disorders* (Vol. 2). New York: Ronald Press, pp. 833–860.

Malcolm X, & Arthur Haley (1973). *The autobiography of Malcolm X*. New York: Ballantine.

Malinowski, B. (1927). *Sex and repression in savage society*. New York: Meridian Press.

Mandler, G. (1982). The structure of value: Accounting for trade. In M. Clark & S. Fiske (Eds.), *Affect and cognition*. Hillsdale NJ: Erlbaum.

Mandler, G. (1984). *Mind and body: Psychology of emotion and stress*. New York: Norton.

Mann, L. (1977). The effect of stimulus queues on queue-joining behavior. *Journal of Personality and Social Psychology*, *35*, 337–342.

Mann, L., Newton, J., & Innes, J. (1982). A test between deindividuation and emergent norm theories of crowd aggression. *Journal of Personality and Social Psychology*, *42*, 260–272.

Manz, W., & Lueck, H. (1968). Influence of wearing glasses on personality ratings: Cross-cultural validation of an old experiment. *Perceptual and Motor Skills*, *27*, 704.

Maranto, G. (1984). Aging: Can we slow the inevitable? *Discover*, *5*, 17–21.

Marcia, J. E. (1980). Identity in adolescence. In J. Adelson (Ed.), *Handbook of adolescent psychology*. New York: Wiley.

Margolis, A. (1971). The black student in political strife. *Proceedings of the 79th Annual Convention of the American Psychological Association*, *6*, 395–396.

Marks, W. B., Dobelle, W. H., & MacNichol, E. F., Jr. (1964). Visual pigments of single primate cones. *Science*, *143*, 1181–1183.

Marshall, J. (1969). *Law and psychology in conflict*. New York: Doubleday.

Martens, R., & Landers, P. (1972). Evalua-tion potential as a determinant of coaction effects. *Journal of Experimental Social Psychology*, *8*, 347–359.

Martin, B. (1981). *Abnormal Psychology: Clinical and scientific perspectives* (2nd ed.). New York: Holt, Rinehart & Winston.

Martindale, D. (1976, April). Torment in the tower. *Chicago*, pp. 96–101.

Martindale, D. A. (1971). Territorial dominance behavior in dyadic verbal interactions. *Proceedings of the American Psychological Association*, 79th Annual Convention, *6*, 305–306.

Maslach, C. (1979). Negative emotional biasing of unexplained arousal. In C. Izard (Ed.), *Emotion, personality and psychopathology*. New York: Plenum.

Maslow, A. H. (1968). *Toward a psychology of being* (2nd ed.). New York: D. Van Nostrand.

Maslow, A. H. (1970). *Motivation and personality* (2nd ed.). New York: Harper & Row.

Massaro, D. W. (1970). Perceptual auditory images. *Journal of Experimental Psychology*, *85*, 411–417.

Masson, M. E. J., & McDaniel, M. A. (1981). The role of organizational processes in long-term retention. *Journal of Experimental Psychology: Human Learning and Memory*, *7*, 100–110.

Masters, J. C., & Yorkin-Levin, K. (Eds.). (1984). *Boundary areas in social and developmental psychology*. New York: Academic Press.

Masters, W. H., & Johnson, V. E. (1966). *Human sexual response*. Boston: Little, Brown.

Masters, W. H., & Johnson, V. E. (1975). *The pleasure bond*. Boston: Little, Brown.

Masters, W. H., & Johnson, V. E. (1970). *Human sexual inadequacy*. Boston: Little, Brown.

Masters, W. H., & Johnson, V. E. (1979). *Homosexuality in perspective*. Boston: Little, Brown.

Mather, J. A., & Lackner, J. R. (1981). Adaptation to visual displacement: Contribution of proprioceptive, visual, and attentional factors. *Perception*, *10*, 367–374.

Matin, L. (1981). Visual location and eye movements. In W. A. Wagenaar, A. H. Wertheim, & H. W. Leibowitz (Eds.), *Symposium on the study of motion perception*. New York: Plenum.

Matin, L., & MacKinnon, E. G. (1964). Autokinetic movement: Selective manipulation of directional components by image stabilization. *Science*, *143*, 147–148.

Matthews, K., & Carra, J. (1982). Suppression of menstrual distress symptoms: A study of type A behavior. *Personality and Social Psychology Bulletin*, *8*, 146–151.

Matthews, K., Helmreich, R., Beane, W., & Lucker, G. (1980). Pattern A., achievement striving, and scientific merit: Does pattern A. help or hinder? *Journal of Personality and Social Psychology*, *39*, 962–967.

Matthews, K. E., & Cannon, L. K. (1975). Environmental noise level as a determinant of helping behavior. *Journal of Personality and Social Psychology*, *24*, 323–350.

Mayer, J. (1955). Regulation of energy intake and body weight: The glucostatic theory and liostatic hypothesis. *Annals of the New York Academy of Sciences*, *63*, 15–43.

Mayer, L. A. (1975, June). That confounding enemy of sleep. *Fortune*.

Mead, M. (1928). *Coming of age in Samoa*. Chicago: University of Chicago Press.

Mead, M. (1935). *Sex and temperament in three primitive societies*. New York: Morrow.

Medvedev, Z. A. (1975). Aging and longevity: New approaches and new perspectives. *The Gerontologist*, *15*, 196–201.

Mee, C. L. (1978). *Seizure*. New York: Jove.

Mehrabian, A. (1971). Nonverbal communication. In M. R. Jones (Ed.), *Nebraska symposium on motivation*. Lincoln, NE: University of Nebraska Press.

Meichenbaum, D. (1977). *Cognitive behavior modification: An integrative approach*. New York: Plenum Press.

Meindl, J., & Lerner, M. (1984). Exacerbation of extreme responses to an outgroup. *Journal of Personality and Social Psychology*, *47*, 71–84.

Meltzoff, J., & Kornreich, M. (1970). *Research in psychotherapy*. New York: Atherton.

Mendel, G. (1955). Letter to Carl Nagele (1867). In M. Gabriel & S. Fogel (Eds.), *Great experiments in biology*. Englewood Cliffs, NJ: Prentice-Hall.

Mendelshon, R., & Orcutt, G. (1979). An empirical analysis of air pollution-does-response curves. *Journal of Environmental Economics and Management*, *6*, 85–106.

Middlemist, R. D., Knowles, E. S., & Matter, C. F. (1976). Personal space invasions in the lavatory: Suggestive evidence for arousal. *Journal of Personality and Social Psychology*, *33*, 541–546.

Milgram, S. (1963). Behavioral study of obedience. *Journal of Abnormal and Social Psychology*, *67*, 376.

Milgram, S. (1965). Liberating effects of group pressure. *Journal of Personality and Social Psychology*, *1*, 127–134.

Milgram, S. (1970). The experience of living in cities. *Science*, *167*, 1461–1468.

Milgram, S. (1977). *The individual in a social world*. Reading, MA: Addison-Wesley.

Miller, A. G. (1977). Actor and observer perceptions of the learning of a task. *Journal of Experimental Social Psychology*, *11*, 95–111.

Miller, A. G. (1982). Historical and contemporary perspectives on stereotypes. In A. G. Miller (Ed.), *In the eye of the beholder: Contemporary issues in stereotyping*. New York: Praeser.

Miller, B. C. (1976). A multivariate developmental model of marital satisfaction. *Journal of Marriage and the Family*, *38*, 643–657.

Miller, G. A. (1956). The magical number seven plus or minus two: Some limits on our capacity for processing information. *Psychological Review*, *62*, 81–97.

Miller, G. A., Galanter, E., & Pribram, K. H. (1960). *Plans and the structure of behavior*. New York: Holt, Rinehart & Winston.

Miller, J. A. (1984, April 21). Looking out for animal research. *Science News*, p. 247.

Miller, M. (1973). *Plain speaking*. New York: Berkeley.

Miller, M. (1982). In J. Roloff, Occupational noise—the subtle pollutant. *Science News*, *121*, 347–350.

Miller, N. E. (1944). Experimental studies of conflict. In J. McV. Hunt (Ed.), *Personality and the behavior disorders* (Vol. 1). New York: Ronald Press.

Miller, N. E. (1978). Biofeedback and visceral learning. *Annual Review of Psychology*, *29*, 373–404.

Miller, N. E. (1983). Behavioral medicine:

Symbiosis between laboratory and clinic. In M. R. Rosenzweig & L. W. Porter (Eds.), *Annual review of psychology*. Palo Alto, CA: Annual Reviews, Inc.

Miller, N. E., & Bugelski, R. (1948). Minor studies of aggression: II: The influence of frustrations imposed by the in-group on attitudes expressed toward the out-group. *Journal of Psychology*, *25*, 437–453.

Miller, N. E., & DiCara, L. (1967). Instrumental learning of heart-rate changes in curarized rats: Shaping and specificity to discriminative stimulus. *Journal of Comparative and Physiological Psychology*, *63*, 12–19.

Millon, T. (1969). *Modern psychopathology*. Philadelphia: Saunders.

Milner, B. (1970). Memory and the medial temporal regions of the brain. In K. H. Pribram & D. E. Broadbent (Eds.), *Biology of memory*. New York: Academic Press, pp. 29–50.

Milner, D. (1981). Racial prejudice. In J. Turner & H. Giles (Eds.), *Intergroup behavior*. Chicago: University of Chicago Press.

Mintz, N. C. (1956). Effects of aesthetic surroundings: II. Prolonged and repeated experience in a "beautiful" and an "ugly" room. *Journal of Psychology*, *41*, 459–466.

Minuchin, S., Rosman, B. L., & Baker, L. (1978). *Psychosomatic families*. Cambridge, MA: Harvard University Press.

Mischel, W. (1968). *Personality and assessment*. New York: Wiley.

Mischel, W. (1973). Toward a cognitive social learning reconceptualization of personality. *Psychological Review*, *80*, 252–283.

Mischel, W. (1976). *Introduction to personality* (2nd ed.). New York: Holt, Rinehart, & Winston.

Mischel, W. (1977). On the future of personality measurement. *American Psychologist*, *32*, 246–254.

Mischel, W. (1981). *Introduction to personality* (3rd ed.). New York: Holt, Rinehart and Winston.

Mischel, W., & Peake, P. K. (1982). Beyond déjà vu in the search for cross-situational consistency. *Psychological Review*, *89*, 730–755.

Mitchell, K. M., Bozarth, J. D., & Krauff, C. C. (1977). A reappraisal of the therapeutic effectiveness of accurate empathy, nonpossessive warmth, and genuineness. In A. S. Gurman & A. M. Razin (Eds.), *Effective psychotherapy: A handbook of research*. New York: Pergamon Press.

Moede, W. (1927). Die Richtlinien der Leisturgs-Psychologie. *Industrielle Psychotechnik*, *4*, 193–207.

Monaham, L., Kuhn, D., & Shuber, P. (1979). Intrapsychic versus cultural explorative of the "fear of success" motive. *Journal of Personality and Social Psychology*, *29*, 60–64.

Monahan, J., & Loftus, E. (1982). The psychology of law. *Annual Review of Psychology*, *33*, 441–475.

Monson, T., & Snyder, M. (1977). Actors, observers, and the attribution process: Toward a reconceptualization. *Journal of Experimental Social Psychology*, *13*, 89–111.

Moody, R. (1975). *Life after life*. New York: Bantam.

Moore, M. L. (1978). *Realities in childbearing*. Philadelphia: Saunders.

Moray, N. (1959). Attention in dichotic listening: Affective cues and the influence of instructions. *Quarterly Journal of Experimental Psychology*, *11*, 56–60.

Morcloud, R. L., & Zajonc, R. (1982). Exposure effects in person perception: Familiarity, similarity and attraction. *Journal of Experimental Social Psychology*, *18*, 395–415.

Morgan, M. J., Fitch, M. D., Holman, J. G., & Lea, S. E. G. (1976). Pigeons learn the concept of an "A." *Perception*, *5*, 57–66.

Morris, W. N., Worchel, S., Bois, J. L., Pearson, J. A., Rountree, C. A., Samaha, G. M., Wachtler, J., & Wright, S. L. (1976). Collective coping with stress: Group reactions to fear, anxiety, and ambiguity. *Journal of Personality and Social Psychology*, *33*, 674–679.

Morrison, F. J., & Lord, C. (Eds.). (1984). *Applied developmental psychology*. New York: Academic Press.

Mortensen, C. (1972). *Communication: The study of human interaction*. New York: McGraw-Hill.

Mosante, L., MacDougall, J., & Dembroski, T. (1984). The type A behavior pattern and attributions for success and failure. *Personality and Social Psychology Bulletin*, *10*, 544–553.

Moscovici, S., & Personnaz, B. (1980). Studies in social influences. Minority influence and conversion behavior in a perceptual look. *Journal of Experimental Social Psychology*, *16*, 270–283.

Moscovici, S., & Zavalloni, M. (1969). The group as a polarizer of attitudes. *Journal of Personality and Social Psychology*, *12*, 125–135.

Moss, M. & Arend, R. (1977). Self-directed contact desensitization. *Journal of Consulting and Clinical Psychology*, *45*, 730–738.

Mowat, F. (1963). *Never cry wolf*. Boston: Atlantic Monthly Press, Little, Brown.

Moyer, K. (1976). *The psychology of aggression*. New York: Harper & Row.

Mueller, C., & Donnerstein, E. (1977). The effects of humor-induced arousal upon aggressive behavior. *Journal of Research in Personality*, *11*, 73–82.

Muhelman, J. T., Bruker, C., & Ingram, C. M. (1976). The generosity shift. *Journal of Personality and Social Psychology*, *34*, 344–351.

Murray, H. (1938). *Explorations in personality*. New York: Oxford University Press.

Murray, J. R., Powers, E. A., & Havighurst, R. J. (1971). Personal and situational factors producing flexible careers. *The Gerontologist*, *11*, 4–12.

Murstein, B. I. (1972). Physical attractiveness and marital choice. *Journal of Personality and Social Psychology*, *22*, 8–12.

Mussen, P. H., & Jones, M. C. (1957). Self-conceptions, motivations, and interpersonal attitudes of late and early maturing boys. *Child Development*, *28*, 243–256.

Myers, D. G. (1982). Polarizing effect of social interaction. In J. Davis & G. Stocker-Kreidgaver (Eds.), *Group decision making*. New York: Academic Press.

Nadler, A., Shapira, R., & Ben-Itzhak, S. (1982). Good looks may help: Effects of helpers' physical attractiveness and sex of helper in males' and females' help-seeking behavior. *Journal of Personality and Social Psychology*, *42*, 90–99.

Nagelman, D. B., Hale, S. L., & Ware, S. (1983). Prevalence of eating disorders in college women. Paper presented at the American Psychology Association, Anaheim.

Nahemow, L., & Lawton, M. P. (1975). Similarity and propinquity in friendship formation. *Journal of Personality and Social Psychology*, *32*, 205–213.

Nail, P., Levy, L., Russin, R., & Crandell, R. (1981). Time estimation and obesity. *Personality and Social Psychology Bulletin*, *7*, 139–146.

Napier, R., & Gershenfeld, M. (1981). *Groups: Theory and experience*. Boston: Houghton Mifflin.

Nash, R. (1967). *Wilderness and the American mind*. New Haven, CT: Yale University Press.

Nathan, P. E. (1976). Alcoholism. In H. Leitenberg (Ed.), *Handbook of behavior modification and behavior therapy*. Englewood Cliffs, NJ: Prentice-Hall.

Nedler, A., & Fisher, J. (1984). Effects of donor-recipient relationships on recipients' reactions to aid. In E. Staub et al. (Eds.), *Development and maintenance of prosocial behavior*. New York: Plenum.

Nelson, L. P., & Nelson, V. (1973). Religion and death anxiety. Paper presented at Society for the Scientific Study of Religion and Religious Research Association, San Francisco.

Nemeth, C. (1985). Intergroup relations between majority and minority. In S. Worchel & W. Austin (Eds.), *Psychology of intergroup relations*. Chicago: Nelson Hall.

Neugarten, B. L. (1968). The awareness of middle age. In B. L. Neugarten (Ed.), *Middle age and aging*. Chicago: University of Chicago Press.

Neugarten, B. L. (1970). Dynamics of transition of middle age to old age. *Journal of Geriatric Psychiatry*, *4*, 71–87.

Neugarten, B. L., & Hagestad, G. O. (1976). Age and the life course. In R. H. Binstock & E. Shanas (Eds.), *Handbook of aging and the social sciences*. New York: Van Nostrand Reinhold.

Neugarten, B. L., & Weinstein, K. K. (1964). The changing American grandparent. *Journal of Marriage and the Family*, *26*, 199–204.

Newcomer, J. (1977). Sonicguide: Its use with public school blind children. *Journal of Visual Impairment and Blindness*, *71*, 268–271.

Newman, O. (1972). *Defensible space*. New York: Macmillan.

Newman, O. (1975). *Design guidelines for creating defensible space*. Washington, DC: U.S. Government Printing Office.

Newman, L. and Hirt, J. (1983). The psychoanalytic theory of depression symptoms as a function of aggressive wishes and level of field articulation. *Journal of Abnormal Psychology*, *92*, 42–48.

New York Times News Service. (1981, November 29). Depression linked to specific gene. *The New York Times*.

Niijima, A. (1969). Afferent impulse charges from glucoreceptors in the liver of the guinea pig. *Annals of the New York Academy of Sciences*, *157* (2) 690–700.

NIMH (1982). *Television and behavior: Ten years of scientific progress and implications for the eighties*. Washington, DC: U.S. Government Printing Office.

Nisbett, R. E. (1968). Taste, deprivation, and weight determinants of eating behavior.

Journal of Personality and Social Psychology, *10*, 107–116.

Nisbett, R. E. (1972). Hunger, obesity, and the ventromedial hypothalamus. *Psychological Review*, *79*, 433–453.

Nisbett, R. E., & Borgida, E. (1975). Attribution and the psychology of prediction. *Journal of Personality and Social Pychology*, *32* (5), 932–943.

Nisbett, R., & Ross, L. (1980). *Human inference: Strategies and shortcomings of social judgment*. Englewood Cliffs, NJ: Prentice-Hall.

Noesjirwan, J. (1977). Contrasting cultural patterns of interpersonal closeness in doctors' waiting rooms in Sydney and Jakarta. *Journal of Cross-Cultural Psychology*, *8*, 359–368.

Norman, D. A. (1973). Memory, knowledge, and the answering of questions. In R. L. Solso (Ed.), *Contemporary issues in cognitive psychology*. Washington, DC: Winston.

Norman, D. A., & Rumelkart, D. E. (1975). *Exploration in cognition*. San Francisco: Freeman.

Normoyle, J., & Lavrokes, P. (1984). Fear of crime in elderly women: Perceptions of control, predictability, and territory. *Personality and Social Psychology Bulletin*, *10*, 191–202.

Nuckolls, K., Caasel, J., & Kaplan, B. (1972). Psychosocial assets, life crisis and the prognosis of pregnancy. *American Journal of Epidemiology*, *95*, 431–441.

Nydegger, C., & Mitteness, L. (1979). Transitions in fatherhood. *Generations*, *4*, 14–15.

Olds, J. (1973). Brain mechanisms of reinforcement learning. In L. D. E. Berlyne & K. B. Masden (Eds.), *Pleasure, reward, preference: Their nature, determinants, and role in behavior*. New York: Academic Press.

Olsen, K. M. (1969). Social class and age-group differences in the timing of family status changes: A study of age norms in American society. Unpublished doctoral dissertation, University of Chicago.

Olson, I. M., & Zanna, M. P. (1983). Attitudes and beliefs. In D. Perlman & P. C. Cozby (Eds.), *Social psychology*. New York: Holt, Rinehart and Winston.

Olshan, N. H. (1980). *Power over your pain without drugs*. New York: Rawson, Wade.

Olszewski, D. A., Rotton, J., & Soler, E. (1976). Conversation, conglomerate noise, and behavioral after-effects. Paper presented at Midwest Psychology Association meeting, Chicago.

Olton, D. S., Becker, J. T., & Handelmann, G. E. (1980). Hippocampal function: Working memory or cognitive mapping. *Physiological Psychology*, *8*, 239–246.

O'Neal, E., Brunault, M., Carifio, M., Trautwine, R., & Epstein, J. (1980). Effect of insult upon personal space. *Journal of Nonverbal Behavior*, *5*, 56–62.

Orne, M. T. (1962). On the social psychology of the psychological experiment: With particular reference to demand characteristics and their implications. *American Psychologist*, *17*, 776–783.

Orne, M. T. (1965). Social control in the psychological experiment: Antisocial behavior and hypnosis. *Journal of Personality and Social Psychology*, *1*, 189–200.

Orne, M. T. (1972). On the simulating subject as a quasi-control group in hypnosis research: What, why, and how. In E. Fromm & R. E. Shor (Eds.), *Hypnosis: Research development and perspectives*. Chicago: Aldine.

Orne, M. T. (1980). In G. D. Burrows & L. Dennerstein (Eds.), *Handbook of hypnosis and psychosomatic medicine*. Amsterdam: Elsevier/North Holland, pp. 29–51.

Ornitz, E. M. (1976). The modulation of sensory input and motor output in autistic children. In E. Scholpler & R. J. Reichler (Eds.), *Psychopathology and child development*. New York: Plenum Press, pp. 115–133.

Ornstein, R. E. (1977). *The psychology of consciousness* (2nd ed.). New York: Harcourt Brace Jovanovich.

Orr, S. P., & Lansetta, J. T. (1984). Extinction of an emotional response in the presence of facial expressions of emotion. *Motivation and Emotion*, *8*, 55–66.

Osgood, C. E. (1966). Dimensionality of the semantic space for communication via facial expressions. *Scandinavian Journal of Psychology*, *7*, 1–30.

Owen, D. R. (1972). The 47, XYY male: A review. *Psychological Review*, *78*, 209–233.

Page, H. A., Elfner, L. B., & Jarnison, N. (1966). Autokinetic effect as a function of intermittency of the light source. *Psychological Record*, *16*, 189–192.

Parke, D., Berkowitz, D., Leyens, J. P., West, S. G., & Sebastian, J. R. (1977). Some effects of violent and nonviolent movies on the behavior of juvenile delinquents. *Advances in Experimental Social Psychology*, *10*, 139–169.

Parkes, C. M., & Brown, R. (1972). Health after bereavement: A controlled study of young Boston widows and widowers. *Psychosomatic Medicine*, *34*, 449–461.

Pasamanick, B., & Lilienfeld, A. (1955). Association of maternal and fetal factors with the development of mental deficiency: I. Abnormalities in the prenatal and perinatal periods. *Journal of the American Medical Association*, *159*, 155–160.

Patterson, F. G. (1978). The gestures of a gorilla: Language acquisition in another pongid. *Brain and Language*, *5*, 72–97.

Patterson, G. R. (1979). A performance theory for coercive family interaction. In R. B. Cairns (Ed.), *Social interaction: Analysis and illustrations*. Hillsdale, NJ: Erlbaum.

Patterson, M. (1977). Interpersonal distance, affect and equilibrium theory. *Journal of Social Psychology*, *101*, 205–214.

Paul, S. M. (1977). Movement and madness: Toward a biological model of schizophrenia. In J. D. Master & M. E. P. Seligman (Eds.), *Psychopathology: Experimental models*. San Francisco: Freeman, pp. 358–386.

Paulus, P., McCain, G., & Cox, V. (1978). Death rates, psychiatric commitments, blood pressure and perceived crowding as a function of institutional crowding. *Environmental Psychology and Nonverbal Behavior*, *3*, 107–116.

Paulus, P., & McLain, G. (1983). Crowding in jails. *Basic and applied social psychology*, *4*, 89–107.

Pavio, A. (1978). Comparisons of mental clocks. *Journal of Experimental Psychology: Human Perception and Performance*, *4*, 61–71.

Pavlov, I. P. (1927). *Conditioned reflexes*. New York: Oxford University Press.

Peake, P., & Mischel, W. (1984). Getting lost in the search for large coefficients: Reply to Conley. *Psychological Review*, *91*, 497–501.

Pellegrini, R. (1973). Impressions of male personality as a function of beardedness. *Psychology*, *10*, 29.

Penfield, W. (1975). *The mastery of the mind: A critical study of consciousness and the human brain*. Princeton, NJ: Princeton University Press.

Penfield, W., & Rasmussen, T. (1950). *The cerebral cortex of man*. New York: Macmillan.

Penick, S. B., Smith, G. P., Wieneke, K., Jr., & Hinkle, L. E. (1963). An experimental evaluation of the relationship between hunger and gastric motility. *American Journal of Physiology*, *205*, 421–426.

Pennebaker, J. W. (1980). Perceptual and environmental determinants of coughing. *Basic and Applied Social Psychology*, *1*, 83–91, 94.

Pennebaker, J. W. (1982). *The psychology of physical symptoms*. New York: Springer-Verlag.

Pennebaker, J. W., & Skelton, A. (1981). Selective monitoring of physical sensations. *Journal of Personality and Social Psychology*, *41*, 213–223.

Pepler, R. (1963). Performance and well-being in heat. In J. Hardy (Ed.), *Temperature: Its measurement and control in science and industry*, *3*, Part 3. New York: Van Nostrand Reinhold.

Perez, J. (1979). *Family counseling*. New York: Van Nostrand.

Perls, F. S. (1969). *Ego, hunger and aggression: The beginning of Gestalt therapy*. New York: Random House.

Perls, F. S. (1969). *Gestalt therapy verbatim*. Lafayette, CA: Real People Press.

Perls, F. S. (1970). Four lectures. In J. Fagan & I. L. Sheperd (Eds.), *Gestalt therapy now*. Palo Alto, CA: Science and Behavior Books.

Perove, D. R., & Spielberger, C. D. (1966). Anxiety and the perception of punishment. *Mental Hygiene*, *50*, 390–397.

Perry, D. G., White, A. J., & Perry, L. C. (1984). Does early sextyping result from children's attempts to match their behavior to sex role stereotypes? *Child Development*, *55*, 2114–2121.

Pessin, J. (1933). The comparative effects of social and mechanical stimulation on memorizing. *American Journal of Psychology*, *45*, 263–270.

Peterson, C., & Seligman, M. (1984). Causal explanations as a risk factor for depression: Theory and evidence. *Psychological Review*, *91*, 347–375.

Peterson, J. A., & Payne, B. (1975). *Love in the later years*. New York: Associated Press.

Peterson, L. R., & Peterson, M. J. (1959). Short-term retention of individual items. *Journal of Experimental Psychology*, *58*, 193–198.

Petri, H. (1981). *Motivation: Theory and research*. Belmont, CA: Wadsworth.

Phares, E. J. (1976). *Locus of control in personality*. Morristown, NJ: General Learning Press.

Phares, E. J. (1984). *Introduction to personality*. Columbus, OH: Merrill.

Piaget, J. (1932). *The moral judgement of the child*. New York: Harcourt Brace Jovanovich.

Piaget, J. (1960). *The child's conception of the world*. London: Routledge.

Piliavin, I., Rodin, J., & Piliavin, J. (1969). Good Samaritanism: An underground phenomenon? *Journal of Personality and Social Psychology, 13*, 289–299.

Planned Parenthood. (1976). 11 million teenagers: What can be done about the epidemic of adolescent pregnancies in the United States? New York: PPFA.

Plomin, R., & DeFries, J. C. (1980). Genetics and intelligence: Recent data. *Intelligence, 4*, 15–24.

Plutchik, R. (1980). *Emotion: A psychoevolutionary analysis.* New York: Harper & Row.

Podd, M. H. (1972). Ego identity status and morality: The relationship between two developmental constructs. *Developmental Psychology, 6*, 497–507.

Pollen, D. A., & Ronner, S. F. (1982). Spatial computation performed by simple and complex cells in the visual cortex of the cat. *Vision Research, 22*, 101–118.

Poon, L. W. (1980). *Aging in the 1980's.* Washington, DC: American Psychological Association.

Poplin, D. (1978). *Social problems.* Glenview, IL: Scott, Foresman.

Population Reference Bureau, 1977. (1977). *World population data sheet.* Washington, DC: Population Reference Bureau.

Porteous, J. D. (1977). *Environment and behavior.* Reading, MA: Addison-Wesley.

Portuges, S. H., & Feshbach, N. D. (1972). The influence of sex and social class upon imitations of teachers by elementary school children. *Child Development, 43*, 981–989.

Potter, R. K., Kopp, G. A., & Kopp, H. G. (1966). *Visible speech.* New York: Dover.

Poulton, E. C. (1970). *Environment and human efficiency.* Springfield, IL: Charles C Thomas.

Poulton, E. C. (1978). A new look at the effects of noise: A rejoinder. *Psychological Bulletin, 85*, 1068–1079.

Poulton, E. C. (1979). Composite model for human performance in continuous noise. *Psychological Review, 86*, 361–375.

Powley, T., & Keesey, R. (1970). Relationship of body weight to the lateral hypothalamic feeding syndrome. *Journal of Comparative and Physiological Psychology, 70*, 25–36.

Premack, A. J., & Premack, D. (1972, November). Teaching language to an ape. *Scientific American, 227*, 25–36.

Premack, D. (1976). *Intelligence in ape and man.* Hillsdale, NJ: Erlbaum.

Prentice-Dunn, S., & Rogers, R. (1980). Effects of deindividuating situational cues and aggressive models on subjective deindividuation and aggression. *Journal of Personality and Social Psychology, 39*, 104–113.

President's Commission on Mental Health, 1978, Report to the President (1978). Washington, DC: U.S. Government Printing Office.

President's Council on Environmental Quality. (1978). Environmental Protection Agency, Washington, DC: U.S. Government Printing Office.

Presser, H. B. (1977). Social consequences of teenage childbearing. In W. Petersen & L. Day (Eds.), *Social demography: The state of the art.* Cambridge, MA: Harvard University Press.

Pribram, K. (1977). Some observations on the organization of studies of mind, brain, and behavior. In N. E. Zinberg (Ed.), *Alternate states of consciousness: Multiple perspectives on the study of consciousness.* New York: Free Press.

Proffitt, D. R., & Cutting, J. E. (1980). An invariant for wheel-generated motions and the logic of its determination. *Perception, 9*, 435–449.

Quattrone, G. (1985). On the perception of a group's variability. In S. Worchel & W. Austin (Eds.), *Psychology of intergroup relations,* Chicago: Nelson-Hall.

Quattrone, G., & Jones, E. (1980). The perception of variability with in-groups and out-groups: Implications for the law of small numbers. *Journal of Personality and Social Research, 38*, 141–152.

Rachman, S., & Hodyson, R. (1980). *Obsessions and compulsions.* Englewood Cliffs, NJ: Prentice-Hall.

Rapoport, R., & Rapoport, R. N. (1971). *Dual career families.* Baltimore: Penguin.

Raven, J. C. (1947). *Progressive matrices.* London: Lewis.

Rayner, K. (Ed.). (1983). *Eye movements in reading: Perceptual and language processes.* New York: Academic Press.

Raynor, J. O. (1970). Relationships between achievement-related motives, future orientation, and academic performance. *Journal of Personality and Social Psychology, 15*, 28–33.

Read, P. P. (1974). *Alive: The story of the Andes survivors.* Philadelphia: Lippincott.

Regan, D. T., Williams, M., & Sparling, S. (1972). Voluntary expiation of guilt: A field experiment. *Journal of Personality and Social Psychology, 24*, 42–45.

Reichel, D., & Geller, E. (1981). Applications of behavioral analysis for conserving transportation energy. In A. Baum & J. Singer (Eds.), *Advances in environmental psychology* (Vol. 3). Hillsdale, NJ: Erlbaum.

Reiser, M. (1980). *Handbook of investigative hypnosis.* Los Angeles: LEHI Publishing Co.

Reiser, M. (1982). Erickson and law enforcement: Investigative hypnosis. In J. K. Zeig (Ed.), *Ericksonian approach to hypnosis and psychotherapy.* New York: Brunner/Mazel.

Reiser, M., & Nielson, M. (1980). Investigative hypnosis: A developing specialty. *American Journal of Clinical Hypnosis, 23*, 75–77.

Rescorla, R. A., & Holland, P. C. (1982). Behavioral studies of associative learning in animals. *Annual Review of Psychology, 33*, 265–308.

Restak, R. (1979). *The brain: The last frontier.* Garden City, NY: Doubleday.

Restak, R. (1984). *The brain.* New York: Bantam Book.

Restle, F. (1962). The selection of strategies in cue learning. *Psychological Review, 69*, 329–343.

Reyaijmakers, J. G. W., & Shiffrin, R. M. (1981). Search of associative memory. *Psychological Review, 88*, 93–134.

Rhodewalt, F. (1984). Self-involvement, self-attribution and the Type A coronary-prone behavior pattern. *Journal of Personality and Social Psychology, 47*, 662–670.

Rice, B. (1974). Rattlesnakes, French fries, and pupillometric oversell. *Psychology Today, 7*, 55–59.

Rice, B. (1978). The new truth machine. *Psychology Today, 12*, 61–78.

Riley, M. W., Johnson, M. E., & Foner, A. (1972). *Aging and society: A sociology of age stratification.* New York: Russell Sage Foundation.

Rimland, B. (1964). *Infantile autism: The syndrome and its implications for a neural theory of behavior.* New York: Appleton-Century-Crofts.

Rimm, D. C., & Masters, J. C. (1979). *Behavior therapy: Techniques and empirical findings.* New York: Academic Press.

Ringness, T. A. (1975). *The affective domain in education.* Boston: Little, Brown.

Ritchie, G. G. (with Elizabeth Sherrill). (1978). *Return from tomorrow.* Waco, TX: Chosen Books.

Rittle, R. M. (1981). Changes in helping behavior: Self versus situational perceptions as mediators of foot-in-the-door effect. *Personality and Social Psychology Bulletin, 7*, 431–437.

Ritzer, G. (1977). *Working: Conflict and change* (2nd ed.). Englewood Cliffs, NJ: Prentice-Hall.

Robertson, J. F. (1976). Significance of grandparents: Perception of young adult grandchildren. *The Gerontologist, 16*, 137–140.

Robinson, F. P. (1941). *Effective behavior.* New York: Harper & Row.

Rock, I. (1977). In defense of unconscious inference. In W. Epstein (Ed.), *Stability and constancy in visual perception: Mechanisms and processes.* New York: Wiley.

Rock, I., & Harris, C. S. (1967). Vision and touch. *Scientific American, 216*, 96–104.

Rodin, J. (1975). Causes and consequences of time perception differences in overweight and normal weight people. *Journal of Personality and Social Psychology, 31*, 808–910.

Rodin, J. (1977). The effects of stimulus-bound behavior on biological self-regulation: Feeding, obesity and external control. In G. Schwartz & D. Shapiro (Eds.), *Consciousness and self-regulation.* New York: Plenum Press.

Rodin, J. (1981). Understanding obesity: Defining the samples. *Personality and Social Psychology Bulletin, 7*, 147–151.

Rodin, J., & Baum, A. (1978). Crowding and helplessness: Potential consequences of density and loss of control. In A. Baum & Y. Epstein (Eds.), *Human response to crowding.* New York: Halsted.

Rodin, J., & Langer, E. (1977). Long-term effects of a control-relevant intervention with the institutionalized aged. *Journal of Personality and Social Psychology, 35*, 891–902.

Rodin, J., Slochower, J., & Fleming, B. (1977). Effect of degree of obesity, age of onset, and weight loss on responsiveness to sensory and external stimuli. *Journal of Comparative and Physiological Psychology, 36*, 988–999.

Rodin, J., Slochower, J., & Fleming, B. (1977). The effects of degree of obesity, age of onset and energy deficit on external responsiveness. *Journal of Comparative and Physiological Psychology, 91*, 586–597.

Rodin, J., Solomon, S., & Metcalf, J. (1978). Role of control in mediating perceptions of density. *Journal of Personality and Social Psychology, 36*, 988–999.

Roethlisberger, F., & Dickson, W. (1939). *Management and the worker.* Cambridge, MA: Harvard University Press.

Rofe, Y. (1984). Stress and affiliation: A utility theory. *Psychological Review, 91*, 251–268.

Rofe, Y., & Lewin, I. (1983). Affiliation among individuals suffering from severe diseases. Bar-Ilan University, Israel, unpublished manuscript.

Rogers, C. (1942). *Counseling and psychotherapy: Newer concepts in practice.* Boston: Houghton Mifflin.

Rogers, C. (1951). *Client-centered therapy.* Boston: Houghton Mifflin.

Rogers, C. (1970). *On becoming a person: A therapist's view of psychotherapy.* Boston: Houghton Mifflin.

Rogers, C. R. (1977). Carl Rogers on personal power: Inner strength and its revolutionary impact. New York: Delacorte Press.

Rogers, C. R. (1980). *A way of being.* Boston: Houghton Mifflin.

Rogers, C., & Dymond, A. (1954). *Psychotherapy and personality change.* Chicago: University of Chicago.

Rogers, C. R., & Truax, C. B. (1967). The therapeutic conditions anticedent to change: A theoretical view. In C. R. Rogers (Ed.), *The therapeutic relationship and its impact: A study of pychotherapy with schizophrenics.* Madison, WI: University of Wisconsin Press.

Rogers, R., & Deckner, C. (1975). Effects of fear appeals and physiological arousal upon emotion, attitudes, and cigarette smoking. *Journal of Personality and Social Psychology, 32,* 222–230.

Roitblat, H. L., Bever, T. G., & Terrance, H. S. (1984). *Animal cognition.* Hillsdale, NJ: Erlbaum.

Roos, P. (1968). Jurisdiction: An ecological concept. *Human Relations,* 75–84.

Rosch, E., & Lloyd, B. B. (Eds.). (1978). *Cognition and categorization.* Hillsdale, NJ: Erlbaum.

Rose, A. (1952). *Union solidarity.* Minneapolis: University of Minnesota Press.

Rose, S. (1973). *The conscious brain.* New York: Knopf.

Rosen, M. A. (1975). A dual model of obsessional neurosis. *Journal of Consulting and Clinical Psychology, 43,* 453–459.

Rosen, R., & Rosen, L. (1981). *Human sexuality.* New York: Knopf.

Rosen, S. (1984). Some paradoxical status implications of helping and being helped. In E. Staub et al. (Eds.), *Development and maintenance of prosocial behavior.* New York: Plenum.

Rosen, S., Bergman, M., Plestor, D., El-Mofty, A., & Satti, M. (1962). Presbycosis study of a relatively noise-free population in the Sudan. *Annals of Otology, Rhinology and Laryngology, 71,* 727–743.

Rosenbaum, D. L., & Seligman, M. (1984). *Abnormal psychology.* New York: Norton.

Rosenblatt, P. C., & Budd, L. B. (1977). Territoriality and privacy in married and unmarried couples. *Journal of Social Psychology, 31,* 240–242.

Rosenfeld, P., Giacalone, R., & Tedeschi, J. (1984). Cognitive dissonance and impression management explanations for effort justification. *Personality and Social Psychology Bulletin, 10,* 394–401.

Rosenhan, D. L. (1973). On being sane in insane places. *Science, 179,* 250–258.

Rosenhan, D. L. (1975). The contextual nature of psychiatric diagnosis. *Journal of Abnormal Psychology, 84,* 462–474.

Rosenthal, D. (1970). *Genetic theory and abnormal behavior.* New York: McGraw-Hill.

Rosenthal, R. (1966). *Experimenter effects in behavioral research.* New York: Appleton-Century-Crofts.

Rosenthal, R. (1973). The Pygmalion effect lives. *Psychology Today,* 56–63.

Rosenthal, R., & Jacobson, L. V. (1968). Teacher expectations for the disadvantaged. *Scientific American, 4,* 19–23.

Rosenthal, R., & Jacobson, L. (1968). *Pygmalion in the classroom: Teacher expectation and pupils' intellectual development.* New York: Holt, Rinehart & Winston.

Rosenthal, T., & Bandura, A. (1978). Psychological modeling: Theory and practice. In S. L. Garfield & A. E. Bergin (Eds.), *Handbook of psychotherapy and behavior change: An empirical analysis* (2nd ed.). New York: Wiley.

Rosenzweig, M. R. (1966). Environmental complexity, cerebral change and behavior. *American Psychologist, 21,* 321–332.

Ross, L. (1977). The intuitive psychologist and his short-comings: Distortions in the attribution process. In L. Berkowitz (Ed.), *Advances in experimental social psychology* (Vol. 10). New York: Academic Press.

Ross, L., Bierbrauer, G., & Hoffman, S. (1976). The role of attribution processes in conformity and dissent: Revisiting the Asch situation. *American Psychologist, 31,* 148–157.

Ross, L. D. (1981). The "intuitive scientist" formulation and its developmental implications. In J. H. Harell & L. Ross (Eds.), *Social cognitive development: Frontiers and possible futures.* Cambridge, England: Cambridge University Press.

Ross, L. D., Lepper, M., Strack, F., & Steinmetz, J. (1977). Social explanation and social expectation: Effects of real and hypothetical explanations on subjective likelihood. *Journal of Personality and Social Psychology, 35,* 817–829.

Ross, M., & Sicoly, F. (1979). Egocentric biases in availability and attribution. *Journal of Personality and Social Psychology, 37,* 322–336.

Ross, N. (1984, November 24). Researchers debate use of animals in studies. Began TX: Eagle. (Syndicated story—Knight-Ruler News Service.)

Rothbart, M. K. (1971). Birth order and mother-child interaction in an achievement situation. *Journal of Personality and Social Psychology, 17,* 113–120.

Rothbart, M., & Birrell, P. (1977). Attitude and the perception of faces. *Journal of Research in Personality, 11,* 209–215.

Rotter, J. (1954). *Social learning and clinical psychology.* Englewood Cliffs, NJ: Prentice-Hall.

Rotter, J. B. (1966). Generalized expectancies for internal vs. external control of reinforcement. *Psychological Monographs, 80* (whole No. 609).

Rotter, J. B. (1975). Some problems and misconceptions related to the construct of internal versus external control of reinforcement. *Journal of Consulting and Clinical Psychology, 43,* 56–67.

Rotter, J. B. (1978). Generalized expectancies for problem solving and psychotherapy. *Cognitive Therapy and Research, 2,* 1–10.

Rotter, J. B. (1982). *The development and application of social learning theory.* New York: Praeger.

Rotter, J., & Frey, J. (1984). Air pollution, weather and psychiatric emergencies: A constructive replication. In J. Fisher et al. (Eds.), *Environmental psychology* (2nd ed.). New York: Holt, Rinehart and Winston.

Rotter, J. B., & Hochreich, D. J. (1975). *Personality.* Glenview, IL: Scott, Foresman.

Rotton, J., Barry, T., Frey, J., & Soler, E. (1978). Air pollution and interpersonal attraction. *Journal of Applied Social Psychology, 8,* 57–71.

Rotton, J., Frey, J., Barry, T., Milligan, M., & Fitzpatrick, M. (1979). The air pollution experience and interpersonal aggression. *Journal of Applied Social Psychology, 9,* 397–412.

Routtenberg, A. (1968). The two-arousal hypothesis: Reticular formation and limbic system. *Psychological Review, 75,* 51–80.

Royce, J. R., Stayton, W. R., & Kinkade, R. G. (1962). Experimental reduction of autokinetic movement. *American Journal of Psychology, 75,* 221–231.

Rozin, P., & Kalat, J. W. (1971). Specific hungers and poison avoidance as adaptive specializations of learning. *Psychological Review, 78,* 459–486.

Rubin, A. (1973). *Liking and loving: An invitation to social psychology.* New York: Holt, Rinehart & Winston.

Rubin, I. (1966). Sex after forty and after seventy. In R. Brecher & E. Brecher (Eds.), *An analysis of human sexual response.* New York: Signet.

Rubin, J. (1967). Increased self-acceptance: A means of reducing prejudice. *Journal of Personality and Social Psychology, 5,* 233–238.

Rubin, J. A., Provenzano, F. J., & Luria, A. (1974). The eye of the beholder: Parents' views on sex of newborns. *American Journal of Orthopsychiatry, 44,* 512–519.

Rubin, Z., Peplau, L. A., & Hill, C. T. (1978). Loving and leaving: Sex differences in romantic attachments. Unpublished manuscript, Brandeis University.

Ruff, H. A., & Birch, H. G. (1974). Infant visual fixation: The effect of concentricity, curvilinearity, and the number of directions. *Journal of Experimental Child Psychology, 17,* 460–473.

Rumbaugh, D. M. (Ed.). (1977). *Language learning by a chimpanzee: The Lana project.* New York: Academic Press.

Rushton, J. P., Bainerd, C., & Pressley, M. (1983). Behavioral development and construct validity: The principle of aggregation. *Psychological Bulletin, 94,* 18–38.

Russek, M. (1971). Hepatic receptors and the neurophysiological mechanisms controlling feeding behavior. In S. Ehrenpreis (Ed.), *Neurosciences research* (Vol. 4). New York: Academic Press.

Russell, F. (1962). *Tragedy in Dedham.* New York: McGraw-Hill.

Rutter, M. (1974). The development of infantile autism. *Psychological Medicine, 4,* 147–163.

Rux, J. M. (1976). Widows and widowers: Instrumental skills, socioeconomic status, and life satisfaction. Unpublished doctoral dissertation, Pennsylvania State University.

Ruys, T. (1971). Windowless offices. *Man-Environment Systems, 1,* 549.

Rykman, R. M. (1979). *Theories of personality.* New York: Van Nostrand.

Sacks, J. S. S. (1967). Recognition memory for syntactic and semantic aspects of connected discourse. *Perception and Psychophysics*, *2*, 437–442.

Safer, M., Tharps, Q., Jackson, T., & Leventhal, H. (1979). Determinants of three stages of delay in seeking care at a medical center. *Medical Care*, *17*, 11–29.

Sakurai, M. M. (1975). Small group cohesiveness and detrimental conformity. *Sociometry*, *38*, 340–357.

Sanders, E. (1974, November). Charlie and the devil. *Esquire*, pp. 105–111.

Sanders, G. (1981). Driven by distinction: An integrative review of social facilitation theory and research. *Journal of Experimental Social Psychology*, *17*, 227–251.

Santee, R., & Maslach, C. (1982). To agree or not to agree: Personal dissent amid social pressure to conform. *Journal of Personality and Social Psychology*, *42*, 690–701.

Sarason, I. G. (1975). Test anxiety and the self-disclosing coping model. *Journal of Consulting and Clinical Psychology*, *43*, 148–153.

Sarason, I. G. (1981). Test anxiety, stress and social support. *Journal of Personality*, *49*, 101–114.

Sarason, I. G., & Sarason, B. R. (1980). *Abnormal psychology* (3rd ed.). Englewood Cliffs, NJ: Prentice-Hall.

Sarnoff, I., & Zimbardo, P. G. (1961). Anxiety, fear and social affiliation. *Journal of Abnormal and Social Psychology*, *62*, 356–363.

Scarr, S., & Weinberg, R. A. (1977). Intellectual similarities within families of both adopted and biological children. *Intelligence*, *1*, 187–191.

Scarr-Salapatek, S. (1971). Race, social class, and IQ. *Science*, *174*, 1285.

Scarr-Salapatek, S. (1975). Genetics and the development of intelligence. In F. Horowitz (Ed.), *Review of child development research* (Vol. 4). Chicago: University of Chicago Press.

Schacht, T., & Nathan, P. (1977). But is it good for psychologists? Appraisal and status of DSM-III. *American Psychologist*, *32*, 1017–1025.

Schacter, D. L. (1976). The hypnagogic state: A critical review of the literature. *Psychological Bulletin*, *83*, 452–481.

Schachter, S. (1951). Deviation, rejection and communication. *Journal of Abnormal and Social Psychology*, *46*, 190–207.

Schachter, S. (1959). *The psychology of affiliation*. Stanford, CA: Stanford University Press.

Schachter, S. (1971). *Emotion, obesity, and crime*. New York: Academic Press.

Schachter, S. (1971). Some extraordinary facts about obese humans and rats. *American Psychologist*, 129–144.

Schachter, S., & Friedman, L. N. (1974). The effects of work and cue prominence on eating behavior. In S. Schachter & J. Rodin (Eds.), *Obese humans and rats*. Hillsdale, NJ: Erlbaum.

Schachter, S., & Gross, L. P. (1968). Manipulated time and eating behavior. *Journal of Personality and Social Psychology*, *10*, 98–106.

Schachter, S., & Latane, B. (1964). Crime, cognition, and the autonomic nervous system. In D. Levine (Ed.), *Nebraska Symposium on Motivation*, 221–273.

Schachter, S., & Singer, J. F. (1962). Cognitive, social and physiological determinants of emotional state. *Psychological Review*, *69*, *337*, 379–399.

Schachter, S., & Wheeler, L. (1962). Epi-

nephrine, chlorpromazine and amusement. *Journal of Applied Social Psychology*, *65*, 121–128.

Schaffer, H. R., & Emerson, P. E. (1964). The development of social attachments in infancy. *Monographs of the Society for Research in Child Development*, *29* (3, Serial No. 94).

Schaie, K. W. (Ed.). (1983). *Longitudinal studies of adult psychological development*. New York: The Guilford Press.

Schaie, K. W., & Labouvie-Vier, G. (1974). Generational and ontogenetic components of change in adult cognitive behavior. A fourteen-year cross-sequential study. *Journal of Developmental Psychology*, *10*, 305–320.

Schaller, M. (1975). Chromatic vision in human infants: Conditioned operant fixation to "hues" of varying intensity. *Bulletin of the Psychonomic Society*, *6*, 39–42.

Schank, R. (1973). Identification of conceptualizations underlying natural language. In R. Schank & K. Colby (Eds.), *Computer models of thought and language*. San Francisco: Freeman.

Schank, R., & Abelson, R. P. (1977). *Scripts, plans, goals, and understanding: An inquiry into human knowledge structures*. New York: Halsted.

Shebilske, W. L. (1977). Visuomotor coordination in visual direction and position constancies. In W. Epstein (Ed.), *Stability and constancy in visual perception: Mechanisms and processes*. New York: Wiley.

Shebilske, W. L. (1980). Structuring an internal representation of text: A basis for literacy. In P. A. Kolers, M. E. Wrolstad, & H. Bouma (Eds.), *Processing of visible language* (Vol. 2). New York: Plenum.

Shebilske, W. L. (1984). Context effects and efferent factors in perception and cognition. In W. Prinz & A. F. Sanders (Eds.), *Cognition and motor processes*. New York: Springer-Verlag.

Shebilske, W. L., & Rotondo, J. H. (1981). Typographical and spatial cues that facilitate learning from textbooks. *Visible Language*, *15*, 41–54.

Scheerer, M. (1963). Problem solving. *Scientific American*, *208*, 118–128.

Schein, E. H. (1975). How "career anchors" hold executives to their career paths. *Personnel*, *52*, 11–24.

Schiller, P., & Wiener, M. (1962). Binocular and stereoscopic viewing of geometric illusions. *Perceptual and Motor Skills*, *15*, 739–747.

Schlenker, B. R. (1985). *The self and social life*. New York: McGraw Hill.

Schlesier-Stropp, B. (1984). Bulimia: A review of the literature. *Psychological Bulletin*, *95*, 247–257.

Schlesinger, A. (1965). *A thousand days*. Boston: Houghton Mifflin.

Schlossberg, H. (1954). Three dimensions of emotion. *Psychological Review*, *61*, 81–88.

Schroeder, D., & Costa, P. (1984). Influence of life event stress on physical illness: Substantive effects or methodological flaws? *Journal of Personality and Social Psychology*, *46*, 853–863.

Schulz, R. (1984). *Human sexuality* (2nd ed.). Englewood Cliffs, NJ: Prentice-Hall.

Schwartz, D., & Barsky, S. (1977). The home court advantage. *Social Forces*, *55*, 641–661.

Schwartz, G. E. (1975). Biofeedback, self-regulation, and the patterning of physio-

logical processes. *American Scientist*, *63*, 314–324.

Schwartz, S. H. (1970). Elicitation of moral obligation and self-sacrificing behavior: An experimental study of volunteering to be a bone marrow donor. *Journal of Personality and Social Psychology*, *15*, 283–293.

Schwartz, S. H., & Howard, J. A. (1984). Internalized values as motivators of helping behavior. In E. Staub et al. (Eds.), *Development and maintenance of prosocial behavior*. New York: Plenum.

Scovern, A. W., & Kilmann, P. R. (1980). Status of electroconvulsive therapy: Review of the outcome literature. *Psychological Bulletin*, *87*, 260–303.

Sears, P. S., & Barbee, A. H. (1977). Career and life satisfactions among Terman's gifted women. In J. C. Stanley, W. C. George, & C. H. Solano (Eds.), *The gifted and the creative: Fifty-year perspective*. Baltimore: Johns Hopkins University Press.

Sears, R. R. (1977). Sources of life satisfactions of the Terman gifted man. *American Psychologist*, *32*, 119–128.

Sears, R. R., Whiting, J. W. M., Nowlis, J., & Sears, P. W. (1953). Child-rearing antecedents of aggression and dependency in young children. *Genetic Psychology Monographs*, *47*, 135–234.

Secunda, S. K., Katz, M. M., Friedman, R. J., & Schuyler, D. (1973). *Special report 1973: The depressive disorders*. Washington, DC: U.S. Government Printing Office (DHEW Publication No. 739157).

Seeman, M., & Evans, J. W. (1962). Alienation and learning in a hospital setting. *American Sociological Review*, *27*, 772–783.

Segal, M. W. (1974). Alphabet and attraction: An unobtrusive measure of the effect of propinquity in a field study. *Journal of Personality and Social Psychology*, *30*, 654–657.

Seghers, C. (1948). Color in the office. *The Management Review*, *37*, 452–453.

Sekuler, R., Kline, D., & Dismukes, K. (1982). *Aging and human visual function*. New York: Alan R. Liss, Inc.

Seligman, C., & Darley, J. (1977). Feedback as a means of decreasing residential energy consumption. *Journal of Applied Psychology*, *62*, 363–368.

Seligman, C., & Hutton, R. (1981). Evaluating energy conservation programs. *Journal of Social Issues*, *37*, 51–72.

Seligman, C., Kriss, M., Darley, J., Fazio, R., Becker, L., & Pryor, J. (1979). Predicting residential energy consumption from homeowners' attitudes. *Journal of Applied Social Psychology*, *9*, 70–90.

Seligman, M. E. P. (1974). Depression and learned helplessness. In R. J. Friedman & M. M. Katz (Eds.), *The psychology of depression: Contemporary theory and research*. Washington, DC: Winston-Wiley.

Seligman, M. E. P. (1975). *Helplessness: On depression development and death*. San Francisco: Freeman.

Seligman, M. E. P., Maler, S. F., & Geer, J. (1968). The alleviation of learned helplessness in the dog. *Journal of Abnormal Psychology*, *78*, 256–262.

Selye, H. (1976). *The stress of life* (rev. ed.). New York: McGraw-Hill.

Seyler, L., Canalis, E., Spare, S., & Reichlin, S. (1978). Abnormal gonadotropin secretory responses to LRH in transsexual women after diethylstibestrol priming. *Jour-*

nal of Clinical Endocrinology Metabolism, 47, 176–183.

Shadish, W. R. (1984). Policy research: Lessons from the implementation of deinstitutionalization. *American Psychologist, 39*, 725–738.

Shakow, D. (1977). Segmental set: The adaptive process in schizophrenia. *American Psychologist, 32*, 129–139.

Shapiro, A. (1971). Placebo effects in medicine, psychotherapy, and psychoanalysis. In A. Bergin & S. Garfield (Eds.), *Handbook of psychotherapy and behavior change*. New York: Wiley.

Shapiro, D. (1977). A biofeedback strategy in the study of consciousness. In N. E. Zinberg (Ed.), *Alternate states of consciousness: Multiple perspectives on the study of consciousness*. New York: Free Press.

Shapiro, D., & Shapiro, D. (1982). Meta-analysis of comparative therapy outcome studies: A replication. *Psychological Bulletin, 92*, 581–604.

Shapiro, D., & Shapiro, D. (1983). Comparative therapy outcome research: Methodological implications of meta-analysis. *Journal of Counseling and Clinical Psychology, 51*, 54–64.

Shapiro, J. (1978). *Methods of group psychotherapy and encounter*. Itasca, IL: Peacock Press.

Shapiro, S. (1981). *Contemporary theories of schizophrenia*. New York: McGraw-Hill.

Shashoua, V. E. (1967). Identification of specific changes in the pattern of brain protein synthesis after training. *Science, 193*, 1264–1266.

Shaver, K. (1973). *An introduction to attribution processes*. Cambridge, MA: Winthrop.

Shaw, M. (1981). *Group dynamics: The psychology of small group behavior* (3rd ed.). New York: McGraw-Hill.

Shaw, M. E. (1955). A comparison of two types of leadership in various communication nets. *Journal of Abnormal and Social Psychology, 50*, 127–134.

Shebilske, W. L. (1977). Visuomotor coordination in visual direction and position constancies. In W. Epstein (Ed.), *Stability and constancy in visual perception: Mechanisms and processes*. New York: Wiley.

Shebilske, W. L. (1980). Structuring an internal representation of text: A basis for literacy. In P. A. Kolers, M. E. Wrolstad, & H. Bouma (Eds.), *Processing of visible language* (Vol. 2). New York: Plenum.

Shebilske, W. L. (1981). Visual direction illusions in everyday situations: Implications for sensorimotor and ecological theories. In D. F. Fisher, R. A. Monty, & J. W. Senders (Eds.), *Eye movements: Cognition and visual perception*. Hillsdale, NJ: Erlbaum.

Shebilske, W. L., & Ebenholtz, S. M. (1971). Ebbinghaus derived-list experiments reconsidered. *Psychological Review, 78*, 553–555.

Shebilske, W. L., & Reid, L. S. (1979). Reading eye movements, macro-structure and comprehension processes. In P. A. Kolers, M. E. Wrolstad, & H. Bouma (Eds.), *Processing visible language* (Vol. 1). New York: Plenum.

Shebilske, W. L., & Rotondo, J. H. (1981). Typographical and spatial cues that facilitate learning from textbooks. *Visible Language, 15*, 41–54.

Sheldon, W. H. (1942). *The varieties of tempera-*

ment: A psychology of constitutional differences*. New York: Harper & Row.

Sheldon, W., Hart, E., & McDermott, E. (1949). *Varieties of delinquent youth: An introduction to constitutional psychiatry*. New York: Harper & Row.

Sheppard, J. J., & Mysak, E. D. (1984). Ontogeny of infantile oral reflexes and emerging chewing. *Child Development, 55*, 831–843.

Sherif, M. (1936). *The psychology of social norms*. New York: Harper & Row.

Sherif, M., Harvey, O., White, B., Hood, W., & Sherif, C. (1961). *Intergroup conflict and cooperation: The Robber's Cove experiment*. Norman, OK: Institute of Group Relations, University of Oklahoma.

Sherman, A. R. (1979). In vivo therapies for phobic reactions, instrumental behavior problems, and interpersonal and communication problems. In A. P. Goldstein & F. H. Kanfer (Eds.), *Maximizing treatment gains: Transfer enhancement in psychotherapy*. New York: Academic Press.

Sherrod, D. (1974). Crowding, perceived control and behavioral aftereffects. *Journal of Applied Social Psychology, 4*, 171–196.

Shertzer, B., & Stone, S. C. (1974). *Fundamentals of counseling* (2nd ed.). Boston: Houghton Mifflin.

Shields, J. (1962). *Monozygotic twins brought up apart and brought up together*. London: Oxford University Press.

Shockley, W. (1972). Dysgenics, geneticity, and raceology: A challenge to the intellectual responsibility of educators. *Phi Delta Kappa, 53*, 297–307.

Shor, R. E., & Orne, E. C. (1962). *The Harvard group scale of hypnotic susceptibility: Form A*. Palo Alto, CA: Consulting Psychologists Press.

Shotland, R. L., & Huston, T. L. (1979). Emergencies: What are they and do they influence bystanders to intervene? *Journal of Personality and Social Psychology, 37*, 1822–1834.

Shotland, R. L., & Straw, M. K. (1976). Bystander response to an assault: When a man attacks a woman. *Journal of Personality and Social Psychology, 34*, 990–999.

Shurley, J. (1963). *Proceedings of the third world congress of psychiatry* (Vol. 3). Toronto, Ontario: University of Toronto Press.

Siegel, R. K. (1977). Hallucinations. *Scientific American, 237*, 132–139.

Siegelman, M. (1974). Parental background of male homosexuals and heterosexuals. *Archives of Sexual Behavior, 3*, 3–18.

Sigall, H., & Ostrove, N. (1975). Beautiful but dangerous: Effects of offender attractiveness and nature of crime on juridic judgements. *Journal of Personality and Social Psychology, 31*, 410–414.

Silverman, L. H. (1976). Psychoanalytic theory: "The reports of my death are greatly exaggerated." *American Psychologist, 31*, 621–637.

Simpson, E. (1974). Moral development research. A case study of scientific cultural bias. *Human Development, 17*, 81–105.

Simpson, M. L. (1984). The status of study strategy instruction: Implications for classroom teachers. *Journal of Reading, 28*, 136–43.

Sinex, F. M. (1974). The mutation theory of aging. In M. Rickstein (Ed.), *Theoretical aspects of aging*. New York: Academic Press.

Singer, J. L. (1975). The inner world of daydreaming. New York: Harper & Row.

Singer, J. L. (1984). *The human personality*. New York: Harcourt Brace Jovanovich.

Singer, J., Brush, C., & Lublin, S. (1965). Some aspects of deindividuation: Identification and conformity. *Journal of Experimental Social Psychology, 1*, 356–378.

Singer, J. E., Lundberg, V., & Frankenhauser, M. (1978). Stress on the train: A study of urban commuting. In A. Baum, J. Singer, & S. Valins (Eds.), *Advances in environmental psychology* (Vol. 1). Hillsdale, NJ: Erlbaum.

Sistrunk, F., & McDavid, J. W. (1971). Sex variable in conforming behavior. *Journal of Personality and Social Psychology, 17*, 200–207.

Sizemore, C., & Pittillo, E. (1977). *I'm Eve*. Garden City, NY: Doubleday.

Skinner, B. F. (1948). *Walden two*. New York: Macmillan.

Skinner, B. F. (1953). *Science and human behavior*. New York: Macmillan.

Skinner, B. F. (1957). *Verbal behavior*. New York: Appleton-Century-Crofts.

Skinner, B. F. (1960). Pigeons in a pelican. *American Psychologist, 15*, 28–37.

Skinner, B. F. (1938, 1966). *The behavior of organisms*. Englewood Cliffs, NJ: Prentice-Hall.

Skinner, B. F. (1974). *About behaviorism*. New York: Knopf.

Skinner, B. F. (1978). The ethics of helping people. In L. Wispe (Ed.), *Sympathy, altruism, and helping behavior*. New York: Academic Press.

Sklar, L., & Anirman, H. (1951). Stress and cancer. *Psychological Bulletin, 89*, 369–406.

Slobin, D. I. (1971). *Psycholinguistics*. Chicago: Scott, Foresman.

Smith, C. P., Ryan, E. R., & Diggins, D. R. (1972). Moral decision making: Cheating on examinations. *Journal of Personality, 40*, 640–660.

Smith, E. E., & Medin, D. L. (1981). Categories and concepts. Cambridge, MA: Howard University Press.

Smith, M. L., & Glass, G. V. (1977). Meta-analysis of psychotherapy outcome studies. *American Psychologist, 32*, 752–760.

Smith, M., Glass, G., & Miller, T. (1980). *The benefits of psychotherapy*. Baltimore: Johns Hopkins University Press.

Smith, P., Kendell, L., & Hulia, C. (1969). *The measurement of satisfaction in worth and retirement*. Chicago: Rand McNally.

Smith, T., & Brehm, S. (1981). Person perception and the type A coronary-prone behavior pattern. *Journal of Personality and Social Psychology, 40*, 1137–1149.

Snowden, C. (1969). Motivation, regulation, and the control of meal parameters with oral and intragastric feeding. *Journal of Comparative and Physiological Psychology, 69*, 91–100.

Soal, S. G., & Bateman, F. (1954). *Modern experiments in telepathy*. New Haven, CT: Yale University Press.

Sobel, E. F. (1980, April). Countertransference issues with the later life patient. *Contemporary Psychoanalysis, 16* (2), 211–222.

Sommer, R. (1969). *Personal space: The behavioral basis of design*. Englewood Cliffs, NJ: Prentice-Hall.

Sommer, R., & Ross, H. (1958). Social interaction on a geriatric ward. *International Journal of Social Psychiatry, 4*, 128–133.

Sommersschield, H., & Reyher, J. (1973). Posthypnotic conflict, repression, and psychopathology. *Journal of Abnormal Psychology*, *82*, 278–290.

Sophian, C. (Ed.). (1984). *Origins of cognitive skills: The eighteenth annual Carnegie symposium on cognition*. Hillsdale, NJ: Erlbaum.

Sorensen, R. C. (1973). *Adolescent sexuality in contemporary America*. New York: World.

Sorrentino, R. M., & Boutillier, R. G. (1956). The effect of quantity and quality of verbal interaction on ratings of leadership ability. *Journal of Experimental Social Psychology*, *52*, 296–305.

Sparacino, S. et al. (1981). Type A behavior and well-being among municipal employees. Paper presented at 89th annual meeting of American Psychological Association, Los Angeles.

Spark, G. M., & Brody, E. M. (1970). The aged are family members. *Family Process*, *9*, 195–210.

Spearman, C. (1927). *The abilities of man*. New York: Macmillan.

Speisman, J. C., Lazarus, R. S., Mordkoff, A. M., & Davidson, L. A. (1964). The experimental reduction of stress based on ego-defense theory. *Journal of Abnormal and Social Psychology*, *68*, 367–380.

Sperling, G. (1960). The information available in brief visual presentations. *Psychological Monographs*, *74* (11, Whole No. 498).

Sperry, R. W. (1970). Perception in the absence of neocortical commissures. In *Perception and its disorders* (Res. Publ. A. R. N. M. D., Vol. 48). New York: The Association for Research in Nervous and Mental Disease.

Spitzer, R. L. (1975). On pseudoscience in science, logic in remission, and psychiatric diagnosis: A critique of D. L. Rosenhan's "on being sane in insane places." *Journal of Abnormal Psychology*, *84*, 442–452.

Spitzer, R. L. (1976). More on pseudoscience in science and the case for psychiatric diagnosis: A critique of D. L. Rosenhan's "on being sane in insane places," and "the contextual nature of psychiatric diagnosis." *Archives of General Psychiatry*, *33*, 459–470.

Sroufe, L. A. (1985). Attachment classification from the perspective of infant-caregiver relationships and infant temperament. *Child Development*, *56*, 1–14.

Sroufe, L. W. (1978). Emotional development in infancy. In J. Osofsky (Ed.), *Handbook of infancy*. New York: Wiley.

Sroufe, L., & Waters, E. (1976). The ontogenesis of smiling and laughter. A perspective on the organization of development in infants. *Psychological Review*, *83*, 173–189.

Stafford, R., Backman, E., & Dibona, P. (1977). The division of labor among cohabiting and married couples. *Journal of Marriage and the Family*, *39*, 43–58.

Stafford-Clark, D., & Smith, A. C. (1978). *Psychiatry for students* (5th ed.). London: Allen & Unwin.

Stapp, J., & Fulcher, R. (1982). The employment of 1979 and 1980 doctorate recipients in psychology. *American Psychologist*, *37*, 1159–1185.

Steck, L., Levitan, D., McLane, D., & Kelley, H. (1982). Care, need, and conceptions of love. *Journal of Personality and Social Psychology*, *43*, 481–491.

Stein, A. (1974). *Lovers, friends, slaves*. New York: Berkley.

Stein, M. (1982). *Jungian analysis*. La Salle, IL: Open Court.

Steiner, I. D. (1972). *Group process and productivity*. New York: Academic Press.

Steiner, I. (1976). Task performing groups. In J. Thibaut, J. Spence, & R. Carson (Eds.), *Contemporary trends in social psychology*. Morristown, NJ: General Learning Press.

Stendler, C. B. (1952). Critical periods in socialization and overdependency. *Child Development*, *23*, 1–2.

Stephan, W. G. (1978). School desegregation: An evaluation of predictions made in *Brown* vs. *Board of Education*. *Psychology Bulletin*, *85*, 217–238.

Sternberg, S. (1966). High-speed scanning in human memory. *Science*, *153*, 652–654.

Stevens-Long, J., & Coff, N. J. (1983). *Adolescence and early adulthood*. Palo Alto, CA: Mayfield.

Stevens, S. S., & Galanter, E. H. (1957). Ratio scales and category scales for a dozen perceptual continua. *Journal of Experimental Psychology*, *54*, 377–411.

Stewart, A., & Salt, P. (1981). Life stress, life-styles, depression and illness in adult women. *Journal of Personality and Social Psychology*, *40*, 1063–1069.

Stinnett, N., Carter, L. M., & Montgomery, J. E. (1972). Older persons' perceptions of their marriages. *Journal of Marriage and the Family*, *34*, 665–670.

Stinnett, N., & Walters, J. (1977). *Relationships in marriage and family*. New York: Macmillan.

Stokols, D. (1972). On the distinction between density and crowding: Some implications for future research. *Psychological Review*, *79*, 275–278.

Stone, J., Cohen, F., & Adler, N. (1979). *Health psychology*. San Francisco: Jossey-Bass.

Stoner, J. (1961). A comparison of individual and group decisions, including risk. Unpublished master's thesis, School of Industrial Management, M. I. T.

Streif, G. F., & Shneider, G. J. (1971). *Retirement in American society: Impact and process*. Ithaca, NY: Cornell University Press.

Strelow, E. R., Kay, N., & Kay, K. (1978). Binaural sensory aid: Case studies of its use by two children. *Journal of Visual Impairment and Blindness*, *72*, 1–9.

Streufert, S., & Streufert, S. C. (1969). Effects of conceptual structure, failure and success: An attribution of causality and interpersonal attitudes. *Journal of Personality and Social Psychology*, *11*, 138–147.

Strodbeck, F., & Mann, R. (1956). Sex-role differentiation in jury deliberations. *Sociometry*, *19*, 3–11.

Stroebe, M., & Stroebe, W. (1983). Who suffers more? Sex differences in health risks of the widowed. *Psychological Bulletin*, *93*, 279–301.

Strongman, K. T. (1973). *The psychology of emotion*. New York: Wiley.

Strube, M. J., Turner, C., Ceiro, D., Stevens, J., & Hincheg, F. (1984). Interpersonal aggression and the Type A coronary-prone behavior pattern: A theoretical distinction and practical implications. *Journal of Personality and Social Psychology*, *47*, 839–847.

Strupp, H. H., & Hadley, S. W. (1979). Specific versus nonspecific factors in psychotherapy: A controlled study of outcome. *Archives of General Psychiatry*, *36* (10), 1125–1136.

Stuart, P., Taylor, A., & Gammon, C. B. (1975). Effects of type and dose of alcohol on human physical aggression. *Journal of Personality and Social Psychology*, *32*, 169–175.

Suedfeld, P. (1975, January-February). The benefits of boredom: Sensory deprivation reconsidered. *American Scientist*.

Suedfeld, P. (1981). Aloneness as a healing experience. In L. A. Peplau & D. Perlman (Eds.), *Loneliness: A sourcebook of current theory, research, and therapy*. New York: Wiley-Interscience.

Sugarman, A., Quinlan, D., & Devenis, L. (1981). Anorexia nervosa as a defense against anaclitic depression. *The International Journal of Eating Disorders*, D. Van Nostrand, Autumn, Vol. 1.

Sugarman, S. (1983). *Children's early thought: Developments in classification*. New York: Cambridge University Press.

Suinn, R. M. (1984). *Fundamentals of abnormal psychology*. Chicago: Nelson-Hall.

Sundstrom, E. (1978). Crowding as a sequential process: Review of research on the effects of population density on humans. In A. Baum & Y. Epstein (Eds.), *Human response to crowding*. Hillsdale, NJ: Erlbaum.

Suomi, S. J. (1977). Peers, play, and primary prevention in primates. In *proceedings of the third Vermont conference on the primary prevention of psychopathology: Promoting social competence and coping in children*. Hanover, NH: University Press of New England.

Suomi, S. J., & Harlow, H. F. (1976). The facts and functions of fear. In M. Zuckermann & C. D. Spielberger (Eds.), *Emotions and anxiety: New concepts, methods, and applications*. Hillsdale, NJ: Erlbaum.

Sussman, M. B., & Burchinal, L. (1962). Kin family network: Unheralded structure in current conceptualization of family functioning. *Marriage and Family Living*, *24*, 231–240.

Swain, D. (1981). The fantasy-reality distinction in televised violence: Modifying influences on children's aggression. *Journal of Research in Personality*, *15*, 323–330.

Swenson, R. (1973). *Interpersonal relations*. Glenwood, IL: Scott, Foresman.

Swets, J. A. (1964). *Signal detection and recognition by human observers*. New York: Wiley.

Szasz, T. S. (1961). *The myth of mental illness: Foundations of a theory of personal conduct*. New York: Harper & Row.

Szasz, T. S. (1970). *Ideology and insanity: Essays on the psychiatric dehumanization of a man*. Garden City, NY: Anchor Books.

Tajfel, H. (1981). Social stereotypes and social groups. In J. Turner & H. Giles (Eds.), *Intergroup behavior*. Chicago: University of Chicago Press.

Tajfel, H., & Turner, J. (1985). The social identity theory of intergroup behavior. In S. Worchel & W. Austin (Eds.), *Psychology of intergroup relations* (2nd ed.). Chicago: Nelson-Hall.

Tanford, S., & Penrod, S. (1982). Biases in trials involving defendants charged with multiple offenses. *Journal of Applied Social Psychology*, *12*, 453–480.

Tanner, J. M. (1978). *Foetus into man: Physical growth from conception to maturity*. Cambridge, MA: Harvard University Press.

Tanner, J. (1972). Sequence, tempo, and individual variation in growth and development of boys and girls aged twelve to sixteen. In J. Kagan & R. Coles (Eds.), *Twelve to sixteen: Early adolescence*. New York: Norton.

Tarler-Benlolo, L. (1978). The role of relaxation in biofeedback training. *Psychological Bulletin*, 85, 727–755.

Tarris, D., & Offir, C. (1977). *The longest war: Sex differences in perspective*. New York: Harcourt Brace Jovanovich.

Tart, C. T. (1977). Putting the pieces together: A conceptual framework for understanding discrete states of consciousness. In N. E. Zinberg (Ed.), *Alternate states of consciousness: Multiple perspectives on the study of consciousness*. New York: Free Press.

Tartter, V. C., & Knowlton, K. C. (1981). Perception of sign language from an array of 27 moving spots. *Nature*, 289, 676–678.

Taylor, R. E. (1981). Hinckley case might revive insanity issue. *Wall St. Journal*, April 28, p. 33.

Taylor, S. (1981, July 27). The plea of insanity and its use in criminal cases. *The New York Times*.

Taylor, S., Lichman, R., & Wood, J. (1984). Attribution, beliefs about control and adjustment to breast cancer. *Journal of Personality and Social Psychology*, 46, 489–502.

Taylor, S. E., & Fiske, S. T. (1975). Point of view and perceptions of causality. *Journal of Personality and Social Psychology*, 32, 439–445.

Taylor, S., & Thompson, S. (1982). Stalking the elusive "vividness" effect. *Psychological Review*, 89, 155–181.

Taylor, S. P., Vardaris, R. M., Rawitch, A. B., Gammon, C. B., & Cranston, J. W. (1976). The effects of alcohol and delta p-tetrahydrocannibol on human physical aggression. *Aggressive Behavior*, 2, 153–162.

Taylor, W., & Martin, M. (1944). Multiple personality. *Journal of Abnormal and Social Psychology*, 39, 281–300.

Teevan, R. C., & McGhee, P. E. (1972). Childhood development of fear of failure motivation. *Journal of Personality and Social Psychology*, 21, 345–348.

Teghtsoonian, R. (1971). On the exponent in Steven's law and the constant in Ekman's law. *Psychological Review*, 18, 71–80.

Templar, D. I. (1972). Death anxiety in very religiously involved persons. *Psychological Reports*, 31, 361–362.

Terman, L. A. (1904). A preliminary study in the psychology and pedagogy of leadership. *Pedagogical Seminary*, 4, 413–451.

Terman, L. M. (1916). *The measurement of intelligence*. Boston: Houghton Mifflin.

Terman, L. M., & Merrill, M. A. (1937). *Measuring intelligence*. Boston, MA: Houghton Mifflin.

Terrance, H. S., Petitto, L. A., Sanders, R. J., & Bever, T. G. (1979). Can an ape create a sentence? *Science*, 206, 891–901.

Thigpen, C. H., & Cleckley, H. M. (1974). *The three faces of Eve*. New York: Popular Library.

Thoman, E. B., Liederman, P. H., & Olson, J. P. (1972). Neonate-mother interaction during breast feeding. *Developmental Psychology*, 6, 110–118.

Thomas, M. H., Horton, R. W., Lippincott, E. C., & Drabman, R. S. (1977). Desensitization to portrayals of real-life aggression as a function of exposure to television violence. *Journal of Personality and Social Psychology*, 35, 450–458.

Thompson, J. (1941). Development of facial expression of emotion in blind and seeing children. *Archives of Psychology*, 37, No. 264.

Thorndike, E. L. (1911). *Animal intelligence*. New York: Macmillan.

Thorndike, E. L. (1913). *The psychology of learning*. New York: Teachers College.

Thorndike, E. L. (1932). *The fundamentals of learning*. New York: Teachers College.

Thorndike, P. W. (1977). Cognitive structures in comprehension and memory of narrative discourse. *Cognitive Psychology*, 9, 77–110.

Thorndike, P. W. (1984). Applications of schema theory in cognitive research. In J. L. Anderson & S. M. Kosslyn (Eds.), *Tutorials in learning and memory*. San Francisco, Freeman.

Thurstone, L. L. (1946). Theories of intelligence. *Scientific Monthly*, 62, 101–112.

Tighe, T. J. (1982). *Modern learning theory: Foundations and fundamental issues*. New York: Oxford University Press.

Timberlake, W., Wahl, G., & King, D. (1982). Stimulus and response contingencies in the misbehavior of rats. *Journal of Experimental Psychology: Animal Behavior Processes*, 8, 62–85.

Time. (1978, December 25). Parental line: Same old birds and bees, p. 60.

Tinbergen, N. (1951). *The study of instinct*. New York: Oxford University Press.

Tolman, E. C., & Honzik, C. H. (1930). Introduction and removal of reward, and maze performance in rats. *University of California Publications in Psychology*, 4, 257–275.

Tomkins, S. (1979). Script theory: Differential magnification of affects. In V. Howe & R. Dienstbier (Eds.), *Nebraska symposium on motivation* (Vol. 26). Lincoln, NE: Nebraska University Press.

Tomkins, S. (1981). The role of facial response in the experience of emotion: A reply to Tourangeau and Ellsworth. *Journal of Personality and Social Psychology*, 40, 355–357.

Tomkins, S. S., & McCorter, R. (1964). What and where are the primary affects? Some evidence for a theory. *Perceptual and Motor Skills*, 18, 119–158.

Toynbee, A. (1965). *A study of history* (Vol. 1). New York: Oxford University Press.

Travis, L. (1925). The effect of a small audience upon eye-hand coordination. *Journal of Abnormal and Social Psychology*, 20, 142–146.

Treiman, D. J., & Hartman, H. I. (1981). *Women, work, and wages: Equal pay for jobs of equal value*. Washington, DC: National Academy Press.

Treisman, A. M. (1960). Contextual cues in selective listening. *Quarterly Journal of Experimental Psychology*, 12, 242–248.

Tribich, D., & Messer, S. (1974). Psychoanalytic character type and status of authority as determiners of suggestibility. *Journal of Consulting and Clinical Psychology*, 42, 842–848.

Triplett, N. (1898). The dynamogenic factors in pace-making and competition. *American Journal of Psychology*, 9, 507–533.

Tripp, C. (1975). *The homosexual matrix*. New York: McGraw-Hill.

Troll, L. E. (1971). The family of later life: A decade review. *Journal of Marriage and the Family*, 33, 263–290.

Truaz, C. B., & Mitchell, A. (1971). Research on certain therapist interpersonal skills in relation to process and outcome. In A. E. Bergin & S. L. Garfield (Eds.), *Handbook of psychotherapy and behavior change*. New York: Wiley, pp. 299–344.

Tryon, R. C. (1940). Genetic differences in maze-learning abilities in rats. In *39th Yearbook, Part I*. National Society for the Study of Education. Chicago: University of Chicago Press.

Tsang, R. C. (1938). Hunger motivation in gastrectomized rats. *Journal of Comparative Psychology*, 1–17.

Tulving, E. (1972). Episodic and semantic memory. In E. Tulving & W. Donaldson (Eds.), *Organization of memory*. New York: Academic Press.

Tulving, E. (1983). *Elements of episodic memory*. New York: Oxford University Press.

Tulving, E., & Pearlstone, Z. (1966). Availability versus accessibility of information in memory for words. *Journal of Verbal Learning and Verbal Behavior*, 5, 381–391.

Turiel, E. (1978). The development of concepts of social structure. In J. Glick & A. Clark-Steward (Eds.), *The development of social understanding*. New York: Gardner Press.

Turner, C. W., & Berkowitz, L. (1972). Identification with film aggressor (overt role taking) and reactions to film violence. *Journal of Personality and Social Psychology*, 21, 256–264.

Turner, J. (1981). The experimental social psychology of intergroup behavior. In J. Turner & H. Giles (Eds.), *Intergroup behavior*. Chicago: University of Chicago Press.

Turner, T. A drink a day keeps the doctor away. In *Family Weekly*. New York: Family Weekly, 23.

Turvey, M. T., & Carello, C. (1985). The ecological approach to perceiving-acting: A pictorial essay. Paper presented at a conference on sensorimotor interactions in space perception and action, February 1985, at the Center for Interdisciplinary Research, Bielefeld, West Germany.

Ubell, E. (1984, November 25). How to prepare for old age. *Parade Magazine*, pp. 13–15.

Udolf, R. (1981). *Handbook of hypnosis for professionals*. New York: Van Nostrand.

Underwood, B. J. (1982). *Studies in learning and memory*. New York: Praeger Press.

Underwood, B., Berenson, J., Bereson, R., Cherget, K., Wilson, D., Kulik, J., Moore, B., & Wenzel, G. (1977). Attention, negative affect, and altruism: An ecological validation. *Personality and Social Psychology Bulletin*, 3, 54–58.

U.S. Riot Commission. (1968). *Report of the national advisory commission on civil disorders*. New York: Bantam Books.

Vaillant, G. E. (1977). *Adaptation to life*. Boston: Little, Brown.

Valins, S. (1966). Cognitive effects of false heart rate feedback. *Journal of Personality and Social Psychology*, 4, 400–408.

Valins, S. (1972). Persistent effects of information about internal reactions: Ineffectiveness of debriefing. In H. London & R. Nisbett (Eds.), *The cognitive alteration of feeling states*. Chicago: Aldine.

Van Beskirk, S. S. (1977). A two-phase perspective on the treatment of anorexia nervosa. *Psychological Bulletin*, *84*, 529–538.

Vance, E., & Wagner, N. (1976). Written descriptions of orgasm: A study of sex differences. *Archives of Sexual Behavior*, *5*, 87.

Van Rossum, E. J., & Schenk, S. M. (1984). The relationship between learning conception, study strategy, and learning outcome. *British Journal of Educational Psychology*, *54*, 73–83.

Veitch, R., & Griffit, W. (1976). Good news, bad news: Affective and interpersonal effects. *Journal of Applied Social Psychology*, *6*, 69–75.

Verinis, J., & Roll, S. (1970). Primary and secondary male characteristics: The hairiness and large penis stereotypes. *Psychological Reports*, *26*, 123–126.

Von Frisch, K. (1974). Decoding the language of the bee. *Science*, *185*, 663–668.

Wagemaker, H., Jr., & Cade, R. (1977). The use of hemodialysis in chronic schizophrenia. *American Journal of Psychiatry*, *134*, 684–685.

Wahba, M., & Birdwell, L. (1976). Maslow reconsidered: A review of research on the response hierarchy. *Organizational Behavior and Human Performance*. *15*, 212–240.

Wain, H. J. (1980). Pain control through use of hypnosis. ASCH, *23*, 41–46.

Walk, R. D., & Gibson, E. J. (1961). A comparative and analytical study of visual depth perception. *Psychological Monographs*, *75*.

Wallace, B. (1979). *Applied hypnosis: An overview*. Chicago: Nelson-Hall.

Wallace, R. (1970). Physiological effects of transcendental meditation. *Science*, *167*, 1751–1754.

Wallace, W. H., Turner, S. H., & Perkins, C. C. (1957). *Preliminary studies of human information storage*, Signal Corps Project No. 132C, Institute for Cooperative Research, University of Pennsylvania, December.

Wallach, H. (1948). Brightness constancy and the nature of achromatic colors. *Journal of Experimental Psychology*, *38*, 310–324.

Wallach, H., & O'Connel, D. N. (1953). The kinetic depth effect. *Journal of Experimental Psychology*, *45*, 205–217.

Wallach, M., Kogan, N., & Bem, D. (1962). Group influence on individual risk taking. *Journal of Abnormal and Social Psychology*, *65*, 75–86.

Wallin, P. (1953). A Guttman scale for measuring women's neighborliness. *American Journal of Sociology*, *59*, 243–246.

Wallin, P., & Vollmer, H. M. (1953). Marital happiness of parents and their children's attitudes to them. *American Sociological Review*, *18*, 424–431.

Walster, E., Aronson, E., & Abrahams, D. (1966). On increasing the persuasiveness of a low prestige communicator. *Journal of Experimental Social Psychology*, *2*, 325–342.

Walster, E., Aronson, E., Abrahams, D., & Rottman, L. (1966). Importance of physical attractiveness in dating behavior. *Journal of Personality and Social Psychology*, *4*, 508–516.

Walter, G. H., & Ashton, P. (1980). The relationship of teacher-offered empathy, genuineness, and respect to pupil classroom behavior. Paper presented at the American Educational Research Association, Boston.

Waterhouse, L., & Fein, D. (1984). Developmental trends in cognitive skills for children diagnosed as autistic and schizophrenic. *Child Development*, *55*, 236–248.

Waters, H. F., & Malamud, P. (1975, March

10). Drop that gun, Captain Video. *Newsweek*, *85*, 81–82.

Watson, J. B., & Rayner, R. (1920). Conditioned emotional reactions. *Journal of Experimental Psychology*, *3*, 1–14.

Watson, J. D., & Crick, F. H. C. (1953). Molecular structure of nucleic acid: A structure for deoxyribose nucleic acid. *Nature*, *171*, 737–783.

Watson, R. I. (1973). Investigation into deindividuation using a cross-cultural survey technique. *Journal of Personality and Social Psychology*, *25*, 342–345.

Waugh, N. C., & Norman, P. A. (1965). Primary memory. *Psychological Review*, *72*, 89–104.

Webb, W. B. (Ed.). (1973). *Sleep: An active process*. Glenview, IL: Scott, Foresman Co.

Wegner, D. M., & Vallicher, R. R. (1981). *The self in social psychology*. New York: Oxford University Press.

Weiner, M. J., & Wright, F. E. (1973). Effects of undergoing arbitrary discrimination upon subsequent attitudes toward a minority group. *Journal of Applied Social Psychology*, *3*, 94–102.

Weingartner, H., Grafman, J., Boutelle, W., Kaye, W., & Martin, P. R. (1983). Forms of memory failure, *221*, 380–382.

Weiss, J. M. (1972, June). Psychological factors in stress and disease. *Scientific American*.

Weitzenhoffer, A. M., & Hilgard, E. R. (1962). *Stanford hypnotic susceptibility scales, form C*. Palo Alto, CA: Consulting Psychologists Press.

Welch, R. B. (1978). *Perceptual modification*. New York: Academic Press.

Wells, A. (1975). *Mass media and society* (2nd ed.). Palo Alto, CA: Mayfield.

Welsh, B. (1979). Extra-auditory health effects of industrial noise: Survey of foreign literature. Aerospace Medical Research Laboratory, Aerospace Medical Division, Air Force Systems Command, Wright-Patterson, June.

West, D. (1967). *The young offender*. Harmondsworth, England: Penguin.

Wetmore, M. E. The relationship between perceived text structure, familiarity of content, and recall of expository text. Unpublished doctoral dissertation, University of Virginia.

Wheeler, L., Deci, E., Reis, H., & Zuckerman, B. (1978). *Interpersonal influence*. Boston: Allyn & Bacon.

White, C. Unpublished doctoral dissertation. Catholic University, Washington, DC.

White, R. W. (1975). *Lives in progress: A study of the national growth of personality* (3rd ed.). New York: Holt, Rinehart & Winston.

Whyte, W. (1956). *The organization man*. New York: Simon & Schuster.

Wickelgren, W. A. (1977). *Learning and memory*. Englewood Cliffs, NJ: Prentice-Hall.

Wickelgren, W. A. (1979). *Cognitive psychology*. Englewood Cliffs, NJ: Prentice-Hall.

Wicker, A. (1979). *An introduction to ecological psychology*. Monterey, CA: Brooks/Cole.

Wicklund, R. A., & Brehm, J. W. (1976). Perspectives on cognitive dissonance. Hillsdale, NJ: Erlbaum.

Wicks-Nelson, R., & Israel, A. (1984). *Behavior disorders of children*. Englewood Cliffs, NJ: Prentice-Hall.

Widom, C. S. (1978). A methodology for studying noninstitutionalized psychopaths. In R. R. Hare & D. Schalling (Eds.), *Psycho-

pathic behavior: Approaches to research*. Chichester, England: John Wiley, pp. 71–84.

Wiel, A. T. (1977). The marriage of the sun and moon. In N. E. Zinberg (Ed.), *Alternate states of consciousness: Multiple perspectives on the study of consciousness*. New York: Free Press.

Wilder, D. A. (1977). Perception of groups, size of opposition, and social influence. *Journal of Experimental Social Psychology*, *13*, 253–268.

Wilder, D. A. (1985). Cognitive factors affecting success of intergroup contact. In S. Worchel & W. Austin (Eds.), *Psychology of intergroup relations*. Chicago: Nelson-Hall.

Wilder, D. A., & Allen, V. L. (1973, May). The effect of absent social support on conformity. Paper presented at the meeting of the Midwestern Psychological Association, Chicago.

Wilkens, W. (1973). Expectancy of therapeutic gain: An empirical and conceptual critique. *Journal of Consulting and Clinical Psychology*, *40*, 69–77.

Willerman, B., & Swanson, L. (1953). Group prestige in voluntary organizations. *Human Relations*, *6*, 57–77.

Wilson, G. (1966). Arousal properties of red versus green. *Perceptual and Motor Skills*, *23*, 947–949.

Winterbottom, M. R. (1953). The relationship of childhood training in independence to achievement motivation. Unpublished doctoral dissertation, University of Michigan.

Wirtenburg, T., & Nakamura, C. (1976). Education: Barrier or boon to changing occupational roles of women. *Journal of Social Issues*, *32*, 165–179.

Wolman, B. B., Dale, L. A., Schmeidler, G. R., & Ullman, M. (Eds.). (1977). *Handbook of parapsychology*. New York: Van Nostrand.

Wolpe, J. (1958). *Psychotherapy by reciprocal inhibition*. Stanford, CA: Stanford University Press.

Wolpe, J. (1962). The experimental foundations of some new psychotherapeutic methods. In A. J. Bachrach (Ed.), *Experimental foundations of clinical psychology*. New York: Basic Books.

Wolpe, J. (1974). *The practice of behavior therapy*. New York: Pergamon Press.

Wood, W., & Eagly, A. (1981). Stages in the analysis of persuasive messages: The role of causal attributions and message comprehension. *Journal of Personality and Social Psychology*, *40*, 246–259.

Woodruff, D. S. (1977). *Can you live to be 100?* New York: Chatham Square Press.

Woodworth, R. S. (1938). *Experimental psychology*. New York: Holt.

Woolfolk, R. L., & Richardson, F. C. (1984). Behavior therapy and the ideology of modernity. *American Psychologist*, *39*, 777–786.

Worchel, P. (1979). Trust and distrust. In W. Austin & S. Worchel (Eds.), *The social psychology of intergroup relations*. Monterey, CA: Brooks/Cole.

Worchel, S. (1984). The darker side of helping: The social dynamics of helping and cooperation. In E. Staub et al. (Eds.), *Development and maintenance of prosocial behavior*. New York: Plenum.

Worchel, S. (1985). Cooperation and the reduction of intergroup conflict: Some determining factors. In S. Worchel & W. Austin (Eds.), *Psychology of intergroup relations*. Chicago: Nelson-Hall.

Worchel, S., & Andreoli, V. (1978). Facilitation of social interaction through deindividuation of the target. *Journal of Personality and Social Psychology*, *36*, 549–557.

Worchel, S., & Andreoli, V., & Folger, R. (1977). Intergroup cooperation and intergroup attraction: The effect of previous interaction and outcome of combined effort. *Journal of Experimental Social Psychology*, *13*, 131–140.

Worchel, S., Axsom, D., Ferris, F., Samaha, G., & Schweitzer, S. (1978). Determinants of the effects of intergroup cooperation on intergroup attraction. *Journal of Conflict Resolution*, *xxii*, 429–439.

Worchel, S., & Brown, E. (1984). The role of plausibility in influencing environmental attractions. *Journal of Experimental Social Psychology*, *20*, 86–96.

Worchel, S., & Burnham, C. A. (1967). Reduction of autokinesis with information about the registration of eye position. *American Journal of Psychology*, *80*, 434–437.

Worchel, S., & Cooper, J. (1983). *Understanding social psychology* (2nd ed.). Homewood, IL: Dorsey Press.

Worchel, S., & Lollis, M. (1982). Reactions to territorial contamination as a function of culture. *Personality and Social Psychology Bulletin*, *8*, 370–375.

Worchel, S., & Teddlie, C. (1976). The experience of crowding: A two-factor theory. *Journal of Personality and Social Psychology*, *34*, 30–40.

Worchel, S., & Yohai, S. M. L. (1979). The role of attribution in the experience of crowding. *Journal of Experimental Social Psychology*, *15*, 91–104.

Wright, H. F. (1967). *Recording and analyzing child behavior*. New York: Harper & Row.

Wright, J. D. (1978). Are working women really more satisfied? Evidence from several national surveys. *Journal of Marriage and the Family*, *40*, 301–313.

Wyden, B. (1971, December). Growth: 45 crucial months. *Life*, pp. 93–95.

Wyer, R., Henninger, M., & Hinkle, R. (1977). An informational analysis of actors' and observers' belief attributions in a role-playing situation. *Journal of Experimental Social Psychology*, *13*, 199–217.

Yalom, I. D. (1975). *The theory and practice of group psychotherapy* (2nd ed.). New York: Basic Books.

Yalom, I. D., & Lieberman, A. (1971). A study of encounter group casualties. *Archives of General Psychiatry*, *25*, 16–30.

Yekovich, F. R., & Thorndyke, P. W. (1981). An evaluation of alternative functional models of narrative schemata. *Journal of Verbal Learning and Verbal Behavior*, *20*, 454–469.

Zager, L., & Megargee, E. (1981). Seven MMPI alcohol and drug abuse scales: An empirical investigation of their interrelationships, convergent and discriminant validity, and degree of racial bias. *Journal of Personality and Social Psychology*, *40*, 532–544.

Zaiden, J. (1982). Psychodynamic therapy: Clinical applications. In A. Rush (Ed.), *Short-term psychotherapies for depression*. New York: Guilford Press.

Zajonc, R. (1968). Attitudinal effects of mere exposure. *Journal of Personality and Social Psychology*, *9*, 1–27.

Zajonc, R. B. (1965). Social facilitation. *Science*, *149*, 269–274.

Zajonc, R. (1970). Brainwash: Familiarity breeds comfort. *Psychology Today*, *13*, 32–35.

Zajonc, R. B. (1976). Family configuration and intelligence. *Science*, *192*, 227–236.

Zanna, M., & Fazio, R. (1982). The attitude-behavior relation: Moving toward a third generation of research. In M. Zanna, E. T. Higgins, & C. Herman (Eds.), *Consistency in social behavior: The Ontario symposium* (Vol. 2). Hillsdale, NJ: Erlbaum.

Zeig, J. K. (Ed.). (1982). *Ericksonian approach to hypnosis and psychotherapy*. New York: Brunner/Mazel.

Ziegler, H., & Karten, H. (1974). Central trigeminal structures and the lateral hypothalamus syndrome in the rat. *Science*, *186*, 636–637.

Zilboorg, G., & Henry, G. W. (1941). *A history of medical psychology*. New York: Norton.

Zillman, D. (1971). Excitation transfer in communication-mediated aggressive behavior. *Journal of Experimental Social Psychology*, *7*, 419–434.

Zillman, D. (1979). *Hostility and aggression*. Hillsdale, NJ: Erlbaum.

Zillman, D. (1983). Arousal and aggression. In R. Green & E. Donnerstein (Eds.), *Aggression: Theoretical and empirical reviews*. New York: Academic Press.

Zillman, D., Johnson, R. C., & Day, K. D. (1974). Attribution of apparent arousal and proficiency of recovery from sympathetic activation affecting excitation transfer to aggressive behavior. *Journal of Experimental Social Psychology*, *10*, 503–515.

Zimbardo, P. (1970). The human choice: Individuation, reason and order versus individuation, impulse and chaos. In W. J. Arnold & D. Levine (Eds.), *Nebraska symposium on motivation*. Lincoln, NE: University of Nebraska Press.

Zimbardo, P. (1971). The psychological power and pathology of imprisonment. Statement prepared for the U.S. House of Representatives Committee on the Judiciary (Subcommittee No. 3, Robert Kastemeyer, Chairman, hearings on prison reform). Unpublished paper, Stanford University.

Zimbardo, P., & Ebbesen, E. (1970). *Influencing attitudes and changing behavior*. Reading, MA: Addison-Wesley.

Zinberg, N. E. (1977). The study of consciousness states: Problems and progress. In N. E. Zinberg (Ed.), *Alternate states of consciousness: Multiple perspectives on the study of consciousness*. New York: Free Press.

Zubek, J. P. L., Bayer, A., & Shepard, J. M. (1969). Relative effects of prolonged social isolation and confinement: Behavioral and EEG changes. *Journal of Abnormal Psychology*, *74*, 625–631.

Zucker, S. H., & Altman, R. (1973). An on-the-job training program for adolescent trainable retardates. *Training School Bulletin*, *70*, 106–110.

Zuckerman, M. (1969). Variables affecting deprivation results. In J. P. L. Zubek (Ed.), *Sensory deprivation: Fifteen years of research*. New York: Appleton-Century-Crofts.

Zuckerman, M. (1979). *Sensation seeking: Beyond the optimal level of arousal*. Hillsdale, NJ: Erlbaum.

Zuckerman, M., Persky, H., Link, K., & Basu, G. (1968). Experimental and subject factors determining responses to sensory deprivation, social isolation and confinement. *Journal of Abnormal Psychology*, *73*, 183–194.

Zurcher, L. (1977). *The mutable self: A self-concept for social change*. Beverly Hills, CA: Sage Publications.

ACKNOWLEDGMENTS

Figures, Tables, Text

Table 1–1: Reprinted by permission of the American Psychological Association.

Chap. 2 story: Excerpt from *Reprieve: A Memoir* by Agnes de Mille. Copyright © 1981 by Agnes de Mille. Reprinted by permission of Doubleday & Company, Inc. **Fig. 2–1 photos:** Peter Brunjes. **Fig. 2–5:** From "The Brain" by David H. Hubel, © September 1979 Scientific American, Inc. All Rights Reserved. **Fig. 2–7:** Reprinted with permission of Macmillan Publishing Company from *The cerebral cortex of man* by W. Penfield and T. Rasmussen. **Fig. 2–16:** (left and right) Photos courtesy of M. M. Grumbach, U. of California, San Francisco.

Fig. 3–1: From D. McBurney & V. Collings, *Introduction to sensation/perception*, 2/e, © 1984, p. 13. Reprinted by permission of Prentice-Hall, Inc., Englewood Cliffs, NJ. **Fig. 3–7:** Spatially quantized images by Ed Manning, c/o Blocpix^R Images, 972 E. Broadway, Stratford, CT 06497. **Fig. 3–8:** American Optical Corporation. **Fig. 3–10:** Fritz Goro, Life Magazine, © Time, Inc. **Fig. 3–15:** After Dunkle, T. (1982, April). The sound of silence. *Science*, pp. 30–33.

Fig. 4–1: William Vandivert. **Fig. 4–6:** M. Elizabeth Wetmore. **Fig. 4–8:** (photo) Baron Wolman/Woodfin Camp & Associates. **Fig. 4–9:** (top, left and right) Marc Anderson; (bottom, left) Louis Goldman/Photo Researchers; (bottom, right) Guy Gillette/Photo Researchers. **Fig. 4–10:** NASA. **Fig. 4–12:** (A) United Nations Photo by John Isaac; (B) Alexander Lowry/Photo Researchers; (C) USDA. **Figs. 4–14 and 4–16:** From R. K. Potter, G. A. Kopp, & H. G. Kopp, *Visible Speech*. New York: Dover Publications, Inc., 1966. Reprinted through the permission of the publisher.

Chap. 5 story: Taken from *Return from tomorrow* by George M. Ritchie, M.D., with Elizabeth Sherrill. Copyright © 1978 by George M. Ritchie, M.D. Used by permission of Zondervan Publishing House. **Table 5–1:** Reprinted with permission of Macmillan Publishing Co., Inc. from *Alternate states of consciousness: Multiple perspectives on the study of consciousness* by Norman E. Zinberg, Ed. Copyright © 1977 by the Free Press, a division of Macmillan Publishing Co., Inc. **Fig. 5–1:** Teri Leigh Stratford, Courtesy Sleep-Wake Disorders Center, Montifiore Medical Center. **Fig. 5–2:** Cotman, C. W., & McGaugh, J. L., *Behavioral neuroscience*. New York: Academic Press, 1980, p. 612. **Fig. 5–3:** Illustration is reprinted from *Some must watch while some must sleep* by William C. Dement, by permission of W. W. Norton and Company, Inc. Copyright © 1972, 1974, 1976 by William C. De-

ment. **Fig. 5–4:** Reprinted from *Alternate states of consciousness: Multiple perspectives on the study of consciousness* by Norman E. Zinberg, Ed. Copyright © 1977 by the Free Press, a division of Macmillan Publishing Co., Inc. **Figs. 5–5—5–8:** *Scientific American*, 1977, *237*, No. 4, p. 134. **Figs. 5–9 and 5–10:** Peter Suedfeld, The benefits of boredom: Sensory deprivation reconsidered. *American Scientist*, 1975, *63*, 60. Reprinted with permission of *American Scientist*.

Chap. 6 story: Excerpts from *The story of my life* by Helen Keller. Copyright © 1902, 1903, 1905 by Helen Keller. Reprinted by permission of Doubleday and Company, Inc. **Fig. 6–5:** Sepp Seitz/Woodfin Camp & Associates. **Fig. 6–8:** Lilo Hess Three Lions, Inc. **Fig. 6–9:** From Tolman, E. C., & Honzik, C. H. *Introduction and removal of reward, and maze performance in rats*. Reproduced by permission of the University of California Press. **Table 6–1:** Luchins, *Psychological Monographs*. **Fig. 6–13:** From *Kit of Factor-Referenced Cognitive Tests*. Copyright © 1962, 1975 by Educational Testing Service. All Rights Reserved. Reprinted by permission. **Fig. 6–14:** Horn, J. L. & Donaldson, G. Cognitive development II: Adulthood development of human abilities. In O. G. Brim, Jr., & J. Kagan (Eds.), *Constancy and change in human development: A volume of review essays*. Cambridge, MA: Harvard University Press, 1980.

Fig. 7–3: Sperling, G. The information available in brief visual presentations. *Psychological Monographs*, 1960, *74* (11, 498). **Fig. 7–4:** From Peterson, L. R., & Peterson, M. J. Short-term retention of individual items. *Journal of Experimental Psychology*, 1959, *58*, 193–198. Copyright © 1959 by the American Psychological Association. Reprinted by permission. **Fig. 7–6:** From Kosslyn et al., Visual images preserve metric spacial information. *Journal of Experimental Psychology: Human Perception and Performance*, 1977, *4*, 47–60. Copyright © 1977 by the American Psychological Association. Reprinted by permission. **Fig. 7–7:** Collins, A. M., & Quillian, M. R. Retrieval time from semantic memory. *Journal of Verbal Learning and Verbal Behavior*, 1969, *8*, 240–247. **Fig. 7–8:** Allport, G. W. *The nature of prejudice*. New York: Doubleday-Anchor, 1958. **Fig. 7–9:** Sternberg, S. High-speed scanning in human memory. *Science*, 1966, *153*, 652–654. Copyright © 1966 by the American Association for the Advancement of Science. **Table 7–2:** Brown, R. W., & McNeill, D. The "tip-of-the-tongue" phenomenon. *Journal of Verbal Learning and Verbal Behavior*, 1966, *5*, 325–337.

Table 8–1: From Apgar, V. A proposal for a new method of evaluation of the newborn infant. *Current Researches in Anesthesia and Analgesia*, 1953, *32*, 260–267. **Fig. 8–1:** Franken-

burg, W. K., & Dodds, J. B. The Denver development screening test. *Journal of Pediatrics*, 1967, *71*, 181–191. **Table 8–2:** From *Psycholinguistics* by Dan I. Slobin. Copyright © 1971 Scott, Foresman and Company. Reprinted by permission. **Fig. 8–2:** Wright, H. F. *Recording and analyzing child behavior*. New York: Harper & Row, 1967.

Fig. 9–1: Tanner, J. M. *Foetus into man: Physical growth from conception to maturity*. Cambridge, MA: Harvard University Press, 1978. **Table 9–1:** From L. Kohlberg, *Stages in the development of thought and action*. New York: Holt, Rinehart and Winston, 1969. Used with permission. **Table 9–3:** Murray, J. R., Powers, E. A., & Havighurst, R. J. Personal and situational factors producing flexible careers. *The Gerontologist*, 1971, *11*, 4–12.

Table 10–1: Schachter, S., & Gross, L. P. Manipulated time and eating behavior. *Journal of Personality and Social Psychology*, 1968, *10*, 98–106. **Fig. 10–2:** Tanner, J. Sequence, tempo and individual variation in growth and development of boys and girls aged twelve to sixteen. In J. Kagan & R. Coles (Eds.), *Twelve to sixteen: Early adolescence*. New York: Norton, 1972. **Table 10–2:** Reprinted by permission of PEI Books, Inc. From *Sexual behavior in the 1970s* by Morton Hunt. Copyright © 1974 by Morton Hunt. **Table 10–3:** Schachter, S. *The psychology of affiliation*. Stanford, CA: Stanford University Press, 1959.

Fig. 11–5: After Speisman, J. C., Lazarus, R. S., Mordkoff, A. M., & Davison, L. Experimental reduction of stress based on ego-defense theory. *Journal of Abnormal and Social Psychology*, 1964, *68*, 367–380. Copyright © 1964 by the American Psychological Association. Reprinted by permission of the author. **Table 11–1:** Reprinted with permission of S. S. Tomkins & R. McCarter and *Psychological Reports*. From Tomkins, S. S., & McCarter, R. What and where are the primary affects? Some evidence for a theory. *Perceptual and Motor Skills*, 1964, *18*, 119–158. **Fig. 11–8:** Selye, H. *The stress of life*. New York: McGraw-Hill, 1956. (Rev. ed., 1976) **Table 11–2:** Reprinted by permission from *Journal of Psychosomatic Research*, 1967, *11*, 213–218. T. H. Holmes & R. H. Rahe, The social readjustment rating scale. Copyright © 1967, Pergamon Press, Ltd.

Fig. 12–2: Cattell, R. B. *The scientific analysis of personality*. Harmondsworth, Eng.: Penguin Books, 1965. **Table 12–1:** Summary of the characteristics of self-actualizing people from *Motivation and personality*, 2nd ed. by Abraham H. Maslow. Copyright © 1954 by Harper & Row, Publishers, Inc. Copyright © 1970 by

Abraham H. Maslow. Reprinted by permission of Harper & Row, Publishers, Inc. **Table 12–2:** Rotter, J. B. Generalized expectancies for internal vs. external control of reinforcement. *Psychological Monographs*, 1966, *80* (1), 1–28.

Chap. 14 story: Excerpts from *I'm Eve* by Chris Costner Sizemore and Elen Sain Pittillo. Copyright © 1970 by Chris Costner Sizemore and Elen Sain Pittillo. Reprinted by permission of Doubleday and Company, Inc. **Table 14–1:** Wolpe, J. *Psychotherapy by reciprocal inhibition*. Stanford, CA: Stanford University Press, 1958. **Fig. 15–2:** Rosenthal, R., & Jacobson, L. F. Teacher expectations for the disadvantaged. *Scientific American*, 1968, *4*, 19–23. **Table 15–1:** Aronson, E., & Linder, D. E. Gain and loss of esteem as determinants of interpersonal attractiveness. *Journal of Experimental Social Psychology*, 1965, *1*, 156–171. Copyright © 1965 by The American Psychological Association. Reprinted with permission of the author. **Table 15–3:** Shotland, R. L., & Huston, T. L. Emergencies: What are they and do they influence bystanders to intervene? *Journal of Personality and Social Psychology*, 1979, 37, 1822–1834. Copyright © 1979 by The American Psychological Association. Reprinted with permission of the author. **Fig. 15–3:** Latane, B., & Darley, J. M. *The unresponsive bystander: Why doesn't he help?* Adapted by permission of Prentice-Hall, Inc.

Highlight Table, p. 547: Milgram, S. Behavioral study of obedience. *Journal of Abnormal and Social Psychology*, 1963, 67, 376. **Table 16–1:** From *The height of your life* by Ralph Keyes. Copyright © 1980 by Ralph Keyes. By permission of Little, Brown and Company.

Table 17–1: Reproduced by permission of the American Anthropological Association from *American Anthropologist*, 65 (5): 1003–1026, 1963. Not for further reproduction. **Fig. 17–2:** From Horwitz, M. J., Duff, D. F., & Stratton, L. O. Redrawn by permission from *Archives of General Psychiatry*, December 1964, Vol. 11. Copyright © 1964, American Medical Association. **Fig. 17–3:** Argyle, M. & Dean, J. Eye-contact, distance and affiliation. *Sociometry*, 1965, *28*, p. 330, fig. 2. Reproduced with permission. **Tables 17–3 and 17–4:** From *Environmental psychology*, 2nd ed. by Jeffrey D. Fisher, Paul A. Bell, and Andrew Baum. Copyright © 1984 by CBS College Publishing. Copyright © 1978 by W. B. Saunders Company. Reprinted by permission of CBS College Publishing. **Fig. 17–4:** Baum, A., & Valins, S. *Architecture and social behavior*. *Psychological studies in social density*. Hillsdale, NJ: Erlbaum, 1977.

Photographs

2 Chris Regas 4 The Bettmann Archive 5 Phyllis Greenberg, Photo Researchers 8 UPI/Bettmann Newsphotos 10 Mary Evans Picture Library, Sigmund Freud Copyrights, Ltd. 12 Kathryn Millan © 1982 13 Ken Karp 14 Atari, Inc. 15 George S. Zimbel, Monkmeyer 17 Kenneth Murray, Photo Researchers 18 Laimute E. Druskis 19 Joan Menschenfreund 23 Ken Karp 24 Mimi Forsyth, Monkmeyer 25 Steve Shames

35 Diana Walker, Gamma-Liaison 40 © Lester V. Bergman & Associates 49 Fred Burrell 51 (left) Sylvia Martin, Photo Researchers; (right) UPI/Bettmann Newsphotos 56 Bruce Roberts, Photo Researchers 58 UPI/Bettmann Newsphotos

64 Wide World Photos 65 Wolfgang Bayer, Bruce Coleman, Inc. 69 Bohdan Hrynewych, Southern Light 76 Jack Finch/SPL/Science Source, Photo Researchers 80 Wolfgang Bayer, Bruce Coleman, Inc. 82 Sansui Electronics Corp. 84 Louis Goldman, Photo Researchers 86 C. Max Dunham, Photo Researchers 87 Suzanne Szasz, Photo Researchers 88 A. I. Parnes, Photo Researchers 89 George and Judy Manna, Photo Researchers 90 (left and right) Sensory Aids Corp. of Bensenville 91 Sensory Aids Corp. of Bensenville

98 NASA 99 NASA 100 (bottom) Hank Morgan, Photo Researchers 101 Suzanne Szasz, Photo Researchers 102 (top) Suzanne Szasz, Photo Researchers; (bottom) David Linton, *Scientific American* 103 Jerry Schad/Science Source, Photo Researchers 114 John G. Ross, Photo Researchers 125 Photo by Jack Jeffers 132 Robert E. Murowchick, Photo Researchers 139 Will McIntyre, Photo Reseachers 141 Charles Gatewood, Stock, Boston 142 Charles Gatewood 148 UPI/Bettmann Newsphotos 150 Charles Gatewood

163 American Foundation for the Blind 166 Tom McHugh, Photo Researchers 175 Billy E. Barnes, Southern Light 176 Springer/Bettmann Film Archive 177 Porterfield-Chickering, Photo Researchers 180 Robert Isear, Photo Researchers 191 R. A. and B. T. Gardner 192 Suzanne Szasz, Photo Researchers

202 UPI/Bettmann Newsphotos 203 The Bettmann Archive 210 Paul Conklin, Monkmeyer 214 Joseph Szabo, Photo Researchers 215 UPI/Bettmann Newsphotos 216 UPI/Bettmann Newsphotos 219 University of Miami 221 AP/Wide World Photos 229 Ken Karp 232 Leon D. Harmon; Bell Laboratories and *Scientific American* 233 © The Photo Works, Photo Researchers

239 By permission of Harper & Row, Publishers, Inc. 241 Mimi Forsyth, Monkmeyer 243 (top, left/top, right/middle, left) Petit Format/Nestle/Science Source, Photo Researchers; (middle, right) Martin M. Rotker, Taurus Photos; (bottom) Petit Format/Nestle/Science Source, Photo Researchers 245 Ken Karp 247 (top, left) Mimi Forsyth, Monkmeyer (top, right) Suzanne Szasz, Photo Researchers; (bottom) George S. Zimbel, Monkmeyer 250 (top, left and right) George S. Zimbel, Monkmeyer; (bottom) Mimi Forsyth, Monkmeyer 253 M. D. Fenton, Taurus Photos 255 W. Zehr, Alpha/FPG 256 (top) L. T. Rhodes, Taurus Photos; (bottom) Harry F. Harlow, University of Wisconsin Primate Laboratory 258 Alan Mercer, Stock, Boston 259 Lenore Weber, Taurus Photos 260 Charles Gupton, Southern Light 261 (left) Susan Johns, Rapho/Photo Researchers; (right) Bob Smith, Rapho/Photo Researchers

267 Dennis Brack, Black Star 269 Strix Pix, Monkmeyer 270 Richard Hutchings, Photo Researchers 274 Mimi Forsyth, Monkmeyer 279 Bruce Roberts, Photo Researchers 280 Jook Leung, Taurus Photos 281 Kenneth P. Davis 283 United Nations Photo by John Isaac 284–285 Photos courtesy of Joyce Turner 286 UPI/Bettmann Newsphotos 287 Irene Bayer, Monkmeyer 289 (top) Tom Tucker, Monkmeyer; (bottom) Mimi Forsyth, Monkmeyer 290 (left) National Institute of Aging; (right) Lynn McLaren, Photo Researchers

296 Jean-Pierre Laffont, Sygma 300 UPI/Bettmann Newsphotos 301 Sybil Shelton, Monkmeyer 305 Tim Gibson, Photo Researchers 306 Bonnie Schiffman, Gamma-Liaison 308 Jan Luka, Photo Researchers 309 Marc Anderson 315 Alex Webb, Magnum 316 Courtesy Harry F. Harlow, University of Wisconsin Primate Laboratory 324 UPI/Bettmann Newsphotos

332 Pictorial Parade, Inc. 333 Ann Meuer, Photo Researchers 336 Bohdan Hrynewych, Southern Light 343 (top) Bonnie Freer, Photo Researchers; (bottom, left) Wide World Photos; (bottom, right) Richard J. Quataert, Taurus Photos 344 Erich Hartmann, Magnum 345 Photo by James Fiedler, Jr., The Washington Times 346 Paul Ekman and Wallace F. Friesen 348 Alec Duncan, Taurus Photos 349 Ken Karp 353 Susan McCartney, Photo Researchers 359 Richard Hutchings, Photo Researchers 360 Baron Wolman, Woodfin Camp & Associates 364 James Steinberg 365 M. Philippot, Sygma

372 Library of Congress 375 UPI/Bettmann Newsphotos 376 Ken Karp 377 National Library of Medicine 380 Mary Evans/Sigmund Freud Copyrights Ltd. 384 Christa Armstrong, Photo Researchers 385 Suzanne Szasz, Photo Researchers 387 The Bettmann Archive 388 Steve Kagan, Photo Researchers 389 (left and right) Wide World Photos 390 Ken Karp 392 Cary Wolinsky, Stock, Boston 394 Bohdan Hrynewych, Southern Light 396 Shirley Zeiberg, Taurus Photos 398 Mimi Forsyth, Monkmeyer 403 Frank Siteman, Taurus Photos

413 UPI/Bettmann Newsphotos 416 Andy Capp by Reggie Smythe © 1980 Daily Mirror Newspaper LTD; Distributor, News America Syndicate 417 Wide World Photos 425 Arthur Tress, Photo Researchers 433 UPI/Bettmann Newsphotos 434 Richard Hutchings, Photo Researchers 436 Allen Green 445 "Schizophrenic Painting"—Painting by Ms. Kathy Stimson. From *The Schizophrenic Bulletin*, 7, no. 2, 1981 (cover). Art reproduced with permission of the bulletin and of the artist, Kathryn Stimson. 448 NYU 449 Barclay Martin, *Abnormal psychology: Clinical scientific perspectives*, 2nd ed. New York: Holt, Rinehart & Winston, 1981. 452 Wide World Photos 453 Douglas Faulkner, Photo Researchers 455 UPI/Bettmann Newsphotos

461 C. Sizemore & E. Petillo, *I'm Eve*. Garden City, NY: Doubleday, 1977 463 (left) The American Museum of Natural History; (right)

Historical Pictures Service, Inc., Chicago **464** UPI/Bettmann Newsphotos **465** Marion Bernstein **469** Culver Pictures **471** Eric Kroll, Taurus Photos **473** Susan Rosenberg **475** The Bettmann Archive **477** Susan Rosenberg **478** Susan Rosenberg **482** David Gonzales, Camarillo State Hospital **484** Bohdan Hrynewych, Stock, Boston **485** Linda Ferrer, Woodfin Camp & Associates **487** Thomas S. England, Photo Researchers **493** Karen R. Preuss, Taurus Photos

498 UPI/Bettmann Newsphotos **499** UPI/Bettmann Newsphotos **502** Anita Duncan **503** Paul Conklin, Monkmeyer **505** Reprinted courtesy of Thermos **509** Hugh Rogers, Monkmeyer **510** USDA Photo by Russell T. Forte, Photo Researchers **511** UPI/Bettmann Newsphotos **515** Michael Kagan, Monkmeyer **519** Eric Kroll, Taurus Photos **521** UPI/Bettmann Newsphotos **523** Mimi Forsyth, Monkmeyer **525** Marc Anderson

535 Photo courtesy of James "Cool Papa" Bell **537** Laimute E. Druskis **538** Josephus Daniels, Photo Researchers **539** Paul Conklin, Monkmeyer **541** Nancy J. Pierce, Photo Researchers **545** William Vandivert **548** Philip G. Zimbardo **550** (left) United Nations; (middle) UPI/Bettman Newsphotos; (right) Alain Nogues, Sygma **552** Walker Research, Inc. **553** Tim Davis, Photo Researchers **559** UPI/Bettmann Newsphotos **560** Mimi Forsyth, Monkmeyer **561** Wide World Photos **562** Photo courtesy of Bill Yancey **563** F. B. Grunzweig, Photo Researchers **566** Louis Fernandez **567** Ken Karp

575 Wide World Photos **576** Wide World Photos **578** Larry Miller, Photo Researchers **579** Russ Kinne, Photo Researchers **580** Michael Philip Manheim, Photo Researchers **583** Chris Reeberg, DPI **586** Tom McHugh, Photo Researchers **593** Barry Lopez, Photo Researchers **596** Wide World Photos **598** Jerry Cooke, Photo Researchers **599** United Press International **601** Jan Halaska, Photo Researchers **603** (left) New York Convention and Visitors Bureau; (right) Steven Frankel, Photo Researchers

NAME INDEX

Stokols, D., 584
Stone, G., 369
Stone, S. C., 485
Stoner, J. A., 557
Storms, M., 315
Straw, M. K., 527
Streif, G. F., 290
Streissguth, A. P., 244
Strelow, E. R., 90
Strickland, L., 260
Strodbeck, F., 561
Stroebe, M., 363
Stroebe, W., 363
Strongman, K. T., 334
Stroud, Robert, 573–576, 577, 580, 587, 592
Strube, M. J., 363t
Strupp, H. H., 491
Suedfeld, P., 152, 153
Sugarman, A., 307
Sugarman, S., 263
Suinn, R. M., 429, 431, 435, 458
Sullivan, Anne, 161–163, 167–168, 169, 170–171, 174–176, 177–179, 181, 182, 191, 199
Sullivan, B., 480
Sundstrom, E., 585
Suomi, S. J., 256, 350
Sussman, M. B., 282
Swanson, L., 536
Swets, John A., 69, 223
Swigert, John L., 97–99, 108
Szasz, T. S., 419, 458
Szucko, J., 336

Tajfel, H., 566
Tanford, S., 561
Tanner, J., 269f, 310
Tart, C. T., 126, 143, 154
Tavris, C., 314
Taylor, D. G., 257
Taylor, S., 367, 504
Taylor, S. E., 514
Taylor, W., 433
Teddlie, C., 583, 588
Teevan, R. C., 326
Teghtsoonian, R., 70, 71
Teitelbaum, P., 303
Templar, D. I., 292
Terman, L. M., 192, 195, 197, 549, 550
Terrace, H. S., 191
Terrance, H. S., 180
Thigpen, C. H., 459, 460, 461, 462, 465, 466, 467, 469, 474–475, 479, 481, 483, 489, 495

Thoman, E. B., 261
Thomas, G. B., Jr., 616
Thomas, M. H., 323
Thompson, J., 347
Thompson, R. F., 61
Thompson, S., 504
Thompson, W. R., 61
Thorndike, E. L., 170, 171, 182, 204
Thorndyke, P. W., 218
Thurstone, L. L., 192
Tighe, T. J., 199
Timberlake, W., 187
Titchener, Edward Bradford, 5
Tobias, L. L., 470
Tolman, E. C., 164, 183–186
Tomkins, S. S., 344
Toynbee, A., 551
Travis, L., 563
Treiman, D. J., 278
Treisman, A. M., 212
Trent, C., 570
Tribich, D., 384
Troll, L. E., 288, 290
Trope, Y., 558
Truax, C. B., 476, 491
Truman, Harry S., 371–374, 375, 386, 391, 393, 409
Tsang, R. C., 302
Tulving, E., 214, 222, 235
Turiel, E., 271
Turnage, T. W., 217
Turner, J., 566
Turner, S., 571
Turner, S. H., 230
Turner, T., 452
Tyron, R. C., 59

Ubell, E., 285
Ulrich, D., 486
Underwood, B., 529
Underwood, B. J., 199

Valins, S., 365, 599
Vallicher, R. R., 393
Van Buskirk, S., 306
Vance, E., 312
Van Itallie, T. B., 307
Veitch, R., 519
Verinis, J., 525
Vernon, P., 409
Villa-Komaroff, L., 58
Vinokur, A., 558
Vlok, L., 492
Voegtlin, W. L., 479
von Békésy, George, 83
von Frisch, K., 190
von Helmholtz, Hermann, 79

Wagemaker, H., Jr., 448
Wagner, N., 312
Wahba, M., 328
Wahl, G., 187
Wain, H. J., 130, 147
Wald, G., 79
Walk, R. D., 100
Walker, Jeff, 3
Wallace, B., 147
Wallace, W. H., 230
Wallach, H., 95, 106, 110, 121
Wallach, M., 557
Wallin, P. A., 354
Walster, E., 354, 369, 522, 524
Walster, G., 369
Walter, G. H., 259
Walters, J., 275
Walters, R. H., 321, 395
Walton, J., 343
Ward, L. M., 121
Washburn, A., 302, 302f
Waterhouse, L., 249
Waters, E., 349
Waters, H. F., 322
Watson, J. B., 169, 170, 312
Watson, J. D., 9, 54, 197
Watson, R. I., 31
Waugh, N. C., 214
Webb, W. B., 133
Weber, Ernst H., 70
Wegener, B., 31
Wegner, D. M., 393
Weil, A., 140, 159
Weinberg, R. A., 197
Weiner, M. J., 570
Weingartner, H., 226
Weinstein, T., 590, 592
Weiss, Jay, 172–173
Weiss, J. M., 362
Weiss, R. S., 291
Weiss, W., 504
Weissmuller, Johnny, 389
Weitzenhoffer, A. M., 147
Welch, R. B., 93
Wells, A., 507
Welsh, B., 592
Wertheimer, Max, 8
Wetmore, M. E., 605
Wever, E. G., 84
Wheeler, J., 571
Wheeler, L., 544
Whitaker, H. A., 61
White, A. J., 259
White, R. W., 276
Whyte, W., 557
Wickelgren, W. A., 187, 209, 212, 224
Wicklund, R. A., 508

Widom, C. S., 451
Wiel, Andrew T., 129
Wiener, M., 111
Wiesel, N., 241
Wiesel, T. N., 78
Wiesenthal, D. L., 544
Wilder, D., 565
Wilder, D. A., 545
Wilkens, W., 490
Willerman, B., 536
Williams, K., 564
Wilson, D. W., 324, 591
Winterbottom, M. R., 326
Wirtenburg, T., 277
Wollheim, R., 409
Wolpe, J., 166, 480, 480t
Wood, W., 505
Woodruff, D. S., 282
Woodsworth, R. S., 117
Woolfolk, R. L., 462
Worchel, Francis, 23
Worchel, S., 111, 348, 464, 500, 506, 509, 526, 530, 531, 568, 569, 571, 582, 583, 586, 588
Wortman, C., 520
Wright, F. E., 570
Wright, H. F., 259
Wundt, Wilhelm, 5
Wyden, B., 244

Yalom, I. D., 484, 493
Yarkin-Levin, K., 263
Yekovich, F. R., 218
Ynille, J. C., 235
Young, J. E., 435
Young, Thomas, 76–79

Zager, L., 404
Zaiden, J., 474
Zajonc, R., 390, 507, 522, 563–64
Zanna, M., 508
Zanna, M. P., 503
Zavalloni, M., 557
Ziemon, G., 595
Zillman, D., 323–24
Zimbardo, P., 548, 555
Zimmerman, R. R., 256
Zinberg, N. E., 126, 127, 127t, 159
Zucker, S. H., 195
Zubek, J., 59
Zubek, J. P. L., 153
Zuckerman, M., 153, 317, 571
Zukier, H., 516
Zusman, J., 489

SUBJECT INDEX

ABOUT THE AUTHORS

STEPHEN WORCHEL is a professor and department head of psychology at Texas A&M University. He received his B.A. at the University of Texas at Austin and his Ph.D. at Duke University. Before coming to Texas A&M, he taught at North Carolina Central University, the University of North Carolina at Chapel Hill, and the University of Virginia. He was a Senior Fulbright Research fellow in Athens, Greece, during 1979–1980. He has held numerous editorial positions, including psychology series editor to Nelson-Hall Publishers, Associate Editor of the *Personality and Social Psychology Bulletin,* Advisory Editor to the *Psychological Abstracts,* and Editorial Consultant to *Basic and Applied Social Psychology* and *Environmental Psychology and Nonverbal Behavior.* Steve Worchel does research on environmental issues, intergroup relations, attitude change, conflict resolution, and group dynamics. He has published more than fifty articles and chapters and co-authored *Understanding Social Psychology* (three editions), *Adjustment and Human Relations* (1981), *Clinical Psychology: A Social Psychological Approach* (1979), *Adjustment: Pathways to Personal Growth* (1985), and *The Psychology of Intergroup Relations* (1986). In his spare time, Steve raises cattle at his Franklin, Texas, ranch.

WAYNE SHEBILSKE is a professor of psychology at Texas A&M University. He received his B.A., M.S., and Ph.D. degrees at the University of Wisconsin. Before coming to Texas A&M, he taught at the University of Virginia where he was honored for excellence in undergraduate advising. While this edition was being revised, he spent two years at the National Academy of Sciences as Study Director of the Committee on Vision and two months at the Center for Interdisciplinary Research in Bielefeld, West Germany, where he participated in an international, multidisciplinary workshop on the relationship between perception and action. His research is on natural event perception (with an emphasis on effects of eye movement anomalies) and on reading (with an emphasis on learning from textbooks).

Wayne Shebilske   Stephen Worchel